FEDERAL INCOME TAXATION

ASPEN CASEBOOK SERIES

FEDERAL INCOME TAXATION

Third Edition

Richard Schmalbeck
Simpson Thacher & Bartlett Professor of Law
Duke University School of Law

Lawrence Zelenak
Pamela B. Gann Professor of Law
Duke University School of Law

Wolters Kluwer
Law & Business

Printed in the United States of America.

1 2 3 4 5 6 7 8 9 0

ISBN 978-0-7355-9251-3

Library of Congress Cataloging-in-Publication Data

Schmalbeck, Richard L.
  Federal income taxation / Richard Schmalbeck, Lawrence Zelenak. — 3rd ed.
     p. cm.
  Includes index.
  ISBN 978-0-7355-9251-3
  1. Income tax — Law and legislation — United States. I. Zelenak, Lawrence. II. Title.
KF6369.S36 2011
343.7305'2 — dc23

                                                                    2011018825

About Wolters Kluwer Law & Business

Wolters Kluwer Law & Business is a leading global provider of intelligent information and digital solutions for legal and business professionals in key specialty areas, and respected educational resources for professors and law students. Wolters Kluwer Law & Business connects legal and business professionals as well as those in the education market with timely, specialized authoritative content and information-enabled solutions to support success through productivity, accuracy and mobility.

Serving customers worldwide, Wolters Kluwer Law & Business products include those under the Aspen Publishers, CCH, Kluwer Law International, Loislaw, Best Case, ftwilliam.com and MediRegs family of products.

CCH products have been a trusted resource since 1913, and are highly regarded resources for legal, securities, antitrust and trade regulation, government contracting, banking, pension, payroll, employment and labor, and healthcare reimbursement and compliance professionals.

Aspen Publishers products provide essential information to attorneys, business professionals and law students. Written by preeminent authorities, the product line offers analytical and practical information in a range of specialty practice areas from securities law and intellectual property to mergers and acquisitions and pension/benefits. Aspen's trusted legal education resources provide professors and students with high-quality, up-to-date and effective resources for successful instruction and study in all areas of the law.

Kluwer Law International products provide the global business community with reliable international legal information in English. Legal practitioners, corporate counsel and business executives around the world rely on Kluwer Law journals, looseleafs, books, and electronic products for comprehensive information in many areas of international legal practice.

Loislaw is a comprehensive online legal research product providing legal content to law firm practitioners of various specializations. Loislaw provides attorneys with the ability to quickly and efficiently find the necessary legal information they need, when and where they need it, by facilitating access to primary law as well as state-specific law, records, forms and treatises.

Best Case Solutions is the leading bankruptcy software product to the bankruptcy industry. It provides software and workflow tools to flawlessly streamline petition preparation and the electronic filing process, while timely incorporating ever-changing court requirements.

ftwilliam.com offers employee benefits professionals the highest quality plan documents (retirement, welfare and non-qualified) and government forms (5500/PBGC, 1099 and IRS) software at highly competitive prices.

MediRegs products provide integrated health care compliance content and software solutions for professionals in healthcare, higher education and life sciences, including professionals in accounting, law and consulting.

Wolters Kluwer Law & Business, a division of Wolters Kluwer, is headquartered in New York. Wolters Kluwer is a market-leading global information services company focused on professionals.

SUMMARY OF CONTENTS

We dedicate this book to our wives, Linda Schmalbeck and Jeanne Moskal, and to our daughters, Suzanne and Sabine Schmalbeck, and Alice Zelenak.

CONTENTS

PREFACE

Most law school casebooks, including most income tax casebooks, contain far more material than can be covered in a course of standard length. The books typically give no indication of which material, if any, is optional; the implicit message seems to be that the class should be able to give careful, and roughly proportional, attention to the entire book. Faced with the unreasonableness of that implicit message, a teacher must make hard choices about which sections of a book to omit or cover lightly. The default approach, of which the authors have been guilty on occasion, is to start the course with unfounded optimism about the ability to cover the entire book, and to march through the book without omissions until the semester ends — an approach that leaves forever unstudied whatever the author happened to put at the end of the book. Our experience is that these editing choices are difficult to make well, and that even when they are made well the omissions may raise student doubts about the casebook, the teacher, or both.

This book does not altogether abandon the tradition of including more material than can be covered in an income tax course of the usual duration. We have attempted, however, to provide more than the usual amount of guidance to the teacher trying to decide what material should be covered, and what material may be in good conscience omitted, through the division of the book into a core text and more specialized "cells." The core text consists of twelve chapters, providing reasonably succinct coverage of the fundamental topics of an introductory income tax course. Following almost all chapters are one or more cells, consisting of deeper examinations of narrower selected topics.

The depth of coverage in selected areas — made possible by the cells — distinguishes this book from other income tax casebooks, which typically provide coverage of approximately uniform depth in all or most of the topics they explore. While even coverage has its virtues, it has an important drawback in an area as complex as federal income tax: Uniform coverage provides few opportunities for students to achieve significant depth of understanding of the materials, and little opportunity to hone the interpretive and problem-solving skills tax lawyers must bring to their work. The cells address this problem by replicating what we, and most other experienced teachers, have learned to do over time: They supplement the core text with materials and exercises intended to give students deeper and more direct experiences with the tax law as it is encountered by lawyers and policymakers.

The cells have a variety of emphases. Some feature problem sets designed to develop students' ability to read and apply moderately complex statutory provisions; some examine policy issues from perspectives informed by legislative dynamics or public finance economics; some focus on the interpretation of ambiguous statutes; and others are case studies in the development of the law over time. While we do not consider any of the substantive material covered in the cells to be essential to an introductory income tax course, we do think it essential that students have the experience of dealing with some material in more-than-survey-course fashion, and of approaching the tax law from the various perspectives embodied in the cells. Accordingly, we encourage every teacher to use at least a few cells, reflecting several different approaches to the law.

The core text is concise enough, we believe, to be covered in its entirety in a four-hour-per-week one-semester course, with enough time left over for some of the cells. We hasten to add that the process of dividing material between main text and cells is more art than science, and that no two teachers have exactly the same set of priorities. Thus, we would expect that many — perhaps most — teachers using the book will decide to skip a few portions of the main text. (This includes the authors themselves, since our decisions about what to include in the main text were driven to some degree by our sense of majority opinion among income tax teachers, rather than solely by our idiosyncratic preferences.)

We recognize as well that many teachers will have developed their own "cells," by whatever name they may call them, to supplement the casebooks they currently use. The core materials in this book should leave ample time for exploration of those teacher-produced materials, instead of or in conjunction with the cells we have provided. Our object has been to provide a flexible package of materials that can be easily customized to provide emphasis in those areas that each teacher finds most useful, interesting, and effective.

The core text, as much as the cells, reflects our conviction that income tax is best taught by a highly eclectic approach. One topic might be approached through the traditional case method, another might present an opportunity to read and apply statutory and regulatory provisions, a third might lend itself to economic analysis, a fourth might call for an exploration of history and politics, and so on. The book includes material using all these approaches (and a few others besides). The problems — more than 150 of them, counting both main text and cells — should be particularly helpful in developing the skills of statutory interpretation and application.

The book also reflects our lack of enthusiasm for full-bore Socratic methodology in teaching tax. While teaching that allows insights to emerge synthetically from class discussion certainly has its merits, our sense is that the complexity of the material in the federal income tax course is such that a "hide the ball" approach isn't generally appropriate. The tax ball is difficult enough to comprehend when it is in plain view. Accordingly, we have tried to explain concepts and rules as clearly as possible throughout this book. When material could be explained more clearly or more efficiently through the use of author-written text than through the presentation of cases, we have not hesitated to use text. We have also made liberal use of notes following cases to reveal what may have been hidden by the opinions themselves. The result is an income tax casebook with a relatively high ratio of author-written pages to case pages.

Despite the considerable extent of explanatory text, the book can still, with more than 75 cases, rulings, and similar materials, be fairly described as a casebook. We have included most of the classic cases, and have made an effort to include as well a fresh selection of interesting cases of more recent vintage. No book can, by itself, create a lively and productive course. But we believe that we have provided materials of sufficient variety, depth, and insight to enable enthusiastic teachers to offer very stimulating experiences to their introductory federal income tax students.

Finally, we are greatly indebted to several tax scholars who reviewed various drafts of this work, and provided a number of helpful comments. To assure the reviewers' candor, this part of the editorial process was designed to be opaque to the authors. As a consequence, we do not know who the reviewers were, and so can thank them only in this anonymous way. We are also grateful to those who adopted the first and second editions of our book — for that fact itself, of course, but also for the helpful comments they have offered. Wayne Gazur, Donald Tobin, Roberta Mann, and Darryll Jones have been particularly helpful in this way. Finally, we acknowledge with gratitude the assistance of our faculty support staff, especially Tiffany Cervi and Mykou Thao.

June 2011   *R.S.*
                                                                               L.Z.

ACKNOWLEDGMENTS

The authors acknowledge the permissions kindly granted to reproduce excerpts from the materials indicated below.

ABC News, This Week with David Brinkley, February 28, 1993.

American Bar Association Formal Ethics Opinion 85-352 (1985). © 2000 by the American Bar Association. All rights reserved. Reprinted by permission of the American Bar Association. Copies of ABA Ethics Opinions are available from Service Center, American Bar Association, 750 North Lake Shore Drive, Chicago, IL 60611, 1-800-285-2221.

Davenport, Charles, Being at the Top at the IRS Is Not So Taxing, 63 Tax Notes 773 (1994). Copyright 1994 Tax Analysts. Reprinted with permission.

Hershey Jr., Robert D., I.R.S. Backs Down on Frequent-Flier Miles, N.Y. Times, Nov. 29, 1995. Copyright © 1995 by The New York Times Co. Reprinted with permission.

Lim, Katherine & Jeffrey Rohaly, The Individual Alternative Minimum Tax: Historical Data and Projections. © 2009 The Tax Policy Center. Reprinted with permission of the Urban Institute and the Brookings Institution.

Slemrod, Joel, & Jon Bakija, Taxing Ourselves: A Citizen's Guide to the Great Debate over Taxes (fourth edition), pages 176-182, 185-188. © 2008 Massachusetts Institute of Technology, by permission of MIT Press.

Zelenak, Lawrence, *I Can Sit on It, But Is It Art?* 70 Tax Notes 99 (1996).

FEDERAL INCOME
TAXATION

Chapter 1

AN INTRODUCTION TO THE INCOME TAX

A. THE GOALS OF THIS COURSE

The complete Internal Revenue Code (IRC, or simply the "Code") occupies nearly 3,600 pages of the United States Code, with more than half of those pages devoted to the income tax. The income tax regulations promulgated by the Treasury Department take up about 10,700 pages of the Code of Federal Regulations. Even "student editions" of the Code and regulations are often well over 1,000 pages, despite being little more than the income tax's greatest hits. As if this prolixity weren't enough, the Code and regulations are moving targets; in the time it would take to read them straight through (if such a feat were possible), the statute would have been amended and the regulations revised. Faced with this welter of ever-changing detail, what can a law student hope to learn about the income tax in a single semester?

Actually, more than one might expect. This book has three pedagogical goals. The first is to introduce students to concepts that are fundamental to the current income tax and to any plausible future versions of the tax. Many of these concepts are implicated in the Introductory Problem that is posed in the following section; all the concepts are examined in detail in later chapters. Despite the mass of statutory and regulatory detail, the concepts are not overwhelming in number. The exact count depends on whether one is a splitter or lumper of concepts, but even a confirmed splitter would probably agree that there are not much more than a couple dozen. Learning these concepts is facilitated by the fact that they actually tend to make sense. To be sure, many details of the Code are arbitrary and capricious, but the basic structure of the income tax is surprisingly coherent.

The second goal of this book is to help students develop the skill of interpreting and applying complex statutes and regulations.[1] The tax laws are not, of course, the only set of complex statutory and regulatory provisions, and the interpretive skills developed by working with income tax materials will serve equally well on non-tax statutes and regulations.

---

1. In order to emphasize that developing this skill is an important goal of the basic income tax course, and that it is a goal distinct from learning the substance of the law, the authors routinely include on their exams questions requiring students to read and apply Code sections and regulations *not* covered in class or in the readings.

The third goal is to help students learn the details of a limited number of income tax provisions of particular practical importance. A few students already know at the beginning of the course that they want to become tax lawyers, and a few more grow to embrace that career path during the course (often to their considerable surprise). To these students, the utility of learning some details of current law is obvious. Most students, however, will not become tax lawyers. The Code provisions examined in detail have been selected with their professional needs in mind. There is probably no field of law practice that is devoid of income tax implications, and income tax considerations are crucial in many non-tax areas of practice — including family law, personal injury law, and advising closely held businesses, to name just a few. Whatever one's eventual area of practice, this course should furnish the background necessary to understand the relevant income tax rules — or, at the very least, to know when to consult a tax specialist, and to comprehend what the specialist has to say.

B.   INTRODUCTORY PROBLEM

The following problem is designed both to introduce many of the basic concepts of the income tax and to begin the development of interpretive skills. At the outset, an explanation of the structure of the problem may be helpful. At a high level of generality, a taxpayer's liability under any tax system can be described in the same way:

$$\text{tax base} \times \text{tax rate} = \text{tax liability}$$

The tax base is usually featured in the name of the tax. For example, the base of a real property tax is the value of real property, the base of a sales tax is the dollar amount of retail purchases, the base of an estate tax is value transferred at death, and the base of an income tax is income. More precisely, in the case of the federal income tax, the base is "taxable income," as defined by §63. The Code uses a three-step process in arriving at taxable income. Section 61 begins by defining gross income, §62 defines adjusted gross income (AGI), and finally §63 defines taxable income. The first three parts of the problem follow the statutory three-step process. The fourth part of the problem involves the application of the regular tax rates (of §1(a)) to the base, and the fifth and final part of the problem takes into account tax credits and the special rates applicable to capital gains.

The problem asks you to find the applicable law by consulting the Code and the Treasury regulations that interpret it. In real life, of course, taxpayers (or their return preparers) are much more likely to rely on Form 1040 and its instructions than to consult the Code and regulations (to say nothing of judicial opinions and legislative histories). The exercise of doing it the hard way is worthwhile, however, for two reasons:

1.   Although the forms and instructions accurately reflect the law in the vast majority of cases, they have no official legal status. The Code and the regulations are law; forms and instructions are not. Thus, any guidance

provided by forms and instructions is not authoritative, despite the fact that it comes from the Internal Revenue Service (IRS).

2. Forms and instructions address a relatively small number of issues — typically those affecting very large numbers of taxpayers. A sophisticated tax practice deals largely with issues not addressed by forms and instructions.

Thus, forms and instructions are never sources of authoritative answers, and in many cases they are not a source of answers at all. Despite the primacy of the Code and regulations, it is also important to understand how Form 1040 reflects the law. Accordingly, a filled-out Form 1040 is provided following the discussion of the problem.[2]

The discussion following the problem includes the answers to the problem. Before reading that discussion, however, take some time to puzzle through the problem on your own. Don't expect to be able to answer every part of every question with perfect accuracy, but you should be able to figure out quite a bit on your own.

PROBLEM

It is March 2011, and you are preparing the 2010 federal income tax return for John and Mary Smith. They are a married couple with two young children (ages one and three). John is an assistant professor; Mary is an associate in a law firm. John's salary last year was $60,000, and Mary's was $70,000. Their expenses last year included the following: $10,000 payments on their home mortgage loan (consisting of $2,000 principal and $8,000 of "qualified residence interest"); $3,500 property tax on their home; $9,000 for child care for times when both John and Mary were at work; and $4,000 they gave to their church. John's employer provided him with free parking at work, with a value of $1,200 for the year; Mary paid $1,500 for the year to park her car at a garage near her office. They paid $3,000 in state income tax. Their state does not have a sales tax. Mary made a $2,000 "qualified retirement contribution" to her individual retirement account (IRA) (a regular IRA, not a Roth IRA). They sold some Microsoft stock last April for $13,000. They had bought it several years before for $8,000. John had been injured in a car accident three years ago. Last year he settled his claim against the driver of the other car, receiving $15,000 from the other driver's insurance company (none of which was attributable to previously deducted medical expenses).

Assuming there are no other relevant facts, answer the following questions with respect to their federal income tax liability for last year:

(a) What is their gross income? *See* §§61, 104(a)(2), 132(a)(5) and (f), 1001, 1011, 1012, and 1016(a).

(b) What is their adjusted gross income? *See* §§62 and 219(a).

(c) What is their taxable income? *See* §§63, 151, 162(a), 163(h)(3), 164(a), 170(a)(1), and 262; Treas. Regs. §§1.151-1(b) and 1.262-1(b)(5). The statutory $6,000 standard deduction amount (under §63(c)(2)) and the statutory

---

2. See pages 16-17. The taxpayers in the Introductory Problem would also be required to file Schedules A and D, and Form 2441; these are not reproduced here.

$2,000 exemption amount (under §151(d)(1)) are adjusted annually to reflect inflation. *See* §§63(c)(4) and 151(d)(4). For 2010, the standard deduction amount for a joint return is $11,400, and the exemption amount is $3,650. Rev. Proc. 2009-50, 2009-2 C.B. 617.

(d) Apply the rate schedule of §1(a) to their taxable income.[3]

(e) Adjust the amount determined in part (d) to reflect the special favorable rates applicable to long-term capital gains, and to reflect the credits to which the Smiths are entitled. *See* §§1(h), 21, 24(a) and (b), 1221, and 1222.[4]

DISCUSSION

(a) *Gross income: $135,000.* Section 61(a) states that gross income includes "all income from whatever source derived," and goes on to provide a nonexhaustive list of 15 items includible in gross income. "Compensation for services" is the first item on the list, so John's $60,000 salary and Mary's $70,000 salary are (not surprisingly) both included in gross income.

What about John's $1,200 worth of free parking at work? Looking just at §61, this would seem to be included in gross income as part of John's compensation for services. Nothing in that section limits gross income to cash receipts, and in fact many in-kind benefits are included in gross income. But the definition of gross income begins with a qualification — "Except as otherwise provided in this subtitle" — and §132 provides otherwise for free parking at work provided to an employee by his

---

3. Section 1 of the Code is now a bit of a mess, due to several temporary changes made by Congress over the last few years, and due to the cumulative effects of inflation since the last permanent rate schedules were added to the Code. The rate schedules now in §1(a)-(e) were enacted into the Code in 1993, effective for that year. But in a series of enactments in the early years of this century, reflected in §1(i), Congress cut the rates applying to the top four rate brackets, and carved out a new 10 percent bracket that applies to a portion of the lowest tax bracket. (These rate changes, however, are temporary, and will expire — unless Congress strikes again, which is highly likely — at the end of 2012.) You could deal with the rate changes easily enough, but as you can see in §1(f), Congress has also mandated annual adjustments in the width of the brackets to account for inflation, as measured by changes in the consumer price index. The effects of these inflation adjustments are found nowhere in the Code; thus, while §1 is the authoritative statement of our federal income tax rates, it cannot be used to calculate tax liabilities in any year after 1993.

The following is the rate structure (set forth in Rev. Proc. 2009-50) that reflects both the temporary rate cuts and the inflation adjustments, for 2010, for married couples filing joint returns:

If taxable income is:	Then tax is:
Not over $16,750	10% of taxable income
Over $16,750 but not over $68,000	$1,675 plus 15% of the excess over $16,750
Over $68,000 but not over $137,300	$9,362.50 plus 25% of the excess over $68,000
Over $137,300 but not over $209,250	$26,687.50 plus 28% of the excess over $137,300
Over $209,250 but not over $373,650	$46,833.50 plus 33% of the excess over $209,250
Over $373,650	$101,085.50 plus 35% of the excess over $373,650

4. The adjustments required by §1(h) are horrifically complex, and rather daunting to new students of our tax system. An acceptable shortcut at this point is to note that §1(h)(1)(C) effectively caps the tax rate for most capital gain income at 15 percent. Because the Smiths' usual marginal tax rate under the rate schedule in the preceding footnote can be seen to be 25 percent (because their taxable income will be more than $68,000 but less than $137,300, after allowance of deductions), the effect of §1(h) is to reduce the tax paid by an amount equal to 10 percent (the difference in applicable rates) times the amount of the capital gain income. A more complete discussion of this issue will follow in Chapter 12.

employer. The exclusion is limited to $230 per month (§132(f)(2)(B), as adjusted for inflation by Rev. Proc. 2009-50), but this ceiling is not a problem for John.

John also benefits from another, more significant, exclusion. Under §104(a)(2), it appears he may exclude the $15,000 cash received in settlement of his personal injury claim. But wait — the §104(a)(2) exclusion applies to "damages" received on account of personal physical injuries. Does the exclusion apply to a *settlement,* or only to damages awarded by the judicial system? Common sense suggests the exclusion should apply to settlements; otherwise the tax system would create a major disincentive to the settlement of personal injury claims. Fortunately, the Code is consistent with common sense in this instance. A parenthetical provides that the exclusion extends to amounts received "by suit or agreement."

What about the $13,000 the Smiths received from the sale of stock? Section 61(a)(3) provides that gross income includes "gains derived from dealings in property," but it does not explain how to compute such gains. For that one must turn to §1001(a), which defines gain on the sale of property as "the excess of the amount realized therefrom over the adjusted basis provided in section 1011." For this definition to be of any use, we need two more definitions — of amount realized and of adjusted basis. Hundreds of Code sections are structured this way; they provide general rules or definitions, which depend on several terms themselves in need of definition. Usually (but not always) finding the needed definitions is simple enough, either because the definitions appear later in the same Code section or because the general rule provides directions to the definitions. Thus, the first rule of reading the Internal Revenue Code is to *keep reading* until you have found all the definitions you need to make sense of the general rule. In this case, the "amount realized" on the sale of property is defined in §1001(b) — a convenient enough location relative to §1001(a) — as the sum of (1) money received by the taxpayer for the property, and (2) the fair market value of any property other than money received by the taxpayer for the property. The Smiths' amount realized is simply the $13,000 cash.[5] A little farther afield, §1011(a) defines "adjusted basis" as the basis determined under §1012, adjusted as provided in §1016. Here we encounter another common feature of the Code — the search for the necessary definitions may extend through several layers of provisions. Continuing with our hunt, we find in §1012 that generally "[t]he basis of property shall be the cost of such property," and glancing at §1016(a) we find that no basis adjustment rules are applicable in this case. Thus the Smiths' §1011(a) basis is their $8,000 cost of the stock, and under §1001(a) their gain realized is $5,000:

$13,000 amount realized − $8,000 adjusted basis = $5,000 gain realized

This $5,000 gain is included in their gross income under §61(a)(3) as a gain from a dealing in property.

That covers the mechanics of their gain calculation, but what is the logic behind the rules? To explore the logic, consider the two following possibilities (each of which the Code rejects):

---

5. If they had to pay a sales commission, their amount realized would be reduced by the commission.

(1) The sale produced $13,000 cash, so shouldn't the Smiths be required to include $13,000 in gross income, instead of only $5,000? In other words, why are they allowed to use the $8,000 they paid for the stock to reduce their gross income from the sale to $5,000? The answer lies in the fact that the $8,000 they used to buy the stock has already been subject to the income tax. It would be unreasonable to tax the same $8,000 twice, just because they converted the cash into stock and later converted the stock back to cash.[6] The concept of *basis* is simply a way of keeping track of amounts that have already been taxed in order to prevent double taxation. When they sold their stock for $13,000, most of their amount realized — $8,000 — constituted a recovery of previously taxed dollars; only $5,000 was never-taxed-before gain. How can we be so sure they have already paid tax on the $8,000 they used to buy the stock? We can't, really. For example, they might have bought the stock using $8,000 cash from an earlier personal injury award excluded from gross income by §104(a)(2). The policy behind that exclusion, however, is that personal injury damages should *never* be taxed — not in the year they are received, and not in some later year. If a taxpayer uses a cash damage award to purchase property, that policy can be implemented only by giving the taxpayer a basis in the stock equal to the cash paid. If the basis were zero instead, the taxpayer would be taxed on the personal injury award when he sold the property, in contravention of the permanent exclusion policy underlying §104(a)(2). Thus, basis represents both amounts already taxed and amounts that are never to be taxed.

(2) Just before the sale, the Smiths owned stock worth $13,000; immediately after the sale they owned $13,000 cash and no stock. Since they were no richer after the sale than before, why should the sale generate *any* gross income inclusion? In other words, why is a taxpayer treated as deriving a *gain* from a property transaction when he merely sells property for what it is worth? Again, the answer involves taking the long view. Over the several years the Smiths owned the stock, it increased in value by $5,000. As long as they continued to own the stock, the income tax ignored all increases in the value of the stock; the Smiths were not required to include the annual increases in value in their gross income. In tax jargon, *unrealized appreciation* is not included in gross income. In an economic sense, the $5,000 gain on the stock accrued over the time the Smiths owned the stock, rather than all at once when they sold it. The tax imposed at the time of sale on the previously accrued gain is the price the Smiths must pay for having been allowed to ignore the appreciation until the sale. The sale itself does not produce an economic gain, but it is the trigger for taxing the gain that the tax system had disregarded before the sale. In tax jargon, such a trigger is a *realization event.* By far the most important trigger provision is §1001(a), which provides that gain or loss is triggered by a "sale or other disposition of property." Strangely enough, nowhere in the Code is the exclusion for unrealized appreciation explicitly set forth — even though the language of §61 seems broad enough to include

---

6. The stock purchase can be analogized to a bank savings account. If a depositor puts $100 of after-tax income into an account, she would certainly not expect to be taxed on that $100 when she later closes the account.

unrealized appreciation in gross income, in the absence of an explicit exclusion provision.[7] Hence another basic rule in reading the Code: Sometimes reading the Code simply isn't enough. The Code comes encrusted with judicial and administrative interpretations, some of which one might not imagine simply from examining the statutory language.

(b) *Adjusted gross income: $133,000.* Section 62 defines AGI as gross income minus the deductions listed in §62(a). That section does not create any deductions, but it does indicate whether deductions authorized by other Code sections may be taken into account in determining AGI, or whether they may be considered only at the later stage of determining taxable income. The practical significance of this distinction — sometimes referred to as the distinction between "above-the-line" and "below-the-line" or itemized deductions — is explained below, in the discussion of taxable income. The Smiths' only above-the-line deduction is for the $2,000 Mary contributed to her IRA. Section 219(a) creates the deduction, and §62(a)(7) allows the deduction in calculating AGI.

The deduction for IRA contributions is peculiar. Most deductions are for actual expenditures by a taxpayer, but in this case Mary gets a deduction for the equivalent of taking cash out of her left pocket and putting it into her right pocket. Moreover, no income tax will be imposed on the IRA's investment return (e.g., interest and dividend income) during Mary's working years. Eventually, however, Mary will pay a price for this favorable tax treatment. Unlike the exclusion for personal injury damages, which is designed as a *permanent* exclusion from income, the tax rules for IRAs are designed only to *defer* taxation of IRA contributions and of IRA investment returns. When Mary retires and begins receiving cash distributions from her IRA, she will be taxed on every dollar distributed to her.

(c) *Taxable income: $99,900.* Section 63 provides two definitions of taxable income. Under §63(b), which applies to taxpayers who *do not* itemize their deductions, taxable income is defined as AGI minus the standard deduction and the deduction for personal exemptions. This can be restated as: gross income minus (1) the deductions allowed under §62 in arriving at adjusted gross income, (2) the standard deduction, and (3) the deduction for personal exemptions. Under §63(a), which applies to taxpayers who *do* itemize their deductions, taxable income is defined as gross income minus all deductions except the standard deduction. This can be restated as: gross income minus (1) the deductions allowed under §62 in arriving at AGI, (2) itemized deductions, and (3) the deduction for personal exemptions.

As is clear from the restated versions of the two definitions of taxable income, the difference between them is in the second subtraction element. Taxpayers may claim the standard deduction or their itemized deductions, but not both. As a couple filing a joint return, the Smiths are entitled to a standard deduction under §63(c)(2)(A)(i), if they do not claim any itemized deductions. For 2010, the inflation-adjusted standard deduction is

---

7. On the other hand, the inclusion in gross income of "[g]ains derived from dealings in property" (§61(a)(3)) arguably creates an inference that in the absence of "dealings" there is no gross income from property. The same inference could be drawn from §1001 — that no gain is realized in the absence of a "sale or other disposition of property."

$11,400.[8] Alternatively, they may forgo the standard deduction and claim their itemized deductions, which are defined by §63(d) as all allowable deductions except above-the-line deductions (i.e., deductions allowed in arriving at AGI) and the deduction for personal exemptions.

The Smiths' strategic response to these rules is simple. They will add up all their itemized deductions. If the sum is greater than $11,400, they will claim their itemized deductions and forgo the standard deduction; if the sum is less than $11,400, they will take the standard deduction and claim no itemized deductions. Thus they are forced to choose between their itemized deductions and the standard deduction. By contrast, taxpayers are not forced to choose between above-the-line deductions and the standard deduction. To see the significance of the distinction, suppose the $2,000 IRA contribution were the Smiths' only deduction for the year (other than the standard deduction and the deduction for personal exemptions). Because the deduction is above-the-line, the Smiths could claim both the $2,000 IRA deduction and the $11,400 standard deduction. If, instead, IRA contributions were relegated to itemized deduction status, the Smiths would have to choose between the standard deduction and the IRA. They would choose the standard deduction, and so would be unable to claim any deduction for Mary's IRA contribution.

What are the Smiths' itemized deductions? Let's start with the $8,000 interest they paid on their home mortgage. Section 163, which governs the deductibility of interest expense, is an instance of the exception-to-the-exception-to-the-exception structure found in many Code sections. Section 163(a) begins by stating, "There shall be allowed as a deduction all interest paid or accrued within the taxable year on indebtedness." This is just the beginning, however, of the Code's version of a "good news, bad news" joke. Follow the first rule of reading the Code, and keep reading. After wading through several irrelevant subsections, we arrive at §163(h)(1), which states that no deduction is allowed for "personal interest." Is home mortgage interest in the disfavored personal interest category? Keep reading. According to §163(h)(2)(D), "qualified residence interest" (as defined in §163(h)(3)) is not personal interest. So their home mortgage interest is deductible after all, under the general rule of interest deductibility set forth in §163(a).[9] (Nothing in §163 or any other Code provision, however, authorizes a deduction for the $2,000 *principal* payment the Smiths made on their mortgage.[10]) Qualified residence interest is not listed in §62(a), so it is an itemized deduction. Since the $8,000 interest deduction is smaller than the $11,400 standard deduction alternative, the Smiths would forgo this deduction if the interest were their only itemized deduction.

---

8. The dollar figures in §63(c)(2) were added to the Code in 1988. Thus, the $11,400 figure for 2010 reflects the cumulative effects of 22 years of inflation.

9. As you would expect by now, the definition of "qualified residence interest" has its own share of complexities (some of which are explored in Chapter 5). The problem puts those complexities aside for now, however, by simply stating that the $8,000 constituted qualified residence interest.

10. Most home mortgage payments consist of at least two elements: an interest amount, to compensate the lender for the use of its money, and a principal amount, which gradually reduces the balance of the loan, so that the loan is fully discharged by the last scheduled payment.

But it is not their only itemized deduction. Contributions to qualifying charities, including churches, are deductible under §170(a). Thus, the $4,000 they gave to their church will hoist the Smiths over the itemizing threshold. If the Smiths were home renters instead of home owners, but their tax situation was otherwise the same, their itemized deductions would be less than their $11,400 standard deduction, and they would get no tax benefit for the donation to their church. It is not quite true that contributions to charity are deductible by taxpayers with home mortgages and not deductible by those without home mortgages, but it is easy to see why this rule of thumb applies to most taxpayers.[11]

What about the Smiths' state and local taxes? Section 164(a)(1) provides for the deductibility of "State and local . . . real property taxes," so the $3,500 property tax they paid on their home qualifies as an itemized deduction. So too does the income tax paid to their state of $3,000, by reason of §164(a)(3). The Smiths' itemized deductions add up to $18,500 ($8,000 home mortgage interest, $4,000 charitable contribution, and $6,500 of state and local taxes).

Section 162(a) allows a deduction for "all the ordinary and necessary expenses paid or incurred during the taxable year in carrying on any trade or business," including the business of being an employee. This provision is crucial to the basic structure of any income tax; without a business expense deduction the tax base would consist of gross receipts rather than net income. Does Mary's $1,500 expenditure for parking at work qualify as a business expense?[12] Is this a deductible business expense because Mary would not have incurred the expense but for her job, or is it a nondeductible personal expense because she would not have incurred the expense if she had chosen to live within walking distance of work or to commute by public transportation? Following the first rule of reading the Code doesn't help in this instance; nothing in §162 specifically addresses the question of the deductibility of commuting expenses in general or of parking at work in particular. Section 262(a) provides that no deduction shall be allowed "for personal, living, or family expenses" (except as expressly permitted by some other Code section), but this vague general statement does not clarify the treatment of Mary's parking expense. It is time, then, to move on to the *second rule* of tax research: When even a careful reading of the Code does not answer the question, turn to the regulations. Income tax regulations begin with the number "1.", which is followed by the number of the Code section to which they relate. Thus, the regulations to consult here would be Reg. §§1.162 and 1.262. The news is not good for Mary. In the spirit of overkill, commuting expenses (of which parking at work is a subset) are declared nondeductible by both Reg. §1.162-2(e) and Reg. §1.262-1(b)(5). A taxpayer can challenge a regulation

---

11. At this point, it appears that they will get a tax benefit from only the last $600 of their $4,000 contribution, because their itemized deductions of $12,000 exceed the standard deduction by only $600. As we shall see, however, their property tax deduction will bring their total housing-related deductions to $11,500, an amount in excess of the standard deduction.

12. Most §162 business expenses are deductible above-the-line. Business expenses of *employees*, however, are not deductible in arriving at AGI, except for expenses reimbursed by the employer and three more specialized exceptions not applicable here. *See* §§62(a)(1) and (a)(2). Thus, if Mary's parking expense is deductible at all, it is deductible only as an itemized deduction.

in court as being inconsistent with the statute it purports to interpret, but such challenges seldom succeed.

The $9,000 of child care costs incurred to enable John and Mary to be employed raise the same basic question as Mary's parking. Are the costs deductible because they would not have been incurred but for the Smiths' jobs, or are the costs nondeductible because they would not have been incurred but for the Smiths' personal decision to have children? In other words, are the child care costs governed by §162 or by §262? This time, even the regulations provide no clear answer. The next step is to research the case law. Research will uncover an unbroken line of cases holding that child care costs do not qualify as business expenses, even if incurred to enable the parents to be employed.[13] As explained below (in the discussion of part (e) of the problem), Congress has implicitly confirmed this interpretation, by providing a limited credit for child care expenses as a sort of consolation prize for the unavailability of a business expense deduction.

The final step in calculating the Smiths' taxable income is determining their personal exemptions under §151. Section 151(d) provides that the exemption amount (which functions as a deduction) is $2,000 for each exemption. Once again, this rather old number has been adjusted almost beyond recognition for the effects of inflation: For 2010, the amount for each exemption is $3,650. But how many exemptions are the Smiths allowed? Section 151(b) allows a deduction for "the taxpayer" and an additional exemption for the taxpayer's spouse if the taxpayer and the spouse do *not* file a joint return (and certain other requirements are satisfied). This seems to imply that spouses filing a joint return are entitled to only one exemption between them, but surely that can't be right. As is often the case, the regulations clarify a confusing statute. According to Reg. §1.151-1(b), there are two taxpayers in the case of a joint return, so "two exemptions are allowed on such return, one for each taxpayer spouse."[14] Under §151(c), the Smiths are also entitled to an exemption for each dependent. Although the definition of the term *dependent* (in §152) has its share of complexities, the Smiths' two children clearly qualify.

With four exemptions of $3,650 each, they are entitled to subtract $14,600 in arriving at their taxable income. Notice a peculiar feature of personal exemptions: While most deductions are based on actual expenditures, and even the IRA deduction is based on the amount of money placed in a special account, personal exemption amounts have nothing to do with the flow of cash. As long as a taxpayer can satisfy the conditions of §152, he need not prove that he spent any particular amount of money in any particular way in order to be entitled to an exemption. What could justify such a deduction? The standard deduction is similarly

---

13. The leading case is Smith v. Commissioner (no relation to the Smith family in our problem), 40 B.T.A. 1038 (1939), *aff'd without opinion*, 113 F.2d 114 (2d Cir. 1940).

14. In the case of an issue like this, which affects literally millions of taxpayers, the easiest place to find the answer may be on Form 1040, or in the accompanying instructions. Although the form does indicate that spouses filing a joint return are entitled to two exemptions, keep in mind that (1) unlike regulations, forms and instructions do not have the force of law, and (2) the answers to many questions involving smaller numbers of taxpayers can be found only in the regulations.

independent of any actual expenditures by the taxpayer. Taken together, the standard deduction and personal exemptions ensure that taxpayers are not taxed on an amount of income roughly equal to the official poverty level, as adjusted for family size.

To sum up, the Smiths' taxable income is $99,900:

$135,000	gross income
−$2,000	above-the-line IRA deduction (§219)
−$8,000	itemized qualified residence interest deduction (§163(h)(3))
−$6,500	itemized state and local tax deduction (§§164(a)(1) and (3))
−$4,000	itemized charitable contribution deduction (§170(a))
−$14,600	four personal exemptions (§151)
$99,900	

(d) *Tax liability under §1(a).* Under the progressive marginal tax rate schedule of §1(a), different dollars of the Smiths' taxable income are taxed at different rates. In particular, their tax under §1(a) for 2010 is computed as shown below.[15]

Income Bracket	Tax Rate	Tax on Income in Bracket
first $16,750 of taxable income ×	10% =	$1,675
next $51,250 of taxable income ×	15% =	$7,687.50
last $31,900 of taxable income ×	25% =	$7,975
		$17,337.50

The crucial point to note about the operation of this (and any) progressive marginal tax rate schedule is that the higher rates apply only to the portion of the taxpayer's income that falls within the higher brackets. For example, if a couple's income increases from $16,750 to $17,750, only the last $1,000 of taxable income is taxed at 15 percent. The other $16,750 still qualifies for the lower 10 percent rate. Although the Smiths are in the 25 percent bracket, in the sense that the 25 percent rate applies to their last dollars of income, most of their income is taxed at rates below 25 percent.

Here's a trick question: Based on the information in the table above (and supposing $17,337.50 were the Smiths' final income tax liability for last year) what is their tax rate? The trick is that "tax rate" has more than one meaning. Their *average* tax rate — that is, their tax liability as a percentage of their taxable income — is 17.4 percent ($17,337.50/$99,900).[16] On the

---

15. Actually, the Form 1040 instructions direct taxpayers with taxable incomes below $100,000 to find their tax in the appropriate tax table (included with the Form 1040 instructions), rather than to perform the multiple-tax-rate calculations indicated by the statute. The tax tables assign tax liabilities according to $50 income ranges, rather than according to precise income amounts. This makes tax return preparation computationally easier, at the loss of some precision in the assignment of tax liabilities. The 2010 joint return tables assign a tax liability of $17,344 to a joint return with taxable income in the $99,900-$99,949 range, and that would be the actual amount of the Smiths' pre-credit tax liability. The discussion in the text calculates the Smiths' tax liability, rather than using the tax table, for pedagogical purposes (i.e., to explain the operation of a tax rate schedule with progressive marginal rates).

16. Arguably, it would make more sense to use their gross income as the denominator in determining their average tax rate, since gross income is closer than taxable income to their real economic income. With respect to gross income, their average tax rate is less than 13 percent ($17,337.50/$135,000). Their average tax rate would be lower still if the denominator were expanded to include economic benefits excluded from gross income, such as John's personal injury damages.

other hand, their *marginal* tax rate — i.e., the tax rate applied to their last dollars of income — is 25 percent. Both tax rates are important, but for different reasons. If you want to complain to your representatives in Congress that you are overtaxed (either in an absolute sense, or compared with other taxpayers), your average tax rate is the crucial figure. For tax planning purposes, however, the marginal tax rate is what matters. Suppose the Smiths had enough information last year to know that their marginal tax rate for the year would be 25 percent, and they wanted to take income tax consequences into account in making some financial decisions. If John was trying to decide whether to earn $1,000 of overtime, and wanted to know how much of the $1,000 they would be able to keep after tax, he would need to know their marginal tax rate. An extra $1,000 of taxable income would generate additional tax of $250 ($1,000 × 25%), so they would get to keep $750. Similarly, if Mary was considering whether to give another $1,000 to charity, and wanted to know the after-tax cost of such a donation, the answer would depend on their marginal tax rate. A deduction of $1,000 would reduce their tax liability by $250; thus, the after-tax cost would be $750 ($1,000 pretax cost, reduced by $250 tax savings).

(e) *Adjustments to the tax liability determined under §1(a).* Before arriving at the Smiths' ultimate tax liability, it is necessary to make several downward adjustments to the $17,337.50 tentative liability determined under §1(a). First, §1(h) provides for special favorable tax rates for "net capital gain," as defined in §1222(11). Oversimplifying a little, this is gain from the sale of investment-type assets held by the taxpayer for more than one year. The Smiths' Microsoft stock meets the §1221(a) definition of a capital asset, and they owned the stock for more than one year, so their $5,000 gain from the sale qualifies for the special rate. The intricacies of §1(h) are too daunting to explore in detail in an introductory chapter, but here is how the provision applies to the Smiths:

1. The statute makes the taxpayer-favorable assumption that the $5,000 of capital gain is stacked on top of the Smiths' other income for purposes of the §1(a) tax calculations, so that the $17,337.50 figure reflects a 25 percent tax rate on their capital gain.
2. Section 1(h) provides that the Smiths' capital gain should be taxed at 15 percent.
3. Since the $17,337.50 tentative tax was derived by taxing the $5,000 of capital gain at 25 percent, implementing the capital gain rate preference requires reducing the tentative tax by the amount the tentative tax overtaxed the capital gain. The amount of the overtaxation is $5,000 (25% − 15%) = $500. Reducing the tentative tax by $500 leaves $16,837.50.[17]

---

17. The Schedule D Tax Worksheet for Form 1040 uses a slightly different procedure to achieve the same result. In the Smiths' case, it would first calculate the §1(a) tax on $94,900 of taxable income ($16,087.50), and then calculate the 15 percent §1(h) tax on $5,000 of capital gain ($750). The sum of the two taxes would be $16,837.50, which is the same number produced by subtracting $500 from $17,337.50.

Why should capital gains be taxed at special low rates, when a dollar of capital gain "spends" just as well as a dollar of wages? The policy arguments for and against special capital gains rates are examined in detail in Chapter 12, but one point is worth noting here. Some or all of a particular capital gain might be the result of inflation, rather than a real economic gain. For example, if the consumer price index had risen by 10 percent during the time the Smiths held the stock, a sale of the stock for $8,800 would not have produced any real economic gain, because $8,800 in the year they sold the stock would be the equivalent in purchasing power of $8,000 in the year they bought the stock ($8,000 × 110% = $8,800). Ideally, the tax system would permit the Smiths to adjust their $8,000 basis upward by 10 percent to reflect inflation, thus taxing them only on their real gain of $4,200 ($13,000 amount realized—$8,800 inflation-adjusted basis). In fact, however, the Code does not permit basis adjustments on account of inflation.[18] The special capital gain tax rates are sometimes explained as being in lieu of a basis adjustment for inflation. It would be the sheerest accident, however, if taxing nominal capital gains (i.e., gains determined without adjusting basis for inflation) at special rates produced the same result as taxing real capital gains (i.e., gains determined after basis adjustments) at regular rates. In the Smiths' case, for example, the Code produces a tax of $750 (15% × $5,000), while an inflation adjustment and a 25 percent rate applied to real gain would produce a tax of $1,050 (25% × $4,200).

The final step in determining the Smiths' tax liability is calculating the amounts of the credits to which they are entitled. They qualify for both the child care credit of §21 and the child credit of §24.

According to §21(a)(1), a taxpayer who maintains a household with one or more "qualifying individuals" is entitled to a credit equal to the "applicable percentage" of the taxpayer's "employment-related expenses" for the year. As always, keep reading: the definitions of all three quoted terms are located elsewhere in §21. Under §21(a)(2), the "applicable percentage" is higher for lower-income taxpayers than for middle- and upper-income taxpayers. It starts at 35 percent, but is reduced by one percentage point for each $2,000 (or fraction thereof) by which the taxpayer's AGI exceeds $15,000. No matter how great the taxpayer's AGI, however, the credit is never reduced below 20 percent. Under this formula, the 20 percent bottom is hit at AGI of $43,001. The Smiths' applicable percentage is 20 percent. According to §21(b)(1)(A), "qualifying individual" includes any dependent of the taxpayer who is under the age of 13, and with respect to whom the taxpayer is entitled to claim an exemption under §151. Both of the Smiths' children are qualifying individuals. Finally, §21(b)(2) includes within the definition of "employment-related expenses" amounts paid for the care of a qualifying individual, if "incurred to enable the taxpayer to be gainfully employed." Based on these three definitions, it appears that the Smiths' child care credit is $1,800 (20% × $9,000). Unfortunately, appearances are deceiving. It is not enough to keep reading §21 only until one finds the three definitions; one must keep reading even

---

18. As noted earlier, the Code does contain adjustments designed to prevent inflation from pushing a larger percentage of a taxpayer's income into higher-rate brackets, but these adjustments do nothing to prevent the taxation of inflationary gains.

after it appears one has found all the relevant rules. Section 21(a) provides no warning of the ceiling on credit-eligible expenses lurking in §21(c). Because of that ceiling, no more than $6,000 of expenses can be taken into account in computing the credit (or no more than $3,000, for taxpayers with only one qualifying individual). Thus, the Smiths' credit is $1,200 (20% × $6,000), not $1,800. Unlike a one-dollar deduction, which reduces *taxable income* by one dollar, a one-dollar credit reduces *tax liability* by one dollar, Accordingly, §21 entitles the Smiths to reduce their tentative tax liability, calculated under §1(a), by $1,200.

Finally, §24 provides a child tax credit, which is a decidedly different creature from the child care credit of §21. The §24 credit resembles the personal exemptions for dependents allowed under §151 in not being premised on actual expenditures by the taxpayers, but it resembles §21 in directly reducing tax liability instead of reducing taxable income. The basic rules of the child tax credit seem simple enough: §24(a) allows the Smiths a $1,000 credit for each "qualifying child,"[19] and §24(c) defines a qualifying child as a dependent (for purposes of §151) under the age of 17. Thus, the Smiths' child tax credit appears to be $2,000. Again, however, it is necessary to read the rest of the Code section. Section 24(b) provides that the amount of the credit is reduced—and the credit is eventually eliminated—as AGI increases above $110,000 (in the case of a joint return). The reduction in "the amount of the credit allowable under subsection (a)" is $50 for each $1,000 (or fraction thereof) by which the Smiths' AGI exceeds $110,000. The Smiths' AGI of $133,000 exceeds $110,000 by $23,000, which means "the credit" must be reduced by $1,150 ($23,000/$1,000 × $50). What the statute does not make clear is whether "the credit" refers to each $1,000 credit—in which case the phaseout eliminates the Smiths' right to claim any child tax credit—or whether "the credit" refers to the total $2,000 two-child credit—in which case the phaseout leaves the Smiths with an $850 credit. The ambiguity is unfortunate, especially in a provision affecting millions of taxpayers, but drafting flaws are inevitable in a statute as complex as the Internal Revenue Code. The first place to look for clarification would be the regulations, but in this case no regulations have yet been issued. The next step, especially in the case of recently enacted provisions such as the child tax credit, is to consult the legislative history. As it happens, the legislative history of IRC §24 indicates Congress intended the more taxpayer-favorable phaseout rule, and the IRS has issued Form 1040 instructions consistent with the legislative history.[20] As a result, the Smiths' child tax credit is $850.

Taking §24 into account, what is the Smiths' true marginal tax rate? To make the question more concrete, what would be the increase in their tax liability if one of them had earned an additional $1,000 last year, thus increasing their taxable income from $99,900 to $100,900, and their AGI from $133,000 to $134,000? Given their 25 percent marginal tax rate under §1(a), the $1,000 increase in taxable income would increase their tax liability by $250. In addition, the $1,000 increase in AGI would trigger the

---

19. This is the amount of the credit through 2012, after which it will revert to $500 per child, unless Congress strikes again.

20. See Chapter 10 for a more detailed discussion of this issue.

elimination of $50 of credit under §24(b)(1). Combining these two effects, the $1,000 increase in income would cost them $300 ($250 in additional tax under §1(a) and $50 in lost credit under §24), producing a true marginal tax rate of 30 percent ($300/$1,000). Although §24 happens to be the only phaseout provision that is operating at the margin on the Smiths, taxpayers at higher and lower income levels, and taxpayers eligible for other credits and deductions, are subject to a number of other phaseout provisions,[21] all of which function as hidden marginal tax rate increases. These phaseout provisions greatly complicate tax return preparation. They also make tax planning difficult. Tax planning requires knowledge of one's true marginal tax rate, and acquiring that knowledge is not a simple matter in the presence of numerous phaseout provisions.

To sum up, the Smiths are entitled to three reductions in their tentative tax liability of $17,337.50: $500 under the special capital gain rate provisions of §1(h), $1,200 under the child care credit of §21, and $850 under the child tax credit of §24. Their final tax liability is $14,787.50. They have already paid most or all of this amount through wage withholding. If the amount withheld from their wages last year exceeded $14,787.50 they will receive a refund; if the amount withheld was less than their actual tax liability, they will include a check for the difference with their tax return.

What is their tax rate, in the final analysis? Their *average* rate, with respect to *taxable* income, is 14.8 percent ($14,787.50/$99,900). Their average rate, with respect to *gross* income, is 11.0 percent ($14,787.50/ $135,000). Their *official marginal* rate is 25 percent, and their *real marginal* rate (taking into account the phaseout of the child credit) is 30 percent.

C. SOME BASIC CONCEPTS AND ISSUES

Don't worry if you do not fully understand every aspect of the Smiths' tax situation. The purpose of the problem was to introduce you to the reading of the Code and regulations, and to some fundamental structural aspects of the income tax. The remaining chapters of this book explain in much greater detail the provisions and concepts introduced here (as well as provisions and concepts not touched upon in this problem). Before turning to those detailed explanations, however, some additional discussion of a few basic concepts and issues completes this introduction to the income tax.

1. *Exclusions, Deductions, and Credits*

The Introductory Problem involved both exclusions from gross income (for damages on account of John's injury, and for John's employer-provided parking

---

21. And phasedown provisions, as in the case of the reduction of the child care credit percentage under §21.

Form **1040**	Department of the Treasury—Internal Revenue Service **U.S. Individual Income Tax Return** 2010	(99)	IRS Use Only—Do not write or staple in this space.

	For the year Jan. 1–Dec. 31, 2010, or other tax year beginning , 2010, ending , 20	OMB No. 1545-0074

Name, Address, and SSN

See separate instructions.

PRINT CLEARLY

Your first name and initial	Last name	Your social security number
Mary	Smith	
If a joint return, spouse's first name and initial	Last name	Spouse's social security number
John	Smith	

Home address (number and street). If you have a P.O. box, see instructions. | Apt. no.

Make sure the SSN(s) above and on line 6c are correct. ▲

City, town or post office, state, and ZIP code. If you have a foreign address, see instructions.

Checking a box below will not change your tax or refund.

Presidential Election Campaign   ► Check here if you, or your spouse if filing jointly, want $3 to go to this fund . . . . . . ► ☐ You ☐ Spouse

Filing Status

Check only one box.

1 ☐ Single
2 ☑ Married filing jointly (even if only one had income)
3 ☐ Married filing separately. Enter spouse's SSN above and full name here. ►
4 ☐ Head of household (with qualifying person). (See instructions.) If the qualifying person is a child but not your dependent, enter this child's name here. ►
5 ☐ Qualifying widow(er) with dependent child

Exemptions

If more than four dependents, see instructions and check here ► ☐

					Boxes checked on 6a and 6b	**2**
6a	☑ **Yourself.** If someone can claim you as a dependent, **do not** check box 6a					
b	☑ **Spouse**				No. of children on 6c who:	
c	**Dependents:**	(2) Dependent's social security number	(3) Dependent's relationship to you	(4) ✓ if child under age 17 qualifying for child tax credit (see page 15)	• lived with you	**2**
(1) First name Last name					• did not live with you due to divorce or separation (see instructions)	
Jason Smith			child	☑	Dependents on 6c not entered above	
Jennifer Smith			child	☑		
				☐	Add numbers on lines above ►	**4**
				☐		
d	Total number of exemptions claimed					

Income

Attach Form(s) W-2 here. Also attach Forms W-2G and 1099-R if tax was withheld.

If you did not get a W-2, see page 20.

Enclose, but do not attach, any payment. Also, please use Form 1040-V.

7	Wages, salaries, tips, etc. Attach Form(s) W-2	7	130,000
8a	**Taxable** interest. Attach Schedule B if required	8a	
b	**Tax-exempt** interest. **Do not** include on line 8a . . .	8b			
9a	Ordinary dividends. Attach Schedule B if required	9a	
b	Qualified dividends	9b			
10	Taxable refunds, credits, or offsets of state and local income taxes	10	
11	Alimony received	11	
12	Business income or (loss). Attach Schedule C or C-EZ	12	
13	Capital gain or (loss). Attach Schedule D if required. If not required, check here ► ☐	13	5,000
14	Other gains or (losses). Attach Form 4797	14	
15a	IRA distributions .	15a		b Taxable amount . . .	15b	
16a	Pensions and annuities	16a		b Taxable amount . . .	16b	
17	Rental real estate, royalties, partnerships, S corporations, trusts, etc. Attach Schedule E	17	
18	Farm income or (loss). Attach Schedule F	18	
19	Unemployment compensation	19	
20a	Social security benefits	20a		b Taxable amount . . .	20b	
21	Other income. List type and amount	21	
22	Combine the amounts in the far right column for lines 7 through 21. This is your **total income** ►	22	135,000

Adjusted Gross Income

23	Educator expenses	23			
24	Certain business expenses of reservists, performing artists, and fee-basis government officials. Attach Form 2106 or 2106-EZ	24			
25	Health savings account deduction. Attach Form 8889 .	25			
26	Moving expenses. Attach Form 3903	26			
27	One-half of self-employment tax. Attach Schedule SE .	27			
28	Self-employed SEP, SIMPLE, and qualified plans .	28			
29	Self-employed health insurance deduction	29			
30	Penalty on early withdrawal of savings	30			
31a	Alimony paid b Recipient's SSN ►	31a			
32	IRA deduction	32	2,000		
33	Student loan interest deduction	33			
34	Tuition and fees. Attach Form 8917	34			
35	Domestic production activities deduction. Attach Form 8903	35			
36	Add lines 23 through 31a and 32 through 35	36	2,000
37	Subtract line 36 from line 22. This is your **adjusted gross income** . . . . . ►	37	133,000

For Disclosure, Privacy Act, and Paperwork Reduction Act Notice, see separate instructions.   Cat. No. 11320B   Form **1040** (2010)

Form 1040 (2010) Page **2**

Tax and Credits	38	Amount from line 37 (adjusted gross income)		38	133,000
	39a	Check { **You** were born before January 2, 1946, ☐ Blind. } **Total boxes** if: { ☐ **Spouse** was born before January 2, 1946, ☐ Blind. } checked ▶ 39a			
	b	If your spouse itemizes on a separate return or you were a dual-status alien, check here ▶ 39b☐			
	40	**Itemized deductions** (from Schedule A) **or** your **standard deduction** (see instructions) . .		40	18,500
	41	Subtract line 40 from line 38		41	114,500
	42	**Exemptions.** Multiply $3,650 by the number on line 6d		42	14,600
	43	**Taxable income.** Subtract line 42 from line 41. If line 42 is more than line 41, enter -0-		43	99,900
	44	**Tax** (see instructions). Check if any tax is from: **a** ☐ Form(s) 8814 **b** ☐ Form 4972 .		44	16,837.50
	45	**Alternative minimum tax** (see instructions). Attach Form 6251		45	
	46	Add lines 44 and 45 . . . . ▶		46	16,837.50
	47	Foreign tax credit. Attach Form 1116 if required	47		
	48	Credit for child and dependent care expenses. Attach Form 2441	48	1,200	
	49	Education credits from Form 8863, line 23	49		
	50	Retirement savings contributions credit. Attach Form 8880	50		
	51	Child tax credit (see instructions)	51	850	
	52	Residential energy credits. Attach Form 5695	52		
	53	Other credits from Form: **a** ☐ 3800 **b** ☐ 8801 **c** ☐	53		
	54	Add lines 47 through 53. These are your **total credits**		54	2,050
	55	Subtract line 54 from line 46. If line 54 is more than line 46, enter -0- . . . . . . ▶		55	14,787.50
Other Taxes	56	Self-employment tax. Attach Schedule SE		56	
	57	Unreported social security and Medicare tax from Form: **a** ☐ 4137 **b** ☐ 8919		57	
	58	Additional tax on IRAs, other qualified retirement plans, etc. Attach Form 5329 if required . .		58	
	59	**a** ☐ Form(s) W-2, box 9 **b** ☐ Schedule H **c** ☐ Form 5405, line 16 . . .		59	
	60	Add lines 55 through 59. This is your **total tax** . . . . ▶		60	14,787.50
Payments	61	Federal income tax withheld from Forms W-2 and 1099 . .	61	15,287.50	
	62	2010 estimated tax payments and amount applied from 2009 return	62		
	63	Making work pay credit. Attach Schedule M	63		
If you have a qualifying child, attach Schedule EIC.	64a	**Earned income credit (EIC)**	64a		
	b	Nontaxable combat pay election	64b			
	65	Additional child tax credit. Attach Form 8812	65		
	66	American opportunity credit from Form 8863, line 14 . . .	66		
	67	First-time homebuyer credit from Form 5405, line 10 . .	67		
	68	Amount paid with request for extension to file	68		
	69	Excess social security and tier 1 RRTA tax withheld . . .	69		
	70	Credit for federal tax on fuels. Attach Form 4136	70		
	71	Credits from Form: **a** ☐ 2439 **b** ☐ 8839 **c** ☐ 8801 **d** ☐ 8885	71		
	72	Add lines 61, 62, 63, 64a, and 65 through 71. These are your **total payments** . . . ▶		72	15,287.50
Refund	73	If line 72 is more than line 60, subtract line 60 from line 72. This is the amount you **overpaid**		73	500
	74a	Amount of line 73 you want **refunded to you.** If Form 8888 is attached, check here . ▶☐		74a	500
Direct deposit? See instructions.	▶ b	Routing number	▶ c Type: ☐ Checking ☐ Savings		
	▶ d	Account number			
	75	Amount of line 73 you want **applied to your 2011 estimated tax** ▶	75		
Amount You Owe	76	**Amount you owe.** Subtract line 72 from line 60. For details on how to pay, see instructions ▶		76	
	77	Estimated tax penalty (see instructions)	77		

Third Party Designee	Do you want to allow another person to discuss this return with the IRS (see instructions)? ☐ **Yes.** Complete below. ☐ **No** Designee's name ▶ Phone no. ▶ Personal identification number (PIN) ▶
Sign Here Joint return? See page 12. Keep a copy for your records.	Under penalties of perjury, I declare that I have examined this return and accompanying schedules and statements, and to the best of my knowledge and belief, they are true, correct, and complete. Declaration of preparer (other than taxpayer) is based on all information of which preparer has any knowledge. Your signature Date Your occupation Daytime phone number Spouse's signature. If a joint return, **both** must sign. Date Spouse's occupation
Paid Preparer Use Only	Print/Type preparer's name Preparer's signature Date Check ☐ if self-employed PTIN Firm's name ▶ Firm's EIN ▶ Firm's address ▶ Phone no.

Form **1040** (2010)

at work) and deductions (for Mary's IRA contribution, for their home mortgage interest expense, for the donation to their church, for their property tax and for their state income tax). Although exclusions and deductions are taken into account at different stages of the process of determining taxable income, they have much in common. The effect of either a $1,000 exclusion or a $1,000 deduction is to reduce taxable income by $1,000, and in either case the tax saving equals the product of $1,000 and the taxpayer's marginal tax rate. If exclusions and deductions have equivalent effects, how does Congress decide which should be used in a particular context? Simply enough, a tax allowance takes the form of an exclusion if qualification for the allowance depends on the *source* of an economic benefit (as with damages *from a tortfeasor*), and an allowance takes the form of a deduction if it depends solely on the *use* of funds by the taxpayer (for example, money used to pay home mortgage interest is deductible regardless of the source of the money).[22]

If the source/use distinction is the only fundamental difference between exclusions and deductions, there is no obvious reason why Congress should be more generous with respect to exclusions than with respect to comparable deductions. For example, if a taxpayer who receives employer-provided free parking at work is allowed to exclude its value from gross income, it would seem that another taxpayer who has to pay for parking at work should be allowed to deduct its cost. As the Introductory Problem demonstrated, however, employees who pay for their own parking are not allowed a deduction. This pattern of greater generosity with respect to exclusions than with respect to deductions is common in the Code. For example, the tax treatment of employer-provided retirement savings is more generous than the tax treatment of IRA contributions. More generally, taxpayers are forced to choose between itemized *deductions* and the standard deduction, but they may claim both *exclusions* and the standard deduction. To some extent, the more favorable treatment of exclusions may be explained by their lower visibility. Deductions appear as entries on tax returns, while exclusions do not. The higher visibility of deductions makes them more obvious targets than exclusions, when Congress is in the mood to impose limitations on tax benefits.

Credits differ fundamentally from both exclusions and deductions. A credit directly reduces tax liability, while a deduction or exclusion reduces tax liability only indirectly—by reducing taxable income. Unlike the tax saving from an exclusion or deduction, which equals the amount of the exclusion or deduction multiplied by the taxpayer's marginal tax rate, the saving from a credit is simply the amount of the credit. A credit equal to 100 percent of a particular expenditure would mean the taxpayer had *no* after-tax cost for the expenditure; the government would pick up the entire tab. One hundred percent credits are rare.[23] Usually, as in the example of the §21 child care credit, the credit is for some specified lower percentage of qualifying expenditures. Even with credit percentages below 100 percent, the difference between a credit and a deduction (or exclusion) is significant. The tax benefit of a $1,000 deduction is a function of the taxpayer's marginal tax rate; the higher the marginal tax rate (and thus the more affluent the taxpayer), the greater the benefit. By contrast, a credit equal to, say, 20 percent of $1,000 of qualifying expenditures will be worth $200 to any

---

22. If a particular tax allowance depends on both the source of the economic benefit and the nature of the economic benefit—as in the case of employer-provided parking—it takes the form of an exclusion.

23. *But see* §901(a), allowing a 100 percent credit for taxes paid to foreign governments with respect to foreign-source income.

taxpayer, regardless of marginal tax rate. If you gave $1,000 to your church, would you prefer that the tax benefit for the contribution took the form of a $1,000 deduction or a 20 percent credit? This is a matter of comparing your marginal tax rate with the credit percentage. If your marginal tax rate is greater than 20 percent a deduction would save you more; if your marginal tax rate is less than 20 percent you would fare better with a credit. There is a wrinkle, though. Credits — like exclusions but unlike many deductions — are allowed regardless of whether one itemizes deductions or claims the standard deduction. Because of this, you would prefer the credit to the deduction even if your marginal tax rate was greater than 20 percent, if you claim the standard deduction.

2.   *The Importance of Deferral*

All issues concerning the definition of the tax base fall into one of two categories. The question is either (1) whether an amount should *ever* be included in income or deducted, or (2) *in what year* an item should be included or deducted. In the Introductory Problem, John's exclusion of the tort settlement is an example of the first type; he will never be taxed on that $15,000. Similarly, John and Mary will never be taxed on the $4,000 they gave to their church. The stock appreciation and the IRA contribution involve questions of the second type. Congress wants appreciation in stock to be taxed eventually, but it defers the tax until the taxpayer sells the stock. Likewise, Congress wants amounts contributed to an IRA to be taxed eventually, but not until the taxpayer retires and receives distributions from the IRA.

When the issue is now or never, it is easy to calculate the amount of money at stake. John's tax saving from excluding the $15,000 settlement, for example, is $15,000 × 25% = $3,750. Understanding what is really at stake when the issue is one of timing is a little more complicated.

To take a simple example, suppose (unrealistically) that the entire $5,000 appreciation in the Smiths' stock occurred in 2005; the stock increased in value from $8,000 to $13,000 in 2005, and its value never changed again before they sold the stock in 2010. Also suppose they had $750 sitting in a savings account in 2005, earning interest at an after-tax rate of 4 percent. If they had been required to pay $750 tax[24] on the appreciation in 2005, they would have used the $750 in the savings account to pay the tax. Because they did not have to pay the tax in 2005, they were able to keep the money in the savings account for five more years, before using it in 2010 to pay the tax due on the sale of the stock. With after-tax interest income compounded at 4 percent, by 2010 their $750 has grown to $912.[25] After paying the $750 tax, they are left with $162. This $162 is money they would not have had in 2010 if they had not been allowed in 2005 to keep and invest the $750 for five years. In *future value* terms, from the perspective of 2010, having been allowed to defer the tax for five years is worth $162 to the Smiths. Alternatively, one can calculate the *present value,* as of 2005, of the deferral. If the Smiths invested $617 in 2005, at a 4 percent after-tax rate of return, it would grow to $750 in five years. They could spend the other $133 ($750 − $617) in 2005, secure in the knowledge that the remaining $617 would be sufficient to fund their $750 tax

24. Fifteen percent (§1(h)) of $5,000 capital gain.
25. The number is rounded, as are later numbers in this example.

liability in 2010. The connection between the $133 present value of the deferral and the $162 future value? Invested at 4 percent, $133 will grow to $162 in five years. A similar analysis could be done with respect to the value of tax deferral on Mary's IRA contribution, or any other tax deferral provision.

One way of thinking about tax deferral is that it resembles an interest-free loan from the government. Suppose the Smiths' $750 tax liability had not been deferred, but that the government had given them a $750 interest-free loan with which to pay the tax, with repayment of the loan due in five years. They would then be able to keep their $750 in the savings account for the next five years, earning an annual after-tax return of 4 percent. They would be in exactly the same economic position as if their tax liability simply had been deferred for five years.

The value of deferral, then, is a function of two things: (1) the length of the deferral period, and (2) the rate of return the taxpayer can earn on investments during the deferral period. If the deferral period is long enough, and the rate of return is high enough, "mere" deferral can be almost as valuable as permanent exclusion. The present value table (Table 1-1) can be used to determine the benefit of deferral for various deferral periods and rates of return. Suppose a taxpayer is able to defer $1,000 of tax liability for 20 years, and to earn an 8 percent after-tax return on investment during the deferral period. Reading down the 8 percent column and across the 20-year row, the present value of $1 at the end of 20 years is 21.5 cents. That means the taxpayer could fully fund his eventual $1,000 liability by investing just $215 today. In other words, being able to defer the tax for 20 years gives the taxpayer 78.5 percent of the benefit he would realize if he were *never* required to pay the tax. When deferral can be that significant, it is a serious mistake to describe a tax issue as involving "merely" a question of timing.

Table 1-1
Present value of $1 at end of specified future year assuming specified discount rate

					Discount Rate					
Years	1%	2%	3%	4%	5%	6%	7%	8%	10%	12%
1	.990	.980	.971	.962	.952	.943	.935	.926	.909	.893
2	.980	.961	.943	.925	.907	.890	.873	.857	.826	.797
3	.971	.942	.915	.889	.864	.840	.816	.794	.751	.712
4	.961	.924	.888	.855	.823	.792	.763	.735	.683	.636
5	.951	.906	.863	.822	.784	.747	.713	.681	.621	.567
6	.942	.888	.837	.790	.746	.705	.666	.630	.564	.507
7	.933	.871	.813	.760	.711	.665	.623	.583	.513	.452
8	.923	.853	.789	.731	.677	.627	.582	.540	.467	.404
9	.914	.837	.766	.703	.645	.592	.544	.500	.424	.361
10	.905	.820	.744	.676	.614	.558	.508	.463	.386	.322
15	.861	.743	.642	.555	.481	.417	.362	.315	.239	.183
20	.820	.673	.554	.456	.377	.312	.258	.215	.149	.104
25	.780	.610	.478	.375	.295	.233	.184	.146	.092	.059
30	.742	.552	.412	.308	.231	.174	.131	.099	.057	.033
35	.706	.500	.355	.253	.181	.130	.094	.068	.036	.019
40	.672	.453	.307	.208	.142	.097	.067	.046	.022	.011
45	.639	.410	.264	.171	.111	.073	.048	.031	.014	.006
50	.608	.372	.228	.141	.087	.054	.034	.021	.009	.003

3.   *Taxing Income, and the Elusive Concept of Ability to Pay*

Although the government obviously needs to tax *something*, it is not so obvious that the major source of general-purpose federal revenues should be a tax on *income*. What makes an income tax a better choice than, for example, a federal sales tax or a federal property tax? The standard justification for using income as the tax base is that (1) taxes should be imposed on individuals in accordance with their relative abilities to pay, and (2) a person's income is the best practical measure of her ability to pay tax.

It is not self-evident, however, that income is the best measure of ability to pay. Consider two hypothetical taxpayers. Alfred has $50,000 income but no wealth; Brenda also has $50,000 income, but owns assets worth $1 million. Do they really have equal abilities to pay tax? If they do not, perhaps a wealth tax would be a better choice than an income tax. Unfortunately, a wealth tax has problems of its own. It would require regular appraisals of untold numbers of assets, and it could create serious cash flow problems for taxpayers owning valuable but illiquid assets.[26] Moreover, the designers of a wealth tax would have to decide how to deal with human capital. For the majority of people, their most valuable asset is their human capital — that is, the present value of the future income stream they can produce by working. If a wealth tax were imposed on human capital, the valuation and liquidity problems would be immense. At a more theoretical level, it is arguable that one's human capital does not give rise to any *present* ability to pay tax, except to the extent the human capital produces wages in the current year.[27] These considerations might lead to the exclusion of human capital from the base of a wealth tax, but it may not make sense to have a wealth tax at all if the most significant kind of wealth is excluded from the tax base. All this suggests that income might be preferable to wealth as a measure of ability to pay, despite its obvious imperfections.

In any event, today's leading candidate to replace the income tax is not a wealth tax. Instead, a number of politicians and academics have advocated replacing the income tax with some type of consumption tax. Consumption taxes can take several different forms. The familiar state or local retail sales tax is a consumption tax, as are the value-added taxes common in much of the world. The "flat tax" championed several years ago by Steve Forbes is actually a version of a value-added tax.

It would be possible to convert the current income tax to a consumption tax. Consider the following equation:

$$\text{Income} = \text{Consumption} + \text{Savings, or } I = C + S$$

There is nothing very profound about this. The equation is based on the fact that there are only two things one can do with one's income — spend it or save it.

---

26. It might also be unconstitutional, as an unapportioned "direct" tax, in violation of Art. I, Sec. 2, cl. 3, and Art. I, Sec. 9, cl. 4 of the U.S. Constitution. The Sixteenth Amendment removes the apportionment requirement only for "income" taxes, and a wealth tax is presumably not an income tax. (The federal estate tax has been interpreted as an excise tax on the transfer of wealth, rather than as a direct tax on the wealth itself.) For more on the constitutional issues, see Chapter 3.

27. Sometimes a person can generate cash by borrowing against the future income stream to be produced by her human capital, but usually the borrowed cash must be used to finance either the person's education or the purchase of a home. If so, the borrowed cash would not be available for the payment of tax.

Income defined in terms of sources (the left side of the equation) must equal income defined in terms of uses (the right side of the equation). It is important to note, however, that savings (S) can be either positive or negative. S will be negative for a particular taxpayer for a particular year if she finances consumption by spending out of existing savings or by borrowing. For example, a taxpayer might consume $80,000, despite having income of only $60,000, if she spends either $20,000 of her savings or $20,000 of borrowed money.

To a consumption tax advocate, the most interesting aspect of the above equation is that it suggests a simple way to turn the income tax into a consumption tax. If $I = C + S$, then it follows that $C = I - S$. All that would be needed to convert the income tax to a consumption tax would be to allow an unlimited deduction for savings (and to tax consumption financed by prior years' savings or by borrowing). It is only a slight exaggeration to say that the income tax could be converted to a consumption tax simply by repealing the dollar ceiling on deductible IRA contributions imposed by §219(b).[28]

While this change might be simple enough as a technical matter, would it be a policy improvement? If the idea is to have a tax base that corresponds to ability to pay, is consumption a better base than income? For many people, the intuitive response is that consumption is inferior to income as an indicator of ability to pay; saved income generates ability to pay to at least the same extent as consumed income. In fact, the idea that saved income generates ability to pay is the most compelling argument for the superiority of an income tax to a consumption tax. Consumption tax proponents usually make their case on other grounds. For some, the fatal flaw of the income tax is that its taxation of saved income, coupled with its taxation of the return on investment (e.g., interest and dividends), encourages taxpayers to consume now rather than to save and invest to finance future consumption. A consumption tax, by contrast, is neutral as between current consumption and saving for future consumption. Other consumption tax proponents seem to believe in the moral superiority of savers over spenders, and so are attracted by a tax imposed on dollars spent but not on dollars saved.

As the explanation of a consumption tax in terms of IRAs suggests, the base of the actual income tax is much narrower than economic income. The classic economist's definition of a person's income for a particular period, commonly known as the Haig-Simons definition, is: "[T]he algebraic sum of (1) the market value of rights exercised in consumption and (2) the change in the value of the store of property rights between the beginning and the end of the period in question."[29] Even in the Introductory Problem, important differences between Haig-Simons income and taxable income are apparent. Haig-Simons income would include the $2,000 contributed by Mary to her IRA. It would also include any unrealized appreciation in the Smiths' stock. Both of these statutory moves away from Haig-Simons income are steps in the direction of a consumption tax. Not taxing unrealized appreciation and retirement savings, although inconsistent with the Haig-Simons definition of *income,* is appropriate under a tax on *consumption* (because a taxpayer has not consumed either unrealized appreciation or money saved for retirement). It is arguable, however, that these departures of the income tax from Haig-Simons purity make sense in terms of ability to pay. Some forms of unrealized appreciation are difficult to convert to cash (albeit not unrealized

---

28. Generally, §219(b) limits the deductible amount of an IRA contribution to $5,000.
29. Henry Simons, *Personal Income Taxation* 50, 61-62, 206 (1938).

appreciation in Microsoft stock), and thus may not give rise to current ability to pay. Similarly, amounts that one must (in the exercise of prudence) save for retirement are not available for current payment of tax. In any event, the consumption tax features of the current income tax — especially the treatments of unrealized appreciation and of the various types of tax-favored retirement savings — are so significant that the "income" tax label is almost arbitrary. Ours is an income tax with significant consumption tax features, but it could nearly as well be described as a consumption tax with significant income tax features.

Designing a tax that fairly allocates burdens among taxpayers according to their relative abilities to pay is not simply a matter of selecting the right tax base. Even assuming taxable income is the right base, there is still the question of rates. If ability to pay rises proportionately with income, then tax liabilities should rise proportionately with income. A person with $100,000 income, for example, should pay twice the tax of a person with $50,000 income. This can be accomplished by imposing tax at a single ("flat") rate on all income. If ability to pay rises more than proportionately with income, then average tax rates should be progressive. For example, a person with $100,000 income should pay more than twice the tax of a person with $50,000 income. The current income tax uses progressive marginal rates to produce progressive average rates.

Try this thought experiment. A country has only two types of residents, with an equal number of each: the Highs, each of whom earns $100,000 a year, and the Lows, each of whom earns $50,000 a year. If the government is going to impose an income tax, and needs to raise $30,000 from each High-Low pair of people, what rate structure would best distribute the tax burden between Highs and Lows according to their relative abilities to pay? Rather than a flat rate (of 20%), or even a moderately progressive marginal rate structure, doesn't a focus on ability to pay suggest the entire $30,000 burden should be placed on the High taxpayer? This could be done by imposing a tax rate of zero on each taxpayer's first $70,000 of income, and a tax rate of 100 percent on all income above $70,000. Even with the 100 percent tax on his last $30,000 of income, a High taxpayer would still have more money after-tax than a Low (non)taxpayer ($70,000 versus $50,000), which suggests that High is more able to pay $30,000 than Low is to pay even $1.

If tax is supposed to be based on ability to pay, why are actual tax rate schedules so different from this 0 percent/100 percent model? There are two answers. First, one may object on moral or ethical grounds to confiscatory marginal tax rates. Under this view, the ability-to-pay principle must be modified to take into account the principle that people are entitled to retain a significant portion of the fruits of their labors. Notice, however, that this principle would reject the 0 percent/100 percent tax rate structure only if the principle applies to the *marginal* fruits of one's labor. After all, a High taxpayer pays the same tax under the 0 percent/100 percent rate structure as he would under a 30 percent flat tax, and a 30 percent flat tax would not violate the principle. The second — and perhaps more persuasive — objection to the 0 percent/100 percent rate structure is merely practical. Faced with a marginal tax rate of 100 percent on income above $70,000, the Highs would respond by earning little or no income above $70,000, and the system would fail to produce significant revenue. Under this view, ability-to-pay concerns would call for a 0 percent/100 percent rate structure, but for the disincentive effects of confiscatory marginal tax rates. The actual rate structure, then, must depart significantly from the 0 percent/100 percent ideal in order to avoid the undesirable behavioral effects of extremely high marginal tax rates.

4. *The Tax Expenditure Budget*

STAFF OF THE JOINT COMMITTEE ON TAXATION, ESTIMATES OF FEDERAL TAX EXPENDITURES FOR FISCAL YEARS 2010-2014

(2010)

I. THE CONCEPT OF TAX EXPENDITURES

"Tax expenditures" are defined under the Congressional Budget and Impoundment Control Act of 1974 ("the Budget Act") as "revenue losses attributable to provisions of the Federal tax laws which allow a special exclusion, exemption, or deduction from gross income or which provide a special credit, a preferential rate of tax, or a deferral of tax liability." Thus, tax expenditures include any reductions in income tax liabilities that result from special tax provisions or regulations that provide tax benefits to particular taxpayers.

Special income tax provisions are referred to as tax expenditures because they may be considered to be analogous to direct outlay programs, and the two can be considered as alternative means of accomplishing similar budget policy objectives. Tax expenditures are similar to those direct spending programs that are available as entitlements to those who meet the statutory criteria established for the programs.

Estimates of tax expenditures are prepared for use in budget analysis. They are a measure of the economic benefits that are provided through the tax laws to various groups of taxpayers and sectors of the economy. The estimates also may be useful in determining the relative merits of achieving specified public goals through tax benefits or direct outlays. It is appropriate to evaluate tax expenditures with respect to cost, distributional consequences, alternative means of provision, and economic effects and to allow policymakers to evaluate the tradeoffs among these and other potentially competing policy goals.

The legislative history of the Budget Act indicates that tax expenditures are to be defined with reference to a normal income tax structure (referred to here as "normal income tax law"). The determination of whether a provision is a tax expenditure is made on the basis of a broad concept of income that is larger in scope than "income" as defined under general U.S. income tax principles. The Joint Committee staff has used its judgment in distinguishing between those income tax provisions (and regulations) that can be viewed as a part of normal income tax law and those special provisions that result in tax expenditures. A provision traditionally has been listed as a tax expenditure by the Joint Committee staff if there is a reasonable basis for such classification and the provision results in more than a de minimis revenue loss, which solely for this purpose means a total revenue loss of less than $50 million over the five fiscal years 2010-14. The Joint Committee staff emphasizes, however, that in the process of listing tax expenditures, no judgment is made, nor any implication intended, about the desirability of any special tax provision as a matter of public policy. . . .

Some provisions in the Internal Revenue Code provide for special tax treatment that is less favorable than normal income tax law. Examples of such provisions include (1) the denial of deductions for certain lobbying expenses, (2) the denial of deductions for certain executive compensation, and (3) the two-percent floor on itemized deductions for unreimbursed employee expenses. Tax provisions that provide treatment less favorable than normal income tax law and are not directly related to progressivity are called negative tax expenditures. . . .

INDIVIDUAL INCOME TAX

Under the Joint Committee staff methodology, the normal structure of the individual income tax includes the following major components: one personal exemption for each taxpayer and one for each dependent, the standard deduction, the existing tax rate schedule, and deductions for investment and employee business expenses. Most other tax benefits to individual taxpayers can be classified as exceptions to normal income tax law.

The Joint Committee staff views the personal exemptions and the standard deduction as defining the zero-rate bracket that is a part of normal tax law. An itemized deduction that is not necessary for the generation of income is classified as a tax expenditure, but only to the extent that it, when added to a taxpayer's other itemized deductions, exceeds the standard deduction.

All employee compensation is subject to tax unless the Code contains a specific exclusion for the income. . . . Each of these exclusions is classified as a tax expenditure in this report.

Under normal income tax law, employer contributions to pension plans and income earned on pension assets generally would be taxable to employees as the contributions are made and as the income is earned, and employees would not receive any deduction or exclusion for their pension contributions. Under present law, employer contributions to qualified pension plans and employee contributions made at the election of the employee through salary reduction are not taxed until distributed to the employee, and income earned on pension assets is not taxed until distributed. The tax expenditure for "net exclusion of pension contributions and earnings" is computed as the income taxes forgone on current tax-excluded pension contributions and earnings less the income taxes paid on current pension distributions (including the 10-percent additional tax paid on early withdrawals from pension plans). . . .

The individual income tax does not include in gross income the imputed income that individuals receive from the services provided by owner-occupied homes and durable goods. However, the Joint Committee staff does not classify this exclusion as a tax expenditure. The measurement of imputed income for tax purposes presents administrative problems and its exclusion from taxable income may be regarded as an administrative necessity. Under normal income tax law, individuals would be allowed to deduct only the interest on indebtedness incurred in connection with a trade or business or an investment. Thus, the deduction for mortgage interest on a principal or second residence is classified as a tax expenditure.

The Joint Committee staff assumes that, for administrative feasibility, normal income tax law would tax capital gains in full in the year the gains are realized through sale, exchange, gift, or transfer at death. Thus, the deferral of tax until realization is not classified as a tax expenditure. However, reduced rates of tax, further deferrals of tax (beyond the year of sale, exchange, gift, or transfer at death), and exclusions of certain capital gains are classified as tax expenditures. Because of the same concern for administrative feasibility, it also is assumed that normal income tax law would not provide for any indexing of the basis of capital assets for changes in the general price level. Thus, under normal income tax law (as under present law), the income tax would be levied on nominal gains as opposed to real gains in asset values. . . .

II. Measurement of Tax Expenditures

TAX EXPENDITURE CALCULATION GENERALLY

A tax expenditure is measured by the difference between tax liability under present law and the tax liability that would result from a recomputation of tax without benefit of the tax expenditure provision. Taxpayer behavior is assumed to remain unchanged for tax expenditure estimate purposes. . . .

Each tax expenditure is calculated separately, under the assumption that all other tax expenditures remain in the Code. If two or more tax expenditures were estimated simultaneously, the total change in tax liability could be smaller or larger than the sum of the amounts shown for each item separately, as a result of inter-actions among the tax expenditure provisions.

Year-to-year differences in the calculations for each tax expenditure reflect changes in tax law, including phaseouts of tax expenditure provisions and changes that alter the definition of the normal income tax structure, such as the tax rate schedule, the personal exemption amount, and the standard deduction. . . .

If a tax expenditure program were eliminated, Congress might choose to continue financial assistance through other means rather than terminate all federal assistance for the activity. If a replacement spending program were enacted, the higher revenues received as a result of the elimination of a tax expenditure might not represent a net budget gain. . . .

TAX EXPENDITURES VERSUS REVENUE ESTIMATES

A tax expenditure estimate is not the same as a revenue estimate for the repeal of the tax expenditure provision [for several reasons, one of which is that] tax expenditure calculations do not incorporate the effects of the behavioral changes that are anticipated to occur in response to the repeal of a tax expenditure provision. . . .

III. Tax Expenditure Estimates

Tax expenditures are grouped in Table 1 in the same functional categories as outlays in the Federal budget. . . .

Notes and Questions

1. *Compared to what?* The basic idea behind the tax expenditure concept is that it is possible to define a normative ("normal") income tax base, and that any narrowing of taxable income relative to the normative tax base should be analyzed as a federal subsidy administered through the tax

system. Is the definition of the normative tax base so arbitrary as to make this exercise pointless? Are you persuaded, for example, by the Joint Committee Staff's explanation of why the deferral of tax on unrealized appreciation is not a tax expenditure? Does "administrative feasibility" require deferral of taxation of appreciation in stock traded on the New York Stock Exchange?

2. *If a consumption tax is the norm.* What difference would it make to the tax expenditure budget if we thought of the current tax as a consumption tax with some income tax features, rather than as an income tax with some consumption tax features? The exclusion of employer-provided pensions is the largest single item in the tax expenditure budget, yet that exclusion would not be a tax expenditure at all if expenditures were defined as deviations from a comprehensive *consumption* tax base.

3. *Lower rate brackets as tax expenditures.* Although the normative income tax used for tax expenditure analysis has a very different *base* from the actual income tax, it has exactly the same *rates* as the actual tax. In other words, nothing in the basic tax rate structure is considered a tax expenditure. Would it make sense to think of all marginal tax rates below the top rate as subsidies for lower and middle income taxpayers?

4. *Alternative non-tax subsidies.* Despite the shaky theoretical underpinnings of the tax expenditure budget, much of the information contained in the budget is undeniably interesting and useful. In evaluating the child care credit, for example, it is helpful to know that repeal of the credit might finance direct federal child care subsidies of about $2.5 billion annually.[30] Alternatively, if one does not favor either indirect or direct federal subsidies for child care, repeal of the credit might finance across-the-board income tax rate cuts totaling about $2.5 billion per year.

5. *Tax expenditures as "upside-down subsidies."* The early proponents of the tax expenditure concept hoped that viewing tax expenditures as an alternative to direct federal expenditures would lead to the repeal of some tax expenditures. In particular, they hoped that many exclusions and deductions would be rejected as "upside-down subsidies." Their point can be illustrated by considering two employees — one with a marginal tax rate of 10 percent, the other with a marginal tax rate of 30 percent — each of whom is allowed to exclude $1,000 worth of employer-provided parking at work. If the exclusion is intended as a subsidy, it seems perverse — "upside-down" — to give a $300 subsidy to the richer employee and only a $100 subsidy to the poorer employee. If a commuting subsidy is desired, but the upside-down feature is not, the exclusion could be replaced by grants administered outside the tax system, or it could be converted to a tax credit. The credit could be based on the same credit percentage for all taxpayers, or it could be a "right-side-up subsidy," with the credit percentage declining as income increases (as in the case of the §21 child care credit). The upside-down subsidy critique applies, however, only to exclusions and deductions that serve as subsidies, rather than as refinements of the concept of net income (i.e., income available for consumption or

---

30. Note, however, the warning of the Joint Committee Staff, that "[a] tax expenditure estimate is not the same as a revenue estimate for the repeal of the tax expenditure provision," because the tax expenditure estimates do not take into account any behavioral changes that might result from repeal.

Table 1
[Selected] Tax Expenditure Estimates by Budget Function, Fiscal Years 2010-2014
[Billions of dollars]

Function	Corporations					Individuals					Total
	2010	2011	2012	2013	2014	2010	2011	2012	2013	2014	2010-14
Housing:											
Deduction for mortgage interest on owner-occupied residences	.....	.....	.....	.....	.....	90.8	93.8	94.1	98.5	106.8	484.1
Deduction for property taxes on real property	.....	.....	.....	.....	.....	15.0	22.8	26.5	27.6	29.1	120.9
Exclusion of capital gains on sales of principal residences	.....	.....	.....	.....	.....	15.0	16.5	17.5	18.2	19.0	86.3
Other business and commerce:											
Reduced rates of tax on dividends and long-term capital gains	.....	.....	.....	.....	.....	77.7	84.2	65.9	90.3	84.9	402.9
Exclusion of capital gains at death	.....	.....	.....	.....	.....	25.4	31.7	39.0	45.6	52.3	194.0
Transportation:											
Exclusion of employer-paid transportation benefits	.....	.....	.....	.....	.....	3.8	4.2	4.4	4.6	4.8	21.8
Education and training:											
Credits for tuition for post-secondary education:											
Hope Credit	.....	.....	.....	.....	.....	9.6	4.7	3.0	3.0	2.9	23.1
Lifetime Learning Credit	.....	.....	.....	.....	.....	2.3	3.0	3.2	3.2	3.1	14.7
Deduction for charitable contributions to educational institutions	0.4	0.4	0.4	0.4	0.4	5.1	6.0	6.5	6.8	7.1	33.3
Employment:											
Exclusion of benefits provided under cafeteria plans[1]	.....	.....	.....	.....	.....	26.4	29.3	32.3	36.1	39.0	163.1
Exclusion of housing allowances for ministers	.....	.....	.....	.....	.....	0.6	0.7	0.7	0.7	0.7	3.4
Exclusion of miscellaneous fringe benefits	.....	.....	.....	.....	.....	6.6	7.5	8.0	8.2	8.5	38.7
Exclusion of income earned by voluntary employees' beneficiary associations	.....	.....	.....	.....	.....	3.2	3.8	4.2	4.4	4.6	20.2
Social services:											
Credit for children under age 17[2]	.....	.....	.....	.....	.....	55.1	24.7	14.2	14.0	13.9	121.9
Credit for child and dependent care and exclusion of employer-provided child care[3]	.....	.....	.....	.....	.....	3.1	2.5	2.5	2.5	2.5	13.1

Deduction for charitable contributions, other than for education and health	1.0	1.0	1.0	1.1	1.1	29.2	34.5	37.8	39.6	41.3	187.5
Health:											
Exclusion of employer contributions for health care, health insurance premiums, and long-term care insurance premiums[4]	.....	.....	.....	.....	.....	105.7	117.3	128.0	147.4	161.0	659.4
Deduction for medical expenses and long-term care expenses	.....	.....	.....	.....	.....	10.8	13.5	16.1	17.5	19.6	77.6
Exclusion of workers' compensation benefits (medical benefits)	.....	.....	.....	.....	.....	3.0	3.2	3.5	3.7	4.0	17.4
Deduction for charitable contributions to health organizations	1.8	1.8	1.9	1.9	2.0	2.5	3.0	3.3	3.5	3.6	25.3
Income Security:											
Exclusion of damages on account of personal physical injuries or physical sickness	.....	.....	.....	.....	.....	1.5	1.6	1.6	1.6	1.6	7.9
Net exclusion of pension contributions and earnings:											
Defined benefit plans	.....	.....	.....	.....	.....	38.9	51.9	62.0	75.8	74.6	303.2
Defined contribution plans	.....	.....	.....	.....	.....	32.5	38.2	44.1	49.1	48.3	212.2
Traditional IRAs	.....	.....	.....	.....	.....	20.1	12.3	13.2	18.4	21.6	85.6
Roth IRAs	.....	.....	.....	.....	.....	3.4	4.0	4.8	5.4	6.3	23.9
Premiums on group term life insurance (excludes payroll taxes)	.....	.....	.....	.....	.....	1.5	1.6	1.7	1.8	1.9	8.5
Earned income credit[2]	.....	.....	.....	.....	.....	56.2	52.4	52.5	53.6	54.0	268.8
General Purpose Fiscal Assistance:											
Exclusion of interest on public purpose State and local government debt	7.5	8.5	9.0	9.9	10.4	19.3	21.9	23.1	25.3	26.7	161.6
Deduction of nonbusiness State and local government income taxes, sales taxes, and personal property taxes	.....	.....	.....	.....	.....	30.7	43.6	50.6	54.1	58.3	237.3

[1] Estimate includes amounts of employer-provided health insurance purchased through cafeteria plans and employer-provided child care purchased through dependent care flexible spending accounts. These amounts are also included in other line items in this table.

[2] [The $121.9 billion total child tax credit for 2010-2014 includes refundable amounts of $56.7 billion, and the $268.8 billion total EIC for 2010-14 includes refundable amounts of $232.2 billion.]

[3] Estimate includes employer-provided child care purchased through dependent care flexible spending accounts.

[4] Estimate includes employer-provided health insurance purchased through cafeteria plans.

saving). Consider, for example, the theft loss deduction of §165(c)(3). The usual rationale for the deduction is that earning money and then losing it to a thief is the practical equivalent of never having earned the money — in either case, nothing is available for consumption or saving. Suppose Carl earns $51,000 and has $1,000 cash stolen from him, while Donna earns $50,000 and suffers no theft loss. If we believe that Carl and Donna have equal abilities to consume and save, and so should bear equal tax burdens, we can accomplish that goal by allowing Carl to *deduct* his $1,000 theft loss.[31] Allowing Carl to claim a theft loss *credit* would achieve the desired equalization of tax liabilities only if the credit percentage happened to equal Carl's marginal tax rate.

6. *Accelerated obsolescence.* The 2010-2014 tax expenditure estimates excerpted above were released by the Joint Committee on Taxation on December 15, 2010. They reflected the fact that many of the temporary tax reductions enacted in 2001 and 2003 (commonly referred to as the "Bush tax cuts") were scheduled to expire at the end of 2010. As it turned out, a mere two days later — on December 17 — President Obama signed legislation extending most of the temporary reductions through the end of 2012. Many of the Joint Committee's tax expenditure estimates for 2011 and 2012 would have been different if they had been issued after the extension of the temporary tax reductions. For example, the dramatic reduction from 2010 to 2011 in the child tax credit estimate was based on the assumption that the 2011 credit would be $500 per child, rather than $1,000 (as in 2010). With the $1,000 credit now extended through 2012, the 2011 and 2012 tax expenditure amounts for the child tax credit should be similar to the 2010 amounts, with the dramatic reduction delayed until 2013. (Actually, it is likely that further legislation will extend the $1,000 credit well beyond 2012.)

5.   *Sources of Tax Law and the Basics of Tax Litigation*

Like all taxes, the income tax is imposed by statute. Although some income tax doctrines (such as the deferral of tax on unrealized appreciation) are loosely referred to as "common law" rules, this only means that the doctrines represent judicial interpretations of vague or general statutory provisions. In the absence of a tax statute, there is no tax.

Moving upward in the hierarchy of authority, the Internal Revenue Code is, of course, subject to any constraints imposed by the U.S. Constitution. Some older Supreme Court cases struck down various income tax provisions on constitutional grounds, but in recent decades the courts have been very reluctant to find constitutional infirmities in the federal income tax. Moving downward in the hierarchy, regulations promulgated by the Treasury Department under the Code (either under the general authority granted by §7805(a), or under a more specific grant of authority with respect to a particular provision) have the force of law unless they

---

31. In fact, §165(c)(3) would not precisely equalize the tax liabilities of Carl and Donna, because of several limitations on the extent to which theft losses are deductible. The limitations are explained in Chapter 5.

are inconsistent with the statute. Although courts invalidate regulations more often than they find constitutional violations in the statute, judicial invalidation of regulations is not common. In some cases, Congress has delegated to the Treasury the authority to establish substantive rules, rather than merely to interpret the Code.[32] Regulations promulgated under such broad grants of authority are commonly referred to as "legislative" regulations, in contrast to "interpretive" regulations. Because the grants of authority are so broad, legislative regulations are seldom invalidated.[33] Interpretive regulations are at greater risk of invalidation, but if a court believes that a Code provision could reasonably be interpreted in more than one way, it will uphold *any* reasonable regulatory interpretation.[34]

Below regulations in the hierarchy of authority are revenue rulings and revenue procedures published by the Internal Revenue Service. A revenue ruling sets forth the Service's view as to how the Code applies to a hypothetical set of facts. Unlike a regulation, a ruling does not have a presumption of validity or correctness, and courts frequently reject IRS positions expressed in rulings. A taxpayer may, however, rely on a factually applicable taxpayer-favorable ruling (unless and until the IRS revokes the ruling). Revenue procedures have the same legal status as revenue rulings, but they resemble regulations in format, in contrast with the use of hypothetical facts typical of rulings.

A taxpayer contemplating a major transaction of uncertain tax consequences may, for a fee, request a private letter ruling from the IRS. The taxpayer submits to the IRS a description of the proposed transaction and the taxpayer's argument as to why favorable tax treatment is warranted under the applicable law. If the IRS issues a favorable ruling, the taxpayer to whom the ruling is issued may rely on it, even if the IRS later decides the legal analysis in the ruling is wrong.[35] A taxpayer may reject the conclusion of an unfavorable ruling and proceed with the planned transaction, although one should expect to be audited if one reports the tax consequences of a transaction inconsistently with an unfavorable ruling.[36] Letter rulings are not officially published, but they are made available to the public (after redaction of taxpayer-identifying information) by the IRS, and they are unofficially published by commercial publishers (both print and electronic). The major difference between a letter ruling and a revenue ruling is that a taxpayer's reliance on a letter ruling issued to another taxpayer is not protected.[37] If a taxpayer desires protected reliance and there is no revenue ruling on point, he must request his own letter ruling.

---

32. *See, e.g.,* §121(c)(2)(B) (authorizing Treasury to issue regulations defining what, if anything, qualifies as "unforeseen circumstances" for purposes of the exclusion of gain from the sale of a principal residence).

33. For a rare invalidation of a legislative regulation (in the rather arcane area of consolidated corporate returns), *see* Rite Aid Corp. v. United States, 255 F.3d 1357 (Fed. Cir. 2001).

34. Chevron U.S.A. v. Natural Resources Defense Council, 467 U.S. 837 (1984) (the leading case on judicial deference to reasonable regulatory interpretations; not a tax case); Mayo Foundation for Medical Education and Research v. United States, 131 S. Ct. 704 (2011). In *Mayo Foundation*, the Supreme Court made clear that interpretive tax regulations are entitled to deference under the usual *Chevron* standard. Despite being entitled to *Chevron* deference, interpretive regulations are at somewhat greater risk of invalidation than legislative regulations, simply because the range of regulatory approaches that would be consistent with the statute is ordinarily narrower for interpretive regulations than for legislative regulations.

35. A taxpayer is not entitled to rely on a private letter ruling, however, if the IRS finds that the facts of the actual case are at variance with the taxpayer's representations in the ruling request.

36. Taxpayers usually withdraw ruling requests once the IRS has indicated a ruling would be unfavorable. This also involves a heightened risk of audit.

37. In fact, §6110(k)(3) provides that letter rulings "may not be used or cited as precedent," although the meaning of "as precedent" is less than perfectly clear.

Tax legislation is commonly accompanied by very detailed reports from the House Ways and Means Committee and the Senate Finance Committee. The Treasury and the IRS rely heavily on these committee reports in interpreting the Code, and most courts are strongly influenced by the reports as well. An old joke among tax lawyers (not terribly funny, but that's typical of tax lawyer jokes) is that one should consult the statute only when the legislative history is unclear. After the enactment of major tax legislation, the Staff of the Joint Committee on Taxation usually publishes a "General Explanation" — a "Bluebook," to aficionados — describing the legislation. Bluebooks are largely compiled from the House and Senate committee reports, but they often contain original material as well. Because they are written after legislation has been enacted, Bluebooks are not really legislative history, and they do not have the authority of preenactment committee reports. Nevertheless, Treasury and the IRS normally interpret Code provisions in accordance with the Bluebook. One practical advantage of Bluebooks for busy practitioners is that they describe the law actually enacted, whereas the preenactment committee reports may describe provisions that never became law, or that were revised before enactment.[38]

In addition to these legislative and regulatory authorities, there are thousands of federal judicial opinions interpreting the Code. If a taxpayer wants to litigate a dispute with the IRS (after having exhausted administrative remedies), he may choose any one of three judicial forums: the U.S. District Court for the district in which the taxpayer resides, the Court of Federal Claims, or the U.S. Tax Court.[39] The taxpayer can gain entry to a district court or the Court of Federal Claims only by paying the disputed tax and suing for a refund. The Tax Court, by contrast, allows the taxpayer to litigate without having first paid the tax. A taxpayer invokes the jurisdiction of the Tax Court by filing a petition within 90 days of the date of a notice of deficiency issued by the IRS.

The Tax Court, which has its headquarters in Washington, D.C., consists of 19 judges. Tax Court judges ride circuit throughout the country, so a taxpayer does not have to travel to Washington to present her case. Most Tax Court opinions are issued by a single judge, but the chief judge of the court may submit cases of particular importance to a panel of all judges, sitting en banc. All Tax Court trials are bench trials; there are no juries in the Tax Court. (There are also no juries in the Court of Federal Claims.) The chief judge designates opinions as either "memorandum" or "regular" opinions. In general, a memorandum opinion applies well-established law to the facts of a particular case, while a regular opinion involves more interesting legal issues. Both types of opinions have precedential value, although regular opinions have somewhat greater weight, and en banc opinions (identified as "reviewed by the Court") have particularly strong precedential value. The appeal from either the Tax Court or a district court is to the U.S. Court of Appeals for the circuit in which the taxpayer resides. An appeal from the Court of Federal Claims, however, lies with the Court of Appeals for the Federal Circuit.

If a taxpayer loses a case begun in Tax Court, he must pay not only the deficiency, but also interest running from the original due date of the return, at

---

38. For further detail on this distinction, see Redlark v. Comm'r in Chapter 4.B, especially note 4 following that case.

39. In addition, if the taxpayer is bankrupt when the IRS asserts a deficiency, the tax dispute may be litigated in bankruptcy court.

the "Federal short-term rate" plus three percentage points.[40] Conversely, if the taxpayer wins a refund case begun in district court or in the Court of Federal Claims, the government will pay the taxpayer both the amount of the overpayment and interest on the overpayment (running from the date of the overpayment, at the same interest rate applicable to underpayments determined in Tax Court).

How should a taxpayer choose among the three forums? For many taxpayers, the ability to litigate in Tax Court without paying first takes precedence over all other considerations. This explains why the bulk of tax litigation occurs in Tax Court. If one is not averse to paying first, however, the choice becomes more interesting. If the taxpayer's case is legally weak but emotionally appealing, district court is probably the best choice because that is the only forum in which a jury trial is available. If a jury trial is not important, the choice should be whichever court has the most taxpayer-favorable precedent on the issue in the case. Since the Tax Court handles many times more tax cases than either the Court of Federal Claims or any district court, often the only relevant precedent is from the Tax Court.[41] In that case, one simply chooses the Tax Court if its precedent is favorable, and another forum if the Tax Court precedent is unfavorable. In evaluating Tax Court precedent, it is important to keep in mind that the Tax Court will decide a case in accordance with controlling precedent in the circuit to which the case is appealable, even if the Tax Court disagrees with that precedent.[42]

---

40. *See* §§6601 and 6621.

41. In searching for precedents outside the Tax Court, one should consult the officially unpublished tax decisions collected by commercial publishers, as well as decisions appearing in the official reporters.

42. This is referred to as the *Golsen* rule, after the case in which this approach was adopted by the Tax Court. Golsen v. Commissioner, 54 T.C. 742 (1970), *aff'd without discussion of this issue*, 445 F.2d 985 (10th Cir.), *cert. denied*, 404 U.S. 940 (1971).

Cell

UNDERSTANDING TAX RATES: AVERAGE RATES, MARGINAL RATES, AND PHASEOUTS

A. Average Rates and Marginal Rates

B. Phaseouts

    1. Personal Exemptions

       Problems 1-2

    2. Other Phaseouts

       Problems 3-6

A. AVERAGE RATES AND MARGINAL RATES

Take a look at the tax rate schedules in §1 for married couples filing joint returns, for heads of households, and for unmarried individuals. All the rate schedules feature progressive marginal rates. This means that the first several thousand dollars of income are taxed at a low rate, a somewhat higher rate applies to the next several thousand dollars of income, and still higher rates apply to additional dollars of income. Although you can't tell it from reading §1, the rate of tax on the first several thousand dollars of income — roughly equaling the official poverty level — is actually zero. This effectively zero-rated bracket is created by the standard deduction of §63 and the personal exemptions of §151. Taken together, the standard deduction and personal exemptions exempt subsistence-level income from tax. The tax rates of §1 apply only to the income that is left after subtraction of the standard deduction and personal exemptions.

    To understand the basic operation of a progressive marginal tax rate structure, consider a very simple two-bracket rate structure, with a 10 percent tax rate on the first $20,000 of income and a 30 percent rate on all additional income. Suppose Tess has a job which pays $20,000 a year, and she has the option to work some overtime and earn an additional $4,000. What will be the tax consequences to her if she chooses to earn the extra $4,000? If she does not earn the extra money, her entire $20,000 income will be taxed at 10 percent, so she will have a tax liability of $2,000. If she earns the extra money, so that her total earnings are $24,000, her tax liability will increase to $3,200. Her first $20,000 of income is still taxed at 10 percent, generating a tax of $2,000, and the last $4,000 is taxed at 30 percent, generating a tax of $1,200. Thus, she will get to keep $2,800 of her $4,000 overtime earnings. These results are summarized in the table below. The crucial point is that Tess's entering a new rate bracket affects the taxation of only her last $4,000 of income. Having some income taxed at 30 percent does *not* cause her to lose the benefit of having her first $20,000 of income taxed at 10 percent rather than 30 percent. Under the hypothetical tax rate structure, even Bill Gates would pay tax at the rate of only 10 percent on his first $20,000 of income.

	Without Overtime	**With Overtime**
Pre-tax income	$20,000	$24,000
Tax	$2,000 (10% × $20,000)	$3,200 (10% × $20,000, plus 30% × $4,000)
After-tax income	$18,000	$20,800

People sometimes say that they don't want to earn any more income in a given year, because doing so would put them into a higher tax bracket. In many cases, such comments reflect a misunderstanding of how the tax rate system works. For example, Tess might mistakenly believe that if she earns $24,000, so that she is in the 30 percent bracket, *all* her income will be taxed at that rate. If that were true, she would actually have less take-home income if she works the overtime than if she does not. Without the overtime her after-tax income would be $18,000 ($20,000 − $2,000), but with the overtime her after-tax income would be only $16,800 ($24,000 − $7,200). To repeat, however, this is *not* how the system works. In fact, her after-tax income with the overtime will be $20,800 ($24,000 − $3,200), so she will have $2,800 more take-home pay if she earns the overtime than if she does not. Of course, a person in Tess's situation might understand perfectly well how the rate structure operates, and still decide not to work the overtime because it would put her in a higher bracket. That person's reasoning would be that she would be willing to put in the extra hours if she were able to take home $3,600 of her extra earnings (i.e., $4,000 reduced by only a 10 percent tax), but not if she is able to take home only $2,800.

If earning $20,001 instead of $20,000 really did change the tax rate on *all* of one's income from 10 to 30 percent, that would be an example of a massive "cliff effect," which is a tax rule under which a very small change in the taxpayer's income (or some other aspect of the taxpayer's pre-tax situation) results in a huge change in tax liability. For obvious reasons, cliff effects are bad tax policy, and for the most part the Internal Revenue Code avoids them — as illustrated by the fact that earning $20,001 instead of $20,000 would increase Tess's tax liability not by more than $4,000, but only by 30 cents. Hundreds of other provisions of the tax laws, of more specialized application than the §1 rate schedules, are also designed to avoid cliff effects. To pick one example more or less at random, §132(a)(2) allows an employee to exclude from gross income a "qualified employee discount" on services purchased from the employer, as long as the discount does not exceed 20 percent. For example, if an employer sells a service to an employee for $80, when the price to the public is $100, the employee does not have to include anything in income. But what if the price to the employee is $79? Is the inclusion then $21 (cliff effect) or just $1 (no cliff effect)? Not surprisingly, the answer is just $1. *See* §132(c)(1) and Treas. Reg. §1.132-3(e). Be aware, however, that cliff effects are merely uncommon, not nonexistent. One example of a cliff effect can be found in §32(i), which denies the earned income tax credit to any person with investment income of more than $2,200 (adjusted annually for inflation). Investment income of exactly $2,200 has no effect on eligibility for the credit, but one more dollar of investment income means the loss of the entire credit (which can be several thousand dollars).[1]

If Tess does earn $24,000, what will be her tax rate? This is a trick question, because there is more than one definition of tax rate. Her *average* tax rate is her $3,200 tax liability divided by her $24,000 income, or 13.3 percent. However, her *marginal* tax rate—the rate that applies to her last dollars of income—is 30 percent. Both types of rates are important, but for different reasons. If Congress is trying to adjust the distribution of tax burdens among taxpayers of differing incomes, its focus should be on average rates. But for tax planning purposes, the marginal rate is the crucial factor. If, like Tess, you are trying to decide whether to take on some extra work and you want to know how much of the extra earnings you will be able to keep, you need to know not your average tax rate, but your marginal rate. Similarly, if you are trying to decide whether to make a $1,000 deductible donation to your favorite charity and you are wondering how much the donation will cost you after taking the tax savings into account, you need to know your marginal tax rate. The tax savings from a deduction is the amount of the deduction multiplied by the taxpayer's marginal rate. Thus a $1,000 deductible contribution by a taxpayer in the 30 percent bracket will reduce her tax liability by $300, resulting in an after-tax cost of $700 for making the gift. Notice that it is possible for a taxpayer to have two marginal tax rates at the same time—one with respect to additional income, the other with respect to deductions. If Tess has $20,000 income and is deciding whether to earn additional income, her marginal rate is 30 percent. But if she has $20,000 income and is deciding whether to spend money in a way entitling her to a $1,000 deduction, her marginal rate is 10 percent.[2]

It is not too difficult to understand the mechanics of progressive marginal tax rates. Evaluating the merits of such a rate structure can be a considerably more difficult matter, as evidenced by decades of both philosophical and political debates between proponents of progressive marginal rates and proponents of a "flat" (i.e., single-rate) tax system. Here is a thumbnail sketch of one way (by no means the only way) to explain why a society might choose a progressive marginal rate tax system. Begin with the utilitarian premise that the costs of government

---

1. The income tax code features a number of miniature cliff effects. Instead of multiplying their taxable incomes by their various tax rates to determine their tax liabilities, taxpayers with taxable incomes below $100,000 use tax tables included with the Form 1040 instructions. The purpose of the tax tables is simply to relieve low and moderate income taxpayers of a computational burden; the tables indicate the tax liabilities that result from applying the §1 rates to various amounts of taxable income. The price of this convenience is numerous small cliff effects, because the tables set forth tax liabilities based on $50 taxable income increments. Suppose, for example, the tables indicate a tax liability of $2,000 for taxable income from $19,951 to $20,000, and a tax liability of $2,010 for taxable income from $20,001 to $20,050. Increasing one's income from exactly to $20,000 to $20,001 would increase one's tax liability by $10. The result is a small cliff effect, with a 1000 percent marginal tax rate on that one dollar of taxable income. Several phaseout provisions involve similar miniature cliff effects. For example, the child credit of §24 is reduced by $50 for every $1,000 *or fraction thereof* by which the taxpayer's adjusted gross income (AGI) exceeds a specified threshold amount. If one's AGI exceeds the threshold by exactly $1,000, the credit is reduced by $50, but if one's AGI exceeds the threshold by $1,001, the credit is reduced by $100. Similar small cliff effects are produced by the phasedown of the §21 child care credit and the phaseout of the §151 personal exemptions.

2. In addition, the marginal rate for a large increment may be a blended rate. If a taxpayer is considering whether to earn an extra $10,000, half of which would fall in the 10 percent bracket and half of which would fall into the 15 percent bracket, the blended marginal tax rate on the $10,000 will be 12.5 percent.

should be funded in the way that inflicts the least possible amount of total pain on taxpayers (given the amount of money that must be raised). If we assume that money has declining marginal utility (i.e., the more money you already have, the less value an additional dollar has for you), and that everyone's utility curve is the same, then at first glance the least-total-sacrifice tax system would seem to feature a zero bracket and a 100 percent tax bracket above it, with the breakpoint between the brackets set at $X, so that there was just enough societal income above the $X level to finance government operations. The problem, of course, is that people faced with a 100 percent marginal tax rate would decide not to earn any income in the 100 percent bracket, and the otherwise ideal system would be a complete disaster. A utilitarian must modify the initial prescription of a two bracket, 0-100 percent system, to take into account the disincentive effects of high tax rates on work and investment. The question then becomes how to raise the required amount of tax revenue while imposing the least possible loss of utility on taxpayers, taking into account *both* the declining marginal utility of money and the disincentive effects of high tax rates. The result might well be an income tax with progressive marginal rates.

Many other explanations of progressive tax rates are possible. For example, one might view the actual—modestly progressive—rate structure of the income tax not as the embodiment of a consistent philosophical approach, but rather as a political compromise between two very different approaches. Egalitarians might favor a highly progressive rate structure (with much of the revenue being devoted to redistribution), while libertarians might object to all taxation beyond the amount necessary to finance a minimal "night watchman" government. Neither group would be happy with our actual tax system, but each might accept it as the best politically attainable compromise. A progressive income tax might also be favored by someone who believes the overall tax burden should be proportional (i.e., flat), if a progressive income tax would offset the regressivity of other taxes (such as state and local sales taxes).

Whether progressive marginal rates further the goals of distributive justice is a question on which tax lawyers have no special expertise. Tax lawyers do have a legitimate claim to expertise, however, on the question of how much of the complexity of the income tax is due to progressive marginal tax rates. One aspect of that question can be answered easily. The purely arithmetical complexity involved in having several different tax rates is trivial. It is no great challenge to multiply several different chunks of taxable income by several different tax rates, rather than multiplying all taxable income by a single rate. In any event, either tables in the Form 1040 instruction booklet or tax return preparation software do the math for the majority of taxpayers. It may be, however, that progressive marginal rates are a source of other—more significant but less obvious—types of complexity. In particular, progressive marginal rates put considerable pressure on the definition of the taxable unit (individual, married couple, or family) and on how to identify the proper taxpayer for various items of income; the definition of the taxable unit and the allocation of income items among taxable units will determine the rates at which income is taxed. Under a flat tax system, by contrast, the rate of tax would depend on neither the definition of the taxable unit nor the allocation of income among taxpayers.[3]

---

3. However, if the flat-tax system includes an exemption of any significance (as most such proposed tax systems do) then taxpayer-identification problems remain in any case in which the income may plausibly be taxable to someone who may not have exhausted his exemption.

B. PHASEOUTS

1. Personal Exemptions

Take a look at §151(d)(3) of the Code. It provides that a taxpayer's personal exemption amount is reduced by 2 percentage points for every $2,500 by which the taxpayer's AGI exceeds the "threshold amount." The threshold amounts in the statute are $150,000 for joint returns, $125,000 for heads of households, and $100,000 for other unmarried taxpayers, but these amounts are annually adjusted for inflation. Section 151(d)(3) does not apply in 2010, 2011, or 2012, but absent further legislation it will apply in 2013 and later years.

Problem 1. Mark and Molly, a married couple with three young children, file a joint return for a year in which §151(d)(3) applies. Before taking into account the §151(d)(3) phaseout, they are entitled to five personal exemptions. Suppose that the inflation-adjusted personal exemption amount (before phaseout) is $3,000, the threshold amount for joint returns is $200,000, and their official marginal tax rate (under §1(a)) is 35 percent. Molly is considering putting in some extra hours at work, which would increase their AGI from $200,000 to $210,000. Taking into account both §§1 and 151(d)(3), how much of that $10,000 would Mark and Molly get to keep, net of federal income tax?

Problem 2.   The facts are the same as in the previous problem, except Mark and Molly's AGI will be increased from $325,000 to $335,000 if Molly puts in the extra hours of work. Determine the hidden marginal tax rate produced by §151(d)(3) on Molly's $10,000 in this situation. (As in the previous problem, assume the phaseout threshold is $200,000.)

There are four major objections to the phaseout of personal exemptions. First, as Problem 1 suggests, calculating the effect of the phaseout is quite complex. Eliminating this phaseout—and the phaseouts of several other tax provisions, discussed below—could greatly simplify tax return preparation for millions of taxpayers. Arguably, mere computational complexity is no longer a major concern, given the fact that about 90 percent of tax returns are now prepared with the assistance of tax return preparation software. The availability of software does not help, however, with the other three objections. The second objection is that the complexity of the phaseout means that most taxpayers probably do not understand its operation well enough to take it into account in making financial decisions. In Problem 1, for example, it is likely that Molly will decide whether or not to earn the extra $10,000 on the assumption that her real marginal tax rate is only 35 percent, rather than more than 39 percent. It seems unfair, then, to blindside her with the higher rate. Third, the phaseout produces some regressivity in marginal tax rates, because the true marginal tax rate drops once the phaseout is completed. In Problem 1, Mark and Molly faced a true marginal tax rate of 39.2 percent at $200,000 AGI. At the substantially higher AGI level of $325,000, by contrast, they would face the *lower* marginal tax rate of 35 percent. Such marginal tax rate "bubbles" may not be unfair (on the premise that fairness is a function of average rates, rather than marginal rates), but they are at least strange.

Finally, there is the objection that family-size adjustments in tax liability are appropriate even at high income levels, so that it is unfair that Mark and Molly with AGI of $325,000 will pay as much tax as a childless couple with the same AGI. The disallowance of personal exemptions to high income taxpayers is sometimes defended on the grounds that tax breaks for children should be targeted at families at low or moderate income levels. It is a mistake, however, to frame this as a question of *vertical* equity — that is, fairness between taxpayers at different income levels. Properly understood, whether Mark and Molly should be entitled to personal exemptions is a question of *horizontal* equity — that is, fairness between taxpayers at the same (high) income level, but with different numbers of children. The cost of allowing Mark and Molly to claim five personal exemptions need not be paid for by taxpayers with lower incomes. Instead, it can be paid for by increasing the tax on high income taxpayers without children. For example, suppose the government could raise the same tax revenue it currently raises from taxpayers at the $325,000 AGI level by repealing the phaseout of personal exemptions and raising their §1 marginal tax rate by a few percentage points. This would decrease the tax owed by Mark and Molly, increase the tax owed by childless taxpayers at the same income level, and have no effect on the liabilities of taxpayers with lower incomes.

There is probably no point in trying to find a principled justification for the phaseout of personal exemptions. Part of what makes the phaseout bad tax policy — its hidden nature — is precisely what makes it attractive to Congress. Congress likes the tax revenue that comes from high marginal tax rates, but it does not like the political heat associated with those rates when the public understands them. What could be better, then, than a marginal tax rate increase imposed in such a convoluted manner that few taxpayers understand what is being done to them? On the other hand, the temporary suspension of the personal exemption phaseout suggests Congress is not completely insensitive to the objections to the provision. Perhaps the provision will be repealed — rather than merely suspended — in the next few years.

2. Other Phaseouts

In fact, Congress has grown so fond of the phaseout strategy in recent years that §151(d)(3) is just the tip of the phaseout iceberg. Other prominent examples of phaseouts or "phasedowns" (a phasedown reduces a tax benefit as income increases, but stops before the benefit is eliminated) include: the phasedown of the §21 child care credit; the phaseout of the §24 child tax credit; the phaseout of the §25A Hope Scholarship and Lifetime Learning Credits; the phaseout of the §32 earned income credit; the §68 phasedown of itemized deductions; and the §86 phasedown of the exclusion of Social Security benefits from gross income. Each of these provisions involves the same sort of hidden marginal tax rate increase as the phaseout of personal exemptions, followed by a decrease in the real marginal tax rate once the phaseout (or phasedown) has been completed. The following problem involves the operation of one of these provisions.

Problem 3. Paul and Patty, a married couple with two young children, file a joint return. Before taking into account any effect of §24(b), they are entitled to two child tax credits of $1,000 each. Paul is considering putting in some extra hours at work, which would increase their AGI from $110,000 to $115,000. If he does, what will be the effect on the amount of their child tax credits? Also, what is the rate of the §24(b) hidden tax?

Section 68 reduces a taxpayer's itemized deductions by the lesser of (1) 3 percent of the excess of AGI over a threshold amount ($100,000 in the statute, but indexed for inflation after 1991), or (2) 80 percent of the total amount of itemized deductions. It is a *phasedown* provision, since a taxpayer is never left with less than 20 percent of the original amount of itemized deductions. (The phase-down may, however, induce the taxpayer to claim the standard deduction rather than the diminished itemized deductions.) Like §151(d)(3), §68 is temporarily inoperative, for 2010, 2011, and 2012. Depending on the taxpayer's situation, the practical impact of §68 may be either to impose a hidden tax rate increase on income over the threshold amount, or to diminish the marginal tax benefit of itemized deductions (with the former effect being much more common). Consider the following problems.

Problem 4.   It is December (of a year in which §68 applies), and Donna is trying to decide whether to earn $10,000 overtime before the end of the year. If she does not, her AGI will be $100,000, and her itemized deductions will be $10,000. How will §68 affect her if she decides to earn the extra $10,000? Assume the §68 threshold amount is simply $100,000 (that is, there has been no inflation adjustment).

Problem 5.   Suppose Donna decided to earn the overtime, so her AGI is now $110,000. It is now very late in December, and she is considering giving $10,000 to her favorite charity before the end of the year. If she does so, will §68 have any effect on the tax benefit she obtains from the contribution?

If you have correctly answered both Problem 4 and Problem 5, you will see that §68 is designed and labeled in a highly misleading way (perhaps intentionally). Although it is advertised as reducing itemized deductions, for most taxpayers within its grasp it will have no effect on the tax benefit derived from marginal dollars of itemized deductions, but it *will* function as a hidden rate increase on marginal dollars of income. Can §68 ever function as it is labeled, and reduce the tax benefit of marginal dollars of deductions, rather than increasing the tax rate on marginal dollars of income? Yes, but only for really high income taxpayers, as illustrated by the following problem.

Problem 6.   In a year in which §68 applies, Gail has AGI of $5.1 million and $100,000 of itemized deductions (before taking into account any §68 reduction). (1) What will be the impact on Gail of §68 if her AGI increases by $1 million, to $6.1 million? (2) What will be the impact on Gail of §68 if her AGI remains $5.1 million, but she gives $50,000 to charity (increasing her itemized deductions, before the application of §68, to $150,000)?[4]

---

4. While barely imaginable, this example is unrealistic, because a taxpayer with this high an income would normally have much greater itemized deductions. To be plausible, this example must implicitly assume this wealthy taxpayer lives in a state with no income tax, owns little or no property subject to property taxes, pays little or no mortgage interest, makes few if any charitable contributions, etc.

Understanding the practical impact of §68 may not be easy, but it is considerably easier than finding a justification for the provision. Justifying an explicit marginal tax rate increase is one thing; justifying a surreptitious increase is a more difficult task. Of course, if one is willing to settle for an explanation, rather than a justification, there is no difficulty. The political attraction of §68 is that few taxpayers will recognize it for what it is — a marginal tax rate increase for most high income taxpayers. As in the case of the phaseout of personal exemptions, it is possible that Congress will see the light and turn the temporary suspension of §68 into a permanent repeal of the provision.

42

Cell

INFLATION AND
THE INCOME TAX

A. Bracket Creep

B. Inflation and Income Measurement

Hellermann v. Commissioner

A. BRACKET CREEP

Imagine a very simple tax rate structure, under which the first $20,000 of income is taxed at 10 percent, and any additional income is taxed at 30 percent. Joe has $40,000 income, so he owes $8,000 tax (10% of the first $20,000, plus 30% of the other $20,000). His average tax rate is 20 percent ($8,000/$40,000). Now suppose it is a year later. There has been 10 percent inflation since last year, and Joe's pre-tax income this year is $44,000—just keeping up with inflation. If the tax rate structure is not adjusted in response to inflation, Joe's tax liability this year will be $9,200 (10% of the first $20,000, plus 30% of $24,000). This gives Joe an average tax rate of about 20.9 percent ($9,200/$44,000). This is an example of "bracket creep." Note that Joe's real (inflation-adjusted) income has not increased, nor has his marginal tax rate; nevertheless his average tax rate has. The reason for the increase is that inflation has pushed a larger portion of his total income into the higher tax bracket. In the first year only half of Joe's income was taxed at 30 percent, but in the second year almost 55 percent of Joe's income ($24,000/$44,000) is in the 30 percent bracket.

The solution to the bracket creep problem is simply to increase the width of the tax brackets by the inflation rate. In the example, this would mean applying the 10 percent bracket to the first $22,000 of income in the second year. If that were done, Joe's tax liability in the second year would be $8,800 (10% of the first $22,000, plus 30% of the other $22,000). This would result in an average tax rate of 20 percent ($8,800/$44,000)—the same average rate as in the previous year. Joe's nominal tax liability has increased from $8,000 to $8,800, but that increase merely keeps pace with inflation, just as his pre-tax income merely kept pace with inflation.

For many decades, the income tax rate brackets were not indexed for inflation, and bracket creep imposed hidden tax increases on people whose real income was not increasing. Congress was understandably fond of a system that produced tax increases without the need to vote for them,[5] but eventually decided to index the

5. Or that resulted in Congress getting credit for cutting taxes when it passed tax reduction legislation that merely offset tax increases caused by bracket creep.

tax rates. Legislation enacted in 1981 provided for annual inflation adjustments to the §1 tax rate schedules, the personal exemption, and the standard deduction. Although this has greatly reduced bracket creep, the phenomenon still exists to a limited extent, because inflation indexing is not comprehensive. A number of tax benefits are phased out for high income taxpayers. As explained in the immediately preceding cell, those phaseouts function as disguised marginal tax rate increases. As such, they should be indexed for inflation, just like the §1 rate schedules. Some of the phaseouts are indexed for inflation (for example, the phaseouts of the earned income tax credit and the personal exemption), but others are not (for example, the phaseout of the child tax credit). In addition, the exemption amounts and the rate brackets of the alternative minimum tax are not indexed for inflation. There is no obvious reason why Congress decided to eliminate most sources of bracket creep, but not all such sources.

Bracket creep results from the differing value of a dollar over time. There is a nontemporal analogue of bracket creep, involving the different value of a dollar in localities with different costs of living. Suppose, as before, a two-bracket tax system, with a 10 percent rate of tax imposed on the first $20,000 of income, and a 30 percent rate on all additional income. Anne has income of $40,000 in City A, and Betty has income of $44,000 in City B, where the cost of living is 10 percent higher. Accepting, for the moment, the premise that Anne's $40,000 is the functional equivalent of Betty's $44,000, they should be subject to equivalent tax burdens. Yet Anne will have an average tax rate of only 20 percent ($8,000/$40,000), while Betty will be subject to an average tax rate of 20.9 percent ($9,200/$44,000). This is the geographic version of bracket creep, and the solution to the problem would be to adjust tax bracket widths according to geographic differences in cost of living, just as the law now adjusts according to temporal differences in living costs. Thus, if Anne's 10 percent bracket continues to apply to the first $20,000 of income, Betty's should apply to the first $22,000. In that case, Betty would owe tax of $8,800, and her average tax rate would be 20 percent ($8,800/$44,000) — the same as Anne's. Betty would still pay more nominal tax dollars than Anne, but that would be appropriate given the assumption that the $8,800 Betty pays is the equivalent of the $8,000 Anne pays (in terms of the burden imposed on the taxpayers, although not in terms of the benefit received by the government), after taking the cost-of-living difference into account.

If the case for geographic adjustments to rate bracket widths is basically the same as the case for temporal adjustments, why has Congress rejected one while embracing the other? There are several possible justifications or explanations. First, the case for a cost-of-living adjustment applies only with respect to income devoted to local consumption. To the extent Anne and Betty spend money on nonlocal consumption (such as vacations, or their children's cost of attending nonlocal colleges), there is no justification for a local cost-of-living adjustment. There is also no justification for a geographic cost-of-living adjustment for the taxation of income that is saved, rather than consumed. In addition, it is possible that City B is more expensive than City A because it is nicer in ways not captured by cost-of-living statistics. For example, suppose Anne can rent an apartment for $1,000 a month, and Betty must pay $1,100 for an apartment that is identical apart from the difference in location. Because of the difference in location, however, Betty enjoys better weather, better proximity to natural and cultural attractions, and a lower crime rate — all differences not reflected by the cost-of-living data. Cost-of-living data to the contrary, Betty may really be better off with her $44,000 than Anne is with her $40,000. If so, it may be appropriate for Betty to have a higher average tax rate than Anne.

There is also the little problem of the Tax Uniformity Clause of the Constitution. Article I, sec. 8, requires that "all Duties, Imposts and Excises shall be uniform throughout the United States." It is possible that different tax rate schedules for taxpayers living in different parts of the country would violate this clause.[6] Finally, there is a probably insuperable political obstacle to regional cost-of-living tax adjustments. The high cost-of-living states, which would benefit from geographic adjustments to the rate brackets, tend to be high-population states. Residents of such states are, of course, greatly underrepresented in the Senate. There are enough senators from low-cost, low-population states to thwart any attempt to lower the average tax rates of Californians and New Yorkers.

B.   INFLATION AND INCOME MEASUREMENT

The effect of bracket creep is not to increase the amount of income subject to tax, but only to increase the average rate at which income is taxed. There is a second way, however, in which inflation affects the tax system, and this second effect does involve the creation of artificial taxable income. Suppose a taxpayer buys raw land as an investment, at a cost of $100,000. Ten years later, the taxpayer sells the land for $150,000. If there has been 50 percent inflation over those ten years, the value of the land has merely kept pace with inflation, and the taxpayer has enjoyed no real gain. It seems that he should be allowed to adjust his basis for inflation to reflect the fact that his $100,000 cost in the dollars of ten years ago is the equivalent of a $150,000 cost in today's dollars. In other words, a tax system is comparing apples with oranges if it defines amount realized in terms of today's dollars, but defines basis in terms of ten-year-old dollars. If the taxpayer were allowed to make a basis adjustment, his amount realized and his inflation-adjusted basis would be equal, and he would not have to pay tax on any capital gain. Despite Congress's solicitude for the victims of bracket creep, it has never seen fit to extend equal sympathy to the victims of tax on inflationary gain. The taxpayer will not be allowed any inflation adjustment to basis; he will have to pay tax on $50,000 of capital gain, despite the fact that the entire gain is an illusion — an artifact of inflation. True, he will be allowed to pay tax at a special favorable capital gains rate, but that is scant consolation when in a better (inflation-adjusted) world he would have no gain and owe no tax at all.

Failing to obtain relief from Congress, victims of tax on inflationary gains have turned to the courts, but to no avail.

---

6. *But see* United States v. Ptasysnski, 462 U.S. 74 (1983), in which the Supreme Court rejected a Uniformity Clause challenge to an Alaska exemption from a windfall profit tax on oil producers, and did so in such a way as to suggest a very limited role for the Clause. Note also that the IRS does allow cost-of-living differentials to be reflected in certain business-expense per diem rates. *See* Regs. §1.274-5 and Rev. Proc. 2010-39, 2010-42 I.R.B. 459.

HELLERMANN v. COMMISSIONER

77 T.C. 1361 (1981)

EKMAN, Judge: Respondent determined a deficiency of $11,206.60 in petitioners' Federal income taxes for 1976. The sole issue for our decision is whether that portion of gain from the sale of property, which is attributable solely to inflation, is income within the meaning of the 16th Amendment.

Petitioners purchased four buildings in 1964 for $93,312. They sold the buildings in 1976 for $264,000, and reported a capital gain of $170,688 on their 1976 return. . . . Petitioners [now claim] that they are . . . entitled to a refund of capital gains tax paid in 1976.

Petitioners claim that much of their reported gain on the sale of the four buildings was due to inflation. They point out that the Consumer Price Index (CPI) had approximately doubled between 1964 and 1976. Thus, even though they received more dollars on the sale than they had paid to purchase the buildings, each 1976 dollar they received was worth less than each 1964 dollar they paid. From this they concluded that their economic gain on the sale was $88,167. However, they concede that they had a nominal gain of $170,688.

Petitioners assert that they should not be taxed on their nominal gain, but only on their economic gain. They argue that the portion of their nominal gain which is attributable solely to inflation does not constitute taxable income within the meaning of the 16th Amendment. Instead, they contend that, economically speaking, such gain is a return of capital. As they correctly observe, tax on a return of capital is a direct tax, subject to apportionment.[7] They maintain that to the extent the Internal Revenue Code permits that portion of nominal gain which is attributable to inflation to be taxed, it is an unconstitutional exercise of the Congress' power. They conclude that the Code must be interpreted in a manner which does not permit such gain to be taxed as income. As an appropriate means to that end, petitioners suggest that we adjust nominal gain to reflect the effects of inflation.

Respondent rejects as irrelevant petitioners' use of the CPI, or other measures of inflation, to calculate taxable income. He contends that nominal capital gain is taxable income whether or not such gain represents an increase in economic value. We agree with respondent, and therefore, need not decide whether the CPI is an appropriate measure with which to adjust taxable income. . . .

We reject petitioners' contention that nominal gain is not taxable income within the meaning of the 16th Amendment on two grounds. First, we rely on the well-established doctrine that Congress has the power and authority to establish the dollar as a unit of legal value with respect to the determination of taxable income, independent of any value the dollar might also have as a commodity. *See* Legal Tender Cases, 79 U.S. 457 (1870). In the Legal Tender Cases, *supra*, the Supreme Court held that Congress had the power to declare treasury notes ("greenbacks"), which were backed by gold, to be legal tender. The Court held that paper money could be on a par with gold coins because both had the same legal value. The Court recognized that the statutory value of the nation's currency might not correspond to the market value of the bullion which backed the paper or from which the gold coins were made. It termed this discrepancy the difference between legal and intrinsic value. However, it did not doubt that Congress had the power to legislate

---

7. U.S. Const. art. I, sec. 2, cl. 3. *See also* U.S. Const. art. I, sec. 9, cl. 4.

such a difference. The Court viewed the Constitution as being "designed to provide the same currency, having a uniform legal value in all the States. . . . [F]or this reason the power to coin money and regulate its value was conferred upon the Federal government," and it reasoned that "Whatever power there is over the currency is vested in Congress." . . .

Petitioners concede that Congress has the power to require that the income tax be paid in dollars as legal tender, but argues [sic] that it does not have the power to measure gain in terms of dollars, because such dollars do not have a constant value. Given the reasoning behind the holding of the Legal Tender Cases, *supra*, and Norman v. Baltimore & Ohio Railroad Co., [294 U.S. 240 (1935),] we must disagree. Dollars have constant legal value under the uniform monetary system created by Congress. When petitioners sold the buildings in 1976, they realized a gain in legal value. The 16th Amendment does not prevent the Congress from taxing such gain as income if it chooses to do so.

As our second ground for rejecting petitioners' arguments, we rely upon the doctrine of common interpretation. As was stated by Judge Learned Hand, "[the] meaning [of income] is . . . to be gathered from the implicit assumptions of its use in common speech." United States v. Oregon-Washington R. & Nav. Co., 251 F. 211, 212 (2d Cir. 1918). Thus, the meaning of income is not to be construed as an economist might, but as a layperson might. Petitioners received many more dollars for the buildings than they had paid for them. The extra dollars they received are well within the common perception of income, even though each 1976 dollar received represents less purchasing power than each 1964 dollar paid. Petitioners' nominal gain may or may not equal their real gain in an economic sense. Nonetheless, neither the Constitution nor tax laws "embody perfect economic theory." See Weiss v. Wiener, 279 U.S. 333, 335 (1929).

Based on the foregoing, we find that petitioners' nominal gain represented a change in legal value. Thus, petitioners' nominal gain is taxable income within the meaning of the 16th Amendment. . . . [B]ecause petitioners have not sustained their burden of proving that they had a lesser capital gain on sale of the buildings than they reported, there is no overpayment of income taxes to which they are entitled.

Decision will be entered for the respondent.

Notes and Questions

1. *Inflation indexing by regulation?* In the early 1990s, the Bush (père) administration gave serious consideration to the possibility of promulgating regulations interpreting the word "cost" in §1012 ("The basis of property shall be the cost of such property") to mean inflation-adjusted cost. There is nothing inherently illogical in interpreting the statute in this way. Commentators argued, however, that such an interpretation would be unreasonable, in light of the long-standing regulatory, judicial, and legislative understanding that §1012 does not refer to inflation-adjusted cost. In fact, Congress has several times indicated in committee reports that special favorable rates for capital gains are appropriate precisely because the law does *not* permit basis adjustments to reflect inflation. For example, a 1934 Ways and Means Committee Report justified low capital gains tax

rates by noting, "In many instances, the capital-gains tax is imposed on the mere increase in monetary value resulting from the depreciation of the dollar instead of on a real increase in value." H. Rep. No. 704, 73d Cong., 2d Sess. 31 (1934). Despite the lack of legitimate *authority* to index basis by regulation, Treasury probably has the *power* to do so (subject only to legislative reversal). The taxpayers who benefitted from regulatory indexing would obviously not complain, and in all likelihood no one else would have standing to object to the Treasury's unduly generous treatment of those taxpayers. On the general unavailability of third-party standing to challenge favorable administrative treatment of taxpayers, *see* Allen v. Wright, 468 U.S. 737 (1984); Simon v. Eastern Kentucky Welfare Rights Org., 426 U.S. 26 (1976). In any event, the Bush administration finally decided not to pursue regulatory indexing of basis, and later administrations have shown no interest in the idea.

2. *Indexing depreciation deductions for inflation.* If Congress were to index basis for inflation, it would make sense to apply the basis adjustments in calculating depreciation deductions, as well as in calculating gain realized under §1001. Suppose a taxpayer buys a depreciable asset for $1,000, the applicable depreciation schedule provides for straight-line depreciation over ten years, and inflation is running at an annual rate of 10 percent. The depreciation deduction for the first year would be simply $100.[8] The second year's depreciation, however, would be $110 — the second year's $100 share of the original $1,000 cost, with an inflation adjustment to translate last year's $100 into this year's $110. The third year's deduction would be $121 (reflecting two years of 10% annual inflation), the fourth year's would be $133, and so on. Congress indicated in 1981 that the enactment of the accelerated cost recovery system was justified, in part, as a correction for the effects of inflation: "Inflation reduces the tax savings from depreciation deductions because the value of the dollar is less when these deductions are claimed than it was when the investment was originally made. As a result, the current [i.e., pre-ACRS] system of depreciation reduces the incentive to invest." S. Rep. No. 144, 97th Cong., 1st Sess. 13 (1981). It might be appropriate, then, to couple inflation indexing of depreciation deductions with the repeal of the accelerated cost recovery system.

3. *Inflation and debt.* Suppose the tax system adjusted asset basis for inflation, but did not make any inflation adjustments with respect to debt. Sara buys some land for $100, financing the entire purchase price with a $100 loan secured by the land. Several years later, when the principal amount of the mortgage is still $100, Sara sells the land for $150. Her amount realized consists of $50 cash and $100 debt relief. There has been 50 percent inflation between the year of purchase and the year of sale. If Sara is permitted to adjust her original $100 basis to $150, to reflect this inflation, she will owe no tax on the sale: $150 amount realized − $150 inflation-adjusted basis = zero gain realized. There's something wrong with that result, though, because Sara has made a real $50 profit on the deal. She invested no money of her own in the land, yet she is able to walk away from

---

8. This disregards the half-year convention of §168(d)(1).

the sale with $50 in her pocket. The way to get the correct tax result is to index debt, as well as basis, for inflation. Thus, Sara would be treated as having borrowed $150 (the $100 amount actually borrowed, adjusted for the 50% inflation between the year of borrowing and the current year), and as having repaid only $100, and she would have to pay tax on $50 of cancellation-of-indebtedness income.[9] The basic point is that if the tax base (as opposed to tax rates) is to be indexed for inflation, doing it comprehensively is considerably more complicated than just adjusting the basis of capital assets, and if inflation indexing is not done comprehensively it is probably better not to do it at all. The ideal solution for the havoc inflation can wreak with a tax system is just to keep inflation under control.[10]

4. *Inflation indexing of interest payments.* The previous note described a simple way of adjusting debt for inflation — treating a borrower as having cancellation-of-indebtedness income when she repays a debt with dollars worth less than the dollars she borrowed years before. (On the other side of the transaction, the lender would realize a loss when, after the inflation adjustment is taken into account, the loan is not fully repaid.) A more comprehensive system for inflation-indexing of loans would apply to all interest payments, rather than waiting until there has been a repayment of principal. Suppose, for example, that Ted borrows $10,000 from the Bank at 10 percent, when the anticipated rate of annual inflation is 4 percent. When Ted makes his first annual interest payment of $1,000, the tax system could recharacterize the payment as consisting of $600 *real* interest, and $400 disguised repayment of principal. Ted's interest expense deduction (assuming he qualifies for an interest expense deduction under §163) would be $600, rather than $1,000, and the Bank's taxable interest income would also be only $600. What if Ted repaid the $10,000 principal of the loan at the same time? After an inflation adjustment, he would be treated as having borrowed $10,400, but he would not have any cancellation of indebtedness income, because he would be treated as having repaid a total of $10,400 — consisting of the $10,000 payment labeled repayment of principal, and the $400 labeled as interest but recharacterized as repayment of principal.

---

9. See Chapter 2.C.2.a.

10. While difficult, comprehensive indexing of asset bases to correct inflation is not impossible, and some countries (Mexico, for example) actually do it.

Cell

COMPLIANCE AND ENFORCEMENT

A. The Case of Tips

> Joint Committee on Taxation, General Explanation of the Revenue Provisions of the Tax Equity and Fiscal Responsibility Act of 1982

B. The Big Picture

> Slemrod & Bakija, Taxing Ourselves

A. THE CASE OF TIPS

Tips received by restaurant employees are clearly taxable under current law. They do not qualify as tax-free gifts under §102, because customers do not tip out of "detached and disinterested generosity."[11] The problem with tips is not the technical legal analysis, but compliance. How can taxpayers be persuaded to report their tip income, and how can the IRS detect unreported tip income?

JOINT COMMITTEE ON TAXATION, GENERAL EXPLANATION OF THE REVENUE PROVISIONS OF THE TAX EQUITY AND FISCAL RESPONSIBILITY ACT OF 1982

JCS-38-82

f. Employer Reporting with Respect to Tips (Sec. 314 of the Act and Sec. 6053 of the Code)

PRIOR LAW

Any employee who receives, in any calendar month and during the course of his employment, any tips which are wages or compensation, must report all such tips to his employer on or before the 10th day following the month of receipt.

Tips are defined as wages or compensation if they are paid in cash during any calendar month, are $20 or more in amount, and are received by an employee in the course of his employment. . . .

---

11. Commissioner v. LoBue, 351 U.S. 243, 246 (1956), *quoted in* Commissioner v. Duberstein, 363 U.S. 278, 285 (1960). For §102 generally, see Chapter 2.A.3.a.

In general, withholding for purposes of the Federal Insurance Contributions Act (FICA) tax and the income tax is required only to the extent tips are reported to the employer and only to the extent collection of the tax can be made by the employer from wages paid to the employee (excluding tips, but including funds turned over by the employee to the employer or under the control of the employer). . . .

Substantial recordkeeping requirements are imposed upon tipped employees and employers. In general, employees, whether or not they receive tips, are required to keep records to establish the amount of their gross income and deductions. Because tips are includible in income, employees must keep records of all tips received and of all deductible tips paid to other employees. . . .

REASONS FOR CHANGE

The compliance rate in 1981 with respect to tip income was approximately 16 percent according to preliminary estimates by the Internal Revenue Service based upon data furnished by the Bureau of Economic Analysis of the Department of Commerce. The only type of income with a lower compliance rate was illegal income which had a compliance rate of only 5 percent.

Congress believed that such a low compliance rate is fundamentally unfair to wage earners and other taxpayers with substantially higher levels of voluntary compliance. Expanded information reporting on tip income will encourage better reporting of such income by its recipients and facilitate Internal Revenue Service efforts to increase compliance in this area. At the same time, Congress recognized that improved compliance rules should not impose unnecessary recordkeeping obligations on taxpayers or employers.

EXPLANATION OF PROVISION

Under the Act, the rules of prior law relating to reporting of tips to employers by their employees and to the resulting withholding of FICA and income taxes are retained. However, to assist the Internal Revenue Service in its examinations of returns filed by tipped employees, the Act provides a new set of information reporting requirements for large food or beverage establishments, including, under certain circumstances, a tip allocation requirement.

Under the Act, each large food or beverage establishment is required to report annually to the Internal Revenue Service (1) the gross receipts of the establishment from food or beverage sales . . . , (2) the amount of aggregate charge receipts, (3) the aggregate amount of tips shown on such charge receipts and (4) reported tip income. . . .

If tipped employees of large food or beverage establishments voluntarily report tips aggregating 8 percent or more of gross receipts . . . , then no tip allocations will need to be made. However, if this 8-percent reporting threshold is not met, then the employer must allocate (as tips for reporting purposes) an amount equal to the difference between 8 percent of gross receipts and the amounts reported by employees for the year to all tipped employees pursuant to either an agreement between the employer and employees or, in the absence of such an agreement, according to regulations issued by the Secretary. The employer will have no liability to employees in connection with any dispute regarding allocations of amounts under this rule.

Regulations under this provision will provide procedures under which a particular establishment, or type of establishment, can show that its tipped employees' average tip rate is less than 8 percent (but not less than 5 percent) and, can therefore, allocate based on that lower amount in the future.

The allocation of the excess of the 8-percent amount over reported tips to employees for reporting purposes will have no effect on the FICA or income tax withholding responsibilities of the employer or on his FUTA obligations. Thus, employers will continue to withhold only on amounts reported to them by their tipped employees. Of course, the allocation also has no effect on the actual entitlement of the employer or employee to gross receipts or tip income. Similarly, this purely informational report to the Internal Revenue Service will not affect the requirements of the Fair Labor Standards Act or any collective bargaining agreement.

The 8-percent figure reflects Congress's judgment that the tip rate in establishments subject to this reporting requirement will rarely be below the 8-percent level. Thus, an employee who reports less than his allocated amount of tips must be able to substantiate his reporting position with adequate books and records (as he had to do under prior law). The Internal Revenue Service can still prove that tipped employees received a larger amount of tip income. For example, as under prior law, the Internal Revenue Service could show from charge tip rates that a particular establishment had a higher tip rate than 8 percent. . . .

It is anticipated that the information statement concerning allocated tips will be integrated into Form W-2 now supplied by employers with respect to wages. If the employer furnishes an employee with a W-2 within 30 days after the employee terminates employment, the employer must also furnish the employee and the Internal Revenue Service with an amended Form W-2 that includes tip allocations in January of the following year.

Notes and Questions

1. *The mechanics.* To see how §6053 works, imagine a restaurant that qualifies as a "large food and beverage establishment," and that has $1 million of gross receipts from food and beverage sales. If employees voluntarily report to the restaurant tips totaling $30,000, then the restaurant must allocate an additional $50,000 of tip income among its tipped employees, and include that $50,000 on the W-2 forms (information returns) the employer furnishes to the employees and to the IRS. If an employee does not include on his tax return tip income equal to at least the amount shown on his W-2, the IRS computers will notice the discrepancy (most of the time) and generate a letter to the taxpayer asking for either the additional tax due (if the taxpayer concedes the W-2 is correct) or an explanation (if the taxpayer claims the W-2 is wrong). After the 1982 amendments to §6053, the estimated compliance rate for tips improved from the miserable 16 percent figure noted in the Joint Committee Staff's *General Explanation* to somewhere in the neighborhood of 60 percent. This is consistent with actual tips averaging 13-14 percent of gross receipts, and §6053's forcing the reporting of tips equaling 8 percent of gross receipts.
2. *The just and the unjust.* Suppose you are a wait person. Your actual tips for the year are about $10,000. You know you are supposed to report the $10,000 to your employer and to the IRS, but you know that if you do not

do so the employer will allocate only $6,000 of tips to you. You also know there will be no meaningful risk that the IRS will attempt to tax you on more than that. In short, the tax on your last $4,000 of tips is a voluntary tax. What would you do? (According to Plato, "When there is an income tax, the just man will pay more, and the unjust less, on the same amount of income."[12] Was he thinking of a situation like this?) The almost — but not quite — universal answer is that people do not report more tip income than the amount they know the employer would allocate to them anyway. Those few who would report more than the $6,000 fall into two categories: the heroically honest, and those who actually *benefit* from reporting additional earned income, because of the earned income tax credit.[13]

3. *So what's the problem?* One can take a glass half-full or a glass half-empty view of tip compliance and enforcement. On the one hand, thanks to §6053 compliance is quite good for tips up to 8 percent. On the other hand, tips in excess of 8 percent are taxable in theory, but in practice are taxable only to the most honest workers. How big a problem is this discrepancy between the law on the books and the law in practice? Beyond the obvious revenue loss from the de facto exemption for tips above 8 percent, there are two arguments that the discrepancy is a significant problem. First, the existence of unenforced rules may foster a general disrespect for the tax system, and thus encourage cheating not only with respect to tips but whenever cheating is not likely to be detected. Winking at underreporting of *tip* income is especially troublesome in this respect, because restaurant jobs are the first jobs — and thus the first encounter with the income tax — for so many people. How honest is a taxpayer likely to be at age 40, if at age 18 she is socialized by her fellow restaurant employees to believe that only a fool reports all her tip income?[14] The second argument that the discrepancy is a serious problem relates to the double tax imposed on the honest restaurant worker. Restaurants pay lower wages to their wait staffs because almost half of tips are de facto tax exempt (for all but the especially honest). Thus the honest wait person pays an implicit tax, in the form of reduced wages, in addition to the explicit tax.

4. *Reconciling the law on the books with the law in practice.* If Congress is unwilling to give the IRS the tools needed to enforce taxation of tips in excess of 8 percent, wouldn't it be better simply to amend the Code to provide that gross income does not include tips above 8 percent? Congress sometimes does amend the Code in order to make de facto exclusions official, thus eliminating a source of disrespect for the tax law. For example, before 1984 the value of free standby flights provided to airline employees (and their families) was theoretically taxable, but no one was reporting such income and the IRS was making no enforcement effort. In 1984, Congress brought the law on the books into line with the law in practice, by providing for an official exclusion for certain "miscellaneous fringe benefits,"

---

12. *Republic* bk. 1.
13. For the earned income tax credit, see Chapter 9.E. In all likelihood, many taxpayers who would benefit by reporting all their tip income are not aware of that fact, and actually lose money by cheating on their taxes.
14. In the words of St. Francis Xavier, "Give me the children until they are seven and anyone may have them afterwards." (Fortunately, child labor laws keep most children of seven off the restaurant payroll.)

including "no additional cost services" (such as standby flights) provided to employees by their employers.[15] At the same time, Congress sent a clear message to taxpayers and to the IRS that it was serious about taxing fringe benefits that did not satisfy the requirements for exclusion under the new provision.[16] Why do you suppose Congress acted to eliminate the conflict between theoretical taxability and de facto exclusion in the case of miscellaneous fringe benefits, but has continued to tolerate the conflict in the case of tips over 8 percent? There are, of course, several possible ways of resolving the tip conflict. Instead of providing an official exclusion for tips over 8 percent, Congress could increase the §6053 magic number from 8 percent to 12 or 13 percent, thereby ensuring the taxation of the vast majority of tip income. Why has Congress failed to adopt either approach?

5. *Excluding all tips from income.* Instead of merely providing an exclusion for tips in excess of 8 percent, Congress could be even more generous and exclude *all* tips from income. Would that be a good idea, because the typical tip recipient is just struggling to get by and has little or no ability to pay tax? Although that may be true of most tip recipients, it is certainly not true of all. Some tip recipients do quite well, and do not deserve a tip exclusion based on the assumption they are poor. As for tip recipients who *are* struggling to get by, they will pay little or no tax even if all their tips are included in their gross incomes, because of the standard deduction, personal exemptions, and the progressive rates of §1. In fact, once the earned income credit and the refundable portion of the child credit are figured in, the tax liability of many low income tip recipients will be *negative* (i.e., they will receive net transfers from the government), even if they report all their tip income.

B. THE BIG PICTURE

Having looked at the details of one area (tips) presenting special problems of compliance and enforcement, we now turn to a consideration of the bigger picture. The following excerpt provides an excellent introduction to the topics of tax evasion and enforcement.

JOEL SLEMROD & JON BAKIJA, *TAXING OURSELVES*
176-182, 185-188 (4th ed. 2008)

HOW MUCH TAX EVASION IS THERE?

Most people don't have to read such anecdotes about tax evasion to be convinced that it exists. Moreover, reciting anecdotes does not convey any sense about

---

15. Section 132, discussed in Chapter 2.B.3.a.

16. However, in the closely related area of frequent flier miles retained by employees for personal use, there continues to be a conflict between theoretical taxability and de facto exclusion. See the Chapter 2 cell on the taxation of frequent flier miles.

whether tax evasion is a big problem or a little problem. For obvious reasons — would you answer honestly survey questions about tax evasion? — it is difficult to determine just how big a problem tax evasion is. Although measuring how much tax is collected is easy enough, measuring what *should* be paid is not at all easy.

The IRS has, though, periodically estimated what it calls the *tax gap*, meaning the amount of income tax that should have been paid but wasn't. The IRS calculates the tax gap by combining information obtained from a special program of intensive random audits with information from special studies about sources of income, such as tips, that are difficult to uncover even in an intensive audit. The procedure for estimating the tax gap is an imperfect one, and even the IRS would admit that its measures are only approximations. In addition, some types of evasion that are difficult to uncover, such as unreported income from illegal activities, are not included in the estimate.

The most recent tax gap study was completed in 2006, based on data from the 2001 tax year. Considering all federal taxes, the overall gross tax gap estimate came to $345 billion, which amounts to 16.3 percent of actual (paid plus unpaid) tax liability. Of the $345 billion, the IRS expects to recover $55 billion, resulting in a "net tax gap" — that is, the tax that should have been paid but that is never collected — of $290 billion for the tax year 2001, which is 13.7 percent of the tax that should have been reported. . . .

The 2001 figures focus on the individual income tax gap, which was estimated at $245 billion. About 10 percent of the individual income tax gap was due to nonfiling, another 10 percent was due to tax underpayment, and the remaining 80 percent was due to underreporting. Of the underreported individual income tax liability, 55 percent is underreported business income, 28 percent is underreported nonbusiness income, and 16 percent is overreported exemptions, deductions, adjustments, and credits.

WHY IS TAX EVASION A PROBLEM?

. . . Evasion creates horizontal inequity because equally well off people end up with different tax burdens. . . .

To the extent that opportunities or predilections for evasion are related to level of well-being (for instance, if the rich could evade more easily than the poor), . . . evasion makes it difficult to achieve whatever degree of progressivity we deem to be consistent with vertical equity.

In part, tax evasion is a gamble like any other, with a chance of coming out ahead and a chance of coming out behind. As you would expect, the lower the chance of getting caught, the more likely people are to try to get away with tax evasion. This is borne out by the data in Table 5.1, which presents information from the IRS's tax gap study about the percentages of several types of income that are reported by individuals. It ranges from 99 percent for wages and salaries (taxes on which are difficult to evade successfully because of employer reports to the IRS) down to 28 percent for farm net income. The reporting percentage for nonfarm sole proprietors is estimated to be only 43 percent, and this category alone accounts for 35 percent of the overall individual tax gap. Tip income, which is not shown in Table 5.1, is also very hard for the IRS to find. An earlier study found the reporting rate for tip income to be just 60 percent. These facts suggest that significant horizontal inequities persist because of evasion, although, as we discuss below, in some cases the market mitigates these inequities.

On average, high-income people evade more. However, some evidence suggests that, contrary to what many may suspect, higher-income people actually evade *less* as a percentage of their income than those with lower incomes.

Table 5.1
Compliance estimates for selected types of personal income, 2001

Type of Personal Income	Reported net income as a percentage of true net income from this source	Percentage of individual income tax gap caused by underreporting of this item
Wages and salaries	99	5
Pensions and annuities	96	2
Interest and dividends	96	2
Capital gains	88	6
Partnerships and S corporations	82	11
Nonfarm proprietor income	43	35
Farm net income	28	3

Source: IRS Office of Research, Analysis, and Statistics (2006a).

Tax evasion not only compromises the equitable sharing of tax burdens; it also imposes economic costs. Other things being equal, evasion requires higher tax rates, which makes extra work and thrift less attractive to honest taxpayers. This is partially offset by lower effective tax rates on the evaders but not enough to make up fully for the distortion to income-earning activities.

More important, because it is easier to get away with tax evasion in certain circumstances, there is an incentive—which is inefficient from a social point of view—to pursue these circumstances. As an example, consider the market for house painting, where payment is often made in cash, to facilitate tax evasion. Because the cash income from house painting is hard for the IRS to detect, this occupation is more attractive than otherwise. The supply of eager house painters bids down the market price of a house-painting job, so that the amount of taxes evaded overstates the benefit of being a tax-evading house painter, and comparing taxes actually paid may overstate the extent of horizontal inequity. The biggest loser in this game is the honest housepainter, who sees his or her wages bid down by the competition but who dutifully pays taxes.

Although a supply of eager and cheap house painters undoubtedly is greeted warmly by prospective buyers of that service, it is also a symptom of an economic cost of tax evasion. The work of the extra people drawn to house painting or to any activity that facilitates tax evasion would have higher value in some alternative occupation. . . . Georgia State University economist James Alm has estimated that the cost of having too many resources diverted into activities (both legal and illegal) that facilitated tax evasion was as high as $100 billion per year.

It's clear that widespread evasion endangers the fairness of how we tax ourselves and may have a substantial economic cost. Thus, an enforcement agency like the IRS is a necessity for any tax system. But how should it be run?

How the IRS Operates

Mention the IRS, and most people think of the dreaded tax audit. But you may be surprised to learn that the IRS now audits only about 1 percent of all individual tax returns. This fraction has declined dramatically over the last three decades; it was typically about 4 percent during the 1960s.

Does this mean that if you file a tax return and omit reporting your wages or capital gains, you have only about a 1 in 100 chance of being caught in the act? Absolutely not, for several reasons.

First of all, the IRS does not just pick out of a hat which returns to audit, which would mean that everyone has the same chance of being audited. Instead, the probability that a return will be examined is influenced by a carefully developed secret formula, called the *discriminant index function* (DIF). This formula assigns a score to each return that reflects the estimated likelihood of significant noncompliance for that taxpayer, based on the amounts stated on the return for each type of income and deduction. Returns that fit the profile of those that have a significant dollar amount of evasion are the most likely to be examined. For example, in fiscal year 2006, the fraction of nonbusiness returns audited was 0.6 percent for people with incomes between $25,000 and $50,000 but [was] 3.6 percent for those with some business income and income above $100,000. Among very large corporations, nearly every single one is audited every year by a team of IRS examiners, although recent events make clear that these audits fail to catch all noncompliance among these firms.

Face-to-face audits are by no means the only way the IRS checks on the accuracy of tax returns. Another important tool for the IRS is *information reporting*. For example, employers are required to send information reports on wages and salaries for all their employees to the IRS. The IRS computers then match up most of these information reports against tax returns. About three-quarters of the audits that go into the 1 percent audit rate mentioned above refer to correspondence by tax examiners generated by computer matching of returns to information reports. If the computer detects a discrepancy, a computer-generated notice is automatically sent out to the taxpayer asking him or her to pay up or provide an explanation. Most interest and dividend income and pensions are also subject to information reporting. It is therefore no accident that these types of income, together with wages and salaries, have near 100 percent compliance rates, as reported in Table 5.1. In fiscal year 2006, the IRS received 1.56 billion information reports, 97 percent of which were transmitted in electronic form. The increased use and efficiency of computer checks based on information reporting has clearly substituted for the decline in face-to-face audits.

Another major enforcement tool of the IRS is withholding of taxes on wage and salary income, a practice it has followed since 1943. All firms above a certain size are required to remit payments directly to the IRS based on an estimate of the personal income taxes owed by their employees on their labor income. In 2004, 88 percent of personal income tax liability was withheld in this manner. The amount withheld for an employee is usually greater than actual tax liability over the course of the year, so the vast majority of individual taxpayers (78 percent in 2004) are eligible for a refund. This creates an added incentive for taxpayers to file their returns in a timely manner. . . .

Together, information reporting and withholding are powerful enforcement mechanisms. A stark illustration of that is provided by the IRS tax gap study. . . . For income subject to both withholding and substantial information reporting, the misreporting rate is just 1.2 percent. . . . Strikingly, the misreporting rate is 53.9 percent for income not subject to withholding and subject to "little or no" information reporting. . . .

<h2 style="text-align:center">WHAT FACILITATES ENFORCEMENT?</h2>

Congress has handed the IRS a difficult if not impossible task—to fairly and efficiently administer a tax system that is plagued with inequities and complexities. Just as bill collectors are never popular, the IRS will never be, but the tax enforcement process could be less painful and costly if the tax system were different. What features of a tax system facilitate enforcement?

As we discussed earlier in this chapter, some of the aspects that make a tax system simpler also facilitate enforcement. Information reporting and also tax withholding and remittance at the source of payment are the best examples. The effectiveness of these measures is amply demonstrated by compliance rates that are vastly higher for income that is subject to them (such as employee wages and salaries) than for income that is not (such as income of informal suppliers), shown in Table 5.1. Another feature that facilitates enforcement is limiting the number of credits, deductions, and other nonrevenue-raising aspects of the tax system that stretch IRS resources. But a number of other factors also strongly influence the effectiveness of tax enforcement. We turn to these next. . . .

Much of the tax evasion in our country occurs on types of income that are difficult for the IRS to monitor. Self-employment income is the most important example. Some types of capital income are also relatively easy to conceal, at least when compared to wages and salaries. The tax system could become considerably easier to enforce if we simply give up on trying to tax some of these types of income. . . .

The more that taxpayers are required to document their incomes and deductions, the easier it is to enforce the tax system. The current requirement that a Social Security number be provided for each dependent exemption is one particularly effective example. But most types of deductions, such as those for charitable contributions or employee business expenses, are generally reported without any documentation; only if the taxpayer is audited must he or she provide the documentation. Requiring documentation for more items would make evasion much more difficult. A potentially even more effective approach would be to have the IRS check most or all returns, requiring taxpayers to provide some justification for each item. This may seem far-fetched, but in the Netherlands, the tax authority annually audits every single personal income tax return, at least briefly.

Of course, requiring more documentation from taxpayers and expanding auditing could make the taxpaying process considerably more complicated for both the taxpayer and the IRS, even as it cuts down on evasion. In this case, there is a clear trade-off among the multiple objectives of tax policy. In other situations, costs of enforcement can be transferred from the government budget to the private sector with substantial flexibility. For example, requiring more documentation of tax-payers who make some personal use of a business car may facilitate an audit, but it certainly increases the taxpayers' cost of compliance. For a given degree of enforcement effectiveness, whether this is a good idea depends on whether the sum of these costs declines. Shifting the costs off the budget onto the taxpayers does not necessarily constitute an improved process.

Notes and Questions

1. *Taxing self-employment income.* As Slemrod and Bakija make clear, the Achilles' heel of income tax enforcement is self-employment income. Self-employment income raises, on a much larger scale, the same kinds of questions discussed above with respect to tips. If Congress is unwilling to give the IRS the tools necessary to enforce the tax liabilities of self-employed housepainters (for example), would it be better to provide an official exclusion for such income? Unlike the case of tips, where compliance could be dramatically improved simply by increasing the 8 percent figure in §6053 to 12 or 13 percent, there is no magic bullet for improving income tax compliance by the self-employed. Only a massive auditing campaign — expensive for the IRS and intrusive for taxpayers — could make a significant dent in tax evasion by the self-employed. That suggests an official exclusion may be the only way to bring the law on the books into line with the law in practice. What do you suppose would happen, though, if Congress declared that all self-employment income was exempt from income tax? Would there be anyone left who did not claim to be self-employed?

2. *Unreported income versus overstated deductions.* Were you surprised that the tax gap due to underreported income on personal returns is more than five times greater than the tax gap due to overstated exemptions, deductions, adjustments, and credits? The huge difference suggests that tax-payers have a good sense of what kinds of cheating are and are not likely to be detected by the IRS. If a taxpayer claims unusually large deductions, the IRS computers can identify the return as a good candidate for audit. In addition, once a return is selected for audit (either randomly or because of unusually large deductions) any competent IRS agent will ask for documentation in support of all claimed deductions. In short, cheating by overstating deductions is dangerous. The standard deduction also helps to reduce overstating of deductions. A taxpayer with no legitimate item-ized deductions could not cheat by falsely claiming he gave $1,000 to his church, because $1,000 would be less than his standard deduction amount. He could cheat only by claiming he gave more than his standard deduction amount, and a charitable deduction that large, claimed by a taxpayer with modest gross income, might trigger an audit. It is much safer to cheat by not reporting income, as long as the income is not reported to the IRS by the payor (on a W-2 in the case of employment income, or on a 1099 in the case of interest, dividends, and other payments subject to payor information reporting). A taxpayer who receives a payment not subject to payor information reporting can omit the payment from income almost

with impunity. Since the omission is not apparent from the face of the return, it furnishes no basis for the IRS computers to identify the return as a good candidate for audit. Even if the return does happen to be selected for audit, nothing on the return will alert the IRS agent to the existence of the unreported income.

3. *Multiple tax bases as a response to cheating.* One partial solution to problems of compliance and enforcement is to raise revenue from several different taxes. For example, a state might have both an 8 percent income tax and a 6 percent sales tax. If taxpayers consume the vast majority of their incomes on items subject to sales tax, it might seem that replacing the two-tax system with a 14 percent income tax would produce a similar distribution of tax burdens more simply. But consider the self-employed housepainter who cheats on his income tax. Under the two-tax system, at least he has to pay a 6 percent sales tax when he spends his earnings. Under a 14 percent income tax, however, he might pay no tax at all. Using several different tax bases, each with its own peculiar enforcement difficulties, can diminish the significance of the enforcement problems of any one tax base. However, the federal tax system, unlike most state tax systems, takes little advantage of this insight. The other major federal revenue source — the social security wage tax — is just as vulnerable as the income tax to cheating by the self-employed.

4. *The arithmetic of noncompliance.* To the extent taxpayers are motivated to comply by fear of getting caught if they cheat, they are interested in both their chances of getting caught and the consequences that they could face. Even if Congress is unwilling to fund an audit rate of more than, say, 2 percent, fear of detection might still generate a high level of compliance if the consequences are serious enough. But how serious would be serious enough? Suppose a taxpayer is considering whether to cheat by not reporting $50,000 of self-employment income, thereby avoiding $10,000 of tax liability. He estimates his chance of getting caught at 2 percent. Assuming he is risk-neutral,[17] how large a potential cheating penalty would he have to face before opting to report the income? If he reports the income, the cost of doing so is simply the $10,000 tax he must pay. If he does not report the income, the expected cost is $2\% \times (\$10,000 + x)$, where x equals the amount of the penalty he will be required to pay if he is caught. He will choose to report the income if the expected cost of cheating is greater than the cost of reporting the income — that is, if $2\% \times (\$10,000 + x) > \$10,000$. In order for the expected cost of cheating to be greater than $10,000, the penalty must be greater than $490,000, which means the penalty must be more than 4,900 percent of the amount of tax evaded. Even assuming the IRS can prove the omission of the income from the return was fraudulent, the actual penalty (under the §6663 civil fraud provision) will be only 75 percent.[18] Thus, the expected cost of cheating will be $2\% \times (\$10,000 + \$7,500) = \$350$, which is far less than the $10,000 cost of not cheating. In short, civil penalties of the magnitude

---

17. For example, he is indifferent between definitely having to pay $10 and running a 10 percent chance of having to pay $100.

18. In the absence of fraud, §6662 imposes a civil penalty for "negligence or disregard of rules or regulations," or for a "substantial understatement" of income tax, equal to 20 percent of the amount of tax involved.

Congress has been willing to impose will have little positive effect on compliance when the chance of audit and detection is low.

5. *Information reporting and compliance.* The taxpayer's analysis will be very different, of course, if the income he is considering not reporting has been reported to the IRS by the payor on a W-2 or 1099. In that case, the perceived chance of detection may be close to 100 percent, assuming the taxpayer is aware of IRS computer matching of information reporting with Form 1040. Even the 20 percent penalty under §6662 (for negligence or substantial understatement of tax liability) would be sufficient to keep the taxpayer honest if he estimates the chance of detection at 90 percent. He would then compare the $10,000 cost of compliance with an expected cost for noncompliance of $90\% \times (\$10{,}000 + \$2{,}000) = \$10{,}800$.

6. *A small chance of a huge penalty?* Even if the risk of getting caught is quite low, compliance may be high if taxpayers believe there is a real (albeit small) chance of a felony conviction for cheating. Unfortunately, many people appear to realize that the risk of criminal prosecution for understating tax liability is very low, unless the amount of tax involved is extremely large, or the situation has unusually high visibility that makes it an attractive target. Of course, even at a near-zero chance of prosecution, compliance might be high if the penalty for conviction was facing a firing squad. The most cost-effective enforcement technique might be to combine a very low audit rate with capital punishment for the rare cheater who is caught, but concerns about proportionality of punishment have ruled out this approach.

Cell

TAX RETURN PREPARATION STANDARDS AND PENALTIES

A. ABA AND TREASURY RETURN PREPARATION STANDARDS

AMERICAN BAR ASSOCIATION FORMAL ETHICS OPINION 85-352

(1985)

A lawyer may advise reporting a position on a tax return so long as the lawyer believes in good faith that the position is warranted in existing law or can be supported by a good faith argument for an extension, modification or reversal of existing law and there is some realistic possibility of success if the matter is litigated.

The Committee has been requested by the Section of Taxation of the American Bar Association to reconsider the "reasonable basis" standard in the Committee's Formal Opinion 314 governing the position a lawyer may advise a client to take on a tax return.

Opinion 314 (April 27, 1965) was issued in response to a number of specific inquiries regarding the ethical relationship between the Internal Revenue Service and lawyers practicing before it. The opinion formulated general principles governing this relationship, including the following:

> [A] lawyer who is asked to advise his client in the course of the preparation of the client's tax returns may freely urge the statement of positions most favorable to the client just as long as there is a *reasonable basis* for this position. (Emphasis supplied.)

The Committee is informed that the standard of "reasonable basis" has been construed by many lawyers to support the use of any colorable claim on a tax return to justify exploitation of the lottery of the tax return audit selection process. This view is not universally held, and the Committee does not believe that the reasonable basis standard, properly interpreted and applied, permits this construction.

However, the Committee is persuaded that as a result of serious controversy over this standard and its persistent criticism by distinguished members of the tax bar, IRS officials and members of Congress, sufficient doubt has been created regarding the validity of the standard so as to erode its effectiveness as an ethical guideline. For this reason, the Committee has concluded that it should be restated. Another reason for restating the standard is that since publication of Opinion 314, the ABA has adopted in succession the Model Code of Professional Responsibility (1969, revised 1980) and the Model Rules of Professional Conduct (1983). Both the Model Code and the Model Rules directly address the duty of a lawyer in presenting or arguing positions for a client in language that does not refer to "reasonable basis." It is therefore appropriate to conform the standard of Opinion 314 to the language of the new rules. . . .

The ethical standards governing the conduct of a lawyer in advising a client on positions that can be taken in a tax return are no different from those governing a lawyer's conduct in advising or taking positions for a client in other civil matters. Although the Model Rules distinguish between the roles of advisor and advocate,[19] both roles are involved here, and the ethical standards applicable to them provide relevant guidance. In many cases a lawyer must realistically anticipate that the filing of the tax return may be the first step in a process that may result in an adversary relationship between the client and the IRS. This normally occurs in situations when a lawyer advises an aggressive position on a tax return, not when the position taken is a safe or conservative one that is unlikely to be challenged by the IRS.

Rule 3.1 of the Model Rules, which is in essence a restatement of DR 7-102(A)(2) of the Model Code, states in pertinent part:

> A lawyer shall not bring or defend a proceeding, or assert or controvert an issue therein, unless there is a basis for doing so that is not frivolous, which includes a good faith argument for an extension, modification or reversal of existing law.

Rule 1.2(d), which applies to representation generally, states:

> A lawyer shall not counsel a client to engage, or assist a client, in conduct that the lawyer knows is criminal or fraudulent, but a lawyer may discuss the legal consequences of any proposed course of conduct with a client and may counsel or assist a client to make a good faith effort to determine the validity, scope, meaning or application of the law.

On the basis of these rules and analogous provisions of the Model Code, a lawyer, in representing a client in the course of the preparation of the client's tax return, may advise the statement of positions most favorable to the client if the

---

19. *See, e.g.,* Model Rules 2.1 and 3.1.

lawyer has a good faith belief that those positions are warranted in existing law or can be supported by a good faith argument for an extension, modification or reversal of existing law. A lawyer can have a good faith belief in this context even if the lawyer believes the client's position probably will not prevail.[20] However, good faith requires that there be some realistic possibility of success if the matter is litigated.

This formulation of the lawyer's duty in the situation addressed by this opinion is consistent with the basic duty of the lawyer to a client, recognized in ethical standards since the ABA Canons of Professional Ethics, and in the opinions of this Committee: zealously and loyally to represent the interests of the client within the bounds of the law.

Thus, where a lawyer has a good faith belief in the validity of a position in accordance with the standard stated above that a particular transaction does not result in taxable income or that certain expenditures are properly deductible as expenses, the lawyer has no duty to require as a condition of his or her continued representation that riders be attached to the client's tax return explaining the circumstances surrounding the transaction or the expenditures.

In the role of advisor, the lawyer should counsel the client as to whether the position is likely to be sustained by a court if challenged by the IRS, as well as of the potential penalty consequences to the client if the position is taken on the tax return without disclosure. Section 6661 [now §6662] of the Internal Revenue Code imposes a penalty for substantial understatement of tax liability which can be avoided if the facts are adequately disclosed or if there is or was substantial authority for the position taken by the taxpayer. Competent representation of the client would require the lawyer to advise the client fully as to whether there is or was substantial authority for the position taken in the tax return. If the lawyer is unable to conclude that the position is supported by substantial authority, the lawyer should advise the client of the penalty the client may suffer and of the opportunity to avoid such penalty by adequately disclosing the facts in the return or in a statement attached to the return. If after receiving such advice the client decides to risk the penalty by making no disclosure and to take the position initially advised by the lawyer in accordance with the standard stated above, the lawyer has met his or her ethical responsibility with respect to the advice.

In all cases, however, with regard both to the preparation of returns and negotiating administrative settlements, the lawyer is under a duty not to mislead the Internal Revenue Service deliberately, either by misstatements or by silence or by permitting the client to mislead. Rules 4.1 and 8.4(c); DRs 1-102(A)(4), 7-102(A)(3) and (5).

In summary, a lawyer may advise reporting a position on a return even where the lawyer believes the position probably will not prevail, there is no "substantial authority" in support of the position, and there will be no disclosure of the position in the return. However, the position to be asserted must be one which the lawyer in good faith believes is warranted in existing law or can be supported by a good faith argument for an extension, modification or reversal of existing law. This requires that there is some realistic possibility of success if the matter is litigated. In

---

20. Comment to Rule 3.11; *see also* Model Code EC 7-4.

addition, in his role as advisor, the lawyer should refer to potential penalties and other legal consequences should the client take the position advised.

Notes and Questions

1. *No legal effect, but considerable influence.* ABA ethics opinions have no legal force. They are likely, however, to be influential with those who do have the power to discipline attorneys for ethical violations — state bar disciplinary committees and, ultimately, state supreme courts. It is unlikely that conduct permissible under Opinion 85-352 would be considered an ethical violation by a disciplinary committee or a supreme court.

2. *Serving aces to an empty court?* According to Opinion 85-352, "In many cases a lawyer must realistically anticipate that the filing of the tax return may be the first step in a process that may result in an adversarial relationship between the client and the IRS." Crucial to the Opinion's analysis, this sentence treats the filing of a tax return as part of the litigation process, so that whatever is ethical in litigation will be ethical in tax return preparation. It is ethical for an attorney to take a litigating position he thinks will probably not prevail because there is another party (represented by counsel, or at least with the right to be represented by counsel) presenting the argument against that position, and there is a judge or jury to decide which side is right. The classic explanation is from Boswell's *Life of Johnson*. Boswell asks Dr. Johnson, "But what do you think of supporting [as a lawyer] a case which you know to be bad?" Johnson replies, "Sir, you do not know it to be good or bad till the Judge determines it." Are you persuaded that the litigation model should apply to the filing of a tax return, when only 1 or 2 percent of all tax returns are audited? If you take a position in litigation that has only a 40 percent chance of prevailing on the merits, you will succeed only if the judge (or jury) decides the issue in your favor. But if you take an undisclosed 40 percent position on a tax return, it is far more likely that you will succeed because the IRS never audits the return (or the IRS agent misses the position, even if the return is audited) than because the position prevails on the merits after audit and litigation. If filing a tax return should be viewed as the first step in an adversary proceeding, then perhaps someone who serves ace after ace because there is no one on the other side of the net should be viewed as a great tennis player. What, if anything, would be wrong with an ethical rule that an attorney may advise a client to take a tax return position with a less than 50 percent chance of prevailing on the merits, but only if the position is fully disclosed on the return in order to facilitate a challenge by the IRS?

3. *The jurat.* The jurat on Form 1040, which must be signed by both the taxpayer and the paid return preparer (if there is one), reads, "I declare that I have examined this return and accompanying schedules and statements, and to the best of my knowledge and belief, they are true, correct, and complete." How can taking a return position that you think would probably lose on the merits be reconciled with the jurat? One would think it could not be reconciled, yet both Treasury and Congress have implicitly acknowledged that some positions that would probably not prevail on the merits can be taken consistently with the jurat. Read on.

B.   STATUTORY PENALTIES FOR INACCURATE TAX RETURNS AND TREASURY STANDARDS OF PRACTICE

Section 6662 imposes a "substantial understatement" penalty on a taxpayer who files a tax return that understates his correct tax liability by more than the greater of $5,000 or 10 percent of the correct tax liability.[21] The penalty is 20 percent of the understatement. An understatement subject to penalty does not arise from either (1) an undisclosed return position for which the taxpayer has "substantial authority," or (2) a position that lacks substantial authority, but that is adequately disclosed and for which there is a "reasonable basis." It is clear from the regulations that in some cases there will be substantial authority for a position with a less than 50 percent chance of prevailing on the merits if challenged.[22] Even if an undisclosed return position lacks substantial authority, §6664(c) provides that the taxpayer will not be subject to penalty if the taxpayer establishes that "there was reasonable cause . . . and that the taxpayer acted in good faith." Good faith reliance on professional advice is the most common route to §6664(c) relief.

Under certain circumstances §6694 imposes a penalty on an income tax return preparer who prepares a return (or provides advice in connection with the preparation of a return)[23] that understates the taxpayer's actual tax liability. The amount of the penalty is the greater of $1,000 or 50 percent of the taxpayer's income from preparing the return. Prior to 2007, an understatement of tax triggered the preparer penalty if (1) the position was not disclosed on the return and the position did not have at least a one-in-three chance of prevailing on the merits if litigated, or (2) the position was adequately disclosed on the return but the position was "frivolous." Legislation enacted in 2007 provided that an undisclosed position was subject to the preparer penalty if the preparer did not reasonably believe that the position "would more likely than not be sustained on its merits." Congress did not, however, change the accuracy standard imposed on *taxpayers* by §6662. The result was a major discrepancy between the accuracy standard for taxpayers and the accuracy standard for their return preparers. A taxpayer could take an undisclosed position without fear of penalty, even if the position would probably not prevail on the merits if litigated, as long as there was substantial authority for the position. A return preparer, however, would be subject to penalty for preparing a return taking such a position. In response to the complaints of return preparers, Congress amended §6694 again in 2008, making the preparer penalty standard consistent with the taxpayer penalty standard. Under the 2008 revision (which remains the law today), (1) an undisclosed position is subject to the preparer penalty "unless there is or was substantial authority for the position," and (2) a disclosed position is subject to the preparer penalty if there is no "reasonable basis" for the position. The taxpayer and preparer penalty provisions are now consistent with one another, with respect to both undisclosed and disclosed positions. Both provisions

---

21. Section 6662 also provides for a 20 percent negligence penalty, which can apply to understatements too small to trigger the substantial understatement penalty. A return position is subject to the negligence penalty only if it lacks a "reasonable basis," and even then only if the taxpayer is not eligible for the "reasonable cause and good faith" exception of §6664(c).

22. Treas. Reg. §1.6662-4(d)(3).

23. It is possible to be a return preparer for purposes of the §6694 penalty without having signed the return. *See* Treas. Reg. §1.6694-1(b)(3).

permit the taking of probably wrong undisclosed positions, as long as the positions satisfy the substantial authority standard. Granting the desirability of consistency between the two penalty standards, should Congress have raised the accuracy standard for taxpayers, rather than lowering the standard for preparers?

Regulations at 31 C.F.R. part 10 (universally referred to by tax practitioners as Circular 230[24]) regulate the practice of taxpayers' representatives before the Treasury Department (including the Internal Revenue Service). Proposed §10.34 of Circular 230, if finalized, will provide that a practitioner may not willfully, recklessly, or through gross incompetence sign a return containing an undisclosed position for which there is not substantial authority, or advise a client to take an undisclosed return position lacking substantial authority. Violation of Circular 230 standards can lead to a practitioner's suspension or the revocation of the practitioner's right to represent clients before the IRS. In addition, 31 U.S.C. §330(b) permits the Treasury to impose monetary penalties for Circular 230 violations. The only statutory limitation on the penalty amount is the practitioner's income from the penalized conduct.

Problem 1. You are an attorney advising a client in connection with the preparation of his income tax return for the year recently ended. You conclude that the correct tax treatment of one of the client's transactions is uncertain. Most likely, the client owes about $100,000 of tax as a result of the transaction. However, there is a reasonable basis (but not substantial authority) for the position that he owes no tax. You inform the client that the position has about a 20 percent likelihood of prevailing on the merits if challenged by the IRS, and that he will be subject to a 20 percent penalty under §6662 if he takes the position without disclosure. The client then asks you to estimate how likely it is that he will be audited (and that the IRS agent will notice this issue) if he takes the position without disclosure. Your educated guess is that the chances of audit and detection, absent disclosure, are about 10 percent.[25] You have no doubt why the client is asking for your estimate: He wants the information in order to decide whether not disclosing would be a smart bet. If you give him the information, he will compare the expected cost of disclosing with the expected cost of not disclosing. If he assumes audit and detection will inevitably follow if he discloses on the return that he is taking a position lacking substantial authority,[26] he will calculate the

---

24. Tax practitioners have no idea what happened to the first 229 circulars; if they exist at all, nobody ever mentions them. For another instance of this sort of thing, see Lewis Carroll, *Alice's Adventures in Wonderland*:

>   At this moment the King . . . read out from his book, "Rule Forty-two. *All persons more than a mile high to leave the court.*" . . .
>   "Well, I shan't go, at any rate," said Alice; "besides, that's not a regular rule: you invented it just now."
>   "It's the oldest rule in the book," said the King.
>   "Then it ought to be Number One," said Alice.
>   The King turned pale, and shut his notebook hastily.

25. In recent years, the overall audit rate has hovered around 1 percent. However, most returns selected for audit are not selected randomly, and your client's tax return has features that make an audit significantly more likely than the overall rate of 1 percent.

26. Actually, there is good reason to think that the IRS has insufficient resources to follow up on all disclosures, so that the chance of audit and detection following disclosure is considerably less than 100 percent. If you estimate that the chance of audit and detection following disclosure is only about 50 or 60 percent, you could give your client that information along with the 10 percent odds in the case of no disclosure. The example in the text assumes disclosure leads to certain detection, in order to keep the calculations simple.

expected cost of disclosure as (80%)($100,000) = $80,000. This follows from a 100 percent chance of detection and an 80 percent chance of having to pay $100,000 tax (but no penalty) after the issue has been litigated.[27] He will calculate the expected cost of not disclosing as (10%)(80%)($100,000 + $20,000) = $9,600. There is a 10 percent chance the IRS will detect the issue, and an 80 percent chance the IRS will win when the issue is litigated. If both those events occur, your client will then have to pay $120,000, representing $100,000 tax and $20,000 penalty. Unless he is very strongly risk-averse,[28] he will easily choose nondisclosure (expected cost $9,600) over disclosure (expected cost $80,000). Should you answer his question about the odds of audit and detection? If you give him the information and he decides to play the audit lottery (i.e., not to disclose), may you continue to help him prepare the return?

C. WHY NOT A HIGHER STANDARD?

Many people are surprised—some are even scandalized—to learn that in some cases it is perfectly permissible to take undisclosed return positions that the taxpayer and the preparer think would probably not prevail on the merits if challenged by the IRS. Can you think of any arguments in favor of the current tax standards? Evaluate the argument set forth in the following paragraph.

> Penalties for "aggressive" return positions will be imposed, of course, only in cases in which it is ultimately determined that the return position was wrong on the merits. (The ultimate determination may be made by either the IRS or a court, depending on whether the taxpayer decides to litigate the issue.) If a penalty is imposed whenever a return takes a position that would probably not prevail on the merits if challenged, and if the penalty determination is made by the same decision-maker (IRS or court) that has just decided that the position loses on the merits, then the penalty will be imposed virtually every time a taxpayer loses on the merits. It would be extremely rare for a court or the IRS to conclude that the taxpayer loses on the merits, but that at the time the return was filed the odds were that the taxpayer would win on the merits. Thus, the practical effect of penalizing every undisclosed less-than-50-percent position would be to penalize every understatement of tax liability—which would obviously be a bad idea.

The argument has a certain appeal, although some may disagree that penalizing every understatement is obviously a bad idea. The bigger problem with the argument, however, is that it disregards the reasonable cause and good faith exception of §6664(c). It would be possible to have a general rule (in a revised §6662) that a substantial understatement attributable to a probably wrong position is subject to

---

27. For simplicity, the problem ignores costs of litigation.
28. A person is risk-neutral if he is indifferent, for example, between running a 10 percent chance of losing $100 and a certain loss of $10. A risk-averse person, by contrast, might be willing to pay $15 for insurance to eliminate a 10 percent chance of losing $100. One could be strongly risk-averse and still prefer an 8 percent chance of losing $120,000 to an 80 percent chance of losing $100,000.

penalty, combined with a §6664(c) exception for any taxpayer who reasonably and in good faith (albeit incorrectly) believed his return position was probably correct.

D. THE SPECIAL CASE OF TAX SHELTERS

As a practical matter, Congress can tolerate the revenue loss from undisclosed aggressive return positions when taxpayers stumble into areas of legal uncertainty — that is, when a taxpayer just happens to engage in a transaction with uncertain tax consequences, and resolves the legal doubt in his own favor on his return. Taxpayers simply don't stumble into such situations all that frequently. The threat to the revenues is of a different magnitude, however, if a taxpayer can, with near-impunity, engage in a dubious tax shelter transaction for the very purpose of saving taxes by playing the audit lottery — that is, hoping to prevail not because the tax shelter really "works," but because the IRS never detects the existence of the shelter. The revenue loss would be enormous if tax shelter promoters could market dubious shelters to thousands of audit-lottery playing taxpayers. Because of the special threat to the fisc posed by the combination of tax shelters and the audit lottery, special disclosure and penalty rules apply to tax shelter investments.

Reg. §1.6011-4, promulgated in 2003, requires disclosure on a taxpayer's annual return of certain information regarding any "listed transaction" or any other "reportable transaction." Both terms are defined in the regulation, and most tax shelters will fall within one definition or the other. Congress subsequently added a specific statutory penalty (contained in §6707A, added to the Code in 2004), for failure to meet the requirements of the regulation. The penalty is $10,000 for each failure (though penalties as high as $100,000 may be imposed if the failure is with respect to a "listed transaction," and higher penalties may be imposed on corporations or other entities). Certain other parties who advise, assist, or derive gross income from such transactions are also potentially subject to penalties, and must file information returns.[29] The disclosure requirements (and the penalties for their violation) are designed to prevent taxpayers from playing the audit lottery with respect to tax shelters. If a taxpayer investing in a reported transaction or listed transaction complies with the disclosure requirements, the IRS will be aware of the shelter and will be able to challenge the validity of the shelter (if it decides to do so).

Section 6662A imposes a penalty equal to 20 percent of the amount of an understatement of tax attributable to a listed transaction. The same penalty applies to a reportable transaction (other than a listed transaction) if tax avoidance or evasion is a significant purpose of the transaction. Failure properly to disclose the transaction can result in an additional 10 percent penalty. Although the reasonable-cause-and-good-faith exception of §6664(c) can be used to avoid the §6662A penalty, the exception applies only if (1) the taxpayer adequately disclosed to the IRS the facts of the transaction, (2) there was substantial authority for the taxpayer's position, and (3) the taxpayer reasonably believed the taxpayer's position was probably correct. Finally, §6662(b)(6), added to the Code in 2010, imposes a 20 percent penalty on "[a]ny disallowance of claimed tax benefits by reason of a

---

29. IRC §6111.

transaction lacking economic substance (within the meaning of §7701(*o*)"; the penalty is increased to 40 percent if the transaction is not disclosed on the tax-payer's return. The reasonable-cause-and-good-faith exception of §6664(c) does not apply to transactions described in §6662(b)(6), with the result that the new penalty provision imposes a form of strict liability.

Chapter 2

T HE SCOPE OF GROSS INCOME

A. CASH RECEIPTS: DOES SOURCE MATTER?

1. Generally, No

COMMISSIONER v. GLENSHAW GLASS CO.

348 U.S. 426 (1955)

MR. CHIEF JUSTICE WARREN delivered the opinion of the Court.

This litigation involves two cases with independent factual backgrounds yet presenting the identical issue. The two cases were consolidated for argument before the Court of Appeals for the Third Circuit and were heard en banc. The common question is whether money received as exemplary damages for fraud or as the punitive two-thirds portion of a treble-damage antitrust recovery must be reported by a taxpayer as gross income under §22(a) of the Internal Revenue Code of 1939 [the predecessor of current §61]. In a single opinion, 211 F.2d 928, the Court of Appeals affirmed the Tax Court's separate rulings in favor of the taxpayers. 18 T.C. 860; 19 T.C. 637. Because of the frequent recurrence of the question and differing interpretations by the lower courts of this Court's decisions bearing upon the problem, we granted the Commissioner of Internal Revenue's ensuing petition for certiorari.

The facts of the cases were largely stipulated and are not in dispute. So far as pertinent they are as follows:

Commissioner v. Glenshaw Glass Co. — The Glenshaw Glass Company, a Pennsylvania corporation, manufactures glass bottles and containers. It was engaged in protracted litigation with the Hartford-Empire Company, which manufactures machinery of a character used by Glenshaw. Among the claims advanced by Glenshaw were demands for exemplary damages for fraud and treble damages for injury to its business by reason of Hartford's violation of the federal antitrust laws. In December, 1947, the parties concluded a settlement of all pending litigation, by which Hartford paid Glenshaw approximately $800,000. Through a method of allocation which was approved by the Tax Court, and which is no longer in issue, it was ultimately determined that, of the total settlement, $324,529.94 represented payment of punitive damages for fraud and antitrust violations. Glenshaw did not report this portion of the settlement as income for the tax year involved. The Commissioner determined a deficiency claiming as taxable the entire sum less only deductible legal fees. As previously noted, the Tax Court and the Court of Appeals upheld the taxpayer.

Commissioner v. William Goldman Theatres, Inc. — William Goldman Theatres, Inc., a Delaware corporation operating motion picture houses in Pennsylvania, sued Loew's, Inc., alleging a violation of the federal antitrust laws and seeking treble damages. After a holding that a violation had occurred, the case was remanded to the trial court for a determination of damages. It was found that Goldman had suffered a loss of profits equal to $125,000 and was entitled to treble damages in the sum of $375,000. Goldman reported only $125,000 of the recovery as gross income and claimed that the $250,000 balance constituted punitive damages and as such was not taxable. The Tax Court agreed, 19 T.G. 637, and the Court of Appeals, hearing this with the Glenshaw case, affirmed. 211 F.2d 928.

It is conceded by the respondents that there is no constitutional barrier to the imposition of a tax on punitive damages. Our question is one of statutory construction: are these payments comprehended by §22(a)?

The sweeping scope of the controverted statute is readily apparent:

Sec. 22. Gross Income.

(a) General Definition. — "'Gross income' includes gains, profits, and income derived from salaries, wages, or compensation for personal service . . . of whatever kind and in whatever form paid, or from professions, vocations, trades, businesses, commerce, or sales, or dealings in property, whether real or personal, growing out of the ownership or use of or interest in such property; also from interest, rent, dividends, securities, or the transaction of any business carried on for gain or profit, *or gains or profits and income derived from any source whatever.* . . ." (Emphasis added.)

This Court has frequently stated that this language was used by Congress to exert in this field "the full measure of its taxing power." Helvering v. Clifford, 309 U.S. 331, 334; Helvering v. Midland Mutual Life Ins. Co., 300 U.S. 216, 223; Douglas v. Willcuts, 296 U.S. 1, 9; Irwin v. Gavit, 268 U.S. 161, 166. Respondents contend that punitive damages, characterized as "windfalls" flowing from the culpable conduct of third parties, are not within the scope of the section. But Congress applied no limitations as to the source of taxable receipts, nor restrictive labels as to their nature. And the Court has given a liberal construction to this broad phraseology in recognition of the intention of Congress to tax all gains except those specifically exempted. . . . [W]e cannot but ascribe content to the catchall provision of §22(a), "gains or profits and income derived from any source whatever." The importance of that phrase has been too frequently recognized since its first appearance in the Revenue Act of 1913 to say now that it adds nothing to the meaning of "gross income."

Nor can we accept respondents' contention that a narrower reading of §22(a) is required by the Court's characterization of income in Eisner v. Macomber, 252 U.S. 189, 207, as "the gain derived from capital, from labor, or from both combined." The Court was there endeavoring to determine whether the distribution of a corporate stock dividend constituted a realized gain to the shareholder, or changed "only the form, not the essence," of his capital investment. Id., at 210. It was held that the taxpayer had "received nothing out of the company's assets for his separate use and benefit." Id., at 211. The distribution, therefore, was held not a taxable event. In that context — distinguishing gain from capital — the definition served a useful purpose. But it was not meant to provide a touchstone to all future gross income questions.

Here we have instances of undeniable accessions to wealth, clearly realized, and over which the taxpayers have complete dominion. The mere fact that the payments were extracted from the wrongdoers as punishment for unlawful conduct cannot detract from their character as taxable income to the recipients. Respondents concede, as they must, that the recoveries are taxable to the extent that they compensate for damages actually incurred. It would be an anomaly that could not be justified in the absence of clear congressional intent to say that a recovery for actual damages is taxable but not the additional amount extracted as punishment for the same conduct which caused the injury. And we find no such evidence of intent to exempt these payments.

Reversed.

Mr. Justice Douglas dissents. Mr. Justice Harlan took no part in the consideration or decision of this case.

Notes and Questions

1. *Two types of reasons.* When a taxpayer is in receipt of an economic benefit, Congress might decide to exclude that benefit from the taxpayer's gross income for either of two types of reasons: because it believes benefits from a particular *source* should not be taxed, or because it believes a particular type of *non-cash benefit* should not be taxed. With *Glenshaw Glass*, we begin by considering the significance of the source of cash receipts. The next part of this chapter will consider the taxability of non-cash benefits.

2. *A page of history.* The language of former §22, and of current §61, could not be any clearer on the irrelevance of source. The old statute spoke of "income derived from any source whatever," and the current statute says that "gross income means all income from whatever source derived." The current statutory language is tautologous as a definition of income (" . . . income means . . . income")—which is why we will need to examine the question of noncash benefits in some detail later—but the statute certainly succeeds in making the point that source does not matter. Lest there be any lingering doubt, the current statute explicitly states that its listing of 15 types of income from 15 types of sources is illustrative, rather than exhaustive ("including (but not limited to) the following items"). In view of the clarity of the statutory language—even in the §22 version at issue in *Glenshaw Glass*—it would seem that there was no room for doubt about the taxability of windfalls. Why, then, was it necessary for the Supreme Court to resolve this issue? As the opinion suggests, the confusion stemmed from prominent dictum in the venerable *Eisner v. Macomber* case,[1] which defined income as being derived from labor or from capital (or from both combined). Under this definition, a pure windfall would arrive *ex nihilo*—derived from neither labor nor capital—and hence would not be taxable. The message of the *Glenshaw Glass* opinion is that the Supreme Court had not been thinking of windfalls when it offered the *Eisner v. Macomber* definition. When windfalls were called to the Court's attention

---

1. *Eisner v. Macomber,* the leading case on the realization doctrine, is set forth in section A of Chapter 3, dealing with the taxation of property transactions.

in *Glenshaw Glass,* the Court easily concluded they were within the scope of the Code's definition of gross income.[2]

3. *Windfalls and efficient taxation.* Is there any policy reason why windfalls should not be taxed? There is one policy reason why windfalls are especially *good* candidates for taxation. When a taxpayer must do something to produce gross income — either working or making an investment — the prospect of a tax on the resulting income discourages the income-producing activity. Faced with a tax on labor income, some people will choose tax-free leisure instead. Faced with a tax on investment income, some people will choose to consume now instead of saving and investing. When work and investment are taxed, but the alternatives of leisure and consumption are not, there is an efficiency cost. Suppose a taxpayer in the 30 percent tax bracket has an opportunity to earn $10,000 of overtime, which would leave him with additional after-tax income of $7,000. If he values the alternative use of his time — leisure — at $8,000, he will decide not to work the overtime. Even though his labor has a social value of $10,000 (as measured by the amount the employer is willing to pay), and even though his leisure has a social value of only $8,000, the tax system has caused him to choose the leisure. The tax system has turned $3,000 of the value of his labor into a positive externality that the taxpayer cannot capture, and that he therefore ignores in making his choice between overtime and leisure. This produces what economists refer to as a "deadweight loss" of $2,000 — the excess of the value of the forgone labor over the value of the leisure. The tax on investment income similarly produces deadweight loss when it causes a taxpayer to spend money now instead of investing it. From an efficiency standpoint (although not necessarily from a fairness standpoint) the best tax is one that does not depend on any choices made by the taxpayer; since such a tax is not based on taxpayer behavior, it cannot inefficiently discourage any behavior. By definition, a windfall arrives without any effort on the taxpayer's part, so a tax on windfalls is especially attractive from an efficiency perspective.

4. *What is a windfall?* If you were representing the government in *Glenshaw Glass,* and the Supreme Court gave you reason to believe (at oral argument) that it was inclined to follow the *Eisner v. Macomber* dictum excluding windfalls from gross income, would you have a fallback argument? You might be able to convince the court that the punitive damages in the two cases were not true windfalls, and thus were within the *Eisner v. Macomber* dictum after all. You could argue that the damages were really produced by the labor of the taxpayers' attorneys, by the capital invested by the taxpayers in pursuing their damage claims, or by a combination of labor and capital. Similarly, under the *Eisner v. Macomber* dictum the taxability of a Publishers' Clearinghouse sweepstakes award would depend on whether licking the envelope and putting it in the mailbox constituted labor, or perhaps on whether the taxpayer had to supply the postage (thus giving the taxpayer a capital investment). If arguments like these seem silly, that strongly suggests that the Supreme Court was right to put such arguments to rest in *Glenshaw Glass* by holding that even pure windfalls are taxable.

---

2. This view is not universal. For example, the Canadian income tax rules insist that income must have a source, and accordingly do not tax windfall gains.

5. *The tax treatment of antitrust defendants.* Some years after the *Glenshaw Glass* decision, Congress enacted §162(g), which denies a deduction for two-thirds of treble damage payments made by an antitrust defendant if the defendant also has been convicted of a criminal antitrust offense. Thus, the rule in such cases is that the plaintiff must include the punitive portion of the damages in income, but the defendant cannot deduct that portion. Is this fair? Does it suggest an argument for excluding the punitive part of the antitrust damages from the plaintiff's gross income?

6. *Tax policy and antitrust policy.* Why do you suppose Congress has authorized treble damage payments in antitrust cases? Does the reason tell us anything useful about whether the payments should be taxable to the recipients?

7. *A caveat.* Although the Supreme Court's holding that windfalls are taxable is itself significant, the more important aspect of *Glenshaw Glass* is its broader holding: Source is always irrelevant under the definition of gross income. A crucial caveat, however, is provided by the introductory phrase of §61. Gross income includes all income regardless of source, "Except as otherwise provided in this subtitle." Thus, source is irrelevant under §61 itself, but source may become relevant because some other Code section excludes receipts from a particular source from gross income. Source-based exclusions for cash receipts are considered in detail later in this chapter.

CESARINI v. UNITED STATES

296 F. Supp. 3 (N.D. Ohio 1969), *aff'd per curiam,* **428 F.2d 812 (6th Cir. 1970)**

YOUNG, District Judge: . . . In 1957, the plaintiffs purchased a used piano at an auction sale for approximately $15.00, and the piano was used by their daughter for piano lessons. In 1964, while cleaning the piano, plaintiffs discovered the sum of $4,467.00 in old currency, and since have retained the piano instead of discarding it as previously planned. Being unable to ascertain who put the money there, plaintiffs exchanged the old currency for new at a bank, and reported the sum of $4,467.00 on their 1964 joint income tax return as ordinary income from other sources. On October 18, 1965, plaintiffs filed an amended return . . . eliminating the sum of $4,467.00 from the gross income computation, and requesting a refund in the amount of $836.51, the amount allegedly overpaid as a result of the former inclusion of $4,467.00 in the original return for the calendar year of 1964. On January 18, 1966, the Commissioner of Internal Revenue rejected taxpayers' refund claim in its entirety, and plaintiffs filed the instant action in March of 1967.

Plaintiffs make three alternative contentions in support of their claim that the sum of $836.51 should be refunded to them. First, that the $4,467.00 found in the piano is not includable in gross income under Section 61 of the Internal Revenue Code. Secondly, even if the retention of the cash constitutes a realization of ordinary income under Section 61, it was due and owing in the year the piano was purchased, 1957, and by 1964, the statute of limitations provided by 26 U.S.C. §6501 had elapsed. And thirdly, that if the treasure trove money is gross income for the year 1964, it was entitled to capital gains treatment under Section 1221 of Title 26. . . .

After a consideration of the pertinent provisions of the Internal Revenue Code, Treasury Regulations, Revenue Rulings, and decisional law in the area, this Court has concluded that the taxpayers are not entitled to a refund of the amount requested, nor are they entitled to capital gains treatment on the income item at issue.

The starting point in determining whether an item is to be included in gross income is, of course, Section 61(a) of Title 26 U.S.C., and that section provides in part: "Except as otherwise provided in this subtitle, gross income means all income from whatever source derived, including (but not limited to) the following items: . . . "

Subsections (1) through (15) of Section 61(a) then go on to list fifteen items specifically included in the computation of the taxpayer's gross income, and Part II of Subchapter B of the 1954 Code (Sections 71 et seq.) deals with other items expressly included in gross income. While neither of these listings expressly includes the type of income which is at issue in the case at bar, Part III of Subchapter B (Sections 101 et seq.) deals with items specifically excluded from gross income, and found money is not listed in those sections either. This absence of express mention in any of the code sections necessitates a return to the "all income from whatever source" language of Section 61(a) of the code, and the express statement there that gross income is "not limited to" the following fifteen examples. Section 1.61-1(a) of the Treasury Regulations, the corresponding section to Section 61(a) in the 1954 Code, reiterates this broad construction of gross income, providing in part: "Gross income means all income from whatever source derived, unless excluded by law. Gross income includes income realized in any form, whether in money, property, or services. . . . "

The decisions of the United States Supreme Court have frequently stated that this broad all-inclusive language was used by Congress to exert the full measure of its taxing power under the Sixteenth Amendment to the United States Constitution. Commissioner of Internal Revenue v. Glenshaw Glass Co., 348 U.S. 426, 429 (1955); Helvering v. Clifford, 309 U.S. 331, 334 (1940); Helvering v. Midland Mutual Life Ins. Co., 300 U.S. 216, 223 (1937); Douglas v. Willcuts, 296 U.S. 1, 9 (1935); Irwin v. Gavit, 268 U.S. 161 (1925).

In addition, the Government in the instant case cites and relies upon an I.R.S. Revenue Ruling which is undeniably on point: "The finder of treasure trove is in receipt of taxable income, for Federal income tax purposes, to the extent of its value in United States currency, for the taxable year in which it is reduced to undisputed possession." Rev. Rul. 61, 1953-1, Cum. Bull. 17. . . .

Although not cited by either party, and noticeably absent from the Government's brief, the following Treasury Regulation appears in the 1964 Regulations, the year of the return in dispute:

§1.61-14 *Miscellaneous Items of Gross Income.*

(a) In general. In addition to the items enumerated in section 61 (a), there are many other kinds of gross income. . . . Treasure trove, to the extent of its value in United States currency, constitutes gross income for the taxable year in which it is reduced to undisputed possession.

Identical language appears in the 1968 Treasury Regulations, and is found in all previous years back to 1958. This language is the same in all material respects as that found in Rev. Rul. [61, 1953-1,] Cum. Bull. 17, and is undoubtedly an attempt to codify that ruling into the Regulations which apply to the 1954 Code. This Court is of the opinion that Treas. Reg. §1.61-14(a) is dispositive of the major issue in this case if the $4,467.00 found in the piano was "reduced to undisputed possession" in the year petitioners reported it, for this Regulation was applicable to returns filed in the calendar year of 1964.

This brings the Court to the second contention of the plaintiffs: that if any tax was due, it was in 1957 when the piano was purchased, and by 1964 the Government was blocked from collecting it by reason of the statute of limitations. Without reaching the question of whether the voluntary payment in 1964 constituted a waiver on the part of the taxpayers, this Court finds that the $4,467.00 sum was properly included in gross income for the calendar year of 1964. Problems of when title vests, or when possession is complete in the field of federal taxation, in the absence of definitive federal legislation on the subject, are ordinarily determined by reference to the law of the state in which the taxpayer resides, or where the property around which the dispute centers is located. Since both the taxpayers and the property in question are found within the State of Ohio, Ohio law must govern as to when the found money was "reduced to undisputed possession" within the meaning of Treas. Reg. §1.61-14 and Rev. Rul. [61, 1953-1,] Cum. Bull. 17. . . .

[Under Ohio property law], if plaintiffs had resold the piano in 1958, not knowing of the money within it, they later would not be able to succeed in an action against the purchaser who did discover it. Under Ohio law, the plaintiffs must have actually found the money to have superior title over all but the true owner, and they did not discover the old currency until 1964. Unless there is present a specific state statute to the contrary, the majority of jurisdictions are in accord with the Ohio rule. Therefore, this Court finds that the $4,467.00 in old currency was not "reduced to undisputed possession" until its actual discovery in 1964, and thus the United States was not barred by the statute of limitations from collecting the $836.51 in tax during that year.

[The Court's rejection of the taxpayers' claim that they were entitled to capital gains treatment is omitted.]

Since it appears to the Court that the income tax on these taxpayers' gross income for the calendar year of 1964 has been properly assessed and paid, this taxpayers' suit for a refund in the amount of $836.51 must be dismissed, and judgment entered for the United States. An order will be entered accordingly.

Notes and Questions

1. *Two piano variations.* In light of *Glenshaw Glass*, *Cesarini* is not a difficult case. Even viewing the money found in the piano as pure windfall (rather than as a spectacular return on a $15 investment), it is clearly taxable. But what about two variations on the *Cesarini* facts? (1) The taxpayers discover a $10,000 diamond necklace inside the piano; or (2) the taxpayers discover that the piano is actually a valuable antique Steinway, once used by Rachmaninoff, and worth at least $10,000. If the *Cesarini* court is right that Treas. Reg. §1.61-14 (the treasure trove regulation) applies to money found in a piano, then jewelry found in a piano presumably is also taxable treasure trove. By contrast, the taxpayers in the Steinway hypothetical merely discovered that property they already owned (and knew they owned) was more valuable than they had thought. That sort of discovery is probably not covered by the treasure trove regulation. Moving from the technical question of the scope of the treasure trove regulation to broader

policy considerations, can you think of any policy justifications for taxing the found money, but not taxing either the necklace or the discovery that the piano is a Steinway? In other words, are there policy arguments for taxing only *cash* windfalls?

2. *Enforcement.* If you found money in an old piano, how would the IRS know about it? The IRS would almost certainly *not* know, unless you decided to tell. The Service was aware of the Cesarinis' find only because they originally reported it as income on their tax return, and then later decided to sue for a refund. Had the Cesarinis been less forthcoming, they almost certainly would have escaped paying tax on the money. More generally, how does the IRS ever find out about a taxpayer's receipt of income if the taxpayer does not choose to report the income on his return? Most income — including wages, interest, and dividends — is subject to "information reporting," which means the payor must notify the IRS that it has made taxable payments to the payee. Information reporting for wages is on Form W-2; for most other reportable types of income, information reporting is on Form 1099. IRS computers then match the payer's information reporting with the payee's tax return. If the payee's tax return omits income items shown on a W-2 or 1099, the payee can expect to hear from the IRS about the discrepancy. Of course, this system depends on honest information reporting by payors, but compliance by payors with information reporting requirements is generally good. Compared with individual taxpayers, payors are few and easy for the IRS to audit; good audit coverage of payors gives them reason to file accurate W-2s and 1099s. There are types of income, however, for which information reporting is not required — including a great deal of self-employment income. It is very difficult for the IRS to detect underreporting of income not subject to information reporting. Accordingly, compliance and enforcement with respect to self-employment income not subject to information reporting (and probably with respect to money found in old pianos) is poor.

2. But Tax-Free Recovery of "Capital" Is Allowed

Section 61(a)(3) states that gross income includes "*Gains* derived from dealings in property." The taxation of property transactions will be explored in depth in Chapter 3, but a basic understanding of the concept of *gain* is needed to understand the scope of the §61 definition of gross income.

Example 1.   Several years ago, Jane bought a tract of raw land as an investment, paying $50,000. This year, she sells it for $80,000. How much gain does she have under §61(a)(3)?

The answer is governed by two Code provisions, §§1001 and 1012. Section 1001(a) defines the gain on the sale of property as the excess of the "amount realized" on the sale over the "adjusted basis" of the property. Section 1001(b) defines a taxpayer's amount realized on a sale as the cash received by the taxpayer plus the fair market value of any non-cash property received. In a sale for cash, the taxpayer's amount realized is simply the amount of cash received. Section 1012 defines a taxpayer's basis in an asset as "the cost of such property." Although the term "cost" is sometimes given a specialized meaning for tax purposes (as we will see later), most of the time §1012 tax "cost" is precisely what a layperson would expect. Here, Jane's tax cost is the $50,000 she paid for the land. Section 1016 provides for certain adjustments in moving from §1012 basis to "adjusted basis," but none of those adjustments are applicable here. Thus, Jane's amount realized is $80,000, her adjusted basis is $50,000, and her gain — the amount included in her gross income on account of the sale — is the $30,000 excess of amount realized over adjusted basis.

Those are the technical rules, and they seem intuitively sensible. Still, it's worth examining the logic supporting the intuition. Why shouldn't Jane have to include $80,000 in gross income as a result of the sale? After all, she ended up with $80,000 cash in her pocket, so why does she have to pay tax on only $30,000? The answer lurks in the tax treatment of the $50,000 Jane used to buy the land. She bought the land with "after-tax" dollars — in other words, with money on which she had already paid tax. Since she has already paid tax on the $50,000 once, she should not have to pay a second tax on the same amount when she sells the land. The concepts of *basis* and *adjusted basis* are tax accounting devices for keeping track of amounts on which the taxpayer has already been taxed, in order to prevent double taxation. In most cases, what a layperson would consider the cost of property is also the amount on which the taxpayer has already paid tax, with the result that §1012 "cost" is exactly what a layperson would suppose. The §1012 definition diverges from the everyday meaning in certain specialized situations, in which there is a difference between the everyday meaning of "cost" and the amount on which the taxpayer has previously paid tax. Several of those situations are examined in detail in the next chapter.

The concept of a tax-free recovery of previously taxed amounts can apply even where there has been no property transaction.

Example 2.   Last year Jane paid $2,000 in state income tax, by way of wage withholding. She took the standard deduction (§63(c)) rather than itemizing her deductions, so she claimed no federal income tax deduction on last year's return with respect to her state income tax payments. (Taxpayers who itemize their deductions are permitted by §164(a)(3) to deduct state and local income tax payments.) The $2,000 withheld last year exceeded Jane's actual state income tax liability for that year by $250, so this year she received a $250 state income tax refund. Must Jane include the refund in gross income on her federal income tax return for this year?

She does not have to include the $250 refund in this year's gross income, for basically the same reason her gain on the sale of the land was only $30,000 (rather than $80,000). Since she did not deduct her state income tax payments on last year's federal tax return, she paid federal income tax last year on the $2,000 of her wages devoted to state income tax withholding. When she receives a $250 refund this year, it represents a return of an amount on which she has already paid federal income tax; thus she is entitled to treat it as a tax-free recovery of a previously taxed amount. As a matter of technical tax analysis, this falls under the rubric of the exclusionary aspect of the tax benefit rule,[3] rather than being treated as an example of tax-free recovery of basis. The result is the same, however, as if Jane's state

---

3. The exclusionary aspect of the rule is codified by §111.

income tax refund claim were treated as an asset in which she had a $250 adjusted basis.

Example 3.   The facts are the same as in the previous example, except that last year Jane itemized her deductions rather than claiming the standard deduction. Her standard deduction last year would have been $5,000. Instead, she was able to claim itemized deductions totaling $7,500 (including a $2,000 deduction for state income tax withheld). This year she receives a $250 state income tax refund, on account of overwithholding last year. Must Jane include the refund in gross income on her federal income tax return for this year?

This time she *does* have to include the $250 refund in this year's gross income. Because she claimed a deduction on last year's federal income tax return for state income tax withholding, she did not pay federal income tax last year on any portion of her $2,000 of withheld wages. As a result, the $250 refund is not a refund of a previously taxed amount, and she must include it in this year's gross income. Technically, this falls under the rubric of the inclusionary aspect of the tax benefit rule.[4] The result is just the same, however, as if Jane's state income tax refund claim were treated as an asset in which she had an adjusted basis of zero.

Example 4.   Last year Jane had $2,000 of state income tax withheld from her wages. She claimed a total of $5,100 of itemized deductions on her federal income tax return for last year, consisting of $2,000 of state income tax withheld during the year and $3,100 of other itemized deductions. If she had not itemized deductions on her return for last year, she could have claimed a $5,000 standard deduction. This year she receives a $250 state income tax refund, on account of overwithholding last year. Must Jane include any or all of the refund in gross income on her federal income tax return for this year?

Although technically Jane deducted the entire $2,000 of state income tax withholding on last year's return, as a practical matter she deducted only $100 of the withholding. If the withholding had been only $1,900 (or any smaller amount) instead of $2,000, she would have claimed the standard deduction—thereby claiming no state income tax deduction. Of the $2,000 technically deducted, then, only $100 was practically deducted. If only $100 was practically deducted, the $250 refund should be treated as consisting of two portions. The first $100 of the refund should be treated as an amount on which she has not already paid tax (because of last year's deduction), so it should be taxable. The remaining $150 of the refund should be treated as an amount on which she has already paid tax (because she did not deduct that amount last year, practically speaking), so it should not be taxable. In other words, she should be treated as if she had a $150 basis in the $250 refund, and so should be taxed on $100. Taken together, the inclusionary and exclusionary aspects of the tax benefit rule produce precisely that result.

Because millions of taxpayers must deal with the tax consequences of state income tax refunds, it is important that the IRS explain the application of these rules in a way that ordinary taxpayers can understand. The instructions to Form 1040 contain a worksheet similar to the one set forth below. Try applying the worksheet to the facts of Examples 2, 3, and 4. Does the worksheet produce the correct results? If it does, do you see *why* it works?

_____

4. See section C.2.d of this chapter.

State and Local Income Tax Refund Worksheet

1. Enter the income tax refund from Form 1099-G.   1. _____
   But do not enter more than the amount you
   claimed as a state and local income tax deduction
   on Schedule A of last year's Form 1040.
2. Enter your total allowable itemized deductions from   2. _____
   last year's Schedule A.
3. Enter the amount of the standard deduction you   3. _____
   would have been allowed on last year's return if
   you had not itemized your deductions.
4. Subtract line 3 from line 2. If zero or less, enter 0.   4. _____
5. **Taxable part of your refund.** Enter the **smaller** of   5. _____
   line 1 or line 4 here and on Form 1040, line 10.

---

3. Source Matters When Congress Says Source Matters: Statutory Exclusions

a. Gifts and Bequests

COMMISSIONER v. DUBERSTEIN

363 U.S. 278 (1960)

Mr. Justice BRENNAN delivered the opinion of the Court.

These two cases concern the provision of the Internal Revenue Code which excludes from the gross income of an income taxpayer "the value of property acquired by gift." They pose the frequently recurrent question whether a specific transfer to a taxpayer in fact amounted to a "gift" to him within the meaning of the statute. The importance to decision of the facts of the cases requires that we state them in some detail.

No. 376, Commissioner v. Duberstein. The taxpayer, Duberstein, was president of the Duberstein Iron & Metal Company, a corporation with headquarters in Dayton, Ohio. For some years the taxpayer's company had done business with Mohawk Metal Corporation, whose headquarters were in New York City. The president of Mohawk was one Berman. The taxpayer and Berman had generally used the telephone to transact their companies' business with each other, which consisted of buying and selling metals. The taxpayer testified, without elaboration, that he knew Berman "personally" and had known him for about seven years. From time to time in their telephone conversations, Berman would ask Duberstein whether the latter knew of potential customers for some of Mohawk's products in which Duberstein's company itself was not interested. Duberstein provided the names of potential customers for these items.

One day in 1951 Berman telephoned Duberstein and said that the information Duberstein had given him had proved so helpful that he wanted to give the latter a present. Duberstein stated that Berman owed him nothing. Berman said that he had a Cadillac as a gift for Duberstein, and that the latter should send to New York for it; Berman insisted that Duberstein accept the car, and the latter finally did so, protesting however that he had not intended to be compensated for the information. At the time Duberstein already had a Cadillac and an Oldsmobile, and felt that he did not need another car. Duberstein testified that he did not think Berman would have sent him the Cadillac if he had not furnished him with information about the customers. It appeared that Mohawk later deducted the value of the Cadillac as a business expense on its corporate income tax return.

Duberstein did not include the value of the Cadillac in gross income for 1951, deeming it a gift. The Commissioner asserted a deficiency for the car's value against him, and in proceedings to review the deficiency the Tax Court affirmed the Commissioner's determination. It said that "The record is significantly barren of evidence revealing any intention on the part of the payor to make a gift. . . . The only justifiable inference is that the automobile was intended by the payer to be remuneration for services rendered to it by Duberstein." The Court of Appeals for the Sixth Circuit reversed.

No. 546, Stanton v. United States. The taxpayer, Stanton, had been for approximately 10 years in the employ of Trinity Church in New York City. He was comptroller of the Church corporation, and president of a corporation, Trinity Operating Company, the church set up as a fully owned subsidiary to manage its real estate holdings, which were more extensive than simply the church property. His salary by the end of his employment there in 1942 amounted to $22,500 a year. Effective November 30, 1942, he resigned from both positions to go into business for himself. The Operating Company's directors, who seem to have included the rector and vestrymen of the church, passed the following resolution upon his resignation: "BE IT RESOLVED that in appreciation of the services rendered by Mr. Stanton . . . a gratuity is hereby awarded to him of Twenty Thousand Dollars, payable to him in equal installments of Two Thousand Dollars at the end of each and every month commencing with the month of December, 1942; provided that, with the discontinuance of his services, the Corporation of Trinity Church is released from all rights and claims to pension and retirement benefits not already accrued up to November 30, 1942."

The Operating Company's action was later explained by one of its directors as based on the fact that, "Mr. Stanton was liked by all of the Vestry personally. He had a pleasing personality. He had come in when Trinity's affairs were in a difficult situation. He did a splendid piece of work, we felt. Besides that . . . he was liked by all of the members of the Vestry personally." And by another: "We were all unanimous in wishing to make Mr. Stanton a gift. Mr. Stanton had loyally and faithfully served Trinity in a very difficult time. We thought of him in the highest regard. We understood that he was going in business for himself. We felt that he was entitled to that evidence of good will."

On the other hand, there was a suggestion of some ill-feeling between Stanton and the directors, arising out of the recent termination of the services of one Watkins, the Operating Company's treasurer, whose departure was evidently attended by some acrimony. At a special board meeting on October 28, 1942, Stanton had intervened on Watkins' side and asked reconsideration of the matter. The minutes reflect that "resentment was expressed as to the 'presumptuous' suggestion that the action of the Board, taken after long deliberation, should be changed." The Board adhered to its determination that Watkins be separated from employment, giving him an opportunity to resign rather than be discharged. At another special meeting two days later it was revealed that Watkins had not resigned; the previous resolution terminating his services was then viewed as effective; and the Board voted the payment of six months' salary to Watkins in a resolution similar to that quoted in regard to Stanton, but which did not use the term "gratuity." At the meeting, Stanton announced that in order to avoid any such embarrassment or question at any time as to his willingness to resign if the Board desired, he was tendering his resignation. It was tabled, though not without dissent. The next week, on November 5, at another special meeting, Stanton again tendered his resignation which this time was accepted.

The "gratuity" was duly paid. So was a smaller one to Stanton's (and the Operating Company's) secretary, under a similar resolution, upon her resignation at the same time. The two corporations shared the expense of the payments. There was undisputed testimony that there were in fact no enforceable rights or claims to pension and retirement benefits which had not accrued at the time of the taxpayer's resignation, and that the last proviso of the resolution was inserted simply out of an abundance of caution. The taxpayer received in cash a refund of his contributions to the retirement plans, and there is no suggestion that he was entitled to more. He was required to perform no further services for Trinity after his resignation.

The Commissioner asserted a deficiency against the taxpayer after the latter had failed to include the payments in question in gross income. After payment of the deficiency and administrative rejection of a refund claim, the taxpayer sued the United States for a refund in the District Court for the Eastern District of New York. The trial judge, sitting without a jury, made the simple finding that the payments were a "gift," and judgment was entered for the taxpayer. The Court of Appeals for the Second Circuit reversed. . . .

The exclusion of property acquired by gift from gross income under the federal income tax laws was made in the first income tax statute passed under the authority of the Sixteenth Amendment, and has been a feature of the income tax statutes ever since. The meaning of the term "gift" as applied to particular transfers has always been a matter of contention. Specific and illuminating legislative history on the point does not appear to exist. . . . The meaning of the statutory term has been shaped largely by the decisional law. With this, we turn to the contentions made by the Government in these cases.

First. The Government suggests that we promulgate a new "test" in this area to serve as a standard to be applied by the lower courts and by the Tax Court in dealing with the numerous cases that arise.[5] We reject this invitation. We are of opinion that the governing principles are necessarily general and have already been spelled out in the opinions of this Court, and that the problem is one which, under the present statutory framework, does not lend itself to any more definitive statement that would produce a talisman for the solution of concrete cases. The cases at bar are fair examples of the settings in which the problem usually arises. They present situations in which payments have been made in a context with business overtones—an employer making a payment to a retiring employee; a businessman giving something of value to another businessman who has been of

---

5. The Government's proposed test is stated: "Gifts should be defined as transfers of property made for personal as distinguished from business reasons."

advantage to him in his business. In this context, we review the law as established by the prior cases here.

The course of decision here makes it plain that the statute does not use the term "gift" in the common-law sense, but in a more colloquial sense. This Court has indicated that a voluntary executed transfer of his property by one to another, without any consideration or compensation therefor, though a common-law gift, is not necessarily a "gift" within the meaning of the statute. For the Court has shown that the mere absence of a legal or moral obligation to make such a payment does not establish that it is a gift. Old Colony Trust Co. v. Commissioner, 279 U.S. 716, 730. And, importantly, if the payment proceeds primarily from "the constraining force of any moral or legal duty," or from "the incentive of anticipated benefit" of an economic nature, Bogardus v. Commissioner, 302 U.S. 34, 41, it is not a gift. And, conversely, "where the payment is in return for services rendered, it is irrelevant that the donor derives no economic benefit from it." Robertson v. United States, 343 U.S. 711, 714.[6] A gift in the statutory sense, on the other hand, proceeds from a "detached and disinterested generosity," Commissioner v. LoBue, 351 U.S. 243, 246; "out of affection, respect, admiration, charity or like impulses." Robertson v. United States, supra, at 714. And in this regard, the most critical consideration, as the Court was agreed in the leading case here, is the transferor's "intention." Bogardus v. Commissioner, 302 U.S. 34, 43. . . .

The Government says that this "intention" of the transferor cannot mean what the cases on the common-law concept of gift call "donative intent." With that we are in agreement, for our decisions fully support this. Moreover, the Bogardus case itself makes it plain that the donor's characterization of his action is not determinative — that there must be an objective inquiry as to whether what is called a gift amounts to it in reality. 302 U.S., at 40. It scarcely needs adding that the parties' expectations or hopes as to the tax treatment of their conduct in themselves have nothing to do with the matter.

It is suggested that the Bogardus criterion would be more apt if rephrased in terms of "motive" rather than "intention." We must confess to some skepticism as to whether such a verbal mutation would be of any practical consequence. We take it that the proper criterion, established by decision here, is one that inquires what the basic reason for his conduct was in fact — the dominant reason that explains his action in making the transfer. Further than that we do not think it profitable to go.

Second. The Government's proposed "test," while apparently simple and precise in its formulation, depends frankly on a set of "principles" or "presumptions" derived from the decided cases, and concededly subject to various exceptions; and it involves various corollaries, which add to its detail. Were we to promulgate this test as a matter of law, and accept with it its various presuppositions and stated consequences, we would be passing far beyond the requirements of the cases before us, and would be painting on a large canvas with indeed a broad brush. The Government derives its test from such propositions as the following: That payments by an employer to an employee, even though voluntary, ought, by and large, to be taxable; that the concept of a gift is inconsistent with a payment's being a deductible business expense; that a gift involves "personal" elements; that a business corporation cannot properly make a gift of its assets. The Government admits that there are exceptions and qualifications to these propositions. We think,

6. The cases including "tips" in gross income are classic examples of this. See, e.g., Roberts v. Commissioner, 176 F.2d 221.

to the extent they are correct, that those propositions are not principles of law but rather maxims of experience that the tribunals which have tried the facts of cases in this area have enunciated in explaining their factual determinations. Some of them simply represent truisms: it doubtless is, statistically speaking, the exceptional payment by an employer to an employee that amounts to a gift. Others are over-statements of possible evidentiary inferences relevant to a factual determination on the totality of circumstances in the case: it is doubtless relevant to the over-all inference that the transferor treats a payment as a business deduction, or that the transferor is a corporate entity. But these inferences cannot be stated in absolute terms. Neither factor is a shibboleth. The taxing statute does not make nondeduct-ibility by the transferor a condition on the "gift" exclusion; nor does it draw any distinction, in terms, between transfers by corporations and individuals, as to the availability of the "gift" exclusion to the transferee. The conclusion whether a transfer amounts to a "gift" is one that must be reached on consideration of all the factors.

Specifically, the trier of fact must be careful not to allow trial of the issue whether the receipt of a specific payment is a gift to turn into a trial of the tax liability, or of the propriety, as a matter of fiduciary or corporate law, attaching to the conduct of someone else. The major corollary to the Government's suggested "test" is that, as an ordinary matter, a payment by a corporation cannot be a gift, and, more specifically, there can be no such thing as a "gift" made by a corporation which would allow it to take a deduction for an ordinary and necessary business expense. As we have said, we find no basis for such a conclusion in the statute; and if it were applied as a determinative rule of "law," it would force the tribunals trying tax cases involving the donee's liability into elaborate inquiries into the local law of corpora-tions or into the peripheral deductibility of payments as business expenses. The former issue might make the tax tribunals the most frequent investigators of an important and difficult issue of the laws of the several States, and the latter inquiry would summon one difficult and delicate problem of federal tax law as an aid to the solution of another. . . . These considerations, also, reinforce us in our conclusion that while the principles urged by the Government may, in nonabsolute form as crystallizations of experience, prove persuasive to the trier of facts in a particular case, neither they, nor any more detailed statement than has been made, can be laid down as a matter of law.

Third. Decision of the issue presented in these cases must be based ultimately on the application of the fact-finding tribunal's experience with the mainsprings of human conduct to the totality of the facts of each case. The nontechnical nature of the statutory standard, the close relationship of it to the data of practical human experience, and the multiplicity of relevant factual elements, with their various combinations, creating the necessity of ascribing the proper force to each, confirm us in our conclusion that primary weight in this area must be given to the conclu-sions of the trier of fact.

This conclusion may not satisfy an academic desire for tidiness, symmetry and precision in this area, any more than a system based on the determinations of various fact-finders ordinarily does. But we see it as implicit in the present statutory treatment of the exclusion for gifts, and in the variety of forums in which federal income tax cases can be tried. If there is fear of undue uncertainty or overmuch litigation, Congress may make more precise its treatment of the matter by singling out certain factors and making them determinative of the matter, as it has done in one field of the "gift" exclusion's former application, that of prizes and awards [now dealt with by §74]. Doubtless diversity of result will tend to be lessened somewhat since federal income tax decisions, even those in tribunals of first instance turning on issues of fact, tend to be reported, and since there may be a natural tendency of professional triers of fact to follow one another's determinations, even as to factual matters. But the question here remains basically one of fact, for determination on a case-by-case basis.

One consequence of this is that appellate review of determinations in this field must be quite restricted. Where a jury has tried the matter upon correct instructions, the only inquiry is whether it cannot be said that reasonable men could reach differing conclusions on the issue. Where the trial has been by a judge without a jury, the judge's findings must stand unless "clearly erroneous." . . .

Fourth. A majority of the Court is in accord with the principles just outlined. And, applying them to the *Duberstein* case, we are in agreement, on the evidence we have set forth, that it cannot be said that the conclusion of the Tax Court was "clearly erroneous." It seems to us plain that as trier of the facts it was warranted in concluding that despite the characterization of the transfer of the Cadillac by the parties and the absence of any obligation, even of a moral nature, to make it, it was at bottom a recompense for Duberstein's past services, or an inducement for him to be of further service in the future. We cannot say with the Court of Appeals that such a conclusion was "mere suspicion" on the Tax Court's part. To us it appears based in the sort of informed experience with human affairs that fact-finding tribunals should bring to this task.

As to *Stanton,* we are in disagreement. To four of us, it is critical here that the District Court as trier of fact made only the simple and unelaborated finding that the transfer in question was a "gift." To be sure, conciseness is to be strived for, and prolixity avoided, in findings; but, to the four of us, there comes a point where findings become so sparse and conclusory as to give no revelation of what the District Court's concept of the determining facts and legal standard may be. . . . While the standard of law in this area is not a complex one, we four think the unelaborated finding of ultimate fact here cannot stand as a fulfillment of these requirements. It affords the reviewing court not the semblance of an indication of the legal standard with which the trier of fact has approached his task. For all that appears, the District Court may have viewed the form of the resolution or the simple absence of legal consideration as conclusive. While the judgment of the Court of Appeals cannot stand, the four of us think there must be further proceedings in the District Court looking toward new and adequate findings of fact. In this, we are joined by Mr. Justice Whittaker, who agrees that the findings were inadequate, although he does not concur generally in this opinion.

Accordingly, in No. 376, the judgment of this Court is that the judgment of the Court of Appeals is reversed, and in No. 546, that the judgment of the Court of Appeals is vacated, and the case is remanded to the District Court for further proceedings not inconsistent with this opinion.

It is so ordered.

Mr. Justice Harlan concurs in the result in No. 376. In No. 546, he would affirm the judgment of the Court of Appeals for the reasons stated by Mr. Justice Frankfurter.

Mr. Justice Whittaker, agreeing with *Bogardus* that whether a particular transfer is or is not a "gift" may involve "a mixed question of law and fact," 302 U.S., at 39, concurs only in the result of this opinion.

Mr. Justice Douglas dissents, since he is of the view that in each of these two cases there was a gift under the test which the Court fashioned nearly a quarter of a century ago in Bogardus v. Commissioner, 302 U.S. 34.

Mr. Justice BLACK, concurring and dissenting.

I agree with the Court that it was not clearly erroneous for the Tax Court to find as it did in No. 376 that the automobile transfer to Duberstein was not a gift, and so I agree with the Court's opinion and judgment reversing the judgment of the Court of Appeals in that case.

I dissent in No. 546, Stanton v. United States. The District Court found that the $20,000 transferred to Mr. Stanton by his former employer at the end of ten years' service was a gift and therefore exempt from taxation under [§102(a)]. I think the finding was not clearly erroneous and that the Court of Appeals was therefore wrong in reversing the District Court's judgment. While conflicting inferences might have been drawn, there was evidence to show that Mr. Stanton's long services had been satisfactory, that he was well liked personally and had given splendid service, that the employer was under no obligation at all to pay any added compensation, but made the $20,000 payment because prompted by a genuine desire to make him a "gift," to award him a "gratuity." . . .

Mr. Justice FRANKFURTER, concurring in the judgment in No. 376 and dissenting in No. 546.

As the Court's opinion indicates, we brought these two cases here partly because of a claimed difference in the approaches between two Courts of Appeals but primarily on the Government's urging that, in the interest of the better administration of the income tax laws, clarification was desirable for determining when a transfer of property constitutes a "gift" and is not to be included in income for purposes of ascertaining the "gross income" under the Internal Revenue Code. As soon as this problem emerged after the imposition of the first income tax authorized by the Sixteenth Amendment, it became evident that its inherent difficulties and subtleties would not easily yield to the formulation of a general rule or test sufficiently definite to confine within narrow limits the area of judgment in applying it. While at its core the tax conception of a gift no doubt reflected the non-legal, nontechnical notion of a benefaction unentangled with any aspect of worldly requital, the divers blends of personal and pecuniary relationships in our industrial society inevitably presented niceties for adjudication which could not be put to rest by any kind of general formulation.

Despite acute arguments at the bar and a most thorough re-examination of the problem on a full canvass of our prior decisions and an attempted fresh analysis of the nature of the problem, the Court has rejected the invitation of the Government to fashion anything like a litmus paper test for determining what is excludable as a "gift" from gross income. Nor has the Court attempted a clarification of the particular aspects of the problem presented by these two cases, namely, payment by an employer to an employee upon the termination of the employment relation and non-obligatory payment for services rendered in the course of a business relationship. While I agree that experience has shown the futility of attempting to define, by language so circumscribing as to make it easily applicable, what constitutes a gift for every situation where the problem may arise, I do think that greater explicitness is possible in isolating and emphasizing factors which militate against a gift in particular situations.

Thus, regarding the two frequently recurring situations involved in these cases — things of value given to employees by their employers upon the termination of employment and payments entangled in a business relation and occasioned by the performance of some service — the strong implication is that the payment is of a business nature. The problem in these two cases is entirely different from the problem in a case where a payment is made from one member of a family to another, where the implications are directly otherwise. No single general formulation appropriately deals with both types of cases, although both involve the question whether the payment was a "gift." While we should normally suppose that a payment from father to son was a gift, unless the contrary is shown, in the two situations now before us the business implications are so forceful that I would apply a presumptive rule placing the burden upon the beneficiary to prove the payment wholly unrelated to his services to the enterprise. The Court, however, has declined so to analyze the problem and has concluded "that the governing principles are necessarily general and have already been spelled out in the opinions of this Court, and that the problem is one which, under the present statutory framework, does not lend itself to any more definitive statement that would produce a talisman for the solution of concrete cases." . . .

Varying conceptions regarding the "mainsprings of human conduct" are derived from a variety of experiences or assumptions about the nature of man, and "experience with human affairs," is not only diverse but also often drastically conflicting. What the Court now does sets fact-finding bodies to sail on an illimitable ocean of individual beliefs and experiences. This can hardly fail to invite, if indeed not encourage, too individualized diversities in the administration of the income tax law. I am afraid that by these new phrasings the practicalities of tax administration, which should be as uniform as is possible in so vast a country as ours, will be embarrassed. By applying what has already been spelled out in the opinions of this Court, I agree with the Court in reversing the judgment in Commissioner v. Duberstein.

But I would affirm the decision of the Court of Appeals for the Second Circuit in Stanton v. United States. I would do so . . . because the very terms of the resolution by which the $20,000 was awarded to Stanton indicated that it was not a "gratuity" in the sense of sheer benevolence but in the nature of a generous lagniappe, something extra thrown in for services received though not legally nor morally required to be given. . . . Thus the taxpayer has totally failed to sustain the burden I would place upon him to establish that the payment to him was wholly attributable to generosity unrelated to his performance of his secular business functions as an officer of the corporation of the Trinity Church of New York and the Trinity Operating Co. Since the record totally fails to establish taxpayer's claim, I see no need of specific findings by the trial judge.

Notes and Questions

1. *Subsequent case history.* On remand, the district court made detailed findings of fact, and again concluded that Mr. Stanton had received a tax-free gift. 186 F. Supp. 393 (E.D.N.Y. 1960). Among other things, the district court found that the payment to Mr. Stanton was "the gratification of a kindly impulse present in the minds of the Vestry," and that the Vestry made the payment out of "a deep sense of appreciation for the way in which Mr. Stanton had

enabled the members of the Vestry to rise to the requirements of their high office." This time the Second Circuit concluded that the district court's findings and conclusion were not clearly erroneous, and affirmed. 287 F.2d 876 (2d Cir. 1961). One of the affirming judges noted that he would have drawn "the contrary inference . . . from the undisputed basic facts."

2. *Jury instructions.* Normally, one would expect the Supreme Court's explication of a key statutory term to be the source of jury instructions in cases in which the term is at issue. If you were a district court judge in a post-*Duberstein* gift case, how would you instruct the jury on the legal meaning of "gift"? Do you think the jury members would find it helpful to be told to consult their "experience with the mainsprings of human conduct," and that they must free themselves of any "academic desire for tidiness, symmetry and precision"? Are there other passages from the opinion that could serve as the basis for more helpful instructions?

3. *The colloquial sense.* The basic problem, on both the *Duberstein* and *Stanton* facts, was that the transfers were gift-like in the sense that the transferors were not legally obligated to make the transfers, but not gift-like in the sense that the transfers occurred in business contexts. In trying to decide whether such borderline cases are within the scope of §102, where should a court look for guidance? In the absence of helpful legislative history or interpretive regulations, the Supreme Court decided that Congress intended the term *gift* to be interpreted in a "colloquial sense." The opinion's extreme deference to the gift or non-gift conclusion of the trier of fact can be understood as letting juries (and trial court judges) decide gift cases based on their own understandings of whether the transfers at issue are gifts in the colloquial sense. Based on your own experience as a speaker of English, would you describe Mr. Duberstein's Cadillac as a gift? If not, what word or phrase would you use to describe it? What about Mr. Stanton's $20,000? Is that a gift, or is there another term in common usage to describe receipts such as his?

4. *The rationale for the exclusion.* Instead of, or in addition to, the colloquial usage approach, a court interpreting §102 might attempt to discern the policy underlying the gift exclusion, and then decide whether applying the exclusion to the transfer in question is consistent with that policy. Although Justice Frankfurter's opinion reflects this interpretive method (to some extent), the majority opinion seems strangely uninterested in this approach. If the Court had been interested in policy-influenced interpretation, it might have begun by noting that the noncontroversial core of §102 is gratuitous transfers between family members and close friends. If Grandmother (GM) gives $10,000 cash to her adult granddaughter (GD), motivated by love and affection, everyone would agree the transfer is excluded from GD's gross income by §102. But what is the policy justification for the exclusion? GM presumably paid tax on the $10,000 at some time in the past, and she is not entitled to claim an income tax deduction for the amount of the gift. These two facts suggest a five-part rationale for GD's exclusion:

  1. Income represents ability to consume (either now or in the future, as the recipient chooses); thus, a tax on income is a tax on potential consumption.
  2. Every dollar of potential consumption should be subject to income tax once, and only once.

3. GM has already paid income tax on the $10,000 of potential consumption represented by the gift.

4. The gift of the $10,000 does not generate additional potential consumption, but merely transfers the potential consumption from GM to GD.

5. Since there is only one potential consumption, there should be only one tax, which has already been paid by GM; thus, there is no reason also to tax GD.

In contrast with the GM to GD gift, consider the case of GM paying $10,000 to her gardener for his work on the flowers and shrubs surrounding her home. In this case, GM has consumed the $10,000 by obtaining $10,000 worth of gardening services, and the gardener will be able to consume the $10,000 again, on whatever he chooses to buy with the money. Because there are two $10,000 potential consumptions, each taxpayer should be taxed on $10,000. In fact, they will both be taxed on $10,000 — GM because the cost of gardening is a nondeductible personal consumption expense (*see* §262(a)), and the gardener because compensation for services is specifically included in gross income by §61(a)(1).

5. *Questioning the rationale.* Two points are worth noting about the above policy analysis of the application of §102 to GM's gift to GD. First, there is another way to achieve the goal of one tax on one potential consumption: The Code might make gifts taxable to recipients, but deductible by donors. GM's $10,000 deduction would then offset her previous $10,000 inclusion, and the single tax on $10,000 would be imposed on GD instead of on GM. Wouldn't this make more sense than current law, considering the fact that GD is the person who actually gets to consume the $10,000? Perhaps it would, but notice that large gifts, like water, tend to flow downhill — that is, from richer to poorer family members. Given that tendency and an income tax with progressive marginal rates, what effect would the deduction-and-inclusion treatment of gifts have on income tax revenues compared with the actual no-deduction-no-inclusion approach? The second point worth noting is that the underlying premise of the one-potential-consumption-one-tax analysis is debatable. The analysis assumes that GM has merely transferred the consumption potential to GD, rather than obtaining $10,000 of actual consumption for herself in making the gift. But one could argue that GM received $10,000 worth of consumption — not fundamentally different from $10,000 worth of gardening services — from the gift. At the very least, she received the warm glow of giving, and she may have received something slightly more tangible as well, such as increased attention and displays of affection from GD. If you think what GM received is substantial enough to count as $10,000 worth of consumption for herself, then you will conclude that this $10,000 has supported two $10,000 consumptions (just as in the gardening example), and there should be two taxes.[7] Under this view, gifts should be nondeductible to donors *and* taxable to donees. Whatever your view of the merits of this two-tax approach, Congress clearly rejected it by enacting §102.

---

7. This was the view of Henry Simons, who was in some ways the godfather of the modern income tax. "[G]ifts are consumption to the donor, and therefore not properly deductible." *Personal Income Taxation*, at 139 (1938).

6. *Applying the rationale.* If the above policy explanation of §102 is correct, it suggests that neither Mr. Duberstein nor Mr. Stanton should have been eligible for the gift exclusion because the transferor had not already paid the tax in either case. Mohawk's business expense deduction for the cost of the Cadillac offset any tax it would otherwise have paid on the value of Duberstein's new car, and the church had not paid tax on Stanton's $20,000 gratuity because it was exempt from income tax (*see* §501(c)(3)). In neither case, then, would gift treatment under §102 result in one potential consumption (by the transferor) being matched with one tax (on the transferee). Instead, treating the transfer as a gift would result in one potential consumption being matched with *no tax* on either transferor or transferee. Under this analysis, the final result in *Duberstein*—taxing Mr. Duberstein on the value of the Cadillac—is correct, although the result should not have been dependent on the intuitions of the trier of fact. Under the same analysis, the final result in *Stanton*—gift treatment upheld on remand—is wrong.

7. *Section 274(b) and surrogate taxation.* Although Congress did not amend §102(a) in response to *Duberstein,* two post-*Duberstein* statutory amendments have greatly reduced the number of situations in which gifts in a business context result in no tax on either the transferor or the transferee. First, §274(b) (enacted in 1962) denies the transferor a business expense deduction for any business gift, to the extent the total value of gifts made by the taxpayer to the recipient during the year exceeds $25. Under this rule, if the Cadillac is a §102 gift to Mr. Duberstein, then Mohawk's business expense deduction for the car is limited to $25. Although §274(b) confirms the Supreme Court's view that a gift is possible in a business context, it avoids the possibility of no tax being imposed on either party (except for $25 per recipient, per year). The deduction disallowance means that the value of the gift will be taxable to the transferor.

Imagine you are Mr. Berman of Mohawk Metal, §274(b) has been added to the Code, and Mr. Duberstein has furnished you so much additional helpful information that you want to give him *another* Cadillac. What do you do if you want to protect Mohawk's ability to claim a business expense deduction for its cost of the car? You know that Mohawk will not be able to deduct the cost of the car (except for $25) if the car is a §102 gift to Mr. Duberstein, and you know that whether the car is a gift to Mr. Duberstein depends on whether Mohawk had the requisite gift-type intent. You can negate the existence of the necessary intent by sending the car along with a letter drafted with the *Duberstein* opinion in mind. The letter might mention that the transfer of the car is "in return for services rendered," is made from "the incentive of anticipated benefit," and is not made out of "detached and disinterested generosity." Such a letter would almost guarantee that Mr. Duberstein would not be able to convince the IRS or a court that the car was a gift. As long as the car was not a gift, Mohawk's deduction would not be limited by §274(b), and Mohawk could deduct the entire cost of the car. Of course, sending Mr. Duberstein the car along with a hefty tax bill may backfire from a non-tax standpoint, if the idea is to generate goodwill with Mr. Duberstein. Your alternative is to send him a letter drafted—again with the *Duberstein* opinion in mind—to indicate that the car *is* a §102 gift. That should be enough to enable Mr. Duberstein to exclude the value of the car under §102 (and to keep his goodwill), but it amounts to an admission by Mohawk that the car is subject to the $25 deduction ceiling imposed on business gifts by §274(b).[8] In light of the tax hit Mohawk will take as a result of the gift letter, you may decide to send Duberstein a Buick instead of a Cadillac. The table below shows how Mohawk might adjust the value of the car to take tax consequences into account.

Mohawk's Choices
(assumes Mohawk and Duberstein are both in the (hypothetical) 40% bracket, and ignores the $25 deduction allowed by §274(b))

	Value of Car	After-tax Cost to Mohawk	After-tax Benefit to Duberstein
Mohawk's letter indicates car is not a gift	$50,000	$30,000 ($50,000 reduced by $20,000 tax savings from deduction)	$30,000 ($50,000 value of car, reduced by $20,000 tax liability)
Mohawk's letter indicates car is a gift	$30,000	$30,000 (no deduction allowed by §274(b))	$30,000 (car treated as gift)

Although §274(b) takes much of the tax fun out of business gifts, it is not a complete solution to the government's problem of tax being imposed on neither transferee nor transferor. Section 274(b) would not change the no-tax result in *Stanton,* for example, because the nontaxability of the church derived from its tax-exempt status, rather than from its ability to claim a business expense deduction. It would also not change the result whenever the transferor is de facto tax exempt — because it has no net income for the year, or because its net income for the year is offset by net operating loss carryovers from other years.[9] And even if the transferor does suffer a tax cost because of the application of §274(b), the transferor's cost will be less than the recipient's gain if the recipient is in a higher marginal tax rate than the transferor. Suppose, for example, that Mr. Duberstein's marginal tax rate is 40 percent, Mohawk's is 25 percent, and the value of the car is $10,000. If not taxing Mr. Duberstein and denying the deduction to Mohawk is supposed to serve as a surrogate for the more theoretically correct result of taxing Mr. Duberstein and allowing Mohawk a deduction, it will be an imperfect surrogate to the extent of the difference in the marginal rates. Under the more theoretically correct approach, the IRS would collect $4,000 of tax (from Mr. Duberstein). Under the §274(b) approach, which can be understood as taxing Mohawk as a surrogate for

8. Of course, the IRS *could* attempt to tax Mr. Duberstein on the value of the car despite Mohawk's letter indicating the car is a gift; the IRS might argue the letter is a self-serving (or, more precisely, Duberstein-serving) document, which does not reflect economic reality. In practice, however, the IRS will usually be happy to let Mr. Duberstein have his §102 exclusion, as long as Mohawk is willing to accept disallowance of its deduction under §274(b).

9. For the net operating loss carryover rules of §172, see section C.1 of this chapter.

Mr. Duberstein, the IRS will collect only $2,500 of tax (ignoring the allowance of a $25 deduction).[10]

8. *No gifts to employees.* The second post-*Duberstein* amendment is §102(c), which was enacted in 1986. This provision declares that §102(a) cannot apply to "any amount transferred by or for an employer to, or for the benefit of, an employee." Section 102(c) would not have had any effect on Mr. Duberstein, because he was not Mohawk's employee. On the other hand, if the *Stanton* facts arose today, the case would be decided in the government's favor under §102(c). Or would it? If the church made the $20,000 payment shortly after the employment relationship had terminated, would §102(c) still apply? How would you argue the case for Mr. Stanton? For the government?

9. *Gratuitous transfer or compensation for services?* Section 102(a) applies to amounts received by "bequest, devise, or inheritance," as well as to gifts. Thus, the provision excludes from gross income gratuitous transfers made by both the quick and the dead. The interpretive issues under §102(a) are largely the same whether or not the transferor is still with us, but one type of problem looms larger for bequests than for inter vivos transfers — distinguishing gratuitous transfers from compensation for care-giving services. In the classic situation, a wealthy elderly person asks a younger person (who may or may not be a family member) to live with her and take care of her, with the understanding that the wealthy person will provide generously for the younger person in her will. If the decedent intended the bequest as belated compensation for services, the *Duberstein* analysis indicates the bequest should not be eligible for the §102(a) exclusion, even if the decedent was under no legal obligation to make the bequest. Most of the pro-government authority in this area, however, involves situations in which the decedent was under a legally enforceable obligation to the person who performed the services. *See, e.g.,* Cotnam v. Commissioner, 263 F.2d 119 (5th Cir. 1959); Braddock v. United States, 434 F.2d 631 (9th Cir. 1970).

10. *Gifts of services.* Suppose, following your exemplary performance in this course, you begin offering tax advice, or perhaps return-preparation services, gratuitously to members of your immediate family. Does §102 allow them to exclude the value of your services from their incomes?

b. Damages on Account of Personal Physical Injuries

Section 104(a)(2) excludes from gross income "any damages (other than punitive damages) received (whether by suit or agreement and whether as lump sums or as periodic payments) on account of personal physical injuries or physical sickness." The exclusion applies to all three major types of compensatory damages: nonpecuniary damages for pain and suffering or loss of enjoyment, damages for medical expenses (past and future), and damages for lost wages (past and future). The policy analysis of the exclusion is different for each of the three types of damages.

Nonpecuniary damages (pain and suffering, loss of enjoyment). Suppose Paul loses his right arm as a result of Don's negligence, and receives $1 million in damages for

---

10. At the present time, the top individual rate under §1 and the top corporate rate under §11 are the same (35%), which is convenient for purposes of surrogate taxation.

"loss of enjoyment" of the arm (in addition to damages for any lost wages or medical expenses). In effect, Paul has sold his arm — albeit involuntarily — for $1 million. Absent §104(a)(2), the tax analysis would be that Paul had an amount realized of $1 million on the sale of a zero basis asset, resulting in $1 million of taxable gain.[11] What is the policy justification for not taxing Paul on this gain? According to the theory underlying compensatory tort damages, the $1 million damage award is intended to make Paul as well off as if the accident had never occurred (obviously, there are limits to what money can do, but that is the theory). In other words, having $1 million and no right arm is supposed to be as good as having a right arm and no damage award. Most people, then, have a right arm with a basis of zero and a value of $1 million, but they never have to pay tax on this unrealized appreciation because they never sell. Just as tort damages are supposed to put Paul in as good a position as if he had not lost his arm, so the §104(a)(2) exclusion puts Paul in the same tax position as if he had not been forced to realize the gain inherent in his arm. The exclusion of the nonpecuniary damages is based on special congressional solicitude for victims of *forced* sales. If one *voluntarily* sells a zero-basis part of one's body (such as hair, blood, or a kidney), the amount realized is not received as "damages," with the result that §104(a)(2) does not apply. Incidentally, §104(a)(2) is not the only instance in the Internal Revenue Code of special concern for taxpayers who involuntarily realize gains. Section 1033 allows a taxpayer who realizes a gain on the "involuntary conversion" of real estate or other property (for example, as a result of a condemnation award) to defer tax on the gain if she invests the amount realized in similar replacement property.[12] While §104(a)(2) provides a permanent exclusion not conditioned on the taxpayer's use of the damage award, §1033 only defers taxation, and it does that only if the taxpayer purchases replacement property.

Although the §104(a)(2) exclusion seems to produce tax equity between a taxpayer who receives tort damages for loss of a limb and a taxpayer who never loses a limb, it may create tax inequity of another sort. Suppose there are three taxpayers: Alan has an intact right arm, worth $1 million; Brenda lost her arm, but received tort damages of $1 million; and Carl lost his arm but received no compensation (either because the accident was not the result of another's negligence, or because the tortfeasor could not be found or was judgment-proof). Under the tort system's heroic assumption that money can adequately compensate for the loss of a limb, Alan and Brenda are equally well off. Carl, of course, is worse off than either of the others. Yet the tax system treats all three exactly the same; there are no arm-related income tax consequences for any of them. The exclusion for tort damages can be defended as treating Brenda fairly vis-à-vis Alan, but doesn't the exclusion treat Brenda too generously vis-à-vis Carl? Is the solution to give Carl a $1 million deduction, despite the fact that under normal tax principles his lack of any basis in his arm would preclude a deduction?

Medical expenses. The policy justification for the exclusion of medical expense damages piggybacks on the §213 deduction for medical expenses.[13] If §104(a)(2)

---

11. The *Garber* opinion, set forth in the cell on the limits of tax-free recovery of capital, suggests that a taxpayer might have a basis in a body part equal to the value of that part, but the suggestion is clearly wrong — as explained in a note following the opinion.
12. See section D.2 of Chapter 3 for a detailed explanation of §1033.
13. See section E of Chapter 4 for the medical expense deduction.

did not apply to damages on account of medical expenses, then a taxpayer would include the damages in gross income but offset the inclusion with a medical expense deduction (although the inclusion and deduction would not necessarily be in the same tax year). By allowing an exclusion for medical expense damages, the Code reaches more simply the result that would otherwise be obtained by inclusion and an offsetting deduction. This policy rationale is apparent on the face of the statute — the introductory language of §104(a) denies the exclusion for damages received as compensation for medical expenses deducted by the taxpayer under §213 in an earlier year. Allowing a taxpayer to exclude compensation for a previously deducted expense would be the equivalent of allowing the taxpayer to deduct the same expense twice. Despite the theoretical equivalence between an exclusion and an inclusion followed by an offsetting deduction, in practice an exclusion under §104(a)(2) usually produces better tax results than would be produced by inclusion and a deduction under §213. The medical expense deduction is allowed only for medical expenses in excess of 7.5 percent (10 percent in 2013 and later years) of the taxpayer's adjusted gross income, and even the excess is deductible only if the taxpayer does not claim the standard deduction. Neither of these limitations applies to the exclusion under §104(a)(2).[14]

Lost wages. The exclusion for damages on account of lost wages is the hardest part of §104(a)(2) to justify. If the taxpayer had not been injured, his actual wages would have been taxable under §61(a)(1). Why, then, should the tort substitute for his wages be excluded from gross income? One possible answer relates to the practical difficulty of determining what portion of a lump sum damage award (or settlement) is properly allocable to lost wages. If the exclusions of nonpecuniary damages and of medical expense damages are justified, and if it is not practical to separate lost wages from the other elements of damages, then the exclusion for lost wages may be an unfortunate but unavoidable consequence of the exclusion for the other damage elements. This depends, of course, on the debatable assumption that a reasonably accurate allocation of a lump sum damage award between lost wages and other elements of damages is not feasible. As currently written, §104(a)(2) assumes that it *is* practical to allocate a lump sum damage award between its nontaxable elements and taxable damages on account of medical expenses deducted in previous years. If that is practical, why wouldn't it also be practical to allocate a lump sum award between lost wages and other elements of damages? The exclusion for lost wages is sometimes explained as a tax subsidy for the tort plaintiff's contingent attorneys' fees. Suppose Pam has lost wages of $99,000. If she had not been injured and had earned the wages, she would have paid income tax of $33,000 on the wages, resulting in take-home pay of $66,000. When she receives a $99,000 damage award in lieu of wages she owes no income tax, but she must pay $33,000 to her attorney under their one-third contingent fee arrangement. Thus, her take-home damages in lieu of wages are $66,000. The government has sacrificed $33,000 of potential tax revenue so that Pam can pay her attorney and still take home the same $66,000 as if she had not been injured. Of course, this works perfectly only if the attorneys' contingent fee percentage

---

14. For a more detailed examination of the interaction between §§104(a)(2) and 213, see the Chapter 4 cell on double tax benefits.

happens to be exactly the same as the tax rate that would have applied if Pam had earned the wages.

If you accept this justification for the lost wages exclusion, does it have any implications for whether the jury in a personal injury case should be informed that actual wages would have been subject to income tax, but that damages in lieu of wages are tax-free? If the jury is given the tax information (but is not given any information about the contingent fee agreement), how would you expect the jury to use that information in determining the appropriate size of the damage award for lost wages? Would the jury's probable response to the tax information defeat the purpose of the §104(a)(2) exclusion for lost wages damages? In the majority of jurisdictions within the United States, the standard practice is *not* to inform the jury of the difference in the income tax treatments of actual wages and damages for lost wages.[15]

Consider three taxpayers, each of whom is injured by another's negligence, and each of whom suffers one year's lost wages as a result. Alice's lost wages are $100,000, and would have generated an income tax liability of $25,000 if she had earned them; she recovers $100,000 damages from her tortfeasor. Brad's lost wages are also $100,000, but he recovers nothing because his tortfeasor has no assets. Chuck had a much lower-paying job. His lost wages are $30,000, and would have generated an income tax liability of $5,000 if he had earned them; he recovers $30,000 damages from his tortfeasor. If the lost wages exclusion is intended as a tax subsidy for tort victims, what are the amounts of the subsidies received by each of the three tort victims? Are the three subsidies positively or negatively correlated with the level of neediness of the three victims?

The physical injury requirement. The word *physical* was added to §104(a)(2) in 1996; before then the exclusion applied to damages on account of "personal injuries," whether physical or not. Under the pre-1996 statute, courts had great difficulty deciding which nonphysical injuries qualified as personal injuries, damages for which were excludable. The Supreme Court addressed this issue twice, and the state of the law was probably more confused after the Supreme Court's efforts than before. *See* United States v. Burke, 504 U.S. 229 (1992); Commissioner v. Schleier, 515 U.S. 323 (1995). The 1996 amendment significantly reduced the confusion, but did it do so at the expense of fairness? Is there any policy justification for allowing the exclusion to physically injured tort victims, while denying the exclusion to (for example) persons who recover damages for defamation, or for violations of federal employment discrimination statutes?[16]

In Murphy v. IRS, 460 F.3d 79 (D.C. Cir. 2006), the Court of Appeals for the District of Columbia Circuit held that the 1996 legislative attempt to tax damages arising from nonphysical personal injuries (such as the emotional distress damages at issue in *Murphy*) was unconstitutional because such damages are not income within the meaning of the Sixteenth Amendment. The opinion was heavily criticized by tax lawyers and tax academics, and the court vacated the opinion a few months later. On reconsideration, the court decided that the 1996 legislation was constitutional after all. Murphy v. IRS, 493 F.3d 170 (D.C. Cir. 2007), *cert. denied,*

---

15. Juries are also not usually informed of attorneys' fee arrangements.
16. In the recent past there was much confusion and litigation over the tax treatment of contingent attorneys' fees paid by taxpayers who received taxable damage awards on account of nonphysical injuries. For an examination of these issues, see section B.2 of Chapter 10.

553 U.S. 1004 (2008). The court did not reach the question of whether damages on account of nonphysical personal injuries constitute income within the meaning of the Sixteenth Amendment. Instead, the court concluded that a tax on such damages was not a direct tax (whether or not it was not an income tax), and thus was not subject to the provisions of the original Constitution (art. I, §2, cl. 3, and art. I, §9, cl. 4) requiring apportionment of direct taxes among the states according to their populations.[17]

A further complication introduced by the distinction between physical and other injuries is that the facts are often messy, involving commingling of damages paid for a variety of reasons. Further, once liability is established (or a settlement amount is agreed to) the precise nature of the cause of action may well not matter for tort law purposes. But measuring precisely what dollars were paid for what reason is critical for tax law purposes, creating a separate tax issue in many cases. The following case provides an example.

AMOS v. COMMISSIONER

86 T.C.M. 663 (2003)

CHIECHI, J.

Respondent determined a deficiency of $61,668 in petitioner's Federal income tax (tax) for 1997.

The only issue remaining for decision is whether the $200,000 settlement amount (settlement amount at issue) that petitioner received in 1997 in settlement of a claim is excludable under section 104(a)(2) from petitioner's gross income for that year. We hold that $120,000 is excludable and that $80,000 is not.

FINDINGS OF FACT

. . . During 1997, petitioner was employed as a television cameraman. In that capacity, on January 15, 1997, petitioner was operating a handheld camera during a basketball game between the Minnesota Timberwolves and the Chicago Bulls. At some point during that game, Dennis Keith Rodman (Mr. Rodman), who was playing for the Chicago Bulls, landed on a group of photographers, including petitioner, and twisted his ankle. Mr. Rodman then kicked petitioner. . . .

On January 15, 1997, shortly after the incident, petitioner was taken by ambulance for treatment at Hennepin County Medical Center. Petitioner informed the medical personnel at that medical center . . . that he had experienced shooting pain to his neck immediately after having been kicked in the groin, but that such pain was subsiding. The Hennepin County medical personnel observed that petitioner was able to walk, but that he was limping and complained of experiencing pain. The Hennepin County medical personnel did not observe any other obvious signs of trauma. Petitioner informed the Hennepin County medical personnel that he was currently taking pain medication for a preexisting back condition. The Hennepin County medical personnel offered additional pain medications to

---

17. For an explanation of the direct tax clauses and the Sixteenth Amendment, see section A.3 of Chapter 3.

petitioner, but he refused those medications. After a dispute with the Hennepin County medical personnel concerning an unrelated medical issue, petitioner left Hennepin County Medical Center without having been discharged by them. . . .

On January 15, 1997, after the incident and petitioner's visit to the Hennepin County Medical Center, petitioner filed a report (police report) with the Minneapolis Police Department. In the police report, petitioner claimed that Mr. Rodman had assaulted him.

On January 16, 1997, petitioner sought medical treatment at the Veterans Affairs (VA) Medical Center. The medical personnel at that medical center (VA medical personnel) took X-rays of petitioner's back. Petitioner complained to the VA medical personnel about his groin area, but he did not advise them that he was experiencing any symptoms related to that complaint. The VA medical personnel determined that there was no swelling of, but they were unable to ascertain whether there was bruising around, petitioner's groin area. The VA medical personnel gave petitioner some pain medication and told him to continue taking his other prescribed medications. The VA medical personnel prepared a report regarding petitioner's January 16, 1997 visit to the VA Medical Center. That report indicated that, except for certain disk problems that petitioner had since at least as early as February 14, 1995, "the vertebrae are intact and the remaining disk spaces are normal."

Very shortly after the incident on a date not disclosed by the record, Andrew Luger (Mr. Luger), an attorney representing Mr. Rodman with respect to the incident, contacted Ms. Pearson [Amos's attorney]. Several discussions and a few meetings took place between Ms. Pearson and Mr. Luger. Petitioner accompanied Ms. Pearson to one of the meetings between her and Mr. Luger, at which time Mr. Luger noticed that petitioner was limping. Shortly after those discussions and meetings, petitioner and Mr. Rodman reached a settlement.

[The opinion incorporates the full text of the lengthy settlement agreement. The agreement referred to "the Incident" in which "Rodman allegedly kicked Amos," but Rodman admitted no wrongdoing. It provided for payment by Rodman to Amos of $200,000, in consideration of which Amos released Rodman, and every other potential defendant in sight or imagination, from any claims "by reason of any damage, loss, or injury" sustained by Amos. The agreement also provided that its terms should be kept confidential, and encouraged courts to be aware that the confidentiality agreement was part of the consideration for the payment — an exhortation that the Tax Court apparently ignored. The agreement also required that the parties refrain from defaming or disparaging each other, and that Amos neither initiate nor cooperate in any criminal actions relating to the incident.]

Petitioner filed a tax return (return) for his taxable year 1997. In that return, petitioner excluded from his gross income the $200,000 that he received from Mr. Rodman under the settlement agreement.

In the notice that respondent issued to petitioner with respect to 1997, respondent determined that petitioner is not entitled to exclude from his gross income the settlement amount at issue.

OPINION

We must determine whether the settlement amount at issue may be excluded from petitioner's gross income for 1997. Petitioner bears the burden of proving that the determination in the notice to include the settlement amount at issue in petitioner's gross income is erroneous.[18]

Section 61(a) provides the following sweeping definition of the term "gross income": "Except as otherwise provided in this subtitle, gross income means all income from whatever source derived." Not only is section 61(a) broad in its scope, exclusions from gross income must be narrowly construed.

Section 104(a)(2) on which petitioner relies provides that gross income does not include:

> (2) the amount of any damages (other than punitive damages) received (whether by suit or agreement and whether as lump sums or as periodic payments) on account of personal physical injuries or physical sickness;

The regulations under section 104(a)(2) restate the statutory language of that section and further provide:

> The term "damages received (whether by suit or agreement)" means an amount received (other than workmen's compensation) through prosecution of a legal suit or action based upon tort or tort type rights, or through a settlement agreement entered into in lieu of such prosecution. [Sec. 1.104-1(c), Income Tax Regs.]

The Supreme Court summarized the requirements of section 104(a)(2) as follows:

> In sum, the plain language of §104(a)(2), the text of the applicable regulation, and our decision in *Burke* establish two independent requirements that a taxpayer must meet before a recovery may be excluded under §104(a)(2). First, the taxpayer must demonstrate that the underlying cause of action giving rise to the recovery is "based upon tort or tort type rights"; and second, the taxpayer must show that the damages were received "on account of personal injuries or sickness." Commissioner v. Schleier, 515 U.S. 323, 336-337 (1995).

When the Supreme Court issued its opinion in *Commissioner v. Schleier, supra*, section 104(a)(2), as in effect for the year at issue in *Schleier*, required, inter alia, that, in order to be excluded from gross income, an amount of damages had to be received "on account of personal injuries or sickness." After the Supreme Court issued its opinion in *Schleier*, Congress amended (1996 amendment) section 104(a)(2), effective for amounts received after August 20, 1996, by adding the requirement that, in order to be excluded from gross income, any amounts received must be on account of personal injuries that are physical or sickness that is physical. The 1996 amendment does not otherwise change the requirements of section 104(a)(2) or the analysis set forth in *Commissioner v. Schleier, supra;* it imposes an additional requirement for an amount to qualify for exclusion from gross income under that section.

Where damages are received pursuant to a settlement agreement, such as is the case here, the nature of the claim that was the actual basis for settlement controls whether such damages are excludable under section 104(a)(2). The determination

---

18. Petitioner does not contend that sec. 7491(a) is applicable in this case. Even if petitioner had advanced such a contention, he has not established that he has complied with the applicable requirements of sec. 7491(a)(2). Under the circumstances presented in this case, we conclude that the burden of proof does not shift to respondent under sec. 7491(a).

of the nature of the claim is factual. Where there is a settlement agreement, that determination is usually made by reference to it. If the settlement agreement lacks express language stating what the amount paid pursuant to that agreement was to settle, the intent of the payor is critical to that determination. Although the belief of the payee is relevant to that inquiry, the character of the settlement payment hinges ultimately on the dominant reason of the payor in making the payment. Whether the settlement payment is excludable from gross income under section 104(a)(2) depends on the nature and character of the claim asserted, and not upon the validity of that claim.

The dispute between the parties in the instant case relates to how much of the settlement amount at issue Mr. Rodman paid to petitioner on account of physical injuries. It is petitioner's position that the entire $200,000 settlement amount at issue is excludable from his gross income under section 104(a)(2). In support of that position, petitioner contends that Mr. Rodman paid him the entire amount on account of the physical injuries that he claimed he sustained as a result of the incident.

Respondent counters that, except for a nominal amount (i.e., $1), the settlement amount at issue is includable in petitioner's gross income. In support of that position, respondent contends that petitioner has failed to introduce any evidence regarding, and that Mr. Rodman was skeptical about, the extent of petitioner's physical injuries as a result of the incident. Consequently, according to respondent, the Court should infer that petitioner's physical injuries were minimal. In further support of respondent's position to include all but $1 of the settlement amount at issue in petitioner's gross income, respondent contends that, because the amount of any liquidated damages (i.e., $200,000) payable by petitioner to Mr. Rodman under the settlement agreement [in the event that petitioner violated the terms of the agreement] was equal to the settlement amount (i.e., $200,000) paid to petitioner under that agreement, Mr. Rodman did not intend to pay the settlement amount at issue in order to compensate petitioner for his physical injuries.

On the instant record, we reject respondent's position. With respect to respondent's contentions that petitioner has failed to introduce evidence regarding, and that Mr. Rodman was skeptical about, the extent of petitioner's physical injuries as a result of the incident, those contentions appear to ignore the well-established principle under section 104(a)(2) that it is the nature and character of the claim settled, and not its validity, that determines whether the settlement payment is excludable from gross income under section 104(a)(2). In any event, we find below that the record establishes that Mr. Rodman's dominant reason in paying the settlement amount at issue was petitioner's claimed physical injuries as a result of the incident.

With respect to respondent's contention that Mr. Rodman did not intend to pay the settlement amount at issue in order to compensate petitioner for his physical injuries because the amount of liquidated damages (i.e., $200,000) payable by petitioner to Mr. Rodman under the settlement agreement was equal to the settlement amount (i.e., $200,000) paid to petitioner under that agreement, we do not find the amount of liquidated damages payable under the settlement agreement to be determinative of the reason for which Mr. Rodman paid petitioner the settlement amount at issue.

On the record before us, we find that Mr. Rodman's dominant reason in paying the settlement amount at issue was to compensate petitioner for his claimed physical injuries relating to the incident. Our finding is supported by the settlement agreement, a declaration by Mr. Rodman (Mr. Rodman's declaration), and Ms. Pearson's testimony.

The settlement agreement expressly provided that Mr. Rodman's payment of the settlement amount at issue

> releases and forever discharges [Mr.] Rodman from any and all claims and causes of action of any type, known and unknown, upon and by reason of any damage, loss or injury sustained by Amos [petitioner] arising, or which could have arisen, out of or in connection with [the incident].

Mr. Rodman stated in Mr. Rodman's declaration that he entered into the settlement agreement "to resolve any potential claims" and that the settlement agreement was intended to resolve petitioner's "claim without having to expend additional defense costs." The only potential claims of petitioner that are disclosed by the record are the potential claims that petitioner had for the physical injuries that he claimed he sustained as a result of the incident. Furthermore, Ms. Pearson testified that Mr. Rodman paid the entire settlement amount at issue to petitioner on account of his physical injuries. As discussed below, Ms. Pearson's testimony that Mr. Rodman paid that *entire* amount on account of petitioner's physical injuries is belied by the terms of the settlement agreement. Nonetheless, her testimony supports our finding that Mr. Rodman's dominant reason in paying petitioner the settlement amount at issue was to compensate him for claimed physical injuries relating to the incident.

We have found that Mr. Rodman's dominant reason in paying petitioner the settlement amount at issue was to compensate him for his claimed physical injuries relating to the incident. However, the settlement agreement expressly provided that Mr. Rodman paid petitioner a portion of the settlement amount at issue in return for petitioner's agreement not to: (1) [d]efame Mr. Rodman, (2) disclose the existence or the terms of the settlement agreement, (3) publicize facts relating to the incident, or (4) assist in any criminal prosecution against Mr. Rodman with respect to the incident (collectively, the nonphysical injury provisions).

The settlement agreement does not specify the portion of the settlement amount at issue that Mr. Rodman paid petitioner on account of his claimed physical injuries and the portion of such amount that Mr. Rodman paid petitioner on account of the nonphysical injury provisions in the settlement agreement. Nonetheless, based upon our review of the entire record before us, and bearing in mind that petitioner has the burden of proving the amount of the settlement amount at issue that Mr. Rodman paid him on account of physical injuries, we find that Mr. Rodman paid petitioner $120,000 of the settlement amount at issue on account of petitioner's claimed physical injuries and $80,000 of that amount on account of the nonphysical injury provisions in the settlement agreement. On that record, we further find that for the year at issue petitioner is entitled under section 104(a)(2) to exclude from his gross income $120,000 of the settlement amount at issue and is required under section 61(a) to include in his gross income $80,000 of that amount.

Notes and Questions

1. *Echoes of* Duberstein. This was anything but a gratuitous transfer, but one hears nevertheless the echoes of the *Duberstein* decision in the court's insistence on finding Mr. Rodman's "dominant reason" for making the transfer. But is that very helpful here? Surely his dominant reason for

making the transfer was to dispose of this action, avoiding both the inconvenience and adverse publicity associated with a trial, and the possibility of a verdict in a larger amount than the settlement. What was or wasn't in Mr. Rodman's mind seems an unpromising source of insight into the nature of the recovery.

2. *Any nonphysical claims here?* It does not appear from the opinion that any tort complaint was ever filed with a civil court that would have had jurisdiction to hear it. And the agreement did not admit that any tort of any sort had been committed. Under those circumstances, what evidence did the Tax Court have of the underlying basis of the claim? It appears to have relied on some mix of common sense inferences from the undisputed facts of the incident, and the testimony of Amos's lawyer about the tort settlement negotiations. In a case of this sort, where nonphysical tort claims (perhaps "intentional infliction of emotional duress") can certainly be imagined, there may be an advantage to taxpayers in handling the tort case in a way that obviates the necessity of disclosing the plaintiff's full range of claims. In this case, anyway, it would appear that the taxpayer would have been able to exclude the full recovery, but for Rodman's insisting (apparently) that Amos be quiet about the incident.

3. *Being quiet.* What do you make of Amos's agreement not to cooperate in any criminal investigations or prosecutions relating to the incident? Can a person legally make such an agreement?

4. *Rodman's tax implications.* There is no public record of how Mr. Rodman may have treated this payment for purposes of his tax return for 1997. It is premature to discuss that question at this point, but perhaps you can tuck away in the back of your mind the question of whether this might have been a deductible business expense for him.

Problem 1.   Peter receives $100,000 damages for Dana's intentional infliction of emotional distress (also known as the tort of "outrage") upon Peter. Under state law, physical symptoms of the distress are a necessary element of the plaintiff's prima facie case; Peter's symptoms included nausea and a severe rash. Of the $100,000 damages, $10,000 was for past medical expenses (which Peter had not deducted), and the other $90,000 was not allocated between lost wages and nonpecuniary damages. How much, if anything, may Peter exclude from gross income?

Problem 2.   Husband is killed in an automobile accident caused by D's negligent driving. Under state law, this entitles Wife to damages for loss of consortium. After the 1996 amendments, is Wife entitled to exclude her damages under §104(a)(2)?

Problem 3.   Phyllis settled her physical injury tort claim against Diane by agreeing to accept Microsoft stock, worth $100,000 at the time of the transfer. If Phyllis sells the stock several years later for $120,000, what is the amount of her taxable gain?

Problem 4.   Pat was physically injured as a result of Drew's negligent driving. During the course of settlement negotiations, Drew's insurer offers Pat two choices. The first is a lump sum settlement of $1 million. The second is a structured settlement under which the insurer would make ten annual payments of $50,000 each, with the first payment to be made one year from now. At the end of ten years, the insurer would make a one-time payment of $1 million (in addition to the final $50,000 payment). If Pat selects the first option, he will invest the entire amount in corporate bonds paying 5 percent annual interest and maturing in ten years. Thus, Pat would experience the same pre-tax cash flow under either option — $50,000 per year for nine years (beginning one year from now), and $1,050,000 in ten years. Pat is indifferent between the two options, apart from any difference in income tax results. Which option should he choose?

Problem 5.   According to Reg. §1.104-1(c), IRC §104(a)(2) applies only to "an amount received . . . through prosecution of a legal suit or action based upon tort or tort type rights, or through a settlement agreement entered into in lieu of such prosecution." Does that regulation foreclose the application of the §104(a)(2) exclusion in all cases of consented-to injuries, or might it leave the door slightly ajar? Consider this problem. Paul suffers from kidney failure and needs a transplant to lead a normal life. His brother Andy is a good match, and agrees to provide the kidney. A kidney donor will ordinarily spend a few days in the hospital, receive significant amounts of expensive antibiotics, and face some risk of infection or other complications that may require expensive treatment. Andy's health insurance does not cover voluntary exposures of this sort. Paul has no insurance, but does have enough assets to cover both his own and Andy's costs. So Paul agrees to pay for all of Andy's medical expenses. Are those amounts excluded from Andy's gross income? (If not, Andy may be able to deduct them, but only if he itemizes his deductions, and even then only to the extent that his unreimbursed medical expenses exceed 7.5 percent (10 percent in 2013 and later years) of his adjusted gross income; see the discussion of medical expenses in Chapter 4 for more details.) What if Paul also pays Andy $5,000 to compensate him for the pain and suffering involved in the major surgery required to extract the donated kidney, making it clear in their contract that the payment will be made regardless of whether Andy's kidney turns out to be in a condition that allows it to be transplanted into Paul's body? What if Paul and Andy heartily dislike each other, the payment described in the preceding sentence is $500,000 instead of $5,000, and Andy would not have agreed to donate the kidney if the payment had been a penny less?

c. Life Insurance

Section 101(a) provides, in general, that gross income does not include "amounts received . . . under a life insurance contract, if such amounts are paid by reason of the death of the insured." In order to understand the implications of this exclusion, one must first understand the non-tax basics of life insurance.

Individuals who have dependents ordinarily wish to make some provision for the possibility that they might be unable to continue supporting those dependents because of their own death. A sizable industry has arisen to satisfy this wish by providing, for a fee, a promise to pay a death benefit to or for the benefit of dependents in the event of the breadwinner's premature death — premature in the sense that it comes before a support obligation has been fully discharged.[19] Life

---

19. Life insurance is available for other purposes as well. For example, a business that was significantly dependent on the talents of one or a few key personnel might buy insurance to cover business losses that might occur because of the unexpected deaths of those personnel.

insurance generally falls into one or another of two broad categories, called "term" life insurance and "whole" life insurance (the latter sometimes called "straight" or "permanent" life insurance). Each of these two forms is favored—in rather different ways—by the Internal Revenue Code, reflecting Congress's sense that it is good public policy to encourage individuals with dependents to make arrangements to continue support of those dependents for as long as support is needed.

Term life insurance. Term life insurance consists generally of a very simple contract, usually called a policy: The insurer promises to pay a death benefit of a specified dollar amount to a beneficiary specified by the insured policyholder, if the latter dies within the stated term of the policy. In turn, the policyholder promises to pay to the insurer, usually at the inception of the term, a "premium" to cover the expected costs of providing insurance. The insurer is usually a large company, heavily regulated by the various insurance commissions in the states in which policies are to be sold. The company takes on the gamble of insuring the insured's life as part of a portfolio of similar risks. By insuring many lives, it can be reasonably certain that most of its policyholders will not die during the terms of their policies, thereby providing enough premium revenue to cover the costs of paying the death benefits to the beneficiaries of the few policyholders who actually do die during the terms of their policies.

A concrete example will illustrate the basic mechanics. Suppose that a very large insurance company sells one-year term insurance, with a $50,000 death benefit, to 100,000 50-year-old policyholders. Death rate data suggest that, if those policyholders are of average health and other risk characteristics, 407 of them will die during the policy year,[20] and that the insurance company will accordingly need to pay that number, times $50,000, in death benefits that year on behalf of this pool of insured lives. Anticipating this, the company will have charged at least $20.35 million, or $203.50 per insured, in premiums, in order to cover the expected costs of paying those death benefits. In reality, the insurance company needs to cover marketing and administrative costs, and profits, and may add a bit of an intentional overcharge to cover unexpected mortality losses (some part of which may be rebated to the policyholders in the subsequent year in what insurance companies call "dividends," though they little resemble the dividends paid by corporations to their shareholders). The actual premium, then, may be nearly twice as much as the $203.50 necessary to cover the expected actuarial risks of insuring the lives of this pool. Even so, many people with dependents are quite willing to pay, say, $400 for the assurance that a $50,000 check will be paid to their beneficiaries in the unfortunate event of their demise during the policy year. It is a gamble, of a sort: The policyholder wins the bet—getting $50,000 of value from the company in exchange for the payment of a $400 premium—only if he dies during the year. The company wins if he does not. The company keeps the premium, along with whatever it may have earned investing the premium, and owes the policyholder nothing. The company will make more profit if it beats the odds represented by the death rate of 407 per 100,000 policyholders, and this is why insurance companies employ "underwriting" standards, in an effort to sell insurance primarily to those whose survival prospects are above average.

---

20. *Statistical Abstract of the United States, 2011,* Table 105 (overall 2007 death rates in the United States).

Whole life insurance. An important and inexorable truth of actuarial science is that death rates increase with age, at least within the age ranges of greatest insurance needs.[21] When our 50-year-old policyholders reach age 60, they will encounter death rates for that age group that are nearly double the rate they had when they were 50 — 801 of 100,000 policyholders will likely die during their sixtieth year.[22] If the premium for $50,000 of insurance was $400 when they were 50, it will likely be around $800 at age 60. Many individuals who would like to have life insurance at that age may find that they cannot afford as much insurance as they would like. They have become high-risk policyholders, and insurance companies will gamble on them only at a high price.

High-risk insurance has another aspect that makes insurance companies nervous. When the risks — and thus the premiums — are high, potential policyholders may take a harder look at the gamble that they are undertaking. Imagine the psychology of our group of 60-year olds, for example. Some may no longer need insurance, because their dependents have matured out of dependency. But among those who still feel a need for life insurance, which among them will be most likely to continue to renew their policies? All else equal, the ones most likely to view the policy terms as attractive will be those who assess their survival chances most pessimistically. If you have high blood pressure and a family history of early death from heart disease or cancer, you are likely to think that if the overall rate of death is a bit over one percent for the next year, your own rate may be several times that percentage. Some of this variation in prospects can be controlled through the underwriting process, which tries to assess the variable elements of risk and assign differential premiums accordingly. But the objective information available to the insurance company in the underwriting can never account for residual risk variability quite as well as the insured herself can. (The ultimate example of this phenomenon is an insured who is suicidal; such an individual is in a much better position to know his intentions than the insurance company ever would be.[23])

This tendency for the highest-risk policyholders to be the most interested in buying insurance is called *adverse selection.* It is a problem of some importance in all insurance contexts, but reaches critical proportions in high-risk insurance situations. Adverse selection problems have a spiraling quality: As the insurer recognizes a high risk, and raises the premium to cover the greater risk, the lower-risk insureds in the pool are disproportionately likely to drop their coverage, which raises the average risk remaining in the pool even further. Further reassessment of risks will yield a still higher premium, and so on. Adverse selection problems can become so severe that no coverage at all can feasibly be offered for some types of risks.

Whole life insurance can be seen as something of a response to the problems of increasing expense, and increasing risk, of life insurance associated with aging.

---

21. Actually, infants during their first year of life have a higher death rate — 676 per 100,000 in the United States in 2007 (*ibid.*) — than even our pool of fifty-year-old policyholders; and death rates decline from that rate during about the first ten years of life. After that, they increase very gradually until middle age, at which point both the year-to-year changes and the absolute rates become, well, noticeable.

22. *Id.*

23. It is for this reason that many policies have an exclusion (a denial of coverage) for deaths by suicide. However, under the regulations of most state insurance agencies, these clauses must expire after the policy has been in force for some period of time, typically one year.

The central idea of whole life policies is to level the premiums for life insurance over the entire (the "whole") life of the insured. This works best if the insurance coverage is begun at relatively young ages, when the actuarial risks are relatively small. The premiums in such cases may be set at levels that are many times the amount necessary to cover the actuarial risk of paying a death benefit for the young insured; yet they are still affordable because the risk is so very low at those early ages. The company then sets aside a significant portion of the premiums in a life insurance reserve fund. This fund, along with the excess premiums paid by other younger policyholders, constitutes a pool of capital that the insurance company can invest, with the earnings on the investment being credited largely to the insurance reserve fund, with perhaps a bit here and there taken off as profit for the company.

As the policyholder ages, she will ultimately reach an age where the actuarial risk that the company might have to pay a death benefit to her beneficiaries exceeds the amount that still constitutes her level premium. No matter; by that time, the insurance company will have set aside enough of her earlier premiums that the amount set aside, together with the earnings generated by the amount set aside during the early policy years, will cover the premium shortfall during the policy-holder's later years. The policyholder also has rights—which vary somewhat from state to state and company to company—to borrow money from the issuing company against the reserve account, and to receive a "surrender value" when and if the policyholder decides to cancel the policy. The amounts that can be borrowed or received upon surrender of the policy are typically not the whole amount of the reserve account for the policy, but do constitute a significant portion of that reserve (at least in the case of a policy that has been in force for several years). The precise amounts available to a policyholder under loan or surrender arrangements are fixed by the contract, and are called the "loan value" and the "cash surrender value," respectively.

There are many variants on the permanent insurance model described. For example, some policies are structured as "single-premium" policies, in which the costs of the policy are fully paid at the inception of the policy by a single large payment. Other policies, typically called "variable life" policies, allow the death benefit and cash surrender value to vary within specified ranges, depending on the returns achieved by the company as it invests the policyholder reserves. So-called universal life policies provide some options to the policyholders to vary the amount and timing of the premium payments, with the death benefits being adjusted accordingly for upward or downward variations in the premiums paid. The policies described in this paragraph are usually purchased to further the investment purposes of the policyholder as much as for traditional insurance purposes; how-ever, they do provide a sizable portion of the insurance coverage in force in recent years, and have become very important products in the lines of business offered by major insurance companies.

The exclusion for life insurance proceeds. Section 101 of the Code provides that amounts received as the "proceeds of life insurance" are not includible in gross income, despite the fact that those proceeds would seem to be "accessions to wealth, clearly realized," in the words of *Glenshaw Glass*. Some would argue that, viewed collectively, §101(a) does not confer any favoritism on life insurance, since the exclusion of death benefits paid is offset by the nondeductibility of the premiums paid by all the insureds, most of whom did not die during any particular tax year.[24] Thus, the system ignores both so-called "mortality gains" and "mortality losses," coming out about right in the aggregate even if not in individual cases. Others point out, however, that the surviving buyers of insurance, even in the case of pure term insurance, received something valuable from the very fact of coverage, even if their beneficiaries did not receive any death benefits. Under this view, those who "lose" their life insurance gamble in any given year (by not dying) made consumption expenditures equal to their premiums, while those who "won" (by dying) did indeed win in financial terms, so that either their estates or their beneficiaries should report income in the amount of the death benefit received.

Consider two possible tax regimes for term life insurance. Under the first regime (which happens to be current law), term life insurance premiums are not deductible and death benefits are not taxable. Under the second regime, premiums are fully deductible (as above-the-line deductions, under §62), and death benefits are fully taxable. Intuitively, it seems that the first regime is more favorable for taxpayers who win their bets with the insurance company (by dying during the term of the policy), while the second is more favorable for taxpayers who lose their bets (by not dying). However, under the reasonable assumption that taxpayers take the tax rules into account in deciding how much insurance coverage to purchase, the difference between the two regimes is less than meets the eye. In fact, if a single rate of tax applies to all income in all years, there is *no* real difference between them.

Example. An income tax of 20 percent applies to all taxable income in all relevant years. At your age, you can buy $100,000 of term coverage for every $1,000 of premium. You want to buy enough coverage so that your family will be left with $1,000,000 (after taxes, if any) if you die during the year. Under the first regime, you simply pay a $10,000 nondeductible premium for $1 million of tax-free coverage. What do you do under the second regime? You want to buy enough coverage so that your family will be left with $1 million after paying a 20 percent tax. Expressed as a formula, you want a death benefit, x, such that

$$x(1-.2) = \$1,000,000, \text{ or } x = \$1,000,000/.8, \text{ or } x = \$1,250,000$$

Thus, you pay a premium of $12,500 to buy $1,250,000 of coverage. The premium is deductible, and deducting $12,500 in the 20 percent bracket reduces your tax liability by $2,500. You have incurred an after-tax premium cost of $10,000 ($12,500 − $2,500) for an after-tax death benefit of $1 million ($1,250,000 − $250,000). The after-tax premium cost and the after-tax death benefit under the second regime are identical with the premium cost and the death benefit under the first regime.

Pre-death benefits. The advantages of exclusion of life insurance death benefits have recently been extended to cover situations in which a dying policyholder

---

24. *See* Reg. §1.262-1(b)(1) (treating life insurance premiums paid by the insured as nondeductible personal expenses), §264(a)(1) (denying a deduction for life insurance premiums paid by a policy beneficiary), and §265(a)(1) (denying a deduction for expenses allocable to tax-exempt income).

receives a pre-death insurance benefit. Many life insurance policies now permit payment of all or a part of the death benefit to the insured himself, prior to death, if he is terminally ill. In addition, so-called viatical settlement providers have arisen to purchase or take assignments of an insured's interest in a life insurance policy if he is terminally ill. Under §101(g), added to the Code in 1996, Congress has allowed such payments — either from the insurance company or from the sale or assignment of rights to a viatical settlement company — to qualify for the exclusion granted by §101(a) for life insurance proceeds. "Terminal illness" is defined in §101(g)(4)(A) as an illness or physical condition that can reasonably be expected to result in death within 24 months of the certification of such illness or condition by a physician.

Payments made to chronically ill patients may also be excluded as death benefits under §101(a) and (g), if the payments are used to defray certain long-term care expenses — a limitation that does not apply to the terminally ill. Chronic illness is defined for this purpose as an illness that leaves the patient unable to perform basic living activities, such as eating, bathing, or dressing, or which leaves the patient so cognitively impaired as to need substantial supervision for his own protection.

Internal earnings on whole life policies. A further, and less equivocal, tax benefit associated with life insurance ownership is that under long-standing IRS administrative practice (with surprisingly little statutory authority), the internal earnings within insurance policies are generally not taxed. By "internal earnings" we mean the amounts earned by the insurance company that are credited to a policy reserve for the insured. Virtually all life insurance policies — even term life policies — involve prepayment of premiums, so that the premium is received before the company has been exposed to the risk it has underwritten. At any given point in the term of the policy, the part of the premium that is still exposed to risk is held in reserve for accounting purposes, but is available for investment by the company, and therefore generates earnings. In turn, this slightly reduces the amounts that the policyholders need to pay for particular amounts of coverage.

The tax advantage associated with the de facto exemption of internal earnings within an insurance policy is clearest, and financially most important, in whole life or similar policies, in which relatively large premiums are paid relatively early in the period of risk exposure, with the sums being actuarially likely to be held by the company for some extended period. In 2009, some $3.62 trillion was held by life insurance companies as reserves on insurance and annuity policies.[25] These funds were generally invested, earning returns amounting to billions of dollars. To the extent those earnings were credited to the policyholder reserves, they would generally not be taxed as income to the insurance company. (Indeed, they are liabilities of the company.) But neither are they taxed to the individual policyholders. If the policyholder dies, the reserves essentially are distributed as proceeds of life insurance and are never taxed, pursuant to §101(a). If all or part of the reserves are distributed to the policyholder — in the event that the policyholder cancels the policy, for example — the earnings are taxable to the policyholder at

25. *Life Insurers Fact Book 2010*, Table 3.2.

that point, but only after what may have been years of deferral while the earnings were building up within the reserve account.

This remarkably favorable tax treatment is not without its counterparts in other corners of the tax system. For example, qualified pension plans of various types receive treatment that is at least as favorable. Even the practice of not taxing unrealized appreciation in the values of corporate stock or real estate involves a similar willingness to permit deferral of tax liabilities. But tax-favored pension plan contributions on behalf of a taxpayer are limited in amount and subject to elaborate antidiscrimination rules. Appreciated stock is not so limited, but typically does involve at least the collection of a corporate income tax on the earnings that contributed to the increase in the value of the stock. Real estate purchases are indeed quite tax-favored in many ways, but they also typically demand more of the taxpayer in terms of selection and management of properties, and those demands tend to somewhat limit the range of abuse. Life insurance involves none of those limitations, risks, management demands, or ongoing tax payments. It is thus exceptional in the ease with which it can be used in tax-avoidance devices.

Universal life. So-called universal life insurance has become very popular within the last generation. (How could it not, with such a wonderful name?) It is available in a wide range of variants, but the forms have in common the fact that substantial investment aspects are combined with a core life insurance element. In some early forms of this insurance, the investment elements predominated the insurance elements, and the policies were transparently intended to use the tax-deferral opportunities of life insurance to shelter otherwise taxable investment income. A simplified form of this type of insurance might involve the following relationships of premium to death benefits and cash values, with comparable numbers for a straight life insurance contract shown for comparison:

	Straight Life	**Universal Life**
Annual premium	$1,000	$2,000
Death benefit		
First year	$100,000	$101,200
Second year	$100,000	$102,900
Cash value		
First year	$200	$1,200
Second year	$800	$2,900

What the universal life contract involves in this case is simply a $100,000 life insurance contract, with an added investment fund, to which the policyholder contributes an extra $1,000 per year. His death benefit is increased by the accumulated additional contributions (and earnings with respect to those contributions), and his cash value similarly reflects those additional elements. In later years, the cash value would grow exponentially, since the part of the premium that is in effect a non-insurance investment would not be encumbered with any actuarial load necessary to cover death benefits to other policyholders.

Congress significantly cut back on the more abusive forms of universal life insurance in 1984, when it added §7703 to the Code. The rules contained in that section are largely unintelligible to readers who are not actuaries, but the gist is to impose, as a definitional property of life insurance, an actuarially sound relationship between the premiums paid and the death benefits offered under the contract. While this limits the possibilities to create large investment accounts within the umbrella of a relatively small life insurance contract, this form of insurance remains popular among new policyholders, presumably because of its greater flexibility, compared with other forms of life insurance.

d. Other Source-Based Exclusions for Cash Receipts

In addition to the exclusions for gifts and bequests, for damages on account of personal physical injuries, and for life insurance proceeds, there are several other important exclusion provisions that can apply to cash receipts, and that do not depend on the use of the receipts. Two of the most important of these provisions are examined in detail elsewhere in this book: the §103 exclusion for interest on municipal bonds, and the §121 exclusion for gain on the sale of a personal residence.[26] Another example, not considered in detail in this book, is the partial exclusion provided by §86 for Social Security benefits.[27] Yet another important exclusion — the "general welfare exclusion" — has no express statutory basis, but has long been recognized by the Internal Revenue Service.[28] This non-statutory exclusion applies to benefits to low income families (such as food stamps and Temporary Assistance for Needy Families payments), and to welfare-type aid to the disabled and the elderly. It has also been applied to disaster relief payments, although §139 (enacted in 2001) now provides an explicit exclusion for "qualified disaster relief payments." There are also a few legislative exclusions that have not been included in the IRC. For example, §803 of the Economic Growth and Tax Relief Reconciliation Act of 2001 provides an exclusion for certain restitution payments received by victims of Nazi Germany.

There are numerous other exclusion provisions, but few that apply to receipts of cash which the taxpayer is free to use for any purpose. In other words, most other exclusion provisions are for non-cash benefits, or for cash earmarked for a particular use. A number of exclusions of this sort are considered in the following section.

---

26. See section A of Chapter 8 for §103, and section D.4 of Chapter 3 for §121.

27. Oversimplifying considerably, §86 excludes 100 percent of Social Security benefits for lower income recipients, excludes 50 percent of Social Security benefits for middle income recipients, and excludes only 15 percent of Social Security benefits for higher income recipients.

28. *See, e.g.,* Rev. Rul. 73-87. 1973-1 C.B. 39 (holding that payments received under a federally funded anti-poverty program are excluded from gross income).

B. IS IT TAXABLE IF IT ISN'T CASH?

1. *Generally, Yes, as Far as §61 Is Concerned*

ROONEY v. COMMISSIONER

88 T.C. 523 (1987)

SIMPSON, J.: . . . David Rooney, Richard Plotkin, and Grafton Willey are partners in Rooney, Plotkin & Willey (the partnership), a certified public accounting firm located in Newport, Rhode Island. . . .

The partners make it a practice to patronize the business establishments of many of their clients because they believe it to be good for business. At times, the partners paid for the goods and services received from a client through a practice known as "cross-accounting." On such occasions, they reduced the client's debt to the partnership by an amount equal to the price normally charged for such goods and services by the client to its retail customers. The partnership then recognized that amount as gross receipts.

During 1981, four of the partnership's clients became delinquent in paying for services rendered in that year. The four clients and their principal businesses were as follows:

Client	Business
Caswell-Massey Pharmacy	Pharmacy
Easton Inn Corp. d.b.a. Greenhouse Restaurant	Restaurant
Henriques Shell Station	Service station
Gary Kirwin	Plumber

The partnership attempted to collect the unpaid balances by making demands for payment and threatening to institute collection proceedings. After such efforts proved unsuccessful, the partnership allowed the petitioners and their families to receive goods and services from such clients in 1981. The Plotkins received toiletry products from the pharmacy. They also had the plumber do some work at their home. Mr. Rooney purchased automobile tires from Henriques Shell station. All of the petitioners took meals at the restaurant. The partnership used its cross-accounting procedure to credit the clients for these goods and services.

The partners became dissatisfied with the cross-accounting arrangement with these four clients. They determined that some of the goods received were overpriced and that some of the services were not satisfactorily performed and that therefore the value to them of the goods and services was less than the normal retail prices charged by such clients. The partners agreed that they patronized the clients only because they were in danger of going out of business and that the only way to reduce the amount owed to the partnership was to cross-account. Consequently, the partners "discounted" the retail prices of the goods and services received by them from the four clients and reduced the partnership's gross receipts account by the amount of the discount. The retail prices charged by the clients and the adjustments made by the partners were as follows:

Client	Retail Price	Adjustment
Caswell-Massey Pharmacy	$1,407.37	$351.84
Easton Inn Corp. d.b.a. Greenhouse Restaurant	$2,021.91	$1,010.95
Henriques Shell Station	$580.82	$480.82
Gary Kirwin — plumber	$250.65	$120.83

The total of such adjustments is $1,964.44, but the partnership actually claimed a total adjustment of $1,963.78. The four clients were never informed that the partnership made such adjustments. . . .

The sole issue for our decision is whether an accounting partnership, in computing its income, may discount the retail prices of goods and services received in exchange for accounting services by considering the partners' subjective determination of value. The petitioners concede that they must report on their individual income tax returns their distributive shares of the income and expenses of the partnership. *See* secs. 701-704. They also concede that the gross income of their accounting partnership includes the fair market value of the goods and services received by them in exchange for accounting services. Sec. 61; sec. 1.61-2(d), Income Tax Regs. However, they challenge the Commissioner's determination of the fair market value of such goods and services. . . .

The Commissioner determined the fair market value of the goods and services received by the petitioners to be equal to the prices normally charged by the clients to their retail customers. He argues that such prices represent the fair market value of such goods and services as established by the marketplace and that the petitioners cannot discount such prices for personal reasons. *See* sec. 1.61-2(d)(1), Income Tax Regs.

Ordinarily, the fair market value of property is "the price at which the property would change hands between a willing buyer and a willing seller, neither being under any compulsion to buy or to sell and both having reasonable knowledge of relevant facts." Sec. 20.2031-1(b), Estate Tax Regs. However, the petitioners argue that their situation calls for a departure from the usual method of measuring fair market value. They claim that they ordinarily did not patronize the four clients but that they did so because such clients were in precarious financial condition and were past due on amounts owed to the partnership. The petitioners contend that they chose to accept goods and services from the clients in order to reduce the amounts owed, rather than risk collecting nothing should the clients go out of business. They claim that circumstances compelled them to accept such goods and services at prices higher than they would otherwise pay. Therefore, the petitioners argue that the value to them of such goods and services was less than their retail prices.

In Koons v. United States, 315 F.2d 542 (9th Cir. 1963), the court considered a situation similar to the one in this case. In *Koons,* a taxpayer accepted employment which required that he relocate to a new home. His new employer paid the cost of moving the taxpayer's household effects to the new home. The taxpayer did not dispute that the value of the moving services constituted taxable income,[29] nor did he dispute the amount paid by his employer for such services. However, he argued that he could have moved himself at much less cost and that therefore the value to him of the moving services was less than the amount paid by his employer. The Ninth Circuit rejected the taxpayer's argument, holding that:

> the use of any such [subjective] measure of value as is suggested is contrary to the usual way of valuing either services or property, and would make the administration of the tax laws in this area depend upon a knowledge by the Commissioner of the state of mind of the individual taxpayer. We do not think that tax administration should be based upon anything so whimsical. . . . We think that sound administration of the tax laws requires that there be as nearly objective a measure of the value of services that are includible in income as possible, and the only such objective measure . . . is fair market value. . . . [315 F.2d at 545.]

We agree with the court's reasoning in *Koons*. In our judgment, section 61 requires an objective measure of fair market value. . . . Under such standard, the petitioners may not adjust the acknowledged retail price of the goods and services received merely because they decide among themselves that such goods and services were overpriced.

We are not persuaded by the petitioners' claims that they were compelled by circumstances to patronize these clients and that they were therefore "forced" to accept prices for the goods and services higher than they would have otherwise paid. We believe that their situation cannot be termed a forced purchase. The petitioners themselves made the decision to accept compensation in a form other than cash. Moreover, although the petitioners claim that they would not have willingly paid the retail prices for the goods and services received from the four clients, those prices were, so far as we know, accepted by other customers of those clients and thus represent the prices established in the marketplace. In our judgment, the petitioners must value their compensation by applying an objective measure of fair market value. For such reasons, we hold that the fair market value of the goods and services received by the petitioners is the prices charged by the partnership's clients to their retail customers. *See* sec. 20.2031-1(b), Estate Tax Regs.

Decision will be entered for the respondent.

Notes and Questions

1. *Preventing a flight from cash.* There are two obvious reasons why taxing cash receipts is more attractive than taxing compensation received in the form of drugs, food, gas, and plumbing services: valuation and liquidity. When compensation for services (or an amount realized on the sale of property) takes the form of cash, there is no difficulty in determining the fair market value of what the taxpayer has received. Moreover, the taxpayer can use a portion of the cash to pay the tax. If in-kind receipts are taxable, however,

---

29. [Under current law, a moving expense reimbursement received from one's employer is excluded from gross income, if certain requirements are satisfied. *See* §§132(a)(6), (g). — Eds.]

taxpayers and the IRS will inevitably quarrel over their value, and taxpayers will have to convert some of their receipts to cash or come up with cash from other sources in order to pay the tax. (The IRS does not accept in-kind tax payments, even if the taxpayer accepts in-kind payments for his services.) Given these serious problems with the taxation of in-kind receipts, why do Congress, the IRS, and the courts insist that in-kind receipts are within the scope of §61? The answer readily emerges if one imagines how taxpayers would respond if §61 applied only to cash. There would be a massive flight from cash compensation (and from cash payments for property). As much as possible, an employee would indicate her consumption wishes to her employer and the employer would do the employee's shopping — instead of giving the employee cash and letting her do her own shopping. That would be a disaster, both because of the loss of the efficiency advantage of a cash economy over a barter economy, and because of the devastating effect on income tax revenues as the cash tax base withered away. The main purpose, then, of including non-cash receipts in the tax base is not to raise revenue from the taxation of non-cash receipts, but to protect the cash tax base by denying any tax advantage to non-cash receipts. In the absence of an in-kind tax advantage, taxpayers will overwhelmingly opt for the non-tax advantages of cash over barter.

2. *Subjective versus objective valuation.* Even if you believe the taxpayers' claim in *Rooney* that their subjective valuation of their barter receipts was far below the fair market value of those receipts, the court's rejection of subjective valuation is obviously correct. A workable tax system cannot be premised on subjective valuations. The court's conclusion is consistent with Treas. Reg. §§1.61-21(b)(1) and (2), which apply to taxable fringe benefits received by employees from their employers. The regulations provide that the amount included in gross income is based on fair market value, and that "an employee's subjective perception of the value of a fringe benefit is not relevant to the determination of the fringe benefit's fair market value." These regulations are not technically applicable on the facts of *Rooney,* because they apply only to non-cash compensation received by employees, and Mr. Rooney was an independent contractor. Nevertheless, the valuation principle enunciated in the ruling applies to all taxable non-cash receipts.

REV. RUL. 57-374

1957-2 C.B. 69

Where an individual refuses to accept an all-expense paid vacation trip he won as a prize in a contest, the fair market value of the trip is not includible in his gross income for Federal income tax purposes.

Notes and Questions

1. *Why so terse?* The above sentence constitutes the entire text of the ruling. Ordinarily a revenue ruling cites and describes the relevant legal authority,

and explains the application of that authority to the facts of the ruling. Why the extreme terseness here? When the IRS believes it has good practical reasons for taking a particular position, but that the position is technically dubious (or worse), it sometimes deals with the problem by issuing an analysis-free ruling. In that way, the IRS is able to take the desired pragmatic position, while limiting the precedential effect of the ruling (on the assumption that a ruling devoid of analysis cannot be easily applied beyond its narrow facts and so has limited precedential value).

2. *Constructive receipt.* So why did the IRS want to take the position it took in Rev. Rul. 57-374, and why was the IRS so embarrassed that it offered no explanation for its conclusion? Suppose a game show contestant wins a cruise. The contestant can only take the cruise herself or turn it down; she cannot sell it or give it to anyone else. The fair market value of the cruise is $10,000, but the contestant's subjective valuation of the cruise (i.e., the most she would be willing to pay for such a vacation) is only $2,000. If the cruise is included in her income, the inclusion will be at the $10,000 fair market value. The contestant's marginal tax rate is 30 percent, so if she takes the cruise her $3,000 tax liability on the $10,000 objective value will be greater than the subjective value she places on the prize. In effect, she would be buying the trip for $1,000 more than it is worth to her. The IRS wanted to give a taxpayer in this situation an escape route, but did not want to suggest that the amount included in gross income could ever be based on subjective valuation. The solution was to let the taxpayer avoid paying a tax greater than the subjective value of the trip by not accepting the trip. The IRS's embarrassment stems from the fact that the ruling is in conflict with the doctrine of constructive receipt. Under that doctrine, a taxpayer who has the right to receive a taxable item cannot avoid the tax by "deliberately turn[ing] his back upon income."[30] Taxpayers seeking to avoid the application of the constructive receipt doctrine in other contexts will find Rev. Rul. 57-374 of little use, because of its lack of analysis.

3. *All or nothing?* Section 119 provides an exclusion from gross income for the value of meals and lodging furnished by an employer to an employee, if the meals and lodging are furnished on the employer's business premises "for the convenience of the employer." The exclusion could apply, for example, to a hotel suite and room service meals provided to the general manager of a hotel, if his job requires that he be on call at all times. As with in-kind game show prizes, it is likely that the hotel manager's subjective valuation of his meals and lodging — the amount he would be willing to pay for them if they did not come with the job — is considerably lower than their fair market value. Why not follow the approach of Rev. Rul. 57-374, and tell the manager that taxation of his room and board is based on fair market value, but that he can avoid taxation by declining to accept the benefits? Can you see why that approach is reasonable for game show contestants, but not for hotel managers? If the approach of the revenue ruling is unacceptable here, and if taxation based on subjective value is administratively

---

30. The quotation is from Hamilton Natl. Bank of Chattanooga v. Commissioner, 29 B.T.A. 63, 67 (1933). *See also* Treas. Reg. §§1.446-1(c)(1)(i), 1.451-2(a) (income is taxable when it is "constructively received"). For more on constructive receipt, see section B.1 of Chapter 7.

impractical, does the §119 exclusion necessarily follow? In effect, §119 assumes the subjective value of the manager's room and board is zero. Can you think of an administratively workable alternative to §119, which would recognize the valuation problems inherent in forced consumption, without being quite so generous as current law? Hint: Look at §274(n) for inspiration.

2. *The Two Great Non-Statutory Exclusions of Non-Cash Economic Benefits*

a. Imputed Income

Imputed income from services. (1) You are a professional housepainter. You paint a customer's house and are paid in cash. Must you include the cash in gross income under §61? (This is not a trick question; it is just setting up the following questions.) The answer, of course, is that you must. This is a classic case of §61(a)(1) compensation for services.

(2) One of your housepainting customers is a divorce lawyer. You need legal services in connection with your divorce, and the value of your housepainting services is approximately the same as the value of the legal services you need. You and the lawyer agree to trade housepainting services for legal services. Must you include in your gross income the value of the legal services you receive in exchange for the work you perform? This question is answered by *Rooney* and by Treas. Reg. §1.61-2(d)(1) ("If services are paid for in exchange for other services, the fair market value of such other services taken in payment must be included in income as compensation").

(3) Your own house needs painting, but you have an aversion to working on your own house.[31] You have a housepainter acquaintance (not really a friend) whose house also needs painting, and who also dislikes the idea of painting his own house. The two jobs are about the same size, so you each agree to paint the other's house. Must you include in your gross income the value of the housepainting services you receive in exchange for the work you perform? This is analytically no different from situation (2); the value of the services you receive is taxable under *Rooney* and Treas. Reg. §1.61-2(d)(1).

(4) You are a professional housepainter whose own house needs painting. You do the painting yourself. Must you include in your gross income the value of your own housepainting services? This time the answer is no. In both situation (3) and situation (4) you do housepainting work, and as a result of your efforts your own house is painted. What explains the different tax results in the two cases? The doctrinal answer is that although non-cash benefits received in an *exchange* are taxable, non-cash benefits you create *for yourself* — that is, in the absence of an exchange — are not. These benefits are referred to as imputed income from services, and they are not within the scope of §61. The language of that section seems broad enough to encompass imputed income from services, and no other

---

31. You are a soulmate of the proverbial cobbler whose children have no shoes.

Code provision expressly excludes imputed income from gross income. Nevertheless, the de facto exclusion is as old as the federal income tax.

Why do you suppose Congress decided to draw the gross income dividing line between situations (3) and (4)? If it is appropriate to include barter receipts in gross income, despite the resulting valuation and liquidity problems, why is it not also appropriate to include imputed income from self-performed services? One answer may be that the two situations differ in their privacy implications. Perhaps it is an unacceptable invasion of privacy to require you to report to the IRS what services you perform for yourself, and to determine the value of those services. In the barter situation, by contrast, the existence of another party to the transaction lessens the privacy objection to taxation. Even more important than the privacy distinction may be that the exclusion for imputed income does not erode the income tax base to nearly the extent of the likely erosion if barter income were made nontaxable. As discussed above, an official exclusion for barter income would likely trigger a massive flight from cash compensation. By contrast, the exclusion for imputed income has not triggered a massive flight from cash (or from barter), because there are major limits to what services most people can or will perform for themselves, even given a tax inducement to self-sufficiency. The exclusion of imputed income means that the income tax can be understood as a tax on specialization of labor and on market exchanges. If you are able and willing to do everything for yourself, you can legitimately avoid paying any income tax. The benefits of specialization of labor and of exchange are so great, however, that hardly anyone takes full advantage of this opportunity.

To a large extent, the effects of the imputed income exclusion even out among individuals. Everyone performs services for himself or herself, and everyone gets to exclude the value of those services from income. (An unusually lazy person may have less imputed income from self-performed services than most other people, but leisure also has its value, and that person has an unusually large amount of imputed income from leisure.) To take an extreme example, suppose everyone in society earned $40,000 cash each year and had $10,000 of imputed income from services (being one's own chauffeur, mowing one's own lawn, brushing one's own teeth, and so on). If the government wanted each person to pay $10,000 income tax, the government could require imputed income to be included in gross income, and impose a 20 percent tax on each person's income of $50,000. It would be simpler, however, to allow everyone to exclude imputed income from gross income, and to impose a 25 percent tax on each person's cash income of $40,000.

In the real world there is one important group of taxpayers who have significantly more imputed income from services than do other taxpayers: married couples in which one spouse is a full-time homemaker. Between these one-earner couples and other taxpayers, things do *not* roughly even out with respect to the nontaxation of imputed income. This raises both fairness and efficiency concerns.

Consider first the fairness problem. Anna and Arnold, a married couple with two young children, have a "traditional" division of responsibilities in their marriage. Anna is a full-time homemaker, and Arnold earns $80,000 at his full-time job. Brenda and Bob, a two-earner married couple, also have two young children; each spouse has a $40,000 job. In the absence of the equivalent of Anna's full-time homemaking services, Brenda and Bob are faced with some difficult choices. They may (1) pay babysitters, house cleaners, and others to do the kind of work Anna does in the other marriage, (2) stagger their work schedules so each can take care of the children while the other is being employed — in effect, each spouse having an exhausting "second shift" at home, or (3) settle for having feral children and a filthy house. Under any of these three options, they will be substantially less well off than Anna and Arnold. For example, if they choose the first option, and it costs them $20,000 to purchase the equivalent of Anna's services, they will have $20,000 less than Anna and Arnold to spend on all types of consumption other than child care and homemaking services. Despite the fact that they are obviously less well off than Anna and Arnold, Brenda and Bob will have the same gross income and the same taxable income as the one-earner couple.

If the goal is tax equity between the two couples, and if taxing the imputed income of Anna and Arnold is not an option, is there another solution? What if a two-earner couple were allowed a deduction for the costs of purchasing the equivalent of a one-earner couple's imputed income? No such deduction is allowed under current law. If Bob and Brenda spend money on child care, §21 will allow them a child care credit equal to 20 percent of their child care expenses, up to a maximum credit of $1,200 (based on maximum credit-eligible expenses of $6,000), but this is not nearly the equivalent of the $20,000 deduction they would need to achieve tax parity with Anna and Arnold. And if Brenda and Bob choose option (2) or option (3), they will have exactly the same tax liability and Anna and Arnold, despite their perpetual exhaustion (option 2) or miserable living conditions (option 3).

Only one couple is needed to illustrate the efficiency problem with the imputed income exclusion. Carla and Chuck are a married couple with a young child. Chuck is firmly committed to his job, which pays $80,000. Carla is trying to decide whether to continue as a full-time homemaker, or to reenter the paid workforce. She has an offer of a job at a salary of $30,000. She estimates that they would have to spend $20,000 to replace her homemaking services if she took the job. Assuming (1) that she is going to make this decision based on the financial bottom line, rather than on any commitment or aversion to full-time homemaking, and (2) that any income she earns will be taxed at the marginal rate of 40 percent, what should she do?[32] If she takes the job, the 40 percent tax bite will reduce her take-home pay to $18,000. Actually, it will not be quite that bad, because they will qualify for a $600 child care credit under §21 (calculated as 20% of their first $3,000 of child care expenses), but even taking the credit into account her take-home pay will be only $18,600. After paying $20,000 to replace Carla's services, Chuck and Carla will be $1,400 poorer if she earns $30,000 (pre-tax) than if she stays home and produces only $20,000 of imputed income. Faced with these numbers, Carla will decide to stay home. If one believes in the market, this is an inefficient result: Carla's work as an employee is $10,000 more valuable than her work as a full-time homemaker, yet the disparate tax treatments of the two options have caused her to choose homemaking. The $11,400 tax liability that the job would generate functions as a positive externality of Carla's employment. Society as a whole would be $10,000 better off if Carla took the job than if she stayed home, but that is the net result of the government's being $11,400 better off and Carla's and Chuck's being $1,400 poorer. Since Carla would not get the benefit of $11,400 of her earnings, she will ignore that amount in making her decision. Of course, if you think that full-time

---

32. The 40 percent rate is roughly realistic, taking into account the combined effects of the federal income tax, the Social Security wage tax (imposed at the flat rate of 7.65 percent), and a state income tax. The marginal federal income tax rate imposed on Carla's income will be relatively high, because Chuck's income has already used up the lower brackets on their joint income tax return.

parental child care is far superior to other forms of child care, you will be pleased that the tax system has pushed Carla in that direction.

Despite the inefficiency of the result described in the previous paragraph, valuation and privacy concerns are thought by most to rule out imposing a tax on the imputed income of full-time homemakers. It does not follow, however, that the exclusion from the tax base of their imputed income has no policy implications. If taxing imputed income is out of the question, but the tax bias in favor of full-time homemaking is considered undesirable, other reforms are possible. At the extreme, the tax bias in favor of full-time homemaking would be eliminated if Carla were allowed to deduct the entire $20,000 cost of replacing her imputed income. In that case, taking the job would increase her taxable income by only $10,000, and even with a 40 percent tax they would come out $6,000 ahead. Short of that extreme, the tax bias in favor of homemaking would be reduced if the child care credit were made more generous — by increasing the credit percentage, the dollar ceiling on credit-eligible expenses, or both. The tax bias in favor of homemaking would also be lessened if the joint return system for married couples were replaced by a system of mandatory separate returns; this would reduce the marginal tax rate applied to Carla's earnings.

Some conservative commentators have complained that the child care credit of §21 — which is calculated as a percentage of child care expenses — is unfairly denied to one-earner couples. If one spouse is a full-time homemaker there is no credit because there are no child care expenses.[33] Their proposed solution is to permit a one-earner couple to claim a credit of some specified amount, despite the absence of any actual expenses. The concept of imputed income from services demolishes the fairness argument for the proposed expansion of the child care credit. If there is unfairness, the victims are two-earner couples, whose modest child care credits are worth much less than the imputed income exclusion enjoyed by one-earner couples. If one wants to encourage full-time homemaking as a matter of social policy, it may make sense to extend the child care credit to one-earner couples with no actual expenses, but such an extension is clearly *not* required as a matter of fairness to one-earner couples.

Problem 6. Karen and Sandra are neighbors and good friends. When Karen goes on vacation, Sandra feeds Karen's cat and waters Karen's lawn. Karen does the same for Sandra when Sandra goes on vacation. They make no attempt to keep score. In some years Karen does more work for Sandra than Sandra does for Karen, and vice versa in other years. Over several years, however, the favors roughly even out. If Karen and Sandra are honest taxpayers, should they each report barter income (under Treas. Reg. §1.61-2(d)(1)) as a result of their arrangement?

Problem 7. Karen and Sandra (from Problem 6) are both single parents with young children. As much as possible, they arrange their work schedules so that one can babysit the other's children while the other is working. No money ever changes hands as a result of this arrangement, but the value of the babysitting services performed by each is in the neighborhood of $5,000 to $10,000 per year.

---

33. Of course, a full-time homemaker might employ babysitters or purchase other day-care services to some extent. Nevertheless, she is ineligible for the credit, which only applies to "employment-related expenses." *See* §21(b)(2).

Although they don't insist on precise equality in the number of babysitting hours performed by each, they have had arguments when the imbalance became significant, and they are now careful to keep the hours of babysitting done by each approximately equal. Should each report barter income in this situation?

Problem 8. Usually the exclusion of imputed income from services is a permanent exclusion. Not only are you not taxed this year on the value of services you performed this year for yourself (or your family or friends), you also will not be taxed on that value in any future years. Can you think of a situation, however, in which the exclusion operates only to defer taxation?

Imputed income from property. As everyone who has ever paid or received rent knows, the right to use property has economic value. This suggests that the right to use property without paying rent might result in the inclusion of the rental value in gross income — as, in fact, it sometimes does. If your employer allows you to live, rent-free, in a house owned by the employer, you must include the rental value of the house in your gross income (unless either of two narrow exclusions applies).[34] Of course, the most common way that people acquire the right to use property without paying rent is by owning the property. When you live rent-free in a house that you own, you are benefitting from imputed rental income. Like imputed income from services, imputed income from owner-used property is implicitly excluded from the scope of §61. In both cases, the key to the exclusion is the absence of any transaction or exchange. Just as you are not taxed on the value of work you do for yourself, so too are you not taxed on the value of the use you make of your own property.

Imputed rental income is produced by all consumer-owned durable goods. Cars, furniture, appliances, and perhaps even pets produce imputed income (although the rental market for pets is thin). As a practical matter, however, the rental value of owner-occupied housing dwarfs the value of all other imputed income from property. Roughly accurate taxation of this form of imputed income might be possible, without either the invasion of privacy or the valuation problems inherent in any attempt to tax imputed income from services. Taxation would be based on periodic appraisals of owner-occupied homes, combined with a semi-arbitrary rule that annual rental value equaled (for example) 5 percent of the appraised value. If periodic appraisals are practical for local property tax purposes, they should also be practical for federal income tax purposes. A system along these lines was actually used in the United Kingdom for several decades. Despite the technical feasibility of this approach, it is politically out of the question in the United States today.

In light of the deduction for home mortgage interest provided by §163(h)(3),[35] many people believe it is a big tax mistake to pay off a home mortgage. This view is based on a failure to appreciate the imputed income exclusion. Consider two situations:

---

34. Section 119 excludes the rental value of employer-provided housing if (1) the housing is located on the business premises of the employer, (2) the employee must accept the housing as a condition of employment, and (3) the housing is furnished "for the convenience of the employer" (e.g., because the employee's job requires that he be on call 24 hours a day). Section 107(1) excludes the rental value of a "parsonage" furnished to a member of the clergy as part of his compensation.

35. See section B.2.b of Chapter 4.

(1) You own your home free and clear. The house is worth $200,000, and its annual rental value is $10,000. Since the imputed rental income is not taxable, your economic income from the house ($10,000) exceeds your taxable income from the house (zero) by $10,000.

(2) Your neighbor owns an identical house, subject to a $200,000 mortgage debt, with an interest rate of 5 percent. From an economic standpoint, the neighbor's $10,000 imputed rental income and $10,000 interest expense cancel out; the neighbor has no *net* economic income from his debt-financed housing. For tax purposes, however, the neighbor has a $10,000 loss, created by the combination of the imputed income exclusion and the home mortgage interest deduction. Like you, the neighbor has economic income that exceeds taxable income by $10,000.[36]

The home mortgage interest deduction preserves the benefit of the imputed income exclusion for homeowners with mortgages. The underlying tax break, however, is the exclusion, not the deduction. The same point can be made in a slightly different way. If the imputed income were taxable, it would make perfect sense to allow the mortgage interest deduction as a cost of producing taxable income; it follows that the real tax break is the exclusion. The reason many people fail to realize this is that the home mortgage interest deduction is highly visible (as an entry on one's income tax return), whereas the imputed income exclusion is invisible (producing no entry on one's Form 1040). The only loser in the story of the income taxation of housing is the renter. Both the outright owner and the owner with a mortgage enjoy the benefit of the exclusion for imputed rental income, but the renter is not permitted a corresponding rent expense deduction.[37]

Although the exclusion is very valuable for homeowners, two limitations on its value are worth noting. *First,* the *net* exclusion may be far less than the gross rental value of the house. If you rented a house to a tenant for cash, you would be allowed deductions for the costs of producing taxable rental income, including maintenance and depreciation. However, no deductions (other than home mortgage interest) are allowed for the cost of producing tax exempt income.[38] Thus, if the gross rental value of your home is $10,000, but annual maintenance and depreciation expenses total $3,000, your net imputed income exclusion is only $7,000. *Second,* it is a rule of thumb for tax breaks that the early bird gets the free worm. Later birds must pay for their worms. When you buy a house, the price reflects the favorable tax treatment of owner-occupied housing. If imputed rental income were taxable, or if home mortgage interest were not deductible, houses would cost less. In other words, the value of a tax break for a particular type of property is largely "capitalized" into the prices of the tax-favored assets. You would have enjoyed a windfall gain if you had owned a house when the tax breaks for housing were introduced, but if you buy a house today you have largely paid for your tax breaks. This is one reason why it is so politically difficult to repeal tax breaks.

---

36. The excess of zero over negative $10,000 is $10,000.

37. Despite the unfavorable tax treatment of renters, however, it does appear that, at some times and in some markets, renting one's home may be advantageous even for high-bracket taxpayers. The economic considerations that can produce this result are beyond the scope of this book (but are suggested in the following paragraph of the text).

38. Section 265(a)(1).

THIS WEEK WITH DAVID BRINKLEY

February 28, 1993

Mr. Brinkley: Finally, a few words about federal taxes and what some of the great minds in the U.S. Treasury are thinking about. The Treasury likes to calculate the American people's ability to pay taxes, based not on how much money we have, but on how much we might have, or could have had. For example, a family that owns a house and lives in it, the Treasury figures if the family didn't own the house and rented it from somebody else, the rent would be $500 a month, so it would add that amount — $6,000 a year — to the family's so-called "imputed income." Imputed income is income you might have had, but don't. They don't tax you on that amount. The IRS does not play this silly game. Instead, the Treasury calculates how much they could take away from us if they decided to. If that were the system, consider the possibility. How about being taxed on Ed McMahon's $10-million magazine lottery? You didn't win it, you say? But you could have. The Treasury must have something better to do. If not, there is a good place for Clinton to cut some spending.

Notes and Questions

1. *Distributional analyses.* From time to time, the Treasury Department publishes "distributional tables," indicating how the tax burden is distributed among taxpayers at different income levels, either under current law or under reform proposals. In the process of assigning taxpayers to income categories, the Treasury considers not only items of §61 gross income, but also the imputed rental income of homeowners. As David Brinkley noted, this does not constitute taxation of imputed income. It is certainly a defensible way of producing distributional tables, as long as the readers of the tables understand the rules.

2. *Comparing Ed McMahon with owner-occupied housing.* Brinkley was probably right that the use of imputed income in distributional analyses is confusing to some readers. His more fundamental objection, however, was to the very concept of imputed rental income. Was he right that money you could have received if you had rented out your house (and lived in a tent) is like money you could have received if you had won the lottery?

3. *Are rights relevant?* People sometimes object to the concept of imputed rental income by saying, "But I own my house; I have a *right* to live in it." Does the existence of a legal right to an economic benefit have anything to do with §61 gross income analysis?

Problem 9.   Two law professors agree to a temporary house swap, while each is teaching as a visiting professor at the other's permanent school. In general terms, what are the income tax consequences of this arrangement?

b.   Unrealized Appreciation

On January 1 of the current year, you bought 1,000 shares of Growth, Inc. at a total cost of $10,000 ($10 per share). On December 31 you still own all 1,000 shares, which are now worth $15,000 ($15 per share). The $5,000 increase in value — referred to in tax circles as "unrealized appreciation" — clearly constitutes an economic benefit to you. The language of §61 seems broad enough to require you to include the $5,000 in gross income, and no other provision excludes unrealized appreciation from gross income. Nevertheless, the $5,000 of unrealized appreciation is *not* included in your gross income; unrealized appreciation is the second of the two great implicit exclusions from gross income. It resembles the other implicit exclusion — of imputed income — in that it is available only in the absence of an exchange. Considering the imputed income and unrealized appreciation exclusions together, the base of the income tax generally does not include any economic benefits not related to transactions or exchanges.

As long as you do not sell (or otherwise dispose of) your shares of Growth, Inc., the income tax will continue to disregard any increases or decreases in the value of the stock. Upon sale, however, the §1001 formula for gain realized (amount realized minus adjusted basis) will cause you to be taxed on what had been unrealized appreciation until the sale. If you sell the stock sometime in the next year, when it is still worth $15,000, your $5,000 of taxable gain ($15,000 amount realized minus $10,000 adjusted basis) is not really gain *created* by the sale. After all, you were not lucky enough to sell the stock for more than it was worth; you had $15,000 worth of stock just before the sale, and you have $15,000 of cash immediately after the sale. The sale is the trigger for taxation of the appreciation that accrued (in an economic sense) but went untaxed in the previous year. Because a sale triggers taxation of previously accrued appreciation, the exclusion of unrealized appreciation usually results only in deferral of taxation (until sale), rather than permanent exclusion of appreciation.

In a later chapter, we examine in detail the history of the exclusion for unrealized appreciation, the policy underlying the exclusion, and some technical aspects of the exclusion.[39] A few basic points, however, are worth noting here.

Policy: valuation and liquidity. The usual policy explanation for the exclusion is that taxation of unrealized appreciation would involve tremendous problems of valuation and liquidity. Taxpayers and the IRS would be constantly arguing about the amounts by which assets had increased (or declined) in value during a year, and unrealized appreciation would generate no cash with which to pay the tax. How might a defender of the exclusion of unrealized appreciation respond to the following critique of the doctrine?

> Although valuation and liquidity concerns justify the exclusion of unrealized appreciation in many types of assets — real estate, for one example — they do not justify the exclusion of appreciation in publicly traded securities (stocks and bonds). A glance at two newspapers will reveal the amount by which listed stock has appreciated during the year, and a taxpayer could readily sell (or borrow against) some of the shares in order to pay a tax on the appreciation. Conversely, sometimes the income tax treats gain as realized (and thus included in gross income) despite the existence of major valuation and liquidity problems. If a taxpayer exchanges raw land for a valuable painting, the exchange is a taxable event (an "other disposition" under §1001 (a)), and the taxpayer realizes gain to the extent the value of the painting exceeds her adjusted basis in the land. The IRS and

---

39. See section A of Chapter 4.

the taxpayer may disagree as to the value of the painting, and the painting is probably a highly illiquid asset; nevertheless the taxpayer's gain in the land is no longer unrealized appreciation. In short, if the nontaxation of unrealized appreciation is a response to problems of valuation and liquidity, it is a response which is both overinclusive (listed stock) and underinclusive (land-for-painting exchange).

Deferral, not exclusion. Mostly. Ordinarily, the exclusion for unrealized appreciation is not permanent. Instead, tax is deferred until the taxpayer sells the appreciated asset.[40] However, the exclusion of unrealized appreciation will be permanent if the taxpayer holds the property until death and the property's basis is then stepped-up to fair market value by §1014.[41]

Unrealized appreciation and the income tax: historically and today. In the famous case of *Eisner v. Macomber*,[42] the Supreme Court ruled that the exclusion of unrealized appreciation from gross income was required by the Constitution. Although the case has never been formally overruled, later Supreme Court opinions appear to have demoted it from constitutional status. There is almost universal agreement among tax experts today that the exclusion survives only as a matter of statutory interpretation. Under this prevailing view, Congress has the power to tax unrealized appreciation to the extent it sees fit. In fact, Congress has done so in a few situations. For example, §475 requires securities dealers to "mark to market" their securities each year, which is a fancy way of saying they must include appreciation in their securities in gross income despite the fact that they have not sold (or otherwise disposed of) the securities.[43] Congress could apply the same treatment to *all* owners of publicly traded securities, and there are serious policy arguments in favor of doing so (given the absence of problems of valuation or liquidity), but there is no reason to believe a large-scale legislative assault on the unrealized appreciation exclusion is imminent.

3. Statutory Exclusions Based on the Non-Cash Nature of the Benefit, or on the Required Use of Cash

Non-cash economic benefits (other than imputed income and unrealized appreciation) are generally includable in gross income in the absence of an explicit exclusion provision. Congress has enacted a number of explicit exclusion provisions for particular types of non-cash receipts. Most of these provisions require both a specified type of non-cash benefit and a specified source of the benefit (usually, one's employer). For example, §§132(a)(5) and 132(f) exclude the value of a transit pass from gross income, but only if the pass is "provided by an employer to an employee."

---

40. You may want to review the material in section C.2 of Chapter 1 on the importance of deferral.
41. For §1014, see section H.2 of Chapter 3.
42. 252 U.S. 189 (1920). See section A of Chapter 3 for the edited text of the opinion.
43. Correspondingly, they are permitted to take into account for tax purposes declines in the value of securities. For more on this provision, and on other legislative forays into the taxation of unrealized appreciation, see section A.2 of Chapter 3.

The limitation of an exclusion to items received from one's employer would not be significant if persons who spent their own money to purchase the same items were allowed to deduct their expenditures. Suppose Alfred is paid a cash salary of $50,000 and also receives a $1,000 annual transit pass from his employer; Billie is paid a cash salary of $51,000 and uses $1,000 of her salary to buy an annual transit pass. If Billie were allowed to deduct her $1,000 expense, these two similarly situated taxpayers — each with $50,000 of salary available for all uses other than commuting — would also have the same taxable income and the same tax liability. In the case of many of the exclusions for employer-provided benefits, however, taxpayer purchases of the same items are either not deductible at all or are deductible subject to severe restrictions (where similar restrictions do not apply to the corresponding exclusion). For example, commuting expenses are not deductible at all, so Billie will not be able to claim any deduction for her $1,000 transit pass expense. Similarly, an employee who receives employer-provided health insurance will be able to exclude the entire value of the insurance (under §106), but a taxpayer who purchases health insurance on her own will be allowed a deduction (under §213) only to the extent that her total medical expenses exceed 7.5 percent (10 percent in 2013 and later years) of her adjusted gross income — and even then, only if she itemizes her deductions rather than claiming the standard deduction.

As you read through the descriptions of the exclusions in the following paragraphs, consider whether there is a sound justification for this tax discrimination against persons who are compensated in cash and then do their own shopping, vis-à-vis persons who receive excludable non-cash compensation. This section will consider in detail three exclusions for in-kind benefits: (1) the exclusion of employer-provided health benefits under §§105 and 106; (2) the exclusion of group-term life insurance coverage under §79; and (3) the exclusion of scholarships under §117. Two more exclusions — the exclusion of forfeitable property under §83 and the exclusion for a miscellany of fringe benefits under §132 — are the topics of cells associated with this chapter. Two other exclusions are considered elsewhere in this book, in connection with their closely related deductions or credits. These are the exclusions for dependent care assistance (§129)[44] and the exclusion for employer-provided retirement savings (§§401 et seq.).[45] Still other exclusions, although interesting and important, are not considered in detail anywhere in this book, in the interests of keeping it to a manageable length. These include the exclusions for parsonage allowances (§107),[46] meals and lodging furnished for the convenience of the employer (§119), and adoption assistance (§137).

a. Employer-Provided Health Insurance

Section 106(a) excludes from the gross income of an employee the value of employer-provided health insurance coverage. A companion provision, §105(b), excludes from gross income the value of benefits received under employer-

---

44. See section A.1.c of Chapter 9.
45. See section A of Chapter 11.
46. But see the cell on double tax benefits (associated with Chapter 5), in which §107 makes an appearance.

provided health insurance, to the extent the benefits constitute reimbursement of medical expenses. Taken together; the two provisions remove employer-provided health insurance — both premiums and benefits — from the base of the income tax.[47] Many people receive health insurance through their employer, but have to pay for some or all of the cost of the coverage by payroll deductions. Does this sort of coverage qualify as employer-provided, so that the amount of the payroll deduction is excluded from gross income? The answer is yes, but only because §125 provides that health insurance coverage may be offered under a "cafeteria plan." Under the cafeteria plan rules of §125, a taxpayer who is offered a choice between cash and health insurance coverage, and who chooses insurance, will not be taxed under the doctrine of constructive receipt.[48]

The §106 exclusion applies not only to employer-provided basic health insurance coverage, but also to so-called Cadillac[49] employer-provided health insurance with small or non-existent deductibles and co-pays, no or very high dollar ceilings on benefits, and broad definitions of covered conditions and treatments. In lieu of limiting the §106 exclusion to the value of basic coverage, the 2010 health care reform legislation introduced an excise tax (§4980I of the Code) — imposed on employers, not employees — equal to 40 percent of the amount by which the cost of employer-provided Cadillac health insurance exceeds the cost of basic health insurance. The provision is not scheduled to become effective until 2018 — a remarkably long delay for a provision enacted in 2010 — and there is good reason to suspect that Congress may have second thoughts before then.

On one crucial point, §106(a) is silent. The statute provides an exclusion for employer-provided coverage, but it does not specify who may be insured. The regulations, however, state that the exclusion applies only to health insurance for the employee, "his spouse, or his dependents, as defined in section 152." Treas. Reg. §1.106-1. If an employer provides health insurance coverage for unmarried partners of its employees, the value of the partner coverage cannot be excluded under the regulatory interpretation (except in the somewhat unusual case where the partner qualifies as a dependent of the employee under §152(a)(9)).[50] Whatever one may think of the merits of this limitation on the scope of the exclusion, it is surprising that Congress has left it to Treasury to decide so important an issue. Unmarried heterosexual couples always have the option to improve their §106 situation by getting married, but same-sex couples are simply out of luck if they cannot satisfy the dependency test of §152(a)(9). Even if a same-sex couple is married for purposes of state law, the marriage will not be recognized for federal income tax purposes, by reason of the Defense of Marriage Act, Pub. L. No. 104-199, 100 Stat. 2419 (1996).

47. Employer-provided health insurance is also excluded from the base of the social security wage tax, by §3121(a)(2).
48. For more on constructive receipt, see section B.1 of Chapter 7.
49. Even if many luxury car buyers today prefer German or Japanese automobiles to American vehicles, for some reason Cadillac remains the unchallenged standard of luxury in the health insurance industry.
50. There are two problems with qualifying an unmarried partner as a dependent under §152(a)(9). First, the partner can qualify as a dependent only if he receives more than half of his support from the taxpayer. The second problem applies only to some relationships in some states; §152(b)(5) denies dependent status if the relationship between the taxpayer and the would-be dependent is "in violation of local law." It is unclear what, if anything, remains of the practical effect of §152(b)(5) following Lawrence v. Texas, 539 U.S. 558 (2003).

What about taxpayers who are not fortunate enough to have health insurance through their employers? Section 213 allows them to claim their medical expenses—including health insurance premiums not excluded under §106—as itemized deductions.[51] There is a big catch, however. Under §213(a), medical expenses are deductible only to the extent they exceed 7.5 percent (10 percent in 2013 and later years) of adjusted gross income. Although health insurance purchased outside the employment context can be expensive, in most cases little or none of it will be deductible after taking into account the 7.5 percent (or 10 percent) floor and the need to itemize to claim the deduction. Self-employed persons receive much better treatment, however. Under §162(*l*), a self-employed person can claim an above-the-line deduction for the cost of health insurance for herself, her spouse, and her dependents.[52]

Prior to the enactment of the health care reform legislation of 2010, the tax rules for health insurance and medical expenses, when considered together with Medicare and Medicaid, left a major gap in the system of federal assistance for health insurance. The elderly and those with very low incomes were eligible for Medicare or Medicaid, while the vast majority of middle income and upper income workers received employer-provided health insurance, not subject to either income tax or social security tax. This left out low wage workers, whose income was too high for Medicaid, and whose employers did not provide health insurance. In theory, these workers could purchase insurance on their own and claim a deduction under §213, but in practice millions did not purchase insurance and so received no tax benefit. Even those who did purchase insurance often received little or no tax benefit, given the 7.5 percent floor of §213 and the below-the-line status of the deduction (making it unavailable to taxpayers claiming the standard deduction). A major purpose of the 2010 health care legislation was to subsidize health insurance for low wage workers. In furtherance of that goal, the legislation created new §36B, which provides a refundable "premium assistance credit" for low and moderate income taxpayers purchasing health insurance through a state-based health insurance exchange. Because the provision does not become effective until 2014 (and may be revised before then), only a brief description is provided here. The credit will be available for a taxpayer with household income of at least 100 percent but not more than 400 percent of the federal poverty level, but only if the taxpayer is not offered "minimum essential coverage" in the form of employer-provided health insurance. The generosity of the credit declines as household income rises from 100 percent to 400 percent of the poverty level. For a taxpayer with income at 100 percent of the poverty level, the credit is (oversimplifying a bit) designed to cover the amount by which the cost of basic health insurance exceeds 2 percent of household income. In other words, the taxpayer is expected to devote 2 percent of household income to the purchase of health insurance, and the government will pick up the rest of the tab. For a taxpayer with income at 300 percent to 400 percent of the poverty level, by contrast, the credit will cover only the amount by which the cost of basic health insurance exceeds 9.5 percent of household income.

For taxpayers with employer-provided health insurance, the §106 exclusion is the equivalent of an above-the-line deduction for the cost of insurance, not subject

51. For a detailed discussion of §213, see section E of Chapter 4.
52. That is, the expense is allowed as a deduction in computing adjusted gross income, rather than being one allowed in computing taxable income. *See* §62(a)(1), and the discussion in section B of Chapter 1.

to any percentage-of-AGI floor. What explains the strikingly less generous treatment under §213 of taxpayers who buy their own health insurance (and who are not eligible for the §36B credit, either because their household income is too high or because 2014 has not yet arrived)? It is common for exclusions for employer-provided fringe benefits to be more generous than the corresponding deductions for taxpayers who purchase similar items with their own money. For example, the ceilings on excludable employer contributions to employees' pensions are much higher than the ceilings on deductible IRA contributions.[53] In some situations, including the case of retirement savings, the explanation for the discrepancy lies in the nondiscrimination rules applicable to employer-provided benefits. Congress wants employers to provide pensions not just to highly compensated employees (who demand pensions), but also to rank-and-file employees (who are often too worried about current expenses to demand pensions). In pursuit of this objective, Congress conditions tax-favored treatment for the executives' pensions on the provision of pensions to rank-and-file employees. This strategy will work, of course, only if the executives cannot receive equally favorable tax treatment for non-employer-provided retirement savings. They cannot, because of the much lower ceiling on deductible IRAs than on employers' pension contributions.[54]

The same sort of analysis could explain why the §213 health insurance deduction is much less generous than the §106 exclusion, but only if §106 included a nondiscrimination requirement. Congress came to the same conclusion in 1986, and added the nondiscrimination rules of §89 to the Code. The following excerpt explains the policy behind this legislation.

JOINT COMMITTEE ON TAXATION, GENERAL EXPLANATION OF THE TAX REFORM ACT OF 1986

Under prior and present law, the tax-favored treatment of employer-provided employee benefits reduces the Federal income tax base and reduces Federal budget receipts. However, Congress believed these costs are justifiable if such benefits fulfill important social policy objectives, such as increasing health insurance coverage among taxpayers who are not highly compensated and who otherwise would not purchase or could not afford such coverage.

In order to achieve these objectives, Congress believed that effective nondiscrimination rules with respect to all employee benefits, including health insurance, were necessary because they permit the exclusion from income of employee benefits only if the benefits are provided to required levels of nonhighly compensated employees. . . .

As a general rule, Congress believed that, to the extent possible, the nondiscrimination rules should require employers to cover nonhighly compensated employees to an extent comparable to the coverage of highly compensated employees.

Congress recognized that employers desire flexibility in designing employee benefit programs. However, Congress believed that flexibility should be provided

---

53. See section A of Chapter 11.
54. *See also* §219(g), which denies a taxpayer the right to make *any* deductible IRA contribution if the employee is an "active participant" in an employer-sponsored pension plan and the employee's AGI is above a specified level (with the level depending on the taxpayer's filing status and on the taxable year in question).

only to the extent not inconsistent with the nondiscrimination rules. For example, if an employer operates, for legitimate economic reasons, multiple lines of business, the employee benefit structures in each line of business may differ because of historical trends within each industry. The Act permits employers to test the new nondiscrimination rules separately with respect to each line of business. Congress is concerned, however, that the line of business exception not be administered in a manner that circumvents Congress' premise that highly-compensated employees should not be permitted to exclude employee benefits unless the employer's plan benefits a nondiscriminatory group of the employer's employees.

Notes and Questions

1. *Retroactive repeal.* In response to complaints that §89 was too burdensome on employers, Congress repealed it in 1989, with the repeal retroactive to the provision's original effective date. Today, nondiscrimination rules apply to employers who self-insure for their employees' medical expenses instead of purchasing coverage from an insurance company (§105(h)), and to cafeteria plans providing health benefits (§125(g)(2)). Except in those two situations, an employer can provide unlimited amounts of tax-favored health insurance to its executives, without having to provide any insurance to its rank-and-file employees. In the absence of a generally applicable nondiscrimination rule under §106, the §213 limitations on the deductibility of health insurance obviously cannot be intended to encourage the provision of health insurance to employees who are not highly compensated. But if that is not the purpose of the §213 limitations, do the limitations serve any legitimate purpose? If Congress is not willing to subject the §106 exclusion to nondiscrimination rules, should it allow taxpayers who buy their own health insurance an above-the-line deduction not subject to a percentage-of-AGI floor?

2. *Health care as a cost of subsistence.* Official tax expenditure budgets[55] treat both the exclusion for employer-provided health insurance and the medical expense deduction as tax expenditure items. In 2010, for example, the Joint Committee on Taxation estimated the five-year (2010 through 2014) revenue cost of the exclusion for employer-provided health benefits at $659.4 billion, and the five-year cost of the medical expense deduction at $77.6 billion. Labeling these provisions tax expenditures implies that they are not part of a theoretically pure income tax base, but instead are intended as health care subsidies administered through the tax system. There is a strong argument, however, that this view of the provisions is mistaken, and that the costs of health insurance and medical expenses should be excluded from the base of a normative income tax. There is general agreement among income tax theorists that tax should be imposed only on "clear income," defined as income in excess of subsistence needs. The costs of subsistence include not only food, clothing, and shelter, but also necessary medical care. Taken together, the standard deduction and personal and dependency exemptions serve to remove most subsistence-level income from the tax base. These provisions are not well adapted,

---

55. See section C.4 of Chapter 1.

however, to removing the cost of basic medical care from the tax base, because the cost of basic medical care varies greatly among persons according to age, sex, and medical condition. Basic health insurance coverage might cost only $2,000 per year for a healthy male in his twenties, but it would cost much more for a woman of child-bearing age, or for a 50-year-old of either sex. Rather than attempting to build the cost of health care into a one-size-fits-all standard deduction, it makes sense to vary the amount of the basic health care exclusion as the cost of basic health care varies from taxpayer to taxpayer. The §106 exclusion makes good sense under this analysis. If an employer provides basic health insurance to two employees, and the coverage for one employee (a man in his 20s) is worth $2,000 while the coverage for the other employee (a woman in her 50s) is worth $6,000, §106 appropriately excludes different amounts from the incomes of the two employees.[56] Under this analysis, it is also appropriate to allow a deduction for the full cost of basic health insurance purchased by taxpayers who do not have employer-provided coverage. This deduction should be above-the-line (conceptually; it is an *adjunct* to the standard deduction, not an allowance *in lieu of* the standard deduction), and it should not be subject to a percentage-of-AGI floor.

b.   Group-Term Life Insurance

Section 79 allows employees to exclude the value of group-term life insurance provided by their employers, for up to $50,000 of insurance. The $50,000, sometimes called the "face amount" of the policy, is essentially its death benefit. Larger amounts of insurance can be provided, but to the extent that the policy exceeds the $50,000 face amount permitted to be received tax-free, §79 provides that the employee has additional wage income in the amount of the premium properly allocable to the excess coverage.

The cap of $50,000 of insurance strikes many people as a rather modest sum. In the aggregate, however, these insurance amounts are an important element in the financial health of American workers. Group-term life insurance coverage is extremely widespread throughout the economy; in 2009, there were about 113 million policies in force, with an aggregate death benefit of nearly $7.7 trillion dollars, or about $68,000 per policy.[57] Some sense of the importance of these amounts can be inferred from noting that the median net worth of American families in 2007 was only $120,300.[58]

Section 79 operates as an exclusion from gross income. In its absence, life insurance premiums paid by an employer would ordinarily be includible in the employee's income under §61.[59] However, it is phrased — rather oddly — as an inclusion section, and arranged among a series of such sections in part II of

---

56. The only criticism of §106, from this perspective, is that it does not attempt to limit the exclusion to the cost of *basic* health insurance. As explained earlier in the text, the §4980I excise tax on Cadillac employer-provided health insurance is a response to that criticism — albeit a response with a 2018 effective date.

57. American Council of Life Insurance, *Life Insurers Fact Book 2010,* Table 7.9.

58. *Statistical Abstract of the United States, 2011,* Table 720.

59. Indeed, Treas. Reg. §1.61-2(d)(2)(ii) specifically provides that premiums paid by employers on such policies are normally included, except to the extent that §79 applies.

sub-chapter B of the IRC. Its exclusion properties emerge almost as an after-thought: It includes amounts paid by employers to provide group-term life insur-ance, but only to the extent that the insurance exceeds the permitted $50,000 face amount.[60] This anomaly is best explained historically. In the early days of the income tax, employee benefits were generally not regarded as income. For the most part, there were no specific exclusion provisions, but rather a pattern of practice that was widely followed by employers, and infrequently challenged by the IRS. Group-term life insurance was among the best established of these exclusions-by-default.

By the 1950s, group-term life insurance had become a major element in most executive compensation packages, with top executives frequently enjoying the benefits of so-called jumbo insurance policies having seven-figure death benefits, free of any tax. In the Revenue Act of 1964, Congress decided to curtail this practice to some degree, and so provided that the cost of coverage in excess of $50,000 would be taxed. Of course, in 1964 the median family income was much lower than it is today, with more than half of all families having incomes below $7,000.[61] That meant that a $50,000 life insurance policy would have provided the family with income replacement of more than seven times the annual family income.[62] By 2008, the median family income had risen to $61,521,[63] but Congress has never even adjusted, much less indexed, the amount of life insurance that can be excluded. At present levels, the maximum tax-free insurance amount provides less than a single year of income replacement for the average family.[64] But in fact, there may be no reason to lament this; it is not as if Congress ever intended specifically to encourage employers to provide group-term insurance. Rather, it is as if Congress never thought about the problem one way or another until it became an item of abuse in designing executive compensation packages, at which point Congress simply moved to curtail the abuse. In a way, by simply failing to act to correct for the effects of inflation, it has been gradually phasing out the value of this benefit over the subsequent decades.

c. Scholarships and Other Tax Benefits for Higher Education Expenses

Scholarships. Section 117(a) excludes from gross income "any amount received as a qualified scholarship by an individual who is a candidate for a degree" at a college

60. An interesting oddity that remains in the Code is the treatment of group-term life insurance provided to disabled employees. Section 79(b) says that the rules of §79(a) do not apply to disabled employees. But §79(a) contains both the inclusion rule for amounts above $50,000 and the exclusion rule for amounts within that sum. By disclaiming applicability of that rule, subsection (b) would seem to leave disabled employees to the complete inclusion rules in the regulations. However, that was not Congress's intent in the Revenue Act of 1964, and the IRS has never applied the rules in that way. Congress meant to exclude disabled employees (and, at the time, retired employees) from the new inclusion rules, allowing them to enjoy the benefits of any amount of insurance tax-free, as had been the de facto rule prior to 1964.
61. *Historical Statistics of the United States, Colonial Times to 1970,* pt. 1 at 289. (Series G 1-15; 54.4 percent of families reported family income below $7,000.)
62. Far more than seven times, actually, in light of the fact that §101(a) excludes the death benefits from gross income, even though the income that the death benefits replace would have been subject to tax.
63. *Statistical Abstract of the United States, 2011,* Table 698.
64. Note though that the insured decedent may not have been the family's sole source of income, and that the insurance proceeds, unlike the income they may replace, would be tax-free under §101(a).

or university. The exclusion applies both to cash scholarships and to scholarships received in-kind (in the form of free or reduced tuition). The exclusion is limited to the amount of the student's tuition and fees, and the cost of course-related books, supplies, and equipment. Thus, a room-and-board scholarship is not eligible for the exclusion. The source of the scholarship may be the educational institution the student is attending, a government agency, a business, a charitable organization, or any other source (even an individual). However, §117(c) provides that the exclusion does not apply to "any amount received which represents payment for teaching, research, or other services by the student required as a condition for receiving the qualified scholarship." This rule obviously applies to a university's teaching and research assistants. It also applies, however, to an employee of an employer of any sort, if the employee receives a "scholarship" from his employer as part of his compensation. Notice the strange contrast with many other exclusions, which apply only if an in-kind benefit *is* received as compensation from an employer.

To examine the policy behind the scholarship exclusion, consider three students. Arnold pays full tuition — $5,000 per year — at State University. He receives no scholarship, but a comparable education at a private university would cost $20,000 per year. Brenda attends Private University, where the annual tuition is $20,000. Because of a $15,000 scholarship, the annual cost to her is only $5,000. Clara attends Private University but receives no scholarship. She works nights and weekends to earn the money to pay her $15,000 of extra tuition expense (compared to Arnold and Brenda). Because the IRS has never attempted to include the bargain element of public university tuition in gross income, the scholarship exclusion can be defended as achieving tax equity for Brenda vis-à-vis Arnold. The exclusion becomes more troubling, however, if we compare Brenda's tax treatment with Carla's. Why should Brenda enjoy her $15,000 scholarship tax-free, when Carla must pay tax on the $15,000 she earns in lieu of a scholarship?

Can Brenda's exclusion be defended on the grounds that even if the scholarship were included in her gross income, it would generate little or no tax liability after the application of the standard deduction, the personal exemption, and the low marginal tax rate on the first dollars of taxable income? The tax system does not generally exclude particular types of receipts from gross income merely because they are associated with low income taxpayers (consider tips, for example). Moreover, not every scholarship recipient is on the edge of poverty. Suppose Dan and Erin both receive $5,000 scholarships. Dan has no other income. If the scholarship were included in his gross income, it would generate no tax liability (because of his standard deduction and personal exemption). Thus, the scholarship exclusion is worthless to Dan. Erin has a large amount of investment income. If the scholarship were included in her income, it would be taxed at the marginal rate of 30 percent. The $5,000 exclusion saves Erin $1,500 in taxes. If the exclusion is intended as a tax subsidy for higher education expenses, it is a strange sort subsidy; the amount of the subsidy is inversely related to need. Impoverished Dan receives no tax reduction, while affluent Erin receives a $1,500 subsidy. This suggests that concerns about appropriate tax liabilities for low income taxpayers are best addressed by the standard deduction, the personal exemption, and the tax rate schedule — not by excluding particular items from gross income because they are disproportionately received by low income taxpayers.

One might believe that most scholarships offered by private universities are really a form of customer-sensitive variable pricing, under which universities try to charge each student the highest net-of-scholarship price the student is willing to pay. Under this view, what universities are trying to do with scholarships is no different from what airlines attempt to do with their Byzantine pricing practices. No one, of course, argues that an air traveler who gets a good price on a promotional rate ticket has income as a result. As long as a purchase at a good price is not a means of providing disguised compensation, it should not and does not result in any gross income inclusion. If the analogy of scholarships to airlines pricing is convincing, it justifies the exclusion of university-provided scholarships. It also explains why a "scholarship" received from a university as compensation for services (rather than as variable pricing) should not be eligible for the exclusion. It does not, however, explain why the exclusion should apply to scholarships received from sources other than the university the student is attending.

REV. PROC. 76-47

1976-2 C.B. 670

SECTION 1. PURPOSE.

. . . The purpose of this Revenue Procedure is to provide guidelines to be used in determining whether a grant made by a private foundation under an employer-related grant program to an employee or to a child of an employee of the particular employer to which the program relates is a scholarship . . . subject to the provisions of section 117(a) of the Code. . . .

SEC. 2. APPLICATION OF GUIDELINES.

These guidelines apply to educational grants made on or after January 1, 1970, by a private foundation under an employer-related grant program to individuals who are employees, or the children of employees, of the employer to which the program relates.

An employer-related program is a program that treats some or all of the employees, or children of some or all of the employees, of a particular employer as a group from which grantees of some or all of the foundation's educational grants will be selected, limits the potential grantees for some or all of the foundation's grants to individuals who are employees, or children of employees, of a particular employer, or otherwise gives such individuals a preference or priority over others in being selected as grantees of such grants. . . .

SEC. 3. BACKGROUND.

Section 117 of the Code provides that gross income does not include any amount received as a scholarship. . . .

Section 1.117-4(c) of the regulations explains that any amount paid or allowed to, or on behalf of, an individual to enable that individual to pursue studies or research is nevertheless not a scholarship . . . for purposes of section 117 of the Code if such amount represents compensation for past, present, or future employment services or if such studies or research are primarily for the benefit of the grantor. . . . By contrast, a grant made for the relatively disinterested purpose of financially assisting an individual to pursue an education for that individual's own benefit may qualify as a section 117 scholarship or fellowship. The determination must, of course, be made in light of all the relevant facts and circumstances.

When educational grants are made available by an employer to its employees on a preferential basis, the employer-employee relationship is immediately suggestive that the grant is compensatory. See Bingler v. Johnson, 394 U.S. 741 (1969), 1969-2 C.B. 17. Such preferential grants by an employer to the children of employees suggests [sic] a purpose to compensate or otherwise provide an employment incentive to the employee-parents. These suggestions are not dispelled simply because the grantor is an independent third party (for example, a foundation). The employer-related preferential treatment does not, of itself, further in any way the requisite (under section 117 of the Code) disinterested purpose of simply making it financially possible for individuals to obtain an education for their own personal benefit, and suggests the presence of a contrary purpose to provide extra compensation, an employment incentive, or an employee fringe benefit. If a grant program by a private foundation is designed or administered to that end, the grants made under it to the employees or their children will not be scholarships . . . subject to the provisions of section 117(a).

The Internal Revenue Service will not, however, treat a private foundation's program as designed or administered for such a purpose if the availability of grants to employees [or] their children fall[s] outside the pattern of employment. In order to be outside the pattern of employment, the availability of grants to employees or their children under the program must be controlled and limited by substantial non-employment related factors to such an extent that the preferential treatment derived from employment does not continue to be of any significance beyond an initial qualifier. Such qualification must not lead to any significant probability that employment will make grants available for a qualified employee or his or her children interested in applying for one. The Service will treat the grants as scholarships . . . if (1) the availability of the grants falls outside the pattern of employment, and (2) the grants do not otherwise represent compensation for past, present, or future services rendered or to be rendered the foundation or employer by the employees or their children, and (3) the grants are not for studies or research undertaken primarily for the benefit of the foundation or the employer or for some other purposes not sanctioned by section 117.

SEC. 4. GUIDELINES.

If a private foundation's program satisfies the seven conditions set forth in sections 4.01 through 4.07, below, and meets the percentage test described in section 4.08 applicable to grants to employees' children, or to grants to employees, or to both, as the case may require, the Service will assume the grants awarded under the program to employees, or their children, or to both (if the percentage test is met for each category) will be scholarships . . . subject to the provisions of section 117(a) of the Code. . . .

.01 INDUCEMENT

The programs must not be used by the employer, the private foundation, or the organizer thereof, to recruit employees or to induce employees to continue their employment or otherwise follow a course of action sought by the employer.

.02 SELECTION COMMITTEE

Selection of grant recipients must be made by a committee consisting wholly of individuals totally independent (except for participation on this committee) and separate from the private foundation, its organizer, and the employer concerned. An individual who is a former employee of either the foundation or the employer concerned will not be considered totally independent. Such committees preferably should consist of individuals knowledgeable in the education field so that they have the background and knowledge to properly evaluate the potential of the applicants. . . .

Grants must be awarded solely in the order recommended by the selection committee. The number of grants to be awarded may be reduced but may not be increased from the number recommended by the selection committee. Only the committee may vary the amounts of the grants awarded.

.03 ELIGIBILITY REQUIREMENTS

The program must impose identifiable minimum requirements for grant eligibility. . . . If an employee must have been employed for some minimum period by the employer to which the program relates to be eligible to receive a grant, or to make that employee's children eligible to receive a grant, the minimum period of employment may not exceed three years. Moreover, eligibility must not be related to any other employment-related factors, such as the employee's position, services, or duties.

.04 OBJECTIVE BASIS OF SELECTION

Selection of grant recipients must be based solely upon substantial objective standards that are completely unrelated to the employment of the recipients or their parents and to the employer's line of business. Such standards as, but not limited to, prior academic performance, performance on tests designed to measure ability and aptitude for higher education, recommendations from instructors or other individuals not related to the potential awardees, financial need, and conclusions drawn from personal interviews as to motivation and character, may be utilized.

.05 EMPLOYMENT

A grant may not be terminated because the recipient or the recipient's parent terminates employment with the employer subsequent to the awarding of the grant regardless of the reason for such termination of employment. . . .

At the time the grant is awarded or renewed, there must be no requirement, condition or suggestion, express or implied, that the recipient or parent is expected to render future employment services for the foundation or the employer, or be available for such future employment, even though such future employment is at the discretion of the foundation or the employer.

.06 COURSE OF STUDY

The courses of study for which grants are available must not be limited to those that would be of particular benefit to the employer or to the foundation. . . .

.07 OTHER OBJECTIVES

The terms of the grant and the courses of study for which grants are available must meet all other requirements of section 117 of the Code and the regulations thereunder, and must be consistent with a disinterested purpose of enabling the recipients to obtain an education in their individual capacities solely for their personal benefit and must not include any commitments, understandings or obligations, conditional or unconditional, suggesting that the studies are undertaken by the recipients for the benefit of the employer or the foundation or have as their objective the accomplishment of any purpose of the employer or the foundation (even though consistent with its exempt status) other than enabling the recipients to obtain an education in their individual capacities and solely for their personal benefit.

.08 PERCENTAGE TEST

In the case of a program that awards grants to children of employees of a particular employer, the program meets the percentage test if the number of grants awarded under that program in any year to such children does not exceed 25 percent of the number of employees' children who, (i) were eligible, (ii) were applicants for such grants, and (iii) were considered by the selection committee in selecting the recipients of grants in that year, or 10 percent of the number of employees' children who can be shown to be eligible for grants (whether or not they submitted an application) in that year. . . .

Notes and Questions

1. *Statutory authority?* Section 117(c) merely says that the scholarship exclusion is not available for amounts that represent payment for services performed by the *student;* it does not deny the exclusion for amounts that represent payment for services performed by the student's *parent.* The rule that a scholarship must not represent payment for services performed by *any-one* — student or parent — is expressly stated only in the regulations (Treas. Reg. §1.117-4(c)(1)). To the extent the regulation goes beyond §117(c), what (if anything) is the statutory authority for the regulation?

2. *Scholarship versus compensation.* Conceding (for the sake of argument) the validity of the regulatory position that compensation for services can never qualify for the scholarship exclusion, are you persuaded that the type of benefits sanctioned by Rev. Proc. 76-47—scholarships paid for by an employer and available only to children of its employees—are not compensation for services?

3. *Other tax benefits for college and university tuition.* Although a "scholarship" received from one's employer as compensation for services cannot qualify for exclusion under §117(a), there are two other possible routes to exclusion: §127 and §117(d). Section 127 provides an exclusion for an employee whose tuition is paid by his employer under an "educational assistance program." However, the exclusion is subject to two significant limitations that do not apply to the scholarship exclusion: (1) the maximum annual exclusion under §127 is $5,250 (compared with the unlimited exclusion available under §117(a)), and (2) the exclusion is subject to a nondiscrimination requirement. Why would Congress enact one tuition exclusion that applies only if the benefit *is not* received from one's employer as compensation (§117(a)), and a second tuition exclusion that applies only if the benefit *is* received from one's employer (§127)?

Under §117(d), a college or university can provide its employees with tax-free "qualified tuition reductions." Although the exclusion is a part of §117, it resembles the various fringe benefits excluded under §132 more than it resembles scholarships excluded under §117(a). The qualified tuition reduction may be provided to the employee himself, or (more commonly) to the employee's dependent child or the employee's spouse. The exclusion is not limited to reductions in the tuition charged by the university that employs the taxpayer; it is also available if the employer-university subsidizes the tuition of an employee's child at another university. The exclusion applies to tuition reductions received by highly compensated employees (and their families) only if the employer-university also provides tuition reductions for non-highly-compensated employees (and their families). What if a university provides tuition reductions for the children of faculty members, but not for the children of other employees? The limitation of the benefit to children of faculty members may or may not violate the nondiscrimination rules (the details of which are quite technical), depending on the university's salary structure. Where a limitation of the benefit to children of faculty members would violate the nondiscrimination rules, different universities have made different choices. Some have provided the benefit for the children of all employees, thereby qualifying the program under §117(d). Others have limited the benefit to faculty children, with the result that faculty members must pay tax on their children's tuition reductions.

If a taxpayer fails to qualify for any of the three tuition exclusions described above, all is not necessarily lost. In recent years Congress has enacted a confusing array of tax credits and deductions for higher education expenses. The Hope Scholarship Credit (§25A(b)) may be as much as $1,500 for each of a student's first two years of college. The credit is equal to 100 percent of the first $1,000 of qualified tuition expense, and

50 percent of the next $1,000.[65] For 2009 through 2012, special temporary rules provide a more generous Hope Scholarship Credit. Under the temporary rules, the credit amount is 100 percent of the first $2,000 of qualified expenses, plus 25 percent of the next $2,000, for a maximum credit of $2,500. The definition of qualifying expenses is expanded to include course materials (such as books), the credit is available for the first *four* years of college, the AGI threshold for the application of the phaseout rules is increased, and 30 percent of the credit is refundable (i.e., allowable even if the taxpayer has no pre-credit tax liability for the credit to offset). There will undoubtedly be pressure on Congress to extend the lives of these temporary rules.

For expenses not eligible for the Hope Scholarship Credit, the Lifetime Learning Credit (§25A(c)) may be as much as $2,000 per taxpayer (not per student) per year. This credit is equal to 20 percent of the first $10,000 of qualified tuition expenses.[66] For years before 2012, a taxpayer may elect to deduct tuition expenses under §222, instead of claiming a credit under §25A. The maximum deduction, however, is only $4,000. Phaseout rules deny the benefits of the two credits and the deduction to upper income taxpayers. The good news for taxpayers is that the two credits and the deduction, unlike the exclusions, do not depend on the source of the funds used to pay the expenses. The bad news is that the credits and the deduction are subject to rather low dollar ceilings on qualifying expenses, and that these benefits are not available at all to more affluent taxpayers.

There are still more higher education tax benefits. Tax-favored treatment for college savings is provided by both §529 (qualified tuition programs) and §530 (Coverdell education savings accounts). For those who borrow instead of saving, §221 provides a deduction for interest on certain education loans. Finally, charitable contributions to colleges and universities are deductible under §170.[67] It may make sense for Congress to use the tax system to subsidize higher education, but it is not easy to defend the current hodgepodge of subsidy provisions.

Problem 10. Doting Grandmother gives Granddaughter $20,000 to help pay Granddaughter's law school tuition, and calls it a scholarship. Is Granddaughter entitled to exclude the $20,000 from gross income?

Problem 11. Tom, a graduate student at Ivy University, is employed by Ivy as a teaching assistant. He taught one class during the past year, for which he was paid $5,000 cash. He also received a $10,000 graduate tuition reduction. The university provides graduate tuition reductions only to students employed as teaching (or research) assistants. The amount of the reduction is a flat $10,000

---

65. The numbers in the text correspond to those in the Code, but the Hope Scholarship Credit is indexed for inflation. The income phaseout thresholds are also indexed. Curiously, the Lifetime Learning Credit described in the following paragraph is *not* indexed.

66. In some cases, it may be to a taxpayer's benefit to claim the Lifetime Learning Credit in lieu of the Hope Scholarship Credit, even though the taxpayer is eligible to claim the Hope Scholarship Credit. This possibility is explored in the problem set below.

67. It is also possible, under rather limited circumstances, for educational costs to qualify as deductible business expenses under §162. This results from the application of the general definition of business expenses, however, rather than as a legislatively intended subsidy for higher education. For more on this possibility, see section G.2 of Chapter 5.

regardless of the number of courses taught. For example, a graduate student who taught three courses during the year would have been paid $15,000 cash, and would have received the same $10,000 tuition reduction received by Tom. Ivy also employs adjunct professors (non-students) to teach classes. It pays them $5,000 cash per class, but no tuition benefits. Is Tom entitled to exclude the $10,000 tuition reduction from his gross income under either §117(a) or §117(d)? Hint: Pay particular attention to the interaction between §§117(c) and 117(d)(5). It may help to consult Prop. Reg. §1.117-6(d).

The next three problems involve the Hope Scholarship Credit and Lifetime Learning Credit provisions of §25A. As explained above, there are two sets of rules for the Hope Scholarship Credit — special rules applicable through the end of 2012, set forth in §25A(*i*), and less generous and supposedly permanent rules set forth in §25A(b). Try to answer the following problems under both the permanent rules and the temporary rules, using the statutory limits as expressed in the Code rather than the inflation-adjusted numbers for any particular year. In some respects the issues in these problems go beyond this book's brief description of §25A, so you will need to examine the statute carefully in order to answer these problems. (Fair warning: Problem 14 involves an ambiguity in the statute, so even careful examination of the provision will not produce a definitive answer to that problem.)

Problem 12.   Wendy and Harold, a married couple, are the parents of Frances, who is in her first year of undergraduate studies at State University. Wendy and Harold have paid Frances's entire $5,000 tuition. Assuming their AGI is low enough that the phaseout rules of §25A(d) do not apply, what is the amount of the credit available to Wendy and Harold under §25A?

Problem 13.   Wilma and Henry, a married couple, are the parents of Fred, who is in his first year of undergraduate studies at Liberal Arts College. Wilma and Henry have paid Fred's entire $10,000 tuition. Assuming their AGI is low enough that the phaseout rules of §25A(d) do not apply, what is the amount of the credit available to Wilma and Henry under §25A?

Problem 14.   Winifred and Howard, a married couple, are the parents of twins, Freda and Frank. Both children are attending Liberal Arts College, and the parents are paying $10,000 tuition per child per year (the remaining tuition is covered by scholarships).

(*a*) Assuming the parental AGI is low enough that the phaseout rules of §25A(d) do not apply, what is the amount of the credit available to Wilma and Henry under §25A in the twins' *first* year of college?

(*b*) On the same AGI assumption, what is the amount of the credit available to Winifred and Howard under §25A in the twins' *third* year of college?

C. INCOME INCLUSIONS AS MISTAKE-CORRECTING DEVICES

Several important categories of gross income inclusions are artifacts of the income tax system's use of an annual accounting period. These inclusions all follow the same basic pattern. A taxpayer receives favorable tax treatment (such as an exclusion or a deduction) in one year, based on certain factual assumptions. In some later year it becomes clear — but only with the benefit of hindsight — that the assumption underlying the favorable tax treatment in the earlier year was mistaken. The usual way of correcting the mistaken assumption is *not* to amend the earlier year's return, but to include an appropriate amount in gross income in the later year. Before examining these mistake-correcting gross income inclusions, some background on the tax system's annual accounting period is necessary.

1.   *The Annual Tax Accounting Period*

A taxpayer has substantial income this year, but claims he shouldn't have to pay any tax on it yet, because he has a feeling he is going to suffer offsetting losses in the next few years. He asks the government to hold in abeyance the tax consequences of this year's income, pending future developments. As the Supreme Court noted in the famous early case of Burnet v. Sanford & Brooks Co., 282 U.S. 359 (1931), the government requires "revenue ascertainable, and payable to [it], at regular intervals." Given that need, the income tax cannot function if taxpayers are allowed to "postpon[e] the assessment of the tax until the end of a lifetime, or for some other indefinite period, to ascertain more precisely whether the final outcome of the period, or of a given transaction, will be a gain or a loss." Instead, income tax liability must be determined based on income received within some relatively short and standardized period of time. For individuals, that time period is the calendar year.[68] There is nothing magical about the exact length of the tax accounting period (9 months or 15 months might have worked just as well as 12), or about the starting and ending points of the period (fiscal years might have worked just as well as calendar years), but the use of *some* standardized accounting period of moderate length was inevitable.[69]

The annual accounting system serves the government's need for closure with respect to tax liabilities. Thus, an individual must pay tax if he has positive net income within the calendar year, regardless of the losses he may foresee in future years. This does not mean, however, that one's tax liability for the current year is determined by considering only events occurring within the year. The income tax cannot leave tax consequences open pending later developments, but the closure requirement is not violated by tax rules that look *back* to earlier years to determine the tax consequences of this year's receipts. The most fundamental backward-looking rule is contained in §1001, which calculates the gain or loss realized on a sale in the current year by subtracting adjusted basis — a product of past years' events — from the amount realized on this year's sale.

Of course, Congress is free to make exceptions to the rule that tax consequences are not left open pending later developments, and it has done so in a few very limited situations. For example, §1033 provides that a gain realized on the involuntary conversion of property (e.g., by condemnation or casualty) can be deferred if the amount realized on the conversion is reinvested in similar property within

---

68. A corporation is also subject to a 12-month tax accounting period, but it need not coincide with the calendar year.

69. Admittedly, there is some advantage in using a period of 12 months (or some multiple of 12) in the case of seasonal businesses. An annual period will capture the peak, off, and shoulder seasons in correct proportion.

two years of the end of the year in which the conversion occurred.[70] A taxpayer who has realized a gain from an involuntary conversion and has not replaced the property by the time he files his tax return for the year of the conversion may tentatively exclude the gain based on his intention to replace the property within the two-year period. The tax consequences of the conversion remain open until the taxpayer either replaces the property or the period for acquiring replacement property expires. Such exceptions to the sanctity of the annual accounting period are rare, however.

Despite the need for an income tax based on regular accounting periods, the periodicity of the tax can produce disturbing results for a taxpayer whose income (positive or negative) varies greatly from year to year. Consider the five-year income histories of two businesses, a regulated utility and a driller of wildcat oil wells. The utility chugs along earning a steady income, while the driller loses money on dry wells in four of the five years, but hits a gusher in the other year, as shown in the table below.

	Year 1	Year 2	Year 3	Year 4	Year 5	Five-Year Total
Utility	$20	$20	$20	$20	$20	$100
Driller	−$10	−$10	$140	−$10	−$10	$100

Suppose each business is subject to a 20 percent flat-rate income tax. The two businesses would have the same tax liability ($20) if the income tax were based on a five-year accounting period. How will they be treated, however, under a system based on annual accounting? One could imagine an annual accounting-based tax system under which the government shared in a taxpayer's losses just as it shared in gains, so that a taxpayer that lost $10 for the year would be the beneficiary of a *negative* income tax — in other words, the government would pay the taxpayer $2. Under such a system, the Utility and the Driller would have the same net tax liability over the five-year period, even with annual accounting. The Utility would pay $4 × 5 years = $20, and the Driller would pay (−$2) + (−$2) + $28 + (−$2) + (−$2) = $20. In fact, however, there is no negative income tax; a taxpayer with a $10 loss has exactly the same tax liability — zero — as a taxpayer that simply breaks even for the year. Given annual accounting and the lack of a negative income tax, it appears that the Utility will pay $20 tax over the five-year period, while the Driller will unfairly be required to pay $28.

The good news for the Driller is that the unfairness of this aspect of annual accounting is greatly ameliorated by the loss carryover provisions of §172, which permit a taxpayer with a "net operating loss" (NOL) in one tax year to use the NOL to offset positive income in other years. In general, an NOL may be used to offset net income in the two years preceding the loss year, and in the 20 years following the loss year. An NOL is carried first to the earliest permissible year; to the extent it exceeds the income in the earliest year, the excess is carried to the following year, and so on until the NOL is fully used or the loss carryover period expires. For example, at the beginning of Year 3 the Driller had $20 of NOL carryforwards

70. Section 1033, the involuntary conversion provision, is considered in detail in section C.3 of Chapter 3.

from Years 1 and 2.[71] From a non-tax point of view, the existence of NOL carryforwards may be a badge of shame, but the NOLs are an attractive tax attribute. In effect, they give the Driller a tax exemption for its first $20 of Year 3 income. In Year 3, then, the Driller carries forward $20 of NOLs, and reduces its Year 3 taxable income from $140 to $120 (resulting in a $24 tax liability). At the end of Year 4, the Driller carries back the $10 NOL from Year 4 to Year 3, files an amended return for Year 3 showing only $110 of taxable income after the carry-back, and receives a $2 refund (without interest) based on the difference between the tax liability on $120 and the tax on $110. At the end of Year 5, the Driller carries back the $10 NOL from Year 5 to Year 3, files another amended return for Year 3 showing only $100 of taxable income after the second carryback, and receives another $2 refund. As a result of the carryovers, the Driller has paid $20 tax on $100 of income over the five-year period, just like the Utility. But what if the Driller loses another $10 in Year 6? It won't be able to carry that NOL back to Year 3, because of the two-year limitation on carrybacks, though it will be allowed to carry the loss forward for up to 20 future tax years, in search of income to offset in those years. If the company is failing, however, that search for future income may be in vain. As a result, §172 does not eliminate *all* the potential unfairness of annual accounting.

In addition to the rather severe restriction on carryback years, the other major limitation of §172 is that §172(d) permits carryovers only of *business* losses. Consider the situations of the two taxpayers below, assuming each taxpayer is entitled to one personal exemption of $3,000, a $5,000 standard deduction, and no other deductions.

Taxpayer	Year 1 Gross Income	Year 2 Gross Income
Andrea	zero	$40,000
Barbara	$20,000	$20,000

Over the two years, Barbara will have taxable income of $24,000.[72] In a sense, Andrea has negative income of $8,000 in Year 1,[73] but under §172(d) that negative income produces no NOL carryover. Section 172(d) disallows personal exemptions in calculating NOLs, and it allows other non-business deductions (such as the standard deduction) only to the extent of the taxpayer's non-business income. Since Andrea has no non-business income in Year 1 (indeed, no income of any sort), she is not allowed to use the standard deduction in calculating her NOL. With both the personal exemption and the standard deduction disallowed for purposes of the NOL calculation, Andrea's Year 1 NOL is zero. In Year 2, Andrea has $32,000 of taxable income,[74] and no NOL carryover from Year 1. Although Andrea and Barbara would have the same taxable income and the same tax liability if the

71. This assumes that the Driller had no income in years before Year 1, to which the Year 1 and Year 2 NOLs could be carried back.
72. The taxable income in each year will be $12,000: $20,000 − $3,000 − $5,000 = $12,000, using the statutory figures for the personal exemption and standard deduction, respectively.
73. $0 − $3,000 − $5,000 = − $8,000.
74. $40,000 − $3,000 −$5,000 = $32,000.

income tax were based on biannual accounting, the result of annual accounting and §172(d) is that Andrea has $8,000 more taxable income than Barbara over the two-year period.

Even when the annual accounting system does not result in mismeasurement of taxable income (compared with some longer accounting period), it can impose unfairly high marginal tax rates on a taxpayer whose income is bunched into one or a few years, rather than being spread evenly over many years. Given progressive marginal tax rates, a taxpayer who has income of $500,000 in one year and zero in the nine surrounding years will pay tax at higher marginal rates than a taxpayer who earns $50,000 in each of ten consecutive years. At one time the Internal Revenue Code contained "income averaging" rules that reduced the marginal tax rates applicable to taxpayers—such as professional athletes and lottery winners—with severely bunched incomes. When Congress greatly reduced the progressivity of the tax rate structure in 1986, it also repealed income averaging on the premise that income bunching was not a serious problem under the less progressive rate structure. Although Congress has increased the progressivity of the §1 rate structure since 1986, it has not reintroduced income averaging.

2. *The Uses of Hindsight*

a. **Loans and Cancellation of Indebtedness Income**

UNITED STATES v. KIRBY LUMBER CO.

284 U.S. 1 (1931)

Mr. Justice HOLMES delivered the opinion of the Court.

In July, 1923, the plaintiff, the Kirby Lumber Company, issued its own bonds for $12,126,800 for which it received their par value. Later in the same year it purchased in the open market some of the same bonds at less than par, the difference of price being $137,521.30. The question is whether this difference is a taxable gain or income of the plaintiff for the year 1923. By the Revenue Act of (November 23,) 1921, c. 136, §213(a) gross income includes "gains or profits and income derived from any source whatever," and by the Treasury Regulations authorized by §1303, that have been in force through repeated reenactments, "If the corporation purchases and retires any of such bonds at a price less than the issuing price or face value, the excess of the issuing price or face value over the purchase price is gain or income for the taxable year." Article 545(1)(c) of Regulations 62, under Revenue Act of 1921. We see no reason why the Regulations should not be accepted as a correct statement of the law.

In Bowers v. Kerbaugh-Empire Co., 271 U.S. 170, the defendant in error owned the stock of another company that had borrowed money repayable in marks or their equivalent for an enterprise that failed. At the time of payment the marks had fallen in value, which so far as it went was a gain for the defendant in error, and it was contended by the plaintiff in error that the gain was taxable income. But the transaction as a whole was a loss, and the contention was denied. Here there was no shrinkage of assets and the taxpayer made a clear gain. As a result of its dealings it made available $137,521.30 assets previously offset by the obligation of bonds now extinct. We see nothing to be gained by the discussion of judicial definitions. The defendant in error has realized within the year an accession to income, if we take words in their plain popular meaning, as they should be taken here.

Judgment reversed.

Notes and Questions

1. *Codification.* The result in *Kirby* is succinctly codified in §61(a)(12), which provides that gross income includes "[i]ncome from discharge of indebtedness."

2. *Why some debts are canceled.* Why did Kirby Lumber not have to repay the entire amount of the loan? There are two possible explanations. First, doubts might have arisen as to Kirby's creditworthiness, so that bondholders decided to take what cash they could get now, rather than run the risk that the bonds would become worthless later. Second — and the much more likely explanation in Kirby's case — the prevailing interest rate might have risen after Kirby issued the bonds, with the result that the bonds carried a below-market interest rate. A bondholder might then be willing to sell a bond back to Kirby for less than its issue price, so that the bondholder could invest the money at the prevailing higher interest rate. To understand the effect of an increase in the prevailing interest rate on the value of a bond bearing a fixed rate of interest, imagine a bond that provides for interest payments in perpetuity, with no provision for repayment of principal. Suppose that when the prevailing interest rate was 8 percent, Kirby had received $10,000 from a lender in return for Kirby's issuance of a $10,000 perpetual bond, which provided for annual interest payments of $800 (8% of the stated principal) forever, with no provision for repayment of principal. If the prevailing interest rate later rose to 10 percent, the right to a perpetual income stream of $800 per year would then be worth only $8,000, and Kirby would be able to buy back its bond for $8,000, despite the fact Kirby had received $10,000 when it issued the bond.

3. *The tax treatment of borrowing and repayment.* Borrowed money is not included in the borrower's gross income because her receipt of funds is offset by her obligation to repay. In other words, borrowed money is excluded from gross income based on the assumption that the taxpayer will eventually repay the loan. The taxpayer is entitled to no deduction when she makes principal payments on the loan; those payments merely serve to justify the original exclusion of the loan proceeds from income. This treatment of loans — with no tax consequences attached to either the receipt of loan proceeds or to repayments of principal — was not inevitable. Instead, the income tax might have included borrowed amounts in income and allowed a deduction for loan repayments. But taxing borrowed funds as income would cause serious income-bunching problems, and the vast majority of loans are in fact repaid, so the no-tax-consequences approach of current law is probably the better choice. The no-tax-consequences approach runs into trouble, however, when the assumption of eventual repayment — on which the original exclusion was premised — later turns out to be mistaken, as in *Kirby.* When that happens, it is clear that the taxpayer should be required to

include in gross income the amount borrowed that will never be repaid ($137,521.30, in *Kirby*). On the facts of *Kirby*, it is also clear that the inclusion must be in the taxpayer's income for 1923, since both the borrowing and the debt cancellation occurred in that year. More commonly, however, the debt cancellation occurs in a year subsequent to the borrowing year, and the question then arises as to the timing of the taxation of the debt cancellation income. One possibility would be to require the taxpayer to amend its return for the year in which it received the loan proceeds, to include $137,521.30 in that year's gross income. That approach, however, would be inconsistent with income tax annual accounting—in particular, with the principle that the tax consequences of events in one year are not held open pending developments in later years. If the return for the borrowing year was correct when originally filed, based on all the facts known or knowable as of the end of that year, then the tax system's response to later inconsistent events is *not* to amend the original return.[75] Instead, the gross income inclusion is in the year in which it becomes apparent that the loan will not be fully repaid. Making the correction in the later year would be the only possible approach if the earlier year were closed by the statute of limitations,[76] but the annual accounting principle requires that the correction be made in the later year even if the statute of limitations has not run on the earlier year.

4. *Mistakes ab initio versus mistakes only in hindsight.* The correction-in-the-later-year approach described above applies if the earlier year's return appears mistaken *only* with the benefit of hindsight—that is, if an event occurs *in a later year* that is fundamentally inconsistent with an assumption on which the original return was based. If the original return was wrong from the beginning, based on information known or knowable as of the end of the earlier year, then the mistake must be corrected in the earlier year—or not corrected at all, if the statute of limitations on the earlier year has expired.

5. *Don't follow the cash flow.* A confusing aspect of *Kirby* debt cancellation income is that the tax treatment is backward in terms of cash flow. Suppose a taxpayer borrows $1,000,000 in Year 1, and in Year 2 the lender accepts $860,000 from the taxpayer and cancels the remaining $140,000 of the debt. The taxpayer included nothing in gross income when he *received* cash, but he must include $140,000 in gross income when he *repays* cash. Notice, however, that he is not taxed on the $860,000 repayment in Year 2. Rather, he is taxed in Year 2 on the other $140,000 of the loan proceeds, which it is now clear he will never be required to repay. Of course, the repayment of the $860,000 was the consideration for the cancellation of the other $140,000 of the debt, so the cash-flow-backward aspect of *Kirby* is typical, and generally unavoidable, in many cases of debt cancellation income.

6. *An imperfect correction?* When the borrowing and the debt cancellation occur in different years, the *Kirby* approach clearly produces the right total amount of income: The taxpayer must include in gross income precisely the amount he borrowed that he will never repay. In terms of overall

---

75. As noted earlier, there are a very few statutory exceptions to this principle, such as the rules applicable to a taxpayer who fails to replace involuntarily converted property within the time period permitted by §1033.

76. For a timely filed return, the statute of limitations generally expires three years after the due date for the return. *See* §6501.

economic effects, however, inclusion of $140,000 in gross income in Year 2 may be a poor substitute for taxing $140,000 in Year 1. Making the correction in Year 2 denies the government any interest on the deferral of tax from Year 1 to Year 2, and the marginal tax rate applicable in Year 2 may be lower or higher than the marginal tax rate in Year 1. These objections have force, however, only if making the correction in Year 1 is the theoretical ideal. One might think, instead, that making the correction in the later year is not just a concession to practicality, but is also theoretically correct. Even at the level of high theory, the taxpayer had no income in the year of borrowing if eventual full repayment of the loan was reasonably anticipated then; the income arose only in the later year in which the taxpayer was able to eliminate $1 million of debt at a cost of only $860,000. If the debt cancellation income was attributable to an increase in the prevailing interest rate (so that the debt bore a below-market rate of interest at the time it was repaid), and if the increase in the prevailing rate occurred in a year after the borrowing year but before the cancellation year, then the debt cancellation income economically accrued in that intervening year — the year in which the taxpayer *could* have settled the debt for less than the amount borrowed, even though the taxpayer did not actually do so until later. In that case, however, the debt cancellation income would have been unrealized appreciation in the intervening year, and the realization event would have occurred only in the year in which $140,000 of the debt was formally canceled.

7. *Insolvency.* In Note 2, above, we explained that one reason that taxpayers are sometimes able to obtain debt discharge on favorable terms is that their creditworthiness has declined, and their creditors are accordingly worried about whether they will be able to collect the full amount of the debt. In such cases, the rationale for inclusion of the debt discharge in income seems less compelling. That is true for practical reasons — if creditors are pessimistic about collection of a debt, does it make sense for Uncle Sam to create additional tax liability at more or less the same time? But it is also true for conceptual reasons. Imagine that you have assets of $1,000, and debts totaling $1,500, consisting of a mortgage loan of $900 and an unsecured note of $600. The holder of the unsecured note agrees to accept a $400 payment in full discharge of the $600 debt. You were $500 in the hole; now you are $300 in the hole. Are you better off? Surely you are slightly better off; it's always easier to climb out of a shallow hole than a deep one. But you may be headed for bankruptcy anyway, in which case the amount that ends up being discharged in bankruptcy won't really matter to you very much.[77]

And in the case of a corporation, negative net worth numbers seem particularly abstract, even artificial. Negative net worth in a corporate setting translates to negative shareholder equity (since shareholders are the owners of the corporate net worth); but the most important defining element of corporate stock ownership is limited liability. The shareholders, absent fraud, do not owe anything to the corporation's creditors, so the amount by which the corporation's debts exceed its assets is not terribly

---

77. It is worth noting, however, that there is no general income tax dispensation for a taxpayer who has a negative net worth. A taxpayer with liabilities in excess of assets must still include his wages (for example) in his gross income.

meaningful to shareholders. All negative numbers are essentially the equivalent of zero, since the value of the shares cannot fall below that number.[78]

Section 108(a) of the Code reflects Congress's judgment that debtors who are insolvent should indeed not be taxed on income from favorable discharge of debt—at least not immediately—and accordingly provides an exclusion for such income in such circumstances. However, it remains true that debtors who obtain favorable debt discharge must have received something initially (usually, the proceeds of the loan) that they have not had to fully pay back. So, insolvency notwithstanding, it seems as though *some* accounting for the favorable discharge is indicated. Congress has responded to this sense as well: Section 108(b), in effect, converts the exclusion into a deferral, by requiring that a debtor who benefits from the exclusion in subsection (a) must reduce his "tax attributes" by a corresponding amount. To illustrate with an example from a situation already discussed, if a taxpayer has net operating losses, or carryovers of such losses from prior years, he must subtract the amount of the income from the discharge of debt excluded by §108(a) from the amount of those losses or loss carryovers.

8. *Qualified principal residence indebtedness.* In response to the recent (and ongoing) home mortgage crisis, Congress enacted special rules applicable to the cancellation of "qualified principal residence indebtedness" (QPRI). Under §108(a)(1)(E), no gross income inclusion results from the cancellation of QPRI (before the end of 2012) if the cancellation is in response to either (1) a decline in the value of the residence securing the debt, or (2) the precarious financial condition of the taxpayer. QPRI is defined by §108(h)(2) as up to $1,000,000 ($2,000,000 for a married couple filing a joint return) of debt incurred to acquire a principal residence. The exclusion does not apply to the cancellation of non-acquisition indebtedness (i.e., a home equity loan), and it does not apply to the cancellation of any indebtedness secured by a secondary residence (such as a vacation home). Section 108(h)(1) reduces the taxpayer's basis in the home by the amount of QPRI excluded from gross income, but in most cases the basis reduction will be of no practical significance. Consider the effect of the basis reduction in the three following situations.

(i) Don bought his home several year ago for $500,000; he made a $50,000 cash down payment and borrowed $450,000 secured by a mortgage on the home (Don is also personally liable on the debt). The home is now worth only $375,000, and the outstanding principal on the mortgage is still $450,000 (i.e., Don has been making interest-only payments on the loan). The bank holding the mortgage cancels

---

78. This is a slight oversimplification, because the value of the shares is not a direct measure of the net worth of the corporation. Rather, it is the value of a probability space reflecting all possible future outcomes for the corporation, including the possibility that its affairs will turn around. And, as noted, it's easier to climb out of a shallow hole.

So one would expect that the stock of an insolvent corporation would still have some minimal value until it is closed in bankruptcy, and one would further expect that any favorable discharge of debt not already reflected in the stock price would nudge the price of the stock marginally higher, because it makes the optimistic scenarios somewhat more probable. Still, the change would likely be only a fraction of the bargain element in the debt discharge.

$75,000 of Don's debt, while allowing Don to retain ownership and occupancy of the home. Don must reduce his basis in the home from $500,000 to $425,000, but that reduction has no effect on Don's tax liability as long as he continues to own the home. As illustrated by the next two examples, he may not have any tax consequences even if he sells (or otherwise disposes of) the home.

(ii) The facts are the same as in (i), except that instead of retaining ownership and occupancy, Don transfers the home to the bank — thus repaying $375,000 of his debt — and the bank cancels the other $75,000. Again, Don excludes the $75,000 of QPRI from his gross income, and reduces his basis in the home from $500,000 to $425,000. As a result of the reduction, Don's loss on the disposition of the home is $50,000 ($375,000 – $425,000), rather than $125,000. This makes no difference to Don's tax liability, however, because losses on the sales of personal residences are nondeductible (*see* §165(c)).

(iii) Several years after the facts described in (i), when the principal amount of the mortgage is still $375,000 and the value of the house has rebounded, Don sells the house for $600,000 (using $375,000 to pay off the mortgage and keeping the other $225,000). Because of the basis reduction, his gain is $175,000 rather than only $100,000. Even in this situation, however, the basis reduction probably won't matter, because he will probably be able to exclude the entire $175,000 gain under §121.[79]

More detail on the features of §108 is contained in the cells relating to debt discharge following this chapter.

b. Proceeds of Embezzlement and Other Illegal Income

COLLINS v. COMMISSIONER

3 F.3d 625 (2d Cir. 1993)

CARDAMONE, Circuit Judge: Mark D. Collins, taxpayer or appellant, appeals from a final decision of the United States Tax Court . . . determining that, as a result of unreported gross income from theft, he had an income tax deficiency for 1988 of $9,359. The theft occurred when the taxpayer, an employee of a betting parlor that accepts bets on horse races, was unable to stop himself from making wagers on his own behalf. He punched his bets on his computer without funds to pay for them. The horses Collins bet on ran like those of the bettor immortalized in Stephen C. Foster's "De Camptown Races" (Robbins Music Corp. 1933) (Song), some of whose horses left the racetrack, others cut across it, and one got stuck "in a big mud hole." Appellant's horses finished out of the money on most of the races he bet on and he lost heavily for the day. That which Collins had stolen is what he most feared to keep, as is so often the case; so he turned himself in. The theft precipitated a chain of events that led to the present appeal.

---

79. Section 121 is discussed in section C.4 of Chapter 3.

BACKGROUND

A. THEFT AND RACETRACK BETTING

Collins was employed as a ticket vendor and computer operator at an Off-Track Betting (OTB) parlor in Auburn, New York. OTB runs a network of 298 betting parlors in New York State that permit patrons to place legal wagers on horse races without actually going to the track. Operating as a cash business, OTB does not extend credit to those making bets at its parlors. It also has a strict policy against employee betting on horse races. Collins, an apparently compulsive gambler, ignored these regulations and occasionally placed bets on his own behalf in his computer without paying for them. Until July 17, 1988 he had always managed to cover those bets without detection. On that date, appellant decided he "would like some money" and on credit punched up for himself a total of $80,280 in betting tickets.

Collins began the day by betting $20 on a horse across the board in the first race at the Finger Lakes Race Track in upstate New York, that is, he bet $20 to win, $20 to place (finish second or better), and $20 to show (finish third or better). The horse finished out of the money (not in the top three racers) and Collins lost $60. On the second race Collins again bet $40 across the board, with the same results. He was now out a total of $180. Appellant repeated this pattern, betting $600 in the third race and $1,500 in the fourth race at Finger Lakes, both of which he lost. Collins did not bet on the fifth race, but he wagered $1,500 in the sixth race, $7,500 in the seventh, and $15,000 in the eighth. Collins' luck continued to hold steady: he lost all of these races and now owed OTB $26,280.

There were only two races left that day and Collins was determined to recoup his losses. Consequently, he gambled $25,500 of OTB's money on the ninth race. This time his horse came in third, and Collins won back $8,925. He then bet $28,500 in the last or tenth race and finally picked a winner. The winning horse paid him $33,250. After this race, Collins was behind $38,105 for the day.

At the close of the races Collins put his $42,175 in winning tickets in his OTB drawer and reported his bets and his losing ticket shortfall to his supervisor, who until then had not been aware of Collins' gambling activities. She called the police, and in police custody Collins signed an affidavit admitting what he had done. On October 27, 1988 he pled guilty to one count of grand larceny in the third degree, a felony under New York law. . . .

B. TAX DEFICIENCY

Collins filed a timely federal income tax return for 1988 in which he reported wages of $11,980 and a corresponding tax liability of $1,054. He did not believe that his illegal activities on July 17, 1988 had any tax consequences, but the Internal Revenue Service (IRS) disagreed. On March 1, 1990 it mailed the taxpayer a deficiency notice resulting from his failure to report $38,136 in "gross income from gambling winnings during the taxable year 1988." It determined that due to this unreported income, Collins owed $9,376 in additional taxes for the calendar year 1988. . . .

The taxpayer objected to these assessments and, on June 4, 1990, filed a petition for relief with the United States Tax Court. . . .

[The Tax Court] first determined that Collins's actions, rather than giving rise to gambling income, had resulted in a $38,105 gambling loss, arrived at by subtracting all the amounts he had earlier lost from his winnings on the last two races. Thus, contrary to the IRS' position, the taxpayer had not received any net income from his betting activities on July 17, 1988. The tax court then turned to what it deemed the more difficult question: whether the $80,280 in unpaid bets placed by Collins constituted theft or embezzlement income. It answered this query in the affirmative after undertaking a two-step inquiry that examined: (1) whether Collins realized economic value from the betting tickets he stole (the Realizable Value Test) and, if so, (2) whether Collins had sufficient control over this stolen property to derive value from it (the Control Test). The tax court found that Collins' larceny met both parts of the test because he had the opportunity to derive gratification and economic gain from using the stolen tickets.

Having concluded that Collins' theft resulted in income, the tax court calculated the amount of that income. It found a proper measure was the $80,280 value of the tickets, because Collins received from the pilfered tickets the same benefit that any legitimate purchaser would have gotten. To calculate tax liability the court then deducted from the $80,280 the $42,175 in winnings that Collins returned to his OTB till, which it characterized as a restitution payment by the taxpayer to his employer.

In sum, the tax court found Collins' unreported taxable income to be that amount which he stole on July 17 but did not return to his OTB till, a total that came to $38,105. . . . We affirm.

DISCUSSION

I. GROSS INCOME

A. General Principles

In addressing the argument Collins raises regarding the tax treatment of his illegal actions, we believe it useful to set out initially the basic principles underlying the definition of gross income. Internal Revenue Code §61 defines gross income broadly as "all income from whatever source derived." It then categorizes 15 common items that constitute gross income, a list that includes interest, rents, royalties, salaries, annuities, and dividends, among others. Gross income, as §61 specifically states, is "not limited to" the enumerated items.

Defining gross income as "all income" is admittedly somewhat tautological. In the early days of the tax code, the Supreme Court recognized this problem and attempted to provide a more workable and perhaps somewhat more limited definition for the term. It defined income in Eisner v. Macomber, 252 U.S. 189 (1920), "'as gain derived from capital, from labor, or from both combined,' provided it be understood to include profit gained through a sale or conversion of capital assets. . . ." Id. at 207 (quoting Doyle v. Mitchell Bros. Co., 247 U.S. 179, 185 (1918)).

It soon became evident that this definition created more problems than it solved. Under the *Eisner* formulation questions arose as to whether gains from cancellation of indebtedness or embezzlement—which do not fall neatly into either the labor or capital categories—constituted gross income. Acknowledging the defects in the *Eisner* definition, the Supreme Court began to steer away from it.

For example, in United States v. Kirby Lumber Co., 284 U.S. 1, 3 (1931), it held that gains from the retirement of corporate bonds by their issuer at less than their issuing price were includable in gross income. Justice Holmes, writing for the Court, reached this conclusion despite the fact that the gains were not clearly derived from either capital or labor. In so doing he adverted to the futility of attempting to capture the concept of income and encapsulate it within a phrase.

The Court finally abandoned the stilted capital-labor formulation of gross income and jettisoned its earlier attempts to define the term in Commissioner v. Glenshaw Glass Co., 348 U.S. 426 (1954). . . . It cast aside *Eisner*'s definition of income stating that it was "not meant to provide a touchstone to all future gross income questions." Instead the Court stated, "Congress applied no limitations as to the source of taxable receipts, nor restrictive labels as to their nature." The legislature intended to simply tax "all gains," which the Court effectively described as all "accessions to wealth, clearly realized, and over which the taxpayers have complete dominion."

Since *Glenshaw Glass* the term *gross income* has been read expansively to include all realized gains and forms of enrichment, that is, "all gains except those specifically exempted." Under this broad definition, gross income does not include all moneys a taxpayer receives. It is quite plain, for instance, that gross income does not include money acquired from borrowings. Loans do not result in realized gains or enrichment because any increase in net worth from proceeds of a loan is offset by a corresponding obligation to repay it.

This well-established principle on borrowing initially gave rise to another nettlesome question on how embezzled funds were to be treated. The Supreme Court once believed that money illegally procured from another was not gross income for tax purposes when the acquirer was legally obligated, like a legitimate borrower, to return the funds. *See* Commissioner v. Wilcox, 327 U.S. 404, 408-09 (1946). In Rutkin v. United States, 343 U.S. 130 (1952), the Court partially and somewhat unsatisfactorily abandoned that view, holding that an extortionist, unlike an embezzler, was obligated to pay tax on his ill-gotten gains because he was unlikely to be asked to repay the money.

Rutkin left the law on embezzlement in a murky state. This condition cleared in James v. United States, 366 U.S. 213 (1961). There the Court stated unequivocally that all unlawful gains are taxable. It reasoned that embezzlers, along with others who procure money illegally, should not be able to escape taxes while honest citizens pay taxes on "every conceivable type of income." Thus, under *James*, a taxpayer has received income when she "acquires earnings, lawfully or unlawfully, without the consensual recognition, express or implied, of an obligation to repay and without restriction as to their disposition. . . ." This income test includes all forms of enrichment, legal or otherwise, but explicitly excludes loans.

Distinguishing loans from unlawful taxable gains has not usually proved difficult. Loans are identified by the mutual understanding between the borrower and lender of the obligation to repay and a bona fide intent on the borrower's part to repay the acquired funds. Accordingly, in Buff v. Commissioner, 496 F.2d 847 (2d Cir. 1974), we found an embezzler who confessed to his crime and within the same year signed a judgment agreeing to make repayment had received a taxable gain as opposed to a loan because he never had any intention of repaying the money. The embezzler's expressed consent to repay the loan, we determined, "was not worth the paper it was written on." The mere act of signing such a consent could not be used to escape tax liability.

It is important to note, in addition, that though an embezzler must under the *James* test include as taxable income all amounts illegally acquired, the taxpayer may ordinarily claim a tax deduction for payments she makes in restitution. Such a deduction is available for the tax year in which the repayments are made. *See* 26 U.S.C. §165(c).

B. Principles Applied

With this outline of the relevant legal principles in mind, we have little difficulty in holding that Collins' illegal activities gave rise to gross income. Under the expansive definitions of income advanced in *Glenshaw Glass* and *James*, larceny of any kind resulting in an unrestricted gain of moneys to a wrongdoer is a taxable event. Taxes may be assessed in the year in which the taxpayer realizes an economic benefit from his actions. In this case, Collins admitted to stealing racing tickets from OTB on July 17, 1988. This larceny resulted in the taxpayer's enrichment: he had the pleasure of betting on horses running at the Finger Lakes Race Track. Individuals purchase racing tickets from OTB because these tickets give them the pleasure of attempting to make money simply by correctly predicting the outcomes of horse races. By punching up tickets on his computer without paying for them, Collins appropriated for himself the same benefit that patrons of OTB pay money to receive. This illegally-appropriated benefit, as the tax court correctly concluded, constituted gross income to Collins in 1988.

The taxpayer raises a series of objections to this conclusion. He first insists that such a holding cannot be correct because at the end of the day he was in debt by $38,105. He asserts that a tax is being assessed on his losses rather than on any possible gain. What may seem at first glance a rather anomalous result is explained by distinguishing between Collins' theft and his gambling activities. Collins took illegally acquired assets and spent them unwisely by betting on losing horses at a racetrack.

Although the bets gave rise to gambling losses, the taxpayer gained from the misappropriation of his employer's property without its knowledge or permission. The gambling loss is not relevant to and does not offset Collins' gain in the form of opportunities to gamble that he obtained by virtue of his embezzlement. Collins' situation is quite the same as that of any other individual who embezzles money from his employer and subsequently loses it at the racetrack. Such person would properly have his illegally-acquired assets included in his gross income. Further, taxpayer would not be able to deduct gambling losses from theft income because the Internal Revenue Code only allows gambling losses to offset gambling winnings. *See* 26 U.S.C. §165(d). Collins is being treated the same way.

The taxpayer next contends his larceny resulted in no taxable gain because he recognized that he had an obligation to repay his employer for the stolen tickets. He posits that recognition of a repayment obligation transformed a wrongful appropriation into a nontaxable transaction. In effect, Collins tries to revive pre-*James* law under which an embezzler's gain could be found nontaxable due to the embezzler's duty to repay stolen funds. Yet, the Supreme Court has clearly abandoned the pre-*James* view and ruled instead that only a loan, with its attendant "consensual recognition" of the obligation to repay, is not taxable. There was no loan of funds, nor was there any "consensual recognition" here: OTB never gave Collins permission to use betting tickets. To the contrary, it has strict rules against employee betting, and Collins could not have reasonably believed that his supervisors would have approved of his transactions. His unilateral intention to pay for the stolen property did not transform a theft into a loan within the meaning of James.

The taxpayer then avers this case is analogous to Gilbert v. Commissioner, 552 F.2d 478 (2d Cir. 1977), in which we found a consensual recognition of the obligation to repay despite the absence of a loan agreement. Taxpayer Edward Gilbert, as president and a director of E. L. Bruce Company, acquired on margin a substantial personal stake in the stock of a rival company, Celotex Corporation, intending to bring about a merger between Celotex and E. L. Bruce. The stock market declined after Gilbert bought these shares, and he was required to meet several margin calls. Lacking personal funds to meet these obligations, Gilbert instructed the corporate secretary of E. L. Bruce to make $1.9 million in margin payments on his behalf. A few days later, Gilbert signed secured promissory notes to repay the funds; but, the corporation's board of directors refused to ratify Gilbert's unauthorized withdrawal, demanded his resignation, and called in his notes. The board also declined to merge with Celotex, and soon thereafter the Celotex stock that Gilbert owned became essentially worthless. Gilbert could not repay his obligations to E. L. Bruce, and he eventually pled guilty to federal and state charges of unlawfully withdrawing funds from the corporation.

The IRS claimed that Gilbert's unauthorized withdrawal of funds constituted income to the taxpayer. It asserted that there was no consensual recognition of a repayment obligation because E. L. Bruce Company's board of directors was unaware of and subsequently disapproved Gilbert's actions. Citing the highly atypical nature of the case, we held that Gilbert did not realize income under the *James* test because (1) he not only "fully" intended but also expected "with reasonable certainty" to repay the sums taken, (2) he believed his withdrawals would be approved by the corporate board, and (3) he made prompt assignment of assets sufficient to secure the amount he owed. Id. at 481. These facts evidenced consensual recognition and distinguished *Gilbert* from the more typical embezzlement case where the embezzler plans right from the beginning to abscond with the embezzled funds.

Plainly, none of the significant facts of *Gilbert* are present in the case at hand. Collins, unlike Gilbert, never expected to be able to repay the stolen funds. He was in no position to do so. The amount he owed OTB was three times his annual salary—a far cry from *Gilbert*, where the taxpayer assigned to the corporation enough assets to cover his unauthorized withdrawals. Also in contrast to Gilbert, Collins could not have believed that his employer would subsequently ratify his transactions. He knew that OTB had strict rules against employee betting. Moreover, while Gilbert was motivated by a desire to assist his corporation, Collins embezzled betting tickets because he wanted to make some money. Collins' purpose makes this a garden variety type of embezzlement case, not to be confused with a loan. *Gilbert* is therefore an inapposite precedent.

Finally, appellant complains of the root unfairness and harshness of the result, declaring that the imposition of a tax on his July 17 transaction is an attempt to use the income tax law to punish misconduct that has already been appropriately punished under the criminal law. Although we are not without some sympathy to the taxpayer's plight, we are unable to adopt his claim of unfairness and use it as a basis to negate the imposition of a tax on his income. The Supreme Court has repeatedly emphasized that taxing an embezzler on his illicit gains accords with the fair administration of the tax law because it removes the anomaly of having the income of an honest individual taxed while the similar gains of a criminal are not. Thus, there is no double penalty in having a taxpayer prosecuted for the crime that resulted in his obtaining ill-gotten gains and subsequently being required to pay taxes on those illegal gains. Such is not an unduly harsh result because Internal Revenue Code §165 provides that once the taxpayer makes restitution payments to OTB or its insurer, he will be able in that year to deduct the amount of those payments from his gross income.

In sum, we hold that under the expansive definition of income adopted in *Glenshaw Glass* and *James,* Collins received gross income from his theft of OTB betting tickets. There is no basis upon which we may hold that the receipt of these opportunities to gamble may be excluded from a calculation of the taxpayer's income. When and if Collins repays the stolen funds, he will be entitled to a deduction from income in the year that the funds are repaid.

II. VALUATION

Having determined that the July 17 transaction resulted in a taxable gain to Collins, we next consider how that gain should be measured. It is well-settled that income received in a form other than cash is taxed at its fair market value at the time of its receipt. . . .

Based on this measure the value of Collins' tickets was the price at which they would have changed hands between legitimate bettors and OTB. This price was the retail price or face value of the tickets. Accordingly, the tax court properly found that the stolen tickets were worth $80,280, their retail price, and this amount was correctly included in the taxpayer's gross income, as a gain from theft. From that figure Collins was entitled to a deduction for restitution he made to OTB in 1988. Collins returned to his till on July 17 winning tickets with a face value of $42,175. Thus, the tax court correctly determined that Collins' total taxable theft income for the year was $38,105 ($80,280 minus $42,175).

Collins, relying upon the Third Circuit's decision in Zarin v. Commissioner, 916 F.2d 110 (3d Cir. 1990), asserts the stolen tickets were essentially valueless for tax purposes. In *Zarin* the taxpayer was a "high roller" at Resorts International Casino in Atlantic City with a $200,000 casino credit line. He incurred over $2.5 million in gambling debt at the casino, which he repaid in full. The New Jersey Casino Control Commission then identified Zarin as a compulsive gambler and enjoined Resorts from advancing him further credit. Resorts effectively ignored the Commission's order and kept lending its customer money. By January 1980 Zarin was spending 16 hours a day at the craps table, and eventually lost a total of $3.4 million, an amount he could not repay. Resorts sued to collect and Zarin asserted as a defense that Resorts' claim was unenforceable because it had violated the Commission's order. Zarin then settled the Casino's claim by agreeing to pay it $500,000.

The IRS subsequently audited Zarin and declared a deficiency in taxpayer's taxes. It claimed that by settling his suit with Resorts, Zarin had cancellation of indebtedness income in the amount of $2.9 million—the difference between his gambling debt of $3.4 million and the $500,000 he paid to settle it. . . . [The Third Circuit] appellate court concluded that Zarin had no income from cancellation of Resorts' debt because he had no "indebtedness," as that term is defined by the Internal Revenue Code. It ruled that in order to demonstrate indebtedness, the IRS had to prove, under 26 U.S.C. §108(d)(1), that Zarin either (1) was liable to

Resorts on the debt or (2) held "property" subject to the debt. The court found the IRS could make neither showing. Under the first part of the test, Zarin was not liable on the debt because Resorts' $3.4 million loan was issued in violation of the New Jersey Casino Control Commission's order and was not enforceable under New Jersey law. Under the second part, the Third Circuit held the gambling chips Zarin acquired with Resorts' loan were not property because they had "no independent economic value." It reached this conclusion because the chips could not be used outside the casino, only having value as a means of facilitating gambling within the casino itself.

Collins seizes on this second point, insisting that like Zarin he stole opportunities to gamble and that his stolen racing tickets — like Zarin's gambling chips — had no intrinsic economic value. He thinks therefore that his taxable gain from the theft of the tickets was zero.

In disposing of that erroneous assumption, we observe that the statement in *Zarin* regarding the value of the casino's gambling chips was offered as part of the appellate court's interpretation of the narrow income exclusion provision of §108(d) of the Code. Section 108(a) excludes from gross income the amount of the discharge of a taxpayer's indebtedness [under narrowly specified circumstances] and §108(d), just discussed, defines indebtedness. We are not convinced that the Third Circuit's reasoning is applicable outside the context of §108 and the specific facts of that case where nothing was stolen and there was no embezzlement. *Zarin* may have been written differently had the Third Circuit been confronted with the separate question of whether to include as gross income under §61 the face value of stolen gambling opportunities.

Zarin we think is also inapposite because it involved a consensual transaction between Resorts Casino and the taxpayer that impacted no other parties. . . . Consequently, we regard the fair market value of the stolen gambling tickets to be the proper measure of Collins' taxable gain in 1988.

Notes and Questions

1. *More on* Zarin. In deciding that the taxpayer in *Zarin* did not realize cancellation of indebtedness income, the Third Circuit relied on the so-called disputed liability doctrine. That doctrine originated with N. Sobel, Inc. v. Commissioner, 40 BTA 1263 (1939). It applies when a taxpayer incurs a debt in order to acquire property (*not* cash), a dispute arises concerning the value of the property, and the dispute is settled by reducing the amount of the acquisition indebtedness. Suppose a taxpayer acquires a car by giving the seller a $10,000 note, but the debt is later reduced to $7,000 because the seller misrepresented facts crucial to the valuation of the car. The disputed liability doctrine makes good sense in that context. If the real value of the car was only $7,000, then the reduction of the debt from $10,000 to $7,000 does not require application of *Kirby* to correct a mistaken assumption. The original tax assumption was that the taxpayer received $10,000 of value for which she would eventually pay $10,000 cash. As it turns out, the taxpayer actually received $7,000 of value for which she will eventually pay $7,000 cash. The taxpayer still has not received any value for which she will not pay. Contrast that with a situation in which a taxpayer borrows $10,000 *cash,* and when the time for repayment arrives

the taxpayer declines to pay on the grounds that the loan was illegal for some reason, and is thus unenforceable. Eventually the taxpayer and the creditor settle the dispute with a $7,000 payment. This might be described as a disputed liability situation, but it is *not* the sort of disputed liability to which the *Sobel* rule should apply. The taxpayer received $10,000 worth of value (cash) and repays only $7,000. The taxpayer clearly has made a $3,000 profit from the loan transaction, and should be taxed on $3,000 of *Kirby* income. In short, the disputed liability rule of *Sobel* should be limited to situations in which there is a dispute about the value of the property the taxpayer received when he incurred the debt; it should not apply when the dispute merely concerns whether the debt is legally enforceable.[80]

2. *An embezzler's obligation to repay.* Mr. Collins' OTB tickets had value despite the fact that they could be used only to gamble. Collins clearly would have been taxed if he had received the OTB tickets as compensation for services.[81] On the other hand, Collins would not have been taxed on the receipt of the tickets if (contrary to fact) OTB had allowed him to buy the tickets on credit. Although Collins was not *allowed* to buy the tickets on credit, he did so anyway, illegally. Since his embezzlement gave rise to a repayment obligation, just as in the case of a loan from a willing lender, why shouldn't Collins' embezzlement be treated as a loan for tax purposes? If the justification for excluding loan proceeds from income is that the taxpayer's obligation to repay means the taxpayer has not been enriched by the loan transaction, shouldn't the same analysis apply to embezzlement proceeds? As the *Collins* opinion explains, the Supreme Court originally decided (in *Wilcox*) that the obligation to repay prevented an embezzler from realizing income from his theft. Later (in *James*) the Court switched to an analysis based not on legal obligations, but on experience. If most true (consensual) loans are repaid, but most embezzlements are not repaid, then it makes sense for the tax system to assume repayment for true loans (thereby excluding loans from gross income), but not to assume that embezzled funds will be repaid (thereby including embezzlement proceeds in gross income). In the case of a true loan, the tax system relies on the lender's determination of the borrower's creditworthiness; if the lender is willing to bet that the borrower will repay, so is the tax system. In the case of embezzlement, however, the involuntary lender (the victim) has made no creditworthiness determination on which the tax system can rely.

3. *"Honest" embezzlers.* Many embezzlers are "honest" in the sense that they are experiencing temporary (so they hope) cash flow problems, and they truly intend to repay before their theft is detected. For example, lawyers who help themselves to their clients' trust accounts (an act frequently punished by disbarment) often intend to put the money back before anyone notices it is missing. Should these "honest" embezzlers be taxed on the money they

---

80. There is an argument to be made in support of the Third Circuit's result in *Zarin*, but that argument does not rely on the disputed liability doctrine. For much more on *Zarin*, including an edited version of the Third Circuit's opinion, see the cell on discharge of gambling debts.

81. The amount of taxable compensation would have been the fair market value of the tickets. If a $2 ticket received as compensation turned into a $5 winner, the taxpayer would have $2 of compensation income and $3 of gambling winnings. If the ticket turned into a loser, the taxpayer would have $2 of compensation income and a $2 gambling loss (the deductibility of which would be subject to §165(d)).

take, or should the taxation of embezzlement proceeds be limited to embezzlers who never intend to repay? To frame the question differently, should the tax exclusion for loans apply only when a willing lender has determined that repayment is likely (a true loan), or should it also apply when a self-help borrower subjectively intends to repay (an "honest" embezzlement)? What, if anything, does the *Collins* opinion tell you about the treatment of "honest" embezzlers under current law? In distinguishing *Gilbert*, the *Collins* opinion states that "Collins, unlike Gilbert, never expected to repay the stolen funds." Is that right? Earlier, in the statement of facts, the court tells us that Collins' past practice had been "to cover those [illegal] bets without detection." The *Gilbert* opinion suggests that at least some "honest" embezzlers may qualify as legitimate borrowers for income tax purposes. Does that seem like a good idea to you? Does the mere fact that the embezzler intends to repay establish that repayment is likely? (For what it's worth, Gilbert himself did not succeed in repaying his unauthorized withdrawals.) Is a test based on the embezzler's state of mind administratively practical? If the result in *Gilbert* seems technically dubious, it is at least understandable why the court might have strained to reach the no-income result. In many cases involving the taxation of embezzlement proceeds, the real question is whether what's left of the taxpayer's assets will go to the taxpayer's victim or to the IRS. If holding the proceeds taxable means the IRS collects its tax and the victim gets nothing (as it sometimes does), a court may be reluctant to cause that result.

4. *Other illegal income.* If illegal income is taxable even when the criminal is under an obligation to repay the victim, *a fortiori* illegal income is taxable when there is no victim entitled to repayment — as with income from drug dealing, prostitution, and illegal gambling, for example. The government does not, of course, collect much tax on income from illegal sources. The major practical significance of the taxation of illegal income is that sometimes it is easier for the government to convict a criminal — a drug kingpin, say — of a tax crime than of the underlying non-tax crime. Although the example is rather long-in-the-tooth by now, the IRS remains proud of the fact that Al Capone was convicted *only* of tax crime. A few sophisticated criminals, impressed by the story of Capone's downfall and by more recent IRS efforts in the same direction, actually file "Fifth Amendment returns," accurately reporting the amount of their income, but declining to reveal the sources on the grounds that source information might tend to incriminate them. In recent years tax prosecutions have focused heavily on failures to report income from illegal sources. With a large portion of the government's criminal enforcement resources devoted to prosecutions of drug kingpins and other all-around bad guys, there are few resources left to prosecute those who criminally evade taxes on legal sources of income. To the extent the public is aware of this, the general deterrence function of the criminal tax law is undermined.

c.   Debt Relief Associated with the Disposition of Property

The *Tufts* case, set forth below, is widely considered one of the most conceptually difficult cases in the basic income tax course. We believe, however, that the analysis in *Tufts* is straightforward and readily comprehensible, once one has the following background information about the tax treatment of debt incurred in order to acquire property, and about the basics of tax depreciation.

Acquisition indebtedness and basis. (1) You buy an apartment building for $1 million, using your own (unborrowed) money. Your basis for the building is, of course, $1 million. *See* §1012 (basis equals cost).

(2) You buy an apartment building for $1 million, financing the purchase with $200,000 of your own money and an $800,000 loan from the bank. The loan is secured by a mortgage on the building, and you are also personally liable on the loan. Personal liability means that the bank is not limited to foreclosing on the mortgage if you default on the loan; the bank may proceed against any of your assets in order to collect the amount due. (A loan on which the debtor is personally liable is called a recourse loan.) Your basis in the building is $1 million — $200,000 on account of your own money, and $800,000 on account of the borrowed money. The same repayment assumption that justifies excluding borrowed funds from gross income also justifies including the part of the purchase price that was financed by debt in the basis of property.

(3) Instead of borrowing $800,000 from the bank, you give the seller of the apartment building a note for $800,000. The note is recourse (that is, you are personally liable on the note), and it is secured by a mortgage on the building. From your point of view, there is no difference between this transaction and the bank loan in (2). In each case, you have incurred an $800,000 recourse debt in order to acquire a building. Just as you are entitled to $800,000 of basis in the case of the bank loan, premised on the assumption you will eventually pay off the loan, you are entitled to $800,000 of basis in the seller financing case, premised on the same assumption.[82]

(4) You again buy an apartment building by investing $200,000 of your own money and incurring an $800,000 debt (via either a bank loan or seller financing), but this time the debt is secured by a *nonrecourse* mortgage on the building. You are not personally liable on the loan; if you default the seller's only remedy is to foreclose on the mortgage. Does it make sense to include the amount of the nonrecourse loan in your basis in the building? The answer is yes, *if* it is reasonable to assume at the outset that you will repay the loan despite its nonrecourse nature. On these facts, it is reasonable to assume eventual repayment, because by paying $800,000 you can become the owner of unencumbered property worth $1 million. In other words, you can be expected to repay the loan when it becomes due, in order to protect your $200,000 equity in the building. But what if the entire $800,000 is due as a single "balloon" payment in, say, five years, and the apartment declines in value to $700,000 by the time the payment is due? In that case, you would not repay. You would rather default on the loan than pay $800,000 in order to become the free-and-clear owner of a building worth only $700,000. The entire

---

82. Although situations (2) and (3) are identical from the *buyer's* standpoint (in terms of both the underlying economics and the tax treatment), the two situations are very different from the *seller's* perspective. In situation (2) the seller immediately receives $1 million cash, while in situation (3) the seller receives $200,000 cash and a note for $800,000. If the seller realizes a gain on the sale, the seller will be required to pay tax on the entire gain in the year of sale in situation (2), but the seller in situation (3) will generally be able to report the gain under the installment method of §453, with gain being taxed only as the seller receives principal payments (i.e., the downpayment and principal payments on the note). For explanation and discussion of the installment method, see section D of Chapter 3.

point of nonrecourse financing, in fact, is that the risk of the decline in value of the property below the principal amount of the nonrecourse mortgage is borne by the creditor, rather than by the debtor. Although it is *possible* that the value of the building will be less than $800,000 by the time the payment becomes due, and that you will accordingly decide not to pay off the loan, it is *probable* that the value of the building will not fall below the principal amount of the loan, and that you will therefore make the payment when due. Based on that probability, nonrecourse acquisition debt is normally included in basis in exactly the same way that recourse debt is included in basis.

(5) Suppose you "purchase" an apartment building worth $1 million, by investing none of your own money, and giving the "seller" a $2.5 million nonrecourse note secured by the building. The entire principal amount is due as a "balloon" payment in five years. Should the nonrecourse loan be included in your basis in this case? Compared with situation (4), the probabilities are now reversed. It is *possible* that you will decide to pay $2.5 million in five years; you would do so, for example, if the building is worth $3 million when the loan becomes due. More likely, however, the building will be worth less than $2.5 million in five years, and you will default rather than pay $2.5 million to become the free-and-clear owner of property worth less than that amount. In this unusual situation, repayment is unlikely — judged from the time that you "purchase" the property — and thus the debt should not be included in your basis. In fact, the best analysis is that you really have not purchased the property at all. All you have is the equivalent of an option — which you may exercise, but probably will not — to buy the building for $2.5 million in five years. Since you do not really own the property, you have no basis in the property. The leading case denying a taxpayer basis in this situation is Estate of Franklin v. Commissioner, 544 F.2d 1045 (9th Cir. 1976). How could such a case ever arise? Why would a lender be so foolish as to make a loan that in all likelihood would never be repaid? The answer is that a bank or other lender of *cash* would not make such a loan. In past decades, however, seller-financed deals like this were not uncommon. If the deal went unchallenged by the IRS, the buyer could claim depreciation deductions based on the inflated purchase price. The buyer did not mind that the nonrecourse debt greatly exceeded the value of the property, because the buyer had no intention of ever paying off the mortgage. The seller did not mind that the excessive debt resulted in excessive gain realized on the sale, because under the installment method of reporting gain (§453) the gain would not be taxed if the buyer never made the principal payments due on the note. The seller knew that he would eventually get the property back (when the buyer defaulted), and in the meantime he pocketed some cash (from a down payment, for example) for helping the buyer claim inflated depreciated deductions.

Such schemes were always subject to IRS attack under the *Franklin* rationale, when the IRS was able to detect the schemes, but the death blow was not delivered until the enactment in 1986 of the passive loss rules of §469.[83]

Situation (5) is the rare case where it is clear from the outset that repayment is unlikely, with the result that alleged acquisition indebtedness should not be included in basis. In all other cases, repayment is assumed, with the result that acquisition indebtedness is included in basis. This is true whether the loan is recourse or nonrecourse, and whether it is third-party cash financing (such as a bank loan) or seller financing.

---

83. See section B.3 of Chapter 8.

Depreciation: the basic concept. The details of tax depreciation are discussed later,[84] but a basic understanding of the concept is needed to appreciate the issue in *Tufts.* Suppose you pay $5,000 (your own money or borrowed money) for a machine you will use in your business. You expect to use the machine for five years, after which it will be worthless. How should the income tax treat your $5,000 investment in the machine? On the one hand, it should not allow you to deduct $5,000 in the year of purchase, because you have acquired a long-lived asset that still has substantial value at the end of that year. On the other hand, it should not require you to wait until you scrap the machine to recover your cost, because it is predictable that the machine will decline in value gradually—through wear and tear—over the years you use it in your business. In theory, you should be allowed to deduct in each of the five years the amount by which the machine declines in value during the year; that decline in value is the cost of using the machine in your business for that year. Because the annual appraisals required by the theoretically correct approach are impractical, §168 of the Code provides cost recovery (depreciation) schedules for various categories of depreciable assets. The applicable schedule will specify the percentage of the cost of the machine that you may deduct in each of the five years. Section 168 can be viewed as an exception to the general rule that unrealized losses are not taken into account for tax purposes.

Suppose the Code provides that the cost of your machine is to be recovered over a five-year period, at the rate of 20 percent per year. You use the machine in your business for two full years, and properly claim a $1,000 depreciation deduction each year. Because the depreciation allowances represent a partial recovery of your basis in the machine, you must decrease the machine's adjusted basis by the amount of depreciation claimed (§1016). At the end of the second year, then, your adjusted basis in the machine is $3,000 ($5,000 original basis minus $2,000 depreciation). What happens if you sell the machine at the beginning of the third year? In the unlikely event that the depreciation deductions accurately reflected the decline in the machine's value, so that you sell the machine for exactly $3,000, there will be no tax consequences: $3,000 amount realized minus $3,000 adjusted basis equals zero gain realized. If the property declined in value more rapidly than the tax depreciation schedule assumed—for example, if you are able to sell the machine for only $2,500—then you will be able to take the additional decline in value into account upon the sale: $2,500 amount realized minus $3,000 adjusted basis equals $500 loss realized. But if the tax depreciation schedule has overstated the actual decline in value—if, for example, you sell the machine for $3,500—then your gain realized on the sale will reflect the amount by which the depreciation deductions were excessive: $3,500 amount realized minus $3,000 adjusted basis equals $500 gain realized. This gain is entirely an artifact of the tax system. In fact, you sold the asset for $1,500 *less* than what you paid for it. You nevertheless must pay tax on $500 gain, because you had been allowed to claim $2,000 of depreciation deductions, and it turns out that the machine really declined in value by only $1,500. As with cancellation of indebtedness income under *Kirby*, $500 taxable gain on the sale of the machine is needed in order to correct a mistaken assumption—in this case, the assumption reflected in the depreciation schedule that the asset declined in value by $2,000 over the two years of use. Unlike

84. See section A of Chapter 6.

debt cancellation income, however, the correction of overly generous depreciation deductions does not depend on judicial doctrine. Instead, the correction happens automatically as a result of the application of the §1016 downward basis adjustment for depreciation claimed and of the §1001 formula for gain realized.

With this background information on acquisition indebtedness and on tax depreciation mechanics, we are ready to consider *Tufts*.

COMMISSIONER v. TUFTS
461 U.S. 300 (1983)

Justice BLACKMUN delivered the opinion of the Court.

Over 35 years ago, in Crane v. Commissioner, 331 U.S. 1 (1947), this Court ruled that a taxpayer, who sold property encumbered by a nonrecourse mortgage (the amount of the mortgage being less than the property's value), must include the unpaid balance of the mortgage in the computation of the amount the taxpayer realized on the sale. The case now before us presents the question whether the same rule applies when the unpaid amount of the nonrecourse mortgage exceeds the fair market value of the property sold.

I

[Tufts was a member of a partnership that financed the entire cost of acquiring an apartment complex with a $1,851,500 loan from the Farm & Home Savings Association (F&H), secured by a mortgage on the complex.] The partnership obtained the loan on a nonrecourse basis: neither the partnership nor its partners assumed any personal liability for repayment of the loan. . . .

The construction of the complex was completed in August 1971. . . . The total of the partners' capital contributions [to the partnership] was $44,212. In each tax year, all partners claimed as income tax deductions their allocable shares of ordinary losses and depreciation. The deductions taken by the partners in 1971 and 1972 totalled $439,972. Due to these contributions and deductions, the partnership's adjusted basis in the property in August 1972 was $1,455,740.

In 1971 and 1972, major employers in the Duncanville area laid off significant numbers of workers. As a result, the partnership's rental income was less than expected, and it was unable to make the payments due on the mortgage. Each partner, on August 28, 1972, sold his partnership interest to an unrelated third party, Fred Bayles. As consideration, Bayles agreed to reimburse each partner's sale expenses up to $250; he also assumed the nonrecourse mortgage.

On the date of transfer, the fair market value of the property did not exceed $1,400,000. Each partner reported the sale on his federal income tax return and indicated that a partnership loss of $55,740 had been sustained.[85] The Commissioner of Internal Revenue, on audit, determined that the sale resulted in a

---

85. The loss was the difference between the adjusted basis, $1,455,740, and the fair market value of the property, $1,400,000. On their individual tax returns, the partners did not claim deductions for their respective shares of this loss. In their petitions to the Tax Court, however, the partners did claim the loss.

partnership capital gain of approximately $400,000. His theory was that the partnership had realized the full amount of the nonrecourse obligation.[86]

Relying on Millar v. Commissioner, 577 F.2d 212, 215 (CA3), *cert. denied*, 439 U.S. 1046 (1978), the United States Tax Court, in an unreviewed decision, upheld the asserted deficiencies. 70 T.C. 756 (1978). The United States Court of Appeals for the Fifth Circuit reversed. 651 F.2d 1058 (1981). That court expressly disagreed with the *Millar* analysis, and, in limiting Crane v. Commissioner, *supra*, to its facts, questioned the theoretical underpinnings of the *Crane* decision. We granted certiorari to resolve the conflict. 456 U.S. 960 (1982).

II

Section 752(d) of the Internal Revenue Code of 1954 specifically provides that liabilities involved in the sale or exchange of a partnership interest are to "be treated in the same manner as liabilities in connection with the sale or exchange of property not associated with partnerships." Section 1001 governs the determination of gains and losses on the disposition of property. Under §1001(a), the gain or loss from a sale or other disposition of property is defined as the difference between "the amount realized" on the disposition and the property's adjusted basis. Subsection (b) of §1001 defines "amount realized": "The amount realized from the sale or other disposition of property shall be the sum of any money received plus the fair market value of the property (other than money) received." At issue is the application of the latter provision to the disposition of property encumbered by a nonrecourse mortgage of an amount in excess of the property's fair market value.

A

In Crane v. Commissioner, *supra,* this Court took the first and controlling step toward the resolution of this issue. Beulah B. Crane was the sole beneficiary under the will of her deceased husband. At his death in January 1932, he owned an apartment building that was then mortgaged for an amount which proved to be equal to its fair market value, as determined for federal estate tax purposes. The widow, of course, was not personally liable on the mortgage. She operated the building for nearly seven years, hoping to turn it into a profitable venture; during that period, she claimed income tax deductions for depreciation, property taxes, interest, and operating expenses, but did not make payments upon the mortgage principal. In computing her basis for the depreciation deductions, she included the full amount of the mortgage debt. In November 1938, with her hopes unfulfilled and the mortgagee threatening foreclosure, Mrs. Crane sold the building. The purchaser took the property subject to the mortgage and paid Crane $3,000; of that amount, $500 went for the expenses of the sale.

Crane reported a gain of $2,500 on the transaction. She reasoned that her basis in the property was zero (despite her earlier depreciation deductions based on

---

86. The Commissioner determined the partnership's gain on the sale by subtracting the adjusted basis, $1,455,740, from the liability assumed by Bayles, $1,851,500. . . .

including the amount of the mortgage) and that the amount she realized from the sale was simply the cash she received. The Commissioner disputed this claim. He asserted that Crane's basis in the property, under [the predecessor of §1014] was the property's fair market value at the time of her husband's death, adjusted for depreciation in the interim, and that the amount realized was the net cash received plus the amount of the outstanding mortgage assumed by the purchaser.

In upholding the Commissioner's interpretation of [the predecessor of §1014], the Court observed that to regard merely the taxpayer's equity in the property as her basis would lead to depreciation deductions less than the actual physical deterioration of the property, and would require the basis to be recomputed with each payment on the mortgage. 331 U.S., at 9-10. The Court rejected Crane's claim that any loss due to depreciation belonged to the mortgagee. The effect of the Court's ruling was that the taxpayer's basis was the value of the property undiminished by the mortgage. Id., at 11.

The Court next proceeded to determine the amount realized under [the predecessor of §1001(b)]. In order to avoid the "absurdity," *see* 331 U.S., at 13, of Crane's realizing only $2,500 on the sale of property worth over a quarter of a million dollars, the Court treated the amount realized as it had treated basis, that is, by including the outstanding value of the mortgage. To do otherwise would have permitted Crane to recognize a tax loss unconnected with any actual economic loss. The Court refused to construe one section of the Revenue Act so as "to frustrate the Act as a whole." Ibid.

Crane, however, insisted that the nonrecourse nature of the mortgage required different treatment. The Court, for two reasons, disagreed. First, excluding the nonrecourse debt from the amount realized would result in the same absurdity and frustration of the Code. Id., at 13-14. Second, the Court concluded that Crane obtained an economic benefit from the purchaser's assumption of the mortgage identical to the benefit conferred by the cancellation of personal debt. Because the value of the property in that case exceeded the amount of the mortgage, it was in Crane's economic interest to treat the mortgage as a personal obligation; only by so doing could she realize upon sale the appreciation in her equity represented by the $2,500 boot. The purchaser's assumption of the liability thus resulted in a taxable economic benefit to her, just as if she had been given, in addition to the boot, a sum of cash sufficient to satisfy the mortgage.

In a footnote, pertinent to the present case, the Court observed:

> Obviously, if the value of the property is less than the amount of the mortgage, a mortgagor who is not personally liable cannot realize a benefit equal to the mortgage. Consequently, a different problem might be encountered where a mortgagor abandoned the property or transferred it subject to the mortgage without receiving boot. That is not this case. Id., at 14, n. 37.

B

This case presents that unresolved issue. We are disinclined to overrule *Crane*, and we conclude that the same rule applies when the unpaid amount of the nonrecourse mortgage exceeds the value of the property transferred, *Crane* ultimately does not rest on its limited theory of economic benefit; instead, we read *Crane* to have approved the Commissioner's decision to treat a nonrecourse mortgage in this context as a true loan. This approval underlies *Crane*'s holdings that the amount of the nonrecourse liability is to be included in calculating both the basis and the amount realized on disposition. That the amount of the loan exceeds the fair market value of the property thus becomes irrelevant.

When a taxpayer receives a loan, he incurs an obligation to repay that loan at some future date. Because of this obligation, the loan proceeds do not qualify as income to the taxpayer. When he fulfills the obligation, the repayment of the loan likewise has no effect on his tax liability.

Another consequence to the taxpayer from this obligation occurs when the taxpayer applies the loan proceeds to the purchase price of property used to secure the loan. Because of the obligation to repay, the taxpayer is entitled to include the amount of the loan in computing his basis in the property; the loan, under §1012, is part of the taxpayer's cost of the property. Although a different approach might have been taken with respect to a nonrecourse mortgage loan, the Commissioner has chosen to accord it the same treatment he gives to a recourse mortgage loan. The Court approved that choice in *Crane*, and the respondents do not challenge it here. The choice and its resultant benefits to the taxpayer are predicated on the assumption that the mortgage will be repaid in full.

When encumbered property is sold or otherwise disposed of and the purchaser assumes the mortgage, the associated extinguishment of the mortgagor's obligation to repay is accounted for in the computation of the amount realized. *See* United States v. Hendler, 303 U.S. 564, 566-567 (1938). Because no difference between recourse and nonrecourse obligations is recognized in calculating basis, *Crane* teaches that the Commissioner may ignore the nonrecourse nature of the obligation in determining the amount realized upon disposition of the encumbered property. He thus may include in the amount realized the amount of the nonrecourse mortgage assumed by the purchaser. The rationale for this treatment is that the original inclusion of the amount of the mortgage in basis rested on the assumption that the mortgagor incurred an obligation to repay. Moreover, this treatment balances the fact that the mortgagor originally received the proceeds of the nonrecourse loan tax-free on the same assumption. Unless the outstanding amount of the mortgage is deemed to be realized, the mortgagor effectively will have received untaxed income at the time the loan was extended and will have received an unwarranted increase in the basis of his property.[87] The Commissioner's interpretation of §1001(b) in this fashion cannot be said to be unreasonable.

C

The Commissioner in fact has applied this rule even when the fair market value of the property falls below the amount of the nonrecourse obligation. Treas. Reg. §1.1001-2(b); Rev. Rul. 76-111, 1976-1 Cum. Bull. 214. Because the theory on

---

87. Although the *Crane* rule has some affinity with the tax benefit rule, the analysis we adopt is different. Our analysis applies even in the situation in which no deductions are taken. It focuses on the obligation to repay and its subsequent extinguishment, not on the taking and recovery of deductions.

which the rule is based applies equally in this situation, we have no reason, after *Crane,* to question this treatment.[88]

Respondents received a mortgage loan with the concomitant obligation to repay by the year 2012. The only difference between that mortgage and one on which the borrower is personally liable is that the mortgagee's remedy is limited to foreclosing on the securing property. This difference does not alter the nature of the obligation; its only effect is to shift from the borrower to the lender any potential loss caused by devaluation of the property. If the fair market value of the property falls below the amount of the outstanding obligation, the mortgagee's ability to protect its interests is impaired, for the mortgagor is free to abandon the property to the mortgagee and be relieved of his obligation.

This, however, does not erase the fact that the mortgagor received the loan proceeds tax-free and included them in his basis on the understanding that he had an obligation to repay the full amount. When the obligation is canceled, the mortgagor is relieved of his responsibility to repay the sum he originally received and thus realizes value to that extent within the meaning of §1001(b). From the mortgagor's point of view, when his obligation is assumed by a third party who purchases the encumbered property, it is as if the mortgagor first had been paid with cash borrowed by the third party from the mortgagee on a nonrecourse basis, and then had used the cash to satisfy his obligation to the mortgagee.

Moreover, this approach avoids the absurdity the Court recognized in *Crane.* Because of the remedy accompanying the mortgage in the nonrecourse situation, the depreciation in the fair market value of the property is relevant economically only to the mortgagee, who by lending on a nonrecourse basis remains at risk. To permit the taxpayer to limit his realization to the fair market value of the property would be to recognize a tax loss for which he has suffered no corresponding economic loss. Such a result would be to construe "one section of the Act . . . so as . . . to defeat the intention of another or to frustrate the Act as a whole." 331 U.S., at 13.

In the specific circumstances of *Crane,* the economic benefit theory did support the Commissioner's treatment of the nonrecourse mortgage as a personal obligation. The footnote in *Crane* acknowledged the limitations of that theory when applied to a different set of facts. *Crane* also stands for the broader proposition, however, that a nonrecourse loan should be treated as a true loan. We therefore hold that a taxpayer must account for the proceeds of obligations he has received tax-free and included in basis. Nothing in either §1001(b) or in the Court's prior decisions requires the Commissioner to permit a taxpayer to treat a sale of encumbered property asymmetrically, by including the proceeds of the nonrecourse obligation in basis but not accounting for the proceeds upon transfer of the encumbered property. . . .

---

88. Professor Wayne G. Barnett, as amicus in the present case, argues that the liability and property portions of the transaction should be accounted for separately. Under his view, there was a transfer of the property for $1.4 million, and there was a cancellation of the $1.85 million obligation for a payment of $1.4 million. The former resulted in a capital loss of $50,000, and the latter in the realization of $450,000 of ordinary income. . . . Although this indeed could be a justifiable mode of analysis, it has not been adopted by the Commissioner. Nor is there anything to indicate that the Code requires the Commissioner to adopt it. We note that Professor Barnett's approach does assume that recourse and nonrecourse debt may be treated identically. . . .

When a taxpayer sells or disposes of property encumbered by a nonrecourse obligation, the Commissioner properly requires him to include among the assets realized the outstanding amount of the obligation. The fair market value of the property is irrelevant to this calculation. We find this interpretation to be consistent with Crane v. Commissioner, 331 U.S. 1 (1947), and to implement the statutory mandate in a reasonable manner. National Muffler Dealers Assn. v. United States, 440 U.S. 472, 476 (1979). . . .

Justice O'CONNOR, concurring.

I concur in the opinion of the Court, accepting the view of the Commissioner. I do not, however, endorse the Commissioner's view. Indeed, were we writing on a slate clean except for the decision in Crane v. Commissioner, 331 U.S. 1 (1947), I would take quite a different approach — that urged upon us by Professor Barnett as amicus.

Crane established that a taxpayer could treat property as entirely his own, in spite of the "coinvestment" provided by his mortgagee in the form of a nonrecourse loan. That is, the full basis of the property, with all its tax consequences, belongs to the mortgagor. That rule alone, though, does not in any way tie nonrecourse debt to the cost of property or to the proceeds upon disposition. I see no reason to treat the purchase, ownership, and eventual disposition of property differently because the taxpayer also takes out a mortgage, an independent transaction. In this case, the taxpayer purchased property, using nonrecourse financing, and sold it after it declined in value to a buyer who assumed the mortgage. There is no economic difference between the events in this case and a case in which the taxpayer buys property with cash; later obtains a nonrecourse loan by pledging the property as security; still later, using cash on hand, buys off the mortgage for the market value of the devalued property; and finally sells the property to a third party for its market value.

The logical way to treat both this case and the hypothesized case is to separate the two aspects of these events and to consider, first, the ownership and sale of the property, and, second, the arrangement and retirement of the loan. Under *Crane,* the fair market value of the property on the date of acquisition — the purchase price — represents the taxpayer's basis in the property, and the fair market value on the date of disposition represents the proceeds on sale. The benefit received by the taxpayer in return for the property is the cancellation of a mortgage that is worth no more than the fair market value of the property, for that is all the mortgagee can expect to collect on the mortgage. His gain or loss on the disposition of the property equals the difference between the proceeds and the cost of acquisition. Thus, the taxation of the transaction in property reflects the economic fate of the property. If the property has declined in value, as was the case here, the taxpayer recognizes a loss on the disposition of the property. The new purchaser then takes as his basis the fair market value as of the date of the sale.

In the separate borrowing transaction, the taxpayer acquires cash from the mortgagee. He need not recognize income at that time, of course, because he also incurs an obligation to repay the money. Later, though, when he is able to satisfy the debt by surrendering property that is worth less than the face amount of the debt, we have a classic situation of cancellation of indebtedness, requiring the taxpayer to recognize income in the amount of the difference between the proceeds of the loan and the amount for which he is able to satisfy his creditor. 26

U.S.C. §61(a)(12). The taxation of the financing transaction then reflects the economic fate of the loan.

The reason that separation of the two aspects of the events in this case is important is, of course, that the Code treats different sorts of income differently. A gain on the sale of the property may qualify for capital gains treatment, while the cancellation of indebtedness is ordinary income, but income that the taxpayer may be able to defer [under certain circumstances]. Sections 108, 1017. Not only does Professor Barnett's theory permit us to accord appropriate treatment to each of the two types of income or loss present in these sorts of transactions, it also restores continuity to the system by making the taxpayer-seller's proceeds on the disposition of property equal to the purchaser's basis in the property. Further, and most important, it allows us to tax the events in this case in the same way that we tax the economically identical hypothesized transaction.

Persuaded though I am by the logical coherence and internal consistency of this approach, I agree with the Court's decision not to adopt it judicially. We do not write on a slate marked only by *Crane*. . . . In the light of the numerous cases in the lower courts including the amount of the unrepaid proceeds of the mortgage in the proceeds on sale or disposition, it is difficult to conclude that the Commissioner's interpretation of the statute exceeds the bounds of his discretion. As the Court's opinion demonstrates, his interpretation is defensible. . . . As long as his view is a reasonable reading of §1001(b), we should defer to the regulations promulgated by the agency charged with interpretation of the statute.

Notes and Questions

1. *Economic benefit.* From one perspective, the taxpayer's argument in *Tufts* is quite reasonable. The argument begins by noting that the definition of amount realized in §1001(b) — "the sum of the money received plus the fair market value of property (other than money) received" — seems to equate amount realized with economic benefit. The argument next considers the amount of economic benefit one would receive if one owned property encumbered by a nonrecourse loan in excess of the value of the property, and the encumbrance was then removed. Suppose you owned property with a fair market value of $1.4 million, subject to a nonrecourse loan of $1.8 million, and Santa Claus offered to use $1.8 million cash to pay off the loan as your Christmas present. (Not a likely scenario, but humor us.) How would you respond to Santa's generous offer? You might point out to Santa that he has $1.8 million cash he wants to use for your benefit, but that his plan would give you a benefit of only $1.4 million. If you own property subject to a nonrecourse mortgage, you always have the option of simply turning the property over to the mortgage holder instead of paying off the loan. Thus, owning property worth $1.4 million and subject to a nonrecourse debt of $1.8 million does *not* decrease your net worth by $400,000; rather, it has no effect — positive or negative — on your net worth. When Santa pays off the mortgage, your net worth increases by $1.4 million. Before Santa's beneficence the property had zero effect on your net worth, but now you have clear title to property worth $1.4 million. Your economic benefit from being relieved of the nonrecourse mortgage,

then, is only $1.4 million.[89] To generalize the point, if a person owns property subject to a nonrecourse mortgage in excess of the value of the property, the person's economic benefit from relief from the nonrecourse obligation cannot exceed the value of the property. If the §1001(b) definition of amount realized is limited to economic benefit, then the amount realized in *Tufts* must be limited to the value of the property (about $1.4 million). The amount by which the mortgage exceeds the value of the property (about $400,000) should *not* be included in amount realized.

2. *Correcting a mistaken assumption.* The Supreme Court's response to the taxpayer's argument is that the taxpayer is right that the economic benefit is only $1.4 million, but that the taxpayer is wrong that the definition of amount realized is limited to economic benefit. The full amount of the loan — $1.8 million — must be included in amount realized not because the debt relief is worth $1.8 million to the taxpayer, but in order to correct a mistaken assumption. The taxpayer was allowed to include the full $1.8 million loan in basis (and to exclude it from income) on the assumption that the taxpayer would eventually repay the loan. Upon the taxpayer's disposition of the property, it becomes clear that the repayment assumption was mistaken. The full $1.8 million must be included in amount realized not because that is the amount of the taxpayer's economic benefit, but to correct the mistaken assumption that produced the taxpayer's original basis of $1.8 million. In short, the analysis is fundamentally the same as the *Kirby* analysis. In each case, the taxpayer received favorable tax treatment based on the assumption the taxpayer would repay a loan, and in each case a correcting tax adjustment is needed when it becomes clear the assumption was mistaken. The only difference is that in *Kirby* the favorable tax treatment was the exclusion of borrowed funds from income and the correction is to include debt cancellation in gross income, whereas in *Tufts* the favorable tax treatment was the inclusion of debt in basis and the correction is to include debt relief in amount realized.

3. *It must come out right in the end.* There is another way of explaining why the Supreme Court was right to reject the taxpayer's argument in *Tufts*. It is a basic principle of income taxation that in the end — when the dust has settled — the tax treatment of a transaction should be consistent with the economics of the transaction (apart from possible differences in timing). Taxes aside, the partnership had only a modest economic loss from its purchase and sale of the apartment building — the partnership invested some $44,000 when it arranged for the construction of the apartments and it received no cash when it sold the building. Thus, its economic loss was limited to its unrecovered $44,000 investment. The tax system, however, allowed the partnership to claim approximately $440,000 of depreciation deductions over the time it owned the building. In other words, the tax system treated the partnership as having suffered a $440,000 loss during the time it owned the building, despite the fact that the partnership really experienced a loss of only one-tenth of that amount.[90] In order for the final

89. What happens to the other $400,000 of Santa's $1.8 million? It benefits the mortgage holder, who receives $1.8 million instead of the $1.4 million he would have received if he had foreclosed on the mortgage.

90. As it happened, the property did decline in value by approximately the amount of the depreciation deductions allowed, but the economic burden of that loss did not fall on the partnership. Because of the nonrecourse nature of the debt, the economic burden fell on the holder of the mortgage.

tax result to match the economic result, the $440,000 loss previously allowed must be largely offset by a $396,000 artificial gain realized upon the disposition of the building. The Supreme Court's analysis produces the appropriate amount of offsetting gain. By contrast, the taxpayer's analysis (which the Fifth Circuit had accepted) would leave the taxpayer with net tax deductions of $440,000 ($440,000 depreciation deductions previously claimed, with no offsetting gain on disposition), despite the fact that the taxpayer suffered an economic loss of only $44,000.

4. *The tax benefit rule.* In footnote 87 (footnote 16 in the original published opinion), Justice Blackmun states that the result in *Tufts* is *not* based on the inclusionary tax benefit rule. The tax benefit rule is considered in detail in the next section, but the basic idea is simple enough. If a taxpayer claims a deduction in one year, and in a later year an event occurs that is fundamentally inconsistent with an assumption on which the deduction was based, then the taxpayer must include the amount of the mistaken deduction (mistaken, that is, with the benefit of hindsight) in income in the later year. It is another example of the approach illustrated by *Kirby* and by *Tufts* — mistaken assumptions are corrected not by amending the return for the original year, but by an offsetting entry in the later year. As the footnote suggests, the Supreme Court might have decided *Tufts* under the tax benefit doctrine. The analysis would have been that the taxpayer had been allowed depreciation deductions based on the assumption that the taxpayer would bear the economic burden of the building's decline in value, and that an offsetting income inclusion is needed when it becomes clear that the assumption was wrong.

5. Tufts *versus the tax benefit rule.* Why do you suppose Justice Blackmun insisted that his analysis was different from the tax benefit rule? Consider this hypothetical. Taxpayer buys undeveloped land for $1.8 million, financing the entire purchase price with a nonrecourse note to the seller. Land is not depreciable for tax purposes. Several years later, the principal amount of the note is still $1.8 million and the taxpayer's basis is still $1.8 million, but the fair market value of the property has declined to $1.4 million. At that point, the taxpayer "walks away" from the property, giving the seller the deed in lieu of foreclosure. (1) Consistent with economic reality, how much gain or loss should the taxpayer realize on the disposition of the property? (2) How much gain or loss would the taxpayer realize if the Supreme Court had accepted the taxpayer's analysis in *Tufts*? (3) How much gain or loss does the taxpayer realize under the Supreme Court's actual analysis in *Tufts*? (4) Would it be possible to reach the economically accurate result via the tax benefit rule, rather than via the *Tufts* analysis?

6. *A surprise.* Although accelerated cost recovery system (ACRS) allowances under §168 are frequently faster than the actual rate of depreciation, on the facts of *Tufts* the tax allowances closely approximated economic depreciation. Over the years the partnership owned the apartment building, both the tax allowances and actual economic depreciation totaled about $400,000. Is there any evidence in the opinion that the parties were surprised that the property actually declined as rapidly as the tax system assumed it would?

7. *Is footnote 37 really most sincerely dead?* The Court quotes footnote 37 of *Crane*, perhaps the most famous footnote in tax jurisprudence, at the end of

section II.A of the opinion. The Court thus decides that the situation described in the footnote — the amount of the nonrecourse debt exceeding the value of the property — does not justify excluding any part of the loan release from the amount realized. After *Tufts*, is there any situation in which the full amount of nonrecourse debt relief would not be included in the amount realized?

REV. RUL. 90-16

1990-1 C.B. 12

ISSUE

A taxpayer transfers to a creditor a residential subdivision that has a fair market value in excess of the taxpayer's basis in satisfaction of a debt for which the taxpayer was personally liable. Is the transfer a sale or disposition resulting in the realization and recognition of gain by the taxpayer under sections 1001(c) and 61(a)(3) of the Internal Revenue Code?

FACTS

X was the owner and developer of a residential subdivision. To finance the development of the subdivision, *X* obtained a loan from an unrelated bank. *X* was unconditionally liable for repayment of the debt. The debt was secured by a mortgage on the subdivision.

X became insolvent (within the meaning of section 108(d)(3) of the Code) and defaulted on the debt. *X* negotiated an agreement with the bank whereby the subdivision was transferred to the bank and the bank released *X* from all liability for the amounts due on the debt. When the subdivision was transferred pursuant to the agreement, its fair market value was 10,000x dollars, X's adjusted basis in the subdivision was 8,000x dollars, and the amount due on the debt was 12,000x dollars, which did not represent any accrued but unpaid interest. After the transaction *X* was still insolvent.

LAW AND ANALYSIS

Sections 61(a)(3) and 61(a)(12) of the Code provide that, except as otherwise provided, gross income means all income from whatever source derived, including (but not limited to) gains from dealings in property and income from discharge of indebtedness.

Section 108(a)(1)(B) of the Code provides that gross income does not include any amount that would otherwise be includible in gross income by reason of discharge (in whole or in part) of indebtedness of the taxpayer if the discharge occurs when the taxpayer is insolvent. Section 108(a)(3) provides that, in the case of a discharge to which section 108(a)(1)(B) applies, the amount excluded under section 108(a)(1)(B) shall not exceed the amount by which the taxpayer is insolvent (as defined in section 108(d)(3)). . . .

Section 1.1001-2(a)(1) of the regulations provides that, except as provided in section 1.1001-2(a)(2) and (3), the amount realized from a sale or other disposition of property includes the amount of liabilities from which the transferor is discharged as a result of the sale or disposition. Section 1.1001-2(a)(2) provides that the amount realized on a sale or other disposition of property that secures a *recourse* liability [emphasis added by editors] does not include amounts that are (or would be if realized and recognized) income from the discharge of indebtedness under section 61(a)(12). Example (8) under section 1.1001-2(c) illustrates these rules as follows:

> Example (8). In 1980, *F* transfers to a creditor an asset with a fair market value of $6,000 and the creditor discharges $7,500 of indebtedness for which *F* is personally liable. The amount realized on the disposition of the asset is its fair market value ($6,000). In addition, *F* has income from the discharge of indebtedness of $1,500 ($7,500 − $6,000).

In the present situation, *X* transferred the subdivision to the bank in satisfaction of the 12,000x dollar debt. To the extent of the fair market value of the property transferred to the creditor, the transfer of the subdivision is treated as a sale or disposition upon which gain is recognized under section 1001(c) of the Code. To the extent the fair market value of the subdivision, 10,000x dollars, exceeds its adjusted basis, 8,000x dollars, *X* realizes and recognizes gain on the transfer. *X* thus recognizes 2,000x dollars of gain.

To the extent the amount of debt, 12,000x dollars, exceeds the fair market value of the subdivision, 10,000x dollars, *X* realizes income from the discharge of indebtedness. However, under section 108(a)(1)(B) of the Code, the full amount of *X's* discharge of indebtedness income is excluded from gross income because that amount does not exceed the amount by which *X* was insolvent.

If the subdivision had been transferred to the bank as a result of a foreclosure proceeding in which the outstanding balance of the debt was discharged (rather than having been transferred pursuant to the settlement agreement), the result would be the same. . . .

Notes and Questions

1. *If the note is nonrecourse.* Under *Tufts*, what is the result if the facts are the same as in Rev. Rul. 90-16, except the note is nonrecourse?
2. *Bifurcation.* Does the analysis in Rev. Rul. 90-16 seem familiar? It is exactly the bifurcation analysis favored by Justice O'Connor in her concurrence in *Tufts.* Consider the facts of *Tufts*, with the numbers slightly rounded. A taxpayer acquires property by incurring a $1.8 million nonrecourse debt. Over several years depreciation deductions reduce the taxpayer's adjusted basis to $1.4 million and the value of the property declines to $1.4 million, while the amount of the loan remains $1.8 million. The taxpayer then abandons the property. Under *Tufts*, the taxpayer simply realizes a gain of $400,000 (which will probably be eligible for the favorable tax rate applicable to long-term capital gains). Under the O'Connor/Barnett bifurcation analysis, the taxpayer would be treated as having (1) persuaded the

lender to accept $1.4 million cash in cancellation of the $1.8 million loan,[91] and (2) sold the property — no longer subject to the mortgage — for its $1.4 million fair market value. The tax treatment of step (1) would be $400,000 of *Kirby* income, and the tax treatment of step (2) would be zero gain or loss on the sale of the property. Try varying the hypothetical by changing the fair market value of the property at the time the taxpayer disposes of it. Under *Tufts* this makes no difference; the fair market value of the property does not figure into the *Tufts* analysis. Under bifurcation, by contrast, the fair market value is crucial in determining both the amount of *Kirby* income and the amount of gain or loss from the property transaction. However, the *net* amount of income under bifurcation steps (1) and (2) will remain unchanged regardless of the property's value. If, for example, the value is $1.5 million, the taxpayer will have $300,000 of *Kirby* income and $100,000 of property gain;[92] if the value is $1.3 million, the taxpayer will have $500,000 of *Kirby* income and a $100,000 *loss* on the property transaction.[93]

3. *Evaluating the two approaches.* Either the *Tufts* approach or bifurcation will produce the economically correct net amount of income (or loss). In that sense, both approaches are correct, and both are distinguishable from the taxpayer's approach — rejected by the Supreme Court in *Tufts* — which would understate the taxpayer's economic gain (or overstate the taxpayer's loss). Given that both *Tufts* and bifurcation produce a plausible bottom line, is there any reason to find one more theoretically attractive than the other? An argument in favor of bifurcation is that it avoids the legal fiction inherent in Justice Blackmun's analysis — that the taxpayer is magically able to sell the property for much more than its fair market value. On the other hand, tax results under bifurcation depend on the fair market value of the property at the time of the disposition, despite the fact that once the taxpayer decides to dispose of the property, it makes no non-tax difference to him whether it is worth $1.3 million, $1.4 million, or $1.5 million.

4. *Inconsistent treatment of recourse and nonrecourse debt.* Is it a point in favor of the O'Connor/Barnett approach that it would achieve consistency with the bifurcation analysis called for by Rev. Rul. 90-16 in the case of a recourse loan? Recall that recourse and nonrecourse acquisition debt is treated identically for basis purposes at the time the debt is incurred. Is there any good reason to treat the two types of debt differently at the disposition stage?

5. *Practical differences.* Do taxpayers fare better under the majority's analysis in *Tufts* than they would under bifurcation? It all depends. It is better to have $400,000 of capital gain (under *Tufts*) than $400,000 of cancellation of indebtedness income (under bifurcation), if the capital gain is taxed at a special low rate and the cancellation of indebtedness income does not qualify for exclusion under §108 (because the taxpayer is not insolvent and none of the other §108 exceptions applies). On the other hand, it is

---

91. The lender should be willing to agree to this, since the lender would acquire property worth only $1.4 million if it foreclosed on the mortgage. Is it a weakness of the bifurcation analysis, however, that it assumes the taxpayer happened to have $1.4 million cash on hand?

92. The premise here is that the lender would accept $1.5 million cash — the value of the property — in cancellation of the debt, and that the taxpayer would then sell the land for its $1.5 million value.

93. The lender would accept $1.3 million cash in cancellation of the debt, and the taxpayer would then sell the land for $1.3 million.

better to have $400,000 of debt cancellation income than $400,000 of capital gain, if the debt cancellation income qualifies for the §108(a)(1)(B) insolvency exception. Note that situations like the one in Rev. Rul. 90-16, where there is favorable discharge of debt even though the loan was *with* recourse, are much more likely to arise if the debtor is insolvent, and hence eligible for an exclusion under §108(a).

6. *Nonrecourse borrowing against unrealized appreciation.* You own a tract of undeveloped land for which you paid $100,000 some years ago. It is now worth about $1 million. What should your tax consequences be if you borrow $700,000 from a bank, secured by a $700,000 nonrecourse mortgage on the land? Notice that you have locked-in $600,000 gain on the land. Imagine the worst case scenario: The land becomes worthless tomorrow. You would then give the bank the deed in lieu of foreclosure, and you would have succeeded in permanently extracting $700,000 from an asset for which you had paid only $100,000. Given this lock-in of gain, it would be reasonable for the tax system to treat nonrecourse borrowing against unrealized appreciation as an event triggering realization of gain. Nothing in the language of the Code, however, suggests that this constitutes a realization event. The crucial language in §1001 — "sale or other disposition of property" — does not seem to include such borrowing within its scope, and the courts have agreed.[94] *See, e.g.,* Woodsam Assocs. v. Commissioner, 198 F.2d 357 (2d Cir. 1952).

   Continuing with the hypothetical in the previous paragraph, suppose that a few years later the property has further appreciated to $1.6 million, and you have made no principal payments on the $700,000 mortgage. You then sell the property subject to the mortgage, receiving $900,000 cash. How much gain should you realize? Without any knowledge of the rules governing amount realized and basis, you could reach the correct result simply by looking at the cash flow. You invested $100,000 in the property, you have managed to get $1.6 million cash out of the property ($700,000 when you took out the loan, and $900,000 on the sale), and you have not previously been taxed on any gain with respect to the property. If tax results are to be consistent with economic results, you must realize a gain of $1.5 million. The technical way to reach that same result is: (1) amount realized includes both the $900,000 cash and the $700,000 debt relief (from the buyer taking the property subject to the mortgage), and (2) your basis is only the $100,000 cash of your original investment.[95]

7. *Burned out tax shelters and negative basis.* Is it possible for a taxpayer to have a negative basis in an asset? Simply as a matter of arithmetic, it could certainly be done. A basis of − $5, for example, would mean that a taxpayer would realize a gain of $7 if the taxpayer sold the asset for $2,[96] or a gain of $5 if the taxpayer sold the asset for $0. Despite the fact that this works arithmetically, the rule is that zero is the lowest possible basis number. This is

---

94. *But see* §72(e)(4)(A), providing that a loan under an annuity contract shall be taxed as a distribution under the contract.

95. The $700,000 mortgage did not increase your basis in the property because it was not a cost of acquiring the property; only *acquisition debt* is included in basis. Of course, if the proceeds of the $700,000 loan were used to acquire other property, then the loan proceeds would be included in the basis of that other property.

96. $2 − (−$5) =$7.

consistent with the commonsense notion that the cost of an asset cannot be less than zero, and it also avoids the liquidity problems that would arise if the amount of gain could exceed a taxpayer's amount realized.

But consider this hypothetical. A taxpayer bought a building in the early 1980s, financing the entire purchase price with a $1.8 million nonrecourse loan. The taxpayer bought the building as a tax shelter investment. In other words, he hoped that the building would produce artificial tax losses—attributable to the generosity of the §168 cost recovery schedule—that he could use to shelter other income from tax. Under the version of §168 applicable to buildings placed in service in the early 1980s, the taxpayer proceeded to deduct the entire $1.8 million over the next 15 years, reducing his adjusted basis to zero. As the taxpayer had hoped, the §168 deductions proved to be artificial. Even as its basis had been reduced to zero, the building's fair market value remained $1.8 million. The outstanding principal amount of the loan also remained $1.8 million. With no more unrecovered basis, and no more §168 deductions, the building is now a "burned out" tax shelter. The taxpayer is no longer having any fun as the owner of the building, and he would like to dispose of it. He could simply give the deed to the lender in lieu of foreclosure, or he could probably find someone who would be willing to take the building subject to the mortgage. But what will be the tax consequences to him if he disposes of the building? His amount realized on the disposition will be $1.8 million of debt relief,[97] and his adjusted basis is zero. Thus, his gain realized will be $1.8 million.

The tax logic supporting this result is impeccable (under both the *Tufts* analysis and the tax benefit rule). Moreover, taking the long view, the taxpayer has received favorable tax treatment for this investment. He has enjoyed tax deferral between the time he claimed the artificial depreciation deductions and the time he realizes the offsetting gain on the disposition, and the offsetting gain will probably be taxed at favorable capital gains rates despite the earlier deductions having been taken against ordinary income. In spite of all this, the tax result of the disposition is the functional equivalent of negative basis. Technically the taxpayer has a $1.8 million amount realized and a zero basis, but it would be more realistic to say the taxpayer has a zero amount realized (the disposition leaves the taxpayer with neither cash nor any property convertible to cash) and a negative basis of $1.8 million. This phenomenon is sometimes referred to as "phantom gain," for obvious reasons. It is the price the taxpayer must finally pay for the phantom depreciation deductions he has previously enjoyed. The only way to avoid taxation of phantom gain is not to dispose of the property.[98] If the taxpayer continues to own the property until he

97. *Tufts* holds that relief from nonrecourse debt must be included in amount realized even when the debt exceeds the fair market value of the property. *A fortiori*, relief from nonrecourse debt must be included in amount realized when the debt does not exceed the value of the property.
98. A disposition of the property by gift will not solve the problem, despite the usual rule that a gift transfers to the donee the potential tax liability on unrealized appreciation (see part C.1 of Chapter 10). According to the regulations under §1001, a taxpayer realizes gain when he makes a gift of property subject to a nonrecourse mortgage in excess of basis. *See* Reg. §1.1001-2(a)(4)(iii) and Reg. §1.1001-2(c), Ex. (6).

dies, §1014 will then apply to increase its basis to its fair market value as of the taxpayer's death. If the property is still worth $1.8 million when the taxpayer dies, his estate or heir can then give the lender the deed in lieu of foreclosure, without realizing any gain.[99]

d.   The Inclusionary Tax Benefit Rule

HILLSBORO NATIONAL BANK v. COMMISSIONER
460 U.S. 370 (1983)

Justice O'CONNOR delivered the opinion of the Court.

These consolidated cases present the question of the applicability of the tax benefit rule to two corporate tax situations. . . . [The two situations both involve highly technical issues, consideration of which in a basic income tax course would confuse more than it would enlighten. The opinion is excerpted here only for its background discussion of tax benefit rule fundamentals. — EDS.] We conclude that . . . the tax benefit rule ordinarily applies to require the inclusion of income when events occur that are fundamentally inconsistent with an earlier deduction. . . .

The Government in each case relies solely on the tax benefit rule — a judicially developed principle that allays some of the inflexibilities of the annual accounting system. An annual accounting system is a practical necessity if the federal income tax is to produce revenue ascertainable and payable at regular intervals. Burnet v. Sanford & Brooks Co., 282 U.S. 359, 365 (1931). Nevertheless, strict adherence to an annual accounting system would create transactional inequities. Often an apparently completed transaction will reopen unexpectedly in a subsequent tax year, rendering the initial reporting improper. For instance, if a taxpayer held a note that became apparently uncollectible early in the taxable year, but the debtor made an unexpected financial recovery before the close of the year and paid the debt, the transaction would have no tax consequences for the taxpayer, for the repayment of the principal would be recovery of capital. If, however, the debtor's financial recovery and the resulting repayment took place after the close of the taxable year, the taxpayer would have a deduction for the apparently bad debt in the first year under §166(a) of the Code. Without the tax benefit rule, the repayment in the second year, representing a return of capital, would not be taxable. The second transaction, then, although economically identical to the first, could, because of the differences in accounting, yield drastically different tax consequences. The Government, by allowing a deduction that it could not have known to be improper at the time, would be foreclosed[100] from recouping any of the tax saved because of the improper deduction.[101] Recognizing and seeking to avoid the possible distortions

---

99. $1.8 million amount realized minus $1.8 million basis (under §1014) equals zero gain.

100. A rule analogous to the tax benefit rule protects the taxpayer who is required to report income received in one year under claim of right that he later ends up repaying. Under that rule, he is allowed a deduction in the subsequent year. *See generally* 26 U.S.C. §1341.

101. When the event proving the deduction improper occurs after the close of the taxable year, even if the statute of limitations has not run, the Commissioner's proper remedy is to invoke the tax benefit rule and require inclusion in the later year rather than to reopen the earlier year.

of income,[102] the courts have long required the taxpayer to recognize the repayment in the second year as income.[103]

Much of Justice Blackmun's dissent takes issue with this well-settled rule. The inclusion of the income in the year of the deductions by amending the returns for that year is not before us in these cases, for none of the parties has suggested such a result, no doubt because the rule is so settled. It is not at all clear what would happen on the remand that Justice Blackmun desires. Neither taxpayer has ever sought to file an amended return. The statute of limitations has now run on the years to which the dissent would attribute the income, §6501(a), and we have no indication in the record that the Government has held those years open for any other reason.

Even if the question were before us, we could not accept the view of Justice Blackmun's dissent. It is, of course, true that the tax benefit rule is not a precise way of dealing with the transactional inequities that occur as a result of the annual accounting system. Justice Blackmun's approach, however, does not eliminate the problem; it only multiplies the number of rules. If the statute of limitations has run on the earlier year, the dissent recognizes that the rule that we now apply must apply. Thus, under the proposed scheme, the only difference is that, if the inconsistent event fortuitously occurs between the end of the year of the deduction and the running of the statute of limitations, the Commissioner must reopen the earlier year or permit an amended return even though it is settled that the acceptance of such a return after the date for filing a return is not covered by statute but within the discretion of the Commissioner. In any other situation, the income must be recognized in the later year. Surely a single rule covering all situations would be preferable to several rules that do not alleviate any of the disadvantages of the single rule.

A second flaw in Justice Blackmun's approach lies in his assertion that the practice he proposes is like any correction made after audit. Changes on audit reflect the proper tax treatment of items under the facts as they were known at the end of the taxable year. The tax benefit rule is addressed to a different problem — that of events that occur after the close of the taxable year.

In any event, whatever the merits of amending the return of the year of the improper deduction might originally have been, we think it too late in the day to change the rule. Neither the judicial origins of the rule nor the subsequent codification permits the approach suggested by Justice Blackmun. . . .

---

102. As the rule developed, a number of theories supported taxation in the later year. . . . All these views reflected that the initial accounting for the item must be corrected to present a true picture of income. While annual accounting precludes reopening the earlier year, it does not prevent a less precise correction — far superior to none — in the current year, analogous to the practice of financial accountants. This concern with more accurate measurement of income underlies the tax benefit rule and always has.

103. Even this rule did not create complete transactional equivalence. In the second version of the transaction discussed in the text, the taxpayer might have realized no benefit from the deduction, if, for instance, he had no taxable income for that year. Application of the tax benefit rule as originally developed would require the taxpayer to recognize income on the repayment, so that the net result of the collection of the principal amount of the debt would be recognition of income. Similarly, the tax rates might change between the two years, so that a deduction and an inclusion, though equal in amount, would not produce exactly offsetting tax consequences. Congress enacted §111 to deal with part of this problem. Although a change in the rates may still lead to differences in taxes due, §111 provides that the taxpayer can exclude from income the amount that did not give rise to some tax benefit. This exclusionary rule and the inclusionary rule described in the text are generally known together as the tax benefit rule. It is the inclusionary aspect of the rule with which we are currently concerned.

The taxpayers and the Government in these cases propose different formulations of the tax benefit rule. The taxpayers contend that the rule requires the inclusion of amounts recovered in later years, and they do not view the events in these cases as "recoveries." The Government, on the other hand, urges that the tax benefit rule requires the inclusion of amounts previously deducted if later events are inconsistent with the deductions; it insists that no "recovery" is necessary to the application of the rule. Further, it asserts that the events in these cases are inconsistent with the deductions taken by the taxpayers. We are not in complete agreement with either view.

An examination of the purpose and accepted applications of the tax benefit rule reveals that a "recovery" will not always be necessary to invoke the tax benefit rule. The purpose of the rule is not simply to tax "recoveries." On the contrary, it is to approximate the results produced by a tax system based on transactional rather than annual accounting. It has long been accepted that a taxpayer using accrual accounting who accrues and deducts an expense in a tax year before it becomes payable and who for some reason eventually does not have to pay the liability must then take into income the amount of the expense earlier deducted. The bookkeeping entry canceling the liability, though it increases the balance sheet net worth of the taxpayer, does not fit within any ordinary definition of "recovery." Thus, the taxpayers' formulation of the rule neither serves the purposes of the rule nor accurately reflects the cases that establish the rule. . . .

The basic purpose of the tax benefit rule is to achieve rough transactional parity in tax, and to protect the Government and the taxpayer from the adverse effects of reporting a transaction on the basis of assumptions that an event in a subsequent year proves to have been erroneous. Such an event, unforeseen at the time of an earlier deduction, may in many cases require the application of the tax benefit rule. We do not, however, agree that this consequence invariably follows. Not every unforeseen event will require the taxpayer to report income in the amount of his earlier deduction. On the contrary, the tax benefit rule will "cancel out" an earlier deduction only when a careful examination shows that the later event is indeed fundamentally inconsistent with the premise on which the deduction was initially based.[104] That is, if that event had occurred within the same taxable year, it would have foreclosed the deduction. In some cases, a subsequent recovery by the taxpayer will be the only event that would be fundamentally inconsistent with the provision granting the deduction. In such a case, only actual recovery by the taxpayer would justify application of the tax benefit rule. For example, if a calendar-year taxpayer made a rental payment on December 15 for a 30-day lease deductible in the current year under §162(a)(3), see Treas. Reg. §1.461-1(a)(1); e.g., Zaninovich v. Commissioner, 616 F.2d 429 (CA9 1980), the tax benefit rule would not require the recognition of income if the leased premises were destroyed by fire on January 10. The resulting inability of the taxpayer to occupy the building would be an event not fundamentally inconsistent with his prior deduction as an ordinary and necessary business expense under §162(a). The loss is attributable to the business and therefore is consistent with the deduction of the rental payment as an ordinary and necessary business expense. On the other hand, had the premises

---

104. Justice Stevens accuses us of creating confusion at this point in the analysis by requiring the courts to distinguish "inconsistent events" from "fundamentally inconsistent events." That line is not the line we draw; rather, we draw the line between merely unexpected events and inconsistent events. . . .

not burned and, in January, the taxpayer decided to use them to house his family rather than to continue the operation of his business, he would have converted the leasehold to personal use. This would be an event fundamentally inconsistent with the business use on which the deduction was based. In the case of the fire, only if the lessor — by virtue of some provision in the lease — had refunded the rental payment would the taxpayer be required under the tax benefit rule to recognize income on the subsequent destruction of the building. In other words, the subsequent recovery of the previously deducted rental payment would be the only event inconsistent with the provision allowing the deduction. It therefore is evident that the tax benefit rule must be applied on a case-by-case basis. A court must consider the facts and circumstances of each case in the light of the purpose and function of the provisions granting the deductions. . . .

[Opinions by Justices Brennan (concurring and dissenting), Stevens (dissenting), and Blackmun (dissenting) are omitted.]

Notes and Questions

1. *The exclusionary tax benefit rule.* You may find it helpful to review the material in section A.2 of this chapter on §111 and the exclusionary tax benefit rule (referred to in note 103 — note 4 in the original numbering — of the *Hillsboro* opinion).

2. *State income tax refunds.* Although a fertile mind can imagine numerous "fundamentally inconsistent events" calling for the application of the inclusionary tax benefit rule, by far the most common application of the rule is to state income tax refunds (to taxpayers who itemized deductions, rather than claiming the standard deduction). For more on state income tax refunds, see the material in section A.2 of this chapter on the exclusionary tax benefit rule.

3. *Kirby and the tax benefit rule.* What is the difference between the *Kirby* doctrine (cancellation of indebtedness income) and the inclusionary tax benefit rule? In both cases, the taxpayer must include an amount in income in the current year to offset favorable tax treatment in a prior year, because it has become clear that the earlier treatment was based on a mistaken assumption. The only difference is that the favorable tax treatment was an exclusion in one case (*Kirby*) and a deduction in the other (tax benefit rule). This is not a fundamental difference, since the only distinction between exclusions and deductions is that exclusions are based on the *source* of funds, while deductions are based on the *use* of funds. It would be possible to state the tax benefit rule in terms sufficiently broad to encompass the *Kirby* result. In other words, cancellation of indebtedness income could be described as simply a special case of the inclusionary tax benefit rule. *Tufts* can also be viewed as a special case of the tax benefit rule, although the later-year correction in *Tufts* takes the form of an inclusion in amount realized, rather than a direct inclusion in gross income.

4. *Tax benefit rule or amended return?* Under the *Hillsboro* opinion, there is a crucial distinction between (1) a deduction that was incorrect based on the facts available (known or knowable) as of the end of the year for which the deduction was claimed, and (2) a deduction that was correct based on the facts available as of the end of the deduction year, but that is

undermined by subsequent developments. The only proper response to the first type of mistaken deduction is to amend the return for the original year; if the original year is closed by the statute of limitations, then there is nothing to be done. The proper response to the second type of "mistaken" deduction — "mistaken" only with the benefit of hindsight — is to require a tax benefit rule inclusion in a later year. Although it is simple enough to state the distinction between the two situations, there are borderline cases where it is not clear which type of mistaken deduction is at issue. Overwithholding of state income tax might seem to be an example of the first type of mistake (to which the tax benefit rule does not apply), because it should be possible to determine whether the withholding was excessive by the end of the year in which the withholding occurred. Nevertheless, the refund of excessive state income tax withholding (or estimated tax payments) is routinely treated as a situation calling for the application of the tax benefit rule. Suppose you are nearing the end of the year, and you are virtually certain that your marginal tax rate next year will be lower than your marginal tax rate this year. Can you accomplish a self-help shifting of income from this year's high bracket to next year's lower bracket, by the use of excessive state income tax estimated tax payments, the state income tax deduction, and the inclusionary tax benefit rule? Can (and should) the IRS foil this plan?

5. *Justice Blackmun's dissent.* What is at stake, as a practical matter, in the O'Connor-Blackmun debate about amending the return for the year of the deduction versus making an offsetting income entry in a later year? Suppose a taxpayer properly claims a $10,000 bad debt deduction (under §166) in 2009, when the taxpayer's marginal tax rate is 30 percent, and that the debt is miraculously paid in full in 2012, when the taxpayer's marginal tax rate is only 15 percent (and the statute of limitations on 2009 has not yet expired). Under Justice Blackmun's approach, the appropriate correction would be to amend the 2009 return to eliminate the deduction. This amendment would cost the taxpayer $3,000 in 2009 tax liability, plus (presumably) three year's worth of interest on the $3,000. Under Justice O'Connor's approach, the inclusion of $10,000 in 2012 costs the taxpayer only $1,500 in tax liability, and there is no interest charge. On these facts, the taxpayer fares better under the majority's approach, with respect to both the marginal tax rate question and the interest question. If the marginal tax rates were reversed — 15 percent in 2009 and 30 percent in 2012 — the majority approach would be unfavorable to the taxpayer on the rate issue, but still favorable on the interest issue. Which Justice has the better of the argument on the relative merits of the two approaches to mistake correction? Is Justice Blackmun's approach fairer because it corrects mistakes more precisely? Even if it does correct mistakes more precisely, can it be reconciled with the sanctity of the annual accounting system and the need for tax finality?

6. *Claim of right and §1341.* The claim-of-right doctrine addresses the mirror image of the tax benefit rule problem. Suppose a taxpayer receives money in 2010 under a "claim of right," but that the taxpayer is later required to repay the money because of unexpected post-2010 developments. For example, an insurance agent receives a $10,000 commission on prepaid insurance premiums in 2010, and includes the commission in gross income on the assumption he will be entitled to retain it. In 2011, however, the

agent is required to repay the commission, because the insured exercised his right to cancel the policy. In situations of this sort, the basic rule is consistent with the inclusionary tax benefit rule. Amounts received under a "claim of right" are taxable in the year of receipt, even if events of later years result in the taxpayer's being required to repay those amounts. The mistaken assumption (that the taxpayer would be allowed to keep the money he received under a claim of right) is corrected not by amending the return for the original year of inclusion, but by allowing the taxpayer a deduction in the repayment year. *See* United States v. Lewis, 340 U.S. 590 (1951). Section 1341, however, gives the taxpayer special favorable treatment if the amount of the deduction on account of the repayment exceeds $3,000. If the taxpayer's marginal tax rate was higher in 2010 than in 2011, then in lieu of a deduction in 2011 the taxpayer's 2011 tax liability is reduced by the amount by which his 2010 tax liability would have been reduced if the $10,000 had not been included in income in 2010. Suppose that the taxpayer repays $10,000 in 2011, when his marginal tax rate is 15 percent, and that his marginal tax rate in 2010 (the year of the inclusion) was 30 percent. What is the result under §1341? What if the marginal tax rates are reversed (30% in 2011, 15% in 2010)? Is there any practical difference between the approach of §1341 and giving the taxpayer an election either to claim the deduction in 2011 or to amend the 2010 return to eliminate the inclusion? (Hint: There is a practical difference, but it does not relate to marginal tax rates.) The taxpayer always wins under §1341, in that he is always able to take the deduction at the higher of the two relevant marginal tax rates. Does fairness require such a taxpayer-favorable rule? If so, why doesn't fairness require an equally favorable tax benefit rule, so that an amount included in income under the tax benefit rule is always taxed at the lower of the two relevant marginal tax rates?

ROSEN v. COMMISSIONER

611 F.2d 942 (1st Cir. 1980)

BONSAL, J.: . . . Mr. and Mrs. Rosen owned real property in Fall River, Massachusetts. On December 20, 1972, they made a gift of the property to the City of Fall River and claimed as a charitable deduction the value of the property, viz., $51,250, on their joint [1972] federal income tax return. On April 30, 1973, the City of Fall River concluded that it could not use the Rosens' property and returned it to them. On June 20, 1973, the Rosens made a gift of all except a small part of the property to the Union Hospital of Fall River, Inc., placing a value on the property of $48,000, which they took as a charitable deduction on their joint [1973] federal income tax return. On August 27, 1974, the Hospital, finding it could not use the property, transferred it back to the Rosens.

The Tax Court, applying the "tax benefit rule," held that since the Rosens had taken charitable deductions when they transferred the property, they were required to treat the value of the property, upon its return, as income in the year in which it was returned. We affirm.

The tax benefit rule provides that if a taxpayer receives a deduction for a charitable contribution in one taxable year and recoups that donation in a later year, the value of the contribution, on recoupment, is treated as income in the year in which it was recouped. . . .

The Rosens contend that the tax benefit rule does not apply because they did not retain a right of reversion in the event that the property was not used for the charitable purpose for which it was given. Consequently, say the Rosens, the return of the property was not a recoupment but in each case was a gift made to them by the City and by the Hospital and thus not taxable to them.

However, the application of the tax benefit rule does not depend on whether the taxpayers retained a right of reversion. As pointed out in Tennessee-Carolina Transportation v. Commissioner of Internal Revenue, 582 F.2d 378, 382 (6th Cir. 1978):

> The tax benefit rule should be applied flexibly in order to counteract the inflexibility of the annual accounting concept which is necessary for administration of the tax laws. The rule should apply whenever there is an actual recovery of a previously deducted amount *or* when there is some other event inconsistent with that prior deduction. (Emphasis in the original.)

Thus, the rationale of the rule is that if the Rosens received a tax deduction in the year in which the conveyance was made and thereafter the property was returned to them, they were subject to taxation to the extent of the value of the property returned, up to the amount of the charitable deduction previously taken. "(T)he principle is well engrained in our tax law that the return or recovery of property that was once the subject of an income tax deduction must be treated as income in the year of its recovery." Alice Phelan Sullivan Corp. v. United States, 381 F.2d 399, 401 (Ct. Cl. 1967).

Notes and Questions

1. *Recovery of property that has declined in value.* In the proceedings below (71 T.C. 226 (1978)), the Tax Court found that in each case the property was worth less when it was returned to the Rosens than it had been worth when the Rosens gave it to the charity. Suppose the charitable contribution deduction, based on the fair market value of the property at the time of the donation, was $50,000, and that the fair market value of the property when it was returned to the Rosens was only $40,000. Should the amount included in income under the tax benefit rule be $50,000, or only $40,000? In *Rosen*, the IRS conceded that the inclusion should be only $40,000, and neither the Tax Court nor the First Circuit questioned that concession. The First Circuit opinion limits the taxable amount to "the value of the property, upon its return." Was the IRS right to make that concession, or should the Rosens have been required to include $50,000 in income? The combined effect of a $50,000 deduction in one year and a $40,000 inclusion in the next year is a net deduction of $10,000. Assuming that the property really did decline in value by $10,000, would the Rosens have been able to deduct that decline in value if they had simply held onto the property (neither giving it away nor recovering it), and it had declined in value by $10,000 from one year to the next? Does the answer depend on *why* the property declined in value? (*See* §165(c)(3), allowing a deduction for certain

casualty losses.) If the $10,000 decline in value would not have been deductible if the Rosens had simply continued to own the property, should they be allowed to deduct the $10,000 because of the happenstance of their rejected gift to charity? What is the Rosens' basis in the property after it is returned to them?

2. *Recovery of property that has appreciated.* What is the proper treatment of a taxpayer who gives a charity property worth $50,000 (properly claiming a $50,000 deduction), and who gets the property back from the charity when the property has appreciated to $80,000? If the *Rosen* approach is applied symmetrically, the amount included should be $80,000. Is that fair? (If the taxpayer had simply continued to own the property, the $30,000 increase in value would have been treated as unrealized appreciation.) If it is not fair, what does that suggest about the correctness of including only $40,000 in income in the *Rosen* situation?

3. *You can't give it away.* What do you think was wrong with their property, anyway? If it really had value, couldn't one of the donees have sold it and kept the proceeds?

e. A Final Note

The doctrines examined in this section are not the only tax rules dealing with corrections of mistaken assumptions. Several specialized statutory provisions, considered in other chapters, can be understood as additional examples of correcting mistaken assumptions by the use of hindsight-based adjustments in later years. For example, the rules concerning "excess front-loading" of alimony (§71(f)) fit this model.[105] Most significantly, perhaps, results consistent with the inclusionary tax benefit rule apply if a taxpayer sells a depreciable asset after having properly claimed cost recovery deductions (under §168) that exceeded the actual decline in value of the asset.[106] These results do not require invocation of the tax benefit rule; they follow mechanically from the statutory definitions of gain realized, amount realized, and adjusted basis.

105. See section C.4 of Chapter 9.
106. See section A of Chapter 7 and the earlier discussion in section C.2.C of this chapter.

Cell

THE LIMITS OF
TAX-FREE RECOVERY
OF CAPITAL

Garber v. United States

The idea that taxpayers should not have to pay tax on previously taxed amounts is sometimes referred to as the principle of tax-free recovery of "capital." This is fine as long as "capital" is understood to mean no more and no less than previously taxed amounts. The use of the "capital" label can produce confusion, however, as illustrated by the following case.

GARBER v. UNITED STATES

607 F.2d 92 (5th Cir. 1979)

CLARK, J. Dorothy Clark Garber was indicted for willfully and knowingly attempting to evade a portion of her income tax liability for the years 1970, 1971, and 1972 by filing a false and fraudulent income tax return on behalf of herself and her husband. A jury found her innocent of the charges for 1970 and 1971 but convicted her under 26 U.S.C.A. §7201 for knowingly misstating her income on her 1972 tax return. . . . The taxability of the money received by Garber presents a unique legal question. Because of trial errors which deprived defendant of her defense on the element of willfulness, we reverse the conviction.

Some time in the late 1960's after the birth of her third child, Dorothy Garber was told that her blood contained a rare antibody useful in the production of blood group typing serum. Dade Reagents, Inc. (Dade Reagents), a manufacturer of diagnostic reagents used in clinical laboratories and blood banks, had made the discovery and in 1967 induced her to enter into a contract for the sale of her blood plasma. By a technique called plasmapheresis, a pint of whole blood was extracted from her arm, plasma was centrifugally separated, and the red cells were returned to her body. The process was then repeated. The two bleeds produced one pint of plasma from two pints of blood, and took a total of from one and a half to two and a half hours.

Plasmapheresis is often preceded by a stimulation of the donor whereby the titre or concentration of the desired antibody in the blood is artificially increased by an injection of an incompatible blood type. Both stimulation and plasmapheresis are accompanied by pain and discomfort and carry the risks of hepatitis and blood clotting.

In exchange for Garber's blood plasma, Dade Reagents agreed to pay her for each bleed on a sliding scale dependent on the titre or strength of the plasma obtained. Dade Reagents then marketed the substance for the production of blood group typing serum.

Because Garber's blood is so rare — she is one of only two or three known persons in the world with this antibody — she was approached by other laboratories which lured her away from Dade Reagents by offering an increasingly attractive price for her plasma. By 1970, 1971, and 1972, the three years covered in the indictment, she was receiving substantial sums of money in exchange for her plasma.[1] For two of those years she was selling her blood under separate contract to Associated Biologicals, Inc. (Associated) and to Biomedical Industries, Inc. (Biomedical), in both cases receiving in exchange a sum of money dependent on the strength of the antibody in each unit sold. In addition, Biomedical offered a weekly salary of $200, provided a leased automobile, and in 1972 added a $25,000 bonus. In that last year Garber sold her plasma to Biomedical exclusively, producing the coveted body fluid as often as six times a month.

For all three years involved, Biomedical had treated the regular $200 weekly payments as a salary subject to withholding taxes and provided Garber with a yearly W-2 form noting the taxes withheld. Every year, Garber attached those W-2 forms to her income tax return (which was filed jointly with her husband whom she has since divorced), declared the $200 per week as income, and paid the taxes due. All other payments, both from Biomedical and from Associated, had been paid directly to defendant by check. No income taxes were withheld by the companies; she received no W-2 forms, and paid no taxes on the money received. Biomedical did, however, file a Form 1099 Information Return with the IRS which showed a portion of Garber's donor fees not subject to withholding. Garber was provided a copy of each 1099, which plainly states that it is for information only and is not to be attached to the income tax return. She had never before received Information Returns, and, while she was receiving checks from both Biomedical and Associated, only Biomedical provided this information.

In this prosecution for the felony of willful evasion of income taxes the government had the burden of proving every element of the crime beyond a reasonable doubt. This required proof of a tax deficiency, an affirmative act constituting evasion or attempted evasion of the tax due, and willfulness. The element we find lacking here was willfulness.

At trial, outside the presence of the jury, the government proffered the testimony of Jacquin Bierman, a professor of law and practicing attorney in the City of New York, who stated his opinion that Garber had made available her bodily functions or products for a consideration which constituted taxable gross income. His conclusion was based on section 61(a) of the Internal Revenue Code. . . . While admitting that this case is the first of its kind, Bierman opined that if the exchanges were considered the sale of a product, there would be no tax basis or original cost for the product sold, and the entire sales price would constitute gain subject to tax under section 61(a)(3). Alternatively, he considered categorizing the transactions as the rendition of a service, in which case he was of the opinion that the entire sales price similarly would be fully taxable under section 61(a)(1).

The defense proffered to the court the testimony of Daniel Nall, a Certified Public Accountant and former revenue agent, who concluded that the money received by Garber was not within the legal definition of income in section 61(a) and that she had therefore participated in tax-free exchanges. He patterned his reasoning on early case law resting on Doyle v. Mitchell Brothers, 247 U.S. 179

---

1. Sale of her plasma allegedly brought her $80,200 in 1970, $71,400 in 1971, and $87,200 in 1972.

(1918), which held that funds obtained by the conversion of capital assets and which represented only the actual value of such assets was not taxable income. According to Nall, the Attorney General in a 1918 opinion considered the human body a kind of capital asset. Following the reasoning in *Doyle,* the opinion held that the proceeds of an accident insurance policy were not subject to tax because the proceeds of the insurance policy represented a conversion of the capital loss which the injured taxpayer had suffered. Nall mentioned similar opinions finding settlements received for personal injury not taxable income. Eventually the Code was amended to include a specific provision covering the tax consequences of compensation for injuries or sickness.[2] Nevertheless, Nall explained, the theory has reappeared in situations involving the exchange of something so personal that its value is not susceptible to measurement. In these transactions — such as property settlements in divorce actions or damage awards for alienation of affection or for defamation of character — the value received is deemed equal to the value given, resulting in no taxable gain. Nall compared blood plasma, a part of the body which no one can value, and concluded that it too must be worth its market value. He therefore reasoned that its exchange produces no gain.

The district court heard the testimony of these two experts but refused to admit either opinion in the evidence which went to the jury because it considered the question of taxability to be one of law for the court and not the jury to decide. However, the court did permit the government to introduce testimony by an Internal Revenue Service agent who qualified as an expert in the field of accounting and taxation. This agent offered his opinion that additional taxable income was due but not reported in the years in question. His testimony was received over defense objection that it was based on his conclusion that the compensation received was income and taxable. During cross examination, the witness conceded that the taxability of money received for giving up a part of one's body is a unique and undecided question in tax law. He also agreed that money received as a return on a capital product is not subject to tax. Yet, he based his calculations on his opinion that the blood plasma donations here were taxable personal services. . . . The court sustained objections to the relevancy of further inquiry regarding the nature or value of blood plasma.

The defense argued to the court that the expert testimony of Daniel Nall should be presented to the jury to rebut the government's expert IRS agent, to show that doubt existed as to whether a tax was due because it was incapable of being computed, and to demonstrate the vagueness of the law, which would preclude a willful intent to violate it. The court recognized that Nall's theory could be relevant to its judicial resolution of the legal conflict. It ruled however that since Nall had never discussed his opinion of the law with the defendant, it had no relevancy to the fact issue of Garber's intent. The jury never heard the testimony. It did, however, hear considerable factual evidence relating to Garber's actual intent.

---

2. Section 104 of the Code now expressly excludes from taxable income certain insurance proceeds and [damages received on account of personal injuries or sickness]. The defendant has alternatively argued that the payments here in question fall within this exclusion from taxable income. Section 104(a)(2) has consistently been applied only to payments resulting from the settlement or prosecution of a tort claim. The only evidence in the record which could possibly support a claim that the payments to Garber were in settlement of a tort liability were medical release of liability forms she signed. We express no opinion on the ultimate merits of this contention.

After hearing all the evidence, the court ruled as a matter of law that the moneys Garber received for her blood plasma, whether considered a personal service or a product, were income subject to federal income taxation. Consistent with that ruling the jury was instructed that the funds Garber received from the sale of her blood plasma were taxable income. The court also instructed the jury extensively on good faith and willfulness but refused the instructions requested by defense to the effect that a misunderstanding as to defendant's liability for the tax is a valid defense to the charge of income tax evasion. . . .

We hold that the combined effect of the trial court's evidentiary rulings excluding defendant's proffered expert testimony and its requested jury charge prejudicially deprived the defendant of a valid theory of her defense. No court has yet determined whether payments received by a donor of blood or blood components are taxable as income. If, as the government contends, by subjecting herself to the plasmapheresis process Garber has performed a service, her compensation would be taxable under section 61(a)(1) of the Code. In some ways, Garber's activity does resemble work: artificial stimulation, which is not a necessary prerequisite to plasma extraction, causes nausea and dizziness; the ordeal of plasmapheresis can be extremely painful if a nerve is struck, can cause nausea, blackouts, dizziness and scarring, and increases the risks of blood clotting and hepatitis. These efforts of production may logically compare to the performance of a service.

On the other hand, blood plasma, like a chicken's eggs, a sheep's wool, or like any salable part of the human body, is tangible property which in this case commanded a selling price dependent on its value. The amount of Garber's compensation for any given pint of plasma was directly related to the strength of the desired antibodies. The greater their concentration, the more she was paid; her earnings were in no way related to the amount of work done, pain incurred, or time spent producing one pint of plasma.

Of course, the product/service distinction is relevant only if the sale of the product results in no taxable gain. The experts testifying for both parties here concede that section 61(a)(3) includes in income only the profit gained through the sale or conversion of capital assets. They do not, however, agree on the computation of gain, because they differ in their theories as to how the value of the product before its sale is to be established. The cost of Garber's blood plasma, containing its rare antibody, cannot be mathematically computed by aggregating the market cost of its components such as salt and water. That would be equivalent to calculating the basis in a master artist's portrait by costing the canvas and paints. No evidence of any original cost exists in the case of Garber's unusual natural body fluid.

In such a situation it may well be that its value should be deemed equal to the price a willing buyer would pay a willing seller on the open market. If this were the proper basis, the exchange would be a wash resulting in no tax consequences. However, we need not and do not undertake the complex task of resolving what the law should be, nor is it necessary to decide whether, as the trial court concluded, the question is purely one of law for the court and not the jury to resolve. Rather, because the district court refused to permit Bierman, the expert for the government, and Nall, the expert for the defense, to testify and because it reserved to itself the job of unriddling the tax law, thus completely obscuring from the jury the most important theory of Garber's defense — that she could not have willfully evaded a tax if there existed a reasonable doubt in the law that a tax was due — her trial was rendered fundamentally unfair.

A tax return is not criminally fraudulent simply because it is erroneous. Willfulness is an essential element of the crime charged. As such, the government must prove beyond a reasonable doubt that the defendant willfully and intentionally attempted to evade and defeat income taxes for each year in question by filing with the IRS tax returns which she knew were false. It is not enough to show merely that a lesser tax was paid than was due. Nor is a negligent, careless, or unintentional understatement of income sufficient. The government must demonstrate that the defendant willfully concealed and omitted from her return income which she knew was taxable.

When the taxability of unreported income is problematical as a matter of law, the unresolved nature of the law is relevant to show that defendant may not have been aware of a tax liability or may have simply made an error in judgment. Furthermore, the relevance of a dispute in the law does not depend on whether the defendant actually knew of the conflict. In United States v. Critzer, 498 F.2d 1160 (4th Cir. 1974), the Fourth Circuit reversed a criminal tax fraud conviction against an Eastern Cherokee Indian who failed to report a portion of her income derived from land held by the United States in trust for the Eastern Cherokee Band. The evidence clearly established that the underreporting was intentional. Whether the income was taxable, however, was a disputed question dependent on the interpretation of certain land allotment statutes, which the court did not resolve. Instead, it reversed the conviction because of the absence of authority definitively governing the situation. . . .

Critzer differs from this case in that the defendant there had been advised by the Bureau of Indian Affairs that the income received from the transactions on the Reservation was exempt from taxation. The fact that Garber did not have the benefit of such official advice does not persuade us that the result here should be different. The *Critzer* court did not so limit its holding: "It is settled that when the law is vague or highly debatable, a defendant actually or imputedly lacks the requisite intent to violate it." 498 F.2d at 1162. To hold otherwise would advocate convicting an unsophisticated taxpayer who failed to seek expert advice as to whether certain income was taxable while setting free a wise taxpayer who could find advice that taxes were not due on the identical type of debatably taxable income. . . .

In the case presently before us, as conceded by all the experts who testified, there is a dearth of authority directly supporting either argument. However, the fact that the question has never before evoked anything more than theories on either side adds to rather than detracts from the critical conflict upon which defendant's criminal liability hinges. Neither position is frivolous, and the fact that both are urged without clear precedential support in law demonstrates that the court should not have restricted the evidence or instructed as it did.

The tax treatment of earnings from the sale of blood plasma or other parts of the human body is an uncharted area in tax law. The parties in this case presented divergent opinions as to the ultimate taxability by analogy to two legitimate theories in tax law. The trial court should not have withheld this fact, and its powerful impact on the issue of Garber's willfulness, from the jury. In a case such as this where the element of willfulness is critical to the defense, the defendant is entitled to wide latitude in the introduction of evidence tending to show lack of intent. The defendant testified that she subjectively thought that proceeds from the sale of part of her body were not taxable. By disallowing Nall's testimony that a recognized theory of tax law supports Garber's feelings, the court deprived the defendant of evidence showing her state of mind to be reasonable.

This error was compounded by the court's instructions to the jury which took from them the question of the validity of the tax. In effect, the court adopted the government's position that a tax was owing as a matter of law. Garber admitted receiving unreported money and disclosed its source; the defense in this case rested entirely on a denial of the necessary criminal intent to evade taxes. The court erred by refusing to instruct the jury that a reasonable misconception of the tax law on her part would negate the necessary intent. By withholding this theory, the court left the jury with the impression that a tax was clearly due and that Garber simply refused to pay it. . . .

[I]n the case before us, the government presented persuasive evidence showing that the defendant knowingly and willfully evaded her taxes. She received a significant amount of money over a three year period, but reported none of it. The proof also showed that those with whom she dealt advised her that they thought the proceeds were taxable. Nevertheless, the tax question was completely novel and unsettled by any clearly relevant precedent. A criminal proceeding pursuant to section 7201 is an inappropriate vehicle for pioneering interpretations of tax law. The conviction is reversed and the cause is remanded for retrial.

Reversed and Remanded.

HILL, Circuit Judge, specially concurring. Because I conclude that the transactions under investigation constituted services and the income derived therefrom taxable under 61(a)(1), I should have preferred that the court say so in positive terms. The question would thus cease to be a novel one for those considering it in the future.

It was a novel question when it arose here, however, and the defendant should have been permitted to demonstrate its novelty, not so that the jury could pass upon the tax consequences of the transactions, but so that the jurors could better determine the question of willfulness. The case should be sent back for retrial with the willfulness issue determined upon consideration of all the evidence.

I take it that, at some length, the majority winds up by doing just that. So, I concur.

AINSWORTH, J., dissenting. This dissent to the majority opinion is made on the basis of two principal issues involved in the trial in district court. The first of these follows.

(1) Did the trial judge err in ruling, as a matter of law, that the income derived by defendant Garber was taxable?

. . . The majority opinion does not resolve the issue of whether defendant Garber's income as a blood donor was taxable but seemingly avoids a clear decision in this regard. It is true that considerable doubt is cast by the opinion on the taxability of the income. If, however, it is the majority's real view that the income was not taxable, it seems the opinion should say so and dismiss the indictment. However, the conviction is reversed and the case remanded for a retrial, a conclusion which thereby impliedly decides that defendant Garber's income was taxable though it holds that the question of willfulness was not properly submitted to the jury by the district court.

It is our view that defendant Garber's income was taxable and that Judge Fulton correctly ruled, as a matter of law, that it was. Further, his instruction to the jury that the income was taxable and withdrawal of that issue from the jury was a correct trial ruling.

Unfortunately, under the majority opinion, when the case goes back to Judge Fulton for retrial, he will be unable to tell from the majority opinion whether he correctly ruled that defendant Garber's income was taxable. The trial court should not be left in such a dilemma.

The primary legal issue involved in this matter is the construction of section 61 of the Internal Revenue Code, the basic provision of which states that "gross income means all income from whatever source derived." . . .

The definition of taxable income is well established, and the income in this case falls within the confines of the income definition enunciated in *Glenshaw Glass.* . . .

The majority suggests that considerable doubt exists about the tax consequences of the income because the money could be considered as having been received in return for the sale of a product. "Blood plasma, like a chicken's eggs, a sheep's wool, or like any salable part of the human body, is a tangible property which in this case commanded a selling price dependent on its value." If her plasma is treated as a product, appellant is entitled to deduct her cost basis in the plasma from her gross receipts in order to determine her taxable income. Yet, the distinction between an exchange for services and the sale of a product is only significant if defendant has a substantial basis in her plasma. If the basis is zero or minimal, then virtually all of the funds would be gain and hence taxable.[3]

Neither the appellant nor the majority has persuasively shown that appellant had anything but a zero basis in her plasma. The majority suggests that appellant may have had a basis equal to the money received for the plasma. But none of the cases cited for this proposition are in point. . . .

The only explanation for the majority's [analysis] is a misunderstanding between the concepts of value and basis. Basis, as defined in section 1012 of the Internal Revenue Code, is equal to "the cost of such property . . . " Value, on the other hand, is set by the market. Gain is the difference between that value realized in a sale, and the cost basis of the property. Uniqueness is not ground for a tax exemption and the fact that appellant may be one of only a few persons with valuable plasma does not entitle her to immunity from payment of taxes on the large and substantial amounts paid to her each year. Her basis in the plasma is the cost of its constituent parts, which in this case is zero. . . .

The second principal issue follows.

(2) Did the trial judge properly submit the question of willfulness to the jury?

On the issue of willfulness, we first consider whether the trial judge erred in declining to permit the proffered testimony of defendant Garber's so-called expert Nall to go to the jury. The majority argues strenuously that this was probably the most serious of the errors committed in the trial since Nall's testimony would have shown that the law was so uncertain as to whether defendant Garber's income was taxable that she could not have had criminal intent to evade payment of taxes.

---

3. Appellant may be entitled to deduct the cost of any special incidental expenses which she required to promote plasma regeneration such as vitamins. There is no evidence, however, suggesting that such incidental expense would offset anything more than an insignificant proportion of her total receipts . . . . Since the amount of tax owing under either the personal service or sale of a product theory is essentially the same, testimony concerning which theory is in fact proper in this case is irrelevant and would serve only to confuse the jury.

Our view is that receipt of opinion testimony of this kind as to pure issues of law invades the province of the district court. It is the trial judge who must make rulings on the law involved in the case, and boilerplate jury instructions have since time immemorial stated that the jury takes the law only from the court. Now a new rule is attempted by the majority which in effect states that the jury must take its instructions on the law from expert witnesses as well as the trial judge.

The majority's views concerning the admissibility of the proffered expert testimony is in conflict with existing precedent. . . . The expert's testimony here involved a question of law properly reserved for the court's decision. Since there was no showing that appellant had consulted the expert or relied on his view, or views of any other accountant or lawyer, the testimony was unrelated to a determination of defendant's intent or willfulness. . . .

Thus . . . it is clear that the inherent confusion which would result from receipt of expert testimony on the state of the law precludes such testimony where the defendant's actual reliance on the expert opinion is not involved.[4] . . .

TJOFLAT, J., dissenting.

I would affirm the conviction of defendant Garber for essentially the reasons stated by Judge Ainsworth. The majority opinion disturbs me more by its analysis than by its result, however. The majority says that the Government should never have prosecuted Garber for tax evasion. The criminal proceedings were "inappropriate," the majority intimates, because it is an open question whether the proceeds of her blood plasma constituted taxable income and because even if they were taxable, the doubt surrounding the taxability issue suggests that Garber could not have had the willfulness that is an essential element of the crime of tax evasion. Notwithstanding the majority's belief that the prosecution was a mistake, it apparently feels trapped by assumption that the Government is entitled to prosecute Garber. The majority's response is to manufacture a rule of evidence that might permit Garber to extricate herself.

The new rule of evidence embraces any case where someone is charged with an offense involving willfulness. If the defendant avers that the requirements of the law were too vague to give adequate notice, the trial court must permit the parties to call to the stand "experts" to give their opinions about the state of the law. I have no doubt that this innovation in trial procedure, by allowing the jury to consider matters irrelevant to factual issues, will spawn unfair convictions and acquittals. In addition, the rule will inevitably lead to a protracted and unmanageable sequence of impeachment and rehabilitation of every expert allowed to present such testimony.

---

4. A brief review of the testimony offered by appellant's expert demonstrates the extreme risk of confusion which would likely occur if introduced to the jury. The expert was not a lawyer, although he was an accountant with some experience in the Internal Revenue Service. In summary, his testimony was vague, and the only direct legal precedent offered involved personal injury cases and other allegedly analogous situations. The precedent cited is relatively old by tax law standards; most are from the beginning years of income tax adjudication. These materials are connected with the evolution of section 104 and thus only marginally related to the legal confusion the majority seemed to find since they left open the section 104 issue. Noticeably absent from the so-called expert's testimony is any mention of the host of more recent Supreme Court opinions construing section 61 broadly to reach any and all accession to wealth. Thus, the proffered testimony is at best a legal jumble whose introduction would in no way serve to edify the jury as to the issue of uncertainty which the majority addressed. . . .

Notes and Questions

1. *The vote.* Fourteen judges participated in the en banc consideration of *Garber;* four dissented.

2. *Computing gain.* According to the majority opinion, the expert witnesses did not "agree on the computation of gain, because they differ in their theories as to how the value of the product before its sale is to be established." Look at the formula in §1001(a) for computing the gain on the sale of an asset. Does the value of the asset figure into the calculation? The answer, of course, is that gain is the excess of amount realized over adjusted basis; there is no need to know the value of the property in order to compute the taxpayer's gain. The majority appears to have labored under the mistaken impression that the Code defines gain as the excess of amount realized over the value of the property, so that a taxpayer would realize gain only in the unusual situation of selling property for more than its fair market value. Under the court's formula, if you bought property for $50,000, and sold it for $80,000 when its value had increased to that amount, you would not be taxed on any gain. It is surprising and disturbing that ten federal appeals judges could subscribe to an opinion based on such a fundamental misunderstanding.

3. *Basis versus value.* The majority opinion states that "the cost of Garber's blood plasma, containing its rare antibody, cannot be mathematically computed by aggregating the market cost of its components such as salt and water. That would be equivalent to calculating the basis in a master artist's portrait by costing the canvas and paints." Again, this is simply wrong, and is based on a confusion of the concepts of value and basis. Absent an heroic effort to find a trivial basis in an allocated portion of her diet, Garber's basis in her plasma is simply zero. And, contrary to the court's impression, a "master artist" who sells one of her paintings does indeed realize a taxable gain to the extent the amount realized exceeds the cost of "the canvas and paints."

4. Mitchell Brothers. The majority opinion cites Doyle v. Mitchell Brothers, 247 U.S. 179 (1918), as holding "that funds obtained by the conversion of capital assets and which represented only the actual value of such assets was not taxable income." The following hypothetical illustrates the issue in *Mitchell Brothers.* The taxpayer (a corporation) bought an asset in 1906 for $10,000. Congress enacted a corporate income tax, to take effect at the beginning of 1909. As of January 1, 1909, the asset was worth $15,000. In 1910, the taxpayer sold the asset for $18,000. The Supreme Court interpreted the corporate income tax statute to apply only to gains accruing after the effective date of the legislation. Thus, the taxpayer was treated as having a basis of $15,000 (the asset's value as of January 1, 1909), rather than $10,000 (the taxpayer's actual cost). The majority opinion grossly mischaracterizes *Mitchell Brothers* as standing for the proposition that selling an asset for its fair market value never results in taxable gain.

5. *Section 104(a)(2).* Section 104(a)(2), which is considered in detail in section A.3.b of Chapter 2, provides an exclusion for "damages . . . received . . . on account of personal physical injuries or physical sickness." As the majority opinion suggests, §104(a)(2) applies to *tort damages,* but it does not apply to *contractual payments* for injuries to which the taxpayer has consented. *See*

Reg. §1.104-1(c), stating that §104(a)(2) applies only to "an amount re-ceived . . . through prosecution of a legal suit or action based upon tort or tort type rights, or through a settlement agreement entered into in lieu of such prosecution." As a result, a taxpayer who receives a tort damage award for loss of a kidney is allowed to exclude her payment from gross income, but another taxpayer who voluntarily sells a kidney will be taxed. (It does not matter if the sale is illegal; the scope of §61 extends to illegal sources of income.) Can you think of any policy justification for this distinction?

6. *Tax crimes.* *Garber* is the only criminal tax case in this book.[5] The IRC contains several criminal provisions. A willful attempt to "evade or defeat" the income tax is made a felony by §7201. Under §7203, a willful failure to file a return, supply required information to the IRS, or to pay tax, is a misdemeanor. Willfully filing a false return, or willfully assisting another to file a false return, is a felony under §7206. The government prosecutes only a tiny fraction of probable tax crimes. The traditional understanding is that the primary purpose of tax prosecutions is general deterrence (that is, putting the fear of the IRS into taxpayers generally). To that end, the government is particularly likely to prosecute famous people, such as Leona Helmsley and Pete Rose. This strategy guarantees wide publicity for the prosecutions, but it may also send the unfortunate message that you are at almost no risk of being charged with a tax crime if you are not famous.

---

5. However, the *Wilcox, Rutkin,* and *James* trilogy discussed in the *Collins* case in section C.2.b. of Chapter 2 consisted exclusively of criminal tax cases.

Cell

DISTINGUISHING GIFTS FROM COMPENSATION FOR SERVICES

Goodwin v. United States

GOODWIN v. UNITED STATES

67 F.3d 149 (8th Cir. 1995)

LOKEN, Circuit Judge: The Reverend and Mrs. Lloyd L. Goodwin appeal the denial of a refund of income taxes they paid on substantial payments received from members of Reverend Goodwin's congregation. The district court upheld the Commissioner of Internal Revenue's decision that the payments were taxable income, not excludable gifts. We reject the government's proposed standard for resolving this question but nonetheless affirm the district court's decision.

When Reverend Goodwin became pastor of the Gospel Assembly Church in Des Moines, Iowa (the "Church"), in 1963, it had a modest congregation of twenty-five members. Under Goodwin's stewardship, the congregation has grown to nearly four hundred persons. During the three tax years at issue, 1987 through 1989, Goodwin's annual salary from the Church was $7,800, $14,566 and $16,835; he also received a Church parsonage valued at $6,000 per year. The Goodwins reported these amounts on their joint income tax returns.[6]

In 1966, members of the Church congregation began making "gifts" to the Goodwins, initially at Christmas and later on three "special occasion" days each year. At first, the contributors purchased items such as furniture and works of art. But after five years, they began to give cash. By 1987, the congregation had developed a regular procedure for making special occasion gifts. Approximately two weeks before each special occasion day, the associate pastor announced—before Church services, when the Goodwins were not present—that those who wish to contribute to the special occasion gift may do so. Only cash was accepted to preserve anonymity. Contributors placed the cash in envelopes and gave it to the associate pastor or a Church deacon. The associate pastor then gathered the cash and delivered it to the Goodwins. The Church did not keep a record of the amount given nor who contributed to each gift. The Goodwins did not report the special occasion gifts as taxable income.

For the tax years 1987-1989, the Commissioner estimated that the Goodwins received $15,000 in "special occasion gifts" each year. The Commissioner assessed deficiencies for the 1987-1989 tax years based upon the estimated unreported special occasion gifts. The Goodwins paid the deficiencies and filed this refund suit in district court, requesting a jury trial. The parties filed cross-motions for summary judgment and a lengthy stipulation that included the following agreed facts:

---

6. [Parsonage allowances are generally excluded from gross income by §107. It is not clear from the opinion why the Goodwins did not claim this exclusion for the rental value of the parsonage. — EDS.]

33. There is no formal written policy or requirement that anyone contribute to the "special occasion gift."

34. No Church member is counseled to give, or encouraged to give specific amounts.

35. All members of the Church deposed or interviewed maintain that the "special occasion gifts" are gifts given to the [Goodwins] out of love, respect, admiration and like impulses and are not given out of any sense of obligation or any sense of fear that [Reverend Goodwin] will leave their parish if he is not compensated beyond his yearly salary.

42. Church members who were deposed or interviewed . . . did not deduct the money they gave the [Goodwins] as a charitable contribution to the Church.

43. The Church trustees, who set [Goodwin's] annual compensation, will testify that they do not know the amount of the "special occasion gifts" received and do not consider those "gifts" in setting his annual compensation.

The district court granted summary judgment in favor of the government, concluding that the special occasion gifts are taxable income to the Goodwins. However, because the parties stipulated and the district court found that the payments totaled $12,750 in 1987, $14,500 in 1988, and $15,000 in 1989, rather than $15,000 each year, as the Commissioner had estimated, the court ordered the government to redetermine the Goodwins' tax liability for 1987 and 1988 and to refund what they had overpaid. . . .

The Goodwins appeal, supported by a brief amicus curiae from The Rutherford Institute. They present two related arguments, that the undisputed evidence of the individual Church members' donative intent proves that the special occasion gifts are not taxable income to the Goodwins, and alternatively that summary judgment was improperly granted because donative intent is a question of fact for the jury. . . .

Congress has defined "gross income" broadly in the Internal Revenue Code: "Except as otherwise provided in this subtitle, gross income means all income from whatever source derived." 26 U.S.C. §61(a). Therefore, unless the Goodwins can prove that the special occasion gifts fall within the statutory exclusion for gifts, these payments are taxable income.

The Code provides that "gross income does not include the value of property acquired by gift, bequest, devise, or inheritance." 26 U.S.C. §102(a). In the leading case of Commissioner v. Duberstein, 363 U.S. 278 (1960), the Supreme Court rejected the government's proposed "test" to distinguish gifts from taxable income. Instead, the Court adhered to its previous, fact-intensive approach to this recurring issue, explaining that "the problem is one which, under the present statutory framework, does not lend itself to any more definitive statement that would produce a talisman for the solution of concrete cases." 363 U.S. at 284-85. The Court clarified, first, that "the statute does not use the term 'gift' in the common-law sense, but in a more colloquial sense"; second, that the transferor's intention is "the most critical consideration"; and third, that "there must be an objective inquiry" into the transferor's intent. Id. at 285-86.

Despite its lack of doctrinal success in *Duberstein*, the government urges that we adopt the following test to govern whether transfers from church members to their minister are gifts:

The feelings of love, admiration and respect that professedly motivated the parishioners to participate in the special occasion offerings arose from and were directly attributable to the services that taxpayer performed for them as pastor of the church. Since the transfers were tied to the performance of services by taxpayer, they were, as a matter of law, compensation.

We reject that test as far too broad. For example, it would include as taxable income every twenty dollar gift spontaneously given by a church member after an inspiring sermon, simply because the urge to give was "tied to" the minister's services. It would also include a departing church member's individual, unsolicited five hundred dollar gift to a long-tenured, highly respected priest, rabbi, or minister, a result that is totally at odds with the opinions of all nine Justices in Bogardus v. Commissioner:

> Has [the payment] been made with the intention that services rendered in the past shall be requited more completely, though full acquittance has been given? If so, it bears a tax. *Has it been made to show good will, esteem, or kindliness toward persons who happen to have served, but who are paid without thought to make requital for the service? If so, it is exempt.*

302 U.S. 34, 45 (1937) (Brandeis, J., dissenting from the Court's decision that unsolicited transfers by shareholders to former employees after a company was sold were gifts) (emphasis added). We thus turn to the facts of this case, applying *Duberstein*'s objective, no-talisman approach to evaluating transferor intent.[7]

The Goodwins argue that they must prevail as a matter of law, or at a minimum that the district court erred in granting summary judgment for the government, because it is stipulated that Church members made the special occasion gifts out of love, admiration, and respect, not out of a sense of obligation or fear that Goodwin might otherwise leave. We disagree.

From an objective perspective, the critical fact in this case is that the special occasion gifts were made by the congregation as a whole, rather than by individual Church members. The cash payments were gathered by congregation leaders in a routinized, highly structured program. Individual Church members contributed anonymously, and the regularly-scheduled payments were made to Reverend Goodwin on behalf of the entire congregation.

Viewing the question of transferor intent from this perspective makes it clear that the payments were taxable income to the Goodwins. The congregation funds the Church, including Reverend Goodwin's salary. The special occasion gifts were substantial compared to Goodwin's annual salary. The congregation, collectively, knew that without these substantial, on-going cash payments, the Church likely could not retain the services of a popular and successful minister at the relatively low salary it was paying. In other words, the congregation knew that its special occasion gifts enabled the Church to pay a $15,000 salary for $30,000 worth of work.[8] Regular, sizable payments made by persons to whom the taxpayer provides services are customarily regarded as a form of compensation and may therefore be

---

7. Many courts nevertheless give talismanic weight to a phrase used more casually in the *Duberstein* opinion — that a transfer to be a gift must be the product of "detached and disinterested generosity." It is the rare donor who is completely "detached and disinterested." To decide close cases using this phrase requires careful analysis of what detached and disinterested means in different contexts. Thus, the phrase is more sound bite than talisman.

8. The parties stipulated that the salaries in 1990-1991 for pastors in the North Central States with church memberships of less than 400 ranged from $5,000 to $43,000, with an average of $24,176.

treated as taxable income. See, e.g., Olk v. United States, 536 F.2d 876, 879 (9th Cir.), *cert. denied,* 429 U.S. 920 (1976) (tips to casino dealers).

We also reject the Goodwins' contention that it was error to grant summary judgment on this issue. Although a transferor's objective intent is a fact question under *Duberstein,* summary judgment may nonetheless be appropriate. The stipulated facts of this case demonstrate that the congregation as a whole made special occasion gifts on account of Reverend Goodwin's on-going services as pastor of the Church. Therefore, no reasonable jury could conclude that these payments were excludable from the Goodwins' taxable income, and summary judgment was appropriate.[9] The judgment of the district court is affirmed.

Notes and Questions

1. *Identifying the transferor.* In the footnote at the end of the opinion, the court expresses doubt as to whether §102(c)(1) would apply on these facts, because "the Church members [who made the special occasion offerings] are not Rev. Goodwin's 'employer.'" Why is the court reluctant to consider the payments as coming from the Church (rather than from the individual members) for purposes of §102(c)(1), when the key to the court's §102(a) analysis is that the special occasion offerings were really made "by the congregation as a whole, rather than by individual Church members"?

2. *Tips.* As the Supreme Court notes in a *Duberstein* footnote, it has long been settled that tips paid by restaurant customers to their servers are not gifts for purposes of §102(a). Despite the lack of legal compulsion to tip, tips are "payment in return for services rendered," and are given out of "the constraining force of [a] moral . . . duty." They are not ordinarily motivated by the "detached and disinterested generosity" required of a gift. For the typical tip, the interesting question is not theoretical taxability, but how Congress and the IRS can enforce that theoretical taxability against tip recipients who do not voluntarily report all their tip income. This question is examined in detail in the Chapter 1 cell on compliance and enforcement. Does the taxability of the typical tip mean that all tips are taxable, or might a truly extraordinary tip qualify as a gift under §102(a)? What if a customer leaves a $1,000 cash tip on a $20 bill? He offers no explanation of his motivation, other than to make clear he did not leave the $1,000 by accident, and the waitress never sees him again. If the waitress asks you (in your capacity as a tax expert) whether she can legitimately omit the $1,000 from her tax return, on the grounds that it was a gift for tax purposes, what do you tell her?

---

9. In the district court, both parties ignored the fact that Congress amended the governing statute in 1986. Section 102(c)(1) of the Code now provides that §102(a) "shall not exclude from gross income any amount transferred by or for an employer to, or for the benefit of, an employee." Although the legislative history suggests that §102(c)(1) was enacted to address other fact situations, its plain meaning may not be ignored in this case. That meaning seems far from plain, however. The Church members are not Rev. Goodwin's "employer," and the question whether their payments to Goodwin were made "for" his employer seems little different than the traditional gift inquiry under *Duberstein* and *Bogardus.* We therefore decline the government's belated suggestion that we affirm on the alternative ground of §102(c)(1).

Cell

ACCELERATED DEATH BENEFITS

NOTICE OF PROPOSED RULEMAKING, QUALIFIED ACCELERATED DEATH BENEFITS UNDER LIFE INSURANCE CONTRACTS

57 Fed. Reg. 59,319 (1992)

. . . In recognition of the needs of individuals who become terminally ill, the proposed regulations . . . allow the payment of benefits prior to death without any income tax liability to the recipient if death is expected to occur within 12 months. . . .

NEW INSURANCE CONTRACTS

Insurance companies have developed insurance contracts which provide both death benefits and "living benefits" designed to assist policyholders with the rising costs of medical care, particularly medical care in the later years of life. . . . The first type of living benefit, an "accelerated death benefit," addresses the needs of terminally ill individuals who may incur substantial medical and living expenses prior to death. This benefit allows the policyholder, under a life insurance contract insuring a terminally ill individual, to "accelerate" the death benefit paid under the contract. Generally, the accelerated death benefit is equal to all or a portion of the death benefit discounted for the remaining life expectancy (generally 12 months or less) of the terminally ill individual. The payment of a benefit is conditioned upon the policyholder surrendering all or a portion of the policyholder's rights under the life insurance contract. . . .

The proposed regulations allow qualified accelerated death benefits under an insurance contract to be treated as amounts paid by reason of the death of the insured for purposes of sections 101(a) and 7702. This proposed treatment allows an insurance contract including these benefits to continue to meet the definition of a life insurance contract under section 7702. The proposed regulations also permit a person who receives a qualified accelerated death benefit to exclude, under section 101(a), the benefit from gross income.

A qualified accelerated death benefit is defined in the proposed regulations as a benefit payable under a contract on the life of an insured who becomes terminally ill, where the amount of the death benefit made available cannot be discounted by more than 12 months at the rate of interest specified in the regulations. Under the proposed regulations an individual is terminally ill if the individual has an illness or physical condition that, notwithstanding appropriate medical care, is reasonably expected to result in death within 12 months from the date of payment of the accelerated death benefit. As the 12 month determination is necessarily subjective to some extent, it is expected that the insurer will act prudently in its determination of whether the person is terminally ill. The Service is considering whether to develop further guidance that would create a presumption of terminal illness in certain circumstances.

Notes and Questions

1. *The limits of the statutory language.* Inspired by the proposed regulations, Congress in 1996 enacted §101(g), which provides an explicit exclusion for "any amount received under a life insurance contract on the life of an insured who is a terminally ill individual." The authority for the 1992 proposed regulations, however, was simply the §101(a)(1) exclusion for life insurance proceeds "paid by reason of the death of the insured." It is easy enough to understand why Treasury believed there was policy justification for the proposed regulations. Suppose a person is dying of cancer or AIDS, has major medical and nonmedical expenses not covered by insurance, and has few significant financial resources except for a life insurance policy. Cashing in the life insurance policy would be the obvious solution to his financial problems, but only if cashing in the policy before death does not result in the loss of the §101(a)(1) exclusion. The proposed regulations demonstrate considerable compassion on the part of Treasury, and there is no obvious policy objection to extending the exclusion to accelerated death benefits. There is the little matter, however, of the language of the statute. Is it really a reasonable interpretation of the statute to say that payments made before the insured has died can be made "by reason of the death of the insured"? Some commentators thought it was not a reasonable interpretation, and sharply criticized the proposed regulations. *See, e.g.,* Lee Sheppard, *The Goldberg Variations, or Giving Away the Store,* 58 Tax Notes 530 (1993). But is it really so implausible to say that a payment made because the insured is going to die very soon is made by reason of his (impending) death? Whether or not Treasury was *justified* in interpreting the statute so creatively, it almost certainly had the *power* to make that interpretation stick (in the absence of congressional intervention). When Treasury or the IRS interprets a Code provision in a manner unduly favorable to some taxpayers, offended third parties have no standing to challenge the giveaway. *See, e.g.,* Allen v. Wright, 468 U.S. 737 (1984); Simon v. Eastern Kentucky Welfare Rights Org., 426 U.S. 26 (1976). There is no busybody standing in tax cases (at least when the Establishment Clause of the First Amendment is not implicated[10]).

---

10. *See* Flast v. Cohen, 382 U.S. 83 (1968) (holding that taxpayers had standing to challenge government spending as in violation of the Establishment Clause); Hein v. Freedom from Religion Foundation, 551 U.S. 587 (2007) (holding that taxpayer standing under *Flast* did not extend to challenges to discretionary expenditures by the executive branch, as contrasted with spending programs explicitly authorized by Congress).

2. *Comparing the proposed regulation with the statutory amendment.* If Congress approved of applying §101 to accelerated death benefits, and if no one would have had standing to challenge the approach of the proposed regulations, why did Congress feel the need to enact §101(g)? To answer that question, look for ways in which §101(g) is even more generous than the proposed regulations. Three aspects of §101(g) stand out in this respect: (1) the statute defines "terminally ill" as being reasonably expected to die in the next *24* months; (2) the statute applies to certain payments to "chronically ill" insureds, as well as to payments to terminally ill insureds; and (3) the statute applies to the proceeds of the sale of a life insurance policy to a "viatical settlement provider," as well as to accelerated death benefits paid by the insurer. Congress thought there was good policy justification for all three of these provisions, but the three provisions went beyond what Treasury was able to accomplish simply by aggressively interpreting "by reason of the death of the insured." Perhaps the 24-month rule could have been accomplished by extremely aggressive interpretation, but there was no way to claim that a payment made by reason of chronic illness was made by reason of death, nor was there any way to claim that amounts received by the *sale* of a life insurance policy were "amounts received . . . under a life insurance contract," as required by §101(a)(1).

3. *Viatical settlement providers.* The exclusion for sales to viatical settlement providers requires some explanation. Viatical settlement providers are in the rather ghoulish business of buying, at a discount, insurance policies on the lives of terminally ill persons, and collecting the proceeds when the insureds die. If an insured dies sooner than the life expectancy used in calculating the discount, the viatical settlement provider has made a profitable investment. As grim as this may seem, the extension of the life insurance exclusion to sales to viatical settlement providers was in the interests of terminally ill insureds. If a terminally ill person can get tax-free cash by selling his life insurance policy either to his insurer or to a viatical settlement provider, he is likely to receive a larger amount than if only the insurer is able to pay tax-free benefits. Extending the exclusion to sales to viatical settlement providers creates a competitive market for policies on the lives of terminally ill persons, to the benefit of those persons.

4. *Miracles and the tax benefit rule.* Suppose a taxpayer is certified by his physician as having an illness that can reasonably be expected to result in death within the next 24 months, the person receives tax-free accelerated death benefits, and later he miraculously recovers. If he is alive and well 25 months after the certification, does he then have income under the inclusionary tax benefit rule?[11] The tax benefit rule normally applies when a later event is "fundamentally inconsistent" with the assumptions on which a *deduction* was based, but the IRS reasonably takes the position that it can also apply when a later event is inconsistent with the assumptions underlying an *exclusion. See, e.g.,* PLR 81-27-020. The exclusion was premised on a physician's certification that the taxpayer had, in the words of §101(g)(4)(A), "an illness or physical condition which can be reasonably expected to result in death in 24 months or less." Is being alive and well 25 months after the

---

11. See section C.2.d of Chapter 2.

certification "fundamentally inconsistent" with the assumption on which the exclusion was based?

There may be a plausible technical argument for applying the tax benefit rule in this case, but would you pursue the issue if you were the Commissioner, assuming you believed the physician's original certification was in good faith?

Cell

THE PERPLEXING CASE OF THE EXTREMELY VALUABLE BASEBALL

Internal Revenue Service Press Release
IR-98-56

INTERNAL REVENUE SERVICE PRESS RELEASE IR-98-56

(September 9, 1998)

In response to press speculation resulting from events in major league baseball, the Internal Revenue Service today provided a brief explanation of the basic income and gift tax principles that would apply to a baseball fan who catches a home run ball and immediately returns it.

In general, the fan in these circumstances would not have taxable income. This conclusion is based on an analogy to principles of tax law that apply when someone immediately declines a prize or returns unsolicited merchandise. There would likewise be no gift tax in these circumstances. The tax results may be different if the fan decided to sell the ball.

Commenting on this situation, IRS Commissioner Charles O. Rossotti said, "Sometimes pieces of the tax code can be as hard to understand as the infield fly-rule. All I know is that the fan who gives back the home run ball deserves a round of applause, not a big tax bill."

Notes and Questions

1. *Imputed income or taxable treasure trove?* As the IRS press release suggests, the taxation of valuable baseballs became an issue of national concern during the Mark McGwire–Sammy Sosa home run derby of 1998. Before the press release calmed the nation, Senate Finance Committee chairman William V. Roth, Jr., had stated that the mere possibility that a fan who caught a record-setting home run ball might be taxed was "a prime example of what is wrong with our current income tax code." Also before the press release, a bill was introduced in the House of Representatives "to clarify the income and gift tax consequences of catching and returning home run baseballs." Although the issue may not have deserved the amount of attention it received, the dollars involved were not trivial. Philip Ozersky, who caught the most valuable ball of all—Mark McGwire's 70th home run—sold it at auction in 1999 for $3,005,000. (In light of Barry Bonds' breaking

of the McGwire record in 2001, and the general decline in interest in steroid-assisted home run records, the purchaser may have paid too much.)

The press release considers two situations. If the fan returns the ball, the press release relies (without citation) on the dubious but sometimes expedient precedent of Rev. Rul. 57-374, dealing with the game show contestant who declines an in-kind prize.[12] If the fan sells the ball, the ruling hints that the fan would be subject to income tax. This is not surprising or controversial; if catching the ball was not itself a taxable event, the fan would have either a zero basis or a trivial basis in the ball (arguably the cost of the fan's ticket or an allocated portion thereof should be treated as the fan's basis in the ball), and thus a large gain when he sells the ball for cash. Strangely missing from the press release, however, is any mention of the fan who simply keeps the ball. Perhaps Commissioner Rossotti decided not to discuss that situation because he believed Treas. Reg. §1.61-14(a) mandated taxation of the fan, but in the political climate of the moment it was not prudent to say so. Treas. Reg. §1.61-14(a) states that the value of "treasure trove" must be included in a taxpayer's gross income "for the taxable year in which it is reduced to undisputed possession."

Although it seems clear enough that the baseball would be covered by the treasure trove regulation, there is a strong argument that the regulation is invalid as applied to all treasure trove other than cash. Everyone agrees that the value of *self-created* property is excluded from gross income as a type of imputed income from services. The taxpayer's basis in self-created property is thus limited to the cost of materials (if any); the value added by the taxpayer's labor will be taxed only if and when the taxpayer sells the property. If property is both self-created and self-consumed (e.g., vegetables from the backyard garden), no tax is ever imposed. Why not treat property one *finds* (or, in the baseball case, *catches*) for oneself the same as property one *creates* for oneself? As with self-created property, found property fits the imputed income model of not involving any transaction or exchange. Moreover, treating found property as tax exempt is not subject to the objection that applies to treating all barter as tax exempt; an exemption for found property does not open the door to large-scale tax avoidance. Few people are likely to become full-time scavengers just for the tax advantage — especially since the tax break would last only as long as you did not sell your treasure trove. Treating found property (including home run baseballs) as a form of imputed income from services (1) avoids the liquidity and valuation problems inherent in taxing non-cash treasure trove, (2) fits comfortably enough within the doctrine of nontaxation of imputed income from services, and (3) does not threaten the fisc in any significant way.

In fact, *Cesarini*[13] is the only reported case applying the treasure trove regulation, and it applied the regulation only to found *cash*. The approach of the regulation makes good sense with respect to cash treasure troves, the taxation of which raises no problems of either liquidity or valuation. In

12. The ruling is set forth in section B.I of Chapter 2.
13. Set out in section A.1 of Chapter 2.

addition, there is an obvious later time to impose tax on finders of in-kind treasures—when they sell—but with a finder of cash the only choices are to impose tax immediately or never. If the IRS were attempting to enforce the treasure trove regulation with respect to non-cash treasures, one would expect to find a number of judicial opinions—involving professional deep-sea treasure hunters, prospectors, rock-hounds, big-game hunters, and so on—discussing the validity of the regulation and determining the value of the found property. In the absence of any such opinions, one suspects that the IRS has decided—sensibly enough—to ignore the treasure trove regulation for all found property other than cash. If this is in fact the IRS position, wouldn't it be better for the Treasury Department to revise the regulation to apply only to cash treasure troves, rather than leaving on the books a regulation that the IRS routinely ignores? For more on this fascinating topic, see Lawrence A. Zelenak & Martin J. McMahon, Jr., *Taxing Baseballs and Other Found Property*, 84 Tax Notes 1299 (1999).

2. *The infield fly rule as legal whipping boy.* Commissioner Rossotti's linkage of "pieces of the tax code" with the infield fly rule, as if both belonged in a museum of arcana that real people could not be expected to understand, may have been irresistible under the circumstances. It nonetheless does a disservice to both the Code and the Rule. As we have argued throughout, the "pieces of the tax code" ordinarily cohere, though perhaps less so in this case following the IRS press release. The infield fly rule is sound as well. With its preconditions (if there are runners on first and second base, or first, second, and third base, and fewer than two outs . . .), it has the meter of something that is arbitrary and needlessly complex (perhaps not unlike pieces of the tax code). But those conditions conform perfectly to the situations in which the Rule finds its purpose. It was intended to prevent infielders from intentionally dropping a fly ball that could have been caught "with ordinary effort," in order to make force-outs of two (or even three) runners who would be frozen to their bases by an easily catchable infield fly. If there are two outs, there can be no double plays; if there are fewer than two runners who can be forced out, there is no need for a rule to prevent conversion of one fly-out to two force-outs. The Rule is clear, and accurately targeted at the problem it addresses, which is why it has survived the test of time, and any number of wisecracks and parodies.[14] Perhaps the same could be said of the Internal Revenue Code, proving, albeit in a rather backward way, the aptness of the Commissioner's analogy.

---

14. *See, e.g., The Common Law Origins of the Infield Fly Rule*, 123 U. Pa. L. Rev. 1474 (1975).

Cell

FREE PARKING, SECTION 132, CONSTRUCTIVE RECEIPT, AND THE IRS

Davenport, Being at the Top at the IRS
Is Not so Taxing

Big State University has 2,000 employees, the vast majority of whom drive to work and park in university-owned lots. The university charges an employee $600 for an annual parking permit. If an employee uses $600 of her cash salary to pay for the permit, the $600 cash is included in her gross income and the cost of the permit is not deductible (pursuant to the rule that commuting expenses are not deductible[15]). The university could reduce everyone's cash salary by $600 and provide each employee with free parking, thus enabling the employees to exclude the value of the parking as a "qualified transportation fringe" under §132(a)(5). There is a problem, however. The few employees who do not drive to work would object to having $600 of cash compensation replaced by a fringe benefit of no value to them. Would this problem be solved if the university gave each employee the option to elect "free" parking, at the cost of a $600 reduction in cash salary? That would satisfy the employees who do not drive to work, but until recently it would not have achieved the desired exclusion for the employees who opt for the parking and the salary reduction. Under the doctrine of constructive receipt, a taxpayer who has the right to receive a taxable payment, but "turns his back" on the payment, is taxed just as if he had actually received the payment.[16] Thus, the employees who chose the parking would still have been taxed on $600 of income, because they turned their backs on the $600 cash option.

Under this state of affairs, there was no satisfactory solution. Either employees who did not value parking would be forced to suffer salary reductions so that other employees could qualify for the §132(a)(5) exclusion without running afoul of the constructive receipt doctrine, or the employees who opted for parking would have to pay tax because the university made the cash option available. Congress finally eliminated this dilemma, however, by enacting §132(f)(4), which renders the constructive receipt doctrine inapplicable to qualified transportation fringes. Under current law, then, the university can make everyone happy by giving each employee a choice between $600 cash and $600 worth of parking. Employees who choose the cash will be taxed, but those who take the parking will not.

The constructive receipt doctrine is also overridden, and on a larger scale, by the "cafeteria plan" rules of §125. This provision permits employees to choose

---

15. See section F of Chapter 5.
16. For more on constructive receipt, see section B.1 of Chapter 7.

between taxable cash and a smorgasbord of tax-free benefits, without having to worry about constructive receipt. Tax-free benefits that may be offered in a cafeteria plan include group term life insurance (§79), health benefits (§§105 and 106), dependent care assistance (§129), and retirement savings (§401(k)). Section 125 is thus much broader than §132(f)(4) in terms of the benefits it covers; unlike §132(f)(4), however, it is subject to a nondiscrimination rule.

CHARLES DAVENPORT, BEING AT THE TOP AT THE IRS IS NOT SO TAXING

63 Tax Notes 773 (1994)

In reading the *New York Times* on Saturday, April 30 (p. 1), I found a story relating how the IRS wants to value the 79 parking spaces at the IRS national headquarters. According to the story, the spaces have in the past been reserved for top IRS personnel, and reserved spaces in the general area of the IRS headquarters have a value of $355 per month. This is some $200 a month more than the $155 exclusion[17] from income for employer-provided parking spaces and would produce additional taxable income of $2,400 for those lucky persons who park at the IRS.

This income might produce an additional tax of $864 a year, so the story alleged. That prospect, however, apparently bothered someone at the IRS, and this clever, imaginative, and inventive person concluded that the value of unreserved spaces would be lower. So, the IRS decided that the spaces would no longer be reserved. Instead, these 79 spaces would be open to the first 79 people who arrived each morning, provided that they had a permit to enter the lot. Of course, permits were issued only to 79 top IRS executives.

Instinctively, I knew that this solution had too much chicanery for top people at the IRS to approve. They daily deal with practitioners who argue that artifice is fact and that punditry is law. Certainly, they would recognize that a plan of this sort at best had less than the square corners that should be turned in dealing with the revenue agency.

Then, I realized that I was reading all the news that's fit to print. Surely, this venerable source would not lead me into error, and in the next few seconds, there flashed before my eyes thoughts that I would think if the story were true. My calm returned. I was sure that the story was false, but I have taken the trouble to set out the thoughts I had in those few minutes when I suspended belief and contemplated that it might be true. What follows is my stream of unconscious. . . .

Come with an IRS revenue agent sent to audit my mythical company that has 150 employees, but only five parking spaces. Previously, the spaces were reserved — by slot — for me and my four top officials. After reading the *Times* article, I tell the company controller to issue five parking passes on an "unreserved" basis.

Suppose the cost of a reserved parking space in the area is $355 per month, while an unreserved space sells for only $178 a month. Tell me by how much does the value of my space exceed the $155 per month [ceiling] enacted by the 1992 Comprehensive National Energy Policy Act? The IRS National Office knows. It's

17. The inflation-adjusted amount for 2011 is $230.

$23. Seemingly, all I have to do to prevail on audit is to cite the *Times* article (even though, oddly enough, I notice that none of the other four officials ever parks in my "former" spot, which happens to be closest to the door).

This little bit of preferential valuation comes in the midst of Compliance 2000, the major IRS initiative aimed at raising the compliance level to 90 percent by 2000. It's founded on the belief that the citizenry will line up to pay its taxes if it has been properly educated about its responsibilities.

Do we need to ask what is taught by the parking example? I don't. But apparently those in power at the IRS have never heard of being a role model, never heard of urging the implausible in the face of the plausible, never thought about what might happen to tax compliance if the IRS appears to bend the tax law a little to favor its top people, never thought how this might sap the fervor of agents in the field. Rather, they sought a tax practitioner who would give them the advice they wanted.

Can they be entirely insensitive to the much larger issues at stake? Apparently so. Or maybe they just do not care given that they might otherwise have to pay an additional $864 a year in taxes.

One does not know how much trouble the IRS brass had in getting a favorable determination from underlings. As any CEO knows, subordinates will eventually see the light. Subordinates understand that, and they frequently do not even tender contrary opinions. In the tax preparation business, there are tax preparer penalties available to assert against those who are too subordinate to the taxpayer's desires. Those penalties are not really available when the taxpayer is the IRS boss making rules for 79 of its top people. . . .

It may be that the IRS executives were jealous of the perks enjoyed by Congress. After all, are they not a co-equal branch of the government? Had not the Congress found a friendly appraiser who is willing to tell the architect of the Capitol, George White, that those covered spaces in the palatial Rayburn Building really are not worth very much? Certainly, less than $155 per month. Want to bet? Let's auction them off! . . .

I generally don't like to be lied to by my public servants. It breeds a lot of cynicism. But better the cynicism that would come from a statement that the commissioner knew nothing about these rules than from the flagrant violation of both the spirit and the rule of the law. No parking space in America will now be worth more than $155 per month, or at the very most $178.

And what kind of snide thoughts will go through the audience's minds as the commissioner addresses the public and IRS employees about the integrity of the tax system? Sure is a wonderful thing until your parking space is up for valuation. As Leona [Helmsley] said, only the little folks pay taxes — at least if you're a big folk at the IRS worried about a tax-free (or at least low tax-cost) parking space.

Notes and Questions

1. *Reserved parking and hunting licenses.* If a reserved parking permit is really worth about twice as much as an unreserved permit ($355 versus $178), why do you suppose the difference is so great? It can't be because some people place an absurdly high value on seeing their name painted on a parking space, can it? If that is the explanation, sellers of unreserved parking are

making a big mistake by not investing in spray paint and stencils. Rather, it must be because a seller of unreserved parking sells many more permits than there are spaces in the lot. An unreserved parking permit is just a hunting license, not a guarantee of a place to park. If that is right, then the 1:1 ratio of spaces to permits means the IRS spaces were still worth $355 per month after the names were removed (even in the unlikely event that one of the lucky 79 had the temerity to park in the Commissioner's "old" space).

2. *Discrimination.* Section 132(j)(1) imposes nondiscrimination requirements on the exclusions for no-additional-cost services and qualified employee discounts. Similarly, §117(d)(3) imposes a nondiscrimination requirement on the exclusion for qualified tuition reductions. An airline executive cannot exclude the value of a free standby flight unless ticket agents are also entitled to free standby flights, and a college dean cannot exclude the value of his daughter's free tuition unless his secretary's daughter is also entitled to free tuition. There are policy justifications for not imposing nondiscrimination requirements on the exclusions for working condition fringes and de minimis fringes. Discrimination in the provision of working condition fringes is justified by different work-related needs of employees with different jobs. As for de minimis fringes, if the fringe itself is de minimis then any discrimination in its provision must also be de minimis, and by definition not worth worrying about. It is not so easy, however, to explain why executives should be able to exclude the value of their free parking (up to a statutory ceiling) if other employees are not entitled to free parking. If the free parking exclusion makes any policy sense to begin with, shouldn't it be subject to a nondiscrimination requirement?

Cell

SECTION 132 FRINGE BENEFITS

Problems 1-14

Section 132 provides exclusions for a miscellany of fringe benefits. If a fringe benefit received as compensation for services does not qualify for exclusion under §132 or some other provision, §61(a)(1) specifically provides for its inclusion in gross income. Try to apply §132 to the following problems. To ensure that the problems are sufficiently challenging, this book does *not* include explanations of the various subsections of §132. It will be just you, the Code, and the regulations. The problems are intended primarily as exercises in reading and applying a Code section of moderate complexity, but some policy issues should emerge in the process. Two general hints as you work through the problems: (1) The answers to some problems may depend on §132(h) (relating to whether an employee's family members are eligible recipients of tax-free fringes); (2) Pay careful attention to §132(j)(1) (concerning whether nondiscrimination rules apply to the various types of excludable fringes). In the case of any benefits not eligible for exclusion under §132, the amount included in income is the fair market value of the benefit, reduced by any amount the employee had to pay in order to receive the benefit. *See* Treas. Reg. §1.61-21(b)(1).

Problem 1. Edgar, a baggage handler employed by Northeast Airlines, received a free ticket for a reserved (i.e., not standby) round trip flight on Northeast. The fair market value of the ticket was $500. As it turned out, both flights were full, and Northeast could have sold Edgar's seats to a paying customer. May Edgar exclude the value of the ticket, or some portion of the value of the ticket, from his gross income?

Problem 2. The facts are the same as in Problem 1, except that there were dozens of empty seats on both of the flights Edgar took using the free ticket. Does this change the tax results?

Problem 3. Francine, a flight attendant on Northeast Airlines, was allowed to take a free flight on a standby basis (after all paying standby customers had been accommodated). She was served an in-flight meal which cost Northeast $5—an expense Northeast would have avoided if Francine had not flown. May Francine exclude the value of her flight as a no-additional-cost service?

Problem 4. Francine's mother and sister accompanied Francine on the flight; their free standby flights were also provided as a fringe benefit of Francine's employment. May Francine exclude the value of those flights from her gross income? If any amounts are not eligible for exclusion, is the tax imposed on Francine or on the relative who took the flight? *See* Treas. Reg. §1.61-21(a)(4)(i).

Problem 5. Marie is a desk clerk employed by Milton Hotels. Marie and her mother go on vacation together, and as a fringe benefit of Marie's job they are allowed to stay for free (each in her own room) in a Milton Hotel. Free rooms are available to Milton employees and their families only on a standby basis — free rooms may not be reserved, and they are available only when it becomes clear that the rooms cannot be rented to paying customers. May Marie exclude the value of the rooms from her gross income?

Problem 6. Conglo Corporation owns both Midair Airlines and Armada Hotels. Gina, a flight attendant for Midair, receives a free "standby" room at an Armada Hotel as a fringe benefit of her employment. May she exclude the value of the room as a no-additional-cost service?

Problem 7. Northeast Airlines has a written agreement with Central Airlines, under which Northeast employees can take free standby flights on Central, and vice versa. Francine, a Northeast flight attendant, takes a free standby flight on Central pursuant to this arrangement. May she exclude the value of the flight as a no-additional-cost service?

Problem 8. The agreement between Northeast and Central, described above, also allows an employee of one airline to purchase a reserved ticket for a flight on the other airline at a 20 percent discount. Under this arrangement, Francine pays Central Airlines $400 for a $500 round trip ticket. May she exclude the $100 bargain element from her gross income?

Problem 9. Big State University is by far the largest employer in the town of Arbor Hill. Without consulting the university, Tom's Sporting Goods decides to offer a 10 percent discount on all purchases by university employees. Will university employees who take advantage of the discount be able to exclude their discounts under §132?

Problem 10. Triangle Airlines provides free standby flights to its pilots, but not to flight attendants, baggage handlers, and ticket agents. Jeanne, a pilot, takes a free standby flight pursuant to this policy. Will she be able to exclude the value of her flight as a no-additional-cost service?

Problem 11. Fred's Department Store, which caters to a rather upscale clientele, allows its employees to purchase apparel items at a 40 percent discount. Fred's "gross profit percentage" (*see* §132(c)(2)) is 30 percent. Joe, a salesperson in men's suits, buys a $1,000 suit for $600. Is Joe entitled to exclude the $400 discount, or some portion of it, from his gross income? If Joe is entitled to an exclusion, can you construct a policy argument in favor of that result?

Problem 12. Sarah is the only tax professor at Ivy Law School. The school provides her with an annual subscription to *Tax Notes*, at a cost to the school of $500. The school does not provide a *Tax Notes* subscription to any other employee, but no other employee wants one. If Sarah had paid for the subscription herself, it would have been an unreimbursed employee business expense, theoretically deductible but subject to the §67 2-percent of adjusted gross income floor on miscellaneous itemized deductions. As a practical matter, Sarah would not have been able to deduct any portion of her $500 expense, after the application of §67. Will Sarah be able to exclude the value of her subscription under §132? Does it matter whether the law school provides comparably priced subscriptions to other faculty members in their areas of academic interest?

Problem 13. Ivy Law School provides a continental breakfast in the faculty lounge every weekday morning. The available goodies include gourmet coffee, fresh orange and grapefruit juice, and a wide range of pastries, including croissants, bagels, and doughnuts. Faculty members are welcome to eat and drink as much as they like, but nothing remotely comparable is provided to other employees of the school. Larry participates in the breakfasts with particular enthusiasm; he consumes at least $1,000 worth of food and beverages during the year. Will he be able to exclude the value of his breakfasts under §132?

Problem 14. Vivian is a secretary with a law firm. Every Christmas the firm gives each secretary a $50 gift certificate to a store that sells nothing but chocolate candy (in fancy boxes of various shapes and sizes). Should the firm include the value of Vivian's gift certificate as taxable compensation on her Form W-2, or does the gift certificate qualify for exclusion under §132?

A Note on Efficiency and Distortion. Tom is moving to a new job in a new city, and he is debating whether to move his pool table (which he seldom uses). A mover would charge $1,000 to move the table. Tom's new employer is willing to either (1) pay for the cost of moving the table and pay Tom a cash salary of $100,000, or (2) not pay for the cost of moving the table and pay Tom a cash salary of $101,000. Tax consequences aside, Tom would not be willing to pay more than $800 to have the table moved. In a tax-free world, then, Tom would obviously take the extra $1,000 cash (worth $1,000 to him) and forget about having the table moved (worth only $800 to him).[18] If there is an income tax, but both cash and moving expense reimbursements are subject to the tax, Tom will again opt for the cash. If his marginal tax rate is 30 percent, for example, choosing the $1,000 cash would leave him with $700 after tax, while choosing the reimbursement would leave him with $500 of subjective after-tax value if the fair market value of the reimbursement is included in income,[19] or with $560 of subjective after-tax value if only the subjective value of the reimbursement is included in income.[20] Since $700 is greater than either $500 or $560, Tom will again take the cash and abandon the pool table.

But what will Tom choose given the actual rules of the federal income tax, under which the $1,000 cash would be included in his tax base (and taxed at 30 percent), while the reimbursement alternative would be excluded from gross income under §132(a)(6)? Taking the cash would leave him with $700 after tax ($1,000 minus $300 tax), but the reimbursement would leave him with $800 of after-tax subjective value ($800 minus zero tax). He will, of course, have the employer pay to have the table moved. The result is an example of what economists refer to as "distortion," or "deadweight loss." The tax system has caused Tom's employer to spend $1,000 to provide a benefit worth only $800 to Tom; the other $200 simply goes up in smoke. If Tom's employer had paid him $1,000 cash, taxed to Tom at 30 percent, the employer would have spent $1,000 to provide Tom with only $700 of benefit.

---

18. The beauty of cash is that its subjective value is always equal to its objective value, since you can spend it on anything you like.
19. If the moving expense reimbursement is included in income at its objective value of $1,000, $800 subjective value minus $300 tax equals $500 of after-tax subjective value.
20. If the moving expense reimbursement is included in income at its subjective value of $800, $800 subjective value minus $240 tax equals $560 of after-tax subjective value.

There would have been no deadweight loss, however. From the point of view of the economy as a whole, no value would have been destroyed; $700 of the employer's $1,000 would have gone to Tom, and the other $300 would have gone to the government. When Tom chooses the reimbursement, however, the employer spends $1,000, Tom gets $800, and the government gets nothing. The type of deadweight loss illustrated by this example is typical of income tax exclusions for in-kind compensation, and many commentators object to the exclusions for this reason.

The above analysis assumed that the employer had to purchase the tax-favored fringe benefit from a third party (the mover) for its fair market value. In a different type of situation, however, §132 can be defended as actually promoting efficiency. Suppose an airline allows Terri, an employee, to fly standby at no charge. Since the seat would otherwise not be used, and since the airline incurs no substantial additional cost by letting Terri occupy the seat, the airline can provide this fringe benefit at virtually no cost to itself. Also suppose the fair market value of the standby flight is $1,000, but that Terri's subjective value (i.e., the most she would be willing to pay for the flight) is only $200. In a tax-free Utopia, Terri would obviously take the trip, since $200 is better than nothing. If she were taxed only on the subjective value — if such an approach were practical — she would again take the trip; $200 reduced by any tax less than 100 percent is still better than nothing. But if Terri would be taxed on the objective value of the flight, and if her marginal tax rate is 30 percent, she would stay home rather than pay $300 tax on a flight she values at only $200. Relative to the result in a no-tax world, taxation of the fringe benefit would cause a deadweight loss of $200 of value. When Terri stays home the employer saves no money, Terri receives no benefit, and the government collects no tax. Thus, the §132(a)(1) exclusion for no-additional-cost services is an efficiency-promoting provision, even though most other gross income exclusions fare poorly under efficiency analysis.

Cell

FREQUENT FLIER MILES AND THE BETTER PART OF VALOR: A DE FACTO ADMINISTRATIVE EXCLUSION

Technical Advice Memorandum 9547001

Hershey, I.R.S. Backs Down on
Frequent-Flier Miles

Announcement 2002-18

TECHNICAL ADVICE MEMORANDUM 9547001

(July 11, 1995)

ISSUE

Whether the Taxpayer's business expense allowance and reimbursement arrangements described below are "accountable plans" within the meaning of section 62(c) of the Internal Revenue Code and the regulations thereunder?

FACTS

The Taxpayer maintains several arrangements through which it reimburses its employees for official business expenses. We have been asked to determine whether . . . the Air Travel Allowance and Reimbursement Arrangement ("Air Travel Arrangement") [is an "accountable plan"] within the meaning of section 62 (c) of the Code. . . .

Until recently, the Air Travel Arrangement required employees to return certain airline incentives, including discount coupons for future air travel, to an appropriate official of the Taxpayer. The Air Travel Arrangement has been amended to provide that "accumulated mileage/points obtained via participation in Frequent Flyer or Frequent Traveler programs sponsored by commercial airlines . . . may be retained and used by you for personal travel. However, official travel arrangements must be made using the most economical accommodations available, commensurate with the needs of the business."

APPLICABLE LAW

Section 62(a) of the Code lists the deductions from gross income allowed in computing "adjusted gross income." Section 62(a)(2)(A) includes among those deductions those allowed by part VI (section 161 through section 196), which consists [sic] of expenses paid or incurred by the taxpayer, in connection with his or her performance of services as an employee, under a reimbursement or other expense allowance arrangement with his or her employer.

Section 62(c) of the Code provides that arrangements will not be treated as "reimbursement or other expense allowance arrangements" for purposes of section 62(a)(2)(A) unless (1) the arrangement requires the employee to substantiate the expenses covered by the arrangement to the person providing the reimbursement and (2) the arrangement requires the employee to return any amount in excess of the substantiated expenses covered under the arrangement.

In enacting section 62(c) of the Code, Congress noted the sharp distinction it had drawn in the Tax Reform Act of 1986 between unreimbursed and reimbursed employee business expenses by subjecting unreimbursed employee expenses and other miscellaneous itemized deductions to the two-percent floor under section 67. The rationale for the limitation is that, under a true reimbursement arrangement, the employer has an incentive to require sufficient substantiation to ensure that the employee's allowance be limited to actual business expenditures. In the case of nonaccountable plans, however, there is no reason to allow the employee an above-the-line deduction. Such amounts more nearly resemble salary payments: the amount received by the employee is not necessarily determined by the actual amount of business expenses incurred by the employee, and the employee may retain amounts that are not spent for business purposes. The Conference Committee stated:

> If an above-the-line deduction is allowed for expenses incurred pursuant to a nonaccountable plan, the two-percent floor enacted in the 1986 Act could be circumvented solely by restructuring the form of the employee's compensation so that the salary amount is decreased, but the employee receives an equivalent nonaccountable expense allowance.

See H.R. Conf. Rep. No. 998, 100th Cong., 2d Sess. 203 (1988).

Under section 1.62-2(c)(1) of the Income Tax Regulations, a reimbursement or other expense allowance arrangement satisfies the requirements of section 62(c) of the Code if it meets the three requirements of business connection, substantiation, and returning amounts in excess of expenses. These requirements are set forth in paragraphs (d), (e), and (f), respectively, of section 1.62-2 ("the three-requirements"). . . .

An arrangement meets the requirements of section 1.62-2(f) of the regulations if it requires the employee to return to the payor within a reasonable period of time any amount paid under the arrangement in excess of the expenses substantiated ("return of excess requirement"). The determination of whether an arrangement requires an employee to return amounts in excess of substantiated expenses will depend on the facts and circumstances. An arrangement under which money is advanced to an employee to defray expenses will satisfy this requirement only if the amount advanced is reasonably calculated not to exceed the amount of anticipated expenses. . . .

DISCUSSION

. . . Under the Air Travel Arrangement, the Taxpayer pays for its employees' official business travel. This arrangement requires all employees to return to the Taxpayer any compensation for involuntarily denied boarding on overbooked flights. By requiring the return of these excess amounts to the Taxpayer, the Air Travel Arrangement satisfies the return of excess requirement of section 1.62-2(f) of the regulations with respect to denied boarding compensation.

In contrast, the Air Travel Arrangement allows the Taxpayer's employees to retain mileage and awards accumulated on business travel. Mileage accrued toward awards constitutes a rebate in consideration of flying on a particular airline. Under generally accepted principles of tax law, a rebate is a purchase price adjustment, i.e., it reduces the purchaser's cost of the property acquired. These purchase price adjustments constitute amounts in excess of the substantiated expenses covered under the Air Travel Arrangement. Accordingly, the Air Travel Arrangement's failure to require the return of such excess means that the Arrangement is a "nonaccountable plan" under section 1.62-2(c)(3)(i) of the regulations.[21] . . .

A copy of this technical advice memorandum is to be given to the Taxpayer. Section 6110(j)(3) [now §6110(k)(3)] of the Code provides that it may not be used or cited as precedent.

Notes and Questions

1. *Unpublished rulings.* When the IRS issues a published revenue ruling, the ruling is addressed to taxpayers generally. Prior to issuance, published rulings are subject to multiple levels of review within the IRS, and ordinarily to outside review by the Treasury Department as well. Published rulings may be cited as precedent, and a taxpayer may rely on a published ruling in structuring a transaction to produce favorable tax results. The IRS also generates a large number of officially unpublished rulings, which go by several names — including letter rulings, determination letters, general counsel memoranda, and technical advice memoranda (or TAM, of which the above is an example). Pursuant to §6110, these unpublished rulings are available for public inspection in redacted form (i.e., with taxpayer-identifying information removed); print and electronic commercial publishers then unofficially publish these rulings. Unlike a revenue ruling, an unpublished ruling is addressed only to the taxpayer described in the ruling, it may be relied on only by that taxpayer, and it may not be cited as precedent by other taxpayers or by the IRS (*see* §6110(k)(3)). The volume of ruling requests processed by the IRS makes it impossible to review each response at the highest levels. Instead, these rulings are usually written by rank-and-file IRS attorneys, and issued after only limited internal review. Despite the lowly status of unpublished rulings, they provide practitioners with insights into what the IRS is thinking and what positions the IRS is likely to take in published rulings, regulations, and litigation. Thus, practitioners were very

---

21. The Service has suggested several acceptable alternatives for the Taxpayer to consider in rendering its plan "accountable." The Taxpayer has been initially amenable to ideas that will assist it in complying with the requirements of section 62(c).

concerned when they realized that TAM 9547001 implied that employee-retained frequent flier miles are included in the employee's gross income under §61.

2. *Section 62 and the TAM.* To understand the implications of the TAM for the taxation of frequent flier miles under §61, it is necessary to understand the §62 context of the ruling. By reason of §62(a)(1), unreimbursed employee business expenses are not deductible above-the-line in arriving at adjusted gross income; instead they are deductible only if the taxpayer itemizes deductions rather than claiming the standard deduction. This rule would apply, for example, to a law professor who used his own money (rather than the law school's) to attend the annual convention of the Association of American Law Schools. Even among itemized deductions, unreimbursed employee business expenses are disfavored, by being classified as miscellaneous itemized deductions under §67. Miscellaneous itemized deductions are deductible only to the extent they exceed 2 percent of the taxpayer's adjusted gross income, and they are not deductible at all for purposes of the alternative minimum tax. None of these unfavorable rules apply, however, to *reimbursed* employee business expenses, because §62(a)(2)(A) classifies these as above-the-line deductions, which may be claimed even by taxpayers who claim the standard deduction. Thus, if the law school reimbursed (or advanced) the law professor's convention expenses, the reimbursement would be included in the professor's gross income, but it would be fully offset by an above-the-line business expense deduction. For a reimbursement arrangement to qualify under §62(a)(2)(A), it must not allow the employee to retain any amount in excess of the substantiated expenses. Suppose an employer gave traveling employees a $200 per night advance for hotel expenses, and required employees to substantiate actual expenses, but allowed an employee who spent only $180 on a particular night to keep the $20 difference. That policy would violate §62(a)(2)(A),[22] with the result that the entire $200 advance would be included in the employee's gross income, and the $180 would be deductible only as an *unreimbursed* employee business expense (and thus subject to all the restrictions on miscellaneous itemized deductions). Even without the special rules for miscellaneous itemized deductions, the employee would have $20 of taxable income ($200 advance minus $180 expense) as a result of this arrangement, but because of the special rules the taxpayer may have much more than $20 of taxable income.

The TAM concludes that employee-retained frequent flier miles are analytically no different from the $20 in the above example; by not requiring the return of the frequent flier miles the employer has created a "nonaccountable plan." If employee-retained mileage credits cannot be ignored for purposes of §62, the implication is that they also cannot be ignored for purposes of the §61 definition of gross income. As a result, the value of the frequent flier miles would be treated just like the $20 in the above example — included in the employee's gross income, and not even partially offset by a miscellaneous itemized deduction. For example, if an employer paid for the employee's $200 plane ticket, and the employee retained frequent flier miles worth $20, the IRS would bifurcate the $200

22. *See* §62(c)(2) and Treas. Reg. §1.62-2(f)(1).

into a payment of $180 for the business flight, and a payment of $20 for the frequent flier miles.[23] The employee would then be taxed on the $20 with no offsetting deduction, and on the other $180 with an imperfectly offsetting deduction. The §61 implications of the TAM for frequent flier miles were doubly obscure—because of the lowly status of TAMs and because the TAM's §61 analysis is obscured by its focus on §62. Nevertheless, practitioners understood the TAM as indicating the IRS wanted to tax frequent flier miles, and they quickly alerted the media.

3. *The §61 analysis.* On the merits, the §61 implications of the TAM seem right. Frequent flier miles available for personal use obviously have substantial economic value. Assuming that under local law an employer has the right to insist that an employee turn over the miles to the employer, the value of the miles the employee is allowed to retain should be taxable under §61(a)(1) as compensation for services. In the unlikely event that the employer does not have the right under local law to require an employee to turn over the miles, the value of the miles might not be taxable under §61(a)(1) (because they are not received from the employer), but the miles would then be in the nature of kickbacks from the airline to the employee, and kickbacks are clearly within the scope of §61.

The analysis is very different, however, in the case of a taxpayer who earns frequent flier miles on personal trips (which he pays for with after-tax dollars). Suppose a taxpayer pays a total of $2,000 for four personal trips ($500 per trip), and then uses the mileage credits from those trips to take a fifth personal trip. In the end, the taxpayer has taken five personal trips at a total cost of $2,000, for an average cost of $400 per trip. If the airline had simply charged $400 per trip and issued no frequent flier miles, the taxpayer would clearly have no income tax consequences. The tax result should not be different because the airline used a more complicated process to arrive at the same end result. The taxpayer may (or may not) have gotten a good deal on his personal travel because of the frequent flier miles, but getting a good price on a consumer purchase is not a taxable event—as every bargain hunter will be relieved to know. Benjamin Franklin was wrong: A penny saved (by buying at a good price) is *better than* a penny earned, because the penny saved is not taxable, but the penny earned is.[24]

Consider two more variations on the frequent flier mile theme. (1) A self-employed taxpayer takes four business trips at a total cost of $2,000 ($500 per trip), all of which he deducts as business expenses under §162. He earns frequent flier miles from the trips, and uses the miles for a fifth business trip (which would have cost $500). There is no personal consumption here, so there should be no §61 tax consequences for the taxpayer. The only tax result is a sort of non-result: Since the taxpayer had no cost for the fifth trip—or, more precisely, he paid for and deducted the cost of the fifth trip when he paid for and deducted the costs of the

---

23. The $180/$20 division is just for purposes of illustration. In fact, the difficulty or impossibility of accurately bifurcating the cost of tickets is at the heart of the argument for not taxing frequent flier miles.

24. Of course, his maxim was accurate enough in his day. He died 123 years before the income tax was added to the U.S. Code.

previous four trips — he is not entitled to any additional business expense deduction on account of the fifth trip. (2) The self-employed taxpayer in the previous example decides to use the frequent flier miles generated by the first four trips for a personal trip. This time there *is* personal consumption, and there should be a tax. The best technical analysis is that the value of the fifth trip is taxable under the inclusionary aspect of the tax benefit rule.[25] As explicated by the Supreme Court in Hillsboro National Bank v. Commissioner, 460 U.S. 370 (1983), the tax benefit rule applies when a taxpayer claims a deduction, and in a later year an event occurs that is "fundamentally inconsistent" with the assumption on which the deduction was based. Here, the taxpayer was allowed to deduct $2,000 on the assumption that the entire cost of the first four flights would be devoted to business travel. The personal use of the frequent flier miles generated by the business trips is fundamentally inconsistent with the assumption on which the $2,000 deduction was based. Under the inclusionary tax benefit rule, then, the taxpayer must correct the mistaken assumption by including in gross income the value of the personal trip.

4. *Practical problems.* Despite the compelling technical argument for taxing employee-retained frequent flier miles, do you foresee any practical problems if the IRS attempts to collect the tax? If tax is to be imposed, should it be imposed when the taxpayer receives mileage credits, or only when the taxpayer "cashes in" the miles for a free trip? If the mileage credits should be taxed immediately, how can their value be determined in the absence of a well-established market in which credits are bought and sold? Even if the tax is postponed until the taxpayer cashes in the miles, how is the value of the free trip to be determined when (to exaggerate slightly) no two paying passengers on the same flight paid the same price for their tickets? Effective enforcement would be impossible unless employers were required to include the value of frequent flier miles (or flights obtained using frequent flier miles) on their employees' W-2 forms, but how can employers determine the value of the mileage credits (if gross income inclusion occurs as credits are earned) or whether an employee has cashed in her credits (if the inclusion is deferred until credits are used)? One would expect massive employer resistance to such burdensome reporting and withholding obligations. One might also expect resistance from employees and airlines, who have grown accustomed to the de facto tax-free status of their kickback arrangement, and who by now view its continuation as an entitlement. In light of all this, you will probably not be surprised by how the story of the TAM ended.

ROBERT D. HERSHEY, JR., I.R.S. BACKS DOWN ON FREQUENT-FLIER MILES

New York Times, November 28, 1995

In a hasty retreat, the Internal Revenue Service suggested today that it did not intend to tax the legions of business travelers whose employers allow them personal use of frequent-flier bonuses arising from company trips.

---

25. For a detailed consideration of the inclusionary tax benefit rule, see section C.2.d of Chapter 2.

"We have no particular compliance activities geared toward the taxation of frequent flier miles and we don't anticipate any," said Frank Keith, a senior spokesman for the agency. "I want to make sure that people don't overreact." The agency was responding to an article in the *Wall Street Journal* today about an advisory document sent from I.R.S. headquarters here to a field auditor who had asked for help in a case in which a particular company, which was not identified, changed its policy to let employees keep the frequent-flier mileage accumulated on the job instead of turning it over to the company.

About 90 percent of the big companies in the nation regard frequent-flier miles as a kind of recompense for being away from home and as not worth keeping strict tabs on.

The issue of taxing frequent-flier mileage has been raised repeatedly over the past decade, with the agency asserting its right to regard such a bonus as a form of taxable income but without writing regulations or otherwise enforcing this view.

But the advisory by the I.R.S. lawyers, whose work was said not to have been reviewed at top levels of the agency, has caused an uproar by declaring specifically that a company plan for treating expense allowances and reimbursements is made "nonaccountable" if it gives employees benefits arising from company-paid tickets. This would not only make employees liable for income taxes on the benefit but would also create an administrative nightmare for companies, specialists said.

"This is almighty trouble," said Mary B. Hevener, a former Treasury official who is now a benefits tax specialist in Washington at the law firm of Weil, Gotshal & Manges. "It really is a bombshell."

She contended that the I.R.S. document, formally called a technical advice memorandum, would likely be taken as an expression of agency policy even though these memorandums are explicitly intended to be applied only to the individual case for which they are solicited.

"They went to great lengths" to expound the position, Ms. Hevener said of the I.R.S. lawyers, whose memorandum consists of seven single-spaced pages and directly addresses not an arcane point but what appeared to be a typical situation.

The lawyers' conclusion said: "Because the air travel arrangement allows employees to retain the purchase price adjustments, the arrangement does not require the taxpayer's employees to return amounts in excess of substantiated expenses and is, thus, a nonaccountable plan."

This would require the value of the bonus tickets to be listed as income on W-2 forms, raising taxable income and subjecting some employees to the alternative minimum tax as well.

While business deductions might also come into play, these are subject to limitation and would probably not offset all the additional liability.

Later today, Mr. Keith, the I.R.S. spokesman elaborated on his earlier statement: "The I.R.S. does not want other employers to be misled by applying the analysis of this technical advice memorandum to their plans. I.R.S. is reconsidering the analysis in this technical advice memorandum in part because it does not address the full range of regulations potentially applicable to employee reimbursement plans involving frequent-flier miles."

One of the strongest protests about the memorandum came from the American Payroll Association, which represents more than 12,000 companies on the issues of wage and employment-tax withholding and reporting.

If adopted as policy, "nearly every employer in America would be exposed to large potential penalties for underpayment of payroll taxes, retroactive to 1990, and a correspondingly large administrative burden" in calculating tax liability and filing corrected payroll tax and information documents, Carolyn M. Kelley, the association's director for Government affairs, complained today in a letter to Margaret Milner Richardson, the I.R.S. Commissioner.

"Similarly, every employee who has traveled on business since 1990 would derivatively be exposed to penalties for underpaid income taxes," Ms. Kelley said.

ANNOUNCEMENT 2002-18

2002-10 I.R.B. 621

Most major airlines offer frequent flyer programs under which passengers accumulate miles for each flight. Individuals may also earn frequent flyer miles or other promotional benefits, for example, through rental cars or hotels. These promotional benefits may generally be exchanged for upgraded seating, free travel, discounted travel, travel-related services, or other services or benefits.

Questions have been raised concerning the taxability of frequent flyer miles or other promotional items that are received as the result of business travel and used for personal purposes. There are numerous technical and administrative issues relating to these benefits on which no official guidance has been provided, including issues relating to the timing and valuation of income inclusions and the basis for identifying personal use benefits attributable to business (or official) expenditures versus those attributable to personal expenditures. Because of these unresolved issues, the IRS has not pursued a tax enforcement program with respect to promotional benefits such as frequent flyer miles.

Consistent with prior practice, the IRS will not assert that any taxpayer has understated his federal tax liability by reason of the receipt or personal use of frequent flyer miles or other in-kind promotional benefits attributable to the taxpayer's business or official travel. Any future guidance on the taxability of these benefits will be applied prospectively.

This relief does not apply to travel or other promotional benefits that are converted to cash, to compensation that is paid in the form of travel or other promotional benefits, or in other circumstances where these benefits are used for tax avoidance purposes. . . .

Notes and Questions

1. *A de facto exclusion.* It seems unlikely the IRS will ever attempt to enforce the taxation of frequent flier miles. Do you see any problems in having a de facto administrative tax exemption for frequent flier miles, which is not consistent with a technical analysis of the Internal Revenue Code? In particular, do you have any objection to Mr. Keith effectively telling the public, "Frequent flier miles are taxable, but we have no intention of enforcing the law"? If the IRS and Congress think that taxing frequent flier miles is a bad idea, should Congress enact an explicit exclusion, instead of tolerating a continuing discrepancy between the law on the books and the law in practice?

2. *Miles converted to cash.* Suppose an employee is allowed by her employer to retain frequent flier miles, and she eventually sells the miles for cash. Does it matter if the sale is (1) to the employer, or (2) to an unrelated third party? In the former case, this is just a complicated way of increasing the employee's compensation income. The IRS should disregard the game with the frequent flier miles, and simply tax the employee on additional cash compensation under the authority of §61(a)(1). *See* Charley v. Commissioner, 91 F.3d 72 (9th Cir. 1996) (applying this analysis on similar facts). In the latter case, the taxpayer had a zero basis in the frequent flier miles (because she paid nothing for them and was not taxed on their value upon receipt), so under §§61(a)(3) and 1001 her gain is her entire amount realized on the sale.

Cell
================

RESTRICTED PROPERTY
AND STOCK OPTIONS
=======================

Alves v. Commissioner

If a taxpayer performs services and property is transferred to her "in connection with" her performance of those services, then generally she is taxed under §83(a) on the fair market value of the property at the time of the transfer (reduced by any amount she paid for the property). For example, if Jane is allowed to buy $10,000 of her employer's stock for only $4,000, she will have $6,000 of gross income under §83(a). This is hardly surprising; it is clear that the same result would be reached under the general definition of gross income in §61, even if §83 did not exist. The interesting part of §83(a) is its *exclusionary* aspect. Transferred property is not taxable to the person performing services if her rights in the property are not substantially vested. A taxpayer's rights are not substantially vested if they are subject to a substantial risk of forfeiture *and* are not transferable. If substantially nonvested property later becomes vested, the tax under §83(a) is imposed at the time of vesting. The amount included in gross income depends on the value of the property at the time of vesting (not at the time of the original transfer). The employer's business expense deduction under §162 is triggered by the employee's inclusion under §83; the employer is allowed a deduction equal in amount to the employee's inclusion, and in the same year as the employee's inclusion.

Example 1. Gail, who works for a high-tech start-up corporation, receives restricted stock — "golden handcuffs" — as part of her compensation in 2010. She does not have to pay anything for the stock, which at the time of the transfer has a fair market value of $10,000 (determined without taking the restriction into account). The restriction is that Gail will forfeit the stock if she does not continue to work for the corporation until July 1, 2013. In the meantime, she can sell the stock (if she can find a buyer), but the buyer would take the stock subject to the same risk of forfeiture if Gail quits before the magic date. Section 83(c)(1) provides that property is subject to a substantial risk of forfeiture if the "rights to full enjoyment of the property are conditioned upon the future performance of substantial services by any individual." Section 83(c)(2) adds that property is not considered transferable if a transferee's rights in the property would be subject to a substantial risk of forfeiture. Under these rules, Gail's stock is both subject to a substantial risk of forfeiture and nontransferable, with the result that she includes nothing in gross income in 2010 on account of her receipt of the stock. If she continues to work for the corporation and to hold the stock until July 1, 2013, and the restriction then lapses, she will have §83(a) income in 2013. The amount of income will be the value of the stock on July 1, 2013. In the unlikely event that she sells the stock before July 1, 2013 (to a buyer who takes the stock subject to the risk of forfeiture), she will have §83(a) income in the year of the sale, equal to her amount realized on the sale.

Example 2.   The facts are the same as in Example 1, except that the employer transfers the restricted stock to Gail's daughter, who will be 24 years old in 2013, when the restriction lapses. The hope is that the §83(a) income expected in 2013 will be taxed to Gail's daughter, who figures to be in a much lower tax bracket than Gail. Will this plan succeed?[26] No, because §83(a) says that a transfer of property to *any person* in connection with the performance of services results in gross income to "the person who performed such services." Thus, Gail will be taxed, despite the fact that her daughter has the stock. As we will see in Chapter 9.B, the great case of *Lucas v. Earl*[27] stands for the general proposition that earned income must be taxed to the earner, even if the earner arranges for the income to be received by a family member, friend, or controlled entity. The statement in §83(a) that the tax is always imposed on the person performing the services is an example of belt-and-suspenders legislation; the same result would be reached under the authority of *Lucas v. Earl* if §83 were silent on this point.[28]

Section 83(b) permits a taxpayer who receives substantially nonvested property to elect to pay tax on the value of the property (determined without regard to restrictions) in the year she receives the property. In Example 1, Gail could elect to pay tax on $10,000 in 2010. Why might someone in Gail's situation decide to waive the benefit of three years of tax deferral? Accelerating Gail's inclusion would also accelerate her employer's business expense deduction, but few employees would elect to take a tax hit for the greater tax glory of their employers. The key to understanding why Gail might make a §83(b) election is the difference between her tax consequences in *2013* without and with an election. Without an election, Gail will have compensation income in that year equal to the value of the stock on July 1, 2013. With an election, there will be no tax consequences to the vesting in 2013.

Example 3.   The facts are the same as in Example 1, with the additional facts that the stock is worth $100,000 on July 1, 2013, when the risk of forfeiture terminates, and that Gail sells the stock in 2017 for $120,000. Without a §83(b) election, Gail will have no income in 2010, $100,000 of ordinary income in 2013, and $20,000 of long-term capital gain in 2017 (the $100,000 she pays tax on in 2013 becomes her basis in the stock). With a §83(b) election, Gail will have $10,000 ordinary income in 2010, no income in 2013, and $110,000 of long-term capital gain in 2017 (the $10,000 she pays tax on in 2010 becomes her basis in the stock). These results are summarized in the first table. If Gail is optimistic in 2010 about the prospects for her employer's stock over the next three years (and she probably is, or she would be working someplace else), she may decide it is worth paying tax on

---

26. The "kiddie tax" of §1(g) will not be a problem, because the daughter will be 24 by the end of 2013.
27. 281 U.S. 111 (1930).
28. Section 83 is far from a complete codification of *Lucas v. Earl*, because §83 "property" does not include cash. Treas. Reg. §1.83-3(e). It may not be a good idea for Congress to codify a judicial doctrine only partially, because partial codification suggests that Congress might intend to abrogate the doctrine in situations not covered by the partial codification. Partial codification has proven harmless in this particular case, because the application of *Lucas v. Earl* to cash compensation is too firmly established to be legislatively overruled by implication, but partial codification of a less well-established doctrine might put the doctrine at risk outside of the situations covered by the statute.

$10,000 of ordinary income in 2010 in order to avoid paying tax on $100,000 of ordinary income three years later.

	2010	2013	2017
Without §83(b) election	no income	$100,000 ordinary income	$20,000 long-term capital gain
With §83(b) election	$10,000 ordinary income	no income	$110,000 long-term capital gain

As you would expect, the total amount taxed by the time Gail has sold the property is the same ($120,000) under either approach. The two approaches differ greatly, however, with respect to both timing and the division of the income between ordinary income (the portion of the $120,000 treated as compensation for services) and capital gain (the portion of the $120,000 treated as appreciation in a stock investment). The second table divides the $120,000 into three elements—the $10,000 value of the stock at the time of the transfer, the $90,000 appreciation between 2010 and 2013, and the $20,000 appreciation between 2013 and 2017—and indicates how each approach taxes each of the three elements, in terms of both timing and characterization as ordinary income or capital gain.

Element of Income	Timing and Character Without §83(b) Election	Timing and Character with §83(b) Election
$10,000 initial value	2013, as ordinary income	2010, as ordinary income
$90,000 2010-2013 appreciation	2013, as ordinary income	2017, as long-term capital gain
$20,000 2013-2017 appreciation	2017, as long-term capital gain	2017, as long-term capital gain

On timing, the results are mixed. The tax timing without the election is more taxpayer-favorable for the initial $10,000, but less taxpayer-favorable for the appreciation between the year of the transfer and the year of vesting. (There is no timing difference between the two approaches with respect to the 2013-2017 appreciation.) Because of these two opposing effects, one cannot say in the abstract whether the election or failure to elect will produce better tax results. In general, however, the case for making the election grows stronger as the anticipated appreciation between the initial transfer and vesting increases. It is also important to note that the results are mixed only with respect to timing. On the characterization issue, the results are unambiguously better with the election, on the assumption that the stock appreciates. In the example, the election produces only $10,000 of ordinary income, compared with $100,000 of ordinary income without the election. On the facts of the example, it seems very likely that the election produces better overall tax results, although we would need more information (about Gail's marginal tax rates in 2010 and 2013, her capital gains tax rate in 2017, and the appropriate discount rate) to be sure.

As the above discussion demonstrates, even if one had a crystal ball it would not always be easy to decide whether to make the election. The decision is harder still in real life, because it must be made without knowing how the stock will perform, and without knowing whether one will forfeit the stock. The following two examples illustrate the results without and with the election if things turn out badly — either because the stock performs poorly, or because Gail quits before the stock vests.

Example 4.   The stock is worth $10,000 when Gail receives it in 2010. It becomes worthless early in 2013. Without a §83(b) election, Gail has no income in 2010 (because the stock is not substantially vested), and no income in 2013 (because the stock is worthless by the time it vests). With a §83(b) election, Gail has $10,000 ordinary income in 2010, and a $10,000 long-term capital loss when the stock becomes worthless in 2013.[29] If she has no other capital gains or losses in 2013, she will be able to deduct only $3,000 of the loss in that year (§1211(b)); the other $7,000 will carry forward to be used in later years against net capital gains in those years, or against ordinary income at the rate of $3,000 per year (§1212(b)). With the benefit of hindsight, Gail clearly should not have made the election.

Example 5.   The stock is worth $10,000 when Gail receives it in 2010. In 2012 she quits her job, thereby forfeiting the stock. Without a §83(b) election, Gail has no income in 2010 (because the stock is not substantially vested), and also no income in 2012 or any other year (because the stock never becomes substantially vested). With a §83(b) election, Gail has $10,000 ordinary income in 2010, and *no offsetting deduction* in 2012 or any other year. Section 83(b) provides that no deduction is allowed if a taxpayer makes an election and the property is later forfeited. In this situation, the election turns out to be a tax disaster for Gail.

As the following case illustrates, there is one situation where it is absolutely clear that the taxpayer should make a §83(b) election: when the election will trigger no current income tax liability because the taxpayer purchased the property for its fair market value.

ALVES v. COMMISSIONER

734 F.2d 478 (9th Cir. 1984)

SCHROEDER, Circuit Judge: Lawrence J. Alves appeals a Tax Court decision sustaining the Commissioner's finding of deficiency for 1974 and 1975. Alves v. Commissioner, 79 T.C. 864 (1982). The appeal raises an unusual question under section 83 of the Internal Revenue Code.

Section 83 requires that an employee who has purchased restricted stock in connection with his "performance of services" must include as ordinary income the stock's appreciation in value between the time of purchase and the time the restrictions lapse, unless at the time he purchased the stock he elected to include as income the difference between the purchase price and the fair market value at that time. The issue here is whether section 83 applies to an employee's purchase

---

29. *See* §165(g)(1), treating a stock's becoming worthless as a deemed sale or exchange of the stock, thus providing the "sale or exchange" needed to trigger capital loss treatment under §1222.

of restricted stock when, according to the stipulation of the parties, the amount paid for the stock equaled its full fair market value, without regard to any restrictions. The Tax Court, with two dissenting opinions, held that section 83 applies to all restricted stock that is transferred "in connection with the performance of services," regardless of the amount paid for it. We affirm.

FACTS

General Digital Corporation (the company) was formed in April, 1970, to manufacture and market micro-electronic circuits. At its first meeting, the company's board of directors . . . voted to sell . . . 264,000 shares of common stock to seven named individuals, including Alves. All seven became company employees.

Alves joined the company as vice-president for finance and administration. As part of an employment and stock purchase agreement dated May 22, 1970, the company agreed to sell Alves 40,000 shares of common stock at ten cents per share "in order to raise capital for the Company's initial operations while at the same time providing the Employee with an additional interest in the Company. . . ." The six other named individuals signed similar agreements on the same day. The agreement divided Alves's shares into three categories: one-third were subject to repurchase by the company at ten cents per share if Alves left within four years; one-third were subject to repurchase if he left the company within five years; and one-third were unrestricted. . . .

On July 1, 1974, when the restrictions on the four-year shares lapsed, Alves still owned 4,667 four-year shares that had a fair market value at that time of $6 per share. On March 24, 1975, the restrictions on the 7,093 remaining five-year shares lapsed with the fair market value at $3.43 per share.

[Alves] did not report the difference between the fair market value of the four- and five-year shares when the restrictions ended, and the purchase price paid for the shares. The Commissioner treated the difference as ordinary income in 1974 and 1975, pursuant to section 83(a).

In proceedings before the Tax Court, the parties stipulated that: (1) General Digital's common stock had a fair market value of 10 cents per share on the date Alves entered into the employment and stock purchase agreement; (2) the stock restrictions were imposed to "provide some assurance that key personnel would remain with the company for a number of years"; (3) Alves did not make an election under section 83(b) when the restricted stock was received; . . . and (5) the four-and five-year restricted shares were subject to a substantial risk of forfeiture until July 1, 1974, and March 24, 1975, respectively.

The Tax Court sustained the Commissioner's deficiency determination. It found as a matter of fact that the stock was transferred to Alves in connection with the performance of services for the company, and, as a matter of law, that section 83(a) applies even where the transferee paid full fair market value for the stock.

DISCUSSION

. . . By its terms, [§83] applies when property is: (1) transferred in connection with the performance of services; (2) subject to a substantial risk of forfeiture; and (3) not disposed of in an arm's length transaction before the property becomes

transferable or the risk of forfeiture is removed. In the present case, it is undisputed that the stock in question was subject to a substantial risk of forfeiture, that it was
not disposed of before the restrictions lapsed, and that Alves made no section 83(b)
election. Alves's contention is that because he paid full fair market value for the
shares, they were issued as an investment, rather than in connection with the
performance of services.

The Tax Court concluded that Alves obtained the stock "in connection with the
performance of services" as company vice-president. To the extent that this conclusion is a finding of fact, it is not clearly erroneous. Although payment of full fair
market value may be one indication that stock was not transferred in connection
with the performance of services, the record shows that [for a period of time the
corporation] issued stock only to its officers, directors, and employees, with the
exception of the shares sold to the underwriter. Alves purchased the stock when he
signed his employment agreement and the stock restrictions were linked explicitly
to his tenure with the company. In addition, the parties stipulated that the restricted stock's purpose was to ensure that key personnel would remain with the
company. Nothing in the record suggests that Alves could have purchased the
stock had he not agreed to join the company.

Alves maintains that, as a matter of law, section 83(a) should not extend to
purchases for full fair market value. He argues that "in connection with" means
that the employee is receiving compensation for his performance of services. In the
unusual situation where the employee pays the same amount for restricted and
unrestricted stock, the restriction has no effect on value, and hence, Alves contends, there is no compensation.

The plain language of section 83(a) belies Alves's argument. The statute applies
to all property transferred in connection with the performance of services. No
reference is made to the term "compensation." Nor is there any statutory requirement that property have a fair market value in excess of the amount paid at the
time of transfer. Indeed, if Congress intended section 83(a) to apply solely to
restricted stock used to compensate employees, it could have used much narrower
language. Instead, Congress made section 83(a) applicable to all restricted "property," not just stock; to property transferred to "any person," not just to employees;
and to property transferred "in connection with . . . services," not just compensation for employment. . . .

Alves suggests that the language of section 83(b) indicates that Congress meant
for that section to apply only to bargain purchases and that section 83(a) should be
interpreted in the same way. Section 83(b) allows taxpayers to elect to include as
income in the year of transfer "the excess" of the full fair market value over the
purchase price. Alves contends that a taxpayer who pays full fair market value
would have "zero excess," and would fall outside the terms of section 83(b).

Section 83(b), however, is not a limitation upon section 83(a). Congress
designed section 83(b) merely to add "flexibility," not to condition section 83(a)
on the presence or absence of an "excess."

Moreover, nothing in section 83(b) precludes a taxpayer who has paid full
market value for restricted stock from making an 83(b) election. Treasury Regulations promulgated in 1978 and made retroactive to 1969 specifically provide that
section 83(b) is available in situations of zero excess:

> If property is transferred . . . in connection with the performance of services, the person
> performing such services may elect to include in gross income under section 83(b) the

excess (if any) of the fair market value of the property at the time of transfer . . . over the amount (if any) paid for such property. . . . *The fact that the transferee has paid full value for the property transferred, realizing no bargain element in the transaction, does not preclude the use of the election as provided for in this section.*

26 C.F.R. §1.83.2(a) (1983) (emphasis supplied). These regulations are consistent with the broad language of section 83 and, as the Tax Court stated, simply make "more explicit a fact which is inherent in the statute itself."

Alves last contends that since every taxpayer who pays full fair market value for restricted stock would, if well informed, choose the section 83(b) election to hedge against any appreciation, applying section 83(a) to the unfortunate taxpayer who made no election is simply a trap for the unwary. The tax laws often make an affirmative election necessary. Section 83(b) is but one example of a provision requiring taxpayers to act or suffer less attractive tax consequences. A taxpayer wishing to avoid treatment of appreciation as ordinary income must make an affirmative election under 83(b) in the year the stock was acquired.

. . . In the present case, the statutory language, legislative history, applicable regulations and the consistent refusal of courts to create exceptions to the statute's coverage, all compel the conclusion that section 83(a) applies to the income Alves received when the restrictions on his stock lapsed in 1974 and 1975. The decision of the Tax Court is affirmed.

Notes and Questions

1. *Statutory interpretation and policy.* As a matter of statutory interpretation, the result in *Alves* seems correct. The statute speaks of property transferred "in connection with the performance of services," not property transferred "as compensation," and Mr. Alves was allowed to purchase stock only because of his employment relationship. In addition, as noted in the opinion, the regulations clearly contemplate the application of §83 even when the fair market value at the time of the transfer does not exceed the amount paid. When a statute could reasonably be interpreted in more than one way, courts will generally defer to any reasonable regulatory interpretation. Having said all that, Mr. Alves has a valid point on the policy question. Requiring him to make a costless §83(b) election in order to avoid the later application of §83(a) is nothing more than a trap for the unwary. Congress has not, however, acted to remove the trap.

2. *Stock options under §83 ("nonqualified" options).* What are the tax consequences if, instead of simply transferring stock to an employee, an employer grants the employee an option to purchase stock of the employer at a specified price within a specified time frame? A special rule (§83(e)(3)) provides that §83(a) does not apply to the grant of an option unless the option has a "readily ascertainable fair market value" at the time of the grant. Under the regulations, an option will almost never have a readily ascertainable fair market value, unless identical options are actively traded on an established market.[30] The great majority of employer-granted options are not actively traded, so it would be unusual for an option to be

30. Treas. Reg. §1.83-7(b)(1).

taxable under §83. Assuming the option does not have a readily ascertainable fair market value, (1) the grant of the option has no tax consequences to the employee (even if the option is transferable, not subject to a risk of forfeiture, or both), and (2) when the employee exercises the option she will be taxed under §83(a) if the stock is substantially vested. The amount taxed is the excess of the value of the stock at the time of exercise over the amount paid by the employee for the stock. If the stock is not substantially vested at the time of exercise, but later becomes vested, the tax will be imposed at the time of vesting (unless the employee makes a §83(b) election), and the amount taxed will be the excess of the stock's value at vesting over the amount paid by the employee for the stock. The timing and amount of the employer's deduction will always match the timing and amount of the employee's inclusion. If the employee does not exercise the option, and the option eventually expires, there are no tax consequences at any time. All this may sound rather complicated, but the bottom line is that §83 ignores the existence of any option without a readily ascertainable fair market value. The tax results are exactly the same as if the option had never existed and the employer had simply allowed the employee to make a bargain purchase of the stock on the date the employee exercised the option.

3. *Incentive stock options under §§421 and 422.* Different rules apply if an option meets the definition of an "incentive stock option" (ISO) under §422. In that case, (1) the grant of the option is not a taxable event, and (2) when the employee exercises the option, the excess of the value of the stock over the option price is *also* not a taxable event, by reason of §421(a). The exercise of an ISO is not a taxable event even if the stock is substantially vested at exercise, so that tax would be imposed if §83(a) applied. The taxpayer's basis in the stock is limited to the price she paid for it. Thus, upon a later sale both the spread at exercise (i.e., the excess of the stock's value over the option price) and any later appreciation will be taxed as capital gain. These rules give the employee two tax advantages, compared with §83: (1) the tax on the spread at exercise is deferred until the taxpayer sells the stock (which might be many years later), and (2) when the spread is finally taxed, it will be taxed as capital gain rather than as ordinary income.

This sounds like a terrific deal, but some details make ISOs less attractive than they initially appear. First, §421(a)(2) provides that the employer is entitled to no business expense deduction, at any time, with respect to an ISO. This can make employers reluctant to grant ISOs. Under §83, the employee's inclusion is always matched by the employer's business expense deduction. Under §§421 and 422, however, the employee eventually has to take the spread at exercise into income (albeit deferred and as capital gain), but the employer never gets to claim a matching deduction.

Second, §422(b) imposes significant restrictions on ISO qualification. For example, the option cannot be outstanding for more than ten years after it is granted, it cannot be granted to a person who owns more than 10 percent of the stock of the corporation, and it cannot be "in the money" at the time it is granted. The last of these limitations may require a little explanation. An option is "in the money" if the exercise price is less than the current fair market value of the stock. Thus, if the stock is trading at $25 per share on the day the option is granted, the exercise price can be no lower than $25 if the option is to qualify as an ISO. Of course, an option may have substantial value even though it is not currently in the money — basically because it permits the option holder to gamble with the house's money. Suppose the stock is worth $25 per share when the option is granted, the exercise price is $30 per share, and the option term is three years. If the stock appreciates to more than $30 per share during the next three years, the option holder will be able to buy the stock for less than its value. But if the stock fails to appreciate to more than $30 per share, the taxpayer will simply decline to exercise the option; he runs no risk of having to buy the stock for more than it is worth.

Section 422(d) adds a third limitation on the attractiveness of ISOs: An employee cannot be granted ISOs with respect to more than $100,000 of stock in any given year. Many corporate executives thus view ISO treatment as being available only for pocket change. The fourth and final problem is that the spread at exercise escapes taxation only under the regular income tax; it is fully taxable under the alternative minimum tax.[31]

---

31. Section 56(b)(3). For the alternative minimum tax, see section C of Chapter 8.

Cell

ANNUAL ACCOUNTING
AND RESCISSIONS

Rev. Rul. 80-58

REV. RUL. 80-58

1980-1 C.B. 181

ISSUE

In the situations described below, what are the federal income tax consequences of a reconveyance to a taxpayer of property previously sold by the taxpayer?

FACTS

Situation 1: In February 1978, *A*, a calendar year taxpayer, sold a tract of land to *B* and received cash for the entire purchase price. The contract of sale obligated *A*, at the request of *B*, to accept reconveyance of the land from *B* if at any time within nine months of the date of sale, *B* was unable to have the land rezoned for *B's* business purposes. If there were a reconveyance under the contract, *A* and *B* would be placed in the same positions they were prior to the sale.

In October 1978, *B* determined that it was not possible to have the land rezoned and notified *A* of its intention to reconvey the land pursuant to the terms of the contract of sale. The reconveyance was consummated during October 1978, and the tract of land was returned to *A,* and *B* received back all amounts expended in connection with the transaction.

Situation 2: Same as above, except that the period within which *B* could reconvey the property to *A* was one year. In January 1979, *B* determined that it was not possible to have the land rezoned and notified *A* of its intention to reconvey the land pursuant to the terms of the contract of sale. The reconveyance was consummated during February 1979, and the tract of land was returned to *A. B* received back all amounts expended in connection with the transaction.

LAW AND ANALYSIS

Section 61(a)(3) of the Internal Revenue Code provides that, except as otherwise provided, gross income means all income from whatever source derived, including gains derived from dealings in property.

Section 1001(c) of the Code provides that, except as otherwise provided, the entire amount of gain or loss, determined under section 1001, on the sale or exchange of property shall be recognized.

The legal concept of rescission refers to the abrogation, canceling, or voiding of a contract that has the effect of releasing the contracting parties from further obligations to each other and restoring the parties to the relative positions that they would have occupied had no contract been made. A rescission may be effected by mutual agreement of the parties, by one of the parties declaring a rescission of the contract without the consent of the other if sufficient grounds exist, or by applying to the court for a decree of rescission.

The annual accounting concept requires that one must look at the transaction on an annual basis using the facts as they exist at the end of the year. That is, each taxable year is a separate unit for tax accounting purposes. *See* Security Flour Mills Co. v. Commissioner, 321 U.S. 281 (1944), Ct. D. 1603, 1944 C.B. 526.

In Penn v. Robertson, 115 F.2d 167 (4th Cir. 1940), the taxpayer was a participant in an employees' stock benefit fund created by the directors of the company without the approval of the shareholders. Under the plan the taxpayer was credited with earnings from the fund for the years 1930 and 1931. In 1931, as a result of suits filed by a shareholder, the directors of the company passed a resolution whereby the plan would be rescinded as to all participants in the plan who agreed to relinquish their previous credits and rights. The United States Court of Appeals held that although the plan was rescinded for 1930, the annual accounting period principle required the determination of income at the close of the taxable year without regard to subsequent events. That is, the rescission in 1931 was disregarded for purposes of determining 1930 taxable income.

With regard to whether the 1931 income should be taxed, the Court of Appeals said in the *Penn* case that the rescission in 1931 extinguished what otherwise would have been taxable income for that year.

The facts of the *Penn* case are similar to those in Situation 1 and Situation 2. In *Penn,* earnings were credited in 1930 and 1931 and there was a rescission in 1931 (that was intended to affect both years). Situation 1 relates to the earnings credited in 1931, the year of the rescission; and Situation 2 relates to the earnings credited in 1930, that is, a year different from the year of the rescission.

In Situation 1 the rescission of the sale during 1978 placed *A* and *B* at the end of the taxable year in the same positions as they were prior to the sale. Thus, in light of the *Penn* case, the original sale is to be disregarded for federal income tax purposes because the rescission extinguished any taxable income for that year with regard to that transaction. . . .

In Situation 2, as Situation 1, there was a completed sale in 1978. However, unlike Situation 1, because only the sale and not the rescission occurred in 1978, at the end of 1978 *A* and *B* were not in the same positions as they were prior to the sale. Again, in light of the *Penn* case, the rescission in 1979 is disregarded with respect to the taxable events occurring in 1978.

In both situations, the annual accounting period principle requires the determination of income at the close of the taxable year without regard to subsequent events.

HOLDINGS

In Situation 1, no gain on the sale will be recognized by *A* under section 1001 of the Code.

In Situation 2, *A* must report the sale for 1978. In 1979, when the property was reconveyed to *A*, *A* acquired a new basis in the property, which was the price paid to *B* for such reconveyance. . . .

Notes and Questions

1. *Two transactions or none.* The ruling provides a dramatic example of the application of the annual accounting doctrine. A contract rescinded on December 31 results in zero transactions for tax purposes, but the same contract rescinded the next day results in two transactions. Can the seeming arbitrariness of these results be defended on the grounds that we have to draw the line somewhere, and the end of the year is as good a place as any?

2. *A stitch in time.* It is not uncommon for a client to wait until he has completed a transaction before consulting an attorney about the transaction's tax consequences. If the tax consequences are terrible, is there anything the attorney can do to clean up the client's mess? As Rev. Rul. 80-58 suggests, it may indeed be possible to clean up the mess if (1) no other party to the transaction objects to unwinding the transaction, and (2) the unwinding is completed before the end of the taxable year in which the original transaction occurred. If the client does not approach the attorney until the taxable year is over, however, nothing can be done to change the tax results for that year.

3. *Better late than never?* Unwinding the transaction in a later year will generally have tax consequences in the later year. What should have been the tax consequences in 1931 of the rescission of the 1930 employees' stock benefit fund in *Penn v. Robertson*? See the discussion of the claim of right doctrine and §1341 in part C.2.d of Chapter 2.

Cell

DEFINING DEBT CANCELLATION INCOME

Bradford v. Commissioner

BRADFORD v. COMMISSIONER

233 F.2d 935 (6th Cir. 1956)

STEWART, J.: The question here is whether the petitioner realized $50,000 income in 1946 when her liability upon a note for $100,000 was discharged for $50,000.

In 1938 the petitioner's husband owed a Nashville bank approximately $305,000. The debt had grown out of investment banking ventures he had engaged in prior to the depression. He had pledged most of his assets to the bank as collateral, but the greater part of the indebtedness was unsecured. The brokerage firm of which he was a member held a seat on the New York Stock Exchange. In October of 1938 the Exchange adopted a rule requiring each general partner of a member firm to submit a detailed report of his indebtedness. Fearing that disclosure of so much indebtedness might impair the position of his firm with the Exchange, he persuaded the bank to substitute the note of his wife, the petitioner, for a portion of his indebtedness. Accordingly, the petitioner executed her note to the bank for $205,000 without receiving any consideration in return.[32] Her husband remained the obligor on two notes to the bank for $100,000 and so reported to the New York Stock Exchange.

About two years later the petitioner at the bank's request executed two notes to replace her $205,000 note, one for $105,000, on which all the collateral was pledged, and another for $100,000 which was unsecured. In 1943 a bank examiner required the bank to write off $50,000 of the petitioner's $100,000 unsecured note. In 1946 the bank advised petitioner that it was willing to sell the $100,000 note for $50,000, its then value on the bank's books. The petitioner's husband accordingly persuaded his half-brother, a Mr. Duval, to purchase the note from the bank for $50,000 with funds furnished by the petitioner and her husband. The Tax Court found that this transaction "was, in essence, a discharge of Mrs. Bradford's indebtedness for $50,000." The petitioner accepts the correctness of that finding, conceding that Duval "purchased the note as agent for the Bradfords and with no

---

32. The Tax Court unequivocally found as a fact that petitioner received no consideration when she executed this note. This finding is not clearly erroneous, and we accept it, despite qualifying language in the Tax Court's subsequent unreported memorandum and order denying petitioner's motion for reconsideration.

intention of enforcing same." The petitioner was solvent both before and after the note was discharged.

Upon these facts the Tax Court concluded that the petitioner had realized unreported ordinary income of $50,000 in 1946 and upheld the Commissioner's determination of deficiency in accordance with that conclusion. The petitioner asks us to reverse the Tax Court's decision upon [the] grounds . . . that because she received nothing when the original note was executed by her in 1938, she did not realize income in 1946 when the note was cancelled for less than its face amount. . . .

It was the view of the Tax Court that . . . the discharge of the $100,000 note for $50,000 clearly resulted in ordinary income in the amount of $50,000. The Commissioner in effect adopts that view in his argument here. "It has become well settled," we are told, "that a profit is realized by a debtor whose obligation is extinguished by payment of an amount less than that which is owing, and that such profit constitutes gain which is taxable income within the broad sweep of Section 22(a) [the predecessor of current §61] of the Internal Revenue Code of 1939."

The statement quoted can be accepted without question as a correct general proposition of tax law. . . .

It is also a well settled general rule that each year's transactions are to be considered separately, without regard to what the net effect of a particular transaction might be if viewed over a period of several years. Burnet v. Sanford & Brooks Co., 1931, 282 U.S. 359.

A mechanical application of these principles would of course support the Tax Court's decision. Looking alone to the year 1946 under the rule of the *Sanford & Brooks Co.* case, it is obvious that when $100,000 of the petitioner's indebtedness was discharged for $50,000 in that year, she realized a balance sheet improvement of $50,000 which would be taxable as ordinary income under the rule of the *Kirby Lumber Co.* case. We cannot agree with the Commissioner, however, that these principles are to be applied so mechanically.

The fact is that by any realistic standard the petitioner never realized any income at all from the transaction in issue. In 1938 "without receiving any consideration in return," she promised to pay a prior debt of her husband's. In a later year she paid part of that debt for less than its face value. Had she paid $50,000 in 1938 to discharge $100,000 of her husband's indebtedness, the Commissioner could hardly contend that she thereby realized income. Yet the net effect of what she did do was precisely the same. We cannot agree that the transaction resulted in taxable income to her. . . .

Courts have not hesitated in appropriate circumstances to look behind the cancellation of indebtedness in a given calendar year, and in doing so to evaluate in its entirety the transaction out of which the cancellation arose. Thus, it has been consistently held that partial forgiveness of indebtedness in a given year does not constitute taxable income to the debtor if the actual effect of the entire transaction was simply to reduce the purchase price of property acquired in a prior year. Hirsch v. Commissioner, 7 Cir., 1940, 115 F.2d 656; Allen v. Courts, 5 Cir., 1942, 127 F.2d 127; Helvering v. A.L. Killian Co., 8 Cir., 1942, 128 F.2d 433. . . .

Before concluding it should be emphasized that there is not before us on this review the question of the tax liability of petitioner's husband either in 1938 when his indebtedness was assumed by his wife, or in 1946 when it was discharged, nor do we have for decision any question as to the petitioner's gift tax liability. We have decided only that the petitioner herself under the circumstances of this case did not realize $50,000 of unreported income in 1946.

For the reasons stated, the decision of the Tax Court is reversed.

Notes and Questions

1. *Don't look back?* The court cites *Sanford & Brooks* for the proposition that courts should not look back to earlier years to determine the tax treatment of this year's transactions, and then looks back anyway. As explained in section C.1 of Chapter 2, the court need not have worried that looking to earlier years would violate the integrity of annual accounting; annual accounting would be violated only if developments in later years were used to reopen earlier years.

2. *No mistake to correct.* Dan's negligent driving resulted in injury to Pat. Pat sued Dan and a $50,000 judgment was entered in Pat's favor in Year 1. At the time of the accident Dan was driving on a personal errand, so he could not deduct the judgment as a business expense (either when entered or when paid). Dan did not have liability insurance, and he made it as difficult as possible for Pat to collect on the judgment. Frustrated by collection difficulties, Pat agreed in Year 2 to accept a $40,000 check from Dan and not to attempt to collect the remaining $10,000. Does Dan have $10,000 of debt cancellation income in Year 2?

   He probably does not. In a *Kirby*-type situation, the taxpayer receives cash (or other items of value) when the debt is incurred, and is allowed to exclude the value from his gross income based on the assumption that he will pay off the debt. When that assumption turns out to be wrong, a tax correction is required. But Dan received nothing of value when he incurred his debt, and so nothing was excluded from his gross income based on an assumption of eventual payment. With payment never having been assumed for tax purposes, there is no mistaken assumption in need of correction. A different answer is possible, however, if one understands *Kirby* to be based not on the need to correct mistaken assumptions, but rather on a balance sheet analysis, which looks solely at the year the debt is canceled. Under this analysis, a taxpayer who is able to remove a $50,000 liability at the cost of only $40,000 of assets has improved his balance sheet by $10,000 and should be taxed on that improvement — even if there is no mistaken assumption in need of correction. While there is some support in the case law for both views of *Kirby*, the better view is probably that cancellation of indebtedness income is limited to corrections of mistaken assumptions. Dan clearly would not have been required to include anything in gross income if the judgment had been for $40,000 and he had paid it. Is there any good reason why his tax treatment should be different if the judgment is for $50,000 but he manages to pay only $40,000? The mistake-correcting approach treats Dan like the $40,000 judgment debtor, but the balance sheet approach would (unreasonably?) tax Dan more heavily than the $40,000 debtor.

3. *Mrs. Bradford.* The analysis in *Bradford* is consistent with the mistake-correcting analysis under which Dan, as we've just seen, would not be taxed.

The court reasons that if Mrs. Bradford received nothing of value tax-free when she incurred her debt, then cancellation of a portion of the debt should not trigger any gross income inclusion for her. The court is probably correct in its understanding of the nature of debt cancellation income, but is it correct in its understanding of the nature of Mrs. Bradford's transaction? The debtor-substitution transaction in 1938 was the functional equivalent of (1) Mrs. Bradford's borrowing $205,000 from the bank, (2) her making a gift of the borrowed money to Mr. Bradford, and (3) Mr. Bradford's using the gift to repay his loan. If the transaction had been structured that way, Mrs. Bradford would have been able to exclude the $205,000 from income only because of the assumption that she would repay the loan, and later cancellation of $50,000 of her debt would result in *Kirby* income. Is there any reason why Mrs. Bradford should be treated differently just because she never actually had the $205,000 cash in her hands?

4. *The court's hypothetical.* What would have been the income tax consequences of the court's hypothetical, in which Mrs. Bradford pays $50,000 in 1938 to discharge $100,000 of Mr. Bradford's indebtedness? The court says it would not have resulted in any *Kirby* income to Mrs. Bradford. Do you agree? What about Mr. Bradford? If you think it would have resulted in *Kirby* income to Mr. Bradford, what is your analysis?

5. *Accrued expenses.* Recall the Dan and Pat hypothetical in Note 2. Vary the facts by assuming that Dan was driving in connection with his business at the time of the accident. Dan's business is on the accrual accounting method for tax purposes, so he takes items into income when the right to receive payment arises (rather than when he receives payment, as under the cash method), and he deducts expenses when the liability arises (rather than when he pays, as under the cash method).[33] Thus, Dan was able to deduct the $50,000 judgment as a business expense in Year 1. What is the result, then, when it becomes clear in Year 2 that Dan will never have to pay $10,000 of the debt? In this situation there *is* a mistaken assumption in need of correction; the $50,000 business expense deduction was based on the assumption that Dan would eventually pay Pat $50,000. The resulting $10,000 gross income inclusion in Year 2 could be described equally well as an application of *Kirby* or as an application of the inclusionary tax benefit rule (discussed in Section C.2.d of Chapter 2).

6. *Cash method taxpayer.* The facts are the same as in Note 5, except this time Dan's business is on the cash method of accounting for tax purposes. In that case, must Dan include $10,000 in gross income in Year 2?

7. *Disputed liabilities.* Mary buys a car from a used car dealer on credit; she gives the dealer a note for $10,000, which she believes to be the fair market value of the car. A short time later, she discovers the car's odometer has been rolled back. She complains to the dealer, and he agrees to tear up the $10,000 note and replace it with a $7,000 note (representing the value of the car given the higher actual mileage). Does Mary have $3,000 of debt cancellation income?

---

33. For the cash and accrual accounting methods, see Chapter 7.

There is no good reason to treat Mary as having *Kirby* income. *Kirby* should apply only when the taxpayer receives more value up front than she is eventually required to repay. Originally, it appeared that Mary would pay $10,000 for a car worth $10,000; now it appears that Mary will pay $7,000 for a car worth $7,000. Even with the reduction in the debt, she has not received any value for which she will not pay. The only tax consequence should be, and is, that her basis in the car is reduced from $10,000 to $7,000. *See* §108(e)(5) and N. Sobel, Inc. v. Commissioner, 40 BTA 1263 (1939).

8. *Section 108(e)(5).* The original transaction is the same as in Note 7 — Mary buys a car for $10,000 on credit — but this time there is no problem with the car. Instead, interest rates rise and the seller-creditor agrees to accept $9,000 cash in cancellation of the debt. Does Mary have $1,000 of debt cancellation income?

   Logically, this is *Kirby* income. Mary has received $10,000 of value at a cost to her of only $9,000. The tax rules would follow this logic and tax Mary on $1,000 of income, if she had borrowed the $10,000 to buy the car from a bank and she later settled the bank loan for $9,000 after interest rates had risen. However, §108 of the Code provides for exceptions to *Kirby* in a limited number of situations, including Mary's. Under §108(e)(5), gross income does not include a debt reduction if the debt is owed by a purchaser of property to a seller of property (but *not* to a financing third party, such as a bank), and the debt arose out of the purchase of such property. The debtor must, however, reduce her basis in the property by the amount of the debt reduction. The §108(e)(5) approach makes good sense when the debt reduction relates to a dispute about the original transaction (as in Note 7), but it is very generous when the debt reduction is attributable to interest rate fluctuations.

   Other §108 exceptions to *Kirby* include debt cancellation income that is realized when the taxpayer is in a Title 11 bankruptcy case or is otherwise insolvent, and debt cancellations that meet the definition of either "qualified farm indebtedness" or "qualified real property business indebtedness." Just as §108(e)(5) requires a basis reduction as a condition of the exclusion, these other §108 exclusions also require a reduction in asset basis or in other favorable tax attributes, such as §172 NOL carryovers and §1211 capital loss carryovers.

9. Kirby *income or wages?* Ted is temporarily short of cash and asks his employer for a $1,000 loan, with the understanding that Ted will "work off" the loan by doing $1,000 worth of overtime work. When Ted does the extra work and his employer cancels the debt, does Ted have $1,000 of *Kirby* income?

   Ted must include $1,000 in his gross income, but it is not income from the cancellation of indebtedness; rather, it is compensation for services. The easiest way to understand this transaction is to recast it as involving two offsetting payments of cash. First, Ted's employer pays Ted $1,000 for his overtime work, and then Ted uses that $1,000 of compensation to repay the loan. Instead of being canceled in the *Kirby* sense, the debt has been repaid in full. Given that §61 includes both compensation for services and debt cancellation within the scope of gross income (§§61(a)(1) and 61(a)(12)), does it really matter which type of income Ted has received?

For income tax purposes, it usually will not matter, although the fact that this is not debt cancellation income means Ted cannot hope to come within any of the §108 exclusions. The major practical significance of the distinction, in most cases, is that Ted's $1,000 of compensation income is subject to the social security wage (FICA) tax, whereas *Kirby* income would not be.

10. Kirby *income or gift?* Carla's Grandmother loaned her $100,000 to help finance her law school education. On Carla's graduation day, Grandmother was so proud and pleased that she told Carla to consider the debt canceled. Does Carla have $100,000 of *Kirby* income?

   As with the previous problem, using the "cash-two-step" approach clarifies the analysis. This is the equivalent of Grandmother's making a $100,000 cash gift to Carla, who then uses it to repay the loan. On these facts, the practical significance of gift treatment, rather than *Kirby* treatment, is obvious. Whereas *Kirby* income is generally taxable under §61 (unless one of the §108 exclusions applies), the gift is excluded from Carla's gross income by §102.

Cell
DISCHARGE OF
GAMBLING DEBTS

Zarin v. Commissioner

ZARIN v. COMMISSIONER

916 F.2d 110 (3d Cir. 1990)

Cowen, Circuit Judge: David Zarin ("Zarin") appeals from a decision of the Tax Court holding that he recognized $2,935,000 of income from discharge of indebtedness resulting from his gambling activities, and that he should be taxed on the income. . . . After considering the issues raised by this appeal, we will reverse.

I

Zarin was a professional engineer who participated in the development, construction, and management of various housing projects. A resident of Atlantic City, New Jersey, Zarin occasionally gambled, both in his hometown and in other places where gambling was legalized. To facilitate his gaming activities in Atlantic City, Zarin applied to Resorts International Hotel ("Resorts") for a credit line in June, 1978. Following a credit check, Resorts granted Zarin $10,000 of credit. Pursuant to this credit arrangement with Resorts, Zarin could write a check, called a marker,[34] and in return receive chips, which could then be used to gamble at the casino's tables.

Before long, Zarin developed a reputation as an extravagant "high roller" who routinely bet the house maximum while playing craps, his game of choice. Considered a "valued gaming patron" by Resorts, Zarin had his credit limit increased at regular intervals without any further credit checks, and was provided a number of complimentary services and privileges. By November, 1979, Zarin's permanent line of credit had been raised to $200,000. Between June, 1978, and December, 1979, Zarin lost $2,500,000 at the craps table, losses he paid in full.

Responding to allegations of credit abuses, the New Jersey Division of Gaming Enforcement filed with the New Jersey Casino Control Commission a complaint against Resorts. Among the 809 violations of casino regulations alleged in the complaint of October, 1979, were 100 pertaining to Zarin. Subsequently, a Casino Control Commissioner issued an Emergency Order, the effect of which was to make further extensions of credit to Zarin illegal.

---

34. A "marker" is a negotiable draft payable to Resorts and drawn on the maker's bank.

Nevertheless, Resorts continued to extend Zarin's credit limit through the use of two different practices: "considered cleared" credit and "this trip only" credit.[35] Both methods effectively ignored the Emergency Order and were later found to be illegal.[36]

By January, 1980, Zarin was gambling compulsively and uncontrollably at Resorts, spending as many as sixteen hours a day at the craps table.[37] During April, 1980, Resorts again increased Zarin's credit line without further inquiries. That same month, Zarin delivered personal checks and counterchecks to Resorts which were returned as having been drawn against insufficient funds. Those dishonored checks totaled $3,435,000. In late April, Resorts cut off Zarin's credit.

Although Zarin indicated that he would repay those obligations, Resorts filed a New Jersey state court action against Zarin in November, 1980, to collect the $3,435,000. Zarin denied liability on grounds that Resort's claim was unenforceable under New Jersey regulations intended to protect compulsive gamblers. Ten months later, in September, 1981, Resorts and Zarin settled their dispute for a total of $500,000. The Commissioner of Internal Revenue ("Commissioner") subsequently determined deficiencies in Zarin's federal income taxes for 1980 and 1981, arguing that Zarin recognized $3,435,000 of income in 1980 from larceny by trick and deception. After Zarin challenged that claim by filing a Tax Court petition, the Commissioner abandoned his 1980 claim, and argued instead that Zarin had recognized $2,935,000 of income in 1981 from the cancellation of indebtedness which resulted from the settlement with Resorts. Agreeing with the Commissioner, the Tax Court decided, eleven judges to eight, that Zarin had indeed recognized $2,935,000 of income from the discharge of indebtedness, namely the difference between the original $3,435,000 "debt" and the $500,000 settlement. Since he was in the seventy percent tax bracket, Zarin's deficiency for 1981 was calculated to be $2,047,245. With interest to April 5, 1990, Zarin allegedly owes the Internal Revenue Service $5,209,033.96 in additional taxes. Zarin appeals the order of the Tax Court.

II

The sole issue before this Court is whether the Tax Court correctly held that Zarin had income from discharge of indebtedness.[38] Section 108 and section 61(a)(12) of the Code set forth "the general rule that gross income includes income from the discharge of indebtedness." I.R.C. §108(e)(1). The Commissioner argues,

35. Under the "considered cleared" method, Resorts would treat a personal check as a cash transaction, and would therefore not apply the amount of the check in calculating the amount of credit extended Zarin. "This trip only" credit allowed Resorts to grant temporary increases of credit for a given visit, so long as the credit limit was lowered by the next visit.

36. On July 8, 1983, the New Jersey Casino Control Commission found that Resorts violated the Emergency Order at least thirteen different times, nine involving Zarin, and fined Resorts $130,000.

37. Zarin claims that at the time he was suffering from a recognized emotional disorder that caused him to gamble compulsively.

38. Subsequent to the Tax Court's decision, Zarin filed a motion to reconsider, arguing that he was insolvent at the time Resorts forgave his debt, and thus, under I.R.C. section 108(a)(1)(B), could not have income from discharge of indebtedness. He did, not, however, raise that issue before the Tax Court until after it rendered its decision. The Tax Court denied the motion for reconsideration. By reason of our resolution of this case, we do not need to decide whether the Tax Court abused its discretion in denying Zarin's motion.

and the Tax Court agreed, that pursuant to the Code, Zarin did indeed recognize income from discharge of gambling indebtedness.

Under the Commissioner's logic, Resorts advanced Zarin $3,435,000 worth of chips, chips being the functional equivalent of cash. At that time, the chips were not treated as income, since Zarin recognized an obligation of repayment. In other words, Resorts made Zarin a tax-free loan. However, a taxpayer does recognize income if a loan owed to another party is cancelled, in whole or in part. I.R.C. §§61(a)(12), 108(e). The settlement between Zarin and Resorts, claims the Commissioner, fits neatly into the cancellation of indebtedness provisions in the Code. Zarin owed $3,435,000, paid $500,000, with the difference constituting income. Although initially persuasive, the Commissioner's position is nonetheless flawed for two reasons.

III

Initially, we find that sections 108 and 61(a)(12) are inapplicable to the Zarin/Resorts transaction. Section 61 does not define indebtedness. On the other hand, section 108(d)(1), which repeats and further elaborates on the rule in section 61(a)(12), defines the term as any indebtedness "(A) for which the taxpayer is liable, or (B) subject to which the taxpayer holds property." I.R.C. §108(d)(1). In order to bring the taxpayer within the sweep of the discharge of indebtedness rules, then, the IRS must show that one of the two prongs in the section 108(d)(1) test is satisfied. It has not been demonstrated that Zarin satisfies either.

Because the debt Zarin owed to Resorts was unenforceable as a matter of New Jersey state law,[39] it is clearly not a debt "for which the taxpayer is liable." I.R.C. §108(d)(1)(A). Liability implies a legally enforceable obligation to repay, and under New Jersey law, Zarin would have no such obligation.

Moreover, Zarin did not have a debt subject to which he held property as required by section 108(d)(1)(B). Zarin's indebtedness arose out of his acquisition of gambling chips. The Tax Court held that gambling chips were not property, but rather, "a medium of exchange within the Resorts casino" and a "substitute for cash." Alternatively, the Tax Court viewed the chips as nothing more than "the opportunity to gamble and incidental services. . . ." We agree with the gist of these characterizations, and hold that gambling chips are merely an accounting mechanism to evidence debt. Gaming chips in New Jersey during 1980 were regarded "solely as evidence of a debt owed to their custodian by the casino licensee and shall be considered at no time the property of anyone other than the casino licensee issuing them." N.J. Admin. Code tit. 19k, §19:46-1.5(d) (1990). Thus, under New Jersey state law, gambling chips were Resorts's property until transferred to Zarin in exchange for the markers, at which point the chips became "evidence" of indebtedness (and not the property of Zarin).

Even were there no relevant legislative pronouncement on which to rely, simple common sense would lead to the conclusion that chips were not property in Zarin's hands. Zarin could not do with the chips as he pleased, nor did the chips have any independent economic value beyond the casino. The chips themselves were of little

---

39. The Tax Court held that the Commissioner had not met its burden of proving that the debt owed Resorts was enforceable as a matter of state law. *Zarin*, 92 T.C. at 1090. There was ample evidence to support that finding. . . .

use to Zarin, other than as a means of facilitating gambling. They could not have been used outside the casino. They could have been used to purchase services and privileges within the casino, including food, drink, entertainment, and lodging, but Zarin would not have utilized them as such, since he received those services from Resorts on a complimentary basis. In short, the chips had no economic substance.

Although the Tax Court found that theoretically, Zarin could have redeemed the chips he received on credit for cash and walked out of the casino, the reality of the situation was quite different. Realistically, before cashing in his chips, Zarin would have been required to pay his outstanding IOUs. New Jersey state law requires casinos to "request patrons to apply any chips or plaques in their possession in reduction of personal checks or Counter Checks exchanged for purposes of gaming prior to exchanging such chips or plaques for cash or prior to departing from the casino area." N.J. Admin. Code tit. 19k, §19:45-1.24(s) (1979). Since his debt at all times equalled or exceeded the number of chips he possessed, redemption would have left Zarin with no chips, no cash, and certainly nothing which could have been characterized as property.

Not only were the chips non-property in Zarin's hands, but upon transfer to Zarin, the chips also ceased to be the property of Resorts. Since the chips were in the possession of another party, Resorts could no longer do with the chips as it pleased, and could no longer control the chips' use. Generally, at the time of a transfer, the party in possession of the chips can gamble with them, use them for services, cash them in, or walk out of the casino with them as an Atlantic City souvenir. The chips therefore become nothing more than an accounting mechanism, or evidence of a debt, designed to facilitate gambling in casinos where the use of actual money was forbidden. Thus, the chips which Zarin held were not property within the meaning of I.R.C. §108(d)(1)(B).

In short, because Zarin was not liable on the debt he allegedly owed Resorts, and because Zarin did not hold "property" subject to that debt, the cancellation of indebtedness provisions of the Code do not apply to the settlement between Resorts and Zarin. As such, Zarin cannot have income from the discharge of his debt.

Instead of analyzing the transaction at issue as cancelled debt, we believe the proper approach is to view it as disputed debt or contested liability. Under the contested liability doctrine, if a taxpayer, in good faith, disputed the amount of a debt, a subsequent settlement of the dispute would be treated as the amount of debt cognizable for tax purposes. The excess of the original debt over the amount determined to have been due is disregarded for both loss and debt accounting purposes. Thus, if a taxpayer took out a loan for $10,000, refused in good faith to pay the full $10,000 back, and then reached an agreement with the lender that he would pay back only $7,000 in full satisfaction of the debt, the transaction would be treated as if the initial loan was $7,000. When the taxpayer tenders the $7,000 payment, he will have been deemed to have paid the full amount of the initially disputed debt. Accordingly, there is no tax consequence to the taxpayer upon payment.

The seminal "contested liability" case is N. Sobel, Inc. v. Commissioner, 40 B.T.A. 1263 (1939). In *Sobel*, the taxpayer exchanged a $21,700 note for 100 shares of stock from a bank. In the following year, the taxpayer sued the bank for rescission, arguing that the bank loan was violative of state law, and moreover, that the bank had failed to perform certain promises. The parties eventually settled the case in 1935, with the taxpayer agreeing to pay half of the face amount of the note. In the year of the settlement, the taxpayer claimed the amount paid as a loss. The Commissioner denied the loss because it had been sustained five years earlier, and further asserted that the taxpayer recognized income from the discharge of half of his indebtedness.

The Board of Tax Appeals held that since the loss was not fixed until the dispute was settled, the loss was recognized in 1935, the year of the settlement, and the deduction was appropriately taken in that year. Additionally, the Board held that the portion of the note forgiven by the bank "was not the occasion for a freeing of assets and that there was no gain. . . ." Id. at 1265. Therefore, the taxpayer did not have any income from cancellation of indebtedness.

There is little difference between the present case and *Sobel*. Zarin incurred a $3,435,000 debt while gambling at Resorts, but in court, disputed liability on the basis of unenforceability. A settlement of $500,000 was eventually agreed upon. It follows from *Sobel* that the settlement served only to fix the amount of debt. No income was realized or recognized. When Zarin paid the $500,000, any tax consequence dissolved.[40]

Only one other court has addressed a case factually similar to the one before us. In United States v. Hall, 307 F.2d 238 (10th Cir. 1962), the taxpayer owed an unenforceable gambling debt alleged to be $225,000. Subsequently, the taxpayer and the creditor settled for $150,000. The taxpayer then transferred cattle valued at $148,110 to his creditor in satisfaction of the settlement agreement. A jury held that the parties fixed the debt at $150,000, and that the taxpayer recognized income from cancellation of indebtedness equal to the difference between the $150,000 and the $148,110 value affixed to the cattle. Arguing that the taxpayer recognized income equal to the difference between $225,000 and $148,000, the Commissioner appealed.

The Tenth Circuit rejected the idea that the taxpayer had any income from cancellation of indebtedness. Noting that the gambling debt was unenforceable, the Tenth Circuit said, "The cold fact is that taxpayer suffered a substantial loss from gambling, the amount of which was determined by the transfer." Id. at 241. In effect, the Court held that because the debt was unenforceable, the amount of the loss and resulting debt cognizable for tax purposes were fixed by the settlement at $148,110. Thus, the Tenth Circuit lent its endorsement to the contested liability doctrine in a factual situation strikingly similar to the one at issue.

The Commissioner argues that *Sobel* and the contested liability doctrine only apply when there is an unliquidated debt; that is, a debt for which the amount cannot be determined. *See* Colonial Sav. Assn. v. Commissioner, 85 T.C. 855, 862-863 (1985) (*Sobel* stands for the proposition that "there must be a liquidated debt"), *aff'd*, 854 F.2d 1001 (7th Cir. 1988). *See also* N. Sobel, Inc. v. Commissioner, 40 B.T.A. at 1265 (there was a dispute as to "liability and the amount" of the debt). Since Zarin contested his liability based on the unenforceability of the entire debt, and did not dispute the amount of the debt, the Commissioner would have us adopt the reasoning of the Tax Court, which found that Zarin's debt was liquidated, therefore barring the application of *Sobel* and the contested liability doctrine. . . .

---

40. Had Zarin not paid the $500,000 dollar settlement, it would be likely that he would have had income from cancellation of indebtedness. The debt at that point would have been fixed, and Zarin would have been legally obligated to pay it.

We reject the Tax Court's rationale. When a debt is unenforceable, it follows that the amount of the debt, and not just the liability thereon, is in dispute. Although a debt may be unenforceable, there still could be some value attached to its worth. This is especially so with regards to gambling debts. In most states, gambling debts are unenforceable, and have "but slight potential. . . ." United States v. Hall, 307 F.2d 238, 241 (10th Cir. 1962). Nevertheless, they are often collected, at least in part. For example, Resorts is not a charity; it would not have extended illegal credit to Zarin and others if it did not have some hope of collecting debts incurred pursuant to the grant of credit.

Moreover, the debt is frequently incurred to acquire gambling chips, and not money. Although casinos attach a dollar value to each chip, that value, unlike money's, is not beyond dispute, particularly given the illegality of gambling debts in the first place. This proposition is supported by the facts of the present case. Resorts gave Zarin $3.4 million dollars of chips in exchange for markers evidencing Zarin's debt. If indeed the only issue was the enforceability of the entire debt, there would have been no settlement. Zarin would have owed all or nothing. Instead, the parties attached a value to the debt considerably lower than its face value. In other words, the parties agreed that given the circumstances surrounding Zarin's gambling spree, the chips he acquired might not have been worth $3.4 million dollars, but were worth something. Such a debt cannot be called liquidated, since its exact amount was not fixed until settlement.

To summarize, the transaction between Zarin and Resorts can best be characterized as a disputed debt, or contested liability. Zarin owed an unenforceable debt of $3,435,000 to Resorts. After Zarin in good faith disputed his obligation to repay the debt, the parties settled for $500,000, which Zarin paid. That $500,000 settlement fixed the amount of loss and the amount of debt cognizable for tax purposes. Since Zarin was deemed to have owed $500,000, and since he paid Resorts $500,000, no adverse tax consequences attached to Zarin as a result.[41]

In conclusion, we hold that Zarin did not have any income from cancellation of indebtedness for two reasons. First, the Code provisions covering discharge of debt are inapplicable since the definitional requirement in I.R.C. section 108(d)(1) was not met. Second, the settlement of Zarin's gambling debts was a contested liability. We reverse the decision of the Tax Court and remand with instructions to enter judgment that Zarin realized no income by reason of his settlement with Resorts.

STAPLETON, Circuit Judge, dissenting.

I respectfully dissent because I agree with the Commissioner's appraisal of the economic realities of this matter.

Resorts sells for cash the exhilaration and the potential for profit inherent in games of chance. It does so by selling for cash chips that entitle the holder to gamble at its casino. Zarin, like thousands of others, wished to purchase what Resorts was offering in the marketplace. He chose to make this purchase on credit

41. The Commissioner argues in the alternative that Zarin recognized $3,435,000 of income in 1980. This claim has no merit. Recognition of income would depend upon a finding that Zarin did not have cancellation of indebtedness income solely because his debt was unenforceable. We do not so hold. Although unenforceability is a factor in our analysis, our decision ultimately hinges upon the determination that the "disputed debt" rule applied, or alternatively, that chips are not property within the meaning of I.R.C. section 108.

and executed notes evidencing his obligation to repay the funds that were advanced to him by Resorts. As in most purchase money transactions, Resorts skipped the step of giving Zarin cash that he would only return to it in order to pay for the opportunity to gamble. Resorts provided him instead with chips that entitled him to participate in Resorts' games of chance on the same basis as others who had paid cash for that privilege.[42] Whether viewed as a one- or two-step transaction, however, Zarin received either $3.4 million in cash or an entitlement for which others would have had to pay $3.4 million.

Despite the fact that Zarin received in 1980 cash or an entitlement worth $3.4 million, he correctly reported in that year no income from his dealings with Resorts. He did so solely because he recognized, as evidenced by his notes, an offsetting obligation to repay Resorts $3.4 million in cash. In 1981, with the delivery of Zarin's promise to pay Resorts $500,000 and the execution of a release by Resorts, Resorts surrendered its claim to repayment of the remaining $2.9 million of the money Zarin had borrowed. As of that time, Zarin's assets were freed of his potential liability for that amount and he recognized gross income in that amount.[43]

The only alternatives I see to this conclusion are to hold either (1) that Zarin realized $3.4 million in income in 1980 at a time when both parties to the transaction thought there was an offsetting obligation to repay or (2) that the $3.4 million benefit sought and received by Zarin is not taxable at all. I find the latter alternative unacceptable as inconsistent with the fundamental principle of the Code that anything of commercial value received by a taxpayer is taxable unless expressly excluded from gross income.[44] I find the former alternative unacceptable as impracticable. In 1980, neither party was maintaining that the debt was unenforceable and, because of the settlement, its unenforceability was not even established in the litigation over the debt in 1981. It was not until 1989 in this litigation over the tax consequences of the transaction that the unenforceability was first judicially declared. Rather than require such tax litigation to resolve the correct treatment of a debt transaction, I regard it as far preferable to have the tax consequences turn on the manner in which the debt is treated by the parties. For present purposes, it will suffice to say that where something that would otherwise be includable in gross

42. I view as irrelevant the facts that Resorts advanced credit to Zarin solely to enable him to patronize its casino and that the chips could not be used elsewhere or for other purposes. When one buys a sofa from the furniture store on credit, the fact that the proprietor would not have advanced the credit for a different purpose does not entitle one to a tax-free gain in the event the debt to the store is extinguished for some reason.

43. This is not a case in which parties agree subsequent to a purchase money transaction that the property purchased has a value less than thought at the time of the transaction. In such cases, the purchase price adjustment rule is applied and the agreed-upon value is accepted as the value of the benefit received by the purchaser; see e.g., Commissioner v. Sherman, 135 F.2d 68 (6th Cir. 1943); N. Sobel, Inc. v. Commissioner, 40 B.T.A. 1263 (1939). Nor is this a case in which the taxpayer is entitled to rescind an entire purchase money transaction, thereby to restore itself to the position it occupied before receiving anything of commercial value. In this case, the illegality was in the extension of credit by Resorts and whether one views the benefit received by Zarin as cash or the opportunity to gamble, he is no longer in a position to return that benefit.

44. As the court's opinion correctly points out, this record will not support an exclusion under §108(a) which relates to discharge of debt in an insolvency or bankruptcy context. Section 108(e)(5) of the Code, which excludes discharged indebtedness arising from a "purchase price adjustment" is not applicable here. Among other things, §108(e)(5) necessarily applies only to a situation in which the debtor still holds the property acquired in the purchase money transaction. Equally irrelevant is §108(d)'s definition of "indebtedness" relied upon heavily by the court. Section 108(d) expressly defines that term solely for the purposes of §108 and not for the purposes of §61(a)(12).

income is received on credit in a purchase money transaction, there should be no recognition of income so long as the debtor continues to recognize an obligation to repay the debt. On the other hand, income, if not earlier recognized, should be recognized when the debtor no longer recognizes an obligation to repay and the creditor has released the debt or acknowledged its unenforceability.

In this view, it makes no difference whether the extinguishment of the creditor's claim comes as a part of a compromise. Resorts settled for 14 cents on the dollar presumably because it viewed such a settlement as reflective of the odds that the debt would be held to be enforceable. While Zarin should be given credit for the fact that he had to pay 14 cents for a release, I see no reason why he should not realize gain in the same manner as he would have if Resorts had concluded on its own that the debt was legally unenforceable and had written it off as uncollectible.

I would affirm the judgment of the Tax Court.

Notes

1. *The commentators. Zarin* has inspired a great deal of commentary from tax academics and tax practitioners—perhaps more than any other non-Supreme Court tax case of the past two or three decades. There are almost as many different technical analyses of the case as there are commentators, with a nearly even division among the commentators on the bottom-line question of whether Mr. Zarin had *Kirby* income. Almost no one, however, defends the route taken by the Third Circuit to reach its no-income conclusion. For a discussion of the problems with the court's reliance on the disputed liability doctrine, see Note 1 following the *Collins* case, in part C.2.b of this chapter.

2. Zarin *as an instance of gambling on credit.* The following analysis supports the court's no-income conclusion in *Zarin*, but reaches that result via a very different route than that taken by the court.[45] Do you find it persuasive?

   (a) Suppose two professional gamblers place a bet on the outcome of a basketball game, each agreeing to pay the other $100,000 if the other's team wins, and each trusting the other sufficiently that neither puts $100,000 in escrow (or "on the table") pending the outcome of the game. Also suppose that the loser is under a legally binding obligation to pay $100,000 to the winner. If the winner eventually agrees to accept $60,000 from the loser and to cancel the loser's debt for the other $40,000 (for reasons that do not qualify the cancellation as a gift under §102), does the loser have $40,000 of *Kirby* income? If one adopts the view that *Kirby* income results from a debt cancellation only if the taxpayer received untaxed value when the debt was created,[46] the crucial question is whether the loser received something of value that would have been taxable but for the existence of the debt. He did not. The loser did have the opportunity to gamble, but if each

---

45. The analysis set forth here is based on Lawrence Zelenak, *Cancellation-of-Indebtedness Income and Transactional Accounting*, 29 Va. Tax Rev. 277 (2009).

46. For an elaboration of this view, see Note 2 following the *Bradford* case above, in the cell, "Defining Debt Cancellation Income."

team was equally likely to win, the expected value of the bet was zero. The opportunity to make a bet with a zero expected value would not produce taxable income even in the absence of a debt obligation (and, indeed, the debt obligation did not exist until sometime after the bet had been made).

(b) Now consider a different situation. Suppose our taxpayer (the eventual loser) wants to make the bet described above, with the same counterparty, but that the counterparty is willing to make the bet only if the taxpayer places $100,000 cash in escrow (on the table). Accordingly, the taxpayer borrows $100,000 from a bank, and uses the borrowed money as escrow for the bet. The taxpayer loses the bet, the counterparty takes the escrowed $100,000, and eventually the taxpayer settles his debt to the bank with a payment to the bank of $60,000 and cancellation by the bank of the other $40,000. Does this taxpayer have $40,000 of *Kirby* income? Clearly he does, because he received cash that would have been taxable but for his repayment obligation.

(c) Now consider an intermediate situation. Suppose our taxpayer borrows $100,000 cash from a person who happens to be his counterparty in the bet and uses the borrowed cash as the escrow payment in the bet, but that it is merely a coincidence that the lender and the counterparty are the same person. In other words, the lender did not lend the $100,000 with the understanding that it would be placed on the table in connection with the bet. The taxpayer was not obligated at the time of borrowing the money to make the bet, and could have used the $100,000 for any number of other purposes. Given the stipulation of no connection between the loan and the bet, the *Kirby* income analysis of this situation should be identical to that of the previous situation; the taxpayer should have $40,000 of *Kirby* income when $40,000 of the debt is cancelled.

(d) Finally, consider a variation in which the counterparty to the bet nominally lends $100,000 to the taxpayer, but does so in direct connection with the bet, with the understanding that the only thing the taxpayer may do with the money is put it in escrow for the bet. When the taxpayer loses the bet and the counterparty/lender pockets the escrowed cash, the taxpayer still owes $100,000 on the so-called loan. If that debt is eventually settled by the taxpayer paying $60,000 and the counterparty/lender writing off the other $40,000, does the taxpayer have $40,000 of *Kirby* income? In other words, is the substance of this situation (d) closer to that of situation (a) (gambling without escrow, which does not result in *Kirby* income), or closer to that of situation (c) (genuine borrowing followed by the use of the borrowed funds in an unrelated bet with the lender, which does result in *Kirby* income)? The answer is clear. The substance of situation (d) is the same as the substance of situation (a), and the tax consequences should also be the same. In both situations, the taxpayer will owe $100,000 to the counterparty if—and only if—he loses the bet, and in neither situation does the taxpayer ever have control over any of the counterparty's cash. In situation (c), by contrast, the taxpayer owes the counterparty $100,000 before he makes the bet, and he has many choices—besides the making of the bet—as to how to use the borrowed funds.

Situation (d) is a simplified version of the facts of *Zarin*. At least according to the Third Circuit's view of the facts, "Zarin could not do with the chips as he pleased, nor did the chips have any independent economic value beyond the casino. The chips themselves were of little use to Zarin other than as a means of facilitating gambling." The IRS argued that the transaction in chips was the functional equivalent of a loan of cash, with the result that Mr. Zarin had *Kirby* income. In other words, the IRS argued the case was an example of hypothetical situation (c). But under the facts as described by the Third Circuit, the case was actually an example of situation (d). Faced with an instance of situation (d), the Third Circuit reached the correct result — despite its highly dubious technical analysis — when it concluded that Mr. Zarin did not have *Kirby* income.

Chapter 3

PROPERTY TRANSACTIONS

A. THE REALIZATION DOCTRINE

1. *The Great Case of* Eisner v. Macomber

EISNER v. MACOMBER

252 U.S. 189 (1920)

Mr. Justice PITNEY delivered the opinion of the Court.

This case presents the question whether, by virtue of the Sixteenth Amendment, Congress has the power to tax, as income of the stockholder and without apportionment, a stock dividend made lawfully and in good faith against profits accumulated by the corporation since March 1, 1913.

It arises under the Revenue Act of September 8, 1916, which, in our opinion, plainly evinces the purpose of Congress to tax stock dividends as income.

The facts, in outline, are as follows:

On January 1, 1916, the Standard Oil Company of California, a corporation of that State, . . . had shares of stock outstanding, par value $100 each, amounting in round figures to $50,000,000. In addition, it had surplus and undivided profits invested in plant, property, and business and required for the purposes of the corporation, amounting to about $45,000,000. . . . In January, 1916, in order to readjust the capitalization, the board of directors decided to issue additional shares sufficient to constitute a stock dividend of 50 percent of the outstanding stock, and to transfer from surplus account to capital stock account an amount equivalent to such issue. Appropriate resolutions were adopted, an amount equivalent to the par value of the proposed new stock was transferred accordingly, and the new stock duly issued against it and divided among the stockholders.

Defendant in error, being the owner of 2,200 shares of the old stock, received certificates for 1,100 additional shares. . . . She was called upon to pay, and did pay under protest, a tax imposed under the Revenue Act of 1916, based upon a supposed income of $19,877 because of the new shares; and an appeal to the Commissioner of Internal Revenue having been disallowed, she brought action against the Collector to recover the tax. In her complaint she alleged the above facts, and contended that in imposing such a tax the Revenue Act of 1916 violated Art. I, §2, cl. 3, and Art. I, §9, cl. 4, of the Constitution of the United States, requiring direct taxes to be apportioned according to population, and that the stock dividend was not income within the meaning of the Sixteenth Amendment. . . .

[I]n view of the importance of the matter, and the fact that Congress in the Revenue Act of 1916 declared (39 Stat. 757) that a "stock dividend shall be considered income, to the amount of its cash value," we will deal at length with the constitutional question. . . .

The Sixteenth Amendment must be construed in connection with the taxing clauses of the original Constitution and the effect attributed to them before the Amendment was adopted. In Pollock v. Farmers' Loan & Trust Co., 158 U.S. 601, under the Act of August 27, 1894, c. 349, §27, 28 Stat. 509, 553, it was held that taxes upon rents and profits of real estate and upon returns from investments of personal property were in effect direct taxes upon the property from which such income arose, imposed by reason of ownership; and that Congress could not impose such taxes without apportioning them among the States according to population, as required by Art. I, §2, cl. 3, and §9, cl. 4, of the original Constitution.

Afterwards, and evidently in recognition of the limitation upon the taxing power of Congress thus determined, the Sixteenth Amendment was adopted, in words lucidly expressing the object to be accomplished: "The Congress shall have power to lay and collect taxes on incomes, from whatever source derived, without apportionment among the several States, and without regard to any census or enumeration." As repeatedly held, this did not extend the taxing power to new subjects, but merely removed the necessity which otherwise might exist for an apportionment among the States of taxes laid on income.

A proper regard for its genesis, as well as its very clear language, requires also that this Amendment shall not be extended by loose construction, so as to repeal or modify, except as applied to income, those provisions of the Constitution that require an apportionment according to population for direct taxes upon property, real and personal. This limitation still has an appropriate and important function, and is not to be overridden by Congress or disregarded by the courts.

In order, therefore, that the clauses cited from Article I of the Constitution may have proper force and effect, save only as modified by the Amendment, and that the latter also may have proper effect, it becomes essential to distinguish between what is and what is not "income," as the term is there used; and to apply the distinction, as cases arise, according to truth and substance, without regard to form. Congress cannot by any definition it may adopt conclude the matter, since it cannot by legislation alter the Constitution, from which alone it derives its power to legislate, and within whose limitations alone that power can be lawfully exercised.

The fundamental relation of "capital" to "income" has been much discussed by economists, the former being likened to the tree or the land, the latter to the fruit or the crop; the former depicted as a reservoir supplied from springs, the latter as the outlet stream, to be measured by its flow during a period of time. For the present purpose we require only a clear definition of the term "income," as used in common speech, in order to determine its meaning in the Amendment; and, having formed also a correct judgment as to the nature of a stock dividend, we shall find it easy to decide the matter at issue.

After examining dictionaries in common use (Bouv. L.D.; Standard Dict.; Webster's Internal. Dict.; Century Dict.), we find little to add to the succinct definition adopted in two cases arising under the Corporation Tax Act of 1909 (Stratton's Independence v. Howbert, 231 U.S. 399, 415; Doyle v. Mitchell Bros. Co., 247 U.S. 179, 185) — "Income may be defined as the gain derived from capital, from labor, or from both combined," provided it be understood to include profit gained through a sale or conversion of capital assets, to which it was applied in the *Doyle* case (pp. 183, 185).

Brief as it is, it indicates the characteristic and distinguishing attribute of income essential for a correct solution of the present controversy. The Government, although basing its argument upon the definition as quoted, placed chief emphasis upon the word "gain," which was extended to include a variety of meanings; while the significance of the next three words was either overlooked or misconceived. *"Derived — from — capital"; —* "the *gain — derived — from — capital,"* etc. Here we have the essential matter: *not* a gain *accruing to* capital, not a *growth* or *increment* of value in the investment; but a gain, a profit, something of exchangeable *value proceeding from* the property, *severed from* the capital however invested or employed, and *coming in,* being *"derived,"* that is, *received or drawn by* the recipient (the taxpayer) for his *separate* use, benefit and disposal; —*that is* income derived from property. Nothing else answers the description.

The same fundamental conception is clearly set forth in the Sixteenth Amendment — "incomes, *from* whatever *source derived"* — the essential thought being expressed with a conciseness and lucidity entirely in harmony with the form and style of the Constitution.

Can a stock dividend, considering its essential character, be brought within the definition? To answer this, regard must be had to the nature of a corporation and the stockholder's relation to it. We refer, of course, to a corporation such as the one in the case at bar, organized for profit, and having a capital stock divided into shares to which a nominal or par value is attributed.

Certainly the interest of the stockholder is a capital interest, and his certificates of stock are but the evidence of it. They state the number of shares to which he is entitled and indicate their par value and how the stock may be transferred. They show that he or his assignors, immediate or remote, have contributed capital to the enterprise, that he is entitled to a corresponding interest proportionate to the whole, entitled to have the property and business of the company devoted during the corporate existence to attainment of the common objects, entitled to vote at stockholders' meetings, to receive dividends out of the corporation's profits if and when declared, and, in the event of liquidation, to receive a proportionate share of the net assets, if any, remaining after paying creditors. Short of liquidation, or until dividend declared, he has no right to withdraw any part of either capital or profits from the common enterprise; on the contrary, his interest pertains not to any part, divisible or indivisible, but to the entire assets, business, and affairs of the company. Nor is it the interest of an owner in the assets themselves, since the corporation has full title, legal and equitable, to the whole. The stockholder has the right to have the assets employed in the enterprise, with the incidental rights mentioned; but, as stockholder, he has no right to withdraw, only the right to persist, subject to the risks of the enterprise, and looking only to dividends for his return. If he desires to dissociate himself from the company he can do so only by disposing of his stock.

For bookkeeping purposes, the company acknowledges a liability in form to the stockholders equivalent to the aggregate par value of their stock, evidenced by a "capital stock account." If profits have been made and not divided they create additional bookkeeping liabilities under the head of "profit and loss," "undivided profits," "surplus account," or the like. None of these, however, gives to the stockholders as a body, much less to any one of them, either a claim against the going concern for any particular sum of money, or a right to any particular portion of the assets or any share in them unless or until the directors conclude that dividends shall be made and a part of the company's assets segregated from the common fund for the purpose. The dividend normally is payable in money, under exceptional circumstances in some other divisible property; and when so paid, then only (excluding, of course, a possible advantageous sale of his stock or winding-up of the company) does the stockholder realize a profit or gain which becomes his separate property, and thus derive income from the capital that he or his predecessor has invested.

In the present case, the corporation had surplus and undivided profits invested in plant, property, and business, and required for the purposes of the corporation, amounting to about $45,000,000, in addition to outstanding capital stock of $50,000,000. In this the case is not extraordinary. The profits of a corporation, as they appear upon the balance sheet at the end of the year, need not be in the form of money on hand in excess of what is required to meet current liabilities and finance current operations of the company. Often, especially in a growing business, only a part, sometimes a small part, of the year's profits is in property capable of division; the remainder having been absorbed in the acquisition of increased plant, equipment, stock in trade, or accounts receivable, or in decrease of outstanding liabilities. When only a part is available for dividends, the balance of the year's profits is carried to the credit of undivided profits, or surplus, or some other account having like significance. If thereafter the company finds itself in funds beyond current needs it may declare dividends out of such surplus or undivided profits; otherwise it may go on for years conducting a successful business, but requiring more and more working capital because of the extension of its operations, and therefore unable to declare dividends approximating the amount of its profits. Thus the surplus may increase until it equals or even exceeds the par value of the outstanding capital stock. This may be adjusted upon the books in the mode adopted in the case at bar — by declaring a "stock dividend." This, however, is no more than a book adjustment, in essence not a dividend but rather the opposite; no part of the assets of the company is separated from the common fund, nothing distributed except paper certificates that evidence an antecedent increase in the value of the stockholder's capital interest resulting from an accumulation of profits by the company, but profits so far absorbed in the business as to render it impracticable to separate them for withdrawal and distribution. In order to make the adjustment, a charge is made against surplus account with corresponding credit to capital stock account, equal to the proposed "dividend"; the new stock is issued against this and the certificates delivered to the existing stockholders in proportion to their previous holdings. This, however, is merely bookkeeping that does not affect the aggregate assets of the corporation or its outstanding liabilities; it affects only the form, not the essence, of the "liability" acknowledged by the corporation to its own shareholders, and this through a readjustment of accounts on one side of the balance sheet only, increasing "capital stock" at the expense of "surplus"; it does not alter the preexisting proportionate interest of any stockholder or increase the intrinsic value of his holding or of the aggregate holdings of the other stockholders as they stood before. The new certificates simply increase the number of the shares, with consequent dilution of the value of each share.

A "stock dividend" shows that the company's accumulated profits have been capitalized, instead of distributed to the stockholders or retained as surplus available for distribution in money or in kind should opportunity offer. Far from being a realization of profits of the stockholder, it tends rather to postpone such realization, in that the fund represented by the new stock has been transferred from surplus to capital, and no longer is available for actual distribution.

The essential and controlling fact is that the stockholder has received nothing out of the company's assets for his separate use and benefit; on the contrary, every dollar of his original investment, together with whatever accretions and accumulations have resulted from employment of his money and that of the other stockholders in the business of the company, still remains the property of the company, and subject to business risks which may result in wiping out the entire investment. Having regard to the very truth of the matter, to substance and not to form, he has received nothing that answers the definition of income within the meaning of the Sixteenth Amendment. . . .

We are clear that not only does a stock dividend really take nothing from the property of the corporation and add nothing to that of the shareholder, but that the antecedent accumulation of profits evidenced thereby, while indicating that the shareholder is the richer because of an increase of his capital, at the same time shows he has not realized or received any income in the transaction.

It is said that a stockholder may sell the new shares acquired in the stock dividend; and so he may, if he can find a buyer. It is equally true that if he does sell, and in doing so realizes a profit, such profit, like any other, is income, and so far as it may have arisen since the Sixteenth Amendment is taxable by Congress without apportionment. The same would be true were he to sell some of his original shares at a profit. But if a shareholder sells dividend stock he necessarily disposes of a part of his capital interest, just as if he should sell a part of his old stock, either before or after the dividend. What he retains no longer entitles him to the same proportion of future dividends as before the sale. His part in the control of the company likewise is diminished. Thus, if one holding $60,000 out of a total $100,000 of the capital stock of a corporation should receive in common with other stockholders a 50 percent stock dividend, and should sell his part, he thereby would be reduced from a majority to a minority stockholder, having six-fifteenths instead of six-tenths of the total stock outstanding. A corresponding and proportionate decrease in capital interest and in voting power would befall a minority holder should he sell dividend stock; it being in the nature of things impossible for one to dispose of any part of such an issue without a proportionate disturbance of the distribution of the entire capital stock, and a like diminution of the seller's comparative voting power — that "right preservative of rights" in the control of a corporation. Yet, without selling, the shareholder, unless possessed of other resources, has not the wherewithal to pay an income tax upon the dividend stock. Nothing could more clearly show that to tax a stock dividend is to tax a capital increase, and not income, than this demonstration that in the nature of things it requires conversion of capital in order to pay the tax. . . .

We have no doubt of the power or duty of a court to look through the form of the corporation and determine the question of the stockholder's right, in order to ascertain whether he has received income taxable by Congress without apportionment. But, looking through the form, we cannot disregard the essential truth disclosed; ignore the substantial difference between corporation and stockholder; treat the entire organization as unreal; look upon stockholders as partners, when they are not such; treat them as having in equity a right to a partition of the corporate assets, when they have none; and indulge the fiction that they have received and realized a share of the profits of the company which in truth they have neither received nor realized. We must treat the corporation as a substantial entity separate from the stockholder, not only because such is the practical fact but because it is only by recognizing such separateness that any dividend — even one paid in money or property — can be regarded as income of the stockholder. If we regard corporation and stockholders as altogether identical, there would be no income except as the corporation acquired it; and while this would be taxable against the corporation as income under appropriate provisions of law, the individual stockholders could not be separately and additionally taxed with respect to their several shares even when divided, since if there were entire identity between them and the company they could not be regarded as receiving anything from it, any more than if one's money were to be removed from one pocket to another.

Conceding that the mere issue of a stock dividend makes the recipient no richer than before, the Government nevertheless contends that the new certificates measure the extent to which the gains accumulated by the corporation have made him the richer. There are two insuperable difficulties with this: In the first place, it would depend upon how long he had held the stock whether the stock dividend indicated the extent to which he had been enriched by the operations of the company; unless he had held it throughout such operations the measure would not hold true. Secondly, and more important for present purposes, enrichment through increase in value of capital investment is not income in any proper meaning of the term.

The complaint contains averments respecting the market prices of stock such as plaintiff held, based upon sales before and after the stock dividend, tending to show that the receipt of the additional shares did not substantially change the market value of her entire holdings. This tends to show that in this instance market quotations reflected intrinsic values — a thing they do not always do. But we regard the market prices of the securities as an unsafe criterion in an inquiry such as the present, when the question must be, not what will the thing sell for, but what is it in truth and in essence.

It is said there is no difference in principle between a simple stock dividend and a case where stockholders use money received as cash dividends to purchase additional stock contemporaneously issued by the corporation. But an actual cash dividend, with a real option to the stockholder either to keep the money for his own or to reinvest it in new shares, would be as far removed as possible from a true stock dividend, such as the one we have under consideration, where nothing of value is taken from the company's assets and transferred to the individual ownership of the several stockholders and thereby subjected to their disposal. . . .

[T]he Government, . . . virtually abandoning the contention that a stock dividend increases the interest of the stockholder or otherwise enriches him, insist[s] as an alternative that by the true construction of the Act of 1916 the tax is imposed not upon the stock dividend but rather upon the stockholder's share of the undivided profits previously accumulated by the corporation; the tax being levied as a matter of convenience at the time such profits become manifest through the stock dividend. If so construed, would the act be constitutional?

That Congress has power to tax shareholders upon their property interests in the stock of corporations is beyond question; and that such interests might be valued in view of the condition of the company, including its accumulated and undivided profits, is equally clear. But that this would be taxation of property because of ownership, and hence would require apportionment under the provisions of the Constitution, is settled beyond peradventure by previous decisions of this court. . . .

Thus, from every point of view, we are brought irresistibly to the conclusion that neither under the Sixteenth Amendment nor otherwise has Congress power to tax without apportionment a true stock dividend made lawfully and in good faith, or the accumulated profits behind it, as income of the stockholder. The Revenue Act of 1916, in so far as it imposes a tax upon the stockholder because of such dividend, contravenes the provisions of Article I, §2, cl. 3, and Article I, §9, cl. 4, of the Constitution, and to this extent is invalid notwithstanding the Sixteenth Amendment.

Mr. Justice HOLMES, dissenting.

. . . I think that the word "incomes" in the Sixteenth Amendment should be read in "a sense most obvious to the common understanding at the time of its adoption." For it was for public adoption that it was proposed. McCulloch v. Maryland, 4 Wheat. 316, 407. The known purpose of this Amendment was to get rid of nice questions as to what might be direct taxes, and I cannot doubt that most people not lawyers would suppose when they voted for it that they put a question like the present to rest. I am of opinion that the Amendment justifies the tax.

Mr. Justice BRANDEIS, dissenting.

Financiers, with the aid of lawyers, devised long ago two different methods by which a corporation can, without increasing its indebtedness, keep for corporate purposes accumulated profits, and yet, in effect, distribute these profits among its stockholders. One method is a simple one. The capital stock is increased; the new stock is paid up with the accumulated profits; and the new shares of paid-up stock are then distributed among the stockholders pro rata as a dividend. If the stockholder prefers ready money to increasing his holding of the stock in the company, he sells the new stock received as a dividend. The other method is slightly more complicated. Arrangements are made for an increase of stock to be offered to stockholders pro rata at par and, at the same time, for the payment of a cash dividend equal to the amount which the stockholder will be required to pay to the company, if he avails himself of the right to subscribe for his pro rata of the new stock. If the stockholder takes the new stock as is expected, he may endorse the dividend check received to the corporation and thus pay for the new stock. In order to ensure that all the new stock so offered will be taken, the price at which it is offered is fixed far below what it is believed will be its market value. If the stockholder prefers ready money to an increase of his holdings of stock, he may sell his right to take new stock pro rata, which is evidenced by an assignable instrument. In that event the purchaser of the rights repays to the corporation, as the subscription price of the new stock, an amount equal to that which it had paid as a cash dividend to the stockholder.

Both of these methods of retaining accumulated profits while in effect distributing them as a dividend had been in common use in the United States for many years prior to the adoption of the Sixteenth Amendment. They were recognized equivalents. . . .

It is conceded that if the stock dividend paid to Mrs. Macomber had been made by . . . issuing rights to take new stock pro rata and paying to each stockholder simultaneously a dividend in cash sufficient in amount to enable him to pay for this pro rata of new stock to be purchased — the dividend so paid to him would have been taxable as income, whether he retained the cash or whether he returned it to the corporation in payment for his pro rata of new stock. But it is contended that, because the simple method was adopted of having the new stock issued direct to the stockholders as paid-up stock, the new stock is not to be deemed income, whether she retained it or converted it into cash by sale. If such a different result can flow merely from the difference in the method pursued, it must be because Congress is without power to tax as income of the stockholder either the stock received under the latter method or the proceeds of its sale; for Congress has, by the provisions in the Revenue Act of 1916, expressly declared its purpose to make stock dividends, by whichever method paid, taxable as income. . . .

Hitherto powers conferred upon Congress by the Constitution have been liberally construed, and have been held to extend to every means appropriate to attain the end sought. In determining the scope of the power the substance of the transaction, not its form has been regarded. Is there anything in the phraseology of the Sixteenth Amendment or in the nature of corporate dividends which should lead to a departure from these rules of construction and compel this court to hold, that Congress is powerless to prevent a result so extraordinary as that here contended for by the stockholder? . . .

If stock dividends representing profits are held exempt from taxation under the Sixteenth Amendment, the owners of the most successful businesses in America will, as the facts in this case illustrate, be able to escape taxation on a large part of what is actually their income. . . . That such a result was intended by the people of the United States when adopting the Sixteenth Amendment is inconceivable.

2.   *Unrealized Appreciation, Stock Dividends, and Cash Dividends*

Consider a miniature version of the facts of *Macomber*. Sara owns both of the outstanding shares of X Corporation. She created X several years before, by transferring $100 to X in exchange for the two shares of stock. Since its creation, X has earned and retained $50, so Sara is now the 100 percent owner of a corporation worth $150. If she causes X to issue her a third share of stock, identical to the two existing shares, will she be any richer after the stock dividend than immediately before it? Obviously not. Before she owned two shares worth $75 each, afterwards she owns 3 shares worth $50 each, and $75 × 2 = $50 × 3. Just as you can't make a pizza bigger by cutting it into more slices, you can't make yourself richer by dividing your ownership of a corporation into a larger number of shares. Before concluding that this proves the Supreme Court was right in *Macomber*, however, consider the alternative of a cash dividend. Suppose that, when X has $50 of retained earnings, Sara decides to have X distribute $50 to her as a cash dividend. Is Sara richer just after the cash dividend than she was just before it? As with the stock dividend, she clearly is not. Before the cash dividend she owned stock worth $150; after the dividend she owns stock worth $100 and $50 cash. Yet the Supreme Court in *Macomber* assumes that a cash dividend constitutes income (under both the Revenue Act and the Sixteenth Amendment).[1] How can even a *cash* dividend be taxable if it does not increase the recipient's net worth?

The answer is that the income tax generally does not tax an increase in the value of a taxpayer's asset, as long as the taxpayer merely continues to hold the asset. Thus,

---

1. Under current law, §61(a)(7) specifies that dividends are included in gross income. Under a temporary provision, scheduled to expire after 2012, most dividends are subject to favorable tax rates of 15 percent or less. Section 1(h)(11).

Sara was not taxed when X's retained earnings caused the value of her stock to increase from $100 to $150. Instead, there is no tax on the gain until the occurrence of a "realization event," such as a cash dividend. Although the cash dividend does not make Sara any richer, it serves as the trigger for taxing the enrichment that the tax system had previously ignored. The same analysis explains why a taxpayer can be taxed on a gain when he merely sells an asset for what it is worth. Gerry owns land that he bought years ago for $20,000, and which is now worth $100,000. If he sells the land for $100,000, the sale does not make him richer — by definition, $100,000 cash is not more valuable than $100,000 worth of land. Nevertheless, the sale will cause Gerry to be taxed on $80,000 gain. The sale is a realization event, which triggers taxation of the gain that had previously accrued without taxation.

As for X Corporation, and the increase in its value from $100 to $150, two things are clear: (1) The mere increase in value of Sara's shares is unrealized appreciation, on which she will not be taxed as long as no realization event occurs,[2] and (2) if Sara receives X's $50 earnings as a cash dividend, she will be taxed on $50 of income. What justifies the differing treatments of unrealized appreciation and cash dividends? The standard answer is based on considerations of valuation and liquidity. In the absence of a realization event, it may be unclear how much (if at all) an asset has increased in value, and in any event a mere increase in value gives the taxpayer no cash with which to pay a tax. Taxing a cash dividend, by contrast, presents no problems of either valuation or liquidity.

A pro rata stock dividend (i.e., a stock dividend that does not increase any shareholder's percentage interest in the corporation) can be viewed as an intermediate case between unrealized appreciation (no dividend at all) and a cash dividend. From a policy (as distinguished from constitutional) perspective, does the stock dividend more closely resemble no dividend or a cash dividend? The answer seems reasonably clear. If problems of valuation and liquidity justify deferring tax on Sara while she simply continues to own two shares of X,[3] those problems are not diminished when Sara receives a third share as a stock dividend. The third share is no easier to value than the first two, and it is no easier to convert to cash. Thus, the result in *Macomber* seems right, *as a matter of policy.* If mere appreciation in the value of stock is not currently taxed, then a simple pro rata stock dividend should also be excluded from gross income.

At the time of *Macomber,* however, Congress had decided — perhaps foolishly — that stock dividends should be analogized to cash dividends rather than to unrealized appreciation; the statute clearly called for the taxation of stock dividends.[4] Only by holding the statute unconstitutional could the Court conclude that stock dividends were not taxable. The constitutional issue is considered below.

Before turning to the constitutional question, though, a non-tax puzzle: If a pro rata stock dividend so closely resembles no dividend at all, why would a corporation

---

2. Most corporations are subject to the income tax in their own right. *See* §11. Although the increase in the value of X's shares attributable to retained earnings is unrealized appreciation *to Sara,* the earnings constitute realized income *to X.* Thus, corporate earnings can be taxed twice under the income tax: once to the corporation when earned, and again to the shareholder when distributed as a dividend.

3. Valuation and liquidity concerns are plausible reasons for not taxing the shareholder of a closely held corporation (such as X) on the increase in value of her shares. Whether these concerns justify deferring tax on the increase in value of publicly traded stock is briefly discussed later in section A.3 of this chapter.

4. Today, §305(a) takes the opposite approach. A pro rata stock dividend, which merely slices the corporate pie into smaller pieces, is generally excluded from gross income.

ever go to the trouble of issuing a stock dividend? On the facts of the hypothetical, Sara might have caused X to issue a third share so that she could give one share of X to a relative without losing her control of X as majority shareholder. Somewhat similarly, a publicly traded corporation (such as the corporation in *Macomber*) might declare a pro rata dividend to reduce the per share price of stock, in order to facilitate trading of shares.

3.   The Constitutional Issue

With the statute clearly requiring taxation of Mrs. Macomber's stock dividend, why did she win her case? Some background is needed to understand the Court's constitutional analysis. Two provisions of the original Constitution (art. I, §2, cl. 3, and art. I, §9, cl. 4) provide that Congress may impose a "direct" tax only if the tax is apportioned among the states according to their populations. The only two taxes that clearly fall into the direct category are a head (capitation) tax and an ad valorem real property tax. What else, if anything, constituted a direct tax within the intent of the framers is a mystery. In fact, James Madison's minutes of the Constitutional Convention record that when one delegate inquired as to the meaning of the term, "No one answ[ere]d."

As applied to a real property tax, the apportionment requirement means that if Congress imposes a national real property tax, and California has ten times the population of Oregon, then the federal tax imposed on California real property must be ten times the tax imposed on Oregon real property. Unless California real property is worth exactly ten times as much as Oregon real property (an unlikely event), the California and Oregon tax rates will have to be different in order to satisfy the apportionment requirement. Multiply the need for different rates by 50 states, and it is clear that apportionment of any tax other than a head tax is a practical impossibility.[5]

In 1894 Congress enacted a federal income tax (with a very high exemption level and very low rates, by modern standards). Not believing an income tax to be a direct tax subject to the apportionment requirement, Congress made no attempt to apportion the tax among the states according to their populations. However, in the 1895 *Pollock* decision (cited by the Supreme Court in *Macomber*), the Supreme Court ruled that an income tax *was* a direct tax, and that the 1894 income tax was therefore unconstitutional for want of apportionment. The Court started from the unexceptionable premise that a tax on the value of real property is a direct tax, and from the more dubious premise that a tax on the value of personal property is also a direct tax. Although the income tax did not purport to tax the value of property, it did tax the income from property. The Court reasoned (very dubiously) that a tax on the income from property was really a tax on the property itself, with the result that the 1894 tax was unconstitutional as an unapportioned direct tax. Technically, *Pollock* did not hold that *any* federal income tax would be unconstitutional. In theory, Congress could have responded to *Pollock* by imposing an unapportioned tax only on income from labor, or by imposing an apportioned tax

5. A head tax is a tax on the privilege of existing (or having a head), imposed as a flat dollar amount on each person within the taxing jurisdiction. As such, it would be automatically apportioned among the states according to their populations.

on income from both labor and property. Understandably, however, Congress had no interest in either of those options.

There the matter rested until 1913, when the Sixteenth Amendment was ratified. Its language reflects its narrow purpose of reversing *Pollock* by removing the apportionment requirement for an income tax: "The Congress shall have power to lay and collect taxes on incomes, from whatever source derived, without apportionment among the several states, and without regard to any census or enumeration." Congress enacted an income tax shortly after the adoption of the Amendment. Despite the Amendment, the *Macomber* Court invalidated Congress's attempt to tax stock dividends. The Court reasoned:

1. Unless the Sixteenth Amendment applies, a tax on stock dividends is unconstitutional as an unapportioned direct tax on personal property;
2. A tax is relieved of the apportionment requirement by the Amendment only if it is a tax on "income";
3. Unrealized appreciation is not "income" within the meaning of the Amendment;
4. Stock dividends are a form of unrealized appreciation; and
5. Therefore, the attempt to tax stock dividends without apportionment was constitutionally invalid, even after the adoption of the Amendment.

So what does it take, according to the *Macomber* Court, to qualify something as "income" within the meaning of the Amendment? Using a technique reminiscent of some Americans traveling abroad, who seem to believe that anyone can understand English if it is spoken very loudly and very slowly, with much repetition, the Court takes a dictionary definition of income, puts the definition in italics, separates the words by dashes, and repeats: "'*Derived — from — capital*;' — 'the *gain — derived — from — capital*,' etc." Although this is not the most sophisticated of interpretive techniques, the Court's bottom line is clear enough. Unless gain is clearly separated from the taxpayer's original invested capital — as it is in the case of a cash dividend, but not in the case of a stock dividend — the gain is not income and it cannot be taxed by Congress without apportionment.

If Congress were not put in a constitutional straitjacket by *Macomber,* it might want to impose tax on unrealized appreciation in situations where the standard policy justifications for not taxing unrealized appreciation apply weakly or not at all. For example, it might decide that unrealized appreciation in publicly traded stocks should be taxed annually, on a so-called "mark-to-market" basis. Determining the value of such stock as of January 1 and again as of December 31 is a simple matter of looking at two newspapers, and illiquidity is not a problem for assets that can be converted to cash by a phone call (or email message) to one's broker. No matter how attractive a mark-to-market regime for publicly traded stock might be as a matter of policy, it would seem to be foreclosed by the *Macomber* Court's view that gain must be severed from capital before it can be taxed without apportionment.

In later cases, however, the Supreme Court has backed away from *Macomber* as constitutional law. Today, the Court describes the realization requirement as being "founded on administrative convenience"[6] — a considerable demotion from being a constitutional requirement. Although the Court has never officially overruled

6. Cottage Savings Assn. v. Commissioner, 499 U.S. 554, 559 (1991), quoting Helvering v. Horst, 311 U.S. 112, 116 (1940).

Macomber, almost all tax lawyers believe the Court no longer takes the case seriously as a matter of constitutional law. In fact, the current Code contains a number of provisions that would seem to be invalid under *Macomber,* but whose constitutionality is not seriously questioned today. For example, §475 imposes an annual mark-to-market requirement on stock held by securities dealers, and §1256 imposes a mark-to-market regime on the holders of certain options and futures contracts. More esoterically, §551 taxes U.S. shareholders on the undistributed earnings of foreign personal holding companies, in direct contravention of *Macomber.* The original issue discount rules of §§1271-1275 would also be of doubtful validity if *Macomber* retained any constitutional force.[7]

Despite having lost most or all of its constitutional significance, *Macomber* remains important for what it says about the basic structure of the income tax. Even if it is only as a matter of administrative convenience, the income tax remains realization-based, rather than accretion-based. Gains are not taxed (and losses are not deducted) unless there has been a realization event. Rather than being subject to constitutional constraints, however, Congress is probably free to define realization events in any way it chooses, without regard to whether an event severs gain from capital. In most cases, Congress is content to defer taxation of gain until there has been a "sale or other disposition of property" (§1001(a)), but it probably has the power to treat anything at all as a realization event—including the mere turning over of the calendar from December 31 to January 1 (a power it has exercised under the annual mark-to-market rules of §§475 and 1256).

One further, rather peculiar, aspect of *Macomber* is worth noting. Suppose Frank owns land that is worth $1 million, with a basis of only $50,000. He trades it for a Matisse painting valued at $1 million. Under §1001(a), the trade is clearly a realization event—an "other disposition of property"—and Frank will realize a gain of $950,000 on the exchange. The predecessor of §1001(a) required the same result at the time of *Macomber.* Would the *Macomber* Supreme Court have had a problem with that result? If gain must be severed from capital before it can be taxed, has any severance taken place here? What part of the Matisse painting represents Frank's $950,000 gain, what part represents his $50,000 basis, and what would happen to the value of the painting if he physically separated the two parts? Although treating Frank's exchange as a taxable event is inconsistent with the stated rationale of *Macomber,* and although taxing such an exchange may involve problems of both valuation (of Frank's amount realized) and liquidity, in a later case the Supreme Court noted that gain from the exchange of property "has always been recognized as realized taxable gain." Helvering v. Bruun, 309 U.S. 461, 469 (1940).

B.   MANIPULATION OF THE REALIZATION RULES

Although there are numerous realization provisions scattered throughout the Code, the most fundamental realization provision is §1001(a), which states that a

---

7. For an explanation of the original issue discount rules, see the cell accompanying this chapter.

taxpayer realizes gain or loss on the "sale or other disposition of property." This rule invites taxpayer manipulation in two directions. If a taxpayer wants to dispose of appreciated property, the game is to find a way to accomplish the economic equivalent of a sale (or a close approximation) without triggering §1001(a). On the other hand, if a taxpayer owns depreciated property that he wants to retain, the game is to find a way technically to sell the property, while retaining the economic equivalent of ownership. The following material examines some taxpayer attempts to manipulate the realization rules, and some of the responses by Congress, the courts, and the IRS.

1. The Substance of a Sale Without Realization of Gain

Nora, who is elderly, owns 100,000 shares of Growth Corporation (a publicly traded corporation), with a value of $100 million and a basis of only $10 million. She would like to sell the stock in order to diversify her portfolio, but she does not like the prospect of realizing a $90 million gain. What can she do? The following plan—a so-called short sale against the box—was popular in the 1990s. First, Nora "shorts" Growth stock by borrowing 100,000 shares of Growth from her broker. In other words, her broker transfers to her 100,000 shares of Growth and she is obligated eventually to repay her broker in kind, with 100,000 shares of stock. Nora now has 200,000 shares of Growth stock, worth $200 million. Next, Nora quickly sells 100,000 Growth shares for their fair market value of $100 million, taking advantage of a regulation (§1.1012-1(c)) that allows her to identify the borrowed shares as the shares she has sold. The sale of the borrowed shares is treated as an "open transaction," with no gain or loss taken into account by the tax system until Nora "closes" the transaction by returning identical shares to the lender. When the dust has settled, Nora is left with $100 million cash and precisely offsetting "long" and "short" positions in 100,000 shares of Growth. The long position is the 100,000 shares she still owns; the short position is her obligation to repay the 100,000 shares she borrowed from her broker.[8] The two positions effectively cancel each other out. Any increase in the value of Growth stock increases the value of her long position and decreases the value of her short position by exactly offsetting amounts; conversely, any decrease in the value of Growth stock decreases the long position value and increases the short position value by offsetting amounts. Thus, she no longer has any interest in the value of Growth stock. She is in the same economic position as if she had simply sold her original shares for cash. Sooner or later she will need to "close out" her short position by using her shares to repay the loan, and that will be a realization event triggering taxation of the appreciation in the shares. Remember, though, that Nora is elderly. If the short position is not closed out until after her death, §1014 will have increased the basis of the shares to their date-of-death value, wiping out the potential taxable gain.[9] Because of high transaction costs, this technique was available only to the very rich. Taxpayers who could afford the fees, however, would

---

8. To say one has a long position in an asset is a fancy way of saying one owns the asset. A short position is the opposite of a long position—that is, having an obligation to transfer an asset (whether or not one currently owns the asset) to someone at sometime in the future. The simplest—and by far the most familiar—example involves cash. To hold cash is to have a long position in cash, and to owe money is to have a short position in cash.

9. For §1014, see section F.2 of this chapter.

never again have to pay tax on appreciation in any asset with respect to which it was possible to take a short position (such as publicly traded stock). This technique came to the attention of Congress when newspapers reported that Estee Lauder was using a short sale against the box to avoid almost $100 million of income tax liability. Faced with the virtual repeal of the capital gains tax on the wealthiest investors, in 1997 Congress responded by enacting §1259, which is described in the following committee report.

SENATE REPORT 105-33

(Senate Finance Committee, 1997)

PRESENT LAW

In general, gain or loss is taken into account for tax purposes when realized. Gain or loss generally is realized with respect to a capital asset at the time the asset is sold, exchanged, or otherwise disposed of. Gain or loss is determined by comparing the amount realized with the adjusted basis of the particular property sold. In the case of corporate stock, the basis of shares purchased at different dates or different prices generally is determined by reference to the actual lot sold if it can be identified. Special rules under the Code can defer or accelerate recognition in certain situations.

The recognition of gain or loss is postponed for open transactions. For example, in the case of a "short sale" (i.e., when a taxpayer sells borrowed property such as stock and closes the sale by returning identical property to the lender), no gain or loss on the transaction is recognized until the closing of the borrowing.

Transactions designed to reduce or eliminate risk of loss on financial assets generally do not cause realization. For example, a taxpayer may lock in gain on securities by entering into a "short sale against the box," i.e., when the taxpayer owns securities that are the same as, or substantially identical to, the securities borrowed and sold short. The form of the transaction is respected for income tax purposes and gain on the substantially identical property is not recognized at the time of the short sale. Pursuant to rules that allow specific identification of securities delivered on a sale, the taxpayer can obtain open transaction treatment by identifying the borrowed securities as the securities delivered. When it is time to close out the borrowing, the taxpayer can choose to deliver either the securities held or newly-purchased securities. . . .

REASONS FOR CHANGE

In general, a taxpayer cannot completely eliminate risk of loss (and opportunity for gain) with respect to property without disposing of the property in a taxable transaction. In recent years, however, several financial transactions have been developed or popularized which allow taxpayers to substantially reduce or eliminate their risk of loss (and opportunity for gain) without a taxable disposition. Like most taxable dispositions, many of these transactions also provide the taxpayer with cash or other property in return for the interest that the taxpayer has given up.

One of these transactions is the "short sale against the box." In such a transaction, a taxpayer borrows and sells shares identical to the shares the taxpayer holds. By holding two precisely offsetting positions, the taxpayer is insulated from economic fluctuations in the value of the stock. . . .

EXPLANATION OF PROVISION

GENERAL RULE

The bill requires a taxpayer to recognize gain (but not loss) upon entering into a constructive sale of any appreciated position in stock, a partnership interest or certain debt instruments as if such position were sold, assigned or otherwise terminated at its fair market value on the date of the constructive sale.

If the requirements for a constructive sale are met, the taxpayer would recognize gain in a constructive sale as if the position were sold at its fair market value on the date of the sale and immediately repurchased. Except as provided in Treasury regulations, a constructive sale would generally not be treated as a sale for other Code purposes. An appropriate adjustment in the basis of the appreciated financial position would be made in the amount of any gain realized on a constructive sale, and a new holding period of such position would begin as if the taxpayer had acquired the position on the date of the constructive sale.

A taxpayer is treated as making a constructive sale of an appreciated position when the taxpayer (or, in certain circumstances, a person related to the taxpayer) does one of the following: (1) enters into a short sale of the same property, (2) enters into an offsetting notional principal contract with respect to the same property, or (3) enters into a futures or forward contract to deliver the same property. A constructive sale under any part of the definition occurs if the two positions are in property that, although not the same, is substantially identical. In addition, in the case of an appreciated financial position that is a short sale, a notional principal contract or a futures or forward contract, the holder is treated as making a constructive sale when it acquires the same property as the underlying property for the position. Finally, to the extent provided in Treasury regulations, a taxpayer is treated as making a constructive sale when it enters into one or more other transactions, or acquires one or more other positions, that have substantially the same effect as any of the transactions described. . . .

DEFINITIONS

An appreciated financial position is defined as any position with respect to any stock, debt instrument, or partnership interest, if there would be gain upon a taxable disposition of the position for its fair market value. A "position" is defined as an interest, including a futures or forward contract, short sale, or option. . . .

A constructive sale does not include a transaction involving an appreciated financial position that is marked to market, including positions governed by section 475 (mark to market for securities dealers) or section 1256 (mark to market for futures contracts, options and currency contracts). . . .

TREASURY GUIDANCE

The bill provides regulatory authority to the Treasury to treat as constructive sales certain transactions that have substantially the same effect as those specified (i.e., short sales, offsetting notional principal contracts and futures or forward contracts to deliver the same or substantially similar property).

It is anticipated that the Treasury will . . . treat as constructive sales other financial transactions that, like those specified in the provision, have the effect of eliminating substantially all of the taxpayer's risk of loss and opportunity for income or gain with respect to the appreciated financial position. Because this standard requires reduction of both risk of loss and opportunity for gain, it is intended that transactions that reduce only risk of loss or only opportunity for gain will not be covered. Thus, for example, it is not intended that a taxpayer who holds an appreciated financial position in stock will be treated as having made a constructive sale when the taxpayer enters into a put option with an exercise price equal to the current market price (an "at the money" option). Because such an option reduces only the taxpayer's risk of loss, and not its opportunity for gain, the above standard would not be met. . . .

It is anticipated that the Treasury regulations, when issued, will provide specific standards for determining whether several common transactions will be treated as constructive sales. One such transaction is a "collar." In a collar, a taxpayer commits to an option requiring him to sell a financial position at a fixed price (the "call strike price") and has the right to have his position purchased at a lower fixed price (the "put strike price"). For example, a shareholder may enter into a collar for a stock currently trading at $100 with a put strike price of $95 and a call strike price of $110. The effect of the transaction is that the seller has transferred the rights to all gain above the $110 call strike price and all loss below the $95 put strike price; the seller has retained all risk of loss and opportunity for gain in the range price between $95 and $110. A collar can be a single contract or can be effected by using a combination of put and call options.

In order to determine whether collars have substantially the same effect as the transactions specified in the provision, it is anticipated that Treasury regulations will provide specific standards that take into account various factors with respect to the appreciated financial position, including its volatility. . . .

Notes and Questions

1. *Taxing Nora.* Under §1259, what would be the tax treatment of Nora's transaction, described in the text before the committee report?
2. *Is §1259 constitutional?* How would the *Macomber* Court have viewed the constitutionality of §1259? If Congress had wanted to shut down short sales against the box, but believed that the approach of §1259 was constitutionally prohibited, is there any other approach it might have taken, to which the *Macomber* Court would not have objected?
3. *"Substantially identical."* The Treasury has not issued regulations under §1259. In the absence of regulations, it is not clear how close a taxpayer can come to cashing out an appreciated financial position without triggering a constructive sale under §1259. In the case of a short sale, how similar can the long and short position assets be without being "substantially identical"?

4. *Tight collars and a grant of regulatory authority.* Notice that the committee report does not say whether the $95/$110 collar on stock trading at $100 is tight enough to qualify as a constructive sale. If there were regulations under §1259 they might answer that question, but the Treasury has never promulgated any regulations under §1259. In the absence of regulations, it appears that no collar, no matter how tight, can trigger a constructive sale. This is because collars are not included in the statutory list of types of constructive sales in §§1259(c)(1)(A)-(D). Instead, they are merely a permissible subject of the authority granted to the Treasury by §1259(c)(1)(E) to promulgate regulations treating as constructive sales "other transactions . . . that have substantially the same effect as a transaction described in any of the preceding subparagraphs." Most provisions of the Internal Revenue Code are self-executing. That is, they have the force of law even if the Treasury never gets around to issuing regulations interpreting them. The list of types of constructive sales in §§1259(c)(1)(A)-(D), for example, is self-executing. Section 1259(c)(1)(E), by contrast, is not self-executing. Unless and until the Treasury bestirs itself to issue regulations pursuant to §1259(c)(1)(E), it seems that no collar can ever constitute a constructive sale. Congress enacted §1259 more than a decade ago. Has the Treasury (the Treasury of three different presidents, no less) been derelict in its duty?

5. *Nonrecourse borrowing against unrealized appreciation.* Randolph owns undeveloped land, unencumbered by any mortgage, with a basis of $100,000 and a value of $1 million. He borrows $900,000, secured by a nonrecourse mortgage on the land. In the worst case scenario — if the land becomes worthless the next day — Randolph has locked in an $800,000 gain on the land. The nonrecourse loan has shifted from Randolph to the lender the risk that the value of the land will fall below $900,000. On the other hand, Randolph still bears the risk that the land will decline in value from $1 million to $900,000, and he still owns the opportunity for gain if the land appreciates further. Should the locking-in of $800,000 of gain be enough to trigger taxation of Randolph? Although it does not apply to real estate, what answer is suggested by analogy to §1259? What does the committee report say about "transactions that reduce only risk of loss or only opportunity for gain"? The leading case on Randolph's situation is Woodsam Associates v. Commissioner, 198 F.2d 357 (2d Cir. 1952), holding that the taking out of a nonrecourse loan against unrealized appreciation is not a "sale or other disposition" within the meaning of §1001(a).[10]

2. The Substance of Continued Ownership with Realization of Loss

Suppose you own an asset whose value has fallen far below its basis. Of course, you could realize the loss if you sold the asset for cash, but suppose that for non-tax reasons you want to continue to own the asset. Is there any way to accomplish a "sale or other disposition" for tax purposes, while retaining the substance of ownership? In some cases, there is. According to Reg. §1.1001-1(a), an exchange of your asset for another asset will qualify as a realization event so long as the exchanged assets "differ[] materially either in kind or in extent."

---

10. For more on *Woodsam*, see Chapter 2.C.2.c.

COTTAGE SAVINGS ASSOCIATION v. COMMISSIONER

499 U.S. 554 (1991)

Justice MARSHALL delivered the opinion of the Court.

The issue in this case is whether a financial institution realizes tax-deductible losses when it exchanges its interests in one group of residential mortgage loans for another lender's interests in a different group of residential mortgage loans. We hold that such a transaction does give rise to realized losses.

I

Petitioner Cottage Savings Association (Cottage Savings) is a savings and loan association (S & L) formerly regulated by the Federal Home Loan Bank Board (FHLBB).[11] Like many S & L's, Cottage Savings held numerous long-term, low-interest mortgages that declined in value when interest rates surged in the late 1970's. These institutions would have benefited from selling their devalued mortgages in order to realize tax-deductible losses. However, they were deterred from doing so by FHLBB accounting regulations, which required them to record the losses on their books. Reporting these losses consistent with the then-effective FHLBB accounting regulations would have placed many S & L's at risk of closure by the FHLBB.

The FHLBB responded to this situation by relaxing its requirements for the reporting of losses. In a regulatory directive known as "Memorandum R-49," dated June 27, 1980, the FHLBB determined that S & L's need not report losses associated with mortgages that are exchanged for "substantially identical" mortgages held by other lenders.[12] The FHLBB's acknowledged purpose for Memorandum R-49 was to facilitate transactions that would generate tax losses but that would not substantially affect the economic position of the transacting S & L's.

This case involves a typical Memorandum R-49 transaction. On December 31, 1980, Cottage Savings sold "90% participation interests" in 252 mortgages to four S & L's. It simultaneously purchased "90% participation interests" in 305 mortgages held by these S & L's.[13] All of the loans involved in the transaction were secured by single-family homes, most in the Cincinnati area. The fair market value

---

11. Congress abolished the FHLBB in 1989.

12. Memorandum R-49 listed 10 criteria for classifying mortgages as substantially identical.

"1. involve single-family residential mortgages,
"2. be of similar type (e.g., conventionals for conventionals),
"3. have the same stated terms to maturity (e.g., 30 years),
"4. have identical stated interest rates,
"5. have similar seasoning (i.e., remaining terms to maturity),
"6. have aggregate principal amounts within the lesser of 2 1/2 % or $100,000 (plus or minus) on both sides of the transaction, with any additional consideration being paid in cash,
"7. be sold without recourse,
"8. have similar fair market values,
"9. have similar loan-to-value ratios at the time of the reciprocal sale, and
"10. have all security properties for both sides of the transaction in the same state."

13. By exchanging merely participation interests rather than the loans themselves, each party retained its relationship with the individual obligors. Consequently, each S & L continued to service the loans on which it had transferred the participation interests and made monthly payments to the participation-interest holders.

of the package of participation interests exchanged by each side was approximately $4.5 million. The face value of the participation interests Cottage Savings relinquished in the transaction was approximately $6.9 million.

On its 1980 federal income tax return, Cottage Savings claimed a deduction for $2,447,091, which represented the adjusted difference between the face value of the participation interests that it traded and the fair market value of the participation interests that it received. As permitted by Memorandum R-49, Cottage Savings did not report these losses to the FHLBB. After the Commissioner of Internal Revenue disallowed Cottage Savings' claimed deduction, Cottage Savings sought a redetermination in the Tax Court. The Tax Court held that the deduction was permissible.

On appeal by the Commissioner, the Court of Appeals reversed. The Court of Appeals agreed with the Tax Court's determination that Cottage Savings had realized its losses through the transaction. However, the court held that Cottage Savings was not entitled to a deduction because its losses were not "actually" sustained during the 1980 tax year for purposes of §165(a).

Because of the importance of this issue to the S & L industry and the conflict among the Circuits over whether Memorandum R-49 exchanges produce deductible tax losses,[14] we granted certiorari. We now reverse.

II

Rather than assessing tax liability on the basis of annual fluctuations in the value of a taxpayer's property, the Internal Revenue Code defers the tax consequences of a gain or loss in property value until the taxpayer "realizes" the gain or loss. The realization requirement is implicit in §1001(a) of the Code, which defines "[t]he gain [or loss] from the sale or other disposition of property" as the difference between "the amount realized" from the sale or disposition of the property and its "adjusted basis." As this Court has recognized, the concept of realization is "founded on administrative convenience." Helvering v. Horst, 311 U.S. 112 (1940). Under an appreciation-based system of taxation, taxpayers and the Commissioner would have to undertake the "cumbersome, abrasive, and unpredictable administrative task" of valuing assets on an annual basis to determine whether the assets had appreciated or depreciated in value. See 1 B. Bittker & L. Lokken, Federal Taxation of Income, Estates and Gifts ¶5.2, p. 5-16 (2d ed. 1989). In contrast, "[a] change in the form or extent of an investment is easily detected by a taxpayer or an administrative officer." R. Magill, Taxable Income 79 (rev. ed. 1945).

Section 1001(a)'s language provides a straightforward test for realization: to realize a gain or loss in the value of property, the taxpayer must engage in a "sale or other disposition of [the] property." The parties agree that the exchange of participation interests in this case cannot be characterized as a "sale" under §1001(a); the issue before us is whether the transaction constitutes a "disposition of property." The Commissioner argues that an exchange of property can be treated as a "disposition" under §1001(a) only if the properties exchanged are

---

14. The two other Courts of Appeals that have considered the tax treatment of Memorandum R-49 transactions have found that these transactions do give rise to deductible losses. See Federal Nat. Mortgage Assn. v. Commissioner, 896 F.2d 580, 583-584 (D.C. Cir. 1990); San Antonio Savings Assn. v. Commissioner, 887 F.2d 577 (5th Cir. 1989).

materially different. The Commissioner further submits that, because the underlying mortgages were essentially economic substitutes, the participation interests exchanged by Cottage Savings were not materially different from those received from the other S & L's. Cottage Savings, on the other hand, maintains that *any* exchange of property is a "disposition of property" under §1001(a), regardless of whether the property exchanged is materially different. Alternatively, Cottage Savings contends that the participation interests exchanged were materially different because the underlying loans were secured by different properties.

We must therefore determine whether the realization principle in §1001(a) incorporates a "material difference" requirement. If it does, we must further decide what that requirement amounts to and how it applies in this case. We consider these questions in turn.

A

Neither the language nor the history of the Code indicates whether and to what extent property exchanged must differ to count as a "disposition of property" under §1001(a). Nonetheless, we readily agree with the Commissioner that an exchange of property gives rise to a realization event under §1001(a) only if the properties exchanged are "materially different." The Commissioner himself has by regulation construed §1001(a) to embody a material difference requirement: "Except as otherwise provided . . . the gain or loss realized from the conversion of property into cash, *or from the exchange of property for other property differing materially either in kind or in extent,* is treated as income or as loss sustained." Treas. Reg. §1.1001-1, 26 CFR §1.1001-1 (1990) (emphasis added).

Because Congress has delegated to the Commissioner the power to promulgate "all needful rules and regulations for the enforcement of [the Internal Revenue Code]," 26 U.S.C. §7805(a), we must defer to his regulatory interpretations of the Code so long as they are reasonable.

We conclude that Treasury Regulation §1.1001-1 *is* a reasonable interpretation of §1001(a). Congress first employed the language that now comprises §1001(a) of the Code in §202(a) of the Revenue Act of 1924, ch. 234, 43 Stat. 253; that language has remained essentially unchanged through various reenactments. And since 1934, the Commissioner has construed the statutory term "disposition of property" to include a "material difference" requirement. As we have recognized, "'Treasury regulations and interpretations long continued without substantial change, applying to unamended or substantially reënacted statutes, are deemed to have received congressional approval and have the effect of law.'" United States v. Correll, 389 U.S. 299 (1967).

Treasury Regulation §1.1001-1 is also consistent with our landmark precedents on realization. In a series of early decisions involving the tax effects of property exchanges, this Court made clear that a taxpayer realizes taxable income only if the properties exchanged are "materially" or "essentially" different. Because these decisions were part of the "contemporary legal context" in which Congress enacted §202(a) of the 1924 Act, and because Congress has left undisturbed through subsequent reenactments of the Code the principles of realization established in these cases, we may presume that Congress intended to codify these principles in §1001(a). The Commissioner's construction of the statutory language to incorporate these principles certainly was reasonable.

B

Precisely what constitutes a "material difference" for purposes of §1001(a) of the Code is a more complicated question. The Commissioner argues that properties are "materially different" only if they differ in economic substance. To determine whether the participation interests exchanged in this case were "materially different" in this sense, the Commissioner argues, we should look to the attitudes of the parties, the evaluation of the interests by the secondary mortgage market, and the views of the FHLBB. We conclude that §1001(a) embodies a much less demanding and less complex test.

Unlike the question of *whether* §1001(a) contains a material difference requirement, the question of *what constitutes* a material difference is not one on which we can defer to the Commissioner. For the Commissioner has not issued an authoritative, prelitigation interpretation of what property exchanges satisfy this requirement. Thus, to give meaning to the material difference test, we must look to the case law from which the test derives and which we believe Congress intended to codify in enacting and reenacting the language that now comprises §1001(a).

We start with the classic treatment of realization in Eisner v. Macomber, 252 U.S. 189 (1920). In *Macomber,* a taxpayer who owned 2,200 shares of stock in a company received another 1,100 shares from the company as part of a pro rata stock dividend meant to reflect the company's growth in value. At issue was whether the stock dividend constituted taxable income. We held that it did not, because no gain was realized. We reasoned that the stock dividend merely reflected the increased worth of the taxpayer's stock, and that a taxpayer realizes increased worth of property only by receiving "something of exchangeable value *proceeding from* the property."

In three subsequent decisions (United States v. Phellis, *supra* [252 U.S. 189 (1921)]; Weiss v. Stearn, *supra* [265 U.S. 242 (1924)]; and Marr v. United States, *supra* [268 U.S. 536 (1925)] — we refined *Macomber*'s conception of realization in the context of property exchanges. In each case, the taxpayer owned stock that had appreciated in value since its acquisition. And in each case, the corporation in which the taxpayer held stock had reorganized into a new corporation, with the new corporation assuming the business of the old corporation. While the corporations in *Phellis* and *Marr* both changed from New Jersey to Delaware corporations, the original and successor corporations in *Weiss* both were incorporated in Ohio. In each case, following the reorganization, the stockholders of the old corporation received shares in the new corporation equal to their proportional interest in the old corporation.

The question in these cases was whether the taxpayers realized the accumulated gain in their shares in the old corporation when they received in return for those shares stock representing an equivalent proportional interest in the new corporations. In *Phellis* and *Marr,* we held that the transactions were realization events. We reasoned that because a company incorporated in one State has "different rights and powers" from one incorporated in a different State, the taxpayers in *Phellis* and *Marr* acquired through the transactions property that was "materially different" from what they previously had. In contrast, we held that no realization occurred in *Weiss.* By exchanging stock in the predecessor corporation for stock in the newly reorganized corporation, the taxpayer did not receive "a thing really different from what he theretofore had." As we explained in *Marr,* our determination that the reorganized company in *Weiss* was not "really different" from its predecessor turned on the fact that both companies were incorporated in the same State.

Obviously, the distinction in *Phellis* and *Marr* that made the stock in the successor corporations materially different from the stock in the predecessors was minimal. Taken together, *Phellis, Marr,* and *Weiss* stand for the principle that properties are "different" in the sense that is "material" to the Internal Revenue Code so long as their respective possessors enjoy legal entitlements that are different in kind or extent. . . . [A]s long as the property entitlements are not identical, their exchange will allow both the Commissioner and the transacting taxpayer easily to fix the appreciated or depreciated values of the property relative to their tax bases.

In contrast, we find no support for the Commissioner's "economic substitute" conception of material difference. According to the Commissioner, differences between properties are material for purposes of the Code only when it can be said that the parties, the relevant market (in this case the secondary mortgage market), and the relevant regulatory body (in this case the FHLBB) would consider them material. Nothing in *Phellis, Weiss,* and *Marr* suggests that exchanges of properties must satisfy such a subjective test to trigger realization of a gain or loss.

Moreover, the complexity of the Commissioner's approach ill serves the goal of administrative convenience that underlies the realization requirement. In order to apply the Commissioner's test in a principled fashion, the Commissioner and the taxpayer must identify the relevant market, establish whether there is a regulatory agency whose views should be taken into account, and then assess how the relevant market participants and the agency would view the transaction. The Commissioner's failure to explain how these inquiries should be conducted further calls into question the workability of his test.

Finally, the Commissioner's test is incompatible with the structure of the Code. Section 1001(c) provides that a gain or loss realized under §1001(a) "shall be recognized" unless one of the Code's nonrecognition provisions applies. One such nonrecognition provision withholds recognition of a gain or loss realized from an exchange of properties that would appear to be economic substitutes under the Commissioner's material difference test. This provision, commonly known as the "like kind" exception, withholds recognition of a gain or loss realized "on the exchange of property held for productive use in a trade or business or for investment . . . for property of like kind which is to be held either for productive use in a trade or business or for investment." 26 U.S.C. §1031(a)(1). If Congress had expected that exchanges of similar properties would *not* count as realization events under §1001(a), it would have had no reason to bar recognition of a gain or loss realized from these transactions.

C

Under our interpretation of §1001(a), an exchange of property gives rise to a realization event so long as the exchanged properties are "materially different" — that is, so long as they embody legally distinct entitlements. Cottage Savings' transactions at issue here easily satisfy this test. Because the participation interests exchanged by Cottage Savings and the other S & L's derived from loans that were made to different obligors and secured by different homes, the exchanged interests did embody legally distinct entitlements. Consequently, we conclude that Cottage Savings realized its losses at the point of the exchange. . . .

IV

For the reasons set forth above, the judgment of the Court of Appeals is reversed, and the case is remanded for further proceedings consistent with this opinion.

Justice BLACKMUN, with whom Justice WHITE joins, . . . dissenting. . . .

I dissent, however, from the Court's conclusions in [*Cottage Savings* and a companion case, to the effect that the institutions] realized deductible losses for income tax purposes when each exchanged partial interests in one group of residential mortgage loans for partial interests in another like group of residential mortgage loans. I regard these losses as not recognizable for income tax purposes because the mortgage packages so exchanged were substantially identical and were not materially different.

The exchanges, as the Court acknowledges, were occasioned by the Federal Home Loan Bank Board (FHLBB) Memorandum R-49 of June 27, 1980, and by that Memorandum's relaxation of theretofore-existing accounting regulations and requirements, a relaxation effected to avoid placement of "many S & L's at risk of closure by the FHLBB" without substantially affecting the "economic position of the transacting S & L's." But the Memorandum, the Court notes, also had as a purpose the "facilit[ation of] transactions that would generate tax losses." I find it somewhat surprising that an agency not responsible for tax matters would presume to dictate what is or is not a deductible loss for federal income tax purposes. I had thought that that was something within the exclusive province of the Internal Revenue Service, subject to administrative and judicial review. Certainly, the FHLBB's opinion in this respect is entitled to no deference whatsoever. . . .

In applying the realization requirement to an exchange, the properties involved must be materially different in kind or in extent. . . .

That the mortgage participation partial interests exchanged in these cases were "different" is not in dispute. The materiality prong is the focus. A material difference is one that has the capacity to influence a decision.

The application of this standard leads, it seems to me, to only one answer — that the mortgage participation partial interests released were not materially different from the mortgage participation partial interests received. Memorandum R-49, as the Court notes, lists 10 factors that, when satisfied, as they were here, serve to classify the interests as "substantially identical." These factors assure practical identity; surely, they then also assure that any difference cannot be of consequence. Indeed, nonmateriality is the full purpose of the Memorandum's criteria. The "proof of the pudding" is in the fact of its complete accounting acceptability to the FHLBB. Indeed, as has been noted, it is difficult to reconcile substantial identity for financial accounting purposes with a material difference for tax accounting purposes.

This should suffice and be the end of the analysis. Other facts, however, solidify the conclusion: The retention by the transferor of 10% interests, enabling it to keep on servicing its loans; the transferor's continuing to collect the payments due from the borrowers so that, so far as the latter were concerned, it was business as usual, exactly as it had been; the obvious lack of concern or dependence of the transferor with the "differences" upon which the Court relies (as transferees, the taxpayers made no credit checks and no appraisals of collateral); the selection of the loans by a computer programmed to match mortgages in accordance with the Memorandum R-49 criteria; the absence of even the names of the borrowers in the closing

schedules attached to the agreements; ... the restriction of the interests exchanged to the same State; the identity of the respective face and fair market
values; and the application by the parties of common discount factors to each
side of the transaction—all reveal that any differences that might exist made no
difference whatsoever and were not material. This demonstrates the real nature of
the transactions, including nonmateriality of the claimed differences.

We should be dealing here with realities and not with superficial distinctions. As
has been said many times, and as noted above, in income tax law we are to be
concerned with substance and not with mere form. When we stray from that
principle, the new precedent is likely to be a precarious beacon for the future.

I respectfully dissent on this issue.

Notes and Questions

1. *A two-edged sword.* It should always be kept in mind that the realization
   requirement cuts both ways: Taxpayers typically want to have realization
   events when they have losses that they may deduct, but want to avoid
   realization events when they have gains that would be taxable. The gain/
   loss landscape is not symmetrical, however, in at least three ways: (1) in an
   economy that is growing, and experiencing inflation (both generally true
   in the United States over the last 40 years or more), there will always be
   more gains than losses overall; (2) severe restrictions on the deduction of
   net capital losses under §1211 truncate the tax advantages associated with
   losses for most taxpayers[15] ; and (3) the taxpayer controls the facts of the
   transaction, and frequently can shape it to fall on whichever side of a line is
   more advantageous. Under these circumstances, the IRS should be careful
   about trying to make it harder to realize losses; any success it achieves will
   likely come at the cost of making it easier for other taxpayers to avoid
   realizing gains. This point will be discussed in greater detail in the materials on nonrecognition immediately following. It will suffice to note here
   that the government's proposed test, as noted in part II.B. of the opinion—that properties were materially different only if they differ in "economic substance"—might have proven a rather unruly standard. It would
   likely have led to any number of efforts by taxpayers to extend the
   boundaries of the range within which no material difference could be
   found. In a tax system with low levels of audit coverage, many of these
   efforts would be destined to win by default.
2. *Did the Court go too far?* Though the IRS should be careful what it wishes for
   in realization cases, it's still true that the dissent has a point: When a
   transaction has been elaborately designed to leave a taxpayer in as nearly
   identical a position after the transaction as he was before, it is something of
   a legal fiction to declare that he has realized his losses. After all, generally
   accepted accounting principles also incorporate something of a realization requirement, and by those standards, there was no realization here.
   And it should be noted that most taxpayers who want to enjoy their gains
   without a realization event really do want to close out their investments,
   not replace them with other investments that are so nearly identical that
   they may as well not have bothered.

15. See Chapter 12, section C.

3. *Back to grammar school.* Does Justice Blackmun's use of the past perfect tense — "I had thought [that tax advice was not the FHLBB's main line of work]" — indicate that he no longer thought this by the time he wrote his dissent? Or is it in what we might call the "sarcastic voice"?

Hilda owns 100 shares of Microsoft, with a basis of $150,000 and a value of $100,000. On the one hand, she would like to realize her $50,000 economic loss. On the other hand, she expects the stock will appreciate, so she would like to continue to own 100 shares of Microsoft. What can she do to accomplish both of her competing objectives? It won't work to exchange her shares for 100 identical shares. Under the regulatory material difference standard, an exchange of *identical* assets is not a realization event. But what if she sells her 100 shares for $100,000 cash, and one minute later uses the cash to buy 100 identical shares? A cash sale clearly constitutes a realization event, so this technique should enable her to realize her loss while retaining the substance of her investment, shouldn't it? This plan *does* work as far as §1001 is concerned, but just as Congress enacted §1259 to deal with manipulation of §1001(a) with respect to gains, Congress long ago enacted the "wash sale" rules of §1091 to deal with manipulation of §1001(a) with respect to losses. Under §1091, if a taxpayer realizes a loss on the sale of stock, no loss deduction is allowed if the taxpayer purchases "substantially identical" stock "within a period beginning 30 days before the date of such sale or disposition and ending 30 days after such date." The disallowed loss is preserved in the new stock, under the special basis rules of §1091(d). The following problems involve the application of the §1091(d) basis rules.

Problem 1. On March 1, 2011, John sells ten shares of X Corporation stock, in which he has a basis of $1,000, for $800. On March 21 of the same year, John buys ten identical shares of X for $825. How much loss (if any) may John deduct on the sale, and what is his basis in the new shares?

Problem 2. Jane owns ten shares of Y Corporation, with a value of $700 and a basis of $1,200. On April 20, 2011, Jane buys ten additional shares of Y for $700. On May 1 of the same year, Jane sells her original ten shares for $740. How much loss (if any) may Jane deduct on the sale, and what is her basis in the shares she still owns?

Frustrated by §1091, John (from Problem 1) wonders if there is some other way to trigger a loss deduction while retaining the economic substance of his investment. He comes up with the idea of selling his stock ($1,000 basis, $800 value) to Debby, his 15-year-old daughter, for $800. Taxes aside, John feels there is not much practical difference between his owning the stock and Debby's owning the stock. Will this plan enable John to deduct his $200 loss? Unfortunately, this doesn't work either. Section 267(a)(1) disallows any loss deduction on a sale or exchange of property between certain related parties, including a parent and child. (*See* §§267(b)(1) and (c)(4) for the relationship test for family members.) Would John fare any better if he sold the loss stock to a closely held corporation that he controlled? *See* §267(b)(2).

Problem 3. Father (F) sells Microsoft stock, in which he has a basis of $150,000, to Daughter (D) for its fair market value of $100,000. Two years later, D sells the stock (outside the family) for $160,000 cash. How much gain or loss does D realize on the sale? What if she sells the stock for $140,000? What about $90,000? *See* §267(d).

3.   "Cherry Picking" and the Capital Loss Limitations of §1211

Harold owns an extensive stock portfolio. The unrealized gains in portfolio assets exceed the unrealized losses, but there are several million dollars of unrealized losses. It is late December, and Harold estimates that his income for the year—from salary, dividends, and interest—will be about $300,000, unless he makes some tax-motivated year-end sales. He sorts through his portfolio looking for stocks with unrealized losses approximating $300,000. He sells those stocks, realizing $300,000 of losses. He hopes to use those losses to offset all his income, thus wiping out his tax liability for the year. Unfortunately for Harold, this is another plan that won't work. The stocks are capital assets (as defined in §1221), and under §1211(b) an individual may deduct capital losses only against capital gains and a piddling $3,000 of non-capital gain income.[16] (Under §1212(b), capital losses disallowed by §1211(b) can be carried forward, to be used against capital gains—and a limited amount of other income—in later years.) If Harold realized no capital gains during the year, he will be able to deduct only $3,000 of his $300,000 of capital losses.

Section 1211(b) is another provision—like §§1091 and 267—aimed at the manipulation of the realization doctrine with respect to losses. In the case of §1211(b), however, the legislative concern is not that the taxpayer has maintained the substance of his investment either through a purchase of identical property (§1091) or a sale to a related person (§267). Rather, the concern is that taxpayers might engage in "cherry picking" — selectively realizing losses in their investment portfolios while making a point of not realizing gains. Although a taxpayer caught by §1211(b) may have genuinely cashed out a particular losing investment, the suspicion is that the realized loss is offset—or more than offset—by unrealized gains in the taxpayer's remaining investments. The target of §1211(b) is the fortunate investor whose realized losses are offset by unrealized gains, but the provision is a blunt instrument; it also limits the capital loss deduction of the unlucky investor who does not have unrealized gains in other assets.

Section 1211(b) is sometimes misunderstood as the price taxpayers must pay for the favorable tax rates applied to long-term capital gains.[17] Actually, the policy behind the provision has nothing to do with capital gains tax rates, and everything to do with cherry picking concerns. In recognition of this fact, Congress left §1211(b) intact in 1986, despite the elimination (for only a few years, as it turned out) of special capital gains tax rates by the Tax Reform Act of 1986. By contrast, if Congress ever replaces §1001(a) with an annual mark-to-market system for taxing appreciation, *then* the capital loss limitations should be repealed; selective

16. Although legislation enacted in 2003 (and scheduled to expire at the end of 2012) makes "qualified dividend income" (QDI) eligible for the same favorable tax rates as long-term capital gain, the legislation does not technically categorize QDI as capital gain. *See* §1(h)(11). As a result, capital losses can be deducted against QDI only under the rule permitting capital losses to offset $3,000 of income other than capital gains.

17. See generally Chapter 12.

realization of losses would be impossible if all gains and losses were automatically treated as realized every year.

C. NONRECOGNITION

1. The Concept of Nonrecognition

Section 1001 generally defines gains and losses—includible under §61 or deductible under §165, respectively—to consist of the difference between the amount realized on a "sale or other disposition" of an asset and the adjusted basis of the asset. While most taxpayers understand that the sale of an asset will ordinarily trigger some sort of tax recognition of profits or losses enjoyed or suffered during the holding of the asset, the notion that an "other disposition" might similarly trigger tax recognition is less familiar. It is true, nevertheless, that such things as barter transactions are normally taxable events. For example, if your neighborhood grocer were accommodating enough to accept a share of corporate stock for groceries of the same value, it would constitute a realization event requiring you to include in income (or, in the case of a loss, take as a deduction) the difference between the market value of the groceries and the adjusted basis of the share of stock. In some situations, however, Congress has decided that immediate tax recognition of particular realization events would be unwise. Accordingly, the Code specifies several types of "nonrecognition transactions" —transactions in which gain or loss is *realized* by the taxpayer engaging in the transaction, but will not be *recognized* for tax purposes (at least not at that time).

The rationale for allowing deferral of the reckoning of gains and losses is that the taxpayer has maintained a substantially continuous investment, only slightly altered in form. As the House Ways and Means Committee put it in a report on some early amendments to the nonrecognition provisions: "[I]f the taxpayer's money is still tied up in the same kind of property as that in which it was originally invested, he is not allowed to compute and deduct his theoretical loss on the exchange, nor is he charged with a tax on his theoretical profit."[18] Generally, this notion of continuity of investment underlies congressional willingness to defer tax recognition.[19]

Two common types of nonrecognition transactions are considered in detail in this chapter: §1031 allows taxpayers to defer taxation of gains on property that is exchanged for other property that is of "like kind" with the transferred property, and §1033 allows taxpayers to defer taxation of gains on property that has been "involuntarily converted," as by condemnation or physical destruction, if the proceeds of the involuntary conversion have been reinvested in other similar property.[20] This chapter also considers in detail §121, which allows taxpayers to avoid taxation—under certain conditions—of up to $250,000 ($500,000 for a married couple) of gain on the sale of a personal residence. Section 121 provides

18. Ways and Means Committee Report on the Revenue Act of 1934, *reprinted in* 1939-2 C.B. (pt. 2) 564.
19. As we shall see, §121 departs from this rationale in not requiring any replacement investment in a principal residence.
20. Another important nonrecognition provision, §1041, is considered in detail in Chapter 9.C.5. Section 1041 allows taxpayers who realize gains on the transfer of property to a spouse or former spouse to avoid recognizing those gains.

for permanent exclusion of gain, rather than deferral. Most tax professionals would not describe it as a nonrecognition provision (they would reserve the nonrecognition label for deferral provisions). But exploring §121 in this chapter, after our consideration of the two deferral provisions, facilitates a comparison of the effects of the two types of provisions.

Before proceeding to descriptions of §§1031 and 1033, a few general observations about nonrecognition sections should be noted:

Electivity. Most taxpayers, most of the time, would like to defer recognition of gains, but not of losses. This is consistent with the general tax planning maxim that it is beneficial to defer income, but to accelerate losses.[21] Some nonrecognition provisions do taxpayers the favor of applying by their terms only to gains.[22] More typically, however, nonrecognition provisions apply to both gain and loss situations. Where that is true, it is also usually true that taxpayers can, with sound planning, arrange their transactions so as to avoid applicability of nonrecognition provisions when those provisions would work to their disadvantage. Occasionally, the IRS will successfully assert the applicability of a nonrecognition provision in order to defer a loss deduction.[23] Such instances are somewhat unusual, however, in part because the IRS can typically win such cases only by arguing for a broad interpretation of the nonrecognition provision in question. Such arguments, if successful, are likely to make it easier for taxpayers to qualify for the nonrecognition provision in future cases where deferral of gain is sought, a fact ordinarily taken into account by the government in making decisions about litigation strategy.[24]

The role of basis. Nonrecognition provisions are designed to defer recognition of gain, but not to forgive taxation of the gain forever. Preservation of gain or loss for future taxability is one of the functions of the basis account maintained for each asset. The mechanisms by which this is accomplished vary among the several nonrecognition provisions, and so will be described in detail within the descriptions of each provision. In general, however, the idea is to maintain a historical basis in one or more of the new assets, so that any differences between that basis and the fair market value of that asset will preserve the opportunity to recognize gain or loss when the asset is sold or otherwise disposed of.

21. See the discussion in Chapter 1.C.2 of the value of tax deferral.

22. Section 1033 is an example.

23. *See, e.g.,* Redwing Carriers, Inc. v. Tomlinson, 399 F.2d 652 (5th Cir. 1968), in which the taxpayer disposed of old vehicles and shortly thereafter purchased new ones from the buyer of the old vehicles. Despite the taxpayer's efforts to separate the two transactions in order to recognize the losses sustained on the old vehicles, the government successfully argued that the transactions should be viewed as "synchronous parts meshed into the same transaction" (399 F.2d at 656), in order to disallow immediate deduction of those losses under the mandatory deferral provisions of §1031. The IRS has also asserted that in certain situations where a taxpayer transfers property but then leases it back, deduction of losses sustained on the property may be barred by §1031. It prevailed on such an argument in Century Elec. Co. v. Commissioner, 192 F.2d 155 (8th Cir. 1951), but not in Jordan Marsh Co. v. Commissioner, 269 F.2d 453 (1st Cir. 1959). Of course, the *Cottage Savings* case in the preceding section was not decided pursuant to a nonrecognition provision, but involved an analogous gambit by the government as to the interpretation of the realization rules under §1001.

24. The government is not always so foresighted, however. In the *Redwing Carriers* case (note 23, *supra*), the government suggested that the disposition of one asset and the receipt of another did not have to be simultaneous for a qualifying like-kind exchange. This outcome was extremely helpful to the taxpayer in a later case, Starker v. United States, 602 F.2d 1341 (9th Cir. 1979), in which the taxpayer transferred property in exchange for the right to designate for up to five years into the future the property or properties to be received in exchange for the transferred property.

For example, if Smith purchases Blackacre for $100,000, and later trades Black-acre for Whiteacre, at a time when each asset is worth $150,000, Smith has *realized* a gain of $50,000. He has received property with a value of $150,000, which is $50,000 more than his basis in the property that he gave up.[25] If a nonrecognition provision allows Smith to avoid *recognition* of this gain, deferring recognition until the subsequent sale or other disposition of Whiteacre, then we can preserve the $50,000 of gain for future taxability by requiring Smith to take a basis in Whiteacre equal to the $100,000 basis of the property disposed of in the swap. Of course, the value of Whiteacre may go up or down following the swap; thus, the gain recognized on a subsequent sale or other disposition of Whiteacre may be more or less than $50,000. But, all other things being equal, the gain recognized on the subsequent sale or other disposition will be $50,000 more (or any loss will be $50,000 less) than it would have been if Smith had taken a basis in Whiteacre that was equal to the $150,000 consideration he provided to acquire Whiteacre.[26]

In some cases, there is no property (in the usual sense) acquired by one of the parties to a nonrecognition transaction. For example, if a person with a good deal of property divorces someone who has little, some of the property of the richer spouse may be transferred to the other, where the only consideration that can be identified would involve the surrender of "marital rights" to such things as support, a manda-tory minimum share of the richer spouse's estate, and other similar rights as provided by state law governing property relationships within marriage. Once surrendered by the spouse who held those rights, the rights cease to exist; they can never be in any meaningful sense transferred again by anyone. Thus, any gain (or loss, as the case may be) on the property transferred in exchange for the surrender of marital rights cannot be preserved by assigning a historical basis to the marital rights. Rather, the gain or loss must be preserved by transferring the historical basis with the property. Thus, the transferee spouse must take a basis in the property that is equal to the transferor's adjusted basis at the time of the transfer.

Whether the basis rule involved is an "exchanged basis" rule (as in the Whiteacre example) or a "transferred basis" rule (as in the divorce example), the basis determinations are critical in ensuring that gain or loss is merely deferred, rather than extinguished forever. In complicated transactions, a number of adjustments of various sorts will be needed to account accurately for the preservation of any gain or loss not recognized because of the nonrecognition provision. It will be useful in working through the adjustment rules to remember the goal: to build into the basis in the assets whatever gain or loss went unrecognized on the nonrecognition transaction, thereby preserving it for tax recognition in the future.

With these prefatory descriptions as background, we can now proceed to exam-ine the nonrecognition provisions in turn.

2. Like-Kind Exchanges

The basic rule. Section 1031 provides nonrecognition of gains and losses incurred on the transfer of property in exchange for other property of "like-kind." For

---

25. Recall that §1001 says that gain equals the amount realized in a transaction, less the adjusted basis of the property disposed of.

26. The usual basis rule for newly acquired property is found in §1012, which provides a so-called cost basis rule: that the basis of such property is equal to value of the consideration provided to acquire it.

reasons that will become clear, the provision is primarily useful in real estate transactions, where it has become a very important tax deferral device. If one looks in the classified advertisements sections of most major newspapers, ads can typically be found that indicate that a seller of real estate (most commonly, undeveloped land) either prefers or insists on a transaction that can be structured as a like-kind exchange.

Section 1031(a)(1) provides the general rule:

> No gain or loss shall be recognized on the exchange of property held for productive use in a trade or business or for investment if such property is exchanged solely for property of like kind which is to be held either for productive use in a trade or business or for investment.

This language provides one indication of the scope of the rule: It is limited to property that is used in a business or held for investment. This leaves out property held for personal use, such as one's personal residence or automobile, and the like. A further limitation on scope is provided by §1031(a)(2), which precludes applicability of this nonrecognition rule to several categories of property, among which are stocks, bonds, and notes; partnership interests; and inventory property. This limits the scope of the section to a relatively small part of the forms of wealth held by taxpayers — essentially to tangible physical property (including real estate) held for use in a business or for investment.[27]

Searching for a policy justification. What is it about like-kind exchanges that justifies exempting them from the general rule that realized gains must be recognized? It is true that taxing the gain on a like-kind exchange would raise problems of valuation of the taxpayer's amount realized and of liquidity (i.e., the taxpayer might not have cash with which to pay the tax). Valuation and liquidity problems may exist in *any* non-cash exchange, however, regardless of whether the exchanged properties are similar. Thus, valuation and liquidity concerns cannot explain the like-kind requirement. Is the real justification, then, that a taxpayer who receives like-kind property should not be taxed because he has not changed the fundamental nature of his investment? But a taxpayer who sells for cash and quickly purchases like-kind replacement property has also not changed the fundamental nature of his investment, yet he cannot take advantage of §1031. Perhaps Congress decided that nonrecognition was justified only when all three considerations in favor of nonrecognition — difficulty of valuation, lack of liquidity, and continuation of the basic nature of the taxpayer's investment — are present, and that only like-kind exchanges involve all three. Non-like-kind exchanges involve the first two considerations but not the third, while the reinvestment of cash proceeds in like-kind property involves the third but not the first two.

The like-kind concept. Section 1031 applies only when the exchange is of like-kind property. Section 1031 is silent as to the meaning of that concept, but the regulations provide some guidance. The regulations say that the concept refers to the "nature

---

27. This is a slight overstatement, but useful in conceptualizing the practical scope of §1031. There are several exceptions. The IRS has ruled, for example, that professional athlete contracts may be subject to the rules of §1031 (Rev. Rul. 67-380, 1967-2 C.B. 291), and has provided in regulations that patents and copyrights of like kind can be swapped without recognition under §1031 (Treas. Regs. §1.1031(a)-2(c)(3)). Similarly, leaseholds might not be considered tangible property, though they convey rights to hold and use such property.

and character" of the property, and not to its "grade or quality."[28] More helpfully, the regulations provide examples, indicating, among other things, that taxpayers may have like-kind exchanges if they exchange "city real estate for a ranch or farm," improved real estate for unimproved real estate, and even fee interests in real estate for long-term leaseholds of at least 30 years duration.[29] As to tangible personal property, the regulations indicate that two properties will be of like kind as long as they are in the same "asset class," as set forth in the regulations.[30] Thus, cars can — within the protection of §1031 — be traded for other cars, light trucks for light trucks, heavy trucks for heavy trucks, and so on. But, conversely, a light truck could not be traded for a bus, nor for any other vehicle outside of the light truck class.[31]

Why are vehicles broken down into classes, between which nontaxable trades are impermissible, while real estate is not so broken down, permitting virtually unlimited nontaxable trades? There is no clear answer. But taxpayers to a considerable degree take these positions as they find them, and the striking liberality of the IRS with respect to real estate transactions has led to heavy use of §1031 in that industry. Because the principal use of §1031 is to avoid immediate taxation of gain on the disposition of investment real estate, the examples in the remainder of this section will involve such transactions.

What qualifies as an "exchange"? Suppose Jones owns highly appreciated real estate, which Andrews is eager to acquire. Jones is willing to trade his real estate for other real estate, but he is unwilling to pay the tax that would be generated by a sale for cash. Andrews, unfortunately, has no real estate suitable for exchanging with Jones. Are the parties out of luck, as far as qualifying under §1031 is concerned? Not necessarily. Andrews can purchase suitable real estate from a third party for cash, and then transfer that real estate to Jones in exchange for Jones's property. Even though such a transaction closely resembles a cash sale by Jones followed by a reinvestment of the cash (which clearly would *not* qualify under §1031), the IRS acknowledges that a properly structured three-party transaction such as this can qualify for nonrecognition (as to Jones) under §1031. If the law did not permit such three-party exchanges, the practical significance of §1031 would be very limited, as few taxpayers are interested in straight two-party exchanges.[32]

Boot in §1031 transactions. What would happen if taxpayer Smith in our earlier hypothetical had found that his target property, Whiteacre, was worth only $140,000, while his own Blackacre was worth $150,000? He might ask the seller of Whiteacre to throw in $10,000 "to boot" — over and above the value of the fee interest in Whiteacre — to equalize the values going in both directions in the swap. (One imagines that two pieces of real estate will rarely be of precisely equal value, so this sort of case must be much more common than a straight swap without any equalization payment.) But recall that §1031(a) allows Smith to avoid recognition of his gain on Blackacre (which was $50,000) if he receives *solely* property that is of like kind. Does this mean that anything thrown in "to boot" will spoil the transaction for §1031 purposes?

28. Treas. Reg. §1.1031(a)-1(b).
29. Treas. Reg. §1.1031(a)-1(c).
30. Treas. Reg. §1.1031(a)-2.
31. See the cell on like-kind exchanges for additional material on the like-kind requirement as applied to personal property.
32. See the cell on like-kind exchanges for additional material on three-party exchanges.

Thankfully, no. Although there may be less confusing ways to express these ideas, Congress has generally chosen to structure nonrecognition rules by stating the rule first to provide complete relief, but only to the purest form of the transaction involved. Typically, the pure rule is followed by provisions that provide partial nonrecognition treatment to transactions that involve some receipt of consideration in forms other than the qualified property. In this case, subsections (b) and (c) do the job of extending partial relief to partially qualified transactions.

Section 1031(b) says that if the taxpayer has gain on the property she transfers, and receives consideration both in the form of qualified (like-kind) property and nonqualified property or cash (generally referred to as "boot" in either case), then the gain realized on the transferred property will be recognized, but only up to the amount of the boot — the amount of cash or the fair market value of the nonqualified property. To put the same rule slightly differently, the taxpayer's gain recognized is the lesser of gain realized or boot received. Thus, in the example immediately above, if Smith receives $10,000 in cash in addition to Whiteacre, his $50,000 gain on Blackacre is taxable to the extent of that boot, in this case $10,000. This is of course still valuable to Smith, because he is able to avoid immediate taxation of the remaining $40,000 of gain. Notice that it is necessary, in order to apply the rule of §1031(b), to determine the taxpayer's gain realized, which in turn requires a determination of the taxpayer's amount realized — *including the fair market value of Whiteacre*. In view of that fact, is it really possible to defend §1031 as a response to valuation difficulties?

Section 1031(c) adds that if the taxpayer has experienced a loss on the transferred property of like kind, then none of the loss is to be recognized if the consideration received is a mix of qualified and nonqualified property or cash. Thus, if Smith's basis in Blackacre had been $200,000 rather than $100,000, and he traded the property for Whiteacre and $10,000 of cash, the receipt of the cash would not trigger recognition of any portion of Smith's loss. Like §1031(a), §1031(c) provides a rule of complete nonrecognition in loss cases; together those subsections proscribe loss deductions in like-kind transactions whether or not there is any boot in the mix. For this reason, most taxpayers with losses on assets that they are disposing of will prefer not to qualify under §1031, and will take care to avoid creating a transaction structure that could be considered an exchange. Ordinarily, the simplest method of doing this will be to sell the loss asset to one buyer and, in a separately negotiated transaction, to buy the target asset (which might be of like kind with the asset sold) from another party.[33]

Basis of the acquired property.[34] Section 1031(d) provides generally that the basis of the acquired property will be an "exchanged basis," meaning that the historic adjusted basis in the transferred property will become the basis in the acquired property. After stating that deceptively simple rule, however, the subsection goes on to describe three adjustments that affect the basis in the acquired property.[35] The adjustments require that the basis of the acquired property be:

33. In all three of the nonrecognition cases cited *supra* in note 23 (*Redwing Carriers, Century Electric,* and *Jordan Marsh*), the transferees of taxpayers' loss properties were the same parties who transferred the like-kind target properties back to the taxpayers.

34. Additional material on the basis of property received in like-kind exchanges is contained in the cell on like-kind exchanges.

35. In addition to the three adjustments, §1031(d) also includes two ancillary rules, which are described in the cell on like-kind exchanges.

1. decreased by the amount of any money received by the taxpayer in the transaction;
2. increased by the amount of any gain recognized by the taxpayer on the transaction; and
3. decreased by the amount of any loss recognized by the taxpayer on the transaction.

The first two adjustments are frequently involved in §1031 transactions, since, as noted, it is often the case that some cash must change hands in these transactions to equalize the value of the consideration going in each direction. Thus, in the §1031(b) transaction described above, in which Smith swaps Blackacre for Whiteacre and $10,000 of cash, Smith's basis in Whiteacre will be his basis in Blackacre of $100,000, decreased by the $10,000 of money received, but increased by the $10,000 of gain recognized on the transaction. In this case (and in a great many simple §1031(b) transactions) the two basis adjustments cancel each other: Precisely because cash was received, gain was recognized in the same amount, leading to perfectly offsetting adjustments.[36] It is easier to understand the logic behind the first two basis adjustments if they are considered in reverse order from their listing in the statute. First, the taxpayer is entitled to increase his basis by the amount of gain recognized, to ensure that he is not taxed on the same gain twice. Thus, the *total* basis to which the taxpayer is entitled is his old basis in the transferred property, plus his gain recognized on the transfer. That basis, however, must be allocated among all the consideration received by the taxpayer in the exchange. In effect, cash always has a basis equal to its face amount.[37] Hence step two: In order to reflect the allocation of basis to the cash received by the taxpayer, the taxpayer's basis *in the nonrecognition property* must be reduced by the amount of cash received.

The third basis adjustment rule noted — decreasing basis by any loss recognized — is initially puzzling. Both subsections (a) and (c), the two that include provisions dealing with losses, specifically say that no losses can be recognized. This basis adjustment rule therefore seems premised on something that cannot happen. But the basis rules of §1031(d) provide comprehensive basis rules for §1031 transactions, including those involving nonqualified property. Suppose, in our continuing example of Smith and Blackacre, that Whiteacre was more valuable than Blackacre, so to even the exchange Smith decided to throw in a tractor having a value of $10,000. If the tractor had an adjusted basis in excess of $10,000, Smith would realize a loss on the tractor, and nothing in §1031(a) or (c) would preclude him from recognizing that loss.[38] That is the sort of loss that would lead to a decrease in basis of acquired property under §1031(d).

36. This result is not inevitable, even in a simple §1031(b) transaction. Occasionally, the boot received may be more than the amount of gain realized, in which case the two adjustments will not perfectly offset each other. For example, if Smith had received $60,000 of cash, his new basis in Whiteacre would start with his old basis of $100,000, decreased by the $60,000 of cash, but increased by only $50,000 of gain recognized (since that is all the gain Smith realized). Thus, he will end up with a $90,000 basis in Whiteacre. In such a case, however, Smith will have enjoyed no tax advantage from engaging in a like-kind exchange. Because it is usually at least mildly burdensome to structure a transaction to qualify for §1031, it is only rarely that transactions qualifying for §1031 treatment involve no benefit.
37. A taxpayer never recognizes gain or loss when he makes a cash purchase, and an asset purchased with cash ordinarily has a basis equal to the amount of cash paid.
38. *See also* Treas. Reg. §1.1031(d)-1(e), confirming that a taxpayer who transfers both qualified and nonqualified property in the same §1031 exchange recognizes gain or loss on the transfer of the nonqualified property.

There is one more adjustment necessary to obtain the correct basis in the acquired property in some cases, which unfortunately is not specified in §1031(d). It is that the basis in the acquired property must be increased by any money paid by the taxpayer as part of the like-kind exchange. For example, if Blackacre is worth $150,000 and Whiteacre is worth $160,000, and the parties agree that Smith will equilibrate the consideration by paying the owner of White-acre $10,000, in addition to conveying Blackacre, what should be Smith's basis in Whiteacre? None of the explicit adjustment rules of §1031(d) seems to apply, which might leave Smith with a simple exchanged basis of $100,000. But that builds in a gain of $60,000 on Whiteacre, which is plainly too much. Smith invested $100,000 in Blackacre, added $10,000 of additional investment at the time of the like-kind exchange, and now has a property worth $160,000. That value represents a gain of only $50,000 over the total of his investments in the property, and $50,000 should be the limit of his gain. We can limit his built-in gain to that amount by increasing his basis by his new investment of $10,000, giving him a $110,000 basis in Whiteacre. But where is the authority for making such an adjustment?

The regulations provide such authority, stating that when additional consideration is given in a §1031 transaction, the basis of the acquired property is the basis of the transferred property, increased by the amount of the additional consideration.[39] The regulations refer to §1016, a general basis adjustment section that says that basis is to be adjusted for "all expenditures . . . properly chargeable to capital account."

Problem 4.   Marie owns Blackacre. Blackacre has a fair market value of $500, and Marie's basis in Blackacre is $200. Fred owns Whiteacre. Whiteacre has a fair market value of $480, and Fred's basis in Whiteacre is $450. Marie and Fred trade properties, with Fred throwing in $20 cash to even up the values in the exchange. How much gain does Marie realize on the exchange, how much gain must she recognize, and what is her basis in Whiteacre after the exchange?

Problem 5.   The facts are the same as in Problem 4. How much gain does Fred realize on the exchange, how much gain must he recognize, and what is his basis in Blackacre after the exchange?

Problem 6.   Chloe owns Greenacre. Greenacre has a fair market value of $200, and Chloe's basis in Greenacre is $230. She transfers Greenacre to Flora in exchange for Blueacre (fair market value $150) and $50 cash. How much gain or loss does Chloe realize, how much gain or loss does she recognize, and what is her basis in Blueacre after the exchange?

Problem 7.   Sophie owns Redacre. Redacre has a fair market value of $400, and Sophie's basis in Redacre is $380. She transfers Redacre to Mark in exchange for Brownacre (fair market value $370) and $30 cash. How much gain or loss does Sophie realize, how much gain or loss does she recognize, and what is her basis in Brownacre after the exchange?

---

39. Treas. Reg. §1.1031(d)-1(a).

3. *Involuntary Conversions*

Section 1031 requires a like-kind *exchange*; it does not apply to a sale for cash followed by a reinvestment of the cash in like-kind property. Section 1033, however, does provide for nonrecognition for a cash sale followed by a reinvestment, if the cash sale qualifies as an involuntary conversion.

Martha's land is condemned to make way for a freeway. Her basis in the land is $300,000 and the condemnation award is $800,000. If Martha does not reinvest the cash in property "similar or related in service or use to the converted property," she will realize and recognize $500,000 gain. If, however, she spends $800,000 or more on replacement property within the statutory replacement period,[40] she can elect not to recognize her gain. Under §1033(b), the taxpayer's cost basis in the replacement property must be reduced by the amount of gain realized but not recognized on the involuntary conversion. As with the basis rules of §1031, the effect is to defer taxation of gain, rather than to permanently exempt the gain from tax. Section 1033 applies to gains realized as a result of involuntary conversions generally, not just condemnations. Thus, a taxpayer can take advantage of the provision if her property is destroyed by a fire, flood, or other disaster, and she receives insurance proceeds or tort damages in excess of her adjusted basis in the property.

Why do you suppose Congress provided nonrecognition of gain for taxpayers who reinvest the proceeds of involuntary conversions, but was not willing to extend the same generosity to those who reinvest the proceeds of voluntary sales? Does this special solicitude for victims of forced sales remind you of any other Code provision?

What if Martha paid only $750,000 for the replacement for her condemned property? In that case, she would have to recognize her gain "to the extent that the amount realized upon [the involuntary] conversion . . . exceeds the cost of [the replacement] property" (§1033(a)(2)(A)). Thus, she would have to recognize $50,000 of her realized gain of $500,000. What should be her basis in the replacement property? The statute (§1033(b)(2)) takes the $750,000 cost of the replacement property as the starting point for the basis calculation, but requires that her basis be reduced by the amount of gain realized but not recognized on the involuntary conversion. Since her gain realized was $500,000 and her gain recognized was $50,000, the gain realized but not recognized was $450,000. Reducing Martha's $750,000 cost by $450,000 leaves her with a basis of $300,000 in the new property. If she were to sell the new property for $750,000, she would then be taxed on the $450,000 gain deferred by §1033.

The mechanical rules of §1033 may seem quite different from those of §1031, with respect to both the amount of gain that must be recognized and the taxpayer's basis in the new property. The differences, however, are simply a result of the difference between an exchange (§1031) and a cash sale followed by a reinvestment (§1033). Martha is in the same economic position as if she had exchanged her old land for new land worth $750,000 and $50,000 cash boot. When Martha receives an $800,000 condemnation award, uses $750,000 to buy replacement property, and pockets the remaining $50,000, that $50,000 is the functional equivalent of

---

40. Generally, the taxpayer must acquire the replacement property within two years of the end of the year in which she realized the gain. Section 1033(a)(2)(B). Longer replacement periods, typically four years, apply if the property was subject to a presidentially declared disaster. *See* §1033(h).

$50,000 cash boot in a like-kind exchange. In recognition of that equivalence, §1033(a)(2)(A) requires recognition of realized gain to the extent Martha has retained the equivalent of boot. Try applying the gain recognition and basis rules of §1031 to a hypothetical like-kind exchange in which Martha receives like-kind property worth $750,000 and $50,000 cash boot. You should reach the same results — $50,000 gain recognized and $300,000 basis in the replacement property — as in Martha's involuntary conversion.

Problem 8.   Carl owned land, not encumbered by any mortgage, with a basis of $250,000. When the land was condemned for a public use, Carl received a cash award of $600,000. He elected to have §1033 apply to the condemnation, and he purchased similar property within the statutory replacement period. The price of the new property was $560,000. Carl used only $400,000 of his own cash in buying the new property; the rest of the cost he financed with a $160,000 bank loan secured by a mortgage on the new property. How much gain (if any) must Carl recognize, and what is his basis in the new property? Notice that after buying the replacement property Carl still has $200,000 of the cash from the condemnation award.

For no particularly compelling reason, §§1031 and 1033 do not use the same similarity standard for the old and new properties. Under §1031 the two properties must be "of like kind," whereas under §1033 the two properties must be "similar or related in service or use." It is not obvious from the statutory language that the §1033 standard is the more demanding of the two, but that is how the standards have been interpreted — at least with respect to real property. Although any two parcels of real property will qualify under the like-kind standard, they will not necessarily qualify as "similar or related in service or use." The §1033 test looks not only to the inherent nature of the properties, but also to the nature of the taxpayer's relationship to each property. Thus, a taxpayer will not qualify for nonrecognition under §1033 if a supermarket that he operated himself burns down, and he uses the insurance proceeds to buy another supermarket building that he leases to a supermarket chain. *See* Rev. Rul. 70-399, 1970-2 C.B. 164 (a similar example involving hotels).

Problem 9.   In the situation just described, would it make any difference if the involuntary conversion of the supermarket building was by a condemnation for public use, rather than by a fire? *See* §1033(g)(1).

4.   *Permanent Exclusion of Gain on the Sale of a Principal Residence*

HOUSE REPORT 105-148

105th Cong., 1st Sess. (1997)

EXCLUSION OF GAIN ON SALE OF PRINCIPAL RESIDENCE (SEC. 313 OF THE BILL AND SECS. 121 AND 1034 OF THE CODE)

Present Law

No gain is recognized on the sale of a principal residence if a new residence at least equal in cost to the sales price of the old residence is purchased and used by the taxpayer as his or her principal residence within a specified period of time (sec. 1034). This replacement period generally begins two years before and ends two years after the date of sale of the old residence. The basis of the replacement residence is reduced by the amount of any gain not recognized on the sale of the old residence by reason of this gain rollover rule.

In general, an individual, on a one-time basis, may exclude from gross income up to $125,000 of gain from the sale or exchange of a principal residence if the taxpayer (1) has attained age 55 before the sale, and (2) has owned the property and used it as a principal residence for three or more of the five years preceding the sale (sec. 121).

Reasons for Change

Calculating capital gain from the sale of a principal residence is among the most complex tasks faced by a typical taxpayer. Many taxpayers buy and sell a number of homes over the course of a lifetime, and are generally not certain of how much housing appreciation they can expect. Thus, even though most homeowners never pay any income tax on the capital gain on their principal residences, as a result of the rollover provisions and the $125,000 one-time exclusion, detailed records of transactions and expenditures on home improvements must be kept, in most cases, for many decades. To claim the exclusion, many taxpayers must determine the basis of each home they have owned, and appropriately adjust the basis of their current home to reflect any untaxed gains from previous housing transactions. This determination may involve augmenting the original cost basis of each home by expenditures on improvements. In addition to the record-keeping burden this creates, taxpayers face the difficult task of drawing a distinction between improvements that add to basis, and repairs that do not. The failure to account accurately for all improvements leads to errors in the calculation of capital gains, and hence to an under- or over-payment of the capital gains on principal residences. By excluding from taxation capital gains on principal residences below a relatively high threshold, few taxpayers would have to refer to records in determining income tax consequences of transactions related to their house.

To postpone the entire capital gain from the sale of a principal residence, the purchase price of a new home must be greater than the sales price of the old home. This provision of present law encourages some taxpayers to purchase larger and more expensive houses than they otherwise would in order to avoid a tax liability, particularly those who move from areas where housing costs are high to lower-cost areas. This promotes an inefficient use of taxpayers' financial resources.

Present law also may discourage some older taxpayers from selling their homes. Taxpayers who would realize a capital gain in excess of $125,000 if they sold their home and taxpayers who have already used the exclusion may choose to stay in their homes even though the home no longer suits their needs. By raising the $125,000 limit and by allowing multiple exclusions, this constraint to the mobility of the elderly would be removed.

While most homeowners do not pay capital gains tax when selling their homes, current law creates certain tax traps for the unwary that can result in significant capital gains taxes or loss of the benefits of the current exclusion. For example, an individual is not eligible for the one-time capital gains exclusion if the exclusion was previously utilized by the individual's spouse. This restriction has the unintended effect of penalizing individuals who marry someone who has already taken the exclusion. Households that move from a high housing-cost area to a low housing-cost area may incur an unexpected capital gains tax liability. Divorcing couples may incur substantial capital gains taxes if they do not carefully plan their house ownership and sale decisions.

EXPLANATION OF PROVISION

Under the bill a taxpayer generally is able to exclude up to $250,000 ($500,000 if married filing a joint return) of gain realized on the sale or exchange of a principal residence. The exclusion is allowed each time a taxpayer selling or exchanging a principal residence meets the eligibility requirements, but generally no more frequently than once every two years. The bill provides that gain would be recognized to the extent of any depreciation allowable with respect to the rental or business use of such principal residence for periods after May 6, 1997.

To be eligible for the exclusion, a taxpayer must have owned the residence and occupied it as a principal residence for at least two of the five years prior to the sale or exchange. A taxpayer who fails to meet these requirements by reason of a change of place of employment, health, or other unforseen circumstances is able to exclude the fraction of the $250,000 ($500,000 if married filing a joint return) equal to the fraction of two years that these requirements are met.

In the case of joint filers not sharing a principal residence, an exclusion of $250,000 is available on a qualifying sale or exchange of the principal residence of one of the spouses. Similarly, if a single taxpayer who is otherwise eligible for an exclusion marries someone who has used the exclusion within the two years prior to the marriage, the bill would allow the newly married taxpayer a maximum exclusion of $250,000. Once both spouses satisfy the eligibility rules and two years have passed since the last exclusion was allowed to either of them, the taxpayers may exclude $500,000 of gain on their joint return.

Under the proposal, the gain from the sale or exchange of the remainder interest in the taxpayer's principal residence may qualify for the otherwise allowable exclusion.

EFFECTIVE DATE

The provision is available for all sales or exchanges of a principal residence occurring on or after May 7, 1997, and replaces the present-law rollover and one-time exclusion provisions applicable to principal residences.

A taxpayer could elect to apply present law (rather than the new exclusion) to a sale or exchange (1) made before the date of enactment of the Act, (2) made after the date of enactment pursuant to a binding contract in effect on the date or (3) where the replacement residence was acquired on or before the date of enactment (or pursuant to a binding contract in effect [as] of the date of enactment) and the rollover provision would apply. If a taxpayer acquired his or her current residence in a rollover transaction, periods of ownership and use of the prior residence would be taken into account in determining ownership and use of the current residence.

Notes and Comments

1. *A limited exclusion versus unlimited deferral.* As the last part of the House Report indicates, there was a brief transition period during which a taxpayer could elect the application of either the old §1034 rollover provision or new §121. Why would anyone elect the mere deferral of §1034, if she was eligible for permanent exclusion under new §121? A different way of posing the same question, which extends its relevance beyond the transition period, is to ask whether there are any persons selling their homes today who would be better off if §1034 were still on the books. Consider an unmarried taxpayer who sells a home, basis $100,000, for $400,000, and buys a replacement home costing $450,000. Under current law, that taxpayer will have to pay tax on $50,000 of his gain (the amount by which the $300,000 gain realized exceeds the $250,000 exclusion ceiling). Under §1034, by contrast, there was no limit on the amount of gain that could be deferred, as long as the new home costs at least as much as the sales price of the old home. True, the taxpayer would have only a $150,000 basis in the new home under §1034, compared with a $450,000 basis under current law, but many taxpayers were unconcerned about the low bases produced by §1034 (for the reasons discussed in note 2).

2. *The victims of a deferral regime.* As the legislative history suggests, few persons paid tax on the sale of a principal residence under prior law. As taxpayers moved from one home to another, they would rollover their gain repeatedly using §1034. If they decided to move into a smaller home upon retirement, they could take advantage of old §121, which permitted a once-in-a-lifetime exclusion of up to $125,000 of gain, with no reinvestment requirement, for a taxpayer at least 55 years old. Although the repeated use of §1034 could create some very large deferred gains, those gains would be wiped out by the §1014 basis step-up, so long as the taxpayer continued to own a home until death. One of the authors used to tell his students that only the "rare unfortunate person" (or he might have used a more colloquial term) ever paid tax on the sale of a principal residence. He stopped doing that after it turned out, for several years in a row, that he had one or more "rare unfortunate persons" in his class. These were typically people in their 30s, who had sold their homes at a profit and then had invested the amount realized in a law school education rather than in a new house. Another type of unfortunate person, under old law, was the elderly person who sold her home, realized a gain in excess of $125,000, and moved into a retirement home. Of course, there will be persons who pay tax on home sales under the new version of §121, but for the most part they will be people whose gain exceeds $250,000 (or $500,000), and arguably anyone with that much gain is not very unfortunate. On the other hand, a gain in excess of the applicable

ceiling is not always a huge windfall. The ceiling amounts do not increase the longer one has owned one's home. A $250,000 ceiling on excludable gain does not seem especially generous in the case of a home owned for 20 or 30 years, especially considering that much of the gain over such a long time period may be inflationary. In addition, the ceiling amounts are not adjusted for inflation, so the real value of the ceilings will erode over time unless Congress adjusts or indexes the ceilings in the future.

3. *Tax-motivated mansions.* In the early and mid-1990s, large numbers of people moved from high housing cost areas in the Northeast and California to lower housing cost areas in the South and the West (other than California). They often bought very large (ridiculously large?) new homes in the process. As hinted at in the House Report, one explanation for the replacement mansions was that if you were moving from (for example) San Jose to Salt Lake City, the only way to defer all the gain from the sale of your modest tract house in San Jose was to buy a mansion in Salt Lake City. Under current §121, by contrast, there is no need to buy a mansion in Salt Lake City just for tax purposes. As it happened, however, mansion building did not decline in the wake of the repeal of §1034. Apparently the mansion-building incentive caused by dot.com economy wealth (while it lasted) overwhelmed any reaction to the tax change.

4. *Tax breaks for one home or two?* Notice one crucial difference between the §121 tax break for sales of personal residences and the §163(h)(3) tax break for home mortgage interest payments. The §121 exclusion is available only for a taxpayer's "principal residence." The §163(h)(3) deduction, by contrast, is available for interest on mortgages on both the taxpayer's principal residence and one other residence (typically a vacation home). There is no provision permitting the exclusion of gain on the sale of a vacation home. The policy justification for the difference in the scope of the two provisions is not immediately obvious.

5. *Patience (and clever tax planning) is rewarded.* If a taxpayer had enjoyed substantial appreciation on a piece of real estate that was not her personal residence, could she use a combination of §§1031 and 121 to achieve not mere deferral, but rather permanent exemption of her gain? Suppose, for example, that a single taxpayer owned an interest in vacant land that had appreciated from $100,000 to $300,000 over a period of some years. Could she swap it for a house that had a value of $300,000, live in the house for two years, and sell it, claiming the benefits of §121 to exempt the gain from tax? Unfortunately, she wouldn't even get to the §121 question, because if she moves into the house immediately after acquiring it in a swap, the IRS would assert that the swap did not qualify for §1031, because that section requires that both of the exchanged properties be held for business or investment purposes.

So she switches to Plan B: She does the swap of vacant land for the house, but rents the house out for a year, making it property that would be, immediately following the exchange, held for business purposes. After a year has gone by, she boots her tenant, moves in, lives in the house for two years, and sells the house for $350,000. Most of that gain accrued while this investment was in the form of vacant land. But can she use §121 to shield all $250,000 of gain from taxation? No. *See* §121(d)(10), a provision added to the Code by Congress in 2004, which denies the benefits of §121 if the property in question had been acquired in a like-kind exchange within the five years preceding its sale.

But what about Plan C, in which she lives in the house for four years (after having rented it for one year) in order to avoid this five-year rule? That apparently works. Congress appears to be willing to allow extremely patient loophole-chasers to use a combination of these two sections to achieve an exemption of gains that wouldn't seem to have been what §121 was designed to achieve.

6. *Personal residence losses.* What if a taxpayer is unfortunate enough to sell her principal residence at a loss? (Until a few years ago this was a rare occurrence, but not anymore.) Section 121 applies to residence gains, but what are the rules for losses? Such losses are realized, and even recognized, but that does not mean they are deductible. Section 165(c) provides that losses of individuals are deductible only if they are incurred in a trade or business, in a transaction entered into for profit, or in connection with a casualty or theft. Although one might reasonably argue that buying a residence can be an investment for profit, in addition to a personal consumption expenditure, the regulations flatly disallow any loss from the sale of "residential property purchased or constructed by the taxpayer for use as his personal residence and so used by him up to the time of the sale." Treas. Reg. §1.165-9(a).[41] The same rule applies to losses on other consumer durables, such as a personal-use automobile, apparently on the theory that the lost value over time was a nondeductible consumption expense. In Haig-Simons terms, sale of a durable good at a loss represents a realized decrement to wealth, but the decrement is offset by the untaxed value of the consumption enjoyed during the ownership and use of the asset.

5. *Other Nonrecognition Provisions*

The Internal Revenue Code contains numerous nonrecognition provisions, in addition to the ones considered in detail above. One important nonrecognition provision — §1041, governing transfers between spouses and certain transfers between former spouses — is considered in detail later in this book.[42] Other nonrecognition provisions are beyond the scope of the basic course, but figure prominently in courses on the income taxation of partners and partnerships, and of shareholders and corporations. The corporate tax course, in particular, is largely a course about nonrecognition. Section 351 provides tax deferral rules for incorporation transactions and other transfers to transferor-controlled corporations, and §368 defines various forms of corporate mergers, acquisitions, and divisions that are eligible for nonrecognition. Although the *definitions* of corporate non-recognition transactions can be quite complex, once a corporate nonrecognition transaction has been identified the *operative rules* (governing boot, gain recognition, and post-transaction basis) are basically the same as the operative rules for like-kind exchanges.

---

41. For more on this topic, see the cell on determining the amount of a loss and the deductible portion of a loss.
42. See Chapter 9.C.5.

D. INSTALLMENT SALES

You own a tract of undeveloped land, which you purchased for $50,000 some years ago. If you sold it for $200,000 cash, you would recognize a gain of $150,000 in the year of sale. But what if, instead of a cash sale, you and the buyer agree to seller financing? Suppose the buyer gives you a $40,000 cash down payment, and his $160,000 note (i.e., an obligation of the buyer providing for principal payments totaling $160,000, and for periodic payments of interest at a reasonable rate). How would you be taxed in that case? Just looking at §1001, the answer would seem to be that the fair market value of the note is included in your amount realized along with the $40,000 cash, and you must realize and recognize gain equal to the amount by which the value of the note plus the cash exceeded your $50,000 basis. Assuming the note was worth $160,000, you would have the same $150,000 gain as with a cash sale. Principal payments on the note would then be received by you free of tax. At the other extreme, Congress might decide to apply a basis-first approach in the case of seller financing. Under that approach, the receipt of the note would be ignored, cash payments of principal would be treated as tax-free recoveries of your basis in the land until the basis was exhausted, and additional principal payments would be taxed as gain. In the example, this would mean the $40,000 down payment would be treated entirely as a recovery of basis, as would the first $10,000 of principal payments received on the note.

Congress considered the first approach too harsh, because it may impose tax before the seller has received any cash with which to pay the tax. That approach also requires determining the fair market value of the note, which can be difficult. On the other hand, Congress considered the second approach too generous, because it permits deferral of all gain even when we know that the taxpayer has sold property at a gain and may have already received substantial cash.[43] Searching for a just-right compromise between too harsh and too generous, Congress came up with the installment sales rules of §453. Under §453(a), gain from an install-ment sale is ordinarily reported on the "installment method," which is defined by §453(c) as "a method under which the income recognized for any taxable year from a disposition is that proportion of the payments received in that year which the gross profit . . . bears to the total contract price." In a simple case such as our example, gross profit is the gain realized on the disposition and the contract price is the amount realized.

One of the constant challenges of reading the Internal Revenue Code, exempli-fied by §453(c), is deciphering mathematical formulas expressed in words. The tax lawyer's life would be simpler if Congress abandoned its insistence that the Code use words to express all mathematical ideas, but until that happens the ability to translate is essential. Section 453(c) requires the comparison of two ratios, or

---

43. The second approach is commonly known as "open transaction" treatment. It is recog-nized by the current regulations, but only in the most grudging manner. The regulations never permit open transaction treatment for an installment sale involving a "fixed amount" installment note. Reg. §15a.453-1(d)(2)(ii). Even in the case of an installment sale involving a "contingent payment" installment note, open transaction treatment is available only if (1) the taxpayer elects out of the installment method of §453, and (2) the situation is one of "those rare and extraordi-nary cases involving sales for a contingent payment obligation in which the fair market value of the obligation . . . cannot reasonably be ascertained." Reg. §15a.453-1(d)(2)(iii). For the origins of open transaction treatment, see Burnet v. Logan, 283 U.S. 404 (1931).

fractions.[44] The goal is to determine the amount of income recognized for a particular taxable year, so we'll use x to indicate income recognized. The three other elements of the formula are payments received in the year (P), the gross profit (GP), and the contract price (CP). After translation, §453(c) tells us that

$$x/P = GP/CP$$

Multiplying both sides of the equation by P, to isolate x,

$$x = P(GP/CP)$$

In our example, the amount realized (and thus the contract price) is $200,000 (the $40,000 down payment and the $160,000 note), and the gain realized (and thus the gross profit) is $150,000. The payment in the year of sale is the $40,000 down payment. Plugging these numbers into the formula, the amount of gain recognized in the year of sale is

$$\$40,000\ (\$150,000/\$200,000) = \$30,000$$

In one or more future years, you should receive $160,000 of principal payments on the note. As those payments are received, they will be multiplied by the $150,000/$200,000 profit ratio, with the result that three-quarters of each payment will be taxed as gain and one-quarter of each payment will be treated as a recovery of basis. If, for example, you received the entire $160,000 in a single year, the gain recognized would be

$$\$160,000\ (\$150,000/\$200,000) = \$120,000$$

Combining the results in the two years in which payments were received, you have paid tax on $150,000 of gain, and have treated $50,000 of payments as tax-free recovery of basis. These results make sense, because you received total payments of $200,000 for property with a basis of $50,000.

The idea behind the installment method is to treat every principal payment as a microcosm of the entire transaction. If, looking at the transaction as a whole, three-quarters of the amount realized is gain and one-quarter is return of basis, then three-quarters of *each payment* is taxed as gain, and one-quarter of each payment is treated as a return of basis. This matches the imposition of tax with the receipt of cash, thus avoiding the liquidity problems inherent in taxing the entire $150,000 gain in the year of sale. At the same time, it treats a portion of each payment as taxable gain, thus avoiding the unduly generous deferral of gain inherent in the basis-first approach.

Because §453 deals only with the gain from the disposition of the property, its rules govern only the tax treatment of the *principal* payments on an installment

---

44. The language of §453(c) is typical of how the Code expresses ratio comparisons. For another example, see the definition of the exclusion ratio for annuities in §72(b)(1). Many Code provisions refer to the "excess" of one amount "over" another amount. *See, e.g.,* §§83(a) and 453(e)(3). The use of the word *over* sometimes misleads people into thinking the Code is calling for a fraction (and thus division). In fact, however, the "excess/over" formula calls for *subtraction* of the second number from the first. This usually involves (explicitly or implicitly) a "but not less than zero" condition; that is, if the statute refers to "the excess of x over y," and the taxpayer's y happens to be larger than the taxpayer's x, the result of the computation is zero, rather than a negative number.

note. The tax consequences of the *interest* payments are governed by other Code provisions. Interest payments received will be included in the gross income of the seller as ordinary income (§61(a)(4)), and interest paid may be deductible by the buyer under §163 (if none of the numerous special rules limiting the interest deduction applies).[45]

Problem 10. Richard owns land with a basis of $80,000. He sells it to Samantha, who gives Richard a cash down payment of $10,000 and her note with a principal amount of $90,000. The note bears adequate stated interest, and provides for a "balloon" payment of the entire principal amount in five years. Assuming §453 applies, how much gain does Richard recognize in the year of the sale, and how much gain will he recognize in the year he receives the $90,000 principal payment on the note?

E. ANNUITIES

A prototypical annuity provides, in exchange for one or more payments by or on behalf of the beneficiary (annuitant), a stream of equal periodic payments for the life of the annuitant, thus protecting the annuitant against the risk of depleting her savings by outliving her life expectancy. While life insurance provides financial protection against the risk of an early demise, a life annuity protects against the danger of an unexpectedly long life. Life insurance and annuities thus represent opposite bets with an insurance company. The life insurance purchaser wins big (on her bet with the insurer) if she dies the day the policy goes into effect; the annuitant wins big if she lives forever.

At her retirement at age 65, Donna buys an annuity from a life insurance company for $100,000. Her actuarial remaining life expectancy is (let us suppose) exactly 20 years. The annuity entitles her to an annual cash payment of $8,000 for the rest of her life. If Donna cooperates with the actuaries by living for exactly 20 years, she will receive total payments of $160,000.[46] In that case, it is clear that she should be taxed on $60,000 of income and that she should be allowed to treat the other $100,000 as a tax-free recovery of her basis in the annuity. The problem is the *timing*, over the 20 years, of basis recovery and taxation of income — a problem that has much in common with the problem of basis recovery and gain taxation on installment sales. As with installment sales, Congress rejected the idea of using a taxpayer-favorable, basis-first rule for annuities. Under the rejected basis-first approach, Donna would treat the first $100,000 of annuity payments (covering the first 12 years and part of the 13th) as tax-free, and all subsequent payments as fully taxable.

Instead of a basis-first rule, Congress has provided for gradual recovery of an annuitant's basis, according to the "exclusion ratio" of §72(b)(1). Under the statutory approach, the portion of an annuity payment treated as a tax-free

45. If the note does not bear adequate stated interest, the original issue discount (OID) rules must be used both (1) to identify the amount of disguised interest, and (2) in calculating the gain recognized under §453. For the details, see the cell on the OID rules.
46. The insurance company can pay out more than she paid for the annuity and still make a profit, because of the investment return it can earn on the $100,000.

recovery of basis "bears the same ratio to [the amount of the annuity payment] as the investment in the contract (as of the annuity starting date) bears to the expected return under the contract (as of such date)." Using our by now well-developed translation skills, this means

nontaxable amount/annuity payment =
investment in the contract/expected return

or, isolating the crucial term,

nontaxable amount =
annuity payment (investment in the contract/expected return)

The next step is to find the definitions of the terms on the right side of the equation. As one would expect, Donna's *annuity payment* for any given year is the $8,000 cash received, but what is her *investment in the contract,* and what is her *expected return*? As always with the Internal Revenue Code, the first rule is to keep reading, because the definitions are probably later in the same section. In this case, §72(c)(1) says that the investment in the contract equals the premium(s) paid by Donna, reduced by any amounts received by Donna before the annuity starting date and excluded from income. Here, Donna's investment in the contract is simply her single premium payment of $100,000. Section 72(c)(3) doesn't quite *define* expected return, but it does say that if the expected return on an annuity depends on the annuitant's life expectancy, the expected return shall be based on actuarial tables prescribed by the Treasury. Assuming the relevant tables give Donna a life expectancy of 20 years as of the annuity starting date, her expected return is simply

$8,000 per year × 20 years = $160,000

Plugging the investment in the contract and expected return numbers into the statutory formula, the nontaxable amount of each annual payment is

$8,000 ($100,000/$160,000) = $5,000

Since $5,000 of the $8,000 is excluded from income as basis recovery, the other $3,000 is taxable.

There is actually a simpler way of calculating the amount of each payment excluded from income, whenever an annuity provides for *equal* annual payments. In that case, the effect of the formula is to allocate the basis recovery evenly over the annuitant's life expectancy. Here, for example, Donna's annual basis recovery could be calculated simply as

$100,000 investment in the contract/20 years =
$5,000 basis recovery per year

However, if the payments are not level over time (or if the payments are level over time but begin or end midyear), the slightly more complicated statutory formula must be used.

There is obviously some similarity between the annuity formula of §72(b)(1) and the installment method formula of §453(c), but just how close is the resemblance?

For no particularly good reason, the §453 formula is designed to produce the amount of each installment payment *included* in gross income, while the §72 formula defines the amount of each annuity payment that is *excluded* from gross income. That is a superficial difference, however. Either formula could be readily restated to be consistent in form with the other. Try restating the §72 formula to define the taxable amount or the §453 formula to define the tax-free amount. If you do, you will see that the two formulas are not merely similar; they are identical under the skin.

What if, instead of waiting until her retirement to buy an annuity, Donna had bought an identical annuity 15 years earlier for only $40,000? (The price was so much lower because the insurance company could invest the $40,000 for 15 years before it would be required to make any payments under the contract.) As a matter of the mechanical application of §72(b)(1), this works just like the previous example. When Donna turns 65, with a life expectancy of 20 years, and receives her first $8,000 annual annuity payment, she will have a $40,000 investment in the contract and an expected return of $160,000. The amount of each payment she can exclude from income will be

$$\$8,000\ (\$40,000/\$160,000) = \$2,000$$

She must include the other $6,000 of each payment in gross income. Although Donna has more taxable income here than in the previous example, she also enjoys a tax deferral advantage not present in the earlier example. Between her purchase of the annuity at age 50 and the annuity starting date 15 years later, the annuity increased in value by $60,000. (Donna had to pay $100,000 for an identical annuity when she waited until age 65 to buy it.) During that 15-year period, the increase in value is treated as unrealized appreciation; not a penny of it is taxed until Donna begins to receive annuity payments.

This pre-starting date deferral is probably the most significant tax advantage afforded to annuitants, but it is not the only one. Although the ratable basis recovery rule of §72(b)(1) may not seem taxpayer-favorable, in fact it is. Consider the simple example of an annuity paying $1,000 per year for a fixed term of three years. It would be easy to construct a self-help version of an annuity like this, featuring payments for a period determined without regard to anyone's survival or demise. Suppose a taxpayer invests $2,673 in a savings account paying 6 percent interest on January 1, and withdraws $1,000 from the account on December 31, making additional $1,000 withdrawals on December 31 of each of the next two years. The table below summarizes the taxpayer's transactions.

Year	Principal Amount at Beginning of the Year	6% Interest for the Year	Year-end Principal plus Interest	Year-end Withdrawal	Balance after Year-end Withdrawal
1	$2,673	$160	$2,833	$1,000	$1,833
2	$1,833	$110	$1,943	$1,000	$943
3	$943	$57	$1,000	$1,000	zero

Without having bought an actual annuity, the taxpayer has created the exact equivalent—from a non-tax perspective—of an annuity paying $1,000 per year for three years. It is not, however, the *tax* equivalent of an annuity. With this self-help approach, the taxpayer will owe tax on each year's interest income: $160 for the first year, $110 for the second year, and $57 for the third year. Compare this with the tax treatment of an equivalent annuity under §72(b)(1). For each year, the amount excluded is

$$\$1,000 \ (\$2,673/\$3,000) = \$891$$

Thus, the taxable annuity income each year is $109 ($1,000 minus $891). The total amount of annuity income over the three years is $327. This is the same as the total interest income over the three years under the self-help approach, but the §72 timing rules avoid the front-loading of income that occurs under the self-help approach. The taxation of interest income under the self-help approach reflects economic reality. Interest income is greatest in the first year because that is when the principal amount is largest; interest income falls in later years as the principal amount declines. By providing for level annual income amounts, rather than front-loaded annual income amounts, §72 confers a tax benefit on annuitants.[47]

Thus, §72 offers two significant tax advantages to owners of annuities: the deferral of tax on the increase in the value of the annuity during the period before payments begin, and the understatement of the income portion of payments in the early years. Aware that these rules are quite generous, Congress has sought to limit their applicability to investments serving the basic non-tax purpose of annuities: providing annuitants with income security. For example, §72(e)(4) provides that most loans under annuity contracts are treated as taxable distributions. This contrasts with the general rule that loans—even nonrecourse loans secured by appreciated property—are not taxable events.[48] In addition, §72(q)(1) imposes a 10 percent penalty tax (on top of the regular income tax) on annuity distributions unless one of the §72(q)(2) exceptions applies. Two of the most significant exceptions are (1) for any distribution to an annuitant at least 59-1/2 years old, and (2) for a distribution "which is part of a series of substantially equal periodic payments . . . made for the life (or life expectancy) of the taxpayer or the joint lives (or joint life expectancies) of such taxpayer and his designated beneficiary."

The basis recovery rules of §72(b)(1) work out neatly if an annuitant dies right on schedule, but what happens in less tidy cases? The following problems explore the tax treatment of less cooperative annuitants. You will need to examine §72(b) carefully in order to answer the questions.

Problem 11.   Oswald buys an annuity from a life insurance company upon his retirement at age 65, when his actuarial life expectancy is 20 years. The annuity costs $100,000 and entitles Oswald to annual cash payments of $8,000 for the rest

---

47. Does the self-help example in the text seem familiar? Can you think of a common example of a debt instrument that is gradually paid off (i.e., amortized) by level payments, with early payments consisting mostly of interest and later payments consisting mostly of principal? The typical home mortgage loan is structured in the same way as the self-help investment described in the text, and the holder of the mortgage must report interest income in the economically accurate front-loaded manner; §72 does not apply.

48. *See* Woodsam Assocs., Inc. v. Commissioner, 198 F.2d 357 (2d Cir. 1952), discussed in Chapter 2.C.2.c.

of his life. If Oswald is still alive 21 years later, and receives a 21st $8,000 annuity payment, how will he be taxed?

Problem 12. The facts are the same as in Problem 11, except Oswald dies after having received only six annual payments. What, if anything, happens to his unrecovered investment of $70,000?

F. BASIS RULES FOR PROPERTY TRANSFERRED BY GIFT OR BEQUEST

1. *Property Transferred by Inter Vivos Gift*

Margaret paid $1,000 for 100 shares of Exxon stock in 1995. In 2010, when the stock was worth $3,000, Margaret gave the shares to her adult son, Steve. In 2012, Steve sold all 100 shares for $3,500. From our previous consideration of §102, we know that a gift is neither taxable to the recipient nor deductible by the transferor. Our focus now, however, is on the tax treatment of the $2,000 of appreciation existing in the stock at the time of the gift. When and to whom should it be taxed? There are three major possibilities:

1. Because the appreciation occurred while Margaret owned the stock, arguably it should be taxed to her. That result could be reached by (a) treating the gift as a §1001(a) "sale or other disposition of the property" with the $3,000 of value Margaret is able to bestow on Steve as her amount realized on the disposition, and (b) giving Steve a $3,000 basis in the stock to ensure that the $2,000 appreciation is taxed only once.
2. Because making the gift does not produce any cash that Margaret could use to pay a tax on the appreciation, and because a tax imposed on appreciation in gifted property could involve serious valuation problems (albeit not in the case of Exxon stock), it might be better to defer the tax on the appreciation until Steve sells the stock. One way of implementing this approach would be (a) not to treat the gift as a realization event for Margaret, and (b) requiring Steve to take the stock with Margaret's $1,000 basis, so that when Steve sells the stock for $3,500 he will be taxed on both the $500 gain that accrued while he held the stock and the $2,000 gain that accrued during Margaret's ownership.
3. As a variation on the second approach, the income tax might (a) defer taxation of gain until Steve sells the stock, but (b) when Steve sells the stock, tax $2,000 of the gain to Margaret and $500 of the gain to Steve. The difference between the second and third approaches is not merely who writes the check for the tax on $2,000 of gain, but also whether the gain is taxed at Margaret's marginal tax rate or at Steve's (possibly lower) tax rate.[49]

---

49. The gain should qualify as long-term capital gain, but a lower income taxpayer may have a lower capital gains tax rate than a higher income taxpayer. Note that an additional complication of this third approach may be that Margaret, who in realistic examples will be a generation or two older than Steve, may not be around to pay her share of the tax by the time—perhaps years later—that Steve sells the stock.

Which of the three approaches seems most reasonable? For better or worse, Congress has chosen the second approach, which is obviously taxpayer-favorable in that it defers taxation of the $2,000 until the sale by Steve. In many cases, it is also taxpayer-favorable in another sense; it allows a high bracket donor to shift the tax liability on unrealized appreciation to a lower bracket donee. The income-shifting aspect of this approach is considered in more detail in Chapter 10.C.1, in connection with the Supreme Court's *Taft v. Bowers* opinion. The focus here is on the timing of the tax on the appreciation.

By analogy to the tax treatment of like-kind exchanges and involuntary conversions, one might expect to find a Code provision expressly providing that the donor does not *recognize* gain (or loss) on a gift of appreciated (or depreciated) property. In fact, however, there is no such provision. Instead, the implicit rule is that a gift of appreciated property does not constitute a *realization* event — despite the statement in §1001(a) that gain or loss is realized on "the sale *or other disposition* of property,"[50] and the fact that a gift certainly seems like a disposition. In contrast with the Code's failure to address explicitly the tax treatment of the donor of appreciated property, §1015 provides that Steve takes the stock with Margaret's $1,000 basis, rather than with a basis of $3,000 (the value of the stock at the time of the gift).

The tax treatment of appreciation in gifted property resembles the treatment of like-kind exchanges in that (1) gain is not taxed even though a taxpayer has transferred appreciated property, and (2) the tax on the appreciation is deferred — rather than being permanently excused — by a special basis rule. A minor difference between the two situations is that the nontaxation of the gain is by express statutory provision in the case of like-kind exchanges, but by way of a dubious (albeit firmly established) interpretation of §1001(a) in the case of gifts. A more significant difference is that §1031 preserves the potential for tax by making the *original taxpayer* take a below-value basis in a *new asset* (the property received in the like-kind exchange), while §1015 makes a *new taxpayer* (the donee) take a below-value basis in the *original asset*. As a matter of official tax jargon, both rules are examples of "substituted basis," but the like-kind rule is an instance of "exchanged basis," while the gift rule is an instance of "transferred basis." *See* §§7701(a)(42), (43), and (44). Don't worry if you have trouble keeping straight the exchanged basis and transferred basis terminology; so do most tax lawyers.

Section 1015 contains a curious exception to the general rule that a donee succeeds to the donor's basis in gifted property. If the donor's basis is greater than the fair market value of the property at the time of the gift — in other words, if the gift is of property with an unrealized loss — then "for the purpose of determining loss the basis shall be such fair market value [at the time of the gift]." As an example, suppose Margaret owns General Motors stock with a basis of $100. She gives the stock to Steve when the stock is worth $90, and Steve later sells the stock for $85. The stock was loss property at the time of the gift, so the special rule applies in determining the amount of Steve's loss. Under the special rule his basis is only $90, and his loss is $5 ($85 amount realized minus $90 basis). Neither Margaret nor Steve is ever allowed any tax benefit for the $10 loss that accrued while Margaret owned the stock; that loss simply disappears for tax purposes.

What is the purpose of the special loss basis rule? Apparently Congress is concerned that, in the absence of a special rule for gifts of property with built-in

---

50. Emphasis added.

losses, a low income donor could make a gift of loss property to a high income donee, who could then sell the property and deduct the loss against income taxed in the donee's higher bracket.[51] If that is the concern, though, Congress seems to be straining at the proverbial gnat while swallowing the proverbial camel. Surely more tax is avoided by the transferring of gains to lower bracket donees than would ever be avoided by the transferring of losses to higher bracket donees—both because investment gains are more common than investment losses and because the natural direction of gifts is from higher bracket to lower bracket taxpayers. Yet Congress blesses the more serious tax avoidance technique while clamping down on the less serious one. For whatever it may be worth, the special loss basis rule for gifts is consistent with the treatment under §267 of *sales* of loss property between related persons. As explained earlier,[52] §267 does not permit the shifting to the related purchaser of the tax loss disallowed to the seller.

To test your understanding of both the general transferred basis rule of §1015 and the special loss basis rule, try the following problems.

Problem 13. Margaret owns General Motors stock with a basis of $100. She gives it to Steve when it is worth $90. GM stock then stages a rally, and Steve eventually sells it for $105. How much gain does Steve realize on the sale?

Problem 14. Margaret owns General Motors stock with a basis of $100. She gives it to Steve when it is worth $90. Steve eventually sells the stock for $93. How much gain or loss does Steve realize on the sale?

2. Property Transferred at Death

Logically, one might expect that the tax treatment of appreciated property gratuitously transferred at death (by bequest or inheritance) would be the same as the treatment of inter vivos gifts: no gain taxed to the decedent-transferor, with the potential for taxation preserved by saddling the transferee with the decedent's below-value basis. The only seemingly plausible alternative would be to treat transfers at death as realization events, with the appreciation taxed to the decedent on her final return and the transferee taking the property with a basis equal to its date-of-death value. Surprisingly, however, the actual treatment is neither of these. Instead, a transfer at death is not treated as a realization event, and §1014 gives the transferee a basis equal to the property's value as of the decedent's death. As a result of this tax-free step-up in basis at death, no one—neither the decedent nor the transferee—is ever taxed on the appreciation that accrued while the decedent owned the property.

Technically, §1014 is a two-way street. If a taxpayer dies owning property with an unrealized loss, he is not allowed to deduct the loss and the transferee takes the property with a basis stepped *down* to the date-of-death value. In practice, however, the angel of §1014 eliminates much more gain than loss—partly because invest-ment gains historically have exceeded investment losses, and partly because

51. A variation on this concern would be that a donor who could not deduct a loss because of the §1211(b) capital loss limitations (see section B.3 of this chapter) would make a gift of the property to a donee who had realized capital gains against which the loss could be deducted.
52. See section B.2 of this chapter.

the tax-conscious elderly sell their loss assets to avoid the step-down in basis while retaining gain assets in anticipation of a basis step-up.

There is no obvious policy justification for the permanent exemption from the income tax of appreciation transferred at death. It is true that §1014 is not as big a loophole as equivalent treatment for gifts during life. A taxpayer can take advantage of §1014 only once, and only by incurring a significant non-tax detriment. Still, the mere fact that §1014 is not the biggest loophole imaginable is hardly a justification for the provision. Some commentators have defended §1014 as a device for preventing double taxation—once under the income tax and once under the estate tax—of gains transferred at death. This justification does not work, however, for two reasons. First, Congress has not adopted a general policy of not subjecting appreciation to both the income tax and the estate tax. If a taxpayer sells appreciated property during her life, retains the after-tax proceeds of the sale, and transfers those proceeds at death, the appreciation may be subject to both the income tax and the estate tax. Second, in many cases §1014 applies even though the gain protected from the income tax is not subject to the estate tax. Under current law, a person can make up to $5 million worth of gratuitous transfers (during life and at death, combined) without incurring any gift or estate tax liability.[53] In addition, a decedent can use the estate tax marital deduction to transfer unlimited value to his or her surviving spouse without incurring any estate tax liability. Although no estate tax is imposed on transfers of appreciated property sheltered by the exemption amount or by the marital deduction, §1014 nevertheless applies to eliminate the potential income tax on the appreciation. In such situations §1014 does not prevent the imposition of a double tax; it ensures there will not be even a single tax.

Section 1014 is difficult to justify even in the presence of the estate tax, but Congress decided that the provision would be impossible to justify in the absence of the estate tax. For political reasons not worth going into here, the estate tax generally did not apply with respect to persons dying in 2010. Congress decided that §1014 should not apply to property acquired from a decedent who died during the 2010 estate tax holiday. Instead, §1022 applies modified transferred basis rules to that property. Although §1022 resembles the gift basis rules in broad outline, it is considerably more generous. Basically, it allows a tax-free basis step-up of $1.3 million per decedent, with an additional $3 million tax-free basis step-up for property transferred to a surviving spouse.[54] With the estate tax reinstated for 2011 and later years, §1014 determines the basis of property acquired from a decedent after 2010.

---

53. This is true for 2011 and 2012. The exemption amount is scheduled to decline to $1 million in 2013, but it is unlikely Congress will allow that to happen.

54. Legislation enacted in December 2010 set the estate tax exemption level at $5 million for 2011 and 2012, and also gave the executor of an estate of a decedent dying in 2010 a choice between the no-estate-tax-plus-§1022 regime and the estate-tax-plus-§1014 regime. If the estate tax regime is chosen for 2010, the exemption amount for that year is also $5 million. Thus, the estate tax and §1014 will apply even with respect to persons dying in the jubilee year of 2010, if the executor opts for that regime. The executor of a billionaire dying in 2010 will elect the no-estate-tax regime, even if the estate has highly appreciated assets. A carryover basis in appreciated assets—with the potential for a 15 percent capital gains tax if and when the assets are sold—is a small price to pay to avoid an estate tax imposed at the rate of 35 percent. But suppose you are the executor of an estate of a person who died in 2010 owning a single asset with a value of $5 million and a basis of zero. If you choose the no-estate-tax regime, there is no estate tax (obviously) and the basis of the asset becomes $1.3 million under §1022. If you choose the estate tax regime, there is again no estate tax (this time because of the $5 million exemption), and the basis of the asset becomes $5 million under §1014.

Section 1014(c) contains an important exception to the general rule permitting tax-free increases in basis at death. No basis increase is allowed for "property which constitutes a right to receive an item of income in respect of a decedent [IRD] under section 691." Oddly, neither §1014 nor §691 defines IRD. Roughly speaking, however, IRD consists of amounts that would have been taxed to the decedent during his lifetime if he had been on the accrual method instead of the cash method. The classic example is compensation paid after death for services performed by the decedent. By far the most important examples of IRD, however, are distributions from tax-deferred retirement savings vehicles. Post-death distributions from an employer-provided pension or from an IRA will be taxed to the distributee (as ordinary income), to the extent the distributions would have been taxed to the decedent if he had lived to receive them.

Problem 15.   Mildred owns stock with a basis of $50,000 and a value of $650,000. Agnes, Mildred's great aunt, is 93 and in poor health. Mildred gives her stock to Agnes, with the understanding that Agnes will leave the stock to Mildred in her will. Despite the understanding, Agnes is under no legal obligation to leave the stock to Mildred; she could sell it and spend the proceeds, or give or bequeath it to someone else. Agnes dies ten months after the gift (when the stock is worth $700,000), and her will gives the stock back to Mildred. What was Mildred trying to accomplish? Did she succeed? Would your answer be different if Agnes had died 13 months after the gift? What if Agnes died 13 months after the gift, but a secret agreement *required* Agnes to leave the stock to Mildred? If a plan like Mildred's has a potential income tax advantage, are there still reasons why few taxpayers would pursue it?

3. Part Gift–Part Sale Transactions

The following problems are exercises in both tax logic and in reading and applying the Code and regulations. As you will see, the Code and regulations are usually — but not always — consistent with tax logic.

Problem 16.   Fred owns land with a basis of $60,000 and a value of $400,000. Intending to make a gift of $300,000 of value, he sells the land to his adult daughter, Deborah, for $100,000. How much gain, if any, does Fred realize on this sale? First try to figure out the logical answer, without consulting the Code or regulations. After that, examine Reg. §1.1001-1(e) for the actual answer, logical or otherwise.

Problem 17.   Given the treatment of Fred under Reg. §1.1001-1(e) (which you determined in solving Problem 16), what should be Deborah's basis in the land? As with Problem 16, first try this as an exercise in tax logic, and then check your logic against the actual rule set forth in Reg. §1.1015-4(a). Assume that the gift portion of the transfer generated no gift tax liability for Fred.

Problem 18.   Instead of giving the land in Problem 16 to Deborah, Fred decides to make a bargain sale of the land to his church. Intending to make a charitable contribution of $300,000, he sells the land to the church for $100,000. How much gain, if any, does Fred realize on this sale? *See* §1011(b). If the answer is different from the amount of gain realized on the noncharitable bargain sale in Problem 16, what is the policy explanation for the difference?

G. BASIS ALLOCATION: PIECEMEAL ASSET DISPOSITIONS AND OTHER CONTEXTS

GAMBLE v. COMMISSIONER

68 T.C. 800 (1977)

RAUM, J.: The Commissioner determined a deficiency . . . in petitioners' 1971 income tax. At issue are first, whether petitioners realized ordinary income or capital gain from the sale of a yearling colt, and second, the proper cost basis of the colt. [The court's discussion of the ordinary income versus capital gain issue is omitted.]

FINDINGS OF FACT

. . . Mr. Gamble's principal occupation consists of seeking out investment opportunities and managing his assets. He owns stocks, bonds, real estate, farming interests, mining interests, oil and gas operations, and cattle ranches. From 1964 through 1974, in addition to the interests described above, he was also engaged in the business of racing thoroughbred horses. During that period, he acquired full or partial ownership of a total of 13 horses for business or investment purposes. . . .

Mr. Gamble and his "agent" studied the catalogue of the annual fall mixed sale at Keeneland, Ky., with a view towards obtaining another broodmare suitable for use in Mr. Gamble's horse racing business. One of the broodmares listed in the catalogue was Champagne Woman. In addition to a description of Champagne Woman's pedigree, racing record, and past production record, the catalogue indicated that Champagne Woman was believed to be carrying a foal sired by Raise A Native.

Upon studying this catalogue, Mr. Gamble recognized the fine qualities of, and the value inherent in, Champagne Woman in her expectant state. Not only did she herself have an impressive record, but also, Raise A Native was known as a particularly successful stud. His offspring included 17 stakes winners, among them Majestic Prince, winner of both the Kentucky Derby and the Preakness Stakes. In 1969 the 19 yearlings sired by Raise A Native sold for a total of $935,000, or an average price of $49,211 per horse. Over the course of his lifetime, a total of 41 Raise A Native yearlings have been sold for an average price of $50,256.

Prior to November 10, 1969, Mr. Gamble did not know the exact amount of Raise A Native's stud fee, although he believed that it was rather high. Subsequent to that date, he ascertained that in 1969 the stud fee for a mare's service by Raise A Native was $27,500 for a shareholder (an owner of an interest in the stud horse), and between $32,500 and $35,000 for a nonshareholder.

Mr. Gamble and his agent both expected that Champagne Woman would sell for a price in excess of $100,000; in fact, they thought that the auction might begin with bids of $100,000 or more. Therefore, because Mr. Gamble had decided that he wanted to purchase a broodmare costing no more than approximately $50,000, Champagne Woman was not included among the horses for which Mr. Gamble's agent was supposed to bid.

However, notwithstanding the considerations referred to above, Champagne Woman was purchased for Mr. Gamble's account on November 10, 1969, at the Keeneland sale, for only $60,000.[55] She was acquired for use in his horse racing business, and was placed in service in that business immediately upon her purchase. . . .

On November 10, 1969, Mr. Gamble purchased "Live Foal Insurance" covering the expected foal of Champagne Woman. The insurance protected him against loss because of the death of the foal at any time from that date until 30 days after foaling. The benefit payable under this policy was $20,000 and the premium for this coverage was $3,600. The "Cover Note" which, pending issuance of a formal policy, served as a temporary contract of insurance stated in respect of the expected foal:

*** If Purchased, give Purchase Price and Date of Sale $20,000, 11/10/69 ***

At about the same time, Mr. Gamble purchased "Full Mortality Insurance" in the amount of $60,000, covering Champagne Woman for the period from November 11, 1969, through November 10, 1970. The cover note issued in connection with this insurance policy . . . was not submitted in evidence. . . .

The Champagne Woman/Raise A Native foal, whose eventual sale gave rise to the amounts now in controversy, was born on April 12, 1970. The foal was a chestnut colt, and will sometimes hereinafter be referred to by that description.

Five days after the foal's birth, Mr. Gamble purchased "Full Mortality Insurance" in the amount of $30,000 covering the foal from May 12, 1970, through May 11, 1971. . . .

As the colt approached the age at which it would normally have begun training for racing, Mr. Gamble entered it in the Saratoga Yearling Sale, held August 10-13, 1971, at Saratoga, N.Y. . . . The colt was in fact sold on the first night of the Saratoga sale for a price of $125,000. By comparison, the average price of the 52 horses sold there that night was $22,754.

In computing for Federal income tax purposes his gain upon the sale of the colt, Mr. Gamble subtracted from the $125,000 gross proceeds of the sale, selling expenses of $12,500 and, in addition, $30,000 as the cost basis of the colt. This basis was derived from the allocation of a portion of the $60,000 purchase price which had been paid to acquire Champagne Woman carrying the colt as a foal. The portion allocated to the foal was determined by reference to Raise A Native's stud fee at the time he sired the foal.

55. The record is somewhat unclear as to precisely how this purchase came about. For instance, the evidence does not reveal whether petitioner or his agent made the decision to purchase Champagne Woman at that price. Nor does it satisfactorily explain why the horse sold for a price so much lower than expected. According to petitioner's testimony the "bargain" price resulted from the fact that the seller (a foundation) did not "support" the price of the horse at the sale. However, even if this were so, it does not explain why competing prospective purchasers did not drive the price up to anywhere near the levels which petitioner had anticipated.

In his notice of deficiency, the Commissioner determined that " . . . the basis of the colt was zero in that $30,000 of a purchase price of $60,000 for Champagne Woman, a broodmare in foal at purchase date November 1969, was erroneously allocated to the unborn foal."

OPINION

. . . What was the basis of the colt? Petitioner paid $60,000 to acquire Champagne Woman in foal to Raise A Native. To the extent that a portion of this purchase price was in fact paid to acquire the unborn foal, that amount became petitioner's cost basis in the foal.

We are fully convinced by the record as a whole that petitioner did pay more for Champagne Woman in foal to Raise A Native than he would have paid to acquire her "open" or in foal to a lesser known stallion. And, although the record was not entirely satisfactory in this respect, it is our best judgment that $20,000 of the purchase price was properly attributable to the unborn foal. First of all, the insurance policy which petitioner obtained to cover the unborn foal indicated that its purchase price had been $20,000. We regard this as far more reliable evidence of petitioner's estimate of how much he had paid for the foal than was his testimony at trial. Secondly, while stud fees actually paid by a taxpayer for the breeding of one of his mares might be the proper cost basis of the foal which was thus conceived (assuming the fee was not deducted as a current expense), it does not follow from that, that when a taxpayer purchases a mare in foal from the owner who has had it serviced by a stallion, the purchase price includes a dollar-for-dollar payment of the stud fee. Therefore, the stud fees actually charged by Raise A Native are only evidence of how much petitioner paid for the unborn foal. And to the extent that petitioner bought the whole package at a bargain price, we think at least part of the discount must be associated with the unborn foal. However, it would be wholly unrealistic to apply the entire bargain element first against the purchase price of the unborn foal so as to reduce its cost to zero, and therefore to conclude that it was acquired at no extra charge.

We do not accept the Government's contention that the foal had no cost basis whatever, nor do we approve the petitioner's position that a cost basis of $30,000 must be allocated to the foal. It is our best judgment . . . that a cost basis of $20,000 must be allocated to the foal and we so find.

Notes and Questions

1. *The problem of basis allocation. Gamble* is an example of the common tax problem of basis allocation. As in *Gamble,* the problem can arise when a taxpayer pays a single unallocated price for two (or more) assets, and later sells one asset while retaining the other. Basis allocation problems also arise when a taxpayer buys what seems to be a single asset — such as a tract of undeveloped land — and later sells only a portion of the asset. In keeping with the Tax Court's approach in *Gamble,* Reg. §1.61-6(a) provides, "When a part of a larger property is sold, the cost or other basis of the entire property shall be equitably apportioned among the several parts, and the gain realized or loss sustained on the part of the entire property sold is the difference between the selling price and the cost or

other basis allocated to such part." This regulation keeps numerous appraisers busy as expert witnesses in tax controversies.

2. *What's at stake?* Suppose Mr. Gamble sold Champagne Woman for $90,000 three years after his sale of the foal for $125,000. The table below shows the tax consequences of the two sales: (1) under the Tax Court's decision allocating $20,000 of Mr. Gamble's purchase price to the foal, and (2) under the IRS's claim that no part of the purchase price was properly allocable to the foal.

	Tax Court Approach	IRS Approach
1. Net amount realized on sale of foal in year one	$112,500	$112,500
2. Basis allocated to foal	−$20,000	−$0
3. Gain realized on sale of the foal	$92,500	$112,500
4. Amount realized on sale of mare in year four	$90,000	$90,000
5. Basis allocated to mare	−$40,000	−$60,000
6. Gain realized on sale of the mare	$50,000	$30,000
7. Total gain realized (line 3 plus line 6)	$142,500	$142,500

In one sense, the fight over basis allocation is much ado about nothing; after Mr. Gamble's sale of Champagne Woman, he will have been taxed on the same total amount of gain — $142,500 — regardless of how much basis is allocated to the foal. Moreover, the total taxed gain of $142,500 is clearly the correct amount, since that is the amount by which Mr. Gamble's combined amounts realized for the two horses ($202,500) exceed his cost for the two horses ($60,000). Both approaches produce the same total gain in the end because both permit the same total basis recovery. The basis allocated to the foal under the IRS's approach is $20,000 less than the basis allocated to the foal under the Tax Court's approach, but the basis allocated to the mare under the IRS's approach is $20,000 more than the basis allocated to the mare under the Tax Court's approach.

But the fight over basis allocation is not *really* much ado about nothing. What is at stake is the timing of the tax on $20,000 of Mr. Gamble's gain. Even assuming that the gain would be taxed at the same rate (e.g., 30 percent) in either year one or in year four, Mr. Gamble will fare better under the Tax Court's approach than under the IRS's alternative. *Gamble* provides another context for examining the importance of timing in taxation, and the economic benefit of being able to defer tax liability to a later year.

3. *The value of deferral (a reprise).* Suppose Mr. Gamble happens to have $6,000 invested at a 5 percent after-tax rate of return, and he plans to use that money to pay his $6,000 tax liability (30 percent of $20,000), the timing of which is at issue. If the $6,000 tax is due in Year One (under the IRS's basis allocation), he pays the tax in that year and that is the end of the story. But if he is able to defer paying the $6,000 tax for three years (under the Tax Court's basis allocation), his $6,000 investment will grow to $6,946 by the time the tax comes due.[56] He will then have to pay the

56. This is based on 5 percent interest, compounded annually, for three years. Some of the numbers in the text's discussion are rounded.

$6,000 tax, but he will be able to keep the $946 after-tax investment return. Thus, he will be $946 richer in Year Four if his basis is allocated $20,000 to the foal and $40,000 to the mare, than if it is all allocated to the mare. That amount — $946 — is the *future value* (in Year Four) of being able to defer the $6,000 tax liability. Alternatively, Mr. Gamble could spend $816 of the $6,000 in year one, secure in the knowledge that the remaining $5,184 invested at 5 percent (after-tax) would grow to $6,000 by the time the tax became due. That $816 is the *present value* of being able to defer the tax for three years. The connection between the $816 present value and the $946 future value is that $816 invested at 5 percent for three years will grow to $946.

4. *Basis allocation problems not involving a disposition.* Problems of basis allocation can arise even when a taxpayer has not disposed of any part of her acquisition. If a taxpayer pays $3 million for an apartment building and the land on which it sits, she will be able to claim cost recovery (i.e., depreciation) deductions on the portion of the $3 million cost allocable to the building, but she will not be entitled to claim any cost recovery deductions with respect to the portion of her basis allocable to the land. Similarly, if one room of a taxpayer's condominium qualifies as a home office (under the stringent rules of §280A), she may claim cost recovery deductions with respect to the portion of her basis in the condominium allocated to that room, but not with respect to the portion of her basis allocated to the other rooms. Perhaps the most difficult basis allocation problems arise in connection with the purchase of an ongoing business, in which a taxpayer pays a lump sum for a collection of hundreds or thousands of different assets. Some of the assets may not be eligible for cost recovery deductions, and the assets that are eligible may be subject to many different cost recovery schedules. In addition, the taxpayer may sell some of the assets of the business (especially inventory) soon after the acquisition, while retaining other assets for many years. Section 1060 and its regulations — the details of which are mercifully beyond the scope of the basic income tax course — provide elaborate rules governing basis allocations in connection with the purchase of an ongoing business.

5. *Installment sales and annuities as problems of basis allocation.* The basis recovery rules for installment sales (§453) and annuities (§72) were examined earlier in this chapter, but it is worth noting here that both sets of rules can be understood as special instances of the general basis allocation principle embodied in Reg. §1.61-6(a). A taxpayer who receives an installment note in exchange for property has a basis in the note equal to her basis in the property (reduced by any basis recovered against the down payment, if there is a down payment). The question is how the taxpayer should be allowed to recover that basis as she in effect gradually disposes of the note by receiving principal payments on it. Section 453 answers that question. Similarly, §72 allows a taxpayer who buys an annuity gradually to recover her basis as she gradually disposes of the annuity (in effect) by receiving periodic annuity payments.

Cell

DETERMINING THE AMOUNT OF A LOSS AND THE DEDUCTIBLE PORTION OF A LOSS

A. Loss Limited to Basis

B. No Deduction for Losses in Transactions Not Entered into for Profit

Problems 1-2

Quite apart from special provisions to prevent manipulation of the realization doctrine, the amount of a *deductible* loss on a property transaction may be less than a taxpayer's economic loss, because of two fundamental income tax principles: (1) a loss is not allowed with respect to amounts on which the taxpayer has never been taxed, and (2) a loss generally is not allowed in connection with a transaction not entered into for profit. These two principles are discussed below.

A. LOSS LIMITED TO BASIS

In 2009 Lisa paid $1,000 for 100 shares of Bubble, Inc. By late 2010, 100 shares of Bubble were trading for $10,000. In 2011 the bubble burst, and Bubble stock lost almost all its value. Lisa sold all her shares for $100. She feels as if she lost $9,900, and so she did — relative to the high-water mark of Bubble stock. As far as §1001(a) is concerned, however, Lisa's loss is only $900: her $100 amount realized minus her $1,000 basis.[1] Under the formula for gain or loss realized — amount realized minus basis — any fluctuations in the value of Bubble stock while Lisa owned the stock are irrelevant. Is it fair to limit Lisa's tax loss to only $900, when she really has suffered an economic loss of $9,900? Yes, because $9,000 of her economic loss was a loss of unrealized appreciation. Since the income tax never treated her as having received the unrealized appreciation, the income tax cannot logically treat her as having lost it. One cannot lose for tax purposes what one never had for tax purposes. Congress did not need to enact a special provision disallowing losses

---

1. The $900 loss is a long-term capital loss, subject to the deducibility limitations of §1211(b).

of unrealized appreciation; the disallowance follows naturally from the basic statutory definition of gain or loss realized, and from the fact that basis is not adjusted upwards on account of unrealized appreciation. (*See* §1016.) Thus the maximum possible tax loss — in the case of an amount realized of zero — is the taxpayer's cost for the property.

The limitation of loss to basis is further explored later in this book in connection with the deduction under §165(c)(3) for nonbusiness casualty losses and in connection with the deduction under §170 for contributions to charity.[2] In the case of contributions to charity, a special rule illogically allows a deduction for some charitable contributions of unrealized appreciation.

B.   NO DEDUCTION FOR LOSSES IN TRANSACTIONS NOT ENTERED INTO FOR PROFIT

Sam buys a house for $200,000 and lives in it for several years before deciding to sell it and move to another city. Because of a downturn in the local economy, he is able to sell the house for only $170,000. He has *realized* a loss of $30,000 ($170,000 amount realized minus $200,000 basis),[3] but the mere fact that he has realized a loss does not mean the loss is taken into account for tax purposes. Under §165(c), a taxpayer may deduct a realized loss only if the loss was incurred in a trade or business, in a nonbusiness transaction entered into for profit, or as a result of a "fire, storm, shipwreck, or other casualty, or from theft." Sam's loss on the house does not fall into any of these three categories, so the loss has no income tax consequences.[4] In reality, most people probably have a dual purpose in owning a home: the nonbusiness and not-for-profit motive of living in the home, and a secondary hope of someday selling the home at a profit. According to the regulations, however, the subsidiary hope of profit is not enough to qualify ownership of one's home as a transaction entered into for profit. *See* Reg. §§1.165-9(a), 1.262-1(b)(4).

The same disallowance rule applies to a loss realized on the sale of any consumer durable — for example, a loss on the sale of a personal-use car or truck. Even if §165(c) were not in the Code, the same result — complete disallowance of losses on the sale of personal use assets — would probably be reached under the authority of §262(a): "Except as otherwise expressly provided in this chapter, no deduction shall be allowed for personal, living, or family expenses." Personal consumption expenditures are generally not deductible — income devoted to consumption constitutes the bulk of the base of the income tax — and a loss on the sale of a consumer durable is just one type of personal consumption expenditure. A taxpayer who pays

---

2. See Chapter 4.D (casualty losses) and Chapter 4.A (charitable contributions).

3. If Sam had used the house as income-producing rental property, he would have been allowed "cost recovery" (i.e., depreciation) deductions under §168, and those deductions would have reduced his basis in the house (pursuant to §1016). No cost recovery deductions are allowed, however, for owner-occupied housing producing imputed income rather than taxable income. *See* §265(a)(1). Cost recovery deductions under §168 are discussed in Chapter 6.A.

4. If the loss did not fall victim to §165(c), it would be a long-term capital loss subject to the deductibility limitations of §1211(b). Because of §165(c), however, §1211(b) never comes into play.

rent for his home is denied a rent expense deduction by §262, and a homeowner's non-deductible loss on the sale of his home is analogous to the tenant's nondeductible rent. Similarly, the cost of a personal vehicle is nondeductible whether one leases a car, or buys a car and later sells it at a loss.

Problem 1.   Arnold pays $20,000 for a car for his personal (nonbusiness) use. He drives it for several years, and then sells it for $6,000. Bill also pays $20,000 for a car for his personal use, drives it for several years, and then sells it. As it turns out, however, collectors have come to treasure cars like Bill's, so Bill is able to sell his car for $20,000. What are the tax consequences of the two sales? Do the results strike you as fair? As reasonable?

   What happens if a taxpayer converts loss property from personal to business use? Consider the following problem.

Problem 2.   After having lived in her house for several years, Tracy decides to move elsewhere and convert the house to a rental property. At the time she converts the house from personal to business use, Tracy's basis in the house is $200,000, and the fair market value of the house is $170,000. Tracy owns and operates the house as a rental for several years, properly claiming cost recovery (i.e., depreciation) deductions of $50,000 under §168.[5] Tracy then sells the house. (a) What are the tax consequences to Tracy if she sells the house for $120,000 cash? (b) For $115,000 cash? (c) For $190,000 cash? (If Tracy realizes a gain in any of these situations, assume she has used the house as a rental for too long for the gain to qualify for the §121 exclusion.) To answer these questions, you will need to consult Reg. §1.165-9(b) and (c). In addition to understanding the mechanical application of the rules, can you explain the logic underlying the rules?

---

5. See Chapter 6.A.

Cell

A LIFE INSURANCE-ANNUITY COMBINATION

Rev. Rul. 65-57

Suppose you are an elderly person, with a life expectancy of ten years. You have $1 million cash. You would like to invest that money in a debt instrument paying 10 percent annual interest (the going interest rate), consume the after-tax interest income, and leave the $1 million principal to your children when you die. If you do this, you will have $100,000 taxable interest income each year — $1 million total taxable interest, if you happen to die exactly when the actuarial tables say you should.

Your tax advisor, however, suggests a different approach. He wants you to buy two products from a life insurance company at the same time: (1) an annuity paying $100,000 annually for as long as you live, and (2) a single premium life insurance policy with a death benefit of $1 million. Based on your ten-year life expectancy and a 10 percent discount rate, the present value of the annuity is $614,460, and the present value of the life insurance policy is $385,540. Thus, the insurance company will sell you the two-product package for $1 million. Viewing the two products together, the insurance company will agree to pay you $100,000 per year for as long as you live, and $1 million upon your death. Ordinarily, a seller of life insurance hopes that the insured will live a long time, and a seller of a life annuity hopes that the annuitant will die soon. Under the proposal, however, the two bets cancel out, and the insurance company should be indifferent whether you die tomorrow or live for another 50 years (at least as long as the prevailing interest rate remains 10 percent). Because the two bets cancel out, the insurance company should be willing to sell you the life insurance policy without the usual requirement of a medical examination and other "evidence of insurability."

Tax consequences aside, your advisor's plan produces results very similar to the results if you simply purchased a debt instrument bearing 10 percent interest. The only non-tax difference is that the advisor's plan locks in the 10 percent interest rate for however long you happen to live, whereas you probably could not find a debt instrument with the maturity date set at the date of your death (whenever that happens to be). Despite the close resemblance of the life insurance-annuity package to a debt instrument, your tax treatment will be very different from the tax treatment of the holder of a debt instrument, *if* the usual tax rules for life insurance and for annuities apply.[6]

---

6. For the rules applicable to life insurance proceeds, see section A.3.c of Chapter 2. For the rules governing annuities, see section E of Chapter 3.

Your investment in the annuity contract is $614,460. Applying the exclusion ratio formula of §72(b)(1), the portion of each annual payment of $100,000 excluded from gross income is

$$\$100,000 \times (\$614,460/\$1,000,000) = \$61,446$$

Thus, the taxable portion of each $100,000 payment is $38,554. If you happen to expire in exactly ten years, you will have received $1 million of annuity payments, and you will have included only $385,540 in gross income. As for the life insurance, §101(a)(1) will exclude from gross income the entire $1 million death benefit. Putting the annuity and life insurance tax results together, you will have paid tax on only $385,540, compared with paying tax on $1 million if you purchased a debt instrument and died after receiving $100,000 annual interest payments for ten years.

REV. RUL. 65-57

1965-1 C.B. 56

. . . Advice has been requested whether the proceeds of a life insurance policy taken out under the circumstances described below will be excludable from the gross income of the beneficiary under section 101(a) of the Internal Revenue Code of 1954.

The taxpayer purchased a life insurance policy which he could not have acquired except in combination with a nonrefund life annuity contract for which he paid a single premium equal to the face value of the life insurance contract. The annuity payments to the taxpayer are to cease at his death. The contracts are the usual form of contracts issued by the insurance company and the premium rates on both are at the regular rates charged by the company for nonparticipating ordinary life insurance on standard lives and life annuity contracts of the type issued to the taxpayer. The taxpayer named his daughter as beneficiary of the life insurance policy. After its issuance, he assigned the policy to the beneficiary by gift.

Section 101(a)(1) of the Code states the general rule that the proceeds of life insurance policies, if paid by reason of the death of the insured, are excludable from the gross income of the recipient.

In order to be an insurance contract, for Federal tax purposes, a contract must involve an element of risk. The risk must be an actuarial one under which the premium cost is based upon the likelihood that the insured will live for a certain period and the insurer stands to suffer a loss if the insured does not in fact live for the expected period.

In Helvering v. Edyth Le Gierse, et al., 312 U.S. 531 (1941), a decedent took out simultaneously an insurance policy on her life and a nonrefund annuity contract entitling her to payments for her life. A single premium was paid for each, the aggregate of the two premiums exceeding the face value of the life insurance policy by an amount representing loading and other incidental charges. Issuance of the insurance policy was expressly contingent upon the simultaneous purchase of the annuity contract. Each contract was in standard form for that type of contract. The Supreme Court of the United States, in holding that the proceeds of the life insurance policy did not qualify as an "amount receivable . . . as insurance" [for purposes of the estate tax] stated, in part, as follows:

. . . the amounts must be received as the result of a transaction which involved an actual "insurance risk" at the time the transaction was executed. Historically and commonly insurance involves risk-shifting and risk-distributing. . . .

Considered together, the contracts wholly fail to spell out any element of insurance risk. It is true that the "insurance" contract looks like an insurance policy, contains all the usual provisions of one, and could have been assigned or surrendered without the annuity. Certainly the mere presence of the customary provisions does not create risk, and the fact that the policy could have been assigned is immaterial since, no matter who held the policy and the annuity, the two contracts, relating to the life of the one to whom they were originally issued, still counteracted each other. . . . The fact remains that annuity and insurance are opposites; in this combination the one neutralizes the risk customarily inherent in the other. . . .

The concept of insurance laid down in *Le Gierse* was predicated not upon elements peculiar to the estate tax but upon fundamental principles of what constitutes insurance. The concept is equally applicable to the term "insurance" found in section 101(a) of the Code in reference to the income tax, as the term is employed in that section not in any specialized sense but with its normal meaning. . . .

In transactions of the type described herein the insurance company has not undertaken to shift the risk of premature death from the insured and to distribute the risk among its other policyholders. On the contrary, by requiring the purchase of a nonrefund annuity contract the company has eliminated this risk. . . .

In the instant case the taxpayer is considered to have purchased two contracts[:] one a life annuity contract and the other a contract which, while designated a life insurance contract, has no element of "insurance" and is, therefore, not a contract of the type contemplated in section 101(a) of the Code.

Accordingly, it is held that the annual payments received under the annuity contract will be subject to the provisions of section 72(b) of the Code. The proceeds of the other contract, even though received by reason of the insured's death, will not be excludable from gross income under section 101(a) of the Code and will be subject to income tax to the extent they exceed the net premiums paid for that contract.

Notes and Questions

1. *A three-act play.* The ruling provides an example of a common type of three-act tax drama. In the first act, Congress provides favorable tax treatment for a particular type of transaction or investment. In this case, the favorable tax rule is the §101 exclusion for life insurance proceeds payable by reason of the death of the insured. In the second act, taxpayers try to take advantage of the favorable tax rule without actually engaging in the type of conduct, or making the type of investment, that Congress intended to favor. In this case, taxpayers tried to obtain the advantage of §101 without actually making an investment involving any mortality risk. In the final act, the IRS challenges the taxpayers, relying on the doctrine of substance-over-form, the sham transaction doctrine, or some other anti-abuse statutory interpretation doctrine. Sometimes the IRS attack on the perceived abuse succeeds, and sometimes it does not. In this instance, the courts were receptive to the IRS position. *See, e.g.,* Kess v. United States, 451 F.2d 1229 (6th Cir. 1971). There is often a fourth act, although there was not in this instance. In the fourth act, Congress gets involved and

amends the Code to shut down the abusive transactions. The fourth act usually follows IRS failure in the third act, but sometimes Congress intervenes even though the IRS is winning in the courts. Much (but certainly not all) of the complexity in the Internal Revenue Code is attributable to fourth act legislation, which means the complexity is indirectly attributable to second-act taxpayer shenanigans. If only taxpayers would behave themselves, the Code could be much simpler.

2. *A loophole not quite closed?* Does Rev. Rul. 65-57 succeed in taking all the fun out of the life insurance-annuity combination? Applying the ruling to the facts of our hypothetical (in which the taxpayer cooperatively dies right on schedule, at the end of ten years), the ruling does produce the correct total amount of income. Without the protection of §101, the taxpayer realizes a gain of $614,460 on the so-called life insurance policy.[7] Combined with the $385,540 of taxable annuity payments, this produces total taxable income over the ten years of $1 million — exactly the same as the $1 million taxable income he would have had over the ten years if he had simply received $100,000 of interest annually. Although the ruling produces the correct total *amount* of taxable income, the *timing* under the ruling is much more taxpayer-favorable than the timing under the debt instrument alternative. The ruling allows the taxpayer to defer more than 60 percent of the income until the end of the ten years.[8] Perhaps the IRS made a tactical error in the ruling. Arguably, the IRS should have refused to treat the annuity and the "life insurance" as separate investments. Instead, it should have ruled that the two contracts, taken together, constituted a single debt instrument paying 10 percent interest and maturing upon the taxpayer's death.[9]

3. *Tax arbitrage.* Pairing the largely offsetting risks of life insurance and annuities is one way to exploit the tax-favored treatment of internal build-up within life insurance and annuity contracts. Another temptation is to engage in "tax arbitrage." Arbitrage generally — that is, non-tax arbitrage — consists of exploiting small differences between or among markets. As an example of non-tax arbitrage, one might identify an opportunity to buy gold bullion in Zurich at one price, and sell it nearly simultaneously in New York at a slightly higher price. Arbitrageurs are also attracted to such things as tender offers, in which a conditional offer is made to buy a block of stock at a particular price somewhat above its current trading level. Typically, the market price rises toward the tender offer price, but does not reach that price because the conditions may fail, in which case the price may revert to its prior level. Arbitrageurs may buy the stock at some price between the previous market price and the tender offer price, gambling that the conditions will not fail, and that they will receive the full value of the tender offer price as soon as the conditions are met.

Tax arbitrage takes many forms, but always involves exploiting asymmetries in the applicable tax rules. In the insurance context,

---

7. $1 million amount realized minus $385,540 basis.

8. It also seems likely, under the ruling's analysis, that the $614,460 gain would qualify for the lower rates applicable to long-term capital gains.

9. Another possibility would be to attack the deferral on the "life insurance" by treating that contract as a contingent debt instrument, subject to the original issue discount rules. *See* Treas. Reg. §1.1275-4. The approach suggested in the text would be much simpler.

policyholders have at various times (now mostly past, since tax reform efforts in this area have been mostly successful) bought insurance largely with borrowed funds.[10] Even if the funds were borrowed at higher rates than those credited to the policyholder's reserve, this was still advantageous if the interest payments on the borrowing were deductible, while the internal buildup within the policy was excludable. For example, a single-premium policy with a $100,000 death benefit might have been purchased by a middle-aged man for perhaps $20,000. The policy may have guaranteed a 5 percent annual increase in the cash surrender value of the policy, yielding a $1,000 increase in the value of the policy in its first year. The policyholder might have borrowed the funds to purchase this policy, and may have promised his creditor 7 percent interest payments, or $1,400 per year. Borrowing at 7 percent to make investments returning 5 percent seems like a losing venture, but if the $1,400 payments were deductible, and the taxpayer faced a marginal tax rate of 50 percent, the net cost of the interest payments would only be $700 per year. If the $1,000 return were untaxed, the policyholder would have profited on the transaction.[11]

The foregoing description is largely historical because Congress long ago identified this sort of transaction as an abuse of the rules that generated deductible interest payments and excludable interest-like earnings within the policy. Congress responded in 1954 with a provision, in §264, disallowing interest deductions for debts "incurred or continued" to purchase permanent life insurance policies. Section 264 includes a blanket prohibition on interest deductions paid with respect to borrowed money used to buy single-premium policies,[12] and a somewhat less air-tight prohibition, added in 1964, disallowing interest deductions as to other policies "which contemplate the systematic direct or indirect borrowing of part or all of the increase in the cash value of [the] contract."[13] Even under pre-1954 law, the courts showed a willingness to step in to control abusive cases where the taxpayer transparently attempted to create interest deductions through highly leveraged purchases of insurance products. In Knetsch v. United States, 364 U.S. 361 (1960), for example, the Supreme Court ruled that a contract, 99.9 percent of the value of which was financed by the insurance company that sold the contract, could be disregarded as a sham.[14]

---

10. For discussion of a wide range of debt-financed tax shelters, based on the combination of tax-preferred income and deductible interest expense, see parts A and B of Chapter 8.

11. Of course, if the policyholder cashes in the policy for its cash surrender value, the income will be taxed at that time; the tax will thus have been deferred, but not avoided altogether. If the policyholder dies while the insurance is still in force, however, the $100,000 death benefit will be completely excluded, even though the benefit reflects in some sense the average expected investment earnings enjoyed by the insurance company during the time it held the life insurance reserve.

12. IRC §264(a)(2).

13. IRC §264(a)(3).

14. *Knetsch* is set out in section B.4 of Chapter 8. The annuity contract in *Knetsch*, which was a combined annuity-life insurance product, showed other evidence of its lack of economic substance. For example, the annuity in question was not scheduled to begin paying annuity benefits until after the annuitant's 90th birthday. Also, the taxpayer borrowed virtually all of the annual increase in the cash value of the policy during each of the years the contract remained in force.

314

Cell

SELECTED TOPICS IN LIKE-KIND EXCHANGES

A. THE LIKE-KIND REQUIREMENT AS APPLIED TO PROPERTY OTHER THAN REAL ESTATE

As the discussion in the main text indicates, the like-kind standard is interpreted much more narrowly for exchanges of personal property than for exchanges of real estate. The following two rulings illustrate the difficulty of satisfying the like-kind requirement outside of the real estate context.

REV. RUL. 79-143

1979-1 C.B. 264

ISSUE

Does an exchange of numismatic-type coins held for investment for bullion-type coins held for investment qualify for nonrecognition of gain under section 1031 of the Internal Revenue Code of 1954?

FACTS

An individual taxpayer who is not a dealer in foreign or domestic coins purchased United States $20 gold coins as an investment. After the coins had appreciated in value, the taxpayer exchanged them for South African Krugerrand gold coins of equal total fair market value. A gain was realized by the taxpayer as a result of the exchange. The taxpayer will hold the South African Krugerrand gold coins as an investment.

The United States $20 gold coins exchanged by the taxpayer are numismatic-type coins. The value of numismatic-type coins is determined by their age, number minted, history, art and aesthetics, condition, and metal content. The South African Krugerrand gold coins received by the taxpayer are bullion-type coins. The value of bullion-type coins is determined solely on the basis of their metal content.

LAW AND ANALYSIS

Section 1031(a) of the Code provides that no gain or loss is recognized upon an exchange of property (not including evidences of indebtedness) held for productive use in trade or business or for investment for property of a like kind to be held either for productive use in trade or business or for investment.

Section 1.1031(a)-1(b) of the Income Tax Regulations provides that as used in section 1031(a) of the Code, the words "like kind" have reference to the nature or character of the property and not to its grade or quality. One kind or class of property may not, under that section, be exchanged for property of a different kind or class.

Section 1031(e) of the Code provides that the exchange of livestock of one sex for livestock of the other sex is not an exchange of property of like kind for purposes of the nonrecognition provision of section 1031(a), because, as the committee report cited below points out, the different sexes of livestock represent investments of different types, in one case an investment for breeding purposes, in the other an investment in livestock raised for slaughter. Section 1031(e) was enacted to clarify what was considered to be the correct interpretation of section 1031(a). See S. Rep. No. 91-552, 91st Cong., 1st Sess. 102 (1969), 1969-3 C.B. 423, 488-489.

Similarly, in this case, although the coins appear to be similar because they both contain gold, they actually represent totally different types of underlying investment, and therefore are not of the same nature or character. The bullion-type coins, unlike the numismatic-type coins, represent an investment in gold on world markets rather than in the coins themselves. Therefore, the bullion-type coins and the numismatic-type coins are not property of like kind.

HOLDING

The exchange of United States $20 gold coins for South African Krugerrand gold coins does not qualify for nonrecognition of gain under section 1031(a) of the Code.

Rev. Rul. 76-214, 1976-1 C.B. 218, which holds that the exchange of Mexican 50-peso gold coins for Austrian 100-corona gold coins, both of which are official government restrikes, qualifies for nonrecognition of gain under section 1031(a) of the Code, is distinguishable because that Revenue Ruling involves only the exchange of bullion-type coins for bullion-type coins.

Notes and Questions

1. *But bullion is bullion?* One might think that any gold coin would be more like any other gold coin than a ranch is like a shopping center, but this ruling indicates that the IRS will insist on examining the investment climate affecting the coins in question. Bullion-type coins will move with the market for the metal from which they are minted; numismatic-type coins will move with whatever crazy things influence the highly unstable collector markets. But at least holders of bullion-type coins can swap those coins for other bullion-type coins, right? Not necessarily, as the following ruling indicates.

REV. RUL. 82-166

1982-2 C.B. 190

ISSUE

Does an exchange of gold bullion held for investment for silver bullion held for investment qualify for nonrecognition of gain under section 1031(a) of the Internal Revenue Code?

FACTS

An individual taxpayer, who is not a dealer in gold or silver bullion, purchased gold bullion in the cash market and held it as an investment. In 1980, after the gold bullion had appreciated in value, the taxpayer exchanged the gold bullion for silver bullion of equal total fair market value A gain was realized by the taxpayer as a result of the exchange. The taxpayer holds the silver bullion as an investment.

LAW AND ANALYSIS

Section 1031(a) of the Code provides that no gain or loss is recognized upon an exchange of property held for productive use in trade or business or for investment solely for property of a like kind to be held either for productive use in trade or business or for investment.

Section 1.1031(a)-1(b) of the Income Tax Regulations provides that as used in section 1031(a) of the Code, the words "like kind" have reference to the nature or character of the property and not to its grade or quality. One kind or class of property may not, under that section, be exchanged for property of a different kind or class.

Rev. Rul. 79-143, 1979-1 C.B. 264, holds that the exchange of United States $20 gold coins (numismatic-type coins) for South African Krugerrand gold coins (bullion-type coins) does not qualify for nonrecognition of gain under section 1031(a) of the Code because the numismatic-type coins and the bullion-type coins represent totally different types of underlying investment and thus are not property of like kind. The bullion-type gold coins, unlike the numismatic-type gold coins, represent an investment in gold on world markets rather than in the coins themselves.

In this case, the values of the silver bullion and the gold bullion are determined solely on the basis of their metal content. Although the metals have some similar qualities and uses, silver and gold are intrinsically different metals and primarily are used in different ways. Silver is essentially an industrial commodity. Gold is primarily utilized as an investment in itself. An investment in one of the metals is fundamentally different from an investment in the other metal. Therefore, the silver bullion and the gold bullion are not property of like kind.

HOLDING

The taxpayer's exchange of gold bullion for silver bullion does not qualify for nonrecognition of gain under section 1031(a) of the Code.

Notes and Questions

1. *Is the only qualifying exchange a pointless exchange?* One is left with the impression that the only exchanges of coins or metals that might be protected by §1031, at least in the eyes of the IRS, would be exchanges of virtually identical properties — such as South African Krugerrands for Canadian Maple Leaf coins. The rule that seems to emerge is that you can have an exchange of metals that will be tax-free under §1031, as long as the exchange would be pointless. But could the IRS sustain this position in court?

B. ANOTHER WAY OF DETERMINING THE BASIS OF QUALIFIED PROPERTY RECEIVED IN AN EXCHANGE

Here is a rule that is useful both in understanding the logic of the basis adjustments and in checking the correctness of your basis calculations: The difference between the fair market value of the new like-kind property and its basis (as determined under §1031(d)) should always equal the difference between the amount of gain the taxpayer realized on the exchange and the amount of gain the taxpayer was required to recognize on the exchange (under §1031(b)). Suppose, for example, you exchange land with a basis of $100 for land worth $140 and $30 cash boot. Under §1031(b), you must recognize $30 of your realized gain of $70. Under §1031(d), your basis in the new land is $100: your old basis of $100, decreased by the $30 cash received and increased by the $30 gain recognized. If you were then to sell the new land for $140 cash, you would realize and recognize a gain of $40; the fair market value of the new like-kind property exceeds its basis by $40. Appropriately, this $40 is precisely the amount of realized gain that went unrecognized on the like-kind exchange: $70 gain realized minus $30 gain recognized. In this example, then,

1. *$140* fair market value of new like kind property minus
   $100 §1031(d) basis =
2. *$70* gain realized on the like-kind exchange minus *$30* gain recognized

If you use this test and the two numbers are not equal, you know you have made a mistake somewhere in your calculations. As this equivalency suggests, Congress could have written the §1031 basis rules in a manner that would look quite different from §1031(d), but that would produce identical results. It could have defined the basis of the new like-kind property as the fair market value of that property, reduced by the amount of gain that the taxpayer realized but did not recognize on the exchange. In fact, this alternative approach to basis determination is reflected in §1033(b)(2), governing the basis of property acquired to replace involuntarily converted property.

C.   TWO ANCILLARY BASIS RULES

An ancillary rule in §1031(d) provides that, if a taxpayer receives both qualified and nonqualified property, then the basis carried over from the property he transferred, as adjusted, is to be allocated between or among the qualified and nonqualified assets acquired in the exchange. In making this allocation basis is to be allocated first to the nonqualified property in the amount of its fair market value, with the residual basis (i.e., that part of the total basis that is not allocated to the nonqualified property) being allocated to the qualified property. The logic of this allocation is exactly the same as the logic described in the main text, with respect to the allocation of basis between property received and cash received. Any consideration received other than like-kind property — whether cash or non-like-kind property — is given a basis equal to its fair market value, while any deferred gain is reflected in the basis of the like-kind property received. For example, suppose Smith transfers Blackacre with a basis of $100,000, in exchange for White-acre (valued at $150,000) and a pickup truck having a market value of $10,000. He will recognize a gain triggered by the $10,000 of boot in the form of the truck. Thus, his total basis in the acquired property will be his basis in Blackacre ($100,000), increased by the amount of gain recognized ($10,000). This $110,000 amount is then allocated first to the truck, in the amount of its market value ($10,000), with the remaining $100,000 being allocated to Whiteacre. As in the case of the cash §1031(b) transaction, the basis adjustments here — increasing the basis to reflect gain already recognized, then reducing it by the amount of basis allocated to the truck — achieve an offset, leaving the taxpayer with the same basis in Whiteacre that he had in Blackacre. Because Whiteacre's like-kindedness is what justified the deferral of recognition of gain, it makes sense that the untaxed gain should be built into its basis rather than into the basis of the truck (the receipt of which triggered recognition of gain).

The final basis rule of §1031(d) is really more than just a basis rule, because it may affect as well the amount of gain recognized in a like-kind exchange. It says that if a liability of the taxpayer is assumed by another as part of the consideration for the transaction, the amount of the liability is to be treated as though that amount of cash had been received by the taxpayer. Thus, returning to our familiar example, assume that Smith transferred, in a like-kind exchange, his property Blackacre, which had at the time an adjusted basis of $100,000 and a market value of $150,000, but was subject to a $40,000 mortgage. The net value of this asset is only $110,000, since there is a $40,000 claim encumbering the property. If Smith exchanges this for Whiteacre, which has a value of $110,000 and no encumbrances, then Smith will be required to recognize $40,000 of gain, since the assumption of the mortgage is treated as equivalent to the receipt of cash under the last sentence of §1031(d). These results are summarized in the table at the end of this paragraph. The cash-equivalence idea carries over to the basis adjustment rules, with Smith's basis in Whiteacre being his basis in Blackacre ($100,000) decreased by the amount of money (constructively) received ($40,000) and increased by the amount of gain recognized ($40,000).

Blackacre		**Whiteacre**
$100,000	Basis	(Irrelevant)
$150,000	Market Value	$110,000
$40,000	Mortgage	$0
$110,000	Net Asset Value	$110,000
$50,000	Gain Realized	(Irrelevant)
$40,000	Gain Recognized	(Irrelevant)

Because investments in real estate are characteristically made with large amounts of mortgage debt, this rule would, if applied literally, be highly inconvenient, if not disastrous, in the one industry most aided by §1031. Fortunately, the Treasury regulations have saved the day. First, they provide, by example, that only *net* liabilities released must be treated as the equivalent of cash received.[15] Thus, in our example above, if Smith had swapped Blackacre, with its $40,000 mortgage, for Whiteacre when the latter property was subject to a mortgage of $30,000, Smith would have a net liability release of only $10,000 (that is, he would have only $10,000 less debt than he had going into the like-kind exchange). Only this amount would be treated as the equivalent of cash received.

The examples in the regulations go a bit further even than that. They provide that if a taxpayer invests additional cash in a like-kind exchange, and also has a net liability release that would, but for this exception, be treated as cash received, then he will be allowed to offset the new cash invested against the net liability release, so that only the net liability release in excess of the new cash investment will be treated as cash received. For example, if Blackacre, worth $150,000, is encumbered by a

15. Reg. §1.1031(d)-2, ex. 2.

$40,000 mortgage, and Smith, its owner, trades Blackacre, plus $20,000 cash, for Whiteacre, when Whiteacre has a value of $145,000 and a mortgage of $15,000, what will be the result? Smith has a net liability release of $40,000 – $15,000, or $25,000. But he is permitted by the regulations to offset his additional investment of $20,000 against this amount, so that only the net-net amount of $5,000 is treated as the receipt of cash. Thus, he will recognize gain only to the extent of this $5,000 of boot. These results are summarized in the table at the end of this paragraph. If his basis in Blackacre had been $100,000, then his basis in Whiteacre will be that sum, decreased by the liability released ($40,000), increased by the liability assumed ($15,000), by the gain recognized ($5,000), and by the additional cash invested ($20,000), yielding a basis in Whiteacre of $100,000. This "builds in" a gain position in Whiteacre of $45,000, which is the amount of gain Smith enjoyed during his ownership of Blackacre ($50,000), less the $5,000 of gain already taxed.[16]

Blackacre		Whiteacre
$100,000	Basis	(Irrelevant)
$150,000	Market Value	$145,000
$40,000	Mortgage	$15,000
$110,000	Net Asset Value	$130,000
–$20,000	Cash	+$20,000
$130,000	Value Exchanged	$130,000
$50,000	Gain Realized	(Irrelevant)
$5,000	Gain Recognized	(Irrelevant)

These are reasonable results, in the sense that Smith might well have been able to use the $20,000 of cash that he invested in the transaction to pay down his mortgage instead. Then he would only have had a $20,000 mortgage and only $5,000 of net liability release. (And if the terms of Smith's mortgage made this impossible or uneconomic, it is still difficult to see why he should face a greater immediate gain on this transaction merely because of that unfortunate financial fact.) Nevertheless, the language of §1031(d) provides that the full amount of the liability release — $40,000 here — is to be treated as cash. Capping the gain recognized at the amount of the net liability release — $25,000 here — or the net-net liability release of $5,000, is quite a reach for the Treasury. But who will complain, unless Congress itself does so, when the Treasury acts in a way that almost invariably favors taxpayers?

16. Curiously, the same example cited in note 15 indicates that, in the reverse situation, the IRS is less generous. That is, if a taxpayer receives cash, but also incurs a net liability *increase* in a like-kind exchange, the IRS will not allow the taxpayer to offset the cash received with the amount of the net liability increase. This is true despite the fact that the act of borrowing money — of which this would seem to be a variant — is generally nontaxable. In addition, this aspect of the §1031 regulations is inconsistent with the more generous treatment accorded to a taxpayer in an analogous situation with respect to an involuntary conversion under §1033.

D. TRIANGULAR EXCHANGES

1. In General

The regulations — and this book — generally assume that Smith has Blackacre and wants Whiteacre, and that, say, Gonzales, the owner of Whiteacre, is in the opposite position. In the real world, however, things seldom work out so neatly. If §1031 applied only to simple two party exchanges — Smith's farm for Gonzales's farm — the provision would be little more than a curiosity, because it would be rare that Smith and Gonzales would each decide, simultaneously, that the other's grass was greener. But suppose Smith's farm (adjusted basis of $100,000), which once was part of a clearly rural area, is now on the edge of an expanding metropolis. As a farm, Smith's property is worth $1 million, but as land for a shopping center or a residential development it is worth three times that amount. Smith would love to sell the farm for $3 million cash and use the proceeds to buy a larger property farther out in the country, which is worth $3 million *as a farm*. If he did that, however, he would have to pay tax on $2.9 million gain; §1031 does not apply to cash sales followed by reinvestments. If Smith could avoid recognition of his gain only by finding an owner of an appropriate replacement farm who wanted to swap with Smith, his situation would be almost hopeless. As it turns out, however, Smith will be able to take advantage of §1031 by artificially structuring his transaction as a three-party exchange rather than as a sale-plus-reinvestment. In fact, virtually all §1031 real estate transactions involve three or more parties.

Typically, Smith will put Blackacre on the market, perhaps noting in his advertising that he hopes to engage in a like-kind exchange. Real estate developer Chang will appear on the scene, offering cash to Smith in exchange for Blackacre. Smith will suggest instead that Chang buy Whiteacre (which is worth $3 million as a farm) from Gonzales, who has also listed his property for sale. If all goes well, Chang will agree to buy Whiteacre first for cash, then engage in a swap with Smith to obtain Blackacre, giving Smith, finally, possession of Whiteacre. Sometimes, however, it may be difficult to reach this structure. For example, Chang may be concerned about the possibility that the deal might fall apart midway through, leaving her with ownership of a property she never wanted.[17] Ordinarily, to minimize the possibility of various disasters, an escrow arrangement is set up to handle all the transactions. But the escrow arrangement may be so complicated that the very attempt to control all contingencies creates a new hazard — namely, the failure to accurately execute all aspects of the deal in the proper order.

Another potential problem for triangular transactions might be that the essential structure of a triangular like-kind exchange suggests a substance-over-form argument for the IRS. The Service could assert that Chang was merely acting as Smith's agent in the purchase of Whiteacre, and that the whole transaction should be recharacterized as a sale and purchase of Whiteacre by Gonzales and Smith,

---

17. Chang might also be concerned about being in the chain of title of Whiteacre, since there may be environmental or other liabilities that might someday be shared among all persons who owned Whiteacre at any time within a relevant period. If Chang has this concern, she will be relieved to read Rev. Rul. 90-34, 1990-1 C.B. 154, which indicates that Smith can qualify under §1031 if Smith transfers Blackacre to Chang, Chang pays cash to Gonzales, and Gonzales transfers Whiteacre directly to Smith. Thus, the exchange can be accomplished without Chang's ever holding legal title to Whiteacre.

respectively, and a sale and purchase of Blackacre by Smith and Chang, respectively. Both transactions would, in that view, be fully and immediately taxable.

However, the IRS has not actively pursued that theory, apparently conceding that the swap portion of these three-party transactions does qualify for §1031 nonrecognition.[18] The IRS has sometimes found other defects in purported like-kind exchanges, and has pursued its objections with mixed success. For example, defects of one sort or another in the escrow arrangements have produced some litigation, though courts have been quite willing to overlook relatively minor errors so long as the taxpayer seeking the protection of §1031 ends up, when the dust clears, with a piece of property rather like the one he transferred, rather than with cash or other nonqualified consideration.[19] The IRS has also taken the position that the requirement that the acquired property be held for investment purposes or for use in a business precludes application of §1031 in cases where an immediate retransfer of the property, by sale or gift, is contemplated.[20]

As the law of triangular exchanges has developed, a well-advised taxpayer can achieve nonrecognition for the functional equivalent of a cash-sale-plus-reinvestment so long as he jumps through the appropriate exchange hoops. What is the policy justification for this state of affairs? Shouldn't Congress either (1) decide that it is serious about the exchange requirement, and amend the statute to treat triangular exchanges as nonqualifying sale-reinvestments, or (2) amend the statute to provide nonrecognition treatment for sales followed by reinvestment in like-kind property? In the typical triangular exchange, the taxpayer could easily have sold for a known amount of cash. In the above example, Chang would have been perfectly willing to buy Blackacre from Smith for the cash she used to buy Whiteacre from Gonzales. That suggests that taxing Smith on his triangular exchange (under the first legislative reform option) would not raise serious problems of either valuation or liquidity.

2. Deferred Exchanges

Triangular like-kind exchanges are the norm, but the triangulation sometimes creates timing problems; it will often be the case that a buyer for the taxpayer's property will be found before suitable replacement properties have been identified. Even if the buyer is generally willing to facilitate the seller's preference to structure the transaction as a like-kind exchange, the buyer may not be willing to wait until the seller finds the property that will be used to accomplish this. For years, the IRS took the position that an "exchange" implied a substantially simultaneous transfer of properties. However, in the famous case of Starker v. United States,[21] the Ninth Circuit found that a taxpayer who transferred property in exchange for his buyer's "exchange value credits," which had to be used within a

---

18. That is, it qualifies for nonrecognition as to Smith. Presumably Chang does not qualify for nonrecognition on the exchange, because she held Whiteacre only in order to exchange it, rather than for "productive use in a trade or business or for investment," as required by §1031(a)(1). Do you see why the inapplicability of §1031 to her side of the exchange will make little or no difference to Chang?

19. See, e.g., Alderson v. Commissioner, 317 F.2d 790 (9th Cir. 1963), and Biggs v. Commissioner, 69 T.C. 905 (1978).

20. This was an issue as to one of the several properties involved in Starker v. United States, 602 F.2d 1341 (9th Cir. 1979).

21. Id.

five-year period to purchase new properties, could qualify under §1031 for non-recognition of his gain on the property he transferred.

The IRS generally acquiesced in the holding that deferred transactions could qualify, but found the five-year window to be excessive, largely because of audit considerations: The statute of limitations ordinarily precludes adjustment of tax liabilities after three years have passed from the filing of the return. Under the arrangement in *Starker*, neither the taxpayer nor the IRS would know for sure whether a transaction qualified by the end of the audit window if the taxpayer had five years to find replacement properties.

A few years after *Starker*, Congress intervened with a solution that is now embodied in §1031(a)(3). This provision gives the taxpayer 45 days after the transfer of his property to identify the property to be acquired in exchange, so long as the actual transfer of the property occurs within the lesser of 180 days of the initial transfer or the due date for the taxpayer's income tax return for the year in which the purported like-kind exchange took place.[22]

3. Deferred Like-Kind Exchanges, Installment Sales, and Constructive Receipt

SMALLEY v. COMMISSIONER

116 T.C. 450 (2001)

THORNTON, Judge: Respondent determined a $139,180 deficiency in petitioners' joint 1994 Federal income tax. After concessions, the sole issue for decision is whether petitioners are required to recognize income in 1994 as the result of a deferred exchange that petitioner husband (petitioner) entered into in 1994 and that was completed in 1995. . . .

In the 1960s, petitioner acquired some 275 acres of timberland in Laurens County, Georgia. By 1994, some of the timber on this land had reached maturity. After attending a seminar on timber exchanges presented by a well-known timber taxation expert and after consulting with his longtime certified public accountant, petitioner decided to undertake an exchange of standing timber for additional acreage containing standing timber. [O]n November 29, 1994, petitioner entered into a series of agreements with Rayonier, Inc. (Rayonier), whereby for a term of two years he granted Rayonier exclusive rights to cut and remove mature timber on some 95 acres of his Laurens County land (the 95 acres), in consideration of $517,076. Pursuant to the agreements, most of the funds were held by an escrow agent and applied toward the purchase of three parcels of land as designated by petitioner. . . .

Pursuant to the escrow agreement and the timber contract, on November 29, 1994, Lewis [the escrow agent] received from Rayonier net proceeds of $504,935 (the escrow funds), which he deposited into a checking account at Farmers & Merchants Bank in Dublin, Georgia. By three separate letters, dated December

---

22. Because April 15 is the date on which calendar-year taxpayers ordinarily must file their returns, this might seem to create a problem for deferred like-kind exchanges occurring toward the end of a calendar year. However, the Code makes clear that the due date in question is evaluated with regard to extensions of the time to file. Since a six-month extension of the filing deadline is routinely available, all that a taxpayer would need to do to ensure that she has a full 180 days to effect the closing on the property to be acquired would be to file a request for such an extension.

18, 1994, December 21, 1994, and January 2, 1995, petitioner identified to Lewis as replacement properties three parcels of land (the replacement properties), ownership of each of which was transferred directly to petitioner by warranty deed from the respective owners [at various dates during 1995].

The replacement properties are all within 30 miles of the 95 acres. When petitioner acquired these replacement properties, they all contained standing timber that accounted for a significant part of their value.

The purchase of these three replacement properties exhausted all but $205.45 of the escrow funds. By check dated May 9, 1995, Lewis paid petitioner the $205.45 balance.

Petitioners are cash basis taxpayers. On their joint 1994 Federal income tax return, filed on or about April 15, 1995, they characterized the subject transaction as a like-kind exchange of "Timber" for "Timber and Land," giving rise to $496,076 realized gain, all of which they treated as deferred gain pursuant to section 1031. . . .

The notice of deficiency states that "the realized gain from the sale of the timber is to be fully recognized [in 1994] because it has not been established that the requirements of section 1031 of the Internal Revenue Code have been met." . . .

Petitioners argue that to continue petitioner's timber investment, he exchanged standing timber for standing timber that necessarily had to have land attached. Petitioners argue that under applicable Georgia law, both the relinquished property and the replacement property are characterized as real property interests, and that under Commissioner v. Crichton, 122 F.2d 181 (5th Cir. 1941), *aff'g* 42 B.T.A. 490 (1940), the subject transaction qualifies as a tax-deferred like-kind exchange within the meaning of section 1031.

Respondent argues that under Georgia law, the 2-year timber cutting contract was personal property and thus not of like kind to the replacement real property. In addition, relying on Oregon Lumber Co. v. Commissioner, 20 T.C. 192 (1953), respondent argues that regardless of how the property interests may be characterized under State law, the property relinquished and the properties received differ so intrinsically that they are not of like kind within the meaning of section 1031.[23] . . .

On brief, petitioners raise an alternative argument that regardless of whether the subject transaction qualifies as a like-kind exchange, respondent has erroneously determined that they realized income from the transaction in 1994. Relying on section 1.1031(k)-1(g)(3) and (j), Income Tax Regs., petitioners argue that they realized no gain in 1994 because they had no actual or constructive receipt of property in 1994.

Respondent contends that petitioners have improperly raised this issue for the first time on brief. Respondent alleges, and petitioners do not dispute, that the 3-year limitations period for respondent to assess tax for taxable year 1995 ran shortly after the trial date of this case and shortly before the date respondent received a copy of petitioners' brief. Respondent contends that because of this

---

23. Respondent does not dispute that petitioners have met all other requirements for a nontaxable exchange of property held for productive use in a trade or business or for investment within the meaning of sec. 1031. In particular, respondent does not dispute that petitioner's transaction with Rayonier constituted an "exchange" within the meaning of sec. 1031 or that petitioners have satisfied the requirements of sec. 1031(a)(3), which in the case of a nonsimultaneous exchange generally requires that the replacement property be identified no more than 45 days after, and the exchange be completed no more than 180 days after, the transfer of the relinquished property.

circumstance, he is "especially prejudiced" by petitioners' delay in raising their alternative arguments. . . .

Respondent does not contend that he has been prejudiced in developing or presenting evidence regarding petitioners' alternative argument. The only prejudice that respondent suggests would arise from our consideration of petitioners' alternative argument relates to respondent's failure to determine a deficiency for petitioners' 1995 taxable year. If such prejudice exists, it is of respondent's own making. Any such prejudice, however, is speculative, premised as it is on the supposed tax consequences in a year not before us of a legal determination that we decline to reach. The only year before us is 1994, and we confine our determinations to that year. . . .

The section 1031 regulations state: "Except as otherwise provided, the amount of gain or loss recognized . . . in a deferred exchange is determined by applying the rules of section 1031 and the regulations thereunder." Sec. 1.1031(k)-1(j)(1), Income Tax Regs. The section 1031 regulations contain special rules for coordinating the determination of gain or loss under section 1031 and under section 453, which generally requires, subject to a host of qualifications not in issue here, that where a taxpayer disposes of property and is to receive one or more payments in a later year, the taxpayer's profit on the sale is to be included in income as the payments are received.

For purposes of section 453, payments include amounts actually or constructively received in the taxable year. *See* sec. 15A.453-1(b)(3)(i). In the context of a deferred exchange where cash or a cash equivalent provides security for the transfer of replacement property and is held in an escrow account or trust, the question arises, whether, for purposes of applying the installment sale rules of section 453, the taxpayer has actually or constructively received property at the commencement of the deferred exchange. To answer this question, the section 453 regulations cross-reference rules contained in section 1.1031(k)-1(j)(2), Income Tax Regs. These section 1031 regulations generally provide that the determination of whether the taxpayer has received payment for purposes of section 453 will be made without regard to the fact that the transferee's obligation to convey replacement property to the taxpayer is secured by cash or cash equivalent, if the cash or cash equivalent is held in a "qualified escrow account" or "qualified trust" as defined in section 1.1031(k)-1(g)(3), Income Tax Regs., provided the taxpayer had a bona fide intent to enter into a deferred exchange of like-kind property at the beginning of the exchange. *See* sec. 1.1031(k)-1(j)(2)(i), (iv), Income Tax Regs.[24]

---

24. The sec. 1031 regulations provide that, as a general rule:

> The taxpayer is in constructive receipt of money or property at the time the money or property is credited to the taxpayer's account, set apart for the taxpayer, or otherwise made available so that the taxpayer may draw upon it at any time or so that the taxpayer can draw upon it if notice of intention to draw is given. . . . [Sec. 1.1031(k)-1(f)(2), Income Tax Regs.]

Strictly construed and without any further refinement, the principles expressed in these regulations might lead to the conclusion that petitioner had actual receipt of property in 1994 (either by virtue of the escrow agent's acting as his agent in receiving the escrow funds or by virtue of petitioner's receipt of a property interest in the escrow account) or constructive receipt of the sale proceeds. *See* Williams v. United States, 219 F.2d 523 (5th Cir. 1955) (taxpayers who sold standing timber and had sale proceeds placed in an escrow account were in constructive receipt of the proceeds at the time of the sale).

Under such an analysis, however, it might be difficult for any deferred exchange involving an escrow account to qualify under sec. 1031, because (1) the actual or constructive receipt might

Accordingly, in such a circumstance, if all other conditions of section 453 are satisfied, the taxpayer must recognize any gain or loss from such a deferred exchange pursuant to the installment sale rules of section 453.

Here, petitioners contend that because they have met all operative conditions for the application of section 1.1031(k)-1(g)(3) and (j)(2), Income Tax Regs., and of section 453, by operation of law they have no actual or constructive receipt of property in 1994, and, under the rules coordinating gain recognition under sections 453 and 1031, they are not required to recognize income in 1994. Respondent takes issue with only one operative condition relative to petitioners' argument—that petitioner had the requisite bona fide intent to enter into a deferred exchange at the beginning of the subject transaction. Accordingly, we turn to consideration of that issue. . . .

Section 1.1031(k)-1(j)(2)(iv), Income Tax Regs., provides:

> BONA FIDE INTENT REQUIREMENT. The provisions of paragraphs (j)(2)(i) and (ii) of this section [which coordinate gain recognition rules under §§453 and 1031 with respect to a deferred exchange involving a qualified escrow account, qualified trust, or qualified intermediary] do not apply unless the taxpayer has a bona fide intent to enter into a deferred exchange at the beginning of the exchange period. A taxpayer will be treated as having a bona fide intent only if it is reasonable to believe, based on all the facts and circumstances as of the beginning of the exchange period, that like-kind replacement property will be acquired before the end of the exchange period.

In arguing that petitioner lacked the requisite bona fide intent, respondent takes issue only with whether it was reasonable for petitioner to believe that the property he relinquished and the properties he received in the subject transaction were of like kind within the meaning of section 1031. Respondent does not contend that petitioner otherwise failed to satisfy the requirements of section 1.1031(k)-1(j)(2)(iv), Income Tax Regs. (the bona fide intent test).[25] Accordingly, we focus our inquiry on that aspect of the bona fide intent test.

On reply brief, respondent argues as follows:

> Here, petitioner's intent was always to acquire precisely the type of replacement property he ultimately acquired. There is no evidence anywhere in the record to suggest that petitioner intended to acquire as replacement property anything but a fee simple interest in timberland. Since the replacement properties and the relinquished property are not like kind, petitioner's intent from the outset was to acquire replacement property that was not of like kind with the relinquished property and Treas. Reg. sec. 1.1031 (k)-1(j)(2)(iv) does not apply. The regulation does not address the situation such as here where the taxpayer actually acquires the replacement property he intended to acquire and which does not qualify as like kind with the relinquished property.

---

indicate a sale rather than an exchange, and (2) the property interest actually or constructively received at the commencement of the deferred exchange would not necessarily be like kind to the property relinquished. *See* 2 Bittker & Lokken, *Federal Taxation of Income, Estates and Gifts*, par. 44.2.5 (3d ed. 2000). To mitigate such problems, sec. 1.1031(k)-1(g), Income Tax Regs., provides various safe harbors. *See id.* One of these safe harbors provides that in the case of a deferred exchange, the taxpayer is not in actual or constructive receipt of money or property merely because cash or a cash equivalent is held in a "qualified escrow account or in a qualified trust." Sec. 1.1031(k)-1(g)(3)(i), Income Tax Regs.

25. For instance, respondent does not contend that petitioner did not reasonably believe that he would acquire replacement property within the requisite 180-day period.

Respondent's argument is at odds with the bona fide intent test as described in his own regulations, which requires only that it be "reasonable to believe" that like-kind replacement property will be acquired within the requisite exchange period. Sec. 1.1031(k)-1(j)(2)(iv), Income Tax Regs.

As explained in greater detail below, we conclude that at the commencement of the exchange period for the subject transaction, petitioner had a bona fide intent that he would satisfy the like-kind deferred exchange requirements. This conclusion is bolstered by the fact that respondent has determined no negligence penalty or other penalty with regard to the subject transaction, from which we infer that respondent does not dispute that petitioners had reasonable cause and acted in good faith in treating the subject transaction as a tax-deferred like-kind exchange within the meaning of section 1031. *See* sec. 6664(c)(1) (no accuracy-related penalty is to be imposed to the extent there was reasonable cause and the taxpayer acted in good faith). . . .

In Oregon Lumber Co. v. Commissioner, 20 T.C. 192 (1953), the taxpayer conveyed to the United States certain land adjoining national forests in Oregon and containing a specified amount of standing timber. In exchange, the United States granted the taxpayer the right to cut and remove national forest timber of equal value on acreage to be definitely designated by the national forest officer before cutting. This Court concluded that under Oregon State law, because an agreement to cut and remove standing timber from the land immediately or within a reasonable time was an agreement for the sale of goods only, the property rights acquired under the agreement were personalty. *See id.* at 196. Accordingly, this Court held that the taxpayer's exchange was of realty for personalty and was thus not an exchange of properties of like kind. *See id.* [The *Oregon Lumber* court also stated that "the right to cut and remove standing timber is so intrinsically different from a fee in land" that the exchange would not qualify under §1031 even if the timber was realty under state law.]

Petitioners argue that Oregon Lumber Co. v. Commissioner, *supra,* is distinguishable because under Georgia State law, both sets of property involved in petitioner's exchange constituted realty. . . .

We agree with petitioners that under Georgia State law, the prevailing view appears to be that a conveyance of standing timber, to be severed by the buyer, generally constitutes a transfer of real property. . . . [26]

In arguing that the properties are of like kind, petitioners rely in part on Commissioner v. Crichton, 122 F.2d 181 (5th Cir. 1941), which held that an undivided fractional interest in mineral rights on unimproved country land was of like kind to undivided interests in improved city lots. Petitioners cite *Crichton* for the proposition that section 1031 is to be liberally construed to effect legislative intent and that the only distinction that would justify disqualification must be "the broad one between classes and characters of properties, for instance, between real and personal property." *Id.* at 182; *see also* sec. 1.1031(a)-1, Income Tax Regs. Petitioners argue that under *Crichton,* "the conveyance of an entire interest in a

---

26. . . . [O]n the issue of whether an agreement for the sale of growing trees is a contract for the sale of an interest in land, Georgia State law is less than a seamless web of jurisprudence. In this regard, Georgia State law is not unique. With regard to this legal issue, among the various States "There is considerable difference of opinion, often in the same jurisdiction, . . . undoubtedly due to diverse theories of the courts with respect to the exact nature of standing trees." Davis, *Annotation, Sale or Contract for Sale of Standing Timber as Within Provisions of Statute of Frauds Respecting Sale or Contract of Sale of Real Property,* 7 A.L.R.2d 517, 518 (1949).

delineated natural resource treated as real property under state law constitutes like kind property ... when exchanged for other real property interests." In support of their position, petitioners also cite Rev. Rul. 68-331, 1968-1 C.B. 352 (leasehold interest in a producing oil lease is like kind to an improved ranch), and Rev. Rul. 55-749, 1955-2 C.B. 295 (perpetual water rights are like kind to land).

On the other hand, not every exchange of real property interests meets the section 1031 like-kind requirement. ... [27] For instance, carved-out oil payments, although characterized as real property under State law, are not like kind to a fee interest in real estate. *See* Fleming v. Commissioner, 24 T.C. 818, 823-824 (1955), *rev'd*, 241 F.2d 78 (5th Cir. 1957), *rev'd sub nom.* Commissioner v. P.G. Lake, Inc., 356 U.S. 260 (1958); *see also* Clemente, Inc. v. Commissioner, T.C. Memo. 1985-367 (8-acre parcel of land was not like kind to gravel extraction rights in another parcel of land). In addition, for purposes of section 1031, a short-term leasehold of real property is not equivalent to a fee interest. *See* Capri, Inc. v. Commissioner, 65 T.C. 162, 181-182 (1975); May Dept. Stores Co. v. Commissioner, 16 T.C. 547, 556 (1951); Standard Envelope Manufacturing Co. v. Commissioner, 15 T.C. 41, 48 (1950).

Because of the posture of this case, it is unnecessary, and we do not undertake, to resolve the legal issue whether the like-kind requirement was satisfied. It suffices to find, as we do, that petitioner had a bona fide intent that the subject transaction would meet the like-kind exchange requirement, taking into account that it constituted an exchange of realty for realty. ...

In light of all the facts and circumstances, we conclude and hold that petitioners have satisfied the bona fide intent test and that under section 1.1031(k)-1(j), Income Tax Regs., petitioners had no actual or constructive receipt of property in 1994 for purposes of applying the installment sale provisions of section 453. We conclude and hold that petitioners recognized no gain from the subject transaction in 1994 and that respondent's determination was in error.

In light of this holding, it is unnecessary to decide the issue of whether the subject transaction qualifies as a like-kind exchange within the meaning of section 1031. ...

Notes and Questions

1. *Other years.* The court concludes that Mr. Smalley did not recognize gain in 1994, either because (1) the transaction qualified as a like-kind exchange, or because (2) the transaction qualified as an installment sale and no payments were received in 1994. Although either analysis produces the same tax result for 1994 (the only year at issue in the case), the two analyses might produce very different results in later years. If §1031 applies, what are the tax consequences of the receipt of replacement property in 1995? If §453 applies instead, what are the tax consequences of the receipt of the property in 1995? In answering the latter question, note the court's

---

27. In Koch v. Commissioner, 71 T.C. 54, 65 (1978), this Court stated that sec. 1031 requires a comparison of all factors bearing upon the "nature and character" of the exchanged properties as opposed to their "grade or quality." These factors include "the respective interests in the physical properties, the nature of the title conveyed, the rights of the parties, [and] the duration of the interests." *Id.*

discussion of the statute of limitations with respect to 1995. Suppose that in 2011 Smalley sells all three parcels he received in 1995 for a total of $700,000. Should he take the position that the 1994 transaction was a deferred like-kind exchange, or should he claim it was an installment sale?

2. *Interpreting the regulation.* Assuming the 1994 transaction did not qualify as a deferred like-kind exchange, Mr. Smalley would have recognized his gain in 1994 if the ordinary rules of constructive receipt applied.[28] The regulations under §1031, however, provide that the constructive receipt doctrine does not apply if the taxpayer reasonably believed "that like-kind replacement property [would] be acquired before the end of the exchange period." Reg. §1.1031(a)-1(j)(2)(iv). The result in *Smalley* turns on the court's acceptance of the taxpayer's broad reading of the scope of this bona fide intent test, rather than the IRS's narrow reading. The IRS argues that the regulation protects a mistaken taxpayer only in the case of a mistake about future factual developments, but the taxpayer argues (and the court agrees) that the regulation also protects a taxpayer who makes a reasonable mistake about the current state of the law (with respect to whether the relinquished property and the intended replacement property satisfy the like-kind standard). Which interpretation of the regulation seems more reasonable to you? Is it relevant that the rules concerning the integrity of the annual accounting system draw a sharp distinction between mistaken expectations about the future and present mistakes?[29] Is the court applying (*sub silentio*) a principle that ambiguities in the regulations should be strictly construed against the government, because the ambiguities are of the government's own making?

3. *The like-kind standard and real estate.* The last part of the opinion provides a useful caution: It is almost true that all real estate is of like kind to all other real estate for purposes of §1031, but not quite. *Physical* differences between different real properties should not cause problems under the like-kind standard, but differences in the nature of the *legal interests* in the physical properties can cause problems. If the contemplated exchange is other than an exchange of a fee interest for a fee interest, one should not assume without research that the exchange will qualify under §1031.

4. *"Reverse" Deferred Exchanges*

RUTHERFORD v. COMMISSIONER

T.C. Memo. 1978-505

TANNENWALD, Judge: . . . At all times pertinent, Bennie D. Rutherford (Rutherford) was engaged in the trade or business of farming, including the raising of cattle.

On November 1, 1973, Rutherford orally agreed with one Wardlaw that Wardlaw would transfer 12 half-blood heifers to Rutherford and that Rutherford would, at his own cost and expense, have such heifers artificially inseminated by the sperm from a registered bull and deliver to Wardlaw the first 12 three-quarter blood

28. On constructive receipt generally, see Chapter 7.B.1.
29. See Chapter 2.C.2.

heifers born to the Wardlaw heifers at such time as they were weaned. A heifer is a young cow.

Wardlaw delivered possession of the half-blood heifers to Rutherford on November 19, 1973. . . . At the time of the transfer of the half-blood heifers to him, Rutherford established his cost for purposes of depreciation and the investment credit at $3,000, representing his judgment as to the then fair market value of each three-quarter blood heifer that he was obligated to deliver to Wardlaw (or a total of $36,000). In November 1973, the fair market value of each such heifer was $2,759.

The half-blood heifers were artificially inseminated during the summer of 1974 and Rutherford delivered three-quarter blood heifers to Wardlaw as follows: 1975, four; 1976, three; 1977, five. The fair market value of each such heifer at the time of delivery was approximately as follows: 1975, $349; 1976, $295; 1977, $516.

Petitioners deducted as expenses the cost of producing the three-quarter blood heifers. Petitioners had a zero basis in such heifers.

The critical issue is the basis to Rutherford of the half-blood heifers transferred to him by Wardlaw. Petitioners contend that such basis is the fair market value, as of November 1973, of the 12 three-quarter blood heifers which Rutherford was obligated to deliver to Wardlaw. Respondent contends that petitioners had no basis because they paid for the half-blood heifers in property, i.e., three-quarter blood heifers, which they raised themselves and in respect of which they had no costs. We agree with respondent, although for a different reason than advanced by him on brief.

With respect to petitioners' contention, Rutherford's obligation to deliver three-quarter blood heifers was dependent upon the success of the contemplated artificial insemination. As such, it was wholly contingent and speculative in November 1973. Such an obligation cannot be included in the determination of basis. On the basis of the foregoing, any deduction for depreciation or allowance of an investment credit for 1973 and 1974 is clearly precluded.

Rutherford did deliver four three-quarter blood heifers in 1975. We do not agree that, simply because Rutherford had no basis in the heifers delivered, petitioners are necessarily not entitled to some allowance for depreciation and for an investment credit. We think that this issue turns upon whether the transaction between Wardlaw and Rutherford constitutes a taxable or nontaxable exchange. Where a taxable exchange of property is involved, a taxpayer may have a gain or loss on the exchange and thereby acquire a basis in the property he receives.

In our opinion, the transaction between Wardlaw and Rutherford is controlled by section 1031(a). . . .

As our findings of fact show, Rutherford was engaged in the trade or business of raising livestock. There is no question but that cattle are considered property for the purposes of section 1031.[30] At least under the circumstances of this case, we do not consider the fact that the three-quarter blood heifers to be delivered by Rutherford were not in existence at the time of the transfer of the half-blood heifers by Wardlaw precludes the applicability of section 1031(a).

We hold that the transaction between Wardlaw and Rutherford constituted a nontaxable exchange under section 1031(a). Under these circumstances, Rutherford's basis for the half-blood heifers acquired from Wardlaw is his basis in the

---

30. The exception contained in section 1031(e), which excludes livestock of different sexes, is inapplicable because the livestock exchanged herein was of the same sex.

three-quarter blood heifers delivered to Wardlaw in exchange. Section 1031(d). As a consequence, the fair market value of the four heifers delivered to Wardlaw in 1975 is without significance. We also note that sections 1031(a) and (d) are equally applicable to the taxable years 1973 and 1974, although there is an additional ground for holding for respondent in respect of those years. See [the earlier discussion of the exclusion from basis of "contingent and speculative" obligations].

We hold that petitioners are not entitled to a deduction for depreciation or for an investment credit for the taxable years 1973, 1974, or 1975 in respect of the half-blood heifers acquired from Wardlaw.

Notes and Questions

1. *A strange exchange.* We have seen simultaneous like-kind exchanges, in which the taxpayer receives replacement property at the same time he relinquishes his property. We have also seen deferred like-kind exchanges, in which the taxpayer relinquishes his property before he receives the replacement property. *Rutherford* indicates there is a third timing possibility — a sort of reverse deferred exchange — in which the taxpayer acquires the replacement property before he has relinquished his property. *Rutherford* goes so far as to apply §1031 when the property the taxpayer will eventually relinquish does not even exist at the time the taxpayer acquires the replacement property.[31]

2. *Broader implications.* Tom owns appreciated real estate that he would like to exchange for other real estate, if he can qualify for nonrecognition under §1031. He finds land he would be happy to receive as replacement property for sale by Sam, who unfortunately is interested only in a cash sale. Moreover, Tom has not yet found anyone who wants to acquire his property. Tom needs to act fast, because he is not the only person interested in acquiring Sam's land. Is it possible for Tom to engineer a three-party variation on *Rutherford*, in which Tom acquires Sam's land as a replacement for Tom's land before Tom has found a taker for his own land? The following revenue procedure says it is, if Tom jumps through the right hoops.

REV. PROC. 2000-37

2000-2 C.B. 308

SECTION 1. PURPOSE

This revenue procedure provides a safe harbor under which the Internal Revenue Service will not challenge (a) the qualification of property as either

---

31. The facts of *Rutherford* took place before the effective date of §1031(a)(3), which imposes time limits on deferred exchanges. Even apart from the effective date issue, however, §1031(a)(3) does not seem to apply in a *Rutherford*-type situation. By its terms, §1031(a)(3) imposes time limits only on the receipt of replacement property after the taxpayer has relinquished his property; it does not apply if the taxpayer receives the replacement property before relinquishing his property.

"replacement property" or "relinquished property" (as defined in §1.1031(k)-1(a) of the Income Tax Regulations) for purposes of §1031 of the Internal Revenue Code and the regulations thereunder or (b) the treatment of the "exchange accommodation titleholder" as the beneficial owner of such property for federal income tax purposes, if the property is held in a "qualified exchange accommodation arrangement" (QEAA), as defined in section 4.02 of this revenue procedure.

SECTION 2. BACKGROUND

.01 Section 1031(a)(1) provides that no gain or loss is recognized on the exchange of property held for productive use in a trade or business or for investment if the property is exchanged solely for property of like kind that is to be held either for productive use in a trade or business or for investment.

.02 Section 1031(a)(3) provides that property received by the taxpayer is not treated as like-kind property if it: (a) is not identified as property to be received in the exchange on or before the day that is 45 days after the date on which the taxpayer transfers the relinquished property; or (b) is received after the earlier of the date that is 180 days after the date on which the taxpayer transfers the relinquished property, or the due date (determined with regard to extension) for the transferor's federal income tax return for the year in which the transfer of the relinquished property occurs.

.03 Determining the owner of property for federal income tax purposes requires an analysis of all of the facts and circumstances. As a general rule, the party that bears the economic burdens and benefits of ownership will be considered the owner of property for federal income tax purposes. *See* Rev. Rul. 82-144, 1982-2 C.B. 34.

.04 On April 25, 1991, the Treasury Department and the Service promulgated final regulations under §1.1031(k)-1 providing rules for deferred like-kind exchanges under §1031(a)(3). The preamble to the final regulations states that the deferred exchange rules under §1031(a)(3) do not apply to reverse-*Starker* exchanges (i.e., exchanges where the replacement property is acquired before the relinquished property is transferred) and consequently that the final regulations do not apply to such exchanges. T.D. 8346, 1991-1 C.B. 150, 151; *see* Starker v. United States, 602 F.2d 1341 (9th Cir. 1979). However, the preamble indicates that Treasury and the Service will continue to study the applicability of the general rule of §1031(a)(1) to these transactions. T.D. 8346, 1991-1 C.B. 150, 151.

.05 Since the promulgation of the final regulations under §1.1031(k)-1, taxpayers have engaged in a wide variety of transactions, including so-called "parking" transactions, to facilitate reverse like-kind exchanges. Parking transactions typically are designed to "park" the desired replacement property with an accommodation party until such time as the taxpayer arranges for the transfer of the relinquished property to the ultimate transferee in a simultaneous or deferred exchange. Once such a transfer is arranged, the taxpayer transfers the relinquished property to the accommodation party in exchange for the replacement property, and the accommodation party then transfers the relinquished property to the ultimate transferee. In other situations, an accommodation party may acquire the desired replacement property on behalf of the taxpayer and immediately exchange such property with the taxpayer for the relinquished property, thereafter holding the relinquished property until the taxpayer arranges for a transfer of such property to the ultimate transferee. In the parking arrangements, taxpayers attempt to arrange the transaction so that the accommodation party has enough of the benefits and burdens relating to the property so that the accommodation party will be treated as the owner for federal income tax purposes.

.06 Treasury and the Service have determined that it is in the best interest of sound tax administration to provide taxpayers with a workable means of qualifying their transactions under §1031 in situations where the taxpayer has a genuine intent to accomplish a like-kind exchange at the time that it arranges for the acquisition of the replacement property and actually accomplishes the exchange within a short time thereafter. Accordingly, this revenue procedure provides a safe harbor that allows a taxpayer to treat the accommodation party as the owner of the property for federal income tax purposes, thereby enabling the taxpayer to accomplish a qualifying like-kind exchange.

SECTION 3. SCOPE

.01 Exclusivity. This revenue procedure provides a safe harbor for the qualification under §1031 of certain arrangements between taxpayers and exchange accommodation titleholders and provides for the treatment of the exchange accommodation titleholder as the beneficial owner of the property for federal income tax purposes. These provisions apply only in the limited context described in this revenue procedure. The principles set forth in this revenue procedure have no application to any federal income tax determinations other than determinations that involve arrangements qualifying for the safe harbor.

.02 No inference. No inference is intended with respect to the federal income tax treatment of arrangements similar to those described in this revenue procedure that were entered into prior to the effective date of this revenue procedure. Further, the Service recognizes that "parking" transactions can be accomplished outside of the safe harbor provided in this revenue procedure. Accordingly, no inference is intended with respect to the federal income tax treatment of "parking" transactions that do not satisfy the terms of the safe harbor provided in this revenue procedure, whether entered into prior to or after the effective date of this revenue procedure. . . .

SECTION 4. QUALIFIED EXCHANGE ACCOMMODATION ARRANGEMENTS

.01 Generally. The Service will not challenge the qualification of property as either "replacement property" or "relinquished property" (as defined in §1.1031(k)-1(a)) for purposes of §1031 and the regulations thereunder, or the treatment of the exchange accommodation titleholder as the beneficial owner of such property for federal income tax purposes, if the property is held in a QEAA.

.02 Qualified Exchange Accommodation Arrangements. For purposes of this revenue procedure, property is held in a QEAA if all of the following requirements are met:

(1) Qualified indicia of ownership of the property is [sic] held by a person (the "exchange accommodation titleholder") who is not the taxpayer or a disqualified person. . . . Such qualified indicia of ownership must be held by the exchange

accommodation titleholder at all times from the date of acquisition by the exchange accommodation titleholder until the property is transferred as described in section 4.02(5) of this revenue procedure. For this purpose, "qualified indicia of ownership" means legal title to the property [or] other indicia of ownership of the property that are treated as beneficial ownership of the property under applicable principles of commercial law (e.g., a contract for deed). . . .

(2) At the time the qualified indicia of ownership of the property is [sic] transferred to the exchange accommodation titleholder, it is the taxpayer's bona fide intent that the property held by the exchange accommodation titleholder represent either replacement property or relinquished property in an exchange that is intended to qualify for nonrecognition of gain (in whole or in part) or loss under §1031;

(3) No later than five business days after the transfer of qualified indicia of ownership of the property to the exchange accommodation titleholder, the taxpayer and the exchange accommodation titleholder enter into a written agreement (the "qualified exchange accommodation agreement") that provides that the exchange accommodation titleholder is holding the property for the benefit of the taxpayer in order to facilitate an exchange under §1031 and this revenue procedure and that the taxpayer and the exchange accommodation titleholder agree to report the acquisition, holding, and disposition of the property as provided in this revenue procedure. The agreement must specify that the exchange accommodation titleholder will be treated as the beneficial owner of the property for all federal income tax purposes. Both parties must report the federal income tax attributes of the property on their federal income tax returns in a manner consistent with this agreement;

(4) No later than 45 days after the transfer of qualified indicia of ownership of the replacement property to the exchange accommodation titleholder, the relinquished property is properly identified. . . .

(5) No later than 180 days after the transfer of qualified indicia of ownership of the property to the exchange accommodation titleholder, (a) the property is transferred . . . to the taxpayer as replacement property; or (b) the property is transferred to a person who is not the taxpayer or a disqualified person as relinquished property; and

(6) The combined time period that the relinquished property and the replacement property are held in a QEAA does not exceed 180 days.

.03 Permissible Agreements. Property will not fail to be treated as being held in a QEAA as a result of any one or more of the following legal or contractual arrangements, regardless of whether such arrangements contain terms that typically would result from arm's length bargaining between unrelated parties with respect to such arrangements: . . .

(2) The taxpayer . . . guarantees some or all of the obligations of the exchange accommodation titleholder, including secured or unsecured debt incurred to acquire the property, or indemnifies the exchange accommodation titleholder against costs and expenses;

(3) The taxpayer . . . loans or advances funds to the exchange accommodation titleholder or guarantees a loan or advance to the exchange accommodation titleholder; . . .

(6) The taxpayer and the exchange accommodation titleholder enter into agreements or arrangements relating to the purchase or sale of the property, including puts and calls at fixed or formula prices, effective for a period not in

excess of 185 days from the date the property is acquired by the exchange accommodation titleholder; and

(7) The taxpayer and the exchange accommodation titleholder enter into agreements or arrangements providing that any variation in the value of a relinquished property from the estimated value on the date of the exchange accommodation titleholder's receipt of the property be taken into account upon the exchange accommodation titleholder's disposition of the relinquished property through the taxpayer's advance of funds to, or receipt of funds from, the exchange accommodation titleholder. . . .

Notes and Question

1. *Why all the hoops?* Taking into account the rules for simultaneous triangular exchanges, "forward" deferred exchanges, and "reverse" deferred exchanges, a well-advised taxpayer should always be able to structure a deal as a §1031 nonrecognition transaction, rather than as a taxable cash-sale-plus-reinvestment. To repeat a question asked earlier, shouldn't Congress either expressly allow nonrecognition for cash sales with reinvestments in like-kind property, or get serious about limiting nonrecognition to true exchanges?

E. PROBLEMS

Problem 1. Andre deTerre owns Mauvehectare, a piece of unimproved land that he bought for $20,000 some time ago. Its current value is $58,000. In the current tax year, he agrees to swap Mauvehectare for Verdant Acres, a field that has been actively used for agricultural purposes for some years. Because Verdant Acres has a value of only $43,000, the owner of that property, Bill Turf, agrees to throw in $8,000 of cash and a tractor worth $7,000. How will Andre be taxed on this transaction, and what bases will he have in the properties he receives? (Note: This exchange is not an "exchange of multiple properties" for purposes of Reg.§1.1031(j)-1, despite appearances to the contrary; you should ignore that regulation.)

Problem 2. What tax treatment will Bill Turf receive on this transaction, and what will be his basis in Mauvehectare? Assume that Bill's basis in Verdant Acres was $30,000, and that his basis in the tractor was $12,000.

Problem 3. Sam Sodd owns Peat Bog Farm, which has a value of $100,000, a basis of $75,000, and is subject to a nonrecourse mortgage in the amount of $70,000. Alex Gwinness owns the Dew Drop Inn, which has a value of $110,000, an adjusted basis of $70,000, and is subject to a nonrecourse mortgage of $90,000. Sam and Alex decide to swap their properties, each taking subject to the existing mortgages, with Alex throwing in $10,000 in cash to even the equity values exchanged. How will they be taxed, and what will be the bases of their respective properties?

Cell

THE PERSONAL RESIDENCE GAIN EXCLUSION

A. Fun and Games with §121

    1. Personal Residence Churning

    2. Section 121 as an Exclusion for Labor Income

B. A Drafting Error and a Dilemma for the IRS

A. FUN AND GAMES WITH §121

1. Personal Residence Churning

Suppose a married couple owns a home with a basis of $300,000 and a current value somewhere between $700,000 and $800,000. Their best guess is that the home will continue to appreciate at a fairly rapid rate. (Housing prices used to behave that way, and someday they may do so again.) Is there a tax strategy they ought to be considering?

They are getting close to the point at which the appreciation in the house will exceed the $500,000 ceiling on the §121 exclusion. If they continue to own the home for a few more years, and then sell it for $1.2 million, they will have to pay tax on $400,000 of gain. But if they sell their home now for $800,000, buy a new home for $800,000, and several years later sell the new home for $1.2 million, they will not have to pay any tax on either sale: This difference arises because the §121 ceiling is applied on a *per residence* basis. There is no limit on the amount of gain that may be excluded *per taxpayer* over a lifetime, as long as the amount excluded per residence never exceeds $500,000 (or $250,000 for an unmarried taxpayer). Selling the old house and buying a new one wipes the tax slate clean, giving the couple the opportunity to exclude up to $500,000 of future appreciation on the new house.

There is an additional income tax advantage to this sort of house churning, if the couple is interested in having the new house more heavily mortgaged than the old house. If the couple wanted to borrow against their equity in the old house and deduct the interest, only $100,000 of the borrowing could qualify as "home equity indebtedness," the interest on which would be deductible under §163(h)(3).[32] By contrast, they could borrow the entire $800,000 to purchase the new home and

---

32. See Chapter 4.B.2.b.

deduct all the interest, because the entire loan would qualify as "acquisition indebtedness." Most taxpayers will find the tax advantages to house churning are not sufficient to overcome the non-tax disadvantages in brokers' fees, moving expenses, and emotional distress. Nevertheless, the heavy tax encouragement for house churning seems questionable.

2.   *Section 121 as an Exclusion for Labor Income*

Stan is handy with tools and doesn't mind living surrounded by sawdust. He also loves the idea of finding a legal way not to pay income tax on earned income. Do you have a suggestion for Stan?

Although the purpose of §121 is to exempt from tax gains due to market appreciation in owner-occupied housing, the provision also applies to gains due to work a taxpayer puts into improving his house. Suppose Stan buys a fixer-upper for $100,000, and lives in it for two years and a day while he is renovating it. He spends $50,000 on the renovation, and he is then able to sell the house for $350,000. His entire $200,000 gain ($350,000 amount realized minus $150,000 adjusted basis) will qualify for exclusion under §121. He can repeat this process every two years.[33] Although some of the gain may be attributable to general appreciation in the local housing market, most of it is due to Stan's sweat equity. Despite the fact that most or all of the $200,000 gain is really a return on Stan's labor, the §121 exclusion clearly applies. This is a terrific tax break. Although it is relatively easy to find ways to avoid income tax on investment income, there are very few ways to avoid income tax on labor income converted to cash. But it can be done in this instance, and on a scale large enough that one could conceivably make a nice tax-free living by doing this and nothing else. By contrast, this plan would not have been very practical under the old rollover rules of §1034. Under the old rules, Stan could have avoided tax on his $200,000 gain only by buying a replacement residence costing at least $350,000. His next replacement residence would have had to be even more expensive. Eventually, he would have had trouble finding a million-dollar fixer-upper. In addition, the only way for Stan to take cash out, without triggering gain recognition, would have been to borrow against the value of a residence.

B.   A DRAFTING ERROR AND A DILEMMA FOR THE IRS

According to §121(a), a taxpayer is entitled to exclude gain on the sale of a home only if the home has been owned and used by the taxpayer as her principal residence for at least two years during the five-year period preceding the sale. In addition, §121(b)(3) provides that the exclusion applies to only one sale every two years. However, §121(c) provides for a limited exclusion despite the failure to satisfy the two-year ownership and use requirement, or the one-sale-every-two-years rule, if the sale is "by reason of a change in place of employment, health, or,

---

33. *See* §121(a) (two-out-of-five-years ownership and use requirement) and §121(b)(3) (one-sale-every-two-years rule).

to the extent provided in regulations, unforeseen circumstances." As the statute was originally enacted in 1997, §121(c)(1) imposed the following limitation on the amount excluded in such a case:

[T]he amount of gain excluded from gross income under section (a) with respect to such sale or exchange shall not exceed—
    (A) The amount which bears the same ratio to the amount which would have been excluded under this section if such requirements had been met, as
    (B) the shorter of—
        (i) the aggregate periods, during the 5-year period ending on the date of such sale or exchange, such property has been owned and used by the taxpayer as the taxpayer's principal residence, or
        (ii) the period after the date of the most recent prior sale or exchange by the taxpayer to which subsection (a) applied and before the date of such sale or exchange,
    bears to 2 years.

Compare this provision with the statement in the House Report, set forth in section C.4 of Chapter 3: "A taxpayer who fails to meet these requirements by reason of a change of place of employment, health, or other unforeseen circumstances is able to exclude the fraction of the $250,000 ($500,000 if married filing a joint return) equal to the fraction of two years that these requirements are met." Consider how the original statutory language, and the rule described in the House Report, would apply to the following situation.

Example. Joe bought his house for $200,000 on January 1, and immediately moved in. Eight months later, on September 1, Joe sold his house and moved out in order to take a new job in a distant city. His amount realized on the sale of the house was $230,000. How much of his $30,000 gain may Joe exclude under §121?

Joe sold his house after having owned and lived in it for one-third (8 out of 24 months) of the two-year period required under §121(a). According to the original statutory language, this entitles him to exclude one-third of his gain. Where x indicates the amount of gain eligible for exclusion, the formula called for by the original statutory language is

$$x/\$30,000 = 8 \text{ months}/24 \text{ months}$$

Thus, Joe could exclude $10,000 of his gain, and he would be required to pay capital gains tax on the other $20,000. Under the description in the House Report, by contrast, what is prorated is not the amount of the gain, but the $250,000 (or $500,000) ceiling on the exclusion. According to this description, Joe's exclusion ceiling would be $83,333,[34] and he would be able to exclude his entire $30,000 gain.

As the example illustrates, the difference in results under the statutory language and the committee report can be significant, with the committee report's approach being more generous to taxpayers in most cases. In a better world, committee reports would not contradict the statutes they purport to describe, but given the complexities of tax legislation occasional snafus of this sort are inevitable. You will

34. $250,000 × 8/24.

recall from Chapter 1 the old tax lawyer's joke that one should consult the language of the statute only when the legislative history is unclear. Because it *is* a joke, the statutory language should obviously prevail over the contradictory description, and Joe's exclusion should be limited to $10,000.

Or should it? Technical mistakes in tax legislation are so common that every major tax act is followed, a year or so later, by a "technical corrections" act, designed to clean up technical flaws in the original legislation. In the case of this particular glitch, Congress soon noticed the inconsistency between the statute and the committee report, and bipartisan support quickly emerged for a technical correction that would conform the statute to the House Report description, with retroactive effect (i.e., as if the statute had always prorated the exclusion ceiling amount, rather than gain realized). Neither approach is obviously more logical or fair than the other. It was more important that the issue be settled than that it be settled in any particular way, and apparently Congress was in a generous mood.

Although it was clear that the technical corrections act would eventually become law, Congress was in no great hurry to pass it, and the IRS was faced with the problem of how to administer the statute in the intervening months. If the IRS enforced the statute as written, in all likelihood it would have to refund Joe's capital gains tax when the statute was retroactively amended in Joe's favor. On the other hand, if the IRS announced that it would apply the law as if the technical correction had already been enacted, it would be sending the message that clear statutory language can be disregarded based on a guess that Congress will retroactively amend the statute to produce a different result. The IRS hit on a rather clever solution to this dilemma. It did not issue a revenue ruling (which would have had precedential value) indicating the law would be applied as if the correction had already been made, but it did describe the law in Publication 523, "Selling Your Home," as if the correction had already been made. Thus it bowed to reality without setting an official precedent that could be used against it on some later occasion.

The current version of §121(c) reflects the technical correction. It provides that "the dollar limitation under paragraph (1) or (2) of subsection (b) [i.e., $250,000 or $500,000], whichever is applicable," shall be prorated according to the fraction of two years during which the taxpayer owned and used the house. Under current law, then, Joe is clearly entitled to exclude his entire $30,000 gain.

Cell

THE INSTALLMENT
METHOD OF §453

A. THE INSTALLMENT METHOD AND DEBT RELIEF

You own land with a basis of $50,000. The land is worth $200,000 and is subject to a mortgage of $40,000. You sell it to a buyer, who takes the property subject to the mortgage, pays you $30,000 cash down, and gives you a $130,000 note. We know from *Crane* and *Tufts* that the $40,000 of debt relief is included in your amount realized,[35] but how is it treated under §453? The statute itself has no special rules for the treatment of debt relief, so the debt relief would seemingly be treated as part of the payment received in the year of sale. If so, the gain recognized in the year of sale, pursuant to the installment method formula of §453(c), would be

$$\$70,000 \, (\$150,000/\$200,000) = \$52,500$$

If the entire $130,000 principal was paid off in a single later year, the gain recognized in that year would be

---

35. See Chapter 2.C.2.c.

$$\$130,000 \ (\$150,000/\$200,000) = \$97,500$$

The \$150,000 total gain recognized and the \$50,000 total basis recovered (\$17,500 in the year of sale, and \$32,500 in the later year) are consistent with a \$200,000 amount realized and a \$50,000 basis. But treating the debt relief as a payment triggering recognition of gain seems inconsistent with the underlying philosophy of §453, which is to match the imposition of tax with the receipt of cash.

Not to worry, however. The Treasury has issued taxpayer-favorable regulations that generally avoid treating debt relief as payment triggering gain — despite the absence of anything in the statute compelling the Treasury to do so. Under Reg. §15a.453-1(b)(3)(i), "payment" generally does not include "the amount of qualifying indebtedness . . . assumed or taken subject to by the person acquiring the property." "Qualifying indebtedness" is defined by Reg. §15a.453-1(b)(2)(iv) to include "a mortgage or other indebtedness encumbering the property." Thus, the payment in the year of the sale is not \$70,000, but only the \$30,000 cash down payment. Of course, the numbers still have to come out right in the end, which means the total amount of gain taxed, by the time the note is paid in full, must still be \$150,000. That will not happen if the only payments multiplied by the 75 percent profit ratio are the \$30,000 cash down payment and the \$130,000 principal amount of the note (75% of \$160,000 is only \$120,000). If the numbers are to come out right, and if payments are to be only \$160,000, there must be an adjustment to the profit ratio. Sure enough, Reg. §15a.453-1(b)(2)(iii) provides that the contract price must be reduced by the amount of the qualifying indebtedness. Thus, the contract price is only \$160,000, and the profit ratio is \$150,000/\$160,000, or 93.75 percent. When the total payments of \$160,000 are multiplied by that ratio, the correct total amount of gain — \$150,000 — will be recognized.[36]

The special treatment of debt relief in the regulations leaves unchanged the total amount of gain eventually recognized, but it changes the timing of gain recognition, in a taxpayer-favorable direction. The regulations treat the entire amount of the debt relief as a recovery of basis, but this means there is less basis left to be recovered against the amounts that are treated as payments. As a result, a smaller percentage of each cash payment must be treated as basis recovery and a larger percentage treated as gain. This is accomplished by the upward adjustment in the profit ratio caused by the reduction in the contract price by the amount of the debt relief.[37]

Here's a variation. Suppose the property again has a basis of \$50,000 and a value of \$200,000, but this time it is subject to a \$70,000 mortgage. The buyer takes the property subject to the mortgage, pays you no cash down, and gives you his

---

36. In the year of sale, the gain recognized is \$30,000 × 93.75% = \$28,125. If the entire \$130,000 principal of the note is paid off in one later year, the gain recognized in that year will be \$130,000 × 93.75% = \$121,875. The total gain recognized, then, will be \$150,000.

37. For the mathematically inclined, here is a more detailed explanation of what is going on. The statute and the regulations are designed so that, by the time the installment note is paid off, the total payments in the installment method formula of §453(c) will equal the contract price in the same formula. Because the gain ultimately recognized under §453 equals *total payments × (gross profit/contract price),* and because total payments always equal contract price, the gain ultimately recognized under §453 is always — appropriately enough — equal to the gross profit. In the example in the text, the regulations provide that the total payments are only \$160,000 (rather than \$200,000). In order to ensure that the correct total amount of gain (\$150,000) is eventually taxed, it is necessary to set the contract price equal to the \$160,000 total payments, so that *\$160,000 x (\$150,000/\$160,000) = \$150,000.*

note for $ 130,000.[38] The regulations have special rules for situations such as this, where qualifying indebtedness exceeds basis. First, Reg. §15a.453-1(b)(3)(i) provides that relief from qualifying indebtedness *is* treated as a payment to the extent the indebtedness exceeds the taxpayer's basis. In the hypothetical, then, there is a $20,000 "payment" in the year of sale ($70,000 debt relief minus $50,000 basis), despite the absence of any cash down payment. Second, Reg.§15a.453-1(b)(2)(iii) provides that the contract price is *not* reduced by the portion of the qualifying indebtedness that exceeds basis. Thus the contract price is $150,000 ($200,000 minus $50,000 of debt relief not in excess of basis), not $130,000. The gain recognized in the year of sale, then, is

$$\$20,000\ (\$150,000/\$150,000) = \$20,000$$

If the entire principal amount of the note is paid in a single subsequent year, the gain recognized in that year will be

$$\$130,000\ (\$150,000/\$150,000) = \$130,000$$

As always, the total gain recognized accurately reflects the economics of the transaction. The taxpayer's gain was $150,000 ($200,000 amount realized minus $50,000 basis), and the taxpayer's total gain under the §453 regulations is $150,000. But why do the regulations require the taxpayer to treat a portion of the debt relief as payment, when the general philosophy of both the statute and the regulations is to treat only the receipt of *cash* as triggering gain recognition? The problem is that the usual approach of the regulations—to treat debt relief as recovery of basis—works only to the extent the taxpayer *has* basis. To the extent debt relief exceeds basis, the usual approach simply will not work. Another way of expressing the same problem is to note that the general approach of the regulations is to match recognition of gain with the receipt of cash, but that when debt relief exceeds basis, gain realized will exceed cash received. In the hypothetical, for example, gain realized is $150,000 but the total cash payments (down payment and principal of the note) are only $130,000. To the extent of the $20,000 excess of gain realized over cash, it is necessary to treat the debt relief as a payment triggering recognition of gain.

But shed no tears for the seller's predicament of being taxed before he receives cash. As explained in footnote 38, he must either have received some loan proceeds at some earlier time that he will now not have to repay, or he took some tax deductions for depreciation, and now is being asked to restore those deductions to

---

38. At the outset, you may be wondering how an asset can possibly be subject to a mortgage in excess of basis, when acquisition indebtedness is included in basis. If the property is subject to a $70,000 debt, shouldn't its basis be at least $70,000? In general, there are two reasons why a mortgage might be greater than basis, although only one of those reasons could apply in the case of undeveloped land. First, the mortgage may not be acquisition indebtedness. Perhaps the taxpayer borrowed $70,000 secured by the land, sometime after he had acquired the land. The borrowed money could still give rise to basis in *some* asset, if the taxpayer used the borrowed money to buy another asset. It is not a part of the cost of acquiring *this* land, however, and so is not included in this land's basis. The other explanation, in the case of depreciable property, is that a mortgage might exceed basis—even if it is acquisition indebtedness—if the taxpayer was able to claim depreciation (ACRS) deductions faster than he paid off the mortgage. This second explanation could not apply in the case of raw land, however, because raw land is not depreciable.

his income, under a theory that resembles the tax benefit rule and the *Tufts* case from earlier in this chapter.

Notice that a portion of the debt relief is treated as payment only when the basis is insufficient to treat the entire debt relief as recovery of basis. Thus, whenever any part of the debt relief is treated as payment, all available basis has been used to offset the remainder of the debt relief. That means there is no basis left to recover against any payments, which in turn means that the profit ratio will always be 100 percent when debt relief exceeds basis. The ratio of $150,000/$150,000 in the hypothetical is an example of this phenomenon.

Problem 1.   You own undeveloped land free and clear (i.e., not subject to any mortgage), with a basis of $50,000. A potential buyer has offered you $200,000 for the land, in the form of a $50,000 cash down payment and an installment note for $150,000. You do some quick calculations and determine that you will have to recognize $37,500 gain in the year of sale if you accept the offer. Can you think of a way to restructure the transaction so that you still end up with $50,000 cash in your pocket and a $150,000 note from the buyer, but you do not have to recognize any gain in the year of sale? What would be the tax consequences if you (1) borrowed $50,000 from a bank, secured by a nonrecourse mortgage on the land, and (2) sold the property, with the buyer taking the property subject to the $50,000 mortgage and giving you a $150,000 note? Hint: Look carefully at Reg. §15a.453-1(b)(2)(iv).

B.   EXPLOITING THE INCONSISTENT TREATMENT OF INSTALLMENT BUYERS AND SELLERS

There is a taxpayer-favorable inconsistency between the tax consequences of installment notes for sellers, on the one hand, and for buyers, on the other. Although the seller is able to avoid recognition of gain until she receives principal payments on the note, the buyer is permitted to treat the installment note like any other acquisition debt—which means the buyer is immediately allowed to include the amount of the note in his basis in the property. This inconsistency becomes important in two situations where the buyer can quickly put his basis to use: if the buyer sells the property, or if the buyer is able to claim depreciation (ACRS) deductions on the property. Congress has responded to both possibilities in §453.

Consider first the situation in which the buyer quickly sells the property, thus taking advantage of the inclusion of the installment note in basis. Suppose Mother (*M*) owns land with a basis of $100,000. Buyer (*B*), who is not related to *M*, has offered to buy the land for $400,000 cash. *M* wants to sell, but is not pleased with the prospect of immediate recognition of $300,000 gain. In an attempt to defer the gain, she sells the land to her adult Daughter (*D*), for *D*'s $400,000 installment note (and no cash down). The note provides for annual interest payments, and a "balloon" payment of the entire $400,000 principal in ten years. *D* is personally liable for the note, but the note is not secured by a mortgage on the land. *D* quickly turns around and sells the property to *B* for $400,000 cash. Ten years later, *D* pays *M* the $400,000 required under the terms of the note. Absent a special rule, (1) *M* would be eligible to report her gain on the installment method, so that her entire gain would be deferred for ten years, and (2) the note would give D a $400,000 basis in the land, so that she would neither realize nor recognize any gain on the sale of the land for $400,000 cash. The result would be to defer recognition of the $300,000 gain on the disposition of the property for ten years beyond the time the Mother-Daughter family unit converted the property to cash.

Congress was understandably troubled by this prospect, so it enacted §453(e) to take the fun out of the Mother-Daughter plan. Section 453(e) is triggered when there is an installment sale between "related persons," and the related buyer turns around and sells the property within two years of the date of the first sale. In that case, the original seller (M, in the example) is treated as having received a payment on the note at the time of the second sale, with the amount of the payment generally being equal to the amount realized by the original buyer (D) on the second sale. Thus, M will be treated as having received a $400,000 payment when D sells the property, resulting in recognition of M's entire $300,000 gain.[39] Given the fact that M has been taxed on a $400,000 deemed payment on the note before she has received any actual payment, what should be the tax consequences to her when she receives the actual payment ten years later? The answer should be clear as a matter of tax logic, and §453(e)(5) reflects that logic.

Obviously, §453 requires a definition of a "related person." Section 453(f)(1) provides that definition by reference to §§267(b) and 318(a). In addition to two human beings, a statutorily recognized relationship can also exist between a person and an entity, or between two entities. Despite being related persons, an unusually patient M and D could avoid §453(e) by the simple technique of having D wait more than two years after her purchase from M before she sells to B. *See* §453(e)(2).

While the general rule is that the original seller's deemed payment equals the amount realized by the second seller, §453(e)(3) will sometimes result in a smaller deemed payment. Try to figure out how §453(e)(3) applies in the following two situations.

Problem 2.   The facts are the same as in the original hypothetical, except D is able to sell the property to B for $425,000 cash.

Problem 3.   On December 1, 2011, M sells the property (with a $100,000 basis) to D for D's $400,000 installment note. On December 1, 2012, D makes a scheduled $150,000 principal payment on the note to M. On March 1, 2013, D sells the property to B for $450,000 cash.

So much for §453(e) and sales to related persons followed by quick sales outside the family. Now consider the possibility of using an installment sale to increase a buyer's basis for depreciation deductions, without the seller having recognized gain. Suppose Alice owns an apartment building worth $1 million, but in which she has a basis of zero (because she has fully depreciated the building). Can she sell the building to a 100-percent-owned corporation for a $1 million installment note, so that the corporation can begin to depreciate the building using a basis of $1 million, even though Alice will not recognize any gain until the corporation makes principal payments on the note? Unfortunately for Alice, this plan won't

---

39. $400,000 payment × $300,000 gross profit/$400,000 contract price.

work. Section 453(g) provides that the installment method does not apply to sales of depreciable property between "related persons," and Alice and her wholly owned corporation are within the definition of related persons (*see* §1239(b), made applicable here by §453(g)(3)). Thus, Alice will have to recognize her entire $1 million gain in the year of sale. To make matters worse, §1239 provides that all of the gain recognized on the sale of depreciable property between related persons will be taxed as ordinary income, rather than as capital gain. Thus, the price of obtaining depreciation deductions against ordinary income for the corporation is the recognition of ordinary income by Alice.

Suppose Alice had sold the apartment building to Steve, her adult son, for a $1 million installment note. Would she still be subject to §453(g) (and §1239)? Perhaps surprisingly, the answer is no. Although both §453(e) and §453(g) are triggered by sales between "related persons," and although Alice and Steve are related persons for purposes of §453(e), they are *not* related persons for purposes of §453(g). The same term is given very different definitions for purposes of two different subsections of the same Code provision. This is a good example of how carefully one must read the Code; never assume you know what a term means simply because you know how the term is defined for purposes of some other Code provision.

The most significant aspect of §453(g) may not be the situations to which it applies, but the many situations to which it does not apply. Two human beings are never "related persons" for purposes of §453(g), so it is always possible for an installment sale of depreciable property between close relatives to generate depreciation deductions for the buyer before the seller has had to recognize gain. For that matter, the ability to create buyer depreciation deductions before the seller has recognized gain is a significant tax advantage even when the buyer and the seller are unrelated by any standard. As long as the buyer and the seller do not push their luck—by engineering a sham "sale" of the property for a nonrecourse installment note with a principal amount far greater than the value of the property[40] —it is perfectly legitimate to take advantage of this inconsistent tax treatment of installment notes.

C. ASSORTED ISSUES

1. *Limitations on the Availability of the Installment Method*

Gain on some sales cannot be reported on the installment method. For example, §453(k)(2) excludes from installment method reporting any gain on the sale of stocks and securities regularly traded on an established market. The rationale for this limitation is that it is always practical to sell publicly traded stock for cash, so any liquidity problem created by an installment sale of marketable assets is a self-inflicted wound. Perhaps the most important exclusions from the installment method are those for sales of inventory items and for sales by dealers in personal or real property. *See* §§453(b)(2), (*l*). Basically, a person who is in the business of

---

40. *See, e.g.,* Estate of Franklin, 544 F.2d 1045 (9th Cir. 1976), discussed in Chapter 2.C.2.c.

selling property on a regular basis cannot use the installment method to defer gain on ordinary business sales. To put the point the other way around, the installment method is available only for casual (non-dealer) installment sales.

2. Recapture

Another important limitation is imposed by §453(*i*), which requires recognition of all recapture gain in the year of sale. Suppose, for example, a taxpayer sold a fully depreciated truck, with an original basis of $20,000 and an adjusted basis of zero, for no cash down and a $12,000 installment note. Under §1245, gain is recapture gain to the extent of depreciation deductions previously taken,[41] so the entire $12,000 gain realized is recapture gain and must be recognized in the year of sale under §453(*i*). It is easy to sympathize with the legislative decision that the tax deferral from depreciation deductions in excess of the actual decline in value of the property should end when the taxpayer disposes of the property. On the other hand, the fact that the gain happens to be recapture gain doesn't magically make the liquidity problem disappear.

What would be the result if we change the above hypothetical by increasing the amount of the installment note to $25,000? (It would be an unusual truck that could be sold for more than its original basis, but humor us.) Then the gain realized would be $25,000, of which $20,000 is due to recapture of depreciation and $5,000 is due to an actual increase in the value of the truck. Section 453(*i*) would require recognition of $20,000 gain in the year of sale, but the other $5,000 gain could be reported on the installment method.

3. A Legislative Frolic

In 1999, Congress decided that the installment method was fundamentally inconsistent with the accrual method of accounting, under which amounts are taken into income when the right to receive income arises, even though payment has not yet been received. Accordingly, Congress amended §453 to prohibit the use of the installment method by taxpayers using an accrual method of accounting for tax purposes. Since most businesses are required to use the accrual method, this was a huge restriction on the availability of §453. The targets of the amendment were casual sales of assets used in a business; sales of inventory items and dealer dispositions were *already* excluded from §453. Understandably, the objections from small businesses were numerous and vociferous. They pointed out that the liquidity problems at which §453 is aimed exist whether the taxpayer is on the accrual method or the cash method, and that requiring accrual of an installment note payable many years in the future is a very different kettle of fish from requiring accrual of accounts receivable likely to be paid in the next few months. Congress quickly saw the error of its ways, and in 2000 retroactively repealed the 1999 amendment.

41. See Chapter 6.A.

4. *Combining §§1031 and 453*

What if a taxpayer receives boot in a like-kind exchange, and some or all of the boot takes the form of an installment note? Can the taxpayer take advantage of both §1031 (nonrecognition of gain on a like-kind exchange) and §453? In other words, can the taxpayer use §1031 to avoid recognizing gain except to the extent of boot, and use §453 to defer recognition of the gain associated with the boot? There is no policy reason not to permit the use of both provisions, and sure enough §453(f)(6) specifically permits the two provisions to be used together. The technical rules are provided in §453(f)(6) and in Prop. Reg. §1.453-1(f)(1). Try applying those rules to the following two problems.

Problem 4.   John owns land with a basis of $50,000. He exchanges it for land with a value of $120,000, $10,000 cash, and a $30,000 installment note. How much gain must John recognize in the year of the exchange? How much gain must he recognize when he receives payment of the entire $30,000 principal amount of the note in a later year?

Problem 5.   The facts are the same as in Problem 4, except John's basis in the land is $125,000.

5. *Charging Interest on Deferral*

As explained earlier,[42] tax deferral can be understood as the equivalent of an interest-free loan from the government of the amount of tax deferred, to last for the length of the deferral period. The deferred tax must be paid eventually, but without an interest charge to reflect the fact that the taxpayer was allowed to keep the money during the period of the deferral. This suggests that Congress might take the analogy and run with it, by continuing to allow deferral to a cash-strapped taxpayer, but treating the deferral as an *interest-bearing* loan from the government to the taxpayer. Congress has done precisely that in §453A, but only with respect to a small number of wealthy taxpayers. The details of the provision are quite complex, but the general idea is that a taxpayer who receives installment notes in excess of $5 million from sales in a single year must pay interest annually on the tax liability deferred under §453 until the notes are paid and the gain is recognized. (There is no cliff effect; a taxpayer with installment notes of $6 million arising from sales in a single year would pay interest only on the deferral associated with $1 million of notes, not $6 million.) Few taxpayers are subject to §453A, and Congress continues to impose no interest charge on the overwhelming majority of tax deferrals. But §453A demonstrates that Congress understands the interest-free loan analogy, and understands that it is possible to provide liquidity relief while imposing an interest charge for the privilege. Could §453A be a camel's nose under the tent?

To the extent a taxpayer is required to pay interest under §453A, is there any real advantage to deferring gain under §453? Wouldn't the taxpayer do just as well to elect out of §453 (*see* §453(d)) and borrow the money to pay the tax from a bank?

---

42. See Chapter 1.C.2.

Not necessarily. The interest charged by the government under §453A may be less than the interest a bank would charge. In addition, the government is always willing to make the loan, which may not be true of the bank.

6. *Electing Out*

Section 453(d) allows a taxpayer to elect out of the installment method. What happens then? The answers are found in Reg. §15a.453-1(d). In the vast majority of cases, the regulations require "closed transaction" treatment. Under this approach, a cash method taxpayer must include the fair market value of the installment obligation in her amount realized in the year of sale, and recognize gain in that year to the extent the total amount realized exceeds the taxpayer's basis. Similarly, an accrual method taxpayer ordinarily must include in amount realized in the year of sale the total amount payable under the installment obligation (not including interest or original issue discount).

The regulations leave the door ajar for "open transaction" treatment (in which all payments are treated as tax-free returns of basis until basis is exhausted) in the case of contingent payment obligations, but just barely: "Only in those rare and extraordinary cases involving sales for a contingent payment obligation in which the fair market value of the obligation . . . cannot reasonably be ascertained will the taxpayer be entitled to assert that the transaction is 'open.'"

Electing out of §453 will improve one's tax situation only if: (1) opting out results in open transaction treatment; or (2) the taxpayer has reason to believe that his marginal tax rate will be higher in the year(s) of payment than in the year of sale (to a degree sufficient to offset the financial advantage of deferral). If the result is closed transaction treatment, generally the taxpayer would have been better off staying with the installment method. Given the strong regulatory bias in favor of closed transaction treatment for taxpayers who opt out, §453(d) elections are rare.

Cell

ORIGINAL ISSUE DISCOUNT, §483 UNSTATED INTEREST, AND MARKET DISCOUNT

A. Original Issue Discount

    1. The Basic Idea

    2. A Little History

    3. Debt Issued for Hard-to-Value Property

B. Section 483 Unstated Interest

C. Market Discount

A. ORIGINAL ISSUE DISCOUNT

1. The Basic Idea

In exchange for $6,140 cash, Big Corporation issues a bond to Ivan Investor. Under the terms of the bond, Ivan is entitled to no interest payments, but he is entitled to receive a single $10,000 payment of "principal" when the bond matures in ten years. Despite the absence of any stated interest, the $3,860 difference between the $6,140 issue price of the bond and the $10,000 redemption price is obviously the functional equivalent of interest. As it happens, this example is based on an annual compound interest rate of 5 percent. In other words, $6,140 invested at 5 percent, compounded annually, will grow to $10,000 in ten years. Under current law, the $3,860 of disguised interest on the Big bond is subject to the original issue discount (OID) rules (§§1271 et seq.), which are described a few paragraphs below. Before examining the details of those rules, it is helpful to understand how Big and Ivan would have been taxed in the years before Congress enacted the OID rules.

Like most corporations, Big is an accrual method taxpayer. This means Big takes an item into income when all events establishing Big's right to receive income have taken place, even if Big has yet to receive payment. Similarly, Big claims a business expense deduction when a liability accrues, even though Big has not yet made payment.[43] Ivan, on the other hand, is a cash method taxpayer. Like

---

43. For a fuller discussion of the accrual and cash methods of tax accounting, see Chapter 7.

individual investors generally, Ivan takes items into income only when he is paid, and deducts expenses only when he makes payments. As an accrual method taxpayer, Big can deduct (under §163) its interest obligations as they economically accrue, without regard to the fact that it has made no payments. The amount of Big's annual interest expense accruals are indicated in the table below.

Year	Principal Amount at Beginning of Year (With Previous Year's Interest Accrual Added to Principal)	Interest for the Year at 5%
1	$6,140	$307
2	$6,447	$322
3	$6,749	$338
4	$7,107	$355
5	$7,462	$373
6	$7,835	$392
7	$8,227	$411
8	$8,638	$432
9	$9,070	$454
10	$9,524	$476

The total amount of interest for the ten years (the sum of the numbers in the third column) is $3,860. The $10,000 payment on maturity represents the sum of the $9,524 augmented principal amount (i.e., the original $6,140 principal amount increased by previous years' interest added to principal) and the final year's $476 interest.

Although Big would deduct its interest expense accruals every year, during the years prior to the enactment of the OID rules Ivan did not have to include corresponding amounts annually as interest income. He was a cash-method tax-payer, and he had not received any cash. Instead, Ivan included $3,860 in income only when he received $10,000 cash upon the note's maturity. The combination of Big's expense accruals and Ivan's income deferral made the federal government the victim of a timing whipsaw. For example, Big was able to deduct $307 of interest expense in the first year, nine years before Ivan was required to include that amount in income.

Congress eventually decided the whipsaw was unacceptable, and put a stop to it by enacting the OID rules. In general, the effect of the rules is to put Ivan on the accrual method with respect to any debt instrument bearing original issue discount, even as he remains a cash-method taxpayer for other purposes. The first step in the application of the OID rules is to identify the amount of OID contained in a particular debt instrument. In the case of a bond issued for cash, this is simple enough. Under §1273(a), the OID is equal to the bond's "stated redemption price at maturity" (here, $10,000) minus the bond's "issue price" (the $6,140 Ivan paid Big for the bond). Although this example involves a bond bearing no stated interest, under §1273 a bond issued for cash will bear OID whenever the redemption price exceeds the issue price, regardless of the amount (if any) of stated interest payable under the terms of the bond.

Having identified the total amount of OID — $3,860 in the example — the next step is to determine *when* Ivan will be required to include this disguised interest in income. This step is governed by the rules of §1272. The tricky part of applying §1272 is identifying the interest rate at which the issue price will grow (with compounding) to the redemption price by the time the bond matures. Don't worry about the details of this process; it's easy with the right calculator (or, better yet, with the help of someone who has the right calculator and knows how to use it). The bond in the example features an implicit interest rate of 5 percent, compounded annually, and Ivan's annual OID income accruals will be the same amounts shown in Big's interest expense accrual table.[44] Ivan must include the indicated amount in income in each of the ten years the bond remains outstanding. Because of the compounding of interest — i.e., the adding of previous years' interest to principal — the amount of OID is smallest in the first year and largest in the final year. Since the timing of Ivan's inclusions under §1272 matches the timing of Big's interest expense accruals, the OID rules eliminate the whipsaw effect. Ivan will owe no tax when he finally receives the $10,000 cash payment on the note (other than the tax on the $476 that represents the interest in the bond's final year). Of the $10,000 payment, $6,140 will represent his original basis in the note, and the other $3,860 will represent interest on which he has already been taxed under the OID rules.

If *Eisner v. Macomber* were still good constitutional law, the OID rules would probably be an unconstitutional attempt to tax unrealized appreciation. In the first year, for example, the amount of Ivan's OID inclusion is the difference between the present value of the right to receive $10,000 in ten years and the present value of the right to receive $10,000 in nine years. The *Macomber* Supreme Court would almost certainly not have considered an increase in value due to the mere passage of time to be income within the meaning of the Sixteenth Amendment. However, as noted in section A.2 of Chapter 3, the Supreme Court has demoted the realization doctrine to a rule of "administrative convenience," and the constitutionality of the OID rules is not in doubt.

2. *A Little History*

The OID rules are an object lesson in how the tax laws become complex. Discount bonds did not originate as a clever attempt to whipsaw the government. Rather, they were a response to the problem of issuing bonds in a previous era, when days or weeks might elapse between a corporation's ordering bonds to be printed and the printer's filling the order. Suppose Big placed a printing order for bonds with a principal amount of $1 million, bearing interest payable annually at the rate of 10 percent — the market rate of interest at the time Big placed the order. By the time the bonds came back from the printer, however, the market rate had risen to 10.1 percent, with the result that the bonds as printed bore a slightly below-market interest rate. What could Big do? It might have ordered new bonds

---

44. Actually, §1272(a)(5) calls for compounding on a semi-annual basis. With semi-annual compounding, the implicit interest rate on the bond would be slightly lower than 5 percent.

to be printed bearing 10.1 percent interest, but the market interest rate would probably change again by the time the replacement bonds arrived. Rather than chasing its tail indefinitely, Big would simply sell the bonds at a small discount—for slightly less than the $1 million stated principal amount—to compensate buyers for the slightly below-market stated interest rate. Thus was original issue discount conceived. Since this kind of OID was used to accommodate interest rate changes over only a few days or weeks, the amount of OID would generally be small relative to the issue price of the bond. In a world of incidental and de minimis OID, it made sense for Congress to accept a little whipsaw so that bondholders could continue to enjoy the simplicity of reporting their interest income under the cash method.

Taxpayers were not content, however, with de minimis amounts of whipsaw. Once they realized the tax avoidance potential of the asymmetrical treatment of OID, corporations began to exploit that potential by issuing "zero coupon bonds" paying *no* stated interest, with the entire return to the investor taking the form of OID. When the whipsaw problem had grown from its de minimis beginnings to major proportions, Congress felt compelled to end the whipsaw—and to complicate the tax laws—by enacting the OID provisions. Similar stories are behind many other complex provisions of the Internal Revenue Code. Congress begins by tolerating an economically inaccurate taxpayer-favorable rule, in the interests of simplicity. Taxpayers, and their lawyers and accountants, then exploit the loophole in ways Congress had neither intended nor foreseen. Congress reacts by enacting new anti-abuse provisions, and the Code grows ever more complex.

3. Debt Issued for Hard-to-Value Property

If a debt instrument is issued in exchange for real estate or other hard-to-value property, instead of being issued in exchange for cash, the rules for determining the amount of OID are different from the rules described above for the Big Corporation bond. Suppose Paula sells land in which she has a $700,000 basis for an installment note with a stated principal amount of $2 million. The note provides for no stated interest, and the principal is payable as a lump sum in ten years. In theory, it would be possible to apply the approach of §1273 in this situation, using the fair market value of the land as the issue price of the note. In practice, the problem is that there is no mechanical way to determine the fair market value of real estate. In order to avoid valuation controversies, §1274 provides that the issue price of a note issued for real estate (or other hard-to-value property) shall be equal to the "imputed principal amount" (IPA), which is determined by discounting to present value all payments due on the note. The discounting is done at the "applicable federal rate" (AFR). The AFR is determined by reference to market yields on U.S. Treasury obligations, and is adjusted monthly as yields change on Treasury bills.[45] Suppose the AFR at the time of Paula's installment sale is 6 percent. Using a present value table or a calculator, one can determine that the present value of the right to receive $2 million in ten years, using a 6 percent discount rate, is $1,160,000 ($2 million × .558).[46] The effect is to

45. *See* §1274(d).
46. Using a 6 percent discount rate with annual compounding, the present value of the right to receive one dollar in ten years is $0.558. Actually, §1274 requires discounting at the AFR, with semi-annual compounding. For ease of illustration, however, the example is based on annual compounding.

use present value analysis to "back into" the issue price of $1,160,000, without having to appraise the real estate that Paula exchanged for the note. The amount of OID on the note, then, is $840,000: the excess of the $2 million redemption price over the $1,160,000 imputed principal amount.

The only difference between OID on an installment note issued in exchange for real estate, and OID on a bond issued for cash, is in the method of determining the issue price and the resulting amount of OID. Once the $840,000 OID amount has been determined under the rules of §1274, it is taxed to Paula under the same §1272 rules applicable to holders of OID bonds issued for cash, with the AFR as the implicit interest rate. Thus, Paula's OID income for the first year will be

$$\$1,160,000 \times 6\% = \$69,600,$$

her income for the second year will be

$$(\$1,160,000 + \$69,600) \times 6\% = \$73,776,$$

and so on.[47]

As long as an installment note provides for "adequate stated interest" — i.e., stated interest at or above the AFR at the time of issuance, payable at least annually — there will be no OID under §1274. Thus, an installment seller intimidated by the complexities of the OID rules can avoid them by insisting on a note bearing adequate stated interest. If an installment note provides for *some* stated interest, but at a rate less than the AFR, then §1274 will identify some disguised interest on the note, but less than if the note bore no stated interest whatsoever. Without going into the gory details, the issue price on a §1274 note bearing less-than-adequate stated interest is determined by discounting to present value (using the AFR) *all* payments due under the note, regardless of whether the payments are denominated principal or interest. The amount of OID, then, will be the excess of the redemption price over the sum of the present values of all payments due under the note.

Notice that the presence of stated interest has very different implications depending on whether a debt instrument is issued for cash or for real estate (or other hard-to-value property). If a bond is issued for cash, the bond will have OID if the stated principal amount exceeds the cash paid for the bond, even if the bond bears stated interest at or above the AFR. By contrast, under the backing-into-OID approach of §1274, the presence of adequate stated interest negates the possibility of unstated interest, and even the presence of less-than-adequate stated interest reduces the amount of unstated interest.

If a taxpayer sells property for an installment note that does not bear adequate stated interest, the determination of the issue price under §1274 will be crucial to the application of the installment sale rules of §453, as well as to the application of the OID rules. Return to the example of Paula, who sold land with a basis of $700,000 for a non-interest-bearing installment note with a stated principal amount of $2 million, payable as a lump sum in ten years. If the issue price of the note, determined under §1274, is $1,160,000, two results follow. First, the issue price is used to determine the amount of OID ($840,000); second, the issue price is treated as Paula's amount realized in applying the installment method to her gain

---

47. To repeat the earlier caveat, the illustration is based on annual compounding of interest, while the statute actually requires semi-annual compounding.

on the sale. For purposes of §453, Paula is treated as having sold the land for nothing down and a $1,160,000 installment note payable in ten years. She will not recognize any installment gain until the note is paid in the tenth year, because she will not receive any payment before then. When the note is paid in the tenth year, $840,000 represents the OID on which Paula has already been taxed over the ten-year life of the note; therefore she receives that amount tax-free. The other $1,160,000 is treated as the payment of the deemed principal amount of the note, and its tax consequences are determined under the installment method formula of §453(c):

$$\$1,160,000\ (\$460,000/\$1,160,000) = \$460,000 \text{ gain recognized}$$

To sum up, the $2 million payment in Year 10 is treated as consisting of three parts: $840,000 of OID that already has been taxed, $700,000 of recovery of the basis in the land, and $460,000 of capital gain on the sale of the land.

B. SECTION 483 UNSTATED INTEREST

Some installment notes bearing unstated interest are not subject to the rigors of the OID rules—for example, a note arising from a sale by an individual of a farm for $1,000,000 or less, and a note arising from any sale involving total payments of $250,000 or less. Most sales exempted from the OID rules, however, are subject to §483. Section 483 uses the same method as §1274 for identifying unstated interest, but unlike the OID rules it does not put the holder of the installment note on the accrual method. Thus, if §483 had applied to Paula's sale, Paula would still have been taxed on $840,000 of unstated interest income, but the tax would have been deferred until she had received the $2 million cash payment on the note.[48] On receipt of the $2 million cash, Paula would be taxed on (1) $460,000 of capital gain under §453, and (2) $840,000 of interest income under §483. Congress tolerates the interest timing whipsaw in situations covered by §483, but does not tolerate the conversion of interest income (taxable at ordinary income rates) into capital gain (taxable at special low rates).

C. MARKET DISCOUNT

Irene Investor owns a Big Corporation bond with a $10,000 principal amount, bearing stated interest at 5 percent. Five percent was the market rate of interest when Irene purchased the bond upon its issuance by Big, so Irene paid $10,000 for the bond. Because there was no difference between the issue price and the redemption price, the bond has no OID. Since the issuance of the bond, the market rate of interest on similar newly issued bonds has risen to 6 percent. Because the

---

48. Section 483 could not actually apply on Paula's facts, even if the land sold was a farm, because the sales price is greater than $1 million.

bond *now* bears a below-market interest rate, it is worth less than $10,000. Bill Buyer purchases the bond from Irene for $9,500, with the $500 market discount on the bond being just enough to compensate Bill for the below-market rate of interest. How should Bill be taxed on the difference between the $9,500 he paid for the bond and the $10,000 principal payment he will receive upon its maturity? On the one hand, there is no timing whipsaw problem here; since this is market discount rather than original issue discount, Big cannot deduct the $500 as an interest expense. On the other hand, it does seem that Bill should not be able to take advantage of the favorable capital gains rates with respect to the economic equivalent (to him) of interest income. These considerations suggest that Bill should be taxed on the $500 as ordinary income rather than as capital gain, but that he should not be taxed until he receives the cash. The market discount rules of §1276 treat Bill in precisely this manner. Section 1276 does not put Bill on the accrual method with respect to market discount, but it does ensure that market discount will not be taxed as capital gain.

Cell

FEDERAL WEALTH TRANSFER TAXES

A. The Federal Estate Tax

B. The Federal Gift Tax

C. The Federal Generation-Skipping Transfer Tax

Law students typically study the federal income tax prior to studying any of the more advanced tax courses, such as federal estate and gift tax. However, many income tax cases involve issues that touch on related issues of inclusion or deduction within the federal wealth transfer tax system. For example, when studying the rules that govern the basis of property received by will or inheritance, we observe that the rule under IRC §1014 gives the transferee a basis in the property equal to the fair market value of the property at the date of the death of the person from whose estate the property was transferred.[49] Because our income tax generally does not tax appreciation (or recognize losses) until there has been some sort of disposition of the asset, the effect of this rule is to cleanse assets of any unrecognized gain or loss that may have accrued during the decedent's lifetime. Tax advisors, being aware of these rules, are able to manipulate them to some degree to ensure that their elderly and critically ill clients manage to realize their losses before death, but retain highly appreciated assets until death. Thus, though the rule is facially neutral, in making accrued gains and losses disappear with equal thoroughly, far more gains than losses are placed beyond the reach of the income tax by §1014.

But, it seems reasonable to ask, doesn't the estate tax reach these appreciated values? The short answer is that the estate tax sometimes reaches these values (though not systematically, in light of the substantial exemptions and deductions available to executors in computing that tax), but that is an insufficient response to the income tax shortcomings. This can be understood by imagining a block of stock worth, say, $10 million that was owned by a decedent and is now part of her estate, which (we will further assume) is fully taxable on that amount. The estate tax payable on that amount represents an excise tax on the transfer of wealth, imposed by Congress out of a combination of motives (including reducing wealth concentration and raising revenue). As an excise tax on the movement of wealth, the estate tax is not concerned with previously accrued gains or losses. Indeed, the estate tax assessed on this $10 million transfer will be the same whether the decedent paid

49. In some cases, the basis is derived from the fair market value on the "alternate valuation date," which is exactly six months following the date of death. Section 2032. This option, however, has little impact on the primary observations offered in the text about the effect of the basis rule of §1014.

$5,000 or $20,000,000 for this block of stock. The estate tax is thus not designed as a general backstop of the income tax, and is not structured to perform that function in any reasonable way.

This issue is muddied by the fact that some defenders of wealth transfer taxes note that, in a tax system in which §1014 allows accrued gains of decedents to go forever untouched by the income tax, the estate tax may prevent that store of pre-tax wealth from forever escaping the clutches of the tax system. But this view of estate taxes as a substitute for income taxes forgone is true in only a very rough way, and does not accurately represent the primary purpose or structure of the wealth transfer taxes.

There are three primary elements in the federal wealth transfer tax system: the estate tax itself, the gift tax, and the tax on certain transfers that pass value to persons more than one generation younger than the transferor. Each of these is explained separately below.

A. THE FEDERAL ESTATE TAX

The centerpiece of the transfer tax system is the federal estate tax, which has in various forms applied to decedents' estates since 1916. (The estate tax was suspended for the single year of 2010,[50] but it is now again in force, and neither another suspension nor permanent repeal seems likely.) The estate tax is imposed on the transfer of assets from an estate to the decedent's heirs and beneficiaries in cases where the value of the taxable estate so transferred exceeds $5 million. The $5 million exemption — which is technically achieved through the use of a "unified credit"[51] equal to the tax on a taxable estate of precisely that size — applies to estates of decedents dying in 2011 and 2012. The exemption amount is scheduled to decline to $1 million for 2013 and later years, but it is unlikely Congress will allow that to happen.[52]

The rate faced by estates subject to the tax in 2011 and 2012 is a flat 35 percent. It will not be at all surprising if Congress extends the 35 percent rate beyond 2012. Absent further legislation, however, in 2013 the top rate will return to its pre-2001 level of 55 percent. A surcharge of 5 percent on estates roughly between $10 and 17 million is also scheduled to return in 2013. That surcharge would bring the maximum marginal rate up to 60 percent on estates within the affected range.

Congress has given the estate tax a fairly broad reach, so that assets may be included in an estate even if the decedent enjoys less than full ownership of those assets at the time of death. For example, if a testator gives away a remainder interest in property, but retains a life estate, the value of the entire property will

---

50. More precisely, an executor of the estate of a person dying in 2010 may choose whether or not the estate tax applies to that estate. See note 54 in the main text of this chapter for an explanation of why some executors of 2010 estates should opt for the estate tax to apply.

51. Although the caption of IRC §2010 still refers to the "unified credit," the actual words of the Code, since 1997, describe the concept as "the applicable credit amount," and this latter term has come into common parlance among estate planners. Because "unified credit" seems more descriptive, we use that term here.

52. The description in this and the subsequent paragraphs borrows heavily from an earlier work by one of the authors. *See* Richard Schmalbeck, "Avoiding Federal Wealth Transfer Taxes," in *Rethinking Estate and Gift Taxation* (2001), at 113.

generally be included in the testator's estate.[53] Similar rules apply to property over which a testator has retained a power of appointment;[54] life insurance owned by the decedent (which ordinarily does not pass through the decedent's probate estate, but is rather paid directly to the beneficiaries);[55] annuities;[56] certain transfers within three years of death;[57] and so on. On the other hand, the reach of the tax is circumscribed by a number of deductions, of which two are particularly important: There is an unlimited marital deduction, so that any part of the estate left to a surviving spouse may be deducted in full;[58] and there is an unlimited charitable deduction, allowing deduction in full of any testamentary gifts to charitable organizations or governmental units.[59] The impact of these deductions can hardly be overstated. For estates of decedents who died in 2004, the aggregate total of reported *gross* estates was close to $194 billion. The $87 billion difference between that number and the aggregate total of *taxable* estates reported in the same year (about $107 billion) is largely explained by the marital deductions claimed of $60 billion, and the charitable deductions of $15 billion.[60] Thus, it may be said that the federal estate tax is intended to apply to a broad sense of the decedent's wealth transferred at or because of death, but only to the extent that that wealth is transferred to someone other than a surviving spouse or a charitable entity.

B.   THE FEDERAL GIFT TAX

If the tax rules are intended to impose significant tax burdens on transfers of wealth at death, attention must be given to the possibility that wealth transfers can — and in the absence of comparable tax burdens, probably will — take place in advance of death. This was apparently not obvious to the Congress that first enacted the federal estate tax, for that tax had no counterpart gift tax. However, the avoidance opportunity had become clear enough by 1924, when Congress finally enacted the first gift tax.[61] For roughly the next half-century, the estate and gift taxes proceeded in parallel but along separate courses, with each having its

---

53. Section 2036. There is, however, a credit for any gift tax paid on the original transfer of the remainder interest during the testator's life.
54. Section 2041.
55. Section 2042.
56. Section 2039. Only annuities having a death benefit or refund feature, or those covering multiple lives, are includable under these provisions. A single-life annuity does not ordinarily pass anything to anyone at the death of the annuitant, and would not be included in a decedent's estate.
57. Section 2035.
58. Section 2056. The marital deduction, like a number of other rules in the estate and gift tax area, applies in this way only if the donee is a U.S. citizen. Life — or more accurately, death — is more complicated for those whose spouses are aliens; but it is possible, through the use of a "qualified domestic trust," the elements of which are described in §2056(d)(2), to achieve similar results in the cases of spouses who are not citizens.
59. Section 2055. This section covers more or less the same ground as §170, which provides the rules for income tax deductibility of charitable gifts.
60. The balance of the deductions are composed largely of the deduction for estate debts ($8 billion) and attorneys' and executors' fees ($2 billion). The total of all other deductions was less than $2 billion.
61. That gift tax was repealed a year later; however, in 1932 Congress enacted another gift tax that has, with important modifications from time to time, been continuously in force since then.

own exemptions and rate structures. The absence of coordination between the two taxes encouraged wealthy individuals to make sizable gifts during life, to use up the gift tax exemption and the lower ranges of the gift tax rates, because the advantages of those features would be lost once the individual died.

Congress unified the estate and gift taxes in the Tax Reform Act of 1976, but somewhat diminished the unity of that structure in 2001 when it phased in higher estate tax exemptions from 2002 to 2009 and suspended the estate tax but not the gift tax for 2010. Unification has been restored, however, for 2011 and later years. Under the unified system, lifetime gifts are accumulated, and became taxable only when the amount effectively exempted by the unified credit is exhausted. Once exhausted through lifetime gifts, the unified credit is no longer available to shelter subsequent transfers during life, or transfers at the decedent's death. If partially exhausted due to lifetime gifts, the credit is reduced to that extent.

This unification is intended to make taxpayers indifferent, in tax terms, between gratuitous transfers during life and those made at death. It doesn't quite achieve this result, however, due to the fact that the payment of a gift tax during life depletes the estate remaining to that extent, leaving less exposed to transfer taxes of either sort. For example, assume (contrary to fact) that there is a flat-rate transfer tax of 50 percent that applies to gratuitous transfers exceeding $1 million. Assume further that a wealthy individual has an estate of $10 million that she wishes to leave to her son. If she makes no more than $1 million of gratuitous transfers during her life, her total transfer tax will be .5 × ($ 10,000,000-1,000,000), or $4,500,000. But if she transfers $5 million during life, her gift tax will be .5 × ($ 5,000,000-1,000,000) or $2,000,000. And her estate will then contain only the $3 million that is left after both the lifetime transfers and the payment of the gift tax. The tax on an estate of $3 million would be $1.5 million (remember that she has used up her unified exemption already), for a total wealth transfer tax of only $3.5 million. Can you figure out the reason for differing tax burdens in the two situations, given the supposed unification of the two systems? Hint: Is the amount of the gift tax included in the base on which the gift tax is imposed? Is the amount of the estate tax included in the base on which the estate tax is imposed?

Like the estate tax, the gift tax was intended to reach broadly all gratuitous property transfers, whether direct or indirect. For example, if a corporation sells property for less than its value to a relative of a major shareholder, the arrangement is subject to recharacterization as a dividend to the shareholder, followed by a potentially taxable gift from the shareholder to the relative.[62] Similarly, arrangements such as interest-free loans may create taxable gifts.[63]

Also like the estate tax, the gift tax permits unlimited deductions for gifts to spouses and charitable entities.[64] In addition, the gift tax rules permit an "annual exclusion" of gifts of up to $13,000 in value to any donee during any year.[65]

---

62. Such recharacterization would depend on a number of circumstances, and would never be automatic. A case in which precisely these facts were presented is Epstein v. Commissioner, 53 T.C. 459 (1969). (Note that a gift is only potentially taxable, because it may be within the donor's lifetime exemption, or eligible for the annual exclusion from the gift tax explained immediately below.)

63. This rule was first determined by the Supreme Court in Dickman v. Commissioner, 465 U.S. 330 (1984). The rule was subsequently codified by Congress in §7872, added to the Code later the same year.

64. Sections 2523 and 2522, respectively.

65. Section 2503(b). The Code specifies an exclusion amount of $10,000, which is to be adjusted, pursuant to §2503(b)(2), in $1000 increments, to reflect inflation after 1998. The inflation-adjusted amount for 2011 is $13,000.

Married taxpayers can, with the consent of both spouses, claim exclusions for gifts of up to $26,000 per year, per donee, regardless of which spouse is the source of the gifted property.[66] This exclusion is subject to one important caveat, however: Gifts will not qualify for the annual exclusion if they are gifts of "future interests," [67] such as a remainder interest in a trust. And, though the point is an obvious one, it is so important that it should be emphasized: While the exclusion is part of the gift tax provisions, it is effectively an exclusion for estate tax purposes as well, since any funds transferred irrevocably during life will not be present in the gross estate when the estate tax liability is computed. Similarly, subsequent earnings generated by property given away during the testator's life will also fall wholly outside the gross estate.

The importance of using the annual exclusion, especially in the case of estates that are not extremely large, can be appreciated by considering that a middle-aged couple with three children and seven grandchildren could give away, free of any transfer tax, over $5 million over a 20-year period simply by giving each of those children and grandchildren $26,000 each year. (You may want to keep this in mind the next time your parents or grandparents ask what you've learned in law school!)

C.   THE FEDERAL GENERATION-SKIPPING TRANSFER TAX

Prior to 1976, there were transfer-tax advantages associated with trusts that would leave an income interest in the trust to one (or more) of the decedent's children for the duration of that beneficiary's life, with a remainder interest to one or more of the decedent's grandchildren. The transfer of property into the trust from the grandparent's estate would be a taxable transfer by the deceased grandparent, but the enjoyment of the remainder interest by the grandchildren at the death of the member(s) of the intermediate generation was not generally subject to a transfer tax. This was typically true even if the trustees had some powers to invade the corpus of the trust for the benefit of the member(s) of the intermediate generation. If the testator so chose, more than one generation could be skipped; that is, a trust could create a series of lifetime income interests cascading down through subsequent generations, each one beginning tax-free at the death of a member of the previous generation, with a remainder interest vesting in a member of the fourth or fifth generation following the testator whose will created the trust.[68] A majority

---

66. Section 2513.
67. Section 2503(b)(1).
68. Historically, trusts could not endure indefinitely as a matter of state property law. Most states limited the duration of trusts by some variant of the "rule against perpetuities," which generally requires that the interests created by the trust must vest within a period measured by the duration of any life existing at the time the trust is created, plus 21 years. See generally the film *Body Heat,* which is thought to be the cinematic debut of this wonderful common law concept. Some form of this rule, which effectively limits trusts to four or five generations, in most cases, continues to apply in most states. However, a handful of states have recently abolished their versions of the rule against perpetuities, and institutions in some of those states (Delaware and Alaska seem to be particularly prominent) have begun actively marketing so-called dynasty trusts that exploit the absence of such limitations. One needn't live in those states to create such trusts; one merely establishes the trust account in one of those jurisdictions, and the law of that jurisdiction will apply to the trust.

of Congress in 1976 believed that the enjoyment of the value of the property by the intermediate generation(s) was sufficient that the passage of value from each generation to the next should be subject to a federal transfer tax. Accordingly, that year Congress enacted the aptly named "generation-skipping transfer tax" (GST tax).[69]

The GST tax can be quite complex, but essentially it treats the termination of the life interests of any intermediate generation in a situation of the sort described above (or certain others deemed equivalent by Congress) as a taxable event, effectively treating the value of the interest passing to the next generation as a part of the estate of the member of the intermediate generation. The GST tax also taxes certain "direct skips" that do not pass through the intermediate generation, such as gifts or bequests made directly to grandchildren. The saving grace of the GST tax is that it applies to transfers within its ambit only to the extent that they exceed $5 million per transferor.[70] The GST tax collects very little revenue — about $69 million in 2001. However, it is a tax whose impact is to discourage taxpayer behavior by imposing strong disincentives. To the extent that the tax succeeds in this effort, its effects would not be reflected in the revenue collected, but rather in the generation-skipping bequests that it discourages, and in the estate or gift tax collected as a result. While the latter impact is not easily measured, the point is that the GST tax should not be regarded as unimportant simply because of its negligible revenue.

---

69. Sections 2601 *et seq.*
70. Section 2631(a). The $5 million exemption applies in 2011 and 2012. After 2012 the exemption will fall to $1 million, absent further legislation.

Chapter 4

PERSONAL DEDUCTIONS

"Personal deductions" is not a term of art. Most commentators use the term simply to refer to those deductions that are available only to individual taxpayers. These deductions fall within several different categories, perhaps best arranged according to their placement on the basic individual tax return, Form 1040. On the first page of that form, after income items have been listed and totaled, the taxpayer is allowed to subtract several specific items from income to reach a total called "adjusted gross income" (AGI), which appears at the very bottom of the page. These items, sometimes called "above-the-line deductions," include certain qualified contributions to individual retirement or medical savings accounts, moving expenses, student loan interest payments, and alimony payments, among others. (The line referred to is the line on which adjusted gross income appears, but it is unclear how that came to be *the* line.) Alimony and retirement savings accounts are discussed elsewhere in this volume, and will not be extensively considered here. Note also that many deductions may not be shown on the main two pages of the Form 1040 at all, but may instead be reflected in net numbers that appear on the main form. For example, business expense deductions are not reported directly on the main Form 1040, but are shown instead on the Schedule C (except for employee business expenses, which are discussed in part F of this chapter), where items of business income and expense are shown. The net number at the end of the Schedule C is carried over to the income items on the front page of the Form 1040. Despite this treatment on the forms provided by the Internal Revenue Service, all items that are allowed as deductions in computing adjusted gross income are listed in §62 of the Code.[1]

The most important categories of personal deductions — and the primary subject matter of this chapter — are referred to collectively as "itemized deductions." This phrase *is* a term of art, defined by exclusion in §63(d) as allowable deductions other than (1) those allowable in calculating adjusted gross income, and (2) those reflecting personal exemptions for the taxpayer(s) and dependents. The most important categories within itemized deductions are charitable contributions, certain interest payments, certain state and local taxes, casualty losses, medical expenses, and "miscellaneous itemized deductions," which, as the name suggests, include a variety of items. Each of these categories is discussed in some detail in this chapter.

Some sense of the importance of itemized deductions in the aggregate, and of each category, can be derived from the table below, which shows for each category

---

1. A relatively recent addition to the items deductible in computing adjusted gross income is the cost of an attorney hired in connection with claims of unlawful discrimination or for disability benefits. *See* §62(a)(20). This deduction, however, cannot exceed the amount of any recoveries for such claims that the taxpayer realizes and includes in gross income in the same year.

the percentage of itemizing taxpayers claiming a particular deduction in 2008, the average (mean) amount of the deduction for each taxpayer who claims that deduction, and the aggregate amount deducted by all taxpayers.

As the table below shows, three categories of expenses are claimed by almost all itemizing taxpayers: state and local taxes, interest, and charitable contributions. Those categories accordingly accounted for almost 90 percent of the total itemized deductions claimed. The other three categories are, for reasons that will become clear, claimed by few taxpayers. Those categories do, however, retain considerable importance to the small number of taxpayers who are in a position to claim them.

Itemized Deductions, 2008[2]

Category	Pct. of Itemizers	Avg./Return	Total Deductions
Interest Paid	81.4%	$12,694	$497.6 bil.
Taxes Paid	99.3%	$9767	$467.2 bil.
Charitable Gifts	81.0%	$4406	$172.9 bil.
Miscellaneous	25.8%	$7230	$89.9 bil
Medical Expenses	21.1%	$7522	$76.4 bil.
Casualty Loss	0.7%	$12,902	$4.3 bil.

The Code offers an alternative to claiming itemized deductions: The taxpayer may instead elect to take a "standard deduction," of varying amounts, depending on the type of return (single, joint, etc.), whether the taxpayer qualifies as blind or aged, and what tax year is involved. The various standard deduction amounts are indexed for inflation, and so are adjusted every year. For 2011, the applicable amounts are $11,600 for a joint return (or return of a surviving spouse of someone who died during the tax year); $8,500 for a head-of-household return; $5,800 for a single return and for a separate return filed by a married taxpayer. A married taxpayer who is over the age of 65 by the end of the tax year, or is blind, gets an additional standard deduction of $1,150; other blind or elderly taxpayers receive additional standard deductions of $1,450. (A taxpayer who is both elderly and blind may take both of the additional deductions for which he qualifies.)

Most taxpayers choose to claim the standard deduction rather than to itemize their deductions, presumably because the total amount of their itemized deductions is less than the applicable standard deduction. No doubt there are a few taxpayers who fail to claim itemized deductions even when it would be to their benefit to do so, simply because they lack the energy or record-keeping skills necessary to determine and document their deductions. However, the largest dollar-value categories are usually easy to keep track of. The largest two categories are home mortgage interest and state and local taxes, and as to these little record-keeping is required. A taxpayer who has a home mortgage will receive Form 1098 from her mortgagee that will report mortgage interest and (usually) real estate taxes paid; the taxpayer's W-2 received from her employer will report any state and local income tax withholding. The third largest category, charitable contributions,

2. Authors' calculations based on Justin Bryan, "Individual Income Tax Returns, 2008," IRS, *Statistics of Income Bulletin*, Fall, 2010, at 5 (Fig. E, at 9).

may be more problematic. Even as to those items, however, gifts of $250 or more must ordinarily be acknowledged by the recipient, so that acknowledgment will usually be all that a taxpayer would need to determine and document the correct deductible amount.

For whatever reasons, in 2008, only 33.8 percent of all individual taxpayers itemized their deductions.[3] However, the significance of itemized deductions is greater than this statistic may suggest. The tendency to itemize is strongly correlated with income, which in turn is of course strongly correlated with the size of the tax liabilities. For taxpayers whose adjusted gross income was below $25,000 (about 41% of all taxpayers in 2008), only about 1 of every 13 itemized his deductions.[4] That rose to 37.9 percent of taxpayers in the income interval between $40,000 and $50,000; and nearly all taxpayers (88.2%) with adjusted gross incomes above $100,000 itemized deductions on their returns.[5]

The correlation between itemization rate and income is hardly surprising. Taxpayers in relatively high income groups are more likely to be homeowners, pay higher state and local taxes, and have more resources from which to make charitable contributions. Still, this correlation is a somewhat troubling feature of our tax system. Congress allows, for example, deductions for charitable contributions in part because it wishes to encourage such contributions, and thus to subsidize the organizations that receive them. But the realities of the choice between standard and itemized deductions dictate that no encouragement is offered to the two taxpayers out of three who do not itemize their deductions, and no deduction-related subsidy is provided to the charitable organizations supported by such taxpayers, except insofar as they are also able to attract wealthier, itemizing donors.

As just mentioned, deductions are sometimes allowed, at least in part, because of a conscious decision on the part of Congress that an activity or behavior pattern should be encouraged. Charitable contributions are the clearest example, though, as will be seen, even that deduction may derive from multiple or mixed congressional motives. In other cases, a deduction may be allowed because it could be called "income-defining." If, for example, an associate in a law firm joins the American Bar Association, subscribes to the *National Law Journal,* and invests in a laptop computer to use while working at home, the expenses associated with those items are costs of producing her salary as an associate and should be accounted for in determining the net income that the income tax is intended to reach.[6]

In some cases, Congress may allow a deduction simply to refine its differential assessment of tax burdens on the basis of the taxpayer's ability to pay. For example, imagine two taxpayers who have equal incomes of, say, $50,000. One enjoys perfect health over the course of the year, while the other is seriously injured and

---

3. *Id.* at 6, 9.

4. Authors' calculations based on *id.* at 22, 61.

5. *Id.* Even among taxpayers with adjusted gross incomes above $1 million, about 3 percent chose not to itemize their deductions. This is presumably due to the effect of §68, which reduces the amount of otherwise-allowable itemized deductions by as much as 80 percent for very high income taxpayers. (Section 68 does not apply, however, in 2010 through 2012.)

6. This assumes, of course, that she pays for these items from her own resources; if paid by the employer, no employee deduction would be appropriate, or allowed. As we shall see, however, despite the clear income-defining property of such expenses, they are in practice rarely deductible because of the floor on miscellaneous itemized deductions, discussed in section F of this chapter.

incurs $15,000 of medical costs in excess of any amounts covered by insurance. The second taxpayer has surely consumed goods and services of value, probably in amounts roughly equal to the first taxpayer. So, in the terms of the Haig-Simons income definition, there would be no reason to distinguish the two taxpayers. But Congress has decided that the second taxpayer's ability to pay tax has been abridged by the large and unexpected medical costs, and has accordingly adjusted the net tax burden imposed on that taxpayer by allowing a deduction for extraordinary medical expenses.

In a number of cases, the rationale for a deduction is somewhat muddled and probably reflects partial acceptance, or acceptance by some members of Congress but not others, of diverse rationales that may be at least mildly inconsistent with each other. A good example is the first of the deductions we will consider here — the deduction for charitable contributions under §170.

A.   CHARITABLE CONTRIBUTIONS UNDER §170

1. *The Rationale*

As noted above, one rationale for the deduction is simply to encourage taxpayers to support charitable organizations (and hence their activities). This can be justified either on the theory that the government is relieved of an obligation it would otherwise have had to meet, or on grounds that the charitable organization in any event provides a general public benefit. Legislative history suggests that this was what Congress had in mind in creating the deduction.[7]

This rationale is somewhat troubling, however, on several grounds. First, the charitable sector includes a number of organizations that a majority of Congress could not be persuaded to support with appropriations (such as organizations with very liberal or very conservative agendas), and many that Congress would not be *permitted* to support directly under the Constitution (such as religious organizations). Second, support in the form of a contributions deduction provides a greater incentive for high bracket taxpayers to contribute than it does for low bracket taxpayers, since the tax savings per dollar donated depends on the taxpayer's marginal tax rate (and on his status as an itemizer). Why would Congress do that, when it could have easily created a more uniform matching-grant program for individuals' contributions? Finally, it is not even completely clear that allowing deductions for contributions actually results in significantly greater charitable giving. A person who considers herself obligated to give one-tenth of her gross income to her church, for example, may give the same amount regardless of the deductibility of the amount given.

For these reasons, some commentators favor an alternative rationale based on the refinement of the concept of income. Under this view, the charitable gift is seen as

7. As a committee report on one of the early amendments to the deduction put it: "The [deduction] . . . is based upon the theory that the government is compensated for the loss of revenue by its relief from the financial burden which would otherwise have to be met by appropriations from public funds, and by the benefits resulting from the promotion of the general welfare." H.R. Rep. No. 1860, 75th Cong., 3d Sess., (1938), *reprinted in* 1939-1 C.B. (pt. 2) 728, 742.

reducing the consumption opportunities of the donating taxpayer by the amount of the charitable gift. Of course, voluntary reductions in consumption opportunities (such as a gift to a nephew) are not ordinarily accounted for by a reduction in the donor's income for tax purposes. But the altruistic aspect of transferring consumption opportunities to charitable organizations (and ultimately to the beneficiaries of those organizations' charitable activities) may justify more generous accounting for charitable gifts.[8]

2. Contributed Services

Treas. Reg. §1.170A-1(g) states flatly that "[n]o deduction is allowed under section 170 for a contribution of services." If, for example, an internal medicine specialist who could earn $200,000 by working five days per week decides instead to work Mondays through Thursdays for a for-profit medical practice group, but spends Fridays each week working without compensation at an AIDS clinic, he will not be allowed to deduct the value — presumably about one-fifth of $200,000, or $40,000 — of the services he contributes. On the other hand, neither will he be required to include any income that might have been imputed to him as a result of his performance of services on Fridays. His income will simply be the $160,000 that he makes from his four-day practice. To allow him both to exclude the $40,000 that he might have made on his Fridays, and to deduct another $40,000 as a charitable contribution, would be to allow the equivalent of a double deduction, taking him down to a taxable income of only $120,000 — what he could have earned in only a three-day week. But, clearly, his cash income is $160,000, undiminished by any charitable contribution, and that amount should remain in his tax base. The rule thus reflects the commonsense notion that one should not be treated as giving away what one was never treated as possessing. And it has the appealing virtue as well of putting our internist on the same footing as another hypothetical doctor who, let us say, specializes in the health problems of the rich — perhaps a plastic surgeon who exclusively performs face-lift operations. She finds no clear need among the poor for her services, but is as charitably inclined as her internist friend. Instead of contributing services, the plastic surgeon simply works all five days of the week in a paying practice, and contributes $40,000 in cash to the AIDS clinic. She *will* get a deduction for her $40,000 contribution, and will be left with the same $160,000 income — both disposable and taxable — as the internist.

3. The Amount of the Deduction — Appreciated Property

The vast majority of the time, the income tax rules follow this logical approach of not allowing a deduction for the loss of an amount that was never taken into income. There is an important exception, however, in the case of contributions to charity of appreciated property. Suppose a taxpayer gives a charity corporate stock with a basis of $10,000 and a value of $100,000. By the logic of the preceding paragraph, the deduction should be only $10,000. The income tax never treated

8. This rationale is far from immune to criticism. Among other things, it ignores the question of whether and when the beneficiaries to whom consumption opportunities have been transferred should be taxed on those receipts. For further discussion of this and the other points raised in this section, see the cell on "Rationale for the Charitable Contributions Deduction."

the taxpayer as having the $90,000 unrealized appreciation, so it makes no sense to treat him now as giving it away. Strangely enough, however, the taxpayer will usually be able to deduct the entire $100,000 value, including the $90,000 he never included in income. This accounting mistake, which has vigorous defenders within the charitable community but no coherent rationale, is not contained in the statute itself, but rather in the regulations, at §1.170A-1(c)(1), which states a background rule that the amount of the deduction for gifts of property is equal to the fair-market value of the property. But what started out as an oversight, or perhaps an act of charity, on the part of the Internal Revenue Service, has fossilized into a rule with enough history, and enough support of the charitable troops, that reversal as a practical matter is now possible only through legislative change.

In fact, Congress has chipped away marginally at the deduction for contributions of unrealized appreciation. In most cases, the unrealized gain in donated property is deductible only if:

- the gain would have been long-term capital gain had the taxpayer sold the property;
- in the case of a contribution of tangible personal property, the use of the property by the charity is related to the charity's tax-exempt purpose,[9] and
- the property is not given to a "private foundation," a category of charities that has been singled out for special treatment in a number of respects.[10]

In addition to violating tax logic, the deduction for unrealized appreciation encourages taxpayers to put unrealistically high values on donated property, and leads to frequent tax litigation over the value of contributed property. This is not a problem for publicly traded stocks and bonds, of course, but it is a serious problem for closely held stock, art objects and other collectibles, and real estate. Section 170(f)(11)(C) requires a taxpayer to obtain an appraisal for donated property with a claimed value of more than $5,000. While helpful, this provision has by no means eliminated disputes over valuation of contributed property.

The following case illustrates some of the difficulties that arise from the differing treatment of contributions of services and of property.

LARY v. UNITED STATES
787 F.2d 1538 (11th Cir. 1986)

Dr. John Lary and Sherry Lary ("Taxpayers") appeal from a decision of the district court holding that the Commissioner of Internal Revenue ("Commissioner") properly disallowed certain deductions on their 1975 and 1976 tax returns. We affirm.

On their 1975 and 1976 joint tax returns, Taxpayers claimed . . . deductions for . . . the value of a pint of blood donated by Dr. Lary to the Red Cross in 1976. The Commissioner disallowed these deductions, and after paying the deficiencies asserted by the Commissioner, Taxpayers filed suit in district court for a refund.

9. For example, a taxpayer could deduct the full fair market value of antique furniture donated to a furniture museum, but the deduction would be limited to basis if the furniture were donated to a college to be sold at a fund-raising auction.
10. The rules noted in this "bullet" paragraph are contained in §170(e). There is an important exception to the last of these for certain publicly traded stock. *See* §170(e)(5).

The district court held . . . that . . . the Commissioner properly disallowed the deduction for the value of the donated blood because the donation of blood constitutes the performance of a service, which expressly does not qualify as a charitable contribution under the regulations.

Taxpayers argue on appeal that they are entitled to deduct the fair market value of the blood donated by Dr. Lary to the Red Cross. The district court held that the blood donation was the contribution of a personal service, and thus not deductible, see Rev. Rul. 162, 1953-2 C.B. 127, but Taxpayers argue that the donation of blood is the contribution of property rather than the performance of a service. We need not decide whether the donation of blood constitutes the performance of a service or the contribution of a product because Taxpayers cannot claim a charitable deduction under either interpretation.[11] If the donation of blood were the performance of a service, then Taxpayers are not entitled to a charitable deduction because the regulations expressly prohibit charitable deductions for the performance of services.

On the other hand, if the donation of blood were the contribution of a product, Taxpayers would still not be entitled to a charitable deduction. Section 170(e)(1)(A) of the Internal Revenue Code of 1954 provides that the amount of any charitable contribution of property shall be reduced by "the amount of gain which would not have been long-term capital gain if the property contributed had been sold by the taxpayer at its fair market value (determined at the time of such contribution)." I.R.C. section 170(e)(1)(A). In other words, if the property donated to charity would have resulted in ordinary income or short-term capital gain to the donor had the property instead been sold, the donor's charitable deduction would not include any amounts attributable to such gain, but rather would be limited to his adjusted basis in the property.

In the instant case, section 170(e)(1)(A)'s limitation on charitable contributions precludes any charitable deduction for the value of the donated blood. Taxpayers have proffered no evidence as to any basis in the donated blood or that the holding period for blood is more than six [now 12] months,[12] which is the required holding period for a capital asset to qualify for long-term capital gain treatment, see I.R.C. section 1222(3). Since Taxpayers have the burden of proof on both issues, and since Taxpayers have made no effort to shoulder that burden, we conclude that Taxpayers are not entitled to a charitable deduction under section 170(e)(1)(A). . . .

The judgment of the district court is therefore Affirmed.

Notes and Questions

1. *Service or property?* What do you think of the IRS's position that a blood donor is really giving the charity his services, rather than tangible personal

---

11. We note that there is authority for both propositions. *Compare* Rev. Rul. 162, 1953-2 C.B. 127 (no charitable deduction for the value of donated blood because the donation of blood constitutes the performance of a service), *with* Green v. Commissioner, 74 T.C. 1229, 1234 (1980) (for purpose of determining taxable income, sale of blood is the sale of a tangible product).

12. Red blood cells have an average finite life of approximately four months, and blood platelets have an average life of approximately ten days. *See* 2 *Encyclopedia Britannica* 1117-21 (15th ed. 1984).

property? Note that the donor and donee may have different viewpoints on this. From the donor's view, the cost of the contribution probably consists of the time it takes to draw the blood and the mild discomfort of having it drawn. The loss of the blood itself is inconsequential, since it is easily and quickly replaced by natural processes. From the viewpoint of the Red Cross, however, it is the acquisition of a product that matters; it is obviously not interested in your act of bleeding *per se*.

2. *Keep those receipts.* As the court notes, if blood is property the taxpayer would be entitled to a deduction for his basis in the blood, even if he had not owned the blood long enough to satisfy the long-term capital gains holding period. How would a taxpayer prove a basis in his own blood? Would it help if he was a regular consumer of Geritol?

3. *Frozen assets.* The opinion seems to turn on the facts set forth in footnote 12 (footnote 3 in the original numbering). Apparently Dr. Lary would have been entitled to a deduction if only red blood cells had had the decency to live a little longer (more than six months would have been required at the time of *Lary;* §1222 now requires more than one year). If Dr. Lary had drawn his own blood and frozen it, could he contribute it at a later date and deduct the fair market value of the blood?

4. *Amount of the Deduction — Introduction to Quid Pro Quo Issues*

Ordinarily, a charitable contributions deduction is available only for the net value that flows to the charitable target. This topic is more fully explored below in a cell on this topic, but the following case will introduce the general nature of the problem.

ROLFS v. COMMISSIONER
135 T.C. 471 (2010)

GALE, Judge: Respondent determined a deficiency of $19,940 in petitioners' Federal income tax for 1998 and an accuracy-related penalty equal to 20 percent of the underpayment under section 6662(a). By their amended petition, petitioners aver that they are entitled to a charitable contribution deduction of $235,350, rather than the $76,000 claimed on their return, as a result of a donation of a house to a local volunteer fire department, resulting in an overpayment of $39,672 for 1998. By answer to the amended petition, respondent asserts that petitioners are liable for a penalty under section 6662(h) for a gross valuation misstatement. The issues for decision are: (1) Whether petitioners are entitled to a deduction for a charitable contribution under section 170(a) in connection with their donation of a house to a local volunteer fire department for training exercises and demolition and (2) whether petitioners are liable for any accuracy-related penalty under section 6662.

FINDINGS OF FACT

. . .

THE LAKE PROPERTY

On November 27, 1996, petitioners paid $600,000 for a fee simple interest in a 3-acre lakefront property at 5892 Oakland Road in the Village of Chenequa, Wisconsin (lake property). The lake property was on Pine Lake in an area known locally as "lake country" — a desirable residential area where lakefront houses have historically commanded premium prices. The lake property was accessed by a private road owned by an association, the members of which were the homeowners living on the road.

At the time of purchase there were several improvements on the lake property including a house (lake house), a detached garage, a boathouse, and a well and septic system. The lake house, originally built in approximately 1900, was a 1 1/2-story structure with 3,138 square feet of living space, including a stone facade addition that was constructed in the 1950s. The lake house was in good condition and habitable, though in need of remodeling in petitioner's view.

For 1998 the Village of Chenequa, Waukesha County, Wisconsin, assessed the lake property at $460,100, allocating $323,000 to the land and $137,100 to the improvements, for local property tax purposes.

After acquiring the lake house, petitioners were initially undecided regarding whether to remodel it or tear it down. Their deliberations were resolved when . . . Beatrice Gallagher [Mr. Rolfs' mother-in-law] suggested in late 1997 that petitioners demolish the lake house, build a new house to her specifications as her residence in its place, and then exchange the lake property for her existing residence. Petitioners agreed to Mrs. Gallagher's proposal, and they carried out the plan as described below. . . .

DEMOLITION OF THE LAKE HOUSE

Sometime in the latter part of 1997 petitioner determined that it would cost $10,000 to $15,000 to demolish the lake house and remove the debris. Around the same time, petitioner learned from his brother of an individual who had claimed a charitable contribution deduction for donating a residence to a local fire department to be burned down. Petitioner decided to donate the lake house to the Village of Chenequa Volunteer Fire Department (VFD) for firefighter training exercises and demolition in a controlled burn and to claim a charitable contribution deduction for the value of the lake house.

In early October 1997 petitioner obtained the necessary approval for the burn from the Wisconsin Department of Natural Resources (DNR), subject to petitioner's notifying the DNR of the actual date of the burn.

On February 10, 1998, petitioner sent a letter to Gary Wieczorek, the chief of the VFD and of the Chenequa Police Department (Chief Wieczorek), which stated:

> As we have discussed, I would like to donate our house located at 5192 Oakland Road in the Village of Chenequa to the Fire and Police departments of the Village for training and eventually demolition. This letter shall serve as an acknowledgment that it is my

intention to donate the house for such purposes. The house is available immediately. If any further approvals are needed please contact me.

Chief Wieczorek understood that petitioners donated the lake house to the Village of Chenequa for the limited purpose of using the structure for training exercises of firefighters and police, and with the ultimate aim of having the VFD burn it down. He also understood that petitioners expected that the lake house would be destroyed within "the first part of that year [1998]." Chief Wieczorek further understood that the VFD could not use the lake house for any other purpose than training exercises that would include its destruction by fire.

Sometime shortly before February 18, 1998, the Chenequa Police Department used the lake house for a training exercise. On February 18, 1998, the VFD conducted an initial training exercise at the lake house. On February 21, 1998, 11 days after petitioner's letter donating the lake house, the VFD conducted a second training exercise and burned the structure to the ground.

The firefighter training exercises at the lake house allowed the VFD to satisfy monthly training requirements imposed under Wisconsin State law. Chief Wieczorek believed the firefighter training exercises conducted at the lake house were superior to the training exercises otherwise available to the VFD. . . .

On March 30, 1998, approximately 5 weeks after the destruction of the lake house, petitioners entered into a contract to have a new residence constructed on the lake property at a cost of approximately $383,000. The construction contract did not itemize the costs of construction.

Petitioners timely filed a joint Federal income tax return for the taxable year 1998. Petitioners attached to the return a Form 8283, Noncash Charitable Contributions, reporting that the lake house had a cost or adjusted basis of $100,000, and that the lake house was appraised at a fair market value of $76,000. The Form 8283 included a "Declaration of Appraiser" signed by Richard S. Larkin and a "Donee Acknowledgment" signed by Chief Wieczorek. Petitioners claimed on Schedule A, Itemized Deductions, a deduction of $12,626 attributable to charitable contributions by cash or check and a deduction of $83,632 attributable to charitable contributions other than by cash or check (which included a $76,000 deduction claimed for the donation of the lake house). Petitioners attached to the return a summary appraisal report prepared by Richard S. Larkin of Larkin Appraisals, Inc., dated December 31, 1997, in support of the charitable contribution deduction claimed with respect to the lake house. [The $76,000 attributable to the lake house was disallowed as a charitable contribution deduction by the IRS, and the taxpayers filed a timely petition for review by the Tax Court. They subsequently amended their petition to claim a higher value — $235,350 — for the lake house.]

. . .

OPINION

I. CHARITABLE CONTRIBUTION DEDUCTIONS

Section 170(a)(1) provides in relevant part that a deduction is allowed for any charitable contribution, payment of which is made within the taxable year. Section 170(c)(1) defines the term "charitable contribution" to include a contribution or gift to or for the use of, inter alia, a political subdivision of a State, but only if the gift is made for exclusively public purposes.

The Supreme Court has defined "contribution or gift" for purposes of section 170 as follows:

> The legislative history of the "contribution or gift" limitation [of section 170], though sparse, reveals that Congress intended to differentiate between unrequited payments to qualified recipients and payments made to such recipients in return for goods or services. Only the former were deemed deductible. The House and Senate Reports on the 1954 tax bill, for example, both define "gifts" as payments "made with no expectation of a financial return commensurate with the amount of the gift." . . . [Hernandez v. Commissioner, 490 U.S. 680, 690 (1989).]

Thus, "A payment of money generally cannot constitute a charitable contribution if the contributor expects a substantial benefit in return." United States v. American Bar Endowment, 477 U.S. 105, 116 (1986).

The Supreme Court has further instructed that in ascertaining whether a given payment or property transfer was made with the expectation of any return benefit or quid pro quo, we are to examine the external, structural features of the transaction, which obviates the need for imprecise inquiries into the motivations of individual taxpayers.

If a charitable contribution is made in property other than money, the amount of the contribution is generally the fair market value of the property at the time of the contribution. Sec. 1.170A-1(c)(1), Income Tax Regs. "[F]air market value" for this purpose "is the price at which the property would change hands between a willing buyer and a willing seller, neither being under any compulsion to buy or sell and both having reasonable knowledge of the relevant facts." Sec. 1.170A-1(c)(2), Income Tax Regs. Restrictions on the property's use or marketability on the date of the contribution must be taken into account in the determination of fair market value.

Respondent contends that petitioners are not entitled to a deduction for a charitable contribution in connection with their donation of the lake house to the VFD because they anticipated and received a substantial benefit in exchange for the contribution; namely, demolition services. Petitioners therefore did not make a charitable contribution within the meaning of section 170(c), as interpreted in United States v. Am. Bar Endowment, *supra,* because the fair market value of the lake house as donated did not exceed the fair market value of the demolition services petitioners received from the VFD in exchange for the donation (quid pro quo argument). Respondent argues in the alternative that (1) the charitable contribution deduction in dispute is disallowed under section 170(f)(3)(A) because petitioners transferred to the VFD less than their entire interest in the lake house; and (2) the lake house as donated to the VFD was worthless.

. . . Petitioners assert that the Court should not consider respondent's quid pro quo argument (to the effect that petitioners received a benefit in exchange for their donation) because this argument constitutes new matter that respondent raised for the first time in his opening brief. However, if respondent is allowed to raise the quid pro quo argument, petitioners contend that they donated property with a fair market value of $76,000 (according to a qualified appraisal) which they have shown should be valued at its reproduction cost of $235,350 and that they received only an "incidental benefit" in return. Petitioners contend that section 170(f)(3)(A) is inapplicable because in transferring the lake house to the VFD with the right to demolish it, they transferred their entire interest in the property. . . .

DEVELOPMENT OF THE QUID PRO QUO TEST

Respondent argues that petitioners are not entitled to a charitable contribution deduction for their donation of the lake house because they anticipated and received a substantial benefit in exchange for the donation; namely, the demolition of the lake house on a site where they intended to rebuild. Respondent contends that the value of the demolition services received exceeded the value of the property petitioners transferred, eliminating any charitable intent from the transaction. As noted, respondent relies on United States v. Am. Bar Endowment, *supra,* and on section 1.170A-1(h)(1), Income Tax Regs.

In United States v. Am. Bar Endowment, *supra* at 116, the Supreme Court set forth the principle that a payment of money generally cannot constitute a charitable contribution if the contributor expects a substantial benefit in return. "The *sine qua non* of a charitable contribution is a transfer of money or property without adequate consideration." *Id.* at 118. However, the Court also recognized that a taxpayer's payment to a charitable organization that is accompanied by his receipt of a benefit may have a "dual character" of a purchase and a contribution" if the payment exceeds the value of the benefit received in return. *Id.* at 117. The Court consequently adopted a two-part test (first articulated in Rev. Rul. 67-246, 1967-2 C.B. 104) for determining when part of a dual payment is deductible. "First, the payment is deductible only if and to the extent it exceeds the market value of the benefit received. Second, the excess payment must be made with the intention of making a gift." *Id.* The *Am. Bar Endowment* test has since been incorporated into the regulations. See sec. 1.170A-1(h), Income Tax Regs.; 11 T.D. 8690, 1997-1 C.B. 68. The test also applies where payment is made in property other than money.

Petitioner had decided to demolish the lake house and construct another residence on the site when he contacted the VFD about donating the lake house to be burned down for training purposes. Consequently, examining the external features of the transaction, as we must, we find that petitioner anticipated a benefit in exchange for the contribution: demolition of the lake house. On similar facts, this Court decided in a Memorandum Opinion, Scharf v. Commissioner, T.C. Memo. 1973-265, that the taxpayer was entitled to a charitable contribution deduction for the donation of a structure, equal to its value for insurance purposes. We reasoned in *Scharf* as follows:

> we conclude . . . that the benefit flowing back to petitioner, consisting of clearer land, was far less than the greater benefit flowing to the volunteer fire department's training and equipment testing operations. . . . We think the petitioner benefited only incidentally from the demolition of the building and that the community was primarily benefited in its fire control and prevention operations. Consequently, on balance, we hold that the petitioner is entitled to a charitable contribution deduction.

The test applied in *Scharf,* which examines whether *the value of the public benefit* of the donation exceeded the value of the benefit received by the donor, differs from the Supreme Court's test announced 13 years later in United States v. Am. Bar Endowment, 477 U.S. 105 (1986). The *Am. Bar Endowment* test examines whether the *fair market value of the contributed property* exceeded the fair market value of the benefit received by the donor. The test applied in *Scharf* has no vitality after *Am. Bar Endowment.* Instead, we must consider whether the value of the lake house as donated exceeded the value of the demolition services petitioners received.

APPLICATION OF THE QUID PRO QUO TEST

a. *Value of the Benefit Received*

Petitioner testified that his investigation revealed that it would cost approximately $10,000 to $15,000 to have the lake house demolished and the debris removed. This estimate is consistent with those of both of respondent's experts. . . .

Petitioners nonetheless dispute the conclusion that they saved demolition costs of at least $10,000 by virtue of their donation of the lake house to the VFD. Petitioner claimed in his testimony that the cost of the contract to construct the new house for Mrs. Gallagher included "$10,000 to $15,000" in excavation charges for clearing the remnants of the burn and the concrete foundation of the lake house. Petitioners argue on brief that these additional excavation costs demonstrate that petitioners did not save anything from the demolition resulting from the burning and therefore received no benefit from their donation of the lake house to the VFD.

We reject this contention. First, the documentary evidence tends to undermine the claim that the construction contract for the new residence included $10,000 or more for excavation charges associated with clearing the remnants of the burn. The construction contract for the new house, as included in the record, does not contain any allocation of the total contract price for any specific cost — excavation, debris removal, or otherwise. Moreover, a preprinted portion of the contract covering "Building Site Conditions" has been lined through by the parties to the contract, creating an inference that the contract price did *not* cover any significant debris or foundation removal services. Second, two experts, plus whomever petitioner consulted, estimated the cost of demolition *and* debris removal for the lake house as at least $10,000. We do not believe that debris removal alone accounted for these estimates. A much more plausible inference is that the cost of the labor and equipment for the demolition constituted a significant portion of the estimate. On this record, we are persuaded that petitioners saved at least $10,000 in the cost of demolition services as a result of their arrangements with the VFD for the donation of the lake house for burning. They accordingly received a benefit with a fair market value in that amount in exchange for the donation.

b. *Value of the Property Donated*

Because petitioners received a substantial benefit in exchange for their donation of the lake house, their entitlement to any charitable contribution deduction under the *Am. Bar Endowment* test depends upon whether the value of the lake house as donated exceeded the value of the demolition services. As noted, the lake house's value for this purpose is its fair market value at the time of the donation, as measured by the willing buyer/willing seller standard in section 1.170A-1(c)(2), Income Tax Regs. Of particular importance here, the fair market value of contributed property must take into account any restrictions or conditions limiting the property's marketability on the date of the contribution. The restrictions or conditions that must be taken into account include those imposed by the donor incident to the contribution of the property.

Petitioners contend, and we agree, that their donation of the lake house to the VFD, without their conveyance of the underlying land on which it was sited, effected a "constructive severance" of the structure from the land, recognized under Wisconsin law, even though the structure remained affixed to the land. By transferring the lake house to the VFD without the underlying land, however, petitioners created a substantial restriction or condition on the property's marketability; namely, the lake house could not remain indefinitely on the land upon which it was sited.

Petitioners attached two additional restrictions or conditions on the lake house incident to its donation; namely, the permissible use of the lake house was restricted to firefighter and police training exercises and there was a condition that the lake house be burned down relatively soon after the conveyance. Petitioner's letter memorializing the transfer, though informal, stated that the lake house was to be used by the VFD "for training and eventually demolition," and VFD Chief Wieczorek testified that he understood he could not use the lake house for any other purpose and that the burndown was to take place during the first part of 1998. Thus, in addition to being severed from its underlying land, the lake house as donated could not be used for residential purposes and was subject to a condition that it be promptly burned down.

Petitioners offered the appraisal of their expert, Mr. Larkin, in support of their claim that the lake house had a fair market value of at least $76,000 when donated. In his appraisal Mr. Larkin opined that the lake house had a "contributory value" of $76,000 on the basis of a "before and after" approach to value, which treated the value of the donated lake house as equal to the difference between the fair market value of the lake property *with* the lake house and the fair market value of the lake property *without* the lake house. . . .

However, since the starting point of Mr. Larkin's calculation was the market value of the lake property as a whole, as measured by sales of comparable properties *where the houses could remain on their sites indefinitely and were available for residential use,* the "contributory value" for the lake house he derived, by subtracting the value of the land and other improvements, necessarily valued the lake house on the basis of its being available for residential use and affixed to the site indefinitely. Thus, the $76,000 "contributory value" of the lake house postulated by Mr. Larkin at best reflects the value of the lake house *before* taking into account its severance from the underlying land, the prohibition on residential use, and the condition that it be burned down promptly. Consequently, the property interest Mr. Larkin appraised is not comparable to the property interest that petitioners donated to the VFD. . . .

The price at which the lake house would change hands would undoubtedly be affected by the condition that the structure could not remain affixed to its underlying land indefinitely. Petitioners offered no evidence concerning the impact of this condition. Respondent offered the testimony of two experts in the field of house moving regarding the price at which the lake house would likely sell if required to be moved from its existing site. Both house moving experts concluded that the likelihood of a buyer's purchasing the lake house to move it from the site was virtually nil, because the characteristics of the lake house and its site rendered a relocation of the structure infeasible. We are persuaded that the expert testimony concerning the market for the lake house as a structure to be moved provides a reasonable basis for estimating the impact on fair market value of the severance of the lake house from its underlying land. We find that the severance rendered the lake house virtually worthless.

As for the impact on the lake house's fair market value of the remaining conditions petitioners imposed incident to the donation (the restriction of use to firefighter and police training exercises and the condition that the structure be promptly burned down), there is insufficient evidence in the record to support anything beyond speculation. We are persuaded, however, that the impact on fair market value of the foregoing encumbrances would be adverse rather than beneficial. Finally, as for the possibility that the lake house as encumbered by petitioners' restrictions had a fair market value equal to its salvage value, respondent's expert Mr. George provided expert testimony to the effect that the lake house's salvage value was zero. On the basis of his examination of photographs and a video of the lake house, and a description of its features, Mr. George opined that the value of any salvageable materials would be offset by the costs of removing them. As a consequence, we are persuaded by the evidence that the lake house had no salvage value.

CONCLUSION

On the basis of the entire record, we conclude that respondent prevails on his quid pro quo argument. We are persuaded by the evidence that petitioners anticipated a substantial benefit in exchange for their donation of the lake house, in the form of demolition services worth approximately $10,000, and that the fair market value of the lake house as donated did not exceed that figure. Petitioners have failed to prove the lake house had a fair market value exceeding $10,000, because the expert testimony they offered to prove value failed to account for substantial conditions and restrictions imposed on the property incident to its donation, including in particular its severance from the underlying land. The remaining evidence supports a conclusion that the fair market value of the lake house as encumbered at the time of the donation was de minimis. The lake house could not remain on the land on which it was sited, could not be used for residential purposes, yet had no value as a structure to be moved or any salvage value. We therefore hold that petitioners are not entitled to any charitable contribution deduction for the donation of the lake house because they have not satisfied the *Am. Bar Endowment* test: they have not shown that the market value of the property they donated exceeded the market value of the benefit they received in exchange.

Notes and Questions

1. *Burnt offerings.* The basic idea reflected in this case had gained considerable popularity among the set of taxpayers in a position to buy an old house in a desirable neighborhood with the intention of tearing it down and replacing it with a McMansion. ESPN commentator and former Ohio State quarterback Kirk Herbstreit apparently decided that this was a play worth calling, as did former NBA player and Oregon gubernatorial candidate Chris Dudley. *Rolfs* is the first of these cases to reach the Tax Court, but there will probably be more. As this edition went to press, the Rolfs had not appealed their case to the Seventh Circuit, but such an appeal would still have been timely. In a portion of the opinion that has been omitted, the Tax Court denied the IRS's assessment of accuracy-related penalties, noting that while *American Bar Endowment* may have cast doubt on the continuing validity of the *Scharf* opinion, no federal court had to that point explicitly reached that conclusion. Now that *Rolfs* has been decided, will courts in the future be more willing to consider imposition of accuracy-related penalties on taxpayers who claim deductions such as these?

2. *Barn razing.* Imagine a variant on the *Rolfs* facts. Suppose Ralph owns a farm that includes an old barn, on a part of the property not visible either from the main farmhouse or any public road. Its condition and obsolescence make it useless to Ralph, but its location means that it isn't an eyesore, either. Ralph had considered donating it to the local fire department for training exercises, but he is not a particularly altruistic or public-spirited person. When he hears that he probably can't deduct anything, he concludes that it is not

worth the trouble of making the contractual and insurance arrangements necessary to authorize the fire department to raze the barn. Suppose further that the fire department would have valued the exercise at $20,000, and that the county had even authorized the department to spend up to that amount acquiring a property for this purpose, if it could not obtain a donation of a suitable building. Should we be concerned that the tax rule adopted by the regulations, and endorsed by the court in *Rolfs*, seems to have denied the fire department an opportunity to save local tax money?

3. *Value received or value given?* As a more general matter, the tax rules in this area seem to vacillate on the question of whether the appropriate inquiry is aimed at evaluating what is received by the donee or what is given up by the donor. In some ways, the rules seem to focus on the donee's situation, as when Congress justified the deduction by saying: "The exemption from taxation of money or property devoted to charitable and other purposes is based upon the theory that the Government is compensated for the loss of revenue by its relief from financial burden which would otherwise have to be met by appropriations from public funds. . . . " H.R. Rep. No. 1860, 75th Cong., 3d Sess. (1938), reprinted in 1939-1 C.B. (pt. 2) 728, 742. (Note that this was in connection with a 1938 amendment of the predecessor of §170, which dates from 1917.) And even in the very recent decision in *Rolfs* itself, the court values the property by looking at the value received by the fire department — prominently including the restrictions on its use of the property — rather than the value given up by the taxpayer, which of course would have involved no such restrictions.

On the other hand, the rules precluding deductions for gifts of services or the use of property described in the text preceding *Rolfs* reflect the view that the value to the donee is irrelevant, and that no deduction should be allowed because the donor either had given up nothing, or, if the donor has given up an opportunity to earn a return on the labor or property donated, he has already been adequately compensated for that by the omission of any imputed income resulting from that donation. Which of these views should predominate our analysis of the amount of the charitable deduction? Or is there a role for both considerations?

5. *Eligible Recipients of Charitable Contributions*

To be deductible, a contribution must be made to an organization that is either a governmental unit, or a corporation, trust, or similar organization that is organized and operated for one of several stated charitable purposes, prominently including religious, charitable, and educational purposes. The language of §170(c), which defines the eligible organizations to which deductible contributions can be made, substantially tracks the language of §501(c)(3), which is the provision providing exemption from federal tax for charitable organizations.

6. *Limitations on Deductions and Carryovers*

Section 170(b) imposes some limits on charitable contribution deductions based on the taxpayer's income. In general, an individual taxpayer's deduction for any given tax year is limited to 50 percent of the taxpayer's "contribution base," which in most cases is simply his adjusted gross income.[13] Other limitations apply in special cases. For example, gifts made to "private foundations" are deductible only to the extent of 30 percent of the contribution base. A 30 percent limit also applies to gifts of appreciated property, and a special 20 percent limit applies to gifts of appreciated property that are made to private foundations. These limits are applied sequentially; that is, the total of all gifts is first compared with the overall 50 percent limit. If it exceeds that limit, the deductions disallowed are considered to come from the least-favored category first.

For example, if a taxpayer with a contribution base of $100,000 makes cash gifts to public charities of $40,000, and cash gifts to private foundations of $30,000, the overall limit will permit only $50,000 to be deducted, and that amount is considered to represent all of the $40,000 given to the public charities, and $10,000 of the $30,000 given to private foundations.[14] In this case, the $10,000 allowed for the private foundation gifts will not itself violate the 30 percent limit applying to such contributions. However, if this taxpayer had given $10,000 to public charities and $60,000 to private foundations, the overall limit would, as before, disallow $20,000 of contributions, leaving $10,000 of contributions to public charities and $40,000 of contributions to private foundations deductible. However, in this alternative case, the 30 percent limit on private foundation contributions would permit the deduction of only $30,000 of such contributions. Thus, the taxpayer would be allowed, after application of both limits, a deduction of $40,000, consisting of the $10,000 of contributions to public charities, and $30,000 of the $60,000 contributed to private foundations.

Any amounts that are disallowed by these rules may be carried over by the taxpayer and deducted in up to five subsequent years, pursuant to the rules of §170(d). The charitable gifts retain their character in the carryover year; that is, the $30,000 of contributions disallowed in the previous example would be considered as contributions to private foundations in the following year. If nondeductible in that year because they were in excess of the contribution limits, they would be carried over to the following year, and so on.

These percentage limitations seem high enough that most taxpayers need not be much concerned with them, and this is largely true. There are a few situations where the limits may become problematic, however. First, taxpayers who are members of certain religious orders may have taken vows of poverty that call for all of their income to be turned over to the order. In some cases, they may be able, in effect, to assign their income to the order, such as by agreeing to work for no compensation. In other cases, they may need to retain enough income to pay the tax on the 50 percent of their income that cannot be shielded by a charitable contribution deduction.[15]

Taxpayers may also encounter difficulty with these limits if they wish to make a single large gift in one tax year. For example, if a taxpayer wanted to give a large

---

13. In the rare case in which an individual taxpayer has a net operating loss carryback in the year of the contribution, the "contribution base" is AGI before application of that carryback.

14. Treas. Regs. §1.170A-8(f), ex. 1.

15. Some curious exceptions to this rule have been made by statute, some of which were drafted so narrowly that they only applied to a single case. For example, in 1924, Congress effectively exempted the income of Mother Katherine Drexel, allowing her a full deduction for the income from a sizable family trust that she had diverted to a foundation created to provide schools for African-American and Native American children. Mother Drexel was canonized by Pope John Paul II in 2002 (presumably for her accomplishments outside the tax-legislation arena).

parcel of appreciated real estate to a college in a single tax year, the amount of the contribution could exceed 30 percent of her adjusted gross income in that year. A very wealthy taxpayer also sometimes finds himself in the position of having an adjusted gross income that is modest relative to his wealth. For example, an entrepreneur in a high-tech company may have huge wealth in the form of the stock of his company. But that stock may pay no dividends, and his salary from the company may be a tiny fraction of his wealth. If he makes gifts commensurate with his wealth, he is likely to find that *any* limitation based on adjusted gross income will reduce the tax benefits of charitable giving. A person with a wealth of $1 billion and an income of $10 million, for example, will find that charitable gifts of as little as half of 1 percent of his wealth will throw him into a range beyond which charitable gifts are no longer deductible.

For whatever reasons, a significant number of taxpayers do find that their charitable contributions are limited by the rules of §170(b). On 2008 returns, taxpayers deducted $26.4 billion of charitable contributions carried forward from earlier years.[16]

Corporate taxpayers are subject to a different limitation: They may deduct up to 10 percent of their taxable income, computed without regard to their charitable gifts, their dividends-received deduction, and any carrybacks for capital or operating losses. Section 170(b)(2). This limitation is somewhat less troublesome than the individual limitations, presumably because most corporate directors believe that their shareholders are the ones who should decide how much of the corporate profits should be paid over to charities. Directors do often believe that some local cultural and benevolent organizations should be supported; however, overall corporate giving amounts to only about 1 percent of net corporate income in most years. The problem in this case is that a corporation may commit to gifts before it has complete information about what its net income in the taxable year will be. But most are presumably conservative in this respect; and the fact that carrybacks of losses do not reduce the amount of income considered for purposes of setting the deductible limit means that reversals of fortune in subsequent years will not retroactively disallow deductions for charitable contributions.

Problem 1.   Henry made gifts to two charitable organizations in 2011. His adjusted gross income that year was $100,000, and he had no net operating loss carryovers. His gifts consisted of:

- 1,000 shares of Starbucks stock, given to his alma mater, Faber College. He had purchased the stock in 1993 for $2000, and it had a market value on the date of contribution of $30,000.
- Weekly checks written to his church of $100 each, totaling $5,200 over the course of the year.

What charitable contribution deduction may Henry claim in 2011?

Problem 2.   What deductions would be allowed in 2011 for the gifts in Problem 1 if Henry's adjusted gross income had been only $80,000?

Problem 3.   Assume the facts of Problem 1, except that Henry sold the vacant lot next to his house in order to make a special gift to the church's building fund. The

16. Bryan, *supra* note 2, at 66.

lot had been purchased several years ago for $10,000, and Henry sold it for $20,000. He then gave the proceeds to the church. What charitable contribution deduction may Henry claim in 2011 given these facts? Could he have improved the outcome by structuring this gift differently?

Problem 4. Julie is preparing her income tax return for the year recently ended. Her AGI for the year was $300,000. She made one charitable contribution during that year — a gift to her church of land (which she had owned for many years) with a value of $150,000 and a basis of $145,000. What is the maximum charitable contribution she can properly claim on the return? Hint: Look at §170(b)(1)(C)(iii).

B. INTEREST EXPENSE

1. History and Rationale

For most of the first 70 or so years of the history of the American income tax, taxpayers could deduct interest payments in most circumstances. Indeed, the general rule allowing interest deductions suggests that this is still the case: §163(a) says simply that taxpayers may deduct "all interest paid or accrued within the taxable year on indebtedness." The broad sweep of this rule had been circumscribed from time to time in a few areas, as needed to close off abuses. Sections 265 and 264 disallow deductions for interest paid on certain loans used to produce tax exempt income — from municipal bond purchases in the first case, and from life insurance and annuity contracts in the second case. And, in 1969, §163(d) was added to disallow deductions for interest with respect to debts incurred to finance investments, but only to the extent that the interest expense exceeded aggregate investment income.

But the biggest blow for interest expense deductions came in the Tax Reform Act of 1986. As part of a general effort by Congress to broaden the tax base by narrowing deductions wherever possible, it added, in §163(h), a rule that disallows deductions for "personal interest." There are a number of important exceptions to the disallowance rule, but it is fair to say that the disallowance rule of §163(h) effectively reverses, for individual taxpayers, the presumption of §163(a) in favor of deductibility.

Whether interest payments *should* generally be deductible is a controversial question. Under the Haig-Simons income definition, where income equals the value of rights exercised in consumption plus (or minus) changes in wealth within each taxable year, it is clear that the payment of interest reduces wealth. However, if interest payments constitute a form of consumption, then any diminution of the wealth term would be offset by a precisely equal increase in the consumption term, suggesting that no net effect on income should be recognized due to the interest payment (and hence no deduction allowed for that payment).

Some commentators argue that interest payments are indeed a form of consumption, in the sense that they reflect taxpayers' tastes regarding the point in time at which consumption takes place. If a taxpayer wishes to take an expensive vacation to Europe that is beyond his means at the moment, he may decide either to borrow money to take the vacation now, or to save money to finance a vacation that he takes only when he has saved enough to pay for it without borrowing. Just as it is more expensive to vacation in Europe than it would be to repair to the nearest beach, so too is it more expensive to take that vacation now rather than later. The choices both of where and when to take the vacation are part of the package that a taxpayer decides to consume, all features of which constitute consumption. At least so this argument goes.[17]

Others have argued that in an income tax system that treats the effect of deferring consumption as something that generally creates taxable income (in the form of interest or other investment income), a reasonable symmetry in the design of the tax requires that the cost of accelerating consumption should be deductible. The force of this argument can perhaps be seen best by considering three taxpayers, each of whom has a salary income of $50,000 in a particular tax year. Taxpayer A also has debts of $100,000, and must pay $10,000 during the tax year to pay interest on those debts. B has neither debts nor investments. C has an investment portfolio consisting of $100,000 of securities that generate income of $10,000 during the tax year. The income tax requires the inclusion of the investment income on C's return, causing him to have a gross income of $60,000, thereby distinguishing him from taxpayer B. This seems sound, since C will indeed either be able to consume that much more than B during the year, or store up the investment income as an increase in wealth.

But having distinguished C from B, should not the tax rules also distinguish A from B? After all, A is worse off than B by precisely the amount that C is better off than B, and for similar reasons: B's freedom from debt means that the whole of his $50,000 income is available for consumption (less any amounts payable as tax, of course), while A will have only $40,000 available for consumption (and taxes) after payment of his interest obligations. In a way, one could say that interest payments constitute negative investment income. If positive investment income is taxed, ought not negative investment income be allowed as a deduction?[18]

While the latter view has generally dominated the scholarly debate on this subject, the former view enjoys the apparent support of Congress, at least as to interest in the abstract — those interest payments that are not mentioned as exceptions to the rules now generally disallowing deductions for personal interest payments. In truth, though, Congress has struck a compromise, since the exceptions to §163(h), while few in number and narrow in scope, are for most taxpayers items with relatively large dollar amounts at stake. This will become clear in the description of the rules that follow.

2. Overview of the Interest Deduction Rules

a. In General

As noted, the rule of §163(h) generally disallows interest deductions for personal interest. As §163(h) is structured, all interest is personal interest unless it falls within a specific statutory exception. Major exceptions include business interest,

17. *See, e.g.,* Calvin H. Johnson, *Is an Interest Deduction Inevitable?* 6 Va. Tax Rev. 123, 160 (1986), for fuller detailing of this argument.
18. *See, e.g.,* William D. Andrews, *Personal Deductions in an Ideal Income Tax,* 86 Harv. L. Rev. 309, 376 (1972), for a description of this argument.

certain amounts of home mortgage interest, investment interest, passive activity interest, and educational loan interest. To determine what payments are and aren't deductible, the payments must be assigned to one of these categories or to the residual, nondeductible category of personal interest, not otherwise described. In general, interest is assigned to a particular category based on the taxpayer's use of the borrowed funds on which the interest is paid. Because the taxpayer often has a good deal of latitude to determine how particular borrowed funds are used, the rules in this area invite manipulation by taxpayers.

For example, a taxpayer may need both a car for personal use and a computer system of roughly equal cost for use in her business. She has enough savings to cover one of these purchases but not both, and expects to borrow money to finance one or the other. Even though the auto loan may be easier to arrange (since financing is routinely available for automobiles at the point of purchase), this taxpayer will find it advantageous to borrow for the computer purchase instead, since interest incurred on business borrowing continues to be deductible, while interest incurred on borrowing to purchase a personal automobile is not. In many cases resembling this one, the taxpayer will have substantial control over which category the borrowing falls into. Think about how a taxpayer's affairs can be structured to maximize interest deductions as we go through the several major exceptions to the general nondeductibility rule of §163(h).

b.   Qualified Residence Interest

Among the explicit exceptions to the disallowance of deductions for personal interest payments, one stands out from the rest: Taxpayers continue to be allowed to deduct most interest on mortgages that are secured by their personal residence. In 1985, the year before the general pruning of the interest expense deduction, about 64 percent of the amount deducted for interest by itemizing taxpayers was for home mortgage interest.[19] Even as to home mortgage interest, Congress made the deduction slightly less general, but not in a way that affects most homeowners. Although Congress did not say so in its committee reports (and is rarely candid in those reports about its motives, especially when those motives are craven), there can be little doubt that the large number of itemizing homeowners who would have been greatly annoyed by the repeal of deductibility of mortgage interest was enough to persuade Congress that the time had not come for this particular reform, despite whatever Congress's views might have been on the general desirability of interest deductions.[20]

---

19. Authors' calculations based on IRS, *Statistics of Income — Individual Income Tax Returns, 1985*, table 2.1 (1988). The table shows that about $115 billion of the $180 billion deducted as interest was for home mortgage interest.

20. There is, of course, always a good reason not to disappoint the reasonable expectations of taxpayers who make long-term investments premised on long-standing features of the tax landscape. Homeowners would have made decisions about how much they could pay for their housing at least in part on the net, after-tax costs of the home. Repealing deductibility of interest payments would have significantly raised those after-tax costs, leaving many homeowners with upwards of 25-year commitments that would be difficult to renegotiate. Still, if Congress really believed in this reform, it could have used long phase-ins, grandfathering existing mortgages, or other devices to ease transition to a world in which interest was not deductible. Congress chose not to do this.

As noted, there are some limitations in this area, expressed in the rules that define "qualified residence interest." First, the number of personal residences whose mortgages can generate deductible interest is limited to two, with married couples who file separately being allowed only one residence each (§163(h)(4)(A)(ii)). The taxpayer's principal residence is automatically qualified; a second home will qualify only if it is designated for this purpose by the taxpayer, and is used as a residence by the taxpayer for at least 15 days during the tax year. (§163(h)(4)(A)(i)(II)).

Second, the home in question must secure the mortgage loan the interest on which the taxpayer seeks to deduct. It would not be sufficient, for example, to get a letter from your banker that averred that the bank considered your home to be the most valuable asset in your portfolio, and that your ownership of it was the deciding factor in making you creditworthy.

Third, the mortgage loan must be either "acquisition indebtedness" or "home equity indebtedness." Acquisition indebtedness is essentially a purchase-money mortgage, used either to buy or to build the residence. It can also include amounts borrowed to improve the residence or to refinance existing acquisition indebtedness. Home equity indebtedness is any debt secured by a residence that is not acquisition indebtedness. By implication, home equity indebtedness need not be invested in improving the property. (Were it to be so invested, it would ordinarily become acquisition debt.) Home equity indebtedness is thus an exception to the general rule that interest is categorized according to the use of the loan proceeds. Thus, a taxpayer who has sufficient equity (the difference between the market value of the residence and the acquisition debt) in the residence may borrow against that equity, use the proceeds for any purpose whatever, and still deduct the interest on the debt. This might be an alternative way for the taxpayer in the example above, who wants to buy both a car and a computer, to finance the purchase of the car on an interest-deductible basis.

Finally, the *loan* amounts generating deductible interest (but not directly the interest itself) are limited by dollar-level maximums: Interest with respect to up to $1 million of acquisition indebtedness can be deducted, as can interest with respect to up to $100,000 of home equity debt. These numbers are not indexed for inflation, and have not been adjusted since these dollar-level maximums were added to §163(h) in 1987.

Problem 5.   Alan lives in a house that he owns. His basis in the house is $275,000, the house is subject to a purchase money mortgage (i.e., acquisition indebtedness) of $250,000, and the house's current fair market value is $400,000. Alan wants to borrow $80,000 to finance the purchase of his dream automobile. Can he structure the financing so that he will be able to deduct the interest on the $80,000 loan?

Problem 6.   The facts are the same as in the previous problem, except that the fair market value of the house is only $300,000. Does this affect Alan's ability to deduct the interest on the $80,000 loan?

Problem 7.   On the same basic facts as the previous problem ($250,000 acquisition indebtedness, $275,000 basis, and $300,000 fair market value), is there any way Alan could borrow $80,000 to purchase a vehicle, and deduct the interest on the entire $80,000? Hint 1: Notice the problem says "vehicle," not "car." Hint 2: Take a look at Temp. Reg. §1.163-10T(p)(3)(ii).

Problem 8. *(a)* Betty owns and lives in a condominium unit that is not subject to any mortgage. Her basis in the unit is $400,000, and its current fair market value is $600,000. Betty wants to borrow $175,000 for a variety of purposes—a big vacation, a new car, and her grandchildren's educations. If she borrows $175,000 using her home as security, will she be able to deduct the interest on the entire loan? *(b)* A virtually identical unit, across the hall from Betty's, is for sale for $600,000. Suppose Betty sold her unit for $600,000, and bought the other unit for the same price, financing the purchase with $425,000 of her own money and a $175,000 loan secured by her new home. Would she then be able to deduct the interest on the entire $175,000?

Problem 9. Carl buys a very nice house for $2 million. He pays for the house with $900,000 of his own money and with the proceeds of a $1.1 million loan secured by the house. Can Carl deduct the interest on the entire $1.1 million principal amount of the loan? For the view of the Tax Court on this question, read on.

PAU v. COMMISSIONER

T.C. Memo 1997-43

PARR, Judge: After concessions, two issues remain regarding petitioners' income tax liability for 1990: . . . (2) Whether section 163(h)(3) limits petitioners' Schedule A deduction for home mortgage interest to interest paid on acquisition debt of $1 million. We hold it does. [All materials relating to the first issue are omitted.]

FINDINGS OF FACT

Until 1989, petitioners owned a condominium in San Mateo, California, that they used as their primary residence. In 1989, after their move, petitioners reclassified the condominium as rental property. In that year, petitioners also purchased a home in Hillsborough, California, for use as their primary residence and they have since lived there at all times. The purchase price of the residence was $1,780,000. Petitioners have a mortgage on the Hillsborough residence, the original principal amount of which was $1,330,000.

In 1990, petitioners claimed a home mortgage interest deduction on Schedule A of $107,226. Despite having actually paid a greater amount of mortgage interest, petitioners limited their deduction to interest on $1.1 million indebtedness based on advice from an accountant. [An IRS official] allowed the Paus a home mortgage interest deduction, but he limited the allowable deduction to the interest on $1 million indebtedness. Consequently, he calculated that the allowable deduction is $99,040 rather than the $107,226 claimed by petitioners, a difference of $8,186.

OPINION

Section 163(a) states the general rule for deductions for interest paid or incurred on indebtedness within the taxable year. Other provisions of section 163 limit such deductions. Section 163(h) disallows personal interest deductions unless they fit within certain narrowly prescribed categories. Among these narrow exceptions is the deduction for interest on a qualified residence. Sec. 163(h)(2)(D). The parties agree that the interest paid on the mortgage for petitioners' home was qualified residence interest, because the Paus paid it on acquisition indebtedness pursuant to section 163(h)(3)(A)(i) and (B)(i). The parties dispute only the amount of acquisition indebtedness petitioners may use in computing their deduction.

Section 163(h) restricts home mortgage interest deductions to interest paid on $1 million of acquisition indebtedness for debt incurred after October 13, 1987. Acquisition indebtedness is defined as that which is "incurred in acquiring, constructing, or substantially improving any qualified residence of the taxpayer, and . . . is secured by such residence." Sec. 163(h)(3)(B). A taxpayer may be entitled to a greater deduction if he has incurred home equity indebtedness up to $100,000, as allowed by section 163(h)(3)(C)(ii). There can be no additional deduction where taxpayers fail to show that they had home equity indebtedness. *See* Notice 88-74, 1988-2 C.B. 385. Home equity indebtedness is defined as "any indebtedness (*other than acquisition indebtedness*) secured by a qualified residence." Sec. 163(h)(3)(C) (emphasis added).

Petitioners, who purchased their home in 1989, did not demonstrate that any of their debt was not incurred in acquiring, constructing or substantially improving their residence and thus have failed to carry their burden of proof. We therefore sustain respondent's determination as to the amount petitioners may properly deduct for home mortgage interest.

REV. RUL. 2010-25

2010-44 I.R.B. 571

FACTS

In 2009, an unmarried individual (Taxpayer) purchased a principal residence for its fair market value of $1,500,000. Taxpayer paid $300,000 and financed the remainder by borrowing $1,200,000 through a loan that is secured by the residence. In 2009, Taxpayer paid interest that accrued on the indebtedness during that year. Taxpayer has no other debt secured by the residence.

LAW

Section 163(a) allows as a deduction all interest paid or accrued within the taxable year on indebtedness. However, for individuals §163(h)(1) disallows a deduction for personal interest. Under §163(h)(2)(D), qualified residence interest is not personal interest. Section 163(h)(3)(A) defines qualified residence interest as interest paid or accrued during the taxable year on acquisition indebtedness or home equity indebtedness secured by any qualified residence of the taxpayer. Under §163(h)(4)(A), "qualified residence" means a taxpayer's principal residence, within the meaning of §121, and one other residence selected and used by the taxpayer as a residence.

Section 163(h)(3)(B)(i) provides that acquisition indebtedness is any indebtedness that is incurred in acquiring, constructing, or substantially improving a qualified residence and is secured by the residence. However, §163(h)(3)(B)(ii) limits the amount of indebtedness treated as acquisition indebtedness to $1,000,000 ($500,000 for a married individual filing separately). Accordingly, any indebtedness described in §163(h)(3)(B)(i) in excess of $1,000,000 is, by definition, not acquisition indebtedness for purposes of §163(h)(3).

Section 163(h)(3)(C)(i) provides that home equity indebtedness is any indebtedness secured by a qualified residence other than acquisition indebtedness, to the extent the fair market value of the qualified residence exceeds the amount of acquisition indebtedness on the residence. However, §163(h)(3)(C)(ii) limits the amount of indebtedness treated as home equity indebtedness to $100,000 ($50,000 for a married individual filing separately). Accordingly, any indebtedness described in §163(h)(3)(C)(i) in excess of $100,000 is, by definition, not home equity indebtedness for purposes of §163(h)(3).

In Pau v. Commissioner, T.C. Memo. 1997-43, the Tax Court limited the taxpayers' deduction for qualified residence interest to the interest paid on $1 million of the $1.33 million indebtedness incurred to purchase their residence. . . .

ANALYSIS

Taxpayer may deduct, as interest on acquisition indebtedness under §163(h)(3)(B), interest paid in 2009 on $1,000,000 of the $1,200,000 indebtedness used to acquire the principal residence. The $1,200,000 indebtedness was incurred in acquiring a qualified residence of Taxpayer and was secured by the residence. Thus, indebtedness of $1,000,000 is treated as acquisition indebtedness under §163(h)(3)(B).

Taxpayer also may deduct, as interest on home equity indebtedness under §163(h)(3)(C), interest paid in 2009 on $100,000 of the remaining indebtedness of $200,000. The $200,000 is secured by the qualified residence, is not acquisition indebtedness under §163(h)(3)(B), and does not exceed the fair market value of the residence reduced by the acquisition indebtedness secured by the residence. Thus, $100,000 of the $200,000 is treated as home equity indebtedness under §163(h)(3)(C).

Under §163(h)(3)(A), the interest on both acquisition indebtedness and home equity indebtedness is qualified residence interest. Therefore, for 2009 Taxpayer may deduct interest paid on indebtedness of $1,100,000 as qualified residence interest. Any interest Taxpayer paid on the remaining indebtedness of $100,000 is nondeductible personal interest under §163(h).

The Internal Revenue Service will not follow [Pau]. The holding in Pau was based on the incorrect assertion that taxpayers must demonstrate that debt treated as home equity indebtedness "was not incurred in acquiring, constructing or substantially improving their residence." The definition of home equity indebtedness in §163(h)(3)(C) contains no such restrictions, and accordingly the Service will determine home equity indebtedness consistent with the provisions of this revenue ruling, notwithstanding [Pau].

HOLDING

Indebtedness incurred by a taxpayer to acquire, construct, or substantially improve a qualified residence can constitute home equity indebtedness to the extent it exceeds $1 million (subject to the applicable dollar and fair market value limitations imposed on home equity indebtedness by §163(h)(3)(C)).

Notes and Questions

1. *Not so fast.* The statutory interpretation issue in *Pau* is subtler and more difficult than either the Tax Court or Rev. Rul. 2010-25 acknowledges. (Although the *Pau* opinion and Rev. Rul. 2010-25 disagree as to how the statute should be interpreted, neither gives any indication that the issue is difficult.) Section 163(h)(3)(C)(i) defines home equity indebtedness as "any indebtedness (other than acquisition indebtedness) secured by a qualified residence," to the extent the amount of such debt does not exceed the lesser of the taxpayer's home equity or $100,000. The interpretive issue turns on the precise meaning of "acquisition indebtedness" in the parenthetical in §163(h)(3)(C)(i). There are two possibilities. First, "acquisition indebtedness" might mean any debt that was in fact incurred in acquiring the residence, even if it is not *deductible* acquisition indebtedness because it exceeds the $1 million ceiling. This was the Tax Court's interpretation. Under this interpretation no portion of the purchase money mortgage in excess of $1 million can qualify as home equity indebtedness, because of the exclusion of acquisition indebtedness from the definition of home equity indebtedness. Under the second possible interpretation, "acquisition indebtedness" in the parenthetical refers only to debt the interest on which is deductible as interest on acquisition indebtedness, after taking the $1 million ceiling into account. Under this interpretation—the one adopted by Rev. Rul. 2010-25—the purchase money mortgage in excess of $1 million would not be acquisition indebtedness, and the Paus would be able to deduct the interest on $100,000 of that excess as home equity indebtedness.

2. *How to decide the issue.* Carefully examine the language of §§163(h)(3)(B) and (C) with this issue in mind. Does the language clearly support one interpretation over the other, or is it hopelessly ambiguous? If the language is hopelessly ambiguous, do policy considerations favor one interpretation over the other?

3. *Is this any way to run a tax system (part I)?* The issue in *Pau* concerns the basic mechanical operation of §163(h)(3), and is an issue that affects a significant number of taxpayers. As a practical matter, Rev. Rul. 2010-25 finally resolves the ambiguity, for the simple reason that no taxpayer will have any reason to argue against the IRS's adoption of the pro-taxpayer interpretation. But why did Congress allow the ambiguity to persist for so many years?

c. Business Debt

While the qualified residence interest deduction may be the most important, the deduction for interest paid on debt incurred in connection with a trade or business is the least circumscribed of the exceptions to §163(h). Unlike several of the other exceptions, interest on business debt may be deducted even if it results in a net loss from the activity in any particular tax year.

What constitutes trade or business debt is for the most part determined by the general parameters of the trade or business concept, which is described in fuller detail in Chapter 5. Some controversy has developed, however, over how proximately related a debt must be to the trade or business to justify deductibility. The Tax Court and the Ninth Circuit disagreed on this point in the following decision.

REDLARK v. COMMISSIONER
141 F.3d 936 (9th Cir. 1998)

FLETCHER, Circuit Judge: The Commissioner of Internal Revenue appeals the decision of the Tax Court striking down Temporary Treasury Regulation §1.163-9T(b)(2)(i)(A). That regulation disallows the deduction of interest paid on overdue individual income taxes, even when the source of the personal income that gives rise to the tax deficiency is a business or trade. Plaintiffs James and Cheryl Redlark claim that the regulation is in conflict with the relevant provision of the tax code, §163(h)(2)(A). A sharply divided tax court accepted the Redlarks's position. The only other circuit to address this question, however, has concluded that the regulation constitutes a permissible construction of a facially ambiguous statutory provision. *See* Miller v. United States, 65 F.3d 687 (8th Cir. 1995). We agree with the Eighth Circuit and reverse the decision of the tax court.

I

The facts in this case are not in dispute, so we summarize them only briefly. Between 1979 and 1985, James and Cheryl Redlark operated an unincorporated business, Carrier Communications, that installed telephone equipment. The Redlarks kept the books and records of the business using the accrual method of accounting. They reported the income and expenses on their joint federal income tax returns, however, using the cash-basis method of accounting. [Following an audit, the IRS insisted on the use of the accrual method for tax purposes, and assessed additional taxes, interest, and penalties for 1982-1984, inclusive.]

The interest on these assessments amounted to $361,345 for 1982, $42,279 for 1984, and $42,126 for 1985. The Redlarks made the interest payments in installments from 1987 to 1990. They then claimed deductions on their personal income tax returns for portions of the interest payments: On their 1989 return, they claimed a business expense of $195,463 based on the interest paid in that year on their 1982, 1984 and 1985 tax deficiencies; and in 1990, they claimed $23,323 as a business expense for the interest paid on their 1985 deficiency. These deductions represented the interest payments on the portions of the deficiencies that the Redlarks determined to have resulted from accounting errors and that were thus (they asserted) allocable to Carrier Communications. During an audit of the Redlarks' 1989 and 1990 returns, however, the Commissioner determined that none of the interest on tax deficiencies was properly deductible. The controlling regulation, Temporary Treasury Regulation §1.163-9T(b)(2)(i)(A), specifies that interest on income tax deficiencies is not attributable to a taxpayer's conduct of trade or business, regardless of the source of the income, but rather is "personal interest" within the meaning of §163(h).

The issue before us is whether §1.163-9T(b)(2)(i)(A) is a permissible interpretation of §163(h). On its face, §163(h) does not address the deductibility of interest payments on business-related personal income tax deficiencies. The statute simply disallows deductions for all "personal interest," unless the interest in question is "paid or accrued on indebtedness *properly allocable* to a trade or business (other than the trade or business of performing services as an employee)." §163(h)(2)(A) (emphasis added). In promulgating Temporary Treasury Regulation §1.163-9T(b)(2)(i)(A), the Commissioner took the position that interest on personal income tax deficiencies always constitutes a personal obligation and so is never "properly allocable to a trade or business." The parties agree that the disputed interest amounts are not deductible under the regulation. The parties disagree vigorously as to whether the regulation constitutes a valid interpretation of the Internal Revenue Code.

II

This dispute centers on the meaning of the words, "properly allocable," in §163(h)(2)(A). The Redlarks argue that those words refer narrowly and unambiguously to questions of accounting practice. Prior to the addition of §163(h)(2)(A) to the tax code in the Tax Reform Act of 1986, they explain, there was a consistent body of case law holding that interest on business-related personal income tax deficiencies was deductible, provided that the deficiencies constituted an ordinary and necessary expense in the conduct of the business. . . . It is the Redlarks' position that Congress incorporated this body of case law into §163(h)(2)(A) when it used the words, "properly allocable." Under their reading, those words refer only to the "propriety," from an accounting standpoint, of "allocating" personal income tax deficiencies to the conduct of a trade or business. The statute must be read, the Redlarks argue, to incorporate the pre-1986 case law and thus to provide unambiguously that interest from income tax deficiencies is deductible when the deficiencies in question constitute an ordinary and necessary expense in the relevant trade or business.

According to the Commissioner, however, the Redlarks' reading of §163(h)(2)(A) is far too narrow. It is the Commissioner's position that the words, "properly allocable," are deliberately ambiguous and constitute a delegation of authority to the Commissioner to determine when an expense may "properly" be "allocated" to a trade or business and when it may not. That determination, the Commissioner argues, may legitimately involve questions of accounting policy, provided that the policies that the Commissioner promotes are consistent with other provisions of the statute and the purpose of the Code as a whole. Thus, while the Redlarks may have provided a reasonable argument for the proposition that their personal income tax deficiencies should "properly" be considered "allocable" to their business as an accounting matter, theirs is not the only reasonable construction of the phrase "properly allocable," its pedigree from earlier tax court decisions notwithstanding. Rather, the Commissioner argues, the I.R.S. has determined, as a matter of general policy, that personal income tax always constitutes a personal obligation so that deficiencies in meeting that obligation are never "properly allocable" to the taxpayer's trade or business. It is the Commissioner's position that such a determination constitutes an appropriate exercise of the authority that Congress delegated to the Commissioner by using a deliberately ambiguous term in the statute.

We agree with the Commissioner. It is not our function to determine what would be the best or most advisable method for the Commissioner to employ in implementing the tax code. "Congress has delegated to the Commissioner, not to the courts, the task of prescribing all needful rules and regulations for the enforcement of the Internal Revenue Code." United States v. Correll, 389 U.S. 299, 307 (1967). So long as the Commissioner issues regulations that "implement the congressional mandate in some reasonable manner," Rowan Cos. v. United States, 452 U.S. 247, 252 (1981), we must defer to the Commissioner's interpretation. Only if the Code has a meaning that is clear, unambiguous, and in conflict with a regulation does a court have the authority to reject the Commissioner's reasoned interpretation and invalidate the regulation. *See* Chevron U.S.A. v. Natural Resources Defense Council, 467 U.S. 837, 841-44 (1984). "If Congress has explicitly left a gap for the agency to fill, there is an express delegation of authority to the agency to elucidate a specific provision of the statute by regulation." *Id.* at 843-44. Where this is so, prior decisions of reviewing courts that seem to have favored a different interpretation of the statute will not override the agency's reasonable construction. *See id.* at 841-42. Rather, "legislative regulations are given controlling weight unless they are arbitrary, capricious, or manifestly contrary to the statute." *Id.* at 844.

As an initial matter, we find untenable the Redlarks' assertion that the words, "properly allocable," unambiguously specify that interest on business-related personal income tax deficiencies should be deductible. . . .

When Congress uses such broad, generalized language in defining an important term in a statute, a claimant must make a compelling argument, based on the language and history of the statute itself, that Congress can only have intended one meaning to attach to that language before we will find that the administering agency has no authority to employ a different construction. The Redlarks have offered no such compelling arguments. . . .

Having determined that the term, "properly allocable," is subject to interpretation by the Commissioner, we now must decide whether Temporary Treasury Regulation §1.163-9T(b)(2)(i)(A) represents a reasonable interpretation of the term. We have little trouble in doing so. As the Eighth Circuit noted, the legislative history that attended the enactment of I.R.C. §163(h) is entirely consonant with the Commissioner's conclusion that personal income tax obligations are always essentially personal in nature. In explaining the import of I.R.C. §163(h), the report of the Conference Committee says that "[p]ersonal interest also generally includes interest on tax deficiencies." H.R. Conf. Rep. No. 841, 99th Cong., 2d Sess. 11-154. There is no suggestion in the report that Congress intended to preserve an exception for interest on income tax deficiencies that arise in the ordinary course of a business.

The General Explanation of the Tax Reform Act of 1986 likewise supports the Commissioner's interpretation of the Code. *See* Staff of the Joint Committee on Taxation, 100th Cong., 1st Sess., *General Explanation of the Tax Reform Act of 1986* 266 (Comm. Print 1987). While such post-enactment explanations cannot properly be described as "legislative history," they are at least instructive as to the reasonableness of an agency's interpretation of a facially ambiguous statute. In this case, the general explanation clearly supports the Commissioner's interpretation, providing that "[p]ersonal interest also includes interest on underpayments of individual Federal, State or local income taxes notwithstanding that all or a portion of the income may have arisen in a trade or business, because such taxes are not considered derived from the conduct of a trade or business." *General Explanation, supra,* at 266. . . .

Temporary Treasury Regulation §1.163-9T(b)(2)(i)(A) represents a reasonable interpretation of a facially ambiguous statute. It is neither arbitrary, capricious, nor in conflict with any other statutory provision or the purposes of the Code as a whole. That being so, our inquiry is at an end. . . .

Notes and Questions

1. *Procedural aspects.* This case is as interesting for its procedural aspects as for its substantive position. Note that the Tax Court decided the case in favor of the taxpayer after the Eighth Circuit had reached a contrary conclusion in *Miller.* The Tax Court, by its own decision, follows precedents decided in the circuit court to which appeal would lie in the case before it. Golsen v. Commissioner, 54 T.C. 742, 756-757 (1970). Thus, if the taxpayer here had lived in Minnesota or Missouri, the Tax Court would have simply followed the Eighth Circuit rule. Because the Redlarks resided in the Ninth Circuit, they were able to get a fresh hearing of the issue; but, as it turned out, to no avail.

2. Redlark *in the Tax Court.* Tax Court cases are ordinarily heard by only one of the 19 judges of that court. However, all opinions are reviewed by the chief judge, who occasionally decides that all of the Tax Court judges should consider an opinion before it is issued. The Tax Court is naturally reluctant to disagree with a prior decision by a higher court, as it did in *Redlark,* which may be why the Tax Court's chief judge asked the entire Tax Court to review the opinion. The Tax Court was not of one mind on this case by any means: Eight judges signed the plurality opinion, with three others concurring in the outcome, but seven judges dissented. The Tax Court noted that the temporary regulation barred the deduction of interest on tax deficiencies in all cases, even though no such flat prohibition could be found in the statute, nor was it suggested by the legislative history. Primarily for that reason, the court held the regulation invalid as an unreasonable, and therefore impermissible, reading of the statute.

3. *The scorecard.* Remarkably, six circuits — the Fourth, Fifth, Sixth, Seventh, Eighth, and Ninth — have now considered this issue, and they have unanimously endorsed the IRS position. After five of those six circuits had weighed in, the Tax Court reversed its position in *Robinson v. Commissioner,* 119 T.C. 44 (2002), and is now in agreement with the several circuits that have considered this question. It thus seems increasingly unlikely that a split in the circuits will develop, though taxpayers in the other circuits are free to make their best case in those circuits.

4. *The Bluebook.* A continuing source of dispute among tax professionals is the status of the reports published by the Joint Committee on Taxation following major congressional enactments. The Staff of the Joint Committee is a highly respected group of professionals, mostly lawyers and economists, who advise both houses of Congress on technical aspects of proposed tax legislation. The Joint Committee also usually publishes a so-called Bluebook (not the one you're thinking of) after a bill has been passed, purporting to explain its provisions. Views vary on the weight that should be accorded to these reports. In the case of the deductibility of interest on tax deficiencies, the relevant Bluebook (or "General Explanation . . . ")

contained language supporting the Commissioner's position, which is noted near the end of the *Redlark* opinion. The Tax Court below in *Redlark* had pointedly refused to rely on this language, on grounds that it was not true legislative history, and was not helpful without corroboration in one of the reports from the House Ways and Means Committee, the Senate Finance Committee, or the Conference Committee charged with putting the two versions of the bill together. Because those reports just named are published prior to the final votes on the legislation, they have a clearer claim to being official and contemporaneous explanations of congressional intent.

When the Tax Court revisited this issue in *Robinson,* the plurality opinion appeared to rely, at least in part, on the Bluebook language noted at the end of the *Redlark* opinion above. But only five judges (of the 19 on the Tax Court) indicated full agreement with Judge Chabot, the author of the opinion. Three others simply concurred without comment, and two concurred in separate opinions. In his concurring opinion, Judge Thornton noted that the court's position generally was to "require some direct corroboration of congressional intentions before we defer to the Blue Book expressions thereof" (119 T.C. at 94). The failure of Judge Chabot's opinion to win endorsement from a majority of the judges on the court would seem to indicate that the somewhat skeptical view of Bluebooks continues to prevail. *See also* Michael Livingston, *What's Blue and White and Not Quite as Good as a Committee Report: General Explanations and the Role of "Subsequent" Tax Legislative History,* 11 Am. J. Tax Policy 91 (1994).

5. *Is the result fair?* Despite its popularity in the circuits, is this decision really fair? What if the taxpayers in this case had incorporated their business prior to the events that gave rise to the dispute? The tax deficiencies would then have been on the corporate tax return. Do you imagine that the corporation would have been barred from deducting interest paid on the deficiencies? What about a pass-through entity, such as a partnership or limited liability company? (These organizations merely report their items of income and expense to the IRS and to their owners, with the latter reporting their appropriate shares of income and deduction items on their own personal returns.) Would the fact that it was an interest obligation of an entity rather than an individual help in sustaining the deduction?

d. Investment and Passive Activity Interest

The rules regarding deductions for interest paid with respect to debts incurred to finance investment activities, and to finance activities that Congress has chosen to call "passive activities" in §469, are facially similar: Interest is deductible to the extent of the income generated by the investments or passive activities.[21] No net loss deductions (as in a case where interest expense exceeds income) are allowed. For somewhat complicated reasons, however, the practical effects of the rules governing these two types of interest are quite different: Most taxpayers are able

---

21. In the case of passive activities, interest is aggregated with all other expenses of engaging in all passive activities, and the sum is deductible up to the amount of the income from all passive activities. Sections 469(a) and (e).

to deduct most of their investment interest, most of the time, while taxpayers who incur interest to finance passive activities usually find that much or all of their interest expense is not effectively deductible when incurred. The reasons for this are explained in some depth in Chapter 8, which discusses tax shelters.

e. Educational Loan Interest

In 1997, in response to concerns that general disallowance of interest deductions was unfair to young adults who were making significant interest payments to discharge educational loan obligations, Congress added §221 to the Code to partially alleviate this burden. Over the following several years, Congress phased in a limited deduction for up to $2,500 of such interest. Assuming an interest rate of 5 percent, this rule would permit the deduction of the interest paid with respect to as much as $50,000 of principal. As an additional bonus, Congress designated this deduction as one that could be claimed "above-the-line," as part of the definition of adjusted gross income, in §62(a)(17). Thus, taxpayers taking this deduction may also claim the benefits of the standard deduction. This is particularly helpful to younger taxpayers, whose lower average earnings make them more likely than older taxpayers to use the standard deduction,

The deductions are available only with respect to interest paid on a "qualified education loan" that was incurred to pay for "qualified education expenses" — terms that are defined in §221(d). The latter term refers primarily to tuition, fees, room and board, and related expenses, reduced by the amounts of scholarships or similar payments from sources other than the taxpayer. The "qualified education loan" definition primarily requires a reasonable nexus between the time the loan is taken out and the time the expense is incurred. It includes loans that are used to refinance other loans that were themselves qualified educational loans.

There are, unfortunately for many law students, significant limitations on the deduction based on the income of the taxpayer. If "modified adjusted gross income" (as defined in §221(b)(2)(B)) exceeds $60,000 for a single taxpayer, or $120,000 for taxpayers filing jointly, deductibility begins to be phased out; by the time modified adjusted gross income reaches $75,000 ($150,000 for a joint return), all deductions for education interest are denied.[22] Thus, for many law students, deductions will be available for their educational interest only if they take government or public interest jobs (or perhaps marry someone who has little or no income, and few if any educational loan obligations).

C. STATE AND LOCAL TAXES

1. History and Rationale

Although their precise parameters have varied over time, deductions for state and local taxes have been available since the very beginning of the modern income

22. These numbers are indexed for inflation pursuant to §221(f). The numbers shown are for 2011.

tax with the Revenue Act of 1913. Deductibility of such taxes is probably best justified as something of a concession to federalism: The federal government (1) recognizes by this deduction that state and local governments have their own revenue needs, and (2) consents to assess federal taxes only against the income that remains after state and local governments have exacted their assessments. It has in this sense something of an income-defining quality, suggesting that "income," for purposes of assessing the reasonableness of tax burdens, should be determined only on the basis of what is actually available for consumption.[23]

An objection to this conclusion, however, could be developed by imagining two states whose citizens have similar income distributions (that is, income distributions with the same mean and standard deviation), but which differ significantly in state and local tax rates. The citizens of the higher-taxed state will presumably enjoy higher levels of state and local government services, which should offset their loss of private consumption opportunities. Yet they will nevertheless enjoy greater state and local tax deductions, and the lower federal tax liabilities that accompany those deductions.

There is thus an element of consumption in the amount of state and local taxes paid, at least in the aggregate for all citizens of a particular state. And consumption ordinarily belongs in the tax base, according to the Haig-Simons income definition discussed previously. One is left under this view with a sense that Congress is accomplishing little more with this deduction than a crude form of revenue sharing,[24] and something of a perverse one at that, with the greatest amount of revenue being shared with the state and local governments that most greedily seek it through their own tax decisions. For reasons of this general sort, this deduction is not a favorite of public finance economists.

In an ideal world, the federal income tax might distinguish between two types of state and local tax payments: (1) tax payments the value of which are returned to the taxpayer in the form of government services, and (2) tax payments that the state uses to accomplish redistribution from the taxpayer to other less affluent (or

23. Note that the *federal* income tax is not deductible in computing federal income tax liabilities, even though it obviously diminishes the amounts available to the taxpayer for consumption. While this may seem to negate the ability-to-pay, income-defining rationale noted in the text, the nondeductibility of the federal income tax is actually a rather trivial matter, since the income tax could be designed to be self-deductible in a way that would perfectly replicate the effect of the current nondeductibility rule. For example, imagine that the first $100,000 of income is to be subject to an income tax of 25 percent, and that the tax would not be deductible. The tax bill for a taxpayer with a taxable income of $100,000 would be $25,000. The same result could be achieved by a tax of $33\frac{1}{3}$ percent, with the tax itself being allowed as a deduction. The only important differences are that the latter tax sounds like it imposes a higher rate (an effect that members of Congress naturally loathe) and is computationally more difficult (which members say they loathe, though that would be hard to prove on the basis of the provisions they have enacted). Computing a tax-exclusive rate (a rate that assumes that the tax itself will be allowed as a deduction) that is equivalent to a given tax-inclusive rate (a rate that assumes that the tax itself will *not* be allowed as a deduction) requires a "grossing-up" calculation: For any tax-inclusive rate t_i, the tax-exclusive rate t_e that raises the same revenue can be computed for any income Y by noting that the revenue raised by each tax can be represented as: $t_e \bullet [Y - (t_i \bullet Y)] = t_i \bullet Y$. Rearranging this equation yields: $t_e = t_i/(1 - t_i)$. So, for example, where $t_i = .25$, then $t_e = .25/.75$, or $33\frac{1}{3}$ %.

24. This seems to be the view of the Staff of the Joint Committee on Taxation, whose tax expenditure budget analysis (excerpted in Chapter 1.C.4) puts the deductions for state and local income taxes, and for personal property taxes, under the heading of "general purpose fiscal assistance." The Staff's assumption is that state and local governments benefit from §164, in that the deduction enables them to impose higher taxes than their voters would otherwise tolerate. Note, however, that the Staff puts the deduction for property taxes on owner-occupied housing in the "housing" category, rather than "general purpose fiscal assistance."

so one would hope) residents of the state. Taxes of the first sort would not be deductible (for the reasons explained above), but there would be a strong argument for a deduction for taxes of the second kind. In our less-than-ideal world, however, the Code makes no attempt to distinguish between the two types.

The deduction seems healthy and robust notwithstanding critical disapproval. In recent years, however, some pruning of the deduction has been accomplished. In the Revenue Act of 1978, Congress repealed deductibility of state and local gasoline taxes, effective the following year. And in the Tax Reform Act of 1986, which reflected a major effort to broaden the base of the income tax to permit lowering of the rate structure, deductibility of state sales taxes was eliminated, even as the general deductibility of most other state and local taxes was reaffirmed. Because states differ with respect to their emphases on particular sources of revenue, eliminating deductibility of one tax but not others introduced some additional unfairness to a deduction that may not be an especially sound one anyway.[25] In 2004, Congress temporarily restored deductibility of sales taxes as an alternative to deduction of income taxes. This temporary provision has been extended several times, and is currently scheduled to expire at the end of 2011.

2. What Taxes Are Deductible?

The previous section has foreshadowed this one in some detail. Generally, §164 provides that state and local income taxes, real property taxes, and personal property taxes are deductible, as are a few less general types of tax, including, for example, half of the taxes paid pursuant to the Self-Employment Contributions Act.[26] Somewhat surprisingly, §164 also allows deduction of foreign income and real property taxes. (But not foreign personal property taxes. Why not, do you suppose?)

Whether a tax is one of these deductible taxes may become the subject of controversy. In the case of income taxes, there are few disputes about state and local taxes, but many about whether a particular foreign tax is an income tax. In large part, this is due to the common practice in mineral-rich countries of imposing extraction taxes that may be called "income taxes," but that are really more like royalties paid for the extraction privilege.[27]

Property taxes present particular difficulties, which can be imagined by generalizing from the common practice of charging the owners of condominium apartments for maintenance of shared facilities and services, such as garbage collection, doorman services, costs of maintaining a lounge or swimming pool, and the like. Clearly these are not "taxes" paid to a government, but rather charges that are part

25. An important architect of the 1986 reforms, Senator Robert Packwood of Oregon, then chair of the Senate Finance Committee, represented one of the few states that imposes no general sales tax. One cannot help but wonder if sales-tax deductibility would have been spared the tax-reform ax if someone from a high-sales-tax state had been wielding it.

26. These are the "contributions" self-employed persons make to the Social Security fund. An employed person is not required to include his employer's share of the contribution in his gross income, and allowing a self-employed person a deduction for half of his contribution gives him the functional equivalent of the employed person's exclusion. To ensure that this equivalence does not depend on the taxpayer's status as an itemizer, Congress made this an above-the-line deduction. See §§164(f)(2) and 62(a)(1).

27. Note that foreign income taxes are generally creditable against U.S. taxes under §901, and for most taxpayers that alternative will be more attractive than a deduction. In some cases, however, full or even partial credits may not be available, in which case deductibility may be of some importance.

of a private network of contracts. But what if the residents of a neighborhood are assessed to pave a street that they will use? What if residents of a gated community are charged for maintenance (and staffing) of the gates, under circumstances where the community association discharges quasi-public law enforcement functions?

These are not always easy questions to answer, but the statute and regulations do offer some guidance. Section 164(c)(1), for example, disallows deductions for assessments that tend "to increase the value of the property assessed." This was clearly intended to bar deductions of assessments for new roads, sidewalks, and the like. Similarly, §164(b)(1) makes it clear that personal property taxes must be of the "ad valorem" type—assessed based on value of the property, rather than, for example, the weight of a vehicle. Presumably the idea is to allow deduction only of taxes imposed for general revenue-raising purposes, rather than to recoup for externalities such as increased road-maintenance costs occasioned by the use of heavy vehicles.

As noted earlier, a temporary provision (currently scheduled to expire at the end of 2011) allows a taxpayer to choose between deducting state and local income taxes, or deducting state and local sales taxes in lieu of income taxes. This provision has already been extended several times, and there is a good chance it will remain in the Code for many years to come. Recognizing that it might be difficult or impossible for taxpayers to keep track of their sales tax payments throughout the year, Congress has directed the IRS to issue state-specific tables indicating the amount of the sales tax deduction that may be claimed, on a no-questions-asked basis, by taxpayers at various levels of adjusted gross income. A taxpayer purchasing a car, boat, or certain other big-ticket items may claim a deduction for both the sales tax amount determined under the applicable table and the actual sales tax on the big-ticket item. Imagine three taxpayers living in three different states. Each taxpayer pays a total of $20,000 in state taxes. The first taxpayer, living in a state with both a sales tax and an income tax, pays $10,000 of each. The second taxpayer, living in a state with only a sales tax, pays $20,000 in sales tax. The third taxpayer, living in a state with only an income tax, pays $20,000 in income tax. Which taxpayer gets the worst federal tax deal under the temporary rule (allowing the deduction of either income tax or sales tax, but not both)? Which taxpayer gets the worst federal tax deal under the permanent rule (allowing a deduction for income tax but not for sales tax)?

3. Who Can Claim the Deduction?

Public finance economists find it useful to identify the "economic incidence" of a tax — that is, who really bears the burden of the tax imposed. One might think that if the deduction for state and local taxes is intended to reflect the impact of those taxes in a refined assessment of the taxpayer's ability to pay federal income tax, then the economic incidence would be the measure of greatest interest. In fact, however, it is usually the legal incidence that matters.[28]

---

28. A prominent exception is the temporary sales tax deduction. Sales taxes are assessed against the seller of goods and services; the state and local collectors generally have legal authority to collect those taxes only from those sellers. But they are generally regarded as being paid by the consumers, and it is indeed the consumer who is allowed a deduction for those taxes under the temporary provision.

This may be largely a matter of administrability, since the legal incidence is ordinarily easily determined, while the economic incidence typically depends on questions such as the shape of the supply and demand curves within the relevant market, which are constantly shifting and difficult to determine even in a static model. Although understandable from an administrative viewpoint, insistence on disallowing deductions by anyone on whom a tax was not legally imposed can create a hardship.

For example, there can be little doubt that some part of the real estate tax paid by landlords is borne by tenants in the form of higher rents. The legal incidence of the tax does not fall on the tenants, however, and, though a number have tried, tenants may not deduct any part of their landlords' property tax bills. The IRS position on this even embodies a nifty "Catch-22": The IRS has ruled, in a case where a local government tried to structure its property tax to permit a tenant's deduction (by assessing the tax directly on the tenants), that the tax payments still weren't deductible by the tenants, because the tax in that case was not assessed on ownership of property, but rather as an excise tax on the use of property.[29]

The harshness of the "legal incidence" rule can be especially acute in situations where none of the parties involved can claim a deduction, because the tax wasn't paid by the one who owed it, and was paid by someone who didn't bear the legal incidence of the tax, as in the following case.

LORIA v. COMMISSIONER

T.C. Memo 1995-420; 70 T.C.M. (CCH) 553 (1995)

CHIECHI, Judge.

FINDINGS OF FACT AND OPINION

Respondent determined a deficiency in petitioner's Federal income tax and an accuracy-related penalty under section 6662(a) for taxable year 1989 in the amounts of $11,036 and $2,207, respectively.

The issues remaining for decision are:

(1) Is petitioner entitled to deduct for 1989 mortgage loan interest, mortgage loan points, and real property taxes with respect to certain real property? We hold that he is not. [Four other issues are omitted.]

FINDINGS OF FACT

Some of the facts have been stipulated and are so found.[30]

At the time the petition was filed and throughout 1989, petitioner resided at 22314 Runnymede, Canoga Park, California (Runnymede property).

---

29. Rev. Rul. 75-558, 1975-2 C.B. 67.

30. On Nov. 9, 1994, respondent filed with the Court a request for admissions, a copy of which she had served on petitioner on Nov. 8, 1994. Petitioner did not file a response to that request within 30 days after it was served on him by respondent. Accordingly, each matter set forth in respondent's request for admissions is deemed admitted pursuant to Rule 90(c).

RUNNYMEDE PROPERTY

Because petitioner did not have adequate credit to purchase the Runnymede property in his own name, his brother Gregg Loria purchased it in 1985. During 1989, Gregg Loria, and not petitioner, was the legal owner of the Runnymede property and was indebted to Freedom Federal Savings Loan (Freedom Federal) on the mortgage loan it had made on that property. The only mortgage loan payments on the Runnymede property during 1989 were made to Freedom Federal, and the interest portion of such payments totaled $13,575.40.

Petitioner paid at least $13,270.02 to Freedom Federal during 1989 on Gregg Loria's mortgage loan on the Runnymede property. Freedom Federal sent Gregg Loria an annual tax and interest statement (a substitute Form 1098) for 1989 that showed, inter alia, that $13,575.40 of interest on the mortgage loan in his name was paid during 1989 and reported to the Internal Revenue Service.

Prior to December 18, 1989, petitioner was not obligated to make mortgage or trust deed payments on the Runnymede property. On that date, petitioner and his brother obtained a 30-year mortgage loan for $129,000 from Wells Fargo Bank (Wells Fargo), which was secured by the Runnymede property. The first payment under the Wells Fargo mortgage loan was not due until February 1, 1990.

[Facts on other issues omitted.]

NOTICE OF DEFICIENCY

[Among other things, the Commissioner disallowed, for the 1989 tax year, $19,175 of home mortgage interest, $3,300 of "points," which are service charges — in the nature of interest, and treated as interest for purposes of §163 — imposed by many mortgage lenders or brokers, and $3,700 of real estate taxes with respect to the property in question. — Eds.]

Opinion

Petitioner has the burden of showing that the determinations in the notice are erroneous. Rule 142(a). Deductions are strictly a matter of legislative grace, and petitioner must meet the statutory requirements for the deductions he claims. Petitioner attempted to satisfy his burden of proof in this case principally through his testimony. He did not call his brother Gregg Loria or a representative of his employer as a witness.[31] Petitioner's testimony was in large part general, conclusory, and/or uncorroborated. We are not required to, and we do not, accept such testimony as sustaining petitioner's burden of establishing error in respondent's determinations.

CLAIMED EXPENSES WITH RESPECT TO THE RUNNYMEDE PROPERTY

As we understand his position, petitioner contends that he is entitled to deduct for 1989 the mortgage loan interest, mortgage loan points, and real property taxes

---

31. Petitioner did not file any briefs in this case.

that he claimed in Schedule A because he paid those expenses and lived at the Runnymede property during 1989. Respondent counters that the mortgage loan interest at issue was paid on the indebtedness of petitioner's brother Gregg Loria (viz., the Freedom Federal mortgage loan), and not on the indebtedness of petitioner, and that, consequently, petitioner is not entitled to deduct that interest. Respondent further contends that petitioner has not established his entitlement to deductions for the mortgage loan points and real property taxes at issue. . . .

The record establishes that during 1989 petitioner's brother, and not petitioner, (1) was the legal owner of the Runnymede property and (2) was indebted to Freedom Federal on the mortgage loan it had made on that property. Petitioner has not established that he was the legal or equitable owner of the Runnymede property. Nor has he presented any evidence relating to the mortgage loan points involved herein.

On the record before us, we find that petitioner has not established that he is entitled to deduct for 1989 either the mortgage loan interest or the mortgage loan points that are at issue in this case.

REAL PROPERTY TAXES

Section 164 allows a deduction for certain taxes, including real property taxes. Section 1.164-1(a), Income Tax Regs., provides that taxes are generally deductible only by the person on whom they are imposed. Petitioner proffered no evidence showing that the real property taxes at issue were imposed on him by local law. Nor has he presented any evidence, other than his general, conclusory, and uncorroborated testimony on which we are unwilling to rely, that he even paid those taxes.

On the record before us, we find that petitioner has not established that he is entitled to deduct for 1989 the real property taxes at issue.

CONCLUSION

Based on the present record, we sustain respondent's determinations that petitioner is not entitled to deduct for 1989 the mortgage loan interest, the mortgage loan points, and the real property taxes that he claimed in Schedule A.

ACCURACY-RELATED PENALTY

Respondent determined that petitioner is liable for 1989 for the accuracy-related penalty under section 6662(a) because his underpayment of tax for that year was due to negligence or disregard of rules or regulations. . . .

Petitioner presented no evidence and makes no argument regarding the accuracy-related penalty determined by respondent. The record thus provides no basis on which we can find that petitioner was not negligent or that he acted with reasonable cause and in good faith with respect to any portion of the underpayment that respondent determined is subject to the accuracy-related penalty.

On the instant record, we sustain respondent's determination that petitioner is liable for 1989 for the accuracy-related penalty with respect to his underpayment of tax for that year.

Notes and Questions

1. *Beneficial ownership?* The taxpayer argued this case *pro se*, and it is clear that the court was unimpressed by the quality of his representation. But did the taxpayer have a reasonable basis for arguing that he was the beneficial owner of the property in question, and that as such he did have sufficient legal incidence in the tax to justify claiming the deduction? What if, as a means of avoiding usury laws limiting interest rates charged to individuals (but not, under some state laws, to corporations), Mr. Loria had taken title to the property in the name of a corporation created simply to avoid the usury laws? *See* Commissioner v. Bollinger, 485 U.S. 340 (1988), for a case in which a corporation holding property as an agent for individual owners was found not to be the owner of the property for tax purposes.

2. *Section 7491.* The court notes that the taxpayer had the burden of showing that the determination of the Commissioner was incorrect. That was true at the time, but the presumptions in this regard have been modified somewhat by the passage of the "Taxpayer Bill of Rights" provisions in the Internal Revenue Service Restructuring and Reform Act of 1998. That Act added §7491 to the IRC, which generally now imposes a burden of persuasion on the Commissioner, though the taxpayer still bears a burden of production of evidence relating to all relevant facts on his return. Would you say that Mr. Loria's problem in this case related to persuading the court or to producing appropriate evidence?

D.   CASUALTY LOSSES

1. History and Rationale

Losses incurred in a trade or business, or in activities engaged in for profit, are generally deductible under §165(a). The usual justification is that an income tax should reach only the net income from business and profit-seeking activities, not the gross receipts from those activities. But what about losses sustained with respect to property that is not used in a trade or business, nor in a profit-seeking activity? Suppose, for example, that your car, which you use solely for personal purposes, is totaled in an accident, and you receive no compensation for the loss of the car (through insurance or tort damages).

Subject to some significant limitations discussed below, §165(c)(3) will allow you to claim a casualty loss deduction. If your car had been stolen, you could also deduct the loss under §165(c)(3). On the other hand, if the car had gradually worn out over a number of years, until it became worthless, or you simply sold it for much less than what it had cost you, you would not be entitled to any deduction. You would not have been allowed depreciation (ACRS) deductions under §168, because you did not use the car in a trade or business, or for the production of income. (*See* §168(a), incorporating the standards of §167(a).) Nor could you have claimed a loss on the sale or abandonment of the car, because §165(c) does not permit individuals to deduct losses — other than casualty and theft losses — on personal use property.

In addition, §262(a) provides a general rule that no deduction shall be allowed "for personal, living, or family expenses," except as expressly provided in some other Code section.

These rules are generally consistent with the Haig-Simons definition of income, though that may not be immediately obvious. Losses of any sort, of course, might plausibly be considered to be decrements to wealth, and therefore deductible from income because of their negative impact on the "change of wealth" term in the Haig-Simons definition. But if that is the test, why are only some losses permitted? The explanation lies in the fact that some losses (the disfavored, nondeductible ones) merely represent the gradual consumption of the item in question. For example, if you use a $20,000 personal automobile for five years, you will not be surprised to know that it has "lost" perhaps $15,000 of its value over that time. This is indeed a decrement to wealth, but it also represents consumption over the five-year period of $15,000 of automobile services. (It would, indeed, approximate the cost of a five-year lease on a $20,000 automobile.) So, in applying the Haig-Simons income definition, the annualized consumption of $3,000 per year is added to income as consumption, just as the annualized $3,000 loss in value is subtracted as a loss in wealth. The net result is that you have neither income nor a deduction for the use of the car. Of course, the amounts in question need not be precisely equal; one could compare, for example, the rental value of an asset with the actual loss in value that the particular taxpayer experienced over any particular time period. But the tax rules disallowing deductions for gradual loss in wealth in effect presume conclusively that the amount by which the value of an asset is diminished over time is itself the best measure of the consumption value enjoyed by the taxpayer over the same period.[32]

Other losses obviously cannot represent consumption of this sort. A pure example would be presented by a taxpayer who cashes a check for $1,000, but has the cash stolen on the way home from the bank. The practical problem is to find a workable way to distinguish losses that should be deductible as casualties from losses that should be nondeductible as ordinary wear and tear.

Section 165 employs no fewer than three approaches to this problem, which have accreted over time. From the beginning, a deductible casualty loss has had to be a sudden and somewhat dramatic event. In the words of §165(c)(3), it must be the result of "fire, storm, shipwreck, or other casualty, or . . . theft." In 1963, Congress added a second requirement, in §165(h)(1): Even if the property damage is the result of an acceptable sort of casualty, a deduction is allowed only if and to the extent that the taxpayer's loss exceeded $100. Finally, Congress added §165(h)(2) in 1982, which provides that the total amount of a taxpayer's casualty losses for the year (after application of §165(h)(1)) is deductible only to the extent it exceeds 10 percent of the taxpayer's adjusted gross income in the same year.[33]

The result of these changes — particularly the last one — has been to make small-to-medium-sized casualty losses essentially nondeductible, with the

---

32. In reality, it isn't quite this tidy, because the consumption, in the form of the rental value, should normally exceed the depreciation of the automobile by an amount equal to the imputed return on the capital that the taxpayer invested in the automobile. That imputed value, however, is generally ignored for all tax purposes. See the discussion of imputed income in Chapter 2.B.2.a.

33. One might think that this last requirement — which for most itemizing taxpayers disallows vastly larger sums than the second requirement — would have obviated the $100 per casualty rule; but Congress concluded otherwise. And this was probably wise. For those taxpayers whose deductible losses do exceed the 10 percent threshold, the $100 per casualty requirement still serves to prevent taxpayers from having a deductible event every time they spill a bottle of milk.

definition of "small-to-medium-sized" being dependent on the adjusted gross income of the taxpayer. This explains why so few taxpayers are actually able to deduct casualty losses.[34]

Congress has occasionally waived the $100, and the 10-percent-of-AGI, nondeductible floors on casualty losses when the casualties are the result of a widespread disaster. For example, losses due to any of three major hurricanes in the fall of 2005 (Katrina, Rita, and Wilma) were deductible in full under §1400S(b), without either of the §165(h) reductions in the deductible amount. Similarly, §165(h)(3) provides that the 10-percent-of-AGI floor does not apply to casualty losses attributable to a federally declared disaster — but only if the disaster occurred before January 1, 2010. These are questionable policy choices, since the decrement to wealth suffered by the taxpayer would not seem to depend on whether the casualty was widespread or more narrowly focused — as it might be, for example, in the case of damage done by a tornado. In either case, if you have $10,000, or perhaps $100,000, of uninsured damage done by a storm, that is the measure of your casualty loss. Nevertheless, as Congress sees it, the measure of your casualty loss *deduction* may depend on whether the damaged property was within or without a designated geographical area (the so-called Gulf Opportunity Zone, in the case of the 2005 hurricanes).

2.   *Computing the Casualty Loss Deduction*

The several thresholds and restrictions embodied in the present form of the casualty loss rules make computation of the deductible amount rather complex, sufficiently so that taxpayers who claim casualty loss deductions must file a separate form — Form 4684, the 2010 version of which has 42 lines, covering two pages — to reflect the necessary calculations. To begin with, the taxpayer must calculate the amount of each casualty loss sustained over the course of the tax year. This involves comparison of the fair market value of the lost or damaged property immediately before the casualty with the fair market value immediately after that event. (The latter figure will, of course, be zero in the case of stolen or totally destroyed property.)

This comparison must be done separately for each piece of property involved in the casualty. A casualty for this purpose is the physical event that created the loss. For example, a minor hurricane — that is, one not named Katrina, Rita, or Wilma — might blow over a tree, damaging both the roof of a taxpayer's house and her personal automobile parked in the driveway. The same storm may also have flooded her basement, destroying personal property stored there. All these losses are considered part of a single casualty for purposes of the $100 per casualty limitation. Reg. §1.165-7(b)(4)(ii).

The economic loss with respect to each piece of property is then compared with that property's adjusted basis. The adjusted basis is actually used for two purposes. First, if the property has been "involuntarily converted" (meaning that it has been lost, destroyed, or sold for salvage value), and the amount of any recoveries from

34. About 337,000 taxpayers claimed casualty loss deductions in 2008 — which is about two-tenths of 1 percent of all taxpayers. Of course, the majority of taxpayers simply don't have any nontrivial casualty losses in any particular year. But the effect of the 10-percent-of-AGI rule is nevertheless quite conspicuous, and can be clearly seen in its effects in the first year following its addition to the Code. IRS *Statistics of Income* data show that in 1982, the last year preceding the imposition of the 10 percent rule, about 2.2 million taxpayers deducted about $2.8 billion in casualty losses; in 1983, only about 200,000 taxpayers were able to take any deduction at all, and those taxpayers deducted less than $1 billion of casualty losses in the aggregate.

insurance coverage, tort awards, or salvage proceeds exceeds the adjusted basis of the property, then the taxpayer is considered to have enjoyed a casualty *gain*, rather than suffering a casualty loss (§165(h)(3)(A)). (While this is relatively rare, it is certainly possible with respect to real estate, where the usual approach is to insure market value rather than original investment; it can also happen in the case of personal property that is insured at "replacement cost" or the like.) Such gains are taxable as long-term capital gains, if the aggregate of such gains exceeds the aggregate of casualty losses for the tax year (§165(h)(2)(B)).[35] If the aggregate of such gains is less that the sum of all casualty losses, the gains merely reduce the amount of the taxpayer's casualty loss deduction.

The second and much more common use of the property's adjusted basis is to limit the amount of the loss that is cognizable for purposes of §165(c)(3) to the amount of that adjusted basis.

After the taxpayer has identified the lower of adjusted basis and loss in value of the property, she must then reduce the amount of the loss by the amounts of any recoveries. The taxpayer then aggregates all casualty losses stemming from a single casualty, and subtracts from that total the $100 deductible mentioned above. Finally, if the unfortunate taxpayer has suffered more than one casualty event during the same year, losses (and gains, if any) from all casualties are totaled. If there is a net loss, only the amount of that loss that exceeds 10 percent of adjusted gross income is deductible.

At the risk of some repetition, the computational steps a taxpayer must go through to determine the allowable deductions are as follows:

1. For each piece of property that was damaged, lost, or destroyed, begin with the fair market value of the property before the casualty;
2. Subtract the value of the property after the casualty (which will be zero if the property is totally lost or destroyed);
3. Compare the result with the adjusted basis of the property, taking the lesser of the two numbers as the tentative casualty loss;[36]
4. Subtract the amount of any recoveries from tortfeasors or insurance coverage;
5. Once that process is complete for each piece of property lost or damaged in the casualty, the tentative casualty losses are added; and
6. Casualty gains, if any, and the statutory $100 deductible are subtracted.
7. If the taxpayer suffered more than one casualty, the steps above must be repeated for each piece of property in each additional casualty suffered.
8. Once the gains and losses from each casualty are computed, the taxpayer adds them together, then subtracts 10 percent of adjusted gross income. This is the amount of the allowable deduction.

To illustrate these rules, suppose that the hurricane mentioned above totally destroyed the car on which the downed tree fell, and that that car had a basis of $20,000, a fair market value of $15,000, and was insured for $14,000. Suppose

35. See discussion of capital gains in Chapter 12. Note that recognition of gains on property lost to casualty can generally be deferred if and to the extent that the taxpayer invests the proceeds of the recovery in property that is "similar or related in service or use" under §1033. See the discussion of §1033 in Chapter 3.C.1.

36. However, if there is a disposition of the property, and the sum of the recoveries from insurance, tortfeasors, and salvage sales, if any, exceeds the adjusted basis of the property, the amount of the excess is a casualty gain under §165(h)(3)(A).

further that the taxpayer's house had an adjusted basis of $75,000, a fair market value of $300,000 immediately before the storm, and a fair market value immediately after the storm of $220,000, because of the structural damage sustained. Assume further that a hurricane exclusion in the taxpayer's homeowner's insurance policy allowed the insurance company to disclaim liability under the policy, so there was no insurance recovery for damage to the house. Finally, assume that the flood-damaged property in the basement was a clothes dryer with a basis of $400, a fair market value before the storm of $300, and no remaining value after the storm; however, assume also that the taxpayer had "replacement cost" insurance on this dryer, which resulted in the receipt by the taxpayer of a $600 check from her insurance carrier. What is covered under §165(c)(3)?

Note first that the taxpayer actually enjoyed a casualty gain on the dryer: Her recovery — the $600 check — exceeded her adjusted basis of $400 in the property destroyed.[37] As to the car, the damage sustained is $15,000 (which does *not* exceed her adjusted basis), reduced by the $14,000 of insurance recovery. Finally, the house damage of $80,000 is limited by the $75,000 adjusted basis that the taxpayer has in the house. No reduction for insurance recovery is required, however, since there was none. Thus, the cognizable losses consist of the $1,000 loss on the car and a $75,000 loss on the house, partly offset by the $200 of casualty gain on the dryer. The total of these is reduced by the $100 deductible. This casualty therefore produced a net cognizable loss of $75,700. The following table summarizes the several computations:

1. Car:	value before:	$15,000
	less value after	$0
	equals gross economic loss:	$15,000
	adjusted basis:	$20,000
	lesser of previous two lines:	$15,000
	less insurance recovery:	$14,000
	equals casualty loss:	$1,000
2. House:	value before:	$300,000
	less value after:	$220,000
	equals gross economic loss:	$80,000
	adjusted basis:	$75,000
	lesser of previous two lines:	$75,000
	less insurance recovery:	$0
	equals casualty loss:	$75,000
3. Dryer:	insurance recovery:	$600
	less adjusted basis:	$400
	equals casualty gain:	$200

Net cognizable loss from this casualty:
$1,000+ $75,000−$200−$100 = $75,700

---

37. Normally, a taxpayer in this situation would replace the destroyed property with similar property, and elect not to recognize this gain under §1033. Let's assume not in this case — perhaps she's decided to save energy by using a clothes line — so that the mechanics of casualty gain offsets can be illustrated.

Even after all these computations, however, we still do not know what the taxpayer may deduct in this tax year. To compute that, we need to know whether there were other casualties experienced by the taxpayer in the same tax year (and, if so, what the amounts of the damages resulting from those casualties were), and we need to know the taxpayer's adjusted gross income, so that we can apply the limitation on overall casualty loss deductions based on the taxpayer's adjusted gross income. If we assume that there were no other casualties during the tax year, and that the taxpayer's adjusted gross income was $150,000, the casualty deduction she could claim would be the $75,700, reduced by 10 percent of $150,000, or $15,000. Thus, she could deduct $60,700.

Problem 10. Suppose that in the scenario just considered, the taxpayer sustained another casualty loss from an incident quite separate from the hurricane, when the vehicle she bought to replace her hurricane-damaged vehicle was itself stolen. It had an adjusted basis of $22,000, and a fair market value of $20,000 at the time of its theft. The car was not found, but her insurance company settled with her for the "bluebook" value of $18,000. Assume further that her adjusted gross income in this tax year was $200,000. What deduction would she be allowed under §165(c)(3)?

3. Interpretive Issues: Notes on Developments in the Case Law and Elsewhere

The major interpretive issue in casualty losses is, of course, the question of what constitutes a casualty. The statute refers, somewhat quaintly, to damages from "fire, storm, shipwreck, or other casualty, or from theft." Four of these are reasonably clear, leaving only the "other casualty" phrase in need of further elaboration. Certainly automobile accidents routinely produce casualty losses; indeed, they might be thought of as the contemporary counterpart of the shipwreck.[38] But in many areas, the case law quickly becomes murky, and it is easy to find cases with apparently similar facts that come to opposite conclusions about the casualty status.

For example, outcomes are split on losses of wedding and engagement rings as deductible casualty losses. Various decided cases report that rings have been lost in bedrooms, bathrooms, kitchens, car doors, and duck blinds (among other places, no doubt). Two cases selected from this sad saga of nuptial-symbol carnage illustrate nothing so much as the unavoidable subjectivity of courts in making fact-based determinations of this sort. In Keenan v. Bowers, 91 F. Supp. 771 (E.D.S.C. 1950), a wife wrapped her ring in a tissue before retiring for the night in the motel room at which she and her husband were staying. Her husband used several tissues

---

38. Note, though, that §165(c)(3) allows a deduction only for losses "of property," and this has been interpreted to apply only to damage to the taxpayer's own property. Thus, tort liability for damage a taxpayer causes to other people's cars will not be deductible as a casualty loss. The limitation of casualty losses to those associated with one's own property is not explained in the legislative history. Perhaps Congress thought it inappropriate to soften the blow of a taxpayer's tort liability, on grounds that it might reduce the incentives for taxpayers to meet their duties of care to potential tort victims. But if this sentiment were strong, one wonders why losses to the taxpayer's own property are allowed as casualty losses if the losses result from the taxpayer's negligence. Yet the rules clearly do permit deductions even when negligence is present. *See* Reg. §1.165-7(a)(3)(i).

during the night, and in the morning gathered them all up, including the one containing his wife's ring, and flushed them down the toilet, from which the ring was never recovered. In Carpenter v. Commissioner, 25 T.C.M. 1186 (1966), the wife put her ring in a glass of water and ammonia to clean it, and left the glass by the kitchen sink. Her husband emptied the glass into the garbage disposal built into the sink, and the ring was completely destroyed. The Carpenters got a deduction, but the Keenans did not. Floundering for a distinction in the facts, one could conclude that electric devices produce "other casualties," but hydraulic ones do not. But by this point in law school, we know better than that.

Generally, the courts, and especially the IRS, are looking for something that does its damage suddenly, presumably under the theory that slow-paced damage is the sort of thing that is more accurately regarded as a result of the aging or consumption of the property, rather than a true, wealth-diminishing casualty. Thus, damage from rust, dry rot, termites, and the like is usually not allowed to generate casualty loss deductions.

Other policy limitations have also been asserted from time to time. For example, according to Treas. Reg. §1.165-7(a)(3)(i), damage to an automobile qualifies as a casualty if "[t]he damage results from the faulty driving of the taxpayer or other person operating the automobile but is not due to the willful act or willful negligence of the taxpayer. . . ." Although the regulations refer only to automobile accidents, the same principles apply to casualties of all sorts. In Blackman v. Commissioner, 88 T.C. 677 (1987), the taxpayer intentionally set fire to his estranged wife's clothes, and accidentally burned down his house in the process. At least that was his story; the court clearly harbored suspicions that he may have intended to burn down the house. In addition to holding that §165(c)(3) does not allow a deduction for a loss caused by the taxpayer's gross negligence, the court reasoned that allowing the Mr. Blackman a deduction would "frustrate the articulated public policy of Maryland against arson and burning." Was the court afraid that people would burn down their houses on purpose, just to get a tax deduction? If so, should it have been worried? Would §165(c)(3) ever turn arson into a profitable activity?

4. Theft Losses from Ponzi Schemes

REV. RUL. 2009-9

2009-1 C.B. 735

ISSUES

(1) Is a loss from criminal fraud or embezzlement in a transaction entered into for profit a theft loss or a capital loss under §165 of the Internal Revenue Code?

(2) Is such a loss subject to either the personal loss limits in §165(h) or the limits on itemized deductions in §§67 and 68?

(3) In what year is such a loss deductible?

(4) How is the amount of such a loss determined?

(5) Can such a loss create or increase a net operating loss under §172?

(6) Does such a loss qualify for the computation of tax provided by §1341 for the restoration of an amount held under a claim of right? . . .

FACTS

A is an individual who uses the cash receipts and disbursements method of accounting and files federal income tax returns on a calendar year basis. *B* holds himself out to the public as an investment advisor and securities broker. In Year 1, *A*, in a transaction entered into for profit, opened an investment account with B, contributed $100x to the account, and provided *B* with power of attorney to use the $100x to purchase and sell securities on *A*'s behalf. *A* instructed *B* to reinvest any income and gains earned on the investments. In Year 3, *A* contributed an additional $20x to the account. *B* periodically issued account statements to *A* that reported the securities purchases and sales that *B* purportedly made in *A*'s investment account and the balance of the account. *B* also issued tax reporting statements to *A* and to the Internal Revenue Service that reflected purported gains and losses on *A*'s investment account. *B* also reported to *A* that no income was earned in Year 1 and that for each of the Years 2 through 7 the investments earned $10x of income (interest, dividends, and capital gains), which *A* included in gross income on *A*'s federal income tax returns. At all times prior to Year 8 and part way through Year 8, *B* was able to make distributions to investors who requested them. A took a single distribution of $30x from the account in Year 7. In Year 8, it was discovered that *B*'s purported investment advisory and brokerage activity was in fact a fraudulent investment arrangement known as a "Ponzi" scheme. Under this scheme, *B* purported to invest cash or property on behalf of each investor, including *A*, in an account in the investor's name. For each investor's account, *B* reported investment activities and resulting income amounts that were partially or wholly fictitious. In some cases, in response to requests for withdrawal, *B* made payments of purported income or principal to investors. These payments were made, at least in part, from amounts that other investors had invested in the fraudulent arrangement. When *B*'s fraud was discovered in Year 8, *B* had only a small fraction of the funds that *B* reported on the account statements that *B* issued to *A* and other investors. *A* did not receive any reimbursement or other recovery for the loss in Year 8. The period of limitation on filing a claim for refund under §6511 has not yet expired for Years 5 through 7, but has expired for Years 1 through 4. *B*'s actions constituted criminal fraud or embezzlement under the law of the jurisdiction in which the transactions occurred. At no time prior to the discovery did *A* know that *B*'s activities were a fraudulent scheme. . . .

LAW AND ANALYSIS

Issue 1. Theft loss. Section 165(a) allows a deduction for losses sustained during the taxable year and not compensated by insurance or otherwise. For individuals, §165(c)(2) allows a deduction for losses incurred in a transaction entered into for profit, and §165(c)(3) allows a deduction for certain losses not connected to a transaction entered into for profit, including theft losses. Under §165(e), a theft loss is sustained in the taxable year the taxpayer discovers the loss. Section 165(f) permits a deduction for capital losses only to the extent allowed in §§1211 and 1212. In certain circumstances, a theft loss may be taken into account in determining gains or losses for a taxable year under §1231. For federal income tax purposes, "theft" is a word of general and broad connotation, covering any criminal appropriation of another's property to the use of the taker, including theft by swindling, false pretenses and any other form of guile. . . .

The character of an investor's loss related to fraudulent activity depends, in part, on the nature of the investment. For example, a loss that is sustained on the worthlessness or disposition of stock acquired on the open market for investment is a capital loss, even if the decline in the value of the stock is attributable to fraudulent activities of the corporation's officers or directors, because the officers or directors did not have the specific intent to deprive the shareholder of money or property. See Rev. Rul. 77-17, 1977-1 C.B. 44. In the present situation, unlike the situation in Rev. Rul. 77-17, *B* specifically intended to, and did, deprive *A* of money by criminal acts. *B*'s actions constituted a theft from *A*, as theft is defined for §165 purposes. Accordingly, *A*'s loss is a theft loss, not a capital loss.

Issue 2. Deduction limitations. Section 165(h) imposes two limitations on casualty loss deductions, including theft loss deductions, for property not connected either with a trade or business or with a transaction entered into for profit. Section 165(h)(1) provides that a deduction for a loss described in §165(c)(3) (including a theft) is allowable only to the extent that the amount exceeds $100. . . . Section 165(h)(2) provides that if personal casualty losses for any taxable year (including theft losses) exceed personal casualty gains for the taxable year, the losses are allowed only to the extent of the sum of the gains, plus so much of the excess as exceeds ten percent of the individual's adjusted gross income. Rev. Rul. 71-381, 1971-2 C.B. 126, concludes that a taxpayer who loans money to a corporation in exchange for a note, relying on financial reports that are later discovered to be fraudulent, is entitled to a theft loss deduction under §165(c)(3). However, §165(c)(3) subsequently was amended to clarify that the limitations applicable to personal casualty and theft losses under §165(c)(3) apply only to those losses that are not connected with a trade or business or a transaction entered into for profit. Tax Reform Act of 1984, Pub. L. No. 98-369, §711 (1984). As a result, Rev. Rul. 71-381 is obsolete to the extent that it holds that theft losses incurred in a transaction entered into for profit are deductible under §165(c)(3), rather than under §165(c)(2). In opening an investment account with *B*, *A* entered into a transaction for profit. *A*'s theft loss therefore is deductible under §165(c)(2) and is not subject to the §165(h) limitations. Section 63(d) provides that itemized deductions for an individual are the allowable deductions other than those allowed in arriving at adjusted gross income (under §62) and the deduction for personal exemptions. A theft loss is not allowable under §62 and is therefore an itemized deduction. Section 67(a) provides that miscellaneous itemized deductions may be deducted only to the extent the aggregate amount exceeds two percent of adjusted gross income. Under §67(b)(3), losses deductible under §165(c)(2) or (3) are excepted from the definition of miscellaneous itemized deductions. Section 68 provides an overall limit on itemized deductions based on a percentage of adjusted gross income or total itemized deductions. Under §68(c)(3), losses deductible under §165(c)(2) or (3) are excepted from this limit. Accordingly, *A*'s theft loss is an itemized deduction that is not subject to the limits on itemized deductions in §§67 and 68.

Issue 3. Year of deduction. Section 165(e) provides that any loss arising from theft is treated as sustained during the taxable year in which the taxpayer discovers the loss. Under §§1.165-8(a)(2) and 1.165-1(d), however, if, in the year of discovery, there exists a claim for reimbursement with respect to which there is a reasonable prospect of recovery, no portion of the loss for which reimbursement may be received is sustained until the taxable year in which it can be ascertained with reasonable certainty whether or not the reimbursement will be received, for example, by a settlement, adjudication, or abandonment of the claim. Whether a reasonable prospect of recovery exists is a question of fact to be determined upon examination of all facts and circumstances. *A* may deduct the theft loss in Year 8, the year the theft loss is discovered, provided that the loss is not covered by a claim for reimbursement or other recovery as to which *A* has a reasonable prospect of recovery. To the extent that *A*'s deduction is reduced by such a claim, recoveries on the claim in a later taxable year are not includible in *A*'s gross income. If *A* recovers a greater amount in a later year, or an amount that initially was not covered by a claim as to which there was a reasonable prospect of recovery, the recovery is includible in *A*'s gross income in the later year under the tax benefit rule, to the extent the earlier deduction reduced *A*'s income tax. See §111; §1.165-1(d)(2)(iii). Finally, if *A* recovers less than the amount that was covered by a claim as to which there was a reasonable prospect of recovery that reduced the deduction for theft in Year 8, an additional deduction is allowed in the year the amount of recovery is ascertained with reasonable certainty.

Issue 4. Amount of deduction. Section 1.165-8(c) provides that the amount deductible in the case of a theft loss is determined consistently with the manner described in §1.165-7 for determining the amount of a casualty loss, considering the fair market value of the property immediately after the theft to be zero. Under these provisions, the amount of an investment theft loss is the basis of the property (or the amount of money) that was lost, less any reimbursement or other compensation. The amount of a theft loss resulting from a fraudulent investment arrangement is generally the initial amount invested in the arrangement, plus any additional investments, less amounts withdrawn, if any, reduced by reimbursements or other recoveries and reduced by claims as to which there is a reasonable prospect of recovery. If an amount is reported to the investor as income in years prior to the year of discovery of the theft, the investor includes the amount in gross income, and the investor reinvests the amount in the arrangement, this amount increases the deductible theft loss. Accordingly, the amount of *A*'s theft loss for purposes of §165 includes *A*'s original Year 1 investment ($100x) and additional Year 3 investment ($20x). *A*'s loss also includes the amounts that *A* reported as gross income on *A*'s federal income tax returns for Years 2 through 7 ($60x). *A*'s loss is reduced by the amount of money distributed to *A* in Year 7 ($30x). If *A* has a claim for reimbursement with respect to which there is a reasonable prospect of recovery, *A* may not deduct in Year 8 the portion of the loss that is covered by the claim.

Issue 5. Net operating loss. Section 172 (a) allows as a deduction for the taxable year the aggregate of the net operating loss carryovers and carrybacks to that year. In computing a net operating loss under §172(c) and (d)(4), nonbusiness deductions of noncorporate taxpayers are generally allowed only to the extent of nonbusiness income. For this purpose, however, any deduction for casualty or theft losses allowable under §165(c)(2) or (3) is treated as a business deduction. Section 172(d)(4)(C). Under §172 (b)(1)(A), a net operating loss generally may be carried back 2 years and forward 20 years. However, under §172(b)(1)(F), the portion of an individual's net operating loss arising from casualty or theft may be carried back 3 years and forward 20 years. . . . To the extent *A*'s theft loss deduction creates or increases a net operating loss in the year the loss is deducted, *A* may carry back up to 3 years and forward up to 20 years the portion of the net operating loss attributable to the theft loss. . . .

Issue 6. Restoration of amount held under claim of right. Section 1341 provides an alternative tax computation formula intended to mitigate against unfavorable tax consequences that may arise as a result of including an item in gross income in a taxable year and taking a deduction for the item in a subsequent year when it is established that the taxpayer did not have a right to the item. . . . To satisfy the requirements of §1341(a)(2), a deduction must arise because the taxpayer is under an obligation to restore the income. . . . When *A* incurs a loss from criminal fraud or embezzlement by *B* in a transaction entered into for profit, any theft loss deduction to which *A* may be entitled does not arise from an obligation on *A*'s part to restore income. Therefore, *A* is not entitled to the tax benefits of §1341 with regard to *A*'s theft loss deduction. . . .

HOLDINGS

(1) A loss from criminal fraud or embezzlement in a transaction entered into for profit is a theft loss, not a capital loss, under §165.

(2) A theft loss in a transaction entered into for profit is deductible under §165(c)(2), not §165(c)(3), as an itemized deduction that is not subject to the personal loss limits in §165(h), or the limits on itemized deductions in §§67 and 68.

(3) A theft loss in a transaction entered into for profit is deductible in the year the loss is discovered, provided that the loss is not covered by a claim for reimbursement or recovery with respect to which there is a reasonable prospect of recovery.

(4) The amount of a theft loss in a transaction entered into for profit is generally the amount invested in the arrangement, less amounts withdrawn, if any, reduced by reimbursements or recoveries, and reduced by claims as to which there is a reasonable prospect of recovery. Where an amount is reported to the investor as income prior to discovery of the arrangement and the investor includes that amount in gross income and reinvests this amount in the arrangement, the amount of the theft loss is increased by the purportedly reinvested amount.

(5) A theft loss in a transaction entered into for profit may create or increase a net operating loss under §172 that can be carried back up to 3 years and forward up to 20 years. . . .

(6) A theft loss in a transaction entered into for profit does not qualify for the computation of tax provided by §1341. . . .

Notes and Questions

1. *B is for Bernie.* Anyone who did not spend late 2008 and most of 2009 living in a cave will not be surprised to learn that the IRS issued this ruling with the victims of Bernard Madoff in mind. The ruling is not so limited, however, and no doubt will apply to victims of other schemes not yet discovered.

2. *The significance of the theft-loss-versus-capital-loss distinction.* As noted earlier,[39] §1211(b) provides that capital losses are deductible only against capital gains, plus $3,000 of non-capital gain income (with currently nondeductible losses carried forward indefinitely). Even when a capital loss is deductible, it will usually serve to offset capital gains that would have been taxed at 15 percent. By holding that the Madoff victims realized theft losses rather than capital losses, the ruling enabled the victims to avoid the limitations of

39. See section B.3 of Chapter 3.

§1211(b) and enabled them to use the losses to offset ordinary income (taxable at rates as high as 35 percent).

3. *But wait, there's more!* And it gets even better. By holding that a theft loss incurred in a transaction entered into for profit is deductible under §165(c)(2) rather than §165(c)(3), the ruling enables Madoff's victims to avoid all the special limitations imposed on §165(c)(3) personal casualty losses. The only remaining limitation is that the Madoff victims cannot deduct their losses if they claim the standard deduction, but one imagines that will not be a problem. No doubt the IRS found it politically convenient to issue a ruling favorable to the Madoff victims, but the ruling's conclusion that the deductions fit under §165(c)(2) — rather than either §1211(b) or §165(c)(3) — seems technically sound.

4. *How could Madoff steal money that never existed?* As discussed in the preceding notes, the ruling is on solid ground with respect to the theft of *A*'s net investment of $90x. The ruling's treatment of the fictitious investment income reported by *A* in earlier years, however, is a different matter. Look again at the fourth sentence of the ruling's discussion of Issue 4. It indicates that the proper tax response to the discovery that *A*'s investment income in prior years was a fiction from the very beginning is (a) to make no adjustment to the tax returns for those prior years, and (b) to allow a theft loss in the year of the discovery of the fraud. Does respect for the sanctity of the annual accounting system require that approach? The general rule is that events occurring after the close of a taxable year do not affect the taxpayer's tax liability for that year,[40] but is that rule implicated here? Why isn't this a situation in which the reporting of investment income was wrong *ab initio*, based on the facts as they existed in those prior years, with the result that the proper tax response to the discovery of the fraud is not a theft loss in the year of the discovery, but either the filing of an amended return eliminating the investment income (in the case of years as to which the statute of limitations has not run) or no response at all (in the case of closed years)? If the ruling's treatment of the fictitious income seems questionable as a technical matter, can you see why the IRS may have felt pressured to take the approach it did? (Hint: Review the ruling's statement of facts regarding the statute of limitations.)

E. MEDICAL EXPENSES

1. History and Rationale

Spending on medical and dental care is clearly a consumption activity, albeit nondiscretionary in many cases. In the early years of the income tax, this category of consumption was treated no differently from any other nonbusiness category. It was regarded as simply part of personal living expenses and was completely nondeductible. In 1942, however, Congress decided that extraordinary medical expenses — those above a certain floor amount — create a hardship that should be

---

40. See section C.1 of Chapter 2.

reflected in the assessment of ability to pay income tax, and a deduction was accordingly added to the Code. Until 1966, the deduction was subject to both a nondeductible floor and a ceiling, capping deductions at the higher end. However, in 1966, the ceiling was removed; in the years since, modifications in the deduction have taken the form of occasional increases in the amount of the floor, and greater refinement in the definition of deductible expenses.

The current form of the medical expense deduction, which has been only lightly modified since 1986, allows taxpayers who itemize their deductions to claim a fairly broad range of expenses in this area, incurred on their own behalf or on behalf of their dependents, but only to the extent that the expenses exceed 7.5 percent of the taxpayer's adjusted gross income in the tax year in which the expenses are paid, and only to the extent that the expenses exceed amounts covered by insurance or other third-party payers (such as a tortfeasor). The 7.5-percent-of-AGI floor is scheduled to rise to 10 percent of AGI for years after 2012 (with the increase delayed until years after 2016 for taxpayers 65 or older).

2. What Is "Medical Care"?

The statutory definition of medical care is found in §213(d)(1)(A), which says that "medical care means amounts paid for the diagnosis, cure, mitigation, or prevention of disease, or for the purpose of affecting any structure or function of the body." Subparagraphs (B) through (D) of this paragraph add transportation costs to access medical care, certain long-term care services, and medical insurance costs, respectively, to the definition of medical care.

This appears to be a definition of rather broad sweep. After all, getting a haircut or a suntan, lifting weights or jogging, or any of a number of other things not conventionally thought to involve "medical care" could be said, with no great stretch, to affect a structure of the body. Unsurprisingly, neither the IRS nor the judiciary takes the view that the costs of such things are deductible under §213, notwithstanding the statutory definition. In regulations, rulings, and positions adopted in litigation, the IRS has made an effort to patrol the boundaries of the medical expense definition closely, especially when it comes to expenses that look like ordinary personal living expenses. Usually, the IRS has been aided in this effort by the courts, which, as in the case below, appear generally to agree that the statute cannot be understood literally.

COMMISSIONER v. BILDER

369 U.S. 499 (1962)

Mr. Justice HARLAN delivered the opinion of the Court.

This case concerns the deductibility as an expense for "medical care," under §213 of the Internal Revenue Code of 1954, of rent paid by a taxpayer for an apartment in Florida, where he was ordered by his physician, as part of a regimen of medical treatment, to spend the winter months.

The taxpayer, now deceased, was an attorney practicing law in Newark, New Jersey. In December 1953, when he was 43 years of age and had suffered four heart attacks during the previous eight years, he was advised by a heart specialist to spend the winter season in a warm climate. The taxpayer, his wife, and his three-year-old daughter proceeded immediately to Fort Lauderdale, Florida, where they resided for the ensuing three months in an apartment rented for $1,500. Two months of the succeeding winter were also spent in Fort Lauderdale in an apartment rented for $829.

The taxpayer claimed the two rental payments as deductible medical expenses in his 1954 and 1955 income tax returns. These deductions were disallowed in their entirety by the Commissioner.[41] The Tax Court reversed the Commissioner's determination to the extent of one-third of the deductions, finding that proportion of the total claimed attributable to the taxpayer's own living accommodations. The remaining two-thirds it attributed to the accommodations of his wife and child, whose presence, the Tax Court concluded, had not been shown to be necessary to the medical treatment of the taxpayer's illness.

On cross-appeals from the decision of the Tax Court, the Court of Appeals held, by a divided vote, that the full rental payments were deductible as expenses for "medical care" within the meaning of §213. Because of a subsequent contrary holding by the Court of Appeals for the Second Circuit, Carasso v. Commissioner, 292 F.2d 367, and the need for a uniform rule on the point, we granted certiorari to resolve the conflict.

The Commissioner concedes that prior to the enactment of the Internal Revenue Code of 1954 rental payments of the sort made by the taxpayer were recognized as deductible medical expenses. This was because §23(x) of the Internal Revenue Code of 1939, though expressly authorizing deductions only for "amounts paid for the diagnosis, cure, mitigation, treatment, or prevention of disease," had been construed to include "travel primarily for and essential to . . . the prevention or alleviation of a physical or mental defect or illness," Treasury Regulations 111, §29.23(x)-1, and the cost of meals and lodging during such travel, I. T. 3786, 1946-1 Cum. Bull. 76.

The Commissioner maintains, however, that it was the purpose of Congress, in enacting §213(e)(1)(A) of the 1954 Code, albeit in language identical to that used in §23(x) of the 1939 Code, to deny deductions for all personal or living expenses incidental to medical treatment other than the cost of transportation of the patient alone, that exception having been expressly added by subdivision (B) to the definition of "medical care" in §213(e)(1).

We consider the Commissioner's position unassailable in light of the congressional purpose explicitly revealed in the House and Senate Committee Reports on the bill. These reports, anticipating the precise situation now before us, state:

> Subsection (e) defines medical care to mean amounts paid for the diagnosis, cure, mitigation, treatment, or prevention of diseases or for the purpose of affecting any structure or function of the body (including amounts paid for accident or health insurance), or for transportation primarily for and essential to medical care. The deduction permitted for "transportation primarily for and essential to medical care" *clarifies existing law* in that it specifically *excludes deduction of any meals and lodging while away from home receiving medical treatment.* For example, if a doctor prescribes that a patient must go to Florida in order to alleviate specific chronic ailments and to escape unfavorable climatic conditions which have proven injurious to the health of the taxpayer, and the travel is prescribed for reasons

---

41. The Commissioner concedes that the taxpayer's sojourn in Florida was not for vacation purposes but was "a medical necessity and . . . a primary part of necessary medical treatment of a disease" from which the taxpayer was suffering, *i.e.*, atherosclerosis. 33 T.C., at 157. The taxpayer also claimed in each of his tax returns a $250 deduction for his transportation between Newark and Fort Lauderdale. Although the Commissioner initially disallowed this deduction, he thereafter acquiesced in its allowance by the Tax Court.

other than the general improvement of a patient's health, the cost of the patient's transportation to Florida would be deductible *but not his living expenses while there.* However, if a doctor prescribed an appendectomy and the taxpayer chose to go to Florida for the operation not even his transportation costs would be deductible. The subsection is not intended otherwise to *change* the existing definitions of medical care, to deny the cost of ordinary ambulance transportation nor to deny the cost of food or lodging provided as part of a hospital bill. H.R. Rep. No. 1337, 83d Cong., 2d Sess. A60 (1954); S. Rep. No. 1622, 83d Cong., 2d Sess. 219-220 (1954).[42] (Emphasis supplied.)

Since under the predecessor statute, as it had been construed, expenses for meals and lodging *were* deductible as expenses for "medical care," it may well be true that the Committee Reports spoke in part inartistically when they referred to subsection (e) as a mere clarification of "existing law," although it will be noted that the report also referred to what was being done as a *pro tanto* "change" in "the existing definitions of medical care." Yet Congress' purpose to exclude such expenses as medical deductions under the new bill is unmistakable in these authoritative pronouncements. It is that factor which is of controlling importance here.

We need not consider whether we would be warranted in disregarding these unequivocal expressions of legislative intent if the statute were so written as to permit no reasonable construction other than that urged on behalf of the taxpayer. Even the initial decision of the Tax Court under the 1939 Code respecting the deductibility of similar expenses under §23(x) recognized that the language of that statute was "susceptible to a variety of conflicting interpretations," Stringham v. Commissioner, 12 T.C. 580, 583. The Tax Court's conclusion as to the meaning of §23(x) of the earlier statute which was affirmed by the Court of Appeals, 183 F.2d 579, and acquiesced in by the Commissioner, necessarily rested on what emerged from a study of the legislative history of that enactment. So too the conclusion in this case, which turns on the construction of the identical words re-enacted as part of §213, must be based on an examination of the legislative history of this provision of the 1954 Code. The Committee Reports foreclose any reading of that provision which would permit this taxpayer to take the rental payments for his Florida apartment as "medical care" deductions.

Reversed.

Mr. Justice Douglas would affirm the judgment below for the reasons given by Judge Kalodner, 289 F.2d 291.

Notes and Questions

1. *Florida as medical care.* Note that the IRS, in effect, conceded that being in Florida during the winter months was itself medical care under the circumstances faced by this particular taxpayer. (The IRS ultimately acquiesced in the Tax Court's allowance below of the travel expenses of getting from New Jersey to Florida in each of the tax years in question.) Would it have done so, do you imagine, in the case of someone who suffered from "seasonal affective disorder," in which the lack of sunlight induces a tendency to depression during the winter months among susceptible individuals living

---

42. The substance of the rule set forth in both Reports has been embodied in the Treasury Regulations interpreting §213. [*See* Reg. §1.213-1(e)(1)(iv), which reads today exactly as it read at the time of this decision.]

well north of the Tropic of Cancer? Or would it only make such a concession in the case of someone who had previously had four heart attacks? In other words, does the severity of the disease affect the determination of what things constitute medical care? Should it?

2. *Travel may be broadening, but §213 isn't.* In 1984, Congress tightened the rules on deduction of travel costs as medical expenses. In §213(d)(2), it has allowed travel expenses to be deducted as medical expenses only if the care for which the travel is incurred is provided "by a physician, in a licensed hospital [or equivalent]" and only if the travel involves "no significant element of personal pleasure." There is a limit on the deduction of $50 per day for each eligible individual (for example, a parent of the patient is an eligible individual). This amount is not indexed for inflation, so its value has eroded over the years since its enactment, and will continue to do so. No deduction is allowed as a medically necessary travel expense for the cost of food consumed during the trip.

3. *Medical and nonmedical consumption.* The IRS and the courts have always been especially vigilant with respect to situations in which a taxpayer claims medical expense deductions for consumption patterns that many taxpayers engage in for purely nonmedical reasons. Although Bilder was able to deduct the travel to Florida, vacations generally hadn't fared well, even before the 1984 changes, as medical expense deductions, even though it would presumably be easy for a person in compromised physical or mental condition to find a doctor who would agree that "a cruise to Tahiti would do you a world of good." *See, e.g.,* Havey v. Commissioner, 12 T.C. 409 (1949). Similarly, taxpayers have sought deductions, as medical expenses, for the cost of private schooling for their children (Ochs v. Commissioner, 195 F.2d 692 (2d Cir. 1952) — deduction denied, even though boarding school appeared necessary to alleviate demands on mother suffering from throat cancer); for household services such as cooking and cleaning (Borgman v. Commissioner, 438 F.2d 1211 (9th Cir. 1971) — deduction denied, even though heart patient's doctor advised getting help with household services); and even for the costs of mowing one's lawn (Taylor v. Commissioner, 54 T.C.M. 129 (1987) — deduction denied, even though taxpayer's allergies led doctor to advise against lawn mowing). Still, occasionally a taxpayer wins one of these cases. In Cherry v. Commissioner, 46 T.C.M. 1031 (1983), a taxpayer was allowed to deduct the costs of maintaining and improving a swimming pool where a doctor had prescribed a regular exercise regimen for a patient who had emphysema and the patient had been unable to find any other acceptable exercise program. But such successes are rare, and probably need to be so in a system that (1) allows taxpayers to make the initial assessments of their qualifications for deductions, and (2) audits only about 1 percent of tax returns.

In a few areas, the IRS position appears to have softened in recent years. For example, it now recognizes that a weight loss program undertaken as treatment for a specific disease (defined to include obesity) can be deductible as a medical expense. *See* Rev. Rul. 2002-19, 2002-1 C.B. 778. The ruling makes even the cost of the food provided as part of the program deductible under §213 for two hypothetical patients, one of whom is being treated for obesity and the other for hypertension, under circumstances where weight loss is prescribed by a doctor as part of the treatment for that disorder.

4. *Cosmetic surgery, on and under §213.* Congress has nipped and tucked the medical care definition explicitly in a few areas. In the Omnibus Budget Reconciliation Act of 1990, Congress tightened the rules on deductibility of cosmetic surgery, which the IRS had generally allowed prior to the effective date of this act. Since 1990, no deductions have been allowed for cosmetic surgery unless it is "necessary to ameliorate a deformity arising from, or directly related to, a congenital abnormality, a personal injury resulting from an accident or trauma, or disfiguring disease." Section 213(d)(9).

5. *Publication 17.* The IRS publishes informal advice regularly on particular expenses that do (and do not) qualify for deduction as medical expenses. The following list is derived from a checklist in the current edition of IRS Publication 17, the extremely useful general guide to the individual income tax:

Expenses You May Deduct	Expenses You May Not Deduct
• birth control pills • fertility enhancement treatments • guide dog costs • lead paint removal costs • legal abortions • laser eye surgery	• nutritional supplements • nonprescription drugs • household help (even if recommended by a doctor) • herbal remedies

6. *Looking for rules in the wrong places.* Sometimes the writers of the tax rules (and taxpayers too, subsequently) seem to be the victims of unfortunate borrowing of rules designed for non-tax purposes. For example, the basic definition of medical care in §213(d) was apparently derived from the definitions that set the jurisdiction of the Federal Trade Commission to regulate the sale of "drugs" (prior to the creation of the Food and Drug Commission). Congressional attempts to draft a comprehensive definition for regulatory purposes may explain the apparently excessive breadth of the definition in the tax deduction context. Similarly, the use of the distinction between prescription and over-the-counter drugs seems unfortunate in the deduction context, since it has more to do with the dangers of drugs than with their medicinal values. See the last word of §213(b) for the effort to repair this defect in the statute as it applies to diabetics, who would otherwise not be able to deduct the cost of insulin (which is not a prescription drug).

As the list in Note 5 above reflects, the fact that expenses may not be entirely necessary (such as the cost of laser eye surgery) does not preclude deductibility, as long as they are not in the nature of cosmetic surgery. In fact, some of the deductible expenses shown (such as the expenses of an abortion) are ones thought to be immoral by a substantial part of the citizenry. The following recent decision by a divided Tax Court struggles in particular with the line between cosmetic surgery and deductible medical expense.

O'DONNABHAIN v. COMMISSIONER
134 T.C. 34 (2010)

GALE, Judge: Respondent determined a deficiency of $5,679 in petitioner's Federal income tax for 2001. After concessions, the issue for decision is whether petitioner may deduct as a medical care expense under section 213 amounts paid in 2001 for hormone therapy, sex reassignment surgery, and breast augmentation surgery that petitioner contends were incurred in connection with a condition known as gender identity disorder.

[Petitioner was born a genetic male, but from an early age was uncomfortable with her gender. She grew up as a man, married, and fathered three children. Her discomfort with her gender persisted, however, and, following termination of her twenty-year marriage, she sought psychiatric treatment for what was diagnosed as "gender identity disorder" (GID). Treatment of this disorder proceeded in several stages, including administration of feminizing hormones and trial periods of living publicly as a woman. The final stage, which is not indicated for every person suffering from GID, but was eventually prescribed for petitioner, was sexual reassignment surgery. This involved surgical modification of the genitals, and, in petitioner's case, breast augmentation surgery, despite evidence in her medical records that her breasts had, presumably through the hormonal therapies, achieved "approximately B cup [size] with a very nice shape." During 2001 petitioner incurred a total of $21,741 of uninsured expenses in connection with the various aspects of her therapy, including $4,500 for breast augmentation surgery.]

On her Federal income tax return for 2001, petitioner claimed an itemized deduction for the foregoing expenditures as medical expenses, which respondent subsequently disallowed in a notice of deficiency. . . .

OPINION

I. MEDICAL EXPENSE DEDUCTIONS UNDER SECTION 213

A.   In General

Section 213(a) allows a deduction for expenses paid during the taxable year for medical care that are not compensated for by insurance or otherwise and to the extent that such expenses exceed 7.5 percent of adjusted gross income. . . .

[The court then reviewed the history of the definition of medical expenses, concluding that the general statutory definition had not changed materially since its initial introduction into the Code in 1942.]

Thus, since the inception of the medical expense deduction, the definition of deductible "medical care" has had two prongs. The first prong covers amounts paid for the "diagnosis, cure, mitigation, treatment, or prevention of disease" and the second prong covers amounts paid "for the purpose of affecting any structure or function of the body."

The regulations interpreting the statutory definition of medical care echo the description of medical care in the Senate Finance Committee report accompanying the original enactment. . . . Notably, the regulations, mirroring the language of the Finance Committee report, treat "disease" as used in the statute as synonymous with "a physical or mental defect or illness." The language equating "mental defect" with "disease" was in the first version of the regulations promulgated in 1943 and has stood unchanged since. In addition, to qualify as "medical care" under the regulations, an expense must be incurred "primarily" for alleviation of a physical or mental defect, and the defect must be specific. "[A]n expenditure which is merely beneficial to the general health of an individual, such as an expenditure for a vacation, is not an expenditure for medical care." Sec. 1.213-1(e)(1)(ii), Income Tax Regs.

Given the reference to "mental defect" in the legislative history and the regulations, it has also long been settled that "disease" as used in section 213 can extend to mental disorders.

In Jacobs v. Commissioner, 62 T.C. 813 (1974), this Court reviewed the legislative history of section 213 and synthesized the case law to arrive at a framework for analysis of disputes concerning medical expense deductions. Noting that the medical expense deduction essentially carves a limited exception out of the general rule of section 262 that "personal, living, or family expenses" are not deductible, the Court observed that a taxpayer seeking a deduction under section 213 must show: (1) "the present existence or imminent probability of a disease, defect or illness — mental or physical" and (2) a payment "for goods or services directly or proximately related to the diagnosis, cure, mitigation, treatment, or prevention of the disease or illness." *Id.* at 818. Moreover, where the expenditures are arguably not "wholly medical in nature" and may serve a personal as well as medical purpose, they must also pass a "but for" test: the taxpayer must "prove both that the expenditures were an essential element of the treatment and that they would not have otherwise been incurred for nonmedical reasons." *Id.* at 819. . . .

The second prong of the statutory definition of "medical care," concerning amounts paid "for the purpose of affecting any structure or function of the body," was eventually adjudged too liberal by Congress. The Internal Revenue Service, relying on the second prong, had determined in two revenue rulings that deductions were allowed for amounts expended for cosmetic procedures (such as facelifts, hair transplants, and hair removal through electrolysis) because the procedures were found to affect a structure or function of the body within the meaning of section 213(d)(1)(A). . . . In 1990 Congress responded to these rulings by amending section 213 to include new subsection (d)(9) which, generally speaking, excludes cosmetic surgery from the definition of deductible medical care. . . .

Section 213(d)(9) defines "cosmetic surgery" as follows:

SEC. 213(d). Definitions. — For purposes of this section —

    (9) Cosmetic surgery. —
        (A) In general. — The term "medical care" does not include cosmetic surgery or other similar procedures, unless the surgery or procedure is necessary to ameliorate a deformity arising from, or directly related to, a congenital abnormality, a personal injury resulting from an accident or trauma, or disfiguring disease.
        (B) Cosmetic surgery defined. — For purposes of this paragraph, the term "cosmetic surgery" means any procedure which is directed at improving the patient's appearance and does not meaningfully promote the proper function of the body or prevent or treat illness or disease.

In sum, section 213(d)(9)(A) provides the general rule that the term "medical care" does not include "cosmetic surgery" (as defined) unless the surgery is necessary to ameliorate deformities of various origins. Section 213(d)(9)(B) then defines "cosmetic surgery" as any procedure that is directed at improving the patient's appearance but excludes from the definition any procedure that "meaningfully [promotes] the proper function of the body" or "[prevents] or [treats] illness or disease." There appear to be no cases of precedential value interpreting the cosmetic surgery exclusion of section 213(d)(9).

Respondent contends that petitioner's hormone therapy, sex reassignment surgery, and breast augmentation surgery are nondeductible "cosmetic surgery or other similar procedures" under section 213(d)(9) because they were directed at improving petitioner's appearance and did not treat an illness or disease, meaningfully promote the proper function of the body, or ameliorate a deformity. Although respondent concedes that GID is a mental disorder, respondent contends . . . that GID is not a disease for purposes of section 213 because it does not arise from an organic pathology within the human body that reflects "abnormal structure or function of the body at the gross, microscopic, molecular, biochemical, or neurochemical levels." Respondent further contends that the procedures at issue did not treat disease because there is no scientific proof of their efficacy in treating GID and that the procedures were cosmetic surgery because they were not medically necessary. Finally, respondent contends that petitioner did not have GID, that it was incorrectly diagnosed, and that therefore the procedures at issue did not treat a disease.

Petitioner maintains that she is entitled to deduct the cost of the procedures at issue on the grounds that GID is a well-recognized mental disorder in the psychiatric field that "falls squarely within the meaning of 'disease' because it causes serious, clinically significant distress and impairment of functioning." Since widely accepted standards of care prescribe hormone treatment, sex reassignment surgery, and, in appropriate circumstances, breast augmentation surgery for genetic males suffering from GID, expenditures for the foregoing constitute deductible "medical care" because a direct or proximate relationship exists between the expenditures and the "diagnosis, cure, mitigation, treatment, or prevention of disease," petitioner argues. Moreover, petitioner contends, because the procedures at issue treated a "disease" as used in section 213, they are not "cosmetic surgery" as defined in that section.

The availability of the medical expense deduction for the costs of hormonal and surgical sex reassignment for a transsexual individual presents an issue of first impression.

A. Statutory Definitions

Determining whether sex reassignment procedures are deductible "medical care" or nondeductible "cosmetic surgery" starts with the meaning of "treatment" and "disease" as used in section 213. Both the statutory definition of "medical care" and the statute's exclusion of "cosmetic surgery" from that definition depend in part upon whether an expenditure or procedure is for "treatment" of "disease." Under section 213(d)(1)(A), if an expenditure is "for the . . . treatment . . . of disease," it is deductible "medical care"; under section 213(d)(9)(B), if a procedure "[treats] . . . disease," it is not "cosmetic surgery" that is excluded from the definition of "medical care."

Because the only difference between the quoted phrases in these two subparagraphs is the use of the noun form "treatment" versus the verb form "treat," we see no meaningful distinction between them. . . . Consequently, the determination of whether something is a "treatment" of a "disease" is the same throughout section 213, whether for purposes of showing that an expenditure is for "medical care" under section 213(d)(1)(A) or that a procedure is not "cosmetic surgery" under section 213(d)(9)(B). A showing that a procedure constitutes "treatment" of a "disease" both precludes "cosmetic surgery" classification under section 213(d)(9) and qualifies the procedure as "medical care" under section 213(d)(1)(A).

Congress's reuse of the terms "treat" and "disease" in defining "cosmetic surgery" in section 213(d)(9)(B) triggers a second principle of statutory construction. Given that the phrase "treatment . . . of disease" as used in the section 213(d)(1)(A) definition of "medical care" had been the subject of considerable judicial and administrative construction when Congress incorporated the phrase into the definition of "cosmetic surgery" in 1990, it had acquired a settled judicial and administrative interpretation. In these circumstances it is proper to accept the already settled meaning of the phrase. Therefore, the pre-1990 caselaw and regulations construing "treatment" and "disease" for purposes of the section 213(d)(1)(A) definition of "medical care" are applicable to the interpretation of those words as used in the section 213(d)(9)(B) definition of "cosmetic surgery."

B.   Is GID a "Disease"?

Petitioner argues that she is entitled to deduct her expenditures for the procedures at issue because they were treatments for GID, a condition that she contends is a "disease" for purposes of section 213. Respondent maintains that petitioner's expenditures did not treat "disease" because GID is not a "disease" within the meaning of section 213. Central to his argument is respondent's contention that "disease" as used in section 213 has the meaning postulated by respondent's expert, . . . namely, "a condition . . . [arising] as a result of a pathological process . . . [occurring] within the individual and [reflecting] abnormal structure or function of the body at the gross, microscopic, molecular, biochemical, or neurochemical levels."

On brief respondent [urges] the foregoing definition . . . upon the Court as the meaning of "disease" as used in section 213; namely, that a "disease" for this purpose must have a demonstrated organic or physiological origin in the individual. Consequently, GID is not a "disease" because it has "no known organic pathology," respondent argues.

However, this use of expert testimony to establish the meaning of a statutory term is generally improper. . . . The meaning of a statutory term is a pure question of law that is exclusively the domain of the judge. . . .

The meaning of "disease" as used in section 213 must be resolved by the Court, using settled principles of statutory construction, including reference to the Commissioner's interpretive regulations, the legislative history, and case law precedent.

As a legal argument for the proper interpretation of "disease," respondent's position is meritless. Respondent cites no authority, other than . . . expert testimony, in support of his interpretation, and we have found none. To the contrary, respondent's interpretation is flatly contradicted by nearly a half century of case law. Numerous cases have treated mental disorders as "diseases" for purposes of section 213 without regard to any demonstrated organic or physiological origin or cause. These cases found mental conditions to be "diseases" where there was evidence that mental health professionals regarded the condition as creating a significant impairment to normal functioning and warranting treatment. . . .

The absence of any consideration of etiology in the case law is consistent with the legislative history and the regulations. Both treat "disease" as synonymous with "a physical or mental defect," which suggests a more colloquial sense of the term "disease" was intended than the narrower (and more rigorous) interpretation for which respondent contends.

In addition, in the context of mental disorders, it is virtually inconceivable that Congress could have intended to confine the coverage of section 213 to conditions with demonstrated organic origins when it enacted the provision in 1942, because physiological origins for mental disorders were not widely recognized at the time. As [respondent's expert] confirmed in his testimony, the physiological origins of various well-recognized mental disorders—for example, panic disorder and obsessive-compulsive disorder—were discovered only about a decade ago. Moreover, [respondent's expert] confirmed that bulimia would not constitute a "disease" under his definition, because bulimia has no demonstrated organic origin, nor would post-traumatic stress disorder. . . . Petitioner's expert . . . testified without challenge that most mental disorders listed in the DSM-IV-TR [the standard psychiatric diagnosis manual] do not have demonstrated organic causes. Thus, under the definition of "disease" respondent advances, many well-recognized mental disorders, perhaps most, would be excluded from coverage under section 213—a result clearly at odds with the intent of Congress (and the regulations) to provide deductions for the expenses of alleviating "mental defects" generally.

In sum, we reject respondent's interpretation of "disease" because it is incompatible with the stated intent of the regulations and legislative history to cover "mental defects" generally and is contradicted by a consistent line of cases finding "disease" in the case of mental disorders without regard to any demonstrated etiology.

Having rejected respondent's contention that "disease" as used in section 213 requires a demonstrated organic origin, we are left with the question whether the term should be interpreted to encompass GID. On this score, respondent, while conceding that GID is a mental disorder, argues that GID is "not a significant psychiatric disorder" but instead is a "social construction"—a "social phenomenon" that has been "medicalized." Petitioner argues that GID is a "disease" for purposes of section 213 because it is well recognized in mainstream psychiatric literature, including the DSM-IV-TR, as a legitimate mental disorder that "causes serious, clinically significant distress and impairment of functioning."

For the reasons already noted and those discussed below, we conclude that GID is a "disease" within the meaning of section 213. We start with the two case law factors influencing a finding of "disease" in the context of mental conditions: (1) A determination by a mental health professional that the condition created a significant impairment to normal functioning, warranting treatment, or (2) a listing of the condition in a medical reference text. Both factors involve deference by a court to the judgment of medical professionals. . . .

Second, GID is a serious, psychologically debilitating condition. Respondent's characterization of the condition on brief as a "social construction" and "not a significant psychiatric disorder" is undermined by both of his own expert witnesses and the medical literature in evidence. All three expert witnesses agreed that, absent treatment, GID in genetic males is sometimes associated with autocastration, autopenectomy, and suicide. . . .

Third, respondent's position that GID is not a significant psychiatric disorder is at odds with the position of every U.S. Court of Appeals that has ruled on the question of whether GID poses a serious medical need for purposes of the Eighth Amendment, which has been interpreted to require that prisoners receive adequate medical care. . . .

In view of (1) GID's widely recognized status in diagnostic and psychiatric reference texts as a legitimate diagnosis, (2) the seriousness of the condition as described in learned treatises in evidence and as acknowledged by all three experts in this case; (3) the severity of petitioner's impairment as found by the mental health professionals who examined her; (4) the consensus in the U.S. Courts of Appeal that GID constitutes a serious medical need for purposes of the Eighth Amendment, we conclude and hold that GID is a "disease" for purposes of section 213.

C. Did Petitioner Have GID?

Respondent also contends that petitioner was not correctly diagnosed with GID, citing his expert's contentions that certain comorbid conditions such as depression or transvestic fetishism had not been adequately ruled out as explanations of petitioner's condition.

We find that petitioner's GID diagnosis is substantially supported by the record. . . .

D. Whether Cross-Gender Hormones, Sex Reassignment Surgery and Breast Augmentation Surgery "Treat" GID

1. Cross-Gender Hormones and Sex Reassignment Surgery

Our conclusions that GID is a "disease" for purposes of section 213, and that petitioner suffered from it, leave the question of whether petitioner's hormone therapy, sex reassignment surgery, and breast augmentation surgery "[treated]" GID within the meaning of section 213(d)(1)(A) and (9)(B).

In contrast to their dispute over the meaning of "disease," the parties have not disputed the meaning of "treatment" or "treat" as used in section 213(d)(1)(A) and (9)(B), respectively. We accordingly interpret the words in their ordinary, everyday sense.

"Treat" is defined in standard dictionaries as: "to deal with (a disease, patient, etc.) in order to relieve or cure," Webster's New Universal Unabridged Dictionary 2015 (2003). . . .

The regulations provide that medical care is confined to expenses "incurred primarily for the prevention or *alleviation* of a physical or mental defect or illness." Sec. 1.213-1(e)(1)(ii), Income Tax Regs. (emphasis added). A treatment should bear a direct or proximate therapeutic relation to the condition sufficient to justify a reasonable belief the treatment would be efficacious. In Starrett v. Commissioner, [41 T.C. 877, 881 (1964),] this Court concluded that the taxpayer's psychoanalysis was a treatment of disease because the taxpayer was "thereby relieved of the physical and emotional suffering attendant upon" the condition known as anxiety reaction.

Hormone therapy, sex reassignment surgery and, under certain conditions, breast augmentation surgery are prescribed therapeutic interventions, or treatments, for GID outlined in the [accepted medical] standards of care. [Those] standards are widely accepted in the psychiatric profession, as evidenced by the recognition of the standards' triadic therapy sequence as the appropriate treatment for GID and transsexualism in numerous psychiatric and medical reference texts. . . .

Respondent also argues that petitioner's sex reassignment surgery did not "treat" disease within the meaning of section 213(d)(9)(B) because there is insufficient scientific evidence of the surgery's efficacy in treating GID. Petitioner's and

respondent's experts disagree regarding the sufficiency of the scientific proof of
the surgery's efficacy. . . .

However, even assuming some debate remains in the medical profession regarding . . . the scientific proof of the therapeutic efficacy of sex reassignment
surgery, a complete consensus on the advisability or efficacy of a procedure is not
necessary for a deduction under section 213. . . . It is sufficient if the circumstances
"justify a reasonable belief the . . . [treatment] would be efficacious." Havey v.
Commissioner, [12 T.C. at 409, 412 (1949)]. That standard has been fully satisfied
here. The evidence is clear that a substantial segment of the psychiatric profession
has been persuaded of the advisability and efficacy of hormone therapy and sex
reassignment surgery as treatment for GID, as have many courts.

Finally, the Court does not doubt that, as respondent's expert points out in his
report, some medical professionals shun transsexual patients and consider cross-
gender hormone therapy and sex reassignment surgery unethical because they
disrupt what is considered to be a "normally functioning hormonal status or
destroy healthy, normal tissue." However, the Internal Revenue Service has not
heretofore sought to deny the deduction for a medical procedure because it was
considered unethical by some. See, e.g., Rev. Rul. 73-201, 1973-1 C.B. 140 (cost of
abortion legal under State law is deductible medical care under section 213). . . .

2. *Breast Augmentation Surgery*

We consider separately the qualification of petitioner's breast augmentation
surgery as deductible medical care, because respondent makes the additional
argument that this surgery was not necessary to the treatment of GID in petitioner's
case because petitioner already had normal breasts before her surgery. Because
petitioner had normal breasts before her surgery, respondent argues, her breast
augmentation surgery was "directed at improving . . . [her] appearance and [did]
not meaningfully promote the proper function of the body or prevent or treat
illness or disease," placing the surgery squarely within the section 213(d)(9)(B)
definition of "cosmetic surgery." Petitioner has not argued, or adduced evidence,
that the breast augmentation surgery ameliorated a deformity within the meaning
of section 213(d)(9)(A). Accordingly, if the breast augmentation surgery meets the
definition of "cosmetic surgery" in section 213(d)(9)(B), it is not "medical care" that
is deductible pursuant to section 213(a).

For the reasons discussed below, we find that petitioner has failed to show that
her breast augmentation surgery "[treated]" GID. The [applicable] standards
provide that breast augmentation surgery for a male-to-female patient "may be
performed if the physician prescribing hormones and the surgeon have documented that breast enlargement after undergoing hormone treatment for 18 months is
not sufficient for comfort in the social gender role." The record contains no
documentation [of the need for breast augmentation]. . . . [A]ll of the contemporaneous documentation of the condition of petitioner's breasts before the surgery
suggests that they were within a normal range of appearance, and there is no
documentation concerning petitioner's comfort level with her breasts "in the social
gender role." . . .

The breast augmentation surgery is therefore "cosmetic surgery" under the
section 213(d)(9)(B) definition unless it "meaningfully [promoted] the proper
function of the body." The parties have stipulated that petitioner's breast augmentation "did not promote the proper function of her breasts." Although petitioner

expressly declined to stipulate that the breast augmentation "did not meaningfully promote the proper functioning of her body within the meaning of I.R.C. section 213," we conclude that the stipulation to which she did agree precludes a finding . . . that the breast augmentation surgery "meaningfully [promoted] the proper functioning of the body". . . . Consequently, the breast augmentation surgery is "cosmetic surgery" that is excluded from deductible "medical care."

E. *Medical Necessity*

Finally, respondent argues that petitioner's sex reassignment surgery was not "medically necessary," which respondent contends is a requirement intended by Congress to apply to procedures directed at improving appearance, as evidenced by certain references to "medically necessary" procedures in the legislative history of the enactment of the cosmetic surgery exclusion of section 213(d)(9). Respondent in effect argues that the legislative history's contrast of nondeductible cosmetic surgery with "medically necessary" procedures evidences an intent by Congress to impose a requirement in section 213(d)(9) of medical necessity for the deduction of procedures affecting appearance. We find it unnecessary to resolve respondent's claim that section 213(d)(9) should be interpreted to require a showing of "medical necessity" notwithstanding the absence of that phrase in the statute. That is so because respondent's contention would not bar the deductions at issue, inasmuch as we are persuaded, as discussed below, that petitioner has shown that her sex reassignment surgery was medically necessary. . . .

The mental health professional who treated petitioner concluded that petitioner's GID was severe, that sex reassignment surgery was medically necessary, and that petitioner's prognosis without it was poor. Given expert testimony, the judgment of the professional treating petitioner, the agreement of all three experts that untreated GID can result in self-mutilation and suicide, and, as conceded by [respondent's expert], the views of a significant segment of knowledgeable professionals that sex reassignment surgery is medically necessary for severe GID, the Court is persuaded that petitioner's sex reassignment surgery was medically necessary. . . .

IV. CONCLUSION

The evidence amply supports the conclusions that petitioner suffered from severe GID, that GID is a well-recognized and serious mental disorder, and that hormone therapy and sex reassignment surgery are considered appropriate and effective treatments for GID by psychiatrists and other mental health professionals who are knowledgeable concerning the condition. Given our holdings that GID is a "disease" and that petitioner's hormone therapy and sex reassignment surgery "[treated]" it, petitioner has shown the "existence . . . of a disease" and a payment for goods or services "directly or proximately related" to its treatment. *See* Jacobs v. Commissioner, 62 T.C. at 818. She likewise satisfies the "but for" test of *Jacobs*, which requires a showing that the procedures were an essential element of the treatment and that they would not have otherwise been undertaken for nonmedical reasons. Petitioner's hormone therapy and sex reassignment surgery were essential elements of a widely accepted treatment protocol for severe GID. The expert testimony also establishes that given (1) the risks, pain, and extensive rehabilitation associated with sex reassignment surgery, (2) the stigma encountered by persons who change their gender role and appearance in society, and (3) the expert-backed but commonsense point that the desire of a genetic male to have his genitals removed requires an explanation beyond mere dissatisfaction with appearance (such as GID or psychosis), petitioner would not have undergone hormone therapy and sex reassignment surgery except in an effort to alleviate the distress and suffering attendant to GID. Respondent's contention that petitioner undertook the surgery and hormone treatments to improve appearance is at best a superficial characterization of the circumstances that is thoroughly rebutted by the medical evidence.

Petitioner has shown that her hormone therapy and sex reassignment surgery treated disease within the meaning of section 213 and were therefore not cosmetic surgery. Thus petitioner's expenditures for these procedures were for "medical care" as defined in section 213(d)(1)(A), for which a deduction is allowed under section 213(a).

Reviewed by the Court.

[Seven other judges signed onto Judge Gale's opinion. Three other judges filed concurring opinions, and five judges dissented (with respect to the deductions allowed by the Court).]

Notes and Questions

1. *A victory for the LGBT community.* The outcome of this case was viewed as a major victory by the LGBT (lesbian/gay/bisexual/transsexual) community, which has many legitimate complaints about the federal income tax rules. (Ms. O'Donnabhain's case was argued by Gay & Lesbian Advocates and Defenders, presumably at little or no direct cost to her.) Among the most prominent complaints is that the federal Defense of Marriage Act denies same-sex couples, even those who are legally married under local law, the opportunity to be treated as married for federal tax purposes. Such treatment is often (though not universally) favorable in terms of filing joint income tax returns, claiming estate tax marital deductions, and numerous other ways.[43] The obvious direct winners in this case are transsexuals who have had or might have sex-change operations. The stakes are not small: It is estimated that between 1,600 and 2,000 such operations are performed each year, and most of the surgical costs do not relate to breast augmentation. (And note that *O'Donnabhain* does not preclude all expenses of breast augmentation — only those incurred under circumstances like those here, where breast augmentation was found as a matter of fact to be medically unnecessary.)

2. *Relaxing the definition of medical care?* The IRS recently reversed its position on the deductibility as a medical expense of breast pumps and supplies that assist lactation. *See* Announcement 2011-14, 2011-9 I.R.B. 532. This appears to have been a response to congressional interest in this question, as evidenced by a letter urging such a position change signed by 11 senators and 34 representatives sent to the IRS in November 2010. While this may

---

43. But see the Chapter 9 cell on "Income Splitting for California Domestic Partnerships," setting forth and discussing a 2010 private letter ruling permitting income-splitting by California domestic partners.

signal a generally more liberal approach to the definition of medical expenses for purposes of §213, in neither case (breast pumps and sex-change operations) did the IRS act on its own motion.

3. *A "John Doe" option?* This edited version has deleted much of the highly personal detail contained in the full, 88-page opinion written by the Tax Court in this case. Ms. O'Donnabhain, who was 57 at the time of her operation, and 65 by the time of the decision, felt strongly about the justice of her cause, and was apparently willing at that stage of her life to subject herself to the exposure that resulted, in order to further the cause. In general, Tax Court opinions are unsparing in publishing information about the highly personal matters (more typically of a financial sort, but not always so limited) of those who choose to litigate their cases in that court. Should the Tax Court consider providing a "John Doe" option in appropriate cases to taxpayers who wish to dispute their tax liabilities without surrendering their privacy? What might be lost if that option were routinely available?

3. Mechanics of the Deduction

Computing the medical expense deduction is reasonably straightforward, but timing rules create some opportunity for manipulation. The deduction is allowed for expenses "paid" during a taxable year, and the regulations make clear that this refers to the actual year of payment, regardless of when the medical services were performed, and regardless of the taxpayer's usual method of accounting. Reg. §1.213-1(a)(1). Reimbursements must be subtracted, and the net amount of medical expense paid by the taxpayer is then compared with an amount equal to 7.5 percent (10 percent in 2013 and later years) of the taxpayer's adjusted gross income. Any excess is deductible. If there is no excess, no amount can be deducted.

In light of this floor, it makes sense for taxpayers who can reasonably do so to bunch their medical expenses, by delaying payment in some years, and paying promptly in others.[44] (They may be tempted to try to manipulate the timing of their reimbursements as well, but the regulations diminish this incentive by making reimbursements received in subsequent years taxable income, to the extent that the reimbursement is with respect to an item that was deducted as a medical expense in a previous year. Reg. §1.213-1(g).) The operation of this rule may also provide a rare instance in which it may be to the advantage of married taxpayers to file separate returns: If only one spouse has significant medical expenses, separate filing will lower the threshold of deductibility by comparing the medical expenses with 7.5 percent (or 10 percent) of only that person's adjusted gross income.

Another favorable timing rule is that the IRS generally permits deductions as medical expenses of the cost of capital improvements necessitated by medical necessities — such as the cost of installing an elevator in the home of a paraplegic taxpayer. The taxpayer must first reduce the expense by the amount of the value added to the property; but, having done so, he can deduct the remainder of the cost of the improvement in the year in which it was purchased. Reg. §1.213-1(e)(1)(iii).

---

44. Bunching medical expenses by way of payments in advance of services is also possible, but the IRS permits this only if the service provider requires prepayment. *See* Rev. Rul. 76-481, 1976-2 C.B. 82 (deduction allowed for advance fee required by retirement home for lifetime medical care). Prepayments not required by the provider are viewed as mere deposits for future care, and are not deductible until the services are provided.

Even with the opportunities for manipulation, however, it turns out that most itemizers in any given year are not able to take any deductions for medical expenses. As shown in the table at the beginning of this chapter, only about one out of five itemizers in 2008 claimed any medical expense deductions. Since virtually every taxpayer has some unreimbursed medical expenses over the course of the year, it must be assumed that the limitation based on adjusted gross income effectively prevents the other four-fifths from claiming medical expense deductions. This is, however, consistent with the rationale for this deduction noted at the outset of this section: Ordinary medical expenses are part of personal living expenses, and unworthy of any special note in the income tax; only extraordinary medical expenses should be considered in assessing a taxpayer's ability to pay.

4. *Health Savings Accounts and Health Flexible Spending Arrangements*

The percentage-of-AGI floor and the itemization requirement severely limit the ability of taxpayers to claim medical expense deductions under §213. Two other provisions of the Code, however, allow taxpayers to avoid the §213 limitations under certain circumstances.

Section 223 allows an eligible taxpayer to claim an above-the-line deduction for cash contributions to the taxpayer's "health savings account" (HSA).[45] To be eligible, a taxpayer must be covered under a "high deductible health plan" (HDHP), defined as health insurance with an annual deductible of at least $1,200 in the case of self-only coverage, or $2,400 in the case of family coverage.[46] The maximum annual HSA deduction is $3,050 in the case of a taxpayer with self-only health insurance coverage, or $6,150 in the case of taxpayer with family coverage.[47] Amounts in the taxpayer's HSA may be used to pay medical expenses not covered by the taxpayer's health insurance (either because of the high deductible, or because of other policy limitations). Amounts in the HSA ordinarily may not be used, however, to pay health insurance premiums. Suppose an employee provides a taxpayer with coverage under an HDHP, and the employee makes fully deductible HSA contributions to cover the plan's high deductible and other amounts not covered by insurance. By excluding the value of the health insurance coverage (pursuant to §106) and deducting all costs not covered by insurance (pursuant to §223), the employee has managed to avoid income taxation of all his economic resources devoted to health care. Of course, a taxpayer with "Cadillac" zero-deductible employer-provided health insurance would achieve the same income tax health care nirvana. But what about a third taxpayer, with employer-provided health insurance with a moderate deductible? She is disfavored compared to the other two. Yes, she is able to exclude the value of the insurance under §106, but she is relegated to §213 (rather than §223) with respect to her medical expenses not covered by insurance.

Actually, there is a way the third taxpayer may be able to avoid the limitations of §213 with respect to her uninsured medical expenses. If her employer offers a §125

---

45. The deduction is taken in arriving at adjusted gross income, and thus may be claimed by both itemizers and non-itemizers. *See* §62(a)(19).
46. Both figures are the inflation-adjusted amounts for 2011.
47. These are also 2011 inflation-adjusted amounts.

"cafeteria plan,"[48] she can agree, at the beginning of the year, to a salary reduction of a specified number of dollars in exchange for the employer's agreement to contribute an equal amount to the employee's "health flexible spending arrangement" (health FSA).[49] Section 125 renders the constructive receipt doctrine inapplicable, with the result that the contributions to the health FSA are excluded from the taxpayer's gross income. Deductibles and other uninsured expenses incurred by the employee during the year can then be paid out of the health FSA with before-tax dollars. Health FSAs are subject to a use-it-or-lose-it rule, however. If the taxpayer is lucky (or unlucky) enough to incur lower uninsured expenses than the amount of the salary reduction, the unused amount of the FSA is lost to the taxpayer forever. Taxpayers unwilling to take this risk are relegated to the much less generous rules of §213 with respect to their uninsured medical expenses.

If Congress is willing to permit these various "end runs" around the limitations of §213 — for taxpayers with HDHPs, for taxpayers with zero-deductible Cadillac employer-provided health insurance, and for taxpayers willing to run the risk inherent in health FSAs — why isn't it willing to reduce or eliminate the restrictions of the deductibility of medical expenses under §213, for taxpayers not eligible for any of the end runs?

F. MISCELLANEOUS ITEMIZED DEDUCTIONS

The Code permits taxpayers to claim a number of other "miscellaneous" itemized deductions, a concept that is defined negatively as all expenses other than (1) those allowed in computing adjusted gross income (the "above-the-line" deductions), and (2) certain other specified deductions, including interest, charitable contributions, taxes, and medical expenses.[50] As a practical matter, miscellaneous itemized deductions thus consist primarily of (1) expenses associated with investment activities, such as investment advice, safe-deposit boxes, and the like; (2) expenses associated with preparing tax returns and defending them, if necessary, in administrative or judicial proceedings; and (3) unreimbursed employee business expenses, such as subscriptions to journals, professional society membership fees, and so on.

Being consigned to a "miscellaneous" category is not so bad in itself. But there are worse consequences than mere disrespect. When the Tax Reform Act of 1986 created the miscellaneous itemized deduction category, it also imposed a floor on these deductions equal to 2 percent of the taxpayer's adjusted gross income.[51] Since most of the items that fall within this category tend to be small, the effect is to disallow these expenses for most taxpayers. Again, as in the medical expense category, IRS statistics show that relatively few — roughly one-quarter of the total number of itemizers — are able to take these deductions.

---

48. For more on cafeteria plans, see the Chapter 2 cell, "Free Parking, Section 132, Constructive Receipt, and the IRS."

49. For more on health FSAs, see Internal Revenue Service, Publication 969, Health Savings Accounts and Other Tax-Favored Health Plans 15-17 (2009).

50. This is not a complete list of items excluded from the miscellaneous itemized deductions category; the complete list is contained in §67(b).

51. In addition, and much worse for some taxpayers, miscellaneous itemized deductions are disallowed for purposes of the alternative minimum tax. Section 56(b)(1)(A)(i). See the cell on the alternative minimum tax following Chapter 8.

Problem 11.   Helen is an associate in a law firm, working in the corporate and securities law department. In 2011, she had an adjusted gross income of $100,000, and incurred the following expenses:

- A subscription to the *Wall Street Journal* costing $300.
- Membership in the American Bar Association, and its Corporate Law section, costing $350.
- Rental of a safe-deposit box at her bank, to store jewelry and stock certificates, of $150.
- Tax-return preparation fees of $400.
- An orthopedic chair, to ease the strain of long hours at the office, which cost $1,200.

What deductions can she claim as a result of these expenses?

G. REDUCTION OF ITEMIZED DEDUCTIONS FOR HIGH INCOME TAXPAYERS

The Tax Reform Act of 1986 did one last thing in furthering Congress's efforts to expand the tax base by reducing itemized deductions. Section 68, added by that Act, provided that deductions must be reduced for taxpayers whose adjusted gross incomes exceeded $100,000 ($50,000 in the case of married taxpayers who file separately). This threshold has been indexed for inflation since 1991, and as of 2009 stood at $166,800 for all returns except married taxpayers filing separately, whose phaseout in that year began at $83,400. Section 68 has been the target of a great deal of criticism over the years (for reasons that may become apparent after you read the following description of its operation). In response to this criticism, Congress eventually added §68(f), which temporarily phased out the phaseout, disallowing only two-thirds of the amounts computed under §68 in 2006 and 2007, and only one-third of the amounts computed under that section in 2008 and 2009. Section 68 does not apply at all in the jubilee years of 2010, 2011, and 2012. Unless Congress takes further action, however, it will return—in full force—in 2013. What follows is an explanation of how §68 is scheduled to apply in 2013 (except that it uses 2009 inflation adjustments).

If the taxpayer's income exceeds the applicable threshold, the total itemized deductions claimed must be reduced by the *lesser* of the two following amounts:

1. 3 percent of the excess of the adjusted gross income over the threshold amount; or
2. 80 percent of itemized deductions otherwise allowable for the tax year.

This disallowance rule can be illustrated by the following example. Suppose a married couple, filing jointly, has an adjusted gross income of $200,000 and itemized deductions of $30,000. Computing the two alternative disallowance figures yields the following:

1. ($200,000 − 166,800) × .03 = $996
2. $30,000 × .8 = $24,000

Since the first figure is less than the second, it becomes the effective reduction amount. The taxpayers in this example are thus able to deduct only $29,004 (that is, $30,000 of actual deductions less the $996 disallowed pursuant to §68).

As a practical matter, the first disallowance "gate" is nearly always the one that effectively reduces the deduction, for somewhat complicated mathematical reasons that stem from the fact that itemized deductions tend to rise with income. When a taxpayer's income barely exceeds the threshold, it is obvious that 3 percent of the excess over the threshold will be a very small number—certainly far less than 80 percent of itemized deductions. As the taxpayer's income continues to rise above the threshold, as long as at least 3.75 percent of any income increment is spent on deductible items, a limitation based on 3 percent of income will always be less than a limitation based on 80 percent of deductions.

For example, imagine that the taxpayers in the previous example had been able to claim only $1,245 of itemized deductions,[52] so that the disallowance rule based on 80 percent of that number would have been equal to the $996 generated by the limitation based on 3 percent of the "excess" adjusted gross income. Imagine further that the taxpayers enjoy an additional $100,000 of income in the following year, for a total of $300,000 of adjusted gross income in that year. And assume that the taxpayers spend 3.75 percent of the incremental income on, say, charitable contributions, so that their total itemized deductions equal $1,245 plus $3,750, or $4,995. In the second year, the two limitations rules generate the following figures:

1. $(\$300,000 - 166,800) \times .03 = \$3,996$
2. $\$4,995 \times .8 = \$3,996$

Almost everyone does in fact spend at least 3.75 percent of incremental income on deductible items (state income taxes alone are usually enough to account for this), so the first gate becomes, by the sheer mechanics of the design of §68, the effective rule reducing deductions in nearly every case.

This is significant in tax planning, because the structural feature worth noting about the first of the two gates is that it is computed on the basis of the taxpayer's adjusted gross income, not his itemized deductions. If, for example, the taxpayers in the first example above (with the $200,000 adjusted gross income and $30,000 of deductions) had made an additional charitable gift of $1,000 at the end of the year, their itemized deductions would total $31,000, and, even after being reduced by $996, the total deductions allowed, $30,004, would be exactly $1,000 more than they could have deducted in the absence of this last charitable gift. Thus, at the margin (where all tax planning takes place), these taxpayers will still obtain the full tax effect of a $1,000 contribution, despite the limitations of §68.

In fact, because the effective limitation of §68 is almost always based on adjusted gross income, rather than on itemized deductions, it is best viewed as simply an increase in the marginal tax rate. Think again about the first example above. Suppose that instead of making a last-minute charitable contribution of $1,000, the taxpayers receive a last-minute income item of $1,000—perhaps unexpected overtime work at the end of the year. This will increase the disallowed itemized deductions from $996 to $1,026 (representing the additional income of $1,000 times 3%). This will have the effect of increasing taxable income by $30. If the taxpayers are in the 25 percent bracket they will end up paying, at the margin, tax

---

52. Ignore for the moment that such a deduction level would have induced them to claim the standard deduction rather than this itemized total.

at the rate of 25 percent on an incremental income of $1,030—the actual income of $1,000 plus the extra $30 of income generated by the §68 disallowance. Twenty-five percent of $1,030 is $257.50, which in turn is equal to 25.75 percent of the $1,000 of actual incremental income. Thus, the effect of §68 is simply a hidden increment of .75 percent of a point to the taxpayers' marginal tax rate. More generally, the incremental change in the marginal tax rate will be equal to whatever the taxpayer's nominal marginal tax rate is, times the 3 percent rule embodied in §68. (Note that .75% is equal to 25% times 3%.)

So, when all is said and done, there are two tax-planning lessons contained in close analysis of §68: First, it doesn't ordinarily diminish incentives to make contributions, undertake mortgages, and so on; second, it does mean that, if your income is relatively high, your marginal tax rate is probably even higher than you thought it was.

H.   PERSONAL CREDITS AS A LEGISLATIVE ALTERNATIVE TO PERSONAL DEDUCTIONS

Although Congress has not been sufficiently persuaded by the "upside-down subsidy" argument against personal deductions to repeal long-standing deductions and replace them with credits, in recent years Congress has tended to favor credits over deductions as vehicles for newly enacted tax subsidies. Several personal credits discussed elsewhere in this book—including the earned income tax credit (introduced in 1975), the child tax credit (1997), and the higher-education credits (1997)[53]—are of recent vintage, at least compared with the venerable deductions for charitable contributions, home mortgage interest payments, and state and local taxes. The tax savings from a credit, unlike the tax savings from a deduction, do not depend on the taxpayer's marginal tax rate. In addition, the availability of a credit—unlike the availability of most personal deductions—does not depend on the taxpayer's not claiming the standard deduction. Many credits are reduced or eliminated (i.e., phased down or phased out) for taxpayers with AGIs above specified levels. This results in "right-side-up subsidies," in sharp contrast with the subsidy pattern for deductions.

Other recent examples of new credits include the now-expired first-time home-buyer credit (§36), the alternative motor vehicle credit (§30B), and the residential energy-efficient property credit (§25D). Like a number of other recently enacted credits, these three credits are temporary. Congress has a tendency, however, to renew (or reintroduce) temporary credits. In all likelihood, other new personal credits—permanent or temporary—will be enacted in the near future.

53. For the earned income tax credit, see section E of Chapter 9. For the child tax credit, see part A.2.b of Chapter 9. For the higher-education credits, see section B.3.c of Chapter 2.

Cell

RATIONALE FOR THE CHARITABLE CONTRIBUTIONS DEDUCTION

Auten, Clotfelter & Schmalbeck, Taxes and Philanthropy Among the Wealthy

According to the tax expenditure budget of the Joint Committee on Taxation, the decrease in federal tax revenues for the year 2010 resulting from the §170 deduction for charitable contributions was about $40 billion. What is the justification for such an expensive provision? The Supreme Court has described the deduction as "a form of subsidy [for charities] that is administered through the tax system," and has explained that, "deductible contributions are similar to cash grants of the amount of a portion of the individual's contributions." Regan v. Taxation with Representation of Washington, 461 U.S. 540, 543 (1983). To understand the Court's point, consider a taxpayer in the 35 percent bracket who gives $1,000 to her favorite charity and properly claims the $1,000 as an itemized deduction. The deduction wipes out what would have been $1,000 of income taxable at 35 percent, thereby saving the taxpayer $350. Net of the tax savings, her cost of giving $1,000 to the charity is $650. After the dust has settled, of the $1,000 the charity receives, only $650 really comes from the taxpayer. The other $350 comes indirectly from the federal government in the form of forgone tax revenue. To put the point slightly differently, the taxpayer is participating in a sort of matching grant program, under which the government will kick in 35 cents for every 65 cents the taxpayer gives to charity.

Although the public benefits of charitable work are commonly cited as justifying the charitable contributions deduction, there are three serious problems with the analysis. First, there is the basic question of whether charities actually merit a program of annual federal grants in the neighborhood of $40 billion. The Red Cross, for example, may relieve the government of a burden it would otherwise have to carry itself, but that is not true of many other charities. Although eligible charities must satisfy the statutory requirements of §170(c), many organizations that would never receive direct grants from Congress are able to qualify under §170(c). Justice Powell listed a few of them in a footnote in his concurrence in Bob Jones University v. United States, 461 U.S. 574, 609 n.3 (1983):

> The 1,100-page list of exempt organizations [recognized by the IRS as eligible to receive deductible contributions] includes — among countless examples — such organizations as American Friends Service Committee, Inc., Committee on the Present Danger, Jehovah's Witnesses in the United States, Moral Majority Foundation, Inc., Friends of the Earth Foundation, Inc., Mountain States Legal Foundation, National Right to Life Educational Foundation, Planned Parenthood Federation of American, Scientists and Engineers for Secure Energy, Inc. and Union of Concerned Scientists Fund, Inc.

The point of Justice Powell's list, of course, is that these organizations are associated with particular points of view on controversial issues, often on opposite sides. It seems unlikely, for example, that the same Congress would give direct grants to both the National Right to Life Educational Foundation and Planned Parenthood—yet that is the effect of §170. On the other hand, perhaps allowing supporters of Right to Life and Planned Parenthood to vote with their dollars to decide the indirect federal subsidies to be granted to each organization is an example of participatory democracy at its best; certainly defenders of the charitable contribution deduction have celebrated its contribution to the hardy pluralism that is thought (at least by those defenders) to be one of the nation's great strengths. Whatever the general merits of this let-a-thousand-flowers-bloom philosophy, however, it runs into trouble in the case of religious organizations. A matching grant program for contributions to churches would seem to raise serious problems (to say the least) under the First Amendment.

The second problem with the matching grant analysis is the difference in the way the contributions of different taxpayers are matched. Imagine four taxpayers, each of whom gives $1,000 to charity: an itemizing taxpayer in the 35 percent bracket, an itemizing taxpayer in the 25 percent bracket, an itemizing taxpayer in the 15 percent bracket, and a non-itemizing taxpayer. The table below summarizes the tax consequences to each.

Taxpayer	1. Contribution	2. Tax Savings to Taxpayer; Cost to Government	3. After-tax Cost to Taxpayer (1-2)	4. Matching Grant Percentage (2/3)
35% bracket	$1,000	$350	$650	54%
25% bracket	$1,000	$250	$750	33%
15% bracket	$1,000	$150	$850	18%
Non-itemizer	$1,000	—	$1,000	—

Although the government contributes 54 cents for every dollar of after-tax cost of the 35 percent bracket taxpayer, the match is about 40 percent less generous for the 25 percent bracket taxpayer. It is even less generous for the 15 percent bracket taxpayer, and the unlucky non-itemizer is excluded from the program altogether. This is an example of the classic critique of tax expenditures in the form of *deductions* as "upside-down subsidies," in which the highest bracket—and therefore highest income—taxpayers receive the most generous subsidies for each dollar of deduction. Congress is well aware of this critique, and is also well aware that a subsidy in the form of a *credit* would not be subject to the same attack. If Congress replaced §170 with a 25 percent credit for charitable contributions, then the generosity of the matching grant would depend on neither one's tax bracket nor on whether one itemized deductions. The analysis for the 25 percent bracket taxpayer in the table would then be the analysis for all four taxpayers. The credit percentage could be set at whatever level is expected to be revenue neutral—that is, to involve the same revenue loss as the current deduction system. Given the persuasiveness of the "upside-down subsidy" critique of the deduction and the obviousness of the credit alternative as a response to the critique, why do you suppose Congress has not converted the deduction to a credit?

The final difficulty with the matching grant justification is that it seems to reflect an assumption that taxpayers respond to the existence of the deduction by increasing the amounts of their contributions. (If they did not, the deduction would convey no incremental public benefit.) Imagine a 35 percent bracket taxpayer who, in the absence of any tax incentive for charitable giving, would have been willing to give $650 to her favorite charity. How will she respond to the news that whatever she gives to charity is, in fact, deductible? A first approximation of her response might be that she will maintain her out-of-pocket cost of giving. She was willing to give $650 when the gift was not deductible; now that the gift to charity is deductible, she might be willing to incur an after-tax cost of $650, which means she will give the charity $1,000 ($1,000 – $350 tax savings = $650 after-tax cost). If she in fact behaves this way, the $350 revenue loss to the government ends up in the coffers of the charity as an increased contribution, and the matching grant analysis makes sense. But suppose the charity is the taxpayer's church, the taxpayer is religiously obligated to give a certain percentage of her income to her church, and the church's teaching is that the numerator in the giving ratio is the amount the taxpayer actually gives to the church, *not* the after-tax cost of that giving. In that case, if $650 was the appropriate amount to contribute without the charitable deduction, $650 will also be the amount to contribute with the deduction. The effect of the deduction is not to increase the amount received by the charity, but to reduce the taxpayer's cost of giving from $650 to $423 ($650 – $227 tax savings = $423 after-tax cost). The $227 revenue loss goes not to the charity in the form of an increased contribution, but to the taxpayer in the form of a decreased after-tax cost of contributing the original amount. Because the taxpayer did not respond to the deduction by increasing the amount of her contribution, there is *no* matching grant.

Not surprisingly, the evidence is that different taxpayers respond differently to the existence of the deduction. Some behave as the first approximation stated above would have them behave, and others behave even better than that. In other words, some taxpayers are sufficiently motivated by the prospect of a matching grant from the federal government that they are willing to incur a greater after-tax cost for a deductible contribution than the amount they would have been willing to give without a deduction. For example, a 35 percent bracket taxpayer who was thinking of endowing a scholarship at his alma mater with a $200,000 gift may decide, in response to the tax incentive, that he can afford to make a $400,000 gift to endow a classroom.[1] This produces the attractive result of an increase of $200,000 in the amount going to charity, at a cost of only $140,000 to the government (the other $60,000, of course, comes from the taxpayer, as measured by the difference between the original cost of $200,000 for the scholarship and the after-tax cost of $260,000 for the classroom). In many other cases, however, the increase (if any) in the contribution amount in response to the deduction will be less than

---

1. His thinking is that a classroom, at an after-tax cost of $.65 \times \$400,000$, or $260,000, is a more attractive self-commemoration idea than the endowed scholarship. The thinking is much like what a consumer would go through if, suddenly, all automobiles were reduced in price by 35 percent as part of an incentive program to encourage the purchase of new automobiles. She may have been about to buy a Honda, but now she springs for the BMW at a slightly higher cost than the Honda carried before the price drop, but with a sense that the value of the BMW makes it worth the increment.

the revenue loss to the government, thus weakening the force of matching grant analysis. This is especially likely in the case of contributions to religious organizations.

The incentive effects of the charitable deduction have been extensively analyzed by economists. Their usual model, which could be inferred from the foregoing, involves treating the deduction as affecting the price of giving: For a taxpayer facing a 35 percent tax rate, the "price" of transferring a dollar to a charity is 65 cents—the dollar transferred less the 35 cents saved on income taxes. The usual "price effect" of a lowered price is increased consumption of the "good," in this case, charitable gifts. However, higher tax rates reduce both the cost of charitable giving and the taxpayer's after-tax income, and the latter effect also would be expected to alter consumption of the good in question; this effect is usually called an "income effect" or "wealth effect." Thus, as tax rates rise, the price of giving is reduced (which should increase giving), but after-tax income is also reduced (which should diminish giving).[2]

The economist's task in using this model is to try to develop "natural experiments" in which tax rates have changed within some period of time, so that the impact of the implicit "price" changes on the amount of giving can be analyzed. The result of such an analysis is usually an estimate of "elasticity," which is the percentage change in consumption of the good, divided by the percentage change in the price.[3] An elasticity of 1, for example, would mean that a 10 percent reduction in the price of giving would be associated with a 10 percent increase in the amount of the charitable giving. Thus, if a taxpayer's marginal tax rate were to increase from 35 percent to 40 percent, the price of giving a dollar to charity would decline by 8.3 percent, from 65 cents to 60 cents; if the elasticity of demand for charitable giving is 1, then we would predict that charitable giving would rise by 8.3 percent.

The following excerpt summarizes the current state of the controversy on this question:[4]

A great deal of empirical research has examined the effect of tax deductibility on individuals' charitable giving.[5] The deduction effectively reduces the price of making

2. All price changes have an income effect embedded in them, since changing the price of a good or service in the consumer's market basket has the effect of increasing or decreasing his real income. For example, if housing costs decline by 10 percent, and consumers generally spend about 20 percent of their income on housing, the decline in price of that commodity increases their real incomes by about 2 percent. Estimates of price effects that include an offsetting adjustment in real income, so as to focus purely on the substitution effect of the price change, are described as "compensated." Note that in the case of price changes of charitable giving caused by changes in the tax rates, there are actually two income effects: the effect on real income caused by the change in the price of charitable giving, and the income effect caused by the change in the taxpayer's tax bill, which leaves more or less real income available for consumption than the taxpayer had before the tax change. Of course, it is possible to change marginal tax rates in ways that leave at least some taxpayers paying the same total tax bill. For these taxpayers, in this situation, there would be no income effect from the changed rates, but only an income effect from the changed price of charitable giving.

3. Because price and consumption are inversely correlated, the price elasticity would ordinarily be negative. In casual discussion of demand elasticity, this is usually simply a given, so the sign is often ignored.

4. Excerpt from *Taxes and Philanthropy Among the Wealthy*, by Gerald E. Auten, Charles T. Clotfelter & Richard Schmalbeck. Published as chapter 12 of *Does Atlas Shrug? The Economic Consequences of Taxing the Rich* (J. Slemrod ed., 2000) (excerpt appears at pp. 414-416).

5. For a brief review of this literature, see Clotfelter, "The Economics of Giving," in *Giving Better, Giving Smarter: Working Papers of the National Commission on Philanthropy and Civic Renewal* (J. Barry & B. Manno, eds.), published by the Commission in 1997.

donations. Although most studies published before the 1990s concluded that the elasticity of giving with respect to the tax-defined price is greater than one in absolute value, several recent studies have challenged this finding, arguing that donors' efforts to time their contributions have been misinterpreted as indicating permanent price effects.[6] Owing to fluctuations in income over time as well as to periodic changes in the tax law, the net-of-tax price faced by a taxpayer may well vary from one year to the next. In a way analogous to the approach that has been taken in some studies of income, analysts have distinguished permanent from transitory changes in price, a distinction with very important implications for tax policy. One possibility is that taxes have an effect on the timing of charitable gifts — donors may bunch their giving into years when their tax rates are highest and thus when the net cost of giving is lowest — but not on the lifetime amount of giving. This case would be comparable to that of a family whose lifetime purchases of lightbulbs are unaffected by price that nonetheless buys all its bulbs when they are on sale. If taxes, by way of the price effect, influence mainly the timing of gifts and not their long-run level, there would be less reason to believe that tax changes have a significant long-term impact on giving. Compared to most previous empirical work, recent estimates based on this model imply a smaller price effect and a larger income effect, with elasticities of about –0.5 and 1.1, respectively.[7]

So the jury is still out on the incentive effects of the contribution deduction, and uncertainty will probably continue for some time, due to the difficulty of distinguishing between temporary and permanent effects of changes in tax rates and other features of the charitable contribution deduction.

Taken together, these three problems — whether all charitable organizations are deserving of public support, whether the incentive effects should be allowed to vary with tax bracket, and whether the incentive effects really operate in the way they are assumed to — constitute a serious critique of the matching grant justification for the charitable contribution deduction. Why, then, does Congress continue to cling to a provision that is so difficult to defend? In addition to inertia and the political power of donors and charities who benefit from the current system, there may be a more principled explanation, based on an entirely different justification for §170. We might think that money one gives to charity is the functional equivalent of money one never had, in terms of its effect on one's ability to pay income tax. Thus, for example, we might think that Taxpayer *A*, who makes $100,000 and gives $10,000 to her church, has the same ability to pay tax as Taxpayer *B*, who makes $90,000 and gives nothing to charity. The appeal of this justification is that it fits quite well with the actual structure of current law. The first problem with matching grant analysis disappears because now the focus is on the taxpayer, not on the charity. The upside-down-subsidy objection also disappears because a

---

6. Randolph, for example, argues [in *Dynamic Income, Progressive Taxes, and the Timing of Charitable Contributions*, 103 J. Pol. Econ. at 709-710 (1995)] that by using annual data on income and prices, most statistical studies of giving incorrectly ascribe permanent significance to variations in prices that are in fact heavily influenced by transitory fluctuations in income. He argues that, although people appear to smooth their giving in response to transitory variations in income, the effect on price is just the opposite: They tend to bunch their gifts into years when transitory income is the highest to take advantage of the unusually high tax rate in those years. He also presents statistical estimates consistent with this argument, although the difficulty in finding appropriate instruments in the instrumental-variables estimation argues for caution in placing undue reliance on any one set of statistical findings. *See also* Barrett, McGuirk & Steinberg, *Further Evidence on the Dynamic Impact of Taxes on Charitable Giving*, 50 Nat'l Tax J. 321 (1997).

7. [These are the numbers from Randolph's 1995 article — EDS.]

deduction (rather than a credit) is precisely the right way to treat money given to charity as the equivalent of money one never had — in the example, to achieve the goal of equalizing the tax liabilities of *A* and *B*. The third problem evaporates as well, because the ability-to-pay defense is not based on any assumptions about the effect of the tax laws on the amount a taxpayer gives to charity.

The ability-to-pay defense of the deduction has problems of its own, however. First, if money you give to charity is the equivalent of money you never had, then charitable contributions should *always* be deductible. The deduction should be above-the-line, so that it would be available to itemizers and non-itemizers alike. In addition, the percentage limitations of §170(b) — which generally limit charitable deductions to 50 percent of a taxpayer's AGI, regardless of the amount actually contributed — should be repealed. The second, and more fundamental, problem is that the basic premise of the ability-to-pay defense is highly debatable. Income one feels obliged to give to one's church out of deep religious commitment may be the functional equivalent of income one never had, but that is hardly the typical charitable contribution. Income devoted to the more typical discretionary contribution would seem to generate ability-to-pay as much as any other income.

A variation on the ability-to-pay justification focuses on identifying the most appropriate person to pay tax on the contributed dollars. The argument is that tax should be imposed not upon, and at the marginal tax rate of, the *donor,* but upon and at the rate of the *beneficiary* of whatever the charity does with the contributed money. In the case of a charity devoted to poverty relief, this analysis fits well with current law (which allows a deduction for the donor and imposes no tax on the beneficiaries of the charity). The money should not be taxed to the donor because she is not the ultimate consumer, and the money should not be taxed to the beneficiaries of the charity because they do not have enough income to be subject to tax. Many charities, however, distribute their largesse primarily among members of the middle and upper classes. Most churches, for example, spend most of their budgets not providing charity to the poor, but providing religious services to their nonpoor members. Most colleges, museums, and performing arts organizations also have primarily nonpoor — even affluent — beneficiaries. If the donor is in the same bracket as the typical beneficiary of the charity, the implication of the identifying-the-right-taxpayer analysis is that there should be no deduction.

Denying the deduction in such a case would achieve an appropriate result through a technique known as surrogate taxation. Suppose a 25 percent bracket taxpayer gives money to a symphony, which will spend the money providing music to symphony-goers who are also in the 25 percent bracket. In theory, the correct tax treatment would be to allow the donor a deduction, but to tax the money to those who benefit by attending the concerts. This would obviously not be practical, but denying the deduction to the donor and not taxing the beneficiaries will achieve the same results, as long as the donor adjusts the amount of the contribution in response to the prevailing tax rules. The table below demonstrates that the theoretically correct (but impractical) approach of allowing the donor a $1,000 deduction and taxing the beneficiaries on $1,000 will be mimicked by the theoretically incorrect (but practical) approach of not allowing the donor a deduction and not taxing the beneficiaries, if the donor reduces the contribution from $1,000 to $750 in response to the denial of the deduction.

Tax Rule	Donor Gives to Charity	Donor's Tax Savings	After-tax Cost to Donor	Pre-tax Benefit to Beneficiaries	Tax on Beneficiaries	After-tax Benefit to Beneficiaries
Deduction to donor, tax on beneficiaries	$1,000	$250	$750	$1,000	$250	$750
No deduction to donor, no tax on beneficiaries	$750	—	$750	$750	—	$750

What this analysis suggests is that a full deduction should be allowed only when the charitable contribution is earmarked for aid to the poor. There should be no deduction when the beneficiaries of the charity are in the same bracket as the donor; and there should be only a partial deduction when the beneficiaries are not poor, but are in a lower bracket than the donor. In short, the analysis which focuses on identifying the ultimate beneficiary as the appropriate taxpayer supports the current charitable contribution deduction in only a limited number of cases.

But that argument raises still another contentious issue: How do we know who the beneficiaries of charitable activities are? In some cases, this may be fairly straightforward. We can reasonably assume, for example, that the beneficiaries of a soup kitchen's activities are those who consume the soup.[8] Note, however, that even in this simplest case, the amount of the receipt associated with the benefit is far from clear, raising familiar problems of income-in-kind discussed at length in Chapter 2. If the soup consumer receives, without charge, soup costing $2.00 per bowl to make, the subjective value of the benefit received may be much less. All that we can confidently infer from the act of consumption is that the soup had some positive value to the consumer.

Matters can be just as complicated even if there *is* a market exchange. Suppose, for example, that it takes $500 to persuade the Houston Opera Company to travel to Durham, N.C. to stage a performance of Gershwin's *Porgy and Bess*. In Durham, there is one wealthy person who really loves opera and who would willingly pay up to $200 to hear the opera. In addition, four college professors of high taste but middling means would pay $50 each to hear it. Let's say that two music students would like to hear it as well, but can't afford to pay anything for luxuries of this sort. In all, the market stands ready to pay $200 plus (4 × $50) for the opera, for a total of $400. In a completely free market, the Houston Opera would remain in Houston. In the market as we have it, it may be possible for the Durham opera lovers to form a tax-exempt entity, sell five tickets for $50 each, and get a $250 contribution from the one wealthy opera lover. This math works if the wealthy

---

8. Even here, there might be an argument. Marxists, or cynics of any stripe, might argue that the wealthy benefit from the soup kitchen's suppression of revolutionary impulses among those who consume its soup. However, the authors infer from the behavior of the wealthy in recent years that revolutionary risks are not much on their collective mind; accordingly, this explanation seems implausible.

opera lover is in a 40 percent tax bracket, and gets a deduction for the contribution. Her $250 contribution costs her only $150 after tax; and, together with the $50 she paid for her own ticket, she has parted with $200, which we assumed she was willing to do.

The question is: Who is subsidized here? One might assume that it is those who attend the opera. But, as Sportin' Life (a character in the opera) would put it, "It Ain't Necessarily So." After all, the wealthy opera lover gets opera worth $200 to her at a cost of exactly $200. The college professors get opera worth $50 each to them, in exchange for cash of exactly that amount. If the opera company decides to give away free tickets to students, then the students would be subsidized; but even if the value of the free tickets were included in their gross incomes, they probably wouldn't actually pay any tax, because they're probably below the taxable threshold. The Houston Opera Company may arguably enjoy a subsidy from this arrangement, but it's a nonprofit organization that is simply trying to cover its costs; no one earns a profit, per se, from its performances. Maybe the singers are subsidized; but they could probably make a good case that they're not in the same league with Placido Domingo, earning economic rents on their enormous talents; they're just barely scraping by on their modest salaries and whatever private singing lessons they can sell. If people stopped buying opera tickets, these singers would just do something else (probably more lucrative) from nine to five, and do their singing in the shower like the rest of us.

Under these circumstances, it's not easy to locate individuals who are in any meaningful sense subsidized. Instead of thinking of this arrangement as a cross-subsidy of some sort, where opera-indifferent taxpayers subsidize those who love opera, one might describe this as a case where the government has determined that there is value (call it preservation of the culture) that is independent of the pleasure any individuals get out of going to the opera. And so the government artificially boosts demand, so that this form of musical expression will not vanish from our society.[9]

Alternatively, one could argue that, under the circumstances described, this does indeed begin to look more like a traditional charitable enterprise (like a soup kitchen) where the only parties who are really subsidized (the two music students) are under the tax threshold, and so taxing them on their subsidies wouldn't make any difference. And a broader point here is that it would be wrong to assume that because five out of the seven people attending the opera are not poor, there must be an inappropriate, "upside-down" subsidy going on here. In this hypothetical, the five who aren't poor also aren't being subsidized: they're paying the maximum they would be willing to pay to hear *Porgy and Bess*.

Finally, it is sometimes argued that many charitable activities are plagued by "free rider" problems that lead to "market failure," which in turn leads to an inefficiently low level of services of the sort that charities provide being available in the market. For example, educational television may provide broad benefits to the public. But, in a situation where support of advertisers is deemed inappropriate (because, for example, it would counter the educational purposes to use the

9. It remains true even under this scenario, however, that the wealthy taxpayer has been put, by virtue of the charitable contribution deduction, in the position of deciding which parts of our cultural heritage are worthy of protection. In a democratic state, a powerful argument arises that it would be preferable to make those determinations through a democratic process, such as legislative appropriations, rather than through charitable contributions deductions that are of greatest benefit to high bracket taxpayers.

programming to attract new users to hyper-sweetened breakfast cereals), such a television station may have little that it can sell. It may ask its viewers for their support in some proportion to the benefit each viewer feels she receives; but such appeals, however irritating and exhausting, are only partly effective. The boost provided by the charitable contribution deduction may help close this gap by allowing donors who do support the station to contribute greater sums, and so deserves our support on those grounds.

That observation is accurate as far as it goes. However, it may still be worth asking whether it would not be wiser in a democratic society to deal with market failure of this sort by direct government appropriation. After all, the primary explanation offered by economists over the centuries for the very existence of government is that it permits collective action, through forcible collection of tax revenues, to overcome free rider and other market failure problems. That is how public schools and public roadways, among many other things, come to exist. Is there any compelling reason why governments couldn't support educational television stations (to a greater degree than they currently do) if those stations are thought to provide broad public benefits, at levels of service that could not be supported by private markets?

Cell

QUID PRO QUO ISSUES

A. The College Football Saga

>Rev. Rul. 84-132
>
>Announcement 84-101
>
>Tax Reform Act of 1986, §1608

B. The Special Case of "Intangible Religious Benefits"

>Rev. Rul. 70-47
>
>Rev. Rul. 78-189
>
>Hernandez v. Commissioner
>
>Rev. Rul. 93-73
>
>Sklar v. Commissioner

A. THE COLLEGE FOOTBALL SAGA

REV. RUL. 84-132

1984-2 C.B. 55

ISSUE

Whether a charitable contribution deduction under section 170 of the Internal Revenue Code is allowable for a payment to a university's athletic scholarship fund under the circumstances described below.

FACTS

Taxpayer, an individual, made a payment of $300 to a particular athletic scholarship program maintained by a university, an organization described in section 170(c)(2) of the Code. This payment entitled the taxpayer to become a "member" of the program. The only benefit afforded members is that, for an additional $120, they are permitted to purchase a season ticket to the university's home football games, with preferred seating. Preferred seating means merely that the season ticket will be for a seat between the 40 yard lines. No tickets for seats between the 40 yard lines are available to nonmembers of the program. The $300 membership fee is paid annually, and a member is required to make a separate $300 payment for each season ticket the member purchases. There are approximately 2,000 people on the waiting list to become members, and a person is made a member only when a season ticket between the 40 yard lines becomes available.

LAW AND ANALYSIS

Section 170(a) of the Code allows, subject to certain limitations, a deduction for contributions and gifts to or for the use of organizations described in section 170(c), payment of which is made within the taxable year.

Rev. Rul. 67-246, 1967-2 C.B. 104, sets forth various examples concerning the deductibility, as charitable contributions under section 170 of the Code, of payments made by taxpayers in connection with admission to or other participation in fund-raising activities for charitable organizations. The revenue ruling provides that to be deductible as a charitable contribution for federal income tax purposes under section 170 of the Code, a payment to or for the use of a qualified charitable organization must be a gift. To be a gift for such purposes there must be, among other requirements, a payment of money or transfer of property without adequate consideration. As a general rule, if a payment to a charitable organization results in the receipt of a substantial benefit the presumption arises that no gift has been made for charitable contribution purposes. *See also* Rev. Rul. 76-185, 1976-1 C.B. 60.

In showing that a gift has been made, an essential element is proof that whatever portion of the payment that is claimed as a gift represents the excess of the total amount paid over the value of the monetary benefits received in return.

In example 7 of Rev. Rul. 67-246, a symphony obtained $20 contributions from its patrons by providing season memberships, the privilege of attending a cocktail party and a motion picture premiere, and reserved seats for concerts that were not otherwise available. The revenue ruling concluded that even apart from the other benefits, the fair market value of the privilege of having choice reserved seats for the concerts would, in all likelihood, exceed the amount of the payment, and thus, no part of the "contribution" was deductible.

Similarly, the taxpayer here can purchase a season ticket between the 40 yard lines only by contributing $300 to the athletic scholarship fund. The fact that there is a waiting list for membership in the program further indicates that this preferred seating has significant value. In view of this, the value of the benefit received as a result of the payment is considered to be commensurate with the amount of the payment made, and therefore no part of the payment constitutes a gift.

HOLDING

On the basis of the facts presented, the preferred seating has significant value, therefore the taxpayer cannot deduct any part of the $300 payment to the athletic scholarship program as a charitable contribution under section 170 of the Code, unless the taxpayer can establish that the $300 payment exceeds the monetary value of the right to purchase a season ticket for $120.

Notes and Questions

1. *The quid pro quo principle.* The ruling applies well-settled law. The mere fact that one transfers money to a charity does not automatically entitle one to a deduction. No deduction is allowed to the extent one receives value back

from the charity. Thus, no charitable deduction is allowed for college tuition, admission to a museum, or an ordinary ticket to the symphony. If the value received is less than the amount given to the charity — for example, if one gives $100 to a public television station and receives a $15 umbrella in return — then only the difference ($85, in the example) is deductible. In order to improve compliance with this rule, §170(f)(8) disallows a deduction for any contribution of $250 or more unless the taxpayer receives a written acknowledgment of the contribution from the charity, including a "description and good faith estimate of the value of any goods or services" received by the donor in exchange for the contribution.

2. *The reaction.* Although the ruling may have seemed like a statement of the obvious to most tax experts, it was not well received in the college football community, as the following IRS announcement suggests.

ANNOUNCEMENT 84-101

1984-45 I.R.B. 21

The Service has announced that Rev. Rul. 84-132 is suspended pending a public session on the implications of Rev. Rul. 84-132 upon the varied athletic scholarship programs in existence throughout the country. The session will be held on Monday, January 7, 1985, beginning at 10:00 A.M., in the I.R.S. Auditorium, Seventh Floor, 7400 Corridor, Internal Revenue Building, 1111 Constitution Avenue N.W., Washington, D.C.

The IRS has a long-standing position that where consideration, in the form of admissions or other privileges or benefits, is received in connection with payments by patrons of fundraising affairs, the presumption is that no gift has been made for charitable contribution purposes. The burden is on the taxpayer to establish that the amount paid is not the purchase price of the privileges or benefits and that part of the payment, in fact, does qualify as a gift.

Rev. Rul. 84-132 holds that no charitable contribution deduction is allowable for a $300 payment to a university athletic scholarship program entitling the contributor to become a "member" of the program. The only benefit afforded members is that, for an additional $120, they are permitted to purchase a season ticket to the university's home football games, with preferred seating. Such preferred seating is available only to members of the scholarship program, and there is a long waiting list of people desiring to become members. The revenue ruling concludes, based upon the specific facts contained therein, that no part of the $300 payment is a deductible gift because the value of the right to purchase the season ticket with preferred seating is considered commensurate with the amount of the payment.

The IRS emphasizes that the suspension has no effect on existing law and anticipates that after comments are received at the session, the IRS will determine whether further guidelines are needed in this area. . . .

Notes and Questions

1. *A political football?* The IRS is not required to hold hearings on revenue rulings, and almost never does so. It not uncommonly issues revenue

rulings that make Fortune 500 corporations very unhappy, yet the corporations do not succeed in forcing suspension of the rulings and public hearings. Announcement 84-101 hints at the extraordinary political power of the supporters of college football.

2. *The next chapter.* To its credit, the IRS stuck to its guns on this issue. In 1986 the Service issued Rev. Rul. 86-63, 1986-1 C.B. 88, superseding Rev. Rul. 84-132. The new ruling recognized that, in some cases, payments to an "athletic scholarship program" may be deductible in whole or in part, because the taxpayer receives no substantial benefits in exchange or because the benefits received are worth less than the amount contributed. It did not, however, back down from the basic point that payments to college football programs are subject to the same quid pro quo rules that apply to payments to all other charitable organizations.

3. *Don't mess with Texas (or LSU).* At this point Congress decided to get involved. Read on.

TAX REFORM ACT OF 1986, §1608

(a) In General. Amounts paid by a taxpayer to or for the benefit of an institution of higher education described in paragraph (1) or (2) of subsection (b) (other than amounts separately paid for tickets) which would otherwise qualify as a charitable contribution within the meaning of section 170 of the Internal Revenue Code of 1986 shall not be disqualified because such taxpayer receives the right to seating or the right to purchase seating in an athletic stadium of such institution.

(b) Described Institutions. —

(1) An institution is described in this paragraph, if—

(A) such institution was mandated by a State constitution in 1876,

(B) such institution was established by a State legislature in March 1881, and is located in a State capital pursuant to a statewide election in September 1981,

(C) the campus of such institution formally opened on September 15, 1883, and

(D) such institution is operated under the authority of a 9-member board of regents appointed by the governor.

(2) An institution is described in this paragraph if such institution has an athletic stadium —

(A) the plans for the renovation of which were approved by a board of supervisors in December 1985 and January 1986, and

(B) the plans for renovation of which were approved by a State board of ethics for public employees in February 1986.

Notes and Questions

1. *Not "in general" at all.* This is an example of a so-called rifle shot tax provision, conferring special benefits on a very narrow class of taxpayers — in this case, the supporters of the football programs of Louisiana State University and the University of Texas. Senator Russell Long of Louisiana and Rep. J.J.

Pickle of Texas reportedly were primarily responsible for the provision. It follows the rifle shot tradition of describing the beneficiaries in obscure technical ways that make it difficult for the uninitiated to determine their identities. Disguising the beneficiaries suggests members of Congress are embarrassed by the practice. Rifle shots have become less widely used since the rifle shots in the Tax Reform Act of 1986 were the subject of a Pulitzer Prize-winning series of muckraking articles in the *Philadelphia Inquirer*.

2. *Sometimes the rifle is a shotgun.* On occasion, the attempt to disguise the beneficiary of a rifle shot provision can have surprising consequences, as illustrated by the following passage from Jeffrey H. Birnbaum & Alan S. Murray, *Showdown at Gucci Gulch* 290-291 (1987):

> [Senator Russell Long] got the better of [Ways and Means Committee Chairman Daniel] Rostenkowski by securing for a Louisiana-based utility company the same kind of favored treatment in the minimum tax that Rostenkowski won for an Illinois utility. The Ways and Means chairman tried to camouflage the recipient of his break by describing the size of the utility's power generator rather than using its name. What Long knew — and what Rostenkowski found out — was that the Louisiana utility had the same size machine and was also eligible for the break. By waiting patiently in the wings until it was too late to turn back, Long secured a $140 million benefit for Middle South Utilities.

3. *Leveling the playing field.* As a result of the 1986 rifle shot, supporters of Texas and Louisiana State football received better tax treatment than those of any other college football programs. Not surprisingly, this situation proved politically unstable. In 1988 Congress repealed the rifle shot provision and enacted what is now §170(*l*). Applying that provision to the facts of Rev. Rul. 84-132, the taxpayer in the ruling would now be entitled to deduct 80 percent of the $300 he paid for the right to buy tickets (but none of the $120 designated as the price of the tickets). If he had contributed $500 to the program, even though only $300 was required to become a "member," then the extra $200 would be fully deductible under normal §170 quid pro quo analysis.

4. *The equity issue.* The 1986 rifle shot provision was unduly generous to the supporters of two football programs, relative to the supporters of other programs. The 1988 legislation removed that violation of horizontal equity, but replaced it with a provision that treats supporters of all college football (and basketball) programs unduly generously, compared with (for example) the patrons of symphonies and opera companies. Which violation of horizontal equity is worse?

5. *How to get into museums for free.* A number of prominent museums offer annual memberships at a cost typically in the low three figures. These memberships usually entitle the member (and sometimes a limited number of family members or guests) to an unlimited number of free admissions to the museum during the year. At least some of these museums provide the members with acknowledgments (required as a condition of deductibility in the case of donations of $250 or more) that state that the member received no goods or services from the museum in exchange for the contribution. A rather generous regulation permits free admission privileges to be valued at zero, when received in exchange for a payment of $75 or less. Treas. Reg.§1.170A-1(h)(3),

through a cross-reference to Treas. Reg. §1.170A-13(f)(8)(i). But many museums value admission privileges at zero, even though the membership "donation" substantially exceeds $75. How can a museum legitimately do this, if the one-time admission charge for a nonmember is $15 or more? The most likely justification is that the $15 admission charge is really (if you read the fine print at the entrance booth) a "suggested donation" and that a nonmember with the chutzpah to decline the suggestion to donate $15 would not be denied admission.

6. *How far can you go?* If the above justification really works, could it be applied by private schools in situations involving much larger amounts of money? Private school tuition is ordinarily not deductible, because the parents of a student receive an educational quid pro quo equal in value to the tuition paid. But suppose a school drops its tuition and replaces it with a "suggested contribution" of the same amount. Parents are told what it costs to educate their children, and tremendous social pressure is placed on parents to pay the full amount of the suggested contribution. There are, however, two or three exceptionally thick-skinned parents who resist the pressure and pay nothing, and their children are allowed to continue at the school. Does this make the "suggested contributions" of the other parents deductible? (If it does, they owe a debt of gratitude to the thick-skinned parents for demonstrating the contributions are really only suggested.) In Rev. Rul. 83-104, 1983-2 C.B. 46, the IRS takes the position that a deduction is "generally" not available in this kind of situation (Situation 4 of the ruling). It is not clear how much wiggle room is created by the "generally" qualification, nor is it clear that all courts would agree with the IRS position.

B. THE SPECIAL CASE OF "INTANGIBLE RELIGIOUS BENEFITS"

REV. RUL. 70-47

1970-1 C.B. 49

Pew rents, building fund assessments, and periodic dues paid to a church (an organization described in section 170(c) of the Internal Revenue Code of 1954) are all methods of making contributions to the church, and such payments are deductible as charitable contributions within the limitations set out in section 170 of the Code.

REV. RUL. 78-189

1978-1 C.B. 68

Advice has been requested whether, under the circumstances described below, amounts paid by a taxpayer to a Church of Scientology are charitable contributions within the meaning of section 170 of the Internal Revenue Code of 1954.

The taxpayer, a member (but not a minister or employee) of the Church of Scientology, a church that propagates a religious faith known as "Scientology" and purports to treat the spirit of human beings by the practice of "auditing" (or "processing"), subscribed to a course of audits in that church. Auditing is described by the church as a pastoral counseling procedure involving the counseling of one parishioner by one minister, through which "a person is enabled to turn his attention to the more spiritual: his awareness of life, death, his relationship to the physical universe, and his relationship to the Supreme Being." In addition, the church states that "The results claimed and benefits obtainable from auditing and training, though they may be observable to others, are personal and are experienced by the individual himself or herself." The counseling and training subjects provided by the Church of Scientology may be divided into three broad categories:

1. General education courses dealing with subjects of general education such as grammar.
2. Religious education courses directed to the training of individuals who intend to be Scientology ministers.
3. Auditing and processing courses intended to acquaint members or prospective members of the church with the history and tenets of the church.

The church expects a participant in a course of study not to proceed with further study until personally satisfied with the result of the courses previously undertaken. However, other courses, often in another category, may be recommended to the participant to help the participant achieve such personal satisfaction.

The auditing courses may be provided at no charge to some individuals, but they were offered to the taxpayer for a specified sum of money described by the church as a "fixed donation." If a course of study is paid for well in advance, a so-called "advance donation discount" will be awarded to reduce the cost of the course to the participant. The church also advises that refunds are made to any dissatisfied participant within certain time limitations. The Church of Scientology to which the taxpayer paid the "fixed donation" for the course of audits in this case is an organization contributions to which are deductible pursuant to section 170 of the Code.

Section 262 of the Code provides that, except as otherwise expressly provided by law, no deduction shall be allowed for personal, living, or family expenses.

Section 170(a) of the Code provides, subject to certain limitations, for the allowance of a deduction for charitable contributions or gifts to or for the use of organizations described in section 170(c), payment of which is made during the taxable year.

A contribution or gift, for the purposes of section 170 of the Code, is a voluntary transfer of money or property made by the transferor without receipt or expectation of commensurate benefits or privileges. *See* H.R. Rep. No. 1337, 83d Cong., 2d Sess. A44 (1954); S. Rep. No. 1622, 83d Cong., 2d Sess. 196 (1954).

In this case, given the nature of the first two categories of subjects, the person subscribing to these audits (or courses) receives (or reasonably expects to receive) individual benefits in the form of general education or vocational training rendered by a minister of the church. Moreover, the discount for early payment for the courses, as well as the refund feature, support the conclusion that the transaction involves a payment in the form of a purchase of something of value.

The third class of course (that is, auditing and processing courses) are religious in nature and nonvocational. Payments for similar auditing and processing courses were held, in Brown v. Commissioner, 62 T.G. 551 (1974), *aff'd per curiam*, 523 F.2d 365 (8th Cir. 1975), to be nondeductible as medical expenses under section 213 of the Code on the ground that they were "somewhat comparable to the payments by a taxpayer of tuition for his child at a regular private educational institution primarily for the child's education."

It has been held that a charitable contribution deduction under section 170 of the Code is not allowable with respect to tuition fees or fixed donations made by a taxpayer to a private or church school, contributions to which are deductible, on behalf of the taxpayer's child or children attending the school. Rev. Rul. 54-580, 1954-2 C.B. 97; Rev. Rul. 71-112, 1971-1 C.B. 93. Such amounts are not gifts to the school, but are consideration between the parties. Oppewal v. Commissioner, 468 F.2d 1000 (1st Cir. 1972). The denial of the deduction has been upheld even though a significant element of the church school curriculum is religious education. DeJong v. Commissioner, 36 T.C. 896 (1961), *aff'd*, 309 F.2d 373 (9th Cir. 1962). *See also* Rev. Rul. 76-232, 1976-1 C.B. 62, which holds that participants in a weekend marriage seminar conducted by a charitable organization are not entitled to a charitable contribution deduction for any part of a donation made to the organization at the conclusion of the seminar unless the participants establish that the amount donated exceeds the value of all benefits and privileges received and that the amount claimed as a charitable contribution is the amount of such excess. *See also* Rev. Rul. 67-246, 1967-2 C.B. 104, holding that a payment to a charitable organization qualifies as a deductible gift only to the extent that it is shown to exceed the fair market value of any consideration received in the form of privileges or other benefits.

Accordingly, the taxpayer is not entitled to a charitable contribution deduction for any part of the "fixed donation" made to the church for payment of the three categories of auditing courses unless the taxpayer establishes that the "fixed donation" exceeded the fair market value of the benefits and privileges received and that the amount claimed as a charitable contribution is the amount of such excess.

HERNANDEZ v. COMMISSIONER
490 U.S. 680 (1989)

Justice MARSHALL delivered the opinion of the Court.

Section 170 of the Internal Revenue Code of 1954 (Code) permits a taxpayer to deduct from gross income the amount of a "charitable contribution." The Code defines that term as a "contribution or gift" to certain eligible donees, including entities organized and operated exclusively for religious purposes. We granted certiorari to determine whether taxpayers may deduct as charitable contributions payments made to branch churches of the Church of Scientology (Church) in order to receive services known as "auditing" and "training." We hold that such payments are not deductible.

I

. . . Scientologists believe that an immortal spiritual being exists in every person. A person becomes aware of this spiritual dimension through a process known as "auditing." Auditing involves a one-to-one encounter between a participant (known as a "preclear") and a Church official (known as an "auditor"). An electronic device, the E-meter, helps the auditor identify the preclear's areas of spiritual difficulty by measuring skin responses during a question and answer session. Although auditing sessions are conducted one on one, the content of each session is not individually tailored. The preclear gains spiritual awareness by progressing through sequential levels of auditing, provided in short blocks of time known as "intensives."

The Church also offers members doctrinal courses known as "training." Participants in these sessions study the tenets of Scientology and seek to attain the qualifications necessary to serve as auditors. Training courses, like auditing sessions, are provided in sequential levels. Scientologists are taught that spiritual gains result from participation in such courses.

The Church charges a "fixed donation," also known as a "price" or a "fixed contribution," for participants to gain access to auditing and training sessions. These charges are set forth in schedules, and prices vary with a session's length and level of sophistication. In 1972, for example, the general rates for auditing ranged from $625 for a 12½-hour auditing intensive, the shortest available, to $4,250 for a 100-hour intensive, the longest available. Specialized types of auditing required higher fixed donations: a 12½-hour "Integrity Processing" auditing intensive cost $750; a 12-hour "Expanded Dianetics" auditing intensive cost $950. This system of mandatory fixed charges is based on a central tenet of Scientology known as the "doctrine of exchange," according to which any time a person receives something he must pay something back. In so doing, a Scientologist maintains "inflow" and "outflow" and avoids spiritual decline.

The proceeds generated from auditing and training sessions are the Church's primary source of income. The Church promotes these sessions not only through newspaper, magazine, and radio advertisements, but also through free lectures, free personality tests, and leaflets. The Church also encourages, and indeed rewards with a 5 percent discount, advance payment for these sessions. The Church often refunds unused portions of prepaid auditing or training fees, less an administrative charge.

Petitioners in these consolidated cases each made payments to a branch church for auditing or training sessions. They sought to deduct these payments on their federal income tax returns as charitable contributions under section 170. Respondent Commissioner, the head of the Internal Revenue Service (IRS), disallowed these deductions, finding that the payments were not charitable contributions within the meaning of section 170. . . .

II

. . . The legislative history of the "contribution or gift" limitation, though sparse, reveals that Congress intended to differentiate between unrequited payments to qualified recipients and payments made to such recipients in return for goods or services. Only the former were deemed deductible. The House and Senate Reports on the 1954 tax bill, for example, both define "gifts" as payments "made with no expectation of a financial return commensurate with the amount of the gift." S. Rep. No. 1622, 83d Cong., 2d Sess., 196 (1954); H.R. Rep. No. 1337, 83d Cong., 2d Sess., A44 (1954). Using payments to hospitals as an example, both

Reports state that the gift characterization should not apply to "a payment by an individual to a hospital in consideration of a binding obligation to provide medical treatment for the individual's employees. It would apply only if there were no expectation of any quid pro quo from the hospital." S. Rep. No. 1622, supra, at 196 (emphasis added); H.R. Rep. No. 1337, supra, at A44 (emphasis added).

In ascertaining whether a given payment was made with "the expectation of any quid pro quo," S. Rep. No. 1622, supra, at 196; H.R. Rep. No. 1337, supra, at A44, the IRS has customarily examined the external features of the transaction in question. This practice has the advantage of obviating the need for the IRS to conduct imprecise inquiries into the motivations of individual taxpayers. The lower courts have generally embraced this structural analysis. . . .

In light of this understanding of section 170, it is readily apparent that petitioners' payments to the Church do not qualify as "contribution[s] or gift[s]." As the Tax Court found, these payments were part of a quintessential quid pro quo exchange: in return for their money, petitioners received an identifiable benefit, namely, auditing and training sessions. The Church established fixed price schedules for auditing and training sessions in each branch church; it calibrated particular prices to auditing or training sessions of particular lengths and levels of sophistication; it returned a refund if auditing and training services went unperformed; it distributed "account cards" on which persons who had paid money to the Church could monitor what prepaid services they had not yet claimed; and it categorically barred provision of auditing or training sessions for free. Each of these practices reveals the inherently reciprocal nature of the exchange.

Petitioners do not argue that such a structural analysis is inappropriate under section 170, or that the external features of the auditing and training transactions do not strongly suggest a quid pro quo exchange. . . . Petitioners argue instead that they are entitled to deductions because a quid pro quo analysis is inappropriate under section 170 when the benefit a taxpayer receives is purely religious in nature. Along the same lines, petitioners claim that payments made for the right to participate in a religious service should be automatically deductible under section 170.

We cannot accept this statutory argument for several reasons. First, it finds no support in the language of section 170. Whether or not Congress could, consistent with the Establishment Clause, provide for the automatic deductibility of a payment made to a church that either generates religious benefits or guarantees access to a religious service, that is a choice Congress has thus far declined to make. Instead, Congress has specified that a payment to an organization operated exclusively for religious (or other eleemosynary) purposes is deductible only if such a payment is a "contribution or gift." The Code makes no special preference for payments made in the expectation of gaining religious benefits or access to a religious service. . . .

Second, petitioners' deductibility proposal would expand the charitable contribution deduction far beyond what Congress has provided. Numerous forms of payments to eligible donees plausibly could be categorized as providing a religious benefit or as securing access to a religious service. For example, some taxpayers might regard their tuition payments to parochial schools as generating a religious benefit or as securing access to a religious service; such payments, however, have long been held not to be charitable contributions under section 170. . . . Taxpayers might make similar claims about payments for church-sponsored counseling sessions or for medical care at church-affiliated hospitals that otherwise might not be deductible. Given that, under the First Amendment, the IRS can reject otherwise valid claims of religious benefit only on the ground that a taxpayer's alleged beliefs are not sincerely held, but not on the ground that such beliefs are inherently irreligious, *see* United States v. Ballard, 322 U.S. 78 (1944), the resulting tax deductions would likely expand the charitable contribution provision far beyond its present size. We are loath to effect this result in the absence of supportive congressional intent.

Finally, the deduction petitioners seek might raise problems of entanglement between church and state. If framed as a deduction for those payments generating benefits of a religious nature for the payor, petitioners' proposal would inexorably force the IRS and reviewing courts to differentiate "religious" benefits from "secular" ones. If framed as a deduction for those payments made in connection with a religious service, petitioners' proposal would force the IRS and the judiciary into differentiating "religious" services from "secular" ones. We need pass no judgment now on the constitutionality of such hypothetical inquiries, but we do note that "pervasive monitoring" for "the subtle or overt presence of religious matter" is a central danger against which we have held the Establishment Clause guards. . . .

Accordingly, we conclude that petitioners' payments to the Church for auditing and training sessions are not "contribution[s] or gift[s]" within the meaning of that statutory expression.

III

We turn now to petitioners' constitutional claims based on the Establishment Clause and the Free Exercise Clause of the First Amendment.

Petitioners argue that denying their requested deduction violates the Establishment Clause in two respects. First, section 170 is said to create an unconstitutional denominational preference by according disproportionately harsh tax status to those religions that raise funds by imposing fixed costs for participation in certain religious practices. Second, section 170 allegedly threatens governmental entanglement with religion because it requires the IRS to entangle itself with religion by engaging in "supervision of religious beliefs and practices" and "valuation of religious services." [The Court goes on to reject both arguments.]

IV

We turn, finally, to petitioners' assertion that disallowing their claimed deduction is at odds with the IRS' longstanding practice of permitting taxpayers to deduct payments made to other religious institutions in connection with certain religious practices. . . . [Petitioners] make two closely related claims. First, the IRS has accorded payments for auditing and training disparately harsh treatment compared to payments to other churches and synagogues for their religious services: Recognition of a comparable deduction for auditing and training payments is necessary to cure this administrative inconsistency.

Second, Congress, in modifying section 170 over the years, has impliedly acquiesced in the deductibility of payments to these other faiths; because payments for auditing and training are indistinguishable from these other payments, they fall within the principle acquiesced in by Congress that payments for religious services are deductible under section 170.

Although the Commissioner demurred at oral argument as to whether the IRS, in fact, permits taxpayers to deduct payments made to purchase services from other churches and synagogues, the Commissioner's periodic revenue rulings have stated the IRS' position rather clearly. A 1971 ruling, still in effect, states: "Pew rents, building fund assessments, and periodic dues paid to a church . . . are all methods of making contributions to the church, and such payments are deductible as charitable contributions within the limitations set out in section 170 of the Code." Rev. Rul. 70-47, 1970-1 Cum. Bull. 49 (superseding A.R.M. 2, Cum. Bull. 150 (1919)). We also assume for purposes of argument that the IRS also allows taxpayers to deduct "specified payments for attendance at High Holy Day services, for tithes, for torah readings and for memorial plaques."

The development of the present litigation, however, makes it impossible for us to resolve petitioners' claim that they have received unjustifiably harsh treatment compared to adherents of other religions. . . .

Perhaps because the theory of administrative inconsistency emerged only on appeal, petitioners did not endeavor at trial to adduce from the IRS or other sources any specific evidence about other religious faiths' transactions. The IRS' revenue rulings, which merely state the agency's conclusions as to deductibility and which have apparently never been reviewed by the Tax Court or any other judicial body, also provide no specific facts about the nature of these other faiths' transactions. In the absence of such facts, we simply have no way (other than the wholly illegitimate one of relying on our personal experiences and observations) to appraise accurately whether the IRS' revenue rulings have correctly applied a quid pro quo analysis with respect to any or all of the religious practices in question. We do not know, for example, whether payments for other faiths' services are truly obligatory or whether any or all of these services are generally provided whether or not the encouraged "mandatory" payment is made.

The IRS' application of the "contribution or gift" standard may be right or wrong with respect to these other faiths, or it may be right with respect to some religious practices and wrong with respect to others. It may also be that some of these payments are appropriately classified as partially deductible "dual payments." With respect to those religions where the structure of transactions involving religious services is established not centrally but by individual congregations, the proper point of reference for a quid pro quo analysis might be the individual congregation, not the religion as a whole. Only upon a proper factual record could we make these determinations. Absent such a record, we must reject petitioners' administrative consistency argument.

Petitioners' congressional acquiescence claim fails for similar reasons. Even if one assumes that Congress has acquiesced in the IRS' ruling with respect to "[p]ew rents, building fund assessments, and periodic dues," Rev. Rul. 70-47, 1970-1 Cum. Bull. 49, the fact is that the IRS' 1971 ruling articulates no broad principle of deductibility, but instead merely identifies as deductible three discrete types of payments. Having before us no information about the nature or structure of these three payments, we have no way of discerning any possible unifying principle, let alone whether such a principle would embrace payments for auditing and training sessions.

V

For the reasons stated herein, the judgments of the Courts of Appeals are hereby affirmed.

Dissent: Justice O'CONNOR, with whom Justice SCALIA joins, dissenting.

The Court today acquiesces in the decision of the Internal Revenue Service (IRS) to manufacture a singular exception to its 70-year practice of allowing fixed payments indistinguishable from those made by petitioners to be deducted as charitable contributions. Because the IRS cannot constitutionally be allowed to select which religions will receive the benefit of its past rulings, I respectfully dissent. . . .

When a taxpayer claims as a charitable deduction part of a fixed amount given to a charitable organization in exchange for benefits that have a commercial value, the allowable portion of that claim is computed by subtracting from the total amount paid the value of the physical benefit received. If at a charity sale one purchases for $1,000 a painting whose market value is demonstrably no more than $50, there has been a contribution of $950. The same would be true if one purchases a $1,000 seat at a charitable dinner where the food is worth $50. An identical calculation can be made where the quid received is not a painting or a meal, but an intangible such as entertainment, so long as that intangible has some market value established in a noncontributory context. Hence, one who purchases a ticket to a concert, at the going rate for concerts by the particular performers, makes a charitable contribution of zero even if it is announced in advance that all proceeds from the ticket sales will go to charity. The performers may have made a charitable contribution, but the audience has paid the going rate for a show.

It becomes impossible, however, to compute the "contribution" portion of a payment to a charity where what is received in return is not merely an intangible, but an intangible (or, for that matter a tangible) that is not bought and sold except in donative contexts so that the only "market" price against which it can be evaluated is a market price that always includes donations. Suppose, for example, that the charitable organization that traditionally solicits donations on Veterans Day, in exchange for which it gives the donor an imitation poppy bearing its name, were to establish a flat rule that no one gets a poppy without a donation of at least $10. One would have to say that the "market" rate for such poppies was $10, but it would assuredly not be true that everyone who "bought" a poppy for $10 made no contribution. Similarly, if one buys a $100 seat at a prayer breakfast — receiving as the quid pro quo food for both body and soul — it would make no sense to say that no charitable contribution whatever has occurred simply because the "going rate" for all prayer breakfasts (with equivalent bodily food) is $100. The latter may well be true, but that "going rate" includes a contribution.

Confronted with this difficulty, and with the constitutional necessity of not making irrational distinctions among taxpayers, and with the even higher standard of equality of treatment among religions that the First Amendment imposes, the Government has only two practicable options with regard to distinctively religious quids pro quo: to disregard them all, or to tax them all. Over the years it has chosen the former course. . . .

There can be no doubt that at least some of the fixed payments which the IRS has treated as charitable deductions, or which the Court assumes the IRS would allow taxpayers to deduct, are as "inherently reciprocal" as the payments for auditing at issue here. In exchange for their payment of pew rents, Christians receive particular seats during worship services. Similarly, in some synagogues attendance at the worship services for Jewish High Holy Days is often predicated upon the purchase of a general admission ticket or a reserved seat ticket. Religious honors such as publicly reading from Scripture are purchased or auctioned periodically in some synagogues of Jews from Morocco and Syria. Mormons must tithe their income as a necessary but not sufficient condition to obtaining a "temple recommend," i.e., the right to be admitted into the temple. A Mass stipend — a fixed payment given to a Catholic priest, in consideration of which he is obliged to apply the fruits of the Mass for the intention of the donor — has similar overtones of exchange. According to some Catholic theologians, the nature of the pact between a priest and a donor who pays a Mass stipend is "a bilateral contract known as *do ut facias.* One person agrees to give while the other party agrees to do something in return." A finer example of a quid pro quo exchange would be hard to formulate.

This is not a situation where the IRS has explicitly and affirmatively reevaluated its longstanding interpretation of section 170 and decided to analyze all fixed religious contributions under a quid pro quo standard. There is no indication whatever that the IRS has abandoned its 70-year practice with respect to payments made by those other than Scientologists. . . .

[T]he Court cannot abjure its responsibility to address serious constitutional problems by converting a violation of the Establishment Clause into an "administrative consistency argument" with an inadequate record. It has chosen to ignore both longstanding, clearly articulated IRS practice, and the failure of respondent to offer any cogent, neutral explanation for the IRS' refusal to apply this practice to the Church of Scientology. Instead, the Court has pretended that whatever errors in application the IRS has committed are hidden from its gaze and will, in any event, be rectified in due time.

In my view, the IRS has misapplied its longstanding practice of allowing charitable contributions under section 170 in a way that violates the Establishment Clause. It has unconstitutionally refused to allow payments for the religious service of auditing to be deducted as charitable contributions in the same way it has allowed fixed payments to other religions to be deducted. . . . [T]he IRS' application of the quid pro quo standard here — and only here — discriminates against the Church of Scientology. I would reverse the decisions below.

REV. RUL. 93-73
1993-2 C.B. 75

Revenue Ruling 78-189, 1978-1 C.B. 68 is obsoleted.

Notes and Questions

1. *Is that all there is?* The sentence above is the entire text of Rev. Rul. 93-73. The ruling was issued as part of a general settlement of the long-running feud between the IRS and the Church of Scientology, which had involved a number of legal and factual disputes. Although the ruling does not mention *Hernandez,* the ruling amounts to a repudiation by the IRS of its victory in

that case, by "obsoleting" (a word not usually thought to have a verb form) the ruling that *Hernandez* endorsed.

2. *The real hierarchy of authority.* Even if one is persuaded by Justice O'Connor's powerful dissent, the majority opinion in *Hernandez* still represents a decision by the Supreme Court of the United States. Does the IRS really have the power to overrule (*sub silentio*, no less) a decision of the Supreme Court? The answer seems to be that the IRS does have the *power* to do so, although it may not have the *right*. At least in the vast majority of situations, if the IRS decides to be more generous to a particular taxpayer (or group of taxpayers) than the Internal Revenue Code dictates, there is no avenue of legal challenge. The taxpayer, of course, is not interested in challenging the IRS's beneficence, and no one else has standing to challenge the giveaway. *See, e.g.,* Allen v. Wright, 468 U.S. 737 (1984); Simon v. Eastern Kentucky Welfare Rights Organization, 426 U.S. 26 (1976). Notice the surprising hierarchy of authority: Although we saw in the previous set of materials that the NCAA is more powerful than the IRS, it now becomes apparent that the IRS is (sometimes) more powerful than the Supreme Court.

3. *Intangible religious benefits.* A few months before the IRS issued Rev. Rul. 93-73, Congress enacted the Omnibus Budget Reconciliation Act of 1993, which included the substantiation requirements of §170(f)(8). Although that provision ordinarily requires a charity to furnish a donor with a good faith estimate of the value of any goods or services given by the charity to the donor in consideration of the contribution, it provides an exception to the valuation requirement for any "intangible religious benefit." Indulging in tautology, the statute defines intangible religious benefit as "any intangible religious benefit which is provided by an organization organized exclusively for religious purposes and which generally is not sold in a commercial transaction outside the donative context." Although Rev. Rul. 93-73 does not cite this new provision (or anything else) in support of its implicit rejection of *Hernandez,* does the enactment of §170(f)(8) nevertheless justify the issuance of the ruling? The aspect of *Hernandez* at issue here involves statutory interpretation, not constitutional law, so Congress *could* overrule *Hernandez* by legislation. Did it implicitly do so by enacting §170(f)(8)? In considering this question, examine carefully the precise context in which §170(f)(8) makes the concept of intangible religious benefit legally significant. Although one should always consult the legislative history in answering a question like this, it may not be very helpful in this case. The Conference Report, H.R. Rep. No. 213, 103d Cong., 1st Sess. 565-566, has only the following to say:

> The provision explicitly provides that, if in return for making a contribution of $250 or more to a religious organization, a donor receives in return [sic] solely an intangible religious benefit that generally is not sold in commercial transactions outside the donative context (e.g., admission to a religious ceremony[10]), then such a religious benefit may be disregarded for purposes of the substantiation requirement.

---

10. This exception does not apply, for example, to tuition for education leading to a recognized degree, travel services, or consumer goods. However, the Senate committee explanation states that it is intended that de minimis tangible benefits furnished to contributors that are incidental to a religious ceremony (such as wine) generally may be disregarded.

For more on the effect (if any) of §170(f)(8) on *Hernandez,* see the *Sklar* opinion set forth below.

4. *Private school tuition redux?* Return to our earlier consideration of whether there is any way to turn private school tuition into a deductible charitable contribution. Does Rev. Rul. 93-73 suggest an argument for deducting a substantial portion of the tuition paid to a religiously affiliated school? Read the following case.

SKLAR v. COMMISSIONER

282 F.3d 610 (9th Cir. 2002)

REINHARDT, Circuit Judge: The taxpayer-petitioners in this action, Michael and Maria Sklar, challenge the Internal Revenue Service's ("IRS") disallowance of their deductions, as charitable contributions, of part of the tuition payments made to their children's religious schools. In the notice of deficiency sent to the Sklars, the IRS explained that "since these costs are personal tuition expenses, they are not deductible." Specifically, the Sklars sought to deduct 55% of the tuition, on the basis that this represented the proportion of the school day allocated to religious education. The Sklars contend that these costs are deductible under section 170 of the Internal Revenue Code, as payments for which they have received "solely intangible religious benefits." They also argue that they should receive this deduction because the IRS permits similar deductions to the Church of Scientology, and it is a violation of administrative consistency and of the Establishment Clause to deny them, as Orthodox Jews, the same deduction. The Tax Court found that under De Jong v. Commissioner, 309 F.2d 375, 376 (9th Cir. 1962), tuition paid for the education of a taxpayer's children is a personal expense which is non-deductible under Section 170. . . .

I. THE PROVISIONS OF THE TAX CODE GOVERNING CHARITABLE CONTRIBUTION DEDUCTIONS DO NOT APPEAR TO PERMIT THE DEDUCTION CLAIMED BY THE SKLARS

The Sklars assert that the deduction they claimed is allowable under section 170 of the Internal Revenue Code which permits taxpayers to deduct, as a charitable contribution, a "contribution or gift" to certain tax-exempt organizations. Not only has the Supreme Court held that, generally, a payment for which one receives consideration does not constitute a "contribution or gift" for purposes of section 170, see United States v. American Bar Endowment, 477 U.S. 105, 118 (1986) (stressing that "the sine qua non of a charitable contribution is a transfer of money or property without adequate consideration"), but it has explicitly rejected the contention made here, by the Sklars: that there is an exception in the Code for payments for which one receives only religious benefits in return. Hernandez v. Commissioner, 490 U.S. 680 (1989). . . .

Despite the clear statutory holding of *Hernandez,* the Sklars contend that recent changes to the Internal Revenue Code have clarified Congressional intent with respect to the deductibility of these payments. We seriously doubt the validity of this argument. The amendments to the Code appear not to have changed the substantive definition of a deductible charitable contribution, but only to have enacted additional documentation requirements for claimed deductions. Section 170(f) of the Code adds a new requirement that taxpayers claiming a charitable contribution deduction obtain from the donee an estimate of the value of any goods and services received in return for the donation, and exempts from that new estimate requirement contributions for which solely intangible religious benefits are received. . . .

Given the clear holding of *Hernandez* and the absence of any direct evidence of Congressional intent to overrule the Supreme Court on this issue, we would be extremely reluctant to read an additional and significant substantive deduction into the statute based on what are clearly procedural provisions regarding the documentation of tax return information, particularly where the deduction would be of doubtful constitutional validity. *Hernandez*, 490 U.S. at 694; *see* Lemon v. Kurtzman, 403 U.S. 602, 612-13 (1971) (holding that a statute is unconstitutional under the Establishment Clause if it fosters "an excessive government entanglement with religion"). We need not, however, decide this issue definitively in this case.

II. THE IRS POLICY REGARDING THE CHURCH OF SCIENTOLOGY MAY NOT BE WITHHELD FROM PUBLIC SCRUTINY AND APPEARS TO VIOLATE THE ESTABLISHMENT CLAUSE; FURTHER, IT APPEARS THAT THE SKLARS HAVE NOT MADE OUT A CLAIM OF ADMINISTRATIVE INCONSISTENCY

Additionally, the Sklars claim that the IRS engages in a "policy" of permitting members of the Church of Scientology to deduct as charitable contributions, payments made for "auditing," "training," and other qualified religious services, and that the agency's refusal to grant similar religious deductions to members of other faiths violates the Establishment Clause and is administratively inconsistent. They assert that the "policy" is contained in a "closing agreement" that the IRS signed with the Church of Scientology in 1993, shortly after the *Hernandez* decision and the 1993 changes to section 170 of the Internal Revenue Code. Because the IRS erroneously asserted that it is prohibited from disclosing all or any part of the closing agreement, we assume, for purposes of resolving this case, the truthfulness of the Sklars' allegations regarding the terms of that agreement. However, rather than concluding that the IRS's pro-Scientology policy would require it to adopt similar provisions for all other religions, we would likely conclude, were we to reach the issue, that the policy must be invalidated on the ground that it violates either the Internal Revenue Code or the Establishment Clause. *See Hernandez*, 490 U.S. at 694; Lemon v. Kurtzman, 403 U.S. at 612-13.

A. THE IRS'S REFUSAL TO DISCLOSE THE TERMS OF ITS CLOSING AGREEMENT WITH THE CHURCH OF SCIENTOLOGY

The IRS insists that the closing agreement in this case cannot be disclosed as it contains return information which the IRS is required to keep confidential under I.R.C. section 6103. Under section 6103, the IRS is prohibited from disclosing "return information," which is defined to include closing agreements. I.R.C. section 6103(b)(2). The prohibitions of section 6103 are subject to section 6104, where that provision applies, and section 6104 mandates public disclosure by each tax-exempt entity of its application for tax exemption (which itself contains detailed financial information about the entity, including revenues and expenses) as well as all documentation in support of that application. [Most of the court's lengthy discussion of the interplay between §§6103 and 6104 is omitted.]

Therefore, we reject the argument that the closing agreement made with the Church of Scientology, or at least the portion establishing rules or policies that are applicable to Scientology members generally, is not subject to public disclosure. The IRS is simply not free to enter into closing agreements with religious or other tax-exempt organizations governing the deductions that will be available to their members and to keep such provisions secret from the courts, the Congress, and the public.[11]

B. THE CONSTITUTIONALITY OF THE IRS'S AGREEMENT WITH THE CHURCH OF SCIENTOLOGY

The Supreme Court has developed a framework for determining whether a statute grants an unconstitutional denominational preference. Under that test, articulated in Larson v. Valente, 456 U.S. 228, 246-47 (1982), the first inquiry is whether or not the law facially discriminates amongst religions. The second inquiry, should it be found that the law does so discriminate, is whether or not, applying strict scrutiny, that discrimination is justified by a compelling governmental interest. *Id.* Applying this test to the policy of the IRS towards the Church of Scientology, the initial inquiry must be whether the policy facially discriminates amongst religions. Clearly it does, as this tax deduction is available only to members of the Church of Scientology.

The second *Larson* inquiry is whether or not the facially discriminatory policy is justified by a compelling governmental interest. 456 U.S. at 246-47. Although the IRS does not concede that it is engaging in a denominational preference, it asserts in its brief that the terms of the settlement agreement cannot be used as a basis to find an Establishment Clause violation because "in order to settle a case, both parties are required to make compromises with respect to points on which they believe they are legally correct." This is the only interest that the IRS proffers for the alleged policy. Although it appears to be true that the IRS has engaged in this particular preference in the interest of settling a long and litigious tax dispute with the Church of Scientology, and as compelling as this interest might otherwise be, it does not rise to the level that would pass strict scrutiny. The benefits of settling a controversy with one religious organization can hardly outweigh the costs of engaging in a religious preference. . . . Because the facial preference for the Church of Scientology embodied in the IRS's policy regarding its members cannot be justified by a compelling governmental interest, we would, if required to decide the case on the ground urged by the Sklars, first determine that the IRS policy

---

11. We believe that the Tax Court's ruling that the closing agreement is not relevant is in all likelihood correct. The Tax Court concluded that the Sklars were not similarly situated to the members of the Church of Scientology who benefitted from the closing agreement. While we have no doubt that certain taxpayers who belong to religions other than the Church of Scientology would be similarly situated to such members, we think it unlikely that the Sklars are. Religious education for elementary or secondary school children does not appear to be similar to the "auditing" and "training" conducted by the Church of Scientology. Again, however, we need not resolve that issue here.

constitutes an unconstitutional denominational preference under *Larson*. 456 U.S. at 230.

The Sklars contend that because "the IRS has admitted that it permits members of the Church of Scientology to deduct their payments for religious instruction . . . in order to avoid violating the First Amendment, [the] IRS must permit adherents of other faiths to deduct their payments for religious instruction." To the extent that the Sklars claim that the Establishment Clause requires that we extend the Scientology deduction to all religious organizations, they are in error for three reasons: First, we would be reluctant ever to presume that Congress or any agency of the government would intend that a general religious preference be adopted, by extension or otherwise, as such preferences raise the highly sensitive issue of state sponsorship of religion. In the absence of a clear expression of such intent, we would be unlikely to consider extending a policy favoring one religion where the effect of our action would be to create a policy favoring all. Second, the Supreme Court has previously stated that a policy such as the Sklars wish us to create would be of questionable constitutional validity under *Lemon*, because the administration of the policy could require excessive government entanglement with religion. *Hernandez*, 490 U.S. at 694; *see Lemon*, 403 U.S. at 612-13. Third, the policy the Sklars seek would appear to violate section 170. *See Hernandez*, 490 U.S. at 692-93. To the extent that the Sklars are also making an administrative inconsistency claim, we reject that claim on two grounds. First, in order to make an administrative inconsistency claim, a party must show that it is similarly situated to the group being treated differently by the agency. United States v. Kaiser, 363 U.S. 299, 308 (1960) (Frankfurter, J., concurring) ("The Commissioner [of the IRS] cannot tax one and not tax another without some rational basis for the difference. And so, . . . it can be an independent ground of decision that the Commissioner has been inconsistent. . . ."). We seriously doubt that the Sklars are similarly situated to the persons who benefit from the Scientology closing agreement because the religious education of the Sklars' children does not appear to be similar to the "auditing" , "training" or other "qualified religious services" conducted by the Church of Scientology. Second, even if they were so situated, because the treatment they seek is of questionable statutory and constitutional validity under section 170 of the IRC, under *Lemon,* and under *Hernandez,* we would not hold that the unlawful policy set forth in the closing agreement must be extended to all religious organizations. In the end, however, we need not decide the Establishment Clause claim or the administrative inconsistency claim as the Sklars have failed to show that their tuition payments constitute a partially deductible "dual payment" under the Tax Code.

III. THE SKLARS' TUITION PAYMENTS DO NOT CONSTITUTE PARTIALLY DEDUCTIBLE "DUAL PAYMENTS" UNDER THE TAX CODE

A "dual payment" (or "quid pro quo payment") under the Tax Code is a payment made in part in consideration for goods and services, and in part as a charitable contribution. . . . The IRS permits a deduction under section 170 for the portion of a dual payment that consists of a charitable contribution, but not for the portion for which the taxpayer receives a benefit in return. Although the Sklars concede that they received a benefit for their tuition payments, in that their children received a secular education, they claim that part of the payment — the part attributable to their children's religious education — should be regarded as a charitable contribution because they received only an "intangible religious benefit" in return. Leaving aside both the issue, discussed in section I, of whether the tax code does indeed treat payments for which a taxpayer receives an "intangible religious benefit" as a charitable contribution, as well as any constitutional considerations, we are left with the Sklars' contention that their tuition payment was a dual one: in part in consideration for secular education, and in part as a charitable contribution. The Sklars assert that because 45% of their children's school day was spent on secular education, and 55% on religious education, they should receive a deduction for 55% of their tuition payments. On the record before this court, the Sklars failed to satisfy the requirements for deducting part of a "dual payment" under the Tax Code. The Supreme Court discussed the deductibility of such payments in United States v. American Bar Endowment, 477 U.S. 105 (1986), and held that the taxpayer must establish that the dual payment exceeds the market value of the goods received in return. . . .

[T]he Sklars have not shown that any dual tuition payments they may have made exceeded the market value of the secular education their children received. They urge that the market value of the secular portion of their children's education is the cost of a public school education. That cost, of course, is nothing. The Sklars are in error. The market value is the cost of a comparable secular education offered by private schools. The Sklars do not present any evidence even suggesting that their total payments exceeded that cost. There is no evidence in the record of the tuition private schools charge for a comparable secular education, and thus no evidence showing that the Sklars made an "excess payment" that might qualify for a tax deduction. This appears to be not simply an inadvertent evidentiary omission, but rather a reflection of the practical realities of the high costs of private education. The Sklars also failed to show that they intended to make a gift by contributing any such "excess payment." Therefore, under the clear holding of *American Bar Endowment,* the Sklars cannot prevail on this appeal.

IV. CONCLUSION

We hold that because the Sklars have not shown that their "dual payment" tuition payments are partially deductible under the Tax Code, and, specifically, that the total payments they made for both the secular and religious private school education their children received exceeded the market value of other secular private school education available to those children, the IRS did not err in disallowing their deductions, and the Tax Court did not err in affirming the IRS's decision. We affirm the decision of the Tax Court on that ground.

SILVERMAN, Circuit Judge, concurring: Why is Scientology training different from all other religious training? We should decline the invitation to answer that question. The sole issue before us is whether the Sklars' claimed deduction is valid, not whether members of the Church of Scientology have become the IRS's chosen people.

The majority states that the Church of Scientology's closing agreement is not relevant because "the Sklars are not similarly situated to the members of the Church of Scientology. . . ." That may or may not be true, but it has no bearing on whether the tax code permits the Sklars to deduct the costs of their children's religious education as a charitable contribution. Whether the Sklars are entitled to the deduction they claim is governed by 26 U.S.C. section 170, *Hernandez v. Commissioner*, 490 U.S. 680 (1989), and *United States v. American Bar Endowment*, 477 U.S. 105 (1986), not by the Church of Scientology closing agreement. . . .

The Sklars receive something in return for their tuition payments—the education of their children. Thus, they are not entitled to a charitable deduction under section 170, as Judge Reinhardt carefully shows. *Hernandez* clearly forecloses the argument that section 170 should not apply because the tuition payments are for religious education. Finally, the Sklars have not demonstrated that what they pay for their children's education exceeds the fair market value of what they receive in return; therefore, they have not shown that they are entitled to a deduction under *American Bar Endowment.* It is as simple as that.

Accordingly, under both the tax code and Supreme Court precedent, the Sklars are not entitled to the charitable deduction they claimed. The Church of Scientology's closing agreement is irrelevant, not because the Sklars are not "similarly situated" to Scientologists, but because the closing agreement does not enter into the equation by which the deductibility of the Sklars' payments is determined. An IRS closing agreement cannot overrule Congress and the Supreme Court.

If the IRS does, in fact, give preferential treatment to members of the Church of Scientology—allowing them a special right to claim deductions that are contrary to law and rightly disallowed to everybody else—then the proper course of "action is a lawsuit to stop to that policy."[12] The remedy is not to require the IRS to let others claim the improper deduction, too.

Notes and Questions

1. *Is the holding persuasive?* The court's actual holding (section III of the opinion) assumes for the sake of argument that intangible religious benefits don't "count" for purposes of quid pro quo analysis. The court concludes that the Sklars lose anyway because they failed to prove that their children's school was more expensive than secular private schools. But is that the right comparison if their children are receiving only 45 percent as much secular education as children in a secular private school? If any quid pro quo in the form of religious instruction is to be ignored, shouldn't the Sklars be entitled to a deduction to the extent their children's tuition exceeds 45 percent (rather than 100 percent) of the cost of a secular private school?

2. *A different rationale.* During the 55 percent of the school day devoted to religious instruction, the school necessarily provided the secular benefit of child care along with religious instruction. Perhaps the school charged no more for child-care-plus-religious-instruction than the market rate for non-educational child care. If so, would that provide a more convincing basis for the court's conclusion?

---

12. *See* Bowen v. Kendrick, 487 U.S. 589 (1988) (allowing a taxpayer group to challenge the constitutionality of the Adolescent Family Life Act under the Establishment Clause); School Dist. of City of Grand Rapids v. Ball, 473 U.S. 373, 380 n.5 (noting and affirming "the numerous cases in which we have adjudicated Establishment Clause challenges by state taxpayers to programs for aiding nonpublic schools"), *rev'd on other grounds,* Agostini v. Felton, 521 U.S. 203 (1997).

3. *Special treatment for Scientology?* The majority opinion assumes the IRS is treating Scientologists more favorably than adherents of other religions, because only Scientology has a favorable closing agreement. The Ninth Circuit must not have read Justice O'Connor's opinion in *Hernandez,* in which she demonstrates that the IRS has a long-established practice of allowing charitable deductions to members of other religions in situations analogous to Scientology auditing. If there is an establishment clause violation, it is not that the IRS has impermissibly favored Scientology over other religions; rather, it would have to be that the IRS has impermissibly favored benefactors of religious charities over benefactors of nonreligious charities, by not similarly disregarding intangible secular benefits (whatever they might be).[13]

4. *Standing.* In his dissent, Judge Silverman assumes the Sklars would be able to challenge the IRS's alleged favoritism toward Scientology, despite the general rule that no one has standing to challenge unduly favorable IRS treatment of other taxpayers.[14] He is relying on the *Flast v. Cohen* doctrine,[15] under which one's status as a taxpayer gives one standing to challenge government expenditures benefiting religion as violations of the Establishment Clause of the First Amendment (even though one's own tax liability is not at issue). Although Judge Silverman's assumption was reasonable in 2002, it has been undermined by two recent Supreme Court opinions. In Hein v. Freedom from Religion Foundation, 551 U.S. 587 (2007), the Court declined to "lower [] the taxpayer standing bar to permit challenges of purely executive actions." 551 U.S. at 661. After *Hein,* it appeared there would be Establishment Clause standing to challenge religious favoritism embodied in a provision of the Internal Revenue Code, but not to challenge religious favoritism embodied only in the administrative practices of the IRS. Even the limited *Hein* version of Establishment Clause standing to challenge religious favoritism in the tax system appears to have been eliminated by the Court's decision in Arizona Christian School Tuition Org. v. Winn, 131 S. Ct. 1436 (2011), in which the Court ruled (by a vote of five to four) that tax credits (under the Arizona state income tax) did not constitute government spending, and thus did not give rise to taxpayer standing under *Flaust v. Cohen.*

5. *Administrative consistency.* What if the IRS properly applies the Code to one unlucky taxpayer, and gives statutorily unauthorized more favorable treatment to all similarly situated taxpayers? According to Justice Frankfurter's concurrence in *Kaiser* (quoted in *Sklar*), such administrative inconsistency can be an "independent ground of decision." In other words, a court should rule in favor of the singled-out taxpayer because of the IRS's inconsistency, even though the statute supports the IRS's treatment of that taxpayer. The Ninth Circuit misses Justice Frankfurter's point when it rejects the Sklars'

13. For the possibility that favorable tax treatment granted to all religions, but only to religions, might violate the Establishment Clause, see Warren v. Commissioner, 282 F.3d 1119 (9th Cir. 2002) (court *sua sponte* questioned the validity, under the Establishment Clause, of the parsonage allowance exclusion of §107, and appointed constitutional law professor Erwin Chemerinsky to brief the issue as an *amicus curiae*), *dismissed pursuant to stipulation of the parties,* 302 F.3d 1012 (9th Cir. 2002).
    14. See Note 2 following *Hernandez, supra.*
    15. Flast v. Cohen, 392 U.S. 83 (1968).

administrative inconsistency argument on the basis that "the treatment they seek is of questionable statutory . . . validity." On the other hand, there is little judicial authority in support of Justice Frankfurter's position; it is far from clear that IRS inconsistency *can* be "an independent ground of decision."

6. Sklar *redux: Did they have a prayer?* Though the Ninth Circuit opinion doesn't seem encouraging, the Sklars persisted, and litigated the same issue for the tax year (1995) immediately following the one involved in the Ninth Circuit decision. Characterizing the Sklars' new arguments as "virtually identical" to their arguments in the earlier litigation, the Ninth Circuit again ruled in favor of the government. Sklar v. Commissioner, 549 F.3d 1252 (9th Cir. 2008), *cert. denied*, 129 S. Ct. 2888 (2009).

Cell

EXEMPT ORGANIZATIONS

Section 501 exempts a wide variety of nonprofit organizations from the corporate income tax to which they would otherwise presumably be exposed.[16] The categories of exempt organizations are listed in the several paragraphs of §501(c). The most prominent category is described in §501(c)(3), which exempts organizations that are "organized and operated exclusively for religious, charitable . . . or educational purposes."[17] These are sometimes referred to as "charitable organizations." With minor exceptions, these are the organizations that are entitled to receive deductible contributions from their supporters.[18] Noncharitable organizations that may enjoy exemption from tax, but not deductible contributions, include civic and business leagues, labor unions, fraternal societies, and many others.

Exemption from income taxes has been labeled as a subsidy of the organizations entitled to receive such exemptions, but one that is justified—at least in the case of charitable organizations—by the public benefits provided by those

---

16. Section 11 of the IRC imposes an income tax on all "corporations," which would presumably include nonprofit corporations, but for §501. Section 7701(a)(3) of the IRC defines corporations to include "associations," so even unincorporated nonprofit organizations might well be exposed to the corporate income tax, unless they qualify for the exemption under §501. A few nonprofit organizations are organized as charitable trusts. They would, but for the exemption under §501, be taxed under the provisions of §1(e).

17. The quoted paragraph also lists a number of other purposes of less general significance that can qualify an organization for exempt status, including testing for public safety and promoting amateur sports competition.

18. Section 501(c)(3) is both underinclusive and overinclusive as a description of organizations that can receive deductible contributions. For example, §170(c) allows deductions for contributions to some organizations that are not within the ambit of §501(c)(3), such as governmental units, certain veterans' organizations, fraternal societies, and cemetery companies; on the other hand, §170(c) does not authorize deductions for contributions to organizations whose purpose is testing for public safety.

organizations.[19] Other commentators, however, have questioned whether this is in fact a subsidy, or is in any case particularly valuable to most organizations.[20] This argument is based on the recognition that nonprofit organizations, as their name suggests, do not ordinarily generate the profits that are the base of the corporate income tax. Their affairs are arranged in such a way that their expenses normally roughly match their revenue; this would be an especially likely result if contributions to such organization are viewed — as they quite plausibly could be — as either gifts or contributions to capital, neither of which is considered as gross income for individuals or corporations.

To be sure, most organizations experience fluctuations in revenues and expenses, so that during at least some accounting periods, they might well show an excess of the former over the latter. And many organizations seek to grow in scope at least partly by not spending all that they receive in any particular year. For such organizations, exemption from income taxes is quite valuable, and for virtually all nonprofits the exemption is a clear source of convenience, relieving them of the obligation to manage their affairs carefully so as never to show an excess of revenues over expenses during any taxable period. Exemption from federal income taxes may also have ancillary benefits to organizations so exempted, because many state and local governmental units base their own decisions about property and sales tax exemptions on an organization's federal tax-exempt status.

A. CHARITABLE ORGANIZATIONS

The charitable[21] sector in the United States is large, both in absolute terms, and — relative to most other developed countries — in terms of the percentage of our economic output that it generates. Charitable organizations constitute large parts of the health care and higher education industries; they dominate fine arts and cultural activities; and, needless to say, are virtually the exclusive providers of religious services and charitable services to the needy. Not including churches and very small organizations (both of which are exempt from mandatory filing requirements), charitable organizations enjoyed $1.25 trillion in revenue — roughly 10 percent of the gross domestic product — and owned over $2.2 trillion in assets in 2005.[22] Curiously, the sector is defined in terms of the tax from which it is largely exempt, and is largely regulated by the IRS, as that agency enforces restrictions imposed by the Internal Revenue Code.

19. Justice Rehnquist, writing in the majority opinion in Regan v. Taxation with Representation, 461 U.S. 540 (1983), flatly described exemption as providing a subsidy. For a collection of arguments for exemption based on the idea of public benefit, see Chauncey Belknap, *The Federal Income Tax Exemption of Charitable Organizations: Its History and Underlying Policy*, in IV *Research Papers of the Filer Commission on Private Philanthropy and Public Needs* 2025, 2038-2039 (1977).

20. *See, e.g.*, Boris I. Bittker & George K. Rahdert, *The Exemption of Nonprofit Organizations from Federal Income Taxation*, 85 Yale L.J. 299 (1976).

21. "Charitable" is used in two senses in the nonprofit context. It is sometimes used to describe narrowly those organizations whose mission is to provide medical services or other alms to the needy. But it is also used more broadly to describe the activities of §501(c)(3) organizations of all types. It is used in both senses in this cell, with reliance on the context to make clear which sense is intended.

22. Paul Arnsberger, *Charities, Labor and Agricultural, and Other Tax-Exempt Organizations, 2005*, 28(2) *Statistics of Income Bulletin* 270 (2008).

1. Qualification for Exemption

To qualify for exempt status under §501(c)(3), a charitable organization must satisfy several requirements. The first is that it must be organized as a "corporation, community chest, fund or foundation."[23] However, the IRS has applied this requirement with a good deal of flexibility, implicitly allowing even unincorporated associations and charitable trusts to qualify.[24] It might be more accurate to think of the statutory language as imposing a requirement that there be some actual entity engaging in the charitable endeavors, not merely one or more persons acting as individuals.

The second requirement is that the organization be organized and operated exclusively for one of the mandated purposes — education, charity, and so on. This is applied by the IRS through the use of its "organizational test," which looks at the organizing documents, and its "operational test," which looks at the actual conduct of the charitable activities.[25]

The third requirement is that the organization must promulgate and enforce an absolute ban on "private inurement," meaning that no person can obtain financial benefit from the operation of the charitable organization. This does not mean, of course, that such organizations cannot contract with either employees or independent contractors for the provision of services to the organization, and compensate them appropriately. It means, rather, that the organization may not make direct distributions of its net proceeds, nor may it otherwise engage in acts that would amount to the equivalent of such a distribution. For example, a charitable organization cannot make an indirect distribution by paying excessive salaries, buying property at prices above the market value of the properties, and the like.[26] Some commentators have referred to the ban on private inurement as imposing a "nondistribution constraint," which nicely captures perhaps the most important distinction between charitable organizations and other entities.[27]

Fourth, charitable organizations must accept restrictions on their political activities. Section 501(c)(3) requires, as a condition of exempt status, that "no substantial part" of the organization's activities consist of "carrying on propaganda, or otherwise attempting, to influence legislation." Nor can charitable organizations engage in any political campaigns for or against candidates for public office.

The last major requirement is one that is not imposed directly by the language of the Code, but has been found by the Supreme Court to be implicit in the concept of charity. It is that the organization must not be operated in a manner that violates public policy. *See* Bob Jones University v. United States, 461 U.S. 574 (1983), excerpted below in the "public policy constraints" section.

---

23. Section 501(c)(3). The second through fourth requirements, detailed below, are also based directly on provisions of this statutory section.

24. *See, e.g.,* Treas. Reg. §1.501(c)(3)-1(b)(2).

25. *See* Treas. Regs. §1.501(c)(3)-1(b) and (c), respectively, explaining these tests in some detail.

26. Whether a salary is excessive is determined by reference to the market rate for the employee's services, not by some absolute standard of excessiveness. If other universities would also be willing — perhaps even eager — to pay an annual salary of $5 million to Whatsammata U.'s football coach, then the coach's $5 million salary is not excessive.

27. *See, e.g.,* Henry Hansman, *The Rationale for Exempting Nonprofit Organizations from the Corporate Income Tax,* 94 Yale L.J. 54 (1981).

Except for the first requirement, each of the foregoing has been the subject of some controversy. A taste of the issues involved in each of these areas is provided in the separate sections below.

a. Exempt Purpose

What constitutes an educational, religious, charitable, or other exempt organization is, like many legal concepts, reasonably clear at the core, but more amorphous at its perimeters. It certainly includes churches, schools, colleges, homeless shelters, and the like. Even as to these relatively easy cases, some circumstances may push the boundaries of these concepts. For example, would a family that conducts religious services in its own home be able to claim that it was a church for purposes of this section? Probably not, but it is difficult to explain why not, and the problems of doing so have been a source of some consternation to the IRS and the courts.[28] But most cases are not problematic.

Some extensions of the exempt status concept outside these core areas have become reasonably well settled. For example, hospitals generally find it possible to qualify as charitable organizations as long as they provide at least some services to indigent patients without regard to their ability to pay.[29] The IRS also recognizes that certain civic and community groups may be engaged in charitable work for purposes of §501(c)(3), such as groups whose purpose is to reduce discrimination and prejudice, combat community decay, or erect public monuments.[30] Symphony orchestras, theaters, museums, and similar cultural groups find it relatively easy to qualify as educational organizations. One might wonder why: A local chamber arts society that arranges a series of performances by well-known string quartets will pay those artists significant sums, rent performance halls in which to stage the performances, buy advertising in local media, and in general behave in a manner not easily distinguishable from that of a nonexempt promoter of rock concerts, except perhaps by reference to the volume at which the music is played.[31]

---

28. *Compare, e.g.,* Universal Life Church of Modesto, California v. United States, 372 F. Supp. 770 (E.D. Cal. 1974), which permitted such a "church" exempt status, *with* any of several subsequent cases (such as Universal Life Church, Inc. (Full Circle) v. Commissioner, 83 T.C. 292 (1984)) in which the IRS was able to persuade the courts that the churches in question should not be recognized as exempt, usually because the churches were operated for a substantial nonexempt purpose.

29. *See, e.g.,* Rev. Rul. 56-185, 1956-1 C.B. 202. Subsequent rulings appear to have relaxed even this rather minimal requirement. Rev. Rul. 69-545, 1969-2 C.B. 117, held that maintenance of an emergency room that was open even to those who could not pay was enough to qualify for an exemption, and Rev. Rul. 83-157, 1983-2 C.B. 94, held that even that requirement did not apply in the case of certain specialty hospitals (a cancer hospital, for example) that did not ordinarily need to operate an emergency room.

30. *See* Treas. Reg. §1.501(c)(3)-1(d)(2).

31. Before students dash off letters to their representatives in Congress protesting this egregious cultural elitism, they may wish to reflect upon the fact that the rock promoter probably wouldn't want to be recognized as an exempt, nonprofit organization, since she hopes her efforts will reap a profit that she can distribute to herself; the more limited hope of the chamber arts society is that it will barely be able to scrape by, offsetting expenses with ticket revenues to the extent possible, and probably still depending on at least a few contributions to make ends meet. (Although we are aware of no cases on this question, it is imaginable that purveyors of rock music could also qualify for exemption if they were willing to accept the constraints that come with exempt status. One imagines that they simply prefer not to, in order to enjoy the profits they hope to achieve.) Also, ticket buyers of the chamber arts recitals are in the same position as the rock fans: Neither can deduct the cost of the price of admission to their chosen performances.

In the opinion that follows, Judge Abner Mikva explores the boundaries of the concept of "educational" in this context, and raises as well some interesting questions about the administrative role of the IRS.

BIG MAMA RAG, INC. v. UNITED STATES
631 F.2d 1030 (D.C. Cir. 1980)

MIKVA, Circuit Judge: Plaintiff, Big Mama Rag, Inc. (BMR, Inc.), appeals from the order of the court below granting summary judgment to defendants and upholding the IRS's rejection of plaintiff's application for tax-exempt status. Specifically, BMR, Inc. questions the finding that it is not entitled to tax exemption as an educational or charitable organization under section 501(c)(3) of the Internal Revenue Code and Treas. Reg. §1.501(c)(3)-1(d)(2) & (3). Appellant also challenges the constitutionality of the regulatory scheme, arguing that it violates the First Amendment and the equal protection component of the Fifth Amendment and that it unconstitutionally conditions tax-exempt status on the waiver of constitutional rights.

Because we find that the definition of "educational" contained in Treas. Reg. §1.501(c)(3)-1(d)(3) is unconstitutionally vague in violation of the First Amendment, we reverse the order of the court below.

I. BACKGROUND

BMR, Inc. is a nonprofit organization with a feminist orientation. Its purpose is "to create a channel of communication for women that would educate and inform them on general issues of concern to them." To this end, it publishes a monthly newspaper, Big Mama Rag (BMR), which prints articles, editorials, calendars of events, and other information of interest to women. BMR, Inc.'s primary activity is the production of that newspaper, but it also devotes a considerable minority of its time to promoting women's rights through workshops, seminars, lectures, a weekly radio program, and a free library.

BMR, Inc. has a predominantly volunteer staff and distributes free approximately 2,100 of 2,700 copies of Big Mama Rag's monthly issues. Moreover, the organization has severely limited the quantity and type of paid advertising. As the district court found, BMR, Inc. neither makes nor intends to make a profit and is dependent on contributions, grants, and funds raised by benefits for over 50 percent of its income.

Because of its heavy reliance on charitable contributions, BMR, Inc. applied in 1974 for tax-exempt status as a charitable and educational institution. That request was first denied by the IRS District Director in Austin, Texas, on the ground that the organization's newspaper was indistinguishable from an "ordinary commercial publishing practice."[32] After BMR, Inc. filed a protest and a hearing was held in the

---

32. The District Director's letter to BMR, Inc. stated: "Based on the information submitted, it appears that your corporate activities, which presumably are within the charter powers, are business activities. They are devoted to publishing a newspaper and selling it to the general public in accordance with ordinary commercial publishing practices. Although the newspaper published articles expressing the Feminist point of view, there is no showing that the operations fulfill a corporate role which in and of itself is exclusively charitable, scientific, literary or educational."

IRS National Office, the denial of tax-exempt status was affirmed on three separate grounds:

1. the commercial nature of the newspaper;
2. the political and legislative commentary found throughout; and
3. the articles, lectures, editorials, etc., promoting lesbianism.

. . . Although the court [below] rejected appellees' argument that BMR, Inc. was not entitled to tax-exempt status because it was a commercial organization, it agreed that appellant did not satisfy the definitions of "educational" and "charitable" in Treas. Reg. §1.501(c)(3)-1(d)(2) & (3). The court found no constitutional basis for disturbing the IRS's decision.

II. THE REGULATORY SCHEME

Tax exemptions are granted under section 501(c)(3) to a variety of socially useful organizations, including the charitable and the educational. The Code forbids exemption of an organization if any part of its net earnings inures to the benefit of private persons or if it is an "action organization" — one that attempts to influence legislation or participates in any political campaign. Treasury regulations impose additional requirements: exempt status is accorded only to applicants whose articles of organization limit their activities to furtherance of exempt purposes (the "organizational test") or [*sic,* should be "and"] whose activities are in fact aimed at accomplishment of exempt purposes (the "operational test"). Treas. Reg. §1.501(c)(3)-1(b)&(c).

The Treasury regulations also define some of the exempt purposes listed in section 501(c)(3) of the Code, including "charitable" and "educational." The definition of "educational" is the one at issue here:

> The term "educational," as used in section 501(c)(3), relates to — (a) The instruction or training of the individual for the purpose of improving or developing his capabilities; or (b) The instruction of the public on subjects useful to the individual and beneficial to the community. An organization may be educational even though it advocates a particular position or viewpoint so long as it presents a sufficiently full and fair exposition of the pertinent facts as to permit an individual or the public to form an independent opinion or conclusion. On the other hand, an organization is not educational if its principal function is the mere presentation of unsupported opinion.

Treas. Reg. §1.501(c)(3)-1(d)(3)(i).

The district court found that BMR, Inc. was not entitled to tax-exempt status because it had "adopted a stance so doctrinaire" that it could not meet the "full and fair exposition" standard articulated in the definition quoted above. Appellant's response is threefold. First, it argues, the "full and fair exposition" hurdle is not applicable at all here because BMR, Inc. is not an organization whose primary activity or principal function is advocacy of change. Second, BMR, Inc. contends that its publication does satisfy the requirements of the "full and fair exposition" standard. Finally, appellant maintains that denial of its application for tax-exempt status on the basis of the "full and fair exposition" standard is unconstitutional for a number of reasons.

Even though tax exemptions are a matter of legislative grace, the denial of which is not usually considered to implicate constitutional values, tax law and constitutional law are not completely distinct entities. In fact, the First Amendment was partly aimed at the so-called "taxes on knowledge," which were intended to limit the circulation of newspapers and therefore the public's opportunity to acquire information about governmental affairs. In light of their experience with such taxes, the framers realized, in the words of Mr. Justice Douglas, that "(t)he power to tax the exercise of a privilege is the power to control or suppress its enjoyment." Thus, although First Amendment activities need not be subsidized by the state, the discriminatory denial of tax exemptions can impermissibly infringe free speech. Similarly, regulations authorizing tax exemptions may not be so unclear as to afford latitude for subjective application by IRS officials. We find that the definition of "educational," and in particular its "full and fair exposition" requirement, is so vague as to violate the First Amendment and to defy our attempts to review its application in this case.[33]

III. Vagueness Analysis

Vague laws are not tolerated for a number of reasons, and the Supreme Court has fashioned the constitutional standards of specificity with these policies in mind. First, the vagueness doctrine incorporates the idea of notice — informing those subject to the law of its meaning. A law must therefore be struck down if "men of common intelligence must necessarily guess at its meaning." Hynes v. Mayor of Oradell, 425 U.S. 610, 620 (1976) (quoting Connally v. General Constr. Co., 269 U.S. 385, 391 (1926)).

Second, the doctrine is concerned with providing officials with explicit guidelines in order to avoid arbitrary and discriminatory enforcement. To that end, laws are invalidated if they are "wholly lacking in 'terms susceptible of objective measurement.'" Keyishian v. Board of Regents, 385 U.S. 589, 604 (1967) (quoting Cramp v. Board of Public Instruction, 368 U.S. 278, 286 (1961)).

These standards are especially stringent, and an even greater degree of specificity is required, where, as here, the exercise of First Amendment rights may be chilled by a law of uncertain meaning. . . . Measured by any standard, and especially by the strict standard that must be applied when First Amendment rights are involved, the definition of "educational" contained in Treas. Reg. §1.501(c)(3)-1(d)(3) must fall because of its excessive vagueness.

We do not minimize the difficulty and delicacy of the task delegated to the Treasury by Congress under section 501(c)(3) of the Code. Words such as "religious," "charitable," "literary," and "educational" easily lend themselves to subjective definitions at odds with the constitutional limitations we describe above. Treasury bravely made a pass at defining "educational," but the more parameters it tried to set, the more problems it encountered.

The first portion of the regulation relied upon to deny BMR, Inc.'s request for tax-exempt status measures an applicant organization by whether it provides

---

33. Given this disposition of the case, we do not, and need not, address the other issues raised by appellant: that the organization satisfies the requirements of Treas. Reg. §1.501(c)(5)-1(d)(2) & (3) and is therefore entitled to tax-exempt status; that the regulation is violative of equal protection; and that exemption is unconstitutionally conditioned on the waiver of constitutional rights.

"instruction of the public on subjects useful to the individual and beneficial to the community." Treas. Reg. §1.501(c)(3)-1(d)(3)(i)(b). The district court rejected that test with barely a murmur of disagreement from appellees. That standard, held the court below, "would be far too subjective in its application to pass constitutional muster."

We find similar problems inherent in the "full and fair exposition" test, on which the district court based affirmance of the IRS's denial of tax-exempt status to BMR, Inc. That test lacks the requisite clarity, both in explaining which applicant organizations are subject to the standard and in articulating its substantive requirements.

A. WHO IS COVERED BY THE "FULL AND FAIR EXPOSITION" TEST?

According to the terms of the Treasury regulation, only an organization that "advocates a particular position or viewpoint" must clear the "full and fair exposition" hurdle. Appellant maintains that the definition of an advocacy organization is to be found in the preceding subsection of the regulation, which defines the term "charitable": The fact that an organization, in carrying out its primary purpose, advocates social or civic changes or presents opinion on controversial issues with the intention of molding public opinion or creating public sentiment to an acceptance of its views does not preclude such organization from qualifying under section 501(c)(3) so long as it is not an "action" organization of any one of the types described in paragraph (c)(3) of this section. Regs. §1.501(c)(3)-1(d)(2).[34]

The district court held that this part of the regulation was designed to cover charitable institutions and that BMR, Inc., an educational rather than a charitable organization, must meet the "full and fair exposition" standard rather than the more lenient "action organization" standard of section 1.501(c)(3)-1(d)(2). Obviously, if BMR, Inc. is an advocacy group and is not a charitable organization, it may not take cover under the "action organization" standard but must instead meet the "full and fair exposition" test.

The initial question, however, is whether or not BMR, Inc. is an advocacy group at all. What appellant turns to Treas. Reg. §1.501(c)(3)-1(d)(2) for is the definition of "advocacy," not for the appropriate standard to be applied to advocacy organizations seeking tax-exempt status. The district court did not deal with that question, and, indeed, it is difficult to ascertain from the language of the regulation defining "educational" exactly what organizations are intended to be covered by the "full and fair exposition" standard and whether or not the definitions of advocacy groups are the same for both educational and charitable organizations.

The uncertainty of the coverage of the "full and fair exposition" standard is evidenced by its application over the years by the IRS. The Treasury Department's Exempt Organizations Handbook has defined "advocates a particular position" as synonymous with "controversial." Such a gloss clearly cannot withstand First Amendment scrutiny. It gives IRS officials no objective standard by which to judge which applicant organizations are advocacy groups—the evaluation is made solely on the basis of one's subjective notion of what is "controversial."

34. [An "action" organization is one that engages in more than de minimis lobbying, or in any political campaigning; such organizations are not entitled to §501(c)(3) status, by the terms of that paragraph.—EDS.]

And, in fact, only a very few organizations, whose views are not in the mainstream of political thought, have been deemed advocates and held to the "full and fair exposition" standard. The one tax-exempt homosexual organization cited by the Government as evidence that the IRS does not discriminate on the basis of sexual preference was required to meet the "full and fair exposition" standard even though it admittedly did not "advocate or seek to convince individuals that they should or should not be homosexuals." Rev. Rul. 78-305, 1978-2 C.B. 172, 173.

The Treasury regulation defining "educational" is, therefore, unconstitutionally vague in that it does not clearly indicate which organizations are advocacy groups and thereby subject to the "full and fair exposition" standard. And the latitude for subjectivity afforded by the regulation has seemingly resulted in selective application of the "full and fair exposition" standard — one of the very evils that the vagueness doctrine is designed to prevent.

B. WHAT DOES THE "FULL AND FAIR EXPOSITION" TEST REQUIRE?

The Treasury definition of "educational" may also be challenged on the ground that it fails to articulate with sufficient specificity the requirements of the "full and fair exposition" standard. The language of the regulation gives no aid in interpreting the meaning of the test:

> An organization may be educational even though it advocates a particular position or viewpoint so long as it presents a sufficiently full and fair exposition of the pertinent facts as to permit an individual or the public to form an independent opinion or conclusion. On the other hand, an organization is not educational if its principal function is the mere presentation of unsupported opinion. Treas. Reg. §1.501 (c)(3)-1(d)(3).

What makes an exposition "full and fair"? Can it be "fair" without being "full"? Which facts are "pertinent"? How does one tell whether an exposition of the pertinent facts is "sufficient . . . to permit an individual or the public to form an independent opinion or conclusion"? And who is to make all of these determinations?

The regulation's vagueness is especially apparent in the last clause quoted above. That portion of the test is expressly based on an individualistic — and therefore necessarily varying and unascertainable — standard: the reactions of members of the public. The Supreme Court has recognized that statutes phrased in terms of individual sensitivities are suspect and susceptible to attack on vagueness grounds. . . .

An additional source of unclarity lies in the relationship between the two sentences comprising the "full and fair exposition" test. Appellant argues that the two should be read as counter-examples — an organization fails to satisfy the test only if "its principal function is the mere presentation of unsupported opinion." The Government, on the other hand, contends that tax-exempt status must be denied BMR, Inc. if a substantial portion of its newspaper consists of unsupported opinion. Again, the language of the regulation does not resolve this issue.

The district court's interpretation of the "full and fair exposition" test, and the one advocated by the Government, is no more precise. The district court found the Treasury regulation "capable of objective application" because "it asks only whether the facts underlying the conclusions are stated." But distinguishing facts, on the one hand, and opinion or conclusion, on the other, does not provide an objective yardstick by which to define "educational." The distinction is not so clear-cut that an organization seeking tax-exempt status — or an IRS official reviewing an application for exemption — will be able to judge when any given statement must be bolstered by another supporting statement.

One of the five examples cited by the Government as evidence of BMR's failure to meet the "full and fair exposition" test may be used to illustrate our point. Most of the article, discussing Susan Saxe's 1975 plea of guilty to charges stemming from a bank robbery in Philadelphia, is simple journalistic reporting. It discusses the terms of the plea bargain, the reaction of local feminists, the differential treatment accorded Saxe supporters and white men who went to observe the pretrial hearing, and police questioning of women in Philadelphia. In return for Saxe's plea, the Government apparently agreed, among other things, to "call off its investigation of the women's and lesbian communities" in the area and not to ask Saxe to testify against "anyone she has known or know (sic) about in the last five years." By forcing Saxe to choose between her own interests and those of other women, the article continues, "the Government has clarified for us, once again, that we, as women, are inextricably bound up with each other in the struggle." Big Mama Rag, July, 1975, at 1, cols. 1-3.

Certainly, the author's viewpoint is not disguised in the last sentence. But is the statement one of fact or opinion? If the latter, is the author's description of the terms of the guilty plea sufficient to inform readers of the basis underlying her opinion? Or is further proof of the existence of "the struggle" necessary? If so, would the article satisfy the "full and fair exposition" test without that final statement? Neither the Treasury regulation nor the proposed fact/opinion distinction is responsive to these questions. And one's answers will likely be colored by one's attitude towards the author's point of view.

The futility of attempting to draw lines between fact and unsupported opinion is further illustrated by the district court's application of that test. The court did not analyze the contents of BMR under its proposed test but merely stated, without further explication, that the publication was not entitled to tax-exempt status because it had "adopted a stance so doctrinaire that it cannot satisfy this standard." Instead of applying the purportedly objective test the court had formulated, it was forced to resolve the case by resorting to the subjective notion of whether the publication was "doctrinaire." We can conceive of no value-free measurement of the extent to which material is doctrinaire, and the district court's reliance on that evaluative concept corroborates for us the impossibility of principled and objective application of the fact/opinion distinction.

Appellees suggest that the Treasury regulation at issue here embodies a related distinction — between appeals to the emotions and appeals to the mind. Material is educational, they argue, if it appeals to the mind, that is, if it reasons to a conclusion from stated facts. Again, the required linedrawing is difficult, a problem which is compounded if the difference between the two relies on the aforementioned fact/opinion distinction.

Moreover, the Treasury regulation does not support such a narrow concept of "educational" and we cannot approve it. Nowhere does the regulation hint that the definition of "educational" is to turn on the fervor of the organization or the strength of its language. As the Supreme Court has recognized in another context, the emotional content of a word is an important component of its message.

An example raised by appellees in their brief and discussed at oral argument is illustrative. The American Cancer Society's cause may be better served by a bumper sticker picturing a skull and crossbones and saying "Smoking rots your lungs" than by one that merely states "Smoking is hazardous to your health." Both are intended to impart the same message, and they are identical in degree of specificity of the underlying facts. Although the first may be said to appeal more to the emotions, and the second to the mind, that distinction should not obscure the similarities between the two. They should be considered equal in educational content.

Even if one could in fact differentiate fact from unsupported opinion, or emotional appeals from appeals to the mind, these proposed distinctions would be inadequate definitions of "educational" because material often combines elements of each. In such cases, appellees suggested at oral argument, a quantitative test would be appropriate. But the Treasury regulation makes no mention of such a test. Even if a quantitative approach were authorized, it is unclear how much of a publication's content would have to be factual, or appeal to the mind, in order to satisfy the "full and fair exposition" standard. Also unanswered is who would apply the test and determine the requisite amount of factual material. Certainly, the Treasury regulation itself gives no clue.

Thus, neither of the distinctions proposed here remedies the imprecise language of the "full and fair exposition" standard or clarifies the requirements imposed by that test.

IV. Conclusion

The definition of "educational" contained in Treas. Reg. §1.501(c)(3)-1(d)(3) lacks sufficient specificity to pass constitutional muster. Its "full and fair exposition" standard, on the basis of which the denial of BMR, Inc.'s application for tax exemption was upheld by the court below, is vague both in describing who is subject to that test and in articulating its substantive requirements.

The history of appellant's application for tax-exempt status attests to the vagueness of the "full and fair exposition" test and evidences the evils that the vagueness doctrine is designed to avoid. The district court's decision was based on the value-laden conclusion that BMR was too doctrinaire. Similarly, IRS officials earlier advised appellant's counsel that an exemption could be approved only if the organization "agree(d) to abstain from advocating that homosexuality is a mere preference, orientation, or propensity on par with heterosexuality and which should otherwise be regarded as normal." Whether or not this view represented official IRS policy is irrelevant. It simply highlights the inherent susceptibility to discriminatory enforcement of vague statutory language.

We are sympathetic with the IRS's attempt to safeguard the public fisc by closing revenue loopholes. And we by no means intend to suggest that tax-exempt status must be accorded to every organization claiming an educational mantle. Applications for tax exemption must be evaluated, however, on the basis of criteria capable of neutral application. The standards may not be so imprecise that they afford latitude to individual IRS officials to pass judgment on the content and quality of an applicant's views and goals and therefore to discriminate against those engaged in protected First Amendment activities.

We are not unmindful of the burden involved in reformulating the definition of "educational" to conform to First Amendment requirements. But the difficulty of the task neither lessens its importance nor warrants its avoidance. Objective standards are especially essential in cases such as this involving those espousing non-majoritarian philosophies. In this area the First Amendment cannot countenance a subjective "I know it when I see it" standard. And neither can we.

This case is accordingly reversed and remanded for further proceedings consistent with this opinion.

Notes and Questions

1. *What would be "full and fair"?* The opinion finds the "full and fair exposition" test impermissibly vague. If you had been before a court that found the test acceptable, what facts would you cite to show either the presence or absence of a full and fair exposition in this case?

2. *Representing Galileo.* The regulations require "full and fair exposition of the pertinent facts," as opposed to "mere presentation of unsupported opinion." Imagine how you would have represented Galileo under this standard, if he had sought exemption for a school formed to explain his view that the earth circled the sun, rather than vice versa. One would expect to find some difficulty in establishing at the time that such a view was supported by anything other than Galileo's own observations and inferences from them. On the other hand, Galileo is obviously a rare exception; most new "ideas" that run contrary to well-accepted views are in fact seriously defective. Do we want to provide tax exemption to organizations that express the idea that, for example, the Holocaust was a hoax? What about ideas that are widely accepted in some communities of discourse, but regarded as completely bogus by others, such as astrology, feng shui, tarot, and the like?

3. *No regulatory revision.* The regulations at issue in *Big Mama Rag* are still on the books. Should the Treasury have revised them after the D.C. Circuit declared them impermissibly vague? Why do you suppose it hasn't?

b. Private Inurement

The regulations provide that an organization will not be considered to be operated exclusively for an exempt purpose if any part of its net earnings inure "to the benefit of any shareholders or individuals."[35] Although both the Code and the regulations refer to net earnings, the IRS extends this analysis to cases in which the expenses of an organization—such as the salaries of its employees and officers—are excessive, leading to the private benefit of those favored by the payments in question.[36] At the same time, it is clear that charitable organizations frequently hire, in one capacity or another, some of the animating spirits of the organization, who may have created it, and seen it through the process of gaining

---

35. Treas. Reg. §1.501(c)(3)-1(c)(2).
36. *See, e.g.,* Church of Scientology of California v. Commissioner, 823 F.2d 1310 (9th Cir. 1987). Of course, the analysis is that the excessive portion of the salaries is really a distribution of net earnings in disguise.

an exemption; so long as the payments in question are not excessive, this is routinely tolerated. The IRS has been reasonably successful in controlling abuses when the organization's insiders are the beneficiaries of the organization's excessive payments. However, as the following case demonstrates, extending this principle to disqualify organizations whose operations unduly benefit outsiders may be very difficult.

UNITED CANCER COUNCIL, INC. v. COMMISSIONER
165 F.3d 1173 (7th Cir. 1999)

POSNER, Chief Judge: The United Cancer Council [UCC] is a charity that seeks, through affiliated local cancer societies, to encourage preventive and ameliorative approaches to cancer, as distinct from searching for a cure, which has been the emphasis of the older and better-known American Cancer Society, of which UCC is a splinter. The Internal Revenue Service revoked UCC's charitable exemption and the Tax Court upheld the revocation, precipitating this appeal.

So far as relates to this case, a charity, in order to be entitled to the charitable exemption from federal income tax, and to be eligible to receive tax-exempt donations, must be "organized and operated exclusively for . . . [charitable] purposes" and "no part of the net earnings of [the charity may] inure[] to the benefit of any private shareholder or individual." §501(c)(3) (exemption); 170(c)(2)(B), (C) (receipt of donations); 26 C.F.R. §1.501(a)-1(c), 1.501(c)(3)-1(d)(1)(i), (ii). The IRS claims that UCC (which is defunct) was not operated exclusively for charitable purposes, but rather was operated for, or also for, the private benefit of the fundraising company that UCC had hired, Watson & Hughey Company (W & H). The Service also claims that part of the charity's net earnings had inured to the benefit of a private shareholder or individual—W & H again. The Tax Court upheld the Service's second ground for revoking UCC's exemption—inurement—and did not reach the first ground, private benefit. The only issue before us is whether the court clearly erred in finding that a part of UCC's net earnings inured to the benefit of a private shareholder or individual.

It is important to understand what the IRS does not contend. It does not contend that any part of UCC's earnings found its way into the pockets of any members of the charity's board; the board members, who were medical professionals, lawyers, judges, and bankers, served without compensation. It does not contend that any members of the board were owners, managers, or employees of W & H, or relatives or even friends of any of W & H's owners, managers, or employees. It does not contend that the fundraiser was involved either directly or indirectly in the creation of UCC, or selected UCC's charitable goals. It concedes that the contract between charity and fundraiser was negotiated at an arm's length basis. But it contends that the contract was so advantageous to W & H and so disadvantageous to UCC that the charity must be deemed to have surrendered the control of its operations and earnings to the noncharitable enterprise that it had hired to raise money for it.

The facts are undisputed. In 1984, UCC was a tiny organization. It had an annual operating budget of only $35,000, and it was on the brink of bankruptcy because several of its larger member societies had defected to its rival, the American Cancer Society. A committee of the board picked W & H, a specialist in raising funds for charities, as the best prospect for raising the funds essential for UCC's survival. Another committee of the board was created to negotiate the contract. Because of UCC's perilous financial condition, the committee wanted W & H to "front" all the expenses of the fundraising campaign, though it would be reimbursed by UCC as soon as the campaign generated sufficient donations to cover those expenses. W & H agreed. But it demanded in return that it be made UCC's exclusive fundraiser during the five-year term of the contract, that it be given co-ownership of the list of prospective donors generated by its fundraising efforts, and that UCC be forbidden, both during the term of the contract and after it expired, to sell or lease the list, although it would be free to use it to solicit repeat donations. There was no restriction on W & H's use of the list. UCC agreed to these terms and the contract went into effect.

Over the five-year term of the contract, W & H mailed 80 million letters soliciting contributions to UCC. Each letter contained advice about preventing cancer, as well as a pitch for donations; 70 percent of the letters also offered the recipient a chance to win a sweepstake. The text of all the letters was reviewed and approved by UCC. As a result of these mailings, UCC raised an enormous amount of money (by its standards) — $28.8 million. But its expenses — that is, the costs borne by W & H for postage, printing, and mailing the letters soliciting donations, costs reimbursed by UCC according to the terms of the contract — were also enormous — $26.5 million. The balance, $2.3 million, the net proceeds of the direct-mail campaign, was spent by UCC for services to cancer patients and on research for the prevention and treatment of cancer. The charity was permitted by the relevant accounting conventions to classify $12.2 million of its fundraising expenses as educational expenditures because of the cancer information contained in the fundraising letters.

Although UCC considered its experience with W & H successful, it did not renew the contract when it expired by its terms in 1989. Instead, it hired another fundraising organization — with disastrous results. The following year, UCC declared bankruptcy, and within months the IRS revoked its tax exemption retroactively to the date on which UCC had signed the contract with W & H. The effect was to make the IRS a major creditor of UCC in the bankruptcy proceeding. The retroactive revocation did not, however, affect the charitable deduction that donors to UCC since 1984 had taken on their income tax returns.

The term "any private shareholder or individual" in the inurement clause of section 501(c)(3) has been interpreted to mean an insider of the charity. A charity is not to siphon its earnings to its founder, or the members of its board, or their families, or anyone else fairly to be described as an insider, that is, as the equivalent of an owner or manager. The test is functional. It looks to the reality of control rather than to the insider's place in a formal table of organization. The insider could be a "mere" employee — or even a nominal outsider, such as a physician with hospital privileges in a charitable hospital, a licensor, or for that matter a fundraiser, *National Foundation, Inc. v. United States*, 13 Cl. Ct. 486, 494-95 (1987) — though the court in that case rejected the argument that the fundraiser controlled the charity.

The Tax Court's classification of W & H as an insider of UCC was based on the fundraising contract. Such contracts are common. Fundraising has become a specialized professional activity and many charities hire specialists in it. If the charity's contract with the fundraiser makes the latter an insider, triggering the inurement clause of section 501(c)(3) and so destroying the charity's tax exemption, the charity sector of the economy is in trouble. The IRS does not take the position that every such contract has this effect. What troubles it are the particular terms and circumstances of UCC's contract. It argues that since at the inception of the contract the charity had no money to speak of, and since, therefore, at least at the beginning, all the expenses of the fundraising campaign were borne by W & H, the latter was like a founder, or rather refounder (UCC was created in 1963), of the charity. The IRS points out that 90 percent of the contributions received by UCC during the term of the contract were paid to W & H to defray the cost of the fundraising campaign that brought in those contributions, and so argues that W & H was the real recipient of the contributions. It argues that because W & H was UCC's only fundraiser, the charity was totally at W & H's mercy during the five-year term of the contract — giving W & H effective control over the charity. UCC even surrendered the right to rent out the list of names of donors that the fundraising campaign generated. The terms of the contract were more favorable to the fundraiser than the terms of the average fundraising contract are.

Singly and together, these points bear no relation that we can see to the inurement provision. The provision is designed to prevent the siphoning of charitable receipts to insiders of the charity, not to empower the IRS to monitor the terms of arm's length contracts made by charitable organizations with the firms that supply them with essential inputs, whether premises, paper, computers, legal advice, or fundraising services.

[The court analyzed the contract at some length, finding that it was negotiated at arm's length, was reasonable at the time it was executed, and was fully enforceable.]

We can find nothing in the facts to support the IRS's theory and the Tax Court's finding that W & H seized control of UCC and by doing so became an insider, triggering the inurement provision and destroying the exemption. There is nothing that corporate or agency law would recognize as control. A creditor of UCC could not seek the satisfaction of his claim from W & H on the ground that the charity was merely a cat's paw or alter ego of W & H, as in *Pepper v. Litton*, 308 U.S. 295, 311-12 (1939). The Service and the Tax Court are using "control" in a special sense not used elsewhere, so far as we can determine, in the law, including federal tax law. It is a sense which, as the amicus curiae briefs filed in support of UCC point out, threatens to unsettle the charitable sector by empowering the IRS to yank a charity's tax exemption simply because the Service thinks the charity's contract with its major fundraiser too one-sided in favor of the fundraiser, even though the charity has not been found to have violated any duty of faithful and careful management that the law of nonprofit corporations may have laid upon it. The resulting uncertainty about the charity's ability to retain its tax exemption — and receive tax-exempt donations — would be a particular deterrent to anyone contemplating a donation, loan, or other financial contribution to a new or small charity. That is the type most likely to be found by the IRS to have surrendered control over its destiny to a fundraiser or other supplier, because it is the type of charity that is most likely to have to pay a high price for fundraising services. It is hard enough for new, small, weak, or marginal charities to survive, because they are likely to have a high expense ratio, and many potential donors will be put off by that. The Tax Court's decision if sustained would make the survival of such charities even more dubious, by enveloping them in doubt about their tax exemption.

We were not reassured when the government's lawyer, in response to a question from the bench as to what standard he was advocating to guide decision in this area, said that it was the "facts and circumstances" of each case. That is no standard at all, and makes the tax status of charitable organizations and their donors a matter of the whim of the IRS.

There was no diversion of charitable revenues to an insider here, nothing that smacks of self-dealing, disloyalty, breach of fiduciary obligation or other misconduct of the type aimed at by a provision of law that forbids a charity to divert its earnings to members of the board or other insiders. What there may have been was imprudence on the part of UCC's board of directors in hiring W & H and negotiating the contract that it did. Maybe the only prudent course in the circumstances that confronted UCC in 1984 was to dissolve. Charitable organizations are plagued by incentive problems. Nobody owns the right to the profits and therefore no one has the spur to efficient performance that the lure of profits creates. Donors are like corporate shareholders in the sense of being the principal source of the charity's funds, but they do not have a profit incentive to monitor the care with which the charity's funds are used. Maybe the lack of a profit motive made UCC's board too lax. Maybe the board did not negotiate as favorable a contract with W & H as the board of a profitmaking firm would have done. And maybe tax law has a role to play in assuring the prudent management of charities. Remember the IRS's alternative basis for yanking UCC's exemption? It is that as a result of the contract's terms, UCC was not really operated exclusively for charitable purposes, but rather for the private benefit of W & H as well. Suppose that UCC was so irresponsibly managed that it paid W & H twice as much for fundraising services as W & H would have been happy to accept for those services, so that of UCC's $26 million in fundraising expense $13 million was the equivalent of a gift to the fundraiser. Then it could be argued that UCC was in fact being operated to a significant degree for the private benefit of W & H, though not because it was the latter's creature. That then would be a route for using tax law to deal with the problem of improvident or extravagant expenditures by a charitable organization that do not, however, inure to the benefit of insiders.

That in fact is the IRS's alternative ground for revoking the exemption, the one the Tax Court gave a bye to. It would have been better had the court resolved that ground as well as the inurement ground, so that the case could be definitively resolved in one appeal. But it did not, and so the case must be remanded to enable the court to consider it. We shall not prejudge the proceedings on remand. The usual "private benefit" case is one in which the charity has dual public and private goals, and that is not involved here. However, the board of a charity has a duty of care, just like the board of an ordinary business corporation, and a violation of that duty which involved the dissipation of the charity's assets might (we need not decide whether it would—we leave that issue to the Tax Court in the first instance) support a finding that the charity was conferring a private benefit, even if the contracting party did not control, or exercise undue influence over, the charity. This, for all we know, may be such a case.

Reversed and remanded.

Notes and Questions

1. *Private inurement versus private benefit.* The IRS primarily argued this case at the Tax Court level on the theory that the United Cancer Council was not operated exclusively for charitable purposes, but also for the benefit of its

fundraisers, who had come to have considerable influence over the organization because of its debts to the fundraisers. Perhaps unfortunately, the Tax Court endorsed the argument that private inurement strictures were violated, but did not reach the "private benefit" argument just described. The reversal by the Seventh Circuit of the private inurement argument also did not reach the "private benefit" argument. Does that possibility remain viable after Judge Posner's opinion?

2. *Fundraising to support fundraising.* Fundraising abuses are a major cause for concern in the charitable sector. As the *United Cancer Council* case demonstrates, devoting more than 90 percent of an organization's budget to the raising of funds is not per se grounds for disqualification. Should it be? A number of states have attempted to regulate the fundraising activities of charitable organizations, and at least some of those efforts have involved limitations on the percentage of funds raised that could be paid to professional fundraisers. However, the Supreme Court dealt a crippling blow to such efforts when it decided, in Riley v. National Federation of the Blind of North Carolina, Inc., 487 U.S. 781 (1988), that such restrictions violated the First Amendment rights of organizations within the scope of the restrictions.

c. Lobbying and Political Activities

Charitable organizations are permitted to engage in lobbying, so long as it does not constitute more than an insubstantial part of their activities. The bar on political activity on behalf of or in opposition to a candidate for office, in contrast, is absolute: any such activity is disqualifying. Both of these restrictions are expressed in the explicit language of §501(c)(3).

The Code offers no elaboration on what may constitute an insubstantial part of an organization's activities, and this has predictably led to a good deal of uncertainty, and some litigation. Partly in response to that situation, Congress added §501(h) to the Code in 1976, permitting organizations to elect a "safe harbor" approach to their lobbying activities. Under this election, an organization is permitted to spend from 5 to 20 percent of its total expenditures on lobbying, depending on the absolute size of those expenditures, up to a total limit of $1 million.[37] Although this provision was intended to lend certainty to this area, its doing so depends on an organization's willingness to make the §501(h) election. Unfortunately, to date, relatively few organizations have done so.

Some organizations have challenged the limitations on lobbying as an unconstitutional abridgement of their First Amendment rights to speak freely and to petition the government for redress of their grievances. The fact that veterans' organizations are exempted from the lobbying restrictions by the words of §501(c)(3) added, in the views of critics, an equal protection problem to the mix. One such challenge, Regan v. Taxation with Representation of Washington, 461 U.S. 540 (1983), reached the Supreme Court, which found no violation of either

---

37. The percentage of total expenditures that can be devoted to lobbying activities is limited by a sliding scale that descends as total expenditures increase. Thus, the smallest organizations can spend up to 20 percent of their total expenditures on lobbying, while larger organizations are allowed to spend more in absolute dollars, but less as a percentage of total expenditures.

First or Fifth Amendment rights. At least some members of the Court relied on the fact that charitable organizations could set up affiliated organizations under §501(c)(4), which does not limit lobbying expenditures, but which also does not allow donors to claim charitable deductions for their gifts. Until this case, there had been some uncertainty about whether charitable organizations could have such affiliates, but, with the apparent endorsement of the idea by the Supreme Court, some organizations that believe that lobbying for legal change is an important part of their exempt purpose have established such affiliates.

Does the *Taxation with Representation* case suggest an approach to regulation of fundraising that might survive First Amendment scrutiny under the *Riley* case noted above?

d. Public Policy Constraints

As explained in the cell on charitable contributions, the deduction of those contributions can be viewed in some ways as the equivalent of a governmental appropriation to the charitable organization receiving any particular contribution. For this reason (among others), Congress and the IRS want organizations operating in ways that violate public policy to be foreclosed from qualification for exempt status under §501(c)(3), even if their ends are otherwise within the range for which qualification for exemption would be available. The practice of racial discrimination is an example of a public policy violation that was intensely controversial during the 1960s and the following years. Congress itself proved unable to enact specific bars on racial discrimination, except for a tepid provision in §501(*i*) relating to social clubs. In the following case, however, a nearly unanimous Supreme Court was able to find such a bar in the history and overall structure of charitable organization regulation in this country.

BOB JONES UNIVERSITY v. UNITED STATES
461 U.S. 574 (1983)

CHIEF JUSTICE BURGER delivered the opinion of the Court.

We granted certiorari to decide whether petitioners, nonprofit private schools that prescribe and enforce racially discriminatory admissions standards on the basis of religious doctrine, qualify as tax-exempt organizations under §501(c)(3).

I

A

Until 1970, the Internal Revenue Service granted tax-exempt status to private schools, without regard to their racial admissions policies, under §501(c)(3) and granted charitable deductions for contributions to such schools under §170 of the Code.

On January 12, 1970, a three-judge District Court for the District of Columbia issued a preliminary injunction prohibiting the IRS from according tax-exempt status to private schools in Mississippi that discriminated as to admissions on the basis of race. Thereafter, in July 1970, the IRS concluded that it could "no longer legally justify allowing tax-exempt status to private schools which practice racial discrimination." IRS News Release (7/10/70). At the same time, the IRS announced that it could not "treat gifts to such schools as charitable deductions for income tax purposes." *Ibid.* By letter dated November 30, 1970, the IRS formally notified private schools, including those involved in this case, of this change in policy, "applicable to all private schools in the United States at all levels of education."

On June 30, 1971, the three-judge District Court issued its opinion on the merits of the Mississippi challenge. Green v. Connally, 330 F. Supp. 1150 (D.D.C.), *aff'd sub nom.* Coit v. Green, 404 U.S. 997 (1971). That court approved the IRS's amended construction of the Tax Code. The court also held that racially discriminatory private schools were not entitled to exemption under §501(c)(3) and that donors were not entitled to deductions for contributions to such schools under §170. The court permanently enjoined the Commissioner of Internal Revenue from approving tax-exempt status for any school in Mississippi that did not publicly maintain a policy of nondiscrimination.

The revised policy on discrimination was formalized in Revenue Ruling 71-447, 1971-2 Cum. Bull. 230: "Both the courts and the Internal Revenue Service have long recognized that the statutory requirement of being 'organized and operated exclusively for religious, charitable, . . . or educational purposes' was intended to express the basic common law concept [of 'charity']. . . . All charitable trusts, educational or otherwise, are subject to the requirement that the purpose of the trust may not be illegal or contrary to public policy." *Id.*, at 230.

Based on the "national policy to discourage racial discrimination in education," the IRS ruled that "a private school not having a racially nondiscriminatory policy as to students is not 'charitable' within the common law concepts reflected in sections 170 and 501(c)(3) of the Code." *Id.*, at 231.[38]

The application of the IRS construction of these provisions to petitioners, two private schools with racially discriminatory admissions policies, is now before us.

B

No. 81-3, *Bob Jones University v. United States*

Bob Jones University is a nonprofit corporation located in Greenville, South Carolina. Its purpose is "to conduct an institution of learning . . . , giving special emphasis to the Christian religion and the ethics revealed in the Holy Scriptures." Certificate of Incorporation, Bob Jones University, Inc., of Greenville, S.C. The corporation operates a school with an enrollment of approximately 5,000 students, from kindergarten through college and graduate school. Bob Jones University is not affiliated with any religious denomination, but is dedicated to the teaching and

---

38. Revenue Ruling 71-447, 1971-2 Cum. Bull. 230, defined "racially nondiscriminatory policy as to students" as meaning that:

[T]he school admits the students of any race to all the rights, privileges, programs, and activities generally accorded or made available to students at that school and that the school does not discriminate on the basis of race in administration of its educational policies, admissions policies, scholarship and loan programs, and athletic and other school-administered programs.

propagation of its fundamentalist Christian religious beliefs. It is both a religious and educational institution. Its teachers are required to be devout Christians, and all courses at the University are taught according to the Bible. Entering students are screened as to their religious beliefs, and their public and private conduct is strictly regulated by standards promulgated by University authorities.

The sponsors of the University genuinely believe that the Bible forbids interracial dating and marriage. To effectuate these views, Negroes were completely excluded until 1971. From 1971 to May 1975, the University accepted no applications from unmarried Negroes, but did accept applications from Negroes married within their race.

Following the decision of the United States Court of Appeals for the Fourth Circuit in McCrary v. Runyon, 515 F.2d 1082 (CA4 1975), aff'd 427 U.S. 160 (1976), prohibiting racial exclusion from private schools, the University revised its policy. Since May 29, 1975, the University has permitted unmarried Negroes to enroll; but a disciplinary rule prohibits interracial dating and marriage. That rule reads:

> *There is to be no interracial dating*
> 1. Students who are partners in an interracial marriage will be expelled.
> 2. Students who are members of or affiliated with any group or organization which holds as one of its goals or advocates interracial marriage will be expelled.
> 3. Students who date outside their own race will be expelled.
> 4. Students who espouse, promote, or encourage others to violate the University's dating rules and regulations will be expelled.

The University continues to deny admission to applicants engaged in an interracial marriage or known to advocate interracial marriage or dating.

Until 1970, the IRS extended tax-exempt status to Bob Jones University under §501(c)(3). By the letter of November 30, 1970, that followed the injunction issued in *Green v. Kennedy, supra,* the IRS formally notified the University of the change in IRS policy, and announced its intention to challenge the tax-exempt status of private schools practicing racial discrimination in their admissions policies.

After failing to obtain an assurance of tax exemption through administrative means, the University instituted an action in 1971 seeking to enjoin the IRS from revoking the school's tax-exempt status. . . . [That suit was found to be procedurally defective under the Anti-Injunction Act provisions of the Code, in §7421(a). Much later, on January 19, 1976, the IRS officially revoked the university's tax-exempt status. The university then filed an employment tax return with respect to a single employee, together with payment of $21 of tax. This was done to establish the jurisdictional basis for a suit to refund that nominal tax payment.]

The United States District Court for the District of South Carolina held that revocation of the University's tax-exempt status exceeded the delegated powers of the IRS, was improper under the IRS rulings and procedures, and violated the University's rights under the Religion Clauses of the First Amendment. The court accordingly ordered the IRS to pay the University the $21.00 refund it claimed and rejected the IRS counterclaim.

The Court of Appeals for the Fourth Circuit, in a divided opinion, reversed. Citing *Green v. Connally, supra,* with approval, the Court of Appeals concluded that §501(c)(3) must be read against the background of charitable trust law. To be eligible for an exemption under that section, an institution must be "charitable in the common law sense, and therefore must not be contrary to public policy. In the court's view, Bob Jones University did not meet this requirement, since its "racial policies violated the clearly defined public policy, rooted in our Constitution, condemning racial discrimination and, more specifically, the government policy against subsidizing racial discrimination in education, public or private." The court held that the IRS acted within its statutory authority in revoking the University's tax-exempt status. Finally, the Court of Appeals rejected petitioner's arguments that the revocation of the tax exemption violated the Free Exercise and Establishment Clauses of the First Amendment. The case was remanded to the District Court with instructions to dismiss the University's claim for a refund and to reinstate the Government's counterclaim.

[The facts of a companion case involving Goldsboro Christian Schools, a K-12 school in North Carolina that explicitly refused to admit African-American, Asian, and Jewish students, are omitted. The Fourth Circuit sustained the IRS's denial of tax-exempt status to the school.]

We granted certiorari in both cases, 454 U.S. 892,[39] and we affirm in each.

II

A

In Revenue Ruling 71-447, the IRS formalized the policy first announced in 1970, that §170 and §501(c)(3) embrace the common law "charity" concept. Under that view, to qualify for a tax exemption pursuant to §501(c)(3), an institution must show, first, that it falls within one of the eight categories expressly set forth in that section, and second, that its activity is not contrary to settled public policy.

Section 501(c)(3) provides that "[c]orporations . . . organized and operated exclusively for religious, charitable . . . or educational purposes" are entitled to tax exemption. Petitioners argue that the plain language of the statute guarantees them tax-exempt status. They emphasize the absence of any language in the statute expressly requiring all exempt organizations to be "charitable" in the common law sense, and they contend that the disjunctive "or" separating the categories in §501(c)(3) precludes such a reading. Instead, they argue that if an institution falls within one or more of the specified categories it is automatically entitled to exemption, without regard to whether it also qualifies as "charitable." The Court

---

39. After the Court granted certiorari, the Government filed a motion to dismiss, informing the Court that the Department of Treasury intended to revoke Revenue Ruling 71-447 and other pertinent rulings and to recognize §501(c)(3) exemptions for petitioners. The Government suggested that these actions were therefore moot. Before this Court ruled on that motion, however, the United States Court of Appeals for the District of Columbia Circuit enjoined the Government from granting §501(c)(3) tax-exempt status to any school that discriminates on the basis or race. Wright v. Regan, No. 80-1124 (CADC Feb. 18, 1982) (*per curiam* order). Thereafter, the Government informed the Court that it would not revoke the revenue rulings and withdrew its request that the actions be dismissed as moot. The Government continues to assert that the IRS lacked authority to promulgate Revenue Ruling 71-447, and does not defend that aspect of the rulings below.

of Appeals rejected that contention and concluded that petitioners' interpretation of the statute "tears section 501(c)(3) from its roots."

It is a well-established canon of statutory construction that a court should go beyond the literal language of a statute if reliance on that language would defeat the plain purpose of the statute: "The general words used in the clause . . . , taken by themselves, and literally construed, without regard to the object in view, would seem to sanction the claim of the plaintiff. But this mode of expounding a statute has never been adopted by any enlightened tribunal — because it is evident that in many cases it would defeat the object which the Legislature intended to accomplish. And it is well settled that, in interpreting a statute, the court will not look merely to a particular clause in which general words may be used, *but will take in connection with it the whole statute . . . and the objects and policy of the law. . . .*" Brown v. Duchesne, 19 How. 183, 194, 15 L. Ed. 595 (1857) (emphasis added).

Section 501(c)(3) therefore must be analyzed and construed within the framework of the Internal Revenue Code and against the background of the Congressional purposes. Such an examination reveals unmistakable evidence that, underlying all relevant parts of the Code, is the intent that entitlement to tax exemption depends on meeting certain common law standards of charity — namely, that an institution seeking tax-exempt status must serve a public purpose and not be contrary to established public policy.

This "charitable" concept appears explicitly in §170 of the Code. That section contains a list of organizations virtually identical to that contained in §501(c)(3). It is apparent that Congress intended that list to have the same meaning in both sections. In §170, Congress used the list of organizations in defining the term "charitable contributions." On its face, therefore, §170 reveals that Congress' intention was to provide tax benefits to organizations serving charitable purposes. The form of §170 simply makes plain what common sense and history tell us: in enacting both §170 and §501(c)(3), Congress sought to provide tax benefits to charitable organizations, to encourage the development of private institutions that serve a useful public purpose or supplement or take the place of public institutions of the same kind.

Tax exemptions for certain institutions thought beneficial to the social order of the country as a whole, or to a particular community, are deeply rooted in our history, as in that of England. The origins of such exemptions lie in the special privileges that have long been extended to charitable trusts.[40]

More than a century ago, this Court announced the caveat that is critical in this case: "[I]t has now become an established principle of American law, that courts of chancery will sustain and protect . . . a gift . . . to public charitable uses, *provided the same is consistent with local laws and public policy. . . .*" Perin v. Carey, 24 How. 465, 501, 16 L. Ed. 701 (1861) (emphasis added). [The Court continued with citations

---

40. The form and history of the charitable exemption and deduction sections of the various income tax acts reveal that Congress was guided by the common law of charitable trusts. *See* Simon, *The Tax-Exempt Status of Racially Discriminatory Religious Schools,* 36 Tax L. Rev. 477, 485-489 (1981) (hereinafter Simon). Congress acknowledged as much in 1969. The House Report on the Tax Reform Act of 1969, Pub. L. 91-172, 83 Stat. 487, stated that the §501(c)(3) exemption was available only to institutions that served "the specified charitable purposes," H.R. Rep. No. 413 (Part 1), 91st Cong., 1st Sess. 35 (1969), U.S. Code Cong. & Admin. News 1969, p. 1645, and described "charitable" as "a term that has been used in the law of trusts for hundreds of years." *Id.,* at 43, U.S. Code Cong. & Admin. News 1969, p. 1688. We need not consider whether Congress intended to incorporate into the Internal Revenue Code any aspects of charitable trust law other than the requirements of public benefit and a valid public purpose.

from a number of late-nineteenth century cases and treatises to the same general effect, concluding:]

These statements clearly reveal the legal background against which Congress enacted the first charitable exemption statute in 1894: charities were to be given preferential treatment because they provide a benefit to society.

. . . In enacting the Revenue Act of 1938, ch. 289, 52 Stat. 447 (1938), Congress expressly reconfirmed this view with respect to the charitable deduction provision:

> The exemption from taxation of money and property devoted to charitable and other purposes is based on the theory that the Government is compensated for the loss of revenue by its relief from financial burdens which would otherwise have to be met by appropriations from other public funds, and by the benefits resulting from the promotion of the general welfare.

H.R. Rep. No. 1860, 75th Cong., 3d Sess. 19 (1938).

A corollary to the public benefit principle is the requirement, long recognized in the law of trusts, that the purpose of a charitable trust may not be illegal or violate established public policy. In 1861, this Court stated that a public charitable use must be "consistent with local laws and public policy," *Perin v. Carey, supra,* 24 How., at 501. Modern commentators and courts have echoed that view.

When the Government grants exemptions or allows deductions all taxpayers are affected; the very fact of the exemption or deduction for the donor means that other taxpayers can be said to be indirect and vicarious "donors." Charitable exemptions are justified on the basis that the exempt entity confers a public benefit—a benefit which the society or the community may not itself choose or be able to provide, or which supplements and advances the work of public institutions already supported by tax revenues. History buttresses logic to make clear that, to warrant exemption under §501(c)(3), an institution must fall within a category specified in that section and must demonstrably serve and be in harmony with the public interest.[41] The institution's purpose must not be so at odds with the common community conscience as to undermine any public benefit that might otherwise be conferred.

B

We are bound to approach these questions with full awareness that determinations of public benefit and public policy are sensitive matters with serious implications for the institutions affected; a declaration that a given institution is not "charitable" should be made only where there can be no doubt that the activity involved is contrary to a fundamental public policy. But there can no longer be any doubt that racial discrimination in education violates deeply and widely accepted views of elementary justice. Prior to 1954, public education in many places still was conducted under the pall of Plessy v. Ferguson, 163 U.S. 537 (1896); racial segregation in primary and secondary education prevailed in many parts of the

---

41. The Court's reading of §501(c)(3) does not render meaningless Congress' action in specifying the eight categories of presumptively exempt organizations, as petitioners suggest. *See* Brief of Petitioner Goldsboro Christian Schools 18-24. To be entitled to tax-exempt status under §501(c)(3), an organization must first fall within one of the categories specified by Congress, and in addition must serve a valid charitable purpose.

country.[42] This Court's decision in Brown v. Board of Education, 347 U.S. 483, (1954), signalled an end to that era. Over the past quarter of a century, every pronouncement of this Court and myriad Acts of Congress and Executive Orders attest a firm national policy to prohibit racial segregation and discrimination in public education.

An unbroken line of cases following *Brown v. Board of Education* establishes beyond doubt this Court's view that racial discrimination in education violates a most fundamental national public policy, as well as rights of individuals.

. . . Few social or political issues in our history have been more vigorously debated and more extensively ventilated than the issue of racial discrimination, particularly in education. Given the stress and anguish of the history of efforts to escape from the shackles of the "separate but equal" doctrine of *Plessy v. Ferguson, supra,* it cannot be said that educational institutions that, for whatever reasons, practice racial discrimination, are institutions exercising "beneficial and stabilizing influences in community life," *Walz v. Tax Comm'n,* 397 U.S. 664, 673 (1970), or should be encouraged by having all taxpayers share in their support by way of special tax status.

There can thus be no question that the interpretation of §170 and §501(c)(3) announced by the IRS in 1970 was correct. That it may be seen as belated does not undermine its soundness. It would be wholly incompatible with the concepts underlying tax exemption to grant the benefit of tax-exempt status to racially discriminatory educational entities, which "exer[t] a pervasive influence on the entire educational process." *Norwood v. Harrison, supra,* 413 U.S., at 469. Whatever may be the rationale for such private schools' policies, and however sincere the rationale may be, racial discrimination in education is contrary to public policy. Racially discriminatory educational institutions cannot be viewed as conferring a public benefit within the "charitable" concept discussed earlier, or within the Congressional intent underlying §170 and §501(c)(3).

C

Petitioners contend that, regardless of whether the IRS properly concluded that racially discriminatory private schools violate public policy, only Congress can alter the scope of §170 and §501(c)(3). Petitioners accordingly argue that the IRS overstepped its lawful bounds in issuing its 1970 and 1971 rulings.

Yet ever since the inception of the tax code, Congress has seen fit to vest in those administering the tax laws very broad authority to interpret those laws. In an area as complex as the tax system, the agency Congress vests with administrative responsibility must be able to exercise its authority to meet changing conditions and new problems. Indeed as early as 1918, Congress expressly authorized the Commissioner "to make all needful rules and regulations for the enforcement" of the tax laws. Revenue Act of 1918, ch. 18, §1309, 40 Stat. 1057, 1143 (1919). The same provision, so essential to efficient and fair administration of the tax laws, has appeared in tax codes ever since; and this Court has long recognized the primary authority of the IRS and its predecessors in construing the Internal Revenue Code.

---

42. In 1894, when the first charitable exemption provision was enacted, racially segregated educational institutions would not have been regarded as against public policy. Yet contemporary standards must be considered in determining whether given activities provide a public benefit and are entitled to the charitable tax exemption. . . .

Congress, the source of IRS authority, can modify IRS rulings it considers improper; and courts exercise review over IRS actions. In the first instance, however, the responsibility for construing the Code falls to the IRS. Since Congress cannot be expected to anticipate every conceivable problem that can arise or to carry out day-to-day oversight, it relies on the administrators and on the courts to implement the legislative will. Administrators, like judges, are under oath to do so.

In §170 and §501(c)(3), Congress has identified categories of traditionally exempt institutions and has specified certain additional requirements for tax exemption. Yet the need for continuing interpretation of those statutes is unavoidable. For more than 60 years, the IRS and its predecessors have constantly been called upon to interpret these and comparable provisions, and in doing so have referred consistently to principles of charitable trust law. In Treas. Reg. 45, art. 517(1) (1921), for example, the IRS denied charitable exemptions on the basis of proscribed political activity before the Congress itself added such conduct as a disqualifying element. In other instances, the IRS has denied charitable exemptions to otherwise qualified entities because they served too limited a class of people and thus did not provide a truly "public" benefit under the common law test. Some years before the issuance of the rulings challenged in these cases, the IRS also ruled that contributions to community recreational facilities would not be deductible and that the facilities themselves would not be entitled to tax-exempt status, unless those facilities were open to all on a racially nondiscriminatory basis. . . .

Guided, of course, by the Code, the IRS has the responsibility, in the first instance, to determine whether a particular entity is "charitable" for purposes of §170 and §501(c)(3). This in turn may necessitate later determinations of whether given activities so violate public policy that the entities involved cannot be deemed to provide a public benefit worthy of "charitable" status. We emphasize, however, that these sensitive determinations should be made only where there is no doubt that the organization's activities violate fundamental public policy.

On the record before us, there can be no doubt as to the national policy. In 1970, when the IRS first issued the ruling challenged here, the position of all three branches of the Federal Government was unmistakably clear. The correctness of the Commissioner's conclusion that a racially discriminatory private school "is not 'charitable' within the common law concepts reflected in . . . the Code," Rev. Rul. 71-447, 1972-2 Cum. Bull., at 231, is wholly consistent with what Congress, the Executive and the courts had repeatedly declared before 1970. Indeed, it would be anomalous for the Executive, Legislative and Judicial Branches to reach conclusions that add up to a firm public policy on racial discrimination, and at the same time have the IRS blissfully ignore what all three branches of the Federal Government had declared. Clearly an educational institution engaging in practices affirmatively at odds with this declared position of the whole government cannot be seen as exercising a "beneficial and stabilizing influenc[e] in community life," *Walz v. Tax Comm'n, supra,* 397 U.S., at 673, and is not "charitable," within the meaning of §170 and §501(c)(3). We therefore hold that the IRS did not exceed its authority when it announced its interpretation of §170 and §501(c)(3) in 1970 and 1971.

D

The actions of Congress since 1970 leave no doubt that the IRS reached the correct conclusion in exercising its authority. It is, of course, not unknown for independent agencies or the Executive Branch to misconstrue the intent of a statute; Congress can and often does correct such misconceptions, if the courts have not done so. Yet for a dozen years Congress has been made aware — acutely aware — of the IRS rulings of 1970 and 1971. As we noted earlier, few issues have been the subject of more vigorous and widespread debate and discussion in and out of Congress than those related to racial segregation in education. Sincere adherents advocating contrary views have ventilated the subject for well over three decades. Failure of Congress to modify the IRS rulings of 1970 and 1971, of which Congress was, by its own studies and by public discourse, constantly reminded; and Congress' awareness of the denial of tax-exempt status for racially discriminatory schools when enacting other and related legislation make out an unusually strong case of legislative acquiescence in and ratification by implication of the 1970 and 1971 rulings.

Ordinarily, and quite appropriately, courts are slow to attribute significance to the failure of Congress to act on particular legislation. We have observed that "unsuccessful attempts at legislation are not the best of guides to legislative intent," Red Lion Broadcasting Co. v. FCC, 395 U.S. 367, 381-382 n.11 (1969). Here, however, we do not have an ordinary claim of legislative acquiescence. Only one month after the IRS announced its position in 1970, Congress held its first hearings on this precise issue. *Equal Educational Opportunity: Hearings Before the Senate Select Comm. on Equal Educational Opportunity,* 91st Cong., 2d Sess. 1991 (1970). Exhaustive hearings have been held on the issue at various times since then. . . .

Non-action by Congress is not often a useful guide, but the non-action here is significant. During the past 12 years there have been no fewer than 13 bills introduced to overturn the IRS interpretation of §501(c)(3). Not one of these bills has emerged from any committee, although Congress has enacted numerous other amendments to §501 during this same period, including an amendment to §501(c)(3) itself. It is hardly conceivable that Congress — and in this setting, any Member of Congress — was not abundantly aware of what was going on. In view of its prolonged and acute awareness of so important an issue, Congress' failure to act on the bills proposed on this subject provides added support for concluding that Congress acquiesced in the IRS rulings of 1970 and 1971.

The evidence of Congressional approval of the policy embodied in Revenue Ruling 71-447 goes well beyond the failure of Congress to act on legislative proposals. Congress affirmatively manifested its acquiescence in the IRS policy when it enacted the present §501(*i*) of the Code. That provision denies tax-exempt status to social clubs whose charters or policy statements provide for "discrimination against any person on the basis of race, color, or religion."[43] Both the House and Senate committee reports on that bill articulated the national policy against granting tax exemptions to racially discriminatory private clubs.

Even more significant is the fact that both reports focus on this Court's affirmance of *Green v. Connally, supra,* as having established that "discrimination on account of race is inconsistent with an *educational institution's* tax exempt status." S. Rep. No. 1318, at 7-8 (emphasis added). These references in Congressional committee reports on an enactment denying tax exemptions to racially discriminatory private social clubs cannot be read other than as indicating approval of the standards applied to racially discriminatory private schools by the IRS subsequent to 1970, and specifically of Revenue Ruling 71-447.

---

43. Prior to the introduction of this legislation, a three-judge district court had held that segregated social clubs were entitled to tax exemptions. McGlotten v. Connally, 338 F. Supp. 448 (D.D.C. 1972). Section 501(*i*) was enacted primarily in response to that decision.

III

Petitioners contend that, even if the Commissioner's policy is valid as to non-religious private schools, that policy cannot constitutionally be applied to schools that engage in racial discrimination on the basis of sincerely held religious beliefs. As to such schools, it is argued that the IRS construction of §170 and §501(c)(3) violates their free exercise rights under the Religion Clauses of the First Amendment. This contention presents claims not heretofore considered by this Court in precisely this context.

This Court has long held the Free Exercise Clause of the First Amendment an absolute prohibition against governmental regulation of religious beliefs, Wisconsin v. Yoder, 406 U.S. 205, 219 (1972); [and other cases.] As interpreted by this Court, moreover, the Free Exercise Clause provides substantial protection for lawful conduct grounded in religious belief. However, "[n]ot all burdens on religion are unconstitutional. . . . The state may justify a limitation on religious liberty by showing that it is essential to accomplish an overriding governmental interest." United States v. Lee, 455 U.S. 252, 257-258 (1982).

On occasion this Court has found certain governmental interests so compelling as to allow even regulations prohibiting religiously based conduct. In Prince v. Massachusetts, 321 U.S. 158 (1944), for example, the Court held that neutrally-cast child labor laws prohibiting sale of printed materials on public streets could be applied to prohibit children from dispensing religious literature. The Court found no constitutional infirmity in "excluding [Jehovah's Witness children] from doing there what no other children may do." Id., at 170. Denial of tax benefits will inevitably have a substantial impact on the operation of private religious schools, but will not prevent those schools from observing their religious tenets.

The governmental interest at stake here is compelling. As discussed in Part II(B), *supra,* the Government has a fundamental, overriding interest in eradicating racial discrimination in education[44] — discrimination that prevailed, with official approval, for the first 165 years of this Nation's history. That governmental interest substantially outweighs whatever burden denial of tax benefits places on petitioners' exercise of their religious beliefs. The interests asserted by petitioners cannot be accommodated with that compelling governmental interest, and no "less restrictive means" are available to achieve the governmental interest.

The remaining issue is whether the IRS properly applied its policy to these petitioners. Petitioner Goldsboro Christian Schools admits that it "maintain[s] racially discriminatory policies," but seeks to justify those policies on grounds we have fully discussed. The IRS properly denied tax-exempt status to Goldsboro Christian Schools.

Petitioner Bob Jones University, however, contends that it is not racially discriminatory. It emphasizes that it now allows all races to enroll, subject only to its restrictions on the conduct of all students, including its prohibitions of association between men and women of different races, and of interracial marriage. Although a ban on intermarriage or interracial dating applies to all races, decisions of this Court firmly establish that discrimination on the basis of racial affiliation and

---

44. We deal here only with religious *schools* — not with churches or other purely religious institutions; here, the governmental interest is in denying public support to racial discrimination in education. As noted earlier, racially discriminatory schools "exer[t] a pervasive influence on the entire educational process," outweighing any public benefit that they might otherwise provide, Norwood v. Harrison, 413 U.S. 455, 469 (1973)."

association is a form of racial discrimination, *see, e.g., Loving v. Virginia,* 388 U.S. 1 (1967). We therefore find that the IRS properly applied Revenue Ruling 71-447 to Bob Jones University.[45]

The judgments of the Court of Appeals are, accordingly, *affirmed.*

[Justice Powell joined in the judgment of the Court, and in part III of Chief Justice Burger's opinion (relating to the free exercise issue), but wrote a separate opinion expressing his concerns about the "broader implications of the Court's opinion with respect to the authority of the Internal Revenue Service. . . ." In particular, Justice Powell was concerned about granting the IRS broad discretion to determine the contours of public policy and their implications for interpretation of the tax laws.

Justice Rehnquist dissented, noting that although there is indeed a strong national policy against racial discrimination, it remains for Congress to determine when and how that policy is to be reflected in the tax laws. He wrote:

> With undeniable clarity, Congress has explicitly defined the requirements for section 501(c)(3) status. An entity must be (1) a corporation, or community chest, fund, or foundation, (2) organized for one of the eight enumerated purposes, (3) operated on a nonprofit basis, and (4) free from involvement in lobbying activities and political campaigns. Nowhere is there to be found some additional, undefined public policy requirement.

Justice Rehnquist's analysis emphasized that the clear language of §501(c)(3) puts "charitable" and "educational" in a disjunctive sequence, suggesting that being either kind of organization is sufficient, if the other conditions are satisfied, for exempt status. He concluded:

> Petitioners are each organized for the "instruction or training of the individual for the purpose of improving or developing his capabilities," 26 CFR §1.501(c)(3)-1(d)(3), and thus are organized for "educational purposes" within the meaning of §501(c)(3). Petitioners' nonprofit status is uncontested. There is no indication that either petitioner has been involved in lobbying activities or political campaigns. Therefore, it is my view that unless and until Congress affirmatively amends §501(c)(3) to require more, the IRS is without authority to deny petitioners §501(c)(3) status. For this reason, I would reverse the Court of Appeals.]

Notes and Questions

1. *Should it be enough to be "educational"?* Are you satisfied with the majority response to the points Justice Rehnquist makes in his dissent? That is, since "educational" and "charitable" are disjunctively listed in §501(c)(3), why wasn't it sufficient that Bob Jones University was merely educational?

2. *The limits of IRS expertise.* Is determining whether the practices of a charitable organization violate public policy a task that is reasonably within the competence of the Internal Revenue Service?

45. Bob Jones University also argues that the IRS policy should not apply to it because it is entitled to exemption under §501(c)(3) as a "religious" organization, rather than as an "educational" institution. The record in this case leaves no doubt, however, that Bob Jones University is both an educational institution and a religious institution. As discussed previously, the IRS policy properly extends to all private schools, including religious schools. *See* n.29 [here, n.44], *supra.* The IRS policy thus was properly applied to Bob Jones University.

3. *Third-party standing.* If an individual believes that a charitable organization has practiced racial discrimination, may the individual challenge a previous IRS determination that the organization qualified for exempt status? Should an individual have such an opportunity?

4. *Exempt status and the charitable contributions deduction.* Note that the language of §170(c)(2)(B) essentially tracks the language of §501(c)(3), so that a determination that an organization is not qualified for exemption under the latter section ordinarily operates to preclude deductibility of contributions made by donors to the organization in question.

5. *Single-sex educational institutions and public policy.* In United States v. Virginia, 518 U.S. 515 (1996), the Supreme Court held that Virginia's maintenance of an all-male military academy (Virginia Military Institute) violated the Equal Protection Clause. Does this opinion establish a public policy against sex discrimination in education, so that single-sex private schools and colleges are ineligible for exempt status under the *Bob Jones* rationale? Justice Scalia, dissenting in *United States v. Virginia,* feared that it might: "[I]t is certainly not beyond the Court that rendered today's opinion to hold that a donation to a single-sex college should be deemed contrary to public policy and therefore not deductible if the college discriminates on the basis of sex." 518 U.S. at 598. The question has not been litigated, because the IRS has shown no interest in denying exempt status to single-sex schools.

2. *Exemption Application and Reporting*

Charitable organizations must apply for recognition of their exempt status, unless they are churches or have very limited operations (with annual revenues of less than $25,000). The application, on IRS Form 1023, requires extensive information about the organization's organizing documents, fundraising, compensation of officers, exempt purposes, and plans for accomplishing them, among many other things. If the IRS denies the request for recognition of the organization's exemption, the organization may seek review of that determination by petitioning the Tax Court to undertake such a review.

Once recognized, a charitable organization must file an annual information return on IRS Form 990. This return essentially updates the application for recognition of exemption, reporting on the revenues of the organization, its expenditures in pursuit of its exempt purposes, the presence of any unrelated business income, fundraising activities and results, and the like. Both Form 1023 and Form 990 are, by law, to be maintained and available for public inspection upon request.

B. NONCHARITABLE EXEMPT ORGANIZATIONS

Many noncharitable, nonprofit organizations are also eligible for exemption from the corporate income tax. The major distinction from charitable nonprofits is that donors to noncharitable nonprofit organizations typically cannot deduct any contributions to such organizations; but in many other respects, the terms of §501 apply with equal force to these noncharitable organizations. The categories of such organizations are described in the several numbered paragraphs of §501(c) (other than (c)(3)). A quick review of those paragraphs reveals that labor unions, civic leagues, recreational clubs, fraternal organizations, and many others are eligible for exempt status.

This may seem inappropriate at first glance, since the argument that such organizations provide general public benefits would be controversial at best, and in many cases — such as exemption of social clubs — could hardly be taken seriously at all. An alternate theory, explained at the beginning of this cell, offers a better rationale, based on the notion that such organizations really don't enjoy income in the usual sense of that word. Consider, for example, the situation of a single individual who decides to build a swimming pool in his backyard. No deductions would be available for either the capital investment in the pool or payment of the annual expenses associated with the maintenance and operation of the pool; but neither would there be any imputation of income resulting from the return on those investments in the form of the pleasure of using the pool.

Similarly, if two neighbors decided to build and operate such a pool jointly, they might create an account, to which each would contribute, to cover the investment in the pool and the maintenance and operating costs. Each neighbor might pay an "initiation fee" to this account, and might annually pay "dues" to this account to cover current expenses. Again, the payments wouldn't be deductible, but neither would the individual members of this tiny consortium have any income imputed with respect to the benefit of using the pool. A swim and tennis club with 2,000 members is not fundamentally different from this two-person example. All that the club involves is a decision to act collectively to create, maintain, and operate facilities that the individual members could have provided for themselves (presumably at a lesser level) without adverse tax implications. Should the tax system then say that the collective action renders the activity taxable?

The tax system might in fact say so. After all, when a dentist performs dental services for his family members without charge, there is normally no income tax consequence. However, if a dentist performs dental services for the family members of a lawyer, in exchange for the lawyer's services in drafting the dentist's will, the (entirely reasonable) view of the IRS is that both parties have income in the amount of the fair market value of the services each has received. Arguably, a large social club could be viewed as a barter club for recreational services.

Congress has not taken that view with respect to the basic operations of social clubs and other noncharitable exempt organizations. Congress has, however, decided that investment income of such organizations should generally be taxable. This rule, and its rationale, are explained in the next section.

C. BUSINESS ACTIVITIES OF EXEMPT ORGANIZATIONS

Tax-exempt organizations — charitable or not — routinely engage in business activities in discharge of their exempt purposes: hospitals treat patients, universities offer academic programs to students, athletic clubs operate athletic programs, and so on. Some exempt organizations also operate businesses whose activities are unrelated to the exempt purposes of the organization. For example, a university might rent its football stadium to a professional sports franchise or a promoter of rock concerts. Because Congress has been concerned about the possibility that nonprofit organizations might compete with profit-seeking businesses on an unfair footing (because of their tax exemption), it decided in 1950 to impose a tax, at regular corporate rates, on the profits earned by charitable organizations from operations of unrelated businesses.[46]

This unrelated business income tax (often called by its acronym, UBIT) generally requires the organization to pay the UBIT on all income from unrelated businesses that are regularly carried on, using the usual rules of accounting for business income, with deductions available for business expenses, depreciation of physical equipment and real estate used in the unrelated business, and so on. The UBIT does not actually generate much revenue, but presumably does discourage some organizations from engaging in business practices that are unrelated to the organization's exempt function.

The UBIT does generate controversy, however, in large part because there is considerable room for argument about whether particular business activities are related to an organization's exempt purpose. *See, e.g.,* Rev. Rul. 73-105, 1973-1 C.B. 264, holding that an art museum's sale of art reproductions was not subject to the UBIT, but that sales of scientific books and city souvenirs were subject to the tax.

The 800-pound gorilla in this area is big-time college athletics. Is sponsoring football and basketball teams of near-professional quality related to a university's exempt educational purposes? Yes, according to the IRS: "The Service has traditionally taken the position that income from paid admissions to college and university athletic events, regardless of the number of persons in attendance or the amount of paid admissions, is not taxable as income from [an] unrelated trade or business because the events themselves are related to the educational purposes of the colleges and universities." Rev. Rul. 80-296, 1980-2 C.B. 195 (applying the same analysis to revenue from the sale of radio and television broadcast rights to college football and basketball games).

Exempt organizations also frequently invest funds that are beyond the current needs of the organization. Indeed, universities in particular undertake considerable efforts to create and preserve endowment accounts that are invested to generate returns that can be used as a source of general or special revenues for the institution. Subject to some important limitations relating mostly to the use of investment income generated by borrowed funds, charitable organizations are permitted to maintain endowment accounts, and to use the income from those accounts in their ordinary operations each year without adverse tax consequences. In contrast, noncharitable organizations are usually taxed on their investment income. This pattern is consistent with other rules distinguishing the two types of organization. For example, if an individual were to hold title to an income-

---

46. Whether such competition would actually be unfair is a matter of some debate, since the advantages of tax exemption may be offset by a number of factors running in the opposite direction. Indeed, one prominent justification for the existence of the tax exemption is to allow for the greater difficulty that charitable organizations have in raising capital, due to the ban on distribution of profits. *See* Henry Hansmann, *The Rationale for Exempting Nonprofit Organizations from Corporate Income Taxation,* 91 Yale L.J. 54 (1981).

generating fund, she could pay the income from that fund to a charitable organization each year, and, subject to some limitations, take deductions for those contributions that would offset the income reported from the fund. In contrast, if the income from such a fund were to be paid to a noncharitable exempt organization, no deduction would be permitted for the contribution, and investment income would remain taxable. Requiring noncharitable exempt organizations to report and pay tax on their investment income approximates the result that would have obtained had the investment funds been held by the individual members.

Cell

▬▬▬▬▬ CASUALTY
▬▬▬▬▬   LOSSES — MATERIALS
             AND PROBLEMS

A. What Constitutes a Casualty?

Chamales v. Commissioner

Rev. Rul. 63-232

B. Casualty Loss Problem Set

Problems 1-5

A. WHAT CONSTITUTES A CASUALTY?

CHAMALES v. COMMISSIONER

T.C. Memo 2000-33 (2000)

NIMS, Judge: Respondent determined a Federal income tax deficiency for petitioners' 1994 taxable year in the amount of $291,931. . . .

Gerald and Kathleen Chamales (petitioners) are married and resided in Los Angeles, California, at the time of filing their petition in this case. In the spring of 1994, petitioners became interested in purchasing a residence in Brentwood Park, an exclusive Los Angeles neighborhood. They were attracted to the beautiful, parklike setting and the quiet peacefulness of the area. Subsequently, on June 2, 1994, petitioners opened escrow on property located in Brentwood Park, at 359 North Bristol Avenue. . . .

At the time petitioners opened escrow, O.J. Simpson (Simpson) owned and resided at the property located directly west of and adjacent to that being purchased by petitioners. . . . During the escrow period, on June 12, 1994, Nicole Brown Simpson and Ronald Goldman were murdered at Ms. Brown Simpson's condominium in West Los Angeles. Simpson was arrested for these murders shortly thereafter. Following the homicides and arrest, the Brentwood Park neighborhood surrounding the Simpson property became inundated with media personnel and equipment and with individuals drawn by the area's connection to the horrific events. The media and looky-loos[47] blocked streets, trespassed on neighboring residential property, and flew overhead in helicopters in their attempts to get close to the Simpson home. Police were summoned to the area for purposes of

---

47. As explained by petitioners' counsel, "looky-loo" is a term developed in Hollywood to describe individuals who gather at places and events in hopes of glimpsing celebrities. The phrase is apparently used in California to denote those who frequent a location not because of its status as a conventional tourist sight but because of its association with a famous or notorious person. We adopt the terminology and spelling as used in petitioners' briefs and by the witnesses at trial.

controlling the crowds, and barricades were installed at various Brentwood Park intersections to restrict traffic. This police presence, however, had little practical effect. Significant media and public attention continued throughout 1994 and 1995. Although Simpson was acquitted on October 4, 1995, civil proceedings in 1996 reignited public interest.

Petitioners closed escrow on June 29, 1994, purchasing the residence on North Bristol Avenue for $2,849,000. Petitioners had considered canceling the escrow and had discussed this possibility with their attorney, but upon being advised that liability would result from a cancellation, they decided to go through with the transaction. Later that summer, as the crowds and disruption persisted, Gerald Chamales (petitioner) inquired of his broker Solton whether the value of his property had declined. Solton indicated that she estimated a decrease in value of 20 to 30 percent.

Petitioners' 1994 tax return was prepared by Ruben Kitay (Kitay), a certified public accountant. In the course of preparing this return, Kitay and petitioner discussed the possibility of claiming a deduction for casualty loss. After preliminary research in the regulations addressing casualty loss, Kitay spoke with two area real estate agents regarding the amount by which petitioners' property had decreased in value. The agents estimated the decline at 30 to 40 percent. Kitay and petitioner decided to use the more conservative 30 percent figure in calculating the deduction to be taken on petitioners' return. . . .

As of early 1999, the area surrounding the former Simpson home was no longer inundated with media personnel or equipment. The police barricades restricting traffic in the immediate vicinity of petitioners' property had been removed. Looky-loos, however, continued to frequent the neighborhood, often advised of the location of Simpson's former residence by its inclusion on "star maps" published for the Los Angeles area. Anniversaries of the murders were also typically accompanied by periods of increased media and public attention. . . .

Petitioners contend that the media and onlooker attention following the murders and focusing on Simpson's home has decreased the value of their adjacent property. They argue that because the homicides were a sudden, unexpected, and unusual event, and because aspects of the public interest precipitated thereby continued at least to the time of trial in this case, they have suffered a permanent casualty loss. Petitioners further allege that the proximity of their residence to that of Simpson has stigmatized their property and rendered it subject to permanent buyer resistance. . . .

Section 165 governs the tax treatment of losses and reads in relevant part as follows:

SEC. 165. LOSSES.
(a) General Rule. — There shall be allowed as a deduction any loss sustained during the taxable year and not compensated for by insurance or otherwise. . . .
(c) Limitation on Losses of Individuals. — In the case of an individual, the deduction under subsection (a) shall be limited to — . . .

> (3) except as provided in subsection (h), losses of property not connected with a trade or business or a transaction entered into for profit, if such losses arise from fire, storm, shipwreck, or other casualty, or from theft.

Subsection (h) of section 165 further limits the allowable deduction to the amount by which the casualty loss exceeds (1) $100 and (2) the sum of personal casualty gains plus 10 percent of the adjusted gross income of the individual.

Regulations promulgated under section 165 additionally provide that, to be allowable as a deduction, a loss must be both "evidenced by closed and completed transactions" and "fixed by identifiable events." Sec. 1.165-1(b), Income Tax Regs.

As interpreted by case law, a casualty loss within the meaning of section 165(c)(3) arises when two circumstances are present. First, the nature of the occurrence precipitating the damage to property must qualify as a casualty. . . . Second, the nature of the damage sustained must be such that it is deductible for purposes of section 165. . . . At issue here then are whether the events surrounding the alleged Simpson murders and affecting petitioners' property can properly be termed a casualty and whether the type of loss suffered by petitioners as a consequence of these events is recognized as deductible. We conclude that both inquiries must be answered in the negative.

A. Nature of Occurrence Constituting a Casualty

The word "casualty" as used in section 165(c)(3) has been defined, through application of the principle of *ejusdem generis,* by analyzing the shared characteristics of the specifically enumerated casualties of fire, storm, and shipwreck. . . . As explained by this Court:

> wherever unexpected, accidental force is exerted on property and the taxpayer is powerless to prevent application of the force because of the suddenness thereof or some disability, the resulting direct and proximate damage causes a loss which is like or similar to losses arising from the causes specifically enumerated in section 165(c)(3). . . . [White v. Commissioner, 48 T.C. 430, 435 (1967).]

. . . Here, we cannot conclude that the asserted devaluation of petitioners' property was the direct and proximate result of the type of casualty contemplated by section 165(c)(3). While the stabbing of Nicole Brown Simpson and Ronald Goldman was a sudden and unexpected exertion of force, this force was not exerted upon and did not damage petitioners' property. Similarly, the initial influx of onlookers, although perhaps sudden, was not a force exerted on petitioners' property and was not, in and of itself, the source of the asserted decrease in the home's market value. Rather, petitioners base their claim of loss on months, or even years, of ongoing public attention. If neither media personnel nor looky-loos had chosen to frequent the Brentwood Park area after the murders, or if the period of interest and visitation had been brief, petitioners would have lacked grounds for alleging a permanent and devaluing change in the character of their neighborhood. Hence, the source of their difficulties would appear to be more akin to a steadily operating cause than to a casualty. Press and media attention extending for months bears little similarity to a fire, storm, or shipwreck and is not properly classified therewith as an "other casualty."

B. Nature of Damage Recognized as Deductible

With respect to the requisite nature of the damage itself, this Court has traditionally held that only physical damage to or permanent abandonment of property will be recognized as deductible under section 165. . . . In contrast, the Court has refused to permit deductions based upon a temporary decline in market value. . . .

Moreover, the Court of Appeals for the Ninth Circuit, to which appeal in the present case would normally lie, has adopted this rule requiring physical damage. . . .

Given the above decisions, we conclude that petitioners here have failed to establish that their claimed casualty loss is of a type recognized as deductible for purposes of section 165(c)(3). They have not proven the extent to which their property suffered physical damage, and their attempt to base a deduction on market devaluation is contrary to existing law. . . .

As regards decrease in property value, petitioners' efforts to circumvent the established precedent repeatedly rejecting deductions premised on market fluctuation, through reliance on Finkbohner v. United States, 788 F.2d 723 (11th Cir. 1986), are misplaced. In Finkbohner v. United States, the Court of Appeals for the Eleventh Circuit permitted a deduction based on permanent buyer resistance in absence of physical damage. The Finkbohners lived on a cul-de-sac with 12 homes, and after flooding damaged several of the houses, municipal authorities ordered seven of the residences demolished and the lots maintained as permanent open space. Such irreversible changes in the character of the neighborhood were found to effect a permanent devaluation and to constitute a casualty within the meaning of section 165(c)(3).

However, as explicated above, this Court has long consistently held that an essential element of a deductible casualty loss is physical damage or, in some cases, physically necessitated abandonment. Furthermore, under the rule set forth in Golsen v. Commissioner, 54 T.C. 742, 756-757 (1970), aff'd, 445 F.2d 985 (10th Cir. 1971), we are in any event constrained to apply the law of the court in which an appeal would normally lie. Since the Court of Appeals for the Ninth Circuit has adopted and has not diverged from a requirement of physical damage for a section 165(c)(3) deduction, to hold otherwise would contravene Golsen.

Moreover, we further note that petitioners' circumstances do not reflect the type of permanent devaluation or buyer resistance which would be analogous to that held deductible in Finkbohner v. United States, supra. The evidence in the instant case reveals that media and onlooker attention has in fact lessened significantly over the years following the murders. Access to petitioners' property is no longer restricted by media equipment or police barricades. Residents of Brentwood Park have continued to invest substantial funds in remodeling and upgrading their homes. Hence, petitioners' difficulties are more akin to a temporary fluctuation in value, which no court has found to support a deduction under section 165(c)(3). We therefore hold that petitioners have failed to establish their entitlement to a casualty loss deduction. Respondent's determination of a deficiency is sustained. . . .

REV. RUL. 63-232

1963-2 C.B. 97

. . . The Internal Revenue Service has re-examined its position with regard to the deductibility of losses resulting from termite damage, as set forth in Revenue Ruling 59-277, C.B. 1959-2, 73.

Revenue Ruling 59-277 stated that the Service would follow the rule of George L. Buist et ux. v. United States, 164 Fed. Supp. 218 (1958); Martin A. Rosenberg v. Commissioner, 198 Fed. (2d) 46 (1952); and Joseph Shopmaker et al. v. United States, 119 Fed. Supp. 705 (1953), only in those cases where the facts were substantially the same. The courts in these cases held that damage caused by termites over periods up to 15 months after infestation constituted a deductible casualty loss under section 165 of the Internal Revenue Code of 1954.

Revenue Ruling 59-277 further stated that in other cases, the Service would follow the rule announced in Charles J. Fay et al. v. Helvering, 120 Fed. (2d) 253 (1941); United States v. Betty Rogers et al., 120 Fed. (2d) 244 (1941); and Leslie C. Dodge et ux. v. Commissioner 25 T.C. 1022 (1956). In the latter cases the termite infestation and subsequent damage occurred over periods of several years.

An extensive examination of scientific data regarding the habits, destructive power and other factors peculiar to termites discloses that the biological background of all termites found in the United States is generally the same, with one notable exception. The subterranean or ground dwelling termite attacks only wood which is in contact with the ground, while the other types of termites attack wood directly from the air.

Leading authorities on the subject have concluded that little or no structural damage can be caused by termites during the first two years after the initial infestation. It has been estimated that under normal conditions, if left unchecked, depending upon climate and other factors, an infestation of three to eight years would be required to necessitate extensive repairs. Even under extreme conditions, the period would be from one to six years. *See* "Our Enemy the Termite" by Thomas Elliott Snyder; "Termite and Termite Control" by Charles A. Kofoid; "Insects Their Ways and Means of Living" by Robert Evans Snodgrass; and other authorities.

Such authorities agree that termite infestation and the resulting damage cannot be inflicted with the suddenness comparable to that caused by fire, storm or shipwreck.

Accordingly, it is the position of the Service, based on the scientific data available in this area, that damage caused by termites to property not connected with the trade or business does not constitute an allowable deduction as a casualty loss within the meaning of section 165(c)(3) of the Code. Such damage is the result of gradual deterioration through a steadily operating cause and is not the result of an identifiable event of a sudden, unusual or unexpected nature. Further, time elapsed between the incurrence of damage and its ultimate discovery is not a proper measure to determine whether the damage resulted from a casualty. Time of discovery of the damage, in some situations, may affect the extent of the damage, but this does not change the form or the nature of the event, the mode of its operation, or the character of the result. These characteristics are determinative when applying section 165(c)(3) of the Code.

The Internal Revenue Service will no longer follow the decisions of *Buist, Rosenberg,* and *Shopmaker, supra.* The only real distinction between these cases and the decisions of *Rogers, Fay,* and *Dodge, supra,* is the time in which the loss was discovered.

Under the authority contained in section 7805(b) of the Code, Revenue Ruling 59-277, C.B. 1959-2, 73, is revoked for all taxable years beginning after November 12, 1963.

Notes and Questions

1. *Something to chew on.* The result in the termite ruling may be defensible as an interpretation of the statutory phrase "other casualty," but does it make any sense as a matter of policy? Why should homeowners be entitled to casualty loss deductions for damage from earthquake, fire, flood, or storm, but not for damage from the lowly termite? Is it appropriate to think of the termite damage as a natural consequence of the aging of the structure, so that it can be considered as nondeductible "consumption"?[48] Would expert opinion to the effect that the probability of a structure's being damaged by termites had nothing to do with its age be sufficient to rebut that notion? And, if so, should that be enough to yield a favorable result for the taxpayers in this situation? Or is the consumption rationale too far removed from the statutory language for this argument to make much difference?

2. *And what about earthquakes?* Apparently the ruling applies even if the house suddenly and unexpectedly collapses from the termite damage; the fact that the termites had been secretly chewing away for years makes the collapse a non-casualty. The IRS recognizes earthquakes as "other casualties," but by the logic of the termite ruling this may be wrong. After all, the earthquake may have been quietly brewing deep in the earth for years, just as the termites were quietly munching for years before the house collapsed. Perhaps the best that can be said for the termite ruling is that the statute requires the drawing of a line between casualties and non-casualties, and that the close calls at the margin will always be somewhat arbitrary.

3. *Tort defendants.* What if you negligently damage the property (or person) of another, and have to pay tort damages? If the damage occurred while you were pursuing your trade or business, you will be able to deduct the damages as a business expense under §162. If not, you are out of luck. Section 165(c)(3) allows a deduction only for losses "of property," and this has been interpreted to apply only to damage to the taxpayer's own property. (This is closely related to the majority rule, followed by the Tax Court in *Chamales*, that §165(c)(3) permits a deduction for a decline in value of the taxpayer's property only if there is physical damage to the *taxpayer's* property.) If you negligently cause a car accident, and you total both your own car and the car you hit, you can claim a casualty loss deduction for the damage to your own car, but you cannot claim a deduction for the money you pay to the owner of the other car. Does this distinction make any policy sense?

4. *Casualty loss deductions as insurance.* The casualty loss deduction functions as partial insurance. If a taxpayer in the 35 percent bracket suffers a $100,000 uninsured casualty loss, he will be allowed to claim a $100,000 deduction (disregarding §165(h)), which will save him $35,000 in taxes. In effect, the federal government provides the taxpayer with 35 percent casualty insurance coverage, without charging any insurance premiums. It is easy to see that this creates a tax incentive *not* to buy actual insurance.[49] If the taxpayer

---

48. It's clearly consumption by the termites; what we mean here is the taxpayer's consumption, in the Haig-Simons sense.

49. There is no offsetting tax benefit for purchasing insurance, because insurance premiums for consumer durables are not deductible. *See* §262(a), denying deductions for "personal, living, or family expenses."

fully insured his $100,000 asset, he would have to pay premiums based on $100,000 of coverage, but he would obtain only $65,000 of additional coverage. In other words, he has to pay for the $35,000 of coverage he is currently enjoying for free, if he wants to obtain coverage for an additional $65,000 of value. Faced with this tax disincentive, he may decide not to purchase insurance.

This insurance analysis suggests that the casualty loss deduction may be a bad idea. There are two types of casualty losses: those for which the taxpayer could have obtained insurance, and those for which insurance was not available. With respect to the first type, the argument is that no casualty loss deduction should be allowed, in order to avoid discouraging persons from insuring. This result should not be disturbing on fairness grounds. After all, the taxpayer could have avoided suffering a casualty loss simply by purchasing insurance. Why should the government bail him out if he did not want to pay the premiums? Under this analysis, the result in the termite revenue ruling is not disturbing, since termite insurance is readily available. Of course, insurance is also readily available for many kinds of casualties that clearly are within the scope of §165(c)(3).

With respect to the second type of losses — those for which insurance was not available — it may be that whatever prevented private insurers from offering coverage should also prevent the federal government from offering quasi-insurance through §165(c)(3). Consider the *Chamales* facts, for example. Private insurers do not offer decline-in-value-due-to-looky-loos insurance. This may be because it is too difficult for insurers to determine the amount of the decline in value. If so, it should also be too difficult for the tax system to determine the decline in value. Alternatively, there may be no looky-loo insurance because there is no demand for it, and there may be no demand because any decline in value is almost always slight and temporary. Again, these are also reasons why a tax deduction would be inappropriate.

The quasi-insurance effect of the casualty loss deduction was more prominent in the 1960s and 1970s, when many upper and upper-middle income taxpayers were in a 50 percent marginal rate bracket, and there was no percentage-of-adjusted-gross-income floor on the deduction. The Tax Reform Act of 1986 reduced the insurance effect in two ways: it reduced top marginal rates; and it introduced a "means-tested" disallowance of the casualty loss deduction, under §165(h), requiring reduction of the deduction by an amount equal to 10 percent of the taxpayer's adjusted gross income. Thus, in the example above, a taxpayer in the 35 percent bracket might have an adjusted gross income of $400,000, and, accordingly, a disallowed amount of $40,000 (plus a statutory $100 deductible from each casualty loss). This would reduce the federal "insurance" to a maximum of $20,965 for the $100,000 loss noted above (($100,000 − $40,000 − $100) × .35). Since the most common casualties that befall taxpayers probably involve losses occasioned by automobile accidents, the 10 percent disallowance frequently greatly reduces or even eliminates any net value of the deduction. While the 1986 changes do not appear to have been motivated by the concerns expressed in this Note (they were part of a general effort to reduce rates and to broaden the tax base by reducing the value of deductions), they do nevertheless ameliorate the concerns described here.

5. *Federally proclaimed disasters.* Section 165(*i*) provides that a taxpayer who suffers a loss attributable to a federally proclaimed disaster may elect to take the deduction for the year *before* the year in which the disaster actually occurred. There can be two advantages to making this election. First, a deduction in the current year might be wasted, because the taxpayer has little or no income in the year of the disaster. By contrast, the taxpayer may have had sufficient income to absorb the loss in the preceding year. Second, a taxpayer making the election can file an amended return for the previous year and receive a quick refund, instead of having to wait for a refund of the current year's taxes. Congress sometimes goes even further to demonstrate its sympathies for taxpayers who have suffered losses as a result of major disasters. For example, victims of Hurricanes Katrina, Rita, and Wilma, which struck various parts of the Gulf Coast (particularly New Orleans) in the fall of 2005, were allowed to calculate their disaster losses without reducing the deductible amounts by either the $100-per-casualty floor or the 10 percent of adjusted gross income floor. *See* §1400S(b). What is the policy justification for treating victims of some disasters differently from the victims of other disasters? Is it constitutionally permissible? (*See* Constitution of the U.S., Art. I, §8.)

B. CASUALTY LOSS PROBLEM SET

Problem 1.   (a) Brian's car is totaled in an accident. Brian had no collision insurance and has no claim for tort damages. His adjusted basis in the car (just before the accident) was $10,000, the fair market value of the car just before the accident was $6,000, and the value of the car after the accident was zero. Before taking the limitations of §165(h) into account, what is the amount of Brian's casualty loss? First try to figure this out as a matter of tax logic; then look at Treas. Reg. §1.165-7(b)(1). Do the regulations give the same answer as your own analysis?

(b) If Brian's AGI is $50,000, and the car is his only casualty loss for the year, what is the amount of his casualty loss after taking §165(h) into account?

(c) Would the analysis be any different if Brian had used the car full-time in his business? *See* Treas. Reg. §1.165-7(b)(1), last sentence. Do you need to know Brian's AGI to determine the amount he will be allowed to deduct in this case?

Problem 2.   Charley owned a 1964 Mustang, which he had lovingly restored with his own hands. It was totaled in an accident, and Charley had neither insurance coverage nor a claim for tort damages. His adjusted basis in the car was $10,000. The value of the car just before the accident was $15,000, and the value after the accident was zero. Before taking the limitations of §165(h) into account, what is the amount of Charley's casualty loss? Again, first try to figure this out as a matter of tax logic; then consult Treas. Reg. §1.165-7(b)(1).

Problem 3.   (a) Donna's vacation home was severely damaged in a flood, and Donna had no flood insurance. Before the flood Donna's adjusted basis in the home was $100,000, and its fair market value was $250,000. After the flood, the home was worth only $150,000. Before the application of §165(h), what is the amount of Donna's casualty loss?

(b) If Donna's AGI for the year of the loss was $200,000, and this was her only casualty loss for the year, what is the effect of the casualty loss on Donna's adjusted basis in the home?

Problem 4. The facts are the same as in Problem 1, except that Brian had collision insurance on the car, with a $1,500 deductible. At the end of the year in which the accident occurred, he had not yet received any insurance proceeds, but the insurer had told him to expect a check for $4,500 in the next few months. Before application of §165(h), what is the amount of Brian's casualty loss? *See* §165(a) and Treas. Reg. §1.165-1(d)(2)(i).

Problem 5. Ellen's beachfront vacation home, with an adjusted basis of $40,000 and a fair market value of $40,000, was destroyed by a hurricane not named Katrina, Rita, or Wilma. The home was insured for its full value against damage, including wind damage. However, the policy specifically excluded coverage for flood damage. Ellen promptly filed a claim with her insurer, but the insurer took the position the entire damage was caused by flooding, and thus denied all liability. Ellen continued to pursue the claim, and even contemplated litigation, but she was not optimistic. On her tax return for the year of the hurricane, she claimed a casualty loss of $40,000 (before reduction by §165(h)), taking the position that she did not have a reasonable prospect of any insurance recovery. A few months later, to Ellen's surprise, the insurer offered to settle her claim for $30,000, and Ellen accepted. What are the tax consequences to Ellen of these events in the year of the hurricane, and in the subsequent year of the partial recovery? *See* Treas. Reg. §1.165-1(d)(2)(iii).

Cell

DOUBLE TAX BENEFITS

A. PERMISSIBLE AND IMPERMISSIBLE DOUBLE TAX BENEFITS

1. *Parsonage Allowances, Property Taxes, and Home Mortgage Interest*

REV. RUL. 83-3

1983-1 C.B. 72

... May a minister deduct interest and taxes paid on a personal residence if the amounts expended are allocable to a rental allowance excluded from gross income under section 107 of the Internal Revenue Code? ...

During the taxable year, a minister of a gospel who is employed as a pastor of a church received $19,000 as compensation from the church and a combined rental and utility allowance of $6,300. The rental and utility allowance is excludable from the gross income of the minister under section 107 of the Code, to the extent used to rent or provide a home.

During the year, the minister used the rental and utility allowance, together with other funds, to make monthly payments for the residence in which the minister lived. Those payments totaled $8,400 and consisted of principal ($500), insurance ($400), real estate taxes ($1,400), interest ($4,000), and utility costs ($2,100).

The minister incurred no other expenses directly related to providing a home during the taxable year. Interest and real property taxes paid are generally deductible expenses under the provisions of §163 and 164 of the Code, respectively, provided the taxpayer elects to itemize deductions. ...

Section 163 of the Code allows as a deduction all interest paid or accrued within the taxable year on indebtedness. [Although §163(h) now generally denies deductions for personal interest, most home mortgage interest continues to be deductible by reason of §163(h)(3). — EDS.]

Section 164 of the Code allows, except as otherwise provided, as a deduction for the taxable year within which paid or accrued, state and local real property taxes.

Section 265(1) [now §265(a)(1)] of the Code provides that no deduction shall be allowed for any amount otherwise allowable as a deduction that is allocable to one or more classes of income . . . wholly exempt from the taxes imposed by subtitle A of the Internal Revenue Code. . . .

The purpose of section 265 of the Code is to prevent a double tax benefit. In United States v. Skelly Oil Co., 394 U.S. 678 (1969), the Supreme Court of the United States said that the Internal Revenue Code should not be interpreted to allow the practical equivalence [sic] of double deductions absent clear declaration of intent by Congress. Section 265(1) [now §265(a)(1)] applies to otherwise deductible expenses incurred for the purpose of earning or otherwise producing tax-exempt income. It also applies where tax exempt income is earmarked for a specific purpose and deductions are incurred in carrying out that purpose. In such event, it is proper to conclude that some or all of the deductions are allocable to the tax exempt income. . . .

In [the hypothetical case at the beginning of the ruling], the taxpayer has incurred expenses for the purposes for which the tax-exempt income was received. Permitting a full deduction . . . would lead to a double benefit not allowed under section 265 of the Code. . . .

[T]he amount of the itemized deductions otherwise allowable for the interest and real estate taxes must be decreased to the extent the expenses are allocable to the rental allowance received from the church.

The following demonstrates one reasonable method of allocation under section 1.265-1(c) of the regulations that will be accepted by the Internal Revenue Service. . . .

[T]he $4,000 of interest otherwise deductible under section 163 of the Code is decreased by $3,000, computed by multiplying $4,000 (the amount of the interest otherwise deductible) by a fraction, the numerator of which is $6,300 (the combined rental and utility allowance) and the denominator of which is $8,400 (the total of all expenditures to which the rental and utility allowance is applicable), or $4,000 × $6,300/$8,400 = $3,000. Therefore, the deduction for interest allowable under section 163 . . . is $1,000 ($4,000 – $3,000).

[T]he $1,400 of real estate taxes otherwise deductible under section 164 of the Code is decreased by $1,050 computed by multiplying $1,400 (the amount of the real estate taxes otherwise deductible) by a fraction, [the numerator of which is $6,300 and] the denominator of which is $8,400 (as indicated in the preceding paragraph), or $1,400 × $6,300/$8,400 = $1,050. Therefore, the itemized deduction for real estate taxes allowable under section 164 . . . is $350 ($1,400 – $1,050).

2. The Analytical Framework

Suppose a minister receives $10,000 from his church, designated as a "parsonage allowance," and uses the money to pay the interest on his home mortgage. If he can exclude the $10,000 from income under §107(2) and deduct the same $10,000 from income under §163(h)(3), the tax result will be *negative* income of $10,000. In other words, the minister's taxable income will be $10,000 lower than if he had received no parsonage allowance and made no mortgage payments.

Excluding an item from income is the equivalent of including the item in income, but then claiming an offsetting deduction. If a tax break applies only to economic benefits received from a particular *source,* the tax break will take the form of an exclusion, since an exclusion is simpler than inclusion and an offsetting deduction. If a tax break depends only on the *use* to which income is devoted, the tax break will take the form of a deduction. If a taxpayer may exclude particular dollars from income based on their source, and then deduct those same dollars based on their use, he has enjoyed the functional equivalent of a double deduction of those dollars. For example, allowing the minister both to exclude and to deduct the same $10,000 is the equivalent of requiring him to include the $10,000 in income (as compensation for services), but then allowing him to deduct it twice.

It is understandable that the IRS is troubled by the prospect of double deductions and their exclusion-plus-deduction equivalents. Allowing both an exclusion and a deduction in the parsonage allowance situation may be especially disturbing if the minister is compared with another (non-clergy) taxpayer who receives $10,000 cash compensation that he uses to pay the rent on his home. Both the minister and the other taxpayer have received $10,000 compensation for services, and both have spent the $10,000 on a place to live, but the minister has *negative* income of $10,000 (if the double tax benefit is permitted), while the other taxpayer has *positive* income of $10,000.

Despite the instinctive reaction that double tax benefits are wrong, the Supreme Court's malediction on double tax benefits in *Skelly Oil,* and a statement in Reg. §1.161-1 that "[d]ouble *deductions* are not permitted,"[50] there is no general rule that a taxpayer may not both exclude and deduct the same dollars. In fact, taxpayers are routinely permitted to exclude and deduct the same dollars, even when there has been no "clear declaration of intent by Congress." Suppose a taxpayer receives $10,000 as a gift (tax-free under §102) and gives the money to charity (deductible under §170). It is absolutely clear that the taxpayer may take advantage of both the deduction and the exclusion, even though this is the equivalent of a double deduction, and even though the result is to treat the taxpayer as if she were $10,000 poorer than if neither the receipt nor the expenditure had ever happened. Or suppose a taxpayer receives $10,000 damages on account of personal physical injuries (excluded from gross income under §104(a)(2)) and uses the $10,000 to pay property taxes on her home (deductible under §164). Again, it is perfectly clear that the taxpayer may take advantage of both the exclusion and the deduction, despite the resulting failure of taxable income to reflect economic reality. Double tax benefits would also be clearly permissible if the gift exclusion were paired with the property tax deduction, or if the damages exclusion were paired with the charitable contribution.[51]

---

50. Emphasis added. For an example of the disallowance of a literal double deduction (as opposed to an exclusion-deduction combination), see Reg. §1.162-15(a)(1), which says that the same dollars cannot be deducted as both a charitable contribution and a business expense.

51. Another, easy-to-overlook, example of a permissible double tax benefit is the deduction for unrealized appreciation in long-term capital gain property donated to charity. The law allows the donor both to exclude the unrealized appreciation from income and to deduct the unrealized appreciation as a charitable contribution. See section A.3 of Chapter 4. This is a case of "clear declaration of intent by Congress" to permit the equivalent of a double deduction.

The underlying principle is clear enough, although it is seldom explicitly stated. Double tax benefits—such as an exclusion and a deduction for the same dollars—*are* permitted (even "absent clear declaration of intent by Congress") so long as the two benefits have independent policy justifications. Thus, a taxpayer may both exclude physical personal injury damages from income and deduct the same dollars when paid as property taxes, because the source-based policy justification for excluding damages from income is unrelated to the use-based justification for allowing a deduction for property taxes, and the taxpayer has met the requirements for both benefits (albeit with the same dollars). On the other hand, sometimes two tax benefits do not have independent policy justifications, in which case the taxpayer is limited to one benefit or the other. For example, §§132(a)(6) and (g) allow an employee to exclude from gross income a "qualified moving expense reimbursement" received from her employer, because if the employee were required to include the reimbursement in gross income she could claim an offsetting moving expense deduction under §217. Since the exclusion is justified as being in lieu of a deduction, it would obviously be inappropriate to allow the taxpayer to exclude and deduct the same moving expense dollars. Sure enough, §132(g) specifically states that the exclusion is not available for "any payment for (or reimbursement of) an expense actually deducted by the individual in a prior year." A similar relationship exists between the §104(a)(2) exclusion for personal physical injury damages and the §213 deduction for medical expenses. Although Congress has indicated it does not want taxpayers to be able to exclude medical expense damage awards under §104(a)(2) *and* deduct the same medical expenses under §213, the IRS has encountered great difficulty in enforcing this particular prohibition of double benefits. This issue is explored in detail later.

The disallowance of double tax benefits is not limited to double deductions, or deduction-and-exclusion situations. Consider, for example, the relationship between the child care credit (§21) and the exclusion of employer-provided dependent care assistance benefits (§129). Both provisions are intended to provide a tax benefit based on dollars expended for child care while parents are at work. Since they share the same basic policy justification, it would seem inappropriate to allow parents to claim both the credit and the exclusion for the same dollars of child care expenditures. As with moving expenses, Congress has acted to prevent double benefits. Section 129(e)(7) provides that no deduction or credit shall be allowed for any amount excluded from gross income by reason of §129. Thus, any amounts excluded under §129 cannot be the basis for a credit under §21. At the taxpayer's election, a particular dollar expended on child care may support either a §21 credit or a §129 exclusion, but it cannot support both.

In light of the above discussion of the general law of double tax benefits, the conclusion in Rev. Rul. 83-3 seems doubtful. The facts in the ruling occupy a murky middle ground between situations where double tax benefits are allowed because they rest on completely unrelated policy justifications and situations where double benefits are disallowed because they share a single justification. It is true that both the §107 parsonage exclusion and the deductions under §§163(h)(3) (for home mortgage interest) and 164 (for property tax) are housing subsidies, but they are very differently targeted. On the one hand, §107 provides a tax benefit very limited in its beneficiaries, but very broad in the housing benefits it excludes for qualified beneficiaries. So long as the benefit is provided to eligible clergy,[52] the exclusion is available regardless of whether the housing is provided in kind or as a cash allowance to be expended on housing. An excluded cash allowance need not be spent on mortgage interest or property tax; it may also be spent on rent, on utilities, on furniture, on a down payment, or on mortgage principal payments. By contrast, the deductions under §§163(h)(3) and 164 are available without regard to the taxpayer's line of work, but only for a much narrower range of expenditures. It is far from clear that the policy justifications for the exclusion (on the one hand) and the two deductions (on the other hand) are so closely related that a double tax benefit should be denied.

In any event, Congress disagreed with the Service's position in Rev. Rul. 83-3. In 1986, Congress overruled the ruling by enacting §265(a)(6)(B), which provides that no deduction for home mortgage interest or property taxes shall be disallowed "by reason of the receipt of an amount as . . . a parsonage allowance excludable from gross income under section 107." In light of the weak connection between the policy underlying the exclusion provision and the policies underlying the two deduction provisions, §265(a)(6)(B) seems consistent with the general law of double tax benefits.

B. THE PERSONAL INJURY DAMAGE EXCLUSION AND THE MEDICAL EXPENSE DEDUCTION: ENFORCING THE DOUBLE BENEFIT PROHIBITION

As noted above, Congress has indicated that a taxpayer should not be permitted a double tax benefit when he receives damages as compensation for medical expenses incurred as a result of a personal physical injury. He may exclude the damages under §104(a)(2) or deduct the medical expenses under §213, but he is not supposed to be able to do both. When the medical expenses are incurred and deducted *before* the damages are received, the applicable double benefit prohibition is contained in §104(a), which states that the exclusion does not apply "in the case of amounts attributable to . . . deductions allowed under section 213 . . . for any prior taxable year." When the medical expenses are incurred *after* the damages have been received and excluded, the applicable double benefit prohibition is contained in

---

52. Despite the rather startling (in light of the First Amendment's Establishment Clause) reference in §107 to "ministers of the gospel," the IRS has interpreted the exclusion as being available to clergy of all faiths, gospel-based or otherwise. Rev. Rul. 78-301, 1978-2 C.B. 103. In Warren v. Commissioner, 282 F.3d 1119 (9th Cir. 2002), the Ninth Circuit raised the issue, *sua sponte*, of whether limiting the housing exclusion to clergy (albeit of all faiths) violates the Establishment Clause. The court requested supplemental briefing by the parties, and appointed Professor Erwin Chemerinsky *amicus curiae* on the issue. The IRS and Reverend Warren later settled the case, and the Ninth Circuit then dismissed the appeal and rejected Professor Chemerinsky's motion to intervene as a private taxpayer. Warren v. Commissioner, 302 F.3d 1012 (9th Cir. 2002). Recently, however, a federal district court has held that third parties (i.e., persons other than taxpayers claiming the benefit of §107 and the government) had "taxpayer standing" under Flast v. Cohen, 392 U.S. 83 (1942), to challenge §107 as a violation of the Establishment Clause of the First Amendment. Freedom from Religion Fdn. v. Geithner, 715 F. Supp. 2d 1051 (E.D. Cal. 2010). The court has not yet decided the case on the merits.

§213(a), which provides that medical expenses are deductible only if they are "not compensated for by insurance or otherwise." The prior receipt of medical expense damages excluded from gross income under §104(a)(2) would be a form of "or otherwise" compensation. The ruling below addresses the situation where the medical expenses come first; the *Niles* case following the ruling addresses the situation where the damages are received before the expenses are incurred.

REV. RUL. 75-230
1975-1 C.B. 93

Advice has been requested whether any portion of an amount received by a taxpayer in settlement of a damage suit for personal injuries, which would otherwise be excludable from his gross income under section 104(a)(2) of the Internal Revenue Code of 1954, is includible in his gross income as being attributable to medical expenses deducted by him in a prior taxable year.

The taxpayer sued for damages for injuries suffered in an automobile accident as a result of another's alleged negligence. The complaint filed in the lawsuit asked for a total judgment of 100x dollars as compensatory damages for personal injuries sustained in the accident; however, the complaint did not state separately the amounts claimed for each of the particular items of damage alleged, such as previously paid medical expenses, and pain and suffering.

The taxpayer, in a taxable year prior to commencing the suit, paid 5x dollars for medical expenses attributable to the accident. He deducted those expenses on his Federal income tax return for that year, within the limitations of section 213 of the Code, and the deduction was allowed.

In a taxable year subsequent to the year in which that deduction was taken, the taxpayer's suit was settled out of court for 20x dollars. In arriving at the amount of the settlement, the taxpayer's previously paid medical expenses were considered as a partial measure of the damages sustained, as well as his pain and suffering, but the settlement contained no allocation of the amount received between the taxpayer's previously paid medical expenses and his pain and suffering.

At the time of settlement the taxpayer executed a standard form of release from all claims or demands for damages, costs, expenses, and consequential damages on account of, or growing out of, all known and unknown injuries as a result of the accident.

Section 104(a)(2) of the Internal Revenue Code of 1954 provides, in part, that except in the case of amounts attributable to (and not in excess of) deductions allowed under section 213 (relating to medical, etc., expenses) for any prior taxable year, gross income does not include the amount of any damages received (whether by suit or agreement) on account of personal injuries.

Under the provisions of section 1.213-1(g)(1) of the Income Tax Regulations, a reimbursement, from insurance or otherwise, for medical expenses received in a taxable year subsequent to a year in which a deduction was claimed on account of such expenses, is includible in gross income in such subsequent year to the extent attributable to (and not in excess of) a deduction allowed under section 213 of the Code for any prior taxable year.

Although the settlement reached in the instant case does not specify the portion thereof that is allocable to the taxpayer's previously paid and deducted medical expenses, the amount of previously paid medical expenses is a sum certain, while the damages sought for his pain and suffering are speculative. Thus, under such circumstances the amount of the taxpayer's previously paid medical expenses is the best evidence available on which to base an allocation of the amount he received in the subsequent settlement.

Accordingly, in the instant case, the Internal Revenue Service will presume that the amount received in settlement of the personal injury suit is attributable first to medical expenses deducted, and thus is includible in the taxpayer's gross income in the taxable year of receipt to the extent of the medical expense deduction allowed in the prior taxable year, that is, 5x dollars.

However, where the settlement of a personal injury suit contains an express allocation of a portion of the amount received in settlement to previously paid medical expenses deducted by the taxpayer under section 213 of the Code in a prior taxable year, the Service will presume the correctness of the allocation to medical expenses, unless it is unreasonable in the light of all the facts, and require inclusion of that allocable amount in gross income in the taxable year of receipt to the extent of the medical expense deduction allowed in the prior taxable year.

Notes and Questions

1. *'Tis more blessed to exclude than to deduct.* Under current law, medical expenses are deductible only to the extent they exceed 7.5 percent (10 percent for years after 2012) of the taxpayer's adjusted gross income. Suppose a taxpayer with adjusted gross income of $100,000 incurs $20,000 of medical expenses in connection with a personal physical injury, and is able (after application of the 7.5% of AGI floor) to deduct $12,500. In a later year, the taxpayer receives a personal injury damage award of $75,000, of which $20,000 is properly allocated to the $20,000 of past medical expenses. How, much, if any, of the award is taxable? Is the taxable portion $20,000 (based on the $20,000 of expenses taken into account in arriving at the $12,500 deduction), or is it only $12,500 (the amount actually deducted)? Sensibly enough, §104(a)(2) denies the exclusion only to the extent of "deductions allowed" in prior years, so the taxable amount is only $12,500. *See also* Reg. §1.213-1(g)(1). Notice that something rather strange is going on here, however. If exclusion of medical expense damages under §104(a)(2) is in lieu of deduction under §213, why is it that an actual §213 deduction is subject to all sorts of restrictions (the 7.5% of AGI floor, the denial of the deduction to non-itemizers, and the §68 phasedown of itemized deductions), none of which applies to the in-lieu-of-deduction exclusion under §104(a)(2)? This difference between severely restricted deductions and unrestricted exclusions is pervasive in the Internal Revenue Code.

2. *Settlement allocations based on hazards of litigation.* Suppose a plaintiff settles a tort claim for $60,000, and the plaintiff has deducted $20,000 of medical expenses in earlier years in connection with the injuries caused by the defendant. The settlement was premised on the belief of both parties that plaintiffs total damages were $100,000, but that there was only a 60 percent chance that a jury would find the defendant liable. If the settlement document does not specify any allocation of the $60,000, Rev. Rul. 75-230 will treat $20,000 as attributable to the past medical expenses, and therefore

taxable. The ruling suggests, however, that the IRS would respect the settlement document if it allocated only $12,000 to past medical expenses, on the theory that the plaintiff was receiving 60 percent of each element of his damages.

3. *Comparative negligence and settlement allocations.* The allocation of only $12,000 to past medical expenses in the previous note might be termed a hazards of litigation allocation. In an appropriate case, it should be possible to reduce the allocation to past medical expenses even more, by combining a hazards of litigation allocation adjustment with a comparative negligence allocation adjustment. Suppose the past medical expenses are $20,000, the parties agree that total damages are about $100,000, but the settlement is for only $42,000. The parties estimated that there was only about a 60 percent chance that a jury would find the defendant liable. They also estimated that, even if a jury found the defendant liable, it would also find the plaintiff negligent, and reduce damages to $70,000 under comparative negligence principles. The settlement reflects an estimate that plaintiff had a 60 percent chance of obtaining $70,000 damages at trial (after a comparative fault reduction from $100,000). In that case, the IRS should respect the settlement document if it allocates only $8,400 to past medical expenses, on the theory that the plaintiff received only 42 percent of each element of damages.

4. *Allocations of damage awards.* Although Rev. Rul. 75-230 does not address allocations to past medical expenses received by suit (rather than by settlement), it is easy to see how the logic of the ruling would apply to court-awarded damages. If there is no reduction in damages on account of the plaintiff's comparative fault, then the award should be allocated to previously deducted medical expenses up to the amount of the deductions. If there is a comparative fault reduction, it should be reflected in the allocation to previously deducted medical expenses. For example, if previously deducted medical expenses were $80,000, the jury allocated 75 percent of the fault to the defendant and 25 percent to the plaintiff, and the jury awarded the plaintiff $300,000 (75% of plaintiff's total damages of $400,000), the plaintiff should be treated as having received only $60,000 of damages (75% of $80,000) on account of the deducted medical expenses.

5. *When the damages come first.* The approach of Rev. Rul. 75-230 seems to have worked out well in practice, partly because it is easy to determine the amount of previously deducted medical expenses, partly because of the flexibility of allocation it permits in the case of settlements, and partly because jury determinations of comparative fault provide the information needed to do allocations for damages received by suit. As the following case demonstrates, however, the IRS has had much worse luck in trying to enforce the prohibition on double tax benefits when the receipt of damages precedes the payment of medical expenses.

NILES v. UNITED STATES
710 F.2d 1391 (9th Cir. 1983)

CHOY, Circuit Judge: In this tax-refund suit, the Internal Revenue Service (IRS) appeals from a summary judgment for taxpayer Niles. The novel issue on appeal is whether the IRS may allocate a portion of a lump-sum personal injury award to future medical expenses (resulting from the injury) and disallow deduction of those medical expenses to the extent of the allocation. The district court ruled that the IRS may not make such an allocation. We affirm.

The facts of this case are not disputed. In 1970, Kelly Niles, then 11 years old, suffered a head injury during a playground scuffle. Subsequent negligent medical care left Niles with irreparable brain damage. He is now a quadriplegic, unable to speak or take care of himself.

Niles' personal injury action in 1973 resulted in a lump-sum jury award of $4,025,000. At trial, Niles presented detailed, substantially unrebutted evidence (including expert testimony) as to each specific component of the total economic loss he claimed as part of the damage award. The verdict was attacked as excessive, but the California Court of Appeal affirmed. During the course of that appeal, in an effort to prove that the award was not excessive, Niles again presented a detailed, hypothetical itemization of the award, allocating $1,588,176 to future medical expenses. Niles collected the personal injury award, but properly excluded it from his gross income under I.R.C. §104(a)(2).

In an unprecedented move, the IRS disallowed the deduction [for medical expenses incurred in a year following the collection of the personal injury award] on the ground that the expenses had already been compensated for within the meaning of I.R.C. §213(a) by virtue of Niles' receipt of the lump-sum award. The IRS reasoned that if Niles were allowed to deduct amounts he received in a personal injury award that were intended as compensation for future medical expenses, he would be getting an exclusion and a deduction for the same monies. The IRS adopted the allocation Niles presented to the California Court of Appeal, and ruled that Niles cannot deduct any future medical expenses until the aggregate amount of such expenses exceeds $1,588,176. Niles paid the deficiency and sued for a refund in district court. At trial, both parties moved for partial summary judgment. The district court granted summary judgment in favor of Niles, holding that he satisfied his burden of proof by demonstrating that the IRS has no authority to allocate lump-sum awards. . . .

Niles must prove that he did not receive compensation within the meaning of §213(a) for the medical expenses he claimed as a deduction on his 1975 tax return. The district court felt that Niles satisfied his burden of proof by showing that he received a lump-sum personal injury award and that there is no basis upon which the IRS may allocate any part of such an award to future medical expenses.

The Government persistently asserts that in order for Niles to meet his burden of proof, he must prove that no part of the lump-sum award was intended as compensation for the medical expenses he claimed on his 1975 tax return. The Government, it is clear, assumes the conclusion that a portion of a lump-sum jury award is in fact allocable as compensation for future medical expenses. If an award is not so allocable, then Niles has satisfied his burden by proving that the alleged compensation for future medical expenses is part of an unapportioned lump-sum personal injury award. The question of allocability is thus at the heart of the dispute.

We initially note that there is no statutory authority or case law supporting the IRS' authority to allocate.[53] Therefore, in determining the propriety of the IRS'

---

53. Revenue Ruling 79-427, 1979-2 C.B. 120, specifically addresses the issue in this case and concludes that although the jury did not allocate a specific amount for future medical expenses, an allocable amount may be determined based on the best evidence available under the circumstances. We do not rely on nor pass judgment on the propriety of Revenue Ruling 79-427 since it was promulgated during the audit, and was based on the facts of the instant case. As the district court noted, we cannot allow the IRS to take advantage of a self-serving ruling.

actions, we must focus on the question of whether such actions are unreasonable or plainly inconsistent with the Internal Revenue Code.

In attempting to allocate a portion of Niles' lump-sum jury award to future medical expenses, the Government is changing an administrative practice almost as old as the income tax itself. It was in 1922 that the Government declared it would not make allocation from lump-sum verdicts. . . .

The continuous administrative practice of nonallocation is illustrated by two letter rulings from the 1960's that sanctioned nonallocation of both lump-sum awards and unallocated settlement payments.[54] It would be no exaggeration to suppose that the nonallocability of lump-sum awards to future medical expenses has been a basic presumption of litigants in thousands of personal injury suits over the years. This court does not look favorably upon an administrative change in "a principle of taxation so firmly entrenched in our jurisprudence," Commissioner v. Greenspun, 670 F.2d 123, 126 (9th Cir. 1982), particularly when that change is sought by means of adjudication in a particular audit.

The Government seeks to distinguish the past administrative precedent, which, the Government concedes, correctly interpreted §213(a). It argues that the past nonallocation is justified by the speculative nature of past lump-sum awards, whereas the present allocation is not speculative in light of the arguments of Niles' counsel before the California Court of Appeal. In other words, Niles is subject to taxation, while other lump-sum recipients are not, because of the success of Niles' attorneys in defending the award. This is a strange basis to distinguish among taxpayers, as well as completely irrelevant to the net-income concept underlying the income tax. . . .

Even if this distinction among recipients of lump-sum awards could be justified by a rational basis such as administrative convenience, it would still be unpersuasive for the reason that there is in fact no difference in the degree of speculation in allocating Niles' award from that of anyone else. The mere defense of the award by Niles on appeal provides no evidence at all of what Niles' jury meant to allocate to Niles' future medical expenses. That, after all, is the only question — what that jury meant to allocate to Kelly Niles' future medical expenses. It is, we suppose, possible that the jury meant to allocate precisely $1,588,176 of its award toward Niles' future medical expenses. It also seems possible that the jury did not decide on any allocation, but merely decided that $4 million would be a nice round sum, upon which $25,000 might be added as a "sweetener." While defending this award on appeal, Niles was merely required to show that the award was not so large as to "shock[] the conscience and suggest[] passion, prejudice or corruption on the part of the jury." Seffert v. Los Angeles Transit Lines, 56 Cal. 2d 498, 507 (1961). As a means to this end, a hypothetical breakdown may be used to illustrate the reasonableness of the award. It was not Niles' burden to prove that any specific allocation was in fact made by the jury. A hypothetical allocation of any personal injury award can always be made, based upon evidence presented to an awarding jury. The allocation in this case is no less speculative than in any other case merely because Niles speculated on the record.[55] The Government's attempt to distinguish this

54. I.e., Letter Rulings 6207314840A (July 31, 1962) (lump-sum award), and 6510284440A (October 28, 1965) (settlement). Letter rulings have no precedential force, but they are competent evidence of administrative practice. *See* Rowan Cos. v. United States, 452 U.S. 247, 261 n.17 (1981).

55. The parties agree that if part of the award had been expressly allocated to future medical expenses, those expenses would not be deductible to the extent compensated for by the award, as per Revenue Ruling 75-232, 1975-1 C.B. 94.

case from all others subsumed under its venerable administrative practice of nonallocation is thoroughly unpersuasive. . . .

Our holding is narrow. Medical expenses of a taxpayer are not "compensated for" within the meaning of I.R.C. §213(a) by any portion of a previous lump-sum personal injury jury award.

Notes and Questions

1. *Double tax benefits for future medical expense damages, but not for past medical expense damages.* The IRS seems to have given up on the *Niles* issue, although it has not officially revoked Rev. Rul. 79-427 (discussed in note 53 of the opinion). Thus, a taxpayer may deduct medical expenses, although in an earlier year he received tort damages and claimed an exclusion under §104(a)(2), and some unspecified portion of the excluded damages was awarded on account of future medical expenses. The same is true if the taxpayer excluded a settlement payment in a prior year, so long as the taxpayer was not so foolish as to agree to an allocation of a specific portion of the settlement payment to future medical expenses. Whether a double tax benefit can be obtained by combining an exclusion under §104(a)(2) with a deduction under §213 thus depends on the happenstance of whether the receipt of the damages (or settlement payments) precedes or follows the payment of the medical expenses. If the payment of the medical expenses comes first, the IRS is able to enforce the §104(a)(2) prohibition on double tax benefits. But if the receipt of the damages comes first, the IRS is generally unable to enforce the §213 prohibition of double benefits.

2. *Bootstrap rulings.* Rev. Rul. 79-427, referred to in note 53 of the opinion, is an example of a "bootstrap ruling." In a bootstrap ruling, the IRS describes a hypothetical version of the facts of a case currently in litigation, resolves the legal issue in favor of the IRS's position in the litigation, and then cites the ruling in the litigation as supporting authority for the IRS's position. This would be a neat trick if it worked, but the *Niles* opinion is typical of judicial attitudes to bootstrap rulings. Courts accord considerably more weight to non-bootstrap revenue rulings, but no revenue ruling has the weight of a Treasury regulation.

3. *More blessed to exclude than to deduct (reprise).* If a taxpayer is unable to achieve the *Niles* result of benefitting from both an exclusion-in-lieu-of-deduction and the deduction itself, would the taxpayer generally be better off taking advantage of the exclusion or the deduction? As noted earlier, the taxpayer generally will prefer to claim the exclusion, because exclusions tend to be much less hedged-about with restrictions than are deductions. By excluding medical expense damages under §104(a)(2), rather than deducting them under §213, the taxpayer avoids the 7.5 percent of AGI floor, the need to itemize deductions to claim the benefit, and the §68 phasedown of itemized deductions.

   The exclusion from gross income of working condition fringe benefits — such as a tax professor's subscription to *Tax Notes,* paid for by his employer — under §§132(a)(3) and (d), provides another example. The statute defines a working condition fringe as "any property or services provided to an employee of the employer to the extent that, if the employee paid for such property or services, such payment would be allowable as a [business expense] deduction." As the definition makes clear, the exclusion is based on an in-lieu-of-deduction rationale. (In keeping with that rationale, a double tax benefit is not permitted; if the employee excludes the benefit under §132(a)(3), he may not also deduct it as a business expense.) In fact, however, if the tax professor had paid for the *Tax Notes* subscription with his own money, he probably would have been entitled to no deduction. The cost of the subscription would have been an unreimbursed employee business expense. Such expenses are deductible in theory, but only as §67 miscellaneous itemized deductions. (*See* §62(a)(1), excluding most unreimbursed employee business expenses from above-the-line status.) Miscellaneous itemized deductions are available only to itemizers (of course), but that is just the first hurdle. In addition, miscellaneous itemized deductions are allowable only to the extent their aggregate amount exceeds 2 percent of AGI. Finally, miscellaneous itemized deductions are completely disallowed for purposes of the alternative minimum tax. None of these hurdles applies, however, under §132. In fact, Reg. §1.132-5(a)(1)(vi) expressly states that an employer-provided benefit may be excluded as a working condition fringe, even though the 2-percent-of-AGI floor of §67 would have barred a deduction if the employee had paid for the item himself.

Although the inconsistent rules for exclusions-in-lieu-of-deductions and their related deductions highlight the tax favoritism for exclusions vis-à-vis deductions, the differing treatment of exclusions and deductions is a much broader phenomenon. Deductions are routinely phased out or phased down for higher income taxpayers, made available only to taxpayers who do not claim the standard deduction, subjected to floors based on percentages of AGI, and disallowed for purposes of the alternative minimum tax (AMT). In the vast majority of cases, exclusions are subjected to no such limitations. Section 86 does phasedown the exclusion of social security benefits from gross income for higher income taxpayers, but this is a rare exception.[56] There is no obvious policy justification for this general disfavoring of deductions relative to exclusions. After all, the basic difference between a deduction and an exclusion is simply that a deduction is based on the *use* to which income is put, while an exclusion is based on the *source* of the income. Nothing in the use-source distinction suggests that tax benefits based on source should be systematically favored over tax benefits based on use. Far from having a principled basis, the favoritism for exclusions is probably based on the happenstance that deductions tend to be more visible than exclusions. Deductions show up as numbers on tax returns, whereas exclusions typically do not show up on returns at all.

---

56. *See also* §56(b)(3), which denies the §421 incentive stock option exclusion for purposes of the alternative minimum tax, and §57(a)(5)(A), which denies for AMT purposes the §103 exclusion for interest on certain private activity bonds.

Being more visible, deductions are easier targets for legislators looking for ways to raise tax revenues by decreasing tax benefits.

What about restrictions on credits? In very general terms, credits tend to be treated less favorably than exclusions, but more favorably than deductions. Credits are commonly subject to phaseouts and phasedowns, and some credits are not allowed for purposes of the alternative minimum tax, but they are never limited to taxpayers who itemize their deductions, nor are they subject to percentage-of-AGI floors.

Chapter 5

BUSINESS EXPENSE DEDUCTIONS

The primary federal taxes on both individuals and corporations are assessed against "income." In the business context, that term is ordinarily understood to represent the net result of the conduct of the business over the course of the tax year, and is thereby distinguishable from the "sales" or "gross receipts" of the business. The proper measurement of income accordingly requires that the business count first its sales, or other gross income, and then deduct the legitimate expenses of conducting the business. Business expense deductions, unlike personal deductions, are thus justified largely by their definitional properties — without a sensible understanding of business expenses, there would be no way of adequately defining business income. With few exceptions, Congress is not trying to encourage any particular behavior in allowing business expenses. The tax rules are simply an attempt to define income properly.

The importance of allowing business expense deductions can hardly be overstated: For most businesses, in most years, expenses will substantially offset receipts, so that net income — the base of the income tax — is only a small fraction of total receipts. As can be easily imagined, this varies greatly among businesses; and even for a single business it varies from one year to another. But Table 5-1, based on a reasonably prosperous year, illustrates of the significance of business expenses overall and of several important categories of business expenses.

As can be seen, even in a good year, the difference between receipts and net income is profound, with the latter accounting for only about 8 percent of the former. Business expenses explain the difference, and essentially define what we mean by "business income."

The Internal Revenue Code embodies this income-defining idea in §162, the primary provision of which says, with deceptive simplicity, that deductions shall be allowed for "all the ordinary and necessary expenses paid or incurred during the taxable year in carrying on any trade or business. . . ." One gets a rough idea from this language, but at least two concepts are insufficiently specific to permit immediate judgment as to whether any particular expense would or would not be deductible: One needs to know what "ordinary and necessary" means, and what "trade or business" means. Each part of this chapter is intended to contribute to the student's understanding of one or both of those concepts, in the several specific contexts in which questions arise.

After the general language quoted above, §162 adds detail in some particular areas. Among the more important of these are paragraphs (1), (2), and (3) of §162(a), which respectively permit deductions for: compensation of employees (and others); traveling expenses while away from home; and rentals paid for the use of property. Section 162(c) deals with the mixed treatment of expenses incurred to pay bribes and kickbacks; 162(e) deals with lobbying expenses; 162(f)

Table 5-1
Business Receipts and Deductions, 2003

Category	Dollar Amounts (in Billions)	Percentage of Total Deductions
Total receipts	$24,462	–
Total business deductions	$23,328	–
Cost of goods sold	$13,180	56.5%
Salaries and wages[*]	$2,390	10.2%
Taxes paid[**]	$471	2.0%
Interest paid	$893	3.8%
Depreciation	$819	3.5%
Net income (less deficit)	$1,354	–

Source: Kelly Luttrell, Patrice Treubert & Michael Parisi, Integrated Business Data, 2003, 26(2) SOI Bulletin 47, 46. tbl. 1 (2006).

[*] Includes executive and officer compensation, salaries of employees, and employee benefits, except to the degree that wages of workers are included in the inventory accounts, and thus reflected in the "cost of goods sold" item.

[**] This figure does not include federal income taxes paid by corporations, which are of course not allowed as deductions in computing taxable income, nor does it include personal federal income taxes paid by partners and sole proprietors.

and (g) deal with fines, penalties, and antitrust award payments. There are a few other specific provisions of less significance.

Other Code sections deal with certain kinds of expenditures that may or may not have been incurred in the interests of advancing a trade or business. Sections 163 (relating to interest expenses), 164 (relating to state and local taxes), 165 (relating to losses), and 167 and 168 (relating to depreciation of capital equipment) are examples of provisions that provide additional detail as to particular types of expenses or allowances.[1] There are also several sections that limit the availability of business expense deductions in particular cases, such as §183 (hobby losses), §274 (travel and entertainment), and §280A (home offices and vacation homes). These too will be discussed in this chapter.[2]

Still, even after due consideration of these provisions, what is striking about the structure of the Code's treatment of business expenses is how much is left unsaid. As to many important categories of expenses, Congress has said nothing beyond the general language quoted above. And even in the areas where Congress has said more, it hasn't said much. This has left the development of important doctrines in this area to the Treasury, acting largely through regulations and litigation positions, and the courts, which are, as in other areas, the ultimate arbiters of what a taxpayer's tax liability turns out to be. Because of the importance of these rules, and the openness of their structure, the Supreme Court itself has felt obliged to step in to provide clarification in many cases. It is no accident that many of the materials you will examine in this chapter are drawn from the U.S. Reports.

1. Note that several of these deductions are also available as personal deductions, the basic rules regarding which are discussed in Chapter 4; §§167 and 168 are discussed in Chapter 6.
2. Several other provisions limiting business expense deductions are discussed in the tax shelter materials in Chapter 8.

A. WHAT IS AN "ORDINARY AND NECESSARY" EXPENSE?

1. Necessary?

In an oft-cited dictum in the famous case of Welch v. Helvering, the Supreme Court described the word "necessary" in §162(a) as requiring only that expenses be "appropriate and helpful" in "the development of the [taxpayer's] business."[3] This substitution of "appropriate and helpful" for "necessary" was itself appropriate and helpful in getting the business expense concept onto solid ground. In fact, "necessary" was probably too strong a word for Congress to use in this context, with its suggestion that an expense could be deducted only if the business could not be effectively conducted without incurring that expense. It would be nearly impossible to show absolute necessity in most cases, simply because there are usually multiple alternative approaches to any business task, among which the business can reasonably choose. Do your office workers need writing implements? Even if they do, can they be said to need the ball-point pens purchased for this purpose, when pencils, felt-tips, roller balls, and fountain pens could perform the same function? This entire line of inquiry invites inappropriate intrusion into business decisions, where the looming presence of tax considerations may already seem overbearing. Even if the government were to concede in such a case that some writing implements were needed, a strong emphasis on the word "necessary" might give it a basis for a determination that only the least expensive writing implements could be deducted; this would hamper business decisions that it might be wiser to buy writing implements that cost more but that work better for the task at hand. A requirement that a business show the absolute necessity of its expenses, in other words, would put the IRS in the position of reviewing every business decision to ensure that no money was spent (and deducted) unnecessarily.

The IRS has occasionally pursued arguments based on the absence of necessity. For example, it argued in Mason Dixon Lines, Inc. v. United States, 708 F.2d 1043 (6th Cir. 1983), that the accident expenses that the taxpayer deducted were not "necessary," because they could have been avoided if the taxpayer had undertaken greater precautions. But the Service's efforts were rebuffed by the court in that case; more generally, the tax jurisprudence has embraced the Welch formulation, and rarely denies an expense because it wasn't "necessary." The following excerpt is typical of the judicial approach to such questions.

PALO ALTO TOWN & COUNTRY VILLAGE, INC. v. COMMISSIONER

565 F.2d 1388 (9th Cir. 1978)

[Commander Aviation, Inc. owned an airplane. The taxpayers paid a fee to Commander, in return for which Commander made the plane available to the taxpayers on a standby basis. — EDS.] The Tax Court permitted the disallowance of

---

3. 290 U.S. 111, 113 (1933). *Welch v. Helvering* deals primarily with the distinction between current and capital expenses; accordingly, it is set forth in full in Chapter 6, on capitalization and cost recovery.

these expenses and allowed them to deduct as an "ordinary and necessary" business expense, under §162(a), only $125 an hour for actual flying time, $125 an hour being the prevailing rate for chartering such a plane. It rejected any deduction for amounts above that, which were paid to operate the plane on a 24-hour standby basis.

An "ordinary" expense is one that is normally to be expected, in view of the circumstances facing the business, and a "necessary" expense is one that is appropriate and helpful to the business. The Tax Court conceded that the plane was useful in the operation of the business, for example, that it was instrumental in obtaining a number of tenants at Palo Alto's shopping centers, since it enabled Williams and other employees to visit several cities in one day for this purpose and return home, and permitted prospective tenants to visit the shopping centers and return to their places of business in a minimum amount of time. The Tax Court, though, said that the plane was not used often enough to justify maintaining it on a permanent standby basis. But the Tax Court didn't deny that on one occasion the immediate availability of the plane, arising from its standby status, led to a saving of almost $1,000,000 in interest on a loan, or that not having the plane on standby would result in delays in getting Palo Alto personnel back home from their business trips, or that chartering a plane and keeping it on standby would be much more expensive than taxpayers' standby arrangement.

In short, incurring the expense of maintaining Commander's plane on a standby basis was certainly appropriate and helpful to the business, and it was a response one would normally expect a business in taxpayers' circumstances to make. Thus, it was an "ordinary and necessary" business expense, and the Tax Court's contrary determination was clearly erroneous and will be set aside. Taxpayers will be allowed to deduct the expense of maintaining the plane on a standby basis.

2.   Ordinary?

The question of whether an expenditure is "ordinary" has been more controversial in the development of business deductions. At the outset, it should be noted that there are two quite distinct meanings that this word could have in this context. It could mean simply that the expenses must be of a normal type; that is, that the expenses must not be extraordinary. The Supreme Court endorsed this view in Deputy v. DuPont, 308 U.S. 488, at 495, when it said that "ordinary" means something that is "normal, usual, or customary" in the trade or business in which the taxpayer is engaged.

A less obvious meaning, but one closer to the actual usage in most cases, is that "ordinary" in this context means something that does not provide continuing value, but is rather used up in the production of income in the current tax year. This interpretation was succinctly expressed by the Supreme Court in Commissioner v. Tellier, 383 U.S. 687, 689-690 (1966), as follows: "The principal function of the term 'ordinary' in section 162(a) is to clarify the distinction, often difficult, between those expenses that are currently deductible and those that are in the nature of capital expenditures, which, if deductible at all, must be amortized over the useful life of the asset."

Many cases reflect some confusion as to which meaning was intended. Indeed, the *Welch* opinion (mentioned in the description of "necessary" immediately above) vacillates between the two concepts without even seeming to notice the distinction. That case was brought by the IRS as one involving an investment, not a current expense; and ultimately the Court appears to have concurred in that view. But much of the language suggests that the ordinary/extraordinary distinction was also on Justice Cardozo's mind in writing the opinion.

Considerable attention is given in the next chapter to the question of what must be capitalized, and, conversely, what may be deducted as an expense in the year it is paid or incurred. Note again that taxpayers' nearly universal preference will be for the immediate deduction, since that will usually minimize the present value of any stream of tax payments. The following case presents an example of the alternate view of the word "ordinary," considering whether the legal expenses of contesting fraud charges can be ordinary expenses in a case where the contest was ultimately unsuccessful.

COMMISSIONER v. HEININGER
320 U.S. 467 (1943)

Mr. Justice BLACK delivered the opinion of the Court.

The question here is whether lawyer's fees and related legal expenses paid by respondent are deductible from his gross income under [the predecessor of §162(a)] as ordinary and necessary expenses incurred in carrying on his business.

The fees and expenses were incurred under the following circumstances. From 1926 through 1938 respondent, a licensed dentist of Chicago, Illinois, made and sold false teeth. During the tax years 1937 and 1938 this was his principal business activity. His was a mail order business. His products were ordered, delivered, and paid for by mail. Circulars and advertisements sent through the mail proclaimed the virtues of his goods in lavish terms. At hearings held before the Solicitor of the Post Office Department pursuant to U.S.C. Title 39, §§259 and 732, respondent strongly defended the quality of his workmanship and the truthfulness of every statement made in his advertisements, but the Postmaster General found that some of the statements were misleading and some claimed virtues for his goods which did not exist. Thereupon, on February 19, 1938, a fraud order was issued forbidding the Postmaster of Chicago to pay any money orders drawn to respondent and directing that all letters addressed to him be stamped "Fraudulent" and returned to the senders. Such a sweeping deprivation of access to the mails meant destruction of respondent's business. He therefore promptly sought an injunction in a United States District Court contending that there was no proper evidential basis for the fraud order. On review of the record that Court agreed with him and enjoined its enforcement. The Court of Appeals drew different inferences from the record, held that the evidence did support the order, and remanded with instructions to dissolve the injunction and dismiss the bill.

During the course of the litigation in the Post Office Department and the courts respondent incurred lawyer's fees and other legal expenses in the amount of $36,600, admitted to be reasonable. In filing his tax returns for the years 1937 and 1938 he claimed these litigation expenses as proper deductions from his gross receipts of $287,000 and $150,000. The Commissioner denied them on the ground that they did not constitute ordinary and necessary expenses of respondent's business. The Board of Tax Appeals affirmed the Commissioner and the Circuit Court of Appeals reversed and remanded. We granted certiorari because of an alleged conflict with the decisions of other circuits.

There can be no doubt that the legal expenses of respondent were directly connected with "carrying on" his business. Our enquiry therefore is limited to the narrow issue of whether these expenses were "ordinary and necessary" within the meaning of [§162(a)]. In determining this issue we do not have the benefit of an interpretative departmental regulation defining the application of the words "ordinary and necessary" to the particular expenses here involved. Nor do we have the benefit of the independent judgment of the Board of Tax Appeals. It did not deny the deductions claimed by respondent upon its own interpretation of the words "ordinary and necessary" as applied to its findings of fact. The interpretation it adopted was declared to be required by the Second Circuit Court's reversal of the Board's view in National Outdoor Advertising Bureau, Inc. v. Commissioner, 32 B.T.A. 1025.[4]

It is plain that respondent's legal expenses were both "ordinary and necessary" if those words be given their commonly accepted meaning. For respondent to employ a lawyer to defend his business from threatened destruction was "normal"; it was the response ordinarily to be expected. Since the record contains no suggestion that the defense was in bad faith or that the attorney's fees were unreasonable, the expenses incurred in defending the business can also be assumed appropriate and helpful, and therefore "necessary." The government does not deny that the litigation expenses would have been ordinary and necessary had the proceeding failed to convince the Postmaster General that respondent's representations were fraudulent. Its argument is that dentists in the mail order business do not ordinarily and necessarily attempt to sell false teeth by fraudulent representations as to their quality; that respondent was found by the Postmaster General to have attempted to sell his products in this manner; and that therefore the litigation expenses, which he would not have incurred but for this attempt, cannot themselves be deemed ordinary and necessary. We think that this reasoning, though plausible, is unsound in that it fails to take into account the circumstances under which respondent incurred the litigation expenses. Upon being served with notice of the proposed fraud order respondent was confronted with a new business problem which involved far more than the right to continue using his old advertisements. He was placed in a position in which not only his selling methods but also the continued existence of his lawful business were threatened with complete destruction. So far as appears from the record respondent did not believe, nor under our system of jurisprudence was he bound to believe, that a fraud order destroying his business was justified by the facts or the law. Therefore he did not voluntarily abandon the business but defended it by all available legal means. To say that this course of conduct and the expenses which it involved were extraordinary or unnecessary would be to ignore the ways of conduct and the forms of speech prevailing in the business world. Surely the expenses were no less ordinary or necessary than expenses resulting from the defense of a damage suit based on malpractice, or fraud, or breach of fiduciary duty. Yet in these latter cases legal expenses have been held deductible without regard to the success of the defense.

4. In that case the taxpayer had incurred legal expenses, defending a suit begun by the United States to enjoin violations of the Sherman Act. It had successfully defended part of the charges against it, but had agreed to the entry of a consent decree of injunction as to the balance. The Board held that all of the legal expenses were ordinary, and were proximately connected with the taxpayer's business, and that to allow them as deductions would not be against public policy. The Circuit Court reversed as to that portion of the expenses attributable to the consent decree. *See also* Helvering v. Superior Wines & Liquors, Inc., [134 F.2d 373 (8th Cir. 1943),] where the Board was reversed for allowing a taxpayer in the liquor business to deduct lawyer's fees incurred in connection with a compromise of liability for civil penalties assessed for improper bookkeeping.

[The Court went on to note that deductions could be denied if the consequence of allowing the deduction would be to frustrate "sharply defined national or state policies proscribing particular types of conduct." But it found no such frustration of public policy in allowing a business to defend itself against charges made by regulatory agents such as the Postmaster General. Accordingly, the Court allowed the taxpayer to deduct his litigation expenses.]

Notes and Questions

1. *Why was the government wrong?* This case explores the IRS contention that legitimate businesses wouldn't have expenses involved in *unsuccessful* defenses against charges of fraud. A successful defense, of course, would suggest that there had been no fraud, as the facts were ultimately determined, but merely a pesky assertion of fraud by an overreaching agency. Does this argument — made by the government here — make sense to you? Why does the Court reject it? Note that under the government's argument the determination of the underlying fact—whether the advertising was fraudulent or not—would also determine the tax treatment of the legal expenses. But it is not especially unusual to have tax consequences turn on legal determinations of various sorts — property ownership, marital status, and a number of other non-tax legal determinations routinely affect tax treatment of the taxpayers involved.

2. *Deductions for losers?* As a more general matter, is an interpretation of "ordinary and necessary" that depends on the success of the taxpayer's endeavors likely to produce sound results? Would we, for example, disallow the expenses incurred by an independent sales agent in soliciting business from a prospect if the solicitations fell on deaf ears, and no sales resulted from the particular expenses?

B.   WHAT IS A "TRADE OR BUSINESS"?

Congress has been no more forthcoming in defining a "trade or business" than it has been in defining "ordinary and necessary." One ancillary issue is clear: There is no distinction anywhere in the tax jurisprudence *between* a trade and a business; rather, the phrase is simply another legal redundancy, reflecting the lawyerly literary taste that causes us to write things like: "I give, devise, and bequeath the rest, residue, and remainder of my estate. . . ."[5] But distinguishing the trade-or-business collective concept from things not falling within this category has proven more elusive.

Before tackling this distinction, it may be worthwhile to explore briefly some of its consequences. Before 1942, the predecessor of §162(a) was the only provision that could be relied upon to support deductions for expenses related to profit-seeking activities. Thus, taxpayers who were found by the IRS (and ultimately a

---

5. In truth, such apparent redundancies often reflect historical distinctions that no longer apply; but lawyers are reluctant to abandon language that has led to predictable interpretation by courts.

court) to be engaged in no more than the mere management of a portfolio of investments were denied deductions for any expenses they may have incurred in performing those management activities. These would typically consist of investment research, accounting costs incurred to report accurately on the investments (and gains and losses therefrom) to regulatory or tax authorities, costs of storage of documents, or, in the case of physical assets, storage of the assets themselves, and so on.[6] For very wealthy taxpayers, who tend to incur substantial portfolio-management costs, a good deal was at stake in the trade or business question.

After a period of some uncertainty on this question, the Supreme Court determined that merely managing a portfolio, no matter how large the portfolio or how expensive the management, could not rise to the status of a trade or business. Higgins v. Commissioner, 312 U.S. 212 (1941). Congress promptly responded in 1942 by adding §212 to the Code, allowing deductions of certain profit-seeking expenses that were not part of a trade or business. While that reduced the stress on the distinction between business and investment activities, it did not eliminate controversies altogether. There continue to be some important differences between trade or business deductions under §162 and nonbusiness profit-seeking expense deductions under §212. The following list, which is not comprehensive, provides some sense of the situation. First, consider several respects in which §162 expenses are treated more favorably than §212 expenses:

- Most §212 deductions have been, since 1986, part of the "miscellaneous itemized deduction" category; §67 imposes a nondeductible floor on these expenses equal to 2 percent of the taxpayer's adjusted gross income. Thus, as a practical matter, many expenses that are hypothetically deductible under §212 are not effectively deductible, in whole or in part, because of the §67 limitations.[7]
- Even when miscellaneous itemized deductions can effectively be claimed for regular tax purposes, they cannot be deducted for purposes of the alternative minimum tax. See §56(b)(1)(A)(i).[8]
- Certain other deductions may depend on whether or not the taxpayer is engaged in a trade or business. For example, the deductibility of expenses associated with a maintaining a home office depends in part on whether the office is used to conduct a trade or business. See §280A(c)(1), and Moller v. United States, 721 F.2d 810 (Fed. Cir. 1983).

At least some distinctions, however, cut the other way, with nonbusiness activities enjoying some favoritism. For example:

- Income from "self-employment," such as when one conducts a trade or business involving active personal participation, is ordinarily subject to self-employment taxes, which are currently equal to 15.3 percent of income from self-employment up to $94,200 (in 2006), and 2.9 percent of income from self-employment beyond that threshold. If the activity is simply managing an investment, it does not generate self-employment tax liabilities.

---

6. The costs of buying or selling portfolio assets, such as brokerage commissions, would normally be capitalized and considered part of the basis of the asset so acquired, or a reduction of the amount realized on assets sold.

7. See the discussion of §67 in Chapter 4.F. Some §212 deductions are not subject to §67, however. It is a useful exercise to work through the provisions of §§62, 63, and 67 to see which §212 expenses are within the miscellaneous itemized deduction category and which are not.

8. See the discussion of the alternative minimum tax in Chapter 9.C.

Some distinctions can cut either way, depending on the circumstances. For example:

- The definition of a "capital asset" under §1221 excludes assets that are held for sale to customers in the ordinary course of business. As we shall see in Chapter 12, individual taxpayers will usually prefer capital asset treatment of investments in which they have enjoyed profits, but prefer to avoid capital asset treatment for investments in which they have suffered losses. Thus, a taxpayer may argue for, or against, business status in the case of asset sales, depending on whether the sale or sales have generated net profits or net losses. *See, e.g.,* Van Suetendael v. Commissioner, 152 F.2d 654 (2d Cir. 1945).

So battles continue over the trade or business issue, notwithstanding the supposed availability of §212 to authorize deductions even when the activity does not qualify as a trade or business. The Supreme Court has, at various times, in various cases, offered a number of definitions or tests, none of which has proven completely satisfactory. The most recent expression of the Court's views on this subject is contained in the following case, which includes a thorough survey of the Court's earlier struggles with this issue.

COMMISSIONER v. GROETZINGER

480 U.S. 23 (1987)

Justice BLACKMUN delivered the opinion of the Court.

The issue in this case is whether a full-time gambler who makes wagers solely for his own account is engaged in a "trade or business," within the meaning of §§162(a) and 62(1) of the Internal Revenue Code of 1954, as amended.

I

There is no dispute as to the facts. The critical ones are stipulated. Respondent Robert P. Groetzinger had worked for 20 years in sales and market research for an Illinois manufacturer when his position was terminated in February 1978. During the remainder of that year, respondent busied himself with parimutuel wagering, primarily on greyhound races. He gambled at tracks in Florida and Colorado. He went to the track 6 days a week for 48 weeks in 1978. He spent a substantial amount of time studying racing forms, programs, and other materials. He devoted from 60 to 80 hours each week to these gambling-related endeavors. He never placed bets on behalf of any other person, or sold tips, or collected commissions for placing bets, or functioned as a bookmaker. He gambled solely for his own account. He had no other profession or type of employment.

Respondent kept a detailed accounting of his wagers and every day noted his winnings and losses in a record book. In 1978, he had gross winnings of $70,000, but he bet $72,032; he thus realized a net gambling loss for the year of $2,032.

Respondent received $6,498 in income from other sources in 1978. This came from interest, dividends, capital gains, and salary earned before his job was terminated.

On the federal income tax return he filed for the calendar year 1978 respondent reported as income only the $6,498 realized from nongambling sources. He did not report any gambling winnings or deduct any gambling losses. He did not itemize deductions. . . .

Upon audit, the Commissioner of Internal Revenue determined that respondent's $70,000 in gambling winnings were to be included in his gross income and that, pursuant to §165(d) of the Code, a deduction was to be allowed for his gambling losses to the extent of these gambling gains. But the Commissioner further determined that, under the law as it was in 1978, a portion of respondent's $70,000 gambling-loss deduction was an item of tax preference and operated to subject him to the minimum tax under §56(a) of the Code. At that time, under statutory provisions in effect from 1976 until 1982, "items of tax preference" were lessened by certain deductions, but not by deductions not "attributable to a trade or business carried on by the taxpayer." §§57(a)(1) and (b)(1)(A), and §§62(1).[9]

These determinations by the Commissioner produced a §56(a) minimum tax of $2,142 and, with certain other adjustments not now in dispute, resulted in a total asserted tax deficiency of $2,522 for respondent for 1978.

Respondent sought redetermination of the deficiency in the United States Tax Court. That court, in a reviewed decision, with only two judges dissenting, held that respondent was in the trade or business of gambling, and that, as a consequence, no part of his gambling losses constituted an item of tax preference in determining any minimum tax for 1978. In so ruling, the court adhered to its earlier court-reviewed decision in Ditunno v. Commissioner, 80 T.C. 362 (1983). . . .

The United States Court of Appeals for the Seventh Circuit affirmed. Because of a conflict on the issue among Courts of Appeals,[10] we granted certiorari. . . .

II

The phrase "trade or business" has been in §162(a) and in that section's predecessors for many years. Indeed, the phrase is common in the Code, for it appears in over 50 sections and 800 subsections and in hundreds of places in proposed and final income tax regulations. The slightly longer phrases, "carrying on a trade or business" and "engaging in a trade or business," themselves are used no less than 60 times in the Code. The concept thus has a well-known and almost constant presence on our tax-law terrain. Despite this, the Code has never contained a definition of the words "trade or business" for general application, and no regulation has been issued expounding its meaning for all purposes.[11] Neither has a broadly applicable authoritative judicial definition emerged.[12] Our task in this case

---

9. This statutory scheme was amended by the Tax Equity and Fiscal Responsibility Act of 1982, §201(a), 96 Stat. 411. For tax years after 1982, gambling-loss deductions explicitly are excluded from the minimum tax base. The Commissioner acknowledges that a taxpayer like respondent for a year after 1982 would not be subject to minimum tax liability because of his gambling-loss deduction.

10. [The Eleventh and Seventh Circuits had held that full-time gambling could be a trade or business; the Second, Third, and Sixth had held that it could not. — EDS.]

11. Some sections of the Code, however, do define the term for limited purposes. . . .

12. Judge Friendly some time ago observed that "the courts have properly assumed that the term includes all means of gaining a livelihood by work, even those which would scarcely be so characterized in common speech." Trent v. Commissioner, 291 F.2d 669, 671 (CA2 1961).

is to ascertain the meaning of the phrase as it appears in the sections of the Code with which we are here concerned.[13]

In one of its early tax cases, Flint v. Stone Tracy Co., 220 U.S. 107 (1911), the Court was concerned with the Corporation Tax imposed by §38 of the Tariff Act of 1909, ch. 6, 36 Stat. 112-117, and the status of being engaged in business. It said: " 'Business' is a very comprehensive term and embraces everything about which a person can be employed." It embraced the Bouvier Dictionary definition: "That which occupies the time, attention and labor of men for the purpose of a livelihood or profit." . . .

With these general comments as significant background, we turn to pertinent cases decided here. Snyder v. Commissioner, 295 U.S. 134 (1935), had to do with margin trading and capital gains, and held, in that context, that an investor, seeking merely to increase his holdings, was not engaged in a trade or business. Justice Brandeis, in his opinion for the Court, noted that the Board of Tax Appeals theretofore had ruled that a taxpayer who devoted the major portion of his time to transactions on the stock exchange for the purpose of making a livelihood could treat losses incurred as having been sustained in the course of a trade or business. He went on to observe that no facts were adduced in *Snyder* to show that the taxpayer "might properly be characterized as a 'trader on an exchange who makes a living in buying and selling securities.' " *Id.*, at 139. These observations, thus, are dicta, but, by their use, the Court appears to have drawn a distinction between an active trader and an investor.

In Deputy v. Du Pont, 308 U.S. 488 (1940), the Court was concerned with what were "ordinary and necessary" expenses of a taxpayer's trade or business, within the meaning of [§162(a)]. In ascertaining whether carrying charges on short sales of stock were deductible as ordinary and necessary expenses of the taxpayer's business, the Court *assumed* that the activities of the taxpayer in conserving and enhancing his estate constituted a trade or business, but nevertheless disallowed the claimed deductions because they were not "ordinary" or "necessary." 308 U.S., at 493-497. Justice Frankfurter, in a concurring opinion joined by Justice Reed, did not join the majority. He took the position that whether the taxpayer's activities constituted a trade or business was "open for determination," *id.*, at 499, and observed:

> " . . . carrying on any trade or business," within the contemplation of [§162(a)], involves holding one's self out to others as engaged in the selling of goods or services. This the taxpayer did not do. . . . Without elaborating the reasons for this construction and not unmindful of opposing considerations, including appropriate regard for administrative practice, I prefer to make the conclusion explicit instead of making the hypothetical litigation-breeding assumption that this taxpayer's activities, for which expenses were sought to be deducted, did constitute a "trade or business." *Ibid.*

Next came Higgins v. Commissioner, 312 U.S. 212 (1941). There the Court, in a bare and brief unanimous opinion, ruled that salaries and other expenses incident to looking after one's own investments in bonds and stocks were not deductible under [§162(a)] as expenses paid or incurred in carrying on a trade or business. While surely cutting back on *Flint*'s broad approach, the Court seemed to do little

---

13. We caution that in this opinion our interpretation of the phrase "trade or business" is confined to the specific sections of the Code at issue here. We do not purport to construe the phrase where it appears in other places.

more than announce that since 1918 "the present form [of the statute] was fixed and has so continued"; that "[no] regulation has ever been promulgated which interprets the meaning of carrying on a business'"; that the comprehensive definition of "business" in *Flint* was "not controlling in this dissimilar inquiry"; that the facts in each case must be examined; that not all expenses of every business transaction are deductible; and that "[no] matter how large the estate or how continuous or extended the work required may be, such facts are not sufficient as a matter of law to permit the courts to reverse the decision of the Board." 312 U.S., at 215-218. The opinion, therefore — although devoid of analysis and not setting forth what elements, if any, in addition to profit motive and regularity, were required to render an activity a trade or business — must stand for the propositions that full-time market activity in managing and preserving one's own estate is not embraced within the phrase "carrying on a business," and that salaries and other expenses incident to the operation are not deductible as having been paid or incurred in a trade or business.[14] It is of interest to note that, although Justice Frankfurter was on the *Higgins* Court and this time did not write separately, and although Justice Reed, who had joined the concurring opinion in *Du Pont*, was the author of the *Higgins* opinion, the Court in that case did not even cite *Du Pont* and thus paid no heed whatsoever to the content of Justice Frankfurter's pronouncement in his concurring opinion. Adoption of the Frankfurter gloss obviously would have disposed of the case in the Commissioner's favor handily and automatically, but that easy route was not followed.

Less than three months later, the Court considered the issue of the deductibility, as business expenses, of estate and trust fees. In unanimous opinions issued the same day and written by Justice Black, the Court ruled that the efforts of an estate or trust in asset conservation and maintenance did not constitute a trade or business. City Bank Farmers Trust Co. v. Helvering, 313 U.S. 121 (1941); United States v. Pyne, 313 U.S. 127 (1941). The *Higgins* case was deemed to be relevant and controlling. Again, no mention was, made of the Frankfurter concurrence in *Du Pont*. Yet Justices Reed and Frankfurter were on the Court. . . .

From these observations, and decisions, we conclude (1) that, to be sure, the statutory words are broad and comprehensive (*Flint*); (2) that, however, expenses incident to caring for one's own investments, even though that endeavor is full time, are not deductible as paid or incurred in carrying on a trade or business (*Higgins; City Bank; Pyne*); (3) that the opposite conclusion may follow for an active trader (*Snyder*); (4) that Justice Frankfurter's attempted gloss upon the decision in *Du Pont* was not adopted by the Court in that case; (5) that the Court, indeed, later characterized it as an "adumbration"; and (6) that the Frankfurter observation, specifically or by implication, never has been accepted as law by a majority opinion of the Court, and more than once has been totally ignored. We must regard the Frankfurter gloss merely as a two-Justice pronouncement in a passing moment and, while entitled to respect, as never having achieved the status of a Court ruling. One also must acknowledge that *Higgins*, with its stress on examining the facts in each case, affords no readily helpful standard, in the usual sense, with which to

---

14. *See, however,* §212. . . . It allows as a deduction all the ordinary and necessary expenses paid or incurred "for the management, conservation, or maintenance of property held for the production of income," and thus overcame the specific ruling in *Higgins* that expenses of that kind were not deductible. The statutory change, of course, does not read directly on the term "trade or business." Obviously, though, Congress sought to overcome *Higgins* and achieved that end.

decide the present case and others similar to it. The Court's cases, thus, give us results, but little general guidance.

III

Federal and state legislation and court decisions, perhaps understandably, until recently have not been noticeably favorable to gambling endeavors and even have been reluctant to treat gambling on a parity with more "legitimate" means of making a living. And the confinement of gambling-loss deductions to the amount of gambling gains, a provision brought into the income tax law as §23(g) of the Revenue Act of 1934, 48 Stat. 689, and carried forward into §165(d) of the 1954 Code, closed the door on suspected abuses, but served partially to differentiate genuine gambling losses from many other types of adverse financial consequences sustained during the tax year. Gambling winnings, however, have not been isolated from gambling losses. The Congress has been realistic enough to recognize that such losses do exist and do have some effect on income, which is the primary focus of the federal income tax. . . .

If a taxpayer, as Groetzinger is stipulated to have done in 1978, devotes his full-time activity to gambling, and it is his intended livelihood source, it would seem that basic concepts of fairness (if there be much of that in the income tax law) demand that his activity be regarded as a trade or business just as any other readily accepted activity, such as being a retail store proprietor or, to come closer categorically, as being a casino operator or as being an active trader on the exchanges.

It is argued, however, that a full-time gambler is not offering goods or his services, within the line of demarcation that Justice Frankfurter would have drawn in *Du Pont.* Respondent replies that he indeed is supplying goods and services, not only to himself but, as well, to the gambling market; thus, he says, he comes within the Frankfurter test even if that were to be imposed as the proper measure. "It takes two to gamble." Surely, one who clearly satisfies the Frankfurter adumbration usually is in a trade or business. But does it necessarily follow that one who does not satisfy the Frankfurter adumbration is not in a trade or business? One might well feel that a full-time gambler ought to qualify as much as a full-time trader, as Justice Brandeis in *Snyder* implied and as courts have held. The Commissioner, indeed, accepts the trader result. In any event, while the offering of goods and services usually would qualify the activity as a trade or business, this factor, it seems to us, is not an absolute prerequisite.

We are not satisfied that the Frankfurter gloss would add any helpful dimension to the resolution of cases such as this one, or that it provides a "sensible test," as the Commissioner urges. It might assist now and then, when the answer is obvious and positive, but it surely is capable of breeding litigation over the meaning of "goods," the meaning of "services," or the meaning of "holding one's self out." And we suspect that — apart from gambling — almost every activity would satisfy the gloss. A test that everyone passes is not a test at all. We therefore now formally reject the Frankfurter gloss which the Court has never adopted anyway.

Of course, not every income-producing and profit-making endeavor constitutes a trade or business. The income tax law, almost from the beginning, has distinguished between a business or trade, on the one hand, and "transactions entered into for profit but not connected with . . . business or trade," on the other. . . . We accept the fact that to be engaged in a trade or business, the taxpayer must be involved in the activity with continuity and regularity and that the taxpayer's primary purpose for engaging in the activity must be for income or profit. A sporadic activity, a hobby, or an amusement diversion does not qualify. . . .

We do not overrule or cut back on the Court's holding in *Higgins* when we conclude that if one's gambling activity is pursued full time, in good faith, and with regularity, to the production of income for a livelihood, and is not a mere hobby, it is a trade or business within the meaning of the statutes with which we are here concerned. Respondent Groetzinger satisfied that test in 1978. Constant and large-scale effort on his part was made. Skill was required and was applied. He did what he did for a livelihood, though with a less-than-successful result. This was not a hobby or a passing fancy or an occasional bet for amusement.

We therefore adhere to the general position of the *Higgins* Court, taken 46 years ago, that resolution of this issue "requires an examination of the facts in each case." 312 U.S., at 217. This may be thought by some to be a less-than-satisfactory solution, for facts vary. But the difficulty rests in the Code's wide utilization in various contexts of the term "trade or business," in the absence of an all-purpose definition by statute or regulation, and in our concern that an attempt judicially to formulate and impose a test for all situations would be counterproductive, unhelpful, and even somewhat precarious for the overall integrity of the Code. We leave repair or revision, if any be needed, which we doubt, to the Congress where we feel, at this late date, the ultimate responsibility rests.

The judgment of the Court of Appeals is affirmed.

Notes and Questions

1. *No help from the dictionary.* The definition that the Court cribbed from *Bouvier's Law Dictionary* in the *Flint* case, which described business activity as "that which occupies the time, attention, and labor of men for the purpose of livelihood or profit," may have been useful for some purposes. Note, however, that it is of no help in making the primary distinction relevant here, since it would seem to embrace investment activities as well as those we now think of as constituting a business.

2. *The Frankfurter gloss.* As the court notes, the concurring opinion by Justice Frankfurter some years after *Flint* offered a definition of "carrying on a *trade* or business" as involving "holding oneself out to others as engaged in the selling of goods or services." Deputy v. Du Pont, 308 U.S. 488, 499 (1940). Arguably, the Frankfurter definition would not embrace employment situations, a type of business activity that has been widely accepted by the courts as constituting a trade or business.[15] But perhaps one could say that all business people engage in one transaction at a time, and that in the case of employees, the "transaction" (i.e., the job) simply takes a long time? And that in any case, employees are participating in a labor market at all times, and are at all points available to whatever opportunities might arise for their services?

---

15. And *see* §62(a)(1), which clearly implies that employees are, or at least can be, engaged in the trade or business of being employees. (Despite that, however, their unreimbursed business expenses end up being treated as they would be under §212. See Chapter 4.F.)

3. *The icing on the gloss.* Even if the Frankfurter definition could have been stretched to cover employees, it *still* seems underinclusive as to some occupations. For example, many traders in commodities markets trade "on their own accounts." They descend each morning into the pits of, say, the Chicago Mercantile Exchange, buying and selling contracts, hoping to squeeze out whatever arbitrage gains they can manage by the end of the trading session. They may do this day after day, over the course of the 240 or so trading days contained in each year. But if they do not perform these services for anyone but themselves, can they be said to hold out their services for sale to the market? Yet they seem to be engaged in a business activity. While they are in some sense making investments in the contracts they buy, they are not primarily earning a return for the use by others of that capital; the capital is invested only for a few moments, in an effort to catch short swings in value. Accordingly, full-time traders of this sort have generally been treated as being engaged in a trade or business. Indeed, it appears that the IRS does not contest this position with respect to full-time commodities traders who are members of regular exchanges.

4. *Goodbye to the gloss.* Where does *Groetzinger* leave this question? The opinion explicitly rejects "the Frankfurter gloss" in the *Du Pont* case. It goes on to say that if an activity is "pursued full time, in good faith, and with regularity" and is involved in "the production of income for a livelihood, and is not a hobby," then it is a trade or business. Does this mean that, contrary to the *Higgins* and *Moller* cases (and a good many others reaching the same result), a taxpayer who is engaged in the management of her investment portfolio on a full-time basis is engaged in a business? And, conversely, does it mean that an activity that does not occupy its practitioner on a substantially full-time basis cannot constitute a trade or business? The answer to both questions appears to be: No, this opinion does not mean that. The court rather explicitly says it is not overruling *Higgins;* and it is clear that the IRS routinely treats a part-time business enterprise as a "trade or business" for purposes of §162.[16] But what then does the opinion mean? Are we left with a state of the law under which someone who manages investments full time isn't engaged in a business, but someone who spends an equivalent amount of time and energy at the dog track is?

5. *A tough way to make a living.* Note that Mr. Groetzinger was not in the gambling business before 1978, and that in that year he actually suffered net losses from his efforts at the track. Is there any reason to think on the basis of this record that his activities could realistically have provided a "livelihood"?

C. PUBLIC POLICY LIMITATIONS

Courts have routinely treated allowance of a deduction in computing taxable income as an extension of legislative grace — even in the area of business expenses,

---

16. For example, the regulations under §469 defining material participation in business activities clearly contemplate less than full-time services of the taxpayer.

where that allowance is really what makes the tax an income tax rather than a tax on gross receipts. Under this conception of deductions, allowance of a deduction constitutes something of a congressional blessing, an indication that Congress regards the expenditure in question as worthy and appropriate. That framework makes certain types of deductions problematic: Should a deduction be allowed for a payment by a bank robber to the driver of the getaway car? More prosaically, should a store-front bookie be allowed to deduct the rent he pays for the store, in a state where gambling (at least that which is not state sponsored!) is illegal? What about the payments of bribes and kickbacks to obtain valuable contracts? Fines paid for highway violations by drivers of business vehicles? Industrial espionage costs? Legal expenses associated with determining whether any of the above actually happened, and, if they did, were against the law?

These and related issues created thorny difficulties for the IRS and the courts during the first 55 years or so of our income tax history (that is, from 1913-1968), before finally receiving some congressional attention. The following case is the last major case within that early period to consider the treatment of fines. Uncertainty in this area ultimately (in 1969) provoked a legislative response that will be detailed following the discussion of this case.

TANK TRUCK RENTALS, INC. v. COMMISSIONER
356 U.S. 30 (1958)

Mr. Justice CLARK delivered the opinion of the Court.

In 1951 petitioner Tank Truck Rentals paid several hundred fines imposed on it and its drivers for violations of state maximum weight laws. This case involves the deductibility of those payments as "ordinary and necessary" business expenses under [the predecessor of §162(a)]. Prior to 1950 the Commissioner had permitted such deductions, but a change of policy that year caused petitioner's expenditures to be disallowed. The Tax Court, reasoning that allowance of the deduction would frustrate sharply defined state policy expressed in the maximum weight laws, upheld the Commissioner, The Court of Appeals affirmed on the same ground, and we granted certiorari. In our view, the deductions properly were disallowed.

Petitioner, a Pennsylvania corporation, owns a fleet of tank trucks which it leases, with drivers, to motor carriers for transportation of bulk liquids. The lessees operate the trucks throughout Pennsylvania and the surrounding States of New Jersey, Ohio, Delaware, West Virginia, and Maryland, with nearly all the shipments originating or terminating in Pennsylvania. In 1951, the tax year in question, each of these States imposed maximum weight limits for motor vehicles operating on its highways. Pennsylvania restricted truckers to 45,000 pounds, however, while the other States through which petitioner operated allowed maximum weights approximating 60,000 pounds. It is uncontested that trucking operations were so hindered by this situation that neither petitioner nor other bulk liquid truckers could operate profitably and also observe the Pennsylvania law. Petitioner's equipment consisted largely of 4,500- to 5,000-gallon tanks, and the industry rate structure generally was predicated on fully loaded use of equipment of that capacity. Yet only one of the commonly carried liquids weighed little enough that a fully loaded truck could satisfy the Pennsylvania statute. Operation of partially loaded trucks, however, not only would have created safety hazards, but also would have been economically impossible for any carrier so long as the rest of the industry continued capacity loading. And the industry as a whole could not operate on a partial load basis without driving shippers to competing forms of transportation. The only other alternative, use of smaller tanks, also was commercially impracticable, not only because of initial replacement costs but even more so because of reduced revenue and increased operating expense, since the rates charged were based on the number of gallons transported per mile.

Confronted by this dilemma, the industry deliberately operated its trucks overweight in Pennsylvania in the hope, and at the calculated risk, of escaping the notice of the state and local police. This conduct also constituted willful violations in New Jersey, for reciprocity provisions of the New Jersey statute subjected trucks registered in Pennsylvania to Pennsylvania weight restrictions while traveling in New Jersey. In the remainder of the States in which petitioner operated, it suffered overweight fines for several unintentional violations, such as those caused by temperature changes in transit. During the tax year 1951, petitioner paid a total of $41,060.84 in fines and costs for 718 willful and 28 innocent violations. Deduction of that amount in petitioner's 1951 tax return was disallowed by the Commissioner.

It is clear that the Congress intended the income tax laws "to tax earnings and profits less expenses and losses," Higgins v. Smith, 308 U.S. 473, 477 (1940), carrying out a broad basic policy of taxing "net, not . . . gross, income. . . . " McDonald v. Commissioner, 323 U.S. 57, 66-67 (1944). Equally well established is the rule that deductibility under [§162(a)] is limited to expenses that are both ordinary and necessary to carrying on the taxpayer's business. Deputy v. Du Pont, 308 U.S. 488, 497 (1940). A finding of "necessity" cannot be made, however, if allowance of the deduction would frustrate sharply defined national or state policies proscribing particular types of conduct, evidenced by some governmental declaration thereof. Commissioner v. Heininger, 320 U.S. 467, 473 (1943); see Lilly v. Commissioner, 343 U.S. 90, 97 (1952). This rule was foreshadowed in Textile Mills Securities Corp. v. Commissioner, 314 U.S. 326 (1941), where the Court, finding no congressional intent to the contrary, upheld the validity of an income tax regulation reflecting an administrative distinction "between legitimate business expenses and those arising from that family of contracts to which the law has given no sanction." 314 U.S., at 339. Significant reference was made in *Heininger* to the very situation now before us; the Court stated, "Where a taxpayer has violated a federal or a state statute and incurred a fine or penalty he has not been permitted a tax deduction for its payment." 320 U.S., at 473.

Here we are concerned with the policy of several States "evidenced" by penal statutes enacted to protect their highways from damage and to insure the safety of all persons using them.[17] Petitioner and its drivers have violated these laws and have been sentenced to pay the fines here claimed as income tax deductions. It is clear that assessment of the fines was punitive action and not a mere toll for use of the highways: The fines occurred only in the exceptional instance when the overweight run was detected by the police. Petitioner's failure to comply with the state laws obviously was based on a balancing of the cost of compliance against the chance of detection. Such a course cannot be sanctioned, for judicial deference

---

17. Because state policy in this case was evidenced by specific legislation, it is unnecessary to decide whether the requisite "governmental declaration" might exist other than in an Act of the Legislature. *See* Schwartz, *Business Expenses Contrary to Public Policy,* 8 Tax L. Rev. 241, 248.

to state action requires, whenever possible, that a State not be thwarted in its policy. We will not presume that the Congress, in allowing deductions for income tax purposes, intended to encourage a business enterprise to violate the declared policy of a State. To allow the deduction sought here would but encourage continued violations of state law by increasing the odds in favor of noncompliance. This could only tend to destroy the effectiveness of the State's maximum weight laws.

This is not to say that the rule as to frustration of sharply defined national or state policies is to be viewed or applied in any absolute sense. "It has never been thought . . . that the mere fact that an expenditure bears a remote relation to an illegal act makes it nondeductible." Commissioner v. Heininger, *supra,* at 474. Although each case must turn on its own facts, the test of nondeductibility always is the severity and immediacy of the frustration resulting from allowance of the deduction. The flexibility of such a standard is necessary if we are to accommodate both the congressional intent to tax only net income, and the presumption against congressional intent to encourage violation of declared public policy.

Certainly the frustration of state policy is most complete and direct when the expenditure for which deduction is sought is itself prohibited by statute. If the expenditure is not itself an illegal act, but rather the payment of a penalty imposed by the State because of such an act, as in the present case, the frustration attendant upon deduction would be only slightly less remote, and would clearly fall within the line of disallowance. Deduction of fines and penalties uniformly has been held to frustrate state policy in severe and direct fashion by reducing the "sting" of the penalty prescribed by the state legislature.

There is no merit to petitioner's argument that the fines imposed here were not penalties at all, but merely a revenue toll. It is true that the Pennsylvania statute provides for purchase of a single-trip permit by an overweighted trucker; that its provision for forcing removal of the excess weight at the discretion of the police authorities apparently was never enforced; and that the fines were devoted by statute to road repair within the municipality or township where the trucker was apprehended. Moreover, the Pennsylvania statute was amended in 1955, raising the maximum weight restriction to 60,000 pounds, making mandatory the removal of the excess, and graduating the amount of the fine by the number of pounds that the truck was overweight. These considerations, however, do not change the fact that the truckers were fined by the State as a penal measure when and if they were apprehended by the police.

Finally, petitioner contends that deduction of the fines at least for the innocent violations will not frustrate state policy. But since the maximum weight statutes make no distinction between innocent and willful violators, state policy is as much thwarted in the one instance as in the other. . . .

Affirmed.

Notes and Questions

1. *Is it a fine or a toll?* Is the Court correct in thinking that allowance of a deduction in this case would frustrate state policy? Note that the fines are not predicated on any moral opprobrium that is attached to driving an overweight truck. Rather, it is that overweight trucks cause measurable physical damages, primarily in the form of greater road repair and

maintenance costs. A well-designed fine would approximate the damage done to the roads, divided by the probability of detection. This approach will both appropriately compensate the state for damage done by overweight trucks and produce economically efficient behavior by trucking companies.

For example, if the damage done by an overweight truck is $5 per trip, and the probability of detecting overweight trucks on any representative trip is 1 out of 100, the appropriate fine would be $5 divided by .01, or $500. The expected value of the fine on any given trip would then be $5 — 1/100th of $500 — which is precisely equal to the damage done. In a tax-free world, if the cost to the trucking company of keeping its trucks under the maximum weight is less than $5 per trip, it will choose to comply with the weight limits. If the cost is greater than $5, it will run its trucks overweight and take its chances. Note that this is not only a descriptive statement of what companies will predictably do, but a prescriptive statement of what they *should* do: If their private costs of compliance with the regulatory statute exceed the public benefit of the compliance with the statute, noncompliance is the efficient course for both the company and the economy as a whole. And the fine ensures that the public will be appropriately compensated for the damages it incurs due to overweight trucks.

To illustrate, consider two companies, each of which expects to make 1,000 trips through the state in any particular year. Assume Company A would incur a cost of $3,000 (or $3 per trip) to ensure that its trucks met the weight requirements. It would incur expected fines of $5,000 (or $5 per trip) if it routinely fails to comply. (It would expect to be detected as overweight ten times, or 1/100th of the 1,000 trips it will make, and would pay a fine of $500 for each violation.) The costs of compliance are less than the costs of noncompliance, so compliance prevails.

In contrast, Company B (more like Tank Truck Rentals) would incur compliance costs of $7 per trip. For B, compliance ($7,000) is more costly than noncompliance ($5,000), so noncompliance would be predicted. This result is both fair and efficient. The state is no worse off, having been compensated for $5,000 of damage to its roads by the payment of $5,000. And the company has saved the $2,000 by which compliance costs would have exceeded the costs of paying the fines.

If both compliance costs and fines are deductible, this state of affairs would be preserved in the face of an income tax. Assume, for example, that a 40 percent tax is imposed on net income. The costs of compliance and noncompliance are now just 60 percent of the gross cost, because of the value of the deduction. So Company A faces a trade-off between $1,800 of after-tax compliance costs ($3,000 × .6) and $3,000 of after-tax noncompliance costs ($5,000 × .6). Company B faces after-tax compliance costs of $4,200 ($7,000 × .6) and after-tax costs of noncompliance of $3,000 ($5,000 × .6). Both companies will make the same choices that they would make in a tax-free state, the efficient outcome is preserved, and the state is still fully compensated for the damage caused by Company B. Public policy is in no way frustrated.

But if compliance costs are deductible, and noncompliance costs are not, then the calculus shifts for Company B. It now faces costs of noncompliance of $5,000 (the gross cost undiminished by any deduction) and costs of compliance of only $4,200. It will presumably now comply, even though that is an inefficient result.[18] This would be a result that would comport with public policy only if that policy were to prevent overweight trucks at any and all costs. But if all the state seeks is compensation for damage done to its roads, then allowing the deduction does nothing to frustrate the achievement of that goal.

2. *The PPUC view of the problem.* That fines for overweight vehicles resembled user fees is buttressed by statements in the record of this case to the effect that the Pennsylvania Public Utility Commission treated fines as operating expenses under its accounting rules for rate-setting purposes. And, in this case, the amount of the fine was very small relative to the revenue of the company, and presumably small compared to the cost of complying with the weight limits. The fine, in other words, was unlikely to affect behavior. Unfavorable tax treatment of the fine added to the effect of the fine, but even at that, the impact of the nondeductible fine was likely too small to actually change the way the taxpayer did business. Should this have influenced the Court?

3. *A Supreme Court trilogy.* The Supreme Court decided a number of cases in the 1950s and 1960s involving possible public policy limitations on the deductibility of business expenses. The first of these, Lilly v. Commissioner, 343 U.S. 90 (1952), involved an optical company that routinely paid fees to doctors who referred patients to the company to be outfitted with corrective lenses. Writing for a unanimous Court, Justice Burton allowed the deductions, and noted: "There is no statement in the [IRC] . . . prohibiting the deduction of ordinary and necessary business expenses on the ground that they violate public policy" (at 94).

In Commissioner v. Sullivan, 356 U.S. 27 (1958), decided the same day as *Tank Truck Rentals*, the Court considered whether expenses of compensating employees, and renting office space, could be deducted by a Chicago bookie, despite the illegal nature of his business. Justice Douglas, noting that if the deductions were disallowed it would "come close to making this type of business taxable on its gross receipts, while all other businesses are taxable on the basis of their net income" (at 29), said that "if that choice is to be made, Congress should do it" (*id.*).

In Commissioner v. Tellier, 383 U.S. 687 (1966), a follow-up of sorts to *Heininger,* the Court again considered the legal expenses of an unsuccessful defendant, this time one who was charged with violations of the federal

---

18. It is interesting to note who bears the cost of this inefficiency in the short run. The state bears no costs, because there is neither road damage nor compensation. But Company *B* bears some costs — the after-tax costs of compliance, $4,200, are greater by $1,200 than the after-tax costs of noncompliance would have been, had those costs been deductible. The other $800 of efficiency loss is actually borne by the federal government. It has allowed a deduction of $7,000 of compliance costs against a 40 percent tax, at a cost of $2,800; under the more efficient rule, a deduction of $5,000 of noncompliance costs would have been permitted instead, at a cost to the government of only $2,000. As usual, the longer-run distribution of costs and benefits is more complex, depending as it does on the adjustments the various actors make to the *Tank Truck* rule. Are companies with high compliance costs forced to withdraw from the market? Or are they able to pass on much of the burden of the extra costs to their customers? One cannot say in general. One can only say that someone will bear the costs of an inefficiency that is not a necessary feature of the tax rules.

securities laws. The Court allowed the deductions, relying on *Heininger* (and, to a lesser degree, on *Lilly* and *Sullivan*), affirming that the deductibility of legal expenses involved in defending business activities, even if unsuccessful, survived the discovery by the courts of public policy limitations in the years between *Heininger* and *Tellier*.

4. *A congressional sequel.* Congress finally stepped in to resolve some of the questions left open by this series of cases in 1969. To disallow deductions of certain bribes and kickbacks, it amended §162(c) (which had been added to the Code in 1958 to prohibit deductions of bribes paid to officials of foreign governments). Section 162(c)(1) now prohibits deduction of illegal bribes or kickbacks to officials or employees of any governmental unit, agency, or instrumentality; if the payment is to an employee or official of a foreign government, it is nondeductible if it violates the Foreign Corrupt Practices Act of 1977. Section 162(c)(2) bars deduction of payments to any other persons if the payment constitutes an illegal bribe or kickback; but if the payment violates only state law, it will be nondeductible only if that law is generally enforced. Section 162(c)(3), added in 1971, denies deductions for kickbacks, rebates, and bribes in connection with the Medicare and Medicaid programs, whether or not the payments are illegal. (Payments for referral of patients are specifically made nondeductible by the language of this paragraph.)

The 1969 Act also added subsection (f), which denies deduction of fines "or similar penalties" paid to a government for a violation of law, and subsection (g), which disallows deductions for two-thirds of any judgments or settlements of private antitrust suits that follow criminal convictions of violations of antitrust laws.

The specific disallowance of *illegal* bribes and kickbacks in paragraphs (c)(1) and (2), coupled with language in the legislative history suggesting that the rules were intended to be comprehensive,[19] would seem to indicate that other payments, such as legal bribes, would be deductible. But, while the 1969 amendments lent greater clarity to a muddy set of doctrines, they didn't remove the particulates altogether.

An interesting pair of cases from the 1980s illustrates some of the continuing difficulties. Both cases involved bribes paid to the same individual, a vice president of a general contractor, by two different subcontractors, as a condition of continuing work on a shopping center in Ohio. Apparently, the bribes in question did not violate Ohio law, which, at least at the time, must have taken a rather tolerant view of buying business in this way. In Raymond Bertolini Trucking Co. v. Commissioner, 736 F.2d 1120 (6th Cir. 1984), the circuit court held that the payments were indeed deductible. But about a year later, a different panel of the same court held, in Car-Ron Asphalt Paving Co., Inc. v. Commissioner, 758 F.2d 1132 (6th Cir. 1985), that the payments were not deductible. The latter panel was of course aware of the earlier decision, but explained the earlier decision as being, in effect, a product of defective pleading: In *Bertolini,* the IRS had

19. The Senate report said that "public policy, in other circumstances, generally is not sufficiently clearly defined to justify the disallowance of deductions." S. Rep. No. 552, 91st Cong., 1st Sess., *reprinted in* 1969-3 C.B. 423, 597.

conceded that the payments in question were "necessary," questioning instead whether they were "ordinary." The *Bertolini* panel said that ordinary meant only that the payments needed to be current expenses, not capital investments, and found that the payments in question were indeed current items. (736 F.2d at 1123.) In *Car-Ron,* the IRS insisted that the payments were not "necessary," persuaded the Tax Court of that point, and won affirmance by the Sixth Circuit on grounds that this was a finding of fact, which could not be reversed because it was not clearly erroneous. The Tax Court and Sixth Circuit opinions avoided direct interpretation of §162(c) by finding that the deductions were not justified in the first place under §162(a), because of an absence of evidence that kickbacks of this sort were commonplace in the construction industry in Ohio at that time.

A sharp dissent in *Car-Ron* noted that the Tax Court in that case had also found that the contract, worth about $1 million to the taxpayer, would not have been awarded without the payment of bribes costing less than 10 percent of this amount, and that that finding was plainly inconsistent with the finding that the payments were not necessary. (758 F.2d at 1135.) But the pair of cases illustrates the continued willingness of the IRS to challenge — sometimes successfully — deductions in this area, by using the general "ordinary and necessary" standard, despite the enactment of the rules in §162(c) that appear to permit deduction of legal bribes and kickbacks.

CALIFORNIANS HELPING TO ALLEVIATE MEDICAL PROBLEMS, INC. v. COMMISSIONER

128 T.C. 173 (2007)

LARO, Judge: [W]e decide whether section 280E precludes petitioner from deducting the ordinary and necessary expenses attributable to its provision of medical marijuana pursuant to the California Compassionate Use Act of 1996, codified at Cal. Health & Safety Code sec. 11362.5 (West Supp. 2007). We hold that those deductions are precluded. We also decide whether section 280E precludes petitioner from deducting the ordinary and necessary expenses attributable to its provision of counseling and other caregiving services (collectively, caregiving services). We hold that those deductions are not precluded.

FINDINGS OF FACT

. . . Petitioner was organized on December 24, 1996, pursuant to the California Nonprofit Public Benefit Corporation Law, Cal. Corp. Code secs. 5110-6910. (West 1990). Its articles of incorporation stated that it "is organized and operated exclusively for charitable, educational and scientific purposes" and "The property of this corporation is irrevocably dedicated to charitable purposes." Petitioner did not have Federal tax-exempt status, and it operated as an approximately break-even (i.e., the amount of its income approximated the amount of its expenses) community center for members with debilitating diseases. Approximately 47 percent of petitioner's members suffered from Acquired Immune Deficiency Syndrome (AIDS); the remainder suffered from cancer, multiple sclerosis, and other serious illnesses. Before joining petitioner, petitioner's executive director had 13 years of experience in health services as a coordinator of a statewide program that trained outreach workers in AIDS prevention work.

Petitioner operated with a dual purpose. Its primary purpose was to provide caregiving services to its members. Its secondary purpose was to provide its members with medical marijuana pursuant to the California Compassionate Use Act of 1996 and to instruct those individuals on how to use medical marijuana to benefit their health. Petitioner required that each member have a doctor's letter recommending marijuana as part of his or her therapy and an unexpired photo identification card from the California Department of Public Health verifying the authenticity of the doctor's letter. Petitioner required that its members not resell or redistribute the medical marijuana received from petitioner, and petitioner considered any violation of this requirement to be grounds to expel the violator from membership in petitioner's organization.

Each of petitioner's members paid petitioner a membership fee in consideration for the right to receive caregiving services and medical marijuana from petitioner. Petitioner's caregiving services were extensive. First, petitioner's staff held various weekly or biweekly support group sessions that could be attended only by petitioner's members. The "wellness group" discussed healing techniques and occasionally hosted a guest speaker; the HIV/AIDS group addressed issues of practical and emotional support; the women's group focused on women-specific issues in medical struggles; the "Phoenix" group helped elderly patients with lifelong addiction problems; the "Force" group focused on spiritual and emotional development. Second, petitioner provided its low-income members with daily lunches consisting of salads, fruit, water, soda, and hot food. Petitioner also made available to its members hygiene supplies such as toothbrushes, toothpaste, feminine hygiene products, combs, and bottles of bleach. Third, petitioner allowed its members to consult one-on-one with a counselor about benefits, health, housing, safety, and legal issues. . . .

Petitioner paid for the services it provided to its members by charging a membership fee that covered, and in the judgment of petitioner's management approximated, both the cost of petitioner's caregiving services and the cost of the medical marijuana that petitioner supplied to its members. Petitioner notified its members that the membership fee covered both of these costs, and petitioner charged its members no additional fee. Members received from petitioner a set amount of medical marijuana; they were not entitled to unlimited supplies. . . .

In a notice of deficiency mailed to petitioner on August 4, 2005, respondent disallowed all of petitioner's deductions and costs of goods sold, determining that those items were "Expenditures in Connection with the Illegal Sale of Drugs" within the meaning of section 280E. Respondent has since conceded this determination except to the extent that it relates to the "Total deductions" of $212,958.[20] Respondent has also conceded that the expenses underlying the $212,958 of total deductions are substantiated. The "Total deductions" were ordinary, necessary, and reasonable expenses petitioner incurred in running its operations during the subject year. . . .

20. In other words, respondent concedes that the disallowance of sec. 280E does not apply to costs of goods sold, a concession that is consistent with the caselaw on that subject and the legislative history underlying sec. 280E. See Peyton v. Comm'r, T.C. Memo 2003-146; Franklin v. Commissioner, T.C. Memo. 1993-184; Vasta v. Commissioner, T.C. Memo. 1989-531; see also S. Rept. 97-494 (Vol. 1), at 309 (1982).

OPINION

The parties agree that during the subject year petitioner had at least one trade or business for purposes of section 280E. According to respondent, petitioner had a single trade or business of trafficking in medical marijuana. Petitioner argues that it engaged in two trades or businesses. Petitioner asserts that its primary trade or business was the provision of caregiving services. Petitioner asserts that its secondary trade or business was the supplying of medical marijuana to its members. As to its trades or businesses, petitioner argues, the deductions for those trades or businesses are not precluded by section 280E in that the trades or businesses did not involve "trafficking" in a controlled substance. Respondent argues that section 280E precludes petitioner from benefiting from any of its deductions. Accrual method taxpayers such as petitioner may generally deduct the ordinary and necessary expenses incurred in carrying on a trade or business. See sec. 162(a). Items specified in section 162(a) are allowed as deductions, subject to exceptions listed in section 261. See sec. 161. Section 261 provides that "no deduction shall in any case be allowed in respect of the items specified in this part." The phrase "this part" refers to part IX of subchapter B of chapter 1, entitled "Items Not Deductible." "Expenditures in Connection With the Illegal Sale of Drugs" is an item specified in part IX. Section 280E provides:

> No deduction or credit shall be allowed for any amount paid or incurred during the taxable year in carrying on any trade or business if such trade or business (or the activities which comprise such trade or business) consists of trafficking in controlled substances (within the meaning of schedule I and II of the Controlled Substances Act) which is prohibited by Federal law or the law of any State in which such trade or business is conducted.

In the context of section 280E, marijuana is a schedule I controlled substance. . . . Such is so even when the marijuana is medical marijuana recommended by a physician as appropriate to benefit the health of the user. See United States v. Oakland Cannabis Buyers' Coop., 532 U.S. 483 (2001). Respondent argues that petitioner, because it trafficked in a controlled substance, is not permitted by section 280E to deduct any of its expenses. We disagree. Our analysis begins with the text of the statute, which we must apply in accordance with its ordinary, everyday usage. . . .

Congress enacted section 280E as a direct reaction to the outcome of a case in which this Court allowed a taxpayer to deduct expenses incurred in an illegal drug trade. See S. Rept. 97-494 (Vol. 1), at 309 (1982). In that case, Edmondson v. Commissioner, T.C. Memo. 1981-623, the Court found that the taxpayer was self-employed in a trade or business of selling amphetamines, cocaine, and marijuana. The Court allowed the taxpayer to deduct his business expenses because they "were made in connection with . . . [the taxpayer's] trade or business and were both ordinary and necessary." Id. In discussing the case in the context of the then-current law, the Senate Finance Committee stated in its report:

> Ordinary and necessary trade or business expenses are generally deductible in computing taxable income. A recent U.S. Tax Court case allowed deductions for telephone, auto, and rental expense incurred in the illegal drug trade. In that case, the Internal Revenue Service challenged the amount of the taxpayer's deduction for cost of goods (illegal

drugs) sold, but did not challenge the principle that such amounts were deductible. On public policy grounds, the Code makes certain otherwise ordinary and necessary expenses incurred in a trade or business nondeductible in computing taxable income. These nondeductible expenses include fines, illegal bribes and kickbacks, and certain other illegal payments. [S. Rept. 97-494 (Vol. 1), supra at 309.]

The report then expressed the following reasons the committee intended to change the law:

There is a sharply defined public policy against drug dealing. To allow drug dealers the benefit of business expense deductions at the same time that the U.S. and its citizens are losing billions of dollars per year to such persons is not compelled by the fact that such deductions are allowed to other, legal, enterprises. Such deductions must be disallowed on public policy grounds. [Id.]

The report explained that the enactment of section 280E has the following effect:

All deductions and credits for amounts paid or incurred in the illegal trafficking in drugs listed in the Controlled Substances Act are disallowed. To preclude possible challenges on constitutional grounds, the adjustment to gross receipts with respect to effective costs of goods sold is not affected by this provision of the bill. [Id.]

Section 280E and its legislative history express a congressional intent to disallow deductions attributable to a trade or business of trafficking in controlled substances. They do not express an intent to deny the deduction of all of a taxpayer's business expenses simply because the taxpayer was involved in trafficking in a controlled substance. We hold that section 280E does not preclude petitioner from deducting expenses attributable to a trade or business other than that of illegal trafficking in controlled substances simply because petitioner also is involved in the trafficking in a controlled substance.

Petitioner argues that its supplying of medical marijuana to its members was not "trafficking" within the meaning of section 280E. We disagree. We define and apply the gerund "trafficking" by reference to the verb "traffic," which as relevant herein denotes "to engage in commercial activity: buy and sell regularly." Webster's Third New International Dictionary 2423 (2002). Petitioner's supplying of medical marijuana to its members is within that definition in that petitioner regularly bought and sold the marijuana, such sales occurring when petitioner distributed the medical marijuana to its members in exchange for part of their membership fees. Accord United States v. Oakland Cannabis Buyers' Coop., supra at 489.

We now turn to analyze whether petitioner's furnishing of its caregiving services is a trade or business that is separate from its trade or business of providing medical marijuana. . . .

We do not believe it to have been artificial or unreasonable for petitioner to have characterized as separate activities its provision of caregiving services and its provision of medical marijuana. Petitioner was regularly and extensively involved in the provision of caregiving services, and those services are substantially different from petitioner's provision of medical marijuana. By conducting its recurring discussion groups, regularly distributing food and hygiene supplies, advertising and making available the services of personal counselors, coordinating social events and field trips, hosting educational classes, and providing other social services, petitioner's caregiving business stood on its own, separate and apart from petitioner's provision of medical marijuana. On the basis of all of the facts and circumstances of this case, we hold that petitioner's provision of caregiving services was a trade or business separate and apart from its provision of medical marijuana. . . .

Given petitioner's separate trades or businesses, we are required to apportion its overall expenses accordingly. Respondent argues that "petitioner failed to justify any particular allocation and failed to present evidence as to how . . . [petitioner's expenses] should be allocated between marijuana trafficking and other activities." We disagree. Respondent concedes that many of petitioner's activities are legal and unrelated to petitioner's provision of medical marijuana. The evidence at hand permits an allocation of expenses to those activities. Although the record may not lend itself to a perfect allocation with pinpoint accuracy, the record permits us with sufficient confidence to allocate petitioner's expenses between its two trades or businesses on the basis of the number of petitioner's employees and the portion of its facilities devoted to each business. Accordingly, in a manner that is most consistent with petitioner's breakdown of the disputed expenses, we allocate to petitioner's caregiving services 18/25 of the expenses for salaries, wages, payroll taxes, employee benefits, employee development training, meals and entertainment, and parking and tolls (18 of petitioner's 25 employees did not work directly in petitioner's provision of medical marijuana), all expenses incurred in renting facilities at the church (petitioner did not use the church to any extent to provide medical marijuana), all expenses incurred for "truck and auto" and "laundry and cleaning" (those expenses did not relate to any extent to petitioner's provision of medical marijuana), and 9/10 of the remaining expenses (90 percent of the square footage of petitioner's main facility was not used in petitioner's provision of medical marijuana).[21] . . .

Notes and Questions

1. *A public policy double whammy?* Why do you suppose the petitioner did not have tax-exempt status under §501(c)(3)? Hint: Review part A.1.d of the cell on tax-exempt organizations in Chapter 4.
2. *What about state law?* The petitioner's medical marijuana activity was permissible under California law (the California Compassionate Use Act of 1996)—hence the petitioner's ability to qualify as a charity under the California Nonprofit Public Benefit Corporation Law. Why, then, did the petitioner run afoul of §280E?
3. *One business or two?* Are you persuaded by the Tax Court's analysis of why supplying medical marijuana was a separate business from everything else done by petitioner? Why wasn't providing medical marijuana simply one aspect of the petitioner's single business of providing a wide range of caregiving services? Might the Tax Court's (unstated) view of the policy merits of §280E, as applied to the petitioner, have something to do with the court's two-business conclusion?

21. While we apportion most of the $212,958 in "Total deductions" to petitioner's caregiving services, we note that the costs of petitioner's medical marijuana business included the $203,661 in labor and $43,783 in other costs respondent conceded to have been properly reported on petitioner's tax return as attributable to cost of goods sold in the medical marijuana business.

4. *Costs of goods sold and §280E.* Although it seems as if costs of goods sold (i.e., inventory costs) should be deductible as business expenses under §162, the regulations under §61 take the position that such costs are deductible from gross receipts in arriving at gross income (rather than deductible from gross income in arriving at taxable income): "In a manufacturing, merchandising, or mining business, 'gross income' means the total sales, less the costs of goods sold. . . ." Treas. Reg. §1.61-3(a). Given this view of inventory costs, Congress was concerned that denying costs of goods sold allowances to drug traffickers might be unconstitutional. The resulting tax on drug dealers might be a gross receipts tax rather than an income tax, and such a tax might be unconstitutional as an unapportioned direct tax (prohibited by the direct tax clauses of the original Constitution, and not within the scope of the Sixteenth Amendment's authorization of an unapportioned *income* tax).[22] Accordingly, Congress indicated in the legislative history of §280E that the provision does not disallow deductions for drug traffickers' costs of goods sold, and both the IRS and the Tax Court have interpreted §280E in accordance with the legislative history. This is a major limitation on the impact of §280E, because the income tax inventory accounting rules define costs of goods sold quite broadly. For example, wages paid to employees to acquire, handle, and store purchased inventory are included in costs of goods sold, as are wages paid to employees to produce self-created inventory. It is not clear from the opinion whether the petitioner's marijuana inventory was purchased or self-created, but the opinion does indicate that a very substantial portion of the petitioner's labor costs ($203,661) was properly allocable to costs of goods sold, and thus not subject to disallowance by §280E.

5. *Other public policy disallowances and costs of goods sold.* Suppose the IRS is asserting that one of the public policy disallowance rules of §162 — the §162(c) rules governing illegal bribes and kickbacks, the §162(f) rules governing fines and penalties, or the §162(g) rules governing antitrust treble damages — applies to a particular taxpayer. If the taxpayer can persuade a court that the expenditures in question are properly classified as part of the costs of goods sold, rather than as business expenses, will the taxpayer thereby avoid the public policy restrictions of §162? The last sentence of §263A(a) indicates this strategy will not succeed: "Any cost which . . . could not be taken into account in computing taxable income for any taxable year shall not be treated as a[n inventory] cost described in this paragraph." Because of this sentence, the public policy disallowances for bribes, kickbacks, fines, penalties, and treble damages apply regardless of whether the expenditures are analyzed as business expenses or as inventory costs. If Congress is so concerned about the possible unconstitutionality of applying §280E to costs of goods sold, why is it not equally troubled by the possible unconstitutionality of the last sentence of §263A(a)?

6. *Who really won this case?* The petitioner lost on the basic issue of whether it was a drug trafficker subject to §280E. Notice, however, that the Court allowed the petitioner to claim about three-quarters of its "total deductions" of $212,958 (by reason of the allocation of those expenses to the caregiving

---

22. For more on the direct tax clauses and the Sixteenth Amendment, see section A.3 of Chapter 3.

business rather than the marijuana business) and all of the $247,444 in labor and other costs attributable to costs of goods sold in the marijuana business. Out of slightly more than $460,000 of expenditures, the Tax Court disallowed only a little more than $50,000.

7. *What about more typical drug traffickers?* Californians Helping to Alleviate Medical Problems made no effort (as far as one can tell from the opinion) to hide its activities from the IRS. That is not true, of course, of the average dealer in illegal drugs. Presumably Congress did not expect §280E to produce significant tax revenues from drug kingpins who dutifully file Forms 1040 and pay tax on their gross income (without claiming any business expense deductions, in obedience to §280E). The main consequence of the provision is to make it easier for the government to prosecute drug dealers for tax evasion, by making it harder for dealers to claim that they had no taxable income after taking their expenses into account. Section 280E would be considerably more effective in this respect, however, if it applied to inventory costs as well as to deductions under §162.

D.   LOBBYING EXPENSES

Expenses incurred to influence legislation, or to help elect officials who may be sympathetic to the needs of particular industries, may seem to business executives to be money well spent. We do not ordinarily think of such payments as bribes, and they are in any event completely legal, so long as they are within the rather liberal rules regulating campaign finance and lobbying. Even so, these expenses have long been viewed unfavorably as deductible business expenses.

As early as 1918, the Treasury issued regulations disallowing lobbying and campaign contributions as business expenses, on the grounds that they weren't "ordinary and necessary" expenses of running a business — this despite the fact that they would often seem to be "appropriate and helpful" in advancing the interests of the business, and seem as well to be ordinary, both in the sense of being fairly common, and in terms of being current expenses rather than capital investments.[23]

The IRS was generally successful in sustaining its position, most notably in Textile Mills Security Corp. v. Commissioner, 314 U.S. 326 (1941), where the Court specifically found the regulations barring deduction of lobbying expenses to be a reasonable interpretation of the language of §162(a), and Cammarano v. United States, 358 U.S. 498 (1959), where the Court extended this finding to disallow the expenses of a grassroots lobbying campaign undertaken by retailers intended to influence public opinion prior to votes on state ballot initiatives that would have affected the sale of alcoholic beverages.

Shortly after *Cammarano*, Congress intervened by adding subsection (e) to §162, which permitted deduction of lobbying expenses with respect to issues "of direct interest" to the taxpayer. However, after several amendments over the following 30

---

23. A case could be made that some part of lobbying and campaign contribution expenses, if recognized by the tax system at all, are of a capital nature. For example, if a corporation makes a contribution to a candidate (or, more likely, both candidates) for a Senate seat that is contested only every six years, the cost should arguably be spread over the six years, rather than deducted in the year incurred.

years, Congress rewrote §162(e) in 1993 to effectively prohibit the deduction of lobbying expenses in virtually all cases, causing the rules to revert to essentially the form they had taken under the pre-1962 regulations. But now the IRS is in the stronger position of having a clear prohibition of the deduction of these expenses in the statute, rather than having to rely on general interpretations of "ordinary and necessary." The following case illustrates the usefulness to the government of having this extra arrow in its quiver.

GEARY v. COMMISSIONER

235 F.3d 1207 (9th Cir. 2000)

O'SCANNLAIN, Circuit Judge: We must decide whether a taxpayer is entitled to an income tax deduction for expenses incurred to place a proposition affecting his working conditions on a local ballot.

I

Robert Geary, a veteran officer of the San Francisco Police Department, appeals a judgment from the Tax Court upholding the Commissioner's determination of a deficiency in his income tax for the 1993 tax year and an assessment of an accuracy-related penalty. The Tax Court disallowed Geary's claimed deduction of $9,711.49 in purported "business expenses" incurred under the following circumstances.

In response to a 1992 San Francisco Police Department policy to encourage creative community policing strategies, Geary began patrolling his beat with a ventriloquist's dummy, whom he named Officer Brendan O'Smarty ("the dummy" or "Officer O'Smarty"). Geary patrolled San Francisco's ethnically diverse North Beach neighborhood and used the dummy to assist him in breaking down language and cultural barriers with neighborhood residents. Geary's unusual approach to community policing attracted national and international media attention, from Turkish television coverage to the front page of the *New York Times*. Geary realized income as a result of this media attention, Geary signed an option contract with Golden Door Productions to develop a story concept for a film and received over $14,000 when his concept was sold to Interscope Communications. Geary also earned income as a hand model.

When Geary's supervisors became aware of his community policing technique, they told him to "get rid of the puppet because it makes the department look stupid." Geary protested and insisted on meeting with department officials about Officer O'Smarty. At the meeting, it was decided that Geary would need prior written departmental approval before taking Officer O'Smarty on future patrols. The plight of Officer O'Smarty stirred the San Francisco Board of Supervisors to pass a resolution urging the mayor to instruct the chief of police to allow Geary to continue patrolling with the dummy. The mayor resisted the Board's entreaty and the resolution was ignored.

At this point, it occurred to Geary that he should let the San Francisco voters decide whether he should be permitted to use the dummy as he saw fit. He formed the Committee to Save Puppet Officer Brendan O'Smarty and circulated a petition to place the issue before the voters. As required by California law, the San Francisco City Attorney certified that the ballot title appearing on the petition was "presented as a true and impartial statement of the proposed measure." The proposed text of the declaration of policy as it appeared on the petition recited that the measure would allow Geary to decide when to team up with Officer O'Smarty in order "to develop greater trust between the community and the Police Department, improve communications between the department and the general public, and help remove barriers which hamper the goals of the department."

Geary secured sufficient signatures to place the measure on the ballot as "Proposition BB" and the public approved the proposition the following November. Geary incurred $11,465 in petition circulation and promotion expenses and deducted this amount from his 1993 income taxes as Schedule C advertising expenses. . . .

The IRS disallowed Geary's entire Schedule C deduction, issued a notice of deficiency in the amount of $3,499, and assessed an accuracy-related penalty under §6662 (a) and (b)(1) in the amount of $700. Geary petitioned for a redetermination of the deficiency and penalty in Tax Court. He contended that these expenses were "ordinary and necessary expenses" of his business, or in the alternative, unreimbursed employee business expenses, and hence deductible under §162(a). Geary was the sole witness to testify at trial. On April 5, 1999, the Tax Court entered judgment for the Commissioner, holding that such expenses were non-deductible under §162(e)(2)(B), which disallows business deductions for expenses incurred "in connection with any attempt to influence the general public, or segments thereof, with respect to elections, legislative matters, or referendums." The court rejected Geary's contention that his primary purpose in placing the measure on the ballot was to inform the voters of his creative community policing efforts and to let them decide whether he should continue to patrol with Officer O'Smarty. The court concluded that "taken as a whole, petitioner's actions show a clear intent to influence the general public." The court also determined that Geary was subject to an accuracy-related penalty under §6662(b)(1) because he negligently claimed a deduction for such expenses.

On appeal, Geary claims that the Tax Court erred in characterizing his effort to place his puppet proposition on the ballot as an attempt to influence the public. He insists that he merely wished to inform the voters in neutral terms about the issue and let them decide for themselves. Geary has conceded that $1,753.51 of his total claimed advertising deduction, not related to petition circulation or signature collection, was incurred in an attempt to influence the public. Thus, only the $9,711.49 in petition-related expenses are at issue in this appeal.

II

Since 1918, regulations promulgated by the Treasury have provided that expenses incurred for the promotion or defeat of legislation are not deductible as business expenses. *See* Cammarano v. United States, 358 U.S. 498, 502-503 (1959). In *Cammarano*, the Supreme Court held that these regulations applied equally to referenda; hence, expenses incurred by liquor retailers and distributors in an effort to encourage voters to vote against a state prohibition initiative were not deductible as ordinary and necessary business expenses. *Id.* at 505-512. In the Revenue Act of 1962, Congress codified this portion of the *Cammarano* decision, adding §162 (e) to the Internal Revenue Code. Section 162(e)(2)(B) provided that there would be no deduction for "any amount paid or incurred . . . in connection with any attempt to influence the general public, or segments thereof, with respect to elections, legislative matters, or referendums." §162(e)(2)(B).[24]

Geary contends that his petition circulation and signature collection expenses were not incurred in an attempt to "influence the public" under §162(e)(2)(B). He insists that his efforts to place Proposition BB on the ballot were borne solely from a desire to inform the public about the police puppet issue and to let the voters decide whether he should continue to patrol with Officer O'Smarty. He relies heavily on the fact that the San Francisco City Attorney certified that the ballot title appearing on the ballot petition was a "true and impartial statement of the purpose of the proposed measure." He also insists that the signature collectors did not tell anyone to vote for or against the measure.

We disagree. The plain language of §162(e)(2)(B) renders non-deductible "*any* amount paid or incurred . . . *in connection with* any attempt to influence the general public. . . ." §162(e)(2)(B) (emphasis added). The expenses at issue here were clearly "in connection with" Geary's attempt to influence the public with respect to the puppet proposition. The circulation of the petition and collection of signatures were necessary first steps in Geary's overall promotion of the proposition. . . .

[T]he Tax Court found that Geary incurred the petition circulation and signature collection expenses for the purpose of influencing the public. This finding is not clearly erroneous. Geary began his efforts to place Proposition BB on the ballot in response to the police department's restrictions on his use of Officer O'Smarty. He paid for the expenses at issue through his "Committee to Save Puppet Officer Brendan O'Smarty," which he formed, according to his own testimony, for the express purpose of getting the proposition passed. The petition he circulated contained the text of the proposed declaration of policy in addition to a "true and impartial" ballot title certified by the City Attorney as required by the California Election Code. After securing Proposition BB's place on the ballot, Geary incurred additional expenses to promote the measure and to ensure its passage. Thus, there can be little doubt that Geary incurred the disputed petition circulation expenses in connection with — and, in fact, as an integral part of — his overall attempt to persuade the public. . . .

In the words of Judge Learned Hand, "political agitation as such is outside the statute, however innocent the aim. . . . Controversies of that sort must be conducted without public subvention; the Treasury stands aside from them." Slee v. Commissioner, 42 F.2d 184, 185 (2d Cir. 1930). Accordingly, we reject Geary's attempt to receive "public subvention" for his campaign on behalf of Officer O'Smarty.

III

[Because of the uncertainty of the law, and the relative inexperience of the taxpayer in tax matters, the court found that Geary had taken the deduction in good faith. Accordingly, it reversed the Tax Court's finding that the accuracy-related penalties asserted by the IRS were appropriate. — EDS.]

24. This provision was meant to disallow deductions "for expenses incurred in connection with what is usually called 'grassroot' campaigns intended to develop a point of view among the public generally. . . ." Senate Report No. 87-1881, 1962 U.S.C.C.A.N. 3297, 3326.

IV

For the foregoing reasons, the judgment of the Tax Court is affirmed in part and reversed in part. No costs to either party.

Notes and Questions

1. *Announcing the decision.* One hopes that the Ninth Circuit panel enlisted the help of Lamb Chop to announce this decision from the bench; but the record is devoid of any such indication.

2. *What's the policy?* Why is it that Congress believes that lobbying expenses ought not to be deductible? If a political body might undertake actions affecting a taxpayer's business, why isn't it "appropriate and helpful" for the taxpayer to attempt to influence the outcome of the legislative deliberations? Doesn't denying the deductions ignore the important income-defining function of the §162 deduction? Aren't business taxpayers—whether corporations or individuals—entitled to petition Congress for redress of their grievances?

   In addressing these questions in the *Textile Mills* and *Cammarano* cases, the Supreme Court has emphasized that (1) §162(e), and the earlier regulations, do not deny rights to speak, but merely opportunities to claim deductions, which are not constitutionally protected; (2) the disallowance is necessary to make sure that the Treasury doesn't finance business lobbying with tax dollars; and (3) the disallowance is necessary to put all taxpayers "on the same footing" with respect to lobbying (the theory being that nonbusiness taxpayers would ordinarily have no grounds on which to deduct any expenses they might incur in lobbying). *Cammarano,* 358 U.S. at 513. Do you agree with these observations?

3. *Officer O'Smarty's short tenure.* Despite the endorsement of San Francisco voters, the shotgun marriage between Officer O'Smarty and the police department that thought he made them look stupid was not to endure. *See* Steve Rubenstein, *He's No Dummy; Ventriloquist Retiring from Police, Considering Showbiz Bow,* San Francisco Chronicle, July 11, 2000, p. A17.

E.   REASONABLE COMPENSATION

One of the small number of specific deductions allowed under §162 is the one authorized by §162(a)(1) for "a reasonable allowance for salaries or other compensation for personal services actually rendered." Curiously, the core business expense deduction language does not include the word "reasonable," though one supposes that such a limitation is always present. But it is just as well that Congress made a particular point of using that word with respect to compensation income, because the reasonableness of compensation turns out to be an important point of contention in one particular context: the tax liability of small corporations.

Why is compensation so troublesome in that context? Because the standard treatment of corporate income under the U.S. income tax is that the earnings of the corporation, after appropriate deductions, are taxable at the corporate level. That is, §11 of the IRC imposes a separate tax on the income of corporations.[25] When and to the extent that after-tax earnings of the corporation are distributed to shareholders as dividends (which are not deductible by the corporation), those individuals are taxed on that dividend income under §61. The normal tax arrangements with respect to corporations thus call for two layers of tax.

For 2003 through 2012, §§1(h)(3)(B) and (h)(11) provide that most dividend income is taxed at the same low rate as long-term capital gains (15%, for most taxpayers). This takes much of the sting out of the double taxation of dividends. Owners of closely held corporations, however, may want to avoid even this limited form of double taxation. If the officers and executives of a corporation are substantially identical with its major shareholders, a temptation may arise to distribute some of the earnings of the corporation under the label of additional compensation for services, rather than under the dividend label. If the compensation label is respected, there will be no double tax; the corporate level tax will be eliminated by the corporation's §162(a)(1) compensation deduction. From 2003 through 2012, this strategy will increase the income tax liabilities of the individuals, by substituting income taxed at ordinary rates for income taxed at capital gains rates,[26] but the strategy may nevertheless reduce the combined corporate-individual tax burden. Suppose, for example, the marginal tax rate of both the corporation and the shareholder-employee is 35 percent, and that the taxpayer's tax rate for dividends is 15 percent. If the corporation is able to distribute $100 to the shareholder-employee as compensation, the corporation will pay no tax on the $100, and the shareholder-employee will pay a tax of $35, leaving her with $65. If the distribution must be characterized as a dividend, the first consequence is that the corporation will be unable to distribute the full $100 to the shareholder-employee. Instead, the corporation must first pay a $35 tax on the $100, and it can then distribute the remaining $65. After paying a tax of $9.75 (15% of $65) on the dividend, the shareholder-employee will be left with only $55.25. The bottom line is that the 2003-2010 reduction in the dividends tax lessens the tax advantage of compensation over dividends, but in many situations a significant tax advantage for compensation remains.

Often, situations arise in which compensation is paid to close relatives of those holding the corporate purse strings — the ne'er-do-well nephew who is given a six-figure salary and a lofty but empty title like "Vice-President for Corporate Development." In such cases, what may be involved is not only a constructive dividend,

---

25. Subchapter S of the IRC, §§1361 et seq., allows certain small corporations to elect "pass-through" treatment of their earnings. (Those not electing, or not eligible to elect, are subject to the rules of subchapter C, §§301 et seq.) Under the subchapter S provisions, the corporation's income is not taxable at the corporate level, but is rather divided among the shareholders in proportion to their holdings, and taxed to them as individuals. In 2003, almost 62 percent of all corporations were subchapter S corporations; however, they collectively accounted for less than 23 percent of all business receipts of corporations in that year. Kelly Luttrell, Patrice Treubert & Michael Parisi, "Integrated Business Data," 2003, 26(2) *SOI Bulletin* 47, 50, fig. B (2006).

26. Compare the 15 percent top rate on dividends with the 35 percent top rate on compensation for services. At the moment, there is also a payroll tax disadvantage to characterizing the distributions as compensation rather than as dividends. Compensation income — no matter how large — is subject to the Medicare portion of the payroll tax, currently imposing rates of 1.45 percent on both employer and employee, for a combined rate of 2.9 percent. The combined rate for high income taxpayers is scheduled to rise to 3.8 percent in 2013. However, a new Medicare-financing tax on the *investment* income (including dividends) of high income taxpayers is also scheduled to be introduced in 2013, at a rate of 3.8 percent. Thus, after 2012, the Medicare tax will be imposed at the rate of 3.8 percent on both the compensation income and the dividends of high income taxpayers.

but possibly a gift that should be subject to wealth transfer taxes. In cases where it considers this appropriate, the IRS will suggest that the purported compensation be recharacterized in precisely those terms.

The case law is crowded with these so-called reasonable compensation cases. The following offers a lucid, if somewhat one-sided, view of the stakes, the guiding principles, and the difficulties the IRS often has in making its case.

EXACTO SPRING CORP. v. COMMISSIONER
196 F.3d 833 (7th Cir. 1999)

POSNER, Chief Judge: This appeal from a judgment by the Tax Court requires us to interpret and apply section 162(a)(1), which allows a business to deduct from its income its "ordinary and necessary" business expenses, including a "reasonable allowance for salaries or other compensation for personal services actually rendered." In 1993 and 1994, Exacto Spring Corporation, a closely held corporation engaged in the manufacture of precision springs, paid its cofounder, chief executive, and principal owner, William Heitz, $1.3 and $1.0 million, respectively, in salary. The Internal Revenue Service thought this amount excessive, that Heitz should not have been paid more than $381,000 in 1993 or $400,000 in 1994, with the difference added to the corporation's income, and it assessed a deficiency accordingly, which Exacto challenged in the Tax Court. That court found that the maximum reasonable compensation for Heitz would have been $900,000 in the earlier year and $700,000 in the later one — figures roughly midway between his actual compensation and the IRS's determination — and Exacto has appealed.

In reaching its conclusion, the Tax Court applied a test that requires the consideration of seven factors, none entitled to any specified weight relative to another. The factors are, in the court's words, "(1) the type and extent of the services rendered; (2) the scarcity of qualified employees; (3) the qualifications and prior earning capacity of the employee; (4) the contributions of the employee to the business venture; (5) the net earnings of the employer; (6) the prevailing compensation paid to employees with comparable jobs; and (7) the peculiar characteristics of the employer's business." It is apparent that this test, though it or variants of it (one of which has the astonishing total of 21 factors) are encountered in many cases, leaves much to be desired — being, like many other multi-factor tests, "redundant, incomplete, and unclear." Palmer v. City of Chicago, 806 F.2d 1316, 1318 (7th Cir. 1986).

To begin with, it is nondirective. No indication is given of how the factors are to be weighed in the event they don't all line up on one side. And many of the factors, such as the type and extent of services rendered, the scarcity of qualified employees, and the peculiar characteristics of the employer's business, are vague.

Second, the factors do not bear a clear relation either to each other or to the primary purpose of section 162(a)(1), which is to prevent dividends (or in some cases gifts), which are not deductible from corporate income, from being disguised as salary, which is. Suppose that an employee who let us say was, like Heitz, a founder and the chief executive officer and principal owner of the taxpayer rendered no services at all but received a huge salary. It would be absurd to allow the whole or for that matter any part of his salary to be deducted as an ordinary and necessary business expense even if he were well qualified to be CEO of the company, the company had substantial net earnings, CEOs of similar companies were paid a lot, and it was a business in which high salaries are common. The multi-factor test would not prevent the Tax Court from allowing a deduction in such a case even though the corporation obviously was seeking to reduce its taxable income by disguising earnings as salary. The court would not allow the deduction, but not because of anything in the multi-factor test; rather because it would be apparent that the payment to the employee was not in fact for his services to the company. Treas. Reg. §1.162-7(a).

Third, the seven-factor test invites the Tax Court to set itself up as a super-personnel department for closely held corporations, a role unsuitable for courts. . . . The test—the irruption of "comparable worth" thinking in a new-context—invites the court to decide what the taxpayer's employees *should* be paid on the basis of the judges' own ideas of what jobs are comparable, what relation an employee's salary should bear to the corporation's net earnings, what types of business should pay abnormally high (or low) salaries, and so forth. The judges of the Tax Court are not equipped by training or experience to determine the salaries of corporate officers; no judges are.

Fourth, since the test cannot itself determine the outcome of a dispute because of its nondirective character, it invites the making of arbitrary decisions based on uncanalized discretion or unprincipled rules of thumb. The Tax Court in this case essentially added the IRS's determination of the maximum that Mr. Heitz should have been paid in 1993 and 1994 to what he was in fact paid, and divided the sum by two. It cut the baby in half. One would have to be awfully naive to believe that the seven-factor test generated this pleasing symmetry.

Fifth, because the reaction of the Tax Court to a challenge to the deduction of executive compensation is unpredictable, corporations run unavoidable legal risks in determining a level of compensation that may be indispensable to the success of their business.

The drawbacks of the multi-factor test are well illustrated by its purported application by the Tax Court in this case. With regard to factor (1), the court found that Heitz was "indispensable to Exacto's business" and "essential to Exacto's success." Heitz is not only Exacto's CEO; he is also the company's chief salesman and marketing man plus the head of its research and development efforts and its principal inventor. The company's entire success appears to be due on the one hand to the research and development conducted by him and on the other hand to his marketing of these innovations (though he receives some additional compensation for his marketing efforts from a subsidiary of Exacto). The court decided that factor (1) favored Exacto.

Likewise factor (2), for, as the court pointed out, the design of precision springs, which is Heitz's specialty, is "an extremely specialized branch of mechanical engineering, and there are very few engineers who have made careers specializing in this area," let alone engineers like Heitz who have "the ability to identify and attract clients and to develop springs to perform a specific function for that client. . . . It would have been very difficult to replace Mr. Heitz." Notice how factors (1) and (2) turn out to be nearly identical.

Factors (3) and (4) also supported Exacto, the court found. "Mr. Heitz is highly qualified to run Exacto as a result of his education, training, experience, and motivation. Mr. Heitz has over 40 years of highly successful experience in the field of spring design." And his "efforts were of great value to the corporation." So factor (4) duplicated (2), and so the first four factors turn out to be really only two.

With regard to the fifth factor—the employer's (Exacto's) net earnings—the Tax Court was noncommittal. Exacto had reported a loss in 1993 and very little taxable income in 1994. But it conceded having taken some improper deductions in those years unrelated to Heitz's salary. After adjusting Exacto's income to remove these deductions, the court found that Exacto had earned more than $1 million in each of the years at issue net of Heitz's supposedly inflated salary.

The court was noncommital with regard to the sixth factor — earnings of comparable employees — as well. The evidence bearing on this factor had been presented by expert witnesses, one on each side, and the court was critical of both. The taxpayer's witness had arrived at his estimate of Heitz's maximum reasonable compensation in part by aggregating the salaries that Exacto would have had to pay to hire four people each to wear one of Heitz's "hats," as chief executive officer, chief manufacturing executive, chief research and development officer, and chief sales and marketing executive. Although the more roles or functions an employee performs the more valuable his services are likely to be, an employee who performs four jobs, each on a part-time basis, is not necessarily worth as much to a company as four employees each working full time at one of those jobs. It is therefore arbitrary to multiply the normal full-time salary for one of the jobs by four to compute the reasonable compensation of the employee who fills all four of them. Anyway salaries are determined not by the method of comparable worth but, like other prices, by the market, which is to say by conditions of demand and supply. Especially in the short run, salaries may vary by more than any difference in the "objective" characteristics of jobs. An individual who has valuable skills that are in particularly short supply at the moment may command a higher salary than a more versatile, better-trained, and more loyal employee whose skills are, however, less scarce.

The Internal Revenue Service's expert witness sensibly considered whether Heitz's compensation was consistent with Exacto's investors' earning a reasonable return (adjusted for the risk of Exacto's business), which he calculated to be 13 percent. But in concluding that Heitz's compensation had pushed the return below that level, he neglected to consider the concessions of improper deductions, which led to adjustments to Exacto's taxable income. The Tax Court determined that with those adjustments the investors' annual return was more than 20 percent despite Heitz's large salary. The government argues that the court should not have calculated the investors' return on the basis of the concessions of improper deductions, because when Heitz's compensation was determined the corporation was unaware that the deductions would be disallowed. In other words, the corporation thought that its after-tax income was larger than it turned out to be. But if the ex ante perspective is the proper one, as the government contends, it favors the corporation if when it fixed Heitz's salary it thought there was more money in the till for the investors than has turned out to be the case.

What is puzzling is how disallowing deductions and thus increasing the taxpayer's tax bill could increase the investors' return. What investors care about is the corporate income available to pay dividends or be reinvested; obviously money paid in taxes to the Internal Revenue Service is not available for either purpose. The reasonableness of Heitz's compensation thus depends not on Exacto's taxable income but on the corporation's profitability to the investors, which is reduced by the disallowance of deductions — if a corporation succeeds in taking phantom deductions, shareholders are better off because the corporation's tax bill is lower. But the government makes nothing of this. Its only objection is to the Tax Court's having taken account of adjustments made after Heitz's salary was fixed. Both parties, plus the Tax Court, based their estimates of investors' returns on the after-tax income shown on Exacto's tax returns, which jumped after the deductions were disallowed, rather than on Exacto's real profits, which declined. The approach is inconsistent with a realistic assessment of the investors' rate of return, but as no one in the case questions it we shall not make an issue of it.

Finally, under factor (7) ("peculiar characteristics"), the court first and rightly brushed aside the IRS's argument that the low level of dividends paid by Exacto (zero in the two years at issue, but never very high) was evidence that the corporation was paying Heitz dividends in the form of salary. The court pointed out that shareholders may not want dividends. They may prefer the corporation to retain its earnings, causing the value of the corporation to rise and thus enabling the shareholders to obtain corporate earnings in the form of capital gains taxed at a lower rate than ordinary income. The court also noted that while Heitz, as the owner of 55 percent of Exacto's common stock, obviously was in a position to influence his salary, the corporation's two other major shareholders, each with 20 percent of the stock, had approved it. They had not themselves been paid a salary or other compensation, and are not relatives of Heitz; they had no financial or other incentive to allow Heitz to siphon off dividends in the form of salary.

Having run through the seven factors, all of which either favored the taxpayer or were neutral, the court reached a stunning conclusion: "We have considered the factors relevant in deciding reasonable compensation for Mr. Heitz. On the basis of all the evidence, we hold that reasonable compensation for Mr. Heitz" was much less than Exacto paid him. The court's only effort at explaining this result when Exacto had passed the seven-factor test with flying colors was that "we have balanced Mr. Heitz' unique selling and technical ability, his years of experience, and the difficulty of replacing Mr. Heitz with the fact that the corporate entity would have shown a reasonable return for the equity holders, after considering petitioners' concessions." But "the fact that the corporate entity would have shown a reasonable return for the equity holders" after the concessions is on the *same side* of the balance as the other factors; it does not favor the Internal Revenue Service's position. The government's lawyer was forced to concede at the argument of the appeal that she could not deny the possibility that the Tax Court had pulled its figures for Heitz's allowable compensation out of a hat.

The failure of the Tax Court's reasoning to support its result would alone require a remand. But the problem with the court's opinion goes deeper. The test it applied does not provide adequate guidance to a rational decision. We owe no deference to the Tax Court's statutory interpretations, its relation to us being that of a district court to a court of appeals, not that of an administrative agency to a court of appeals. The federal courts of appeals, whose decisions do of course have weight as authority with us even when they are not our own decisions, have been moving toward a much simpler and more purposive test, the "independent investor" test. We applaud the trend and join it.

Because judges tend to downplay the element of judicial creativity in adapting law to fresh insights and changed circumstances, the cases we have just cited prefer to say that the "independent investor" test is the "lens" through which they view the seven (or however many) factors of the orthodox test. But that is a formality. The new test dissolves the old and returns the inquiry to basics. The Internal Revenue Code limits the amount of salary that a corporation can deduct from its income primarily in order to prevent the corporation from eluding the corporate income tax by paying dividends but calling them salary because salary is deductible and dividends are not. (Perhaps they should be, to avoid double taxation of corporate earnings, but that is not the law.) In the case of a publicly held company, where the salaries of the highest executives are fixed by a board of directors that those executives do not control, the danger of siphoning corporate earnings to executives in the form of salary is not acute. The danger is much greater in the case of a closely held corporation, in which ownership and management tend to coincide; unfortunately, as the opinion of the Tax Court in this case illustrates, judges are not competent to decide what business executives are worth.

There is, fortunately, an indirect market test, as recognized by the Internal Revenue Service's expert witness. A corporation can be conceptualized as a contract in which the owner of assets hires a person to manage them. The owner pays the manager a salary and in exchange the manager works to increase the value of the assets that have been entrusted to his management; that increase can be expressed as a rate of return to the owner's investment. The higher the rate of return (adjusted for risk) that a manager can generate, the greater the salary he can command. If the rate of return is extremely high, it will be difficult to prove that the manager is being overpaid, for it will be implausible that if he quit if his salary was cut, and he was replaced by a lower-paid manager, the owner would be better off; it would be killing the goose that lays the golden egg. The Service's expert believed that investors in a firm like Exacto would expect a 13 percent return on their investment. Presumably they would be delighted with more. They would be *overjoyed* to receive a return more than 50 percent greater than they expected — and 20 percent, the return that the Tax Court found that investors in Exacto had obtained, is more than 50 percent greater than the benchmark return of 13 percent.

When, notwithstanding the CEO's "exorbitant" salary (as it might appear to a judge or other modestly paid official), the investors in his company are obtaining a far higher return than they had any reason to expect, his salary is presumptively reasonable. We say "presumptively" because we can imagine cases in which the return, though very high, is not due to the CEO's exertions. Suppose Exacto had been an unprofitable company that suddenly learned that its factory was sitting on an oil field, and when oil revenues started to pour in its owner raised his salary from $50,000 a year to $1.3 million. The presumption of reasonableness would be rebutted. There is no suggestion of anything of that sort here and likewise no suggestion that Mr. Heitz was merely the titular chief executive and the company was actually run by someone else, which would be another basis for rebuttal.

The government could still have prevailed by showing that while Heitz's salary may have been no greater than would be reasonable in the circumstances, the company did not in fact intend to pay him that amount as salary, that his salary really did include a concealed dividend though it need not have. This is material (and the "independent investor" test, like the multi-factor test that it replaces, thus incomplete, though invaluable) because any business expense to be deductible must be, as we noted earlier, a bona fide expense as well as reasonable in amount. The fact that Heitz's salary was approved by the other owners of the corporation, who had no incentive to disguise a dividend as salary, goes far to rebut any inference of bad faith here, which in any event the Tax Court did not draw and the government does not ask us to draw.

The judgment is reversed with directions to enter judgment for the taxpayer.

Notes and Questions

1. *Multifactor tests.* The tax law is full of tests for reaching a determination based on all of the relevant "facts and circumstances." Typically, the tests

involve a list of "factors," not unlike the list that so troubles Judge Posner in this case. Many are found in the Treasury regulations. For example, in determining whether an activity is "engaged in for profit" under §183 (discussed later in this chapter), the regulations require examination of nine listed factors that purportedly distinguish profit-seeking activities from those that are not. Reg. §1.183-2(b). Similarly, the IRS seeks to distinguish employment situations (for wage-withholding and social security tax purposes) from independent contractor situations on the basis of a 20-factor test that is published in its internal manuals for examining agents. Some tests of this sort are even sanctioned by the Code itself. For example, in a context similar to that involved in the reasonable compensation area, the spectacularly unsuccessful §385 of the Code directs the Treasury to promulgate regulations, based on five factors specified in the statute, to distinguish corporate payments of interest with respect to debt (which are deductible) from payments that constitute dividends with respect to stock ownership (which are not).[27] Sometimes a court, especially the Supreme Court or Courts of Appeals, may specify its own set of factors to explain its decision and to provide guidance to taxpayers, the IRS, and lower courts in deciding subsequent cases. For example, the *Winthrop* case in Chapter 12 sets forth the Fifth Circuit's multifactor test for determining when subdivided land is a capital asset in the hands of a taxpayer.

Virtually all tests of this sort suffer from the several defects that Judge Posner notes. Most importantly, because the tests fail to specify weights to be attached to the factors, they provide no guidance on how a factfinder should proceed from determinations as to each factor to a determination of the ultimate outcome of the case.

In defense of such tests, however, it can be said that they do provide an indication of what the proponent of the test regards as significant. And the difficulty of assigning weights to each factor that can be generalized over the wide range of variant factual situations can easily be appreciated. If taken as rough guides, within which considerable judgment and discretion must be exercised, they seem helpful; if one approaches them, as Judge Posner does, as prescriptions that are intended to produce determinate outcomes if scrupulously followed, disappointment will follow.

2. *An old question.* Despite the suggestion in the opinion that these cases represent an "irruption of 'comparable worth' thinking," the reasonable compensation controversy substantially antedates the relatively recent development of "comparable worth" analysis. The IRS began bringing cases under the reasonable compensation clause of §162 shortly after that language was added to the Code with the Revenue Act of 1918, with the first cases reaching the court in the mid-1920s. *See, e.g.,* Gustafson Manufacturing Co. v. Commissioner, 1 B.T.A. 508 (1925). And the flow of cases continues unabated: A database search for "reasonable compensation" cases produced 3,878 "hits," most of which appear to be genuine reasonable compensation disputes. Does the "independent investor" test offer promise in reducing the number of disputes? Is it troubling that the context in which these cases come up is one

---

27. Though this provision was added to the Code in 1969, the regulations the Treasury was directed to promulgate have never been adopted. After twice proposing regulations that were so bitterly criticized that they were withdrawn, it appears that the Treasury is no longer even trying to comply with this directive.

in which the investors are hardly ever actually independent of the managers? What, exactly, does that test appear to involve?

3. *Did the Tax Court pass its test?* Judge Posner seems incredulous that the Tax Court could find that none of the seven factors favored the IRS in this case, and yet still conclude that a reduction in Mr. Heitz's salary was appropriate. But an employee like Heitz would always do well on this sort of test. He clearly was central to the company's success, well-qualified for his role, and uniquely suited to provide the services he was paid to provide. Does that mean that *any* salary would be reasonable? Or can a court plausibly find that a manager of this sort indeed deserved a high salary, but not one as high as the company (typically controlled by this same individual) was willing to pay?

4. *Section 162(m).* Congress has also expressed concern from time to time about excessive salaries in the context of publicly held corporations. In 1993, it added subsection (m) to §162, disallowing deductions for salary payments in excess of $1 million to a chief executive officer or any other of a corporation's four highest paid officers. There is, however, a rather broad exception for "performance based" compensation. Since most corporations do in fact compensate their senior officers with a mix of salary, bonus, and stock options, with the latter two types being ordinarily exempt from the cap, deductible compensation can and frequently does exceed the $1 million mark. Indeed, a cynic might conclude that this legislation was about *seeming* to do something about excessive compensation, rather than actually doing anything about it.

5. *Cliff effect or no cliff effect?* If a corporation pays a purported salary of $300,000 to a shareholder-employee, and a court later determines that only $250,000 of the $300,000 qualifies as reasonable compensation, the corporation gets to keep $250,000 of its deduction; only the deduction for the last $50,000 is lost. This seems sensible enough, and it is consistent with the usual tendency of the income tax to avoid cliff effects. On the other hand, this approach does nothing to discourage corporations and their shareholder-employees from pushing the limits of reasonable compensation. Oddly enough, the rule is different in the closely analogous area of distinguishing deductible interest from nondeductible dividends, in the case of payments made to shareholder-creditors. An attempt to generate excessive interest deductions will generally lead to the loss of *all* interest deductions, including the portion that would not have been excessive. Although cliff effects generally seem like bad policy, is there something to be said for the deterrent effect of this approach?

F. TRAVEL AND ENTERTAINMENT

1. Travel

Section 162(a)(2) allows deduction of "traveling expenses (including amounts expended for meals and lodging . . .) while away from home in pursuit of a trade or business. . . ." Taken literally, this provision would seem to authorize deductions for a wide range of items that might appear to be primarily personal living expenses. For example, consider a typical business taxpayer, who lives in the suburbs and commutes daily to his office in the downtown business district of his city. As soon as the wheels of his oversized SUV hit the pavement at the end of his driveway, he is in some sense away from home, in hot pursuit of his trade or business. Does this mean that his gasoline costs, his parking, and his lunch downtown would be deductible?

Sadly for our businessman, the IRS, with uneven but ultimately sufficient backing from the courts, does not believe that §162(a)(2) means that these costs are deductible. The Service reaches this position by the addition of two requirements to those explicitly stated in the Code: The taxpayer must be away from his "tax home" in order to qualify for these deductions, by which the IRS means away from the general vicinity of his work place; and the taxpayer must satisfy the "overnight" rule, meaning that any trip that doesn't involve a substantial rest period, approximating the usual eight hours in bed, doesn't put the taxpayer in travel status for purposes of this provision.[28]

These rules will be explained in some detail in the following materials, but it can be said as a general matter that they reflect the viewpoint that commuting costs and meal costs are ordinarily personal consumption expenditures, not business expenses. Commuting, it is said, reflects personal choices about where to live; meals would have been consumed in any event, and so lack the business nexus necessary to support a business expense deduction.

This view is of course not beyond debate: But for the need to be at work, commuting costs would not be incurred; and meals consumed in a downtown restaurant are likely to be more expensive than the meal that might have been consumed at home instead. Perhaps the best view is that these expenses are jointly caused by the decision to accept a particular job (a business decision) and the decision not to live at the job location (a personal decision). Analytically, it would not seem that either set of reasons could be assigned a primary importance over the other. But it may be that protection of the tax base justifies resolving this issue against taxpayers. It preserves a larger tax base, which permits a lower set of tax rates, and at the same time relieves taxpayers of the cost of documenting, and the government of the costs of verifying, commuting and lunch expenses.

On the other hand, one could make a strong case on the basis of American patterns of urban development that many, perhaps most, taxpayers really have no choice but to incur commuting (with lunch-away-from-home) costs. Most jobs are located in downtown business districts or office parks, or in airport, manufacturing, or warehouse districts. What little housing is available near these dense employment nodes is typically either very expensive or dilapidated. (In some cities, the lucky taxpayer can find housing that is both!) If the taxpayer cannot find reasonable housing options that are within walking distance of her job, can the commuting expenses really be regarded as anything but a cost associated with earning a living?

But this viewpoint has never enjoyed much acceptance in congressional or administrative policy analysis. And perhaps all that's called for in answering this objection is a reorientation of the argument stated above: If nearly everyone incurs some minimum level of commuting expenses, then we can safely ignore that minimum without perpetrating an inequity; and if taxpayers incur expenses above that

---

28. However, certain local travel costs are deductible under some circumstances. See the discussion in Note 6 following the *Hantzis* case *infra*.

minimum, one could probably identify some significant elements of personal choice that largely account for the excess, such as the cleaner air, better schools, or quieter streets that are associated with the more bucolic suburbs of most cities.[29]

One aspect of travel expense deductions that initially confuses students lies in the suggestion that lunch costs cannot be deducted without an overnight stay at some distant location. This seems contrary to the widely known fact that the "business lunch" is routinely deductible.[30] The resolution of this apparent inconsistency is that while meal costs that are to be deducted as *travel* expenses under §162(a)(2) must meet the overnight and tax home conditions, certain other lunch costs can be deducted under the more general language of §162(a).[31]

For example, a lawyer who flies from Chicago to Washington one evening in order to attend a hearing at a regulatory agency the following morning will be able to deduct her dinner the night before the hearing and her lunch immediately after the hearing (assuming both are consumed after the trip begins and before it ends), as part of her travel expenses. She could do this even if the meals were eaten alone, and had no connection — other than the one established by the purpose of the trip as a whole — to any business motives. If, on the other hand, the hearing had been held in the agency's Chicago regional office, her dinner and lunch expenses in Chicago (her home town) would not be deductible as travel expenses, but could be deductible nevertheless as business expenses if she took an opportunity to discuss the upcoming (or immediately preceding) hearing with professional colleagues or clients during the meal.

It may seem from the above description that the tax home and overnight rule are of rather marginal importance, only occasionally rising to disallow a deduction of the odd lunch or dinner for which the taxpayer has failed to demonstrate any independent business connection. This is not the case, however. For a lawyer who tries a complicated case in some distant city for a few months, or for a college teacher who takes a visiting professorship at a distant institution for a semester, what is at stake is typically the deductibility of all or most of the meal and housing costs while on that assignment, which can aggregate to several thousand dollars. Because the stakes are not trivial, and because the law in this area continues to suffer from some vagueness and incompleteness, this is a frequently litigated issue.

The leading case in the area, Commissioner v. Flowers, 326 U.S. 465 (1946), involved a railroad lawyer who lived in Jackson, Mississippi, but who worked primarily at the railroad's headquarters in Mobile, Alabama, some 175 miles away from his home. He commuted between the two cities (by train, of course!) on an irregular basis during the tax years in issue, making some 33 trips in 1939 and 40 in 1940. While the railroad paid his travel expenses when he was needed in a city other than the two mentioned, it covered none of the costs of trips between the two, nor any lodging costs in Mobile. Mr. Flowers sought deductions for the costs of the trips to Mobile, and his meals and lodging while there, but did not seek

29. On the other hand (if we still have a hand left at this point in the argument), there are millions of persons who have significant income, but who are not employed and who do not incur commuting expenses. Arguably, the failure to allow a deduction for commuting expenses overtaxes workers relative to retirees and the idle rich, and overtaxes two-earner couples relative to one-earner couples.

30. More precisely, *half* of the cost of a business lunch is routinely deductible. Business meal expenses — away from home or not — are subject to the 50 percent disallowance rule of §274(n), which is described in Note 3 following the *Cohan* case *infra*.

31. The same is true of certain business transportation costs; while not *travel* costs, they may be deductible under certain circumstances. See the notes and questions following the *Hantzis* case *infra*.

deductions for his trips back to Jackson. He thus appears to have recognized the mixed motivation of his travel, taking the implicit position that trips to his office in Mobile were for business purposes, but trips to his home in Jackson were personal.

The IRS argued this case on the basis of its tax home theory, saying that Mr. Flowers's "home" for purposes of §162(a)(2) was his place of business in Mobile, so the travel expenses incurred in getting to Mobile, and the meals and lodging while there, were not "away from home" for purposes of the statute. The Supreme Court declined to accept or reject this view, but decided the case instead on the grounds that expenses were deductible only if they were incurred to advance the business interests of the employer. Since Mr. Flowers's decision to live in Jackson advanced no interest of the railroad, it could not be said that his expenses were incurred in pursuit of a trade or business.

The IRS came closer to judicial endorsement of its tax home theory in the following case, which involved travel expenses of a summer law clerk.

HANTZIS v. COMMISSIONER
638 F.2d 248 (1st Cir.), *cert. denied,* 452 U.S. 962 (1981)

CAMPBELL, Circuit Judge: The Commissioner of Internal Revenue (Commissioner) appeals a decision of the United States Tax Court that allowed a deduction under section 162(a)(2) for expenses incurred by a law student in the course of her summer employment. The facts in the case are straightforward and undisputed.

In the fall of 1973 Catharine Hantzis (taxpayer), formerly a candidate for an advanced degree in philosophy at the University of California at Berkeley, entered Harvard Law School in Cambridge, Massachusetts, as a full-time student. During her second year of law school she sought unsuccessfully to obtain employment for the summer of 1975 with a Boston law firm. She did, however, find a job as a legal assistant with a law firm in New York City, where she worked for ten weeks beginning in June 1975. Her husband, then a member of the faculty of Northeastern University with a teaching schedule for that summer, remained in Boston and lived at the couple's home there. At the time of the Tax Court's decision in this case, Mr. and Mrs. Hantzis still resided in Boston.

On their joint income tax return for 1975, Mr. and Mrs. Hantzis reported the earnings from taxpayer's summer employment ($3,750) and deducted the cost of transportation between Boston and New York, the cost of a small apartment rented by Mrs. Hantzis in New York and the cost of her meals in New York ($3,204). The deductions were taken under section 162(a)(2). . . .

The Commissioner disallowed the deduction on the ground that taxpayer's home for purposes of section 162(a)(2) was her place of employment and the cost of traveling to and living in New York was therefore not "incurred . . . while away from home." The Commissioner also argued that the expenses were not incurred "in the pursuit of a trade or business." Both positions were rejected by the Tax Court, which found that Boston was Mrs. Hantzis' home because her employment in New York was only temporary and that her expenses in New York were "necessitated" by her employment there. The court thus held the expenses to be deductible under section 162(a)(2).

In asking this court to reverse the Tax Court's allowance of the deduction, the Commissioner has contended that the expenses were not incurred "in the pursuit of a trade or business." We do not accept this argument; nonetheless, we sustain the

Commissioner and deny the deduction, on the basis that the expenses were not incurred "while away from home."

I

Section 262 of the Code declares that "except as otherwise provided in this chapter, no deductions shall be allowed for personal, living, or family expenses." Section 162 provides less of an exception to this rule than it creates a separate category of deductible business expenses. This category manifests a fundamental principle of taxation: that a person's taxable income should not include the cost of producing that income. . . .

The test by which "personal" travel expenses subject to tax under section 262 are distinguished from those costs of travel necessarily incurred to generate income is embodied in the requirement that, to be deductible under section 162(a)(2), an expense must be "incurred . . . in the pursuit of a trade or business." In [Commissioner v. Flowers, 366 U.S. 465 (1946),] the Supreme Court read this phrase to mean that "(t)he exigencies of business rather than the personal conveniences and necessities of the traveler must be the motivating factors." 326 U.S. at 474.[32] Of course, not every travel expense resulting from business exigencies rather than personal choice is deductible; an expense must also be "ordinary and necessary" and incurred "while away from home." But the latter limitations draw also upon the basic concept that only expenses necessitated by business, as opposed to personal, demands may be excluded from the calculation of taxable income.

With these fundamentals in mind, we proceed to ask whether the cost of taxpayer's transportation to and from New York, and of her meals and lodging while in New York, was incurred "while away from home in the pursuit of a trade or business."

II

The Commissioner has directed his argument at the meaning of "in pursuit of a trade or business." He interprets this phrase as requiring that a deductible traveling expense be incurred under the demands of a trade or business which predates the expense, i.e., an "already existing" trade or business. Under this theory, section 162(a)(2) would invalidate the deduction taken by the taxpayer because she was a full-time student before commencing her summer work at a New York law firm in 1975 and so was not continuing in a trade or business when she incurred the expenses of traveling to New York and living there while her job lasted.[33] The Commissioner's proposed interpretation erects at the threshold of deductibility under section 162(a)(2) the requirement that a taxpayer be engaged in a trade or business before incurring a travel expense. Only if that requirement is satisfied would an inquiry into the deductibility of an expense proceed to ask whether the

---

32. *Flowers* denied a deduction claimed by the taxpayer as not involving expenses required by the taxpayer's employer's business. It is now established, however, that a taxpayer may be in the trade or business of being an employee. . . .

33. The taxpayer has not argued that being a law student constitutes a trade or business and so we do not address the issue. *See generally* Reisinger v. Commissioner, 71 T.C. 568 (1979); Rev. Rul. 68-591, 1968-2 C.B. 73.

expense was a result of business exigencies, incurred while away from home, and reasonable and necessary.

Such a reading of the statute is semantically possible and would perhaps expedite the disposition of certain cases.[34] Nevertheless, we reject it as unsupported by case law and inappropriate to the policies behind section 162(a)(2).

[The court's further discussion of this issue is omitted.]

III

As already noted, *Flowers* construed section 162(a)(2) to mean that a traveling expense is deductible only if it is (1) reasonable and necessary, (2) incurred while away from home, and (3) necessitated by the exigencies of business. Because the Commissioner does not suggest that Mrs. Hantzis' expenses were unreasonable or unnecessary, we may pass directly to the remaining requirements. Of these, we find dispositive the requirement that an expense be incurred while away from home. As we think Mrs. Hantzis' expenses were not so incurred, we hold the deduction to be improper.

The meaning of the term "home" in the travel expense provision is far from clear. When Congress enacted the travel expense deduction now codified as section 162(a)(2), it apparently was unsure whether, to be deductible, an expense must be incurred away from a person's residence or away from his principal place of business. *See* Note, *A House Is Not a Tax Home*, 49 Va. L. Rev. 125, 127-128 (1963). This ambiguity persists and courts, sometimes within a single circuit, have divided over the issue.[35] It has been suggested that these conflicting definitions are due to the enormous factual variety in the cases. . . . We find this observation instructive, for if the cases that discuss the meaning of the term "home" in section 162(a)(2) are interpreted on the basis of their unique facts as well as the fundamental purposes of the travel expense provision, and not simply pinioned to one of two competing definitions of home, much of the seeming confusion and contradiction on this issue disappears and a functional definition of the term emerges.

We begin by recognizing that the location of a person's home for purposes of section 162(a)(2) becomes problematic only when the person lives one place and works another. Where a taxpayer resides and works at a single location, he is always home, however defined; and where a taxpayer is constantly on the move due to his work, he is never "away" from home. (In the latter situation, it may be said either that he has no residence to be away from, or else that his residence is always at his place of employment. *See* Rev. Rul. 60-16, 1960-1 C.B. 58, 62.) However, in the present case, the need to determine "home" is plainly before us, since the taxpayer resided in Boston and worked, albeit briefly, in New York.

---

34. We do not see, however, how it would affect the treatment of this case. The Commissioner apparently concedes that upon starting work in New York the taxpayer engaged in a trade or business. If we held as we do not that an expense is deductible only when incurred in connection with an already existing trade or business, our ruling would seem to invalidate merely the deduction of the cost of taxpayer's trip from Boston to New York to begin work (about $64). We would still need to determine, as in any other case under section 162(a)(2), whether the expenses that arose subsequent to the taxpayer's entry into her trade or business were reasonable and necessary, required by business exigencies and incurred while away from home.

35. The Tax Court has, with a notable exception, consistently held that a taxpayer's home is his place of business. [Citations omitted.] The exception, of course, is the present case.

We think the critical step in defining "home" in these situations is to recognize that the "while away from home" requirement has to be construed in light of the further requirement that the expense be the result of business exigencies. The traveling expense deduction obviously is not intended to exclude from taxation every expense incurred by a taxpayer who, in the course of business, maintains two homes. Section 162(a)(2) seeks rather "to mitigate the burden of the taxpayer who, *because of the exigencies of his trade or business,* must maintain two places of abode and thereby incur additional and duplicate living expenses." *Kroll, supra,* 49 T.C. at 562 (emphasis added). Consciously or unconsciously, courts have effectuated this policy in part through their interpretation of the term "home" in section 162(a)(2). Whether it is held in a particular decision that a taxpayer's home is his residence or his principal place of business, the ultimate allowance or disallowance of a deduction is a function of the court's assessment of the reason for a taxpayer's maintenance of two homes. If the reason is perceived to be personal, the taxpayer's home will generally be held to be his place of employment rather than his residence and the deduction will be denied. If the reason is felt to be business exigencies, the person's home will usually be held to be his residence and the deduction will be allowed. We understand the concern of the concurrence that such an operational interpretation of the term "home" is somewhat technical and perhaps untidy, in that it will not always afford bright line answers, but we doubt the ability of either the Commissioner or the courts to invent an unyielding formula that will make sense in all cases. The line between personal and business expenses winds through infinite factual permutations; effectuation of the travel expense provision requires that any principle of decision be flexible and sensitive to statutory policy.

Construing in the manner just described the requirement that an expense be incurred "while away from home," we do not believe this requirement was satisfied in this case. Mrs. Hantzis' *trade or business* did not require that she maintain a home in Boston as well as one in New York. Though she returned to Boston at various times during the period of her employment in New York, her visits were all for personal reasons. It is not contended that she had a business connection in Boston that necessitated her keeping a home there; no professional interest was served by maintenance of the Boston home as would have been the case, for example, if Mrs. Hantzis had been a lawyer based in Boston with a New York client whom she was temporarily serving. The home in Boston was kept up for reasons involving Mr. Hantzis, but those reasons cannot substitute for a showing by *Mrs.* Hantzis that the exigencies of *her* trade or business required her to maintain two homes. Mrs. Hantzis' decision to keep two homes must be seen as a choice dictated by personal, albeit wholly reasonable, considerations and not a business or occupational necessity. We therefore hold that her home for purposes of section 162(a)(2) was New York and that the expenses at issue in this case were not incurred "while away from home."

We are not dissuaded from this conclusion by the temporary nature of Mrs. Hantzis' employment in New York. Mrs. Hantzis argues that the brevity of her stay in New York excepts her from the business exigencies requirement of section 162(a)(2) under a doctrine supposedly enunciated by the Supreme Court in Peurifoy v. Commissioner, 358 U.S. 59 (1958). The Tax Court here held that Boston was the taxpayer's home because it would have been unreasonable for her to move her residence to New York for only ten weeks. At first glance these contentions may seem to find support in the court decisions holding that, when a taxpayer works for a limited time away from his usual home, section 162(a)(2) allows a deduction for the expense of maintaining a second home so long as the employment is "temporary" and not "indefinite" or "permanent." . . .

The temporary employment doctrine does not, however, purport to eliminate any requirement that continued maintenance of a first home have a business justification. We think the rule has no application where the taxpayer has no business connection with his usual place of residence. If no business exigency dictates the location of the taxpayer's usual residence, then the mere fact of his taking temporary employment elsewhere cannot supply a compelling business reason for continuing to maintain that residence. Only a taxpayer who lives one place, works another and has business ties to both is in the ambiguous situation that the temporary employment doctrine is designed to resolve. In such circumstances, unless his employment away from his usual home is temporary, a court can reasonably assume that the taxpayer has abandoned his business ties to that location and is left with only personal reasons for maintaining a residence there. Where only personal needs require that a travel expense be incurred, however, a taxpayer's home is defined so as to leave the expense subject to taxation. *See supra.* Thus, a taxpayer who pursues temporary employment away from the location of his usual residence, but has no business connection with that location, is not "away from home" for purposes of section 162(a)(2).

On this reasoning, the temporary nature of Mrs. Hantzis' employment in New York does not affect the outcome of her case. She had no business ties to Boston that would bring her within the temporary employment doctrine. By this holding, we do not adopt a rule that "home" in section 162(a)(2) is the equivalent of a taxpayer's place of business. Nor do we mean to imply that a taxpayer has a "home" for tax purposes only if he is already engaged in a trade or business at a particular location. Though both rules are alluringly determinate, we have already discussed why they offer inadequate expressions of the purposes behind the travel expense deduction. We hold merely that for a taxpayer in Mrs. Hantzis' circumstances to be "away from home in the pursuit of a trade or business," she must establish the existence of some sort of business relation both to the location she claims as "home" and to the location of her temporary employment sufficient to support a finding that her duplicative expenses are necessitated by business exigencies. This, we believe, is the meaning of the statement in *Flowers* that "(b)usiness trips are to be identified *in relation to* business demands and the traveler's business headquarters." 326 U.S. at 474 (emphasis added). On the uncontested facts before us, Mrs. Hantzis had no business relation to Boston; we therefore leave to cases in which the issue is squarely presented the task of elaborating what relation to a place is required under section 162(a)(2) for duplicative living expenses to be deductible.

Reversed.

KEETON, District Judge, concurring in the result. [Judge Keeton's concurrence suggests that the same result in this case could be achieved without resort to the somewhat artificial "tax home" concept that the IRS argues for. He would have held that Boston was indeed Mrs. Hantzis's home, but that she nevertheless was entitled to no deductions, because her travel and duplicative housing expenses were not dictated by the exigencies of business. As far as her *business* life was concerned, she could have severed all ties to Boston, and simply moved to New York. — EDS.]

Notes and Questions

1. *Spouses with jobs in different cities.* The court ruled against Mrs. Hantzis because it found that she had no trade or business connection to Boston. But her *husband* certainly had a business connection to Boston. Should her husband's business connection to Boston be attributed to her, for purposes of determining whether she is entitled to business travel deductions? The duplication of living expenses for a business reason seems central to the policy goals of the "away from home" deductions. Is there any doubt that couples who have jobs in different and distant cities will encounter duplicative living expenses? Would it do any violence to the goals of the "tax home" rule to say that such couples could designate either residence as a primary residence and deduct the costs associated with the other, as well as the travel costs to and from that "home away from home"? Is the fact that marriage is a personal choice reason enough to reject this proposal? Does your answer depend on whether the tax system makes joint filing for married couples the norm (as in the United States), or whether the system requires each spouse to file a separate return (as in Canada and many other countries)?

2. *Distinguishing* Hantzis. Because Mrs. Hantzis had no permanent *business* connection to Boston, the court did not consider the duplication of living expenses while she was in New York to be attributable to the exigencies of business. Would the court have ruled differently if Mrs. Hantzis had had a work-study job (15 hours per week, $10 per hour) in the law school library during the school year before her summer in New York, and she had returned to that job after her summer in New York? What if she had been attending a law school program at night in the Boston area (not at Harvard, presumably) while working full-time during the day (in a job paying $50,000 per year), had taken an unpaid leave of absence from her full-time job to work in New York for the summer, and had returned to her full-time job in Boston after the summer in New York?

3. *Temporary versus indefinite jobs.* The *Peurifoy* rule discussed in the *Hantzis* opinion distinguishes between jobs that are "temporary," for which travel expenses are generally deductible, and ones that are "indefinite," for which travel costs are generally not deductible. The IRS view was that jobs that were reasonably expected to last one year or less were "temporary," while jobs that were expected to last longer than that, or jobs whose duration was not reasonably known, were indefinite. This approach was endorsed by Congress in 1992, when it added a sentence to the flush language of §162(a) to the effect that temporary jobs must have a duration no greater than one year. While the sentence that was added to the Code does not itself make clear the significance of the "temporary" category, the legislative history confirms that Congress was adopting the IRS's position on travel expense deductions for short-term assignments.

4. *Visiting professors.* What if one of Mrs. Hantzis's tenured professors at Harvard Law School spent the summer living in New York and doing "of counsel" work with a New York law firm? The professor would be allowed to deduct the kinds of expenses that Mrs. Hantzis was not allowed to deduct. A tenured job at Harvard certainly constitutes a substantial permanent business connection with the Boston area, and a temporary summer job fits comfortably within the one-year limitation described in the preceding

Note. The result would be the same if the Harvard professor spent an academic year (nine months, more or less) working as a visiting professor at NYU Law School. Law students considering careers in academia should note that this is a very sweet deal, considering the facts that (1) the visiting professor may actually incur little or nothing in the way of duplicate housing expenses, if she is able to rent her Boston-area residence — perhaps to a visiting professor at Harvard — while she is in New York, and (2) she will not have to eat restaurant meals in New York if she would rather eat in her apartment, so her meal expenses should not be appreciably higher than they would have been in Boston. By the way, if the professor chooses not to keep records of her meal expenses in New York, the IRS will allow her to claim meal expenses of $58 per day (50% of which is deductible, after the application of §274(n)), no questions asked. *See* Rev. Proc. 2006-41, 2006-43 I.R.B. 777. All the expenses are unreimbursed employee business expenses, and thus are subject to the 2-percent-of-AGI floor of §67, but the good news is that the cost of living in Manhattan for nine months is way more than 2 percent of a law professor's salary. A slightly tricky technical question: If the professor has the option of visiting at NYU for either one academic year (say, September to July) or one calendar year (say, January to November) is there any *tax* reason to prefer one option over the other?

5. *Why doesn't attending law school count as a business connection to Boston?* As much fun as law school can be, most people seem to attend it primarily to increase their future earnings potential, rather than for the sheer pleasure. If that's right, why didn't attending law school give Mrs. Hantzis a business connection with Boston, which would justify away-from-home business travel deductions for her summer in New York? See footnote 33 in the opinion, indicating that the court did not consider this argument because Mrs. Hantzis did not raise it. If she had, the court almost certainly would have rejected the argument. The analysis would closely resemble the analysis (described in section G.2 of this chapter) under which deductions are not allowed for the cost of a law school education. That argument is essentially that a taxpayer cannot deduct trade or business expenses until she is actually engaged in that trade or business.

6. *Noncommuting local transportation expenses.* Cases frequently arise concerning more ordinary transportation expenses of taxpayers who live and work in the same general vicinity, such as a door-to-door salesperson might have. Such taxpayers do not have duplicative living expenses, but may face considerable transportation costs over the course of a year. The general IRS position on these expenses is that pure commuting costs — the costs of travel to and from work, and parking in the vicinity of work — are not deductible. But transportation costs incurred over the course of a workday for taxpayers who must travel locally as part of their jobs generally are deductible. For example, a lawyer who travels from her office to appear in court, interview witnesses, and the like may deduct the costs of using her car to perform those functions.

These rules are straightforward enough, but it is easy to imagine the difficulties that can arise around the boundaries between these situations and ordinary commuting. For example, what if the lawyer in the previous example drives directly from her home to a court in which she must make an early appearance? Does it make a difference if she goes to her office later in the day, or instead spends all day at the court and then drives home directly from the court? What if the taxpayer is an independent sales agent who has no office outside of his home, but spends the day driving around his metropolitan area making sales calls on potential customers?

The IRS has published a number of rulings on variations of these facts. In one relatively recent ruling, Rev. Rul. 99-7, 1999-1 C.B. 361, 362, it summarized its position on deductions for local transportation costs of this sort as follows:

> In general, daily transportation expenses incurred in going between a taxpayer's residence and a work location are nondeductible commuting expenses. However, such expenses are deductible under the circumstances described in paragraph (1), (2), or (3) below.
>
> (1) A taxpayer may deduct daily transportation expenses incurred in going between the taxpayer's residence and a *temporary* work location *outside* the metropolitan area where the taxpayer lives and normally works. However, unless paragraph (2) or (3) below applies, daily transportation expenses incurred in going between the taxpayer's residence and a *temporary* work location *within* that metropolitan area are nondeductible commuting expenses.
>
> (2) If a taxpayer has one or more regular work locations away from the taxpayer's residence, the taxpayer may deduct daily transportation expenses incurred in going between the taxpayer's residence and a *temporary* work location in the same trade or business, regardless of the distance. (The Service will continue not to follow [Walker v. Commissioner, 101 T.C. 537 (1993)].)
>
> (3) If a taxpayer's residence is the taxpayer's principal place of business within the meaning of sec. 280A(c)(1)(A),[36] the taxpayer may deduct daily transportation expense incurred in going between the residence and another work location in the same trade or business, regardless of whether the other work location is *regular* or *temporary* and regardless of the distance.
>
> For purposes of paragraphs (1), (2), and (3), the following rules apply in determining whether a work location is *temporary*. If employment at a work location is realistically expected to last (and does in fact last) for 1 year or less, the employment is *temporary* in the absence of facts and circumstances indicating otherwise. If employment at a work location is realistically expected to last for more than 1 year or there is no realistic expectation that the employment will last for 1 year or less, the employment is *not temporary*, regardless of whether it actually exceeds 1 year. If employment at a work location initially is realistically expected to last for 1 year or less, but at some later date the employment is realistically expected to exceed 1 year, that employment will be treated as temporary (in the absence of facts and circumstances indicating otherwise) until the date that the taxpayer's realistic expectation changes, and will be treated as *not temporary* after that date. . . .

36. [See discussion of this provision in Note 5 following the *Keanini* case *infra* — Eds.]

Problem 1.   Willie Loman sells hosiery to department stores and specialty shops in the Boston area as an independent sales agent of several hose manufacturers located in China and Thailand. Willie has an office in his home in Boston, in which he deals with contract matters, scheduling appointments, and correspondence. During a typical week, he spends much of his time traveling by car to meet with buyers for retailers throughout the area. If Willie logs 200 miles per week on such travel, and relevant IRS guidelines allow deduction of 30 cents per mile for business travel by automobile, may Willie deduct $60 per week for his automobile use?

Problem 2.   Paul Bunyan IV is a logger in South Dakota. He lives in Hill City, which is the closest town to the Black Hills National Forest. Paul spends each work day in the National Forest cutting trees, pursuant to permits from the National Forest Service, and contracts with a local timber company. He has long since traded up from oxen to a pickup truck, which he uses to transport himself and his tools to the various places within the forest where he cuts the logs. (Other contractors then load the logs for shipment to the saw mill.) He maintains a log (the other kind) in which he records his mileage each day. Based on the log, he knows that about 40 percent of his annual mileage relates to the distances from his home to the first cutting site each day, and his return to his home from the last cutting site each day. The other 60 percent relates to trips within the work day between cutting sites. He also spends about seven hours per week in a shop in his garage, maintaining and repairing his chainsaws and other equipment. If his total mileage for logging purposes was 10,000 miles in 2011, and the allowable mileage rate is 30 cents per mile, how much may Paul deduct for his transportation costs in 2011? (*See* Walker v. Commissioner, 101 T.C. 537 (1993), but note as well that this is the case that the IRS disagrees with in Rev. Rul. 99-7 excerpted above.)

2. Entertainment

The conduct of business has always been an intensely social phenomenon: Sellers of goods and services are always seeking buyers or clients, and frequently do so in settings where food, beverages, and entertainment are present or lurking in the vicinity. That these activities have something to do with business motivations is usually clear; however, those activities may involve so much personal consumption that the IRS, and sometimes the courts, are unwilling to allow §162(a) deductions. The following early (and now legislatively overruled) case reveals some of the causes of concern.

COHAN v. COMMISSIONER
39 F.2d 540 (2d Cir. 1930)

L. HAND, Circuit Judge: [George M. Cohan was a legendary theatrical composer, director, and producer during the early 1900s. His larger-than-life life was the subject of a well-known Jimmy Cagney movie *Yankee Doodle Dandy,* and the later Broadway production *George M!* Judge Hand's understated recitation of the facts, however, identified the taxpayer simply as "a theatrical manager and producer." Some sense of Cohan's extravagant lifestyle nevertheless comes through in the following passages, especially if we remember that the sums mentioned would be about 15 times as large if expressed in current dollars. — EDS.] . . .

In the production of his plays Cohan was obliged to be free-handed in entertaining actors, employees, and, as he naively adds, dramatic critics. He had also to travel much, at times with his attorney. These expenses amounted to substantial sums, but he kept no account and probably could not have done so. At the trial before the Board he estimated that he had spent eleven thousand dollars in this fashion during the first six months of 1921, twenty-two thousand dollars, between July first, 1921, and June thirtieth, 1922, and as much for his following fiscal year, fifty-five thousand dollars in all. The Board refused to allow him any part of this, on the ground that it was impossible to tell how much he had in fact spent, in the absence of any items or details. The question is how far this refusal is justified, in view of the finding that he had spent much and that the sums were allowable expenses. Absolute certainty in such matters is usually impossible and is not necessary; the Board should make as close an approximation as it can, bearing heavily if it chooses upon the taxpayer whose inexactitude is of his own making. But to allow nothing at all appears to us inconsistent with saying that something was spent. True, we do not know how many trips Cohan made, nor how large his entertainments were; yet there was obviously some basis for computation, if necessary by drawing upon the Board's personal estimates of the minimum of such expenses. The amount may be trivial and unsatisfactory, but there was basis for some allowance, and it was wrong to refuse any, even though it were the traveling expenses of a single trip. It is not fatal that the result will inevitably be speculative; many important decisions must be such. We think that the Board was in error as to this and must reconsider the evidence. . . .

Notes and Questions

1. *An administrative catastrophe.* Though facially reasonable, Judge Hand's opinion in this case was a disaster for the IRS. It amounted to a partial reversal of the long-standing notion that a taxpayer bore the burden of production of evidence as to every material matter involved in his return.[37] This decision gave taxpayers who were sloppy (or shady) an opportunity to negotiate with the IRS for at least some of the deductions that they claimed, even in the absence of significant evidence that could be reviewed. This is, of course, particularly troublesome in a system in which relatively few taxpayers are audited, so that only a handful of these claims ever come to light in any administrative proceeding.

2. *A belated legislative response.* Intolerable as it was, this situation prevailed for some 30 years, until it was substantially reversed by the addition of §274 to the IRC in 1962. Section 274 operates as a limitation on §162(a) and, to a

---

37. Section 7491, which was added to the Code in 1998, provides that the government "shall have the burden of proof" on a factual issue if the "taxpayer introduces credible evidence" with respect to that issue. It is clear from a careful reading of §7491 that it does not reverse to any significant extent the general rule that the taxpayer bears the burden of production on factual issues. Rather, §7491 shifts the burden of *persuasion* to the government, once the taxpayer has satisfied the burden of *production*. Except to the extent of *Cohan*'s limited continued vitality (as described in Note 4 *infra*), taxpayers continue to bear the burden of production even after the enactment of §7491.

lesser degree, §212; §274 authorizes no deductions, but limits, conditions, or prohibits certain deductions that §162 or 212 would otherwise permit. Section 274 contains a number of substantive limitations, the more important of which are described below. Perhaps of even greater significance, however, are the requirements of §274(d) imposing an obligation on taxpayers to document their travel and entertainment expenses. The legislative history makes clear that these rules were intended flatly to overrule the *Cohan* case.

3. *An overview of §274.* The key provisions of §274 may be briefly summarized as follows:

(1) If an activity is "of a type generally considered to constitute entertainment, amusement, or recreation," its expense may be deducted only if (1) the activity is "directly related" to the taxpayer's business, or (2) the activity is "associated with" the conduct of the taxpayer's business and it immediately precedes or follows a "substantial business discussion." Section 274(a)(1)(A). The regulations elaborate on the "directly related" and "associated with" concepts. Reg. §1.274-1(c) and (d). In general, entertainment can qualify as "directly related" only if the entertainment is of a sort conducive to a business discussion—the regulations cite a "hospitality room" at a convention as an example. If the nature of the entertainment is not conducive to a business discussion—because it is too loud, or because talking during the entertainment is frowned on—then it is relegated to the "associated with" category. Reg. §1.274-2(c)(7). Thus, entertaining a client at a basketball game or at the opera qualifies for a deduction only if there was a substantial business discussion before or after the entertainment. If the taxpayer claims there was a substantial business discussion before or after the "associated with" entertainment, and if the persons entertained support the taxpayer's story, how can the IRS hope to disprove it? One can imagine the sort of "substantial and bona fide business discussion" that might precede or follow a World Series game, or an evening at a nightclub.

Perhaps this rule is useful in requiring some minimal nexus between the expense and the conduct of the business, thereby limiting the ability of a business to claim deductions simply for currying the favor of their clients and customers. A darker view would be that taxpayers of a certain type can *always* find the nexus they need, if they put their minds to it; if that's true, this rule is simply an example of the tendency of an income tax to impose heavier burdens on honest taxpayers than on dishonest ones.

(2) Deductions for facilities used in connection with entertainment (such as yachts, clubs, and the like) are denied, unless the facility is used primarily for the furtherance of the taxpayer's business, and was "directly related to the active conduct of such trade or business." Section 274(a)(1)(B) and 274(a)(2). Section 274(a)(3) flatly prohibits deduction of club dues.

(3) Section 274(b) severely limits the deduction for "business gifts" to individuals, whether they are customers, clients, or even employees. The limitation is set at $25 per recipient, per year. Having been set at that level in 1962, and left unadjusted for inflation in the intervening 40 or so years, the value of this exclusion has been allowed to erode to about one-sixth its value as of the year of its enactment. Thus, customers who may have

received a case of wine in 1963 can now be given only a bottle or two, if the donor's deduction is to be preserved.[38]

(4) Section 274(c) requires allocation between business-related (and deductible) expenses and nonbusiness-related expenses in the case of certain foreign travel—basically, travel for longer than one week, during which at least 25 percent of the trip is not related to business. Under previous rules, transportation expenses for foreign travel that was primarily related to business could be deducted in full, even though up to half of the time spent on the trip may have been personal. (This continues to be the rule for domestic travel, however.) Section 274(h) also imposes limitations on deductions for conventions that are not in North America, or are on cruise ships.

(5) Section 274(n) limits deductions for both types of deductible business meal expenses—travel and non-travel—to 50 percent of the amount actually spent. This rule makes good sense if we assume that it costs twice as much to eat "on the road" (in the case of business travel meals) as it does to eat at home, and that the taxpayer obtains no extra personal gratification for the extra cost. In that case, the $30 cost of a business dinner consists of $15 attributable solely to personal consumption (i.e., the amount the taxpayer would have spent to eat dinner absent the business trip), and $15 attributable solely to the business (i.e., the excess over what the taxpayer would have spent otherwise), and the 50 percent disallowance accurately identifies the personal and business portions of the expense.[39] As explained below (in Note 5), §274(n) also applies to entertainment expenses, such as tickets for concerts and sporting events. It does not, however, apply to lodging expenses incurred on a business trip. Can you explain why the 50 percent disallowance applies to meals but not to lodging?

(6) Section 274(e) provides a number of exceptions to the other rules of §274. For example, §274(e)(3) makes it clear that an employee who receives reimbursement for a business meal is eligible for a deduction in full of the reimbursement amount, creating a perfect offset to the income inclusion from the reimbursement.[40] Similarly, §274(e)(4) makes it clear that the expenses associated with company picnics and Christmas parties will continue to be fully deductible under most circumstances.

(7) Section 274(d) imposes substantiation rules for travel (including meals and lodging) and entertainment expenses, which require that the taxpayer document, "by adequate records or by sufficient evidence corroborating the taxpayer's own statement," (a) the amount of the expense; (b) the time and place that the expense was incurred; (c) the business purpose for which the expense was incurred; and (d) the business relationship to the taxpayer of the party whose entertainment, etc., was in issue. The voluminous regulations relating to this provision provide some

---

38. Section 274(b) is also discussed following the *Duberstein* case in Chapter 2.

39. This approach works in the business meal context, where a portion of the expense can be identified as caused solely by the taxpayer's nonbusiness life, and another portion as caused solely by the taxpayer's business. It would not work in the commuting expense context, where both the taxpayer's personal life and the taxpayer's job are but-for causes of the entire expense.

40. In that case, however, §274(n) denies the employer a deduction for 50 percent of the reimbursement.

exceptions from its application, allowing such things as payment of per diem allowances in some cases without substantiation. *See* Reg. §1.274-5T. As discussed above, in connection with §274(a), there is reason to doubt that §274 has been very effective in identifying expenditures with insufficient business nexus to justify a deduction. By contrast, it appears that §274(d) has been quite effective in denying deductions for amounts that were never spent at all — and deductions for nonexistent expenditures had been a serious problem indeed in the years between the *Cohan* decision and the enactment of §274.

4. *The ghost of* Cohan. Despite the fact that it no longer has any precedential value as to its own subject matter, the *Cohan* case continues to be one of the most widely cited tax cases in the jurisprudence, mostly by taxpayers who cannot adduce adequate evidence to support whatever position they may have taken. Taking some liberties, it could be said to stand for the proposition that in any situation where it's clear that *some* expenses were incurred that might be eligible for a deduction or credit under some section of the IRC, it is permissible to estimate the dollar amounts of those expenditures for purposes of claiming those deductions or credits, unless an explicit provision, such as §274(d) itself, conditions the deduction or credit on satisfying specific documentation requirements. Needless to say, it is not good practice to keep poor records and then hope for the best under the *Cohan* "rule" stated above. However, if a lawyer finds herself with a client who fits this description, the *Cohan* case may still provide some leverage in negotiations with the IRS (but only if the question is beyond the reach of §274).

5. *Why allow any deduction for entertainment expenses?* The deductibility of entertainment expenses is somewhat limited by the "directly related" and "associated with" rules of §274(a), and is more seriously limited by the 50 percent disallowance rule of §274(n). But why should such expenses be allowed at all? A taxpayer and his client or customer could hold their conversation over peanut-butter-and-jelly sandwiches in the taxpayer's office. What *business* purpose is served by holding the discussion over dinner at a fancy restaurant instead? Similarly, the lawyer and the client could simply have their "substantial and bona fide" business discussion and skip the baseball game afterward. What is it about the baseball game that justifies a business expense deduction? Is there a principled argument in favor of these deductions, based on some notion of business-bonding-through-filet-mignon-and-box-seats, or is this just an unprincipled legislative giveaway to affluent business people and to the restaurant, sports, and entertainment industries?

6. *Luxury travel and entertainment.* In the case of business travel expenses, §162(a)(2) specifically disallows deductions for food and lodging expenses that are "lavish or extravagant under the circumstances," and a court could easily find the same limitation to apply to entertainment expenses under the general "ordinary and necessary" language in the first phrase of §162(a). The IRS, however, seldom disallows either travel or entertainment expenses on grounds of extravagance, and the courts do not always support it when it does.[41] The IRS never questions the deductibility of the excess of the cost of

---

41. *See, e.g.,* Kurzet v. Commissioner, 222 F.3d 830 (10th Cir. 2000), involving a taxpayer who claimed business travel expense deductions for the costs of operating his private Lear jet. The Tax Court supported the IRS's limitation of the deduction to the cost of first-class airfare on commercial flights, but the Tenth Circuit reversed.

first-class airfare over coach, the excess of the cost of the Ritz-Carlton over the Marriott, or the excess of the cost of Le Cirque over McDonalds (or even the Olive Garden). Similarly, if the requirements for deductibility of "associated with" entertainment are satisfied, the IRS will not disallow a deduction for the $200 or so by which the cost of a seat in the Metropolitan Opera's Grand Tier exceeds the cost of a seat in the Family Circle. The same is true of the difference between the box seats and the bleachers at the old ball game, except that Congress has (strangely enough) put its foot down in the case of luxury sky boxes (*see* §274(*l*)(2)). Of course, the 50 percent disallowance of §274(n) applies in the case of meals and entertainment, but it does not apply in the case of first-class airfare or expensive hotel rooms. Even when §274(n) does apply, its effect is very different from the effect of a limitation aimed at extravagant expenditures. Just as the law, in its majesty, prohibits both the rich and the poor from sleeping under bridges, so §274(n) denies a deduction for 50 percent of the cost of both a Big Mac and a seven-course meal at Adour Alain Ducasse. By contrast, a limitation on extravagance would disallow much of the cost of the Alain Ducasse meal without affecting the Big Mac at all. If Congress really wanted to limit extravagant expenditures, it might replace the vague "lavish or extravagant under the circumstances" rule with a series of bright-line rules, such as a dollar ceiling on the deductible cost of a meal, hotel room, or sporting event (perhaps adjusted for location), or a rule denying a deduction for the excess of first-class airfare over coach. Such an approach could be used instead of §274(n) or in combination with it — for example, there might be a $100 ceiling on dinner costs taken into account for tax purposes, and §274(n) might then limit the deductible portion of that $100 to $50. Should Congress enact a series of rules along these lines? If it does, should first-class airfare be one of the targets of the legislation, or should it continue to be fully deductible even if expensive meals and entertainment are not?

7. *Airline clubs.* The regulations state that airline clubs are indeed clubs for purposes of the §274(a)(3) denial of deductions for club dues. Reg. §1.274-(2)(a)(2)(iii)(a). Does this result make sense as a matter of policy? The policy argument for the deductibility of airline club dues for business travelers would seem to be essentially the same as the policy argument for the deductibility of first class airfare. Like flying in the first-class section, spending time between flights at the "club" enables one to do more business *en route*, and to arrive at the destination in a condition more conducive to conducting business. Why, then, is a deduction allowed for the excess of first class over coach, but not for club dues? The businessperson who flies first class, and who receives club privileges automatically as a first-class perk, is allowed to deduct the cost of his ticket, including the portion of the first-class airfare allocable to the club privileges. By unfair contrast, the more frugal businessperson, who flies coach but pays club dues, gets no deduction for his dues. As unfair as this may be, was Treasury forced to this result by the language of §274(a)(3)? Is an airline club really a "club organized for business, pleasure, recreation, or other social purposes"? Is there a secret handshake?[42] Do the existing members get to vote on whom to admit as new members? Would the result change if the airlines stopped calling them "clubs"?

_____

42. This is not a rhetorical question; the authors have no idea.

8. *Section 274(n) and surrogate taxation.* It is easy enough to understand the policy behind the 50 percent disallowance of the cost of the taxpayer's own meal, or of the taxpayer's own ticket to the baseball game. But §274(n) also denies the taxpayer a deduction for half the cost of his guest's meal or entertainment. Presumably this is not based on the assumption that the host eats a substantial portion of his guest's food, but what *is* the explanation for the scope of the disallowance rule? The most plausible explanation is that extending §274(n) to the cost of the guest's meal or entertainment is an instance of surrogate taxation. Suppose our taxpayer takes his business guest to dinner and spends a total of $200, $100 for each of the two meals. With respect to his own $100 meal, the limitation of the deduction to $50 means the taxpayer will have to include the other half of the cost of his meal in his taxable income — an appropriate result, on the assumption that half of the cost of the meal represents personal consumption value and half represents a legitimate business expenditure. By the same logic, the theoretically appropriate treatment of the guest would be to require the guest to include the $50 personal consumption value of his meal in his own taxable income. This would not be administratively practical, so instead §274(n) overtaxes the host by $50, by denying him a deduction for half of the guest's meal. From the government's point of view, the overtaxation of the host and the undertaxation of the guest cancel out (assuming host and guest have the same marginal tax rate), and the government collects the appropriate amount of tax. Is the result fair to the host? Maybe not, but things may even out in the long run, if our taxpayer plays the guest role about as often as he plays the host role.

G. PATROLLING THE BUSINESS-PERSONAL BORDERS

Section 162 allows deduction of business expenses. Section 262 specifically disallows deduction of "personal, living, or family expenses." The tension between these two provisions in the case of expenses that have both business and personal aspects has surfaced in several of the cases presented earlier in this chapter, and is one of the most persistently difficult issues in any income tax system.

Consider what may be an extreme case by looking at a typical day in the life of a hypothetical CEO of the International Widget Company. His day begins when he is picked up at his Upper East Side apartment by a company chauffeur. (His efficiency apartment is provided by the company; the executive's home is in Fairfield County, Connecticut, but he spends most weekday evenings in New York, since his long hours and long commute make it more convenient to stay in the city.) He spends the ride reading the *Wall Street Journal* and some midday reports that have been sent to him from the managers of Asian subsidiaries of his company. He arrives at his office, which is beautifully furnished with a huge mahogany desk, several chairs and couches, and a spectacular view of the Manhattan skyline. In an alcove behind his antique credenza is a treadmill for his late-morning workout.

When he enters his office, he is met by his morning muffin and coffee, delivered by his secretary, who then takes letters dictated between the executive's bites and gulps. After a few important calls, the executive continues dictation while his hair is trimmed and his shoes are shined by a barber and valet, respectively, who are under contract with the company to provide these services to a handful of senior executives. Meetings, more calls, and 20 minutes on the treadmill follow. After a shower in his office lavatory, he has lunch in the company's executive dining room with the sales manager of a troubled division, then returns to his office for more meetings and calls. Finally, at about 6:30, he heads to the roof of the building for a 40-minute helicopter ride to Southampton, where he attends a dinner party. In the course of the party, he talks to the managing partner of an investment banking firm about the timing of the company's next stock offering; to an actor who will appear in a new series of commercials for the company's consumer products division; and to a publisher who is trying to interest our executive in writing a book (working title: *Wizard of Widgets*). More rides in the helicopter and the limo, and he's finally "home," at the company apartment where his day began 16 hours earlier.

The executive is likely to believe that virtually his entire waking life is devoted to his business; and he is not clearly wrong in that assessment. Most companies provide a great deal of personal assistance to their highest executives, partly because their jobs are so demanding, and their time so valuable, that it is cost-effective to hire, for example, a barber to come to the office and cut the executive's hair, rather than having the executive spend 30 or 45 minutes of the day getting his hair cut like everyone else. And if the executive is frequently in the public eye, representing the company, his good grooming may be more important than, say, the grooming of a sales clerk, a sanitation worker, or a law school professor. The provision of services, in other words, advances the interest of the company, and is probably not provided primarily for compensatory purposes. Nevertheless, a good deal of personal consumption is going on here.

What is true at the top of the economic ladder is also present throughout the ranks, in somewhat attenuated forms. A lawyer in a prestigious law firm needs a good wardrobe for business use, but he may also wear his suits to weddings and funerals. A stock broker needs subscriptions to business periodicals to provide good advice to her clients, but she may also benefit from those materials in structuring her own investment portfolio (and even the *Wall Street Journal* has a nice wine column). An actor may need to have his teeth capped and bleached to look good on camera, but he may also enjoy private benefits of a good appearance off-camera.

In this section, we look at this problem as it manifests itself in three major areas: so-called hobby losses, educational expenses, and clothing expenses.

1. Hobby Losses

KEANINI v. COMMISSIONER
94 T.C. 41 (1990)

NIMS, Chief Judge: Respondent determined deficiencies in petitioners' Federal income taxes in the amounts of $3,964.00 and $3,875.55 for 1982 and 1983, respectively. . . .

The issues for decision are whether petitioners (1) engaged in dog breeding and grooming for profit within the meaning of section 183(a); and (2) are entitled to deduct certain expenses incurred in their dog breeding and grooming operation.

FINDINGS OF FACT

At the time of filing their petition, petitioners [Samuel Keanini and Moanikeala Jellinger] resided in Honolulu, Hawaii. Petitioners were married and filed joint Federal income tax returns for 1982 and 1983.

During the late 1970's, petitioners became interested in starting a dog breeding and grooming business. In 1979, petitioner Moanikeala Jellinger (Jellinger) worked on a part-time basis at a dog grooming shop and attended a three-month seminar at an entrepreneur training school learning how to start and manage a new business. In 1980, petitioners purchased two poodles and began breeding the poodles on a part-time basis at their personal residence.

In 1982, petitioners built a kennel at their personal residence (the kennel) and started breeding poodles, grooming dogs and sponsoring dogs in quarantine on a full-time basis.

In January 1982, petitioners began breeding, selling and showing black miniature poodles (the breeding operation) under the name of "Pua's Poodles" at the kennel.

Petitioners acquired quality breeding stock from the mainland for the breeding operation at a reduced cost by entering into "co-ownership agreements" with mainland dog owners. Under a co-ownership agreement, petitioners and a mainland dog owner would agree to share the cost of purchasing and breeding a poodle equally. Although the mainland dog owner would actually raise and breed the poodle, petitioners were entitled to half the poodle's litters.

Petitioners sold every poodle from the breeding operation under a written contract which included two provisions. The first provision (the puppy-back provision) required that the poodle purchaser give petitioners, at no cost, a puppy from the poodle's first litter. The second provision required that the poodle purchaser retain petitioners to groom the poodle.

Petitioners showed their poodles at dog shows on the mainland and kept records of their breeding stock as required by the American Kennel Club. Petitioners hired professional dog handlers to show their poodles at dog shows on the mainland that they did not attend. Nine of petitioners' poodles have won national championship titles, and petitioners have established a national reputation as breeders of quality miniature poodles. Petitioners substantially increased the value of their breeding stock by winning national championship titles and estimate that their breeding stock is worth between $20,000 to $25,000.

From January 1982 to September 1983, petitioners groomed dogs at the kennel and at the homes of other dog owners. In September 1983, petitioners opened a dog-grooming shop (the grooming shop) called the "Hair Apparent" to groom dogs and sell dog care products. Petitioners could groom up to 12 dogs a day at the grooming shop. Petitioners hired part-time employees to assist in grooming dogs and purchased supplies for the grooming shop from wholesalers on the mainland.

Since January 1982, petitioners have been listed by the Hawaii Quarantine station (quarantine station) as individuals who are willing to sponsor dogs in quarantine. Animals brought into the state of Hawaii must be placed under quarantine for 120 days in a kennel at the quarantine station. Petitioners, as sponsors, agreed to feed and groom dogs held in quarantine under written contracts entered into with dog owners. By sponsoring dogs in quarantine, petitioners came in contact with dog owners interested in purchasing grooming services from the grooming shop and poodles from the breeding operation.

Petitioners operate what is referred to in the dog business as a fully "integrated" operation because breeding and grooming are carried on within a single business. (Hereinafter the fully integrated operation will be referred to as "the dog operation.")

Ms. Gold, a dog industry expert, testified that breeding and grooming is commonly carried on within a single integrated business because the same customer that purchases a puppy also needs grooming services and dog care products.

Petitioners advertised the breeding operation and the grooming shop in the yellow pages, local newspapers and national dog publications.

Before starting the dog operation, Jellinger had worked as a geologist for the state of Hawaii on a full-time basis. From 1982 to 1988, Jellinger has worked exclusively in the dog operation averaging between 80 to 100 hours a week. From 1982 to 1988, petitioner, Samuel Keanini (Keanini) has worked full-time for the Honolulu Police Department and 20-30 hours a week in the dog operation.

Petitioners are the only dog groomers in the state of Hawaii certified by the Pet Groomers Association of America (PGAA). To be certified by the PGAA, petitioners had to pass a written, oral and hands-on exam. Petitioners regularly attend trade shows, retail marketing shows and grooming seminars and subscribe to a number of dog publications. Jellinger is an active member of the American Kennel Club, the Obedience Training Club of Hawaii and the Poodle Club of Hawaii. During the summer of 1983, Jellinger attended a seminar on the mainland to learn how to more efficiently manage the dog operation.

From January 1982 to September 1983, Jellinger paid the expenses of the dog operation with checks drawn on her personal checking account. In September 1983, a separate checking account was opened to pay expenses of the grooming shop. Petitioners prepared monthly and quarterly income and expense statements for the dog operation. Jellinger kept a daily log in which she recorded the local mileage and expenses incurred in using her automobile in the dog operation.

Petitioners reported the following amounts in connection with the dog operation on Schedule C of their joint Federal income tax returns:

Year	Income	Deductions	Profit/(Loss)
1982	$1,304	$18,323	(17,019)
1983	4,875	21,741	(16,866)
1984	12,528	23,458	(10,930)
1985	20,100	28,154	(8,054)
1986	19,273	23,628	(4,355)
1987	26,114	24,913	1,201

... Respondent determined that petitioners were not entitled to deduct (1) the losses incurred by the dog operation in 1982 and 1983 because petitioners were not engaged in the dog operation for profit within the meaning of section 183(a); and (2) certain miscellaneous expenses incurred in the dog operation because these expenses were not adequately substantiated.

OPINION

As a general rule, individuals are not allowed to deduct losses attributable to an activity not engaged in for profit. Sec. 183(a). Section 183(c) defines an "activity not engaged in for profit" as an "activity other than one with respect to which deductions are allowable for the taxable year under section 162 or under paragraph (1) or (2) of section 212." A taxpayer must engage in an activity with the objective of making a profit in order to fully deduct expenses under either section 162 or section 212.

Respondent contends that breeding operation and grooming shop are separate activities for purposes of section 183(a) and that the breeding operation is not an activity engaged in for profit. We do not agree.

In determining whether a taxpayer engages in two or more separate activities for purposes of section 183, section 1.183-1(d)(1), Income Tax Regs. provides that:

> all the facts and circumstances of the case must be taken into account. Generally, the most significant facts and circumstances in making this determination are the degree of organizational and economic interrelationship of various undertakings, the business purpose which is (or might be) served by carrying on the various undertakings separately or together in a trade or business or in an investment setting, and the similarity of various undertakings. Generally, the Commissioner will accept the characterization by the taxpayer of several undertakings either as a single activity or as separate activities. The taxpayer's characterization will not be accepted, however, when it appears that his characterization is artificial and cannot be reasonably supported under the facts and circumstances of the case.

We find that petitioners' characterization of the dog operation as a single activity for purposes of section 183 to be fully supported by the facts of this case. A close organizational and economic relationship exists between the breeding operation and the grooming shop. Dog breeding and grooming are similar undertakings and are commonly carried on within a single "integrated" business. Petitioners initially carried on both breeding and grooming at the kennel. The goodwill derived from winning national championship titles benefits both the breeding operation and the grooming shop. By retaining, under contract, the right to groom every poodle sold, every customer of the breeding operation becomes a customer of the grooming shop. The breeding operation and grooming shop were carried on as a single integrated business and shared common customers, goodwill and physical facilities. Thus, we find that a close organizational and economic relationship exists between the breeding operation and grooming shop. Accordingly, we determine that for purposes of section 183 the dog operation was a single activity.

We next consider whether petitioners engaged in the dog operation with the objective of making a profit. Petitioners do not need to establish that their expectation of profit was reasonable provided they had an "actual and honest objective of making a profit." Dreicer v. Commissioner, 78 T.C. 642, 644-645 (1982), *aff'd without opinion*, 702 F.2d 1205 (D.C. Cir. 1983). Whether petitioners engaged in the dog operation with the requisite objective of making a profit is one of fact to be resolved on the basis of all the surrounding facts and circumstances. In making this determination, more weight is accorded to objective facts than to the taxpayer's mere statement of intent. The burden of proving the requisite objective is on petitioners.

Section 1.183-2(b), Income Tax Regs., provides a nonexclusive list of factors, which is in large part a synthesis of prior case law, to be considered in determining whether an activity is engaged in for profit. These factors include: (1) The manner in which the taxpayer carried on the activity; (2) the expertise of the taxpayer or his advisors; (3) the time and effort expended by the taxpayer in carrying on the activity; (4) the expectation that assets used in the activity may appreciate in value; (5) the success of the taxpayer in carrying on other similar or dissimilar activities; (6) the taxpayer's history of income or loss with respect to the activity; (7) the amount of occasional profit, if any, which is earned; (8) the financial status of the taxpayer; and (9) whether elements of personal pleasure or recreation are involved. No single factor is controlling. Rather the facts and circumstances of the case taken as whole are determinative. Abramson v. Commissioner, 88 T.C. 360, 371 (1986); sec. 1.183-2(b), Income Tax Regs.

The facts and circumstances of the present case show that petitioners engaged in the dog operation for profit. From 1982 to 1988, petitioners were breeding championship poodles, grooming dogs and sponsoring dogs in quarantine. Jellinger left her profession as a geologist, and from 1982 to 1988 she worked 80-100 hours a week and Keanini worked 20-30 hours a week in the dog operation. Initially, petitioners were able to carry on the dog operation at the kennel using only their own labor. As the dog operation expanded, petitioners opened a separate grooming shop and hired part-time groomers and professional dog handlers. Although the dog operation suffered losses during its start-up years, the losses decreased steadily each year and in 1987 a profit was realized. The profit earned after years of hard work convinces us that petitioners were engaged in the dog operation for profit.

As their experience grew, petitioners implemented business practices designed to make the dog operation more profitable. Petitioners reduced the cost of purchasing supplies for the grooming shop by purchasing these supplies directly from wholesalers on the mainland. Petitioners reduced the cost of acquiring breeding stock from the mainland by entering into co-ownership agreements. Petitioners increased grooming revenues by retaining, under contract, the right to groom every poodle they sold. Petitioners obtained quality breeding stock, at no cost, by selling every poodle under a contract with a puppy-back provision.

Petitioners used a number of marketing techniques to generate revenue and goodwill for the dog operation. Petitioners advertised the grooming shop and breeding operation in the yellow pages, local newspapers and national dog journals. Petitioners listed their names at the quarantine station as sponsors. As quarantine sponsors, petitioners came in contact with dog owners interested in purchasing grooming services at the grooming shop and poodles from the breeding operation. By hiring professional dog handlers to show their poodles and winning national championship titles, petitioners established a national reputation as quality breeders, thus increasing the value of their breeding stock and creating goodwill for their grooming shop.

Petitioners possessed the experience needed to successfully carry on the dog operation. Jellinger had worked at a dog grooming shop prior to starting the dog operation. Petitioners regularly attend seminars and clinics on dog marketing, breeding, and grooming and are the only nationally certified dog groomers in the state of Hawaii. Jellinger is an active member of three dog clubs and subscribes to numerous dog periodicals. Jellinger spent the summer of 1983 attending a seminar on the mainland learning how to manage the dog operation more efficiently.

Considering all the facts and circumstances, we find that petitioners engaged in the dog operation with the objective of making a profit.

[Discussion of documentation of miscellaneous deductions for automobile and telephone use, and seminar attendance, are omitted.]

Notes and Questions

1. *Thoroughbred losses.* Breeders of dogs and horses have litigated many §183 cases, and have generally fared poorly.[43] Typically, they show long, unbroken strings of losses from these activities, leaving the IRS and judicial factfinders free to conclude that the taxpayers engaged in these activities because they love dogs or horses enough to absorb large and continuing losses in these activities. Under those circumstances, the tax system is probably justified in insisting that the taxpayers absorb those losses without assistance from the federal Treasury.

   The taxpayers in this case benefited from the fact that they were able to convince the court that their profit possibilities should be considered on the basis of aggregating their grooming activities (which were apparently profitable) with their breeding activities (which were not). The disaggregated figures are not disclosed in the opinion; the aggregated figures show a fairly normal curve for a new business, with significant losses in early years but continuous improvement in subsequent years, leading to net profits in the sixth year of the business. Had the IRS known that the court would aggregate the two parts of the business, it is doubtful that it would have denied the loss deductions under these financial circumstances.

2. *The structure of §183.* Examine the draftsmanship and structure of §183. Note that it begins, in §183(a), with a provision that claims to eliminate all deductions otherwise available in the case of an activity that is not engaged in for profit. However, the provision is not in fact intended to be so draconian, as the next subsection reveals: §183(b) restores deductibility for two categories of deductions in turn. The first category consists of items that do not depend on any business or profit-seeking purpose. For example, state and local property taxes are generally deductible, even when assessed against property that is not held for business or investment purposes. Such taxes do not become nondeductible simply because the taxpayer happens to use them in an activity that is not engaged in for profit. Section 183(b)(1) makes this clear.

   The second category consists of those deductions that *do* depend on a profit-seeking purpose, such as the deduction for ordinary and necessary

---

43. This appears to be true despite the special favoritism shown to the horse business by subsection (d) of §183. This subsection creates a favorable presumption of deductibility for purported businesses whose gross income exceeds their deductions in any three of the preceding five tax years; however, those engaged in breeding, training, showing, or racing horses enjoy the same presumption if they have shown profits in any two of the preceding seven years. This may reflect: (1) the extraordinary importance of this industry to the American economy; (2) a legitimate allowance for an industry that is by its nature slower to show profits than all other American lines of business; (3) a personal predilection for the ponies on part of a requisite proportion of the members of the 91st Congress, which enacted these provisions in 1969; or (4) the influence of the horse lobby with that same Congress. You may take your guess, but if this were a horse race, it wouldn't be a close one.

Chapter 5. Business Expense Deductions

business expenses under §162(a), or the deduction for depreciation of real or personal property under §§167 and 168. These expenses (or allowances) may be deducted under §183(b)(2), but only to the extent that they do not exceed the income from the activity, after that figure has been reduced by the amount of any deductions claimed under §183(b)(1) above.[44]

3. *Hobbies versus tax shelters.* Section 183 is popularly known as the "hobby loss" provision, but the language of the Code section itself does not speak in those terms, but rather in terms of "activities not engaged in for profit." The IRS has in fact used §183 primarily in two types of cases. In the first type, the IRS believes that substantial elements of personal consumption are involved in an activity that may occasionally generate some incidental income, but the circumstances indicate that the incidental income, while no doubt welcome, is not the *raison d'etre* of the activity. These are the cases most aptly described as "hobby loss" cases. In addition to animal breeding, the case law is filled with car-, yacht-, and speedboat-racing losses; losses from efforts to produce salable works of art or literature; losses from attempts to be discovered as actors or musicians; losses from efforts to develop valuable collections of stamps, coins, carpets, and antiques; losses from engaging in golf or bowling tournaments; and the like. Rarely (except in cases of the sort described in the next paragraph) does the IRS assert that activities that do not have obvious recreational elements are subject to §183. (Though future lawyers should note that, in four or five reported cases, the IRS has asserted that the law practices of the lawyer-taxpayers in those cases were not engaged in for profit. *See, e.g.,* Cohen v. Commissioner, T.C. Memo 1984-237.)

In cases of the second type, the IRS employs §183 in an attempt to deny loss deductions of a taxpayer who has structured an activity with the express purpose of generating an accounting loss (which is usually not a real economic loss, but may be facially deductible anyway). In these tax shelter cases, the IRS may argue that the loss should be disregarded, and the activity considered as one not engaged in for profit, because tax-avoidance, not profit, was the primary motive.

Although the IRS has achieved some success using §183 in the second sort of case, Congress has repeatedly tried to assist the Service in curtailing tax shelter activity by adding more specific provisions targeted at particular types of abuse. In 1976, for example, Congress added §465 to the Code, which limits deductions to the portion of an investment in which the taxpayer is "at-risk," meaning that the taxpayer either has invested her own money in the activity or has invested borrowed money with respect to which she has a personal obligation to repay the debt. (Exceptions to §465 for real estate investments, however, have substantially limited its effectiveness from its inception.)

Section 469, added to the Code in 1986, limits deductions for expenses associated with all of a taxpayer's "passive activities" to the amount of

---

44. Although §183 is generally understood as a *deduction-limiting* provision, the better technical view is that it is a *deduction-creating* provision. Section 162 authorizes business-expense deductions only for taxpayers with profit motives; were it not for §183(b)(2), there would be no authority for any business-related deductions in the context of an activity not engaged in for profit.

582

income generated by those passive activities. The definition of "passive activities" is such that they rarely generate enough income to absorb all of the expenses associated with those activities, and §469 has proven to be quite effective in limiting deductions over a broad range of individual tax shelter investments.[45]

Even so, a role remains for §183; indeed, both of its historical roles continue to have some vitality. If a taxpayer materially participates in an activity, then it would not fall within §469's ambit. So activities like animal breeding, antique restoration, and the like continue to be most accessible to §183. And if tax shelter activities escape the reach of §469 for some reason (such as the fact that the taxpayer is a publicly held corporation, which is not subject to the passive activity rules), then §183 continues to be available to deny deductions on grounds that the activity in question was not pursued for the purpose of achieving a profit.

4. *Vacation homes.* Section 280A imposes limits on deductions that apply to rental income from buildings that are "used as a residence" by a taxpayer, which generally means used by the taxpayer or his family for more than 14 days during any particular tax year. Deductions for rental activities in such cases cannot exceed the amount of income generated by the activities, less any deductions that might be available for interest, taxes, casualty losses, or other business deductions (those not directly related to the rental property.)[46] The mechanics of §280A thus resemble those of §183, on which they were based.

5. *Home offices.* Section 280A also applies to deductions for the use of part of a personal residence as a business facility, such as a studio, clinic, or, most commonly, an office that is located in the taxpayer's home. Prior to the enactment of this section, many professional and managerial taxpayers had claimed that, because they often did work for their employers (or to advance their own trades or businesses) in their homes, they should be allowed to deduct a portion of the costs of maintaining those homes. The costs typically included a portion of the utilities and maintenance costs for the unit, plus an allowance for depreciation. Of course, in many such cases, the amount of work done at home was quite minimal, and the room supposedly set aside for this purpose often served other, more personal purposes as well. Because the IRS was rarely in a position to rebut the taxpayer's own testimony about the relative magnitudes of business and personal use, it had considerable difficulty in controlling these deductions.

Section 280A was designed to attack this problem, along with the vacation home problem. But Congress did not want to limit deductions for the much smaller number of taxpayers who actually did conduct their trade or business activities out of their homes. Although it is relatively rare today, in the 1970s it was not unusual for doctors, dentists, psychotherapists, and other professionals to conduct their professions in a room (or two) in their homes.

To separate the deserving latter group from the undeserving former group, §280A first disallows all deductions related to the use of the dwelling unit in subsection (a), then restores deductibility in subsection (b) for expenses—like home mortgage interest and local property taxes—that would ordinarily be deductible whether or not there was a business use of

---

45. See Chapter 8.B.3.
46. For more detail on §280A, see the cell on this subject.

the residence, and finally restores deductibility selectively in subsection (c) for certain business or profit-seeking uses of the property. In the case of a home office, the operative rules are in §280A(c)(1), which allows deductions[47] relating to a portion of a dwelling unit that is used exclusively and regularly for business, if it meets one of the three following conditions:

1. It is used as the principal place of business for any trade or business of the taxpayer.
2. It is a place of business routinely used by patients, clients, or customers.
3. It is located in a separate structure, such as a garage, which is not attached to the dwelling unit.

In the case of an employee (as distinguished from a self-employed person), there is an additional, and not easily satisfied, requirement: The employee's use of the home office must be "for the convenience of his employer." These rules have generally proven adequate to separate the taxpayers who make significant business use of their homes from those who simply take home an occasional briefcase of business reading material. Taxpayers who practice their professions out of their homes will be able to meet either the first or second tests, or both.[48] But, despite the disjunctive phrasing of the tests, which means that a taxpayer need only satisfy one of the three, most taxpayers who simply do occasional work at home will have difficulty meeting any of the tests.

Problem 3.   C. Garrett races speedboats, and wins $5,000 doing so in a particular tax year. Suppose that the expenses she incurred during the year were as follows: $2,000 in personal property taxes with respect to the speedboat; $3,500 in transportation expenses to get to the places at which the contests would be held; and $3,000 in allowable depreciation with respect to her investment in the speedboat. Suppose further that this year was typical of her experience in racing speedboats over the last several years. What will be the tax effect of the income and expense items described?

2.   Education Expenses

NAMROW v. COMMISSIONER
288 F.2d 648 (4th Cir. 1960), *cert. denied,* **368 U.S. 914 (1961)**

SOPER, Circuit Judge: Upon this petition for review we must decide whether there is sufficient evidence to sustain the ruling of the Tax Court that expenditures made by two psychiatrists in order to qualify themselves to practice psychoanalysis

---

47. Technically, §280A(c)(1) operates as an exception to the disallowance rule of §280A(a). The Code section governing the deduction is thus §162(a), the provision authorizing business expense deductions generally.
48. The third test seems qualitatively different from the first two, which are focused on the nature and extent of the business use of the dwelling. Congress apparently thought that separate structures were less likely to be the object of abusive deductions than the family study.

are not deductible in computing their taxable income. The Commissioner of Internal Revenue determined a deficiency against Dr. Arnold Namrow and his wife for the year 1954 in the sum of $376.84. [The facts as to the second taxpayer are omitted.] The cases were consolidated for trial and the determinations of the Commissioner were sustained. In each case the taxpayer was engaged in the practice of psychiatry in Washington, D.C. during the tax years and paid certain fees as a student in the Washington Psychoanalytic Institute for training in psychoanalysis. The deductibility of these expenditures gives rise to the instant controversy.

Psychiatry is a medical specialty which deals with the study and treatment of mental disorders and is recognized as a specialty by the American Medical Association, the American Psychiatric Association, and the American Neurological Association. The minimum qualification of a doctor as a psychiatrist consists of graduation from a recognized medical school, one year of general internship, and one year of specialized residency in an institution for the treatment of mental disorders which has been approved by the American Medical Association and the American Psychiatric Association. In actual practice full recognition as a psychiatrist is obtained only by additional years as a resident psychiatrist in a mental institution and passing an examination set by the American Board of Psychiatry and Neurology.

Still further training is required if a psychiatrist desires to obtain general recognition as one qualified to practice in the special field of psychoanalysis. This method for the treatment of mental disorders derives its importance from the studies of Sigmund Freud, who conceived the idea of the unconscious mind and developed a method of analyzing a person's mental life which is now widely-accepted by psychiatrists as a form of psychotherapeutic treatment. Psychotherapy is a general term which includes, according to qualified witnesses in this case, sitting down with the patient and encouraging him to talk freely to the doctor about himself so as to discover his history and his emotional and personal difficulties. It is sometimes described as the "talking cure," which is generally employed by psychiatrists and more or less consciously by ministers of religion and laymen whose work involves consultation with persons in difficult situations. The most intensive form of this treatment is psychoanalysis, which is described by the taxpayers in this case as "the revolutionary technique originated by Freud in which emotionally maladjusted but otherwise intelligent adults explore deeply into the workings of their conscious and unconscious minds by talking freely with the psychiatrist until they ultimately are able to recognize and re-examine rationally those intense feelings and experiences which theretofore were buried in and distorted by the unconscious mind."

It is generally recognized by psychiatrists that the technique originated by Freud demands an exceptional degree of emotional objectivity and control on the part of the doctor. On this account specialized institutes for the training and supervision of prospective analysts have been set up in fourteen cities in the United States and organized in accordance with regulations and standards of the American Psychoanalytic Association. The Washington Psychoanalytic Institute attended by the taxpayers was one of these institutes and a description of its operations demonstrates the special training which, in the opinion of the medical profession in general and of its psychiatric branch in particular, is needed to qualify a psychiatrist to practice psychoanalysis. . . .

The bulletin of the Washington Psychoanalytic Institute describes the three general divisions of the training program. This includes, first, a preparatory analysis of the applicant himself, the duration of which may require several years. Its objective is freedom from personality factors that would interfere with the ability to conduct psychoanalytic treatment. The second division of the training, called "Theoretical Instruction," consists of a graduated series of lectures and seminars covering the theory and technique of psychoanalysis. The third division of the training program requires the student to conduct a minimum of four analyses of patients under supervision. . . .

Since the students of the Washington Psychoanalytic Institute must be qualified psychiatrists they customarily engage in the private practice of psychiatry while taking the training at the Institute and both taxpayers in this case were so engaged during the tax periods. . . . During 1954 [Dr. Namrow] paid Dr. Cohen $2,250 for his personal analysis, and also paid $375 for services [of a] supervising analyst. He expected to finish his training at the Institute in 1960 and thereupon become eligible for membership in the psychoanalytic associations.

Each taxpayer claims that his expenditures for personal analysis and for the services of supervising analysts were deductible as ordinary and necessary expenditures under §162, but the Commissioner disallowed these claims.

The Tax Court, five judges dissenting, upheld the Commissioner's determinations. Its decision is based largely on the interpretative application of §162 of the Code, which is contained in §1.162-5 of the Treasury Regulations entitled "Expenses for Education." The gist of this section of the regulations is that expenditures for education are deductible if the education is undertaken primarily for the purpose of maintaining or improving skills required by the taxpayer in his trade or business, but are not deductible if they are for education undertaken for the purpose of obtaining a new position or substantial advancement in position or in order to meet the minimum requirements for qualification in his intended trade or business or specialty therein.

The validity of the regulation is not disputed. The question is whether, under the undisputed facts, the cases fall into one category or the other. We think there is sufficient evidence to support the Tax Court's position. The preponderance of the evidence plainly shows that neither an ordinary physician nor one who has had sufficient additional training to practice psychiatry is considered qualified to practice psychoanalysis unless he has submitted to long and intense additional education and training in the psychoanalytic field. These requirements are not based on statute but on the body of medical opinion that finds expression in representative and recognized medical societies and particularly in the formation of the psychoanalytic institutes in great centers of population which set the standards that are accepted in practice.

Most persuasive of the existence of these requirements is the conduct of the taxpayers themselves in making substantial expenditures of money and devoting long periods of time in intensive training while practicing psychiatry in order to secure the recognition of their professional brethren as competent to engage in the practice of psychoanalysis. It is admitted that their general purpose was to secure referrals from other physicians, which are necessary in the successful practice of psychoanalysis. To this end each of them pledged himself not to administer psychoanalytic treatment or represent himself as a psychoanalyst until he had been authorized to do so by the faculty of the Institute, and each acknowledged that seven years will have passed before his training at the Institute is complete. It was explained by psychiatrists testifying on their behalf that the purpose of the pledge was to make sure that the student is competent before he goes into practice and that a reliable psychiatrist did not hold himself to be an analyst without completing the Institute's course. Thus there is solid ground for the conclusion of the Tax Court that the expenditures were made in order to acquire a special skill not possessed by ordinary psychiatrists. In this respect the Tax Court said:

> We think it fairly appears from this record that a psychiatrist cannot establish himself as a psychoanalyst without completing an Institute. This becomes more evident from other testimony to the effect that psychiatrists obtain most all of their patients by referrals from other doctors, principally other psychiatrists, because they prefer not to treat people with whom they are acquainted. In view of this, it is extremely unlikely that a psychiatrist could ever establish a psychoanalytic practice without attendance at an Institute. Namrow testified he received the majority of his referrals, and Maxwell, a substantial number of his referrals, from colleagues at the Institute.

In opposition the taxpayers point to evidence given on their behalf by qualified psychiatrists and psychoanalysts to the general effect that the dividing line between psychiatry and psychoanalysis is very thin. They say that psychoanalysis is merely an intensive form of psychotherapeutic treatment customarily administered by psychiatrists and that psychiatry is recognized as a specialty by the American Medical Association but psychoanalysis is not. They add that sometimes practicing psychiatrists or even ordinary physicians subject themselves to personal psycho-analysis, since it enables them to practice their profession more effectively; that candidates for training in the Washington Psychoanalytic Institute sometimes come to the Institute after they have already engaged in psychoanalytic practice and that trainees in the Institute are allowed to call themselves psychoanalysts (under supervision) after they have undergone personal analyses for a period of one year. Moreover, it is said that a general practitioner of medicine without analytic training may legally practice psychoanalysis, although he would not be considered qualified by psychiatrists and would not get referrals from them. For all of these reasons it is said that the Institute does not teach a new skill but merely improves the skill which every psychiatrist possesses.

It is contended in addition, in this aspect of the case, that the fees paid by the taxpayers were deductible as business expenses under §162(a)(1) because the personal psychoanalysis to which candidates in an institute are subjected and the supervision of their analyses of patients during their course of training consti-tute professional consultations similar to those which occur when one physician calls in another for diagnosis and treatment of a patient. It is said, moreover, that the fees paid are business expenses in a very practical sense as the cost of obtaining new business, since the training produces referrals that the candidates would not otherwise obtain.

This evidence and these arguments are not without persuasive force, but they are not so weighty as to compel us to conclude that the findings of fact of the Tax Court are so clearly untenable and erroneous that under the rule the judgment of the Tax Court must be reversed. To some extent at least the evidence produced by the taxpayers support[s] the Tax Court's determination. It cannot be disputed that all of the activities for which the fees were paid, including the psychoanalyses of patients under supervision after completion of the first year of training, were parts of a course of training which, in the opinion of psychiatrists generally, is needed to qualify a psychiatrist to engage in a certain type of psychiatric practice. These activities do not lose their quality as training techniques because they were similar to those used by qualified practitioners. The true purpose and effect of an expense govern its deductibility. The experts produced by the taxpayers clearly held the opinion that a psychiatrist should not hold himself as a psychoanalyst unless he had completed long years of training at a psychoanalytic institute. The basic question of fact, whether psychoanalysis requires the acquisition of a new skill or the improvement of one already possessed, still remains to be answered; and the existence throughout the country of psychoanalytic institutes and societies and the organization of the American Psychoanalytic Association on a national scale support the view that even if psychoanalysis is not formally recognized as a specialty by the American Medical Association, it is in effect so regarded by a large body of medical opinion without whose approval it cannot be successfully practiced. . . .

Affirmed.

Notes and Questions

1. *The education regulations.* The Treasury regulations have unusually broad authority over the deduction of education expenses connected with a taxpayer's business, largely because the relevant statute (§162) is silent on this particular question. The basic outline of the regulation's rules on this can be summarized as follows: First, the education in question must satisfy either of two requirements: (1) It must maintain or improve skills required by the individual in his employment or other trade or business; or (2) it must meet the express requirements of the individual's employer or applicable licensing regulations imposed as a condition to the retention of the individual's status. Reg. §1.162-5(a). Second, however, it must *not* be education of either of two other sorts (even if it meets one or both of the requirements above): (1) the education must not meet minimum entry-level requirements for qualification in the particular trade or business the taxpayer is entering; and (2) the education must not qualify the taxpayer for a new trade or business. Reg. §1.162-5(b)(2) and (3), respectively. The logical structure of the regulation's rules could be described as: "Either a or b, but neither c nor d."

2. *A change of mind.* Because the regulations place great emphasis on the idea that the education must be within the taxpayer's already established field, and not in some new field, the definition of the taxpayer's field is heavily freighted with tax consequences. The definition of the field of psychotherapy at issue in *Namrow* provides a nice example, and one in which much may be at stake, since the costs in question include not only institute tuition, but also the costs of a rather drawn out "training analysis" —which may involve four or five sessions per week for several years—of the would-be analyst. One notes in passing that it is hard to imagine anything more intensely personal for a taxpayer than his own psychoanalysis, with its emphasis on childhood relationships to parents, early sexual experiences, and the like. Yet the business connection is reasonably clear as well.

Curiously, after a number of cases in which the IRS successfully asserted the distinction between psychiatry and psychoanalysis insisted on in

Namrow, it reversed its position on this particular issue in 1967, and modified the regulations to include a specific example indicating that, upon further review, there was no distinction of any importance between the two. Reg. §1.162-5(b)(3)(ii), ex. 4. We wish we could ask the Commissioner at the time: "And how did you feel about that?"

3. *Section 67 strikes again.* Many taxpayers will find that the cost of an occasional course or two to improve their performance in their existing fields of employment, while theoretically deductible, is in fact limited by §67, which makes "employee business expenses" a miscellaneous itemized deduction. Thus, only to the extent that the educational expenses, together with any other miscellaneous items the taxpayer may have had that year, exceed 2 percent of the taxpayer's adjusted gross income, will the expenses be effectively deductible.

4. *Other tax benefits for educational costs.* While §67 has made business expense deductions for education less widely available, other Code sections have been added or amended in recent years to provide an extensive array of exclusions, deductions, and credits. *See* §§117, 25A, and 127, all of which are discussed in Chapter 2.B.3.e, and §221, which is discussed in Chapter 4. B.2.d.

5. *Personal or capital?* Educational expenses are usually analyzed in terms of whether they relate primarily to the business or personal interests of the taxpayer. But shouldn't the real issue be whether they should be capitalized or expensed? Take, for example, a law school education. It is almost invariably nondeductible, because it will almost invariably qualify the student for a new occupational field. But if we refer back to our general understanding of the role of business expenses in the definition of income, should the deduction be denied? A few students may find the study of law so fascinating that all they want to do is study it. Their lot in life may be to become impecunious law professors. Most, however, study law because they intend to become lawyers, an occupation that is reasonably well compensated. The tuition expense, in other words, is very closely related to the expected generation of business income upon graduation.

A better argument for denying deductions for law school costs is not that they are personal, but rather that they are capital expenditures, providing as they do useful intellectual capital that is likely to be productive over many years. (This could, of course, be said as well of many of the educational expenses that are found to be deductible in the current year.) But that response does not explain why the deduction should be permanently barred. If the education costs shouldn't be deducted because the benefits last longer than the current year, shouldn't they be amortized over the useful life of the education, namely, the expected career of the new lawyer? It might be objected that the duration of the career (or in any case, of the education) is too uncertain to permit amortization. But this seems dubious in a system that routinely permits deductions for wasting value of railroad tunnels, hydroelectric facilities, subscription lists, and a variety of other assets of substantial but uncertain longevity.[49]

---

49. For more on capitalization and cost recovery, see Chapter 6.

Problem 4. Applying the rules of Reg. §1.162-5, which of the following taxpayers, if any, would be entitled to a deduction?

(a) A lawyer incurs expenses of taking an estate planning update course, as a means of meeting the mandatory continuing legal education requirements imposed by her state bar.

(b) A lawyer takes the same course because he wants to improve his knowledge of estate planning. (Assume either that his state imposes no mandatory CLE requirement or that he has already met the relevant requirement for this time period.)

(c) A fifth-grade teacher takes two courses toward his master's degree in elementary education over the summer; the state teacher-certification requirement imposes a mandate that progress be made toward such a degree at some time within the five-year period of provisional certification of all teachers, but does not impose any requirement that the courses be taken this year.

(d) Another fifth-grade teacher takes the last semester of courses needed for her bachelor's degree; she has been provisionally certified to be a student-teacher, and has been doing so for the last ten months. That provisional certification expires one year after it is issued unless the teacher finishes her bachelor's degree.

(e) A lawyer takes courses toward an LL.M. degree in tax.

(f) A lawyer takes courses in accounting to improve her skills in understanding financial information.

(g) A journalist attends law school in the hopes of becoming the next Supreme Court reporter for the *New York Times.*

(h) An assistant sales manager for a hardware manufacturer enrolls in a full-time MBA program at a local university, with the encouragement of his employer, but no financial support. The employer hopes that the employee will return following the two-year program, and says that it will consider the additional education in evaluating the sales manager's fitness for the next regional sales manager position that becomes open following his return to the company. Before answering, consider the following case.

ALLEMEIER v. COMMISSIONER

90 T.C.M. 197 (2005)

Kroupa, J.

Respondent determined a $4,872 deficiency in petitioner's Federal income tax for 2001 and a $974 accuracy-related penalty. After concessions, the issues for decision are:

1. Whether petitioner may deduct expenses incurred to earn a master's degree in business administration (MBA). We hold that he may deduct education-related, but not parking, expenses. . . .

Findings of Fact . . .

Petitioner has been a Selane Products, Inc. (Selane Products) employee since 1996. Selane Products is an orthodontic and pediatric laboratory that specializes in making removable orthodontic appliances. It employed about 75 people at the time of trial and is located in Chatsworth, California.

When Selane Products hired petitioner, it needed salespeople with expertise to sell a newly manufactured mouth guard. Petitioner, with his educational background in sports medicine, was an ideal fit. . . .

While originally hired to sell a single product, petitioner's duties expanded to encompass other dentistry products and services of Selane Products. For instance, petitioner was tasked with designing marketing strategies to sell company products, organizing informational seminars, and traveling extensively to meet new staff, set up seminars, and promote Selane Products in talks he delivered at dentistry-related conventions. Petitioner performed these duties before obtaining a graduate degree.

Petitioner decided to pursue an MBA about 3 years into his employment with Selane Products. Dr. Veis [Selane's CEO] told petitioner that pursuing the MBA would speed his advancement within the company and enhance his business skills. Selane Products, however, had a strict policy of not reimbursing employees for education costs or other business expenses. Nor did Selane Products require petitioner to obtain the MBA.

Petitioner decided to pay for the MBA personally, and in 1999 he commenced studies at Pepperdine University. He finished the degree in late 2001, the year at issue. His MBA concentration was in business management, and his courses included accounting for managers, statistics, managerial finance, marketing management, quantitative methods, negotiation and conflict resolution, organizational theory and management, and business strategy.

Shortly after petitioner enrolled in, but before he completed, the MBA program, he was promoted to several new positions at Selane Products. Petitioner was promoted to Marketing Manager, Managing Director of the Appliance Therapy Practitioners Association, Head of the SMILE Foundation, Practice Development Consultant, and Project Development Consultant. In these new capacities, petitioner's duties expanded and included analyzing financial reports, designing action plans for sales, and evaluating the effectiveness of marketing campaigns. Petitioner performed many of these same functions before he earned his MBA. Petitioner remained a full-time employee of Selane Products while in the MBA program.

Petitioner deducted his MBA-related expenses on his Schedule A, Itemized Deductions, on Form 2016-EZ, Unreimbursed Employee Business Expenses, which he timely filed along with his electronic Federal income tax return for 2001. Petitioner also incurred substantial business expenses traveling for Selane Products that he deducted on his Schedule A.

Specifically, petitioner deducted $17,500 of tuition expenses and $231 of parking fees associated with his education. . . .

OPINION

Respondent disallowed the claimed employee business expenses and determined that petitioner was liable for an accuracy-related penalty. Petitioner asserts that he may deduct MBA-related expenses and other non-education business expenses, and that he is not liable for the penalty because he acted with reasonable cause and in good faith in taking the deductions. We address each issue in turn. . . .

We first determine whether petitioner's MBA-related expenses qualify as deductible business expenses. A taxpayer may deduct all ordinary and necessary expenses paid or incurred during the taxable year in carrying on a trade or business. Sec. 162(a). Educational expenses, specifically, are deductible if the education maintains or improves skills required by the individual in his or her employment or other trade or business or meets the express requirements of the individual's employer. Sec. 1.162-5(a)(1) and (2), Income Tax Regs.

No deduction is allowed, however, if the taxpayer's expense is for education that enables him or her to meet the minimum educational requirements for qualification in his or her employment or if the education leads to qualifying the taxpayer for a new trade or business. Sec. 1.162-5(b)(2) and (3), Income Tax Regs.

Because the parties agree that the MBA improved petitioner's skills, we focus on whether the MBA met the minimum education requirement of Selane Products or qualified petitioner for a new trade or business. In other words, petitioner's MBA-related expenses are not deductible if the MBA was a condition precedent to his employment. Nor are the expenses deductible if the MBA qualified petitioner for a new trade or business, regardless of his intent to enter a new trade or business, and regardless of whether his duties significantly changed after he obtained the MBA.

1. Whether the MBA Met Minimum Education Requirements of Selane Products

Determining whether an employee meets the minimum education requirement typically means that an employee must have a particular degree before being hired or obtain the degree within a certain period after being hired. *See* sec. 1.162-5(b)(2)(iii), *Examples* (*1*), (*2*), and (*3*), Income Tax Regs. Here, respondent argues that Selane Products had a minimum education requirement, not for petitioner to begin employment but for petitioner to be promoted after he was hired, and that requirement was for petitioner to obtain an MBA. We disagree.

We first note that the parties both stipulated on the record that Selane Products did not expressly require that petitioner obtain an MBA to continue employment with Selane Products. We must determine, therefore, whether Selane Products conditioned promotions, rather than employment generally, on petitioner beginning the MBA program.

Petitioner's boss at Selane Products strongly encouraged him to obtain the MBA. Petitioner's boss also speculated that petitioner might advance faster within Selane Products with the MBA. The record does not support respondent's contention, however, that petitioner's promotions were contingent on his beginning the MBA program. Encouraging petitioner to obtain the MBA and speculating that he might advance faster with the MBA is not tantamount to a requirement that petitioner obtain the MBA. Moreover, we decline to find that a minimum education requirement existed merely because petitioner's promotions happened to coincide with his enrollment in the MBA program.

We find no evidence in the record that petitioner was required to begin the MBA program to receive the promotions at issue. Nor do we discern that a requirement existed on the facts and circumstances, particularly where petitioner was promoted *before* he completed the MBA program. We hold therefore that neither petitioner's enrollment in the MBA program nor his completion of the program met a minimum education requirement of Selane Products. The more difficult question, rather, is whether the MBA qualified petitioner for a new trade or business.

2. Whether the MBA Qualified Petitioner for a New Trade or Business

We must next determine whether petitioner's MBA qualified him to perform a trade or business that he was unqualified to perform before he earned the MBA. Whether an education qualifies a taxpayer for a new trade or business depends upon the tasks and activities he or she was qualified to perform before the education and those that he or she was qualified to perform afterwards. The Court has repeatedly disallowed education expenses where the education qualifies the taxpayer to perform "significantly" different tasks and activities. The relevant inquiry is whether the taxpayer is objectively qualified in a new trade or business.

Respondent claims that petitioner's evolving duties and promotions after he enrolled in the MBA program demonstrate that petitioner was qualified for and indeed entered a new trade or business at Selane Products once he began the MBA program. Respondent argues that petitioner's trade or business before the MBA was principally sales related and involved only limited managerial and financial duties, but that once petitioner began the MBA program he advanced to numerous other jobs and was given advanced managerial, marketing, and financial duties, all of which were "significantly" different from the duties he performed before enrolling. In sum, respondent argues that the MBA qualified petitioner for the specific new trade or business of "advanced marketing and finance management."

Petitioner disagrees and argues that the MBA enhanced and maintained skills he already used in his job, but did not qualify him for a new trade or business or for any particular promotions. Petitioner argues that the MBA merely capitalized on his abilities that he had before beginning the program, giving him a better understanding of financials, costs analyses, marketing, and advertising. After careful consideration, we agree with petitioner.

Petitioner was hired by Selane Products for his experience in sports medicine, and he was hired, at first, to sell a sports-related product. Petitioner excelled in his duties and was rewarded with increased responsibility, including management, marketing, and finance-related tasks. The record establishes that he performed these myriad tasks before he enrolled in the MBA program. Once he enrolled, but before he finished the MBA program, he was promoted to new positions involving more complex tasks, but still involving the same marketing, finance, and management duties.

Simply acquiring new titles or abilities does not necessarily constitute the entry into a new trade or business. The "commonsense approach," rather, requires that a comparison be made between the types of activities that the taxpayer was qualified to perform before acquiring a particular title or degree with those that he or she was qualified to perform afterwards. If the activities are significantly different, then the educational expenses are disallowable. This is an objective test.

Petitioner's business after enrolling in the MBA program did not significantly change. After completing the MBA program, petitioner established with testimony that his business involved the same general activities that he performed before enrolling in the program, activities involving sales, marketing, and management. While petitioner was awarded with new positions and titles after he enrolled in the program and while the MBA may have sped his advancement within Selane Products, the basic nature of his duties did not significantly change. The MBA rather improved preexisting skills that petitioner used before enrolling in the MBA program.

We also distinguish our facts from cases involving taxpayers embarking on a course of study that qualified them for a professional certification or license. Courts considering those factors have often found that the education expenses were not deductible, even where the taxpayer performed many of the same activities before the education. For instance, the Court denied taxpayers' deduction for law school expenses on four occasions because law was a field of study that led the taxpayers to qualify for the new trade or business of being an attorney. Petitioner's MBA was not a course of study leading him to qualify for a professional certification or license.

We find two cases particularly instructive. On one occasion, our Court considered whether an MBA degree qualified a taxpayer for a new trade or business. *See* Blair v. Commissioner, T.C. Memo. 1980-488. In that case, the taxpayer was employed as a personnel manager while taking courses toward an MBA. We found that the taxpayer was entitled to deduct tuition expenses because the courses improved the taxpayer's job skills and did not qualify the taxpayer for a new trade or business.[50] *Id.* Similarly, in another case before our Court, we held that a taxpayer was allowed to deduct the educational expenses associated with a master of science degree in administration where the studies provided the taxpayer with a broad general background in management and business administration, activities that were already components of the taxpayer's work activities. *See* Beatty v. Commissioner, T.C. Memo. 1980-196. As in *Blair* and *Beatty*, petitioner's MBA courses provided him with a general background to perform tasks and activities that he had performed previously at Selane Products. . . .

Accordingly, we find that petitioner's MBA did not meet a minimum education requirement of Selane Products. Nor do we find that the MBA qualified petitioner to perform a new trade or business. Petitioner therefore may deduct the amount of MBA tuition expenses that he substantiated. . . .

To reflect the foregoing and the concessions of the parties,

Decision will be entered under Rule 155.

Notes and Questions

1. *The penalty flag, upon further review.* Because he won his case on the merits, the taxpayer's position was obviously sound in the view of the Tax Court, so it refused to sustain the penalties that the IRS had sought for filing a substantially inaccurate return under §6662. That section was added to the Code to provide disincentives to the filing of returns that are based on unreasonable legal positions, inaccurate valuations, and the like.[51] Why

---

50. We denied deductions for MBA expenses in two other cases on the basis that the taxpayer had not already been established in a trade or business. This is distinguishable from our case where petitioner had worked for Selane Products prior to and throughout the MBA program. In addition, our facts are distinguishable from a case in which we denied MBA expense deductions where the taxpayer's duties were technical before enrolling in the MBA program and managerial afterwards.

51. See the Chapter 1 cell on Tax Return Preparation Standards and Penalties.

do you suppose that the IRS had sought penalties in a case in which the amounts in issue were stipulated, and the taxpayer had, at the very least, a plausible argument that his educational expenses met the standards for deductibility under the regulations?

2. *The MBA irony.* It helped the taxpayer in *Allemeier* that many managers manage to manage without an MBA, or indeed any degree at all. So if any of your business-school friends tease you about the fact that their graduate program may be deductible while your own is not, you might remind them that the reason for the distinction is that their program apparently doesn't qualify them to do anything that they aren't already qualified to do. They may get a valuable tax deduction, but you'll have scored a nice debater's point. (Why does this outcome seem so appropriate?)

3. *Not all MBAs are created equal.* The footnote in this case describing the mixed results in other cases involving MBA degrees illustrates the rather fine line that is being drawn here. If the education doesn't improve one's skills, it wouldn't be deductible on those grounds. But if it improves the taxpayer's skills to a degree that permits a significantly different type of work assignment, that may disqualify the expense from deduction on grounds that it qualifies the taxpayer for a new field. Perhaps the real irony in the educational expense deduction area is that, to be deductible, the education can change the taxpayer's working life only marginally; too fundamental a change (too effective an education?) will disqualify the deduction. Why should this be so?

3. Work-Related Clothing

PEVSNER v. COMMISSIONER
628 F.2d 467 (5th Cir. 1980)

JOHNSON, Circuit Judge: This is an appeal by the Commissioner of Internal Revenue from a decision of the United States Tax Court. The tax court upheld taxpayer's business expense deduction for clothing expenditures in the amount of $1,621.91 for the taxable year 1975. We reverse.

Since June 1973 Sandra J. Pevsner, taxpayer, has been employed as the manager of the Sakowitz Yves St. Laurent Rive Gauche Boutique located in Dallas, Texas. The boutique sells only women's clothes and accessories designed by Yves St. Laurent (YSL), one of the leading designers of women's apparel. Although the clothing is ready to wear, it is highly fashionable and expensively priced. Some customers of the boutique purchase and wear the YSL apparel for their daily activities and spend as much as $20,000 per year for such apparel.

As manager of the boutique, the taxpayer is expected by her employer to wear YSL clothes while at work. In her appearance, she is expected to project the image of an exclusive lifestyle and to demonstrate to her customers that she is aware of the YSL current fashion trends as well as trends generally. Because the boutique sells YSL clothes exclusively, taxpayer must be able, when a customer compliments her on her clothes, to say that they are designed by YSL. In addition to wearing YSL apparel while at the boutique, she wears them while commuting to and from work, to fashion shows sponsored by the boutique, and to business luncheons at which she represents the boutique. During 1975, the taxpayer bought, at an employee's discount, the following items: four blouses, three skirts, one pair of slacks, one trench coat, two sweaters, one jacket, one tunic, five scarves, six belts, two pairs of shoes and four necklaces. The total cost of this apparel was $1,381.91. In addition, the sum of $240 was expended for maintenance of these items.

Although the clothing and accessories purchased by the taxpayer were the type used for general purposes by the regular customers of the boutique, the taxpayer is not a normal purchaser of these clothes. The taxpayer and her husband, who is partially disabled because of a severe heart attack suffered in 1971, lead a simple life and their social activities are very limited and informal. Although taxpayer's employer has no objection to her wearing the apparel away from work, taxpayer stated that she did not wear the clothes during off-work hours because she felt that they were too expensive for her simple everyday lifestyle. Another reason why she did not wear the YSL clothes apart from work was to make them last longer. Taxpayer did admit at trial, however, that a number of the articles were things she could have worn off the job and in which she would have looked "nice."

On her joint federal income tax return for 1975, taxpayer deducted $990 as an ordinary and necessary business expense with respect to her purchase of the YSL clothing and accessories. However, in the tax court, taxpayer claimed a deduction for the full $1,381.91 cost of the apparel and for the $240 cost of maintaining the apparel. The tax court allowed the taxpayer to deduct both expenses in the total amount of $1,621.91. The tax court reasoned that the apparel was not suitable to the private lifestyle maintained by the taxpayer. This appeal by the Commissioner followed.

The principal issue on appeal is whether the taxpayer is entitled to deduct as an ordinary and necessary business expense the cost of purchasing and maintaining the YSL clothes and accessories worn by the taxpayer in her employment as the manager of the boutique. This determination requires an examination of the relationship between Section 162(a), which allows a deduction for ordinary and necessary expenses incurred in the conduct of a trade or business, and Section 262 of the Code, which bars a deduction for all "personal, living, or family expenses." Although many expenses are helpful or essential to one's business activities — such as commuting expenses and the cost of meals while at work — these expenditures are considered inherently personal and are disallowed under Section 262.

The generally accepted rule governing the deductibility of clothing expenses is that the cost of clothing is deductible as a business expense only if: (1) the clothing is of a type specifically required as a condition of employment, (2) it is not adaptable to general usage as ordinary clothing, and (3) it is not so worn. Donnelly v. Commissioner, 262 F.2d 411, 412 (2d Cir. 1959).[52]

In the present case, the Commissioner stipulated that the taxpayer was required by her employer to wear YSL clothing and that she did not wear such apparel apart from work. The Commissioner maintained, however, that a deduction should be denied because the YSL clothes and accessories purchased by the taxpayer were adaptable for general usage as ordinary clothing and she was not prohibited from using them as such. The tax court, in rejecting the Commissioner's argument for

---

52. When the taxpayer is prohibited from wearing the clothing away from work a deduction is normally allowed. *See* Harsaghy v. Commissioner, 2 T.C. 484 (1943). However, in the present case no such restriction was placed upon the taxpayer's use of the clothing.

the application of an objective test, recognized that the test for deductibility was whether the clothing was "suitable for general or personal wear" but determined that the matter of suitability was to be judged subjectively, in light of the taxpayer's lifestyle. Although the court recognized that the YSL apparel "might be used by some members of society for general purposes," it felt that because the "wearing of YSL apparel outside work would be inconsistent with . . . [taxpayer's] lifestyle," sufficient reason was shown for allowing a deduction for the clothing expenditures.

In reaching its decision, the tax court relied heavily upon Yeomans v. Commissioner, 30 T.C. 757 (1958). In *Yeomans*, the taxpayer was employed as fashion coordinator for a shoe manufacturing company. Her employment necessitated her attendance at meetings of fashion experts and at fashion shows sponsored by her employer. On these occasions, she was expected to wear clothing that was new, highly styled, and such as "might be sought after and worn for personal use by women who make it a practice to dress according to the most advanced or extreme fashions." 30 T.C. at 768. However, for her personal wear, Ms. Yeomans preferred a plainer and more conservative style of dress. As a consequence, some of the items she purchased were not suitable for her private and personal wear and were not so worn. The tax court allowed a deduction for the cost of the items that were not suitable for her personal wear. Although the basis for the decision in *Yeomans* is not clearly stated, the tax court in the case sub judice determined that

> [a] careful reading of *Yeomans* shows that, without a doubt, the Court based its decision on a determination of Ms. Yeomans's lifestyle and that the clothes were not suitable for her use in such lifestyle. Furthermore, the Court recognized that the clothes Ms. Yeomans purchased were suitable for wear by women who customarily wore such highly styled apparel, but such fact did not cause the court to decide the issue against her. Thus, *Yeomans* clearly decides the issue before us in favor of the petitioner.

Notwithstanding the tax court's decision in *Yeomans*, the Circuits that have addressed the issue have taken an objective, rather than subjective, approach. An objective approach was also taken by the tax court in Drill v. Commissioner, 8 T.C. 902 (1947). Under an objective test, no reference is made to the individual taxpayer's lifestyle or personal taste. Instead, adaptability for personal or general use depends upon what is generally accepted for ordinary street wear.

The principal argument in support of an objective test is, of course, administrative necessity. The Commissioner argues that, as a practical matter, it is virtually impossible to determine at what point either price or style makes clothing inconsistent with or inappropriate to a taxpayer's lifestyle. Moreover, the Commissioner argues that the price one pays and the styles one selects are inherently personal choices governed by taste, fashion, and other unmeasurable values. Indeed, the tax court has rejected the argument that a taxpayer's personal taste can dictate whether clothing is appropriate for general use. An objective test, although not perfect, provides a practical administrative approach that allows a taxpayer or revenue agent to look only to objective facts in determining whether clothing required as a condition of employment is adaptable to general use as ordinary streetwear. Conversely, the tax court's reliance on subjective factors provides no concrete guidelines in determining the deductibility of clothing purchased as a condition of employment.

In addition to achieving a practical administrative result, an objective test also tends to promote substantial fairness among the greatest number of taxpayers. As the Commissioner suggests, it apparently would be the tax court's position that two similarly situated YSL boutique managers with identical wardrobes would be subject to disparate tax consequences depending upon the particular manager's lifestyle and "socio-economic level." This result, however, is not consonant with a reasonable interpretation of Sections 162 and 262.

For the reasons stated above, the decision of the tax court upholding the deduction for taxpayer's purchase of YSL clothing is reversed. Consequently, the portion of the tax court's decision upholding the deduction for maintenance costs for the clothing is also reversed.

Notes and Questions

1. *Dummy prongs.* The court in *Pevsner* sets forth a three-pronged test for the deductibility of work-related clothing, which, in slightly simplified form, could be stated as follows: (1) the clothing in question must be required as a condition of employment; (2) it must not be suitable for general wear; and (3) it must not be so worn. In practice, however, this test usually has only one working prong: that the clothing not be suitable for general wear. Why do you suppose that might be so?

2. *Mrs. Pevsner's credibility.* The opportunity to buy fashionable clothing at a significant discount is usually regarded by garment-industry employees as one of the more attractive perquisites of the job. And, further, it is usually the case that the value of perquisites is partly or wholly "captured" by the market, in the sense that, all other things being equal, a job with valuable perquisites will pay a lower wage than one without them. If Mrs. Pevsner didn't value the perquisites available to her as a manager of the YSL boutique (and her representations in this case strongly suggest that she did not), wasn't she accepting, in effect, a below-market wage? Does this insight lead you to doubt her credibility on this point? Why do you suppose the IRS didn't raise this point? Didn't the government attorney miss an opportunity for a Perry Mason moment, with a tearful Mrs. Pevsner admitting on cross-examination that, yes, she had worn a YSL dress to opening night at the opera?

3. A Perry Mason moment of this sort actually did arise in a recent case involving the deductibility of clothing items: In Nicely v. Commissioner, T.C. Memo. 2006-172 (2006), the taxpayer, a welder, sought to deduct the cost of several items of work-related clothing, including a pair of Rocky Wolverine boots. But he committed a fatal tactical error: as the opinion drily noted, the petitioner acknowledged that he was wearing the Rocky Wolverine boots during the trial (presumably in response to a question from the bench, which knew its boots!). Perhaps they were suitable only for welding, Tax Court trials, and other high-heat environments.

4. *All is not lost.* Although Mrs. Pevsner did not get her deduction, a taxpayer in her situation today would be entitled to a limited tax benefit. If her employer *allowed* her to purchase clothes at a discount, she would be allowed to exclude the value of the discount under §§132(a)(2) and (c)(1), so long as

the discount did not exceed the employer's "gross profit percentage."[53] Although the qualified employee discount under §132 was not added to the Code until after the tax year involved in *Pevsner,* the administrative practice of the IRS had not been to seek to include the amount of such discounts even before this amendment.

H.   THE DEDUCTION FOR INCOME ATTRIBUTABLE TO DOMESTIC PRODUCTION ACTIVITIES

Section 199 allows a taxpayer engaged in "qualified production activities" to claim a deduction equal to 9 percent of the lesser of (a) the taxpayer's "qualified production activities income" (QPAI) or (b) the taxpayer's taxable income. Because the deduction is based on a formula rather than on any actual expenditures, it functions as a disguised reduction in the taxpayer's marginal tax rate. Suppose, for example, a taxpayer has $1,000,000 of taxable income, all of which is QPAI. Suppose further that the statutory marginal tax rate is 35 percent on the entire $1,000,000. After the §199 deduction is taken into account, the taxpayer's taxable income will be $910,000, and the tax on that $910,000 (at 35%) will be $318,500. The effect is the same as if no deduction were allowed and the $1,000,000 of income were taxed at the rate of 31.85 percent.

The statute defines QPAI as the excess of the taxpayer's gross receipts from domestic production activities over the deductions allocable to those activities. Domestic production activities include the production (or construction) within the United States of tangible personal property, computer software, sound recordings, films, electricity, natural gas, and buildings and structures. The deduction is not available, however, with respect to income from food and beverages prepared at a retail establishment, or from the transmission or distribution (as contrasted with the production) of electricity or natural gas. A footnote in the legislative history elaborates on how these rules apply to Starbucks (although Starbucks is not mentioned by name), which both roasts coffee and sells coffee drinks.[54] The sale of roasted coffee produces deduction-eligible income, while the sale of barista-prepared coffee drinks generally does not (pursuant to the food-and-beverage establishment exception). However, Starbucks may claim a deduction based on the sale of barista-prepared coffee drinks, "to the extent of the value of the [Starbucks coffee beans] used to brew the coffee."

---

53. For more on §132, see the problem cell associated with Chapter 2.
54. H. Rep. No. 108-755, at 13, note 27 (2004).

Cell

========= VACATION HOMES

A. The §280A Remedy

B. Use as a Residence

C. The Limitations on Deductibility

Bolton v. Commissioner

When taxpayers engage in activities that generate income, but also provide personal consumption benefits to the taxpayers and their families, Congress and the IRS are suspicious that the income-generation aspects may be merely incidental, and are being used in an effort to justify deduction of expenses associated with an activity that is primarily personal in nature. Vacation homes present a common form of this problem. According to the Census Bureau, there were almost 4.7 million "seasonal" homes in the United States in 2009.[1] Obviously, taxpayers with larger incomes (and higher marginal tax rates) are in a better position to afford multiple homes, so this — like many tax problems — is one that is heavily concentrated among higher income taxpayers.

Congress tightened the rules on deductions for losses claimed with respect to vacation homes in the Tax Reform Act of 1976. To understand the operation and importance of those rules, it is helpful first to consider some of the more significant features of the pre-1976 landscape. As an example of the pre-1976 financial dynamics of owning a second home that is sometimes occupied by the taxpayer and her family, and sometimes by unrelated tenants, consider the following income and expense statement for a hypothetical vacation condominium that was purchased in 1970 for $100,000, financed by an $80,000 mortgage and $20,000 of the taxpayer's own cash:

Income	Expenses	
Rent $7,000	Mortgage Interest	$6,000
	Property Tax	$2,000
	Maintenance	$1,000
	Depreciation[2]	$5,000
	Net income (loss) ($7,000)	

1. *Statistical Abstract of the U.S. 2011*, table 977.
2. This is a hypothetical figure for depreciation. Depreciation rules have varied widely over time, and the number shown is realistic for depreciation of a unit placed in service prior to 1986; after the Tax Reform Act of that year, the minimum recovery period for real property of 27.5 years, and the required use of the straight-line method, would cap depreciation deductions for this unit at $3,636 per year (or less, depending on the portion of the purchase price allocated to the nondepreciable land).

At first blush, the sizable net loss makes this appear to be an unattractive investment. Unless the taxpayer gets a good deal of personal use out of the unit, $7,000 per year is a steep toll for having your own vacation home. However, several factors should be noted:

(a) The depreciation deduction is an accounting allowance; it does not represent actual out-of-pocket expenditures of the taxpayer, but is rather what is sometimes called a "paper loss." The actual out-of-pocket loss is thus only $2,000.[3]

(b) If the accounting loss of $7,000 were deductible by a taxpayer who was exposed to a marginal rate of tax of 50 percent or more, it would yield a tax savings of at least $3,500. Offsetting the $2,000 cash loss nets to a cash-flow return of $1,500 on the taxpayer's net investment of $20,000.[4]

(c) If the taxpayer had not invested the $20,000 in this condo, but rather in a currently taxable investment, she would have had to earn a return of $3,000, or 15 percent — unrealistic in most markets — to yield an after-tax return of $1,500.[5]

(d) The expenses incurred on the vacation home had the ancillary benefit of providing the taxpayer and her family with a home at the beach, in the mountains, or, depending on their tastes, a *pied-à-terre* in their favorite big city, that could be used for recreational purposes for significant parts of the year, during which the family occupied the unit themselves, rather than renting it out.

(e) Contrary to the implicit assumption of the depreciation deduction, most real estate investments have tended to appreciate over time, rather than losing value.

Putting all these factors together, one can see why, prior to the tax reform efforts that will be detailed below, it was thought that taxpayers in the higher brackets were almost irrational if they did *not* invest some of their capital in a vacation home.

The IRS rightly viewed many of the loss deductions claimed for such properties as abusive, largely because of the substantial personal use of the properties. Its first weapon for attacking them was §183,[6] which limits deductions for "activities not engaged in for profit." It was added to the Code in 1969, just as the tax shelter problem that was to plague the tax system for the better part of two decades was beginning to take shape. While the IRS used §183 with occasional success in this area, it often failed to persuade courts that deductions should be limited on grounds that an activity was not engaged in for profit.[7] When Congress gave the IRS a new weapon to combat the vacation home problem in 1976 (described below), it removed vacation homes from the ambit of §183 under most circumstances.[8]

---

3. Of course, any payments of principal on the mortgage would worsen the negative cash flow. Some mortgages do not require any principal payments during the term of the loan, but require instead the repayment of the full principal amount of the mortgage — a so-called balloon payment — at the maturity of the loan. But even if this were a fully amortized mortgage rather than a balloon mortgage, the payments of principal in the early years of this mortgage would be only about $500 per year, assuming (as this example does) an interest rate of about 8 percent.

4. The highest marginal rate during the 1970s was 70 percent; it fell to 50 percent in 1981. Because the golden age of the real estate tax shelter was roughly from 1970 until 1986, this example is based on the rates then prevailing. An interesting exercise would be to replicate this example using the current highest marginal tax rate of 35 percent. How much of the favorable tax treatment of this investment is lost under today's lower tax rates?

5. A 15 percent return on an investment would have earned $3,000, half of which would have been paid as tax under the assumed 50 percent marginal tax rate.

6. Section 183 is discussed in section G of this chapter.

7. *See, e.g.,* Nickerson v. Commissioner, 700 F.2d 402 (7th Cir. 1983).

8. *See* §280A(f)(3).

A. THE §280A REMEDY

In 1976, Congress decided to adopt an approach more specifically targeted at two problems whose only link was that they both involved the use of a taxpayer's residence in activities that could generate income. One of those problems was the vacation home problem.[9] Both sets of rules are combined, somewhat awkwardly, in the provisions of §280A, typically rendered orally as "280-cap A," to make clear that the "A" designation does not denote a subsection.

Section 280A operates as a limitation on deductions for business and profit-seeking expenses. Its operative rule — subject to several exceptions — is to disallow deductions otherwise allowable "with respect to the use of a dwelling unit which is used by the taxpayer during the taxable year as a residence."[10] It is specifically intended to be more objective than its §183 forebearer and accordingly does not inquire into the taxpayer's motivation in using his dwelling unit in particular ways.

B. USE AS A RESIDENCE

Generally, a taxpayer is considered to use a dwelling unit as a residence if his personal use exceeds 14 days in any tax year.[11] If the unit is rented for more than 140 days during the tax year, then the taxpayer is considered to "use the dwelling as a residence" only if he uses the unit more than 10 percent of the number of days during the year that the unit is rented by others at a fair market rental.[12] The taxpayer's personal use of the unit for this purpose includes use, for any part of a day, by himself, his family members, or anyone else (such as a guest) who is allowed to use the unit without paying the fair rental value of the unit.[13]

The "use as a residence" rules are rounded out by some rules designed to control taxpayer manipulation. For example, if two taxpayers engage in reciprocal arrangements whereby they use each other's vacation homes, as a means of avoiding more than 14 days of use of their own units, they will nevertheless be found to have used their units as residences under §280A(d)(2)(B).

There are also taxpayer-favorable rules designed to prevent the "use as a residence" rules from disallowing deductions in cases where there is a true, market-rent arrangement with someone who happens to be a family member, or where the unit is the taxpayer's primary residence during part of the year but is rented out during another part of the year.[14] Finally, Congress authorized the IRS to make regulations that would provide that days spent repairing or maintaining the unit wouldn't count as days of personal use.[15]

---

9. The other was the home office problem described in section G of this chapter.
10. Section 280A(a).
11. Section 280A(d)(1)(A).
12. Section 280A(d)(1)(B).
13. Section 280A(d)(2).
14. Section 280A(d)(3) and (d)(4), respectively.
15. Section 280A(d)(2) (flush language).

C. THE LIMITATIONS ON DEDUCTIBILITY

Immediately after §280A says that no deductions will be allowed for use of a personal residence except as provided in that section, it follows with just such an exception: §280A(b) says that deductions are allowable if they would be allowable without regard to any business or profit-seeking connection. Thus, things like mortgage interest, real property taxes, and casualty losses, to the extent that they do not depend on a business or profit-seeking connection, remain fully deductible.[16]

On the other hand, all business or profit-seeking deductions involving a personal residence are subject to a limitation based on allocation of use. Section 280A(e) says that expenses relating to the dwelling must be allocated between (nondeductible) personal use and (potentially deductible) rental use according to the ratio of the days of rental use to the total days of use in each tax year. Thus, if a unit is rented 100 days during the year, and used by the taxpayer personally on 50 days, no more than two-thirds (100 days of rental use divided by 150 days of use for any purpose) of any business or profit-seeking expense would be deductible. This rule does not depend on whether the unit is "used as a residence" under §280A(d); thus, even if a unit is used by the taxpayer for only ten days (so that most of §280A will not apply), she still must make an allocation under §280A(e) between the personal and the rental use.

In addition, §280A(c)(5) imposes a limitation on business and profit-seeking expenses that is related to the income that the vacation-home rental activities generate in any tax year. Stated somewhat too simply (as we shall see), the rule is that expenses for items such as maintenance and depreciation are deductible only to the extent of the rental income. There is thus built into §280A(c)(5) a similar problem to the one Congress addressed in §183: In what order does one deduct the various expenses associated with the dwelling, some of which are deductible without any business or profit-seeking connection, and others of which require such a nexus to be deductible? The answer is similar to the one provided in §183: The taxpayer must first deduct expenses allocable to the rental use, but which do not depend on a business or profit connection; then, if any income remains following that subtraction process, the business or profit-seeking expenses can be deducted to that extent.

Unfortunately, Congress did not specify in §280A(c)(5) any formula for determining how expenses like mortgage interest and property tax should be allocated between the rental use and the personal use. This ambiguity has turned out to be crucial in a number of cases, one of which follows.

BOLTON v. COMMISSIONER
694 F.2d 556 (9th Cir. 1982)

COPPLE, District Judge: This appeal from the United States Tax Court presents a question involving the interpretation of statutes governing deductibility of expenses incurred in the rental of a vacation home. Dorance and Helen Bolton (taxpayers) owned a vacation home in Palm Springs, California. In 1976, taxpayers rented the unit for 91 days, used it personally for 30 days, and left it unoccupied for 244 days. During that year, taxpayers made interest payments totalling $2,854 and

---

16. Of course, as noted in Chapter 4.B, deductions for interest paid with respect to mortgages on personal residences are limited to deductions for the taxpayer's principal residence and up to one additional residence.

paid property taxes of $621. In addition, taxpayers incurred $2,693 in maintenance expenses (excluding taxes and interest). Taxpayers received $2,700 gross rents from the unit in 1976.

Section 280A, enacted in 1976, limits a taxpayer's business deductions for expenses incurred with respect to a dwelling unit if that unit was used as a personal residence during the tax year. If §280A applies, as it does in this case, a general rule is invoked that no business deductions are allowable with respect to the unit. The statute, however, provides several exceptions.

Section 280A(b) provides that non-business expenditures otherwise deductible (i.e., taxes, interest, and casualty losses) are not barred by the statute. Further, §280A(c)(3) allows a deduction for "any item attributable to rental of the unit" (i.e., maintenance expenses). But this latter exception to the general rule is limited. In computing deductible maintenance expenses, the taxpayer must first comply with §280A(e) and §280A(c)(5), respectively.

This section was enacted as a response to congressional concern that rental of property used personally by the taxpayer as a residence afforded unwarranted opportunities to obtain deductions for expenses of a personal nature. With respect to vacation homes, the legislative history behind the statute expresses the view that rental activities were often undertaken merely to defray the cost of maintaining a vacation home for the taxpayer's personal use, rather than for the purpose of turning a profit. Although §183 could generally have been expected to apply to such rentals of vacation homes as activities not engaged in for profit, thereby limiting deductions with respect to maintenance of a vacation home to the amount of gross income received from its rental, Congress was concerned that §183 and the related regulations did not provide sufficiently specific rules as to the degree of personal use of a vacation home which would result in its rental being classified as an activity not engaged in for profit. Section 280A was thus intended to provide "definitive rules . . . to specify the extent to which personal use [of a vacation home] would result in the disallowance of certain deductions in excess of gross income" from the property. H.R. Rep. No. 94-658, 94th Cong., 2d Sess. at 162-66.

Section 280A(e) requires that a preliminary computation be undertaken to determine the unit's maintenance expenses which are attributable to rental and thus can be deducted. The statute provides that the following ratio be used in making this calculation:

> Number of days the unit is actually rented [divided by]
> Total number of days during the year the unit is used.

The figure obtained through use of this ratio is then multiplied against the total maintenance expenses of the unit to arrive at a tentative deduction figure. This formula, as applied to the above facts, generates the following calculation:

$$91(\# \text{ days rented})/121(\# \text{ days used}) =$$
$$75\% \times \$2,693 \text{ (total maintenance expenses)} = \$2,020$$

the tentative amount of maintenance expenses deductible as attributable to rental.[17]

---

17. Throughout their presentations the parties have used rounded percentage figures as well as the nearest dollar figures in applying such percentages in their calculations. This opinion follows the same practice.

Having arrived at a tentative maintenance deduction figure, there remains §280A(c)(5) to be complied with. This section provides first that deductions allowed for expenses attributed to rental of the unit (i.e., deductions of any kind — maintenance, taxes, interest) cannot exceed an amount equal to the amount of gross rental income received from the property for that year ($2,700 on the instant facts). Second, this section requires that deductions allowable whether or not the unit was used as a rental (i.e., interest and taxes in this case) be allocated between rental and non-rental use. The amount of otherwise deductible interest and taxes allocated to rental use of the property is then to be counted toward the gross rentals maximum deduction ceiling ($2,700). The statute, however, provides no formula for allocating such "always deductible" expenses (taxes and interest) between rental and non-rental use of the unit.

The primary issue in this case concerns the method by which this latter allocation is to be achieved. Taxpayers contend, and the tax court agreed, that the allocation be based on a ratio of number days rented/number days in a year. The percentage figure derived from this ratio would be the percentage of taxes and interest paid which is allocable to rental use of the unit, and in turn applied toward the gross rentals deduction limit. The Commissioner, on the other hand, takes the position that interest and taxes should be allocated to rental use by using the same fraction as that used for maintenance expenses under §280A(e). The ratio to use under this method would accordingly be number days rented/number days the property was actually used. The percentage derived from this ratio would be the percent of taxes and interest which, in the Commissioner's view, would be applied toward the rental use deduction limit.[18]

---

18. To clarify and illustrate the impact of the competing positions in this appeal, the following calculations based on the facts in this case are presented:

Taxpayer's Position:

Gross rental income		$2,700
Total interest and property taxes	$3,475	
Allocation fraction 91/365 = 25%		$868
(attributable to rental use)		
Rental income in excess of interest		$1,832
and property taxes		
Total maintenance expenses	$2,693	
Allocation fraction 91/121 = 75%		$2,020
Maximum allowable deduction for maintenance		

Given the above, the taxpayer may deduct $1,832 of the $2,020 in potentially deductible maintenance expenses as derived from §280A(e)(1).

Commissioner's Position:

Gross rental income		$2,700
Total interest and property taxes	$3,475	
Allocation fraction 91/121 = 75%		$2,606
(attributable to rental use)		
Rental income in excess of interest and		$94
property taxes		
Total maintenance expenses	$2,693	
Allocation fraction 91/121 = 75%		$2,020
Maximum allowable deduction for maintenance		

Given the above, the taxpayer may deduct $94 of the $2,020 in potentially deductible maintenance expenses as derived from §280A(e)(1). The Commissioner's position, by allocating a

The United States Tax Court held that the deduction for interest and real estate taxes attributable to the rental unit is to be computed as per the taxpayer's method, i.e., the ratio to use for the §280A allocation for taxes and interest is number days unit rented/number days in a year. One basis for the tax court's decision was the premise that interest and property taxes, unlike maintenance-type expenses, are expenses that continue on a daily basis throughout the year. The tax court recognized that a computation based on the period the unit was actually used (121 days in this case) is useful in determining the amount of otherwise nondeductible maintenance expenses, ordinarily associated with actual use of the property, which are to be attributed to rental use. Interest and property taxes, however, accrue ratably over the entire year. The tax court accordingly found that the annual nature of tax and interest expenses as well as the legislative intent shown both by the legislative history and the language of §280A supported the taxpayer's interpretation rather than that of the Commissioner. Despite the tax court's decision, the Commissioner's position in this matter is currently the subject of a Proposed Treasury Regulation, §1.280A-3(d).

This Court is essentially faced with deciding whether to give deference to the Commissioner's interpretation of the statutes in question or to affirm the tax court in finding the Commissioner's position unreasonable. The United States Supreme Court has recently set forth the approach to follow in such a situation. In United States v. Vogel Fertilizer Co., 455 U.S. 16, (1982), the Court stated with regard to Treasury Regulations that:

> Deference is ordinarily owing to the agency construction if we can conclude that the regulation "implements the congressional mandate in some reasonable manner." But this general principle of deference, while fundamental, only sets "the framework for judicial analysis; it does not displace it."
>
> The framework for analysis is refined by consideration of the source of authority to promulgate the regulation at issue. The Commissioner has promulgated Treas. Reg. 1.1563-1(a)(3) interpreting this statute only under his general authority to "prescribe all needful rules and regulations." §7805(a). Accordingly, "we owe the interpretation less deference than a regulation issued under a specific grant of authority to define a statutory term or prescribe a method of executing a statutory provision. . . . " United States v. Vogel Fertilizer Co., *supra,* 455 U.S. 16, 24.

The approach taken by the *Vogel* Court is applicable to the situation faced by this Court even as to the source of the Commissioner's power to propose the regulation involved in this case.[19] This Court must therefore consider the reasonableness of the Commissioner's interpretation of §280A as applied to taxpayers and as put forth in the Proposed Regulation. Consideration must first be made of whether the

---

greater proportion of otherwise deductible interest and taxes to rental of the unit, leaves less room under the gross rentals ceiling for deduction of maintenance expenses of the rental. By contrast, taxpayer's position allows a greater percentage of the §280A(e) maintenance expenses to be deducted. Since interest and taxes paid on the property are deductible whether or not connected to business use of the property, it is to the taxpayer's advantage to have as small a percentage as possible of taxes and interest allocated to rental use and applied toward the gross rentals deduction limit for the unit.

19. Power to propose the Treasury Regulation in issue in this case originates from the Commissioner's general authority to prescribe helpful rules under 26 U.S.C. §7805(a). It should also be noted that while a proposed regulation constitutes a body of informed judgment to which courts may draw on for guidance in the interpretation of relevant statutes, cf. Ricards v. United States, 652 F.2d 897, 902 n.12 (9th Cir. 1981), the Commissioner nevertheless concedes that a proposed regulation still is not entitled to the deference due a final regulation.

Commissioner's interpretation "harmonizes with the statutory language." United States v. Vogel Fertilizer Co., *supra,* at 25. The legislative history and purpose behind the statute are also to be considered in determining whether the Commissioner has acted reasonably. Should the Commissioner's as well as the taxpayer's interpretation of the statute be seen as reasonable, the rule in such a situation is that "the choice among reasonable interpretations is for the Commissioner, not the courts." For the reasons outlined below, however, we conclude that the Commissioner overstepped the bounds of reasonableness in this case, and that the decision of the tax court should therefore be affirmed.

THE STATUTORY LANGUAGE

The Commissioner's position is to allocate interest and taxes to gross rental receipts through use of the same fraction as that used for maintenance expenses specified in §280A(e)(1): number of days rented/total number of days used. Yet subsection (e)(2) of §280A continues: "(2) Exception for Deductions Otherwise Allowable. This subsection shall not apply with respect to deductions which would be allowable under this chapter for the taxable year whether or not such unit . . . was rented." On the very face of the statute, then, it is apparent that the "number of days rented/total number of days used" fraction is not appropriate for allocating expenses such as interest and property taxes. The Commissioner argues, on the other hand, that the meaning of subsection (e)(2) is not plain, and that other interpretations are possible.[20] Thus, the Commissioner argues, the IRS interpretation should be accepted.

There is a major difficulty with the Commissioner's argument, however. Even if it is accepted that this subsection is subject to some different interpretation, the one fact that is clear is that subsection (e)(2) is not, from the face of the statute, subject to an interpretation along the lines of that sought by the Commissioner. Since this Court's task in the first instance is to determine the reasonableness of the Commissioner's interpretation, the Commissioner's argument as to the existence of other possible interpretations misses the focus of the analysis. The question is whether the Commissioner's interpretation is reasonable in the context of the language, legislative history and purpose of the statute. When solely the language on the face of the statute is considered, the Commissioner's interpretation cannot be upheld as reasonable.

---

20. The Commissioner suggests several alternate interpretations of subsection (e)(2). Each construction, however, appears highly unlikely when the plain language of this subsection, along with the language in the remainder of the statute, are considered. The Commissioner first suggests that subsection (e)(2) could be interpreted to mean either that the taxpayer is to apply the entire amount of the interest and tax deductions against the gross income from rentals, or that none of the taxes and interest deductions should be applied against the gross rental income. This argument, however, ignores the language in §280A(c)(5) that deductions for interest and property taxes be allocated between rental and non-rental use. The Commissioner further suggests that subsection (e)(2) could be interpreted to mean that the ratio should be determined by dividing all the days in the year when the unit was not actually used for personal purposes by the total number of days in the year (in this case resulting in a fraction of 335/365, or 92% of taxes and interest being allocated to business use). But this construction ignores the statute's obvious equating of business use with days rented, and therefore cannot be accepted.

II. The Legislative History

The legislative history behind the statutory provisions at issue in this appeal does not adequately address the problem of the proper way to allocate interest and tax expenses. Indeed, both parties in their briefs admit that the legislative history is unclear on this point. . . .

III. Harmony with the Legislative Purpose: Tax Court v. Commissioner

The Commissioner finally argues that the tax court's method of computing the interest and tax allocation actually rewards the taxpayer with a higher deduction the less the unit is used for any purpose. As an example, the Commissioner points out that in the instant case, the taxpayers rented the unit for 91 days, or 25 percent of the time in 1976. He then contends that under the tax court's computation, taxpayers would be allowed to deduct a higher amount of maintenance expenses than they would have been allowed if the unit were rented for 120 days, or 33 percent of the year. The Commissioner maintains that this result would be counter to the congressional purpose behind §280A that taxpayers not be allowed to convert personal expenses, such as maintenance and utilities, into deductible business items.

The Commissioner's example, however, fails to consider the fact that if the unit were rented an additional 30 days as in his example, the gross rental figure for the unit, and likewise the ceiling on maximum deductions, would be higher. Thus, 33 percent of the interest and taxes (allocable to rental under the tax court's approach) would be taken from a higher gross rentals limit, not the same limit as the Commissioner's example assumes. The amount of allowed deductions for maintenance and depreciation expenses under the deduction limit would therefore increase in proportion to the increase in days the unit is rented.[21]

Accordingly, taxpayers are not, as the Commissioner contends, rewarded with higher deductions for letting their unit stand idle. The Commissioner's argument as to legislative purpose is consequently misplaced. The argument further fails to

---

21. To illustrate:

	90 Days Rented		120 Days Rented	
	Tax Court	Comm'r	Tax Court	Comm'r
Rental Income	2,700	2,700	3,600	3,600
Interest & Taxes	(868)	(2,606)	(1,157)	(2,780)*
Ded. Maint. Expenses	(1,832)	(94)	(2,154)**	(820)
Ded. Depreciation	0	0	(289)***	0
Net Income	0	0	0	0

* Days rented (120) divided by total days occupied (150) times total interest and taxes ($3,475) equals $2,780.
** Days rented (120) divided by total days occupied (150) times total maintenance ($2,693) equals $2,154.
** After subtracting the allocation for taxes and interest, there remains room under the gross rentals deduction ceiling for $2,443 in deductions. Since potentially deductible maintenance expenses come to only $2,154, there is room left to deduct $289 in depreciation on the rental unit. Using the tax court's allocation method, the amount of deductible maintenance and depreciation expenses under the deduction limit increase (from $1,831 to $2,443) in proportion to the increase in days rented. As taxpayers point out, it is also interesting to note in the above example that the Commissioner's method allows the deduction for maintenance expenses to increase lopsidedly as a result of increasing the rental days by 33.3% (from $94 to $820, or 772%).

consider that maintenance and utility expenses are first allotted between deductible rental/business and nondeductible personal expenses as per the fraction in §280A(e)(1) prior to taking into account interest and taxes under the deduction limit. Any maintenance expenses deductible after allocated interest and taxes are accounted for therefore have already been deemed potentially deductible business expenses. Personal expenses are not converted into business expenses under the tax court's formula.

As pointed out earlier, neither the statute itself nor its legislative history address the issue of the proper approach to follow in making the §280A interest and tax allocation. The only clear point to be derived from these sources is the incorrectness of the Commissioner's interpretation. The tax court's approach, however, is consistent with the legislative purpose of setting up a scheme whereby personal expenses are separated from the business expenses of rental homes. Following the Commissioner's approach, the facts in this case would allow a deduction of only $94 of maintenance expenses for three months' worth of rental expenses, when the maintenance expenses on the unit for the year were $2,693. The tax court's approach more evenly makes the allocation by determining that maintenance expenses, which tend to vary with occupancy rate, be allocated in accordance with occupancy (*see* §280A(e)(1)) whereas those expenses which are allowable without regard to whether they are personal or not be allocated giving due regard to the method in which they accrue—in this case, taxes and interest accrue on a daily basis, regardless of property use. At least one commentator feels that the allocation of taxes and interest over the entire year may have been so obvious to Congress that Congress did not believe it needed stating. *See* W. Lathen, *Bolton: IRS "Bizarre" On Section 280A(e)*, 60 Taxes 237, 239 (1982). In summary, the Commissioner's interpretation of the statute is at odds with the language, history and legislative purpose behind §280A. "[A] challenged regulation is not a reasonable statutory interpretation unless it harmonizes with the statute's 'origin and purpose.'" United States v. Vogel Fertilizer Co., *supra*, at 26. The approach of the tax court, on the other hand, is reasonable and consistent with the purpose and history behind the statute and the language of the statute itself. The Commissioner's interpretation must accordingly be rejected, and the approach of the tax court given deference. The decision of the tax court is therefore affirmed.

Notes and Questions

1. *Do the Boltons want smaller deductions?* An initially confusing aspect of this case is that the taxpayer seems to be arguing for lesser deductions and the IRS for greater ones. That would surely be unusual (though not unimaginable), but it is not in fact the case. The taxpayer simply wants less of the interest and property tax expenses—*which he is sure to be able to deduct in full, in any event*—taken off the gross rental income, because what remains after reducing gross rental income by those amounts will effectively cap the amounts he can take for maintenance and depreciation.[22] Thus, by arguing

22. Even under the taxpayer's approach to the arithmetic of this case, there is not enough income to permit deduction of depreciation; the deduction of maintenance expenses exhausts the total permissible rental deductions. Prop. Reg. §1.280A-3(d)(3)(ii) requires that deductions that do not affect the basis of property be taken before basis-adjusting deductions, such as depreciation.

for smaller interest and property tax deductions in computing the (c)(5) limitations, the taxpayer is arguing for a larger (c)(5) limit, and hence larger deductions for maintenance.

2. *The analysis of §280A(e).* Much of the analysis of this case turns on the court's understanding of §280A(e). The IRS argued that the problem before the court involved determining the appropriate allocation of expenses between business and personal use, and that the one place Congress indicated that it had considered that question was in §280A(e)(1), where it suggested using a ratio of days rented to total days of use. But the Ninth Circuit objected to this, noting that §280A(e)(2) says that "this subsection" — that is, all of subsection (e) — shall not apply to deductions that would be allowable whether or not the unit was rented, namely, the interest and property tax deductions, which are precisely the expenses the court is trying to allocate. From (e)(2), the court concluded that using the (e)(1) formula is "on the very face of the statute . . . not appropriate for allocating expenses such as interest and property taxes."

But is this the only interpretation of (e)(2)? Might Congress have simply used the language in (e)(2) to remind readers that the limitation on deductions of (e)(1) wasn't meant ultimately to limit the deduction of interest and property tax? After all, the language of subsection (e) closely parallels the language of §§183(a) and (b), and 280A(a) and (b), both of which similarly seem to deny deductibility across the board in subsection (a), but then restore deductibility for expenses whose deductibility doesn't depend on business or profit-seeking use in subsection (b). If all that Congress meant in §280A(e)(2) was simply to reiterate, in case there was any doubt, that interest and property taxes continued to be fully deductible, then it was not necessarily conveying any sort of opinion on the appropriate allocation formula to use for purposes of (c)(5).

In that case, the Commissioner's argument becomes much stronger. He can say: "True, Congress wasn't thinking about the (c)(5) allocation when it wrote (e)(1), but it was thinking about how to separate rental expenses from personal expenses, and doing so on the basis of the relative amounts of use in those two categories seemed sensible. So all we are doing by regulation is extending Congress's principle into an area that it did not specifically cover. And, in any case, since we have the authority to make necessary regulations, as long as they represent a reasonable interpretation of the statute, we don't have to prove that this is the only reasonable interpretation, but merely that it is a reasonable interpretation." Should that have been a winning argument?

3. *Another circuit adds its voice.* The following year the Tenth Circuit considered the same issue, and came to the same conclusion as the Ninth Circuit had, in McKinney v. Commissioner, 732 F.2d 414 (10th Cir. 1983). The IRS, however, has neither withdrawn nor finalized the proposed regulations that were the subject of these cases. Prop. Reg. §280A-3(d)(3) continues to insist that the appropriate formula for purposes of allocating interest and property tax expenses in applying the (c)(5) limitations is one that compares the days of rental use to the total days of rental and personal use.

Generally, the IRS will follow precedents decided by a circuit court in dealing with other taxpayers in the same circuit. It will not necessarily follow them in other circuits, however, reserving the right to try again in litigating the same issue before another court. In this way, it sometimes develops a split between or among circuits, which in turn generates grounds for the grant of certiorari by the Supreme Court.

4. *Strategic considerations.* For many taxpayers in the years since 1976, the best response to these rules has been to limit personal use to 14 days. If they are able to do so, taxpayers can avoid most of the disallowance provisions of §280A.[23] However, changes in the deductibility of mortgage interest and property taxes for so-called passive activities made in 1986 have changed this dynamic for some taxpayers. Taxpayers can now avoid the passive loss rules by falling within the ambit of §280A, which they do only if they use the vacation home as a residence for purposes of §280A.[24] Depending on the facts of each case, avoiding the passive loss limitations may be more important than avoiding the vacation home rules of §280A.[25]

5. *Going for the gold.* Section 280A(g) contains a de minimis rule that provides that units that are rented for less than 15 days in a tax year are not allowed any deductions "because of the rental use," meaning that those deductions that depend on a profit-seeking purpose, such as maintenance and depreciation deductions, are flatly disallowed. But the same subsection also allows such taxpayers to exclude from income any rent they may receive for up to 14 days of rental use. This has been something of a bonanza to people who live near an Olympic venue, who may be able to rent their homes for two weeks for several thousand dollars. (And homeowners who live near the Augusta National Golf Club, Churchill Downs, or the Rose Bowl benefit to a lesser degree (because the premium rental period is shorter) but are able to do so year after year.)

---

23. The exception is §280A(e), discussed above, which applies whether or not the taxpayer uses the unit in question as a residence during the tax year.

24. *See* §469(j)(10).

25. Note, however, that §280A(b) does not *authorize* a mortgage interest deduction; it simply excepts such deductions from the disallowance rule in §280A(a). The deduction is authorized by §163(h)(3). Because that paragraph limits mortgage interest deductions to those arising from mortgages on the taxpayer's principal residence and up to one additional home, taxpayers who have more than one vacation home may not care very much whether the second and subsequent vacation homes are subject to §280A or §469.

Chapter 6

CAPITALIZATION AND COST RECOVERY

A. CAPITALIZATION AND DEPRECIATION: THE BASICS

The owner of a pizza parlor pays $10,000 for a car that he plans to use for deliveries for the next few years. If he uses the car only for business, how much (if any) of the $10,000 should he be allowed to deduct in the year he buys the car? Under an income tax, it is clear that he should not be allowed to deduct the entire $10,000 in the first year. He is not $10,000 poorer as a result of the purchase; he still has the car — and most of its original value — at the end of the year. If his taxable income is to measure accurately his profit or loss for the year, he should be allowed a deduction for the amount by which the car has declined in value during the year. If the car is worth $8,000 at the end of the year, he should be able to claim a $2,000 depreciation deduction for the decline in value of the car during the year. If the car was worth $6,500 at the end of the second year, he should be able to claim a $1,500 depreciation deduction for that year — and so on in later years until the car becomes worthless or he disposes of it. The cost of using the car for a particular year offsets that year's gross income, thus matching expenses with the income that those expenses help to produce.

As the example suggests, the theoretically correct measure of depreciation requires yearly appraisals of business assets in order to determine their annual declines in value. Obviously this would not be practical. Instead, §168 provides various cost recovery formulas — from which cost recovery schedules can be derived — for different kinds of tangible assets used in business. Under the "accelerated cost recovery system" (ACRS) of §168[1] the cost recovery schedule for a particular asset depends on three things — the total amount of cost to be recovered, the number of years over which the cost is to be recovered, and the rate at which the cost is to be recovered over those years.

In theory, the total amount of cost to be recovered is the total expected decline in value while the asset is used in the taxpayer's business, as measured by the difference between the original cost and the salvage value. If our taxpayer expects to be able to sell the car for $1,200 when he is done with it, the total depreciable amount should be only $8,800. In the interests of simplicity, however, §168(b)(4)

---

1. Although depreciation allowances are as old as the income tax, the ACRS rules of §168 were introduced in 1981, and significantly modified in 1986. Tax professionals frequently refer to the post-1986 cost recovery regime as the "*modified* accelerated cost recovery system," or MACRS, but the Code does not use the "modified" terminology.

provides that salvage value is always treated as zero. The taxpayer will be able to claim a total of $10,000 of ACRS deductions on his car. However, as explained below, there will be an eventual price to pay if he depreciates the car below its actual salvage value.

Section 168 provides "recovery periods" for many different types of assets, ranging from three years (for some horses, and a few other types of assets) to 50 years (for railroad grading and tunnel bores). For cars and light trucks, the recovery period is five years. This is shorter than the actual useful lives of most cars, but consistent with the congressional intent to create an *accelerated* cost recovery system.

So far we know that the taxpayer is entitled to deduct a total of $10,000 over a five-year period. We still need to know how much of the $10,000 he will be allowed to deduct each year. There are innumerable possible ways of distributing $10,000 of deductions over five years, of which the simplest is straight line — $2,000 each year. Although §168 requires straight line depreciation for buildings and a few other types of assets, most assets are eligible for an accelerated schedule, under which larger deductions are allowed in the earlier years. According to §168(b)(1), the depreciation method for cars (and many other assets) is "the 200 percent declining balance method," with a switch to straight line when straight line recovery of the remaining basis produces a larger deduction than continued use of 200 percent declining balance. That may sound like gibberish, but the idea is not all that complicated. Under the 200 percent (or "double") declining balance method, the first step is to calculate the percentage of cost the taxpayer could recover each year under the straight line method. For property with a five-year recovery period, the straight line method would produce 20 percent cost recovery each year. The next step is to determine the rate which is double (200 percent of) the straight line rate. Here, that is 40 percent. That percentage is then applied each year to the *unrecovered* basis of the asset, to produce the ACRS deduction for that year. Thus, the ACRS schedule for the car for the first three years would look like this:

Year	Unrecovered Basis at Beginning of Year	40% of Unrecovered Basis
One	$10,000	$4,000
Two	$6,000	$2,400
Three	$3,600	$1,440

Of course, continuing on in this fashion — deducting 40 percent of the remaining basis each year — would never result in recovery of the entire basis. At the beginning of Year 4, there is $2,160 remaining basis. Continued application of the double declining balance method would produce a deduction of only $864, but a switch to straight line — depreciating $2,160 over two years — would produce a deduction of $1,080 in Year 4 and another $1,080 deduction in Year 5. Since these amounts are larger than those produced by continued use of double declining balance, the switch to straight line takes place in Year 4.

This cost recovery schedule is not quite the one actually called for by §168, because of something known as the "half-year convention." If an asset is not placed in service at the very beginning of Year 1, the deduction for that year should be based on less than an entire year's use of the asset. Rather than requiring taxpayers to keep track of the exact date each asset is placed in service, §168(d)(1) treats most assets as being placed in service in the middle of the year, with the result that only a half-year's worth of depreciation is allowed for the first year.[2] Because of the half-year convention, the first year deduction for the car is only $2,000. This also affects the amount of the deduction for all other years. In the second year, for example, the unrecovered basis is now $8,000 (rather than $6,000), so the deduction is $3,200. There will also be a half-year's worth of depreciation in Year 6, since there was only a half-year's worth in Year 1.

The good news, for those who do not enjoy number crunching, is that it is not necessary to do the work of deriving cost recovery schedules from the rules of §168, because the IRS has done the number crunching for us. Rev. Proc. 87-57, 1987-2 C.B. 687, contains a number of tables indicating the percentage of unadjusted basis that is deductible each year for various types of ACRS property. For five-year property, for example, the table provides the following:

Year	Percentage of Unadjusted Basis
One	20.00
Two	32.00
Three	19.20
Four	11.52
Five	11.52
Six	5.76

The percentages add up to 100 percent of the original cost of the asset. To use the table, all the taxpayer has to do each year is multiply the car's unadjusted basis of $10,000 by that year's percentage. Thus, the first year deduction is $2,000, the second year's is $3,200, the third year's is $1,920, and so on. One thing to watch out for: Although the double declining balance method multiplies the asset's *adjusted* basis by a fixed percentage each year, the table translates this into multiplication of the asset's *unadjusted* basis by percentages that change from year to year.

As far as most taxpayers are concerned, the sooner they can take their cost recovery deductions the better. To accelerate a deduction is to defer income, and taxpayers ordinarily benefit from deferral. By ignoring salvage value, by providing for cost recovery periods typically shorter than actual useful lives, and by providing for accelerated depreciation methods (such as double declining balance), Congress has intentionally permitted cost recovery allowances that will usually be significantly faster than the actual declines in value of business assets.[3] Why? Three explanations are commonly given. First, Congress may intend §168 as a subsidy provision;

---

2. Section 168(d)(2) applies a half-month convention for buildings. The idea is that buildings are typically bigger ticket items than other cost recovery property, so a more accurate convention for buildings is worth the extra trouble.

3. There may be cases, however, in which cost recovery allowances are no faster than — or even slower than — economic depreciation. A possible example is the case of computers and peripheral equipment, whose five-year recovery period may underestimate their rate of obsolescence. In addition, the 39-year recovery period for nonresidential real property (§168(c)) does not seem to be accelerated.

the tax deferral it produces encourages businesses to invest in physical plant and equipment. Second, ACRS may compensate for the fact that depreciation deductions are not adjusted for inflation. For example, a $1,000 deduction taken in an asset's fifth year of business use is a recovery of $1,000 invested five years ago, which may be the equivalent (because of inflation) of $1,200 of this year's dollars. By failing to increase the deduction to $1,200, the system understates depreciation deductions in inflationary periods. Thus, too-generous *timing* of deductions may compensate for insufficient generosity with respect to the *amount* of deductions. It would be an accident, of course, if the two wrongs happened to cancel out each other in a particular case.

The third explanation views ACRS as a compromise between proponents of an income tax and proponents of a consumption tax. As discussed later in this book,[4] a number of tax policy experts think it would be better — fairer, more efficient, or both — to tax consumption instead of income. Consumption taxes can take several different forms, including one that superficially seems very similar to an income tax. If taxpayers are allowed immediate deductions for all savings and investments, then income saved or invested will not be subject to tax. (This approach is often referred to as "expensing," because it treats investments identically with current business expenses.) What remains in the tax base under the expensing approach will be consumed income — that is, consumption. In short, under the type of consumption tax with the greatest surface resemblance to an income tax — sometimes referred to as a "cash flow" tax — taxpayers would be allowed immediate deductions for all investments in business assets, regardless of how long-lived those assets might be. Any depreciation system that allows deductions slower than immediate expensing, but faster than actual declines in value, can be understood as a compromise between proponents of an income tax and proponents of a consumption tax. Under present law, with most cost recovery schedules only modestly faster than actual declines in value, the compromise is tilted in the income tax direction. The version of ACRS that applied in the early 1980s, however, was considerably closer to a consumption tax. The recovery period for cars, for example, was just three years, and the recovery period for buildings was 15 years (compared with the current periods of 27.5 years for residential rental property and 39 years for other buildings).[5]

Until the recent rude awakening, the experience across most of the United States for many decades had been that the value of housing moved in only one direction — up. In that environment, did it make any sense for §168 to allow cost recovery deductions (straight line, over 27.5 years) for residential rental property? Arguably, it did. Suppose you buy a condominium unit for $275,000, and become a landlord. You fully expect that the unit will appreciate, and sure enough it is worth about $290,000 one year later. The fact that the unit has appreciated is irrelevant under §168; you are still entitled to a $10,000 ACRS deduction. Although this seems very generous, it actually makes a certain amount of sense. Suppose that, when your one-year-old unit is worth $290,000, a new unit has just been

---

4. See Chapter 11.

5. It may be worth noting that inflation, as measured by the consumer price index, had proceeded at an average annual rate of 8.4 percent over the decade from 1971-1981, immediately preceding the enactment of the original, more generous form of ACRS. In the five years between 1981 and the enactment of less generous depreciation rules in 1986, inflation had abated to an average annual rate of 3.8 percent. So congressional decisions might be explained in terms of the second factor noted in the text, rather than by any shift in the terms of compromise between income and consumption tax advocates.

constructed across the courtyard. The new unit is identical to yours in all respects except age, and it is worth $300,000. In that case, the $15,000 appreciation in your unit is really the net of two effects moving in opposite directions. Wear and tear has decreased the value of your unit by $10,000, and market forces have increased its value by $25,000. The decline in value on account of wear and tear is predictable (in a rough sort of way), so §168 treats that decline as sufficiently realized to merit a current deduction. By contrast, the change in value due to market forces is classic unrealized appreciation, too unpredictable to be built into the §168 schedules. The happy result, from your point of view, is that you are able to turn a $15,000 economic gain into a $10,000 tax loss, by combining $10,000 of ACRS deductions with $25,000 of unrealized appreciation. Of course, in a period of declining real estate values, the result is not so happy — §168 allows a deduction for the predictable decline in value due to wear and tear, but not for the decline in value attributable to market forces.

As long as a taxpayer continues to hold a §168 asset, the tax system assumes the asset declines in value in accordance with the applicable ACRS schedule. When the taxpayer disposes of the asset, however, the system can measure the extent to which that assumption was mistaken, and require an appropriate correction. First consider the usual situation, in which the asset does not decline in value by as much as the asset's ACRS deductions. For example, suppose the taxpayer with the pizza delivery car (which cost $10,000) sells it in the third year for $7,000, after the taxpayer has properly claimed $6,160 of ACRS deductions with respect to it.[6] At this point, it is clear that the ACRS deductions have overshot the mark by $3,160 — the property actually declined in value by only $3,000, but the taxpayer has been allowed deductions based on the assumption that it declined in value by $6,160. It looks as if the IRS might need to invoke the tax benefit rule to include $3,160 in the taxpayer's income.[7] The IRS's argument would be (1) that the ACRS deductions were based on the assumption the car had declined in value by $6,160, (2) that the sale of the car for $7,000 is an event fundamentally inconsistent with that assumption (to the extent of $3,160), and (3) that upon the happening of the inconsistent event the tax benefit rule requires an inclusion (of $3,160) to correct the mistaken assumption.

The IRS does not need to invoke the tax benefit rule here, however, because mechanical application of §§1016 and 1001 automatically produces the same result as would be produced by the tax benefit rule. Since ACRS is a method of recovering a taxpayer's cost, §1016(a)(2) provides that the taxpayer's adjusted basis in an ACRS asset must be reduced by the amount of the deductions allowed under §168. Thus, the taxpayer's adjusted basis in the asset is $3,840 ($10,000 minus $6,160), and the taxpayer's §1001 gain on the sale is $3,160 ($7,000 minus $3,840) — precisely the amount by which the ACRS deductions overstated the actual decline in value. If the taxpayer can be persuaded to look at the big picture — instead of just the tax hit in the year of sale — he should not be unhappy about these results. He has been allowed artificial deductions of $3,160 in previous years, on the condition that he accept an artificial inclusion of $3,160 this year. In other words, he has been allowed to use §168 to defer the taxation of $3,160.

---

6. The half-year convention allows ACRS deductions for half of the year in which the taxpayer disposes of the asset. *See* §168(d)(4)(A).

7. For the tax benefit rule, see section C.2.d of Chapter 2.

The taxpayer might hope for one more tax advantage from the artificial depreciation deductions: conversion of ordinary income to capital gain. The taxpayer used the $3,160 of artificial deductions to offset ordinary income, taxable at high rates. Can the later $3,160 inclusion qualify for the special low rates applicable to long-term capital gains?[8] The answer is no, because of the recapture rules of §1245. Basically, §1245 provides that any gain that represents the recapture of overly generous ACRS deductions on tangible personal property will be treated as ordinary income. Under §1245, the taxpayer's entire $3,160 gain will be ordinary income. The amount of gain treated as ordinary under §1245 is the lesser of (1) the total gain realized on the disposition of the asset or (2) the ACRS deductions previously taken with respect to the asset.

How would §1245 apply in the car example, in the unlikely event that the taxpayer was able to sell the car (adjusted basis, $3,840) for $12,000? The total gain would be $8,160, but §1245 would apply to only the lesser of $8,160 or $6,160 (the amount of ACRS deductions). Thus, $6,160 of the gain would be ordinary income, but the other $2,000 could qualify as capital gain.[9] To the extent the gain results from artificial depreciation deductions, §1245 applies; to the extent the gain results because the taxpayer sells the property for more than he paid for it, §1245 does not apply.

Logically, the same recapture rules should apply to buildings. In most cases, however, §1250 does not require depreciation recapture for buildings. Section 1250 applies recapture principles to gain on the sale of a building only if there is "additional depreciation," defined as depreciation allowances in excess of straight line depreciation. Because buildings placed in service after 1986 must be depreciated using the straight line method, taxpayers disposing of buildings will usually escape §1250 unscathed.[10] Of course, buildings are long-lived assets, and taxpayers who sell buildings they placed in service long ago still must contend with §1250.

What about the other (less common) possibility—that the ACRS deductions have *understated* the actual decline in value of the asset? Suppose the taxpayer sells the car for only $3,000. Then he will realize a loss of $840 ($3,000 amount realized minus $3,840 adjusted basis) on the sale. The loss will be a §1231 loss, which means that the loss will be treated as ordinary (rather than capital) as long as the taxpayer's §1231 gains do not exceed his §1231 losses. Thus, the taxpayer will be able to claim an ordinary loss deduction for the amount by which §168 understated the decline in value of the car. The result is that the taxpayer is allowed ordinary deductions for the entire actual decline in value of the car, but not until he disposes of it.

Partial or complete expensing under §168(k)—a sometimes thing. Section 168(k) allows a taxpayer to deduct 50 percent of the cost of most §168 assets (other than real estate) in the year the assets were placed in service, but only for assets placed in service in 2008, 2009, 2010 (on or before September 8, 2010), or 2012. For eligible property placed in service after September 8, 2010, and before 2012, the deal is

8. As is explained in Chapter 12, favorable capital gains rates are available only to individual taxpayers. Corporations, which own much of the total of depreciable assets, pay tax on capital gains at the same rates applicable to their other income.

9. The car would be a §1231 asset, and gain on the sale of §1231 assets frequently qualifies for long-term capital gain treatment. See section C of Chapter 12.

10. However, capital gain that represents "unrecaptured §1250 gain" is subject to a higher rate than most other long-term capital gain, under §1(h).

even better: §168(k) allows a first-year deduction of the entire cost of the property. An earlier version of §168(k), applicable to property placed in service after September 10, 2001, and before January 1, 2005, had allowed an immediate deduction for 30 percent of the cost of most non–real estate §168 assets. All these versions of §168(k) have been intended as short-term measures to stimulate the economy, and it is likely that §168(k) will be revived in future economic downturns. If a taxpayer has deducted some but not all of the cost of property under §168(k), the remainder of the cost is recovered under normal §168 rules. Suppose in 2012 a taxpayer acquires five-year ACRS property at a cost of $100,000 and places it in service. The taxpayer's ACRS deduction for 2012 would be $60,000: $50,000 under §168(k), and $10,000 (20% of $50,000) under normal ACRS rules.

Expensing under §179. In lieu of gradual cost recovery under §168, §179 allows a taxpayer an immediate deduction for the cost of "§179 property" placed in service during the year, up to a maximum annual amount of $500,000 in 2010 and 2011, and $125,000 in 2012.[11] In general, §179 property is property eligible for ACRS under §168, with the exception of buildings. In 2010 and 2011 the $500,000 ceiling is reduced, dollar-for-dollar, as the total cost of §179 property placed in service during the year exceeds $2 million; in 2012 the $125,000 ceiling is reduced dollar-for-dollar as the total cost of §179 property placed in service exceeds $500,000.[12] For example, if a taxpayer placed in service $520,000 worth of §179 property in 2012, it would be able to deduct only $105,000 under §179.[13] If a taxpayer placed in service §179 property costing $625,000 or more in 2012, it would not be able to deduct any amount under §179. As a result, §179 is of little or no benefit to most large corporate taxpayers.

Notes and Questions

1. *A loophole you could drive an SUV through.* Section 280F, which was added to the Code in 1984, imposes special limitations on the deductions that may be claimed under §§168 and 179 with respect to an expensive automobile used by a taxpayer in her business. Section 179 is of little benefit to most purchasers of cars for business use, after §280F has done its work. According to the legislative history, Congress enacted §280F because it believed that "the investment incentives afforded by . . . ACRS should be directed to capital formation, rather than to subsidize the element of personal consumption associated with the use of very expensive automobiles." H. Rep. No. 98-432, at 1387 (1984). Thinking that no one would be crazy enough to derive personal consumption from vehicles as heavy as trucks—which was true enough in 1984—Congress provided that the limitations of §280F did not apply to vehicles weighing more than three tons. A purchaser of such a behemoth could often deduct its entire cost in the first year, under §179. What Congress didn't anticipate, of course, was that the entire country would soon become crazy enough to view sport utility vehicles—which routinely weight more than three tons—as *the* luxury vehicles of choice.

---

11. After 2012 the temporary statutory provisions augmenting the deductible amount will expire, with the permanent statutory amount of $25,000 returning to applicability.
12. This amount will revert to $200,000 in 2013.
13. $520,000 – $500,000 = $20,000. $125,000 – $20,000 = $105,000.

In this state of affairs, a person about to purchase an expensive vehicle for business use had a choice. She could buy a luxury sedan for $50,000 and be relegated to the piddling deductions permitted by §280F, or she could buy a luxury SUV and deduct the entire $50,000 up front under §179. SUV dealers often emphasized this in their advertising. From an environmental standpoint the effects were perverse, to put it mildly. As this bizarre situation began to attract media attention, Congress decided it had to act. Its response, in 2004, was to enact §179(b)(6), providing that the cost of an SUV that may be written off under §179 is limited to $25,000. This is still a much better deal than is available for purchasers of luxury sedans. Why do you suppose Congress merely narrowed the loophole, rather than shutting it completely?

Problem 1.   On August 1 of the current year, Short Line Railroad Corp. places in service a new stretch of railroad track, for which Short Line pays $1 million. On the assumption that neither §168(k) nor §179 applies, what is Short Line's current year ACRS deduction amount on account of the track? Assume the $1 million was exclusively for "railroad track," and not for "railroad grading or tunnel bore." Hint 1: The first step is to consult the statute to see how railroad tracks are classified under §168. Hint 2: Although the statute contains all the rules necessary to calculate the amount of the deduction, it is much easier to use the applicable table in Rev. Proc. 87-57.

Problem 2.   In the current year, Mega Corp. sells a machine that it bought several years ago for $100,000. As a result of $70,000 of ACRS deductions properly claimed over the years, Mega's adjusted basis in the machine as of the sale is $30,000. If Mega's amount realized on the sale is $45,000, how much gain or loss does Mega realize on the sale, and what is the character (ordinary or capital) of that gain or loss?

Problem 3.   The facts are the same as in Problem 2, except Mega's amount realized on the sale is only $25,000. In that case how much gain or loss does Mega realize on the sale, and what is the character (ordinary or capital) of that gain or loss?

Problem 4.   The facts are the same as in Problem 2, except Mega's amount realized on the sale is $105,000. In that case how much gain or loss does Mega realize on the sale, and what is the character (ordinary or capital) of that gain or loss?

B.   WHAT IS DEPRECIABLE?

1.   Nondepreciable Assets

When a taxpayer is denied a current business expense deduction for a long-lived business asset, the usual consolation prize is permission to deduct the cost of the asset over a number of years. Not every long-lived business asset is depreciable, however, because not every asset can be expected to decline in value due "to wear and tear, to decay or decline from natural causes, to exhaustion, [or] to obsolescence."[14] Land is by far the most important example of nondepreciable tangible property. If a taxpayer acquires land and a building for use in his business, he must allocate his cost between the depreciable building and the nondepreciable land.

What about art or antiques used in a business, such as valuable paintings displayed in the lobby of a luxury hotel or a fancy law firm? The IRS's position, which has generally been upheld by the courts, is that such assets are not subject to sufficient wear and tear to justify depreciation deductions. Thus, the taxpayer can recover the cost of the painting only as an offset against amount realized (under §1001), when and if the taxpayer sells the painting. There is a disagreement between the IRS and two Courts of Appeals, with respect to the depreciability of antique musical instruments — a viol in one case, and violin bows in the other — used by professional musicians. According to the courts, an asset is eligible for ACRS so long as it is subject to wear and tear in use, even if the taxpayer cannot prove that the asset has a determinable useful life, and even if the asset is an antique likely to increase in value. Simon v. Commissioner, 68 F.3d 41 (2d Cir. 1995), *nonacq.* 1996-2 C.B. 2; Liddle v. Commissioner, 65 F.3d 329 (3d Cir. 1995), *nonacq.* 1996-2 C.B. 2.[15]

An intangible business asset is also eligible for depreciation (usually called "amortization," in the case of intangible assets) if it will be used in the business "for only a limited period, the length of which can be estimated with reasonable accuracy."[16] Thus, patents and copyrights, which have finite legal lives, are eligible for depreciation. The taxpayer may be able to recover the cost of a patent or copyright over a shorter period than its legal life if he can prove its income-producing value will be exhausted before the legal protection has expired. What about an intangible business asset that does not have an ascertainable useful life? Under Treas. Reg. §1.167(a)-3(b), promulgated in 2004, such assets may generally be amortized over 15 years, using the straight line method. This 2004 regulation does not apply to assets the amortization of which is "specifically prescribed or prohibited" by any Code section (such as §197, described immediately below).

Problem 5.   What is the ACRS status (eligible or ineligible) of an antique oriental carpet displayed in a law firm's lobby? Does it matter whether the carpet is on the floor (where it is regularly walked on, although experts say it could be walked on for decades with only slight wear, and with little or no negative effect on its value) or hanging on the wall? Does it matter what circuit has jurisdiction over the carpet?

2. Section 197 Intangibles

For years, the IRS took the position that goodwill — the going concern value of a business, based on established customer relationships, good reputation, and the like — was nondepreciable because it had no ascertainable useful life. Taxpayers

---

14. Treas. Reg. §1.167(a)-2.

15. A "nonacquiescence" published in the Internal Revenue Bulletin (and in the Cumulative Bulletin) indicates that the IRS disagrees with a judicial opinion and will continue to contest the issue in other courts.

16. Treas. Reg. §1.167(a)-3(a).

had considerable success, however, in convincing courts that certain intangibles resembling goodwill had ascertainable useful lives and could be depreciated. This series of cases culminated in Newark Morning Ledger Co. v. United States, 507 U.S. 546 (1993), in which the Supreme Court decided that a newspaper could depreciate its customer list upon a factual showing that the list had an ascertainable useful life (because customers on the list would die, move away, complete the training of their puppy, or otherwise drop their subscriptions, in a statistically predictable manner). Fearing an endless stream of litigation about the useful lives of goodwill-like intangibles, Congress responded to *Newark Morning Ledger* by enacting §197. Under that section, taxpayers are allowed to recover the cost of a wide range of purchased intangibles, including goodwill and other "customer-based intangibles," on a straight line basis over 15 years, without regard to the actual useful life of the asset. Section 197 refers to this cost recovery as "amortization," which is nothing more than a term sometimes used for the depreciation of intangible assets. With a few exceptions, §197 does not apply to intangibles created by the taxpayer itself,[17] such as goodwill created by the taxpayer's own advertising. This exclusion is of little practical significance, however, because taxpayers are allowed to deduct the vast majority of the costs of creating goodwill as current business expenses under §162; thus, taxpayers will usually have no basis in self-created goodwill. Section 197 does apply, however, when a taxpayer purchases an ongoing business and part of the purchase cost is allocated to goodwill and other §197 intangibles.[18]

3. Depletion

The Code permits gradual cost recovery in the case of exhaustible natural resources, such as mines, wells, and other natural deposits. The deductions are called "depletion allowances," and the rules are quite different from those governing depreciation. Taxpayers are generally able to choose between two different cost recovery methods: cost depletion under §612, and percentage depletion under §613. A taxpayer may go back and forth between the two depletion methods with respect to the same mine in different years, using whichever method produces the larger deduction in a particular year. Under cost depletion, a taxpayer operating a mine divides the mine's basis by the estimated number of recoverable units of mineral to arrive at a per-unit depletion allowance. The allowance for a particular year is the number of units mined during the year multiplied by the per-unit allowance. As you would expect, cost depletion ceases when the taxpayer's adjusted basis has been reduced to zero.

The percentage depletion alternative does not require an estimate of the number of recoverable units in the mine. Rather, the taxpayer claims a cost recovery allowance equal to a statutorily fixed percentage of the taxpayer's gross income from mining. The allowable percentages range from a low of 5 percent (applicable to gravel, peat, sand, and stone, among other things) to a high of 22 percent (applicable to sulphur and uranium, among other things).[19] For example, a

---

17. Section 197(c)(2).
18. Section 1060 provides detailed rules for the allocation of a lump sum purchase price for a business among the various assets of the business, including §197 intangibles.
19. *See* §613(b).

taxpayer with $1 million of gross income from mining uranium would be entitled to a percentage depletion deduction of $220,000. Under tax logic, percentage depletion deductions should cease when deductions have reduced the taxpayer's adjusted basis in the mine to zero. In fact, however, nothing in §613 limits percentage depletion to basis, and it continues merrily along even after the taxpayer's basis has been reduced to zero. Moreover, percentage depletion in excess of basis does not result in negative basis. On the other hand, a taxpayer with a non-zero basis must decrease the basis by the amount of percentage depletion. Because it is not limited to basis, percentage depletion is better understood as a reduction in the effective tax rates applicable to extractive industries than as a true cost recovery allowance. Section 613A restricts the availability of percentage depletion for oil and gas wells to certain small producers; large oil and gas producers must be content with cost depletion limited to basis.

C.   WHAT COSTS MUST BE CAPITALIZED?

Up to this point, the focus has been on assets that are clearly long-lived, so that their cost must be capitalized rather than currently expensed. The issues have been the timing of cost recovery deductions, and whether cost recovery deductions are available at all. The focus now shifts to situations where the requirement of capitalization is not so clear, and taxpayers hope to be able to claim a current deduction in lieu of capitalization and cost recovery over time.

1. Self-Produced Property

COMMISSIONER v. IDAHO POWER CO.
418 U.S. 1 (1974)

Mr. Justice BLACKMUN delivered the opinion of the Court.

This case presents the sole issue whether, for federal income tax purposes, a taxpayer is entitled to a deduction from gross income, under §167(a) of the Internal Revenue Code of 1954, for depreciation on equipment the taxpayer owns and uses in the construction of its own capital facilities, or whether the capitalization provision of §263(a)(1) of the Code bars the deduction.

The taxpayer claimed the deduction, but the Commissioner of Internal Revenue disallowed it. The Tax Court . . . upheld the Commissioner's determination. 29 T.C.M. 383 (1970). The United States Court of Appeals for the Ninth Circuit . . . reversed. 477 F.2d 688 (1973). . . .

I

Nearly all the relevant facts are stipulated. The taxpayer-respondent, Idaho Power Company, is a Maine corporation organized in 1915, with its principal place of business at Boise, Idaho. It is a public utility engaged in the production, transmission, distribution, and sale of electric energy. The taxpayer keeps its books and files its federal income tax returns on the calendar year accrual basis. . . .

For many years, the taxpayer has used its own equipment and employees in the construction of improvements and additions to its capital facilities. The major work has consisted of transmission lines, transmission switching stations, distribution lines, distribution stations, and connecting facilities.

During 1962 and 1963, the tax years in question, taxpayer owned and used in its business a wide variety of automotive transportation equipment, including passenger cars, trucks of all descriptions, power-operated equipment, and trailers. . . . The transportation equipment was used in part for operation and maintenance and in part for the construction of capital facilities having a useful life of more than one year.

On its books, the taxpayer used various methods of charging costs incurred in connection with its transportation equipment either to current expense or to capital accounts. To the extent the equipment was used in construction, the taxpayer charged depreciation of the equipment, as well as all operating and maintenance costs . . . to the capital assets so constructed. . . .

For federal income tax purposes, however, the taxpayer treated the depreciation on transportation equipment differently. It claimed as a deduction from gross income all the year's depreciation on such equipment, including that portion attributable to its use in constructing capital facilities. . . . The other operating and maintenance costs the taxpayer had charged on its books to capital were not claimed as current expenses and were not deducted.

To summarize: On its books, in accordance with Federal Power Commission-Idaho Public Utilities Commission prescribed methods, the taxpayer capitalized the construction-related depreciation, but for income tax purposes that depreciation increment was claimed as a deduction under §167(a).

Upon audit, the Commissioner of Internal Revenue disallowed the deduction for the construction-related depreciation. He ruled that that depreciation was a nondeductible capital expenditure to which §263(a)(1) had application. He added the amount of the depreciation so disallowed to the taxpayer's adjusted basis in its capital facilities, and then allowed a deduction for an appropriate amount of depreciation on the addition, computed over the useful life (30 years or more) of the property constructed. A deduction for depreciation of the transportation equipment to the extent of its use in day-to-day operation and maintenance was also allowed. . . .

The Court of Appeals . . . concluded that a deduction expressly enumerated in the Code, such as that for depreciation, may properly be taken and that "no exception is made should it relate to a capital item." Id., at 693. Section 263(a)(1) of the Code was found not to be applicable because depreciation is not an "amount paid out," as required by that section. . . .

The taxpayer asserts that its transportation equipment is used in its "trade or business" and that depreciation thereon is therefore deductible under §167(a)(1) of the Code. The Commissioner concedes that §167 may be said to have a literal application to depreciation on equipment used in capital construction, but contends that the provision must be read in light of §263(a)(1) which specifically disallows any deduction for an amount "paid out for new buildings or for permanent improvements or betterments." He argues that §263 takes precedence over §167 by virtue of what he calls the "priority-ordering" terms (and what the taxpayer describes as "housekeeping" provisions) of §161 of the

Code,[20] and that sound principles of accounting and taxation mandate the capitalization of this depreciation. . . .

The issue, thus comes down primarily to a question of timing, . . . that is, whether the construction-related depreciation is to be amortized and deducted over the shorter life of the equipment or, instead, is to be amortized and deducted over the longer life of the capital facilities constructed.

Our primary concern is with the necessity to treat construction-related depreciation in a manner that comports with accounting and taxation realities. Over a period of time a capital asset is consumed and, correspondingly over that period, its theoretical value and utility are thereby reduced. Depreciation is an accounting device which recognizes that the physical consumption of a capital asset is a true cost, since the asset is being depleted. As the process of consumption continues, and depreciation is claimed and allowed, the asset's adjusted income tax basis is reduced to reflect the distribution of its cost over the accounting periods affected. . . . When the asset is used to further the taxpayer's day-to-day business operations, the periods of benefit usually correlate with the production of income. Thus, to the extent that equipment is used in such operations, a current depreciation deduction is an appropriate offset to gross income currently produced. It is clear, however, that different principles are implicated when the consumption of the asset takes place in the construction of other assets that, in the future, will produce income themselves. In this latter situation, the cost represented by depreciation does not correlate with production of current income. Rather, the cost, although certainly presently incurred, is related to the future and is appropriately allocated as part of the cost of acquiring an income-producing capital asset.

Accepted accounting practice and established tax principles require the capitalization of the cost of acquiring a capital asset. . . . This principle has obvious application to the acquisition of a capital asset by purchase, but it has been applied, as well, to the costs incurred in a taxpayer's construction of capital facilities. . . .

There can be little question that other construction-related expense items, such as tools, materials, and wages paid construction workers, are to be treated as part of the cost of acquisition of a capital asset. The taxpayer does not dispute this. Of course, reasonable wages paid in the carrying on of a trade or business qualify as a deduction from gross income. Section 162(a)(1) of the 1954 Code. But when wages are paid in connection with the construction or acquisition of a capital asset, they must be capitalized and are then entitled to be amortized over the life of the capital asset so acquired. . . .

Construction-related depreciation is not unlike expenditures for wages for construction workers. The significant fact is that the exhaustion of construction equipment does not represent the final disposition of the taxpayer's investment in that equipment; rather, the investment in the equipment is assimilated into the cost of the capital asset constructed. Construction-related depreciation on the equipment is not an expense to the taxpayer of its day-to-day business. It is, however, appropriately recognized as a part of the taxpayer's cost or investment in the capital asset. The taxpayer's own accounting procedure reflects this treatment, for on its books the construction-related depreciation was capitalized by a credit to the equipment account and a debit to the capital facility account. By the

---

20. "*§161. Allowance of deductions.* In computing taxable income under section 63(a), there shall be allowed as deductions the items specified in this part, subject to the exceptions provided in part IX (sec. 261 and following, relating to items not deductible)."

same token, this capitalization prevents the distortion of income that would otherwise occur if depreciation properly allocable to asset acquisition were deducted from gross income currently realized. . . .

An additional pertinent factor is that capitalization of construction-related depreciation by the taxpayer who does its own construction work maintains tax parity with the taxpayer who has its construction work done by an independent contractor. The depreciation on the contractor's equipment incurred during the performance of the job will be an element of cost charged by the contractor for his construction services, and the entire cost, of course, must be capitalized by the taxpayer having the construction work performed. The Court of Appeals' holding would lead to disparate treatment among taxpayers because it would allow the firm with sufficient resources to construct its own facilities and to obtain a current deduction, whereas another firm without such resources would be required to capitalize its entire cost including depreciation charged to it by the contractor. . . .

The presence of §263(a)(1) in the Code is of significance. Its literal language denies a deduction for "[any] amount paid out" for construction or permanent improvement of facilities. The taxpayer contends, and the Court of Appeals held, that depreciation of construction equipment represents merely a decrease in value and is not an amount "paid out," within the meaning of §263(a)(1). We disagree.

The purpose of §263 is to reflect the basic principle that a capital expenditure may not be deducted from current income. It serves to prevent a taxpayer from utilizing currently a deduction properly attributable, through amortization, to later tax years when the capital asset becomes income producing. The regulations state that the capital expenditures to which §263(a) extends include the "cost of acquisition, construction, or erection of buildings." Treas. Reg. §1.263(a)-2(a). This manifests an administrative understanding that for purposes of §263(a)(1), "amount paid out" equates with "cost incurred." . . . There is no question that the cost of the transportation equipment was "paid out" in the same manner as the cost of supplies, materials, and other equipment, and the wages of construction workers. The taxpayer does not question the capitalization of these other items as elements of the cost of acquiring a capital asset. We see no reason to treat construction-related depreciation differently. In acquiring the transportation equipment, taxpayer "paid out" the equipment's purchase price; depreciation is simply the means of allocating the payment over the various accounting periods affected. . . .

Finally, the priority-ordering directive of §161 . . . requires that the capitalization provision of §263(a) take precedence, on the facts here, over §167(a). . . . The clear import of §161 is that, with stated exceptions . . . , none of which is applicable here, an expenditure incurred in acquiring capital assets must be capitalized even when the expenditure otherwise might be deemed deductible under Part VI. . . .

We hold that the equipment depreciation allocable to taxpayer's construction of capital facilities is to be capitalized.

Mr. Justice DOUGLAS, dissenting. . . .

I suspect that if the life of the vehicle were 40 years and the life of the building were 10 years the Internal Revenue Service would be here arguing persuasively that depreciation of the vehicle should be taken over a 40-year period. That is not to impugn the integrity of the IRS. It is only an illustration of the capricious character of how law is construed to get from the taxpayer the greatest possible return that is permissible under the Code. . . .

Notes and Questions

1. *Justice Douglas's dissent.* Do you share Justice Douglas's suspicion that the IRS would be singing a different tune if the life of the vehicle were 40 years and the life of the building were ten years? Suppose, in Justice Douglas's hypothetical, that the vehicle cost $40,000, and that §168 calls for straight line cost recovery for the vehicle over 40 years. If the taxpayer uses the vehicle for a full year in constructing a facility with a ten-year recovery period, how would the $1,000 ACRS allowance on the vehicle be treated under *Idaho Power*?

2. *The uniform capitalization rules.* In 1986 Congress enacted the "uniform capitalization" (unicap) rules of §263A, which apply the principle of *Idaho Power* with a vengeance. In general, §263A denies a taxpayer an immediate deduction for the costs of producing property that the taxpayer will either use in its business or sell as inventory.[21] Costs that must be capitalized (or added to the cost of inventory) include depreciation on equipment used in producing the property, employees' wages allocable to production of the property, and an appropriate share of the rent and utilities expenses of the facility where the property is produced. Compliance with the unicap rules can involve a significant accounting burden, but this is largely accounting that should be done anyway, for non-tax reasons. Without cost allocation accounting, a taxpayer will be unable to determine which of its projects are profitable and which are losing money.

   When a taxpayer produces a depreciable asset that it will *use* in its business, the operation of the unicap rules basically follows the *Idaho Power* approach. The example below illustrates the operation of the rules when a taxpayer produces inventory—that is, property that it will *sell* in its business.[22]

   Example. Mary is a self-employed maker of jewelry. She makes one item of jewelry each month in her studio. Her monthly studio rent is $1,000, and her monthly studio utilities bill is $200. Of the 12 pieces she made last year, she had sold eight by the end of the year. The other four were still in inventory at year's end. Assuming the unicap rules apply to Mary (more on that in Note 3), §263A requires Mary to treat each month's $1,200 rent and utilities as part of the cost of the jewelry item produced that month. Thus Mary's tax cost for each item will reflect not only the cost of materials, but also the rent and utilities expenses. When Mary sells an item, she will then be able offset the $1,200 studio costs against the sales proceeds. She will be able to recover $9,600 ($1,200 x 8) of her studio expenses on her tax return for last year, but recovery of the other $4,800 must await sale of the remaining four items.

3. *Is it art?* Mary could escape the clutches of the unicap rules, and claim current deductions for all her studio expenses, if she met the criteria for the "qualified creative expense" exemption in §263A(h). To qualify, she must be an individual in the business of being "a writer, photographer, or artist." Does a

---

21. In addition to applying to self-produced property, §263A also disallows a current deduction for any costs allocable to purchased inventory, but only for taxpayers with gross receipts in excess of $10 million.

22. For additional coverage of §263A, see section A.3 of Chapter 7, on inventory accounting.

maker of fine jewelry qualify as an artist? Although the Internal Revenue
Code may not be the first place most people would look for a definition of an
artist, §263A(h)(3)(C)(i) defines an artist as a person who creates "a picture,
painting, sculpture, statue, etching, drawing, cartoon, graphic design, or
original print edition." The statute also provides that the determination of
whether a person is an artist should take into account the "originality and
uniqueness of the item created" and "[t]he predominance of aesthetic value
over utilitarian value of the item." This sounds fairly promising for Mary.
Jewelry could be considered a kind of sculpture, her jewelry is highly original, and it has *only* aesthetic value (at least if she makes no watches). Unfortunately, the legislative history of the unicap rules is unfavorable. According
to a Committee Report, persons who produce "jewelry, silverware, pottery,
[and] furniture" are "generally" not considered artists for tax purposes.[23]
Perhaps Mary could argue that the legislative history is inconsistent with
the statute, insofar as the legislative history lumps nonutilitarian jewelry with
utilitarian silverware, pottery, and furniture. Or she could simply argue that
the word "generally" in the report leaves some wiggle room for makers of
exceptionally beautiful and useless items of jewelry.

4. *Kiss writing goodbye?* How did the Internal Revenue Service get charged with
determining who is an artist (or writer or photographer)? As explained in the
following passage, the exception for qualified creative expenses is a classic
example of the squeaky — that is, articulate — wheel getting the grease.[24]

> The Tax Reform Act of 1986 applied its uniform capitalization rules broadly, to
> producers of "real or tangible personal property," with "tangible personal
> property" defined to include "a film, sound recording, video tape, book, or
> similar property." Writers and artists soon realized that this meant, among
> other people, them. Rather than immediately deducting costs such as studio
> rent and utilities, they would have to capitalize those costs to their artistic
> inventory. They were deeply troubled by this realization. One painter
> explained, "We're making art, not lawn mowers," and a sculptor added, "I'm
> not a bicycle manufacturer. I'm dealing with dreams here." An art gallery
> assistant director noted that the new law made artists "feel as if someone were
> stabbing them." An artist complained that "for the first time we are obliged to
> think, before we make something, 'How saleable will it be?'" A writer cut
> through the complexities to the heart of the matter: "Simply, this means the
> public can kiss writing, and therefore reading, goodbye." Faced with the immi-
> nent demise of both art-for-art's-sake and written communication, Congress
> saw reason, and in 1988 exempted "qualified creative expenses" from the
> uniform capitalization rules.

It is possible that art-for-art's sake and written communication would
have survived even without §263A(h). Successful artists and writers could
have afforded both the accounting and tax costs of compliance with the
unicap rules, and unsuccessful artists and writers would owe little or no
income tax (at least with respect to their creative endeavors) regardless of
whether §263A applied to them. Nevertheless, Congress was eager to

23. H.R. Rep. No. 1104, 100th Cong., 2d Sess., 145 (1988).
24. The excerpt is from Lawrence Zelenak, *I Can Sit on It, But Is It Art?*, 70 Tax Notes 99
(1996). Citations for the quotations (all taken from newspaper stories) may be found in the article.

appease the wrath of the creative community, leaving the IRS with the job of separating the creative wheat from the uncreative chaff.

Problem 6. For many decades, Charles Chisel made his highly acclaimed sculptures without any assistance. In recent years he has been severely afflicted with Parkinson's disease, making it impossible for him to do any actual sculpting. He continues, however, to design sculptures and minutely supervise the actual sculpting by his assistants. Does Charles qualify for the benefits of §263A(h)?

Problem 7. Rocky Granite is also a sculptor. Rocky has no disabilities, but the demand for his work exceeds his ability to produce sculptures by his own efforts. In response to the high demand, he hires ten sculptors to produce art in his workshop, all of which he sells under his own name. He gives general direction and advice to his employees, but he does not perform detailed design work for most of the sculptures produced in his workshop, and he seldom does any actual sculpting. Does Rocky qualify for the benefits of §263A(h)?

2. INDOPCO: *Taking Capitalization Seriously?*

INDOPCO, INC. v. COMMISSIONER
503 U.S. 79 (1992)

Justice BLACKMUN delivered the opinion of the Court.

In this case we must decide whether certain professional expenses incurred by a target corporation in the course of a friendly takeover are deductible by that corporation as "ordinary and necessary" business expenses under §162(a) of the Internal Revenue Code.

I

. . . Petitioner INDOPCO, Inc., formerly named National Starch and Chemical Corporation and hereinafter referred to as National Starch, is a Delaware corporation that manufactures and sells adhesives, starches, and specialty chemical products. In October 1977, representatives of Unilever United States, Inc., also a Delaware corporation (Unilever), expressed interest in acquiring National Starch, which was one of its suppliers, through a friendly transaction. . . . Frank and Anna Greenwall were the corporation's largest shareholders and owned approximately 14.5% of the common. The Greenwalls, getting along in years and concerned about their estate plans, indicated that they would transfer their shares to Unilever only if a transaction tax free for them could be arranged.

Lawyers representing both sides devised a "reverse subsidiary cash merger" that they felt would satisfy the Greenwalls' concerns. [Under this plan, National Starch would become a subsidiary of Unilever.] . . .

In November 1977, National Starch's directors were formally advised of Unilever's interest and the proposed transaction. At that time, Debevoise, Plimpton, Lyons & Gates, National Starch's counsel, told the directors that under Delaware law they had a fiduciary duty to ensure that the proposed transaction would be fair to the shareholders. National Starch thereupon engaged the investment banking firm of Morgan Stanley & Co., Inc., to evaluate its shares, to render a fairness opinion, and generally to assist in the event of the emergence of a hostile tender offer.

Although Unilever originally had suggested a price between $65 and $70 per share, negotiations resulted in a final offer of $73.50 per share, a figure Morgan Stanley found to be fair. Following approval by National Starch's board and the issuance of a favorable private ruling from the Internal Revenue Service that the transaction would be tax free under §351 for [the Greenwalls], the transaction was consummated in August 1978.

Morgan Stanley charged National Starch a fee of $2,200,000, along with $7,586 for out-of-pocket expenses and $18,000 for legal fees. The Debevoise firm charged National Starch $490,000, along with $15,069 for out-of-pocket expenses. National Starch also incurred expenses aggregating $150,962 for miscellaneous items — such as accounting, printing, proxy solicitation, and Securities and Exchange Commission fees — in connection with the transaction. No issue is raised as to the propriety or reasonableness of these charges.

On its federal income tax return for its short taxable year ended August 15, 1978, National Starch claimed a deduction for the $2,225,586 paid to Morgan Stanley, but did not deduct the $505,069 paid to Debevoise or the other expenses. Upon audit, the Commissioner of Internal Revenue disallowed the claimed deduction and issued a notice of deficiency. Petitioner sought redetermination in the United States Tax Court, asserting, however, not only the right to deduct the investment banking fees and expenses but, as well, the legal and miscellaneous expenses incurred.

The Tax Court, in an unreviewed decision, ruled that the expenditures were capital in nature and therefore not deductible under §162(a) in the 1978 return as "ordinary and necessary expenses." National Starch and Chemical Corp. v. Commissioner, 93 T.C. 67 (1989). . . . The United States Court of Appeals for the Third Circuit affirmed, . . . 918 F.2d 426, 432-433 (1990). In so doing, the Court of Appeals rejected National Starch's contention that, because the disputed expenses did not "create or enhance . . . a separate and distinct additional asset," *see* Commissioner v. Lincoln Savings & Loan Assn., 403 U.S. 345, 354 (1971), they could not be capitalized and therefore were deductible under §162(a). We granted certiorari to resolve a perceived conflict on the issue among the Courts of Appeals.

II

Section 162(a) of the Internal Revenue Code allows the deduction of "all the ordinary and necessary expenses paid or incurred during the taxable year in carrying on any trade or business." In contrast, §263 of the Code allows no deduction for a capital expenditure — an "amount paid out for new buildings or for permanent improvements or betterments made to increase the value of any property or estate." Section 263(a)(1). The primary effect of characterizing a payment as either a business expense or a capital expenditure concerns the timing of the taxpayer's cost recovery: While business expenses are currently deductible, a capital expenditure usually is amortized and depreciated over the life of the relevant asset, or, where no specific asset or useful life can be ascertained, is deducted upon dissolution of the enterprise. . . . Through provisions such as these, the Code endeavors to match expenses with the revenues of the taxable period to which they are properly attributable, thereby resulting in a more accurate calculation of net income for tax purposes. . . .

In exploring the relationship between deductions and capital expenditures, this Court has noted the "familiar rule" that "an income tax deduction is a matter of legislative grace and that the burden of clearly showing the right to the claimed deduction is on the taxpayer." Interstate Transit Lines v. Commissioner, 319 U.S. 590, 593 (1943); Deputy v. Du Pont, 308 U.S. 488, 493 (1940); New Colonial Ice Co. v. Helvering, 292 U.S. 435, 440 (1934). The notion that deductions are exceptions to the norm of capitalization finds support in various aspects of the Code. Deductions are specifically enumerated and thus are subject to disallowance in favor of capitalization. *See* §§161 and 261. Nondeductible capital expenditures, by contrast, are not exhaustively enumerated in the Code; rather than providing a "complete list of nondeductible expenditures," *Lincoln Savings,* 403 U.S. at 358, §263 serves as a general means of distinguishing capital expenditures from current expenses. . . . For these reasons, deductions are strictly construed and allowed only "as there is a clear provision therefor." New Colonial Ice Co. v. Helvering, 292 U.S. at 440; Deputy v. Du Pont, 308 U.S. at 493. . . .

National Starch contends that the decision in *Lincoln Savings* changed these familiar backdrops and announced an exclusive test for identifying capital expenditures, a test in which "creation or enhancement of an asset" is a prerequisite to capitalization, and deducibility under §162(a) is the rule rather than the exception. We do not agree, for we conclude that National Starch has overread *Lincoln Savings.*

In *Lincoln Savings,* we were asked to decide whether certain premiums, required by federal statute to be paid by a savings and loan association to the Federal Savings and Loan Insurance Corporation (FSLIC), were ordinary and necessary expenses under §162(a), as Lincoln Savings argued and the Court of Appeals had held, or capital expenditures under §263, as the Commissioner contended. We found that the "additional" premiums, the purpose of which was to provide FSLIC with a secondary reserve fund in which each insured institution retained a pro rata interest recoverable in certain situations, "serve to create or enhance for Lincoln what is essentially a separate and distinct additional asset." 403 U.S. at 354. "As an inevitable consequence," we concluded, "the payment is capital in nature and not an expense, let alone an ordinary expense, deductible under §162(a)." Ibid.

Lincoln Savings stands for the simple proposition that a taxpayer's expenditure that "serves to create or enhance . . . a separate and distinct" asset should be capitalized under §263. It by no means follows, however, that *only* expenditures that create or enhance separate and distinct assets are to be capitalized under §263. We had no occasion *in Lincoln Savings* to consider the tax treatment of expenditures that, unlike the additional premiums at issue there, did not create or enhance a specific asset, and thus the case cannot be read to preclude capitalization in other circumstances. In short, *Lincoln Savings* holds that the creation of a separate and distinct asset well may be a sufficient, but not a necessary, condition to classification as a capital expenditure. . . .

Nor does our statement in *Lincoln Savings,* 403 U.S. at 354, that "the presence of an ensuing benefit that may have some future aspect is not controlling" prohibit reliance on future benefit as a means of distinguishing an ordinary business expense from a capital expenditure.[25] Although the mere presence of an incidental future benefit—"some future aspect"—may not warrant capitalization, a taxpayer's realization of benefits beyond the year in which the expenditure is incurred

---

25. Petitioner contends that, absent a separate-and-distinct-asset requirement for capitalization, a taxpayer will have no "principled basis" upon which to differentiate business expenses from capital expenditures. We note, however, that grounding tax status on the existence of an asset would be unlikely to produce the bright-line rule that petitioner desires, given that the notion of an "asset" is itself flexible and amorphous. . . .

is undeniably important in determining whether the appropriate tax treatment is immediate deduction or capitalization. . . . Indeed, the text of the Code's capitalization provision, §263(a)(1), which refers to "permanent improvements or betterments," itself envisions an inquiry into the duration and extent of the benefits realized by the taxpayer.

III

In applying the foregoing principles to the specific expenditures at issue in this case, we conclude that National Starch has not demonstrated that the investment banking, legal, and other costs it incurred in connection with Unilever's acquisition of its shares are deductible as ordinary and necessary business expenses under §162(a).

Although petitioner attempts to dismiss the benefits that accrued to National Starch from the Unilever acquisition as "entirely speculative" or "merely incidental," the Tax Court's and the Court of Appeals' findings that the transaction produced significant benefits to National Starch that extended beyond the tax year in question are amply supported by the record. For example, in commenting on the merger with Unilever, National Starch's 1978 "Progress Report" observed that the company would "benefit greatly from the availability of Unilever's enormous resources, especially in the area of basic technology." . . .

In addition to these anticipated resource-related benefits, National Starch obtained benefits through its transformation from a publicly held, freestanding corporation into a wholly owned subsidiary of Unilever. . . . Following Unilever's acquisition of National Starch's outstanding shares, National Starch was no longer subject to what even it terms the "substantial" shareholder-relations expenses a publicly traded corporation incurs, including reporting and disclosure obligations, proxy battles, and derivative suits. . . .

IV

The expenses that National Starch incurred in Unilever's friendly takeover do not qualify for deduction as "ordinary and necessary" business expenses under §162(a). The fact that the expenditures do not create or enhance a separate and distinct additional asset is not controlling; the acquisition-related expenses bear the indicia of capital expenditures and are to be treated as such. . . .

Notes and Questions

1. *A kinder, gentler IRS.* The tone of the *INDOPCO* opinion — as reflected in statements such as "deductions are exceptions to the norm of capitalization" — suggested that the Supreme Court would support an IRS campaign to capitalize a wide range of expenditures producing benefits in future years — regardless, of course, of whether the expenditures produced "separate and distinct" assets. The Court's acknowledgment that "the mere presence of an incidental future benefit" might not require capitalization seemed grudging, at best. The opinion could be read as inviting the IRS to

reconsider a number of doctrines that had allowed taxpayers to claim current business expense deductions for expenditures with obvious future benefits. Taxpayers and their advisors waited anxiously to see how aggressively the IRS would react to *INDOPCO*. They were relieved when the Service began to publish revenue rulings such as the following.

REV. RUL. 92-80
1992-2 C.B. 57

ISSUE

Does the Supreme Court's decision in Indopco, Inc. v. Commissioner, 503 U.S. 79 (1992), affect the treatment of advertising costs as business expenses which are generally deductible under section 162 of the Internal Revenue Code?

LAW AND ANALYSIS

Section 162(a) of the Code allows a deduction for all the ordinary and necessary expenses paid or incurred during the taxable year in carrying on any trade or business.

Section 1.162-1(a) of the Income Tax Regulations expressly provides that "advertising and other selling expenses" are among the items included in deductible business expenses under section 162 of the Code.

Section 1.162-20(a)(2) of the regulations provides, in part, that expenditures for institutional or goodwill advertising which keeps the taxpayer's name before the public are generally deductible as ordinary and necessary business expenses provided the expenditures are related to the patronage the taxpayer might reasonably expect in the future.

Section 263(a) of the Code provides that no deduction is allowed for any amount paid out for permanent improvements or betterments made to increase the value of any property.

In Indopco, Inc. v. Commissioner, 503 U.S. 79 (1992), the Supreme Court concluded that certain legal and professional fees incurred by a target corporation to facilitate a friendly acquisition were capital expenditures. The Court stated that the acquisition costs created significant long-term benefits for the taxpayer. In reaching this decision, the Court specifically rejected the argument that its decision in Commissioner v. Lincoln Savings & Loan Association, 403 U.S. 345 (1971), should be read as holding "that *only* expenditures that create or enhance separate and distinct assets are to be capitalized under §263." *Indopco* at 86-87. (Emphasis in original.)

The *Indopco* decision does not affect the treatment of advertising costs under section 162(a) of the Code. These costs are generally deductible under that section even though advertising may have some future effect on business activities, as in the case of institutional or goodwill advertising. *See* section 1.162-1(a) and section 1.162-20(a)(2) of the regulations. Only in the unusual circumstance where advertising is directed towards obtaining future benefits significantly beyond those traditionally associated with ordinary product advertising or with institutional or goodwill advertising, must the costs of that advertising be capitalized. *See, e.g.,* Cleveland Electric Illuminating Co. v. United States, 7 Cl. Ct. 220 (1975) (capitalization of advertising costs incurred to allay public opposition to the granting of a license to construct a nuclear power plant).

HOLDING

The *Indopco* decision does not affect the treatment of advertising costs as business expenses which are generally deductible under section 162 of the Code.

Notes and Questions

1. *More of the same.* Following the advertising revenue ruling, the IRS issued a series of rulings holding that the ability to claim a current deduction for various types of expenses was not affected by *INDOPCO. See* Rev. Rul. 94-12, 1994-1 C.B. 36 (repairs); Rev. Rul. 94-77, 1994-2 C.B. 19 (severance pay); Rev. Rul. 96-62, 1996-2 C.B. 9 (costs of training employees). *INDOPCO* could be a powerful tool in the hands of the IRS, but the Service has been sparing in its use, both to protect settled expectations and to avoid the complexity involved in a more aggressive approach to capitalization. In December 2003 the Treasury Department issued new regulations (Treas. Reg. §§1.263(a)-4, 1.263(a)-5) which come close to relegating the future benefits test of *INDOPCO* to the dustbin of history, so far as expenditures relating to intangible assets are concerned. The best explanation of the general approach and rationale of the new regulations is contained in the preamble — excerpted immediately below — which accompanied the regulations when they were issued in proposed form in 2002. (The final version of the regulations differs in a number of details from the proposed regulations described in the preamble, but the basic approach and rationale are unchanged.)

DEPARTMENT OF THE TREASURY, GUIDANCE REGARDING DEDUCTION AND CAPITALIZATION OF EXPENDITURES
67 Fed. Reg. 77701 (2002)

II. GENERAL PRINCIPLE OF CAPITALIZATION

A. OVERVIEW

The proposed regulations require capitalization of amounts paid to acquire, create, or enhance an intangible asset. For this purpose, an *intangible asset* is defined as (1) any intangible that is acquired from another person in a purchase or similar transaction . . . ; (2) certain rights, privileges, or benefits that are created or originated by the taxpayer . . . ; (3) a separate and distinct intangible asset . . . ; or (4) a future benefit that the IRS and Treasury Department identify in subsequent published guidance as an intangible asset for which capitalization is required. . . .

Through this definition of *intangible asset,* the IRS and Treasury Department seek to provide certainty for taxpayers by identifying specific categories of rights, privileges, and benefits, the costs of which are appropriately capitalized. In determining the categories of expenditures for which capitalization is specifically required, the IRS and Treasury Department considered expenditures for which the courts have traditionally required capitalization. These categories will help promote consistent interpretation of section 263(a) by taxpayers and IRS field personnel.

B. SEPARATE AND DISTINCT INTANGIBLE ASSET

The proposed regulations define the term *separate and distinct intangible asset* based on factors traditionally used by the courts to determine whether an expenditure serves to acquire, create, or enhance a separate and distinct asset. Courts have considered (1) whether the expenditure creates a distinct and recognized property interest subject to protection under state or federal law; (2) whether the expenditure creates anything transferrable or salable; and (3) whether the expenditure creates anything with an ascertainable and measurable value in money's worth. . . .

The IRS and Treasury Department note that the separate and distinct asset standard has not historically yielded the same level of controversy as the significant future benefit standard. . . .

C. SIGNIFICANT FUTURE BENEFITS IDENTIFIED IN PUBLISHED GUIDANCE

A fundamental purpose of section 263(a) is to prevent the distortion of taxable income through current deduction of expenditures relating to the production of income in future years. Thus, in determining whether an expenditure should be capitalized, the Supreme Court has considered whether the expenditure produces a significant future benefit. INDOPCO, Inc. v. Commissioner, 503 U.S. 79 (1992). A "significant future benefit" standard, however, does not provide the certainty and clarity necessary for compliance with, and sound administration of, the law. Consequently, the IRS and Treasury Department believe that simply restating the significant future benefit test, without more, would lead to continued uncertainty on the part of taxpayers and continued controversy between taxpayers and the IRS. Accordingly, the IRS and Treasury Department have initially defined the exclusive scope of the significant future benefit test through the specific categories of intangible assets for which capitalization is required in the proposed regulations. The future benefit standard underlies many of these categories. . . .

V. TRANSACTION COSTS

D. SIMPLIFYING CONVENTIONS APPLICABLE TO TRANSACTION COSTS

1. Salaries and Overhead

Much of the recent debate surrounding section 263(a) has focused on the extent to which capitalization is required for employee compensation and overhead costs that are related to the acquisition, creation, or enhancement of an asset. Generally, courts and the Service have required capitalization of such costs where the facts show that the costs clearly are allocable to a particular asset. *See* Commissioner v. Idaho Power Co., 418 U.S. 1 (1973) (requiring capitalization of depreciation on equipment used to construct capital assets and noting that wages, when paid in connection with the construction or acquisition of a capital asset, must be capitalized and amortized over the life of the capital asset); Louisville and N.R. Co. v. Commissioner, 641 F.2d 435 (6th Cir. 1981) (requiring capitalization of overhead costs associated with building and rebuilding railroad freight cars); Lychuk v. Commissioner, 116 T.C. 374 (2001) (requiring capitalization of employee compensation where employees spent a significant portion of their time working on acquisitions of installment obligations); Rev. Rul. 73-580 (1973-2 C.B. 86) (requiring capitalization of employee compensation reasonably attributable to services performed in connection with corporate mergers and acquisitions).

In the context of intangible assets, some courts have allowed taxpayers to deduct employee compensation and overhead where there is only an indirect nexus between the intangible asset and the compensation or overhead. *See* Wells Fargo v. Commissioner, 224 F.3d 874 (8th Cir. 2000) (deduction allowed for officers' salaries allocable to work performed by corporate officers in negotiating a merger transaction because the salaries "originated from the employment relationship between the taxpayer and its officers" and not from the merger transaction); PNC Bancorp v. Commissioner, 212 F.3d 822 (3rd Cir. 2000) (deduction allowed for compensation and other costs of originating loans to borrowers); Lychuk v. Commissioner, 116 T.C. 374 (2001) (capitalization not required for overhead costs allocable to the taxpayer's acquisition of installment loans because the overhead did not originate in the process of acquiring the installment notes, and would have been incurred even if the taxpayer did not engage in such acquisition).

To resolve much of this controversy, and to eliminate the burden on taxpayers of allocating certain transaction costs among various intangible assets, the proposed regulations provide a simplifying assumption that employee compensation and overhead costs do not facilitate the acquisition, creation or enhancement of an intangible asset. The rule applies regardless of the percentage of the employee's time that is allocable to capital transactions. For example, capitalization is not required for compensation paid to an employee of the taxpayer who works full time on merger transactions. . . .

Notes and Questions

1. *Do the new regulations overrule* INDOPCO? To get a sense of how the approach of the new regulations works in a few concrete situations, examine Treas. Reg. §1.263(a)-4(*l*), Examples 4, 5, and 6. As the preamble states and the examples illustrate, for the most part the new regulations abandon the future benefits test of *INDOPCO* in favor of the separate-and-distinct asset test that the Supreme Court rejected in *INDOPCO*. Do the new regulations effectively overrule the Supreme Court? The Treasury Department may not have the *authority* to overrule the Supreme Court, but as a practical matter it has the *power* to turn its back on Supreme Court victories. The taxpayers directly affected will not complain that the Treasury is treating them more

generously than is called for by *INDOPCO,* and in all likelihood no one else will have standing to challenge the Treasury's generosity. Is the Treasury's rejection of its *INDOPCO* victory an unprincipled giveaway, or an appropriate concession in the interests of administrative practicality (or a little of each)?

2. *Intangible versus tangible assets.* The new regulations address only the capitalization of costs related to *intangible* assets. As a result of the new regulations, there are now much more rigorous capitalization requirements for tangible assets than for intangible assets. The new regulations are particularly generous with respect to employee compensation costs. Compare the deductibility of employee compensation costs relating to intangible assets (as described in the preamble) with the capitalization of such costs required in the case of tangible assets subject to §263A.

3. Repairs

Repairs are an important area where the IRS continues to allow current deductions under §162 for expenditures with obvious future benefits. The revenue ruling below represents a very generous post-*INDOPCO* application of the repair doctrine.

REV. RUL. 2001-4
2001-1 C.B 295

ISSUE

Are costs incurred by a taxpayer to perform work on its aircraft airframe, including the costs of a "heavy maintenance visit," deductible as ordinary and necessary business expenses under §162 of the Internal Revenue Code, or must they be capitalized under §§263 and 263A?

FACTS

X is a commercial airline engaged in the business of transporting passengers and freight throughout the United States and abroad. To conduct its business, *X* owns or leases various types of aircraft. As a condition of maintaining its operating license and airworthiness certification for these aircraft, *X* is required by the Federal Aviation Administration ("FAA") to establish and adhere to a continuous maintenance program for each aircraft within its fleet. These programs, which are designed by *X* and the aircraft's manufacturer and approved by the FAA, are incorporated into each aircraft's maintenance manual. The maintenance manuals require a variety of periodic maintenance visits at various intervals during the operating lives of each aircraft. The most extensive of these for *X* is termed a "heavy maintenance visit" (also known in the industry as a "D check," "heavy C check," or "overhaul"), which is required to be performed by *X* approximately every eight years of aircraft operation. The purpose of a heavy maintenance visit, according to *X*'s maintenance manual, is to prevent deterioration of the inherent safety and reliability levels of the aircraft equipment and, if such deterioration occurs, to restore the equipment to their inherent levels.

In each of the following three situations, *X* reasonably anticipated at the time the aircraft was placed in service that the aircraft would be useful in its trade or business for up to 25 years, taking into account the repairs and maintenance necessary to keep the aircraft in an ordinarily efficient operating condition. In addition, each . . . aircraft in the following three situations is fully depreciated for federal income tax purposes at the time of the heavy maintenance visit.

SITUATION 1

In 2000, *X* incurred $2 million for the labor and materials necessary to perform a heavy maintenance visit on the airframe of Aircraft 1, which *X* acquired in 1984 for $15 million (excluding the cost of engines). To perform the heavy maintenance visit, *X* extensively disassembled the airframe, removing items such as its engines, landing gear, cabin and passenger compartment seats, side and ceiling panels, baggage stowage bins, galleys, lavatories, floor boards, cargo loading systems, and flight control surfaces. As specified by *X*'s maintenance manual for Aircraft 1, *X* then performed certain tasks on the disassembled airframe for the purpose of preventing deterioration of the inherent safety and reliability levels of the airframe. These tasks included lubrication and service; operational and visual checks; inspection and functional checks; restoration of minor parts and components; and removal, discard, and replacement of certain life-limited single cell parts, such as cartridges, canisters, cylinders, and disks.

Whenever the execution of a task revealed cracks, corrosion, excessive wear, or dysfunctional operation, *X* was required by the maintenance manual to restore the airframe to an acceptable condition. This restoration involved burnishing corrosion; repairing cracks, dents, gouges, punctures, or scratches by burnishing, blending, stop-drilling, or applying skin patches or doublers over the affected area; tightening or replacing loose or missing fasteners, rivets, screws, bolts, nuts, or clamps; repairing or replacing torn or damaged seals, gaskets, or valves; repairing or replacing damaged or missing placards, decals, labels, or stencils; additional cleaning, lubricating, or painting; further inspecting or testing, including the use of sophisticated non-destructive inspection methods; repairing fiberglass or laminated parts; replacing bushings, bearings, hinges, handles, switches, gauges, or indicators; repairing chaffed or damaged wiring; repairing or adjusting various landing gear or flight surface control cables; replacing light bulbs, window panes, lenses, or shields; replacing anti-skid materials and stops on floors, pedals, and stairways; replacing floor boards; and performing minor repairs on ribs, spars, frames, longerons, stringers, beams, and supports.

In addition to the tasks described above, *X* also performed additional work as part of the heavy maintenance visit for Aircraft 1. . . .

None of the work performed by *X* as part of the heavy maintenance visit . . . for Aircraft 1 resulted in a material upgrade or addition to its airframe or involved the replacement of any (or a significant portion of any) major component or substantial structural part of the airframe. This work maintained the relative value of the aircraft. The value of the aircraft declines as it ages even if the heavy maintenance work is performed.

After 45 days, the heavy maintenance visit was completed, and Aircraft 1 was reassembled, tested, and returned to *X's* fleet. *X* then continued to use Aircraft 1 for the same purposes and in the same manner that it did prior to the performance of the heavy maintenance visit. The performance of the heavy maintenance visit did not extend the useful life of the airframe beyond the 25-year useful life that *X* anticipated when it acquired the airframe. . . .

[Situations 2 and 3, involving even more extensive work, are omitted.]

LAW

Section 162 and §1.162-1(a) of the Income Tax Regulations allow a deduction for all the ordinary and necessary expenses paid or incurred during the taxable year in carrying on any trade or business, including "incidental repairs."

Section 1.162-4 allows a deduction for the cost of incidental repairs that neither materially add to the value of the property nor appreciably prolong its useful life, but keep it in an ordinarily efficient operating condition. However, §1.162-4 also provides that the cost of repairs in the nature of replacements that arrest deterioration and appreciably prolong the life of the property must be capitalized and depreciated in accordance with §167.

Section 263(a) provides that no deduction is allowed for (1) any amount paid out for new buildings or permanent improvements or betterments made to increase the value of any property or estate or (2) any amount expended in restoring property or in making good the exhaustion thereof for which an allowance has been made. *See also* §1.263(a)-1(a).

Section 1.263(a)-1(b) provides that capital expenditures include amounts paid or incurred to (1) add to the value, or substantially prolong the useful life, of property owned by the taxpayer, or (2) adapt property to a new or different use. However, that regulation also provides that amounts paid or incurred for incidental repairs and maintenance of property within the meaning of §162 and §1.162-4 are not capital expenditures under §1.263(a)-1. . . .

The United States Supreme Court has specifically recognized that the "decisive distinctions [between capital and ordinary expenditures] are those of degree and not of kind," and a careful examination of the particular facts of each case is required. Deputy v. du Pont, 308 U.S. 488, 496 (1940), quoting Welch v. Helvering, 290 U.S. 111, 114 (1933). . . .

Any properly performed repair, no matter how routine, could be considered to prolong the useful life and increase the value of the property if it is compared with the situation existing immediately prior to that repair. Consequently, courts have articulated a number of ways to distinguish between deductible repairs and nondeductible capital improvements. For example, in Illinois Merchants Trust Co. v. Commissioner, 4 B.T.A. 103, 106 (1926), *acq.,* V-2 C.B. 2, the court explained that repair and maintenance expenses are incurred for the purpose of keeping the property in an ordinarily efficient operating condition over its probable useful life for the uses for which the property was acquired. Capital expenditures, in contrast, are for replacements, alterations, improvements, or additions that appreciably prolong the life of the property, materially increase its value, or make it adaptable to a different use. In Estate of Walling v. Commissioner, 373 F.2d 190, 192-193

(3rd Cir. 1966), the court explained that the relevant distinction between capital improvements and repairs is whether the expenditures were made to "put" or "keep" property in ordinary efficient operating condition. In Plainfield-Union Water Co. v. Commissioner, 39 T.C. 333, 338 (1962), *nonacq. on other grounds,* 1964-2 C.B. 8, the court stated that if the expenditure merely restores the property to the state it was in before the situation prompting the expenditure arose and does not make the property more valuable, more useful, or longer-lived, then such an expenditure is usually considered a deductible repair. In contrast, a capital expenditure is generally considered to be a more permanent increment in the longevity, utility, or worth of the property. The Supreme Court's decision in INDOPCO Inc. v. Commissioner, 503 U.S. 79 (1992), does not affect these general principles. . . .

The characterization of any cost as a deductible repair or capital improvement depends on the context in which the cost is incurred. Specifically, where an expenditure is made as part of a general plan of rehabilitation, modernization, and improvement of the property, the expenditure must be capitalized, even though, standing alone, the item may be classified as one of repair or maintenance. United States v. Wehrli, 400 F.2d 686, 689 (10th Cir. 1968). . . .

ANALYSIS

In Situation 1, the heavy maintenance visit on Aircraft 1 primarily involved inspecting, testing, servicing, repairing, reconditioning, cleaning, stripping, and repainting numerous airframe parts and components. The heavy maintenance visit did not involve replacements, alterations, improvements, or additions to the airframe that appreciably prolonged its useful life, materially increased its value, or adapted it to a new or different use. Rather, the heavy maintenance visit merely kept the airframe in an ordinarily efficient operating condition over its anticipated useful life for the uses for which the property was acquired. . . . The fact that the taxpayer was required to perform the heavy maintenance visit to maintain its airworthiness certificate does not affect this determination. . . .

Although the heavy maintenance visit did involve the replacement of numerous airframe parts with new parts, none of these replacements required the substitution of any (or a significant portion of any) major components or substantial structural parts of the airframe so that the airframe as a whole increased in value, life expectancy, or use. . . . Moreover, the heavy maintenance visit also did not restore the airframe, or make good exhaustion for which an allowance had been made, within the meaning of §263(a)(2). . . . Thus, the costs of the heavy maintenance visit constitute expenses for incidental repairs and maintenance under §1.162-4.

Finally, the costs of the heavy maintenance visit are not required to be capitalized under §§263 or 263A as part of a plan of rehabilitation, modernization, or improvement to the airframe. Because the heavy maintenance visit involved only repairs for the purpose of keeping the airframe in an ordinarily efficient operating condition, it did not include the type of substantial capital improvements necessary to trigger the plan of rehabilitation doctrine. . . . Accordingly, the costs incurred by X for the heavy maintenance visit in Situation 1 may be deducted as ordinary and necessary business expenses under §162. . . .

[In Situation 2, involving more extensive work than Situation 1, the ruling holds that some costs can be currently deducted and some must be capitalized. In

Situation 3, involving even more extensive work, the ruling holds that all costs must be capitalized. — EDS.]

Notes and Questions

1. *Future benefits.* You are an executive of the airline in Rev. Rul. 2001-4, and it is time for the $2 million "heavy maintenance visit" for one of your planes. In deciding whether to spend the money (instead of retiring the plane or selling it), will you consider only the revenue the plane will produce this year, or will you consider the likely revenue from the plane for the next eight years? Of course, you will look to the eight-year revenue stream. Given the *INDOPCO* decision, and the obvious future benefits from the heavy maintenance visit, why should the $2 million be currently deductible? Even assuming the maintenance can be fairly described as a repair, what is the tax magic in the "repair" label? Some repairs, no doubt, should be currently deductible under a de minimis rationale. Even if a $2 replacement light bulb has an expected useful life of three years, there is no point in requiring the taxpayer to deduct 67 cents a year for three years. But this ruling involves $2 million, so the de minimis rationale cannot explain its holding.

2. *Repairs and casualties.* In some cases, repairs are a response to casualty damage, and a deduction for the repairs can be justified as a substitute for a casualty loss deduction — even if the repair is not trivial and clearly produces benefits beyond the current year. Suppose the taxpayer's factory is damaged in a storm, and the taxpayer spends $1 million to repair the damage. Immediately before the storm, the taxpayer's adjusted basis in the building was $3 million. The most theoretically attractive treatment would be to allow the taxpayer an immediate deduction of $1 million for the casualty loss sustained in the current year,[26] and then to require the taxpayer to capitalize the long-lived repair. The deduction would reduce the taxpayer's adjusted basis in the building to $2 million, but the repair would restore the adjusted basis to $3 million. The same result — $1 million deduction and $3 million adjusted basis — can be reached more simply by taking no deduction for the casualty but deducting the repair.[27] A number of cases allowing deductions for major repairs fit this pattern.[28] Again, however, this rationale cannot explain the repair deduction in Rev. Rul. 2001-4, since the scheduled heavy maintenance is not in response to any casualty. Even assuming Rev. Rul. 2001-4 properly interprets the long-standing repair regulation that it cites (Reg. §1.162-4), this merely shifts the focus from the justification for the ruling to the justification for the

---

26. Technically, the casualty loss deduction of §165(c)(3) applies only to losses resulting from *non*business casualties. Business losses are deductible under §165(c)(1). The existence of a casualty of a type recognized by §165(c)(3) is nevertheless important for business losses, because the casualty serves as a loss realization event. *See* Reg. §1.165-7, providing rules for the deduction of both personal and business casualty losses.

27. The taxpayer cannot deduct *both* the casualty loss and the repair. *See* Reg. §1.161-1, disallowing "double deductions." This is equally true whether the casualty loss and the repair occur in different years, or in the same year.

28. *See, e.g.,* Midland Empire Packing Co. v. Commissioner, 14 T.C. 635 (1950) (*acq.*); American Bemberg Corp. v. Commissioner, 10 T.C. 361 (1948) (*nonacq.*), *aff'd per curiam,* 177 F.2d 200 (6th Cir. 1949).

regulation. Was the broad scope of the repair regulation ever justified? If it was once justified, does it remain justified after *INDOPCO*?

3. *Does it all come out right in the end?* Can the repair deduction in Rev. Rul. 2001-4 be justified on the grounds that it produces results identical to those produced by capitalization and amortization of repair expenditures, in the case of an airline with a number of aircraft of different ages? Suppose an airline owns three planes, each of which receives heavy maintenance (at a cost of $300,000) once every three years. The airline staggers the maintenance of the planes, so that one plane receives heavy maintenance each year. If the airline is allowed to deduct heavy maintenance as a current repair expense, its annual deduction will be $300,000 (all for the plane maintained that year). If the airline is required to recover the cost of each heavy maintenance over three years, its annual deduction will still be $300,000 ($100,000 for each of the three planes). Given the equivalency of the results, why require capitalization? The argument is seductive, but it does not stand up to scrutiny. Assume the three planes were placed in service in three consecutive years, so that the first heavy maintenance visits for the three planes occur in three consecutive years. Also assume, to keep things simple, that the planes will last forever if the maintenance is performed on schedule. The following table shows the resulting deductions (1) under the repair doctrine, and (2) under capitalization and amortization over three years,[29] beginning with the year in which the first plane receives heavy maintenance.

	Year 1	Year 2	Year 3	Year 4 (and All Subsequent Years)
Current repair deduction	$300,000	$300,000	$300,000	$300,000
Capitalization and 3-year amortization	$100,000 (first plane)	$200,000 ($100,000 each for first two planes)	$300,000 ($100,000 each for all three planes)	$300,000 ($100,000 each for all three planes)

There is no difference in the annual deduction amounts under the two approaches in Year 3 and later years, but the current deduction approach overstates deductions by $200,000 in Year 1 and by $100,000 in Year 2. Even if this overstatement of deductions merely resulted in deferral of income, it would be a significant unwarranted tax break. On the facts of the example, however, the understatement of income resulting from the repair deductions in the first two years is permanent. The mere fact that the two approaches produce identical results after the first two years does not mean that they are functional equivalents.

---

29. The table assumes the planes are maintained at the beginnings of years, so that one-third of the cost of the maintenance is properly allocated to the year of the repair.

4. *A doctrine with a life of its own.* In short, there is no apparent justification for an immediate repair deduction in Rev. Rul. 2001-4. The repair doctrine may have originated partly as response to de minimis concerns and partly as a substitute for a casualty loss, but it has taken on a life of its own, applying even where its justifications do not. If a taxpayer can plausibly describe an expenditure as a repair, there is a good chance of a current deduction, even if the cost is large and there is no related casualty.

5. *The proposed regulations.* In 2008 the Treasury published a proposed replacement for the current repair regulation of Treas. Reg. §1.162-4. The current regulation is two sentences long; the proposed replacement contains 15,511 words. The basic rule of the proposed regulations is that amounts paid to "improve" property must be capitalized, with "improve" defined as "result in a betterment" to the property, "restore" the property, or "adapt . . . the property to a new or different use." The defining terms are themselves in need of definitions, and the proposed regulations provide those further definitions. For the most part, the proposed regulations are based on existing case law and rulings—a sort of restatement of the repair doctrine. Despite the great length of the proposed regulations their finalization might actually simplify the law, by enabling taxpayers to find answers in the regulations themselves rather than by wading through dozens (or even hundreds) of cases and rulings. The proposed regulations would make a few changes in established doctrine. For example, they would eliminate the rehabilitation doctrine (briefly described in Rev. Rul. 2001-4), under which otherwise deductible repair costs must be capitalized if the repairs are made as part of a general plan of rehabilitation. As this book goes to press, it is unclear when (if ever) the proposed regulations will be finalized.

Problem 8. Widget Corp. owns a factory building. Because Widget has owned the building for a number of years, its adjusted basis in the building is only $100,000. The building is damaged by a flood (for which Widget had no insurance), and Widget spends $500,000 to repair it. Both before the flood and after the repair, the fair market value of the building is $2 million. The law permits Widget either to deduct the casualty loss and capitalize the cost of repair, or to forgo the casualty loss deduction and deduct the repair. Does it make a difference which option Widget chooses?

4. Expenses to Create or Maintain a Business Reputation

WELCH v. HELVERING
290 U.S. 111 (1933)

Mr. Justice CARDOZO delivered the opinion of the Court.

The question to be determined is whether payments by a taxpayer, who is in business as a commission agent, are allowable deductions in the computation of his income if made to the creditors of a bankrupt corporation in an endeavor to strengthen his own standing and credit.

In 1922 petitioner was the secretary of the E. L. Welch Company, a Minnesota corporation, engaged in the grain business. The company was adjudged an involuntary bankrupt, and had a discharge from its debts. Thereafter the petitioner made a contract with the Kellogg Company to purchase grain for it on a commission. In order to reestablish his relations with customers whom he had known when acting for the Welch Company and to solidify his credit and standing, he decided to pay the debts of the Welch business so far as he was able. In fulfilment of that resolve, he made payments of substantial amounts during five successive years. In 1924, the commissions were $18,028.20, the payments $3,975.97; in 1923, the commissions $31,377.07, the payments $11,968.20; in 1926, the commissions $20,925.25, the payments $12,815.72; in 1927, the commissions $22,119.61, the payments $7,379.72; and in 1928, the commissions $26,177.56, the payments $11,068.25. The Commissioner ruled that these payments were not deductible from income as ordinary and necessary expenses, but were rather in the nature of capital expenditures, an outlay for the development of reputation and good will. The Board of Tax Appeals sustained the action of the Commissioner (25 B.T.A. 117), and the Court of Appeals for the Eighth Circuit affirmed. 63 F.2d 976. The case is here on certiorari. . . .

We may assume that the payments to creditors of the Welch Company were necessary for the development of the petitioner's business, at least in the sense that they were appropriate and helpful. . . . He certainly thought they were, and we should be slow to override his judgment. But the problem is not solved when the payments are characterized as necessary. Many necessary payments are charges upon capital. There is need to determine whether they are both necessary and ordinary. Now, what is ordinary, though there must always be a strain of constancy within it, is none the less a variable affected by time and place and circumstance. Ordinary in this context does not mean that the payments must be habitual or normal in the sense that the same taxpayer will have to make them often. A lawsuit affecting the safety of a business may happen once in a lifetime. The counsel fees may be so heavy that repetition is unlikely. None the less, the expense is an ordinary one because we know from experience that payments for such a purpose, whether the amount is large or small, are the common and accepted means of defense against attack. . . . The situation is unique in the life of the individual affected, but not in the life of the group, the community, of which he is a part. At such times there are norms of conduct that help to stabilize our judgment, and make it certain and objective. The instance is not erratic, but is brought within a known type.

The line of demarcation is now visible between the case that is here and the one supposed for illustration. We try to classify this act as ordinary or the opposite, and the norms of conduct fail us. No longer can we have recourse to any fund of business experience, to any known business practice. Men do at times pay the debts of others without legal obligation or the lighter obligation imposed by the usages of trade or by neighborly amenities, but they do not do so ordinarily, not even though the result might be to heighten their reputation for generosity and opulence. Indeed, if language is to be read in its natural and common meaning . . . we should have to say that payment in such circumstances, instead of being ordinary is in a high degree extraordinary. There is nothing ordinary in the stimulus evoking it, and none in the response. Here, indeed, as so often in other branches of the law, the decisive distinctions are those of degree and not of kind. One struggles in vain for any verbal formula that will supply a ready touchstone. The standard set up by the statute is not a rule of law; it is rather a way of life. Life in all its fullness must supply the answer to the riddle.

The Commissioner of Internal Revenue resorted to that standard in assessing the petitioner's income, and found that the payments in controversy came closer to capital outlays than to ordinary and necessary expenses in the operation of a business. . . . Unless we can say from facts within our knowledge that these are ordinary and necessary expenses according to the ways of conduct and the forms of speech prevailing in the business world, the tax must be confirmed. But nothing told us by this record or within the sphere of our judicial notice permits us to give that extension to what is ordinary and necessary. Indeed, to do so would open the door to many bizarre analogies. One man has a family name that is clouded by thefts committed by an ancestor. To add to his own standing he repays the stolen money, wiping off, it may be, his income for the year. The payments figure in his tax return as ordinary expenses. Another man conceives the notion that he will be able to practice his vocation with greater ease and profit if he has an opportunity to enrich his culture. Forthwith the price of his education becomes an expense of the business, reducing the income subject to taxation. There is little difference between these expenses and those in controversy here. Reputation and learning are akin to capital assets, like the good will of an old partnership. . . . For many, they are the only tools with which to hew a pathway to success. The money spent in acquiring them is well and wisely spent. It is not an ordinary expense of the operation of a business.

Many cases in the federal courts deal with phases of the problem presented in the case at bar. To attempt to harmonize them would be a futile task. They involve the appreciation of particular situations, at times with borderline conclusions. . . .

The decree should be Affirmed.

Notes and Questions

1. *Did Mr. Welch lose because his expenditures were capital or because they were weird?* In some parts of the opinion, Justice Cardozo focuses — sensibly enough — on the distinction between current and capital expenditures, as when he remarks that "[m]any necessary payments are charges upon capital." This distinction supports not allowing Mr. Welch a deduction, since he made his payments with the hope of increasing his income-producing ability for years to come. In other parts of the opinion, however, Justice Cardozo focuses on the supposed strangeness of Mr. Welch's payments: "[P]ayment in such circumstances, instead of being ordinary is in a high degree extraordinary." It is clear why a current deduction should not be allowed for capital expenses, but should a deduction be disallowed merely because an expenditure strikes a judge as bizarre? Perhaps in an extreme case a strange expenditure could be attributed to the personal idiosyncrasies of the taxpayer rather than to the needs of the taxpayer's business, and thus disallowed as a personal expense. It does not seem, however, that Mr. Welch's debt repayments belong in that category. Most later cases have read *Welch* as being based on the current-versus-capital distinction, and have paid little attention to Justice Cardozo's distrust of bizarre expenses.

There are, however, a few cases disallowing deductions for particularly odd expenditures.[30]

2. *Poor Mr. Welch.* If Mr. Welch's payments were for business purposes, and the deduction was disallowed only because they were capital expenditures, was he allowed to amortize the payments over some period of time — perhaps the expected length of his new career? Logically, he should have been allowed to do so, but in fact he was not — and probably would not be allowed to do so even today. The payments were made to generate goodwill, and goodwill does not have the ascertainable useful life necessary to support depreciation deductions. *See* Treas. Reg. §1.167(a)-3(a), which states, "No deduction for depreciation is allowable with respect to goodwill."[31] Section 197 would not help, because although he spent money to *generate* goodwill, he did not *purchase* goodwill. A taxpayer in Mr. Welch's situation today might cite *Newark Morning Ledger*, and argue that he was paying for a customer-based intangible with a determinable useful life, but unfortunately this looks like classic non-depreciable goodwill. The end result is that Mr. Welch has spent money for a business purpose, but he may *never* be allowed any tax recognition for that expenditure — not now (because it is capital), not through depreciation (because there is no ascertainable useful life), and perhaps not even as an offset to amount realized on a sale of the business (because the goodwill may be too personal to Mr. Welch to be transferable). If he had attempted to generate goodwill by advertising that he was an honest businessperson, instead of by paying the debts, he probably would have been entitled to an immediate deduction under Reg. §1.162-20(a)(2). Life is not fair.

JENKINS v. COMMISSIONER

T.C. Memo. 1983-667

IRWIN, Judge: ... The sole issue presented for our decision is whether payments made by petitioner to investors in a failed corporation known as Twitty Burger, Inc., are deductible as ordinary and necessary business expenses of petitioner's business as a country music performer. ...

The question presented is whether one person (Conway Twitty) may deduct the expenses of another person (Twitty Burger). In order to determine whether the disallowed expenditures are deductible by petitioner under section 162 we must (1) ascertain the purpose or motive of the taxpayer in making the payments and (2) determine whether there is a sufficient connection between the expenditures and the taxpayer's trade or business. ...

The relevant facts are as follows: Petitioner Conway Twitty [real name Harold L. Jenkins] is a well-known country music entertainer. Most of his income is derived from his performances, songwriting, and record royalties. [The opinion does not

30. *See, e.g.,* Goedel v. Commissioner, 39 BTA 1 (1939) (premiums for insurance on the life of the president of the United States, paid by a stock dealer who feared the president's death would be catastrophic for the stock market); Trebilcock v. Commissioner, 64 T.C. 852 (1975) *(acq,) aff'd by order,* 557 F.2d 1226 (6th Cir. 1977) (payments to a minister to give the taxpayer spiritually based business advice).

31. Presumably this result is not changed by Treas. Reg. §1.167(a)-3(b), which was promulgated in 2003. The new regulation provides for 15-year amortization of some intangible assets without readily ascertainable useful lives, but it does not remove the regulatory language quoted in the text, prohibiting depreciation deductions for goodwill.

reveal Twitty's total income for the years in question, but it states that his music business was "doing very well" during those years.] In 1968, Conway and several of his friends decided to form a chain of fast food restaurants and incorporated Twitty Burger under the laws of Oklahoma. [The restaurant menus featured a picture of Twitty, a message from Twitty, and the Twitty Bird logo—a small yellow bird strumming a guitar.] During 1968 and 1969, approximately 75 of petitioner's friends and business associates invested money in Twitty Burger. Subsequently it was determined that it would be some time before the requirements of the Security and Exchange Commission could be met and a public offering of stock made. It was determined, therefore, that debentures should be issued to those persons who had invested money in the undertaking as interim evidence of their investments.

By late 1970, Twitty Burger was experiencing financial difficulties and it was determined by Twitty Burger's attorney that further attempts to obtain registration of the corporate stock would be futile. Shortly thereafter it was decided that Twitty Burger should be shut down. Except for one independently-owned franchise operating in Texas, the last Twitty Burger restaurant was closed in May 1971. Subsequently, Conway Twitty decided that the investors should be repaid the amount of their investments in the failed corporation. As Twitty Burger had no assets with which to satisfy the debentures, Conway Twitty decided he would repay the investors from his future earnings. During the years in issue, 1973 and 1974, Conway Twitty made payments to the investors of $92,892.46 and $3,600, respectively.

Respondent argues that the payments Conway Twitty made to the investors in Twitty Burger are not deductible by him as ordinary and necessary business expenses under section 162 because there was no business purpose for the payments and, additionally, there was no relationship between his involvement in Twitty Burger and his business of being a country music entertainer. Respondent argues that the payments in question here were made by Conway Twitty gratuitously in that petitioner had no personal liability to the holders of the debentures and made the payments merely out of a sense of moral obligation. Relying on Welch v. Helvering, and certain of its progeny, respondent concludes that while it was "very nice" of petitioner to reimburse the investors in Twitty Burger, the required nexus between the expenditures and Conway Twitty's career as a country music entertainer does not exist and therefore the payments were not "ordinary and necessary" within the meaning of section 162.

Petitioner argues that the rule of Welch v. Helvering is not applicable to the case at bar because petitioner made the payments in question to protect his reputation and earning capacity in his ongoing business of being a country music entertainer whereas in *Welch* the Supreme Court held that the payments made there were capital expenditures of the taxpayer's new business. Petitioner maintains that . . . the expenditures in issue here are deductible under section 162 if the payments were made primarily with a business motive and if there is a sufficient connection between the payments and the taxpayer's trade or business. . . . The question presented for our resolution is purely one of fact. While previously decided cases dealing with this issue are somewhat helpful there is, quite understandably, no case directly on point with the facts before us. As the Supreme Court recognized in Welch v. Helvering, [290 U.S.] at 116, "Many cases in the federal courts deal with phases of the problem presented in the case at bar. To attempt to harmonize them would be a futile task. They involve the appreciation of particular situations, at times with border-line conclusions."

There is no suggestion in the record that any of the payments were made in order to protect petitioner's investment in Twitty Burger or to revitalize the corporation. . . . It is petitioner's contention that Conway Twitty repaid the investors in Twitty Burger from his personal funds in order to protect his personal business reputation. While it is clear from the facts that Conway was under no legal obligation to make such payments, (at least in the sense that the corporate debentures were not personally guaranteed by him), the law is clear that the absence of such an obligation is not in itself a bar to the deduction of such expenditures under section 162. . . . In addition, the fact that the petitioner also felt a moral obligation to the people who had entrusted him with their funds does not preclude the deductibility of the payments so long as the satisfaction of the moral obligation was not the primary motivation for the expenditures. . . .

After a thorough consideration of the record we are convinced that petitioner Conway Twitty repaid the investors in Twitty Burger with the primary motive of protecting his personal business reputation. There was the obvious similarity of the name of the corporation and petitioner's stage name. . . . There is no doubt that the corporation's name was chosen with the idea of capitalizing on Conway Twitty's fame as a country music performer. Additionally, many of the investors were connected with the country music industry.[32] While there is no doubt that part of petitioner's motivation for making the payments involved his personal sense of morality, we do not believe that this ethical consideration was paramount.

Petitioner testified as follows concerning his motivations for repaying the Twitty Burger investors:

> I'm 99 percent entertainer. That's just about all I know. The name Conway Twitty, and the image that I work so hard for since 1955 and '56 is the foundation that I, my family, and the 30 some odd people that work for me stand on. They depend on it, and they can depend on it.
>
> I handle things the way I did . . . for more than one reason. First of all, because of the way I perceive myself and my image. It may not be the same as this guy over here or that one over there, but to me if Conway Twitty does some little old something, it's different than somebody else doing something because everybody has got a different relationship with whoever their fans are.
>
> I handled it that way because of that. Because of the image. And second and very close to it, I handled it that way because I think it is morally right, and if you owe a man something, you pay him. . . .
>
> When we got the letter from Walter Beach and from Haggard's lawyer and from a couple other places, and my people said, hey, you know, we've got some letters from people saying they are going to sue you, and that you might have done something wrong as far as securities and all that stuff goes. It just scares you to death.
>
> I mean it did me. And it would most people. I know it would. And so you — you don't want any part of that. A law suit like that with — say if Merle Haggard sued Conway Twitty or if Walter Beach sued Conway Twitty and you're in court, and they are saying it's fraud and something to do with the securities thing, and, you know, all the years I've worked for are gone. If my fans didn't give up on me, it would warp me psychologically. I couldn't function anymore because I'm the type of person I am. I remember it. . . .
>
> The country music fan . . . will stay right with you as long as you stay within a certain boundaries. They expect a lot out of you because you — a country singer deals with — they deal with feelings and things inside of people — you know — you can listen to the words in a country song, and you're dealing with emotions and feelings that — it's kind of

32. For example, Harlan Howard, Don Davis, Merle Haggard, Steve Lake, and Jimmy Loden, a/k/a/ Sonny James. Petitioner's counsel aptly remarked in his opening statement: "Imagine trying to keep a band together where somebody has stiffed the drummer's mother." We note, however, that "Pork Chop's" mother, Lucibelle Markham, was repaid in a year not at issue in this case.

like a doctor, you know. I'm not comparing myself with a doctor certainly, but when a person gets to trust a doctor, that's all they need is that trust. . . .

We conclude that there was a proximate relationship between the payments made to the holders of Twitty Burger debentures and petitioner's trade or business as a country music entertainer so as to render those payments an ordinary and necessary expense of that business. Although, as respondent argues, the chances of a successful lawsuit against Conway Twitty by any of the investors or the Securities and Exchange Commission was remote we agree with petitioner that the possibility of extensive adverse publicity concerning petitioner's involvement with the defunct corporation and the consequent loss of the investors' funds was very real. We do not believe it is necessary for us to find that adverse publicity emanating from Conway Twitty's failure to repay the investors in Twitty Burger would have ruined his career as a country music singer. Rather, we need only find that a proximate relationship existed between the payments and petitioner's business. We find that such relationship exists. It is not necessary that the taxpayer's trade or business be of the same type as that engaged in by the person on whose behalf the payments are made. . . .

In making these payments petitioner was furthering his business as a country music artist and protecting his business reputation for integrity. The mere fact that they were voluntary does not deprive them of their character as ordinary and necessary business expenses. . . . Under the unique circumstances presented in this case, we hold that the payments in issue are deductible as business expenses under section 162.[33]

Notes and Questions

1. *Distinguishing* Welch. The facts of *Jenkins* bear a striking resemblance to those of *Welch*. In each case, the taxpayer pays debts for which he is not liable, for

---

33. We close with the following "Ode to Conway Twitty":

Twitty Burger went belly up
But Conway remained true
He repaid his investors, one and all
It was the moral thing to do.

His fans would not have liked it
It could have hurt his fame
Had any investors sued him
Like Merle Haggard or Sonny James.

When it was time to file taxes
Conway thought what he would do
Was deduct those payments as a business expense
Under section one-sixty-two.

In order to allow these deductions
Goes the argument of the Commissioner
The payments must be ordinary and necessary
To a business of the petitioner.

Had Conway not repaid the investors
His career would have been under cloud,
Under the unique facts of this case
Held: The deductions are allowed.

the sake of his business reputation. How, then, does Judge Irwin distinguish *Welch*? He doesn't really try. Instead, he quotes the statement in *Welch* that an "attempt to harmonize [cases in this area] would be a futile task," and he limits the holding to "the unique circumstances presented in this case." It is possible, however, to distinguish the two cases by considering whether the expenditures in each case are analogous to deductible repair expenses for physical assets. Mr. Welch lost his case because his business reputation was more or less *destroyed,* and he was spending money to rebuild it from scratch. Conway Twitty, by contrast, never lost his good reputation among country music fans; it was just slightly *damaged,* and he spent money to repair it. Mr. Welch was trying to establish himself in a new business; Twitty was just protecting the reputation he had already established in the music business. Judge Irwin might also have pointed out that Mr. Welch's payments were about 40 percent of his commissions for five years, which is a very high figure to analogize to the "incidental repairs" which are deductible under Reg. §1.162-4. Unfortunately, the *Jenkins* opinion does not provide the information necessary to determine how Twitty's payments related to his music income, but it seems likely the percentage was far lower. In short, there is a strong argument that Twitty's expenses are analogous to deductible repair expenses for physical assets, while Mr. Welch's expenses were not. There are, of course, serious objections to repair deductions for nontrivial repairs not associated with realized casualty losses, but given the existence of the repair doctrine it seems reasonable to allow Twitty a deduction.

2. *Judicial poetry.* Based on the persuasiveness of the taxpayer's testimony, as quoted in the opinion, it seems likely that Conway Twitty could have been a pretty good lawyer. One is less sanguine about Judge Irwin's prospects as a songwriter. If Judge Irwin had asked your advice, would you have recommended including the poem (or song lyrics) in the opinion? Putting aside any questions of literary merit, does the poem give the impression that the judge might be a Conway Twitty fan? (Notice also more than one reference in the opinion to the taxpayer as simply "Conway.") The result in the case is certainly defensible on the merits, and being a fan of the taxpayer is not necessarily grounds for judicial disqualification. Still, it might have been better if Judge Irwin had kept the poem in his desk.[34]

3. *Irresistible impulses.* But once this sort of thing gets started, it can be hard to stop. See the IRS's response below.

Action on Decision 1984-022
Re: Harold L. and Temple M. Jenkins v. Commissioner

[After quoting Judge Irwin's ode, the IRS responded with one of its own:]

Harold Jenkins and Conway Twitty
They are both the same
But one was born
The other achieved fame.

---

34. If you like the "Ode," it can be sung to the tunes of "The Yellow Rose of Texas," "Love Me Tender," and about half the hymns ever written.

The man is talented
And has many a friend
They opened a restaurant
His name he did lend.

They are two different things
Making burgers and song
The business went sour
It didn't take long.

He repaid his friends
Why did he act?
Was it business or friendship?
Which is the fact?

Business the court held
It's deductible they feel
We disagree with the answer
But let's not appeal.

Recommendation: Nonacquiescence.

5. *Job Hunting Expenses*

As a matter of logic, is money spent looking for a new job a current business expense or a capital expenditure? As long as you are looking for a job that will last for more than one year, the answer seems clear: The expenses are associated with the income you will earn over the life of the job, and they should be amortized over that period. The actual rules, however, do not follow that logic. Instead, the position of the IRS is that job hunting expenses are currently deductible if the taxpayer is "seeking new employment in the same trade or business" in which he is currently employed. Rev. Rul. 75-120, 1975-1 C.B. 55. In other cases—where the taxpayer is seeking his first job, or employment in a new trade or business—no current deduction is allowed. As with Mr. Welch's payments to generate goodwill, there is no authority permitting these nondeductible expenditures to be amortized over the life of the job.[35] The treatment of nondeductible job hunting expenses seems too hard, the treatment of deductible job hunting expenses seems too soft, and no job hunting expenses seem to be treated just right. The line between deductible and nondeductible expenses is not easy to draw, as demonstrated by the following ruling.

REV. RUL. 78-93
1978-1 C.B. 38

The taxpayer was engaged in the full-time practice of law and also was a part-time lecturer at a law school. The taxpayer contracted with an agency specializing

---

35. Section 195 permits deduction of up to $5,000 of business "start-up expenditures." The remainder of a taxpayer's start-up expenses can be amortized over 15 years. There is a weak argument that job hunting expenses might fall within the scope of §195, but that does not appear to have been the legislative intent, and there are no cases or rulings in support of that interpretation.

in career counseling in an effort to secure new employment either practicing or teaching law full-time.

The contract specified that the agency would provide the taxpayer with the following: (1) a job evaluation that is an appraisal of the taxpayer's strongest capabilities, personality characteristics, motivating factors, education, training, and experience; (2) the ability to pinpoint immediate and long-range objectives, consisting of possible self-improvement, and the establishment of practical and attainable goals consistent with the taxpayer's motivated abilities and aspirations; (3) interviewing preparations, including counseling on all written resumes and graphic material to present the taxpayer's strengths including competitive techniques for interviews; and (4) implementation counseling, which includes offer evaluation, negotiating salary and fringe benefits, and job acceptance protection procedures. In addition, the contract specifically provided that the fees to be paid to the agency by the taxpayer were for job counseling services and not for any specific contacts, interviews, or guarantees of employment.

After obtaining the career counseling services, the taxpayer secured a new position as a full-time law school assistant professor due to the taxpayer's own employment seeking efforts. The taxpayer was directly assisted in the job seeking efforts as a result of the services provided by the agency. The full-time assistant professor position at another law school did not involve the taxpayer's having to perform tasks or activities substantially different from the tasks and activities performed by the taxpayer as a part-time law school lecturer. In addition, the taxpayer was not required to obtain additional education prior to accepting the full-time position as assistant professor of law.

Section 162(e) of the Code provides that there shall be allowed as a deduction all the ordinary and necessary expenses paid or incurred during the taxable year in carrying on any trade or business.

Section 1.162-1 of the Income Tax Regulations provides that the business expenses deductible under section 162 of the Code include the ordinary and necessary expenditures directly connected with or pertaining to the taxpayer's trade or business.

Section 1.162-5(b)(3) of the regulations further provides that a change of duties does not constitute a new trade or business if the new duties involve the same general type of work as is involved in the taxpayer's present employment.

Rev. Rul. 75-120, 1975-1 C.B. 55, holds that bona fide expenses, incurred in seeking new employment in the same trade or business in which a taxpayer is presently engaged, are deductible under section 162 of the Code, if directly connected with such trade or business as determined by all the objective facts and circumstances. . . .

Although an isolated or occasional activity is not a trade or business, a taxpayer may engage in several trades or businesses either independent of, or in connection with, the taxpayer's principal trade or business. . . . Criteria used in determining the existence or nonexistence of a trade or business include continuity and regularity of business activities by a taxpayer.

As determined by the objective facts and circumstances in the instant case, the taxpayer was engaged in two trades or businesses; one being a practicing attorney and the other being a law school teacher. Thus, the taxpayer was not changing the taxpayer's trade or business by seeking a full-time position as an assistant professor of law, but was seeking employment in the same trade or business.

Accordingly, the taxpayer may deduct, under section 162 of the Code, the expenses paid or incurred for the career counseling services, because the counseling directly assisted the taxpayer in the taxpayer's efforts to obtain new employment in the same trade or business.

Notes and Questions

1. *An arbitrary ruling?* In the interests of full disclosure, one of the authors has a soft spot for this ruling, since it was issued just a few years before the author found himself in the same position as the taxpayer in the ruling, and the author relied on the ruling in deducting his job hunting expenses. Nevertheless, there is an air of arbitrariness to the ruling's conclusions that (1) law school teaching is a different trade or business from practicing law, and (2) the taxpayer was already in the law school teaching business by reason of his work as an adjunct professor. The ruling would seem just about as reasonable — or unreasonable — if each conclusion had been reversed. With respect to the second conclusion, why does the IRS not bother to tell us how much teaching the taxpayer had done as an adjunct, or how much he had been paid for it?

2. *Diminished significance.* Because of the intervening enactment of §67, the deductibility of job hunting expenses is not as significant today as it was in 1978. Job hunting expenses are unreimbursed employee business expenses, and thus are among the "miscellaneous itemized deductions" subject to the 2 percent of AGI floor of §67.[36]

Problem 9. Ralph and Ruth are third-year law students, looking for their first jobs as lawyers. Ralph is interested only in jobs with impecunious public interest organizations, none of which can afford to reimburse him for his interview travel expenses. Ruth interviews only for jobs with high-powered law firms, which pay all of her interview travel expenses. (Incidentally, she stays at much nicer hotels and eats at much nicer restaurants than does Ralph.) What are the tax consequences to Ralph of his interview trips? What are the tax consequences to Ruth of hers?

---

36. For §67, see section F of Chapter 4.

Cell

Frontier Chevrolet Co. v. Commissioner

Problems 1-2

FRONTIER CHEVROLET CO. v. COMMISSIONER

329 F.3d 1131 (9th Cir. 2003)

TROTT, Circuit Judge: Frontier Chevrolet Company ("Frontier") appeals the tax court's decision that I.R.C. §197 applied to a covenant not to compete entered into in connection with Frontier's redemption of 75% of its stock. We agree with the tax court that Frontier's redemption was an indirect acquisition of an interest in a trade or business; therefore Frontier had to amortize the covenant under §197.

BACKGROUND

A

The facts are set forth as stipulated by the parties before the tax court. At the time Frontier filed its petition with the tax court, it was a corporation with its principal place of business in Billings, Montana. Frontier engaged in the trade or business of selling and servicing new and used vehicles. Roundtree Automotive Group, Inc. ("Roundtree") was a corporation engaged in the trade or business of purchasing and operating automobile dealerships and providing consulting services to those dealerships. Frank Stinson ("Stinson") was the President of Roundtree and participated in Frontier's management from 1987 to 1994.

In 1987, Roundtree purchased all of Frontier's stock. Consistent with Roundtree and Stinson's policy of management, Frontier filled the position of its executive manager with one of Stinson's long-term employees, Dennis Menholt ("Menholt"). From 1987 to 1994, Roundtree allowed Menholt to purchase 25% of Frontier's stock as part of his employment by Frontier. Before August 1, 1994, Roundtree owned 75% and Menholt owned 25% of Frontier's stock.

Frontier entered into a "Stock Sale Agreement" with Roundtree effective August 1, 1994. Pursuant to the Stock Sale Agreement, Frontier redeemed its stock owned by Roundtree using funds borrowed from General Motors Acceptance Corporation ("GMAC"). Menholt became the sole shareholder of Frontier because of the redemption.

Roundtree, Stinson, and Frontier also entered into a "Non-Competition Agreement" ("covenant") in connection with the redemption. The covenant was effective August 1, 1994, and stated in part:

To induce [Frontier] to enter into and consummate the Stock Sale Agreement and to protect the value of the shares of stock being purchased, Roundtree and Stinson covenant, to the extent provided in Section 1 hereof, that Roundtree and Stinson shall not compete with the automobile dealership, stock of which was sold to Frontier pursuant to the Stock Sale Agreement.

Section 1 provided that Roundtree and Stinson would not compete with Frontier in the car dealership business for five years. Furthermore, in Section 1, Roundtree and Stinson acknowledged that the non-compete restrictions "are reasonable and necessary to protect the business and interest which Frontier . . . is acquiring pursuant to the Stock Sale Agreement, and that any violation of these restrictions will cause substantial injury to [Frontier] or its assignees." Frontier agreed to pay Roundtree and Stinson $22,000 per month for five years as consideration for the non-compete restrictions.

Frontier's GMAC loan caused it to be leveraged with large interest expenses. During the summer of 1994, Frontier fell below the minimum working capital requirements of its franchisor and had to obtain a special waiver of working capital requirements to continue holding its franchise. In addition, Stinson and Roundtree had the ability and knowledge to compete with Frontier in the Billings, Montana automobile dealership market. Accordingly, Frontier had no known alternative to a non-compete agreement with Stinson and Roundtree to protect it from their competition. Without the covenant, Frontier may not have been able to raise capital or pay its GMAC loan.

Frontier amortized the covenant payments under §197 on its 1994 through 1996 federal income tax returns. In 1999, Frontier filed a claim for refund for the 1995 and 1996 taxable years, asserting that the covenant should be amortized over the life of the agreement and not under §197. Frontier and the Internal Revenue Service stipulated that the only issue for the tax court was whether Frontier must amortize the covenant not to compete under §197.

B

Section 197 provides, in relevant part: [The opinion sets forth the texts of §§197(a), (c)(1), and (d)(1)(E).]

C

As a matter of first impression, the tax court held that the covenant was a §197 intangible because Frontier entered into the covenant in connection with the indirect acquisition of a trade or business. The tax court applied the plain meaning of §197 using dictionary definitions of "acquisition" and "redemption." According to the tax court, "acquisition" means "gaining possession or control over something" and "redemption" in the context of securities means "the reacquisition of a security by the issuer." Putting the definitions together, the tax court concluded that Frontier's redemption was an acquisition within the meaning of §197 because Frontier regained possession and control over 75% of its stock.

The tax court also noted that §197's legislative history stated that an acquisition of stock of a corporation engaged in a trade or business is an indirect acquisition of an interest in a trade or business. In addition, the tax court pointed out in a footnote that Treas. Reg. §1.197-2(b)(9), issued after the transaction at issue, and therefore not applicable to this case, specifically provides that taxpayers can make an acquisition under §197 in the form of a redemption. . . .

DISCUSSION

We agree with the tax court that Frontier's redemption was an indirect acquisition of an interest in a trade or business under §197. Frontier, however, argues that it did not acquire an interest in a trade or business pursuant to the redemption because, both before and after the redemption, Frontier was engaged in the same trade or business and it acquired no new assets. There are three problems with Frontier's arguments. First, Frontier's argument reads a requirement into §197 that taxpayers must acquire an interest in a new trade or business. Section 197, however, only requires taxpayers to acquire an interest in a trade or business. Although Frontier continued its same business, acquired no new assets, and redeemed its own stock, Frontier acquired an interest in a trade or business because it acquired possession and control over 75% of its own stock. In addition, the effect of the transaction was to transfer ownership of the company from one shareholder to another. Menholt, who previously owned only 25% of the shares, become the sole corporate shareholder.

Second, §197's legislative history makes clear that "an interest in a trade or business includes not only the assets of a trade or business, but also stock in a corporation engaged in a trade or business." H.R. Rep. No. 103-111, at 764, *reprinted in* 1993 U.S.C.C.A.N. 378, 995. Here, Frontier acquired stock of a corporation engaged in the trade or business of selling new and used vehicles. The result does not change merely because the acquisition of stock took the form of a redemption. Indeed, the substance of the transaction was to effect a change of controlling corporate stock ownership.

Finally, before enactment of §197, taxpayers could amortize covenants not to compete over the life of the agreement. Treas. Reg. §1.167(a)-3. On August 10, 1993, however, Congress enacted §197 to govern the amortization of intangibles. Congress passed §197 to simplify amortization of intangibles by grouping certain intangibles and providing one period of amortization:

> The Federal income tax treatment of the costs of acquiring intangible assets is a source of considerable controversy between taxpayers and the Internal Revenue Service. . . .
>
> It is believed that much of the controversy that arises under present law with respect to acquired intangible assets could be eliminated by specifying a single method and period for recovering the cost of most acquired intangible assets. . . .

H.R. Rep. No. 103-111, at 760, *reprinted in* 1993 U.S.C.C.A.N. 378, 991. Thus, Congress' intent to simplify the treatment of intangibles indicates that §197 treats stock acquisitions and redemptions similarly—both stock acquisitions and redemptions involve acquiring an interest in a trade or business by acquiring stock of a corporation engaged in a trade or business.

CONCLUSION

Because Frontier entered into the covenant in connection with the redemption of 75% of its stock, the covenant was a §197 intangible and Frontier must amortize it over fifteen years under §197. Accordingly, we affirm the tax court.

Notes and Questions

1. *Why so slow?* The Ninth Circuit's holding is that a corporation can acquire itself, for purposes of §197, by redeeming most of its stock. That is intriguing enough, but the opinion also touches on a second, equally interesting question: Why does §197 require amortization of the covenant not to compete over 15 years, when the actual useful life of the covenant is clearly only five years? Remember that §197 applies to a covenant not to compete only if the taxpayer acquires the covenant "in connection with an acquisition . . . of an interest in a trade or business or a substantial portion thereof." In that situation, the taxpayer will typically be acquiring goodwill in addition to the covenant not to compete. By requiring 15-year amortization for both the covenant and the goodwill, the statute eliminates the incentive for the taxpayer and the IRS to argue about how much of the purchase price of the business is properly allocable to goodwill and how much is properly allocable to the covenant.[1]

Problem 1.   A corporation pays $7 million for a patent with a remaining legal (and economic) life of seven years. Over how many years will the taxpayer's amortization deductions be spread? Does it make a difference whether the taxpayer buys the patent as part of the purchase of a business, or buys the patent alone? Hint: Look at §§197(d)(1)(C) and 197(e)(4).

Problem 2.   Media Corp. purchases a newspaper, with $3 million of the purchase price properly allocated to the subscription list (a §197 "customer-based intangible"). The rules of §197 happen to reflect economic reality for Media Corp., in the sense that subscribers would dwindle to about zero in 15 years if Media made no efforts to replace departing subscribers with new ones. In fact, however, Media spends $200,000 each year on advertising efforts to attract new subscribers, and over the next 15 years Media succeeds in attracting just enough new subscribers to replace the lost ones. Media is allowed to deduct all its advertising costs as current business expenses under §162.[2] At the end of 15 years, therefore, the well-maintained subscription list is still worth $3 million. How much will Media have been allowed to deduct with respect to the list, and what will be Media's adjusted basis for the list? Do you see the rather argumentative point of this problem?

---

1. Note, however, that because §197 applies only to intangibles, arguments about allocation of the purchase price of a business among its various tangible and intangible assets are often unavoidable. Is a marginal reduction in the range of those arguments adequate justification for the unfairness to the taxpayer in this case?

2. *See* Reg. §§1.162-1(a) (including "advertising and other selling expenses" in a list of types of deductible business expenses) and 1.162-20(a)(2) (permitting a §162 deduction for "institutional or 'goodwill' advertising").

Cell

================ THE REPAIR DOCTRINE

Y2K Software Costs

Rev. Proc. 97-50

================

Y2K SOFTWARE COSTS

REV. PROC. 97-50

1997-2 C.B. 525

SECTION 1. PURPOSE

.01 This revenue procedure provides guidelines to be used in connection with the examination of federal income tax returns involving the costs paid or incurred by a taxpayer in its trade or business to convert or replace computer software to recognize dates beginning in the year 2000. . . .

SECTION 2. BACKGROUND

Many computer systems use two digits rather than four digits to represent the year in a date field (for example, "97" to represent 1997). A two-digit year field, however, may be inadequate to represent years after 1999. For data involving the year 2000, for example, computer systems may not recognize "00" as a year, or may treat that year as 1900 instead of 2000. Thus, many computer systems may fail to operate, or may operate improperly, if the software is not converted or replaced to recognize four-digit years (i.e., made "year 2000 compliant"). In order to ensure that their computer systems are year 2000 compliant, taxpayers may pay or incur costs to manually convert their existing software, to develop new software to replace their existing software, to purchase . . . new software to replace their existing software, or to develop or purchase software tools to assist them in converting their existing software to be year 2000 compliant ("year 2000 costs").

SECTION 3. TREATMENT OF YEAR 2000 COSTS

Rev. Proc. 69-21, 1969-2 C.B. 303, provides guidelines to be used in connection with the examination of federal income tax returns involving the costs paid or incurred to develop, purchase, or lease computer software. Year 2000 costs fall within the purview of Rev. Proc. 69-21. Accordingly, the Internal Revenue Service will not disturb a taxpayer's treatment of its year 2000 costs if the taxpayer treats these costs in accordance with section 3 of Rev. Proc. 69-21 (in the case of developed software, including converted software) [or] section 4 of Rev. Proc. 69-21 (in the case of purchased software). . . .

Notes and Questions

1. *Self-developed versus purchased software.* The cited sections of Rev. Proc. 69-21 have been superseded by §§5 and 6 of Rev. Proc. 2000-50, 2000-2 C.B. 601. Under §5 of Rev. Proc. 2000-50, the IRS "will not disturb" a taxpayer's treatment of software development costs if the taxpayer consistently treats such costs as currently deductible expenses. Thus, Rev. Proc. 97-50 authorizes a current deduction for Y2K compliance costs, in the case of compliance software developed or converted by the taxpayer. On the other hand, §6 of Rev. Proc. 2000-50 requires the cost of purchased software to be amortized over a 36-month period. Thus, Rev. Proc. 97-50 does *not* permit an immediate deduction for the cost of purchased Y2K compliance software. Obviously, self-developed and purchased Y2K software serve the same purpose. Why is there a difference in tax treatment? Although Rev. Proc. 97-50 is short on rationale, presumably the deductibility of self-developed software is based on the repair doctrine. Is that an appropriate application of the doctrine? If it is, why does the doctrine not also apply to purchased software?[3] According to §167(f)(1), "If a depreciation deduction is allowable . . . with respect to any computer software, such deduction shall be computed by using the straight line method and a useful life of 36 months." Does this provision preclude an immediate deduction for any purchased software costs? Notice that the provision applies only *if* a depreciation deduction is allowable.

2. *Is it possible to "repair" software that never was Y2K compliant?* In the leading case of Plainfield-Union Water Co. v. Commissioner, 39 T.C. 333, 338 (1962), *nonacq. on other grounds*, 1964-2 C.B. 8 (cited with approval in Rev. Rul. 2001-4, which is set forth in section C.3 of this chapter), the court stated that a repair deduction is appropriate if an expenditure merely restores property to the condition it was in before the occurrence of the situation necessitating the expenditure. Do Y2K compliance costs qualify as repair deductions under this standard? In Norwest Corp. v. Commissioner, 108 T.C. 265, 283 (1997), the government successfully argued that *Plainfield Union* did not apply to the taxpayer's costs of removing asbestos from its building:

> Respondent [the IRS] contends that the *Plainfield-Union* test does not apply herein because a comparison cannot be made between the status of the building before it contained asbestos and after the asbestos was removed; since construction, the building has always contained asbestos. In cases where the *Plainfield-*

---

3. For an argument that the repair doctrine should apply to purchased Y2K software, see Jeffrey H. Kahn, *Deducting Year 2000 Costs*, 79 Tax Notes 1621 (1998).

Union test has been applied . . . respondent continues, the condition necessitating the repair resulted from a physical change in the property's condition. In this case, no change occurred to the building's physical condition that necessitated the removal expenditures. Accordingly, respondent argues that the *Plainfield-Union* test is inapplicable. . . .

What does the IRS's argument in *Norwest* imply about the proper treatment of Y2K expenses? Typically, software was Y2K noncompliant from the start; it did not start out Y2K compliant and somehow become noncompliant as the year 2000 approached.

Chapter 7 ## TAX ACCOUNTING

An income tax based on annual accounting requires rules for determining the year in which an item is taken into income, or an expense is deducted. These rules — commonly referred to as "tax accounting" rules — are the subject of this chapter. Issues of timing are pervasive in the income tax, and in this book. Any tax timing issue *could* be described as an aspect of tax accounting, but a number of important timing issues are traditionally viewed as separate topics rather than as subtopics within tax accounting, and this book follows that tradition. For example, the realization doctrine and the timing of the taxation of appreciation are the concern of Chapter 3, and the capitalization doctrine and the timing of deductions for the cost of long-lived business assets are the concern of Chapter 6. This chapter provides an introduction to the timing issues that traditionally are considered questions of tax accounting.

A. CASH AND ACCRUAL ACCOUNTING

1. The Basic Methods

In reporting their income and deductions, all taxpayers must use either the cash method of accounting or the accrual method of accounting. Under the cash method,

> [A]ll items which constitute gross income (whether in the form of cash, property, or services) are to be included in the taxable year in which actually or constructively received. Expenditures are to be deducted for the taxable year in which actually made.

Treas. Reg. §1.446-1(c)(1)(i).

By contrast, under the accrual method,

> [I]ncome is to be included for the taxable year, when all the events have occurred that fix the right to receive the income and the amount of the income can be determined with reasonable accuracy. [A] liability is incurred . . . in the taxable year in which all the events have occurred that established the fact of the liability, the amount of the liability can be determined with reasonable accuracy, and economic performance has occurred with respect to the liability.

Treas. Reg. §1.446-1(c)(1)(ii).

The cash method has the virtue of simplicity, while the accrual method more accurately measures a taxpayer's economic income for any given year. The accrual method is especially superior to the cash method in matching income inclusions with deductions for the costs of producing that income. Most taxpayers would prefer to use the cash method — not only because it is simpler, but also because it usually provides a deferral advantage. Although the cash method is symmetrical, in the sense that it tends to defer both income and deductions relative to the accrual method, for any taxpayer making a profit deferral of both income and deductions constitutes a deferral of positive net income.

Problem 1.   Wendy operates a pet store as a sole proprietorship. She employs Debby, her adult daughter, as her bookkeeper. Wendy is an accrual method taxpayer (with respect to her business), and Debby is a cash method taxpayer. Wendy does not pay Debby $10,000 of Debby's wages earned in 2010 until January 2011. In which year does Wendy deduct the $10,000, and in which year must Debby include the $10,000 in income? *See* §267(a)(2).

2.   Mandatory Accrual Accounting

In their capacities as employees and investors, individuals are cash method taxpayers.[1] Individuals (and partnerships and corporations) operating businesses, however, may be required to use the accrual method for their business income and expenses. Subject to two significant exceptions noted below, a taxpayer must use the accrual method if "the production, purchase, or sale of merchandise is an income-producing factor" in the taxpayer's business. Treas. Reg. §§1.446-1(c)(2)(i) (imposing accrual accounting requirement on taxpayers using inventories), 1.471-1 (rules for when inventories are required; source of quoted language). Roughly speaking, this means a taxpayer must use the accrual method if the taxpayer's business has an inventory. It is not always clear whether a taxpayer's business is subject to this accrual accounting mandate, and for a time the issue was heavily litigated.[2] However, exceptions sanctioned by revenue procedures issued in 2001 and 2002 have taken much of the pressure off this issue. Rev. Proc. 2001-10, 2000-1 C.B. 272, permits a taxpayer with average annual gross receipts of $1 million or less to elect (1) not to account for inventories, and (2) to use the cash method of accounting. Rev. Proc. 2002-28, 2002-1 C.B. 815, extends this relief to taxpayers with average annual gross receipts of up to $10 million, in a limited range of industries. Types of businesses eligible for the $10 million ceiling include custom manufacturers and businesses whose provision of property to customers is incidental to the provision of services.

3.   Inventory Accounting

For a manufacturer or merchandiser, gross income equals "total sales less the cost of goods sold." Reg. §1.61-3(a). The purpose of inventory accounting is to

---

1. But see the discussion of the original issue discount (OID) rules in the cell accompanying Chapter 3. The OID rules put individual investors on the accrual method with respect to OID income on bonds.
2. *See, e.g.,* Jim Turin & Sons, Inc. v. Commissioner, 219 F.3d 1103 (9th Cir. 2000), reprinted in the cell accompanying this chapter; RACMP Enters., Inc. v. Commissioner, 114 T.C. 211 (2000).

identify the taxpayer's cost of goods sold during the year. This requires two types of rules: (1) rules concerning which costs must be included in inventory, and (2) rules for determining which items of inventory the taxpayer is deemed to have sold during the year. Both types of rules are described below.

Inventoriable costs. Taxpayers must always include "direct costs" in inventory. In the case of merchandise purchased by the taxpayer for resale, the direct cost is simply the price the taxpayer paid for the merchandise. In the case of products manufactured by the taxpayer, direct costs include costs of raw materials, supplies, and of "labor that can be identified or associated with particular units produced." Reg. §1.263A-1(e)(2)(i). Under the uniform capitalization rules of §263A, most producers and resellers must also include in inventory "indirect costs" properly allocable to inventory items. According to the regulations, "Indirect costs are properly allocable to [inventory] when the costs directly benefit or are incurred by reason of the performance of production or resale activities." Reg. §1.263A-1(e)(3)(i). For a reseller, major indirect costs include expenses of handling, insuring, and storing merchandise, and salaries of employees in the purchasing department. For a manufacturer, major indirect costs include factory expenses that cannot be identified with particular units of production; examples are factory electricity bills, depreciation on factory plant and equipment, and factory labor not directly identified with particular units of production. A manufacturer subject to the uniform capitalization rules cannot simply deduct the cost of factory electricity as a business expense under §162. Instead, it must allocate the utility bill among the inventory items produced in the factory during the period to which the bill relates, and recover the cost (as an offset against gross sales) as it sells the inventory. Not every taxpayer with inventory is subject to §263A. The most important exemption is for resellers (but not manufacturers) with annual gross receipts of $10 million or less.[3] An exempted reseller may claim current deductions for indirect costs, rather than including indirect costs in inventory. It must still, however, include direct costs in inventory.

Inventory flow rules. The basic formula for determining a reseller's annual inventory cost is deceptively simple:

$$\begin{array}{r} \text{opening inventory} \\ +\,\text{purchases during the year} \\ -\,\text{closing inventory} \\ \hline \text{cost of goods sold} \end{array}$$

Suppose a business starts the year with an opening inventory of 1,000 identical items, in which it has a per-item cost of $3. The opening inventory amount, then, is $3,000. During the year the business adds 1,000 items (identical to the items in opening inventory) to inventory, at a cost of $5 per item. At year's end, the taxpayer counts its inventory and discovers it still has 1,000 items. Opening inventory is $3,000, and purchases during the year are $5,000, but what is the closing inventory? That depends on whether the items in the closing inventory are considered to be the low-cost items on hand at the beginning of the year, the high-cost items added to inventory during the year, or some combination of the two.

---

3. Additional aspects of §263A, including an exemption for "qualified creative expenses," are examined in section C.1 of Chapter 6.

The business may determine the cost of goods sold under either the first-in, first-out (FIFO) method, or the last-in, first out (LIFO) method.[4] Under the FIFO method, the taxpayer is treated as selling the oldest inventory items first—or, equivalently, the items in the closing inventory are considered to be the most recently acquired items. Thus,

$$
\begin{array}{rl}
\$3,000 & \text{opening inventory} \\
+\$5,000 & \text{purchases} \\
-\$5,000 & \text{closing inventory} \\
\hline
\$3,000 & \text{cost of goods sold}
\end{array}
$$

Under the LIFO method, the items in closing inventory are considered to be the earliest-acquired items—or, equivalently, the taxpayer is treated as selling the newest items first. Thus,

$$
\begin{array}{rl}
\$3,000 & \text{opening inventory} \\
+\$5,000 & \text{purchases} \\
-\$3,000 & \text{closing inventory} \\
\hline
\$5,000 & \text{cost of goods sold}
\end{array}
$$

The taxpayer's chosen inventory accounting method need not correspond to the actual physical flow of goods. A seller of perishable items will make actual sales on a FIFO basis (one hopes), but that does not disqualify it from using LIFO inventory accounting. Conversely, a seller of nonperishables that puts its inventory in a big pile and sells from the top of the pile is not foreclosed from using FIFO inventory accounting.

During a period of rising costs, the LIFO method will generally produce lower tax liabilities than the FIFO method, since LIFO will identify higher-cost, recently acquired items as the goods sold. Since rising costs are the norm, it follows that most businesses would prefer to use LIFO most of the time.[5] Changes in accounting methods require approval of the IRS, and "it would lower my taxes this year" is not ordinarily the justification that wins approval. So the LIFO-versus-FIFO decision is typically made when the business sets up its accounting, and can be revisited only under compelling circumstances. A business that initially chooses LIFO may rue the choice during a later period of declining costs.

Even assuming constantly rising costs, taxpayers must pay a price—two prices, really—for the joys of LIFO. First, a business that uses LIFO for tax purposes must also use LIFO for financial accounting purposes.[6] For the same reason LIFO tends to lower taxable income, it also tends to lower the stated income of a business for purposes of bonus computations, annual reports, and the like. That is unappealing

---

4. In some cases, specific identification of items sold during the year can be used to determine the cost of goods sold. A car dealer, for example, can easily keep track of each car sold during the year, and the dealer's cost for each car. Specific identification is required for sellers of real estate, and it is common (but not required) in the case of car dealers and other sellers of identifiable and expensive items. Where fungibility or commingling makes specific identification impossible, however, one of the approaches described in the text must be used.

5. Inflation, as measured by the consumer price index, has been positive in every year since 1955. The prices faced by producers in particular industries, however, are more variable.

6. In other words, the tax law permits a firm to use LIFO for tax purposes only if the firm also uses LIFO for financial accounting purposes.

to many businesses, and businesses frequently choose to pay more tax rather than present anything less than the rosiest possible picture to the world at large. Second, taxpayers using LIFO are ineligible for a very attractive inventory valuation method available to FIFO taxpayers. Although the normal rule is that inventory dollar amounts must be based on the taxpayer's cost, a taxpayer using FIFO may elect to value inventory at the lower of cost or market value at the end of the tax year, instead of simply at cost. §472(b)(2); Reg. §§1.471-2(c), 1.471-4. Thus, a decline in inventory value during the year results in a lower closing inventory, which leads to correspondingly higher cost of goods sold, and (the bottom line) correspondingly lower gross income. The effect is to allow a taxpayer using FIFO and lower-of-cost-or-market valuation to claim a deduction for a decrease in the value of unsold inventory due to changing market conditions. This pro-taxpayer exception to the general rule that the income tax ignores unrealized gains and losses is not available to businesses using LIFO inventory accounting.

The two important options in valuing inventory — LIFO versus FIFO, and market versus lower-of-cost-or-market — can be illustrated by the following problems:

Problem 2. *A* is a wholesaler of copper pipe, which it buys in six-foot units. In December 2010, *A* buys 1,000 such units at $3.00 per unit. In January 2011, *A* sells 600 units at $4.00 per unit. In December 2011, *A* buys 800 units at $3.50 per unit. Finally, in January 2012, it sells 1,000 units at $4.50 per unit. Assume no other income or costs. What is *A*'s income in 2011 and 2012 if it uses FIFO accounting? What if it uses LIFO?

Problem 3. In the foregoing problem, suppose that at the end of 2012 a competitor company begins offering, at similar prices, copper pipe with an improved finish that permits the copper to retain its coppery glow indefinitely, and that this depresses the price of the old, oxidation-prone pipe to $2.00 per six-foot unit. How will this affect the income statement of *A* in 2012?

The following case explores one aspect of the lower-of-cost-or-market method of valuing the closing inventory.

THOR POWER TOOL CO. v. COMMISSIONER
439 U.S. 522 (1979)

Justice BLACKMUN delivered the opinion of the Court.

This case, as it comes to us, presents two federal income tax issues. One has to do with inventory accounting. The other [omitted from this excerpt] relates to a bad-debt reserve.

The Inventory Issue. In 1964, petitioner Thor Power Tool Co. (hereinafter sometimes referred to as the taxpayer), in accord with "generally accepted accounting principles," wrote down what it regarded as excess inventory to Thor's own estimate of the net realizable value of the excess goods. Despite this write-down, Thor continued to hold the goods for sale at original prices. It offset the writedown against 1964 sales and thereby produced a net operating loss for that year; it then asserted that loss as a carryback to 1963 under §172. The Commissioner of Internal Revenue, maintaining that the write-down did not serve to reflect income clearly for tax purposes, disallowed the offset and the carryback.

On the taxpayer's petition for redetermination, the Tax Court, in an unreviewed decision by Judge Goffe, upheld the Commissioner's exercise of discretion in both respects. As a consequence, and also because of other adjustments not at issue here, the court redetermined the following deficiencies in Thor's federal income tax:

calendar year 1963 — $494,055.99
calendar year 1965 — $59,287.48

The United States Court of Appeals for the Seventh Circuit affirmed. We granted certiorari, to consider these important and recurring income tax accounting issues.

I. THE INVENTORY ISSUE

A

Taxpayer is a Delaware corporation with principal place of business in Illinois. It manufactures hand-held power tools, parts and accessories, and rubber products. At its various plants and service branches, Thor maintains inventories of raw materials, work-in-process, finished parts and accessories, and completed tools. At all times relevant, Thor has used, both for financial accounting and for income tax purposes, the "lower of cost or market" method of valuing inventories. *See* Treas. Reg. §1.471-2(c).

Thor's tools typically contain from 50 to 200 parts, each of which taxpayer stocks to meet demand for replacements. Because of the difficulty, at the time of manufacture, of predicting the future demand for various parts, taxpayer produced liberal quantities of each part to avoid subsequent production runs. Additional runs entail costly retooling and result in delays in filling orders.

In 1960, Thor instituted a procedure for writing down the inventory value of replacement parts and accessories for tool models it no longer produced. It created an inventory contra-account and credited that account with 10% of each part's cost for each year since production of the parent model had ceased. The effect of the procedure was to amortize the cost of these parts over a 10-year period. For the first nine months of 1964, this produced a write-down of $22,090.

In late 1964, new management took control and promptly concluded that Thor's inventory in general was overvalued. After a physical inventory taken at all locations of the tool and rubber divisions, management wrote off approximately $2.75 million of obsolete parts, damaged or defective tools, demonstration or sales samples, and similar items. The Commissioner allowed this writeoff because Thor scrapped most of the articles shortly after their removal from the 1964 closing inventory. Management also wrote down $245,000 of parts stocked for three unsuccessful products. The Commissioner allowed this write-down too, since Thor sold these items at reduced prices shortly after the close of 1964.

This left some 44,000 assorted items, the status of which is the inventory issue here. Management concluded that many of these articles, mostly spare parts, were "excess" inventory, that is, that they were held in excess of any reasonably foreseeable future demand. It was decided that this inventory should be written down to its "net realizable value," which, in most cases, was scrap value.

Two methods were used to ascertain the quantity of excess inventory. Where accurate data were available, Thor forecast future demand for each item on the basis of actual 1964 usage, that is, actual sales for tools and service parts, and actual usage for raw materials, work-in-process, and production parts. Management assumed that future demand for each item would be the same as it was in 1964. Thor then applied the following aging schedule: the quantity of each item corresponding to less than one year's estimated demand was kept at cost; the quantity of each item in excess of two years' estimated demand was written off entirely; and the quantity of each item corresponding to from one to two years' estimated demand was written down by 50% or 75%. Thor presented no statistical evidence to rationalize these percentages or this time frame. In the Tax Court, Thor's president justified the formula by citing general business experience, and opined that it was "somewhat in between" possible alternative solutions.[7] This first method yielded a total write-down of $744,030.

At two plants where 1964 data were inadequate to permit forecasts of future demand, Thor used its second method for valuing inventories. At these plants, the company employed flat percentage write-downs of 5%, 10% and 50% for various types of inventory. Thor presented no sales or other data to support these percentages. Its president observed that "this is not a precise way of doing it," but said that the company "felt some adjustment of this nature was in order, and these figures represented our best estimate of what was required to reduce the inventory to net realizable value." This second method yielded a total write-down of $160,832.

Although Thor wrote down all its "excess" inventory at once, it did not immediately scrap the articles or sell them at reduced prices, as it had done with the $3 million of obsolete and damaged inventory, the write-down of which the Commissioner permitted. Rather, Thor retained the "excess" items physically in inventory and continued to sell them at original prices. The company found that, owing to the peculiar nature of the articles involved,[8] price reductions were of no avail in moving this "excess" inventory. As time went on, however, Thor gradually disposed of some of these items as scrap; the record is unclear as to when these dispositions took place.

Thor's total write-down of "excess" inventory in 1964 therefore was:

Ten-year amortization of parts for discontinued tools	$22,090
First method (aging formula based on 1964 usage)	$744,030
Second method (flat percentage write-downs)	$160,832
Total	$926,952

7. "So here is where I fell back on my experience of 20 years in manufacturing of trying to determine a reasonable basis for evaluating this inventory in my previous association. We had generally written off inventory that was in excess of one year. In this case, we felt that that would be overly conservative, and it might understate the value of the inventory. On the other hand, we felt that two years . . . would be too optimistic and that we would overvalue the inventory [in view of] the factors which affect inventory, such as technological change, market changes, and the like, that two years, in our opinion, was too long a period of time. So what we did is we came up with a formula which was somewhat in between . . . writing off, say, everything over one year as compared to writing everything [off] over two years, and we came up with this formula that has been referred to in this Court today."

8. The Tax Court found that the finished tools were too specialized to attract bargain hunters; that no one would buy spare parts, regardless of price, unless they were needed to fix broken tools; that work-in-process had no value except as scrap; and that other manufacturers would not buy raw materials in the secondary market.

Thor credited this sum to its inventory contra-account, thereby decreasing closing inventory, increasing cost of goods sold, and decreasing taxable income for the year by that amount. The company contended that, by writing down excess inventory to scrap value, and by thus carrying all inventory at "net realizable value," it had reduced its inventory to "market" in accord with its "lower of cost or market" method of accounting. On audit, the Commissioner disallowed the write-down in its entirety, asserting that it did not serve clearly to reflect Thor's 1964 income for tax purposes.

The Tax Court, in upholding the Commissioner's determination, found as a fact that Thor's write-down of excess inventory did conform to "generally accepted accounting principles"; indeed, the court was "thoroughly convinced . . . that such was the case." The court found that if Thor had failed to write down its inventory on some reasonable basis, its accountants would have been unable to give its financial statements the desired certification. The court held, however, that conformance with "generally accepted accounting principles" is not enough; §446(b), and §471 as well, prescribe, as an independent requirement, that inventory accounting methods must "clearly reflect income." The Tax Court rejected Thor's argument that its write-down of "excess" inventory was authorized by Treasury Regulations, and held that the Commissioner had not abused his discretion in determining that the write-down failed to reflect 1964 income clearly.

B

Inventory accounting is governed by §§446 and 471 of the Code. Section 446(a) states the general rule for methods of accounting: "Taxable income shall be computed under the method of accounting on the basis of which the taxpayer regularly computes his income in keeping his books." Section 446(b) provides, however, that if the method used by the taxpayer "does not clearly reflect income, the computation of taxable income shall be made under such method as, in the opinion of the [Commissioner], does clearly reflect income." Regulations promulgated under §446 and in effect for the taxable year 1964, state that "no method of accounting is acceptable unless, in the opinion of the Commissioner, it clearly reflects income." Treas. Reg. §1.446-1(a)(2).

Section 471 prescribes the general rule for inventories. It states:

> Whenever in the opinion of the [Commissioner] the use of inventories is necessary in order clearly to determine the income of any taxpayer, inventories shall be taken by such taxpayer on such basis as the [Commissioner] may prescribe as conforming as nearly as may be to the best accounting practice in the trade or business and as most clearly reflecting the income.

As the Regulations point out, §471 obviously establishes two distinct tests to which an inventory must conform. First, it must conform "as nearly as may be" to the "best accounting practice," a phrase that is synonymous with "generally accepted accounting principles." Second, it "must clearly reflect the income." Treas. Reg. §1.471-2(a)(2).

It is obvious that on their face, §§446 and 471, with their accompanying Regulations, vest the Commissioner with wide discretion in determining whether a particular method of inventory accounting should be disallowed as not clearly reflective of income. This Court's cases confirm the breadth of this discretion. In construing §446 and its predecessors, the Court has held that "[t]he Commissioner has broad powers in determining whether accounting methods used by a taxpayer clearly reflect income." Commissioner of Internal Revenue v. Hansen, 360 U.S. 446, 467 (1959). Since the Commissioner has "[m]uch latitude for discretion," his interpretation of the statute's clear-reflection standard "should not be interfered with unless clearly unlawful." . . .

As has been noted, the Tax Court found as a fact in this case that Thor's write-down of "excess" inventory conformed to "generally accepted accounting principles" and was "within the term, 'best accounting practice,' as that term is used in section 471 of the Code and the regulations promulgated under that section." Since the Commissioner has not challenged this finding, there is no dispute that Thor satisfied the first part of §471's two-pronged test. The only question, then, is whether the Commissioner abused his discretion in determining that the write-down did not satisfy the test's second prong in that it failed to reflect Thor's 1964 income clearly. Although the Commissioner's discretion is not unbridled and may not be arbitrary we sustain his exercise of discretion here, for in this case the write-down was plainly inconsistent with the governing Regulations which the taxpayer, on its part, has not challenged.

It has been noted above that Thor at all pertinent times used the "lower of cost or market" method of inventory accounting. The rules governing this method are set out in Treas. Reg. §1.471-4. That Regulation defines "market" to mean, ordinarily, "the current bid price prevailing at the date of the inventory for the particular merchandise in the volume in which usually purchased by the taxpayer." §1471-4(a). The courts have uniformly interpreted "bid price" to mean replacement cost, that is, the price the taxpayer would have to pay on the open market to purchase or reproduce the inventory items. Where no open market exists, the Regulations require the taxpayer to ascertain "bid price" by using "such evidence of a fair market price at the date or dates nearest the inventory as may be available, such as specific purchases or sales by the taxpayer or others in reasonable volume and made in good faith, or compensation paid for cancellation of contracts for purchase commitments." §1.471-4(b).

The Regulations specify two situations in which a taxpayer is permitted to value inventory below "market" as so defined. The first is where the taxpayer in the normal course of business has actually offered merchandise for sale at prices lower than replacement cost. Inventories of such merchandise may be valued at those prices less direct cost of disposition, "and the correctness of such prices will be determined by reference to the actual sales of the taxpayer for a reasonable period before and after the date of the inventory." *Ibid.* The Regulations warn that prices "which vary materially from the actual prices so ascertained will not be accepted as reflecting the market." *Ibid.*

The second situation in which a taxpayer may value inventory below replacement cost is where the merchandise itself is defective. If goods are "unsalable at normal prices or unusable in the normal way because of damage, imperfections, shop wear, changes of style, odd or broken lots, or other similar causes," the taxpayer is permitted to value the goods "at bona fide selling prices less direct cost of disposition." §1.471-2(c). The Regulations define "bona fide selling price" to mean an "actual offering of goods during a period ending not later than 30 days after inventory date." *Ibid.* The taxpayer bears the burden of proving that "such exceptional goods as are valued upon such selling basis come within the classifications indicated," and is required to "maintain such records of the disposition of the goods as will enable a verification of the inventory to be made." *Ibid.*

From this language, the regulatory scheme is clear. The taxpayer must value inventory for tax purposes at cost unless the "market" is lower. "Market" is defined as "replacement cost," and the taxpayer is permitted to depart from replacement cost only in specified situations. When it makes any such departure, the taxpayer must substantiate its lower inventory valuation by providing evidence of actual offerings, actual sales, or actual contract cancellations. In the absence of objective evidence of this kind, a taxpayer's assertions as to the "market value" of its inventory are not cognizable in computing its income tax.

It is clear to us that Thor's procedures for writing down the value of its "excess" inventory were inconsistent with this regulatory scheme. Although Thor conceded that "an active market prevailed" on the inventory date, it "made no effort to determine the purchase or reproduction cost" of its "excess" inventory. Thor thus failed to ascertain "market" in accord with the general rule of the Regulations. In seeking to depart from replacement cost, Thor failed to bring itself within either of the authorized exceptions. Thor is not able to take advantage of §1.471-4(b) since, as the Tax Court found, the company failed to sell its excess inventory or offer it for sale at prices below replacement cost. Indeed, Thor concedes that it continued to sell its "excess" inventory at original prices. Thor also is not able to take advantage of §1.471-2(c) since, as the Tax Court and the Court of Appeals both held, it failed to bear the burden of proving that its excess inventory came within the specified classifications. Actually, Thor's "excess" inventory was normal and unexceptional, and was indistinguishable from and intermingled with the inventory that was not written down.

More importantly, Thor failed to provide any objective evidence whatever that the "excess" inventory had the "market value" management ascribed to it. The Regulations demand hard evidence of actual sales and further demand that records of actual dispositions be kept. The Tax Court found, however, that Thor made no sales and kept no records. Thor's management simply wrote down its closing inventory on the basis of a well-educated guess that some of it would never be sold. The formulae governing this write-down were derived from management's collective "business experience"; the percentages contained in those formulae seemingly were chosen for no reason other than that they were multiples of five and embodied some kind of anagogical symmetry. The Regulations do not permit this kind of evidence. If a taxpayer could write down its inventories on the basis of management's subjective estimates of the goods' ultimate salability, the taxpayer would be able, as the Tax Court observed, "to determine how much tax it wanted to pay for a given year."

For these reasons, we agree with the Tax Court and with the Seventh Circuit that the Commissioner acted within his discretion in deciding that Thor's write-down of "excess" inventory failed to reflect income clearly. In the light of the well-known potential for tax avoidance that is inherent in inventory accounting, the Commissioner in his discretion may insist on a high evidentiary standard before allowing write-downs of inventory to "market." Because Thor provided no objective evidence of the reduced market value of its "excess" inventory, its write-down was plainly inconsistent with the Regulations, and the Commissioner properly disallowed it.

C

[In this section of the opinion, the Court considered the taxpayer's argument that the regulations create a presumption that accounting that conforms to generally accepted accounting principles (GAAP) — as their inventory practices here were conceded to do — clearly reflects income. This was based primarily on the language in Reg. §1.471-2(b) that inventory accounts taken in conformity with best accounting practice "can, as a general rule, be regarded as clearly reflecting . . . income."[9]

The Court rejected this argument for several reasons, noting that the specific extensions of authority to the Commissioner to determine what practices clearly reflect income was inconsistent with any contrary presumption; that there was no support in the case law for the existence of such a presumption; and that there was too much tension between the goals and biases of financial accounting and tax accounting to permit the former to create presumptive treatment for purposes of the latter. — Eds.]

D

Thor complains that a decision adverse to it poses a dilemma. According to the taxpayer, it would be virtually impossible for it to offer objective evidence of its "excess" inventory's lower value, since the goods cannot be sold at reduced prices; even if they could be sold, says Thor, their reduced-price sale would just "pull the rug out" from under the identical "non-excess" inventory Thor is trying to sell simultaneously. The only way Thor could establish the inventory's value by a "closed transaction" would be to scrap the articles at once. Yet immediate scrapping would be undesirable for demand for the parts ultimately might prove greater than anticipated. The taxpayer thus sees itself presented with "an unattractive Hobson's choice: either the unsalable inventory must be carried for years at its cost instead of net realizable value, thereby overstating taxable income by such overvaluation until it is scrapped, or the excess inventory must be scrapped prematurely to the detriment of the manufacturer and its customers."

If this is indeed the dilemma that confronts Thor, it is in reality the same choice that every taxpayer who has a paper loss must face. It can realize its loss now and garner its tax benefit, or it can defer realization, and its deduction, hoping for better luck later. Thor, quite simply, has suffered no present loss. It deliberately manufactured its "excess" spare parts because it judged that the marginal cost of unsalable inventory would be lower than the cost of retooling machinery should demand surpass expectations. This was a rational business judgment and, not unpredictably, Thor now has inventory it believes it cannot sell. Thor, of course, is not so confident of its prediction as to be willing to scrap the "excess" parts now; it wants to keep them on hand, just in case. This, too, is a rational judgment, but there is no reason why the Treasury should subsidize Thor's hedging of its bets. There is also no reason why Thor should be entitled, for tax purposes, to have its cake and to eat it too.

The judgment of the Court of Appeals is affirmed.

_____

9. This language was deleted from the regulations in 1973, but it applied to the tax years at issue in this case.

Notes and Questions

1. *What to do?* The dilemma facing Thor Power Tool is real. It intentionally overproduces spare parts, because at the margin it is very inexpensive to do so, and it wants to have sufficient spare parts in inventory to meet demand, in order to maintain customer goodwill. Having overproduced the spare parts, it realizes that many of them will probably never be sold, except perhaps eventually as scrap metal. But the demand curve for spare parts is highly inelastic, meaning that it is relatively insensitive to price changes. This is a fundamental fact about spare parts markets: the people who need a replacement part may need it very badly, and be willing to pay a rather high price for it, because without it they may have to junk the machine for lack of one working part. But those who don't need the spare part would be disinclined to maintain a large inventory of spare parts, just in case they might ever need one. So the expectation will be that you can maintain a fairly high price for the parts, but will not be able to sell very many of them; and cutting prices won't help much, because additional buyers are hard to come by at any price. This means that the company may be stuck with a good bit of expensive inventory, the cost of which cannot be deducted until it is sold or scrapped. Do you see any resolution to the dilemma following the Supreme Court decision in this case?

2. *Book publishers.* This inventory problem has counterparts in other industries; a good deal of tax liability was at stake in this case, which is why groups like the U.S. Chamber of Commerce filed *amicus* briefs on behalf of the taxpayer. Book publishers, for example, also generally print more copies of books than they reasonably expect to sell, because printing too many, when the marginal cost per book is low, is less costly than the possible loss of sales (or the costs of gearing up the presses for a second edition) if they print too few. This decision makes it more likely that a publisher will dispose of remaining inventories of each book to clearing houses within a year or two of publication. This permits the sort of bulk sales that allow recovery of printing costs, but at some loss to the reading public. Instead of being able to order slightly out-of-date books directly from the publisher (who is easy to find), bookstores and customers may have to search among clearing houses to find who has copies of the book. Then, again, the Internet may have more or less solved that problem.

B.   THE CASH METHOD: SELECTED TOPICS

1.   Constructive Receipt

Under the cash method, a taxpayer must include an item in income when it is actually *or constructively* received. Under the doctrine of constructive receipt, "a taxpayer may not deliberately turn his back upon income and thus select the year for which he will report it." Hamilton National Bank of Chattanooga v. Commissioner, B.T.A. 63, 67 (1933). For example, if your employer tells you on December

31 that your paycheck is in the accounting office and you can pick it up whenever you want, you cannot defer tax to the next year by not picking up the check until January.

Congress has provided legislative relief for some victims of the constructive receipt doctrine. Section 451(h), described in the following committee report, is an example.[10]

STAFF OF THE JOINT COMMITTEE ON TAXATION, GENERAL EXPLANATION OF TAX LEGISLATION ENACTED IN 1998

(1998)

E. TAX TREATMENT OF PRIZES AND AWARDS (SEC. 5301 OF THE ACT)

PRESENT AND PRIOR LAW

A taxpayer generally is required to include an item in income no later than the time of its actual or constructive receipt, unless the item properly is accounted for in a different period under the taxpayer's method of accounting. If a taxpayer has an unrestricted right to demand the payment of an amount, the taxpayer is in constructive receipt of that amount whether or not the taxpayer makes the demand and actually receives the payment.

Under the principle of constructive receipt, the winner of a contest who is given the option of receiving either a lump-sum distribution or an annuity is required to include the value of the award in gross income, even if the annuity option is exercised. Alternatively, the principle of constructive receipt does not apply if, prior to the declaration of a winner (such as at the time of purchase of a lottery ticket), a taxpayer designates whether he or she chooses to receive a lump-sum distribution or an annuity. This is the case because the taxpayer does not have an unrestricted right to demand the payment of the winnings, since the taxpayer has not yet in fact won.

EXPLANATION OF PROVISION

The existence of a "qualified prize option" is disregarded in determining the taxable year for which any portion of a qualified prize is to be included in income. A qualified prize option is an option that entitles a person to receive a single cash payment in lieu of a qualified prize (or portion thereof), provided such option is exercisable not later than 60 days after the prize winner becomes entitled to the prize. Thus, a qualified prize winner who is provided the option to choose either cash or an annuity not later than 60 days after becoming entitled to the prize is not required to include amounts in gross income immediately if the annuity option is exercised merely by reason of having the option. . . .

---

10. See the Chapter 2 cell on employer-provided free parking for another example.

Qualified prizes are prizes or awards from contests, lotteries, jackpots, games or similar arrangements that provide a series of payments over a period of at least 10 years, provided that the prize or award does not relate to any past services performed by the recipient and does not require the recipient to perform any substantial future service. The provision applies to individuals on the cash receipts and disbursements method of accounting. Income and deductions resulting from this provision retain their character as ordinary, not capital. In addition, the Secretary is to provide for the application of this provision in the case of a partnership or other pass-through entity consisting entirely of individuals on the cash receipts and disbursements method of accounting. . . .

REVENUE EFFECT

The provision is estimated to increase Federal fiscal year budget receipts by $170 million in 1999 and by $1,618 million in 2000, and to reduce receipts by $99 million in 2001, $348 million in 2002, $397 million in 2003, $384 million in 2004, $367 million in 2005, $346 million in 2006, and by $321 million in 2007.

Notes and Questions

1. *The revenue effect.* If §451(h) is a taxpayer-favorable provision, why does the committee report indicate that it was expected to *increase* tax revenues in its first two years?
2. *"Nonqualified" deferred compensation.* Avoiding the constructive receipt doctrine is crucial if an employer wants to provide "nonqualified" deferred compensation to some or all of its highly compensated employees. As long as an employee's current interest in nonqualified deferred compensation consists of a mere unsecured contractual right to receive payment in some future year, the employee will not be in constructive receipt of income in the current year. For more on nonqualified deferred compensation, see section B of Chapter 11.

2. Prepaid Expenses

When there is a timing difference between the cash method and the accrual method, the cash method usually defers both inclusions and deductions, relative to the accrual method. This is because rights to receive income usually arise before payments are received, and obligations to pay usually arise before payments are made. Is it possible, however, for a cash method taxpayer to manipulate the system by paying a deductible expense *before* the obligation to pay has arisen? Consider the following problem.

Problem 4.   Marty, a lawyer with a solo practice and a cash method taxpayer, prepays his office rent for all 12 months of 2011, on December 15, 2010. Does the fact that Marty has paid cash entitle him to deduct all of his 2011 rent expense in 2010? *See* Reg. §§1.461-1(a)(1) and 1.263(a)-4(f)(1).

C. THE ACCRUAL METHOD: SELECTED TOPICS

1. *The All Events Test, Clear Reflection of Income, and Economic Performance*

FORD MOTOR CO. v. COMMISSIONER
71 F.3d 209 (6th Cir. 1995)

Milburn, Circuit Judge. Petitioner Ford Motor Company ("Ford") appeals the decision of the United States Tax Court upholding respondent Commissioner of Internal Revenue's ("Commissioner") reduction of petitioner's deductions for its obligations under agreements it entered into in settlement of tort lawsuits against it. On appeal, the issue is whether respondent Commissioner abused her discretion in determining that petitioner's method of accounting for its structured settlements was not a clear reflection of income under §446(b) and in ordering petitioner to limit its deduction in 1980 to the cost of the annuity contracts it purchased to fund the settlements. For the reasons that follow, we affirm.

Petitioner Ford Motor Company is engaged in a number of businesses, including the manufacture of cars and trucks, and it maintains its books and records and files its income taxes using the accrual method of accounting. In the years preceding 1980, some of Ford's cars and trucks were involved in automobile accidents, and in 1980, Ford entered into 20 structured settlement agreements in settlement of personal injury or accidental death claims with persons who were injured in the accidents and with survivors of persons who died as a result of the accidents. In these structured settlement agreements, Ford agreed to make periodic payments of tort damages, yearly or monthly, in exchange for a release of all claims against it. The payments were to be made over various periods of time, the longest of which was 58 years. All but three of the settlements provided for payments over a period of 40 years or more. The agreements were of three types: (I) those that required petitioner to make periodic payments for a period certain ("Type I settlements"); (II) those that required petitioner to make periodic payments for the remainder of a claimant's life ("Type II settlements"); and (III) those that required petitioner to make periodic payments for the longer of a period certain or the remainder of a claimant's life ("Type III settlements"). In total, the structured settlement agreements provided for payments of $24,477,699.[11]

To provide it with funds to cover the periodic payments, Ford purchased single premium annuity contracts at a cost of $4,424,587. The annuity contracts were structured so that the yearly annuity payments would equal the yearly amount owed to the claimants under the structured settlement agreements. None of the settlement agreements released petitioner from liability following the purchase of the annuity contract, and, in the event of a default on an annuity, petitioner would be required to pay the remaining balance owed to the tort claimants. The parties stipulated that the present value of the deferred payments that petitioner agreed to make to the claimants did not exceed the cost of the annuity contracts.

On its 1980 tax return, petitioner claimed deductions for the various types of structured settlements as follows: for the Type I settlements, it claimed the total

---

11. In order to reach this figure, petitioner presumed that the claimants receiving payments for life would survive to their life expectancies.

amount of all periodic payments due; for the Type II settlements, it claimed the amounts it actually paid during 1980; and for the Type III settlements, it claimed the total amount of all payments due for the period certain portion of the settlement. These deductions totaled $10,636,994, which petitioner included as part of a product liability loss that it carried back to its 1970 taxable year pursuant to §172(b)(1)(I). It also reported the annuity income on its 1980 federal income tax return under §72. For financial accounting purposes, petitioner reported the 1980 structured settlements by expensing the cost of the annuity in the year of the settlement. For other settlements not funded by annuities, of which there were none in 1980, petitioner expensed the present value of the payments to be made to the claimants in the year of the settlement.

Respondent Commissioner determined that Ford's method of accounting for its structured settlements did not clearly reflect income under §446(b) and disallowed the deductions petitioner claimed in excess of the cost of the annuities petitioner purchased. Respondent also excluded from petitioner's income the amounts required to be reported as income from annuity contracts, which was $323,340 in 1980. As a result, respondent determined a deficiency in petitioner's 1970 federal income tax liability of $3,300,151.

Petitioner Ford challenged this deficiency determination by filing a petition in the United States Tax Court. In its amended petition, Ford claimed that it was entitled to deduct in 1980 the full amount of all payments to be made under the structured settlements, basing its valuation of the life settlements on the life expectancies of the claimants. The total deduction Ford claimed was $24,477,699.

The parties submitted the case to the United States Tax Court with all facts fully stipulated. A divided court upheld the Commissioner's position. . . . This timely appeal followed.

Section 446 of the Internal Revenue Code provides the general rule governing use of methods of accounting by taxpayers. Section 446(b) provides that, if the method of accounting used by the taxpayer to compute income does not clearly reflect income, "the computation of taxable income shall be made under such method as, in the opinion of the Secretary or his delegate, does clearly reflect income." The Commissioner has broad discretion under §446(b) to determine whether a particular method of accounting clearly reflects income. . . . Once the Commissioner has determined that a method of accounting does not clearly reflect income, she may substitute a method that, in her opinion, does clearly reflect income. . . .

There are three stages to our analysis in this case: first, we decide whether the application of §446(b) was appropriate; second, we decide whether the tax court correctly determined that petitioner's method of accounting did not clearly reflect income; and third, we address the appropriateness of the method of accounting that the Commissioner imposed in its place.

First, petitioner argues that the tax court erred in allowing the Commissioner to require Ford to change its method of accounting because, in the absence of abuse or manipulation, an accrual method taxpayer clearly reflects its income when its reporting satisfies the "all events" test. Therefore, it argues that, because its accrual of deductions satisfied the all events test, the Commissioner had no authority to invoke §446(b).

Ford Motor Company is an accrual method taxpayer. The accrual method of accounting takes income into account when the right to payment is earned, even if payment is not received until later, and expenses into account when they are incurred, even if payment is not made until a later time. Financial accounting systems differ regarding the time that an expense is "incurred" and therefore should be accrued, but, under the tax law, the standard for determining when an expense is "incurred" is the "all events" test. Treas. Reg. §1.466-1(c)(1)(ii); United States v. Hughes Properties, Inc., 476 U.S. 593, 600 (1986). This test provides that an accrual method taxpayer must deduct an expense in the taxable year when all the events have occurred that establish the fact of liability giving rise to the deduction and the amount of the liability can be determined with reasonable accuracy. *Id.* The tax court assumed for purposes of discussion that Ford's deductions satisfied the all events test, and for purposes of our review, we will make this assumption as well. . . .

[W]e hold that satisfaction of the all events test by an accrual method taxpayer does not preempt the Commissioner's authority under §446(b) to determine that a taxpayer's method of accounting does not clearly reflect income.

Section 446(c) of the Internal Revenue Code provides that, subject to the provisions of subsections (a) and (b), a taxpayer may compute taxable income under the accrual method of accounting. The all events test, which is merely a means devised to define the years in which income and deductions accrue, clearly is subordinate to the clear reflection standard contained in subsection (b). . . .

The language of §446 is clear on its face, and we agree with the tax court's interpretation of the statute. *See* Mooney Aircraft, Inc. v. United States, 420 F.2d 400, 406 (5th Cir. 1969) ("The 'all events test,' however, is not the only basis upon which the Commissioner can disallow a deduction. Under §446(b) he has discretion to disallow any accounting method which does not clearly reflect income.").

Petitioner argues that Congress acknowledged that the Commissioner's discretion under §446(b) does not extend to situations such as the present case when it changed the Internal Revenue Code, effective in 1984, to provide in §461(h)(2)(c) that accrual method taxpayers cannot deduct tort liabilities until the year in which payment is made. Ford points to the legislative history of §461, which states that "the rules relating to the time for accrual of a deduction by a taxpayer using the accrual method of accounting should be *changed* to take into account the time value of money." Brief of Petitioner at 22 (citing H.R. Rep. No. 432, 98th Cong., 2d Sess., pt. II, at 1254 (1984)) (emphasis added). It argues that this statement indicates a recognition by Congress that the Commissioner was not authorized to deny the sort of accrual that Ford is attempting prior to 1984.

The tax court held that the change in prior law to which the legislative history refers is the all events test contained in the Income Tax Regulations and that Congress did not intend "to limit respondent's authority under section 446(b) in any way by enacting section 461(h) in 1984." We agree that the change that this passage references is a modification of the all events test and conclude that nothing in the legislative history of §461(h) limits the Commissioner's authority under §446(b). Section 461(h) was a Congressional effort to remedy an accounting distortion by placing all accrual method taxpayers on the cash method of accounting for tort liabilities, regardless of the length of the payout period and without any consideration of whether accrual of an expense in an earlier year would distort income. Its enactment does not preclude the Commissioner from applying the clear reflection standard of §446(b) on a case-by-case basis to taxpayers in tax years prior to 1984.

Having determined that expenses that satisfy the all events test can be disallowed when accrual would not result in a clear reflection of income, we now examine the correctness of the Commissioner's determination that Ford's method of accounting for its tort obligations did not clearly reflect income. In its opinion, the tax court used an example to "highlight the distortion [of petitioner's income] about which respondent complains." It utilized the numbers from one settlement agreement under which Ford agreed to pay the claimant $504,000 in 42 equal, annual installments of $12,000. The annuity contract that Ford purchased to fund the payments cost $141,124, demonstrating an implicit rate of return of 8.19 percent. Ford claimed a deduction in 1980 in the amount of $504,000 for this obligation. The tax court used these numbers to create three scenarios, assuming that but for the settlement agreement in question, petitioner would have had taxable income in 1980 of at least $504,000.

In the first scenario, the tax court assumed that the accident in question did not occur and that, as a result, petitioner received an additional $504,000 of currently-taxable income. The tax court further assumed that petitioner would have been subject to a 40 percent marginal tax rate, leaving it with $302,400. The tax court then noted that, if the after tax proceeds were invested over 42 years at a rate of 8.19 percent, the $302,400 would grow to $8,249,751.

In the second scenario, the tax court assumed that the accident occurred but that Ford discharged its liability in full by paying and deducting $141,124 and investing the remainder over 42 years. Its current deduction of the $141,124 it paid for the annuity would leave it with $362,876 of taxable income on which it would pay tax of $145,150, leaving $217,726. If it invested the $217,726 over the 42 year period at a 8.19 percent rate of return, it would grow to $5,939,756.

In the third scenario, the tax court assumed that the events occurred as they did in the present case, with Ford deducting the full $504,000 it was required to pay the tort claimants and paying no tax. Investing the $504,000 at a rate of return of 8.19 percent and taking into account the annual payments of $12,000, the tax court found that petitioner would have $9,898,901 remaining after 42 years.

The tax court pointed out that Ford is claiming scenario three treatment and that comparing scenario three to scenario one demonstrates that petitioner is better off with the accidents than if they never occurred. The tax court held that fully deducting payments extending over a long period of time leads to a distortion of income and "the incongruous result that the greater a taxpayer's nominal liability for negligence, the more it benefits." It therefore concluded that petitioner's method of accounting did not clearly reflect income.

Petitioner challenges the tax court's approval of the Commissioner's determination that its accounting method did not clearly reflect income on several grounds. First, it argues that the tax court's numerical example was flawed by its use of a 8.19 percent rate of return. It asserts that the 8.19 percent rate of return that the tax court found implicit in one of the annuity contracts is a pre-tax rate of return because Ford is required to pay tax on amounts received as an annuity under §72 and that the tax court instead should have used the after-tax rate of 4.91 percent. Recomputing the investment growth over 42 years using this rate of return in the three scenarios, petitioner asserts that in scenario one it would be $2,267,705; in scenario two it would be $1,632,729; and in scenario three it would be $2,192,446. Thus, petitioner argues: "Ford did not 'fare[] better than if the accident never occurred'; the tax court's apparent reason for invalidating Ford's tax treatment rests on a misconception." In her brief, respondent acknowledges the flaw in the tax court's numerical example and presents an example of her own, arguing that Ford was in a 46 percent tax bracket rather than a 40 percent tax bracket. In respondent's example, petitioner again fares better under scenario three treatment than under scenario one.

Petitioner's brief suggests that the tax court's determination that its accounting method did not clearly reflect income was based solely on the fact that, in the tax court's example, petitioner fared better with the accident than without. We conclude, however, that this factor was not determinative, and that, even viewing petitioner's numerical example as correct, the gross distortion of income that it demonstrates between the economic and tax results persuades us that the tax court's decision was not improper. Given the length of the payment periods, allowing a deduction for the full amount of liability in 1980 could lead to the result that the tax benefit from the deduction would fund the full amounts due in future years and leave petitioner with a profit. Such a result extends the accrual method of accounting beyond its inherent limitations.

Our task on appeal is to determine whether there is an adequate basis in law for the Commissioner's conclusion that Ford's method of accounting did not clearly reflect income. We find several cases from other circuits that support our finding that the Commissioner's exercise of her discretion was proper. First, in Mooney Aircraft, Inc. v. United States, 420 F.2d 400 (5th Cir. 1969), the Fifth Circuit upheld the Commissioner's denial of the taxpayer's use of an accounting method based on his §446(b) authority. In that case, Mooney manufactured airplanes, and each purchaser of an airplane received a "Mooney Bond," redeemable for $1,000 when the airplane was permanently retired from service. Retirement of the aircraft usually occurred 20 or more years from the date of purchase. Mooney, an accrual method taxpayer, argued that the sale of an aircraft and corresponding issuance of a bond satisfied the all events test for the liability, and, therefore, it attempted to deduct the $1,000 redemption price of the bonds in the year of sale. Conversely, the government argued that the all events test was not satisfied until the aircraft was retired and that the deduction was improper prior to such time. The Fifth Circuit disagreed with the government, holding that the all events test was satisfied at the time of sale. *Id.* at 405-06. However, it concluded that the taxpayer's method of accounting did not clearly reflect income, emphasizing that the long time period between the deduction for the bonds and their date of redemption was problematic and caused a distortion of income. *Id.* at 409-10. . . .

Petitioner also argues that the tax court's decision that petitioner's method of accounting did not clearly reflect income was improper because it "authorizes arbitrary and unprincipled use of the Commissioner's section 446(b) power." It asserts that the tax court failed to provide any principles "to delineate the scope of section 446(b)," and that, in doing so, it created an "arbitrary system . . . that requires all accrual taxpayers to account for their liabilities when they become fixed, yet makes the validity of that reporting method subject to the unconstrained whim of the Commissioner."

We are not persuaded by this policy-based argument. . . .

As the tax court observed, "the issue of whether the taxpayer's method of accounting clearly reflects income is a question of fact to be determined on a case-by-case basis." We find the tax court's language sufficient to limit its holding to extreme cases such as this one in which the economic results are grossly different from the tax results and therefore conclude that the tax court's decision does not allow the Commissioner arbitrary or unprincipled discretion.

Given that a change was necessary because Ford's accrual of its settlement obligations in 1980 did not clearly reflect income, Ford argues that the method of accounting that the Commissioner imposed in its place was improper. Ford asserts that the Commissioner lacked the authority to impose the method of accounting that she did because it is "inconsistent with the plain dictates of the Code and regulations and the undisputed facts of this case."

The method of accounting that the Commissioner imposed was to allow Ford a deduction for the amount that it paid for the annuities with no further deductions for the future payments that Ford will make to the claimants. To offset her disallowance of future deductions, the Commissioner will permit Ford to exclude its income from the annuity contracts. Petitioner asserts that this scheme violates established tax law for several reasons and forces Ford to use a tax treatment that it could not have adopted on its own.

First, petitioner argues that the Commissioner is imposing on it a present value method of accounting which should only be imposed in the presence of a directive by Congress to do so. Ford additionally argues that this method impermissibly allows it only to deduct the approximately $4 million it paid for the annuities without ever allowing a deduction for the additional approximately $20 million it will pay to the claimants and that the Commissioner's method is arbitrary because it is not a method that Ford could have adopted on its own.

Respondent counters that its method of accounting is a modified cash basis method that allows Ford "a dollar for dollar deduction, albeit in the form of an offset against its annuity income, for the full face amount of its future payments of approximately $24 million." Respondent points out that, because she allowed Ford to deduct the full cost of the annuity contracts in 1980, it has no basis in the contracts and would be fully taxable on the annuity income of $24,477,699 as it is received. However, the payments Ford is required to make to the tort claimants, which correspond exactly to the amount of its annuity income, give rise to deductions that offset the income and create a wash. Respondent argues that, because she has relieved taxpayer of the obligation to report the annuity income as it is received, she should not allow Ford any deductions for the required payments.

We find no merit in petitioner's assertion that this methodology is improper because it reduces the amount of the deductions to the present value of the payments petitioner is obligated to make. The Commissioner reduced petitioner's deduction to the cost of the annuity contracts. The stipulated facts provided only that the present value of the payments petitioner is obligated to make did not exceed this amount. There is no indication that respondent was imposing a present value method of accounting on petitioner.

Furthermore, we find no authority that prohibits the tax accounting treatment that the Commissioner and the tax court imposed here. The Commissioner's discretion to impose an alternate method of accounting under §446(b) is not limited to methods that Ford could have adopted on its own. While we recognize that to require Ford to account for its tort obligations on the cash method might have been a more logical alternative, we cannot find that the Commissioner's exercise of her discretion was arbitrary because it resulted in an accounting treatment more favorable to Ford [than] a straight cash method would be. The only difference between the Commissioner's method of accounting and the cash basis method is that petitioner receives an immediate deduction for the cost of its annuities rather than recovering that cost over the terms of the annuities under 26 U.S.C. §72, and this difference inures to Ford's benefit. We therefore conclude that the tax court's decision regarding the accounting method the Commissioner imposed was proper.

Notes and Questions

1. *Simpler numbers.* The Tax Court's numerical example is unnecessarily complex. Here is a simpler version. Suppose Ford agrees to pay a claimant $500,000 in 40 equal annual installments (of $12,500 each), and that Ford fully funds its obligation by buying an annuity for $140,000. If Ford is allowed an immediate deduction of $500,000, Ford will make a profit from the transaction if its marginal tax rate is higher than 28 percent. If Ford's marginal tax rate is 40 percent, for example, the tax savings from a $500,000 deduction will be $200,000. Since this exceeds the cost of the annuity by $60,000, Ford will be $60,000 better off, after taxes, than if it had never committed the tort.[12] An accounting method producing such an absurd result obviously does not clearly reflect income, but the Sixth Circuit correctly notes that there is nothing magic about whether the taxpayer actually profits from its liability. Suppose Ford's marginal tax rate was only 25 percent. In that case, the $140,000 cost of the annuity would exceed the $125,000 tax savings from a $500,000 deduction, so Ford would not actually profit from its tort. Nevertheless, a deduction of $500,000 for a liability that Ford fully funds for only $140,000 would not clearly reflect income; indeed, it would clearly *not* reflect income.

2. *Economic performance.* Although the IRS won in *Ford,* the vagueness of the clear reflection of income rule makes it an unreliable defense against taxpayers accruing expenses greatly in excess of the present values of their obligations. Rather than relying solely on the clear reflection rule and the vigilance and litigating success of the IRS, Congress in 1984 enacted the "economic performance" rules of §461(h).[13] Under §461(h), an accrual method taxpayer may not deduct an expense, even though the all events test has been satisfied, until "economic performance with respect to such item occurs." The statute defines "economic performance" for various sorts of liabilities. If the liability is for services or property provided to the taxpayer by another person, economic performance occurs only as the other person provides the services or property; if the liability requires the taxpayer to provide property or services to another, economic performance occurs only as the taxpayer provides the property or services; and if the liability is for workers' compensation or in tort, economic performance occurs only as the taxpayer actually makes payments. Under these rules, it is generally impossible for an accrual taxpayer legitimately to claim a deduction for an amount significantly greater than the present value of the taxpayer's obligation.

12. This is not quite as good as it sounds, because the annuity would produce a modest amount of additional income in the subsequent years. See section E of Chapter 3. The total taxable income so received would be $360,000, which would produce a tax (at the assumed 40 percent rate) of $144,000. Discounting this amount to present value (using the same discount rate assumed in the annuity itself) yields a current cost associated with the future tax liability of about $40,320.

13. Section 461(h) was enacted after the facts of *Ford* had taken place, but before the case reached the Sixth Circuit. Thus, the court had to consider whether the enactment of the economic performance rules had any implications for the interpretation of pre-1984 law.

2. *Early Cash Receipts of Accrual Method Taxpayers*

Confusion can result when a prepayment reverses the normal timing relationship between cash and accrual accounting. Problem 4 explored this confusion from the perspective of a cash method payor, but what about an accrual method payee? Suppose Marty's landlord (from Problem 4) is an accrual method taxpayer. In the absence of Marty's prepayment in 2010 of the rent for 2011, the landlord would not accrue the 2011 rental income until 2011. Under the all events test, the landlord's right to rental income would accrue only as the landlord actually provided the use of the office to Marty throughout 2011. Does the prepayment in 2010 change this result? According to generally accepted accounting principles (GAAP), the answer is no. For the Supreme Court's answer, read on.

SCHLUDE v. COMMISSIONER
372 U.S. 128 (1963)

Mr. Justice WHITE delivered the opinion of the Court. . . .

Taxpayers, husband and wife, formed a partnership to operate ballroom dancing studios (collectively referred to as "studio") pursuant to Arthur Murray, Inc., franchise agreements. Dancing lessons were offered under either of two basic contracts. The cash plan contract required the student to pay the entire down payment in cash at the time the contract was executed with the balance due in installments thereafter. The deferred payment contract required only a portion of the down payment to be paid in cash. The remainder of the down payment was due in stated installments and the balance of the contract price was to be paid as designated in a negotiable note signed at the time the contract was executed.

Both types of contracts provided that (1) the student should pay tuition for lessons in a certain amount, (2) the student should not be relieved of his obligation to pay the tuition, (3) no refunds would be made, and (4) the contract was noncancelable.[14] The contracts prescribed a specific number of lesson hours ranging from five to 1,200 hours and some contracts provided lifetime courses entitling the student additionally to two hours of lessons per month plus two parties a year for life. Although the contracts designated the period during which the lessons had to be taken, there was no schedule of specific dates, which were arranged from time to time as lessons were given.

Cash payments received directly from students and amounts received when the negotiable notes were discounted at the bank or fully paid were deposited in the studio's general bank account without segregation from its other funds. The franchise agreements required the studio to pay to Arthur Murray, Inc., on a weekly basis, 10% of these cash receipts as royalty and 5% of the receipts in escrow, the latter to continue until a $20,000 indemnity fund was accumulated. Similarly, sales commissions for lessons sold were paid at the time the sales receipts were deposited in the studio's general bank account.

---

14. Although the contracts stated they were noncancelable, the studio frequently rewrote contracts reducing the number of lessons for a smaller sum of money. Also, despite the fact that the contracts provided that no refunds would be made, and despite the fact that the studio discouraged refunds, occasionally a refund would be made on a canceled contract.

The studio, since its inception in 1946, has kept its books and reported income for tax purposes on an accrual system of accounting. In addition to the books, individual student record cards were maintained showing the number of hours taught and the number still remaining under the contract. The system, in substance, operated as follows. When a contract was entered into, a "deferred income" account was credited for the total contract price. At the close of each fiscal period, the student record cards were analyzed and the total number of taught hours was multiplied by the designated rate per hour of each contract. The resulting sum was deducted from the deferred income account and reported as earned income on the financial statements and the income tax return. In addition, if there had been no activity in a contract for over a year, or if a course were reduced in amount, an entry would be made canceling the untaught portion of the contract, removing that amount from the deferred income account, and recognizing gain to the extent that the deferred income exceeded the balance due on the contract, i.e., the amounts received in advance. The amounts representing lessons taught and the gains from cancellations constituted the chief sources of the partnership's gross income. The balance of the deferred income account would be carried forward into the next fiscal year to be increased or decreased in accordance with the number of new contracts, lessons taught and cancellations recognized. . . .

Three certified public accountants testified that in their opinion the accounting system employed truly reflected net income in accordance with commercial accrual accounting standards. . . .

The question remaining for decision, then, is this: Was it proper for the Commissioner, exercising his discretion under [§446(b) and its predecessor] to reject the studio's accounting system as not clearly reflecting income and to include as income in a particular year advance payments by way of cash, negotiable notes and contract installments falling due but remaining unpaid during that year? We hold that it was since we believe the problem is squarely controlled by *American Automobile Association*, 367 U.S. 687 (1961).

The Court there had occasion to consider the entire legislative background of the treatment of prepaid income. The retroactive repeal of §452 of the 1954 Code, "the only law incontestably permitting the practice upon which [the taxpayer] depends," was regarded as reinstating long-standing administrative and lower court rulings that accounting systems deferring prepaid income could be rejected by the Commissioner.

> The fact is that §452 for the first time specifically declared petitioner's system of accounting to be acceptable for income tax purposes, and overruled the longstanding position of the Commissioner and courts to the contrary. And the repeal of the section the following year, upon insistence by the Treasury that the proposed endorsement of such tax accounting would have a disastrous impact on the Government's revenue, was just as clearly a mandate from the Congress that petitioner's system was not acceptable for tax purposes. 367 U.S., at 695.

. . . The *American Automobile Association* case rested upon an additional ground which is also controlling here. Relying upon Automobile Club of Michigan v. Commissioner, 353 U.S. 180 (1957), the Court rejected the taxpayer's system as artificial since the advance payments related to services which were to be performed only upon customers' demands without relation to fixed dates in the future. The system employed here suffers from that very same vice, for the studio sought to defer its cash receipts on the basis of contracts which did not provide for lessons on fixed dates after the taxable year, but left such dates to be arranged from time to time by the instructor and his student. Under the contracts, the student could arrange for some or all of the additional lessons or could simply allow their rights under the contracts to lapse. But even though the student did not demand the remaining lessons, the contracts permitted the studio to insist upon payment in accordance with the obligations undertaken and to retain whatever prepayments were made without restriction as to use and without obligation of refund. At the end of each period, while the number of lessons taught had been meticulously reflected, the studio was uncertain whether none, some or all of the remaining lessons would be rendered. Clearly, services were rendered solely on demand in the fashion of the *American Automobile Association* and *Automobile Club of Michigan* cases.

. . . Consequently, the Commissioner was fully justified in including payments in cash or by negotiable note[15] in gross income for the year in which such payments were received. If these payments are includible in the year of receipt because their allocation to a later year does not clearly reflect income, the contract installments are likewise includible in gross income, as the United States now claims, in the year they become due and payable. For an accrual basis taxpayer "it is the right to receive and not the actual receipt that determines the inclusion of the amount in gross income," Spring City Co. v. Commissioner, 292 U.S. 182, 184 (1934); Commissioner v. Hansen, 360 U.S. 446 (1959), and here the right to receive these installments had become fixed at least at the time they were due and payable. . . .

Mr. Justice STEWART, with whom Mr. Justice DOUGLAS, Mr. Justice HARLAN, and Mr. Justice GOLDBERG join, dissenting.

[T]his case is but the most recent episode in a protracted dispute concerning the proper income tax treatment of amounts received as advances for services to be performed in a subsequent year by a taxpayer who is on an accrual rather than a cash basis. The Government has consistently argued that such amounts are taxable in the year of receipt, relying upon two alternative arguments: It has claimed that deferral of such payments would violate the "annual accounting" principle which requires that income not be postponed from one year to the next to reflect the long-term economic result of a transaction. Alternatively, the Government has argued that advance payments must be reported as income in the year of receipt under the "claim-of-right doctrine," which requires otherwise reportable income, held under a claim of right without restriction as to use, to be reported when received despite the fact that the taxpayer's claim to the funds may be disputed.

[N]either of these doctrines has any relevance to the question whether any reportable income at all has been derived when payments are received in advance of performance by an accrual-basis taxpayer. The most elementary principles of accrual accounting require that advances be considered reportable income only in the year they are earned by the taxpayer's rendition of the services for which the payments were made. The Government's theories would force upon an accrual-basis taxpayer a cash basis for advance payments in disregard of the federal statute

---

15. Negotiable notes are regarded as the equivalent of cash receipts, to the extent of their fair market value, for the purposes of recognition of income.

which explicitly authorizes income tax returns to be based upon sound accrual accounting methods.

Apparently the Court agrees that neither the annual accounting requirement nor the claim-of-right doctrine has any relevance or applicability to the question involved in this case. For the Court does not base its decision on either theory, but rather, as in two previous cases, upon the ground that the system of accrual accounting used by these particular taxpayers does not "clearly reflect income" in accord with the statutory command. This result is said to be compelled both by a consideration of legislative history and by an analysis of the particular accounting system which these taxpayers employed.

. . . [T]o rely on the repeal of §452 . . . as indicating congressional disapproval of accrual accounting principles is conspicuously to disregard clear evidence of legislative intent. The Secretary of the Treasury, who proposed the repeal . . . made explicitly clear that no inference of disapproval of accrual accounting principles was to be drawn from the repeal of the sections. So did the Senate Report. The repeal of these sections was occasioned solely by the fear of temporary revenue losses which would result from the taking of "double deductions" during the year of transition by taxpayers who had not previously maintained their books on an accrual basis.

The Court's decision can be justified, then, only upon the basis that the system of accrual accounting used by the taxpayers in this case did not "clearly reflect income" in accordance with the command of §446(b). In the *Automobile Club of Michigan* case the taxpayer allocated yearly dues ratably over 12 months, so that only a portion of the dues received during any fiscal year was reported as income for that year. In the absence of any proof that services demanded by the Automobile Club members were distributed in the same proportion over the year, the Court held that the system used by the taxpayer did not clearly reflect income. In the *American Automobile Association* case the taxpayer offered statistical proof to show that its proration of dues reasonably matched the proportion of its yearly costs incurred each month in rendering services attributable to those dues. The Court discounted the validity of this statistical evidence because the amount and timing of the services demanded were wholly within the control of the individual members of the Association, and the Court thought that the Association could not, therefore, estimate with accuracy the costs attributable to each individual member's demands.

In the present case the difficulties which the Court perceived *in Automobile Club of Michigan* and *American Automobile Association* have been entirely eliminated in the accounting system which these taxpayers have consistently employed. The records kept on individual students accurately measured the amount of services rendered — and therefore the costs incurred by the taxpayer — under each individual contract during each taxable year. . . .

It seems to me that this decision, the third of a trilogy of cases purportedly decided on their own peculiar facts, in truth completes the mutilation of a basic element of the accrual method of reporting income — a method which has been explicitly approved by Congress for almost half a century.

Notes and Questions

1. *The Supreme Court's trilogy and the landlord with prepaid rent.* In the "trilogy of cases" referred to by Justice Stewart (*Automobile Club of Michigan*, *American Automobile Association*, and *Schlude*), the Supreme Court in effect redefined

the accrual method *with respect to income items* as the earlier-of-cash-or-accrual method. Applying this approach to landlords, Reg. §1.61-8(b) provides that "gross income includes advance rentals, which must be included in income for the year of receipt regardless of the period covered or the method of accounting employed by the taxpayer."

2. *The quality of mercy, somewhat strained.* The IRS has not, however, exploited its Supreme Court victories to the fullest. It has issued a revenue procedure providing that an accrual method taxpayer who receives a payment in Year 1 for services to be performed by the taxpayer in one or more future years may defer inclusion of the payment until Year 2 (but not beyond Year 2, even if the performance of services by the taxpayer is not completed in Year 2). Rev. Proc. 2004-34, 2004-1 C.B. 991. The revenue procedure applies to several other categories of advance payments in addition to advance payments for services, including payments for the use of intellectual property and for memberships in organizations. However, it does not generally apply to prepaid rent, so it would be of no use to Marty's landlord from Problem 4 in this chapter.

3. Later Events Inconsistent with Accruals

Suppose an accrual method taxpayer properly accrues an item of deduction or income in one year, and in a later year it becomes clear that the taxpayer will never have to pay the expense for which a deduction was previously allowed, or will never receive the payment accrual of which was previously required. Situations of this sort are explored in the following problems.

Problem 5.   X Corporation, an accrual method taxpayer, receives a $10,000 utility bill on December 20, 2010, for electricity it used from November 16 to December 15. X does not pay the bill before its tax year ends on December 31, but it nevertheless accrues and deducts the $10,000 expense on its income tax return for 2010. Early in 2011, before X has paid the bill, the state public utility commission determines that the electric company had charged impermissibly high rates in late 2010, and the commission orders the electric company to reduce its customers' bills, or to pay refunds in the case of bills already paid. X's unpaid bill is reduced to $9,000, and X pays the $9,000 in 2011. Do these events have any tax consequences for X in 2011? (Assume that at the end of 2010 X did not know and could not have known that its bill would later be reduced.) Hint: The answer may be lurking in section C of Chapter 2.

Problem 6.   On December 22, 2010, X Corporation billed a customer $5,000 for services performed by X during 2010. Although the customer had not paid the bill by the end of 2010, as an accrual method taxpayer X included the $5,000 in income on its tax return for 2010. The customer declared bankruptcy early in 2011, and it soon became clear X would never be paid a penny of the $5,000. What are the 2011 tax consequences (if any) for X of these events? *See* §166.

Problem 7.   The facts are the same as in Problem 6, except X is a cash method taxpayer. Do the events described in Problem 6 have any tax consequences for X in 2011 in that case? Hint: It is possible to figure this out either by carefully reading §166, or by thinking through the tax logic of the situation.

Cell

================

INVENTORIES AND MANDATORY ACCRUAL ACCOUNTING

================

Jim Turin & Sons, Inc. v. Commissioner

Rev. Proc. 2002-28

================

JIM TURIN & SONS, INC. v. COMMISSIONER
219 F.3d 1103 (9th Cir. 2000)

TASHIMA, Circuit Judge: The Commissioner of Internal Revenue ("Commissioner") appeals the Tax Court's decision that he abused his discretion in requiring Jim Turin & Sons, Inc. ("taxpayer"), to use the accrual method of accounting to compute its federal taxes for the tax years at issue. In particular, the Commissioner contests the Tax Court's finding that emulsified asphalt is not "merchandise," as that term is used in 26 C.F.R. §1.471-1. . . .

Taxpayer is a corporation that provides paving services. Taxpayer purchases its asphalt from a sister manufacturing corporation. When bidding on a contract, taxpayer prices the asphalt at its cost. The sister company ships the asphalt just hours before a paving job. Because of the physical properties of emulsified asphalt, taxpayer must use it within several hours of shipment, otherwise it hardens and becomes useless. Once a job is completed, taxpayer is generally paid within 10 to 30 days of billing.

For the tax years at issue, taxpayer used a cash method of accounting for federal tax purposes, taking deductions for the cost of the asphalt for a job immediately upon its payment to the sister corporation and recognizing income for a job when it received payment. The Commissioner determined that asphalt was "merchandise," under Treas. Reg. §1.471-1, such that taxpayer had inventories and thus was required to use the accrual method of accounting. The accrual method would require the taxpayer to recognize income upon the completion of a job, as opposed to when it received payment for a job.

The Tax Court concluded that the Commissioner abused his discretion in so requiring. . . .

The Commissioner timely appealed.

The Supreme Court has held that the Commissioner's decision to require the use of a particular method of inventory accounting is a discretionary one and that "his interpretation of the statute's . . . standard 'should not be interfered with unless clearly unlawful.'" Thor Power Tool Co. v. Commissioner, 439 U.S. 522, 532 (1979) (quoting Lucas v. American Code Co., 280 U.S. 445,449 (1930)). "The Commissioner's disallowance of an inventory accounting method is not to be set aside unless shown to be 'plainly arbitrary.'" 439 U.S. at 532-33 (quoting Lucas v. Structural Steel Co., 281 U.S. 264, 271 (1930)). Thus, we independently review for abuse of discretion, and our task is to determine whether the Commissioner's decision to require taxpayer to use the accrual method of accounting is clearly unlawful or plainly arbitrary.

Under Treas. Reg. §1.471-1, a taxpayer must use inventories and the accrual method of accounting[1] when the "production, purchase or sale of merchandise is an income-producing factor" in order to "reflect taxable income correctly." The rationale behind §1.471-1, and the underlying statute, I.R.C. §471, is straightforward. If a taxpayer held sizable inventories for resale, under a cash method, the taxpayer could defer income by purchasing all of its goods at the end of one year and taking deductions for the purchase at that time, then selling the goods in subsequent years without recognizing income until its receipts of proceeds from the sales. For example, in Knight-Ridder Newspapers, Inc. v. United States, 743 F.2d 781 (11th Cir. 1984), the court stated that:

> According to accounting wisdom, the income realized from the sale of merchandise is most clearly measured by matching the cost of that merchandise with the revenue derived from its sale. In order to achieve such a matching of revenue and cost, it is necessary to keep an inventory account reflecting the costs of merchandise, raw materials, and manufacturing expenses. These costs are not deducted immediately when paid but are deferred until the year when the resulting merchandise is sold.
>
> To make the matching complete, the taxpayer must report income on the accrual method. That method helps to ensure that income from the sale (like the inventory costs) is reflected in the year of the sale. For example, if the sale is made on credit, the accrual method nevertheless treats the income as accrued and reflects it when the sale occurs. . . .
>
> By contrast, the primal cash method is unable to achieve such a mystical joinder of inventory deductions and credit sale income. To be sure, the cash method could theoretically operate in tandem with inventories. The beast could conceivably close its eyes to deductions until the year of the sale. It could never learn, however, to prophesy future cash payments. If there were a credit sale, the beast could not grasp income and deductions simultaneously in its rugged paw. The goal of matching costs and revenues would fail.

Id. at 789 (footnotes and internal citations omitted). . . .

A paving company that lays asphalt immediately upon purchase cannot delay income or accelerate deductions by inventorying its asphalt, because there is no inventory that can be purchased late in one tax year and held over to the next. Thus, given the rationale of §1.471-1, we agree with the Tax Court that asphalt is not merchandise, and that taxpayer should not have been required to use the accrual method because §1.471-1 does not apply.

The Commissioner's argument that taxpayer failed to adopt an accounting method that clearly reflected income is wholly unrelated to the inventory issues of §1.471-1. Rather, the disparity in taxable income calculated by the Commissioner relating to the paving jobs stems from the mismatch of deductions and income due to the fact that taxpayer had outstanding accounts receivable at the end of each tax year that were not immediately recognized under the cash method of

---

1. Under Treas. Reg. §1.446-1(c)(2)(i), a taxpayer who is required to use inventories must also use the accrual method of income reporting.

accounting. These accounts receivable did not stem from taxpayer's misuse of inventories, but were merely run-of-the-mill debts for collection. The failure of a taxpayer to include accounts receivable in taxable income is not a sufficient basis for the Commissioner to require the use of the accrual method. . . . We thus agree with the Tax Court that the Commissioner abused his discretion in requiring taxpayer to adopt the accrual method.

The Tax Court properly relied upon its earlier decision in Galedrige [v. Commissioner, 1997 T.C. Memo. 240], where it held that "the peculiar physical properties of emulsified asphalt make it impossible" for the taxpayer to hold it in inventory. On this basis, the Tax Court held that the paving company was not required to use an accrual method with respect to the asphalt. Recently, in RACMP Enters., Inc. v. Commissioner, 114 T.C. 211 (2000) (en banc), the Tax Court reaffirmed *Galedrige* in deciding that a contractor who poured cement was not subject to the requirements of §1.471-1, because mixed cement, like asphalt, changes its physical state rapidly so as quickly to become useless.

Galedrige and *RACMP Enterprises* represent the sound principle that §1.471-1 does not apply where the item in question cannot be warehoused in inventory, especially where traditional service providers are involved. . . .

The Commissioner's attempt to force asphalt into the cubby-hole of "merchandise" disregards the purpose of §1.471-1. The Commissioner argues that the transfer of title from the manufacturer of asphalt to the taxpayer is determinative, as opposed to whether the asphalt has the "physical properties necessary for it to be held for sales 'at the end of the day.'" The Commissioner further contends that possessing title for an instant is sufficient to require a taxpayer to inventory its goods, so long as the goods are acquired and held for sale. The Commissioner cites a number of Tax Court cases in support of his contentions; however, all of them are distinguishable. . . .

None of the cases on which the Commissioner relies is on point because all involved goods that were or could be stored in inventory. They have no application to the case at bench because, to repeat, taxpayer is physically unable to manipulate the matching or non-matching of deductions and income. . . .

Because asphalt cannot be stored, it is not susceptible to being inventoried. We thus agree with the Tax Court that asphalt is not "merchandise" within the scope of Treas. Reg. §1.471-1. The Commissioner therefore abused his discretion in requiring taxpayer to use the accrual method of accounting.

Notes and Questions

1. *Corporations and accrual accounting.* Even apart from the accrual accounting mandate for businesses that produce or sell "merchandise," most *corporations* are required by §448 to use the accrual method. The *Turin* opinion does not explain why the taxpayer was not subject to §448, but there are two possibilities. First, the taxpayer may have been an "S corporation," to which §448 does not apply. An S corporation is a small business corporation (as defined by statute) that does not pay tax on its income because its shareholders have agreed to be taxed on their pro rata shares of corporate income, including earnings retained by the corporation. *See* §§1361 et seq. Second, the taxpayer may have qualified for the §448 exemption for

corporations with annual gross receipts of $5 million or less. "Qualified personal service corporations" are also exempt from the accrual method requirement of §448, but this exemption applies only to corporations "substantially all of the activities of which involve the performance of services in the fields of health, law, engineering, architecture, accounting, educational services, performing arts, or consulting." §448(d)(2)(A).

2. *Policy concerns.* What is the policy justification for requiring businesses with inventories to use the accrual method? According to *Turin,* accrual accounting is needed to prevent taxpayers with inventories from deferring income by immediately deducting large year-end purchases of inventory. If that is the only concern, might there be a less draconian solution? Why not allow a taxpayer with an inventory to use the cash method for reporting income from sales, so long as the taxpayer does not deduct the cost of inventory items until the year the taxpayer actually provides the items to a customer?[2] The answer, simply enough, is that the concern noted by the *Turin* court is *not* the only concern. Even without taxpayer manipulation, and even if a deduction is not allowed until the year the taxpayer provides an inventory item to a customer, the use of the cash method by a business with inventories will produce a timing mismatch whenever the business provides an inventory item to a customer in one year and is not paid until the next year. Under the cash method, the inventory cost would be deducted in the first year, but the related income would be deferred until the following year. On the other hand, perhaps such mismatches are tolerable in the name of simplification, in the case of smaller businesses. As the following revenue procedure shows, the IRS has come around to this point of view, for many small and medium-sized businesses.

REV. PROC. 2002-28
2002-1 C.B. 815

SECTION 1. PURPOSE

In order to reduce the administrative and tax compliance burdens on certain small business taxpayers and to minimize disputes between the Internal Revenue Service and small business taxpayers regarding the requirement to use an accrual method of accounting (accrual method) under §446 of the Internal Revenue Code because of the requirement to account for inventories under §471, this revenue procedure provides that the Commissioner of Internal Revenue will exercise his discretion to except a qualifying small business taxpayer (as defined in section 5.01 of this revenue procedure) from the requirements to use an accrual method of accounting under §446 and to account for inventories under §471. This revenue procedure also provides the procedures by which a qualifying small business taxpayer may obtain automatic consent to change to the cash receipts and disbursements method of accounting (cash method) and/or to a method of accounting for

2. As the Eleventh Circuit noted in the passage from *Knight-Ridder* quoted in *Turin,* "The [cash method] beast could conceivably close its eyes to deductions until the year of sale."

inventoriable items as materials and supplies that are not incidental under §1.162-3 of the Income Tax Regulations.

SECTION 2. BACKGROUND

.01   Section 446(a) provides that taxable income must be determined under the method of accounting on the basis of which the taxpayer regularly computes its income in keeping its books.

.02   Section 446(c) generally allows a taxpayer to select the method of accounting it will use to compute its taxable income. A taxpayer is entitled to adopt any one of the permissible methods for each separate trade or business, including the cash method or an accrual method, subject to certain restrictions. For example, §446(b) provides that the selected method must clearly reflect income. In addition, §1.446-1(c)(2)(i) requires that a taxpayer use an accrual method with regard to purchases and sales of merchandise whenever §471 requires the taxpayer to account for inventories, unless otherwise authorized by the Commissioner under §1.446-1(c)(2)(ii). Under §1.446-1(c)(2)(ii), the Commissioner has the authority to permit a taxpayer to use a method of accounting that clearly reflects income even though the method is not specifically authorized by the regulations.

.03   Section 447 generally requires the taxable income from farming of a C corporation engaged in the trade or business of farming . . . to be determined using an accrual method, unless the C corporation meets the $1,000,000 ($25,000,000 for family corporations) gross receipts test.

.04   Section 448 generally prohibits the use of the cash method by a C corporation (other than a farming business and a qualified personal service corporation) . . . unless the C corporation . . . meets a $5,000,000 gross receipts test. Section 448 also prohibits tax shelters from using the cash method.

.05   The cash method generally requires an item of income to be included in income when actually or constructively received and permits a deduction for an expense when paid. Section 1.446-1(c)(1)(i). Other provisions of the Code or regulations applicable to cash method taxpayers may change these general rules, including, for example, §263 (requiring the capitalization of expenses paid out for a new building or for permanent improvements or betterments made to increase the value of any property or estate, or for restoring property or making good the exhaustion of property for which an allowance is or has been made); [and] §263A (requiring capitalization of direct and allocable indirect costs of real or tangible personal property produced by a taxpayer or real or personal property that is acquired by a taxpayer for resale). . . .

.06   Section 471 provides that whenever, in the opinion of the Secretary, the use of inventories is necessary to clearly determine the income of the taxpayer, inventories must be taken by the taxpayer. Section 1.471-1 generally requires a taxpayer to account for inventories when the production, purchase, or sale of merchandise is an income-producing factor in the taxpayer's business.

.07   Section 1.162-3 requires taxpayers carrying materials and supplies (other than incidental materials and supplies) on hand to deduct the cost of materials and supplies only in the amount that they are actually consumed and used in operations during the taxable year. In the case of incidental materials and supplies on hand for which no record of consumption is kept or of which physical inventories at the beginning and end of the year are not taken, taxpayers may include in their expenses and deduct from gross income the total cost of such incidental supplies and materials as were purchased during the taxable year for which the return is made, provided the taxable income is clearly reflected by this method.

.08   Section 263A generally requires direct costs and an allowable portion of indirect costs of certain property produced or acquired for resale by a taxpayer to be included in inventory costs, in the case of property that is inventory, or to be capitalized, in the case of other property. However, resellers with gross receipts of $10,000,000 or less are not required to capitalize costs under §263A, and certain producers with $200,000 or less of indirect costs are not required to capitalize certain costs under §263A. *See* §§263A(b)(2)(B) and 1.263A-2(b)(3)(iv).

.09   Sections 446(e) and 1.446-1(e) state that, except as otherwise provided, a taxpayer must secure the consent of the Commissioner before changing a method of accounting for federal income tax purposes. . . .

SECTION 3. SCOPE

.01   Applicability. This revenue procedure applies to a qualifying small business taxpayer as defined in section 5.01.

.02   Taxpayers Not within the Scope of this Revenue Procedure. Notwithstanding section 3.01 of this revenue procedure, this revenue procedure does not apply to a farming business . . . of a qualifying small business taxpayer. . . . A taxpayer engaged in the trade or business of farming generally is allowed to use the cash method for any farming business, unless the taxpayer is required to use an accrual method under §447 or is prohibited from using the cash method under §448.

SECTION 4. QUALIFYING SMALL BUSINESS TAXPAYER EXCEPTION

.01   Pursuant to his discretion under §§446 and 471, and to simplify the record keeping requirements of a qualifying small business taxpayer, the Commissioner, as a matter of administrative convenience, will allow a qualifying small business taxpayer to use the cash method as described in this revenue procedure for a trade or business described in this section 4.01 (eligible trade or business).

(1) A qualifying small business taxpayer may use the cash method as described in this revenue procedure for all of its trades or businesses if the taxpayer satisfies any one of the following three tests. . . .

(a) The taxpayer reasonably determines that its principal business activity (as defined in section 5.04, below) is described in a North American Industry Classification System ("NAICS") code other than one of the ineligible codes listed below. The ineligible NAICS codes are as follows:

(i) mining activities within the meaning of NAICS codes 211 and 212;

(ii) manufacturing within the meaning of NAICS codes 31-33;

(iii) wholesale trade within the meaning of NAICS code 42;

(iv) retail trade within the meaning of NAICS codes 44 and 45; and,

(v) information industries within the meaning of NAICS codes 5111 and 5122. . . .

(b) Notwithstanding that a taxpayer's principal business activity is described in one of the ineligible NAICS codes listed above in section 4.01(1)(a), the taxpayer reasonably determines that its principal business activity is the provision of services, including the provision of property incident to those services.

    (c) Notwithstanding that a taxpayer's principal business activity is described in one of the ineligible NAICS codes listed above in section 4.01(1)(a), the taxpayer reasonably determines that its principal business activity is the fabrication or modification of tangible personal property upon demand in accordance with customer design or specifications. . . .

.02   A taxpayer who satisfies the qualifying small business taxpayer exception described in section 4.01 and chooses not to use an overall accrual method with inventories being accounted for under §471 has the following three options for an eligible trade or business under this revenue procedure:

    (1) The taxpayer can use the overall cash method and account for inventories under §471; . . .

    (3) The taxpayer can use the overall cash method and account for inventoriable items in the same manner as materials and supplies that are not incidental under §1.162-3 (*see* sections 4.04 and 4.05 below).

.03   Notwithstanding §1001 and the regulations thereunder, qualifying small business taxpayers that use the cash method for an eligible trade or business under section 4.01 of this revenue procedure shall include amounts attributable to "open accounts receivable" (as defined in section 5.10) in income as such amounts are actually or constructively received. . . .

.04   Qualifying small business taxpayers that are permitted to use the cash method for an eligible trade or business under section 4.01 of this revenue procedure and that do not want to account for inventories under §471 must treat all inventoriable items in such trade or business in the same manner as materials and supplies that are not incidental under §1.162-3. For purposes of this revenue procedure, taxpayers are not required to apply §263A to inventoriable items that are treated as materials and supplies that are not incidental. . . .

.05   Under §1.162-3, materials and supplies that are not incidental are deductible only in the year in which they are actually consumed and used in the taxpayer's business. For purposes of this revenue procedure, inventoriable items that are treated as materials and supplies that are not incidental are consumed and used in the year the qualifying small business taxpayer provides the items to a customer. Thus, the cost of such inventoriable items are deductible only in that year, or in the year in which the taxpayer actually pays for the goods, whichever is later. A qualifying small business taxpayer may determine the amount of the allowable deduction for non-incidental materials and supplies by using either a specific identification method, a first in, first out (FIFO) method, or an average cost method, provided that method is used consistently. *See* §1.471-2(d). A taxpayer may not use the last in, first out (LIFO) method described in §472 and the regulations thereunder to determine the amount of the allowable deduction for non-incidental materials and supplies. . . .

SECTION 5. DEFINITIONS

.01   Qualifying Small Business Taxpayer. A qualifying small business taxpayer is any taxpayer with "average annual gross receipts" of $10,000,000 or less that is not prohibited from using the cash method under §448.

.02   Average Annual Gross Receipts. A taxpayer has average annual gross receipts of $10,000,000 or less if, for each prior taxable year ending on or after December 31, 2000, the taxpayer's average annual gross receipts for the three taxable-year period ending with the applicable prior taxable year do not exceed $10,000,000. If a taxpayer has not been in existence for three prior taxable years, the taxpayer must determine its average annual gross receipts for the number of years (including short taxable years) that the taxpayer has been in existence. . . .

.09   Inventoriable Item Defined. An inventoriable item is any item either purchased for resale to customers or used as a raw material in producing finished goods.

.10   Open Accounts Receivable Defined. For purposes of this revenue procedure, open accounts receivable is defined as any receivable due in full in 120 days or less.

SECTION 6. EXAMPLES . . .

Example 10 — Taxpayer Does Not Satisfy the NAICS Code Exception in Section 4.01(1)(a), the Service Exception in Section 4.01(1)(b), or the Custom Manufacturing Exception in Section 4.01(1)(c). Taxpayer is a sofa manufacturer that only produces sofas upon receipt of a customer order. Customers are allowed to pick among 150 different fabrics offered by the Taxpayer or to provide their own fabric, which the Taxpayer will use to finish the customer's sofa. Taxpayer's principal business activity is described in the ineligible NAICS code 33. Taxpayer does not provide sofas incident to the performance of services for purposes of section 4.01(1)(b). Rather, Taxpayer performs certain services (upholstering) incident to the sale of sofas. Taxpayer also does not fabricate or modify tangible personal property for purposes of section 4.01(1)(c) because customers merely choose among pre-selected options offered by Taxpayer and Taxpayer only makes minor modifications to the basic design of its sofa. Taxpayer may not use the cash method under this revenue procedure. . . .

Example 14 — Application of Accounts Receivable 120-Day Rule in Section 4.03. Taxpayer is eligible to use the cash method under this revenue procedure, Taxpayer chooses to use the cash method and to account for inventoriable items as non-incidental materials and supplies under §1.162-3. In December 2001, Taxpayer transfers property to a customer in exchange for an open accounts receivable (due in full in 120 days or less). In February 2002, the customer satisfies the accounts receivable when it pays cash to Taxpayer. As provided by section 4.03 of this revenue procedure, Taxpayer would not include any amount attributable to the accounts receivable in income in 2001. Rather, Taxpayer would include the full amount of the accounts receivable in income in 2002 when it actually receives the cash payment from the customer.

Example 15 — Timing of Deduction for Inventoriable Items Treated as Non-Incidental Materials and Supplies under §1.162-3-Construction. Taxpayer is a roofing contractor that is eligible to use the cash method under this revenue procedure. Taxpayer chooses to use the cash method and to account for inventoriable items as non-incidental materials and supplies under §1.162-3. Taxpayer enters into a contract with a homeowner in December 2001 to replace the homeowner's roof. Taxpayer purchases roofing shingles from a local supplier and has them delivered to the homeowner's residence. Taxpayer pays the supplier $5,000 for the shingles upon their delivery later that month. Taxpayer replaces the homeowner's roof in December 2001, and gives the homeowner a bill for $15,000 at that time. Taxpayer receives a check from the homeowner in January 2002. The shingles are non-incidental materials and supplies. The cost of the shingles is deductible in the year Taxpayer uses and consumes the shingles or actually pays for the shingles, whichever is later. In this case, Taxpayer both pays for the shingles and uses the shingles (by providing the shingles to the customer in connection with the performance of roofing services) in 2001. Thus, Taxpayer deducts the $5,000 cost of the shingles on its 2001 federal income tax return. Taxpayer includes the $15,000 in income in 2002 when it receives the check from the homeowner.

Example 16 — Timing of Deduction for Inventoriable Items Treated as Non-Incidental Materials and Supplies under §1.162-3-Construction. Same as in Example 15, except that Taxpayer does not replace the roof until January 2002 and is not paid until March 2002. Because the shingles are not used until 2002, their cost can only be deducted on Taxpayer's 2002 federal income tax return notwithstanding that Taxpayer paid for the shingles in 2001. Thus, on its 2002 return, Taxpayer must report $15,000 of income and $5,000 of deductions. . . .

SECTION 9. EFFECTIVE DATE

This revenue procedure is effective for taxable years ending on or after December 31, 2001. However, the Service will not challenge a taxpayer's use of the cash method under §446 or a taxpayer's failure to account for inventories under §471 for a trade or business in an earlier year if the taxpayer, for that year, would have been a qualifying small business taxpayer as described in section 5.01 of this revenue procedure and would have been eligible to use the cash method in such year under section 4 of this revenue procedure if this revenue procedure had been applicable to that taxable year.

Notes and Questions

1. *More relief.* Rev. Proc. 2001-10, 2000-1 C.B. 272, provides the same relief from the rigors of inventory accounting and the accrual method for a taxpayer with average annual gross receipts of $1 million or less, regardless of the nature of the taxpayer's business. Thus, a retailer with average annual gross receipts of $800,000 would not qualify for relief under Rev. Proc. 2002-28, but would qualify under Rev. Proc. 2001-10. Conversely, a contractor with average annual gross receipts of $5 million would not qualify under Rev. Proc. 2001-10, but would qualify under Rev. Proc. 2002-28.

2. *Taxpayer manipulation.* Is the concern about taxpayer manipulation identified in *Turin* (and discussed in Note 2 following *Turin*) adequately dealt with in the revenue procedure by the requirement that even a cash method taxpayer must "account for inventoriable items in the same manner as materials and supplies that are not incidental under [Reg.] §1.162-3"?

3. *Section 448.* Rev. Proc. 2002-28 does not override §448. Thus, a corporation might have gross receipts of $10 million or less, in a trade or business to which the revenue procedure applies, and still be unable to use the cash method because of §448. Section 448 is not generally a problem, however, for sole proprietors, partnerships, and S corporations, or for any corporation with gross receipts of $5 million or less.

Chapter 8

TAX PREFERENCES, TAX SHELTERS, AND THE ALTERNATIVE MINIMUM TAX

This chapter explores the concepts of tax preferences and tax shelters. By *tax preference*, we mean any exclusion or deduction that results in taxable income understating a taxpayer's true economic income. The §103 exclusion of municipal bond interest income is an example (one of many) of an exclusion preference; the allowance of faster-than-economic cost recovery under §168 is an example (again, one of many) of a deduction preference. By *tax shelter* we mean an investment that produces artificial tax losses — that is, tax losses in excess of actual economic losses (if any), which can be used to eliminate the tax on income from sources unrelated to the tax shelter investment. Most tax shelter investments are debt-financed; the artificial loss is created by the combination of a tax preference (for example, accelerated cost recovery system (ACRS) deductions under §168) and an interest expense deduction. Over the decades Congress, the IRS, and the courts have all acted to restrict the ability of taxpayers to create tax shelters, but their efforts have never been completely successful.

The first part of this chapter considers, as an example of a tax preference, the §103 exclusion for municipal bond interest income. It explains some of the economic effects of the exclusion, and how the exclusion might be used as the basis for a debt-financed tax shelter investment. The focus on §103, rather than some other tax preference, is for pedagogical reasons. The simplicity of the basic exclusion, and the existence of an investment alternative (corporate bonds) that is nearly identical except for the lack of an exclusion, make §103 an especially good vehicle for illustrating some fundamental aspects of tax preferences and tax shelters. (If §103 did not exist, tax professors might have to invent it.) As we explain below, however, Congress long ago enacted legislation that makes it impossible (more or less) to use §103 as the foundation of a tax shelter. After consideration of §103, we turn to the somewhat messier real world examples of tax shelters based on other preferences, and to the responses — legislative, administrative, and judicial — to those shelters.

A. TAX PREFERENCES AND IMPLICIT TAXES: THE CASE OF MUNICIPAL BONDS

1. *The Economics of the Exclusion*

Section 103(a) provides that gross income does not include the interest on a bond issued by a state or local government (so-called municipal bonds). A taxpayer who wants to buy bonds has a choice. He can invest in corporate bonds (or debt of the federal government) and receive taxable interest, or he can invest in municipal bonds and receive tax-exempt interest.

To explore the possible economic effects of the tax exemption for municipal bond interest, imagine an income tax system with three rate brackets, of 10 percent, 20 percent, and 30 percent. Suppose that the market interest rate on corporate bonds (paying taxable interest) is currently 10 percent. The significance to a taxpayer of §103 depends, of course, on the taxpayer's marginal tax rate, but it also depends on the relationship between the 10 percent interest rate on taxable bonds and the interest rate on tax-exempt bonds.[1] At one extreme, there might be no difference — municipal bonds might pay the same 10 percent interest rate as taxable bonds. In that case, §103 would have accomplished nothing except a windfall for taxpayers who buy municipal bonds. A taxpayer in the 30 percent bracket, for example, would be able to achieve only a 7 percent after-tax rate of return if he invested $100 in a corporate bond,[2] but he could increase his after-tax return to 10 percent simply by investing his $100 in a municipal bond instead. It would be hard to justify the §103 exemption if it benefited high income investors, but did nothing to help state and local governments.

The story in the previous paragraph is not realistic, however. Investors in the 30 percent bracket will accept a lower pre-tax interest rate on municipal bonds, because of the tax advantage. If a corporate bond and a municipal bond are identical in terms of risk and maturity, a 30 percent bracket investor should be indifferent between a corporate bond paying 10 percent interest and a municipal bond paying only 7 percent interest. With either investment, the investor's after-tax rate of return is 7 percent. If demand for tax-favored municipal bonds among top-bracket taxpayers drives the interest rate on municipal bonds down to 7 percent, then it becomes much easier to justify §103. In that case, the top-bracket investors are only the *nominal* beneficiaries of the exclusion. In fact, they have to pay for their tax break by accepting a lower pre-tax rate of return on their investment. The *real* beneficiaries of §103 are then state and local governments, which are able to borrow at 7 percent instead of at 10 percent. If this is the way the market responds to the existence of §103, then the exemption is an efficient subsidy, in the sense that the federal government's revenue loss is captured by state and local governments in the form of reduced borrowing costs, rather than by high bracket investors in the form of higher after-tax returns than they could earn on other investments.

1. The analysis in the text assumes that municipal bonds and corporate bonds are identical investments in terms of risk and time to maturity; the only differences are the differing tax treatments of the interest income and (perhaps) differing interest rates attributable to the differing tax treatments.
2. $10 interest income minus $3 tax leaves a $7 after-tax return on a $100 investment.

When a top-bracket taxpayer invests $100 in a municipal bond paying 7 percent, instead of in a taxable bond paying 10 percent, the federal government loses $3 of tax revenue, the borrowing government enjoys a $3 reduction in borrowing costs, and the taxpayer reaps no windfall. The reduced pre-tax rate of return the taxpayer must accept in order to obtain the tax preference is sometimes referred to as an *implicit tax,* or a *putative tax.* In the example, the taxpayer who buys the municipal bond paying 7 percent interest has replaced a 30 percent explicit tax with a 30 percent implicit tax. The reason the taxpayer enjoys no windfall, of course, is that the implicit tax rate is as high as the explicit tax rate.

The sort of efficiency described above might be labeled "delivery efficiency." Delivery efficiency simply means that the federal government's revenue loss from a subsidy ends up in the pockets of the intended beneficiary of the subsidy (in this case, the borrowing state or local government), rather than in the pockets of some lucky third party (in this case, the municipal bond investor). Even if a particular tax subsidy features perfect delivery efficiency, there may be good reasons to object to it. Section 103, in particular, can be criticized as being inefficient in a different sense. If the prevailing taxable interest rate in the economy is 10 percent, then a corporation would never make an investment with an expected rate of return of 9 percent. (The corporation would be facing a pre-tax loss of 1 percent per year if the corporation borrowed to make the investment, and if the corporation is considering making the investment with its own money it would be better off lending its money at 10 percent.) By contrast, a state or local government faced with a borrowing cost of only 7 percent would be willing to borrow to make an investment with an expected return of, say, 8 percent. The allocation of resources in society is not efficient if corporations are turning down 9 percent investment opportunities while local governments are happy to invest at 8 percent.

Another plausible objection to §103 is that it is not a *general* federal subsidy for state and local governments; instead it subsidizes only *borrowing* by state and local governments. Why should the federal government provide a generous subsidy for extravagant debt-financed spending by local governments, but not provide a subsidy for more frugal local governments that pay as they go? A possible response is that the nonborrowing government may be the indirect beneficiary of the §164 deduction for state and local taxes (on the theory that the federal deductibility of state and local income and property taxes makes it possible for states to impose higher taxes than their residents would be willing to accept without the deduction). The response is not entirely convincing, however, since many state and local taxes are *not* deductible under §164—most notably, sales taxes and all taxes paid by non-itemizers.

One might also object that, if the federal government is going to subsidize borrowing by state and local governments, it ought to pay some attention to whether the borrowing is for a purpose worthy of subsidy. Actually, Congress has attempted to build such a requirement into §103. Section 103(b)(1) denies the exemption for interest on "[a]ny private activity bond which is not a qualified bond." This limits the extent to which a state or local government can share its ability to borrow on a tax-favored basis with private businesses within its jurisdiction. In addition, §103(b)(2) denies the exemption for interest on "[a]ny arbitrage bond." This prevents a state or local government from borrowing at 7 percent, and then turning around and investing the borrowed funds in corporate bonds paying 10 percent.

Earlier we imagined that §103 might feature perfect delivery efficiency, with 30 percent bracket taxpayers having only the choice between a 30 percent explicit tax on corporate bond interest and a 30 percent implicit tax on municipal bond interest. But suppose the appetite of state and local governments for borrowed funds is so voracious that there are not enough taxpayers in the 30 percent bracket to buy all the bonds they want to issue.[3] In that case, the borrowing governments would have to offer an interest rate high enough to attract taxpayers in the 20 percent bracket. Those taxpayers can always earn an after-tax return of 8 percent by investing in corporate bonds paying 10 percent, so they will not be interested in municipal bonds paying anything less than 8 percent. There is no way to price-discriminate among different buyers of municipal bonds (in contrast with different buyers of airline tickets). If state and local governments must pay 8 percent interest to attract investors in the 20 percent bracket, then they must also pay 8 percent interest to investors in the 30 percent bracket. But in that case, the 30 percent bracket taxpayer is faced with a choice between corporate bonds paying interest subject to a 30 percent explicit tax rate, and municipal bonds paying interest subject to an implicit tax of only 20 percent. Now §103 does not feature delivery efficiency. If a 30 percent bracket taxpayer invests $100 in a municipal bond paying 8 percent tax-exempt interest, instead of in a corporate bond paying 10 percent taxable interest, the federal government loses $3 of tax revenue, the borrowing local government enjoys a $2 reduction in borrowing cost, and the taxpayer captures a $1 windfall.

If the governmental appetite for borrowed money is even greater, then state and local governments must induce taxpayers in the 10 percent bracket to buy their bonds, which means the interest rate must be at least 9 percent. At an interest rate of 9 percent, the implicit tax is only 10 percent. Even 20 percent bracket investors enjoy a windfall, and the windfall to 30 percent bracket taxpayers is larger than before.

The situation in the real world is similar to the example of municipal bonds paying 8 percent when taxable bonds are paying 10 percent. There is a significant implicit tax, but the rate of the implicit tax is decidedly below the top explicit tax rate. The result is that the benefit of §103 is shared by borrowing governments and by high bracket investors in municipal bonds.

2. *What Qualifies as a Municipal Bond?*

Suppose a state government owes you money and pays you interest on the debt, but the debt does not take the form of a bond. For example, the state might pay you interest on a state tax refund, on a lottery prize paid in installments, or on an installment note arising from the state's purchase of property from you. Can you exclude such interest from gross income under §103? Section 103(a) provides for the exclusion only in the case of interest on a government *bond*, but §103(c)(1) defines bond as simply "an obligation" of a state or local government. The broad definition of bond suggests you can exclude the interest on your state tax refund. But consider the following case.

3. In the real world, the limited demand for municipal bonds among top-bracket investors may have more to do with their many other opportunities for tax-favored investments (for example, investments in assets expected to produce profits in the form of unrealized appreciation), than with any scarcity of top bracket investors.

UNITED STATES TRUST CO. OF NEW YORK v. ANDERSON

65 F.2d 575 (2d Cir. 1933), *cert. denied,* **290 U.S. 683**

AUGUSTUS N. HAND, Circuit Judge. The interests in real estate belonging to the decedent, Isham, were condemned by the city of New York under section 976 of the Greater New York Charter. By virtue of that section, title to the interest in the first plot passed to the city on April 1, 1925, and to the second plot on June 2, 1926. Upon the making of the award in the condemnation proceedings, interest at 6 per cent. was allowed to the property owner from the dates when the city took title. In the case of the first plot condemned, the decedent received his award, with interest, in 1927, and in the case of the second plot in 1928. . . .

The [question before us is] whether the statutory exemptions from taxation of "the obligations of a State . . . or any political subdivision thereof. . ." covered the interest received by the decedent in 1927 and 1928 upon the condemnation awards. . . .

There is no doubt that the clause exempting from taxation "obligations of a State. . .or any political subdivision thereof" may be so interpreted as to embrace almost anything which a state or municipality is bound to pay and may thus exempt income which is within the taxing power of the United States. The question is how broadly the word "obligations" is to be construed and just what income is covered by the exemption. . . .

The phrase exempting "interest upon . . . the obligations of a state. . . or any political subdivision thereof" has been used in every Revenue Act since the adoption of the Sixteenth Amendment to the Constitution of the United States. At the time that amendment was proposed, it was argued that it would place the borrowing capacity of the states at the mercy of the federal taxing power. On February 8, 1910, Senator Borah submitted to the Senate a resolution No. 175 directing the Judiciary Committee to report whether "the proposed amendment . . . would if adopted authorize Congress to lay a tax upon incomes derived from state bonds and other municipal securities or would authorize Congress to tax the instrumentalities or means and property of the state or the salary of state officers." Cong. Rec. vol. 45, p. 1585.

It is clear from the wording of the foregoing resolution that the author had particularly in mind the question whether the amendment would adversely affect the power of the states and their political subdivisions to borrow money. . . .

[T]axation of the interest received upon [a condemnation] award [cannot] in any way affect the borrowing power of the state. There is no bargaining by the municipality in connection with the matter. The owner of the property condemned is obliged to sell it because of the exercise of the right of eminent domain. There was no competition between the city and other prospective purchasers, for the city had a prior right to the property and one that was subject only to the requirement that it pay a fair price. On the other hand, state and municipal bonds and securities issued to borrow money, if tax exempt, will command a better price in the market than if they are subject to taxation, because the purchaser is not compelled to buy them and, being a free agent, may be induced by the tax exemption feature to prefer them to private bonds for investment. It disregards the whole purpose of the exemption to apply it to interest upon obligations of a state which it can compel a citizen to take in exchange for the fair value of his property. The rate of interest is fixed by law, and neither it, nor the amount of the award adjudged as of the time of taking, is a matter over which he has any control.

Not only is the meaning which we attribute to "obligations of a state" in accord with the evident purposes of granting the exemption, but this meaning has been given to similar words in various decisions rendered by the Circuit Courts of Appeal and the Board of Tax Appeals. . . .

Decree affirmed.

Notes and Questions

1. *Purposive statutory interpretation. United States Trust* is still good law, and the same analysis applies to (for example) interest on state lottery prizes (Rev. Rul. 78-140, 1978-1 C.B. 27) and interest on state tax refunds. The case is noteworthy as much for its approach to statutory interpretation as for its result. Where the crucial statutory language ("obligations") is ambiguous, the interpretation should be guided by the policy behind the statute. The court identifies that policy as reducing the borrowing costs of state and local governments, and reasons that §103 will have the desired effect only when the borrowing government must compete with other borrowers for a limited supply of lenders' funds. When a state is faced with an involuntary lender — such as the owner of condemned property, or someone who has overpaid his taxes — the state does not have to offer a competitive interest rate. Instead, the state can present the involuntary lender with whatever interest rate it chooses, on a take-it-or-leave-it basis. In that situation, making the interest tax exempt would not inure to the benefit of the state, and Judge Hand reasonably concludes that such interest is outside the scope of the §103 exclusion.

2. *Installment obligations of state and local governments.* It does not follow from *United States Trust,* however, that §103 applies only to interest on what one would normally think of as bonds. In Rev. Rul. 60-179, 1960-2 C.B. 27, a state made an installment purchase of a building from the taxpayer, *not* pursuant to the state's power of eminent domain, and paid interest on the installment obligation. The IRS ruled that §103 applied to interest on an "obligation evidenced by an ordinary written agreement of purchase and sale." The crucial distinction between the revenue ruling and *United States Trust* is that there was bargaining between the state and the seller-creditor in the ruling, but not in *United States Trust.* Because the state and the creditor bargained in the shadow of §103,[4] it was reasonable to assume that they agreed to a lower rate of interest as a result of the exclusion.

3. *Not every preference produces an implicit tax.* The *United States Trust* opinion recognizes that there will be a reduction in the state's borrowing cost — and thus an implicit tax on the recipient of the interest — only if there is bargaining or competition influenced by the preference. We can take that insight in another direction, using it to distinguish between tax preferences that are and are not subject to implicit taxes. If favorable tax treatment is an attribute of a particular type of *asset* (such as a municipal bond), and taxpayers must compete with one another for a limited supply of tax-favored assets, then there will be an implicit tax. But what if the favorable tax treatment is

4. Or at least states and installment sellers would bargain in the shadow of §103 after the issuance of Rev. Rul. 60-179.

an attribute of the *taxpayer,* rather than of a particular asset? For example, tax exemption for the investment income of a Roth individual retirement account (Roth IRA) is based not on the nature of the assets in the Roth IRA,[5] but on the circumstances of the taxpayer. The taxpayer does not have to compete with anyone else for his Roth IRA preference. He does not have to pay a premium for the assets he invests in his Roth IRA because the tax-favored status of the Roth IRA does not depend on any attributes of those assets. Thus, there is no implicit tax on investments in Roth IRAs. Do you see why it would be a bad idea to invest your Roth IRA in municipal bonds rather than corporate bonds?

B. TAX SHELTERS

1. *A Hypothetical Debt-Financed Shelter Using Municipal Bonds*

When tax professionals refer to a tax shelter, they generally mean an investment or transaction that produces *artificial* tax losses, which can be used to avoid tax on income from other *unrelated* sources. The first critical point is that the losses must be *artificial.* Suppose there were a provision in the Internal Revenue Code that allowed you a deduction for as much money as you cared to set on fire. If you are willing to burn $1,000 of your own money, you can get a $1,000 deduction. This would not be an attractive proposition. Sure, a deduction of $1,000 would save $300 for a taxpayer in the 30 percent bracket, but that would merely reduce the after-tax cost of burning the money from $1,000 to $700. What *would* be attractive would be a provision that allowed you to treat $1,000 *as if* it were burned, without actually having to burn it—perhaps by waving a match over it, and chanting "I deem thee burned" three times. In that case, the deduction would save $300 in taxes, without any non-tax cost. Tax shelters are nothing more than fancy versions of "I deem thee burned."

The second critical point in the tax shelter concept is that the income being sheltered is *unrelated* to the shelter investment or transaction. (Taxpayers are most eager to find shelters for salaries and other forms of personal service income, but they are also interested in shelters for unrelated investment income.) Investing your own money in municipal bonds is certainly a tax-saving strategy. Most tax professionals would not consider it a tax shelter, however, because it results in avoiding tax on the income from the investment itself rather than sheltering unrelated income from tax. On the other hand, it would be possible to use §103 as the foundation for a tax shelter if one could borrow money to invest in municipal bonds, and deduct the interest expense (under §163) without having to include the municipal bond interest in income. Suppose (unrealistically) there is no implicit tax, and the prevailing interest rate is 10 percent (on both municipal bonds and debt paying taxable interest). In that case, a taxpayer in the 30 percent bracket might decide to borrow $100 at 10 percent in order to invest $100 in municipal bonds paying 10 percent. Obviously, this would be a pointless exercise apart from

5. An IRA may hold a wide range of investment-type assets, although investments in life insurance contracts and most "collectibles" are not permitted. *See* §§408(a)(3), 408(m).

tax consequences. It would make a great deal of sense, though, if the tax result is a $10 artificial loss, produced by the combination of no taxable interest income (§103) and a $10 interest expense deduction (§163). The loss is artificial — the equivalent of "I deem thee burned" — because the pre-tax result of $10 interest income and $10 interest expense is a wash, not a loss.

But let's be more realistic. Can the tax shelter work if there is an implicit tax? What if the taxpayer has to borrow $100 at 10 percent in order to buy a municipal bond paying only 8 percent? This is no longer the *ideal* tax shelter, because there is a $2 pre-tax loss involved in paying $10 interest in order to earn $8 interest income. The plan is still attractive, however, because the $10 tax loss (zero taxable interest income minus $10 interest expense) is much larger than the $2 pre-tax loss. The $10 tax loss is worth $3 to a taxpayer in the 30 percent bracket. Since the $3 tax saving from the deduction is greater than the $2 pre-tax loss, this still works as a shelter — although not as well as if there were no pre-tax loss. One way of understanding this deal is that the taxpayer has managed to replace his 30 percent explicit tax rate with a 20 percent implicit tax.

This description of the mechanics of a tax shelter is based on the assumption that one can borrow to invest in municipal bonds and deduct the interest expense. In fact, Congress has decided that this should not be permitted. We'll examine the details of the prohibition in a moment, but first consider whether Congress *should* permit taxpayers to use municipal bonds in tax shelters.

There are two important points in favor of allowing taxpayers to combine §§103 and 163 to create a tax shelter, once Congress has made the basic decision to allow the §103 exclusion to taxpayers who buy municipal bonds with their own (not borrowed) money. First, using a municipal bond in a tax shelter does not give the taxpayer any greater benefit — either in terms of net benefit or in terms of the amount by which taxable income understates economic income — than another taxpayer who buys an identical municipal bond with his own money. The taxpayer in the example above, who used borrowed money to buy a $100 municipal bond paying 8 percent, realized a net benefit of $1 ($3 reduction in tax liability minus $2 pre-tax loss). His taxable income from the shelter transaction (negative $10) understated his economic income from the transaction (negative $2) by $8. If another taxpayer buys an identical bond using his own money, he will also save $1 (the difference between the $3 explicit tax avoided and the $2 implicit tax on the municipal bond), and his taxable income from the bond (zero) will also understate his economic income from the bond ($8) by $8. (These comparisons are summarized in the following table.) It is not obvious, then, why Congress should be concerned about the use of municipal bonds in shelters, if it is happy with the use of municipal bonds outside of shelters.

The above argument merely claims that the use of §103 in shelters is not fundamentally different from its use outside of shelters. A second argument, however, claims that there is a significant *advantage,* in terms of delivery efficiency, to permitting the use of preferences in shelters. Remember the reason that §103 lacks delivery efficiency: There is not enough demand for municipal bonds among 30 percent bracket taxpayers, so borrowing governments need to offer an interest rate high enough to attract 20 percent bracket taxpayers. But suppose 30 percent bracket taxpayers could use municipal bonds in tax shelters. In that case, demand for municipal bonds among 30 percent bracket taxpayers would increase, and borrowing governments would no longer have to offer an 8 percent interest rate in order to attract 20 percent bracket taxpayers. The borrowing governments could drop the interest rate to just above 7 percent and sell all the bonds they wanted to top-bracket taxpayers. For example, a 30 percent bracket taxpayer could profit by borrowing $100 at 10 percent and investing in a municipal bond paying 7.1 percent. The $3 tax savings from the interest deduction would more than offset the $2.90 pre-tax loss, leaving the taxpayer with 10 cents of profit. Of the federal government's $3 revenue loss, $2.90 would be realized by the borrowing government as a reduction in borrowing costs, and only 10 cents would go as a windfall to the taxpayer. In short, allowing taxpayers to use municipal bonds in shelters would significantly improve the delivery efficiency of §103.

Comparison of Equity-Financed and Debt-Financed Municipal Bond Investments If Interest Expense Were Deductible (i.e., If §265(a)(2) Did Not Exist)

	1. Income (Loss) from Investment	**2. Taxable Income (Loss) from Investment**	**3. Amount by Which Taxable Income Understates Economic Income (Col. 1 Minus Col. 2)**	**4. After-tax Benefit to Taxpayer of Investment (for *A*, Relative to Investment in Corporate Bond, for *B* Relative to Doing Nothing)**
Taxpayer *A*: 30% bracket taxpayer invests his own $100 in 8% municipal bond when taxable bonds are paying 10%	$8 interest income	zero interest income	$8 − $0 = $8	$1 (excess of $8 tax-free return over $7 after-tax return on 10% corporate bond)
Taxpayer *B*: 30% bracket taxpayer borrows $100 at 10% to buy 8% municipal bond	$2 loss (excess of $10 interest expense over $8 interest income)	$10 loss (excess of $10 interest expense deduction over zero taxable interest income)	−$2 − (−$10) = $8	$1 (excess of $3 tax saving from $10 deduction over $2 pre-tax loss from col. 1)

Why, then, does Congress not permit taxpayers to deduct the interest expense on amounts borrowed to finance purchases of municipal bonds? The main reason is the great revenue cost that would be associated with municipal bond tax shelters. An implicit tax may be just as burdensome to the taxpayer as an explicit tax, but it does not remotely resemble an explicit tax from the point of view of the federal government. If the taxpayer in the above example is able to replace $3 of explicit tax with $2.90 of implicit tax, the benefit to the taxpayer is small, but the detriment to the Treasury is much greater (30 times greater, to be precise). Permitting the use of municipal bonds in shelters would make §103 a more delivery-efficient subsidy, but the resulting increased demand among high bracket taxpayers would also make it a much larger subsidy. Congress could reasonably conclude that the increase in delivery efficiency would not justify the tremendous increase in the size of the subsidy.

The prohibition on the use of municipal bonds in shelters is contained in §265(a)(2), which provides that no deduction shall be allowed for "[i]nterest on indebtedness incurred or continued to purchase or carry obligations the interest on which is wholly exempt from the taxes imposed by this subtitle." This obviously disallows the interest expense deduction when a taxpayer uses borrowed money to buy municipal bonds. It also applies when a taxpayer who already owns municipal bonds takes out a loan secured by the bonds, and uses the money to pay some unrelated expense or to make some unrelated purchase. In that case, the loan is viewed as enabling the taxpayer to continue to "carry" the municipal bonds. On the other hand, §265(a)(2) does not apply merely because a taxpayer happens to have outstanding debts at the same time he owns municipal bonds. The statute requires some nexus between the bonds and the debt before the disallowance kicks in. Beyond the two situations described above—purchase of bonds with borrowed money and pledging bonds as security for a loan—it is not entirely clear when the nexus requirement will be satisfied.

2. *Beyond Municipal Bonds: Tax Shelters Based on Other Tax Preferences*

The municipal bond tax shelter illustration can be generalized. Whenever the Code provides a tax break for a particular type of investment income, that break can be converted to a tax shelter—that is, an artificial loss to shelter unrelated income from tax—*if* taxpayers are allowed to buy the tax-favored asset with borrowed money and deduct the interest expense. Does Congress permit shelters based on tax breaks other than §103? The short answer is usually not, but sometimes.

One important tax preference for investment income is the deferral of taxation on unrealized appreciation. Can a taxpayer borrow money at 10 percent to buy an asset that he expects will produce unrealized appreciation at an annual rate of 10 percent, and create an artificial loss by combining the exclusion of the unrealized appreciation with a deduction for the interest expense? As with municipal bonds, the answer is no. Section 163(d) provides that "investment interest"—generally, interest on debt incurred to buy investment assets—is deductible only to the extent of investment income.[6]

Example.   A taxpayer borrows $100 at 10 percent to invest in stock of Growth Corporation (which pays no dividends, but which he expects to appreciate at an annual

---

6. Whether interest expense is classified as investment interest under §163(d) is determined under the interest expense allocation rules of Reg. §1.163-8T, which are described *infra* in Note 7 of section B.3 of this chapter (relating to the passive loss rules of §469). In general, the interest expense allocation rules provide for tracing of the use of loan proceeds, so that interest expense is treated as investment interest (subject to §163(d)) only if the interest is on a debt, the proceeds of which were used by the taxpayer to acquire investment assets. Notice a significant difference between the rule of Reg. §1.163-8T and the "purchase or carry" rule for associating interest expense with municipal bonds under §265(a)(2): The rule of §1.163-8T includes no equivalent to the "or carry" prong of the §265(a)(2) rule. Thus, it is easier for a taxpayer owning growth stock to avoid §163(d) than it is for a taxpayer owning municipal bonds to avoid §265(a)(2).

rate of 10 percent), and he has no other debts or investments. If the corporation pays no dividends, the taxpayer will not be able to deduct any of his $10 interest expense. (The disallowed expense would carry forward, however, to be deductible against investment income in future years.) If the corporation pays $4 of dividends, the taxpayer can use $4 of his investment interest expense to offset the investment income,[7] but the other $6 will not be deductible against noninvestment income.

Section 163(d) is based on a presumption that any excess of investment interest expense over investment income is an artificial loss, because it is offset (or more than offset) by unrealized appreciation in investment assets. The rule operates as a *conclusive* presumption. The disallowance of the $10 interest expense deduction in the first part of the example is fair enough, if the taxpayer's Growth Corporation stock really appreciated $10 or more during the year. The disallowance will be a bitter pill, however, if the Growth Corporation stock failed to appreciate. In that case the $10 loss is not artificial, but the §163(d) disallowance nevertheless applies.

Another important tax preference is the accelerated cost recovery system (ACRS) of §168. To the extent ACRS allows cost recovery faster than the actual decline in value of business assets, it results in the understatement of economic income for tax purposes. Before 1986, the Code generally permitted tax shelters based on the combination of ACRS and the interest expense deduction, and tax shelters based on that combination were extremely popular. Tax shelter promoters sold limited partnership tax shelter investments, involving debt-financed purchases of buildings and other ACRS assets, to thousands of doctors, lawyers, and other taxpayers with large amounts of personal service income. The mass-market tax shelter industry was brought to a screeching halt, however, by the 1986 enactment of the §469 passive loss rules. Those rules are examined in detail below, but their basic thrust is to prohibit the deduction of passive losses — defined as losses from businesses in which the taxpayer does not "materially participate" — against either income from personal services or "portfolio income" (such as dividends, royalties, and interest income). Although §469 does not explicitly focus on interest expense deductions, in practice most disallowed passive losses will be produced by the combination of ACRS (or some other asset-based tax preference) and an interest expense deduction.

So what is left of interest-based tax shelters? Is there any place in the Code where taxpayers can still create tax shelters by combining a tax preference with an interest expense deduction? It is still possible to use ACRS deductions in a debt-financed tax shelter, for those few taxpayers who materially participate in a business, and thus avoid the restrictions of §469. Of more general interest, however, is §163(h)(3), which allows a deduction for "qualified residence interest," which covers the interest on most home mortgages. The mechanics of §163(h)(3) are discussed in detail elsewhere,[8] but the crucial point is that §163(h)(3) sanctions a classic interest deduction-based tax shelter, of precisely the sort that is *not* permitted by §§265(a)(2), 163(d), and 469. Owner-occupied housing qualifies for two important exclusions from income. The rental value of an owner-occupied home is excluded as imputed income from property, and most appreciation in residences is permanently excluded from income (initially as unrealized appreciation, and later

---

7. In that case, the dividend income will not be eligible for the favorable tax rates applicable to "qualified dividend income." *See* §1(h)(11)(D)(i).

8. See section B.2.b of Chapter 4.

as gain eligible for exclusion under §121). These tax breaks do not create a tax shelter — in the sense of an artificial deduction eliminating tax on unrelated income — for a taxpayer who owns his house free-and-clear. But a taxpayer who owns a mortgaged home can combine these tax breaks with an interest expense deduction — thereby creating an artificial loss from his home — which he can use to shelter some of his salary from tax. Owner-occupied housing is the last great interest-based tax shelter.

Problem 1.   Diane owns the house in which she lives. Her basis in the house is $150,000, the house is subject to a purchase money mortgage of $120,000, and the fair market value of the house is $190,000. Diane is considering borrowing $60,000, secured by a second mortgage on the house, and investing the borrowed money in municipal bonds paying tax-exempt interest. If she goes through with this plan, will she be able to deduct some or all of the interest on the second mortgage? Consult §§163(h)(3)(C) and 265(a)(2) (and the regulations thereunder, if necessary).

3. The Passive Loss Rules of §469

The most important restriction on the ability of taxpayers to create tax shelters by borrowing money to invest in tax-favored assets is imposed by the passive loss rules of §469. These rules generally prohibit taxpayers from deducting losses from "passive activities" — a wonderfully oxymoronic term — against either salary income or portfolio income (such as interest and dividends). The passive loss rules are described in the following excerpt from the "Bluebook" for the Tax Reform Act of 1986.

STAFF OF THE JOINT COMMITTEE ON TAXATION, GENERAL EXPLANATION OF THE TAX REFORM ACT OF 1986

(1987)

LIMITATIONS ON LOSSES AND CREDITS FROM PASSIVE ACTIVITIES (SECS. 501 AND 502 OF THE ACT AND NEW SEC. 469 OF THE CODE)

PRIOR LAW

In general, no limitations were placed on the ability of a taxpayer to use deductions from a particular activity to offset income from other activities. Similarly, most tax credits could be used to offset tax attributable to income from any of the taxpayer's activities.

There were some exceptions to this general rule. For example, deductions for capital losses were limited to the extent that there were not offsetting capital gains. . . .

In the absence of more broadly applicable limitations on the use of deductions and credits from one activity to reduce tax liability attributable to other activities, taxpayers with substantial sources of positive income could eliminate or sharply reduce tax liability by using deductions and credits from other activities, frequently by investing in tax shelters. Tax shelters commonly offered the opportunity to reduce or avoid tax liability with respect to salary or other positive income, by making available deductions and credits, possibly exceeding real economic costs or losses currently borne by the taxpayer, in excess or in advance of income from the shelters.

REASONS FOR CHANGE

Congress concluded that it had become increasingly clear that taxpayers were losing faith in the Federal income tax system. This loss of confidence resulted in large part from the interaction of two of the system's principal features: its high marginal rates (in 1986, 50 percent for a single individual with taxable income in excess of $88,270), and the opportunities it provided for taxpayers to offset income from one source with tax shelter deductions and credits from another.

The increasing prevalence of tax shelters — even after the highest marginal rate for individuals was reduced in 1981 from 70 percent to 50 percent — was well documented. For example, a Treasury study revealed that in 1983, out of 260,000 tax returns reporting "total positive income" in excess of $250,000, 11 percent paid taxes equaling 5 percent or less of total positive income, and 21 percent paid taxes equaling 10 percent or less of total positive income. Similarly, in the case of tax returns reporting total positive income in excess of $1 million, 11 percent paid tax equaling less than 5 percent of total positive income, and 19 percent paid tax equaling less than 10 percent of total positive income.

Congress determined that such patterns gave rise to a number of undesirable consequences, even aside from their effect in reducing Federal tax revenues. Extensive shelter activity contributed to public concerns that the tax system was unfair, and to the belief that tax is paid only by the naive and the unsophisticated. This, in turn, not only undermined compliance, but encouraged further expansion of the tax shelter market, in many cases diverting investment capital from productive activities to those principally or exclusively serving tax avoidance goals.

Congress concluded that the most important sources of support for the Federal income tax system were the average citizens who simply reported their income (typically consisting predominantly of items such as salaries, wages, pensions, interest, and dividends) and paid tax under the general rules. To the extent that these citizens felt that they were bearing a disproportionate burden with regard to the costs of government because of their unwillingness or inability to engage in tax-oriented investment activity, the tax system itself was threatened.

Under these circumstances, Congress determined that decisive action was needed to curb the expansion of tax sheltering and to restore to the tax system the degree of equity that was a necessary precondition to a beneficial and widely desired reduction in rates. So long as tax shelters were permitted to erode the Federal tax base, a low-rate system could provide neither sufficient revenues, nor sufficient progressivity, to satisfy the general public that tax liability bore a fair relationship to the ability to pay. In particular, a provision significantly limiting the use of tax shelter losses was viewed as unavoidable if substantial rate reductions were to be provided to high-income taxpayers without disproportionately reducing the share of total liability under the individual income tax borne by high-income taxpayers as a group.

Congress viewed the question of how to prevent harmful and excessive tax sheltering as not a simple one. One way to address the problem would have been to eliminate substantially all tax preferences in the Internal Revenue Code. For two reasons, however, this course was determined by Congress to be inappropriate.

First, while the Act reduces or eliminates some tax-preference items that Congress decided did not provide social or economic benefits commensurate with their cost, there were many preferences that Congress concluded were socially or economically beneficial. It was determined that certain preferences were particularly beneficial when used primarily to advance the purposes upon which Congress relied in enacting them, rather than to avoid taxation of income from sources unrelated to the preferred activity.

Second, Congress viewed as prohibitively difficult, and perhaps impossible, the task of designing a tax system that measured income perfectly. For example, the statutory allowance for depreciation, even under the normative system used under the Act for alternative minimum tax purposes, reflects broad industry averages, as opposed to providing precise item-by-item measurements. Accordingly, taxpayers with assets that depreciate less rapidly than the average, or that appreciate over time (as may be the case with certain real estate), could engage in tax sheltering even under the minimum tax, in the absence of direct action regarding the tax shelter problem. . . .

The question of what constituted a tax shelter that should be subject to limitations was viewed as closely related to the question of who Congress intends to benefit when it enacts tax preferences. For example, in providing preferential depreciation for real estate or favorable accounting rules for farming, it was not Congress's primary intent to permit outside investors to avoid tax liability with respect to their salaries by investing in limited partnership syndications. Rather, Congress intended to benefit and provide incentives to taxpayers active in the businesses to which the preferences were directed. . . .

Congress determined that, in order for tax preferences to function as intended, their benefit should be directed primarily to taxpayers with a substantial and bona fide involvement in the activities to which the preferences related. Congress also determined that it was appropriate to encourage nonparticipating investors to invest in particular activities, by permitting the use of preferences to reduce the rate of tax on income from those activities; however, such investors were viewed as not appropriately permitted to use tax benefits to shelter unrelated income. . . .

A material participation standard identified an important distinction between different types of taxpayer activities. It was thought that, in general, the more passive investor seeks a return on capital invested, including returns in the form of reductions in the taxes owed on unrelated income, rather than an ongoing source of livelihood. A material participation standard reduced the importance, for such investors, of the tax-reduction features of an investment, and thus increased the importance of the economic features in an investor's decision about where to invest his funds.

Moreover, Congress concluded that restricting the use of losses from business activities in which the taxpayer did not materially participate against other sources of positive income (such as salary and portfolio income) would address a fundamental aspect of the tax shelter problem. Instances in which the tax system applies simple rules at the expense of economic accuracy encouraged the structuring of transactions to take advantage of the situations in which such rules gave rise to undermeasurement or deferral of income. Such transactions commonly were marketed to investors who did not intend to participate in the transactions, as devices for sheltering unrelated sources of positive income (e.g., salary and portfolio income). Accordingly, by creating a bar against the use of losses from business activities in which the taxpayer does not materially participate to offset positive income sources such as salary and portfolio income, Congress believed that it was possible significantly to reduce the tax shelter problem.

Further, in the case of a nonparticipating investor in a business activity, Congress determined that it was appropriate to treat losses of the activity as not realized by the investor prior to disposition of his interest in the activity. The effort to measure, on an annual basis, real economic losses from passive activities gave rise to distortions, particularly due to the nontaxation of unrealized appreciation and the mismatching of tax deductions and related economic income that could occur, especially where debt financing was used heavily. Only when a taxpayer disposes of his interest in an activity was it considered possible to determine whether a loss was sustained over the entire time that he held the interest. . . .

EXPLANATION OF PROVISION

1. *Overview*

The Act provides that deductions from passive trade or business activities, to the extent they exceed income from all such passive activities (exclusive of portfolio income), generally may not be deducted against other income. Similarly, credits from passive activities generally are limited to the tax attributable to the passive activities. Suspended losses and credits are carried forward and treated as deductions and credits from passive activities in the next year. Suspended losses from an activity are allowed in full when the taxpayer disposes of his entire interest in the activity.

The provision applies to individuals, estates, trusts, and personal service corporations. A special rule limits the use of passive activity losses and credits against portfolio income in the case of closely held corporations. Special rules also apply to rental activities. Losses from certain working interests in oil and gas property are not limited by the provision. Losses and credits attributable to a limited partnership interest generally are treated as arising from a passive activity. . . .

Losses and credits from a passive activity (taking into account expenses such as interest attributable to acquiring or carrying an interest in the activity) may be applied against income for the taxable year from other passive activities or against income subsequently generated by any passive activity. Such losses (and credits) generally cannot be applied to shelter other income, such as compensation for services or portfolio income (including interest, dividends, royalties, annuities, and gains from the sale of property held for investment). For this purpose, property held for investment generally does not include an interest in a passive activity.

Salary and portfolio income are separated from passive activity losses and credits because the former generally are positive income sources that do not bear deductible expenses to the same extent as passive investments. Since taxpayers commonly can rely upon salary and portfolio income to be positive (and since, when economically profitable, these items generally yield positive taxable income), they are susceptible to sheltering by means of investments in activities that predictably give rise to tax losses (or credits in excess of the tax attributable to income from such investments). The passive loss provision ensures that salary and portfolio income, along with other non-passive income sources, cannot be offset by tax losses from passive activities until the amount of real economic losses from such activities is determined upon disposition.

Under the provision, suspended losses attributable to passive activities are allowed in full upon a taxable disposition of the taxpayer's entire interest in the activity. The full amount of gain or loss from the activity can then be ascertained. To the extent the taxpayer's basis in the activity has been reduced by suspended deductions, resulting in gain on disposition, the remaining suspended deductions will, in effect, offset such gain. However, the character of any gain or loss (i.e., as ordinary or capital gain or loss) is not affected by this provision.

Notes and Questions

1. *Is the rationale persuasive?* According to the Bluebook, "It was determined [by Congress] that certain preferences were particularly beneficial when used primarily to advance the purposes upon which Congress relied in enacting them, rather than to avoid taxation of income from sources unrelated to the preferred activity." Are you persuaded by this explanation of why tax preferences outside of shelters are good, but preferences in shelters are bad? If Congress wants to use ACRS to encourage construction of office buildings (for some strange reason), what difference does it make whether the investment is made with the taxpayer's own money or with borrowed money? In this connection, review the discussion of what would happen if taxpayers could use municipal bonds in tax shelters.

2. *The basic mechanics of the passive loss rules.* To understand the basic mechanics of §469, consider the following example. Ellen borrows $1,000, at 5 percent interest, and uses the borrowed money to finance the entire cost of purchasing an apartment building (with the loan secured by a mortgage on the building). Operating the apartment building is a passive activity. (*See* §469(c)(2).) During her first year of ownership, Ellen receives $100 of rental income (net of all expenses except depreciation and interest), is entitled to a $90 depreciation (ACRS) deduction under §168, and pays $50 interest on the loan. She also makes a nondeductible principal payment of $90 on the loan. The apartment is Ellen's only passive activity for the year, but she has substantial income from her job and from investments in stocks. Before taking §469 into account, Ellen has a $40 tax loss from the apartment ($100 rental income minus $90 depreciation minus $50 interest expense). That $40 is a passive activity loss, and §469(a)(1) prohibits Ellen from using the loss to shelter $40 of earned income or portfolio income.[9] Instead, §469(b) provides that the loss is carried forward. If Ellen has $40 of passive activity income in a future year (either from the apartment or from some other passive activity), she will then be able to deduct the suspended loss. Even without passive activity income, Ellen will be allowed to deduct the suspended loss when she finally disposes of her entire interest in the building (§469(g)).

---

9. This assumes that Ellen's income is sufficiently high that she is unable to take advantage of the "small landlord" exception in §469(*i*). See Note 5 below.

Unlike the investment interest rules of §163(d), §469 does not specifically identify interest deductions as the target of the disallowance rule. In Ellen's case, however, the effect of §469 is the same as if the statute provided that passive activity interest is deductible only to the extent of passive activity income. In that case, Ellen's passive activity income (before taking into account her interest expense) would be $10 ($100 − $90), $10 of her interest expense would be deductible, and the other $40 would not. In the vast majority of cases to which §469 applies, the provision operates in this fashion — as a de facto limitation on the deductibility of interest associated with passive activities.

3. *Passive income generators.* Section 469 does not prohibit the deduction of a loss from a passive activity against *any* unrelated income; a loss from one passive activity can be used to shelter income from another passive activity. (This follows from the definition of passive activity loss in §469(d)(1).) As a result, a taxpayer with a loss-producing passive activity would do well to purchase an interest in a "PIG" — a passive income-generator. Finding a good PIG can be difficult. First, the PIG must qualify as a trade or business; a nonbusiness investment (in stocks or bonds, for example) will not do. A nonbusiness investment will produce portfolio income, which cannot be sheltered by passive losses. Second, the PIG must be passive. A business in which the taxpayer materially participates is not passive, and thus cannot be a PIG. (The material participation standard is discussed below.) Finally, the business must be a reliable source of taxable income rather than tax losses.

4. *Suspended losses and dispositions.* One way of understanding the policy behind the passive loss rules, as applied to Ellen's situation, is that her $40 tax loss is conclusively presumed to be artificial (that is, not reflective of a real economic loss), and thus it is disallowed. As we have seen, the whole idea of tax shelters is that the losses are *supposed* to be artificial — a deduction for a real economic loss isn't much fun. However, the passive loss rules don't bother to investigate whether a particular disallowed loss really is artificial. If Ellen's building really declined in value by the full amount of her ACRS deduction ($90), then her loss wasn't artificial at all. Unfortunately for Ellen, §469 doesn't care. Her loss is disallowed regardless of whether it is artificial or real. Congress decided it was too difficult to distinguish between real and artificial losses, so it decided to treat all passive losses as artificial.

All is not lost for Ellen, however. Recall that a real economic loss *is* deductible when the taxpayer disposes of her entire interest in the passive activity. Suppose Ellen's disallowed loss is real — that is, the building really declined in value by $90 during the year — and that at the beginning of the next year Ellen disposes of the building. The building is worth $910 and it is subject to a $910 mortgage, so Ellen's only amount realized on the disposition will be $910 of debt relief. Since her adjusted basis is also $910 ($1,000 original basis, reduced by $90 of ACRS deductions), her gain realized will be zero. The disposition of the building frees up the suspended loss, so in the year of disposition Ellen can deduct the loss against income of any sort, including earned income. Once she has disposed of her entire interest, it is possible to determine that her suspended loss was real. Since the loss is clearly real, there is no reason not to allow Ellen to deduct it at this point.

But §469(g) says that *all* suspended losses are deductible upon disposition of a taxpayer's entire interest in a passive activity. Does that mean that even artificial losses are then deductible? Technically yes, but really no. Consider a variation on the Ellen example in which the building declines in value by only $50 during the first year. In that case, the economic reality is that she had zero net income during the first year ($100 rental income minus $50 interest expense minus $50 depreciation); the $40 suspended tax loss is completely artificial. At the beginning of the next year, she sells the building for $950, with her amount realized consisting of $40 cash and $910 of debt relief. Section 469(g) allows her to deduct the $40 suspended loss at that point. But why should it, given that the loss is clearly artificial?[10] The key to the mystery is in the determination of her gain on the disposition under §1001. With an amount realized of $950 and an adjusted basis of only $910,[11] she realizes a gain on the sale of $40. Thus, her $40 artificial loss is allowed by §469(g), but it is precisely offset by $40 of artificial gain under §1001.[12]

5. *Material participation.* What makes an activity "passive," so as to be subject to §469? Passive activities occupy a middle ground on a continuum between active businesses and nonbusiness portfolio investments (such as investments in stocks or bonds). In a nutshell, a passive activity is a business in which the taxpayer does not materially participate. The definition of "material participation" is thus central to §469. The statute itself provides limited guidance. The general rule of §469(h)(1) tells us only that material participation must be "regular, continuous, and substantial." In addition, §469(h)(2) provides that a limited partner cannot materially participate in a limited partnership. This is significant, since the vast majority of pre-1986 tax shelters were limited partnerships, and many potential tax shelter investors are interested in investing only if their liability will be limited. The regulations (Treas. Reg. §1.469-5T) define material participation in great detail, but the basic idea is pretty simple. In most cases, a taxpayer will not satisfy the material participation standard unless he participates in the activity for more than 500 hours during the year. No busy doctor or lawyer is interested in spending 500-plus hours a year just to legitimize his tax shelter losses, so this stringent regulatory definition of material participation has been very effective in destroying the market for tax shelters.

Section 469(c)(2) provides that any rental activity is passive, but two special rules provide limited relief for some real estate investors. Under §469(*i*), moderate-income taxpayers who "actively participate" (a less demanding standard than material participation) in rental real estate activities can deduct up to $25,000 of their losses. The typical beneficiary

10. Perhaps the easiest way to see the artificiality of the loss is to follow the flow of cash. Ellen received total cash of $140 ($100 as rental income and $40 cash on sale), and paid total cash of $140 ($90 principal and $50 interest).

11. A taxpayer subject to §469 must reduce her basis in ACRS property by the amount of the cost recovery allowance determined under §168, even if the taxpayer has not been able to enjoy the full benefit of the cost recovery allowance because her passive loss has been suspended under §469(a).

12. On these facts, Ellen's $40 artificial loss will be deductible against ordinary income, while her $40 of artificial gain may be taxed at favorable long-term capital gains rates. This result seems unduly generous, but that is not the fault of §469. The culprit is §1250, which does not apply §1245 recapture principles to most real estate depreciation deductions. See the discussion of recapture in section A of Chapter 5.

of this provision is a taxpayer who owns and manages one or two rental houses. In addition, real estate professionals (such as developers and brokers) who devote more than 750 hours per year to real estate businesses are not subject to the rule that rental activities are automatically passive.

6. *One activity or two?* Suppose a taxpayer is involved in two related undertakings (to use a word that is not a §469 term of art), which might plausibly be considered either a single activity or two activities for purposes of the passive loss rules. Will the taxpayer be better off if the two undertakings are classified as a single activity, or as two activities? It depends. Consider two different situations.

(a) The taxpayer materially participates in Undertaking #1, but does not materially participate in Undertaking #2. Both undertakings produce tax losses. Here, the taxpayer would like to treat the two undertakings as a single activity. If they are separate activities, then Undertaking #2 is passive, and the taxpayer cannot deduct any loss it generates. But if they are a single activity, then the taxpayer's material participation with respect to #1 also constitutes material participation in #2. Since #2 is then part of an active business, it is not subject to §469.

(b) The taxpayer does not materially participate in Undertaking #1 or Undertaking #2, and he has thousands of dollars of suspended losses from prior years with respect to both undertakings. This year he disposes of his entire interest in #1, but he retains his interest in #2. This time the taxpayer would be better off if the undertakings are considered two separate activities. In that case, the disposition of #1 would constitute the disposition of his entire interest in a passive activity, so that §469(g) would allow him to deduct his suspended loss with respect to #1. If they are a single activity, disposition of #1 would not be a disposition of his entire interest, and §469(g) would not be triggered.

The regulations governing the treatment of undertakings as one or several activities give taxpayers a great deal of freedom in deciding whether to aggregate or separate their related undertakings. In fact, Treas. Reg. §1.469-4(c)(2) permits a taxpayer to "use any reasonable method of applying the relevant facts and circumstances in grouping activities." The only catch is that once a taxpayer has selected a particular grouping, he is stuck with it. If a regrouping would produce better tax results in a later year, that is just too bad: "[O]nce a taxpayer has grouped activities under this section, the taxpayer may not regroup those activities in subsequent taxable years." Treas. Reg. §1.469-4(e)(1).

7. *Allocating interest expense.* Suppose that, before taking into account $15,000 of interest expense, a taxpayer has $13,000 of active business income, $10,000 of portfolio income (such as dividends), and $2,000 of income from a passive activity. Calculating the taxpayer's tax liability requires an allocation of the interest expense to one or more of the three income sources. Think of the taxpayer as having three different income baskets; the tax treatment of the interest expense will depend on the basket in which it is put. If the interest goes in the active business basket, it will be deductible under §163(a), without being subject to either §163(d) or §469.[13] This is true even if—as in the example—allocating the interest expense to the active business produces a tax loss from the business. If the interest goes in

---

13. In some cases, however, it might have to be capitalized under §263A. *See* §263A(f).

the portfolio basket, §163(d) will apply to limit the interest expense deduction. In the example, only $10,000 of the interest would be deductible. If the interest is placed in the passive activity basket, it creates a nondeductible $13,000 passive activity loss. In effect, the first $2,000 of the interest is deductible against the $2,000 of passive activity income, and the other $13,000 is disallowed.

Given the fungibility of money, it is not obvious what sort of rules should govern the allocation of interest expense among the various tax baskets. The Treasury has opted for a tracing approach. Without going into the gory details, the basic idea behind Treas. Reg. §1.163-8T is to allocate debt — and hence the interest on the debt — among baskets according to the use of loan proceeds. Thus, if the taxpayer used the borrowed funds (on which he paid the $15,000 of interest) in his active business, no anti-shelter limitations will apply. If he used the borrowed funds to buy portfolio investments, §163(d) will apply. And if he used the borrowed funds to purchase an interest in a passive activity, §469 will apply. This tracing approach gives sophisticated taxpayers considerable flexibility in planning their affairs so as to put their interest expense in the best possible tax basket.

8. *At-risk rules.* In addition to the passive loss rules, §465 — which antedates §469 by a decade — acts as a constraint on tax shelters. Section 465 limits deductions from an activity to the amount the taxpayer has "at risk" in the activity. In general, a taxpayer is at risk with respect to investments made with his own money, and with respect to debt on which he is personally liable. In some cases, a taxpayer will escape the passive loss frying pan only to jump into the at-risk fire. Suppose a taxpayer materially participates in an activity that produces a $25 tax loss. The taxpayer's basis in the activity is $100, attributable to $10 of the taxpayer's own money and a $90 nonrecourse loan. Because the taxpayer materially participates, he is not subject to the passive loss rules. He still must deal, however, with the at-risk rules. The taxpayer's at-risk amount is only $10, so §465 will disallow $15 of the $25 loss. The loss is suspended, so that the taxpayer can deduct it in a later year if his at-risk amount increases (for example, on account of principal payments on the nonrecourse debt). It sounds as if the at-risk rules would have had a major chilling effect on tax shelter activity, even before the enactment of the passive loss rules. Actually, their effectiveness was quite limited, because they did not apply to real estate. In 1986 Congress extended the at-risk rules to real estate, but only in a half-hearted way. A taxpayer involved in a real estate activity is considered at risk with respect to "qualified nonrecourse financing," as defined in §465(b)(6)(B).

9. *Two types of complexity.* The story of tax shelters and the passive loss rules illustrates two different ways of evaluating the complexity of the tax system. Section 469 is an undeniably long and complex provision, and the regulations promulgated under it are even longer (*much* longer) and more complex. Does it follow that the enactment of §469 complicated the income tax? Not necessarily. The Code may have looked simpler before 1986, but the proliferation of tax shelters greatly complicated the administration of the tax system. Tax professionals, the IRS, and the courts devoted countless hours to controversies over the legitimacy of thousands of aggressive (or

worse) tax shelters. With §469 on the books, it was clear that most would-be tax shelters wouldn't work. The result was a major decrease in tax shelter controversies following the enactment of §469.[14] Think of §469 as a fence with a sign: "Anti-Tax Shelter Rules: Keep Out." The rules inside the fence may be complex, but to the extent that the sign serves its purpose and taxpayers keep out, nobody has to deal with the complexity. Strangely enough, then, a more verbose Internal Revenue Code may be simpler in practice, if the verbosity deters enough complexity-generating behavior.

10. *Comparing the investment interest and passive loss rules.* Both §§163(d) and 469 allow interest expense deductions only to the extent of the income generated by the investments (§163(d)) or passive activities (§469). No net loss deductions (as in a case where interest expense exceeds income) are allowed. However, the practical consequences of the two provisions can be quite different. With respect to investment activities, the taxpayer aggregates all such activities and compares the income generated by the portfolio of investments with any interest expense occasioned by indebtedness associated with the portfolio. The most common form of such interest is that paid with respect to so-called margin loans that are routinely extended by stock brokerages to finance some of the costs of acquiring stocks and bonds. Usually, lenders are unwilling to extend loans that much exceed half of the value of the investments bought, because of the volatility of portfolio investments.

Because the interest on margin loans will typically be accruing only with respect to about half as much capital as the portfolio represents, it is ordinarily rather easy to arrange to have enough current income generated by the portfolio to absorb the interest expense. Up to half of the portfolio could still be invested in "growth stocks" that pay little or no dividend income, so long as the other half is invested in stocks and bonds that pay dividends or interest at roughly the rate assessed on the margin loan. Thus, as a practical matter, the rule limiting investment interest deductions to the amount of investment income need not result in the loss or suspension of any such deductions, so long as the portfolio mix is reasonably managed. In contrast, Congress has defined "passive activities" in such a way that the activities rarely achieve positive net income. The interest deduction rule as to passive activities requires that interest expenses associated with such activities be combined with all other passive activity expenses, and that deductions be allowed only up to the amount of the income from the activities. Under these circumstances, it is usually the case that limiting deductions to the amount of income is a severe limitation indeed — one that renders much of the interest expense nondeductible. Of course, as explained in detail above, the expense deductions denied by §469 are not completely lost. They are held in suspense until the disposition of the passive activity to which they relate, and can be deducted in the year of that disposition.

---

14. However, as described in the cell accompanying this chapter, "Corporate Tax Shelters," a new generation of tax shelter controversies eventually emerged.

Problem 2.   Mary is a surgeon with a high-six-figure income from her practice. On January 1 of Year 1, she buys an office building and the land on which it sits for $2.5 million. She pays $500,000 cash, and finances the other $2 million with a nonrecourse loan (which is "qualified nonrecourse financing" within the meaning of §465(b)(6)). The building is Mary's only §469 passive activity. Mary's Year 1 interest expense on the note is $100,000, her ACRS allowance for the building is $50,000, and her rental income from the building (net of all expenses other than interest and depreciation) is $100,000. She makes no principal payments on the loan. What effect, if any, will §469 have on Mary in Year 1?

Problem 3.   On January 1 of Year 2, Mary (from the previous problem) sells the office building and the land. The buyer takes the property subject to the nonrecourse debt (the principal amount of which is still $2 million), and also pays Mary $600,000 cash. Assume that in Year 2 Mary received no rental income from the building, had no interest expense on the note, and was entitled to no ACRS allowance with respect to the building. On those simplifying assumptions, how much gain or loss does Mary realize on the sale of the property, and what effect (if any) will §469 have on Mary in Year 2?

Problem 4.   Undertakings #1 and #2 are related. The taxpayer materially participates in #1, but not in #2. Both #1 and #2 produce taxable income. Undertaking #3, in which the taxpayer does not materially participate, is unrelated to both #1 and #2, and so is clearly a separate activity. Undertaking #3 produces large tax losses. Would the taxpayer prefer that #1 and #2 be classified as a single activity, or as separate activities? Why?

Problem 5.   At the beginning of this year, John borrowed $100,000, at an interest rate of 6 percent. He paid $6,000 of interest on the loan during the year. John made two $100,000 investments during the year, financing one investment with his own money and the other with the borrowed funds. One investment was in the stock of Growth Corporation. His Growth Corporation stock increased in value by $14,000 during the year, but the stock paid no dividends. The other investment was in a limited partnership, the only asset of which was an apartment building. John's share of the partnership rental income for the year was $10,000, and his share of the partnership's ACRS deduction for the year was $8,500. John also owned some corporate bonds, which he had purchased several years earlier, which paid $5,000 of taxable interest income during the year. Of John's $6,000 interest expense, how much may he deduct this year if he used the borrowed $100,000 to purchase the Growth Corporation stock? (Disregard any possible effect of the at-risk rules of §465.)

Problem 6.   The facts are the same as in Problem 5, except that John used the borrowed $100,000 to buy the limited partnership interest rather than to buy the stock. In that case, how much of his $6,000 interest expense may he deduct this year? (Again, disregard §465.)

4. *Judicial Anti-Abuse Doctrines*

Congress has enacted a number of anti-tax shelter provisions, including the at-risk rules and the passive loss rules. Even in the absence of specific anti-tax shelter legislation, however, the courts—urged on by the IRS—have used a number of "common law" doctrines to restrain the use of particularly aggressive tax shelter strategies. The following case is one of the Supreme Court's major efforts in this area.

KNETSCH v. UNITED STATES

364 U.S. 361 (1960)

Mr. Justice BRENNAN delivered the opinion of the Court.

This case presents the question of whether deductions from gross income claimed on petitioners' 1953 and 1954 joint federal income tax returns, of $143,465 in 1953 and of $147,105 in 1954, for payments made by petitioner, Karl F. Knetsch, to Sam Houston Life Insurance Company, constituted "interest paid . . . on indebtedness" within the meaning of . . . §163(a) of the Internal Revenue Code of 1954. The Commissioner of Internal Revenue disallowed the deductions and determined a deficiency for each year. . . .

On December 11, 1953, the insurance company sold Knetsch ten 30-year maturity deferred annuity savings bonds, each in the face amount of $400,000 and bearing interest at 2½% compounded annually. The purchase price was $4,004,000. Knetsch gave the Company his check for $4,000, and signed $4,000,000 of nonrecourse annuity loan notes for the balance. The notes bore 3½% interest and were secured by the annuity bonds. The interest was payable in advance, and Knetsch on the same day prepaid the first year's interest, which was $140,000. Under the Table of Cash and Loan Values made part of the bonds, their cash or loan value at December 11, 1954, the end of the first contract year, was to be $4,100,000. The contract terms, however, permitted Knetsch to borrow any excess of this value above his indebtedness without waiting until December 11, 1954. Knetsch took advantage of this provision only five days after the purchase. On December 16, 1953, he received from the company $99,000 of the $100,000 excess over his $4,000,000 indebtedness, for which he gave his notes bearing 3½% interest. This interest was also payable in advance and on the same day he prepaid the first year's interest of $3,465. In their joint return for 1953, the petitioners deducted the sum of the two interest payments, that is $143,465, as [interest under §163].

The second contract year began on December 11, 1954, when interest in advance of $143,465 was payable by Knetsch on his aggregate indebtedness of $4,099,000. Knetsch paid this amount on December 27, 1954. Three days later, on December 30, he received from the company cash in the amount of $104,000, the difference less $1,000 between his then $4,099,000 indebtedness and the cash or loan value of the bonds of $4,204,000 on December 11, 1955. He gave the company appropriate notes and prepaid the interest thereon of $3,640. In their joint return for the taxable year 1954 the petitioners deducted the sum of the two interest payments, that is $147,105, as "interest paid . . . within the taxable year on indebtedness," under §163(a) of the 1954 Code.

The tax years 1955 and 1956 are not involved in this proceeding, but a recital of the events of those years is necessary to complete the story of the transaction. On December 11, 1955, the start of the third contract year, Knetsch became obligated to pay $147,105 as prepaid interest on an indebtedness which now totalled $4,203,000. He paid this interest on December 28, 1955. On the same date he received $104,000 from the company. This was $1,000 less than the difference between his indebtedness and the cash or loan value of the bonds of $4,308,000 at December 11, 1956. Again he gave the company notes upon which he prepaid interest of $3,640. Petitioners claimed a deduction on their 1955 joint return for the aggregate of the payments, or $150,745.

Knetsch did not go on with the transaction for the fourth contract year beginning December 11, 1956, but terminated it on December 27, 1956. His indebtedness at that time totalled $4,307,000. The cash or loan value of the bonds was the $4,308,000 value at December 11, 1956, which had been the basis of the "loan" of December 28, 1955. He surrendered the bonds and his indebtedness was canceled. He received the difference of $1,000 in cash.

The contract called for a monthly annuity of $90,171 at maturity (when Knetsch would be 90 years of age) or for such smaller amount as would be produced by the cash or loan value after deduction of the then existing indebtedness. It was stipulated that if Knetsch had held the bonds to maturity and continued annually to borrow the net cash value less $1,000, the sum available for the annuity at maturity would be $1,000 ($8,388,000 cash or loan value less $8,387,000 of indebtedness), enough to provide an annuity of only $43 per month.

The trial judge made findings that "there was no commercial economic substance to the. . .transaction," that the parties did not intend that Knetsch "become indebted to Sam Houston," that "no indebtedness of [Knetsch] was created by any of the . . . transactions," and that "no economic gain could be achieved from the purchase of these bonds without regard to the tax consequences. . . ." His conclusion of law, based on this Court's decision in Deputy v. du Pont, 308 U.S. 488, was that "while in form the payments to Sam Houston were compensation for the use or forbearance of money, they were not in substance. As a payment of interest, the transaction was a sham."

We first examine the transaction between Knetsch and the insurance company to determine whether it created an "indebtedness" within the meaning of . . . §163(a) of the 1954 Code, or whether, as the trial court found, it was a sham. We put aside a finding by the District Court that Knetsch's "only motive in purchasing these 10 bonds was to attempt to secure an interest deduction."[15] As was said in Gregory v. Helvering, 293 U.S. 465, 469 (1935): "The legal right of a taxpayer to decrease the amount of what otherwise would be his taxes, or altogether avoid them, by means which the law permits, cannot be doubted. . . . But the question for determination is whether what was done, apart from the tax motive, was the thing which the statute intended."

When we examine "what was done" here, we see that Knetsch paid the insurance company $294,570 during the two taxable years involved and received $203,000 back in the form of "loans." What did Knetsch get for the out-of-pocket difference of $91,570? In form he had an annuity contract with a so-called guaranteed cash value at maturity of $8,388,000, which would produce monthly annuity payments of $90,171, or substantial life insurance proceeds in the event of his death before maturity. This, as we have seen, was a fiction, because each year Knetsch's annual borrowings kept the net cash value, on which any annuity or insurance payments would depend, at the relative pittance of $1,000. Plainly, therefore, Knetsch's

---

15. We likewise put aside Knetsch's argument that, because he received ordinary income when he surrendered the annuities in 1956, he has suffered a net loss even if the contested deductions are allowed, and that therefore his motive in taking out the annuities could not have been tax avoidance.

transaction with the insurance company did "not appreciably affect his beneficial interest except to reduce his tax. . . ." Gilbert v. Commissioner, 248 F.2d 399, 411 (dissenting opinion). For it is patent that there was nothing of substance to be realized by Knetsch from this transaction beyond a tax deduction. What he was ostensibly "lent" back was in reality only the rebate of a substantial part of the so-called "interest" payments. The $91,570 difference retained by the company was its fee for providing the facade of "loans" whereby the petitioners sought to reduce their 1953 and 1954 taxes in the total sum of $233,297.68. There may well be single-premium annuity arrangements with nontax substance which create an "indebtedness" for the purposes of . . . §163(a) of the 1954 Code. But this one is a sham.

The petitioners contend, however, that the Congress in enacting §264 of the 1954 Code authorized the deductions. They point out that §264(a)(2) denies a deduction for amounts paid on indebtedness incurred to purchase or carry a single-premium annuity contract, but only as to contracts purchased after March 1, 1954. The petitioners thus would attribute to Congress a purpose to allow the deduction of pre-1954 payments under transactions of the kind carried on by Knetsch with the insurance company without regard to whether the transactions created a true obligation to pay interest. Unless that meaning plainly appears we will not attribute it to Congress. "To hold otherwise would be to exalt artifice above reality and to deprive the statutory provision in question of all serious purpose." Gregory v. Helvering, *supra,* p. 470. We, therefore, look to the statute and materials relevant to its construction for evidence that Congress meant in §264(a)(2) to authorize the deduction of payments made under sham transactions entered into before 1954. We look in vain. . . .

The judgment of the Court of Appeals is affirmed.

Mr. Justice DOUGLAS, with whom Mr. Justice WHITTAKER and Mr. Justice STEWART concur, dissenting.

. . . It is true that in this transaction the taxpayer was bound to lose if the annuity contract is taken by itself. At least the taxpayer showed by his conduct that he never intended to come out ahead on that investment apart from this income tax deduction. Yet the same may be true where a taxpayer borrows money at 5% or 6% interest to purchase securities that pay only nominal interest; or where, with money in the bank earning 3%, he borrows from the selfsame bank at a higher rate. His aim there, as here, may only be to get a tax deduction for interest paid. Yet as long as the transaction itself is not hocus-pocus, the interest charges incident to completing it would seem to be deductible under the Internal Revenue Code as respects annuity contracts made prior to March 1, 1954, the date Congress selected for terminating this class of deductions. The insurance company existed; it operated under Texas law; it was authorized to issue these policies and to make these annuity loans. While the taxpayer was obligated to pay interest at the rate of $3\frac{1}{2}\%$ per annum, the annuity bonds increased in cash value at the rate of only $2\frac{1}{2}\%$ per annum. The insurance company's profit was in that 1-point spread.

Tax avoidance is a dominating motive behind scores of transactions. It is plainly present here. Will the Service that calls this transaction a "sham" today not press for collection of taxes arising out of the surrender of the annuity contract? I think it should, for I do not believe any part of the transaction was a "sham." To disallow the "interest" deduction because the annuity device was devoid of commercial substance is to draw a line which will affect a host of situations not now before us and which, with all deference, I do not think we can maintain when other cases reach here. The remedy is legislative. Evils or abuses can be particularized by Congress. We deal only with "interest" as commonly understood and as used across the board in myriad transactions. Since these transactions were real and legitimate in the insurance world and were consummated within the limits allowed by insurance policies, I would recognize them tax-wise.

Notes and Questions

1. *The structure of Mr. Knetsch's would-be tax shelter.* What was Mr. Knetsch hoping to gain by borrowing at 3.5 percent in order to invest at 2.5 percent? That's a losing proposition apart from taxes, but as we have seen in other tax arbitrage schemes, it can turn into a winning proposition if the interest expense is deductible and the investment return is not taxable. The plan depended on the 2.5 percent investment return not being subject to tax, because (1) increases in the value of annuity contracts, due to the passage of time, are treated as unrealized appreciation,[16] and (2) borrowing against unrealized appreciation is not treated as a realization event.[17] If Mr. Knetsch borrowed $4 million at 3.5 percent to invest in annuity bonds paying 2.5 percent, his pre-tax loss (for one year) would be $40,000.[18] However, if his marginal tax rate was, say, 40 percent,[19] the $56,000 tax savings from the $140,000 interest expense deduction would turn the $40,000 pre-tax loss into a $16,000 after-tax profit. In short, Mr. Knetsch was attempting to use the debt-financed purchase of an annuity to create the same sort of combination of tax-exempt income and deductible interest expense that one could create by a debt-financed purchase of municipal bonds, but for the interest disallowance rule of §265(a)(2).[20]

2. *The tax consequences of the events of 1956.* Suppose the Supreme Court had ruled that Mr. Knetsch was entitled to his tax shelter interest deductions. What, then, would have been the tax consequences of the termination of the annuity arrangement in 1956? Mr. Knetsch had a basis in the annuity bonds of $4,004,000 (the 1953 purchase price, financed by a $4 million loan and $4,000 of his own money). When he surrendered the bonds in 1956 his amount realized was $4,308,000, consisting of $1,000 cash and $4,307,000 of debt relief.[21] Thus, his taxable gain would have been $304,000—despite the fact that the *cash* he received in 1956 was a mere $1,000. Recall that Mr. Knetsch had received $307,000 of tax-free cash from the insurance company in the form of loans ($99,000 in 1953, and $104,000 in each of the next two years). The effect of the $304,000 inclusion in 1956 would have been to require him, belatedly, to pay tax on that cash. The $304,000 gain can be understood as the sum of the $307,000 cash received as loans, and the

16. See section E of Chapter 3.

17. See section B.1 of Chapter 3. Although borrowing against unrealized appreciation is not generally treated as a taxable event, under current §72(e)(4)(A) (a provision not in existence at the time of *Knetsch*) loans under annuity contracts are generally taxable.

18. $4,000,000 × (3.5% − 2.5%) = $40,000.

19. Actually, the top marginal tax rate at the time of the *Knetsch* facts was 91 percent(!), and Mr. Knetsch was probably in or near the top bracket.

20. See section B.1 of this chapter.

21. On debt relief as amount realized, see section C.2.c of Chapter 2.

$1,000 cash received on the surrender of the bonds, reduced by the $4,000 of his own money Mr. Knetsch had paid when he purchased the annuity bonds. The large "phantom gain" in 1956 would have offset the artificial losses generated by the tax shelter in the earlier years; when he closed out the deal in 1956 he would have been required to include in income an amount equal to the amount by which the tax system had overstated his losses in the earlier years.

The moral? Some tax shelters are based on permanent tax preferences, and some are based on deferral tax preferences. With a permanent tax preference (such as the §103 exclusion for municipal bond interest income), items of economic income are *never* subject to tax. With a deferral preference (such as accelerated cost recovery under §168, or the treatment of annuity loans in *Knetsch*), income is not taxed as it economically accrues, but it is taxed eventually. When a shelter is based on a deferral preference, there is an eventual price to pay for the artificial tax shelter losses — an offsetting amount of artificial gain when the taxpayer disposes of the shelter property. Even with the offsetting gain on disposition, however, the deferral created by this type of shelter can be very valuable. Moreover, some taxpayers fail (innocently or otherwise) to report the phantom gain on the disposition of a deferral-type shelter, and other taxpayers find a new shelter to offset the gain on the disposition of the old one.[22]

3. *A job for Congress or for the courts?* When taxpayers discover and exploit a loophole in the Internal Revenue Code, Congress can always close the loophole by legislation. As the Supreme Court notes in *Knetsch*, the enactment of §264(a)(2) clearly shut down *Knetsch*-type deals for contracts purchased after March 1, 1954.[23] Given the demonstrated ability of Congress to invalidate particular shelter schemes by explicit legislation, why should the courts give themselves a roving commission to identify and invalidate "sham transactions"? Does the old story about the Dutch boy and the dike suggest an answer?

4. *What's a sham?* Exactly what does it take, according to the Supreme Court in *Knetsch,* to make a transaction a "sham"? Is there genuine analytical content to the Court's approach, or is Justice Douglas right to hint that "sham" is just a conclusory label applied to deals that offend a judicial sense of tax propriety? Later opinions of the Supreme Court and lower courts have applied the general approach of *Knetsch* in a variety of contexts, but the scope of the sham transaction doctrine (and of related anti-abuse doctrines) remains uncertain. The following case represents one court's attempt to apply the approach of *Knetsch* to a tax shelter typical of those that flourished in the 1970s and 1980s, prior to the enactment of the passive loss rules (§469) in 1986. As with most shelters of that period, this one was based on the combination of accelerated depreciation (a deferral preference) and the interest expense deduction.

---

22. For a discussion of these concepts from a different angle, see the material on burned-out tax shelters in section C.2.c of Chapter 2.

23. In fact, the deal in *Knetsch* has been legislatively shut down several times over. In addition to §264(a)(2), *see* §72(e)(4)(A) (treating annuity policy loans as taxable distributions) and §163(d) (denying deductions for investment interest in excess of investment income).

RICE'S TOYOTA WORLD, INC. v. COMMISSIONER

752 F.2d 89 (4th Cir. 1985)

PHILLIPS, Circuit Judge: Rice's Toyota World (Rice) appeals the Tax Court's decision upholding the Commissioner's disallowance of interest and depreciation deductions that Rice took on income tax returns filed for 1976, 1977 and 1978 on the basis that underlying sale and leaseback transactions were, for tax purposes, a sham. . . .

I

In form the transactions in issue involved the sale and leaseback of a used computer and financing of the purchase by secured recourse and nonrecourse notes payable to the seller. The principal officer of Rice, a company primarily engaged in the sale of automobiles, learned about computer purchase-and-lease-back transactions through a friend who had already entered into a similar transaction through Finalco, a corporation primarily engaged in leasing capital equipment. Rice's accountant contacted Finalco to request information, and Finalco mailed Rice literature describing potential transactions. Finalco's literature noted that the transactions generate large tax losses in early years because the purchaser could claim depreciation deductions calculated under accelerated depreciation provisions as well as interest expense deductions. The transactions produce income in later years as depreciation deductions decrease.

After meeting with a Finalco representative, Rice purchased a used computer from Finalco in 1976 for a total purchase price of $1,455,227, giving Finalco a recourse note in the amount of $250,000 payable over three years, and two nonrecourse notes in the amount of $1,205,227 payable over eight years. Finalco had recently purchased the used computer for $1,297,643.

Rice leased the computer back to Finalco for a period of eight years, beginning in 1976. Under the lease, rental payments exceeded Rice's obligations on the nonrecourse debt by $10,000 annually. Finalco's obligations to pay rent were made contingent on its receiving adequate revenues in subleasing the computer. At the time of Rice's purchase and leaseback of the computer, Finalco had arranged a five-year sublease of the computer. Finalco was entitled to 30 percent of proceeds generated if it arranged re-lease or sale of the computer after expiration of the five year sublease.

Rice paid off the $250,000 recourse note in three years along with $30,000 in interest on the deferred installments. On its income tax returns for 1976, 1977, and 1978, it claimed accelerated depreciation deductions based upon its ownership of the computer, and interest deductions for its payments on the notes.

The tax court upheld the Commissioner's disallowance of all the depreciation deductions and the interest expense deductions based on both the recourse and nonrecourse notes because the court found that the sale and leaseback was a sham transaction that the Commissioner is entitled to ignore for tax purposes. The tax court found as fact that Rice was not motivated by any business purpose other than achieving tax benefits in entering this transaction, and that the transaction had no economic substance because no reasonable possibility of profit existed. The court accordingly held as a matter of law that the transaction should be treated for tax purposes as if Rice paid Finalco a fee, in the form of the cash payment of $62,500 made on the recourse note in the year of purchase, in exchange for tax benefits. . . .

II

The tax court read Frank Lyon Co. v. United States, 435 U.S. 561 (1978), to mandate a two-pronged inquiry to determine whether a transaction is, for tax purposes, a sham. To treat a transaction as a sham, the court must find that the taxpayer was motivated by no business purposes other than obtaining tax benefits in entering the transaction, and that the transaction has no economic substance because no reasonable possibility of a profit exists. We agree that such a test properly gives effect to the mandate of the Court in *Frank Lyon* that a transaction cannot be treated as a sham unless the transaction is shaped solely by tax avoidance considerations. *See* 435 U.S. at 583-84.

Whether under this test a particular transaction is a sham is an issue of fact, and our review of the tax court's subsidiary and ultimate findings on this factual issue is therefore under the clearly erroneous standard. Boyter v. Commissioner, 668 F.2d 1382, 1388 (4th Cir. 1981). Applying that standard, we affirm the tax court's findings on the sham issues.

A

The business purpose inquiry simply concerns the motives of the taxpayer in entering the transaction. The record in this case contains ample evidence to support the tax court's finding that Rice's sole motivation for purchasing and leasing back the computer under the financing arrangement used was to achieve the large tax deductions that the transaction provided in the early years of the lease.[24]

First, the record supports the court's subsidiary finding that Rice did not seriously evaluate whether the computer would have sufficient residual value at the end of the eight-year lease to Finalco to enable Rice to earn a profit on its purchase and seller-financed leaseback. Under the purchase and lease agreements with Finalco, Rice was obligated to pay (and did pay) $280,000 to Finalco in the form of principal and interest on the recourse note. Finalco's rental payments provided Rice with a return on the investment of $10,000 annually after payment of Rice's principal and interest obligations under the nonrecourse notes. At the time of the lease, Rice could therefore be certain of receiving a $50,000 return since Finalco had subleased the computer for five years, but Rice could recover the additional $230,000 of its investment only if it could re-lease the computer after five years or realize a substantial amount by its sale. Profit on the transaction

---

24. Finalco's literature projected losses of $782,063 during the first five years of the transaction, and Rice reported net losses of approximately $600,000 during the three years following his purchase. During the years immediately following Rice's purchase depreciation deductions are much larger than in later years due to accelerated depreciation provisions. In addition, interest expense deductions fall as the debt balance falls during the course of the lease. However, the transaction would produce net income for Rice in later years, and therefore, if Rice saw the transaction through to completion, it would receive a mere deferral of tax liability.

therefore depended upon re-lease or sale because Finalco had no obligation to pay rent under its lease unless it received adequate revenues in subleasing the computer. Moreover, the sale and leaseback agreement gave Finalco a "marketing fee" of 30 percent of re-lease or sale proceeds if Finalco arranged the subsequent deal, thereby increasing further the amount Rice had to receive on re-leasing or selling the computer to earn a profit.

Residual value of the computer (either in selling or releasing) should therefore have been the crucial point of inquiry for a person with a business purpose of making a profit on this transaction. However, Rice's principal officer knew virtually nothing about computers, and relied almost exclusively on the representations of a Finalco salesperson regarding expected residual value. Despite the Finalco representative's frank concession that he was not an expert in predicting residual values, Rice did not pursue the representative's offer to provide an expert appraisal of likely residual value. Rice's accountant advised that the transaction appeared to be profitable, but the record does not reveal that the accountant's opinion reflects anything more than the fact that the transaction, if successful, would generate large tax deductions. Although Rice had in its possession a report containing a chart that showed a possibility that the computer would have sufficient residual value to earn Rice a profit, the report warned of great risk in predicting residual values, and also showed a large possibility of losses on the transaction.

The record contains additional support for drawing the ultimate inference that Rice was not motivated by potential profit. First off, Finalco's literature emphasized the large tax deductions the transaction would produce, not the potential for profit. To the contrary, the literature warned of great difficulty in predicting residual values.

More critical is the evidence that Rice paid an inflated purchase price for the computer: $1,455,227 for a used computer that Finalco had recently purchased, in an already declining market, for only $1,297,643. Considering that Finalco had a right to 30 percent of re-leasing or sale proceeds after five years. Rice can more accurately be said to have purchased for this amount only 70 percent of a computer, then worth less than $1,000,000. Because Rice paid so obviously inflated a purchase price for the computer and financed the purchase mainly with nonrecourse debt, it was properly inferable by the tax court that Rice intended to abandon the transaction down the road by walking away from the nonrecourse note balance before the transaction ran its stated course. See Estate of Franklin v. Commissioner, 544 F.2d 1045, 1048-49 (9th Cir. 1976). The inference is amply supportable that this intended course of conduct explains Rice's apparent lack of concern with residual value or profitability of the transaction apart from tax benefits. . . .

All in all, Rice's failure seriously to evaluate the likely residual value of the computer, its willingness to pay an inflated purchase price, and its use of nonrecourse debt that would facilitate abandonment of the transaction provide ample support for the tax court's finding that Rice did not have profit motivation apart from tax benefits. We cannot declare that finding clearly erroneous.

B

The second prong of the sham inquiry, the economic substance inquiry, requires an objective determination of whether a reasonable possibility of profit from the transaction existed apart from tax benefits. As noted, the transaction carried no hope of earning Rice a profit unless the computer had residual value sufficient to recoup the $280,000 in principal and interest that Rice paid Finalco on the recourse note less the $10,000 net annual return to Rice under the lease agreement. Even assuming that Finalco paid Rice $10,000 annually for the full eight-year term, which is by no means assured, and ignoring the time value of Rice's money invested, Rice would have to realize $200,000 in residual value to earn a profit. If Finalco re-leased or sold the computer for Rice, the more likely development in view of Rice's lack of computer marketing experience, Rice would receive only 70 percent of the proceeds and would profit only if residual value exceeded approximately $286,000.

The record contains estimates of residual value made by several experts that range from a low of $18,000 to a high of $375,000. Although Rice's experts presented a range of predicted residual values with a high end sufficient to earn Rice a profit, the tax court found the Commissioner's experts to be more credible and to have used more reliable forecasting techniques. The tax court's finding that residual value was not sufficient to earn Rice a profit is amply supported by the record and is not clearly erroneous. This finding, in conjunction with the tax court finding that Rice would not find it imprudent to walk away from the transaction, abandoning the property subject to the sale and leaseback, supports the ultimate inference drawn by the tax court that the transaction lacked economic substance.

Hence, we affirm as not clearly erroneous the tax court's finding that Rice's transaction is a sham because Rice subjectively lacked a business purpose and the transaction objectively lacked economic substance.

C

We turn next to the consequences of the finding of a sham. Where a transaction is properly determined to be a sham, the Commissioner is entitled to ignore the labels applied by the parties and tax the transaction according to its substance. *See* Gregory v. Helvering, 293 U.S. 465, 469-70 (1935). We find no error in the tax court's determination that after stripping away the labels, Rice did not purchase or lease a computer, but rather, paid a fee to Finalco in exchange for tax benefits.

Since Rice's nonrecourse debt was similarly without economic substance, it cannot be relied upon to support the claimed interest deductions. *See* Knetsch v. United States, 364 U.S. 361, (1960); *cf.* Odend'hal v. Commissioner, 748 F.2d 908, 912 (4th Cir. 1984) (taxpayer may not deduct interest expense on portion of nonrecourse debt that he lacks incentive to pay off). Rice was therefore not entitled to depreciation deductions based upon inclusion of the amounts representing the nonrecourse notes in its basis on the computer because Rice had not truly made an investment in the computer. *See Odend'hal*, at 912 (nonrecourse loans not representing "a real investment" in property may not be included in basis to calculate depreciation); *Estate of Franklin*, 544 F.2d at 1049. Moreover, the amount of the recourse note was also not properly includable in basis to support depreciation deductions because, as the tax court properly held, the note did not represent an investment in property. *Cf. Odend'hal*, slip op. at 10 (taxpayer not allowed to include loan in basis since loan did not represent a "real investment" in property); *Estate of Franklin*, 544 F.2d at 1049 (depreciation is predicated upon an investment in property).

Therefore, we affirm the tax court in its disallowance as a matter of law of depreciation deductions reflecting inclusion of the amounts of the recourse and the nonrecourse notes in basis and in its disallowance of interest deductions based on the nonrecourse loans. [The court went on, however, to rule that the taxpayer was entitled to deduct interest payments on the recourse note. — EDS.]

Notes and Questions

1. *Some clarification, but how much?* *Rice's Toyota World* is an improvement over *Knetsch* insofar as it gives some analytical content to the judicial policing of abusive tax shelters. Rather than simply relying on an I-know-it-when-I-see-it approach, the court explains that a transaction is a tax sham if "the taxpayer was motivated by no business purposes other than obtaining tax benefits . . . and . . . the transaction has no economic substance because no reasonable possibility of a profit exists." The business purpose prong of the test inquires into the subjective motivation of the taxpayer, while the economic substance prong considers the objective profit potential of the transaction. As the opinion demonstrates, applying the two-pronged test requires a close examination of the taxpayer's behavior and of the economics of the transaction. Despite being more structured than the *Knetsch* approach, the *Rice's Toyota World* approach still involves considerable uncertainty. Intent-based tests are notoriously difficult to apply, and even the "objective" economic substance prong depends on debatable judgments (such as the residual value question in *Rice's Toyota World*).

2. *A disjunctive or conjunctive test?* Although the courts have generally agreed on the two-pronged test of subjective business purpose and objective economic substance, there has been disagreement as to whether the test is disjunctive or conjunctive. Some courts, including the Fourth Circuit in *Rice's Toyota World,* have stated that a transaction is not a sham if it has *either* a business purpose *or* economic substance. Other courts, however, have stated that a transaction is a sham unless it possesses *both* a business purpose *and* economic substance. *See, e.g.,* Pasternak v. Commissioner, 990 F.2d 893, 898 (6th Cir. 1993). For transactions occurring after March 30, 2010, the issue has been resolved by the codification of the economic substance doctrine in §7701(*o*) (described in part B.6 of this chapter). Under the new provision, a transaction has economic substance only if it satisfies both prongs of the two-pronged test. The choice between the conjunctive and disjunctive versions of the test may be less important than it seems, since a court seldom finds that a transaction satisfies one prong of the test but fails the other.

3. *Tax benefits clearly contemplated by Congress.* A taxpayer buys municipal bonds paying 5 percent interest, with the expectation that the interest income will be tax-free under §103. He could have bought comparable corporate bonds paying 7 percent interest, but he was willing to accept the lower pre-tax interest rate in order to obtain the tax exemption. Could the IRS argue that the investment is a sham, and that he should be taxed on the interest under the logic of *Rice's Toyota World*? The argument would be that the taxpayer had no non-tax business purpose for buying municipal bonds rather than corporate bonds, and that buying municipal bonds offered no objective potential for profit if profit is measured relative to a corporate bond baseline. The IRS would not make the argument, and if it did it would lose in court. It makes no

sense to interpret the sham transaction doctrine so expansively that it repeals tax benefits expressly legislated by Congress. The IRS and the courts agree that the business purpose and economic substance tests do not apply to disallow tax benefits clearly contemplated by Congress. This leaves room for argument in some cases as to whether Congress clearly contemplated particular taxpayer-favorable results.

4. *Not every tax shelter is a sham. Rice's Toyota World* and similar cases were as important for what they did not do as for what they did do. They did not call into question the basic pre-1986 tax shelter strategy of creating artificial losses through the use of debt-financed investments in tax-favored assets (most commonly assets eligible for accelerated cost recovery deductions). The taxpayer lost in *Rice's Toyota World* because it got greedy and claimed depreciation deductions based on an inflated purchase price; the lack of business purpose and economic substance followed from the unrealistically high price. During the pre-1986 era, less greedy taxpayers routinely succeeded in deducting artificial losses from their debt-financed investments in depreciable assets. No amount of IRS success in litigating cases like *Rice's Toyota World* could have put an end to the debt-financed tax shelter phenomenon; for that the passive loss rules of §469 were needed.

5. *The incentive to inflate the purchase price.* What explains the inflated purchase price phenomenon in *Rice's Toyota World* (and many other tax shelters of the same era)? Depreciation deductions are a function of basis; a higher basis means larger deductions. Did it really make sense, though, to pay more for an asset than it was worth, just to obtain larger depreciation deductions? It would not, if you were paying cash for the asset or financing the purchase with a recourse loan. Suppose you paid $100 more than fair market value for an asset. If your marginal tax rate was 30 percent, the tax savings from an extra $100 of depreciation deductions would be only $30, leaving you with a $70 after-tax loss on the overpayment.[25] If the overpayment were financed by a nonrecourse loan of cash from a bank, the taxpayer might not object to the inflated purchase price, but no bank would be willing to make a nonrecourse loan of (for example) $300 cash secured only by a mortgage on property worth $200. Tax shelters with intentionally inflated purchase prices made sense only in the context of nonrecourse financing provided by the seller (as in *Rice's Toyota World*). The buyer was willing to agree to the inflated price because he knew he would never have to make the payments on the under-secured nonrecourse note. The seller did not care that the buyer would never pay off the note, because the deal was structured for the seller to make a nice profit even with the buyer defaulting on the note. Finally, the seller could use the installment method of §453 to avoid paying tax on the gain generated by the inflated purchase price.[26]

25. Actually, the after-tax loss would be as small as $70 only if you could claim the entire $100 deduction in the year of purchase. With the extra $100 deduction spread out over the asset's cost recovery period, in present value terms the after-tax loss would be more than $70.

26. Notice the inconsistent treatment of the two sides of a seller-financed transaction. The buyer is allowed to include the debt to the seller in basis, and can immediately start claiming depreciation deductions based on the debt. The seller, however, can use §453 to defer tax on the gain until the buyer makes principal payments on the note.

5. *Post-1986 Tax Shelters*

The enactment of the passive loss rules in 1986 virtually eliminated the traditional type of tax shelter, based on the combination of a tax preference and an interest expense deduction, and mass-marketed to individual taxpayers of moderate affluence. Beginning in the 1990s, however, the IRS struggled with a new generation of tax shelters. These were commonly referred to as "corporate shelters," because tax shelter promoters originally marketed them only to large corporations. Eventually, however, shelter promoters expanded their marketing efforts to very high income individuals. The very complicated transactions involved in these shelters had such high transaction costs that they could not feasibly be marketed to any taxpayers who did not have very high incomes. (This description uses the past tense because, as will be described more fully below, Congress and the IRS seem to have won their battle against the post-1986 tax shelter industry, at least for the moment.)

Whereas all the shelters attacked by §469 were based on the same theme, the post-1986 shelters were more varied and more sophisticated. These shelters often used literal interpretations of highly technical statutory and regulatory provisions to produce results that Congress never intended or even imagined. When the validity of a post-1986 shelter is litigated (post-1986 shelters are still being litigated, although few if any new ones are being created), the taxpayer argues that the statute or regulation must be applied literally regardless of the consequences, while the government calls upon the business purpose and economic substance tests — developed in response to earlier generations of tax shelters — in arguing that the literal language should be ignored when it would produce unreasonable results not contemplated by Congress.[27]

Many post-1986 shelters were based on specialized provisions beyond the scope of a basic income tax course. The shelter in the case below, however, is based on a reasonably easy-to-understand provision in the regulations governing §453 installment sales.[28] As you may recall, gradual basis recovery under the installment method formula of §453(c) is straightforward when the principal amount of the installment note is fixed. However, the statute does not explain how to apply the installment method if the principal amount is subject to one or more contingencies. Filling the gap in the statute, the regulations provide rules so that gain from contingent payment installment sales can be reported on the installment method. If there is a stated maximum selling price, then the installment method is applied by treating that price as the selling price in the installment method formula. Treas. Reg. §15a.453-1(c)(2). The regulations provide for appropriate adjustments if it turns out that the actual payments are less than the stated maximum amount. If there is no stated maximum selling price, but there is a maximum number of years over which payments may be made, then the taxpayer's basis is recovered ratably over that number of years (again, with appropriate later adjustments, if necessary). Treas. Reg. §15a.453-1(c)(3). Finally, if there is neither a stated maximum selling

---

27. The IRS has no choice but to accept provisions producing unreasonable results clearly contemplated by Congress — of which there are more than a few.
28. See section D of Chapter 3 for §453.

price nor a maximum number of payment years, then the taxpayer generally recovers his basis ratably over a 15-year period. Treas. Reg. §15a.453-1(c)(4).

The regulations recognize that application of these rules might, in a particular case, "substantially and inappropriately defer or accelerate recovery of the taxpayer's basis," and so provide special rules for such cases. Treas. Reg. §15a.453-1(c)(7). If the normal rules would inappropriately defer basis recovery — and thus inappropriately accelerate gain recognition — the taxpayer may apply to the IRS for permission to use an alternative method of basis recovery. If the normal rules would inappropriately accelerate basis recovery — and thus inappropriately defer gain recognition — the IRS may, on its own initiative, require the taxpayer to use an alternative method of basis recovery.

Nothing in the regulations permits the IRS to act on its own initiative if the normal rules would accelerate recognition of gain. After all, if the taxpayer doesn't object to acceleration of gain recognition, why should the IRS? At first glance, this hardly seems like a tax loophole. But the major accounting firms (and, to a lesser degree, some law firms) employed people whose entire job was to pore over the Internal Revenue Code in the spirit of W.C. Fields's deathbed reading of the Bible — looking for loopholes. Once they found a good one, they sold it for a hefty fee to corporations and high income individuals in need of tax shelters. Someone figured out how to turn the seemingly innocuous rules for contingent payment installment sales into a tax shelter, and the following case is the result.

ACM PARTNERSHIP v. COMMISSIONER
157 F.3d 231 (3d Cir. 1998), *cert. denied,* **526 U.S. 1017 (1999)**

GREENBERG, Circuit Judge: [Colgate had over $100 million of long-term capital gains (mostly from the sale of a subsidiary), on which it preferred not to pay tax. Merrill Lynch proposed a tax shelter partnership (ACM) among Colgate, a foreign entity not subject to United States taxation (ABN), and Merrill Lynch, for the purpose of generating capital losses to offset Colgate's capital gains. Colgate accepted the proposal. The following description somewhat simplifies the actual transaction, and uses numbers rounded for computational convenience. Using money contributed by the partners, ACM bought $180 million of short-term debt securities (Citicorp notes), and then quickly sold the Citicorp notes for $140 million cash and contingent payment installment notes (LIBOR notes) providing for payments over the next five years, with a present value of $40 million. The amount realized on the sale roughly equaled ACM's basis in the notes, so the total gain realized was minimal.

Because the LIBOR notes provided for contingent payments with no maximum stated amount but with a fixed payment period (six years), ACM took the position that Treas. Reg. §15a.453-1(c)(3) governed the sale, and required ACM to recover its $180 million basis at the rate of $30 million per year over a six-year period (consisting of the year of sale, and the five subsequent years in which payments were due on the notes). Under this approach, the result in the year of sale would be a capital gain of $110 million ($140 million cash down payment minus $30 million basis). After the first year, the remaining basis in the LIBOR notes would be $150 million, despite the notes being worth only about $40 million. Thus, there would be an artificial loss of $110 million built into the notes, offsetting the $110 million artificial capital gain recognized in the year of sale. Although the contingent payment regulations do not permit recognition of a loss while the taxpayer continues to hold the installment notes, the partnership was able to recognize the loss by selling the notes two years after the installment sale.

The partnership was designed so that ABN was the majority partner in the year of the installment sale. Thus the bulk of the $110 million of capital gain was allocated to ABN. ABN had no objection to this allocation, because it was not subject to U.S. taxation. By the time the partnership recognized the offsetting artificial loss in the later year, Colgate's interest in the partnership was greater than 99 percent. As a result, virtually all the loss was allocated to Colgate, and Colgate used that loss to shelter most of its capital gains from tax. (*See* §1212(a), which allows a corporation to carry a capital loss back three years.) Although application of the contingent payment regulations resulted in inappropriate acceleration of gain, ACM of course did not request permission to use a different method of basis recovery, and the regulations did not give the IRS authority to impose a different method unilaterally. — EDS.]

We must decide whether the Tax Court erred in disallowing ACM's claimed . . . capital loss which the [Tax Court] characterized as a "phantom loss from a transaction that lacks economic substance." . . .

ACM contends that, because its transactions on their face satisfied each requirement of the contingent installment sale provisions and regulations thereunder, it properly deducted the losses arising from its "straightforward application" of these provisions, which required it to recover only one-sixth of the basis in the Citicorp notes during the first of the six years over which it was to receive payments. . . .

While ACM's transactions, at least in form, satisfied each requirement of the contingent installment sale provisions and ratable basis recovery rule, ACM acknowledges that even where the "form of the taxpayer's activities indisputably satisfies the literal requirements" of the relevant statutory language, the courts must examine "whether the substance of those transactions was consistent with their form," because a transaction that is "devoid of economic substance . . . simply is not recognized for federal taxation purposes." . . .

[W]e find that both the objective analysis of the actual economic consequences of ACM's transactions and the subjective analysis of their intended purposes support the Tax Court's conclusion that ACM's transactions did not have sufficient economic substance to be respected for tax purposes.

In assessing the economic substance of a taxpayer's transactions, the courts have examined "whether the transaction has any practical economic effects other than the creation of income tax losses," and have refused to recognize the tax consequences of transactions that were devoid of "nontax substance" because they "did not appreciably affect [the taxpayer's] beneficial interest except to reduce his tax." Knetsch v. United States, 364 U.S. 361, 366 (1960). . . .

Viewed according to their objective economic effects rather than their form, ACM's transactions involved only a fleeting and economically inconsequential investment in and offsetting divestment from the Citicorp notes. . . .

While ACM contends that "it would be absurd to conclude that the application of the Commissioner's own [ratable basis recovery] regulations results in gains or losses that the Commissioner can then deem to be other than 'bona fide,'" its argument confounds a tax accounting regulation which merely prescribes a method for reporting otherwise existing deductible losses . . . with a substantive deductibility provision authorizing the deduction of certain losses. In order to be deductible, a loss must reflect actual economic consequences sustained in an economically substantive transaction and cannot result solely from the application of a tax accounting rule to bifurcate a loss component of a transaction from its offsetting gain component to generate an artificial loss which, as the Tax Court found, is "not economically inherent in" the transaction.[29] Based on our review of the record regarding the objective economic consequences of ACM's short-swing, offsetting investment in and divestment from the Citicorp notes, we find ample support for the Tax Court's determination that ACM's transactions generated only "phantom losses" which cannot form the basis of a capital loss deduction under the Internal Revenue Code. . . .

McKEE, Circuit Judge, dissenting.

By finding that ACM's sales of the Citicorp notes for cash and LIBOR Notes "satisfied each requirement of the contingent installment sales provisions and the ratable basis recovery rule," yet, simultaneously subjecting these transactions to an economic substance and sham transaction analysis, the majority has ignored the plain language of IRC §1001, and controlling Supreme Court precedent. We have injected the "economic substance" analysis into an inquiry where it does not belong. Therefore, I respectfully dissent. . . .

I can't help but suspect that the majority's conclusion to the contrary is, in its essence, something akin to a "smell test." If the scheme in question smells bad, the intent to avoid taxes defines the result as we do not want the taxpayer to "put one over." However, the issue clearly is not whether ACM put one over on the Commissioner, or used LIBOR notes to "pull the wool over his eyes." The issue is whether what ACM did qualifies for the tax treatment it seeks under §1001. The fact that ACM may have "put one over" in crafting these transactions ought not to influence our inquiry. Our inquiry is cerebral, not visceral. To the extent that the Commissioner is offended by these transactions he should address Congress and/or the rulemaking process, and not the courts. . . .

Notes and Questions

1. *The business purpose and economic substance doctrines.* As the disagreement between Judge Greenberg and Judge McKee suggests, it is hard to predict whether a court faced with a tax shelter gimmick designed to exploit an unintended loophole will congratulate the taxpayer for its resourcefulness and suggest the IRS might seek legislative relief, or will instead use the

---

29. Because the ratable basis recovery rule simply provides a method for reporting otherwise existing economically substantive losses, we find it irrelevant that the rule recognizes that its application could "inappropriately defer or accelerate recovery of the taxpayer's basis, resulting in 'substantial distortion'" of the tax consequences realized in any particular year of a transaction. While the rule contemplates some distortion as to the timing of when actual gains or losses are reported over the span of a contingent installment sale, it does not contemplate the reporting of losses which are not the bona fide result of an economically substantive transaction. Thus, contrary to ACM's argument, the tax losses it reported are not "precisely what the [regulations] intended."

business purpose and economic substance doctrines (or a "smell test") to deny the taxpayer the hoped-for tax shelter losses. Because of the doctrines, the mere fact that a tax shelter plan complies with the literal requirements of the Code or regulations is no guarantee that the plan will survive an IRS challenge. As applied by the Third Circuit in *ACM*, the doctrines constitute a significant limitation on aggressive tax planning.

2. *The mills of the gods grind slowly, if at all.* In response to *ACM*-type tax shelters, in 1990 the IRS announced that it was planning to amend Reg. §15a.453-1(c)(7) "to clarify that the Service may require an alternative method of basis recovery with respect to installment obligations where basis is inappropriately deferred." Notice 90-56, 1990-2 C.B. 344. Two decades later, the regulation remains unchanged. It is easy to understand why the IRS does not want to rely *solely* on loophole-closing amendments (regulatory or statutory) in its fight against tax shelters; like the Dutch boy trying to plug the leaks in the dike, the IRS cannot close discovered loopholes as fast as tax planners can discover new ones. Hence the need for the economic substance and business purpose doctrines. None of this explains, however, why a regulation clearly in need of amendment has not been revised.

3. *The audit lottery.* The IRS's litigation record against post-1986 tax shelters has been good, but well short of perfect (as demonstrated by the *IES* opinion below). Many—but by no means all—of the tax shelter losses challenged by the IRS in court have been disallowed under the business purpose and economic substance doctrines or under related anti-abuse doctrines. The biggest problem for the IRS, however, is not the corporate tax shelter cases it litigates, but the tax shelters it never finds. If the odds of detection of a shelter are low, and if the penalties in the case of detection are mild,[30] there is little to deter taxpayers from engaging in highly dubious tax shelter transactions and playing the "audit lottery" in the hopes of avoiding detection.

4. *The odds have changed.* In the wake of recent statutory and regulatory developments, however, taxpayers should assume that the odds are very high that the IRS will detect their shelters.[31] Treas. Reg. §1.6011-4(a) (promulgated in 2003) requires any taxpayer who has participated in a "reportable transaction" to file a "reportable transaction disclosure statement" with the IRS as a tax return attachment. Reportable transactions are defined broadly enough to include most tax shelters. In 2004 Congress enacted a series of tax shelter compliance provisions on the foundation of the 2003 regulatory reform. If a taxpayer fails to comply with the regulatory disclosure requirements, §6707A imposes substantial penalties. If the taxpayer fails to disclose despite the threat of the non-disclosure penalty, the IRS is still likely to receive notice of the taxpayer's shelter from the tax shelter promoter. Section 6111 requires a "material advisor with respect to any reportable transaction" to disclose the details of the transaction to the IRS, and §6112 requires the advisor to maintain and make available to the IRS for inspection a list of the taxpayers investing in the shelter. Section 6707 penalizes

30. *See* §6662, which imposes a 20 percent penalty on a substantial understatement of tax.
31. This note is adapted from Lawrence Zelenak, *Tax Enforcement for Gamers: High Penalties or Strict Disclosure Rules?*, 109 Colum. L. Rev. Sidebar 55 (2009).

failures of material advisors to comply with the disclosure requirements of §6111. Finally, §6708 penalizes failures of material advisors to comply with the list maintenance and inspection requirements of §6112. If either the taxpayer or the tax shelter promoter complies with these disclosure requirements, the taxpayer will assume — probably correctly — that the IRS will almost certainly detect the shelter and challenge the claimed tax benefits. With the audit lottery thus nearly eliminated as a factor in the cost-benefit calculations, taxpayers should reject many shelters that would have attracted them before the imposition of the disclosure requirements. Of course, the disclosure requirements solve the government's audit lottery problem only if taxpayers, their material advisors, or both, comply with the requirements. The new disclosure regime would fail if taxpayers and their advisors were to perform cost-benefit analyses indicating that the optimal strategy is to ignore the disclosure requirements and hope the IRS remains oblivious. Judging from the comments of top-level Treasury and IRS officials, however, it appears that strategic non-compliance has not been a major problem. In 2006, then-IRS Commissioner Mark Everson told a Senate panel, "No longer are abusive tax shelters being marketed by top level accounting firms."[32] Similarly, in late 2008 outgoing IRS Chief Counsel Donald Korb remarked that "we — the IRS, Treasury, and [the] Justice [Department] — have really turned the corner on tax shelters."[33] Tax shelter promoters have been remarkably resilient in the past, however, and it would be a mistake to assume the government has slain the tax shelter dragon once and for all.

As noted above, the IRS has not won all its post-1986 tax shelter cases. The *IES* opinion below is one of the government's defeats. It considers a corporate tax shelter involving the foreign tax credit (FTC). The case is included here not for any light it sheds on the operation of the FTC (a topic far beyond the scope of an introductory income tax course), but because it illustrates a judicial attitude to corporate tax shelters very different from the attitude illustrated in *ACM*. To follow the court's analysis, a little background on the FTC is necessary. If a U.S. taxpayer (an individual or a corporation) has foreign source income, that income will generally be subject to income tax in both the source country and the United States. To alleviate the burden of double taxation, the taxpayer may claim a foreign tax credit, under IRC §27, in determining its U.S. tax liability. The amount of the credit is the lesser of (1) the foreign tax paid on the income subject to tax in both jurisdictions, or (2) the amount of U.S. tax liability (pre-credit) generated by the income subject to tax in both jurisdictions. For example, if a taxpayer has $100 of income subject to U.S. and foreign income taxation, the foreign tax rate is 30 percent, and the U.S. tax rate is 40 percent, then the taxpayer is entitled to a $30 FTC (and so will pay $30 of foreign tax and $10 of U.S. tax on the $100). On the other hand, if the foreign tax rate is 30 percent and the U.S. rate is 25 percent, the taxpayer is entitled to an FTC of only $25 (and so will pay $30 of foreign tax and no

---

32. Mark Everson, *Everson Testimony Calls for "Fundamental Reform" to Deal with Tax Gap*, Tax Notes Today, September 27, 2006, 2006 TNT 187-36.
33. Jeremiah Coder, *Korb Reflects on Long Tenure as Chief Counsel*, 122 Tax Notes 20, 21 (2009).

U.S. tax on the $100). Because the amount of the FTC is limited to the amount of the U.S. tax liability generated by the income in question, the FTC is of no value to an entity exempt from U.S. tax (such as a pension fund).

IES INDUSTRIES, INC. v. UNITED STATES
253 F.3d 350 (8th Cir. 2001)

BOWMAN, Circuit Judge: IES Industries, Inc. appeals from the order of the District Court granting the United States summary judgment on IES's claim for tax refunds to which IES contends it is entitled as a result of securities trades that the court held to be sham transactions. . . .

[A pension fund owned stock of a publicly traded foreign corporation[34] which was about to pay a dividend subject to foreign income tax. The resulting FTC would be of no use to the pension fund, but Twenty-First Securities Corporation (a securities broker) devised a plan that it claimed would, in effect, enable IES—a taxable U.S. corporation that could use the FTC—to purchase the FTC from the pension fund. The essence of the plan was as follows (using illustrative, rather than actual, dollar amounts). IES bought stock of the foreign corporation from the pension fund after the corporation had declared a dividend but before the dividend had been paid. The amount of the declared dividend was $100, but the dividend was subject to a 15 percent foreign withholding tax, so the amount to be received by the shareholder as of the dividend payment date was $85. IES paid $285 for the stock—$85 for the right to receive the dividend, and $200 for the stock apart from the dividend right. IES collected the $85 net dividend, and then immediately sold the stock ex-dividend for $200. The plan was premised on IES's ability to claim both a $15 foreign tax credit and an $85 capital loss on the sale of the stock (purchased cum-dividend for $285, sold ex-dividend for $200). IES would use the $85 capital loss to offset an $85 capital gain it had realized in an unrelated transaction. If the plan succeeded, the tax savings would be $15(1 − t), where t = IES's marginal tax rate. If the rate was 35 percent, for example, the tax savings would be $15 × .65 = $9.75. This is the sum of the tax savings from the credit ($15), the tax burden of the tax on the $100 dividend (−$35), and the tax savings from the $85 capital loss ($29.75). —EDS.]

The [District Court] granted the government's motion for summary judgment, concluding that the transactions "were shaped solely by tax avoidance considerations, had no other practical economic effect, and are properly disregarded for tax purposes." IES appeals and we reverse.

The District Court viewed "the question presented" as "whether these transactions are a sham and therefore to be disregarded for tax purposes." In determining whether a transaction is a sham for tax purposes, the Eighth Circuit has applied a two-part test set forth in Rice's Toyota World, Inc. v. Commissioner, 752 F.2d 89, 91-92 (4th Cir. 1985), which the Fourth Circuit ostensibly found in the Supreme Court's opinion in Frank Lyon Co. v. United States, 435 U.S. 561 (1978). *See*

---

34. [More precisely, the pension fund owned American Depository Receipts (ADRs). As the opinion explains, "ADRs are publicly traded securities, or receipts, fully negotiable in U.S. dollars, that represent shares of a foreign corporation held in trust by a U.S. bank." —EDS.]

Shriver v. Comm'r, 899 F.2d 724, 725-726 (8th Cir. 1990). Applying that test, a transaction will be characterized as a sham if "it is not motivated by any economic purpose outside of tax considerations" (the business purpose test), and if it "is without economic substance because no real potential for profit exists" (the economic substance test). *Id.* at 725, 725-726. The *Shriver* court analyzed the transaction at issue in that case under both parts of the test, but then said in dictum, "We do not read *Frank Lyon* to say anything that mandates a two-part analysis." *Id.* at 727. The Court suggested that a failure to demonstrate either economic substance *or* business purpose — both not required — would result in the conclusion that the transaction in question was a sham for tax purposes. As in *Shriver,* we do not decide whether the *Rice's Toyota World* test requires a two-part analysis because we conclude that the ADR trades here had both economic substance and business purpose.

The District Court dealt with the sham transaction issue summarily and did not apply, or even mention, the *Rice's Toyota World* test iterated in *Shriver.* After a cursory review of the facts and the law, the court simply concluded that the only change in IES's "economic position" as a result of the ADR transactions was "the transfer of the claim to the foreign tax credit to IES," and therefore that the transactions were shams. Assuming this was an application of the objective economic substance test, we will first consider whether there was a "reasonable possibility of profit . . . apart from tax benefits," that is, whether the transactions had economic substance. *Shriver,* 899 F.2d at 726 (quoting *Rice's Toyota World,* 752 F.2d at 94).

The government insists that, "absent the tax benefits that were the sole reason for the transactions, each series of ADR trade pairs resulted, as pre-planned, in an economic loss." According to the government's view of the transaction, "IES purchased only the right to the net dividend — not the gross dividend." Under that view, economic benefit accrues to IES *only* if it receives the foreign tax credit. In other words, the government would have us regard only 85% of the dividends as income to IES, notwithstanding that the IRS treats 100% as income for tax purposes.

We reject the government's argument and agree with IES that the law supports our contrary conclusion: the economic benefit to IES was the amount of the *gross* dividend, before the foreign taxes were paid. IES was the legal owner of the ADRs on the record date. As such, it was legally entitled to retain the benefits of ownership, that is, the dividends due on the record date. While it received only 85% in cash, 100% of the amount of the dividends was income to IES. "'Income' may be realized by a variety of indirect means." Diedrich v. Comm'r, 457 U.S. 191, 195 (1982) (analyzing, and ultimately agreeing with, IRS's position that payment of gift tax by donee, which was obligation of donor, constituted income to donor). In this case, income was realized by the payment of IES's foreign tax obligation by a third party. The fact that the taxes were withheld, and then paid, by the foreign corporation that issued the stock represented by the ADRs, so that IES received only 85% of the dividend in cash, is of no consequence to IES's liability for the tax. "The discharge by a third person of an obligation to him is equivalent to receipt by the person taxed." *Id.* (quoting Old Colony Trust Co. v. Comm'r, 279 U.S. 716, 729 (1929)). The foreign corporation's withholding and payment of the tax on IES's behalf is no different from an employer withholding and paying to the government income taxes for an employee: the full amount before taxes are paid is considered income to the employee. *See id.* Because the entire amount of the ADR dividends was income to IES, the ADR transactions resulted in a profit, an economic benefit to IES.

As for the business purpose test, the *Shriver* court explained that the proper inquiry is "whether the taxpayer was induced to commit capital for reasons only relating to tax considerations or whether a non-tax motive, or legitimate profit motive, was involved." *Shriver*, 899 F.2d at 726. In other words, the business purpose test is a subjective economic substance test. The *Shriver* court considered the District Court's "subjective analysis of the taxpayer's intent" and the court's review of such factors as the depth and accuracy of the taxpayer's investigation into the investment. *Id.* To the extent the taxpayer's subjective intent is material, we too will consider factors that are arguably relevant to the inquiry. We do so, however, mindful of the fact that "the legal right of a taxpayer to decrease the amount of what otherwise would be his taxes, or altogether avoid them, by means which the law permits, cannot be doubted." Gregory v. Helvering, 293 U.S. 465, 469 (1935). A taxpayer's subjective intent to avoid taxes thus will not by itself determine whether there was a business purpose to a transaction.

In their briefs, both parties discuss the risk of loss inherent in the trades, evidently presuming that the degree of risk goes to IES's subjective intent in engaging in the transactions. The government argues that the transactions must be characterized as shams because there was no risk of loss. We disagree. The risk may have been minimal, but that was in part because IES did its homework before engaging in the transactions.... We are not prepared to say that a transaction should be tagged a sham for tax purposes merely because it does not involve excessive risk. IES's disinclination to accept any more risk than necessary in these circumstances strikes us as an exercise of good business judgment consistent with a subjective intent to treat the ADR trades as money-making transactions....

The fact that IES took advantage of duly enacted tax laws in conducting the ADR trades does not convert the transactions into shams for tax purposes.

We hold, considering all the facts and circumstances of this case, that the ADR trades in which IES engaged did not, as a matter of law, lack business purpose or economic substance. Accordingly, IES is entitled to summary judgment on its claim for a tax refund. The judgment is reversed and the case is remanded to the District Court for further action consistent with this opinion.

Notes and Questions

1. *The* Compaq *case.* Later in the same year, the Fifth Circuit reached the same pro-taxpayer conclusion, on almost identical facts, in Compaq Computer Corp. v. Commissioner, 277 F.3d 778 (2001).

2. *A formalistic test for substance.* Review the court's consideration of the objective economic substance test, which the court states as "whether there was a reasonable possibility of profit apart from tax benefits." One might think the answer would be no; after all, the plan was to buy stock for $285 and then to collect a net-of-foreign-tax dividend of $85 and sales proceeds of $200. Sounds like a wash, doesn't it? But the court holds that the economic substance analysis should disregard the $15 of foreign tax, and with that expense disregarded the taxpayer has made a

$15 profit.[35] The irony is that this approach — foreign taxes don't count for purposes of economic substance analysis — is a highly *formalistic* approach to a doctrine that is supposed to be about substance. If courts are going to apply the economic substance doctrine in that manner, is there any point to having the doctrine at all?

3. *More formalism.* Review the court's consideration of the subjective business purpose test. The court concludes that the transactions exposed IES to a "minimal" risk of loss, and that exposure to a minimal risk of loss constitutes a business purpose. How can taking a risk of a loss constitute, in and of itself, a business purpose? Shouldn't the test be about expectation of profit? Even assuming that taking a risk of loss can satisfy the business purpose test, should a minimal risk be enough? In any event, the idea that the business purpose test is about "minimal" anything (whether risk of loss or hope of profit) is in keeping with the formalism of the court's approach to the economic substance doctrine.

6. *Codification of the Economic Substance Doctrine*

Opinions such as *IES* and *Compaq* gave rise to considerable concern in Congress that the courts might be in the process of eviscerating the judge-made anti-abuse doctrines, with very serious revenue consequences. In 2003, the Senate passed a bill that would have codified and clarified the economic substance doctrine, but the bill did not become law. Other efforts to codify the doctrine in subsequent years also failed. In 2010, however, the proponents of codification finally succeeded. The explanation of the 2010 legislation by the Staff of the Joint Committee on Taxation is set forth below.

STAFF OF THE JOINT COMMITTEE ON TAXATION, TECHNICAL EXPLANATION OF THE REVENUE PROVISIONS OF THE "RECONCILIATION ACT OF 2010," AS AMENDED, IN COMBINATION WITH THE "PATIENT PROTECTION AND AFFORDABLE CARE ACT"

(2010)

EXPLANATION OF PROVISION

The provision clarifies and enhances the application of the economic substance doctrine. Under the provision, new section 7701(*o*) provides that in the case of any transaction to which the economic substance doctrine is relevant, such transaction is treated as having economic substance only if (1) the transaction changes in a meaningful way (apart from Federal income tax effects) the taxpayer's economic position, and (2) the taxpayer has a substantial purpose (apart from Federal income tax effects) for entering into such transaction. The provision provides a

---

35. $100 gross dividend plus $200 sales proceeds minus $285 purchase price.

uniform definition of economic substance, but does not alter the flexibility of the courts in other respects.

The determination of whether the economic substance doctrine is relevant to a transaction is made in the same manner as if the provision had never been enacted. Thus, the provision does not change present law standards in determining when to utilize an economic substance analysis.[36]

The provision is not intended to alter the tax treatment of certain basic business transactions that, under longstanding judicial and administrative practice are respected, merely because the choice between meaningful economic alternatives is largely or entirely based on comparative tax advantages. Among these basic transactions are (1) the choice between capitalizing a business enterprise with debt or equity; (2) a U.S. person's choice between utilizing a foreign corporation or a domestic corporation to make a foreign investment; (3) the choice to enter a transaction or series of transactions that constitute a corporate organization or reorganization under subchapter C; and (4) the choice to utilize a related-party entity in a transaction, provided that the arm's length standard of section 482 and other applicable concepts are satisfied. Leasing transactions, like all other types of transactions, will continue to be analyzed in light of all the facts and circumstances. As under present law, whether a particular transaction meets the requirements for specific treatment under any of these provisions is a question of facts and circumstances. Also, the fact that a transaction meets the requirements for specific treatment under any provision of the Code is not determinative of whether a transaction or series of transactions of which it is a part has economic substance.

The provision does not alter the court's ability to aggregate, disaggregate, or otherwise recharacterize a transaction when applying the doctrine. For example, the provision reiterates the present-law ability of the courts to bifurcate a transaction in which independent activities with non-tax objectives are combined with an unrelated item having only tax-avoidance objectives in order to disallow those tax-motivated benefits.

CONJUNCTIVE ANALYSIS

The provision clarifies that the economic substance doctrine involves a conjunctive analysis — there must be an inquiry regarding the objective effects of the transaction on the taxpayer's economic position as well as an inquiry regarding the taxpayer's subjective motives for engaging in the transaction. Under the

---

36. If the realization of the tax benefits of a transaction is consistent with the Congressional purpose or plan that the tax benefits were designed by Congress to effectuate, it is not intended that such tax benefits be disallowed. See, e.g., Treas. Reg. sec. 1.269-2, stating that characteristic of circumstances in which an amount otherwise constituting a deduction, credit, or other allowance is not available are those in which the effect of the deduction, credit, or other allowance would be to distort the liability of the particular taxpayer when the essential nature of the transaction or situation is examined in the light of the basic purpose or plan which the deduction, credit, or other allowance was designed by the Congress to effectuate. Thus, for example, it is not intended that a tax credit (e.g., section 42 (low-income housing credit), section 45 (production tax credit), section 45D (new markets tax credit), section 47 (rehabilitation credit), section 48 (energy credit), etc.) be disallowed in a transaction pursuant to which, in form and substance, a taxpayer makes the type of investment or undertakes the type of activity that the credit was intended to encourage.

provision, a transaction must satisfy both tests, i.e., the transaction must change in a meaningful way (apart from Federal income tax effects) the taxpayer's economic position and the taxpayer must have a substantial non-Federal-income-tax purpose for entering into such transaction, in order for a transaction to be treated as having economic substance. This clarification eliminates the disparity that exists among the Federal circuit courts regarding the application of the doctrine, and modifies its application in those circuits in which either a change in economic position or a non-tax business purpose (without having both) is sufficient to satisfy the economic substance doctrine.

NON-FEDERAL-INCOME-TAX BUSINESS PURPOSE

Under the provision, a taxpayer's non-Federal-income-tax purpose for entering into a transaction (the second prong in the analysis) must be "substantial." For purposes of this analysis, any State or local income tax effect which is related to a Federal income tax effect is treated in the same manner as a Federal income tax effect. Also, a purpose of achieving a favorable accounting treatment for financial reporting purposes is not taken into account as a non-Federal-income-tax purpose if the origin of the financial accounting benefit is a reduction of Federal income tax.

PROFIT POTENTIAL

Under the provision, a taxpayer may rely on factors other than profit potential to demonstrate that a transaction results in a meaningful change in the taxpayer's economic position or that the taxpayer has a substantial non-Federal-income-tax purpose for entering into such transaction. The provision does not require or establish a minimum return that will satisfy the profit potential test. However, if a taxpayer relies on a profit potential, the present value of the reasonably expected pre-tax profit must be substantial in relation to the present value of the expected net tax benefits that would be allowed if the transaction were respected. Fees and other transaction expenses are taken into account as expenses in determining pre-tax profit. In addition, the Secretary is to issue regulations requiring foreign taxes to be treated as expenses in determining pre-tax profit in appropriate cases.

PERSONAL TRANSACTIONS OF INDIVIDUALS

In the case of an individual, the provision applies only to transactions entered into in connection with a trade or business or an activity engaged in for the production of income.

OTHER RULES

No inference is intended as to the proper application of the economic substance doctrine under present law. The provision is not intended to alter or supplant any other rule of law, including any common-law doctrine or provision of the Code or regulations or other guidance thereunder; and it is intended the provision be construed as being additive to any such other rule of law.

As with other provisions in the Code, the Secretary has general authority to prescribe rules and regulations necessary for the enforcement of the provision.

PENALTY FOR UNDERPAYMENTS AND UNDERSTATEMENTS ATTRIBUTABLE TO TRANSACTIONS LACKING ECONOMIC SUBSTANCE

The provision imposes a new strict liability penalty under section 6662 for an underpayment attributable to any disallowance of claimed tax benefits by reason of a transaction lacking economic substance, as defined in new section 7701(*o*), or failing to meet the requirements of any similar rule of law. The penalty rate is 20 percent (increased to 40 percent if the taxpayer does not adequately disclose the relevant facts affecting the tax treatment in the return or a statement attached to the return). An amended return or supplement to a return is not taken into account if filed after the taxpayer has been contacted for audit or such other date as is specified by the Secretary. No exceptions (including the reasonable cause rules) to the penalty are available. Thus, under the provision, outside opinions or in-house analysis would not protect a taxpayer from imposition of a penalty if it is determined that the transaction lacks economic substance or fails to meet the requirements of any similar rule of law. . . .

EFFECTIVE DATE

The provision applies to transactions entered into after the date of enactment [March 30, 2010] and to underpayments, understatements, and refunds and credits attributable to transactions entered into after the date of enactment.

Notes and Questions

1. *How much has really changed?* Will courts decide cases differently under the codified version of the economic substance doctrine than they would have under the judge-made version? Notice that, in the words of the *Technical Explanation*, "The determination of whether the economic substance doctrine is relevant to a transaction is made in the same manner as if the provision had never been enacted." Thus, a court is still free to decide a tax shelter case in the taxpayer's favor by determining that the doctrine is not relevant to the taxpayer's transaction. If a court does determine that the doctrine is relevant, the codified version of the doctrine closely resembles the version applied by most courts before codification. The codification does resolve the conflict between the conjunctive and disjunctive versions of the test, by specifying that the test is conjunctive (that is, that a tax shelter transaction must satisfy both prongs of the test). As noted earlier, however, the choice between the conjunctive and disjunctive versions is seldom significant, because only rarely does a court determine that a transaction satisfies one prong but not the other. More significant, perhaps, is the new

provision's directive to the Treasury to issue regulations reversing the result in *IES* and *Compaq*, by providing that foreign taxes are to be treated as expenses in determining pre-tax profit potential. Aside from that directive and the new strict liability penalty, it is not clear that much has really changed.

2. *The demise of tax shelters (at least for now).* It is a bit ironic that Congress finally got around to codifying the economic substance doctrine *after* the IRS, Treasury, and Congress had won the war against tax shelters. By the later years of the last decade, the tax shelter industry had virtually disappeared. The passive loss rules were a silver bullet aimed at the heart of pre-1986 tax shelters, but there was no silver bullet for the post-1986 shelters. Rather, their demise was caused by a combination of four factors: (1) The new tax shelter disclosure requirements, and the penalties for non-disclosure (described above), more or less eliminated the ability of taxpayers to use tax shelters without detection and challenge by the IRS. (2) Around the middle of the last decade, the government started to win almost all its tax shelter cases, whereas in earlier years it had lost a significant number of cases. This sudden change in the government's success rate was somewhat mysterious. No doubt the government attorneys became more skilled at tax shelter litigation over time. It is also possible, however, that federal judges came to realize that tax shelters posed an almost existential threat to the tax system, and became less willing to decide in favor of taxpayers as they became more aware of the extent of the threat. (3) The government began to prosecute some tax shelter promoters, and obtained convictions in a few cases. The cases selected for prosecution generally involved fraud — such as claims of tax benefits based on transactions never actually carried out — rather than mere disputes over the applicability of the economic substance doctrine. In any event, even a small chance of ending up in a federal prison seemed to have a deeply chilling effect on would-be tax shelter promoters. (4) Taxpayers who had their hoped-for tax shelter benefits disallowed (either in litigation or in settlements with the IRS) brought malpractice suits against the accounting firms and law firms that advised them with respect to the shelters. Almost all malpractice claims are resolved by settlement or in arbitration, so there are very few reported cases. It appears, however, that taxpayers have been quite successful in pursuing their malpractice claims, and that the threat of such claims has convinced almost all tax shelter promoters to get out of the tax shelter business.

C. THE ALTERNATIVE MINIMUM TAX

Congress is of two minds about many of the exclusion and deduction provisions that narrow the income tax base. On the one hand, Congress must approve of the provisions, or it would not have enacted them. On the other hand, Congress thinks it is inappropriate — or at least bad public relations for the legislative branch — for taxpayers to use tax preference items so aggressively that they pay little or no tax despite having substantial economic income. This love-hate relationship with tax preferences is the explanation for the existence of the alternative minimum tax (AMT). The AMT, which is codified in IRC §§55 through 59, amounts to a shadow tax system running alongside the regular tax. The base of the AMT is "alternative minimum taxable income" (AMTI), which is defined so as to disallow many exclusions and deductions that are allowed under the regular tax. After the allowance of a large exemption amount — in effect, a zero rate tax bracket — AMTI is subject to a moderate rate, semi-flat tax. The exemption amounts for the 2010 tax year are $72,450 for joint returns and $47,450 for unmarried taxpayers; for the 2011 tax year the amounts are $74,450 for joint returns and $48,450 for unmarried taxpayers.[37] The tax rate is 26 percent for the first $175,000 of income above the exemption amount, and 28 percent for all other income. (As you might expect by now, there is also a phaseout of the exemption amount, which functions as a marginal tax rate bubble over the phaseout range.) Applying these tax rates to AMTI produces what the statute calls "tentative minimum tax."

The AMT features a broader base than the regular tax,[38] combined with tax rates that are sometimes lower and sometimes higher than the applicable rates under the regular tax.[39] As a result, the AMT may produce either a higher or a lower tax liability than the regular tax. A taxpayer who has reason to suspect her AMT liability will be higher than her regular tax liability must calculate her AMT liability as well as her regular tax; she must then pay whichever tax liability is greater. Technically, the statute (§55(a)) says that she must pay her regular tax and the amount by which her tentative minimum tax exceeds her regular tax liability, but it does not take advanced mathematical training to see that this is the equivalent of having to pay whichever tax is greater. The "alternative" label in the name of the tax suggests the taxpayer has some choice in the matter, but there is nothing elective about the AMT: If the calculations produce an AMT liability, the tax is just as mandatory as the regular income tax.

It is common for a taxpayer who is subject to the AMT to have no suspicions of that fact, and so to file a return without any AMT calculations. The IRS computers can usually detect from the information provided on the return that there is an AMT liability; the IRS will then send a friendly AMT inquiry to the surprised taxpayer. For taxpayers using tax return preparation software, the unhappy surprise will come sooner, because the software will generally calculate the AMT liability even if the taxpayer never asked it to do so.

The classic AMT taxpayer (and the originally intended target of this tax regime) is someone with large amounts of tax preferences, for sophisticated investment and business activities, such as ACRS deductions (*see* §56(a)(1)), incentive stock options (*see* §56(b)(3)), percentage depletion deductions in excess of basis (*see* §57(a)(1)), and tax-exempt interest income from private activity bonds (*see* §57(a)(5)). In recent years, however, AMT demographics have changed, and many of its victims do not fit the classic profile of taxpayers with large amounts of economic income

---

37. The exemption amounts are scheduled to decrease to $45,000 and $33,750 in 2012, although it seems unlikely Congress will allow that to happen.

38. Despite the generally broader base of the AMT, in one significant respect — the higher exemption levels under the AMT than under the regular tax — the AMT base is actually narrower.

39. At the top of the income distribution, regular tax rates (topping out at 35%) are higher than AMT rates (topping out at 28%). At more modest income levels, however, AMT rates are often higher than regular tax rates. Note, for example, that the upper boundary of the 25 percent rate bracket for joint returns in 2010 is, at $137,300, much higher than the AMT exemption amount ($72,450) above which a 26 percent AMT rate applies for joint returns in that year.

and heavy use of investment tax preferences. This change is due in part to a decrease in available investment tax preferences under the regular income tax, thus decreasing the effect of the AMT on the traditional fat cat. The increasing effect on moderate income taxpayers without investment tax preferences is explained partly by the fact that the regular tax brackets are indexed for inflation while the AMT brackets and exemption amounts are not, and partly by the fact that many of the differences between AMTI and regular taxable income do *not* relate to investment-type preferences, but to such plebeian tax breaks as employee business expenses (and other miscellaneous itemized deductions), the itemized deduction for state and local taxes, and personal and dependency exemptions.

Consider the following example, which uses regular tax inflation adjustments for 2010. A married couple with six children has $120,000 wages, a $12,000 qualified residence interest deduction (consisting of $7,000 of interest on acquisition indebtedness and $5,000 of interest on home equity indebtedness), and a $10,000 deduction for state and local taxes. For purposes of the regular tax, their taxable income is $74,900:

Compensation for services		$120,000
Less:		
Qualified residence interest	$12,000	
State and local taxes	$10,000	
Eight personal exemptions ($3,650 each)	$29,200	
Total deductions and exemptions		$51,200
Taxable income		$68,800

Applying the 2010 tax rate schedule for married couples filing joint returns yields a pre-credit regular tax liability of $9,562.50. Of all their regular tax deductions, the only one allowed for AMT purposes is the $7,000 deduction for home mortgage interest on acquisition indebtedness. They may not deduct the interest on the home equity loan (§56(e)(1)), the state and local taxes (§56(b)(1)(A)(ii)), or the personal exemptions (§56(b)(1)(E)). Thus, their AMTI is $113,000. Of that $113,000, $72,450 is sheltered from tax by the AMT exemption amount. The remaining $40,550 is taxed at 26 percent, resulting in a tentative minimum tax of $10,543. The minimum tax increases their tax liability by $980.50 ($10,543 minus $9,562.50). After taking into account their $5,500 child tax credit under §24 ($1,000 for each of the six children, but reduced from $6,000 to $5,500 by §24(b)), which is allowed against both the regular tax and the minimum tax (*see* §26(a)(1)), their final tax liability is $5,043.[40] They are not a particularly high income couple, and they have only the most garden-variety regular tax deductions, yet the AMT has cost them nearly $1,000 and has increased their total tax liability by 24.1 percent.[41] Far from being pushed into the AMT because of sophisticated tax shelter investments, they have been pushed into the AMT by their children. The following case is a real-world example of the same phenomenon.

40. $9,562.50 regular tax liability plus $980.50 minimum tax liability minus $5,500 child tax credit.

41. In the absence of the AMT, their post-credit tax liability would be $4,062.50. The AMT increases their liability by $980.50, which is 24.1 percent of $4,062.50.

KLAASSEN v. COMMISSIONER

83 A.F.T.R.2d (RIA) 1750 (10th Cir. 1999) (not officially reported)

ANDERSON, Circuit Judge: David R. and Margaret J. Klaassen appeal from the Tax Court's ruling that they are liable for an alternative minimum tax (AMT) in the amount of $1,085 for the 1994 tax year. The Klaassens contend that the tax court erred (1) by applying the AMT provisions to them in violation of congressional intent; or, alternatively (2) by applying the AMT provisions to them in violation of their First and Fifth Amendment rights. We affirm.

The facts are undisputed. During the 1994 tax year, the Klaassens were the parents of ten dependent children. According to their 1994 joint tax return, they earned an adjusted gross income (AGI) of $83,056.42. On Schedule A, the Klaassens claimed deductions for medical expenses and for state and local taxes in the respective amounts of $4,767.13 and $3,263.56. Including their claimed deductions for interest and charitable contributions, their total Schedule A itemized deductions equaled $19,563.95. Therefore, they subtracted that amount from their AGI, and on line 35 of their Form 1040, they showed a balance of $63,492.47. On line 36, they entered a total of $29,400 for twelve personal exemptions—one each for themselves and their ten children. After subtracting that amount, they showed a taxable income of $34,092.47 on line 37 of their Form 1040, and a resulting regular tax of $5,111.00 on line 38. They did not provide any computations for AMT liability.

Following an audit, the IRS issued a notice of deficiency, advising the Klaassens that they were liable for a $1,085.43 AMT. According to the IRS's interpretation, subsection 56(b)(1)(A)(ii) required the entire $3,263.56 deduction for state and local taxes to be added back. Next, subsection 56(b)(1)(B) reduced the deduction allowable for medical expenses by setting a 10% floor in lieu of the 7.5% floor normally allowed under §213(a)—resulting in a net adjustment of $2,076.41. Finally, §56(b)(1)(E) deprived the Klaassens of the entire $29,400 deduction they claimed on line 36 of their Form 1040. After adjusting the taxable income by these three amounts, the IRS set the alternative minimum taxable income at $68,832.44. After deducting the $45,000 exemption, the tentative minimum tax was computed on the excess: 26% × $23,832.44 = $6,196.43. The difference between that figure and the Klaassens' regular tax was $1,085.43. The Tax Court upheld the IRS's position, and the Klaassens brought this appeal.

The Klaassens do not dispute the numbers or the mechanics used to calculate the AMT deficiency. Rather, they claim that, as a matter of law, the AMT provisions should not apply to them.

I.R.C. §56(b)(1)(E) plainly states that, in computing the alternative minimum taxable income, "the deduction for personal exemptions under section 151... shall not be allowed." Nonetheless, the Klaassens argue that Congress intended the AMT to apply only to very wealthy persons who claim the types of tax preferences described in I.R.C. §57. Essentially, the Klaassens contend that Congress did not intend to disallow personal exemptions for taxpayers at their income level when no §57 preferences are involved. Although they cite no legislative history to support their contention, the Klaassens argue that their entitlement to their personal exemptions is mandated by I.R.C. §151-153. In particular, they note that for 1994, I.R.C. §151(d) allowed taxpayers filing joint returns to claim the full exemption so long as their AGI was less than $167,700. They then argue that the §151(d) threshold amount should be interpolated as a threshold for the AMT provisions. We disagree.

In the absence of exceptional circumstances, where a statute is clear and unambiguous our inquiry is complete. The AMT framework establishes a precise method for taxing income which the regular tax does not reach. In creating this framework, Congress included several provisions, "marked by a high degree of specificity," by which deductions or advantages which are allowed in computing the regular tax are specifically disallowed for purposes of computing the AMT. Instead of permitting those separate "regular tax" deductions, Congress specifically substituted the $45,000 fixed exemption for purposes of AMT computations. If, as the Klaassens claim, Congress had intended the AMT to apply only to taxpayers whose incomes reached a certain threshold, or only to taxpayers with §57 tax preferences, it could have easily drafted the statute to achieve that result. Instead, as the tax court correctly held, the statute's plain language unequivocally reaches the Klaassens, and our inquiry is therefore complete. While the law may result in some unintended consequences, in the absence of any ambiguity, it must be applied as written. It is therefore from Congress that the Klaassens should seek relief.

As their second, alternative, point of error, the Klaassens contend that applying the AMT provisions to them violates their First Amendment rights, as well as their equal protection and due process rights. First, the Klaassens contend that, by disallowing the personal exemptions for their children, the statute impermissibly burdens their free exercise of religion. [The Klaassens' religious beliefs prohibited birth control.] Second, they contend that their equal protection and due process rights are violated, because the statute deprives them of full deductions for medical and local taxes, whereas those deductions are allowed for families with similar incomes, but fewer than eight children. . . .

The uniform application of the AMT provisions furthers a compelling governmental interest, and we therefore conclude that it does not violate the Free Exercise Clause of the First Amendment.

For similar reasons, we find that the AMT provisions "bear a rational relation to a legitimate governmental purpose." Consequently, we find no equal protection or due process violation.

Affirmed.

KELLY, Circuit Judge, concurring.

Although I agree with the court that the taxpayers cannot prevail on the theories advanced, we are not precluded from examining the legislative history of the alternative minimum tax (AMT), despite the clarity of the statute. The legislative history supports an argument that the original purpose of the AMT, one of the more complex parts of the Internal Revenue Code, was to insure that taxpayers with substantial economic income pay a minimum amount of tax on it. *See* S. Rep. No. 97-494 (1982), *reprinted in* 1982 U.S.C.C.A.N. 781, 876;[42] S. Rep. No. 99-313, at 518, *reprinted in* 1986-3 C.B. 518. The regular income tax may be insufficient to

---

42. "The committee has amended the present minimum tax provisions applying to individuals with one overriding objective: no taxpayer with substantial economic income should be able to avoid all tax liability by using exclusions, deductions and credits. Although these provisions provide incentives for worthy goals, they become counterproductive when individuals are allowed to use them to avoid virtually all tax liability. The ability of high-income individuals to pay little or no tax undermines respect for the entire tax system and, thus, for the incentive provisions themselves."

achieve that objective because it favors certain types of income and allows deductions, exclusions and credits for certain types of expenses.

For a variety of reasons, the number of moderate income taxpayers subject to the AMT has been steadily increasing. From a tax compliance and administration perspective, many of these taxpayers simply are unaware of their AMT obligations. If aware, they probably would need the assistance of a tax professional to comply with the separate rules and computations (apart from regular tax) and additional record keeping essential for the AMT. From a fairness perspective, many of these taxpayers have not utilized I.R.C. §57 preferences (or other more arcane AMT adjustment items) to reduce regular taxable income but are caught up in the AMT's attempt to impose fairness. That certainly seems to be the case here. In the interest of progressivity, the regular tax already reduces or phases out itemized deductions and personal exemptions based upon income, *see, e.g.,* §151(d)(3) (phaseout of personal exemptions); §213(a) (medical and dental expenses deduction only for amounts beyond 7.5% floor); surely Congress never intended a family of twelve that still qualified for these items under the regular tax to partly forfeit them under the AMT.

That said, we must apply the law as it is plainly written, despite what appears to be the original intent behind the AMT. As the tax court has explained, neither the statutory language nor unequivocal legislative history support[s] the argument that the AMT is limited to individuals with tax preferences. The solution to this inequity, whether it be (1) eliminating itemized deductions and personal exemptions as adjustments to regular taxable income in arriving at alternative minimum taxable income, (2) exempting low and moderate income taxpayers from the AMT, (3) raising and indexing the AMT exemption amount, or (4) some other measure, must come from Congress, as the tax court rightly concluded.

Cell

THE ALTERNATIVE MINIMUM TAX AND ITS DISCONTENTS

A. The Impending Storm

Lim & Rohaly, The Individual Alternative Minimum Tax: Historical Data and Projections

B. The AMT and Miscellaneous Itemized Deductions

C. The AMT Credit

Problems 1-2

A. THE IMPENDING STORM

As the following discussion suggests, the Klaassens (from section C of this chapter) will soon have lots of company in their status as unlikely victims of the AMT, unless Congress makes one or more of the changes mentioned by Judge Kelly. Lim and Rohaly wrote their paper before Congress, in late 2010, "patched" the AMT for 2010 and 2011 by enacting increases in the AMT exemption amounts for those two years. (The details of the 2010 and 2011 patches are described in part C of this chapter.) Because of the 2010 legislation, the dramatic increase in the impact of the AMT described below is now scheduled to occur in 2012 rather than 2010.

KATHERINE LIM & JEFFREY ROHALY, THE INDIVIDUAL ALTERNATIVE MINIMUM TAX: HISTORICAL DATA AND PROJECTIONS

(October 2009)

Congress originally enacted a minimum tax in 1969 to guarantee that high-income individuals paid at least a minimal amount of tax each year. Due to design flaws, however, the current alternative minimum tax (AMT) requires annual congressional action to prevent it from affecting tens of millions of taxpayers each year. One reason for the expansion of the AMT is that—unlike the regular income tax system—the AMT brackets and exemption are not indexed for inflation. In addition, the tax cuts passed during the Bush administration exacerbate the AMT problem because they reduce regular income taxes without a corresponding permanent reduction in the AMT. Absent another temporary fix or other change in law, the tax cuts and lack of indexation will combine to push more than 27 million taxpayers onto the AMT in 2010. If Congress extends the Bush tax cuts, that number would swell to almost 52 million by 2020. Alternatively, if Congress allows all of the tax cuts to expire—which is highly unlikely—the number of AMT taxpayers would fall dramatically in 2011, but then trend back upward over time to hit more than 37 million taxpayers by 2020. Regardless of how Congress deals with the coming expiration of the Bush tax cuts, policymakers will also need to address the explosive growth of the AMT from an obscure tax affecting only 20,000 filers in 1970 to one that could affect nearly a third of all taxpayers in 2010.

The Tax Policy Center (TPC) has written extensively about the AMT. This paper briefly describes how the AMT works and provides the TPC's latest estimates of AMT coverage, revenue, and distribution.

1. How the AMT Works

. . .

Exemptions in the AMT are neither indexed for inflation nor adjusted for family size. Under current law for tax years after 2009, the AMT exemption will be $45,000 for married couples filing jointly, $33,750 for unmarried individuals, and $22,500 for married individuals filing separately. Since 2001, Congress has enacted temporary measures—on an annual basis in recent years—to increase the exemptions, but the latest "patch" expires at the end of 2009. The 2009 exemption is $70,950 for married couples filing jointly, $46,700 for unmarried individuals, and $35,475 for married individuals filing separate returns. Those exemptions phase out for high-income taxpayers at a 25 percent rate, beginning at AMTI of $150,000 for married couples filing jointly ($112,500 for singles). Like the exemptions themselves, the phaseout thresholds are not indexed for inflation. . . .

2. Aggregate AMT Projections and Recent History, 1970–2020

In 1970, the minimum tax affected only 20,000 taxpayers and generated $100 million in revenue. Barring congressional action, the AMT will hit more than 27 million taxpayers in 2010 and bring in more than $100 billion in revenue. The 2001–2006 tax cuts are responsible for much of the AMT explosion because they reduce regular tax liability without a corresponding permanent change to the AMT rules. But even without those tax cuts, 14.8 million households would have paid $38.5 billion in AMT in 2010, primarily because the AMT is not indexed for inflation.

As part of the American Recovery and Reinvestment Tax Act of 2009 (ARRA), Congress "patched" the AMT for 2009, raising the AMT exemption and allowing taxpayers to claim certain personal nonrefundable credits regardless of their AMT situation. As a result, we estimate that the AMT will affect just 4 million taxpayers — about 1 in 20 — in 2009. The AMT will generate $33.5 billion, roughly 4 percent of total individual income tax revenue. If Congress does not extend the temporary fix or otherwise modify the AMT, the tax will affect nearly a third of all taxpayers in

2010. AMT revenue will balloon to $102.2 billion, more than 10 percent of total individual income tax revenue.

If Congress lets the Bush tax cuts expire after 2010 (as scheduled under current law), the number of AMT taxpayers would drop sharply to 15.9 million in 2011, but then resume an upward march to 37.5 million by 2020. The amount of revenue raised by the AMT would similarly drop in 2011 to $42.1 billion or just over 3 percent of individual income tax revenue — only to increase throughout the coming decade to reach $114.5 billion by 2020, almost 5 percent of income tax revenue.

Under the administration baseline — which would make the Bush tax cuts and the AMT patch permanent — the AMT would affect 4.6 million households in 2011 and 8 million by 2020. Without the patch, extending the Bush tax cuts would result in 29.7 million AMT taxpayers in 2011 and close to 52 million by 2020.

One indicator of the immense scope of the AMT is that under current law in 2010, tax returns that owe AMT will account for more than half of all adjusted gross income. If Congress extends the Bush tax cuts without an AMT patch, that figure would rise to close to two-thirds by 2020. Even if the tax cuts expire as scheduled, without a change to the AMT, by 2020 it would affect returns reporting 43 percent of AGI.

3. CHARACTERISTICS OF AMT TAXPAYERS

Although Congress originally enacted the AMT to prevent high-income individuals from sheltering all of their income and paying no tax, it now affects more tax filers in lower income classes than at the top of the income scale. Just 40 percent of taxpayers earning more than $1 million will pay the AMT in 2009, compared with more than half of those earning between $200,000 and $1 million. Since the 35 percent top statutory rate in the regular income tax exceeds the top 28 percent statutory rate in the AMT, individuals with high incomes who do not engage in substantial sheltering end up in the regular tax system.

Despite the temporary AMT patch, almost half of filers with incomes between $200,000 and $500,000 and nearly two-thirds of those making between $500,000 and $1 million will pay the AMT in 2009. The patch's higher exemption provides the greatest protection to taxpayers with incomes between $75,000 and $200,000, leaving less than 5 percent of them subject to the AMT in 2009. But these households will be hit hard if Congress fails to extend the patch or otherwise reform the AMT. Under current law, the share of filers earning $100,000 to $200,000 who are affected by the AMT will explode from 4 percent in 2009 to 75 percent in 2010, and the share of filers with incomes between $75,000 and $100,000 affected by the AMT will soar from less than 1 percent to 37 percent.

Barring legislative action, the AMT will become the de facto tax system in 2010 for taxpayers with incomes between $200,000 and $500,000, affecting 92 percent of them. Three-fourths of filers with incomes between $100,000 and $200,000 and between $500,000 and $1 million will also fall prey to the AMT next year. If Congress extends the Bush administration tax cuts without fixing the AMT, more than 80 percent of taxpayers earning between $100,000 and $1 million would pay the tax by 2020. In addition, the tax would extend down the income distribution, affecting 56 percent of those making between $75,000 and $100,000. Even if Congress lets the Bush tax cuts expire after 2010, 44 percent of filers with incomes between $75,000 and $200,000 — and 78 percent of those with incomes between $200,000 and $500,000 — will be paying the AMT by 2020.

The share of taxpayers affected by the AMT varies widely depending on number of children, state tax level, and filing status. Because the AMT disallows dependent exemptions, it affects filers with many children more than those without children. In 2009, only 2 percent of childless taxpayers will owe AMT, compared with 8 percent of those with three or more children. If Congress does not extend the patch, those shares will jump to 13 percent and 42 percent, respectively, in 2010.

The state and local tax deduction accounts for about two-thirds of all exemption preferences, making it the largest AMT preference item. Although residents of high tax states are consistently more likely to pay AMT than residents of low tax states, the differential will fall as AMT coverage expands. In 2009, residents of high-tax states will be almost three times as likely to pay AMT as people in low-tax jurisdictions. In 2010, under current law, residents of high-tax states will be only 47 percent more likely to be on the AMT (24 percent vs. 17 percent).

Because the AMT exemption for married couples is less than double that for singles and because the AMT brackets are the same regardless of filing status, married couples are much more likely to pay the AMT than single or head of household filers. In 2009, 5 percent of joint returns will owe the AMT, compared with only 1 percent of single returns. In 2010 under current law, the share of joint returns paying AMT will reach 40 percent, whereas only 3 percent of single returns will owe the tax.

Absent a change in law, the AMT will become an almost universal tax for upper-middle class families. In 2009, just 1 in 1,000 married couples with two or more kids and cash income between $75,000 and $100,000 will pay the AMT. That share will rise to 59 percent in 2010 and to 84 percent by 2020.

. . .

8. CONCLUSION

The individual AMT operates parallel to the regular income tax: it defines income differently, imposes different tax rates, and allows different deductions, exemptions, and credits. Taxpayers must pay the larger of their regular income tax or the tax calculated under the AMT rules. Because the AMT is not indexed for inflation, and because the Bush tax cuts reduced regular income tax liability without adjusting the AMT to match, the tax threatens to hit tens of millions of taxpayers each year. To avoid the AMT explosion, Congress has enacted temporary AMT "patches" on an annual basis that raise the AMT exemption and allow certain credits against the AMT. The current AMT patch expires at the end of 2009.

The AMT will affect 4 million taxpayers in 2009. Barring extension of the patch, that number will rise to more than 27 million in 2010 and nearly 38 million in 2020. The AMT will become the de facto tax system for taxpayers with incomes between $200,000 and $500,000 in 2010, affecting 92 percent of them. Because the AMT disallows dependent exemptions and the state and local tax deduction, it affects filers with many children more than those with no children and hits more taxpayers in high-tax states. The AMT also imposes significant marriage penalties: in 2010 under current law, 40 percent of joint filers will pay AMT, compared with only 3 percent of single filers.

The AMT fails on efficiency grounds: for the majority of affected taxpayers, the AMT taxes less income and imposes higher marginal rates than does the regular income tax. The share of AMT taxpayers with less income subject to AMT than to the regular income tax will rise from 56 percent in 2009 to 87 percent in 2010. The share with higher marginal tax rates under the AMT than under the regular tax will rise from 78 percent in 2009 to 90 percent in 2010.

Because the Bush tax cuts did not permanently reform the AMT, the alternative tax claws back a substantial portion of the tax reduction that individuals would otherwise receive. Without congressional action, the AMT will completely eliminate the tax cuts for about 2 percent of all taxpayers in 2010 and will reclaim a quarter of the potential tax cut overall.

Notes and Questions

1. *The Tax Policy Center.* The Lim and Rohaly paper excerpted above is a product of the Tax Policy Center. The Center, which is a joint venture of the Urban Institute and the Brookings Institution, describes itself as "provid[ing] timely, accessible analysis and facts about tax policy to policymakers, journalists, citizens, and researchers." The products of the Center are generally of very high quality, and are often quite influential with policymakers.

2. *Inflation indexing and the AMT.* As noted by Lim and Rohaly, much of the increasing impact of the AMT is due to the inconsistent treatment of inflation under the regular tax and the AMT. The rate structure, standard deduction, and personal exemption of the regular tax are adjusted annually for inflation, while the AMT exemption amounts are eroded by inflation. Can you think of any policy reason for indexing the regular tax rate structure for inflation, but not doing the same for the AMT? If not, why do you suppose Congress has allowed this inconsistency to continue for so long?

3. *What to do?* Which, if any, of the possible fixes for the AMT mentioned in Judge Kelly's dissent in *Klaassen* should be enacted? Some of the suggestions could be enacted together. For example, it would be possible both to index the exemption amounts for future inflation (after, perhaps, a one-time increase to reflect past inflation) and also to remove some or all the itemized deductions from the AMT hit list. It would also be possible, of course, simply to repeal the AMT in its entirety.

4. *AMT marriage penalties.* Because the AMT exemption amount in §55(d) for joint returns ($72,450, for 2010) is less than twice as large as the exemption amount for unmarried taxpayers ($47,450, for the same year), the AMT creates its own marriage penalties. For example, if two unmarried persons had AMTI of $47,450 each, neither would have any tentative minimum tax liability. But if the same two people were married, their combined income of $94,900 would exceed their exemption amount by $22,450, and their tentative minimum tax liability would be $5,837. So far, AMT marriage penalties have been mostly ignored in the political discussions of tax reforms aimed at reducing or eliminating marriage penalties. If the AMT begins to affect millions of moderate income taxpayers, however, AMT marriage penalties will surely become a significant issue.

B. THE AMT AND MISCELLANEOUS ITEMIZED DEDUCTIONS

Among the many targets of the AMT are §67 miscellaneous itemized deductions—most significantly, unreimbursed employee business expenses and §212 expenses for the production or collection of income. For moderate income taxpayers with significant miscellaneous itemized deductions, this disallowance can be the main culprit in subjecting them to the AMT. One of the authors discovered this the hard way, when he found himself subject to the AMT—despite being a moderate income taxpayer, having a small family, and having no investment-type tax preference items—solely because of the AMT disallowance of the unreimbursed expenses of being a visiting professor.[1] Until Congress acted in 2004, the AMT disallowance of miscellaneous itemized deductions created severe tax problems for taxpayers who receive taxable damage awards, but had to pay attorneys' fees as a cost of collecting such awards. In a number of cases taxpayers won large gross verdicts and were taxed on those recoveries. But they had to pay large fractions of their awards—40 percent was a typical figure—to their attorneys. Deduction of the fees was disallowed for AMT purposes because the deduction was a miscellaneous itemized deduction, and hence not allowed for purposes of that tax.[2]

This problem was addressed in 2004, when Congress added §62(a)(20) to the Code, making the legal expenses of successful "discrimination suits" deductible in defining adjusted gross income, rather than as itemized deductions. This automatically takes the costs of such suits out of the miscellaneous deduction nondeductible floor, and out of the line of fire of the AMT. It remains true, however, that the cost of recovering on claims not described under §62(a)(20), such as claims grounded in defamation, will continue to be miscellaneous itemized deductions, subject to nondeductible floors on deductibility under the regular tax, and complete bars on deductibility under the AMT.

C. THE AMT CREDIT

Many of the differences between taxable income under the regular tax and AMTI are permanent differences. In other words, some deductions and exclusions allowed under the regular tax are never allowed under the AMT. On the other hand, some differences between the two tax bases are only differences of timing. For example, the total amount of ACRS deductions for any given asset will be the same under both tax systems, but the deductions will be more front-loaded under the regular tax. These timing differences give rise to the possibility that the same income could be taxed twice. Suppose a particular income item is includable in AMTI in Year 1, and the taxpayer is subject to the AMT that year. If the same item is includable in regular taxable income in Year 2, and the taxpayer is subject only to the regular tax in Year 2, the result is that the same income has been taxed in both

---

1. For the regular tax treatment of unreimbursed employee business expenses, see section F of Chapter 4.
2. The *Banks* case in Chapter 10 is an example of such a case.

years. The legislative response to this possible unfairness is embodied in §53, which in this situation would provide a credit in year two for the AMT paid on the income item in year one. The operation of §53 is complicated by the need to distinguish between (1) AMT paid on account of *timing* differences between AMTI and regular taxable income (for which the credit should be, and is, allowed), and (2) AMT paid on account of *permanent* differences between AMTI and regular taxable income (for which the credit should not be, and is not, allowed).

As an exercise in reading and applying a moderately complex Code provision, try to determine the amount of credit that would be allowed under §53 based on the following facts.

Problem 1.   Anne had never been subject to the AMT before Year 1. In that year, she has a tentative minimum tax liability of $55,000, which compares with her regular tax liability of $40,000. Thus, she pays an AMT of $15,000. There are three differences between her regular taxable income and her AMTI: (1) her personal exemption is allowed under the regular tax but not under the AMT; (2) her itemized deductions for state and local taxes are allowed under the regular tax but not under the AMT; and (3) her income from the exercise of an incentive stock option (*see* §§421, 422) is excluded under the regular tax but is included in AMTI (*see* §56(b)(3)). If the incentive stock option had not existed, so that the difference between regular taxable income and AMTI was due solely to the personal exemption and the state and local taxes, her tentative minimum tax liability would have been $43,000. She was able to purchase stock worth $80,000 at a price of only $35,000 pursuant to the incentive stock option. The amount included in AMTI on account of the option is the $45,000 bargain element in the purchase. The next year (Year 2), Anne sells the same stock for $90,000. Because of the different treatments of the option under the two tax systems in the previous year, Anne has two bases in the stock—a $35,000 regular tax basis and an $80,000 AMT basis. (*See* §56(b)(3).) Thus, she realizes a regular tax gain of $55,000 on the sale, but an AMT gain of only $10,000. Anne's regular tax liability for Year 2 is $48,000. Because her Year 2 tentative minimum tax liability is only $30,000, she simply pays the regular tax. In effect, Anne has paid tax twice on the $45,000 bargain element in the stock purchase—once under the AMT in Year 1, and again under the regular tax in Year 2. This is an example of the kind of unfairness the §53 credit is designed to prevent. What is the amount of the credit to which Anne is entitled?

Problem 2.   The facts are the same as in Problem 1, except Anne's tentative minimum tax liability in Year 2 is $42,000. What is the amount of the §53 credit to which Anne in entitled?

Chapter 9

TAXATION OF THE FAMILY

This chapter examines the numerous rules dealing with the income tax treatment of familial relationships. It begins with a consideration of tax allowances for parents of dependent children. After that, it considers the rules governing marriage and divorce, and the rules (or absence of rules) applicable to unmarried couples. It concludes with coverage of the earned income tax credit (EITC), which serves as a wage subsidy for low income parents.

A. TAX ALLOWANCES FOR FAMILY RESPONSIBILITIES

The income tax provides two types of benefits for parents with dependent children. Benefits of the first type are based on actual dollars paid for child care while parents are at work. The two provisions in this category are §21, which provides a credit for a limited amount of child care expenditures, and §129, which allows an exclusion for benefits (including cash) received from an employer pursuant to a "dependent care assistance program." The second type of benefit is based simply on the fact that the taxpayer is a parent of dependent children. Benefits of this type are available without regard to the amount of money the taxpayer actually spends on the children. The two most obvious examples are the §151 dependency exemption and the §24 child credit. However, the favorable rules associated with head-of-household filing status also belong in this category (as do the rules for computing the amount of the earned income tax credit, which are considered later in this chapter). These materials begin with an examination of the tax treatment of child care expenses, and then turn to allowances not based on actual expenditures.

1. Allowances for Child Care Expenses

a. Child Care as a Business Expense

It has long been settled that child care is not deductible as a business expense under the U.S. income tax. The leading case is an old one. Smith v. Commissioner, 40 B.T.A. 1038 (1939), *aff'd without opinion*, 113 F.2d 114 (2d Cir. 1940). Child care and commuting are the two classic examples of jointly caused business-and-personal expenses. Both one's personal life (the fact that one has children) and one's business life are but-for causes of child care expenses. Remove either the children or the job, and the entire child care expense disappears. In the same way, both one's personal life (the fact that one lives in one place) and one's business (the fact that one works in another place) are but-for causes of commuting expenses. Remove either the home (by sleeping on the couch in the office) or the job and the commuting expense vanishes. The appropriate tax treatment of such jointly caused expenses is a puzzle. This is a fundamentally different sort of problem than that presented by, for example, restaurant meals while away from home on a business trip. If we make the factual assumption that you have to spend twice as much on the restaurant meal as you would have spent if you had been able to eat at home, then the appropriate tax treatment readily follows. Half the cost of the meal is a purely personal expense, because you would have spent that half whether or not you were on a business trip; the other half is caused solely by the fact of the business trip. With your personal life as the sole but-for cause of half the restaurant expense, and the business trip as the sole but-for cause of the other half, it seems clear (given our convenient factual assumption) that half the cost should be deductible and half should not. But child care and commuting are not like this. For child care and commuting, your business life is a but-for cause of 100 percent of the expense, and so is your personal life. The kind of causal apportionment that works so neatly for business meals does not work here.

Whatever one's view on the appropriate treatment of these jointly caused expenses, the U.S. tax system at least deserves credit for consistency. Neither child care costs nor commuting costs are treated as business expenses. The underlying principle seems to be: If we can imagine another taxpayer with the same job, but with a different personal life (no child in one case, a home across the street from work in the other), who would not incur the expense, then the expense is not treated as a business expense. Of course, one might view this as an instance of Emersonian foolish consistency ("the hobgoblin of little minds"). A deduction for child care expenses raises very different policy issues from a deduction for commuting expenses, so Congress is not logically compelled to allow a deduction for both or for neither.

b. The §21 Child Care Credit

Section 21 provides a credit equal to a percentage of a taxpayer's child care expenses, if the expenses are "incurred to enable the taxpayer to be gainfully employed." Expenses eligible for the credit are capped at $3,000 for a taxpayer with one "qualifying individual" (generally, a child under the age of 13, or another individual unable to care for himself), and at $6,000 for a taxpayer with two or more qualifying individuals.[1] For a taxpayer with adjusted gross income (AGI) of $15,000 or less, the credit is 35 percent of the credit-eligible expenses. The rate of credit is reduced by one percentage point for each $2,000 (or fraction thereof) by which AGI exceeds $15,000, but the credit is never reduced below 20 percent. The credit rate hits the 20 percent floor at AGI of $43,001. Thus, for most taxpayers of middling incomes or above, the credit rate is simply 20 percent.

---

1. The rules described in the text are scheduled to terminate at the end of 2012, after which the rules are to become less generous (with respect to both the ceilings on credit-eligible expenses and credit percentages). It seems likely, however, that Congress will extend the current rules beyond 2012.

The fact that the credit is available only for child care expenses incurred in order to enable the taxpayer to be employed (or self-employed) may suggest that Congress is sympathetic to the idea that work-related child care is a legitimate business expense. In fact, however, the credit is far less valuable for many taxpayers than a business expense deduction would be. Consider, for example, a taxpayer with a marginal rate of 28 percent who spends $10,000 on work-related child care for her only child. If she were allowed a $10,000 business expense deduction, her tax savings would be $2,800. By contrast, her credit is only $600 (20% of $3,000). The credit amount is smaller than the savings from a deduction both because the credit rate is lower than her marginal tax rate and because credit-eligible expenses are capped at only $3,000. On reflection, then, the structure of §21 suggests Congress does *not* believe that child care costs are legitimate business expenses. Instead, it appears that Congress has decided to use the tax system to subsidize the cost of child care for working parents. From a subsidy point of view, both the use of a credit rather than a deduction and the low ceiling on eligible expenditures can be explained as attempts to ensure that the largest subsidies do not go to higher income taxpayers. Not only does the use of a credit avoid the "upside-down" aspect of subsidies designed as deductions (where a $ 1,000 deduction is worth more to a 28% bracket taxpayer than to a 15% bracket taxpayer); the use of a credit rate that *declines* as income rises produces a "right-side-up" subsidy.

Problem 1. Martha asks her child's babysitter to do some laundry and dishwashing while the child is sleeping. Assuming all other requirements of §21 are satisfied, can Martha claim a credit with respect to the entire amount she pays the babysitter, or must she allocate her expense between child care and housework, and claim a credit only for the expense allocated to child care? To answer this question, consult both §21 and Reg. §1.21-1(d).

Problem 2. Marvin hires a maid to clean his house while Marvin is at work and his only child (who is eight years old) is at school. Can Marvin claim a §21 credit based on the amount he pays the maid? Again, you will need to consult both the statute and Reg. §1.21-1(d).

Problem 3. Ted and Tina pay tuition for their child to attend preschool at a private school while they both work. Can they claim a credit under §21 based on their tuition expense? If you cannot find a clear answer in the statute, take a look at Reg. §1.21-1(d).

Problem 4. The following year, Ted and Tina of Problem 3 again pay tuition for their child to attend the same school while they both work, but now the child is in kindergarten. Can they claim a §21 credit for the cost of tuition?

Problem 5. Sally and Sam both work full-time. They pay a babysitter to watch their child while they go out for dinner and a movie. Can they claim a child care credit for the cost of the babysitter? Do you need to consult the regulations, or is the answer clear from the statute itself? If they are not entitled to claim the credit, but they claim it anyway, how will the IRS ever discover their cheating?

Problem 6. The facts are the same as in the previous problem — babysitting for dinner and a movie — except that Sally is a full-time homemaker. Are they entitled to claim the credit in this case? If they are not, will they nevertheless be able to claim the credit with impunity?

Problem 7. Don and Donna spend $6,000 for day care for their two young children while Donna is at work and Don is attending graduate school (as a full-time student). Donna earns $40,000 a year, and Don has no earned income. Assuming Don is a student for all 12 months of the year, how much (if any) of their $6,000 of child care expenses are eligible for the credit? You can answer this question from the statute itself; no need to look at the regulations.

Problem 8. Barbara, a single parent, has AGI of $31,100. She spends $5,000 on day care for her only child so that she can be gainfully employed. Calculate the amount of the child care credit to which Barbara is entitled.

c. The §129 Dependent Care Assistance Exclusion

Section 129 provides an exclusion for "dependent care assistance" received by an employee from his employer, if the employer has a qualifying "dependent care assistance program" (DCAP). The exclusion is subject to a ceiling of $5,000, regardless of how many children the taxpayer has. At first reading, this may seem to be designed to cover employer-operated on-site child care facilities. In fact, it does cover child care services provided in-kind, but its more frequent application is to cash reimbursements of employees' child care expenses.

Here's how §129 operates in the case of cash reimbursements. Late in the calendar year, an employer asks its employees if they want to participate in the employer's DCAP for the following year. For an employee who answers yes, the employer will reduce the employee's salary for the upcoming year by the amount the employee chooses (but not by more than $5,000). During the next year, as the employee incurs and pays child care expenses, he submits receipts to the employer (or to the employer's plan administrator), and the employer reimburses the employee for the expenses, up to the amount of the salary reduction. While amounts received as salary would have been taxable, amounts received in lieu of salary under a DCAP are tax-free under §129.[2] When the taxpayer and the employer have jumped through all the required hoops — the salary reduction agreement, the submission of receipts, and the reimbursements — the net tax effect is the same as if the taxpayer had included the $5,000 (or any lesser amount chosen by the taxpayer) in income, and then had deducted the $5,000. The exclusion is the equivalent of a child care deduction, but only for taxpayers whose employers are willing to go to the trouble and expense of setting up and administering a DCAP, and who are themselves willing to deal with all the DCAP red tape. As you would expect, a taxpayer cannot use the same dollars of child care expenses to generate both an exclusion under §129 and a credit under §21; §129(e)(7) provides that any expenditure used to support an exclusion under §129 cannot be the basis of a credit under §21. However, a taxpayer whose employer offers DCAP benefits can choose between the benefits of § 129 and the benefits of §21.[3]

---

2. The tax-free status of the reimbursements also depends on the "cafeteria plan" provisions of §125. Absent §125, the constructive receipt doctrine would treat a taxpayer who was entitled to receive taxable salary as if he had actually received it, even if he renounced it in favor of benefits under a DCAP. For the constructive receipt doctrine, see section B.1 of Chapter 7.

3. This choice is available for up to $5,000 of qualifying expenses. Because of the higher cap on the §21 credit, even taxpayers who maximize their §129 exclusion may claim a $1,000 credit under §21, assuming that they have at least two qualifying children and at least $6,000 of qualifying expenses.

The coexistence of the two child care tax benefits raises three policy questions. First, why should Congress give some taxpayers a choice between a deduction-equivalent and a credit? Shouldn't Congress decide which type of benefit is more appropriate, and allow only that type? Second, assuming that it is appropriate to give taxpayers a choice between the two benefits, why should only some taxpayers get that choice? Because there is considerable trouble and expense involved in setting up a DCAP, few small employers offer DCAP benefits. Year after year, the tax expenditure budget shows that §21 generates much more revenue loss than §129. This is not because the credit generally provides a greater tax savings than the exclusion — in fact, for many taxpayers the opposite is true. Rather, it is because §21 is available to working parents generally, whereas only parents with the right employers can take advantage of §129. Third, what possible justification could there be for the difference in the ceiling amounts? Why should the ceiling on credit-eligible expenses be either $3,000 or $6,000, depending on the number of children, while the ceiling on excludable benefits is $5,000 in all cases? All three questions are largely rhetorical. It may be possible to explain the coexistence of the two provisions with a page or two of history, but not with even a volume of logic.

Problem 9.   Alice spends $10,000 on day care for her only child, and she would like a tax benefit for as much of the $10,000 as possible. If her employer has a DCAP, can she exclude $5,000 under §129 and claim a credit for another $3,000 under §21? Notice that this is *not* an attempt to obtain both an exclusion and a credit for the same dollars, which would be prohibited by §129(e)(7).

Problem 10.   Felicia and Fred, who both work full-time, have two young children. They expect to incur $15,000 of work-related child care expenses in the upcoming year. They expect their AGI for next year to be about $60,000, and their marginal tax rate to be 25 percent. Felicia's employer has a DCAP. Should she elect to participate in the DCAP for the upcoming year or would they be better off simply claiming the credit?

Problem 11.   The facts are the same as in the previous problem, except that Felicia and Fred have only one child, and they expect to spend $9,000 on day care for that child during the upcoming year. Should Felicia elect to participate in her employer's DCAP?

2.   *Child Tax Benefits Not Based on Expenditures*

a.   **Exemptions**

Section 151 allows a taxpayer to claim one personal exemption for himself (two exemptions for a married couple filing a joint return) and an additional exemption for each dependent. The amount of the exemption is indexed for inflation; the exemption amount for 2011 is $3,700. As used in this context, "exemption" is just another word for deduction. A taxpayer would generally be entitled to a §151 deduction equal to the inflation-adjusted exemption amount multiplied by the number of people in his household.

The personal and dependency exemptions serve two functions. First, they work together with the standard deduction to prevent the imposition of income tax liability on persons living at or below the poverty level. In 2011, a married couple with no children is entitled to a standard deduction of $11,600, and two exemptions of $3,700 each. As a result, they could earn $19,000 — an amount somewhat higher than their official poverty level — before having any taxable income.[4] The official poverty level increases with family size, and so does the amount of income sheltered from tax. A couple with two children, for example, could earn $26,400 ($11,600 plus 4 times $3,700) before having any taxable income.[5]

Exemptions are not available, however, only to persons living at or near the poverty level. A taxpayer with $100,000 of income is still entitled to claim personal and dependency exemptions. The policy explanation is that exemptions serve a second purpose — to adjust tax liabilities for differences in family size, across a wide range of income levels. Suppose two couples each have $150,000 of adjusted gross income, but one couple has no dependent children while the other couple has five. It seems fair that the first couple, whose $150,000 is used to support only two people, should pay more tax than the second couple, whose income must support seven. Section 151 accomplishes that differentiation by giving the second couple a deduction $18,500 ($3,700 times 5) greater than the first couple's deduction. This is consistent with the notion that people have ability to pay tax only out of their "clear income" — that is, income in excess of the amount needed to cover basic subsistence needs. Assuming the cost of family subsistence increases by $3,700 for each additional family member, then the first couple has $18,500 more clear income than the second couple; §151 ensures that the first couple will also have $18,500 more income subject to tax.

As with any deduction, the tax savings from an exemption is the amount of the exemption multiplied by the taxpayer's marginal tax rate. Thus, a $3,700 exemption is worth more to an affluent taxpayer in the 35 percent bracket than it would be worth to a 15 percent bracket taxpayer struggling to make ends meet. Because of this, exemptions have been criticized as being unfairly skewed to the benefit of upper income taxpayers. Two provisions described and discussed below — the §151(d)(3) phaseout of personal exemptions and the §24 child credit — represent legislative responses to this criticism of exemptions.

The criticism, however, is misguided. It is based on the misconception that exemptions are about vertical equity (fairness between rich and poor taxpayers), when in fact exemptions are about horizontal equity (fairness between taxpayers at the same income level, but with different family sizes). Consider the four couples in the table below.

Couple	Income (before exemptions)	Number of Children
A. Alice and Andy	$40,000	0
B. Betty and Barney	$49,000	3
C. Carla and Carl	$150,000	0
D. Donna and Don	$159,000	3

4. The 2011 poverty threshold used for most federal purposes for a family of two is $14,710.
5. The official poverty threshold for a family of four in 2011 is $22,350.

Assume $3,000 is an accurate measure of the per-child increase in the cost of subsistence living. In that case, couples *A* and *B* have exactly the same amount of clear income, and thus should have the same amount of taxable income. Similarly, couples *C* and *D* have the same clear income, and should have the same taxable income. Horizontal equity between the *A*s and the *B*s, and between the *C*s and the *D*s, is achieved by giving each three-child couple a §151 deduction $9,000 larger than the deduction allowed to the childless couples. In a tax system with progressive marginal rates, the *D*s' $9,000 deduction will decrease their tax liability by more than the *B*s' $9,000 deduction will reduce their tax liability, but so what? If there is a legitimate vertical equity objection to the distribution of tax burdens among the four couples, it must be that the upper middle class taxpayers (the *C*s and the *D*s) do not pay enough tax relative to the lower middle class taxpayers (the *A*s and the *B*s). But if that is the objection, the solution is to redesign the tax rate schedule — lowering marginal rates at the bottom and raising them at the top — not to phase out exemptions for high income taxpayers, or to replace or supplement exemptions with credits.

Despite the strong argument that exemptions are appropriate at all income levels, §151(d)(3) phases out exemptions for upper income taxpayers. The statute indicates that the phaseout begins at AGI of $150,000 (for joint returns) and ends at $272,501.[6] The phaseout range is adjusted for post-1992 inflation. The phaseout does not apply in the jubilee years of 2010, 2011, and 2012, but it is scheduled to return in full force in 2013. (It would not be surprising, however, if Congress extended the §151(d)(3) holiday for a few more years, or even repealed it once and for all.) The phaseout is apparently based on the view that exemptions are subsidies, and that very high income parents do not need subsidies. If exemptions are viewed as subsidies, however, the resulting subsidy pattern is very strange. The amount of subsidy per child *increases* with income until the phaseout begins; the amount of per child subsidy does not begin to decrease as income increases until AGI has reached the phaseout threshold. The policy justification for this pattern is far from obvious.

In the case of a child of divorced parents, §152(e) generally allocates the dependency exemption to the parent who has custody of the child for most of the year, but the custodial parent can waive the right to the exemption in favor of the noncustodial parent. Because the value of an exemption depends on the circumstances of the particular taxpayer, and because allocation of the §24 child credit follows the allocation of the exemption, the analysis of whether the custodial parent should waive the exemption can be quite complicated.[7]

b.   The Child Credit

Rather than declare a victor in the great debate between proponents of dependency exemptions and proponents of credits, in 1997 Congress decided to make everyone a winner by enacting the §24 child credit — in addition to, rather than as a replacement for, the §151 dependency exemption. In contrast to the exemption, the value of the credit is independent of the taxpayer's marginal tax rate. For most

6. For a detailed explanation of the mechanics of the phaseout, and for additional policy critique, see the Chapter 1 cell on understanding tax rates.

7. For a detailed consideration of this question, see section C.2 of this chapter.

taxpayers, the calculation of the credit could not be simpler: By the terms of §24(a), just multiply $1,000 by the number of the taxpayer's "qualifying children."[8] Like the dependency exemption, however, the credit is phased out for higher income taxpayers. This phaseout operates over a lower income range than the exemption phaseout.

The child credit phaseout begins at $110,000 for married couples filing joint returns and at $75,000 for unmarried taxpayers. (These phaseout thresholds are *not* adjusted for inflation.) The credit phaseout serves as a way of means-testing the subsidy embodied in the credit. It is easy enough to understand why Congress might subject such a subsidy to means-testing, but it is not easy to understand why the means-testing should be so minimal. It is true that the phaseout prevents a couple with $150,000 AGI from receiving the subsidy, but why should a couple with $110,000 AGI receive just as large a per-child subsidy as a couple with $30,000 AGI?

If the phaseout makes credit calculations somewhat complex for higher income parents, there is even more complexity in the rules applicable to low income parents. Most tax credits, with the very important exception of the earned income credit, are nonrefundable. That means they are of value to a particular taxpayer only to the extent that the taxpayer has a before-credit income tax liability. For example, if a taxpayer has a pre-credit income tax liability of $300, and is theoretically entitled to a nonrefundable credit of $1,000, $700 of the credit will be unusable. On the other hand, if the credit were refundable, the taxpayer could use $300 of the credit to reduce income tax liability to zero, and would be entitled to receive the other $700 as a check from the government.

To oversimplify the political debate a bit, liberals and conservatives have differing views as to whether the child credit should be refundable. The liberal view is that the credit is intended as a subsidy for parents and their children, and that there is no good reason why eligibility for a subsidy should depend on having income tax liability to offset — in fact, poor parents with little or no pre-credit income tax liability are in greatest need of the subsidy. Under this view, the credit should be fully refundable. To conservatives, however, there is a great moral gulf between the last dollar of tax reduction (good) and the first dollar of transfer payments (bad). Under this view, it is one thing to allow the credit to reduce or eliminate the income tax burden on low income parents, but it is a very different thing to use the credit to give low income parents a handout (on top of the already refundable earned income credit).

Each of these positions is philosophically coherent, and either would be simple to implement. Unfortunately, the legislative compromise between the two makes little policy sense and imposes considerable complexity on taxpayers who cannot afford expensive professional assistance in dealing with it. The messy compromise, embodied in §24(d), is a version of partial refundability. According to the statute, the credit is refundable to the extent of 15 percent of the amount by which earned income exceeds $10,000. The $10,000 amount is adjusted for post-2000 inflation, and a special rule reduces the threshold amount to $3,000 for 2009 through 2012. For example, assume the $10,000 threshold applies, and a particular parent's earned income is $14,000. In that case, $600 of the taxpayer's §24 credit would be refundable.[9] The partial refundability is determined on a per-taxpayer basis rather than a per-child basis. Thus, the parent in the example would be entitled to

---

8. The per-child credit amount is scheduled to decline to $500 for 2013 and later years, but Congress is likely to extend the $1,000 credit for years beyond 2012.

9. ($14,000 − $10,000) × .15 = $600.)

only $600 of refundable credit, regardless of the number of qualifying children.[10] The partial refundability rule acts as a *negative* 15 percent marginal tax rate, beginning at $10,000 earned income. This negative tax rate operates over much of the same income range as the hidden *positive* marginal tax rate imposed by the phaseout of the earned income credit of §32,[11] and serves to counteract the high marginal tax rates otherwise caused by the combination of the §1 rate schedule and the earned income tax credit phaseout. For example, if a taxpayer is simultaneously subject to a 10 percent rate under §1, a 21.06 percent earned income credit phaseout rate (the rate applicable to taxpayers with two or more qualifying children), and a 15 percent negative rate under §24, the taxpayer's overall marginal tax rate (ignoring social security tax and state income tax) is 16.06 percent. The negative marginal tax rate under the child credit does not fully offset the earned income credit phaseout, both because the §24 negative rate is lower than the phaseout rate for the earned income credit and because the income range for phaseout of the earned income credit extends well beyond the end of the negative tax rate under §24. Of course, there is value in having §24 even partially offset the high marginal tax rates imposed by §32. It might be better yet, however, to redesign the system to eliminate both the negative tax of §24 and the positive tax imposed by §32. Why would anyone design a tax system under which a low income parent with one child is simultaneously subject to a 15.98 percent positive tax under §32 and a 15 percent negative tax under §24?[12] Depending on your taste in literary references, the system must have been designed either by the Duke of York[13] or Alice's White Knight.[14] Rather than having the positive tax and the negative tax virtually cancel out each other, wouldn't it be simpler to get rid of both?

Most of the time, if a child qualifies as a taxpayer's dependent for exemption purposes, the child will also be a "qualifying child" for purposes of the child credit. There is, however, one important difference: The credit is allowed only with respect to a child who is 16 or younger at the end of the taxable year.[15] Thus, parents will often be unable to claim the credit with respect to children attending high school. The legislative history provides no explanation for this rather strange cut-off age.

Problem 12.   Gina and George, whose adjusted gross income is $118,000, have two "qualifying children" for purposes of the child credit. But for the §24(b)(2) phaseout provision, they would be entitled to a $2,000 child credit ($1,000 for each child). How large a credit are they entitled to, taking the phaseout into account?

---

10. For taxpayers with three or more children, the partial refundability calculations are even more complicated. Basically, they can calculate the amount of refundable credit using either the method described in the text, or a method that makes the credit refundable to the extent the taxpayer's social security taxes exceed the taxpayer's earned income credit. If this sounds like a complicated mess, it is. At least it is a pro-taxpayer mess, since the taxpayer is entitled to use whichever method produces the larger refundable amount.

11. For the earned income tax credit, see section E of this chapter.

12. The phase-out rate for taxpayers with only one qualifying child is 15.98 percent. *See* §32(b)(1).

13. "He had ten thousand men/He marched them up to the top of the hill/and marched them down again."

14. "But I was thinking of a plan/To dye one's whiskers green/And always use so large a fan/That they could not be seen."

15. *See* §24(c)(1).

Problem 13.   Helen, a single parent, has two "qualifying children" for purposes of the child credit. Her earned income for the year is $18,000. If the child credit did not exist, she would have an income tax liability of $200. A $2,000 credit is generally available to a taxpayer with two children, but what will be the amount of Helen's §24 credit? (Assume no inflation adjustment applies to the $10,000 threshold in §24(d)(1)(B)(i).)

c. Head-of-Household Status

A single parent who lives with one or more dependent children will usually qualify as a head of household for purposes of the income tax.[16] Head-of-household status carries with it two important tax benefits. First, a head of household is entitled to a substantially larger standard deduction than that available to other unmarried taxpayers. In 2011 the head-of-household standard deduction is $2,700 larger than the single taxpayer standard deduction. Second, a head of household pays tax under a §1 rate schedule with wider brackets than the §1 rate schedule for other unmarried taxpayers. In 2011 the top of the 15 percent bracket for heads of households is $11,750 higher than the top of the 15 percent bracket for other unmarried taxpayers. Taken together, the two benefits of head of household status can be worth several thousand dollars. These rules make the *first* dependent child of an unmarried taxpayer uniquely valuable for tax purposes. No child of married taxpayers, and no additional child of unmarried taxpayers, have any effect on the amount of the standard deduction. Similarly, in no other situation does the existence of a dependent child determine the applicable §1 tax rate schedule. The head-of-household rules are easier to explain by history than by logic. In 1948, Congress provided for joint return income-splitting by married couples. Although this tax benefit for married couples was not premised on the existence of dependent children, single parents viewed it as an allowance for family responsibilities and demanded similar consideration. Congress responded to their demands in 1951, by creating the head-of-household rules.

There *is* a plausible argument for widening the rate brackets as the number of dependents increases, but the argument does not suggest that this should be done only for the first child of an unmarried parent. Suppose we are designing a tax system, and our first decision is that a single adult, with no family responsibilities, should pay tax at the rate of 10 percent on his first $20,000 of taxable income, and at the rate of 30 percent on all additional income. We also decide that we want families, of whatever size, to pay tax according to the standard of living that their income will support. We then need to decide how much additional income is needed to support a particular standard of living as family size increases. To keep it simple, suppose we decide there are no economies of scale, so that two adults living together need $40,000 to live as well as a single adult can live on $20,000. Finally, we determine that children are more efficient consumers than adults; a child can live as well on $10,000 as an adult can live on $20,000. Based on all this, we make the household the taxable unit, and we give each household a 10 percent bracket equal to $20,000 × (number of adults + number of children/2). The table below illustrates the resulting 10 percent brackets for households of

---

16. *See* §2(b) for the definition of "head-of-household."

various compositions. The idea is that the amount of income in the 10 percent bracket will support the same standard of living in each case, taking family size into account.

Household Composition	Adults + Children/2	Width of 10% Bracket
1 adult	1	$20,000
1 adult, 1 child	1 + .5	$30,000
1 adult, 2 children	1 + 1	$40,000
2 adults	2	$40,000
2 adults, 3 children	2 + 1.5	$70,000

A strong case can be made that a tax system that allowed this sort of family income-splitting would be well designed to adjust income tax liability according to ability to pay. This does not explain, however, why the current system generally fails to permit family income-splitting (i.e., to widen rate brackets based on family size), with the two exceptions of joint returns and head-of-household status. If brackets should be widened on account of the first child of a single parent, it would seem that brackets should be widened on account of every child—regardless of the number of children in the family, and regardless of whether the parents are single or married.[17]

B.   THE INCOME TAX TREATMENT OF MARRIAGE

LUCAS v. EARL

281 U.S. 111 (1930)

Mr. Justice HOLMES delivered the opinion of the Court.

This case presents the question whether the respondent, Earl, could be taxed for the whole of the salary and attorney's fees earned by him in the years 1920 and 1921, or should be taxed for only a half of them in view of a contract with his wife which we shall mention. . . .

By the contract, made in 1901, Earl and his wife agreed "that any property either of us now has or may hereafter acquire . . . in any way, either by earnings (including salaries, fees, etc.), or any rights by contract or otherwise, during the existence of our marriage, or which we or either of us may receive by gift, bequest, devise, or inheritance, and all the proceeds, issues, and profits of any and all such property shall be treated and considered and hereby is declared to be received, held, taken, and owned by us as joint tenants, and not otherwise, with the right of survivorship." The validity of the contract is not questioned, and we assume it to be unquestionable under the law of the State of California, in which the parties lived. Nevertheless we are of opinion that the Commissioner and Board of Tax

---

17. This idea is developed in greater detail in the cell on family income-splitting by statute.

Appeals were right [in ruling that Mr. Earl should be taxed on all of his earned income]. . . .

A very forcible argument is presented to the effect that the statute seeks to tax only income beneficially received, and that taking the question more technically the salary and fees became the joint property of Earl and his wife on the very first instant on which they were received. We well might hesitate upon the latter proposition, because however the matter might stand between husband and wife he was the only party to the contracts by which the salary and fees were earned, and it is somewhat hard to say that the last step in the performance of those contracts could be taken by anyone but himself alone. But this case is not to be decided by attenuated subtleties. It turns on the import and reasonable construction of the taxing act. There is no doubt that the statute could tax salaries to those who earned them and provide that the tax could not be escaped by anticipatory arrangements and contracts however skillfully devised to prevent the salary when paid from vesting even for a second in the man who earned it. That seems to us the import of the statute before us and we think that no distinction can be taken according to the motives leading to the arrangement by which the fruits are attributed to a different tree from that on which they grew.

Judgment reversed.

Notes and Questions

1. *What's at stake?* At the time of *Lucas v. Earl*, the income tax treated a married couple as two separate taxpayers.[18] To understand the stakes in *Earl*, imagine a tax system under which the individual (rather than the couple) is always the taxable unit, and which imposes two rates of tax: a 10 percent tax rate on the first $40,000 of income and a 30 percent tax rate on all income above $40,000. Suppose Mr. Earl had earned $80,000 from his job and Mrs. Earl was a full-time homemaker with no earned income of her own. Mr. Earl's argument was that $40,000 of his earnings should be taxed to him, but that the other $40,000 should be taxed to Mrs. Earl because of their agreement. If his argument had prevailed, the entire $80,000 would have been taxed at the rate of 10 percent, and the combined tax bill would have been only $8,000. The government's position, with which the Supreme Court agreed, was that all the income should be taxed to Mr. Earl, resulting in a total tax bill of $16,000 (10% of the first $40,000, plus 30% of the second $40,000).

2. *A different sort of controversy.* *Earl* represents a peculiar sort of tax controversy, in which there is no disagreement between the government and the taxpayer about the amount of income that should be taxed in the current year. The only disagreement is over the identity of the proper taxpayer. The identity of the correct taxpayer can be crucial, however, in a tax system with progressive marginal rates. When Mr. Earl's second $40,000 of income is stacked on top of his first $40,000 of income — in Mr. Earl's income pile — it is taxed at 30 percent. If, instead, it had been treated as the only income in Mrs. Earl's income pile, the rate would have been just 10 percent.

18. This assumes that each partner had income in excess of the threshold of taxability, thus qualifying as a taxpayer.

3. *Two branches*. Post-*Earl* developments branch off in two directions. One branch is the law of income-shifting, which deals with the question of when a taxpayer can shift the liability for income to a related lower bracket taxpayer, such as a child or a controlled entity. Basically, the answer is that *Earl* remains good law with respect to *earned* income, but that a taxpayer can shift the tax liability on income *from property* by making a gift of the income-producing property. That is an oversimplification, of course, and we will examine income-shifting in detail in the next chapter. The second branch, and the one followed in this chapter, is the taxation of married couples. The first post-*Earl* development concerning the taxation of marriage followed in a matter of months.

POE v. SEABORN

282 U.S. 101 (1930)

Mr. Justice ROBERTS delivered the opinion of the Court.

Seaborn and his wife, citizens and residents of the State of Washington, made for the year 1927 separate income tax returns as permitted by the Revenue Act of 1926.

During and prior to 1927 they accumulated property comprising real estate, stocks, bonds and other personal property. While the real estate stood in his name alone, it is undisputed that all of the property real and personal constituted community property and that neither owned any separate property or had any separate income.

The income comprised Seaborn's salary, interest on bank deposits and on bonds, dividends, and profits on sales of real and personal property. He and his wife each returned [i.e., reported] one-half the total community income as gross income and each deducted one-half of the community expenses to arrive at the net income returned.

The Commissioner of Internal Revenue determined that all of the income should have been reported in the husband's return, and made an additional assessment against him. Seaborn paid under protest, claimed a refund, and on its rejection, brought this suit. . . .

The case requires us to construe Sections 210(a) and 211(a) of the Revenue Act of 1926 (U.S.C. App., Tit. 26, secs. 951 and 952), and apply them, as construed, to the interests of husband and wife in community property under the law of Washington. These sections lay a tax upon the net income of every individual. The Act goes no farther, and furnishes no other standard or definition of what constitutes an individual's income. The use of the word "of" denotes ownership. It would be a strained construction, which, in the absence of further definition by Congress, should impute a broader significance to the phrase.

The Commissioner concedes that the answer to the question involved in the cause must be found in the provisions of the law of the State, as to a wife's ownership of or interest in community property. What, then, is the law of Washington as to the ownership of community property and of community income, including the earnings of the husband's and wife's labor?

The answer is found in the statutes of the State, and the decisions interpreting them.

These statutes provide that, save for property acquired by gift, bequest, devise or inheritance, all property however acquired after marriage, by either husband or wife, or by both, is community property. On the death of either spouse his or her interest is subject to testamentary disposition, and failing that, it passes to the issue of the decedent and not to the surviving spouse. While the husband has the management and control of community personal property and like power of disposition thereof as of his separate personal property, this power is subject to restrictions which are inconsistent with denial of the wife's interest as co-owner. . . .

Without further extending this opinion it must suffice to say that it is clear the wife has, in Washington, a vested property right in the community property, equal with that of her husband; and in the income of the community, including salaries or wages of either husband or wife, or both. . . .

The taxpayer contends that if the test of taxability under Sections 210 and 211 is ownership, it is clear that income of community property is owned by the community and that husband and wife have each a present vested one-half interest therein.

The Commissioner contends, however, that we are here concerned not with mere names, nor even with mere technical legal titles; that calling the wife's interest vested is nothing to the purpose, because the husband has such broad powers of control and alienation, that while the community lasts, he is essentially the owner of the whole community property, and ought so to be considered for the purposes of Sections 210 and 211. He points out that as to personal property the husband may convey it, may make contracts affecting it, may do anything with it short of committing a fraud on his wife's rights. And though the wife must join in any sale of real estate, he asserts that the same is true, by virtue of statutes, in most States which do not have the community system. He asserts that control without accountability is indistinguishable from ownership, and that since the husband has this, *quoad* community property and income, the income is that "of" the husband under Sections 210-211 of the income tax law.

We think, in view of the law of Washington above stated, this contention is unsound. The community must act through an agent. . . .

The reasons for conferring such sweeping powers of management on the husband are not far to seek. Public policy demands that in all ordinary circumstances, litigation between wife and husband during the life of the community should be discouraged. Law-suits between them would tend to subvert the marital relation. The same policy dictates that third parties who deal with the husband respecting community property shall be assured that the wife shall not be permitted to nullify his transactions. The powers of partners, or of trustees of a spendthrift trust, furnish apt analogies.

The obligations of the husband as agent of the community are no less real because the policy of the State limits the wife's right to call him to account in a court. Power is not synonymous with right. Nor is obligation coterminous with legal remedy. The law's investiture of the husband with broad powers, by no means negatives the wife's present interest as a co-owner.

We are of opinion that under the law of Washington the entire property and income of the community can no more be said to be that of the husband, than it could rightly be termed that of the wife. . . .

The Commissioner urges that we have, in principal, decided the instant question in favor of the Government. He relies on . . . Lucas v. Earl, 281 U.S. 111. . . .

In the *Earl* case . . . the very assignment . . . was bottomed on the fact that the earnings would be the husband's property, else there would have been nothing on which it could operate. That case presents quite a different question from this, because here, by law, the earnings are never the property of the husband, but that of the community.

Finally the argument is pressed upon us that the Commissioner's ruling will work uniformity of incidence and operation of the tax in the various states, while the view urged by the taxpayer will make the tax fall unevenly upon married people. . . .

The District Court was right in holding that the husband and wife were entitled to file separate returns, each treating one-half of the community income as his or her respective income, and its judgment is affirmed.

Notes and Questions

1. *What about the fruit and the tree?* So what happened to attributing the fruit to the tree on which it grew? Are you persuaded by the Court's explanation that *Earl* is different from this case, "because here, by law, the earnings are never the property of the husband," or is that exactly the sort of "attenuated subtlety" scorned by Justice Holmes in *Earl*? Although the *Seaborn* holding clearly permits splitting of both earned income and income from property by spouses in community property states, the opinion seems to focus more on the taxation of income from property. Perhaps the government would have done better to have conceded the case with respect to investment income, but to have argued more forcefully that *Earl* governed the taxation of earned income even in community property states.

2. *State marital property law and federal income tax liabilities.* Using the same hypothetical tax rate schedule as in the note following *Earl* (10% on the first $40,000 of income, 30% on all additional income), what will be the tax liability of the Seaborns if Mr. Seaborn earns $80,000 and Mrs. Seaborn earns nothing? Because the diversion of income from husband to wife is by operation of state community property law, rather than by private agreement, under the *Seaborn* opinion half the income will be taxed to Mrs. Seaborn. As a result, none of the income will be subject to the 30 percent rate, and their combined tax liability will be only $8,000. After *Earl* and *Seaborn*, if two husbands had equal salaries and had wives with no income of their own, and one couple lived in a common-law property state and one lived in a community property state, the salary of the common-law property husband would be more heavily taxed.

3. *Community property sweeps the nation, but not for long.* In the years following the *Earl* and *Seaborn* decisions, a wave of enthusiasm for community property swept the nation. A number of states abandoned centuries of tradition and adopted community property regimes, in order to obtain the benefits of *Seaborn* for their married residents. The enthusiasm was shortlived, however. In 1948 Congress provided for automatic income-splitting between spouses as a matter of federal law. Under this new system, any married couple — regardless of state marital property law — had a tax liability equal to the tax liabilities of two single persons, each with half of the couple's

income. This was accomplished by allowing a married couple to file a joint return, combining the incomes (and deductions) of the spouses, and then taxing that income under a rate schedule with brackets twice as wide as the brackets applicable to unmarried taxpayers. Thus, if the 10 percent bracket encompassed the first $40,000 of income for unmarried taxpayers, it would cover the first $80,000 of income for a married couple filing a joint return. Under this system, both the Earls and the Seaborns would report $80,000 of income on a joint return, with the entire $80,000 fitting (just barely) into the 10 percent bracket. Each couple's tax liability would be only $8,000. The 1948 approach extended to couples in common-law property states the income-splitting benefit already enjoyed by couples in community property states. Not surprisingly, all the states that had adopted community property after 1930 quickly reverted to common-law property regimes following the 1948 legislation.

4. *The rise of singles penalties.* Was everyone happy after the 1948 reforms? Of course not. Married couples in common-law property states were now mollified, but the new tax victims were single people. Using the same hypothetical tax rate schedules (with the 10% bracket covering $40,000 for single taxpayers, but $80,000 for couples), consider the plight of a single person earning $80,000. His tax liability is $16,000, because half of his income is taxed in the 30 percent bracket. But suppose he has a married coworker, with an identical job and an identical salary, and a homemaking wife with no income of her own. The coworker's tax liability will be only $8,000, because his entire salary will fit within the 10 percent bracket for joint returns. In the mind of the unmarried worker, this amounts to a massive singles penalty. Single taxpayers complained that their married coworkers were allowed to use their homemaking spouses as a sort of human tax shelter. In 1969 Congress responded to complaints about singles penalties by widening the brackets for unmarried taxpayers, while leaving the joint return brackets unchanged. In our hypothetical, this might mean extending the 10 percent bracket to $50,000 for unmarried taxpayers, while leaving it at $80,000 for joint returns. The unmarried taxpayer with income of $80,000 would still have $30,000 of income taxed at 30 percent, compared with no income taxed at 30 percent for his equal-income married coworker, but at least his singles penalty had been reduced.

5. *And here come marriage penalties.* So was everyone finally satisfied after the 1969 reforms? Of course not. Not only were there still singles penalties to complain about; for the first time there were also *marriage* penalties. It was now possible for a two-earner couple to have a higher tax bill because they were married, than they would have had as unmarried cohabitants. For example, two single people, each earning $50,000, would pay a combined tax of $10,000 under our hypothetical unmarried taxpayer rate schedule. The entire income of each would just squeeze into the 10 percent bracket for unmarried taxpayers. But if they were married, and they combined their incomes on a joint return, their tax bill would be $14,000. The $4,000 marriage penalty would result because they would then have $20,000 of income taxed at 30

percent.[19] Could a two-earner married couple do anything to avoid this sort of marriage penalty? As the following case demonstrates, one should never underestimate the ingenuity of the American taxpayer.

BOYTER v. COMMISSIONER
668 F.2d 1382 (4th Cir. 1981)

WINTER, Chief Judge: Taxpayers (H. David Boyter and his sometime wife, Angela M. Boyter), both of whom are domiciled in Maryland, ask us to reverse the Tax Court and to rule that for the tax years 1975 and 1976 they successfully avoided the "marriage penalty" of the Internal Revenue Code. The "marriage penalty" results from the fact that a man and woman who are husband and wife on the last day of the taxable year, each having separate income, are taxed, in the aggregate, in a greater amount if they file either joint or separate income tax returns than would be the case if they were unmarried. The Tax Court ruled that the Boyters were legally married at the end of tax years 1975 and 1976, and therefore were subject to the higher tax rate, since their purported Haitian and Dominican Republic divorces (granted on December 8, 1975 and November 22, 1976, respectively) were invalid under the law of Maryland, the state of the Boyters' domicile. The Tax Court therefore sustained the Commissioner's deficiency assessments for unpaid taxes. In view of this conclusion the Tax Court apparently thought it unnecessary to decide the Commissioner's alternative argument that even if the divorces would be recognized in Maryland, the taxpayers should be treated as husband and wife for federal income tax purposes under the "sham" transaction doctrine.

Without expressing a view on the correctness of what was actually decided, we remand the case to the Tax Court for further findings as to the applicability of the sham transaction doctrine.

I

Taxpayers were married in Maryland in 1966 and were domiciled in Maryland during the tax years in issue, 1975 and 1976. Both are employed as federal civil service employees and have not insubstantial earnings. They filed joint federal income tax returns and reported their income as married individuals filing separately from 1966 to 1974.

Probably as a result of dinner table conversation with a friend who had been recently divorced, taxpayers came to the realization that their combined federal income tax liability would be lower if they were able to report their respective incomes as unmarried individuals. They were also aware that the Internal

---

19. Married persons have the option to file separate returns. If they do, however, they must use the special unfavorable tax rate schedule of §1(d), which has rate brackets only half as wide as the joint return rate brackets. If the two-earner couple described in the text elected this option, each would have $40,000 of income taxed at 10 percent and $10,000 taxed at 30 percent, resulting in a combined tax liability of $14,000. Obviously, this would not solve their tax problem. Section 1(d) is used by spouses who distrust each other too much to sign a joint return (which would result in joint and several liability for all tax due on their combined income); it does not provide marriage penalty relief. On rare occasions there may be a tax advantage to separate filing under §1(d), but not because of the tax rate schedule. Rather, separate filing may reduce the impact of a provision that allows a particular sort of deduction only to the extent expenses exceed some specified percentage of AGI. Deductions subject to percentage-of-AGI floors include medical expenses, miscellaneous itemized deductions, and casualty losses.

Revenue Code provides that the determination of whether an individual is married shall be made as of the close of the taxable year. 26 U.S.C. sec. 143(a)(1) [now §7703(a)(1)].

Taxpayers thus concluded that if they obtained a divorce decree at the end of the taxable year (here, December 31) they would be entitled to file their returns as unmarried individuals. It seems clear, as the Tax Court found, that at least through 1976 taxpayers never intended to and never did physically separate from each other prior to or subsequent to either of the divorces that they obtained. Rather, they continued to reside together through the tax years in question in the home they purchased in 1967.

Late in 1975 taxpayers traveled to Haiti. Through an attorney, whose name they had obtained from a Baltimore public library and who in correspondence had quoted them an attractive estimate of his fee and expenses, they obtained a decree of divorce. The action was instituted by Angela Boyter and the divorce decree was granted on the ground of incompatibility of character notwithstanding that the parties occupied the same hotel room prior to and immediately after the granting of the decree. Moreover, Angela Boyter testified before the Tax Court that her character was not incompatible to that of David Boyter. She testified also that the sole reason for her obtaining the divorce was "because the tax laws, as currently written, caused us to pay a penalty for being married." Indeed she testified that she advised her Haitian counsel "that we got along quite well and planned to continue to live together. . . ." Shortly after the Haitian court granted the divorce, taxpayers returned to their matrimonial domicile in Maryland and were remarried in Howard County, Maryland on January 9, 1976. For the calendar year 1975 taxpayers filed separate income tax returns claiming the rates applicable to unmarried individuals.

In November of 1976 taxpayers traveled to the Dominican Republic where David Boyter, as the moving party, obtained a divorce decree on November 22, 1976. Again the parties traveled together to and from the Dominican Republic. Whether they occupied the same hotel room is not shown by the record. The record does show, however, that although the Dominican decree was granted on the ground of "incompatibilities of temperaments existing between (the parties) that has made life together unbearable," Angela Boyter denied that she had ever said anything which would serve as a basis for such a finding by the Dominican Republic court. David Boyter testified before the Tax Court that he would not characterize the grounds as "totally" true. As he explained it: "I understood that these were strictly legalistic terms."

The taxpayers returned to Maryland to their matrimonial domicile and they were remarried on February 10, 1977. For calendar year 1976 they filed separate federal income tax returns claiming the rates applicable to unmarried individuals.

The Commissioner determined a deficiency in income taxes for each of the taxpayers for 1975 and 1976 and taxpayers sought review in the Tax Court. The Tax Court sustained the deficiencies. Although the government argued that the divorce decrees should be disregarded for federal income tax purposes because a year-end divorce whereby the parties intend to and do in fact remarry early in the next year is a sham transaction, the Tax Court expressed no view on this argument. Rather, it undertook an elaborate analysis of Maryland law with respect to the validity of the divorce decrees and concluded that Maryland would not recognize the foreign divorces as valid to terminate the marriage. On this basis, the Tax Court entered judgment for the government.

II

We agree with the government's argument that under the Internal Revenue Code a federal court is bound by state law rather than federal law when attempting to construe marital status. . . . The difficulty with this approach in this case, however, is that the Maryland authorities do not establish beyond peradventure of doubt that the two divorces with which we are concerned are invalid under Maryland law. As the Tax Court stated, "the law in Maryland with regard to the recognition of migratory divorces obtained in a foreign country by Maryland domiciliaries has not been explicitly declared by either the legislature or the highest court of that state," although, as the taxpayers have demonstrated, a number of Maryland trial courts, explicitly and implicitly, have recognized the validity of migratory foreign divorces.

In this ambiguous state of the Maryland law, we would ordinarily be disposed to invoke the certification procedure authorized by Ann. Code of Md., Cts. & Jud. Proc. sec. 12-601 (1980), and ask the Maryland Court of Appeals for a definitive pronouncement on the validity of these bilateral foreign migratory divorces.[20]

But there are other factors which must be considered. The Commissioner has made it clear to us both in his brief and in oral argument that he intends to press the contention, advanced in the Tax Court but not decided by it, that under the sham transaction doctrine taxpayers must be treated as husband and wife in computing their federal income taxes for the years 1975 and 1976 even if Maryland recognizes the validity of their migratory foreign divorces. Of course, if the issue of their validity were certified to the Maryland Court of Appeals and that court ruled them invalid, that decision would decide this case. Significantly, however, if the Maryland Court of Appeals ruled them valid, further proceedings would still be necessary in a federal tribunal and those proceedings might result in an adjudication which would render the certification and the opinion of the Maryland court a futile, academic exercise with respect to final disposition of this case.

We think that certification is inappropriate here. Considerations of comity lead us to conclude that we ought not to request the Maryland Court of Appeals to answer a question of law unless and until it appears that the answer is dispositive of the federal litigation or is a necessary and inescapable ruling in the course of the litigation. . . . We hold that that discretion ought not to be exercised to certify a question of state law where a question of federal law is present and undecided, the decision of which may be wholly dispositive of the case.

III

We therefore turn to the question of whether in principle the sham transaction doctrine may be dispositive in this case. Although we hold that the doctrine may be applicable, we do not decide that the divorces in question are in fact shams.

The sham transaction doctrine has its genesis in Gregory v. Helvering, 293 U.S. 465 (1935). . . .

The Court conceded that the [transaction in *Gregory*] was conducted in technical compliance with applicable statutes [governing tax-free corporate reorganizations]

---

20. This option was not available to the Tax Court because the Maryland statute does not permit a certification from that tribunal.

and that taxpayers are entitled to arrange their affairs so as to decrease their tax liability. It held nonetheless that the "whole undertaking . . . was in fact an elaborate and devious form of conveyance masquerading as a corporate reorganization" and should be disregarded for income tax purposes. 293 U.S. at 470. . . . The Court concluded: "The rule which excludes from consideration the motive of tax avoidance is not pertinent to this situation, because the transaction upon its face lies outside the plain intent of the statute. To hold otherwise would be to exalt artifice above reality and to deprive the statutory provision in question of all serious purpose." *Id.* at 470.

Gregory has been subsequently invoked by the courts to disregard the form of a variety of business transactions and to apply the tax laws on the basis of the substance or economic reality of the transactions. . . .

In evaluating the substance of a transaction, the courts take care to examine the transaction as a whole, not as the sum of its component parts. Accordingly, the liquidation of a corporation will be disregarded when it reincorporates subsequently and the business enterprise remains in substantially continuous operation. Atlas Tool Co. v. Commissioner, 614 F.2d 860, 866-67 (3d Cir. 1980). . . .

Although the sham transaction doctrine has been applied primarily with respect to the tax consequences of commercial transactions, personal tax consequences have often served as the motive for those transactions. . . . The principles involved, moreover, are fundamental to the system of income taxation in the United States and should be applicable generally.

Thus Revenue Ruling 76-255 applies the sham transaction doctrine to the divorce of taxpayers who promptly remarry. The underlying purpose of the transaction, viewed as a whole, is for the taxpayers to remain effectively married while avoiding the marriage penalty in the tax laws. It is the prompt remarriage that defeats the apparent divorce when assessing the taxpayers' liability, just as the prompt reincorporation of a business enterprise in continuous operation defeats the apparent liquidation of the predecessor corporation. *Atlas Tool Co.*, 614 F.2d at 866-67. Thus, the sham transaction doctrine may apply in this case if, as the record suggests, the parties intended merely to procure divorce papers rather than actually to effect a real dissolution of their marriage contract.

Having decided in principle that the sham transaction doctrine may apply to the conduct of the parties, we make no finding that the conduct in fact constituted a sham. In our view, the Tax Court as the trier of fact is the only body competent to make that determination in the first instance. . . .

In summary, we conclude that the correctness of the Tax Court's basis of decision cannot be determined under the present state of Maryland law without certifying the precise question to the Maryland Court of Appeals. Certification should not now be undertaken because there is present and undecided a federal issue which may be dispositive of the litigation, and it is proper that the federal issue be decided before certification is made. The sham transaction doctrine is not inapplicable to this case as a matter of law, but whether the two divorces with the subsequent marriages were shams for income tax purposes are questions of fact which must be determined by the Tax Court and not by us in the first instance.

Accordingly we remand the case to the Tax Court to determine whether the divorces, even if valid under Maryland law, are nonetheless shams and should be disregarded for federal income tax purposes for the years in question.

Remanded.

WIDENER, Circuit Judge, dissenting: I respectfully dissent.

I think the Tax Court had the proper thought in mind when it treated the case as one under Maryland law. I express no opinion on the correctness of the Tax Court's decision that the divorces in question were invalid under Maryland law, but note, as does the majority, that various inferior Maryland courts have held similar divorces obtained in foreign countries to be valid.

I think the case should be certified to the Maryland courts under the applicable statutes of that State. . . .

Whether or not a divorce may be a sham transaction under federal tax law in the face of a ruling by a State court of competent jurisdiction that the very divorce in question is valid is a question of first impression. This court now answers that question in the affirmative without even permitting the Tax Court an opportunity to rule on the question in the case at hand, and without considering applicable Supreme Court and circuit precedent.

I think the necessity of obtaining a ruling from the Maryland court is evident from the opinion of the majority itself, with only little outside reference needed.

It is only simple logic to say that a divorce which is not a sham under Maryland law would have harder going when sought to be treated as a sham under federal tax law, if indeed that is possible at all. . . .

If the majority had simply remanded to the Tax Court, I would have less objection to the opinion. The remand, however, has unnecessarily, and I think unreasonably, restricted the decision of the Tax Court on remand. That court may not now decide because of our preemption whether a divorce may be a sham in the face of a State court decision that it is valid, which, after all, is the most important aspect of the case.

Notes and Questions

1. *Do you know a sham when you see it?* The sham transaction doctrine is a brooding omnipresence in the tax law, but—as the dispute between the majority and dissent in *Boyter* suggests—no one knows exactly what it means.[21] Roughly speaking, it means that if the judge is convinced the taxpayer is trying to get away with something, and the judge doesn't admire that sort of thing (some judges do), the taxpayer will lose and the official explanation will be "sham transaction." As Judge Widener remarks, it is not easy to understand how the Boyters' divorces could be tax shams if they were valid under Maryland law. Assuming the divorces were valid under state law, they would have had real consequences, in terms of probate law, if either spouse had died during the few weeks between divorce and remarriage. Why isn't that enough to make the divorces non-shams?

2. *Of divorces and corporate liquidations.* According to the majority opinion, "It is the prompt remarriage that defeats the apparent divorce." The implication is that the Boyters would have been free to avoid the marriage penalty by obtaining a divorce and *remaining* divorced, even if they continued to live together. The IRS agrees with this view of the law. Notice the reference in the opinion to the *Atlas Tool* case, in which the court disregarded the liquidation of a corporation when the business was quickly reincorporated.

21. For much more on the sham transaction doctrine and related "common law" anti-abuse doctrines, in a very different context, see section B.4 of Chapter 8, and the Chapter 8 cell on corporate tax shelters.

Under the corporate income tax law as it existed before 1986, liquidations of corporations were subject to very favorable tax rules — basically, appreciation in the assets of a liquidating corporation was permanently exempted from corporate tax. The question in *Atlas Tool* was whether this tax benefit was available when the business was promptly reincorporated, and the answer (in *Atlas Tool* and in a number of other cases) was no. To most tax lawyers, the analogy between a liquidation-reincorporation and a divorce-remarriage is obvious, which suggests what a strange thing it is to think like a tax lawyer.

   3. *The Boyters in later years.* There is no reported decision in *Boyter* on remand; apparently the case was settled. Several newspapers reported, however, that the Boyters avoided marriage penalties in later years by taking the divorce-without-remarriage route, while continuing to live happily together.

   4. *A constitutional issue?* Is the marriage penalty so perverse as to be unconstitutional? Apparently not; equal protection challenges to the marriage penalty have been consistently rejected by the courts. *See, e.g.,* Druker v. Commissioner, 697 F.2d 49 (2d Cir. 1982).[22]

C. THE INCOME TAX CONSEQUENCES OF DIVORCE

When one former spouse makes cash payments to the other, those payments will usually qualify as alimony under the definition of §71(b). Payments meeting the definition of alimony are taxable to the payee (§71(a)) and are deductible by the payor (§215(a)). By reason of §62(a)(10), the deduction is allowed in arriving at adjusted gross income, so it is available even to a payor claiming the standard deduction.

   When the person who earns income is not the person who consumes the income, the question arises whether the income should be taxed to the earner or to the consumer. The usual answer is to tax the earner,[23] but the alimony rules represent a departure from that approach. Is this departure justified? Is it relevant that (1) the alimony transfer by the payor is involuntary, and (2) the payee has unfettered discretion over the use of the money?

1. Alimony: The Basic Strategy

   Suppose Husband (*H*) and Wife (*W*) are negotiating the amount of alimony *H* will pay *W*. After the divorce, *W* expects to have annual income of $30,000 (not including any alimony received), and *H* expects to have annual income of $80,000 (before reduction on account of any alimony paid). After the divorce, each will file as a single taxpayer under a rate schedule that taxes the first $60,000 of income at 20 percent and all additional income at 30 percent.[24] *H* and *W* are not aware of the

---

   22. To help yourself decide whether the marriage penalty has any rational basis (for purposes of equal protection analysis), consult the cell on marriage penalty causes and cures.
   23. *See* Lucas v. Earl, 281 U.S. 111 (1930), set forth in section B of this chapter.
   24. The departure from the usual hypothetical lower bracket of 10 percent makes the arithmetic tidier.

alimony tax rules, and they negotiate under the mistaken assumption that alimony paid is not deductible and alimony received is not taxable. They tentatively agree on annual alimony payments of $7,000. They then ask an attorney to put their agreement in writing, but the attorney informs them that they need to renegotiate because of their misunderstanding of the tax rules.

Armed with this new information, *W* proposes that *H* pay her $10,000 annual alimony. Her reasoning is that a deduction of $10,000 in the 30 percent bracket will save *H* $3,000 in taxes, resulting in an after-tax cost of only $7,000—an amount *H* has already indicated his willingness to pay. *H*, however, notices that *W*'s proposal would leave *W* with $8,000, after she pays a 20 percent tax on $10,000. He makes a counterproposal, for annual alimony of $8,750. His reasoning is that this will leave *W* with $7,000, after paying a 20 percent tax,[25] and that *W* has already indicated her willingness to accept this amount. *W* objects that this is too favorable to *H*, because his after-tax cost would be only $6,125.[26] Eventually they settle on an alimony amount that leaves them both winners, relative to a $7,000 payment with no tax consequences. Any number greater than $8,750 and less than $10,000 will produce this result, although a number close to $8,750 will make *H* the bigger winner, while a number close to $10,000 will make *W* the bigger winner. If they settle on $9,000, for example, *H*'s after-tax cost will be $6,300, and *W*'s after-tax benefit will be $7,200. The results under various alimony agreements are summarized in the table below. Notice the relationship between the first and last columns in the table. The net tax savings is always 10 percent of the alimony payment. This makes sense, because the effect of the alimony tax rules is to shift an amount of income equal to the alimony payment from *H*'s 30 percent bracket to *W*'s 20 percent bracket. The net tax savings, then, is the amount of the payment multiplied by the 10 percentage point difference in the brackets. At any payment amount greater than $8,750 but less than $10,000, the net tax savings are shared between the ex-spouses, in the sense that each is better off than under the alternative of a nondeductible, nontaxable, payment of $7,000.

**Tax Consequences of Alimony Payments from 30% Bracket
Payor to 20% Bracket Payee**

1. Alimony Payment	2. After-tax Cost to *H*	3. After-tax Benefit to *W*	4. Net Tax Savings (column 3 minus column 2)
$10,000	$7,000	$8,000	$1,000
$8,750	$6,125	$7,000	$875
$9,000	$6,300	$7,200	$900

Two important points follow from this analysis of alimony tax planning strategy. First, §71(b)(1)(B) is, in most cases, a trap for the unwary. It permits the spouses to opt out of alimony tax treatment, by providing in the divorce or separation instrument that payments otherwise qualifying as alimony are not to be treated as alimony for tax purposes. At first glance, it might seem that the payee spouse should push hard for a non-alimony designation, in order to avoid having to include payments in income. As the analysis demonstrates, however, as long as

25. $8,750 alimony − $1,750 tax = $7,000.
26. $8,750 alimony − $2,625 tax savings = $6,125.

the payee is in a lower tax bracket than the payor, he or she will actually fare better if the payment *is* taxable, assuming the amount of the payment is increased (relative to the payment amount if there are no tax consequences) so that the ex-spouses share the benefit of the income-shifting.

Second, the alimony income-shifting game is self-limiting. At some point, the alimony payments will be large enough so that any additional payments would be taxed to W in the 30 percent bracket, would be deductible by H against 20 percent bracket income, or both. When that point has been reached, there is no tax advantage (and there may even be a tax disadvantage) to additional alimony payments. In the example, that point would be reached at alimony of $20,000. A $20,000 deduction would be enough to eliminate all 30 percent bracket income for H. Another $1,000 of alimony would produce only $200 of tax savings for H, at a $200 tax cost to W. Thus the maximum net alimony tax savings for H and W *is* $20,000 (30% − 20%) = $2,000. This is not trivial, but it is also not the stuff of which great fortunes are made. The maximum amount to be gained from alimony income-shifting under the actual §1 rate schedules varies from year to year (as the rate schedules are adjusted for inflation or amended by legislation), but is generally in the low five-figure range.

2. Who Gets the Dependency Exemption?

Another divorce tax planning question, closely related to alimony, is which ex-spouse should claim the dependency exemption for a child of the marriage. The default rule (expressed in §152(c)(4)(B)) is that the parent with whom the child resides for the larger portion of the year is entitled to the exemption. However, §152(e)(2) permits the custodial parent (i.e., the winner under the default rule) to waive the exemption in favor of the noncustodial parent. Suppose (as is often the case) that the custodial parent is in a lower bracket than the noncustodial parent. A $3,000 exemption would be worth $900 to the 30 percent bracket noncustodial parent, but only $600 to the 20 percent bracket custodial parent. There is a $300 net tax savings to be gained if the custodial parent waives the exemption. She should be willing to do so as long as the noncustodial parent agrees to share the tax savings with her (for example, by increasing the amount of alimony he is obligated to pay).

Unfortunately, the analysis of whether the noncustodial parent should waive the exemption has become more complex in recent years. Although a $3,000 exemption is, of course, more valuable to the higher bracket parent, that parent may not be entitled to the same dependency exemption amount as the lower bracket parent, because of the §151(d)(3) phaseout of personal exemptions. In some cases, the dependency exemption may actually produce a larger tax benefit for the *lower* bracket parent, after the phaseout does its work. There is one more reason why it may be better for the custodial parent not to waive the exemption. Section 24(c)(1) provides that the child tax credit goes to the parent who is entitled to the dependency exemption. Thus, a §152(e)(2) waiver of the exemption also waives the credit. The value of the credit is independent of one's tax bracket, but the credit is (like the exemption) phased out for higher income taxpayers. Because of the phaseout of the credit, the custodial parent's loss from waiving the credit will not always be the noncustodial parent's gain. In short, §§151(d)(3) and 24 greatly complicate the question of whether the custodial parent should make a §152(e)(2) waiver. Considering the limited amount of money involved, the analysis can become almost ridiculously complex.

3.   Fun and Games with the Alimony Deduction?

Problem 14.   Harry and Wilma are married. Harry has a salary of $120,000; Wilma is a full-time homemaker with no income. The (hypothetical) §1(a) tax rate schedule for joint returns imposes a 10 percent tax on the first $80,000 of income, and a 30 percent tax rate on all additional income. The (equally hypothetical) §1(c) tax rate schedule for unmarried taxpayers applies the 10 percent rate to the first $60,000 of income, and the 30 percent bracket to all additional income. As things now stand, are *H* and *W* victims of the marriage penalty, or recipients of a marriage bonus?

Problem 15.   Not content with their current tax situation, Harry and Wilma come up with a plan intended to produce better results. They get divorced, but continue to live together, and Harry pays Wilma $60,000 as alimony. What are they trying to accomplish? Will it work? Hint: Consult §71(b)(1)(C).

4.   Distinguishing Alimony from Other Transfers

There are three basic reasons why one ex-spouse might make transfers to the other: (1) to satisfy a continuing obligation of spousal support; (2) to support children of the marriage living with the other parent; and (3) to settle claims relating to marital property rights. Congress has decided that the income-shifting rules of §§71 and 215 should apply only to transfers of the first type. If a taxpayer's income is being used to support his children, there is no good reason to allow him to shift the tax liability on that income to his ex-spouse, merely because the children are living with the ex-spouse. As for property settlements, Congress has concluded that income-shifting opportunities should be limited to ongoing *diversions* of income streams; one-time *divisions* of assets should not qualify.

It is one thing to state the general principle that alimony should qualify for income-shifting but child support and property settlements should not; it is another thing to write clear and workable rules embodying that principle. The legislative attempts to do so are examined below.

Alimony versus child support. To solve the following problems, look at §71(c) and Reg. §1.71-1T(c).

Problem 16.   Henry and Wanda are divorced. Clara, their only child, is ten years old. Clara lives with Wanda. The terms of their divorce instrument require Henry to pay Wanda $30,000 per year, with $18,000 designated as alimony and $12,000 designated as child support. Of the $30,000, how much qualifies as alimony for tax purposes?

Problem 17.   Henry decides to be more creative. He has the divorce instrument amended to require him to pay Wanda $30,000 "alimony" per year, to be reduced to $18,000 when Clara reaches the age of 19. Now how much of the $30,000 will qualify as alimony for tax purposes?

Problem 18.   Not one to give up easily, Henry tries a third approach. It occurs to
him that he can predict with reasonable accuracy when Clara will turn 19, so that
the divorce instrument can provide for reduced payments on Clara's nineteenth
birthday without actually mentioning Clara. This time the instrument is amended
to provide for annual "alimony" payments of $30,000, to be reduced to $18,000
on a date nine years in the future, which just happens to be Clara's nineteenth
birthday. Has Henry's persistence finally paid off? Hint 1: Nineteen is not the
local age of majority. Hint 2: Look at the regulations under §71, as well as at the
statute itself.

Alimony versus property settlement. Two mechanical aspects of the §71(b) definition
of alimony are designed, in a rough sort of way, to weed out property settlements
masquerading as alimony. First, §71(b)(1) provides that only payments "in cash"
can qualify as alimony. No non-cash transfer between former spouses ever
generates an alimony deduction for the transferor or taxable alimony income for
the recipient.[27] Second, §71(b)(1)(D) provides that payments cannot qualify as
alimony if the payor spouse would be required to continue to make payments
even after the death of the payee spouse. For example, if the divorce instrument
requires the payor spouse to pay $30,000 annual "alimony" for the next ten years,
even if the payee spouse dies before the end of the ten-year period, *none* of the
payments would qualify as alimony. This is true even if the payee spouse in fact
survives the ten-year period. The policy explanation is that payments that would
continue beyond the death of the payee spouse cannot really be for the support of
the (possibly deceased) spouse; they must be in the nature of a property settlement,
payable in installments. There is potential for malpractice liability here, if the
divorce instrument fails to say anything about whether payments would continue
beyond the death of the payee spouse, and a court interprets the instrument to
require continued payments in the case of the payee's death. Notice, however, that
§71(b)(1)(D) does not require that the terms of the divorce instrument specifically
negate liability for continued payments after the death of the payee spouse; if state
law negates such liability when the instrument is silent on the point, that is good
enough.

   Nothing in the §71(b) definition of alimony would prevent a large one-time cash
payment — say, $100,000 in the year of the divorce — from qualifying as alimony,
even though such a payment obviously has a strong flavor of property settlement.
Instead of policing payments of this sort through the definition of alimony, the
Code subjects such payments to the alimony recapture rules of §71(f). In general
terms, these rules provide that, if annual alimony payments decrease sharply
during the first three "post-separation years," then tax benefit rule principles will
apply in the third year.

Example.   Alimony payments in the first post-separation year were $100,000;
payments were zero in both the second year and the third year.

27. If there is a difference between the basis and the value of the transferred property, §1041
(discussed in detail below) provides that the transferor recognizes no gain or loss and that the
transferee takes the property with the transferor's basis.

Answer. According to §71(f)(3), the "excess payments" for the first year are $85,000: the $100,000 payment minus the sum of (i) $15,000 and (ii) the average of the second and third year payments (zero). Since there were no payments in the second year, it is not surprising that the §71(f)(4) excess payments for the second year are zero. The basic idea behind §71(f) is that we know, with the benefit of hindsight, that $100,000 should not have been treated as tax alimony in the first year. Instead, only $15,000 of the first-year payment should have been treated as alimony. The other $85,000 was really (we now know) in the nature of a property settlement. This can be determined only with hindsight; treating the entire $100,000 first-year payment as alimony would have been correct if there had also been (for example) payments of $100,000 in each of the next two years. In keeping with the usual tax benefit rule approach, the mistake is not corrected by amending the returns for the first year. Instead, §71(f)(1)(A) requires the payor spouse to correct the mistake in the *third* year, by including $85,000 of phantom income on his Year 3 return. Section 71(f)(1)(B) allows the payee spouse a corresponding $85,000 above-the-line deduction in Year 3. If she happens to have insufficient income in Year 3 to enable her to use the entire deduction, that is just her bad luck.

If the ex-spouses in the above example do not like the tax results when the alimony recapture rules apply, but they really want to keep the one-time payment of $100,000 in the first year, is there anything they can do? They could take advantage of the opting-out rule of §71(b)(1)(B) by specifying in the divorce instrument that $85,000 of the $100,000 payment is not to be treated as alimony for tax purposes. If the portion of the first year payment treated as alimony is only $15,000, there will be no alimony recapture in the third year. It is not clear, however, that the payor spouse should favor this approach. Confronted with a choice between a $15,000 deduction in the first year, and the combination of a $100,000 deduction in the first year and $85,000 of phantom income in the third year, the payor actually ought to prefer the latter (assuming his marginal tax rate is the same in both years). The latter treatment allows the payor to defer tax liability on $85,000 of income for two years, without having to pay interest on the deferral. On the other hand, the payor spouse may prefer to avoid phantom income — even at the cost of forgoing a deferral opportunity. In addition, the payee spouse would generally fare better if $85,000 is designated as non-alimony.[28]

Problem 19.   Harold pays Winnie $100,000 alimony in the first post-separation year, $60,000 in the second, and $20,000 in the third. What is the total amount of §71(f) "excess payments" in the third year? Hint: You will need to do the §71(f)(4) calculation for the second year *before* doing the §71(f)(3) calculation for the first year. Do you see why?

The maximum permissible reductions in payments, which will *not* trigger alimony recapture under §71(f), are $7,500 from Year 1 to Year 2, and $15,000 from Year 2 to Year 3. If X is the payment in Year 1, the smallest Year 2 and

---

28. This is especially true if the payee spouse would be unable to use some or all of the phantom deduction in Year 3 (if the entire Year 1 payment is initially treated as alimony, and §71(f) applies in Year 3). Even assuming the payee spouse is able to use the entire deduction in Year 3, at the same tax rate that applied to the inclusion in Year 1, the payee spouse will have made the equivalent of an interest-free loan to the government.

Year 3 payments which will not trigger recapture are $X - \$7,500$ in Year 2, and $X - \$22,500$ in Year 3. Taxpayers who want to avoid §71(f) while front-loading payments as much as possible can design their alimony schedules accordingly. As noted earlier, they can also use §71(b)(1)(B) to designate payments as non-alimony to the extent necessary to avoid recapture.

5.   Transfers of Property between Spouses and Former Spouses: §1041

In United States v. Davis, 370 U.S. 65 (1962), Mr. Davis transferred appreciated stock to the former Mrs. Davis as part of their divorce property settlement. According to the Supreme Court, Mr. Davis owed a debt to Mrs. Davis (pursuant to Delaware marital property law), and he used appreciated property to pay the debt. Under that analysis, the tax result to Mr. Davis was clear. Under standard "cash two-step" analysis, he was treated as if he had sold the stock for cash and used the cash to pay the debt. He thus realized and recognized a gain equal to the amount of appreciation in the stock.

Although the result in *Davis* was defensible as a matter of tax logic, as a practical matter *Davis* imposed tax at an unfortunate time. When he transferred his stock, Mr. Davis did not receive any cash with which to pay the resulting tax; he did not even receive anything he could sell to generate cash. In addition to being harsh on taxpayers who complied with the law, *Davis* also failed to produce much tax revenue. Many taxpayers in Mr. Davis's situation honestly did not know that they had a taxable gain, or less honestly decided that the IRS would never notice if they failed to report the gain. In 1984 Congress finally enacted legislation rejecting the *Davis* approach. Under §1041(a), no gain or loss is recognized on any transfer of property to one's spouse, or to one's former spouse if the transfer is "incident to the divorce." The unrecognized gain or loss does not disappear. Instead, §1041(b)(2) gives the transferee spouse a basis in the property equal to the transferor's adjusted basis.

Problem 20.   You are the attorney representing Wendy in connection with her divorce from Hank. You have tentatively agreed that Hank will pay Wendy $1 million cash, as a property settlement (to be designated as non-alimony pursuant to §71(b)(1)(B)). Before the deal is signed, Hank's attorney proposes replacing the cash with $1 million of stock, in which Hank has a basis of only $200,000. Assuming Wendy is willing to accept stock instead of cash, how do you respond to the proposal?

Problem 21.   You are the attorney for a software billionaire who is engaged to be married. He and his fiancee want to enter into a prenuptial agreement, under which he will transfer to her stock worth $100 million, in which he has a basis of approximately zero, in exchange for her relinquishment of all marital property rights. Do you have any advice as to how they should carry out this agreement?

Problem 22.   Hubert transfers stock to Wilhelmina in connection with their divorce. The stock is worth $100,000, and Hubert's basis in the stock is $150,000. If Wilhelmina later sells the stock for $120,000, what will be the amount of her realized gain or loss? Hint: Compare §1041(b)(2) with §1015(a).

D. TAX ISSUES RELATING TO UNMARRIED COUPLES

Imagine two cohabiting unmarried persons with very unequal incomes, whose combined tax liability would be reduced if they were able to file a joint return as a married couple. Do they have a valid complaint that they are the victims of a singles penalty? For a heterosexual couple, the easy answer is that the penalty is of their own making; if they don't like it they should get married. For a same-sex couple without the marriage option, however, the complaint has more force.[29] It may be that most same-sex couples have two earners with roughly equal incomes, and so pay less tax as singles than they would pay if married. Even if that is true, same-sex couples as a group still have a plausible complaint. Heterosexual couples may choose whichever status — married or unmarried — results in a lower income tax liability,[30] but same-sex couples are not given this choice.

For many same-sex couples, the inability to file joint returns is a less serious problem than the fact that a number of fringe benefit exclusions apply to benefits received by spouses of employees but not to benefits received by unmarried partners of employees. Some of these exclusions are for benefits of small value or of interest to only a few taxpayers, but that is not the case with respect to the exclusion of employer-provided health insurance. According to Reg. §1.106-1, the exclusion is available only for coverage of the employee, "his spouse, or his dependents." Unless the nonemployee partner qualifies as a dependent of the employee partner (an issue discussed below), an employee must pay tax on the value of health insurance provided by her employer to her unmarried partner.[31] This limitation on the exclusion is imposed only by the regulation; nothing in the language of §106 of the Code requires the limitation. Congress is well aware of the regulation, however, and has not chosen to overrule it.

In the case of a one-earner unmarried couple, may the earning partner claim a dependency exemption for the homemaking partner, assuming the earning partner provides over half of the support of the homemaking partner? Pursuant to §152(a)(2) and §152(d)(2), the answer would seem to be yes, so long as they share the same home. However, §152(f)(3) denies the exemption if "the relationship between such individual and the taxpayer is in violation of local law." There are few litigated cases involving §152(b)(5) — presumably because the IRS seldom asserts that it is applicable — and the scope of the provision is far from clear. There may be little or nothing left of §152(b)(5) in the aftermath of Lawrence v. Texas, 539 U.S. 558 (2003) (invalidating, under the Due Process Clause, a Texas statute criminalizing sexual conduct between two persons of the same sex).

Suppose A earns $200,000 annually, and A's unmarried partner, B, is a full-time homemaker. What is the proper income tax treatment of the portion of A's income that is consumed by B? The IRS could take the position that A is buying B's

---

29. Even if a same-sex couple is allowed to marry under state law, the marriage will not be recognized for federal income tax purposes, by reason of the Defense of Marriage Act, Pub. L. No. 104-199, 100 Stat. 2419 (1996). Early in 2011, the Obama administration indicated that it would no longer defend the Defense of Marriage Act in court, believing it to be unconstitutional. However, until it is invalidated by Congress or a federal court, the IRS will continue to apply its provisions.

30. For many heterosexual couples, however, moral or religious concerns effectively eliminate the unmarried option.

31. *See* Private Letter Ruling 9850011 (so holding).

homemaking services, with the results that (1) *A*'s purchase of *B*'s services is a nondeductible personal consumption expenditure (by reason of §262), and (2) the value of *B*'s consumption is earned income to *B* that must be included in *B*'s gross income. Under this view, the combined incomes of *A* and *B* would be considerably more than their combined $200,000 cash income. If *A* also transferred appreciated property to *B* as compensation for *B*'s services, the tax consequences would be even worse; without the protection of §1041 *A* would be taxed on the appreciation at the time of transfer (with the value of *B*'s services as *A*'s amount realized). Fortunately for unmarried couples, the IRS does not generally assert liabilities in these situations, preferring instead to assume that *A*'s transfers to *B* qualify as gifts under §102.[32] The technical merits of the gift analysis are debatable, however, and a change in the IRS position is possible. As the following case demonstrates, even now the IRS may attempt to treat transfers in connection with the breakup of a cohabiting relationship as taxable events.

REYNOLDS v. COMMISSIONER
T.C. Memo. 1999-62

LARO, Judge: . . . Petitioner and Gregg P. Kent (Mr. Kent) were involved in a close personal relationship from 1967 until 1991, and they cohabited as an unmarried couple during the last 24 years of the relationship. Mr. Kent told petitioner early in the relationship that she should not work and that he would provide for her financially. Petitioner generally was not employed during the relationship. She took care of the house and grounds in and on which she and Mr. Kent lived, and she took care of a boat that was acquired during their 25 years together. She also acted as hostess for their parties and as Mr. Kent's nurse when he was ill. Her relationship with Mr. Kent resembled that of a husband and wife, including, but not limited to, the sharing of affection and the presence of sexual relations.

Several items of real and personal property were purchased during their relationship. Each item was placed in the name of Mr. Kent or in the name of KENCOR, a California corporation in which Mr. Kent was the majority shareholder. The property included a house, an automobile, furniture, and boats. The house was purchased in 1980, and, following the purchase, Mr. Kent and petitioner lived there for the next 11 years.

Mr. Kent purchased clothing and jewelry for petitioner and gave her a weekly allowance. When Mr. Kent and petitioner traveled together, they would hold themselves out as husband and wife.

In July 1991, Mr. Kent moved out of the house and broke off the relationship. He asked petitioner to leave the house and return the vehicle she was driving (a 1987 Lincoln Town Car), which was in the name of KENCOR. Petitioner refused, and Mr. Kent and KENCOR (collectively, the plaintiffs) sued petitioner for ejectment, trespass, and conversion (the lawsuit). The plaintiffs prayed mainly for a judgment stating that petitioner had no interest in the property that was purchased during their relationship. Petitioner, in answering the plaintiffs' claim, asserted as a "First Affirmative Defense" that she had an equitable interest in the property. . . . She stated in a "Declaration" filed in the lawsuit:

---

32. *See* United States v. Harris, 942 F.2d 1125, 1135 (7th Cir. 1991) ("[W]e have not found a single case finding tax liability for payments that a mistress received from her lover, absent proof of specific payments for specific sex acts").

... 26. In 1968, Mr. Kent and I entered into an agreement whereby he was to be the provider and I was to take care of our nest. That agreement subsequently became more involved and included my taking care of him, the home, the interior of the boat, acting as a hostess for all parties and entertaining he wanted to do for personal and business reasons, doing laundry, housekeeping, ironing, cooking, shopping, supervising the service people who occassionaly [sic] worked on the home and acting as nurse for Mr. Kent when he had health problems. In turn Mr. Kent agreed to provide for all of my living expenses. ... For over 20 years we have lived according to our agreement ... Mr. Kent wants to throw me out with nothing to show for the many years we spent together.

In October 1991, the lawsuit was settled, Petitioner and Mr. Kent (both individually and on behalf of KENCOR) signed the Release and Settlement Agreement (settlement agreement). The settlement agreement provided in pertinent part:

... 1. In consideration for the full and complete release by REYNOLDS of any claims of any nature, including but not limited to, any sums of money, and/or claims to any real and/or personal property of KENT, KENT agrees to pay REYNOLDS the following sums, on the following terms:

A. Cash in the sum of Fifty-seven Thousand Five Hundred Dollars ($57,500), payable after REYNOLDS has delivered all items she has removed from KENT, whether removed from the property ... or any other items belonging to KENT whether removed from the Subject Property or any other location, and after KENT has verified all items have been returned to the Subject Property ... and

B. The sum of Two Thousand Dollars ($2,000) per month for a period of three (3) years payable to the first day of each month commencing November 1, 1991; and

C. Thereafter, the sum of One Thousand Dollars ($1,000) per month for a period of two (2) years, payable on the first day of each month commencing November 1, 1994 to and including October 1, 1996.

2. In addition to said sums, KENT will transfer all right, title, and interest in and to the following personal property:

A. That certain 1987 Lincoln Town Car automobile ... ;

B. All clothing and jewelry in Reynolds's possession;

C. ... miscellaneous household furniture and furnishings. ...

In accordance with the payment plan set forth in the settlement agreement, petitioner received $22,000 in 1994. This amount was received from KENCOR, and KENCOR issued a Form 1099-MISC, Miscellaneous Income, to petitioner reporting the amount as miscellaneous income. Petitioner did not perform services for KENCOR during that year, nor did she sell it any property during that year. Petitioner, allegedly relying on advice from her attorney and accountant, did not report this amount on her 1994 Federal income tax return.

We must decide whether the $22,000 amount is includable in petitioner's 1994 gross income. Respondent argues it is. Petitioner argues it is not. Respondent contends that petitioner received the disputed amount as compensation for her homemaking services.[33] Petitioner contends that she received the disputed amount as a gift.

We agree with petitioner that the $22,000 amount is not includable in her 1994 gross income, but we do so for a reason slightly different than she espouses. The

---

33. In this regard, respondent states, petitioner's homemaking services do not include sex.

taxability of proceeds recovered in settlement of a lawsuit rests upon the nature of the claim for which the proceeds were received and the actual basis of recovery. Ascertaining the nature of the claim is a factual determination that is generally made by reference to the settlement agreement in light of the facts and circumstances surrounding it. Key to this determination is the "intent of the payor" in making the payment. We must ask ourselves: "In lieu of WHAT was the payment received?" Although the payee's belief is relevant to this inquiry, the payment's ultimate character depends on the payor's dominant reason for making the payment. Commissioner v. Duberstein, 363 U.S. 278, 286 (1960).

The settlement agreement indicates that Mr. Kent paid the disputed amount to petitioner in surrender of her rights in most of the property purchased during their relationship.[34] Respondent agrees with this characterization, but extrapolates therefrom that Mr. Kent paid petitioner the disputed amount to compensate her for past services that she rendered to him. We do not agree. Nothing in the record persuades us that petitioner ever sought in the lawsuit remuneration for services that she may have rendered to Mr. Kent during their relationship, let alone that Mr. Kent intended to compensate her for any such services by paying her the disputed amount. The written judgment sought by Mr. Kent and the settlement agreement both indicate that the only reason Mr. Kent commenced the lawsuit and paid the disputed amount to petitioner was to retain possession of most of the assets acquired during their relationship.

Although petitioner did refer in her Declaration to an agreement under which she would provide services to Mr. Kent in exchange for support, the facts of this case do not support an inference that she ever sought in the lawsuit to recover remuneration for these services, or, more importantly, that Mr. Kent paid her the disputed amount intending to compensate her for any services that she may have rendered to him. The payor's intent controls the characterization of settlement payments, and, as we have found, Mr. Kent intended to perfect his sole possession of most of their joint property when he paid petitioner the disputed amount. . . .

Our conclusion that Mr. Kent paid petitioner the disputed amount for her interest in the property does not end our inquiry. Petitioner's sale of her property interest to Mr. Kent is a taxable event for which she must recognize gain to the extent that the selling price exceeds her basis in the property. Sec. 1001(a). As to her basis, the record indicates that petitioner received her interest in the property by way of numerous gifts that Mr. Kent made to her throughout their relationship. Petitioner's declaration depicts a setting under which Mr. Kent repeatedly "gave" her property, and the facts of this case support the conclusion that he made these "gifts" with the "detached and disinterested generosity, . . . affection, respect, admiration, charity, or the like" required by Commissioner v. Duberstein, *supra* at 285. Given the fact that petitioner and Mr. Kent for a long period of time lived as husband and wife in most regards, but for the obvious fact that they were not legally

34. We recognize that KENCOR paid petitioner the $22,000 amount and that KENCOR issued petitioner a Form 1099-MISC reporting that the amount was paid as miscellaneous income. The record, however, tends to disprove such a characterization. The more likely explanation of the payment, and the one we find from the facts herein, is that Mr. Kent, as principal shareholder of KENCOR, caused KENCOR to pay petitioner the $22,000 amount on his behalf.

married, we find it hard to believe that their relationship was actually akin to a business arrangement.[35]

Our conclusion herein that the property received by petitioner from Mr. Kent was by way of a gift, rather than as compensation for her services, is consistent with prior decisions of this Court. First, in Starks v. Commissioner, T.C. Memo 1966-134, the taxpayer, a young unmarried, nonworking woman was involved with a much older man. The man, in return for the woman's companionship, gave her money to buy a house and to spend on her living expenses. He also gave her an automobile, jewelry, furniture, fur coats, and other clothing. Respondent determined that the money and other assets were taxable to the woman as compensation for services rendered to the man. We disagreed. We held that the woman received the money and other assets as gifts. *See also* Libby v. Commissioner, T.C. Memo 1969-184 (similar holding as to cash and property given to a young mistress by her older paramour).

Later, in Pascarelli v. Commissioner, 55 T.C. 1082, 1090-1091 (1971), *aff'd without published opinion*, 485 F.2d 681 (3d Cir. 1973), we held to the same effect. There, the taxpayer was a woman who lived with a man who was not her husband. The man gave money to the woman in exchange for "wifely services." Respondent determined that the money was taxable to the woman as compensation that she earned for her services. We disagreed. We held that the payments were gifts. We found that the man paid the money to the woman "motivated by sentiments of affection, respect, and admiration." *Id.* at 1091.

And later, in Reis v. Commissioner, T.C. Memo 1974-287, the taxpayer was a young female nightclub dancer who met an older man when he bought dinner and champagne for the performers in the show. The man paid each person at the table, other than the woman, $50 to leave the table so that he and she would be alone. The man gave the woman $1,200 for a mink stole and another $1,200 so that her sister could have an expensive coat too. Over the next 5 years, the woman saw the man "every Tuesday night at the [nightclub] and Wednesday afternoons from approximately 1:00 p.m. to 3:00 p.m. . . . at various places including . . . a girl friend's apartment and hotels where [he] was staying." He paid her living expenses, plus $200 a week, and he provided her with money for other things, such as investing, decorating her apartment, and buying a car. We held that none of the more than $100,000 that he gave her over the 5 years was taxable to her. We concluded that she received the money as a gift. We reached this conclusion notwithstanding the fact that the woman had stated that she "earned every penny" of the money.

Given our conclusion in this case that petitioner received her interest in the property as gifts from Mr. Kent, her basis in the property equals Mr. Kent's basis immediately before the gifts, to the extent that his basis is attributable to the gifted property. Sec. 1015(a). Although the record does not indicate with

---

35. We are mindful that all property acquired during the relationship was placed in the name of Mr. Kent or that of a corporation that he controlled. We do not find this fact to negate the presence of a gift under the facts herein. Federal law answers the question of whether a gift has occurred for Federal income tax purposes, Commissioner v. Duberstein, 363 U.S. 278, 286 (1960), and we believe that Mr. Kent's requested judgment and the settlement agreement speak loudly to the effect that he gave petitioner interests in property under the test set forth in *Duberstein*. To the extent that State law is relevant to this inquiry, applicable State (California) law does provide that a nonmarital partner may have an equitable interest in property titled solely in the other partner's name. *See* Marvin v. Marvin, 18 Cal. 3d 660, 684 n.24 (1976), and the cases cited therein at 669-670.

mathematical specificity the amount of Mr. Kent's basis that passed to petitioner as a result of the gifts, we are satisfied from the facts at hand that her basis equaled or exceeded the amount that she realized on the sale; i.e., $153,500. We conclude that petitioner had no gain to recognize upon receipt of the disputed payment.

Notes and Questions

1. *Aggregating or disaggregating assets for tax analysis.* In the last paragraph of the opinion the court lumps together all the assets sold by Ms. Reynolds to Mr. Kent in connection with their breakup, and concludes that she has no taxable gain because her basis in those assets equaled or exceeded her total amount realized of $153,500. The aggregation of assets implied in that paragraph is improper; rather, the tax consequences of the sale of each asset should be determined separately. Suppose, for example, Ms. Reynolds sold two assets to Mr. Kent: a personal-use car with a basis of $75,000, which she sold for its fair market value of $40,000; and land with a basis of $100,000, which she sold for its fair market value of $113,500. The correct analysis would be that she had a nondeductible personal loss of $35,000 on the car, and a taxable gain of $13,500 on the land. She should not be able to avoid paying tax on the gain on the land, on the grounds that her combined basis in the two assets exceeded her combined amount realized for the two assets.

2. *What about Mr. Kent?* The opinion is not concerned with Mr. Kent's tax consequences, but the facts raise two interesting issues with respect to him. First, what are the tax consequences to Mr. Kent when he transfers his interest in appreciated property (such as the jewelry, perhaps) to Ms. Reynolds in connection with the settlement? His state of mind is obviously not one of "detached and disinterested generosity," so he cannot take advantage of the deferral provided by §1015 for gifts of appreciated property. He also, of course, cannot take advantage of the deferral provided by §1041 for appreciated property transferred incident to a divorce. Probably he will be taxed on the excess of the value of the transferred property over its adjusted basis. *See, e.g.*, Rev. Rul. 79-44, 1979-1 C.B. 265, in which *A* and *B* jointly owned two assets, and agreed to an exchange whereby *A* became sole owner of one asset and *B* became sole owner of the other. The ruling held the exchange was a §1001(a) realization event to both taxpayers. On the other hand, there is some authority predating §1041 that does not treat similar divorce-related exchanges as realization events, and perhaps Mr. Kent could persuade the IRS or a court to apply those authorities in this quasi-divorce context. *See, e.g.*, Rev. Rul. 76-83, 1976-1 C.B. 213. If Ms. Reynolds had merely had creditor-type rights against Mr. Kent's property, rather than being an equitable co-owner, presumably Mr. Kent would be taxed on the transfer of appreciated property to Ms. Reynolds under the reasoning of Davis v. United States, 370 U.S. 65 (1962). *Davis* remains good law where it has not been overruled by §1041, and §1041 does not apply here.

3. *A disguised dividend.* Second, what are the tax consequences to Mr. Kent of the payments made to Ms. Reynolds on his behalf by KENCOR? The answer to this question is clear. A shareholder is taxed on dividends received from a corporation (§61(a)(7)), and the payments to Ms. Reynolds

are indirect dividends to Mr. Kent. Mr. Kent is taxed as if he had received cash dividends from KENCOR and used the dividends to make settlement payments to Ms. Reynolds.

E. THE EARNED INCOME TAX CREDIT

1. An Idealized Version of the Credit

Suppose the federal government decided to implement a policy that no person working full-time should have to live below the official poverty level. If the poverty level for an adult living alone is $10,000 (for example), and if full-time is defined as 2,000 hours a year, then it would seem to follow that the minimum wage should be $5 per hour. But what about a single parent living with one child? If the poverty level for a one-adult, one-child family is $12,000, then the parent should be entitled to a minimum wage of $6 per hour. If the poverty level for a one-adult, two-child family is $14,000, then that parent should be entitled to a $7 minimum wage. It would not be easy, however, to vary the minimum wage according to each worker's family responsibilities. Even if it were practical, it would have the unfortunate effect of discouraging employers from hiring workers with children for low wage jobs, since workers with children would be more expensive.

Perhaps a different strategy is superior to the minimum wage approach. The government could set the minimum wage at $5 per hour (based on the needs of a childless worker), but provide a subsidy for workers with children sufficient to bring the wage-plus-subsidy up to the poverty level. If, for example, each child in a family increases the poverty level by $2,000, and n represents the number of children in a family, then the subsidy formula for a full-time minimum-wage parent should be, simply enough, $2,000 \times n$. A full-time minimum wage worker with one child would be entitled to a $2,000 subsidy, a worker with two children would claim a $4,000 subsidy, and so on. If the subsidy were contained in the Internal Revenue Code and administered by the IRS, it could be described as a tax credit. It would be a special sort of credit, however. Most tax credits are nonrefundable; in other words, they can be used to reduce or eliminate one's tax liability, but they cannot be used to obtain a net transfer from the government. By contrast, this credit would have to be refundable, since the goal is to give the recipient after-"tax" income greater than pre-"tax" income. Since the personal exemptions and the standard deduction already exempt poverty-level income from tax, the entire credit would take the form of a cash transfer from the government to the credit recipient, rather than a reduction in tax liability. To describe the proposal slightly differently, the credit would function as a kind of negative income tax, under which the tax rate on the first $10,000 of income would be *minus* 20 percent (for a recipient with one child). Instead of *taking* 20 cents for each dollar earned, the government would *give* the "taxpayer" 20 cents for each dollar earned.

From the worker's perspective, the credit would serve the same function as a family-size adjustment to the minimum wage. For several reasons, it is arguably superior to requiring *employers* to pay different minimum wages to workers in different family circumstances. First, it may be easier for the government to determine a worker's family circumstances (through the tax system) than it would be for an employer. Second, any minimum wage functions as a quasi-tax on the party required to pay the wage, and it may be fairer to use a credit to impose much of that burden on society at large, rather than using differential minimum wage laws to impose the entire burden on employers. Finally, using a credit avoids the disincentive to hire workers with children, which would be inevitable under a system requiring employers to pay those workers higher wages.

2. *The Real Thing*

The earned income tax credit (EITC) set forth in §32 of the Code bears a general resemblance to the above proposal, and can be understood as serving the goal of increasing the after-tax incomes of low wage workers with family responsibilities. The details of the EITC, however, are considerably less tidy than the proposal.

Like the proposal, the actual EITC is refundable, and in fact the credit is largely received as transfer payments rather than as reductions in tax liability. It is debatable whether a refundable credit should be considered part of the tax system at all. It would certainly be possible to have a subsidy program identical in substance to the EITC, but not contained in the Internal Revenue Code and not administered by the IRS. Nevertheless, the EITC is generally considered part of the income tax system because it is contained in the Code, is administered by the IRS, and is defined by reference to a number of income tax concepts (such as adjusted gross income). The amount of the credit depends in part on the number of the taxpayer's "qualifying children." Contrary to the above proposal, the actual EITC provides a small credit for childless workers. For 2011, the childless worker credit is 7.65 percent of the first $6,070 of earned income, producing a maximum credit of $464. The credit is reduced by 7.65 percent of the amount by which AGI (or earned income, if greater) exceeds $7,590. The phaseout is completed — and the credit is thus eliminated — at AGI of $13,660.[36] The dollar amounts are adjusted annually for inflation. Obviously, the purpose of the credit for childless workers cannot be to adjust the minimum wage on account of family responsibilities. Rather, the key to the purpose can be found in the rate of the credit. The employee's share of the federal payroll tax (for social security and Medicare) is imposed at the rate of 7.65 percent; thus the credit functions as a rebate of the payroll tax on the first $6,070 of earned income.

A special rule provides that the childless EITC is available only to taxpayers who are at least 25 years old, but no older than 64, at the close of the taxable year. What could be the point of that rule? Ideally, Congress might like the credit to be based on one's hourly wage rate, rather than on annual income. Thus, the credit would not be available to a worker with a moderate or high wage rate, whose annual income is low only because she chooses to work few hours during the year. All the IRS has the capacity to measure, however, is the taxpayer's annual income. The age-based eligibility rule serves as an imperfect substitute for limiting the credit to low wage workers. The rule amounts to a conclusive presumption that very low

36. Both the beginning point and the end point of the phaseout range are higher in the case of joint returns — $5,080 higher in 2011. Absent further legislation, the upwards adjustment in the phaseout range for joint returns will no longer apply after 2012.

incomes earned by childless workers under 25 or over 64 are due to low hours worked (by students or by retirees), rather than to low wage rates. While this rule is effective in denying a credit for the summer earnings of most undergraduates, a childless law student 25 or older will be able to claim the credit for her summer earnings, if those earnings are less than $13,660.

For a taxpayer with one qualifying child, the credit is much more generous, because this portion of the credit does serve as a family-responsibility adjustment to the minimum wage. In 2011 the credit is 34 percent of the first $9,100 of earned income, resulting in a maximum credit of $3,094. The credit is reduced by 15.98 percent(!) of the amount by which AGI (or earned income, if greater) exceeds $16,690. The phaseout is completed at AGI of $36,052.[37] Still in keeping with the theme of adjusting the minimum wage for family responsibilities, the credit is more generous for a taxpayer with two qualifying children. In that case, the credit is 40 percent of the first $12,780 of earned income, producing a maximum credit of $5,112. The credit is reduced by 21.06 percent(!) of the amount by which AGI (or earned income, if greater) exceeds $16,690, and the phaseout is completed at AGI of $40,964.[38] A special rule, scheduled to expire at the end of 2012, increases the credit rate to 45 percent in the case of a taxpayer with three or more qualifying children. Under this special rule, the maximum credit amount is $5,751. After the special rule expires, the credit computation rules for taxpayers with two children will also apply to taxpayers with three or more children. A taxpayer with a qualifying child may claim the credit regardless of the taxpayer's age. Thus, in the case of taxpayers with children, Congress makes no attempt to distinguish between genuinely low wage workers and moderate or high wage workers who work few hours during the year.

Despite the fact that the poverty level continues to rise as a family expands beyond a second child, the amount of the EITC is not increased on account of children beyond the first two (apart from the temporary rule described above). This is in striking contrast with the rules for dependency exemptions (§151) and the child tax credit (§24); both of those benefits are available with respect to an unlimited number of children. Why should the rules be different under the EITC? Apparently Congress believes there is a great policy difference between tax benefits that merely reduce the amount the taxpayer owes the government (such as dependency exemptions) and benefits that can exceed tax liability (such as the EITC).[39] Under this view, there should be no limit to the number of children that can be used to reduce tax liability, but the number of children that can be used to obtain subsidies should be limited to two (or, temporarily, the first three). Congress's position, embodied in the design of the EITC, is that if low income workers have more than two (or three) children, they must find some way to pay for the additional children without help from the federal government.

The earned income tax credit is, by far, the most significant federally administered anti-poverty program (Medicaid is administered by the states). The annual total cost of the program is over $50 billion. Less than 20 percent of the cost of the program takes the form of reductions in income tax liability; the remainder of the cost represents transfers in excess of income tax liability.

---

37. The same joint return adjustments to the beginning and ending points of the phaseout range apply as in the case of the no-child credit.
38. The same joint return adjustments to the beginning and ending points of the phaseout range apply as in the case of the no-child and one-child credits.
39. The child tax credit of §24 does not fit neatly into this framework, since it *is partially* refundable. See the discussion in section A.2.b of this chapter.

Cell

A COMPARATIVE PERSPECTIVE ON CHILD CARE AS A BUSINESS EXPENSE

Symes v. Canada

The following case, from the Supreme Court of Canada, considers whether child care costs should be deductible as business expenses, and whether a failure to allow full deductibility of child care expenses constitutes discrimination against women. The case is included here partly because there is no modern case from the United States that seriously considers these important questions, and partly as a corrective against the insularity of most thinking about tax in the United States. Few questions of income tax policy are unique to the United States. Much can be learned by examining how other countries have designed and implemented their income tax systems.

Mrs. Symes, the taxpayer in the case below, claimed that she should be able to deduct as a business expense the entire amount she spent on child care, thereby avoiding the low dollar ceiling ($2,000 per child) in the provision expressly allowing a child care deduction. Most of the background information you will need to understand the issue in *Symes* is set forth in the opinion, but you should be aware at the outset of two significant differences between the U.S. and Canadian income tax systems that are implicated in *Symes*. First, married couples in Canada are not allowed to file joint returns. Thus, if a business expense deduction is allowable, it must be allowed to one spouse or the other, rather than taken by both spouses on a joint return. Second, the Canadian income tax allows no deductions whatsoever for employee business expenses.[1] For this reason, it is crucial to Mrs. Symes's argument for a child care business expense deduction that she is self-employed. If she were an employee, she would clearly be unable to claim a business expense deduction for her child care costs (although she would be entitled to claim a deduction under the child care deduction provision, subject to the low ceiling on eligible expenses).

SYMES v. CANADA

4 S.C.R. 695 (Supreme Court of Canada, 1993)

IACOBUCCI J.: The basic issue in this appeal is whether child care expenses, on the facts of this case, are deductible as business expenses in the determination of profit under the Income Tax Act, R.S.C. 1952, c. 148, as amended (the "Act").

---

1. Compare this with the U.S. rule, which allows a deduction for unreimbursed employee business expenses, subject to §67's 2-percent-of-AGI floor on miscellaneous itemized deductions.

I. FACTS

The appellant taxpayer, Elizabeth Symes, is a lawyer and a mother. During the relevant period, she practised law full-time as a partner in a Toronto law firm. During that same period, she was initially the mother of one child (in taxation years 1982, 1983 and 1984), and was later the mother of two children (in taxation year 1985). The appellant is married.

The appellant employed a nanny, Mrs. Simpson (Simpson), during these taxation years. Simpson's only employment function was to care for the appellant's children in the appellant's home. During 1982, 1983 and 1984 respectively, the appellant paid Simpson $10,075, $11,200 and $13,173 to care for her one child. During 1985, the appellant paid Simpson $13,359 to care for her two children. . . .

In her personal income tax returns for 1982 to 1985, the appellant deducted the wages paid to Simpson as business expenses. . . . The expenses were characterized [by Revenue Canada] as personal or living expenses. In place of the disallowed deductions, Revenue Canada allowed the appellant revised child care deductions of $1,000 for 1982, $2,000 for each of 1983 and 1984, and $4,000 for 1985, pursuant to s. 63 of the Act. . . .

II. RELEVANT CONSTITUTIONAL AND STATUTORY PROVISIONS

A. CONSTITUTIONAL PROVISIONS

1. *Canadian Charter of Rights and Freedoms, ss. [1 and 15]*

1. The Canadian Charter of Rights and Freedoms guarantees the rights and freedoms set out in it subject only to such reasonable limits prescribed by law as can be demonstrably justified in a free and democratic society.

15. (1) Every individual is equal before and under the law and has the right to the equal protection and equal benefit of the law without discrimination and, in particular, without discrimination based on race, national or ethnic origin, colour, religion, sex, age or mental or physical disability.

(2) Subsection (1) does not preclude any law, program or activity that has as its object the amelioration of conditions of disadvantaged individuals or groups including those that are disadvantaged because of race, national or ethnic origin, colour, religion, sex, age or mental or physical disability. . . .

B. STATUTORY PROVISIONS

Income Tax Act, R.S.C. 1952, c. 148, as amended and applicable in taxation years 1983 to 1985, ss. [9(1), 18(1), and 63]

9. (1) Subject to this Part, a taxpayer's income for a taxation year from a business or property is his profit therefrom for the year.

18. (1) In computing the income of a taxpayer from a business or property no deduction shall be made in respect of

(a) an outlay or expense except to the extent that it was made or incurred by the taxpayer for the purpose of gaining or producing income from the business or property; . . .

(h) personal or living expenses of the taxpayer except travelling expenses (including the entire amount expended for meals and lodging) incurred by the taxpayer while away from home in the course of carrying on his business; . . .

63. (1) Subject to subsection (2), in computing the income of a taxpayer for a taxation year the aggregate of all amounts each of which is an amount paid in the year as or on account of child care expenses in respect of an eligible child of the taxpayer for the year may be deducted. [The expenses must be incurred in order to enable the taxpayer to earn income, and the deduction may not exceed the smallest of (i) $2,000 per child, (ii) $8,000 total, or (iii) two-thirds of the taxpayer's earned income; in the case of a married couple, the deduction must generally be taken by the spouse with the lower earned income. — EDS.] . . .

V. ANALYSIS

1. *Are child care expenses deductible as part of the determination of profit under s. 9(1) of the Act? . . .*

In essence, [appellant] argues that the Act is capable of comprehending a business expense deduction for child care as part of its ordinary determination of business income. This argument, therefore, mandates a discussion of how the Income Tax Act ordinarily determines what constitutes business income. . . .

[I]n a deductibility analysis, one's first recourse is to s. 9(1), a section which embodies, as the trial judge suggested, a form of "business test" for taxable profit. . . .

This appeal presents a particular expense which has been traditionally characterized as personal in nature. If, in coming to a decision, this Court stated that since such expenses have always been personal, they must now be personal, the conclusion could be easily and deservedly attacked. For this reason, proper analysis of this question demands that the relationship between child care expenses and business income be examined more critically, in order to determine whether that relationship can be sufficient to justify the former's deductibility. . . .

Why, in this case, is it appropriate to re-examine extensively whether child care expenses are appropriately characterized as personal expenses? Relying upon the evidence of the expert witness, Armstrong, the trial judge had this to say:

> . . . there has been a significant social change in the late 1970's and into the 1980's, in terms of the influx of women of child-bearing age into business and into the workplace. This change post-dates the earlier cases dismissing nanny expenses as a legitimate business deduction and therefore it does not necessarily follow that the conditions which prevailed in society at the time of those earlier decisions will prevail now.

I consider the existence of the trend discussed in this paragraph to be relatively non-controversial, such that the point could have been accepted even without the assistance of an expert.

The decision to characterize child care expenses as personal expenses was made by judges. As part of our case law, it is susceptible to re-examination in an appropriate case. . . .

[N]o test has been proposed which improves upon or which substantially modifies a test derived directly from the language of s. 18(1)(a). The analytical trail leads back to its source, and I simply ask the following: did the appellant incur child care expenses for the purpose of gaining or producing income from a business? . . .

First, it is clear on the facts that the appellant would not have incurred child care expenses except for her business. It is relevant to note in this regard that her choice of child care was tailored to her business needs. As a lawyer, she could not personally care for her children during the day since to do so would interfere with client meetings and court appearances, nor could she make use of institutionalized daycare, in light of her working hours. These are points which were recognized by the trial judge.

Second, however, it is equally clear that the need which is met by child care expenses on the facts of this case, namely, the care of the appellant's children, exists regardless of the appellant's business activity. The expenses were incurred to make her available to practise her profession rather than for any other purpose associated with the business itself.

Third, I note that there is no evidence to suggest that child care expenses are considered business expenses by accountants. There is, however, considerable reason to believe that many parents, and particularly many women, confront child care expenses in order to work. . . . [T]he intervener the Canadian Bar Association presented this Court with survey information which specifically addresses the experience of lawyers in Ontario. That information suggests that for lawyers with children, a significant proportion of child care responsibility is borne by paid child care workers, and the mean proportion is over 250 percent greater for women (25.56 hours per week) than for men (9.53 hours per week): Law Society of Upper Canada, Transitions in the Ontario Legal Profession (1991). This demographic picture may increase the likelihood that child care expenses are a form of business expense.

Finally, as a fourth point of analysis, I am uncomfortable with the suggestion that the appellant's decision to have children should be viewed solely as a consumption choice. . . . The appellant and her husband freely chose to have children, and they further determined that the costs of child care would be paid by the appellant. However, it would be wrong to be misled by this factual pattern. Pregnancy and childbirth decisions are associated with a host of competing ethical, legal, religious, and socioeconomic influences, and to conclude that the decision to have children should—in tax terms—be characterized as an entirely personal choice, is to ignore these influences altogether. While it might be factually correct to regard this particular appellant's decision to have children as a personal choice, I suggest it is more appropriate to disregard any element of personal consumption which might be associated with it. . . .

The factors so far analyzed suggest that, considering only ss. 9, 18(1)(a) and 18(1)(h), arguments can be made for and against the classification of the appellant's child care expenses as business expenses. In another case, the arguments might be differently balanced, since the existence of a business purpose within the meaning of s. 18(1)(a) is a question of fact, and that the relative weight to be given to the factors analyzed will vary from case to case. However, in general terms, I am of the view that child care expenses are unique: expenditures for child care can represent a significant percentage of taxpayer income, such expenditures are generally linked to the taxpayer's ability to gain or produce income, yet such expenditures are also made in order to make a taxpayer available to the business, and the expenditures are incurred as part of the development of another human life. It can be difficult to weigh the personal and business elements at play. . . .

I am aware that if I were compelled to reach a conclusion with respect to the proper classification of child care expenses with reference to only ss. 9, 18(1)(a) and 18(1)(h) of the Act, such a conclusion would involve competing policy considerations. On the one hand, there is value in the traditional tax law test which seeks to identify those expenses which simply make a taxpayer available to the business, and which proceeds to classify such expenses as "personal" for the reason that a "personal need" is being fulfilled. On the other hand, however, it is inappropriate to disregard lightly the policy considerations which suggest that choice and consumption have no role to play in the classification of child care expenses. . . .

However, I find it unnecessary to determine whether reconceptualization is appropriate having regard to the presence of s. 63 in the Act. . . .

In fact, as I will now attempt to demonstrate, I do not believe that ss. 9, 18(1)(a) and 18(1)(h) can be interpreted to account for a child care business expense deduction, in light of the language used in s. 63. . . .

Considering first the language of s. 63, it is readily apparent that the Act's definition of "child care expenses" specifically comprehends the purpose for which the appellant incurred her nanny expenses. . . .

The fact that this language accurately describes the situation at hand — i.e., a law partner paying child care in order to work — is itself persuasive reason to suppose that ss. 9, 18(1)(a) and 18(1)(h) cannot be interpreted to permit a child care business expense deduction. . . .

One such reason is the structure of s. 63 itself. Section 63 places a number of limitations upon the child care deduction. It varies the deduction according to the taxpayer's earned income, or according to the product obtained when a fixed sum is multiplied by the number of children requiring care, subject to an annual ceiling. In addition, when two or more taxpayers have contributed during a year to the support of a child, the scheme established by s. 63 ordinarily limits the deduction in a further way: it makes the deduction available only to the lower earning supporter — see s. 63(2). . . .

I cannot imagine that a system which allowed some parents to deduct expenses under general provisions respecting business income, but which confined others to a s. 63 regime, would permit deductibility "under carefully controlled terms" within the meaning of the above quotation [from the legislative history]. Further, I am not impressed by the suggestion that Parliament intended s. 63 to limit deductibility only for employees. The proposals do not specify the kind of "work" which is to be encouraged, and the language of s. 63 clearly addresses income from business.

For these reasons, a straightforward approach to statutory interpretation has led me to conclude that the Act intends to address child care expenses, and does so in fact, entirely within s. 63. It is not necessary for me to decide whether, in the absence of s. 63, ss. 9, 18(1)(a) and 18(1)(h) are capable of comprehending a business expense deduction for child care. Given s. 63, however, it is clear that child care cannot be considered deductible under principles of income tax law applicable to business deductions. . . .

2. *If child care expenses are not deductible as part of the determination of profit under s. 9(1) of the Act, has there been a violation of s. 15(1) of the Charter?*

. . . The appellant argues that she has been denied the equal benefit of the law in this case, and she further argues that this inequality constitutes sex-based discrimination. More particularly, in light of my interpretation of the Act, the appellant would seem to argue two related points. First, she seems to argue that an Income Tax Act deduction may be characterized as a benefit of which she can be deprived. Second, she seems to argue that s. 15(1) of the Charter is infringed by s. 63 of the Act to the extent that s. 63 prevents her from fully deducting her child care expenses under s. 9. . . .

The relevant question is, therefore, the following: does s. 63 of the Act infringe the right to equality guaranteed by s. 15(1) of the Charter?

[T]he answer to this question must come in parts. First, it must be determined whether s. 63 establishes an inequality: does s. 63 draw a distinction (intentionally or otherwise) between the appellant and others, based upon a personal characteristic? Second, if an inequality is found, it must be determined whether the inequality results in discrimination: does the distinction drawn by s. 63 have the effect of imposing a burden, obligation or disadvantage not imposed upon others or of withholding or limiting access to opportunities, benefits and advantages available to others? Finally, assuming that both an inequality and discrimination can be found, it must be determined whether the personal characteristic at issue constitutes either an enumerated or analogous ground for the purposes of s. 15(1) of the Charter.

With respect to whether s. 63 creates a distinction, the language of s. 63 must be separated from its effect. Clearly, the language of that provision does not include terms which expressly limit the child care expense deduction to one sex or the other. . . .

What, however, is the effect of the distinction created by s. 63? Does s. 63 have an effect which draws a distinction on the basis of sex? More particularly, in light of the manner in which this appeal has been framed, does s. 63 have an adverse effect upon women who must incur child care expenses to enable the pursuit of business income?

An abundance of information was placed before this Court which conclusively demonstrates that women bear a disproportionate share of the child care burden in Canada. For example, at trial, the expert witness asserted this point, and stated further that the burden is disproportionate whether or not women work outside the home. Similarly, Statistics Canada reports that working men are primarily responsible for child care in only six percent of families. . . .

Based upon this information—indeed, even based upon judicial notice—I have no doubt that women disproportionately incur the social costs of child care. Whether or not such costs are imposed by society upon women, however, is not the s. 15(1) issue. The s. 15(1) issue is whether s. 63 of the Act has an adverse effect upon women in that it unintentionally creates a distinction on the basis of sex. In my view, in order to establish such an effect, it is not sufficient for the appellant to show that women disproportionately bear the burden of child care in society. Rather, she must show that women disproportionately pay child care expenses. Only if women disproportionately pay such expenses can s. 63 have any effect at all, since s. 63's only effect is to limit the tax deduction with respect to such expenses.

Unfortunately, the factual background of this case tends to obscure the problem faced by the appellant with respect to s. 15(1). [T]he appellant and her husband made a "family decision" to the effect that the appellant alone was to bear the financial burden of having children. If, extrapolating from this circumstance, it could be said that women, far more than men, pay child care expenses, the limitations imposed by s. 63 might well create the adverse effect the appellant must demonstrate. However, it is difficult to imagine how such statistics could arise.

I say this because the "family decision" made by the appellant and her husband is not mandated by law and public policy. . . .

Stated another way, I believe that the appellant has presented this Court with evidence of the social burden of child care, and has asked that from this burden, we infer that a positive child care expense burden is also placed directly upon women, and particularly upon businesswomen, including businesswomen who are married. . . .

In order to demonstrate a distinction between the sexes within an adverse effects analysis, one therefore needs to prove that s. 63 disproportionately limits the deduction with respect to actual expenses incurred by women.

In my opinion, the appellant taxpayer has failed to demonstrate an adverse effect created or contributed to by s. 63, although she has overwhelmingly demonstrated how the issue of child care negatively affects women in employment terms. Unfortunately, proof that women pay social costs is not sufficient proof that women pay child care expenses. Those social costs, although very real, exist outside of the Act. . . .

I conclude, therefore, that the appellant is unable to demonstrate a violation of s. 15(1) of the Charter with respect to s. 63 of the Act, since she has not proved that s. 63 draws a distinction based upon the personal characteristic of sex. In reaching this conclusion, however, I wish to note that I do not reject that such a distinction might be proved in another case. The appellant in this case belongs to a particular subgroup of women, namely, married women who are entrepreneurs. It is important to realize that her evidentiary focus was skewed in this direction.

I pause to note that the appellant's focus upon self-employed women to the exclusion of women employees is a very curious aspect of this case. . . .

Undoubtedly, it was the juxtaposition of s. 8(2) with s. 9 of the Act which led the appellant to take the position she took. By virtue of s. 8(2) of the Act, employees are generally prohibited from making any deductions from employment income. Accordingly, the appellant thought it desirable to distance herself from employees in this case. When considering her arguments with respect to statutory interpretation, this approach is understandable. When considering her Charter arguments, it is less so.

In another case, a different subgroup of women with a different evidentiary focus involving s. 63 might well be able to demonstrate the adverse effects required by s. 15(1). For example, although I wish to express no opinion on this point, I note that no particular effort was made in this case to establish the circumstances of single mothers. If, for example, it could be established that women are more likely than men to head single-parent households, one can imagine that an adverse effects analysis involving single mothers might well take a different course, since child care expenses would thus disproportionately fall upon women. . . .

Given the evidentiary focus of this case, I have concluded that the appellant has not proved that s. 63 of the Act involves a distinction between men and women, as required by the equality challenge she has brought under s. 15(1) of the Charter. Accordingly, the limitations upon child care deductions in that section have not been proved to be unconstitutional in this case. Revenue Canada's reassessment of the appellant's deductions in respect of taxation year 1985 is affirmed. . . .

L'Heureux-Dube J. (dissenting): . . . This appeal concerns the statutory interpretation of the Act and, in particular, ss. 9, 18(1)(a), 18(1)(h) and 63. It also requires that we ask fundamental and complex questions about the visions of equality and inclusivity that mould our legal constructs. . . .

The basic question which must be asked is whether the appellant incurred child care expenses for the purpose of gaining or producing income from employment.

At this time, I would like to make a brief comment on the gendered analysis entangled in the statutory interpretation in this case. While it happens that the appellant is a woman lawyer claiming child care expense deductions as a business expense, s. 9 of the Act is gender neutral. Such a claim may also have been made by a businessman in the same situation as Ms. Symes. If such a businessman were, for example, the primary caretaker of his children, the rationale as well as the end result would have been the same. The ability to deduct a legitimate business expense that one incurs in order to gain or produce income from business should not be based on one's sex. Any businessperson would be entitled to a deduction if he or she can prove that such expenses have been incurred for business purposes. The reality, however, is that generally women, rather than men, fulfil the role of sole or primary caregiver to children and, as such, it is they alone who incur and pay for such expenses. Men, until very recently, have rarely been primary care-givers, nor single parents and, as a result, they have not incurred direct child care expenses. In many traditional family situations child care issues were not concrete business expenses for men in business, as most often their wives stayed home to care for their children or made such child care arrangements. Consequently, such a businessman would have no basis on which to claim child care expenses as a business expense. However, in light of our changing society, in which men are being called upon to bear a greater burden of child care responsibilities and expenses, which may impede their ability to earn a profit, it is quite possible that businessmen will accordingly be entitled to claim such expenses should they meet the criteria for business expense deductions, as set out in s. 18(1)(a). Regardless of this future possibility, however, at this time the reality is that it is primarily women who incur the cost, both social and financial, for child care and this decision cannot, as such, ignore the contextual truth when examining whether child care may be considered a business expense.

As my colleague asserts, child care expenses have traditionally been viewed as expenses that were not incurred for the purpose of gaining or producing income, as they were considered personal in nature and accordingly, could not be regarded as commercial. . . .

In the past, the scope of deductible business disbursements has been expanded constantly. It has been held to include a wide array of expenditures, such as club dues, meals and entertainment expenses, car expenses, home office expenses, legal and accounting fees, to name only a few. In order that the expense the appellant claims as a business expense be analyzed in the context of other "business expenses," I will briefly examine some of the many deductions that have been held to be legitimately expended for the purpose of gaining or producing income from business. . . .

Self-employed persons are also able to deduct 80 percent of their entertainment and meal expenses that are expended for the purpose of gaining or producing income. Section 67.1 of the Act limits the deductible portion of an expense in recognition of the partly personal benefit which is received from these expenses. . . .

In Royal Trust Co. v. Minister of National Revenue, 57 D.T.C. 1055, the Exchequer Court of Canada held that the appellant trust company should be able to deduct club dues and initiation fees paid on behalf of its executives and senior personnel. The court held that the evidence proved conclusively that the practice of paying the club dues resulted in business from which the appellant gained or produced income.

In Friedland v. The Queen, 89 D.T.C. 5341 (F.C.T.D.), the taxpayer was allowed to deduct the expenses which he incurred for his Rolls Royce and BMW, to the extent that these automobiles were used for business. . . .

When we look at the case law concerning the interpretation of "business expense," it is clear that this area of law is premised on the traditional view of business as a male enterprise and that the concept of a business expense has itself been constructed on the basis of the needs of businessmen. This is neither a surprising nor a sinister realization, as the evidence well illustrates that it has only been in fairly recent years that women have increasingly moved into the world of business as into other fields, such as law and medicine. The definition of "business expense" was shaped to reflect the experience of businessmen, and the ways in which they engaged in business. As Dorothy Smith points out in *A Peculiar Eclipsing: Women's Exclusion from Man's Culture* (1978), 1 Women's Studies Int. Quart. 281, when only one sex is involved in defining the ideas, rules and values in a particular domain, that one-sided standpoint comes to be seen as natural, obvious and general. As a consequence, the male standard now frames the backdrop of assumptions against which expenses are determined to be, or not to be, legitimate business expenses. Against this backdrop, it is hardly surprising that child care was seen as irrelevant to the end of gaining or producing income from business but rather as a personal non-deductible expense.

[T]he world of yesterday is not the world of today. In 1993, the world of business is increasingly populated by both men and women and the meaning of "business expense" must account for the experiences of all participants in the field. This fact is enhanced by expert evidence which indicates that the practices and requirements of businesswomen may, in fact, differ from those of businessmen. When we look at the current situation, it becomes clear that one of the critical differences in the needs of businessmen and businesswomen is the importance of child care for business people with children, particularly women. . . . In my view, Ms. Symes' child care expenses come within the definition of "the purpose of gaining or producing income" and, as a result, are not prevented by the wording of s. 18(1)(a) from deduction under s. 9(1).

The second point, to which I will now turn, is whether child care expenses may be disallowed as a business expense pursuant to s. 18(1)(h) as being personal in nature. . . .

If we survey the experience of many men, it is apparent why it may seem intuitively obvious to some of them that child care is clearly within the personal realm. This conclusion may, in many ways, reflect many men's experience of child care responsibilities. In fact, the evidence before the Court indicates that, for most men, the responsibility of children does not impact on the number of hours they work, nor does it affect their ability to work. Further, very few men indicated that they made any work-related decisions on the basis of child-raising responsibilities. The same simply cannot currently be said for women. For women, business and family life are not so distinct and, in many ways, any such distinction is completely unreal, since a woman's ability to even participate in the work force may be completely contingent on her ability to acquire child care. The decision to retain child care is an inextricable part of the decision to work, in business or otherwise. . . .

The reality of Ms. Symes' business life necessarily includes child care. The 1993 concept of business expense must include the reality of diverse business practices and needs of those who have not traditionally participated fully in the world of business.

[O]ne must ask whether the many business deductions available, for cars, for club dues and fees, for lavish entertainment and the wining and dining of clients and customers, and for substantial charitable donations, are so obviously business expenses rather than personal ones. Although potentially personal, each one of these expenses has been accepted as a legitimate business expense and, as each reflects a real cost incurred by certain kinds of business people to produce income from business, a deduction has been allowed. The real costs incurred by business-women with children are no less real, no less worthy of consideration and no less incurred in order to gain or produce income from business. . . .

[C]hild care may be held to be a business expense deductible pursuant to ss. 9(1), 18(1)(a) and 18(1)(h) of the Act, all other criteria being respected. This result leads me to the most crucial consideration in this appeal, that is whether s. 63 of the Act precludes the deduction of child care expenses as a business expense. Here, I part company with my colleague since, in my view, s. 63 of the Act, properly interpreted, is no such bar. . . .

Section 63 of the Act, reproduced earlier, provides a limited deduction for child care expenses. The deduction is available, in most circumstances, to the lower income earning spouse in a family unit. . . .

According to my colleague, . . . since the wording of s. 63 of the Act clearly includes the appellant's nanny expenses, s. 63 acts as a complete bar, rendering the appellant Symes ineligible to deduct her child care expenses as a business expense. I do not interpret s. 63 of the Act in such a fashion. Sections 63 and 9(1), in my view, may co-exist. The fact that Parliament enacted a section to benefit all parents in the paid work force without distinction does not prevent a taxpayer who is in business from deducting an expense which can be legitimately claimed as a business expense. Section 63 provides general relief to parents, but nothing in its wording implies that deductions available under s. 9(1) are abolished or restricted in this respect. Had Parliament intended to submit the deduction of child care expenses to the application of s. 63 it would have expressed it in clear language. . . .

Deductions under s. 63 of the Act, as opposed to business expense deductions, clearly require that different criteria be met for one to be eligible for the deduction under one or the other section. In addition, each has its own purpose. Working parents, to whom the deduction under s. 63 applies, would not be eligible for any such deduction had s. 63 not been enacted. Businesspersons, however, may be eligible to deduct child care as they would any other business expense, provided they were able to meet the requirements for a deduction under ss. 9 and 18 of the Act. . . .

The definition of a business expense under the Act has evolved in a manner that has failed to recognize the reality of businesswomen. It is thus imperative to recognize that any interpretation of s. 63 which prevents the deduction of child care as a business expense may, in fact, be informed by this partisan perspective. . . .

Since I have reached the conclusion that, on the basis of statutory interpretation, Ms. Symes is entitled to deduct her child care expenses as a business expense pursuant to ss. 9(1), 18(1)(a) and (h) and 63 of the Act, the constitutional questions do not have to be answered. However, since my colleague, Iacobucci J., has raised many areas of concern and difficulty with respect to the effect and application of s. 15 of the Charter on the Act, I wish to make the following comments. . . .

Ms. Symes is asking that she be treated equally, independently of her sex, under the Act. She has provided ample evidence that women suffer the social cost of child care and that the expense of child care which she incurs, and has paid, is not a purely personal expense but is incurred for the purpose of gaining or producing income from business. In my view, Ms. Symes suffers an actual and calculable loss as a result of not being able to deduct a legitimate business expense which she incurs. The goal and the requirement of equality, as set out by s. 15 of the Charter, makes it unacceptable that Ms. Symes be denied the right to deduct her business expenses merely because such expenses are not generally incurred by business-men. Denial of these deductions would constitute discrimination under the Act. . . .

This is not a case about the advantageous position in society some women garner as opposed to other women, but, rather, an examination of the advantaged position that businessmen hold in relation to businesswomen. . . . The fact that Ms. Symes may be a member of a more privileged economic class does not by itself invalidate her claim under s. 15 of the Charter. She is not to be held responsible for all possible discriminations in the income tax system, nor for the fact that other women may suffer disadvantages in the marketplace arising from child care. As the appellant argues, we cannot "hold every woman to the position of the most disadvantaged women, apparently in the name of sex equality." . . .

The divergent effect of a different contextual approach can be significant to the outcome of a case such as the appeal at hand. As Professor Audrey Macklin describes, the contrasting contextual approaches to this case taken by the trial judge and the Court of Appeal played a pivotal role in the outcome [Macklin, Symes v. M.N.R.: *Where Sex Meets Class*, 5 C.J.W.L. 498, 508-09 (1992)]:

> The simplest way to decipher the diverging views of Mr. Justice Cullen and Mr. Justice Decary on the Charter issue is to imagine the judges peering at Beth Symes through different pairs of glasses. When the trial judge looked at her, he saw a business woman standing next to a business man. When the judges of the Court of Appeal looked at her, they saw a self-employed, professional woman standing next to a salaried woman. In the former scenario, Symes was disadvantaged by her sex contrary to section 15 and deserved to have her business expenses treated the same as a businessman's. In the latter, she was privileged by her class and made a mockery of section 15 of the Charter by attempting to use her status as a business woman to obtain greater benefits than those available to salaried women.
>
> The gist of Mr. Justice Decary's position is that it is absurd to grant Symes parity with businessmen if, in so doing, she is placed in a superior position to other women. To put it another way, it is preferable that all women be equally disadvantaged relative to men if the alternative is to improve the situation of the best-off women.

The proper interpretive approach to issues of equality must recognize that a real solution to discrimination cannot be arrived at without incorporating the perspective of the group suffering discrimination. In this case, s. 15 of the Charter demands that the experience of both women and men shape the definition of business expense. . . .

Notes and Questions

1. *Just a coincidence?* The seven justices in the majority in *Symes* were all men; the two dissenting justices were both women.

2. *The "very curious aspect" of the case.* The real stakes in *Symes* are rather subtle. Ms. Symes was clearly entitled to a $4,000 child care deduction ($2,000 per child) under §63 of the Canadian Income Tax Act, but she could deduct the remainder of her nanny expenses only if she could convince the court that they qualified as business expenses. Given the rule that no deduction whatsoever was allowable for employee business expenses, she had a plausible argument for an uncapped deduction only because she was self-employed (as a principal in a law firm). Even if she had won, *employed* mothers would still have been unable to deduct child care expenses in excess of $2,000 per child. This is what Justice Iacobucci describes as the "very curious aspect" of the case. If Ms. Symes had won, a high income law partner could deduct $20,000 of child care costs, but employees (including low and moderate income employees) would still be limited to a deduction of $2,000 per child. Do you agree with Justice L'Heureux-Dube that, from the point of view of women's rights, that would be a better result than limiting the child care deduction to $2,000 per child in all cases?

3. *Male and female business expenses?* Justice L'Heureux-Dube argues that, because the Canadian income tax allows uncapped business expense deductions for some typically male expenses with a strong personal consumption element (such as a Rolls Royce used for business travel, club dues, and 80 percent of the cost of business meals), it would be sex discrimination not to allow an uncapped deduction for the typically female expense of child care. Do you agree that the typically male expenses are sufficiently like child care, apart from the gender difference, that they should be subject to equivalent tax treatment? Do you agree with her characterization of child care as a basically female expense, and of the other expenses as basically male?

4. *An underlying gender-neutral principle?* As explained in the main text,[2] the nondeductibility of child care expenses under the U.S. income tax is consistent with the treatment of commuting expenses. Both types of expenses are jointly caused by business and personal aspects of a taxpayer's life, and the U.S. income tax denies a business expense deduction for both. The principle seems to be that an expense does not qualify as a deductible business expense if it would not be incurred by another taxpayer in the same business situation, but with different personal circumstances. If the tax treatment of both child care and commuting is based on the same underlying principle, if the principle itself is not gender-biased, and if the application of the principle to commuting is not gender-biased, does that help to defend the nondeductibility of child care (as a business expense) from the sex discrimination charge?

5. *Whose responsibility?* Would you guess that Ms. Symes and her husband agreed that Ms. Symes was solely responsible for all child care expenses because that reflected their view of the proper division of responsibilities in their marriage, or do you think the agreement was a tax-motivated gimmick? The tax motivation, of course, would be to avoid the standing problem that her husband

---

2. Section A.1.a of Chapter 9.

would have had in arguing that the denial of a business expense deduction for child care discriminated against women. Is it your experience or impression that most two-earner couples even think about which spouse's financial resources are being used to pay for child care, or is child care more often paid out of a common pot? Even for couples that do think about individual responsibility for paying for child care, do you think very many couples assign the entire responsibility to the wife? This was the sticking point for Justice Iacobucci in his Charter analysis; he was unconvinced that the burden of paying for child care was disproportionately shouldered by women.

6. *The cost of child care and wives' employment decisions.* But perhaps a revised version of Ms. Symes's complaint would have avoided Justice Iacobucci's objection. Imagine a married couple with young children. The husband and wife pool all their economic resources; all income and all expenses are shared 50-50. The husband has a job and is firmly committed to the work force. The wife is deciding (with input from the husband) between being a full-time homemaker and reentering the paid work force. If the wife takes the job (which pays $30,000), the husband and wife will share the resulting child care expenses ($20,000) evenly between them. Despite this perfect sharing, they will naturally think of child care as a cost associated with the wife's job when they are deciding whether she should take the job. If the child care expenses are not deductible, a job that produces net income (after child care expenses) of only $10,000 will generate $30,000 of taxable income. This overtaxation may lead the wife to decide not to take the job. In this way, the failure to allow an adequate tax benefit for child care expenses can discourage married mothers from taking paying jobs, arguably in violation of §15 of the Charter (or the Equal Protection Clause, in the United States). Like the argument in *Symes*, this argument is based on assumptions about how married couples typically behave. It assumes that the typical husband with young children is strongly committed to his job and that the typical wife is on the margin between unpaid and paid labor. (If the wife were strongly committed to her job and the husband were on the margin, not allowing a tax benefit for child care expenses would discourage the *husband* from working.) The difference, however, is that it is more plausible that wives are commonly on the work-home margin than that wives commonly pay all child care expenses in two-earner marriages.

7. *Equal protection and the income tax.* Even though the taxpayer's constitutional challenge was ultimately rejected in *Symes*, the Canadian Supreme Court clearly took the challenge seriously. By contrast, equal-protection-type challenges to the U.S. income tax are seldom taken seriously by the courts, and virtually never succeed. A rare exception is Moritz v. Commissioner, 496 F.2d 466 (10th Cir. 1972), *cert. denied*, 412 U.S. 906 (1973). The challenged statute allowed a dependent care deduction (the predecessor of the current §21 dependent care credit) to women regardless of marital status, but denied the deduction to never-married men. The court held that this discrimination violated equal protection principles, and allowed the taxpayer—a never-married man—to claim the deduction. The taxpayer was represented by (now Supreme Court Justice) Ruth Bader Ginsburg and her husband Martin Ginsburg, a prominent tax attorney and professor. The current Internal Revenue Code does not feature any provisions so blatantly discriminatory.

Cell

FAMILY INCOME-SPLITTING BY STATUTE

Congress could have declined to accept the government's victory in *Lucas v. Earl*; it is not inevitable that income should be taxed to the earner rather than the consumer, when those are different people.[3] Suppose Congress decided that income should be taxed to the consumer, rather than to the earner, within nuclear families. Although this might be accomplished by legislatively overruling *Lucas v. Earl*, or by making gifts deductible by the donor and taxable to the donee, a better approach might be to continue formally to tax income to the earner, and to retain the current treatment of gifts, but to adjust the earner's tax rate schedule to provide the functional equivalent of family income-splitting.

Family income-splitting through the rate schedules would be based on the premise that families with incomes supporting the same standard of living should pay income tax at the same average rate, regardless of the number of persons in each family. Implementing this policy requires information (or at least assumptions) about how families share consumption resources, and about how family size and composition affect the amount of income needed to maintain any given standard of living. For ease of illustration, suppose the best evidence is that the typical family shares consumption resources according to a formula under which each adult is given a weight of 1, and each child is given a weight of ½. Thus, a family of two adults and one child, with $25,000 available for consumption, allocates $10,000 (1/2.5) to each adult's consumption, and $5,000 (.5/2.5) to the child's consumption. Also assume that sharing according to this pattern equalizes the standards of living of all of the members of the family (in other words, assume that children as consumers are twice as efficient as adults). Finally, assume (somewhat unrealistically) that living together creates no consumption economies—for example, that one of the adults in the above family has exactly the same standard of living as an adult living alone on $10,000.

Armed with these assumptions, we can construct a standard-of-living-equivalency scale for families of various sizes and compositions, as shown in the table below.

---

3. *Lucas v. Earl* was a statutory interpretation case, not a constitutional case, so Congress is free to overrule it.

Family Composition	Consumption Units (Adult = 1, Child = ½)	Standard-of-Living-Equivalent Incomes
One adult	1	$X
Two adults	2	$2X
One adult, two children	2	$2X
Two adults, one child	2.5	$2.5X
Two adults, two children	3	$3X

For example, the same standard of living would be enjoyed by (1) a one-adult household living on $10,000, (2) a one-adult, two-children household living on $20,000, and (3) a two-adult, one-child household living on $25,000.

The next step is to construct a reference tax rate schedule applicable to an adult living alone. To keep it simple, imagine a two-bracket rate schedule that imposes a rate of 10 percent on the first $10,000 of income, and a rate of 30 percent on all additional income. For any larger household, the width of the 10 percent bracket is increased by multiplying $10,000 by the number of "consumption units" (as indicated in the above table) in the family. Thus, a two-adult family would have a 10 percent bracket of $20,000, a two-adult, one-child family would have a 10 percent bracket of $25,000, and so on. Consider a two-adult, one-child family with $25,000 of taxable income, all earned by one of the adults. The entire $25,000 is formally taxed to the earner (thus leaving *Lucas v. Earl* technically intact), but the effect of the widening of the 10 percent bracket is the same as allowing the earner to shift tax liability on $10,000 to the other adult, and tax liability on $5,000 to the child.

Under this approach, any two families with incomes supporting the same standard of living will pay tax at the same average rate, regardless of the size of each family. The table below demonstrates that result for one set of standard-of-living-equivalent incomes, but the system will produce equal average tax rates for *any* set of standard-of-living equivalent incomes.

Family Composition	Consumption Units	10% Bracket Width	Income (All Incomes Are Standard-of-Living-Equivalent)	Tax on Income in Previous Column (Income Above 10% Bracket Taxed at 30%)	Average Tax Rate (Tax/Income)
One adult	1	$10,000	$30,000	$7,000	23.3%
Two adults	2	$20,000	$60,000	$14,000	23.3%
One adult, two children	2	$20,000	$60,000	$14,000	23.3%
Two adults, one child	2.5	$25,000	$75,000	$17,500	23.3%
Two adults, two children	3	$30,000	$90,000	$21,000	23.3%

A family income-splitting regime quite similar to the hypothetical one described above has long been a feature of the French income tax. Although the actual U.S. income tax falls far short of full-fledged family income-splitting, three aspects of current law represent steps in that direction. (1) A dependency exemption (§151(c)) for the taxpayer's child eliminates all tax liability on an amount of income intended to approximate the cost of supporting that child at a subsistence level. This has the same effect as shifting to the child income equal to the amount of the exemption, and taxing that income at the rate of zero. This does not, however, permit a taxpayer to shift any above-subsistence income to a child, to be taxed at the child's lower marginal rates. (2) A version of bracket-widening is embodied in the relationship between the tax rate schedule for unmarried taxpayers (§1(c)) and the tax rate schedule for married couples filing joint returns (§1(a)). The joint return brackets are considerably wider than the unmarried taxpayer brackets, although in most cases less than twice as wide.[4] This statutory income-splitting is permitted only between spouses. (3) The §1(b) tax rate schedule for heads of households (roughly speaking, single parents) features wider brackets than the §1(c) tax rate schedule for other unmarried taxpayers. This can be viewed as allowing family income-splitting between a single parent and the parent's first child for all income (not just for subsistence-level income, as in the case of the dependency exemption). Strangely, however, this bracket-widening on account of a dependent child is limited to the first child of a single parent; no bracket-widening is permitted on account of additional children of a single parent, or on account of *any* children of a married couple.

To summarize, consideration of family income-splitting by statute suggests three lessons:

(*1*) There are three ways the tax system might allow income-shifting from the earner of the income (or the owner of income-producing property) to the consumer of the income. One would be by legislatively overruling *Lucas v. Earl*, thus permitting tax-effective self-help assignments of income. The second would be to change the tax treatment of gifts, making gifts deductible by donors and taxable to donees. The third would be to keep *Lucas v. Earl* and the existing gift rules on the books, but to design the earner's tax rate schedule (and dependency exemptions) in such a way that the taxpayer is *effectively* allowed to split his income with the family members who share in its consumption.

(*2*) The U.S. income tax has taken a few steps in the direction of statutory income-shifting (the third approach described above). Dependency exemptions, the joint return tax rate schedule, and the head of household tax rate schedule can all be viewed as practical (although not technical) exceptions to *Lucas v. Earl*.

(*3*) If Congress so desired, it could go much further in the direction of family income-splitting by rate schedule adjustments; the French system provides a working model.

---

4. The fact that they are less than twice as wide may reflect implicit judgments about the efficiencies involved in sharing a household. For much more on the taxation of married couples, marriage bonuses, and marriage penalties, see section B of Chapter 9, and the cell on marriage penalty causes and cures.

INCOME TAX MARRIAGE PENALTIES: CAUSES AND CURES

For millions of two-earner couples who are unwilling to follow the Boyters'[5] lead and tear up their marriage certificates, the marriage penalties created by the 1969 singles penalty relief legislation remain an unpleasant fact of life. On the other hand, millions of other married couples enjoy substantial marriage *bonuses*. The Congressional Budget Office (CBO) estimated that in 1996 more than 21 million married couples paid a total of $29 billion in marriage penalties (an average of nearly $1,400 per couple), but that another 25 million couples enjoyed tax marriage bonuses totaling $33 billion (averaging about $1,300 per couple).[6] Here we first explain the basic nature of the legislative dilemma concerning the income tax treatment of marriage, and then discuss several possible ways of amending the law to reduce or eliminate marriage penalties.

A. THE DILEMMA

Despite frequent claims to the contrary, the existence of marriage penalties is not the result of legislative perversity or ineptitude. Rather, marriage penalties are unfortunate by-products of the pursuit of other policy goals. Given the basic policy decisions to have (1) a progressive tax rate structure and (2) joint returns for

---

5. Boyter v. Commissioner, 668 F.2d 1382 (4th Cir. 1981), set forth in section B of Chapter 9.
6. CBO, *For Better or Worse: Marriage and the Federal Income Tax* 1 (1997). Temporary changes to the standard deduction provisions and the rate brackets have reduced marriage penalties — and increased marriage bonuses — but only through 2012. See section B.6 *infra*.

married taxpayers, it is inevitable that there will be marriage penalties, marriage bonuses, or both. At the outset, it is worth noting that the justification usually offered today for joint returns is not the same as the historical explanation for the creation of the joint return system in 1948. The joint return system originated as a sort of historical accident; it was a response to the geographic discrimination (between married taxpayers in separate property states and married taxpayers in community property states) created by the interaction of the Supreme Court's *Lucas v. Earl* and *Poe v. Seaborn* opinions. It is usually defended today, however, as being based on the principle of "couples neutrality." This principle assumes that the typical married couple functions as a single economic unit, and that any two married couples with the same total income have the same taxpaying ability. According to proponents of couples neutrality, it follows that any two married couples with the same total income should have the same tax liability regardless of how marital income is distributed between the spouses in each marriage.

A simple example illustrates the nature of the policy dilemma. Imagine a tax system that imposes two rates of tax on unmarried individuals: a 10 percent tax rate on the first $40,000 of income, and a 30 percent tax rate on all income above $40,000. The following table indicates how this rate schedule would apply to four unmarried taxpayers.

Taxpayer	Income	Tax Liability
Andy	$80,000	$16,000[7]
Betty	$0	$0
Carl	$40,000	$4,000[8]
Donna	$40,000	$4,000

Now suppose Andy and Betty get married, as do Carl and Donna. If their incomes remain unchanged, each couple will, of course, have $80,000 of combined spousal income. The commitment to couples neutrality (as implemented by joint returns) means two couples with the same combined income should have the same tax liability. Since the combined unmarried tax liabilities of Andy and Betty ($16,000) were higher than the combined unmarried tax liabilities of Carl and Donna ($8,000), equal tax liabilities for the two married couples can be achieved only if marriage changes the tax liabilities of one or both couples. In general terms, there are three possibilities (which are summarized in the table below):

(1) Make the joint return tax rate schedule identical to the unmarried taxpayer tax rate schedule, with the 10 percent bracket covering only the first $40,000 of income. Under this approach, marriage would have no effect on the combined tax liabilities of Andy and Betty, but there would be a very large marriage penalty of $8,000 ($16,000 married liability minus $8,000 combined unmarried liabilities) on Carl and Donna.

(2) The other extreme would be to make the 10 percent bracket for joint returns twice the width of the 10 percent bracket for unmarried taxpayers. With a 10 percent bracket of $80,000, marriage would have no effect on the combined

---

7. This results from a 10 percent tax imposed on Andy's first $40,000 of income ($4,000 tax), and a 30 percent tax imposed on the remaining $40,000 of income ($12,000 tax).

8. This results from a 10 percent tax imposed on $40,000 of income.

tax liabilities of Carl and Donna, but there would be an $8,000 marriage *bonus* ($16,000 unmarried liability minus $8,000 married liability) for Andy and Betty. This was the approach of the 1948 legislation.

(3) A compromise approach would be to make the joint return 10 percent bracket larger than the unmarried taxpayer 10 percent bracket, but less than twice as large. Suppose, for example, the joint return 10 percent bracket covers the first $60,000 of income. Then each couple, when married, would owe tax of $12,000.[9] Andy and Betty would then enjoy a marriage bonus of $4,000, while Carl and Donna would suffer a marriage penalty of $4,000.

Couple	Combined Unmarried Tax Liabilities	Marriage Bonus or Penalty with $40,000 10% Bracket for Joint Returns	Marriage Bonus or Penalty with $80,000 10% Bracket for Joint Returns	Marriage Bonus or Penalty with $60,000 10% Bracket for Joint Returns
Andy-Betty	$16,000	$0	$8,000 bonus	$4,000 bonus
Carl-Donna	$8,000	$8,000 penalty	$0	$4,000 penalty

In general terms, current law follows the third approach, thus producing both marriage penalties (for two-earner couples with relatively equal incomes) and marriage bonuses (for one-earner couples and two-earner couples with very unequal incomes).[10] The break-even division of spousal income varies by income levels, but it is commonly somewhere between 80-20 percent and 70-30 percent. In other words, a married couple with an income division more unequal than 80-20 percent will generally enjoy a marriage bonus, and a married couple with an income division more nearly equal than 70-30 percent will generally suffer a marriage penalty.

B.   THE CURE?

The available evidence suggests that the behavioral effects of the marriage penalty are slight. Despite the example of the Boyters, very few people decide not to marry or to obtain a divorce out of concern for the marriage penalty.[11] Of course, the

---

9. This is the sum of a 10 percent tax on the first $60,000 ($6,000) and a 30 percent tax on the remaining $20,000 ($6,000).

10. A close comparison of the breakpoints between the brackets under the §1(a) joint return rate schedule, and the breakpoints under the §1(c) rate schedule for unmarried taxpayers, reveals a rather odd pattern. The 10 percent and 15 percent brackets are twice as wide for married couples as for unmarried taxpayers (but only through 2012, absent legislative extension), with the result that those brackets produce substantial marriage bonuses and never produce marriage penalties. On the other hand, the 35 percent top bracket begins at exactly the same income level for joint filers as for unmarried taxpayers—an approach which, if applied throughout the rate schedule, would produce substantial marriage penalties and never produce marriage bonuses. For the intermediate brackets—25 percent, 28 percent, and 33 percent—the breakpoints for joint filers are higher than for unmarried taxpayers, but less than twice as high. This approach produces both marriage penalties and marriage bonuses.

11. It is not uncommon, however, for two-earner couples to take the marriage penalty into account in selecting a wedding date in January rather than in December, thus postponing the onset of the penalty for one year.

marriage penalty may be unfair even (or perhaps especially) if its behavioral effects are minor. Many ways of amending the Code to lessen or eliminate marriage penalties have been proposed in recent years. Some of the leading candidates are described below.

1. *Return to 1948*

As explained in the main text, the system that existed between 1948 and 1969 produced substantial marriage bonuses, but no penalties.[12] Such a system could be reintroduced, by providing married taxpayers with rate brackets twice as wide as the brackets for unmarried taxpayers and with a standard deduction twice as large as the standard deduction for unmarried taxpayers.[13] What are the objections to this approach? The obvious objection is that it was tried before and it didn't work, because it created unacceptably large singles penalties. It is not clear, however, that complaints about singles penalties have the same political force today that they had in 1969. The singles penalty complaint — that a coworker's homemaking spouse is a kind of tax shelter — is persuasive only when homemaking spouses are the norm. That was the case in 1969, when only about 40 percent of married women were in the labor force. Today, however, over 60 percent of wives are in the labor force.[14] A single person's married coworker probably has an employed spouse, and marriage to an employed spouse may well subject that coworker to a tax penalty. Without the ability to appeal to a married coworker's homemaking spouse as the social norm, much of the force of the singles penalty complaint is lost.

On the other hand, a related argument against this form of marriage penalty relief has been politically powerful in recent years — namely, that a return to the 1948 system is not narrowly targeted at elimination of marriage penalties. It would also create new marriage bonuses and enlarge existing ones. In fact, the CBO estimated in 1997 that slightly more than half of the revenue loss from this reform would benefit couples already enjoying marriage bonuses under then-current law.[15]

Not only would this approach provide tax reductions for some couples who *are not* marriage penalty victims; it would also fail to provide complete relief for many couples who *are* subject to marriage penalties. This may be surprising, since the same approach in 1948 resulted in no marriage penalties. The explanation is that changes in the structure of the income tax since 1948 have created new sources of marriage penalties, which a return to 1948 would not address. First, the proposals do not eliminate marriage penalties for couples with dependent children. If a husband and wife with children were not married, one parent could file as a head of household, and benefit from the special head-of-household tax rate schedule in §1(b) and the special head-of-household standard deduction in §63(c)(2)(B). A joint return standard deduction twice as large as the single taxpayer standard deduction would still be less than the combination of one head-of-household standard deduction and one single taxpayer standard deduction; the same goes for bracket widths. This was not an issue in 1948 because head-of-household status did not exist. Second, there are substantial marriage penalties in the design of the earned income tax credit (EITC) that would not be alleviated by a return to

12. See the Notes following *Poe v. Seaborn*, in section B of Chapter 9.

13. In fact, Congress took several steps in this direction in legislation enacted in 2001 and 2003. For a description of this legislation, see section B.6 *infra*.

14. *Statistical Abstract of the U.S.: 2009*, table 576, at p. 375. (The labor-force participation rate for married women was 61.0 percent in 2007.)

15. CBO, *supra* Note 6, at 50.

the 1948 approach.[16] Again, this was not a problem in 1948 because the EITC did not exist. Finally, a return to 1948 would have no effect on marriage penalties created by the design of the phaseouts (or phasedowns) of various tax benefits, such as personal exemptions, the child tax credit, higher education tax credits, the partial exclusion for social security benefits, and itemized deductions. None of these phaseouts existed in 1948.

2. Optional Separate Filing

Under this approach, a married couple could file a joint return or two separate returns as if unmarried, depending on which choice resulted in a lower combined tax liability. The great attraction of this approach is its precision in attacking marriage penalties without increasing existing marriage bonuses or creating new ones. Couples already enjoying marriage bonuses would, of course, elect to continue filing joint returns. Thus, their tax liabilities would be unaffected.

There are two major objections to this approach. The first is complexity. Many couples would have to prepare three tentative returns in order to determine which filing strategy resulted in the lower tax burden. (This may not be a major problem, however, if all the computational heavy lifting is handled by tax return preparation software.) Also, there would be some complexity in allocating items of income and deduction between spouses who elect to file separately. The second objection is that the approach is philosophically incoherent. The standard justification for joint returns is that married couples function as economic units. Under that view, two couples with equal incomes should pay equal taxes, regardless of how the earning of the incomes is distributed between the spouses in each marriage. Optional filing will result in equal tax on the two couples *if* both couples file joint returns. But if either couple (or both) files separate returns, the two couples generally will have different liabilities. Hence the philosophical incoherence. The purpose of joint filing is to impose equal tax on equal income couples, but *optional* joint filing defeats that purpose.

3. A Two-Earner Deduction

From 1981 to 1986, a two-earner couple was allowed a deduction of 10 percent of the earned income of the lower-earner spouse, with a maximum deduction of $3,000 (in the case of earned income of $30,000 or more). There have been calls for the return of a two-earner deduction. Although the benefit of the deduction would be limited to two-earner couples, it would not be perfectly targeted to victims of the marriage penalty. For some two-earner couples with very unequal incomes, the two-earner deduction would enlarge an existing marriage bonus; for other two-earner couples, the savings from the deduction would be insufficient to eliminate the marriage penalty.

A possible objection to this approach is that it violates the principle of equal-tax-on-equal-income-couples (couples neutrality), by resulting in the imposition of a higher tax on (for example) a one-earner couple earning $60,000 than on a two-earner couple with each spouse earning $30,000. This might even be provocatively described as "a homemaker penalty." Interestingly, however, no objections of this sort were made against the two-earner deduction in its previous incarnation. Perhaps this was because even most one-earner couples perceived the deduction as accomplishing a sort of rough justice, in light of the extra nondeductible

---

16. For a description of EITC marriage penalties and bonuses, see the cell on the EITC.

expenses of being a two-earner household (for example, for commuting, for work clothes, and for replacing the imputed income of a full-time homemaker).

4. *Mandatory Separate Returns*

Marriage penalties, marriage bonuses, or both, are inevitable by-products of the simultaneous pursuit of couples neutrality and progressive marginal rates. One cure for marriage penalties, then, would be to abandon the goal of couples neutrality, by abolishing joint returns. Each individual, married or unmarried, would simply pay tax on his or her own income. There are two objections to this approach. The first is that couples neutrality is too important a principle to abandon. This objection will not be compelling to people who think that marriage neutrality — that is, a system with neither marriage penalties nor bonuses — is more important than couples neutrality. The second objection is that the approach would generate more complexity than current law, because of the need to allocate items of income and deduction between spouses. This is not a trivial problem, but many other countries (including Canada) have successfully administered mandatory separate returns for decades.

5. *A Truly Flat Tax*

Just as marriage penalties disappear once we abandon the goal of couples neutrality, marriage penalties also disappear if we abandon the goal of progressive marginal rates. If all income is taxed at the rate of, say, 20 percent, regardless of the taxpayer to whom it is assigned, then marriage can never affect the rate at which income is taxed. The problem with this approach is that hardly anyone favors a truly flat tax. Most so-called flat tax proposals are really proposals for two-bracket systems, with a zero bracket for poverty-level income and a flat rate for all other income. As illustrated by the hypothetical tax rate schedule with a 10 percent bracket and a 30 percent bracket, even a two-bracket rate schedule violates marriage neutrality, if combined with joint returns.

On the other hand, it is possible to use the combination of a single marginal tax rate and a universal cash transfer program (a "demogrant") to produce progressive *average* tax rates, marriage neutrality, and couples neutrality. Imagine a tax-and-transfer system with a flat rate tax of 25 percent and a demogrant of $5,000 per person, as illustrated in the table below. When the effects of the tax and the demogrant are considered together, this system features progressive average tax rates, even though it has only one marginal tax rate. As shown in the table, average rates are negative at incomes below $20,000 (that is, the demogrant exceeds the tax), and as income rises above $20,000 the average rate rises — approaching, but never quite reaching, 25 percent. Despite this average rate progressivity, the system would feature both marriage neutrality and couples neutrality. Administered on a separate return basis, it obviously would be marriage neutral. It also would have couples neutrality: Regardless of how income was distributed between spouses, any couple with $X of income would have a tax liability (positive or negative) of $X (25%) − 2($5,000). This seems like such a neat solution to the dilemma of the income tax treatment of marriage, that it may seem surprising it has not been seriously considered. For better or worse, this approach seems to have no political constituency. Conservatives object to the universal cash grant, while liberals object to the inability to impose higher marginal rates on high income taxpayers.

1. Income	2. Net Tax Liability (or Net Transfer Payment)	3. Average Tax Rate (Column 2 ÷ Column 1)
$0	($5,000)	Infinitely negative
$20,000	$0	0%
$50,000	$7,500	15%
$100,000	$20,000	20%
$1,000,000	$245,000	24.5%

6. A Semi-Symbolic Response?

After several years of intense legislative worrying about tax marriage penalties, Congress provided limited marriage penalty relief in 2001. That legislation gives married taxpayers twice the standard deduction available to single taxpayers (other than heads of households), and makes the two lowest tax brackets (10% and 15%) twice as wide for married taxpayers as for singles.[17] In effect, this is a limited version of a return to the 1948 approach — limited because it does not also apply to marriage penalties in the higher tax brackets. Although the approach provides too much relief to be described as purely symbolic, it does leave the bulk of tax marriage penalties in place. Given the intractability of the problems in this area, there is something to be said in favor of a semi-symbolic legislative response.

A more ambitious attack on marriage penalties would probably have proven unstable. With respect to the income tax treatment of marriage, taxpayers divide into three interest groups: unmarried taxpayers, two-earner couples, and one-earner couples. Under every possible tax treatment of marriage, at least one of these groups will have a plausible claim that it is being treated unfairly. It is easy to imagine Congress's becoming caught in an endless recycling of unstable solutions. The 1948 system of only marriage bonuses led to complaints about singles penalties, which led to legislative relief for singles in 1969, which in turn led to complaints about marriage penalties for two-earner couples. If Congress responded to those complaints with optional separate filing — the reform precisely targeted at relief for two-earner couples — one-earner couples would undoubtedly complain about being taxed more heavily than equal-income two-earner couples. Congress might respond to this complaint about homemaker penalties by returning to the 1948 approach, whereupon the next cycle would begin.

C.   THE STACKING EFFECT

In many marriages the wife is the marginal earner, in the sense that the husband's job is a given, and the question is whether the wife should be a full-time homemaker or take a paying job. Under the current joint return system, the wife will view her earnings as stacked on top of the husband's for tax purposes, so that even her first dollars of income will be taxed at high marginal rates. There is nothing in the

17. Subsequent legislation has extended the temporary patch described in the text through 2012.

Code, of course, that decrees that the husband's income soaks up the standard deduction and the lower rate brackets, and the wife's income is taxed in the higher brackets, but this will be the effect in any marriage where the wife is the marginal earner. In light of this stacking effect, the wife may decide to stay home. Like the marriage penalty, the stacking effect is a phenomenon of joint returns, but it is not the *same* phenomenon. Marriage penalty analysis takes the income of each person as given, and their marital status as the question to be decided. By contrast, stacking effect analysis takes the marriage and the husband's job as givens, and the wife's earnings as the open question. To see the difference, consider the joint return system in effect from 1948 to 1969. This system produced no marriage penalties (only bonuses), but it nevertheless featured the stacking effect.

When the stacking effect is combined with the facts that (1) the imputed income produced by a full-time homemaker is not taxable, (2) only very limited tax benefits are available for expenses incurred to replace such imputed income if the wife takes a paid job, and (3) most work-related expenses — such as commuting costs and work clothes — are nondeductible, the tax system can strongly discourage wives from employment. Suppose Jane, a married woman with two young children, is debating whether to be a full-time mother or to take a job. Because of the income of her husband, John, the federal income tax rate on any income she earns will be 28 percent. In addition, suppose the combined burden of the social security wage tax and state income tax is 12 percent. Her salary would be $40,000, but she would have expenses of $5,000 for commuting and work clothes, and $20,000 for child care, housecleaning, and more restaurant meals (this $20,000 is the cost of re-placing her imputed income). After taking into account taxes and expenses, how much of the $40,000 salary would Jane get to keep? The new expenses are all nondeductible. Jane's and John's tax liability (federal and state income, and federal wage tax) will increase by $14,800. This represents 40 percent of $40,000, reduced by a $1,200 child care credit under §21.[18] After the $40,000 salary is reduced by $25,000 for work-related expenses and the costs of replacing imputed income, and by $14,800 for taxes, the couple will have a net gain of $200 if their gross income increases by $40,000.

This dramatic result is not caused solely by the stacking effect; it is also caused by the fact that their taxable income increases by $40,000 while their economic income (i.e., new income net of new expenses) increases by only $15,000. If they were entitled to deduct the $25,000 of expenses, they would come out significantly ahead as a result of Jane's job, even if her net income of $15,000 were all taxed at 28 percent. On the other hand, the stacking effect also plays a major role in producing the result. The tax burden on $40,000 would be much lower in a separate return system, under which part of the income would be sheltered from tax by Jane's standard deduction and the rest would be taxed in the lowest brackets.

The recent legislative attention to the tax treatment of marriage has focused entirely on alleviating marriage penalties. Congress has expressed no interest in reducing the stacking effect, although the two-earner deduction — marketed as an attack on the marriage penalty — would ameliorate the stacking effect. The only reform that would eliminate the stacking effect would be the abolition of joint returns, and that does not appear to be on the legislative horizon.

---

18. No matter how much they actually spend on child care, the credit-eligible expenses will be limited to $6,000 by §21(c)(2). Under §21(a)(2), their credit percentage will be 20 percent. Multiplying $6,000 by 20 percent produces a $1,200 credit.

Cell

INCOME-SPLITTING FOR CALIFORNIA DOMESTIC PARTNERSHIPS

Private Letter Ruling 201021048

PRIVATE LETTER RULING 201021048
(May 5, 2010)

FACTS

Taxpayer uses the cash method of accounting and files federal income tax returns on a calendar year basis.

Since 1999, California law has granted certain civil and property rights to domestic partners who register their partnership with California. California has maintained a registry of domestic partnerships since 2000. On Date 1 (after 2000), Taxpayer and Domestic Partner registered with California as registered domestic partners by filing a Statement of Domestic Partnership. Their registration is still valid.

On September 19, 2003, California enacted Assembly Bill 205, the California Domestic Partner Rights and Responsibilities Act of 2003 (AB 205), adopting California Family Code (CFC) Section 297.5, which became effective on January 1, 2005. AB 205 significantly expanded the rights and obligations of persons entering into a California domestic partnership. In relevant part, CFC Section 297.5 provides as follows:

(a) Registered domestic partners shall have the same rights, protections, and benefits, and shall be subject to the same responsibilities, obligations, and duties under law, whether they derive from statutes, administrative regulations, court rules, government policies, common law, or any other provisions or sources of law, as are granted to and imposed upon spouses.

(e) To the extent that provisions of California law adopt, refer to, or rely upon, provisions of federal law in a way that otherwise would cause registered domestic partners to be treated differently than spouses, registered domestic partners shall be treated by California law as if federal law recognized a domestic partnership in the same manner as California law.

However, CFC section 297.5(g) provided that "[e]arned income may not be treated as community property for state income tax purposes."

On September 29, 2006, California enacted Senate Bill 1827. Senate Bill 1827, effective January 1, 2007, repealed CFC section 297.5(g), which provided that earned income was not to be treated as community property for state income tax purposes. Consequently, as of January 1, 2007, California treats the earned income of registered domestic partners as community property for both property law purposes and state income tax purposes.

Finally, California gives registered domestic partners the right to enter into agreements identical to premarital agreements between prospective spouses, to modify or avoid the application of the community property laws. Taxpayer and Domestic Partner have not entered into such an agreement.

LAW AND ANALYSIS

ISSUE #1

Whether Taxpayer must report on his individual federal income tax return one-half of the combined income that Taxpayer and Domestic Partner earn from the performance of personal services and one-half of the combined income derived from their community property assets.

Section 61(a)(1) of the Internal Revenue Code provides that gross income includes all income from whatever source derived including compensation for services, including fees, commissions, fringe benefits, and similar items.

Federal tax law generally respects state property law characterizations and definitions. U.S. v. Mitchell, 403 U.S. 190 (1971), Burnet v. Harmel, 287 U.S. 103 (1932). In Poe v. Seaborn, 282 U.S. 101 (1930), the Supreme Court held that for federal income tax purposes a wife owned an undivided one-half interest in the income earned by her husband in Washington, a community property state, and was liable for federal income tax on that one-half interest. Thus, the Court concluded that husband and wife must each report one-half of the community income on his or her separate return regardless of which spouse earned the income. U.S. v. Malcolm, 282 U.S. 792 (1931), applied the rule of *Poe v. Seaborn* to California's community property laws.

California community property law developed in the context of marriage and originally applied only to the property rights and obligations of spouses. The law operated to give each spouse an equal interest in each community asset, regardless of which spouse is the holder of record. d'Elia v. d'Elia, 58 Cal. App. 4th 415 (1997).

By 2007, California had extended *full community property treatment* to registered domestic partners. Applying the principle that federal law respects state law property characterizations, the federal tax treatment of community property should apply to California registered domestic partners. Consequently, Taxpayer, a registered domestic partner in California, must report one-half of the community income, whether received in the form of compensation for personal services or income from property, on his federal income tax return.

[The discussions of issues 2 and 3, relating to withholding tax credits and gift tax, are omitted.]

Notes and Questions

1. *Private letter rulings.* As explained in part C.5 of Chapter 1, a favorable private letter ruling may be relied upon only by the taxpayer who requested the ruling. The IRS must have been aware, however, that the issue addressed in this ruling is relevant to thousands of taxpayers, and the IRS must have anticipated that news of the ruling would reach many of those taxpayers. As a practical matter, then, it seems unlikely that the IRS will challenge taxpayers who take return positions consistent with the ruling — at least unless and until the IRS issues a contrary ruling. In the interests of sound tax administration, however, shouldn't the IRS either promulgate a regulation or issue a revenue ruling on the question addressed by this private letter ruling, so that all similarly situated taxpayers can rely on the regulation or revenue ruling?

2. *What's at stake?* As the ruling notes, *Poe v. Seaborn* is still good law. For federal income tax purposes, all income of a married couple living in a community property state (and not opting out of the community property regime) is taxed half to one spouse and half to the other. The allocation of income between spouses makes a practical difference only if the spouses do not file a joint return — a rather rare occurrence, because of the unfavorable §1(d) rate structure for married persons filing separately. But California domestic partners are not considered married for purposes of the federal income tax, and so file separate returns under the §1(c) tax rate schedule for unmarried taxpayers (or possibly under the §1(b) tax rate schedule for heads of households). Imagine a California domestic partnership in which one partner earns $200,000 and the other has no earnings. If the private letter ruling had taken the opposite position (that is, that the entire $200,000 is taxed to the partner who earned it) what would be the tax liability of the partner with the income? The answer depends on whether the earning partner is able to claim the nonearning partner as a dependent — which should be possible if the earning partner provides over half of the support of the nonearning partner. *See* §152(d)(1) and §152(d)(2)(H). If the earning partner was entitled to claim the nonearning partner as a dependent, the earning partner would also be eligible to use the head of household tax rate schedule of §1(b). The resulting tax, in 2011, would be $42,733.50.[19] If the earning partner cannot claim the nonearning partner as a dependent, the 2011 tax on the earning partner income under the §1(c) rate schedule for unmarried taxpayers would be $47,762.[20] What is the combined 2011 tax liability of the two partners under the private letter ruling, with each partner reporting $100,000 of income and filing under §1(c)? Each partner would have a tax liability of $18,957, for a combined liability of $37,914. The tax reduction produced by community property income-splitting is either nearly $5,000 or nearly $10,000 (depending on the resolution of the dependent issue).

---

19. This assumes the taxpayer claims a standard deduction of $8,500 and two exemptions totaling $7,400, and files under §1(b).

20. This assumes the taxpayer claims a standard deduction of $5,800 and one exemption of $3,700, and files under §1(c).

3. *Compared to a married couple.* What would be the 2011 tax liability of a one-earner married couple with income of $200,000? Filing a joint return under §1(a), they would have a tax bill of $38,749.50.[21] (They cannot do better — and in fact would do worse — filing separately, because they would be relegated to the unfavorable tax rate schedule of §1(d).) This is $835.50 *higher* than the combined tax liabilities of the domestic partners under the private letter ruling. The result is that the private letter ruling, by permitting the domestic partners to take advantage of the income-splitting of *Poe v. Seaborn* without being relegated to the unfavorable rate schedule of §1(d), provides better tax treatment for one-earner domestic partnerships than that provided to one-earner marriages. This is a surprising result, and would surely not be approved by many members of Congress. Is the ruling, nevertheless, clearly correct in its interpretation of the law as it currently stands?

4. *Who can take advantage?* As the preceding Note explains, many one-earner California marriages would have lower federal tax liabilities if they converted from marriages to domestic partnerships. California domestic partnership law, however, provides the domestic partnership option only for same-sex couples, and for opposite-sex couples in which at least one of the partners is at least 62 years of age.

---

21. This assumes the taxpayers claim a standard deduction of $11,600 and two exemptions totaling $7,400, and file under §1(a).

822

Cell

WHEN IS A TRANSFER "INCIDENT TO THE DIVORCE"?

Craven v. United States

In the case of a transfer between former spouses, §1041 applies only if the transfer is "incident to the divorce." As the following case demonstrates, the courts have had some difficulty determining when a transfer is incident to a divorce. As we explain in the Notes following the *Craven* opinion below, the result in that case would be different under new Reg. §1.1041-2, promulgated in 2003. The opinion is included here because the decision and the regulation together illustrate a common evolutionary process in the interpretation of new tax statutes. When the process works well (as it did in this instance), the litigated cases serve to identify important ambiguities in the statute, and the Treasury is then able to resolve the ambiguities by regulation.[22]

CRAVEN v. UNITED STATES
215 F.3d 1201 (11th Cir. 2000)

CYNTHIA HOLCOMB HALL, Senior Circuit Judge: The United States appeals an order granting summary judgment in favor of Linda Craven ("Linda"). Linda had sued the Internal Revenue Service ("IRS") seeking a refund of certain proceeds she had received from her divorce settlement which she claimed were not taxable to her. . . .

I

The following facts are undisputed by both parties: Linda married Billy Joe Craven ("Billy Joe") in 1966. In 1971, the couple started their own pottery business, in which they both worked. In 1975, Billy Joe incorporated the business under the name of Craven Pottery, Inc. ("the corporation"). The corporation was formed with Billy Joe owning 51% of the stock, Linda owning 47% of the stock, and the remaining 2% being owned by their two children at 1% each respectively. Billy Joe became the corporation's president. . . .

In 1991, a divorce decree was entered into. This decree contained a settlement agreement between Billy Joe, Linda, and the corporation, and settled all matters

22. There are, of course, other possible outcomes. Sometimes courts are able to resolve the uncertainty on their own, sometimes Congress solves the problem by legislation, and sometimes the problem never gets solved.

between the parties. By terms of this agreement, Billy Joe and Linda agreed to divide their marital property. In relevant part, Linda agreed to sell to the corporation, and the corporation agreed to buy, her stock pursuant to a consent in lieu of special joint meetings of directors and shareholders of the corporation. The divorce was the sole reason for Linda's agreement to transfer the stock.

The corporation gave Linda a promissory note in the face amount of $4.8 million for her stock. Billy Joe guaranteed the note and expressly acknowledged that its terms were of "direct interest, benefit and advantage" to him. . . .

Four prepayments of the note were made, the first by Billy Joe in 1991 and the remaining three prepayments by the corporation in 1992, 1993, and 1998. Linda . . . filed disclosure statements taking the position that the redemption qualified for nonrecognition under 26 U.S.C. sec. 1041. . . .

After an audit, the IRS determined that the redemption did not qualify for nonrecognition treatment under sec. 1041 and that, consequently, Linda had capital gains based on the principal of the prepayments on the note. . . . Linda paid the resulting tax and interest due, filed a timely claim for refund, and after that claim was denied, sued for the refund in federal district court. . . .

The central issue of this case is whether Linda can avoid recognition of gain on the redemption of her stock in Craven's Pottery, Inc. in accordance with a property settlement incident to a divorce.

The income tax consequences that would normally ensue from this transaction are clear when sec. 1041 does not apply. Where a redemption of stock completely terminates the shareholder's interest in the corporation, the Internal Revenue Code treats the redemption as a sale of stock. *See* 26 U.S.C. secs. 302(a) & (b)(3). The amount by which the payment of principal received by the shareholder from the sale of the stock exceeds the taxpayer's basis in the stock constitutes gain, which is ordinarily taxed as capital gain. *See* 26 U.S.C. sec. 1001(a). . . . Section 1041 was enacted as a response to the Supreme Court case of United States v. Davis, 370 U.S. 65 (1962). In that case, a husband owned 1,000 shares of stock in the du Pont company, which he transferred to his wife as part of a divorce settlement. In return, she relinquished her marital rights in the stock, including a right of intestate succession; her interest in the stock was governed by the law of Delaware, which is not a community property state. The value of the stock at the time of transfer exceeded the husband's basis therein. The Supreme Court had "no doubt" that Congress intended that the appreciation or "economic growth" in the stock be taxed. *See id.* at 68. Rather, the question was whether the transfer from husband to wife was an appropriate occasion for triggering the tax:

> The problem confronting us is simply *when* is such accretion to be taxed. Should the economic gain be presently assessed against . . . [the husband], or should this assessment await a subsequent transfer of the property by the wife?

Id. (emphasis in the original). The husband argued that the conveyance should occasion no tax to him, invoking the principle that a division of jointly owned or community property is not a taxable event. But after examining Delaware law, the Supreme Court concluded that the wife's inchoate marital rights in the stock did not rise to the level of making her a co-owner. The Court held that the transfer was a taxable event, generating gain to the husband. In addition, the Court ruled that the wife acquired a stepped-up basis in the stock equal to such fair market value. *See id.* at 69.

Davis spawned considerable controversy and litigation, in part because the Court's opinion left open the possibility that the tax consequences of a divorce settlement might be different in a community property jurisdiction, or even in a common law jurisdiction that (unlike Delaware) treated spouses as co-owners of marital property. Congress entered the field in 1984, enacting sec. 1041 to modify the rules of *Davis*. . . .

Section 1041 provides a broad rule of nonrecognition for sales, gifts, and other transfers of property between one spouse (or former spouse) and another. It provides in relevant part, that:

> No gain or loss shall be recognized on a transfer of property from an individual to (or in trust for the benefit of) —
>   (1) a spouse, or
>   (2) a former spouse, but only if the transfer is incident to the divorce.

26 U.S.C. sec. 1041. Thus, the provision is not limited to transfers in divorce, but also applies to conveyances between spouses who are not contemplating divorce. Under sec. 1041(b), property received in a transfer subject to sec. 1041 is excluded from the recipient's gross income as if it were a gift, even if the transfer is a cash sale or is made without donative intent as part of a contested divorce. The recipient takes a "carryover" basis for the property equal to the transferor's basis, even if it exceeds the value of the property at the time of the transfer.

Shortly after the enactment of sec. 1041, the Treasury department published a temporary regulation, which is still in effect, to provide guidance to taxpayers. The Ninth Question of 26 C.F.R. sec. 1.1041-1T, which is relevant to the present appeal, states in pertinent part:

> Q-9 May transfers of property to third parties on behalf of a spouse (or former spouse) qualify under sec. 1041?
>
> A-9 Yes. There are three situations in which a transfer of property to a third party on behalf of a spouse (or former spouse) will qualify under sec. 1041. . . . The first situation is where the transfer to the third party is required by a divorce or separation instrument. The second situation is where the transfer to the third party is pursuant to the written request of the other spouse (or former spouse). The third situation is where the transferor receives from the other spouse (or former spouse) a written consent or ratification of the transfer to the third party. . . . In the three situations described above, the transfer of property will be treated as made directly to the nontransferring spouse (or former spouse) and the nontransferring spouse will be treated as immediately transferring the property to the third party. The deemed transfer from the nontransferring spouse (or former spouse) to the third party is not a transaction that qualifies for nonrecognition of gain under sec. 1041.

An example of such an occurrence is where the husband owes a debt to a bank, and the wife, as part of the divorce settlement, transfers appreciated stock of her own directly to the bank in discharge of husband's debt. Such a transfer would fall within the first "situation" described in the regulation, i.e., the transfer would be one "required by a divorce or separation instrument" and would be treated as made by the wife "on behalf of" the husband. Therefore, the stock would be deemed to go first from wife to husband in a nonrecognition transaction covered by sec. 1041, with husband acquiring a carryover basis in the stock, and then from husband to the bank, which would trigger gain to husband measured by the excess of the discharged debt over the carryover basis. The effect of this would be to preserve the element of gain, but to shift the incidence of the tax from wife to husband, "on behalf of" whom wife made the transfer to the "third party" bank.

Linda contends that her transfer of stock qualified for nonrecognition treatment under sec. 1041 as interpreted in Temp. Reg. sec. 1.1041-1T(c). She argues that the transfer of the stock to the corporation was done pursuant to her divorce agreement and therefore was on behalf of her former spouse within the language and purposes of the temporary regulations. The IRS disputes that the transfer was "on behalf of" Billy Joe so as to come within the regulation and shield Linda from recognizing gain. It is undisputed that the transfer occurred incidental to the Cravens' divorce. Therefore, the central question is whether the transfer was made by Linda "on behalf" of Billy Joe. Linda offered the district court three main reasons, which the district court agreed with, for why sec. 1041 would apply to her redemption of the stock: (1) because Georgia law obligates the equal distribution of marital assets pursuant to a divorce agreement, Linda was obligated to redeem her stock to the corporation; (2) Billy Joe was the guarantor of the corporation's payments that were due on the note, and because Georgia law makes guarantors jointly and severally liable for any debts incurred on the note, her redemption of the stock was "on behalf" of Billy Joe; and (3) because the corporation is a closely held one where, after the redemption, Billy Joe owned 98% of the stock, Linda's transfer was, in effect, to her husband.

[The court discusses the judicial precedents concerning the application of sec. 1041 to stock redemptions in connection with divorce, paying particular attention to Read v. Commissioner, 114 T.C. 14 (2000).—EDS.] As illustrated above, the meaning of the phrase "on behalf" reflects the notion that a transfer from *A* to *C* is treated for tax purposes as a transfer from *A* to *B* to *C*, when *A* is in fact transferring on behalf of *B* to *C*. . . . The facts of this case show that the transfer from Linda to the corporation squarely comports with this understood definition of "on behalf."

The three facts that place Linda within the framework outlined by the *Read* court are: (1) she was redeeming her stock pursuant to the divorce settlement; (2) Billy Joe guaranteed the note; and (3) in that note Billy Joe acknowledged that its terms were of "direct interest, benefit and advantage" to him. The first fact enumerated above would be enough on its own to qualify Linda's transfer to the corporation for nonrecognition under sec. 1041. The other two facts simply add strength to this conclusion. When the Cravens settled their divorce, they agreed to this redemption, and subscribed to a document that obligated Linda to transfer her stock to the corporation. In so doing, Linda was acting "on behalf" of Billy Joe because the divorce settlement reflected Billy Joe's wishes on the matter. . . .

We hold that the proceeds of Linda's transfer to the corporation fit within the terms outlined by sec. 1041 and Q&A 9, and therefore qualify for nonrecognition. This holding follows the rationale behind the adoption of sec. 1041 because it "facilitates the division of a marital estate incident to divorce without taxation to the spouse who is withdrawing assets from the marital estate." *See Read* at 42 (Colvin, J., concurring). As such, Congress' stated purpose of broadly applying sec. 1041 to transactions between divorcing spouses incident to their divorce is properly served.

Notes and Questions

1. *The need for certainty.* Imagine a situation like the hypothetical described by the court in *Craven*, in which former *W* transfers appreciated property to a creditor of former *H*, in satisfaction of *H*'s debt. If §1041 applies to the transfer (as the court says it would), then *W* is not taxed on the appreciation, but *H* is taxed. He is treated as if he received the property in a §1041 transfer from *W*, and then used the property to pay his creditor. If §1041 did *not* apply to the transfer, then W would be taxed on the appreciation (under *Davis*), but *H* would not be. *H* would still be treated as having received the property from *W* and as having used it to pay his creditor, but he would have a §1012 basis in the stock equal to its value at the time of the transfer. In this sort of situation, it makes no difference to the IRS whether or not §1041 applies, so long as *H* and *W* are in the same capital gains tax bracket. It should not even matter to *H* and *W* whether §1041 applies, as long as it is *clear* which of them owes the tax. If the tax result is certain, they can adjust the amount of transfers between them to take into account the nominal incidence of the tax. If the law is not clear, however, the parties cannot adjust the amount of transfers to reflect the incidence of the tax. It is important, then, that the parties be able to determine with reasonable certainty whether or not §1041 will apply to a particular transaction. Until the promulgation in 2003 of Reg. §1.1041-2 (described *infra* in Note 3), the law was far from clear concerning when §1041 would apply in *Craven*-type stock redemption situations. The uncertainty was well illustrated by the Tax Court's *en banc* opinion in *Read*. Of the 16 tax-specialist judges involved in *Read*, nine thought §1041 applied and seven dissented. The most upsetting situation for the IRS resulted from the application of different interpretations of §1041 to the same facts by two different courts, with the result that neither ex-spouse was taxed on the stock redemption. *See* Arnes v. United States, 981 F.2d 456 (9th Cir. 1992) (regarding the tax treatment of the former wife); Arnes v. Commissioner, 102 T.C. 522 (1994) (regarding the tax treatment of the former husband).

2. *The tax stakes.* Of course, the IRS will not be indifferent as to whether or not §1041 applies if the parties are in different tax brackets. In the case of stock redemptions, whether or not §1041 applies may also determine whether the redemption is taxed as a sale (with basis recovery and favorable capital gains tax rates) or as a dividend (also taxed at capital gains rates through 2010, but with no basis recovery). Under §302, a redemption that terminates a taxpayer's interest in a corporation is generally taxed as a sale, but a redemption that leaves a taxpayer still owning a majority of the stock of the corporation is taxed as a dividend. If the court had held that §1041 did not apply to Linda Craven, the redemption of the stock from Linda would have terminated her interest in the corporation, and so would have been taxed as a sale. The court's holding—that §1041 did apply—implies that Billy Joe Craven should be treated as having received Linda's stock in a §1041 transfer, and as then having had the stock redeemed from him by the corporation. *That* redemption is taxed as a dividend, because Billy Joe remains in control of the corporation after the redemption.

3. *Treasury to the rescue.* In response to the confusion created by the cases involving §1041 and stock redemptions, in 2003 the Treasury promulgated

Reg. §1.1041-2. Under the new regulation, §1041 applies to a divorce-related stock redemption in only two situations: (1) if the nontransferor spouse (Billy Joe) also owns stock in the redeeming corporation, and the nontransferor spouse had a "primary and unconditional obligation" to purchase the stock owned by the transferor spouse (Linda), or (2) the spouses jointly elect to have §1041 apply. If the redemption involves neither of these situations, then §1041 does not apply, with the result that the tax consequences follow the form of the transaction (i.e., the taxed spouse is the spouse whose stock is redeemed). There was no indication in *Craven* that Billy Joe had a "primary and unconditional obligation" to purchase Linda's stock, so the new regulation produces the opposite result from *Craven* on identical facts (barring a joint election by the spouses to have §1041 apply). The regulation represents a significant advance over the case law, but not because the result under the regulation (taxation of Linda) is inherently superior to the *Craven* result (taxation of Billy Joe). Rather, the regulation is an improvement because it supplies a reasonably clear rule, which the parties can rely on in planning their transactions. As Justice Brandeis observed in an income tax case long ago, "[I]n most matters it is more important that the applicable rule of law be settled than that it be settled right." Burnet v. Coronado Oil & Gas Co., 285 U.S. 393, 406 (1932) (Brandeis, J., dissenting).

Cell

THE EARNED INCOME TAX CREDIT AND PROBLEMS OF ANTI-POVERTY PROGRAM DESIGN

A. THE EITC AND MARGINAL TAX RATES

In combination with the standard deduction, the personal and dependency exemptions, and the income tax rates of §1 of the Code, the EITC produces a strange collection of marginal tax rates. Consider a single parent with two qualifying children. Using the inflation adjustments for 2011, the first $19,600 of her earnings will be sheltered from income tax by the head-of-household standard deduction ($8,500) and three exemptions ($3,700 each). The §1 tax rate on the next $12,150 (the first $12,150 of taxable income) will be 10 percent, and the §1 rate on the $34,100 after that will be 15 percent. Under the EITC, the tax rate on the first $12,780 of earnings is *negative* 40 percent, the tax rate on earnings between $12,780 and $16,690 is zero, and the tax rate between $16,690 and

$40,964 (i.e., over the phaseout range) is 21.06 percent. Combining the EITC with the standard deduction, the personal exemptions, and the §1 rates produces the marginal rate structure set forth in the table below.

Earned Income	EITC/Income Tax Marginal Tax Rate
$0-$12,780	-40%
$12,780-$16,690	0%
$16,690-$19,600	21.06%
$19,600-$31,750	31.06%
$31,750-$40,964	36.06%
$40,964-$65,850	15%

The troubling aspect of this, of course, is the high marginal rates — over 30 percent — that the combination of the §1 rates and the EITC 21.06 percent phaseout rate imposes between about $20,000 and $40,000 of earned income. This is sometimes described as a marginal tax rate "bubble," since the marginal tax rate drops after the phaseout is completed. Adding the 7.65 percent federal payroll tax and a state income tax in the neighborhood of 5 or 6 percent, workers in this wage range — just struggling to enter the middle class — are faced with a combined marginal tax rate of around 50 percent. Some amelioration of these high marginal rates is provided by the partial refundability of the §24 child tax credit.[23]

Problem 1. Jane is a single mother with two young children. She has a part-time job at a supermarket, which pays $20,000 per year. The supermarket has just offered her the chance to increase her weekly hours, which would increase her annual earnings to $27,000. If she accepts the offer, how much of her additional $7,000 of wages will she be able to keep, after taking into account both the EITC and the §1 tax rates? (Disregard the child tax credit, the federal payroll tax, and state income tax.)

Problem 2. Carla is a single mother with two young children. She is currently unemployed and living with her parents, who have been supporting her and her children. She has an offer of a full-time (40 hours a week) job at a supermarket, paying $10 per hour. If she accepts the offer, how much of her $20,000 wages will she be able to keep, after taking into account both the EITC and the §1 tax rates? (Disregard the child tax credit, the federal payroll tax, and state income tax.)

In addition to providing some practice in working with the EITC rules, the Problems illustrate that whether the high marginal tax rates created by the phaseout discourage work depends on the nature of the decision a particular taxpayer is facing. In Problem 1, where Jane's decision is between earning $20,000 and $27,000, the effect of the EITC is to *reduce* substantially the after-tax return from the additional work, and this may cause Jane to decide not to take on the extra hours. In Problem 2, where Carla's decision is between earning nothing and $20,000, the effect of the EITC is to *increase* significantly the after-tax return from taking the job. To use some economics jargon, Jane is making a decision at

23. See section A.2.b of Chapter 9.

the *intensive margin,* where the work disincentive effect of the phase out operates. Carla, by contrast, is making her decision at the *extensive margin,* so she simply views the EITC as a benefit equal to her net credit amount. If her decision is that "lumpy"—between earning nothing and $20,000—it will not matter to her that the amount of her EITC is arrived at by a set of calculations including a phaseout. All that will matter is the bottom line, and for her the EITC bottom line is a work incentive, not a disincentive. In short, not every taxpayer whose earned income ends up in the phaseout range has in fact been subject to the work disincentive effect of the phaseout. Taxpayers making decisions at the intensive margin will have been subject to that effect, but taxpayers making decisions at the extensive margin will not have been.

No one really knows whether the overall effect of the EITC is to encourage paid labor, to discourage it, or neither. Like any tax or subsidy, the EITC will have two different kinds of effects on work effort. First, there is an *income effect.* This simply means that the more income (or wealth) one has, the less one is inclined to work.[24] Since the EITC always increases the disposable income of an EITC recipient (even if the amount of the credit is reduced by the phaseout), the income effect of the EITC will discourage work effort, although the strength of the effect is far from clear. Second, there is the *substitution effect.* All else being equal, people will work more hours when their wage rate is higher and fewer hours when it is lower. The substitution effect encourages work effort for taxpayers making work decisions within the phasein range of the EITC, where the effect of the credit is to increase after-tax wages. As explained above, the substitution effect of the EITC encourages work effort even for taxpayers who end up with income in the phaseout range, if they made their decisions at the extensive margin. On the other hand, the substitution effect discourages work effort for taxpayers who have earned income in the phaseout range and are making decisions at the intensive margin. In sum, the income effect of the EITC discourages work effort, and the substitution effect of the EITC sometimes encourages and sometimes discourages work effort. No one is sure of the relative strengths of these effects, or whether the net result is more or less work.

The above analysis of incentives and disincentives assumes that workers understand the EITC, so they can take it into account in making their labor supply decisions. It may be that the credit is so complicated that its effects are a mystery to many low income workers. What if Jane, in Problem 1, fails to consider the effect of the EITC phaseout in deciding whether to work the extra hours? Purely from the point of view of economic efficiency, that would be a good thing. Jane would not be discouraged from working by a tax she did not realize existed. However, there is a fairness cost to achieving the efficiency gain. If Jane made her decision to work the extra hours under the reasonable misapprehension that her federal income tax rate was only 10 percent, it may be unfair to increase her rate to over 31 percent by means of a stealth tax.

---

24. This is not true for every person, under any and all circumstances. Some people so enjoy their work that they would continue doing it without compensation, if necessary. But, in general, people prefer leisure to work, and will substitute the former for the latter to the degree that they can afford to do so.

B. THE ACCURACY OF EITC DELIVERY: CHEATING AND NONPARTICIPATION

TREASURY INSPECTOR GENERAL FOR TAX ADMINISTRATION, THE EARNED INCOME TAX CREDIT PROGRAM HAS MADE ADVANCES; HOWEVER, ALTERNATIVES TO TRADITIONAL COMPLIANCE METHODS ARE NEEDED TO STOP BILLIONS OF DOLLARS IN ERRONEOUS PAYMENTS

(December 31, 2008)

BACKGROUND

. . .

The Internal Revenue Service (IRS) is charged with administration of the EITC, which includes developing strategies to improve the EITC Program, managing the Program's outcomes, and coordinating activities of support functions within the IRS. In 2003, the IRS established a centralized function, the EITC Program Office, to oversee administration of the Program. The mission of the Program Office is to ensure that all eligible individuals receive the EITC, while reducing the number of erroneous EITC claims. To accomplish its mission, the EITC Program Office coordinates with multiple functions within the IRS, including those involving tax return processing, communication and media relations, electronic tax administration, and compliance.

Although participation and dollars claimed have continued to increase, the EITC Program continues to be vulnerable to a high rate of noncompliance, including incorrect or erroneous claims for the EITC caused by taxpayer error and resulting from fraud. For example:

— In February 2002, the IRS estimated that between $8.5 billion and $9.9 billion (27 percent to 32 percent) of the $31.3 billion in EITC claims made by taxpayers in Tax Year (TY) 1999 should not have been paid.
— In 2005, the IRS estimated that between $9.6 billion and $11.4 billion (23 percent to 28 percent) of the $41.3 billion in EITC claims paid for TY 2004 returns were paid in error. . . .

THE IRS CONTINUES TO FACE CHALLENGES IN IMPROVING THE EITC PROGRAM

EITC eligibility rules are complicated and cause taxpayers to make errors while attempting to interpret and apply the tax laws to their individual situations. An analysis performed by the National Taxpayer Advocate identified that many low-income taxpayers struggle to determine their eligibility for the EITC. Some taxpayers lack an understanding of the eligibility issues related to family status, such as the dependency exemption and Head of Household filing status.

In addition, the changing population of taxpayers who claim the EITC increases the difficulty the IRS faces in improving EITC compliance. The IRS has conducted numerous studies showing how taxpayers move in and out of the EITC Program and has plans to conduct more. [A]pproximately one-third of EITC claimants each year are intermittent or first-time claimants.

A large part of EITC compliance depends on the taxpayers' understanding of the EITC eligibility rules and how to properly claim the Credit. In programs with a stable population, compliance should improve as more taxpayers become familiar with program rules. However, EITC rules are frequently revised as a result of changes to the tax law. The ever-changing EITC population and changes in eligibility requirements reduce the effectiveness of the IRS' education and outreach efforts because the IRS must continually educate new claimants. . . .

RESULTS OF REVIEW

. . . [T]he IRS established two long-term goals for the [administration of the EITC] Program: 1. Increasing Program participation. 2. Reducing erroneous payments. These goals relate directly to the mission of the EITC Program Office. However, processes have not been developed to consistently measure progress in meeting these goals, and methodologies used to measure EITC compliance were inconsistent, resulting in the inability to compare yearly results. Although the IRS does not have a process to consistently measure progress in increasing participation, indicators show that improvements have been made. Specifically, the IRS has implemented a number of initiatives that appear to have resulted in increases to the numbers of (1) taxpayers who claim the EITC from year to year and (2) new EITC claimants from one year to the next.

In addition, the IRS has established a number of processes to identify and prevent the issuance of erroneous EITC payments. However, resource constraints prevent the IRS from making any significant impact on stopping the billions of dollars in erroneous payments identified by these processes annually.

. . .

THE IRS HAD NOT ESTABLISHED A CONSISTENT METHOD TO MEASURE EITC PARTICIPATION AND COMPLIANCE

The IRS had not developed a consistent method to quantify its progress in meeting its two Program goals. The inability to measure progress in meeting these goals results from delays in obtaining necessary data and inconsistent measurement methods. The IRS has since developed a methodology that it believes will allow it to consistently measure its progress in meeting Program goals once the needed data are available. The IRS plans to be able to report on Program participation late in 2008 and reducing erroneous payments in 2009. . . .

Although the IRS is unable to measure the increase in EITC participation and the reduction in erroneous payments, indicators show some increase in EITC participation and the development of processes to successfully identify billions of dollars in potentially erroneous EITC payments.

INDICATORS SHOW SOME INCREASE IN EITC PARTICIPATION

. . .

The IRS recognizes that the EITC-eligible population is constantly changing and has developed a strategic research plan to gain a better understanding of taxpayers' movement within the EITC Program. These projects will be useful in identifying new areas in which the IRS can focus its continued efforts to improve EITC participation. Projects include updating and analyzing trends for return characteristics and behavioral trends of EITC filers to determine why taxpayers move in and out of the EITC claimant population. Further, the IRS has initiated a number of actions to increase EITC participation, including:

— Partnering to conduct outreach with more than 300 coalitions, which represent hundreds of nonprofit organizations, financial institutions, and government agencies. These coalitions conduct their own local EITC outreach through direct mail and media efforts.
— Holding an annual National EITC Awareness Day to create national awareness of the EITC and educate the diverse EITC population. Actions include public appearances by members of Congress and key IRS executives to discuss the benefits of the EITC and focused assistance at IRS Taxpayer Assistance Centers.
— Improving information and tools available on the IRS web site (IRS.gov) to provide assistance to taxpayers, tax preparers, and the IRS EITC partners. For example, the IRS has updated the EITC Assistant, the EITC Electronic Toolkit for Tax Preparers, and the Electronic Toolkit for EITC Partners and has launched EITC Marketing Express.
— Providing key EITC Program information during annual Nationwide Tax Forums. Presentations were made to 14,800 tax preparers nationwide in 2007.
— Sending computer-generated notices proactively to taxpayers who file tax returns and appear to be eligible for the EITC but did not claim the Credit. For example, the IRS sent more than 650,000 notices based on information reported on TY 2006 returns.

**PROCESSES HAVE BEEN DEVELOPED TO SUCCESSFULLY IDENTIFY
BILLIONS OF DOLLARS IN ERRONEOUS EITC PAYMENTS**

Prior to 2004, the IRS focused on ways to identify EITC noncompliance. As a result, it has successfully developed a number of processes to identify erroneous EITC payments. All of the efforts listed below, except for document matching, are performed prior to issuance of a potentially erroneous EITC payment.

— Electronic Filing Filters—The IRS reviews electronically filed tax returns before they are accepted for processing to ensure that specific information on the tax returns is accurate. For example, filters verify whether a valid Social Security Number (SSN) is present for each qualifying child being claimed for the EITC. Tax returns that do not have a valid SSN are rejected to the taxpayer for correction.

- Math Error—Congress authorized the IRS to correct certain mathematical or clerical errors on a tax return without opening an audit. This authority was later expanded to allow the IRS to adjust or disallow the EITC when a valid SSN is missing for a child claimed for the EITC or when earned income is above the maximum level for the EITC.
- Dependent Database Audits—The Dependent Database is made up of a collection of information databases that include birth certificate information and court documents used to establish a relationship and residency between the taxpayer and the qualifying children claimed on the tax return. Taxpayers must meet a relationship and a residency test to claim the EITC for the qualifying children listed on the tax return. Tax returns with an EITC claim are processed through the Dependent Database when the tax return is filed. . . . Two of the primary sources of information included in the Dependent Database are the Social Security Administration KIDLINK and the Department of Health and Human Services Federal Case Registry. The KIDLINK database includes birth records that associate the name and SSN of the birth parents with the name and SSN of the child. The Federal Case Registry is a collection of information provided by the States that includes divorce decrees and other child custody orders established in the United States court system.
- EITC Recertification Audits—Because of the potential EITC compliance problems, Congress passed legislation requiring taxpayers who had the EITC denied during examinations to prove eligibility before receiving the EITC again. The IRS initiated the EITC Recertification Program to implement this legislation and to address the compliance issues. If a taxpayer does not provide adequate support to prove that he or she is entitled to receive the EITC during an examination, the IRS will deny the EITC and place a "recertification" indicator on the taxpayer's account. This indicator prevents the taxpayer from receiving the EITC until the taxpayer can prove he or she is entitled to receive the Credit. Once the taxpayer provides the IRS Examination function with supporting documentation to prove that he or she is entitled to receive the EITC, the IRS will remove the recertification indicator from the taxpayer's account and issue the EITC. The IRS refers to this process as "recertification." These audits are conducted prior to payment of the EITC claim.
- Document Matching—Subsequent to the filing and processing of tax returns containing an EITC claim, the IRS matches third-party information documents to information reported on the tax return to identify unreported or underreported income that—if included on the tax return—would reduce the amount of EITC a taxpayer is entitled to.

Implementation of the above enforcement tools has protected billions of dollars in EITC revenue.

   . . .

ALTERNATIVES TO TRADITIONAL COMPLIANCE METHODS ARE NEEDED TO REDUCE THE BILLIONS OF DOLLARS IN IDENTIFIED ERRONEOUS EARNED INCOME TAX CREDIT PAYMENTS

The IRS continues to report that $10 billion to $12 billion in erroneous EITC payments are issued each year. Compliance resources are limited and additional alternatives to traditional compliance methods have not been developed, resulting in the majority of the potentially erroneous EITC claims identified being paid in error. . . .

IRS management recognizes the limitations faced in significantly reducing noncompliance using the traditional process of auditing tax returns. The IRS Commissioner stated that he did not believe that the IRS could audit its way to full compliance and needed to drive for innovation in its enforcement efforts. . . .

Although the IRS has developed better ways to identify EITC noncompliance, it has not pursued additional alternatives to address the identified potentially erroneous EITC claims. For example, the IRS has spent millions of dollars developing probability filters to improve its selection of cases for audit using information contained in the Dependent Database. These filters [help] to determine the likelihood that an EITC claim is in fact erroneous. Use of probabilities allows the IRS to maximize the benefit gained from its examination resources by working the most productive audits. By combining the use of probability filters with external data included in the Dependent Database, the IRS increased its EITC audit change rate from 89.7 percent on TY 2004 tax returns to 93.9 percent on TY 2005 tax returns. . . .

To address erroneous EITC claims, the IRS conducts audits and, in some limited situations, uses math error processing. For example, the IRS has the authority to address EITC claims with an invalid SSN. When this condition is identified, the IRS can systemically adjust the amount being claimed for the EITC to disallow all or a portion of the EITC claim based on identification of the invalid SSN. . . .

If further expansion of the math error authority is not possible to cover cases identified using probability filters, the IRS needs to develop alternative processes that are less costly than an audit to protect revenue associated with erroneous EITC claims. These alternatives might require legislative changes. The IRS should work with the Assistant Secretary of the Treasury for Tax Policy to obtain legislative authority for an improved process that can make use of its success in combining external data with probability filters. If the IRS does not move beyond traditional compliance methods, it will be unable to significantly reduce the amount of erroneous EITC payments, which is estimated to be $10 billion to $12 billion annually. As technology and data sharing among Federal Government agencies improve, the IRS must continually evaluate its ability to ensure that taxpayers are filing accurate tax returns and paying the correct amount of tax. . . .

Notes and Questions

1. *Encouraging participation and discouraging cheating.* The Report describes a distressing level of inaccuracy in the delivery of the EITC. Erroneous EITC payments total $10 billion to $12 billion annually. At the same time, many persons entitled to the credit fail to claim it. The EITC enforcement efforts of the IRS may be hampered by the fact that the IRS has little experience in dealing with people who cheat on their taxes by overstating their actual income. Consider the following problem.

Problem 3. You are an IRS agent auditing the tips reported by the employees of a large restaurant. You notice that one waiter, who received wages of only $3,000, reported receiving $7,000 of tips. No other waiter or waitress reported receiving tips equal to more than one-third of wages. Have you discovered the world's most honest taxpayer, or do you have suspicions of wrongdoing?

C. THE EITC AND MARRIAGE PENALTIES AND BONUSES

The following two Problems demonstrate that the EITC, in its current form, produces both marriage penalties and marriage bonuses. Are these marriage effects objectionable? If so, is there a way to redesign the credit to avoid marriage effects such as those illustrated by the Problems?

Problem 4. Joe, who has earned income of $16,000 and two qualifying children, marries Sara, who also has earned income of $16,000 and two qualifying children. What is the effect of their marriage on the size of their EITC?

Problem 5. Betty, who has $16,000 of earned income and no qualifying children, marries Bob, who has no earned income but two qualifying children. Does marriage increase or decrease their EITC?

D. THE EXCESSIVE INVESTMENT INCOME RULES

To answer the following problem, you will need to look at the "excessive investment income" rules of §32(i). What seems to be the policy behind these rules? Do you agree with that policy, and do you agree that the rules of §32(i) are the best way to effectuate that policy?

Problem 6. Dan has one qualifying child, and his earned income last year was $16,000. He is not a low wage worker, but he was unemployed for much of last year. He owns about $50,000 of corporate bonds, which produced $3,500 of taxable interest income last year. Determine the amount of the EITC to which Dan is entitled for last year. Would your answer be any different if, instead of owning $50,000 of corporate bonds paying $3,500 taxable interest, Dan owned $50,000 of municipal bonds paying $3,000 interest?

E. ALTERNATIVES TO THE EITC: FOUR BASIC MODELS OF CASH TRANSFER PROGRAMS

In designing a cash transfer program, a fundamental question is how (if at all) the amount of the transfer should vary based on recipients' incomes. The EITC reflects decisions that (1) the amount of the transfer should be positively associated with the amount of earned income at very low earnings levels, and (2) as earnings increase to moderate levels, the transfer amount should be decreased and eventually eliminated. Neither of these choices is inevitable. The alternative to the first choice is not to condition eligibility for the cash transfer on the existence of earned income. Under this alternative (sometimes referred to as the "demogrant" approach), even a person with no earned income would be eligible for a cash grant in some specified amount, and the amount of the grant would not increase as earned income rose above zero. The alternative to the second choice, of course, is not to phaseout eligibility for the grant as income increases above the poverty level.

Thus, there are two basic decisions to be made in designing a cash transfer program: (1) between a demogrant and a subsidy based on the existence and amount of earned income; and (2) between a grant available only to the poor and near-poor, and a grant available even to persons with moderate or high levels or income. Either choice on the first issue can be combined with either choice on the second issue, so four basic designs are possible, as illustrated in the table below.

	Credit Eligibility Based on Earned Income	**Credit Available Even to Non-Earners**
Credit phased out	**Type 1 program:** credit phased in with earned income, credit phased out as earned income increases above the poverty level (e.g., the EITC)	**Type 2 program:** cash grant (available even to those with no earned income), phased out as earned income increases above some specified low level (e.g., traditional welfare)
Credit not phased out	**Type 3 program:** credit phased in with earned income, credit never phased out	**Type 4 program:** demogrant (available even to those with no earned income), never phased out

As the table indicates, the EITC and traditional welfare are familiar examples of the two types of phased-out transfer programs.[25] There are no familiar examples in the United States, however, of either type of non-phased-out transfer program. The discussion below briefly describes some of the factors to consider in making the two basic design decisions.

Demogrant versus subsidy only to those with earned income. From the standpoint of targeting antipoverty transfers where the need is greatest, the phasein of the EITC—as contrasted with a demogrant—is perverse. A single parent with two

---

25. When most people think about differences between traditional welfare and the EITC, they probably focus on the difference between administration by welfare system bureaucrats and administration by tax system bureaucrats. Although that is certainly an important difference, the even more fundamental difference is that the EITC is available only to persons with earned income, whereas having earned income is not a condition of eligibility for traditional welfare. The current choices of administrators for each type of program are not inevitable. It would certainly be possible to have a Type 2 program administered by the IRS. Similarly, a Type 1 program administered by a welfare agency might be feasible.

children and no income is obviously in greater need than a single parent with two children and $10,000 earned income, yet the EITC gives nothing to the first parent and $4,000 to the second. What could possibly justify designing the subsidy so that it is, at the lowest income levels, *inversely* related to need? The explanation must be that Congress was troubled by the significant work disincentive effect of a demogrant. As explained in section A of this cell, the income effect of any cash transfer will be to decrease work effort. During the phasein range, the substitution effect of the EITC counteracts the income effect,[26] making the net effect of the EITC on work effort uncertain. By contrast, the effect of a demogrant on work effort is clearly to discourage it. Whether the better incentive effects of the EITC justify its less attractive distributional effects depends partly on the strength of the income and substitution effects, and partly on value judgments about the relative importance of providing well-targeted poverty relief versus not discouraging work effort. Notice that this does not have to be an either-or question; it would be possible to have both a demogrant and a phased-in credit based on earned income. Under such a system, even a person with no earned income would receive the demogrant, but a person with earned income would be entitled to both the demogrant and an earned income credit.

Phased-out benefit versus benefit available at all income levels. The high marginal tax rates caused by the phaseout of the EITC are perhaps the most troubling aspect of the credit. It is inefficient, and arguably unfair as well, to impose combined marginal tax rates approaching 50 percent on taxpayers working hard to escape poverty and enter the middle class. Nevertheless, it is commonly assumed that the credit *must* be phased out, because otherwise middle income and high income taxpayers would benefit from a credit intended to help the working poor. Without a phaseout, even Bill Gates would be entitled to claim the EITC! On reflection, however, perhaps there is nothing wrong with allowing high income earners (even Bill Gates) to claim an earned income credit or a demogrant. The crucial step in the analysis is to view the credit (or demogrant) as a part of an integrated tax-and-transfer system, rather than as a freestanding program. Consider, for example, a system in which the first $10,000 of wages are eligible for a 20 percent EITC, and wages in excess of $10,000 are taxed at a flat rate of 25 percent, with no explicit phaseout of the credit. Even without an explicit phaseout, when wages reach $18,000 the credit will have been fully offset by $2,000 of tax. Those earning less than $18,000 receive a net transfer and those earning more pay a net tax. It is true that even a taxpayer who earns $110,000 (for example) is still entitled to calculate a $2,000 credit on his first $10,000 of wages, but there is nothing wrong with that so long as his net tax burden of $23,000 is deemed appropriate. The $110,000 earner is nominally entitled to the EITC, but the value of the credit has been taxed away — and then some — simply by the 25 percent tax rate, without the need for a special mar-ginal tax rate bubble on income slightly above the poverty level. If a $23,000 tax burden on $110,000 income is deemed insufficient, there is still no need to impose a high marginal rate bubble just above the poverty level; instead, simply impose a higher marginal tax rate on the *last* few tens of thousands of dollars of the high earner's income.

---

26. As explained earlier, this can be true even for a person whose actual income falls in the phaseout range of the credit, if the person made his labor supply decision at the extensive margin.

Chapter 10

IDENTIFYING THE PROPER TAXPAYER

A. INTRODUCTION

Reread the Supreme Court's opinion in *Lucas v. Earl*, which is set forth in the material on the income taxation of married couples in Chapter 9.B. The government and the taxpayer agreed on the amount of income to be taxed and on the year in which the income should be taxed. The only question was the identity of the proper taxpayer. Given Mr. Earl's anticipatory assignment of half of his earned income to Mrs. Earl, should Mrs. Earl's share be taxed to Mr. Earl because he earned it or to Mrs. Earl because she was entitled to receive it? The question can be restated more broadly. When one person earns income but another person consumes the income (or saves it for future consumption), should the tax be imposed on the earner or on the consumer? In *Lucas v. Earl*, one of the most important cases in the history of the income tax, the Supreme Court held that earned income must be taxed to the earner: The "fruits" may not be "attributed to a different tree from that on which they grew."

If everyone agrees on the amount to be included in income and on the timing of the inclusion, why does the identity of the taxpayer matter? Obviously, identity would be crucial if the question were whether some item of income should be taxed to you or to some stranger. Even if the IRS were indifferent to taxing you versus taxing the stranger (because it would collect the same amount of tax either way), you would much prefer that the tax be paid by the stranger. In practice, however, income attribution controversies are never like that. Instead, the controversies resemble *Lucas v. Earl*, in that the candidates for the status of the proper taxpayer are closely related individuals or entities with a commonality of economic interest. The Earls, for example, would probably not have cared who was taxed on Mrs. Earl's share of Mr. Earl's earnings, if the total amount of tax would have been the same either way. If the issue had been merely whether Mr. Earl or Mrs. Earl owed the IRS $10,000 tax on $50,000 income (for example), Mr. Earl almost certainly would not have bothered to litigate. Because of progressive marginal tax rates, however, the identification of the proper taxpayer may affect the amount of tax owed on the income in question. Mr. Earl had substantial other income (from his share of his own earnings and perhaps from investments) that had used up his lower tax brackets. When Mrs. Earl's $50,000 share of his earnings was taxed to him, it was stacked on top of that other income and thus was subject to high marginal tax rates. If Mrs. Earl had no income apart from the $50,000 at issue, the $50,000 would have been taxed to her at lower marginal tax rates (perhaps as low as zero), because her lower brackets would not have been used up by other income. To pull some numbers out of a hat, if Mr. Earl's marginal tax rate was 30 percent and Mrs. Earl's was 10 percent, and the amount of income at issue was $50,000, then the amount of tax liability at stake would have been $10,000 — the difference between the $15,000 tax (at 30%) on Mr. Earl and the $5,000 tax (at 10%) on Mrs. Earl.

In the typical income attribution case, the candidates for taxation are closely enough related that they do not care *who* pays the tax; they only care *how much* total tax must be paid, by whomever. It follows that income attribution is worth arguing about only in a tax system with progressive marginal tax rates, because only in such a system does the identity of the taxpayer affect the amount of tax owed. If all taxpayers were subject to a tax at a flat rate of 20 percent on all their income, then $50,000 income would have generated $10,000 tax liability for either Mr. or Mrs. Earl, and the great case of *Lucas v. Earl* would never have been litigated. It is worth noting, however, that income attribution issues would not be eliminated under the specific proposal known as *the* flat tax,[1] because that proposal (and any similarly realistic variant) actually has two rates: a zero tax bracket (an exemption amount) designed to protect subsistence income from tax, and a single ("flat") positive tax rate on all income above the exemption amount. Taxpayers would still have incentive to shift income from a taxpayer with no unused exemption amount to a taxpayer whose exemption amount had not been exhausted by other income.

Despite the very significant limitations imposed on income-shifting by *Lucas v. Earl* and its progeny, some opportunities remain (and are discussed below). A taxpayer's goal in the income-shifting game is to transfer the tax liability on an item of income to a related taxpayer in a lower bracket. That person may be in a lower bracket because she has little or no other income, because she is subject to a less burdensome tax rate schedule,[2] or both. Assuming a tax-effective income shift requires giving the lower bracket taxpayer a real economic interest in the income (as it generally does), income-shifting will be attractive only when the higher bracket taxpayer identifies closely with the financial interests of the taxpayer to whom the income is shifted. Despite the net tax savings, taxpayers in the 40 percent bracket would not be terribly interested in a rule that allowed them to reduce the tax bite on their income to 15 percent by making a gift of their income to a stranger in the 15 percent bracket. (The §170 deduction for charitable contributions can be viewed as allowing high bracket taxpayers to shift their income to taxpayers in the zero bracket by giving their income to charity; despite this opportunity, most high income taxpayers do not donate major portions of their earnings to charity.)

B.   EARNED INCOME

1.   The Basic Rules

So much for what is a stake in the income attribution game. What are the rules? As noted above, the basic rule for earned income is pretty simple. Earned income

---

1. Robert E. Hall & Alvin Rabushka, *The Flat Tax* (2d ed. 1995).
2. For example, compare the §1(c) tax rate schedule for most unmarried individuals with the less burdensome §1(b) tax rate schedule for heads of households. Of more practical importance, an individual may attempt to shift income to a controlled corporation to take advantage of the relatively low rates on the first $75,000 of corporate income (*see* §11). This possibility is discussed in section C.2.g of this chapter.

must be taxed to the earner, even if the earner is not also the consumer. The apple is attributed to owner of the tree, not to the person who comes to own, or ultimately eat, the apple. For example, the regulations on taxable fringe benefits (i.e., fringe benefits not excluded under §132 or any other exclusion provision) state:

> A taxable fringe benefit is included in the income of the person performing the services in connection with which the fringe benefit is furnished. Thus, a fringe benefit may be taxable to a person even though that person did not actually receive the fringe benefit. . . . For example, the provision of an automobile by an employer to an employee's spouse in connection with the performance of services by the employee is taxable to the employee.[3]

Recall the income tax treatment of gifts.[4] Section 102 excludes gifts from recipients' gross income, and there is no provision allowing a donor a deduction for gifts made. A different system is possible; gifts might be taxable to recipients and deductible by donors. Under that alternative system, however, a taxpayer could do an end run around *Lucas v. Earl* by making a gift of a portion of her earned income to a lower bracket relative. The taxpayer's entire earned income would still be included in her *gross* income, but the gift deduction would remove the gifted portion of her income from her *taxable* income, and the gift inclusion would shift the tax liability to her relative in a lower bracket. Thus, it was necessary for Congress to reject the donor-deduction, donee-inclusion treatment of gifts in order to protect the integrity of *Lucas v. Earl*.

Suppose you are an associate in a law firm, with an annual salary of $125,000. The firm bills clients (and succeeds in collecting) $500,000 for your services during the year. Are you the metaphorical tree with respect to that $500,000, so that under *Lucas v. Earl* you must pay tax on your $500,000 of billings, rather than on your $125,000 salary? Thankfully, the answer is clearly no.[5] The integrity of the progressive marginal tax rate structure is not threatened by arm's-length agreements between unrelated parties. Similarly, if two unrelated attorneys form a law partnership, and enter into an arm's-length agreement to share future profits 50-50, the partnership profits will be taxed according to the agreement. This would be true even if the firm's entire profits for the year were attributable to the efforts of only one of the partners (for example, because the other partner spent the entire year on an unsuccessful contingent fee case). On the other hand, what if a very successful attorney, with a track record of earning about $500,000 per year as a sole practitioner, forms a 50-50 law partnership with her son who has just graduated from law school? In light of the close family relationship, and the inconsistency between the 50-50 agreement and the very different income-producing abilities of the two partners, *Lucas v. Earl* will have a role to play in analyzing this partnership.

2.   *Exploring the Limits of the Doctrine: The Case of Contingent Attorneys' Fees*

The *Lucas v. Earl* doctrine is designed to police the shifting of earned income to family members and controlled entities; it is far from clear that it should have any

---

3. Reg. §1.61-21(a)(4)(i).
4. See section A.3.a of Chapter 2.
5. *See, e.g.,* Rev. Rul. 69-274, 1969-1 C.B. 36 (doctors who were employed as medical school professors were not taxable on Medicare payments received by their employer for services rendered by the doctors).

application to allocations of income pursuant to arms'-length agreements between unrelated taxpayers. Most of the time, as in the above example of the associate with $500,000 billings and a $150,000 salary, it is clear that *Lucas v. Earl* does not apply where unrelated taxpayers are involved. As the opinion set forth below demonstrates, however, some courts—including the Supreme Court—have invoked *Lucas v. Earl* in situations where it is of doubtful relevance.

COMMISSIONER v. BANKS
COMMISSIONER v. BANAITIS

543 U.S. 426 (2005)

Justice KENNEDY delivered the opinion of the Court.

The question in these consolidated cases is whether the portion of a money judgment or settlement paid to a plaintiff's attorney under a contingent-fee agreement is income to the plaintiff. The issue divides the courts of appeals. In one of the instant cases, Banks v. Commissioner, 345 F.3d 373 (2003), the Court of Appeals for the Sixth Circuit held the contingent-fee portion of a litigation recovery is not included in the plaintiff's gross income. The Courts of Appeals for the Fifth and Eleventh Circuits also adhere to this view. . . . In the other case under review, Banaitis v. Commissioner, 340 F.3d 1074 (2003), the Court of Appeals for the Ninth Circuit held that the portion of the recovery paid to the attorney as a contingent fee is excluded from the plaintiff's gross income if state law gives the plaintiff's attorney a special property interest in the fee, but not otherwise. Six Courts of Appeals have held the entire litigation recovery, including the portion paid to an attorney as a contingent fee, is income to the plaintiff. . . . We granted certiorari to resolve the conflict.

We hold that, as a general rule, when a litigant's recovery constitutes income, the litigant's income includes the portion of the recovery paid to the attorney as a contingent fee. We reverse the decisions of the Courts of Appeals for the Sixth and Ninth Circuits.

I

A. COMMISSIONER v. BANKS

In 1986, respondent John W. Banks, II, was fired from his job as an educational consultant with the California Department of Education. He retained an attorney on a contingent-fee basis and filed a civil suit against the employer in a United States District Court. The complaint alleged employment discrimination in violation of 42 U.S.C. §§1981 and 1983. The original complaint asserted various additional claims under state law, but Banks later abandoned these. After trial commenced in 1990, the parties settled for $464,000. Banks paid $150,000 of this amount to his attorney pursuant to the fee agreement.

Banks did not include any of the $464,000 in settlement proceeds as gross income in his 1990 federal income tax return. In 1997 the Commissioner of Internal Revenue issued Banks a notice of deficiency for the 1990 tax year. The Tax Court upheld the Commissioner's determination, finding that all the settlement proceeds, including the $150,000 Banks had paid to his attorney, must be included in Banks' gross income.

The Court of Appeals for the Sixth Circuit reversed in part. It agreed the net amount received by Banks was included in gross income but not the amount paid to the attorney. Relying on its prior decision in Estate of Clarks v. United States, 202 F.3d 854 (2000), the court held the contingent-fee agreement was not an anticipatory assignment of Banks' income because the litigation recovery was not already earned, vested, or even relatively certain to be paid when the contingent-fee contract was made. A contingent-fee arrangement, the court reasoned, is more like a partial assignment of income-producing property than an assignment of income. The attorney is not the mere beneficiary of the client's largess, but rather earns his fee through skill and diligence. This reasoning, the court held, applies whether or not state law grants the attorney any special property interest (*e.g.*, a superior lien) in part of the judgment or settlement proceeds.

B. COMMISSIONER v. BANAITIS

After leaving his job as a vice president and loan officer at the Bank of California in 1987, Sigitas J. Banaitis retained an attorney on a contingent-fee basis and brought suit in Oregon state court against the Bank of California and its successor in ownership, the Mitsubishi Bank. The complaint alleged that Mitsubishi Bank willfully interfered with Banaitis' employment contract, and that the Bank of California attempted to induce Banaitis to breach his fiduciary duties to customers and discharged him when he refused. The jury awarded Banaitis compensatory and punitive damages. After resolution of all appeals and post-trial motions, the parties settled. The defendants paid $4,864,547 to Banaitis; and, following the formula set forth in the contingent-fee contract, the defendants paid an additional $3,864,012 directly to Banaitis' attorney.

Banaitis did not include the amount paid to his attorney in gross income on his federal income tax return, and the Commissioner issued a notice of deficiency. The Tax Court upheld the Commissioner's determination, but the Court of Appeals for the Ninth Circuit reversed. In contrast to the Court of Appeals for the Sixth Circuit, the *Banaitis* court viewed state law as pivotal. Where state law confers on the attorney no special property rights in his fee, the court said, the whole amount of the judgment or settlement ordinarily is included in the plaintiff's gross income. Oregon state law, however, like the law of some other States, grants attorneys a superior lien in the contingent-fee portion of any recovery. As a result, the court held, contingent-fee agreements under Oregon law operate not as an anticipatory assignment of the client's income but as a partial transfer to the attorney of some of the client's property in the lawsuit.

II

To clarify why the issue here is of any consequence for tax purposes, two preliminary observations are useful. The first concerns the general issue of deductibility. For the tax years in question the legal expenses in these cases could have been taken as miscellaneous itemized deductions subject to the ordinary requirements, but doing so would have been of no help to respondents because of the operation of the Alternative Minimum Tax (AMT). For noncorporate individual taxpayers, the AMT establishes a tax liability floor equal to 26 percent of the taxpayer's "alternative minimum taxable income" (minus specified exemptions) up to $175,000, plus 28 percent of alternative minimum taxable income over $175,000. Alternative minimum taxable income, unlike ordinary gross income, does not allow any miscellaneous itemized deductions.

Second, after these cases arose Congress enacted the American Jobs Creation Act of 2004. Section 703 of the Act amended the Code by adding [§62(a)(20)]. The amendment allows a taxpayer, in computing adjusted gross income, to deduct "attorney fees and court costs paid by, or on behalf of, the taxpayer in connection with any action involving a claim of unlawful discrimination." The Act defines "unlawful discrimination" to include a number of specific federal statutes, any federal whistle-blower statute, and any federal, state, or local law "providing for the enforcement of civil rights" or "regulating any aspect of the employment relationship . . . or prohibiting the discharge of an employee, the discrimination against an employee, or any other form of retaliation or reprisal against an employee for asserting rights or taking other actions permitted by law." These deductions are permissible even when the AMT applies. Had the Act been in force for the transactions now under review, these cases likely would not have arisen. The Act is not retroactive, however, so while it may cover future taxpayers in respondents' position, it does not pertain here.

III

The Internal Revenue Code defines "gross income" for federal tax purposes as "all income from whatever source derived." The definition extends broadly to all economic gains not otherwise exempted. A taxpayer cannot exclude an economic gain from gross income by assigning the gain in advance to another party. The rationale for the so-called anticipatory assignment of income doctrine is the principle that gains should be taxed "to those who earn them," a maxim we have called "the first principle of income taxation." The anticipatory assignment doctrine is meant to prevent taxpayers from avoiding taxation through "arrangements and contracts however skillfully devised to prevent [income] when paid from vesting even for a second in the man who earned it." The rule is preventative and motivated by administrative as well as substantive concerns, so we do not inquire whether any particular assignment has a discernible tax avoidance purpose. As [*Lucas v. Earl*] explained, "no distinction can be taken according to the motives leading to the arrangement by which the fruits are attributed to a different tree from that on which they grew."

Respondents argue that the anticipatory assignment doctrine is a judge-made antifraud rule with no relevance to contingent-fee contracts of the sort at issue here. The Commissioner maintains that a contingent-fee agreement should be viewed as an anticipatory assignment to the attorney of a portion of the client's income from any litigation recovery. We agree with the Commissioner.

In an ordinary case attribution of income is resolved by asking whether a taxpayer exercises complete dominion over the income in question. In the context of anticipatory assignments, however, the assignor often does not have dominion over the income at the moment of receipt. In that instance the question becomes whether the assignor retains dominion over the income-generating asset, because the taxpayer "who owns or controls the source of the income, also controls the disposition of that which he could have received himself and diverts the payment from himself to others as the means of procuring the satisfaction of his wants." [Helvering v. Horst, 311 U.S. 112, 116-117 (1940).] Looking to control over the income-generating asset, then, preserves the principle that income should be taxed to the party who earns the income and enjoys the consequent benefits.

In the case of a litigation recovery the income-generating asset is the cause of action that derives from the plaintiff's legal injury. The plaintiff retains dominion over this asset throughout the litigation. We do not understand respondents to argue otherwise. Rather, respondents advance two counterarguments. First, they say that, in contrast to the bond coupons assigned in *Horst*, the value of a legal claim is speculative at the moment of assignment, and may be worth nothing at all. Second, respondents insist that the claimant's legal injury is not the only source of the ultimate recovery. The attorney, according to respondents, also contributes income-generating assets — effort and expertise — without which the claimant likely could not prevail. On these premises respondents urge us to treat a contingent-fee agreement as establishing, for tax purposes, something like a joint venture or partnership in which the client and attorney combine their respective assets — the client's claim and the attorney's skill — and apportion any resulting profits.

We reject respondents' arguments. Though the value of the plaintiff's claim may be speculative at the moment the fee agreement is signed, the anticipatory assignment doctrine is not limited to instances when the precise dollar value of the assigned income is known in advance. Though *Horst* involved an anticipatory assignment of a predetermined sum to be paid on a specific date, the holding in that case did not depend on ascertaining a liquidated amount at the time of assignment. In the cases before us, as in *Horst*, the taxpayer retained control over the income-generating asset, diverted some of the income produced to another party, and realized a benefit by doing so. As Judge Wesley correctly concluded in a recent case, the rationale of *Horst* applies fully to a contingent-fee contract. That the amount of income the asset would produce was uncertain at the moment of assignment is of no consequence.

We further reject the suggestion to treat the attorney-client relationship as a sort of business partnership or joint venture for tax purposes. The relationship between client and attorney, regardless of the variations in particular compensation agreements or the amount of skill and effort the attorney contributes, is a quintessential principal-agent relationship. The client may rely on the attorney's expertise and special skills to achieve a result the client could not achieve alone. That, however, is true of most principal-agent relationships, and it does not alter the fact that the client retains ultimate dominion and control over the underlying claim. The control is evident when it is noted that, although the attorney can make tactical decisions without consulting the client, the plaintiff still must determine whether to settle or proceed to judgment and make, as well, other critical decisions. Even where the attorney exercises independent judgment without supervision by, or consultation with, the client, the attorney, as an agent, is obligated to act solely on behalf of, and for the exclusive benefit of, the client-principal, rather than for the benefit of the attorney or any other party.

The attorney is an agent who is duty bound to act only in the interests of the principal, and so it is appropriate to treat the full amount of the recovery as income to the principal. In this respect Judge Posner's observation is apt: "[T]he contingent-fee lawyer [is not] a joint owner of his client's claim in the legal sense any more than the commission salesman is a joint owner of his employer's accounts receivable." Kenseth v. Commissioner, 259 F.3d 881, 883 (7th Cir. 2001). In both cases a principal relies on an agent to realize an economic gain, and the gain realized by the agent's efforts is income to the principal. The portion paid to the agent may be deductible, but absent some other provision of law it is not excludable from the principal's gross income.

This rule applies whether or not the attorney-client contract or state law confers any special rights or protections on the attorney, so long as these protections do not alter the fundamental principal-agent character of the relationship. . . . State laws vary with respect to the strength of an attorney's security interest in a contingent fee and the remedies available to an attorney should the client discharge or attempt to defraud the attorney. No state laws of which we are aware, however, even those that purport to give attorneys an "ownership" interest in their fees, . . . convert the attorney from an agent to a partner. . . .

IV

The foregoing suffices to dispose of Banaitis' case. Banks' case, however, involves a further consideration. Banks brought his claims under federal statutes that authorize fee awards to prevailing plaintiffs' attorneys. He contends that application of the anticipatory assignment principle would be inconsistent with the purpose of statutory fee shifting provisions. . . . In the federal system statutory fees are typically awarded by the court under the lodestar approach, and the plaintiff usually has little control over the amount awarded. Sometimes, as when the plaintiff seeks only injunctive relief, or when the statute caps plaintiffs' recoveries, or when for other reasons damages are substantially less than attorney's fees, court-awarded attorney's fees can exceed a plaintiff's monetary recovery. . . . Treating the fee award as income to the plaintiff in such cases, it is argued, can lead to the perverse result that the plaintiff loses money by winning the suit. Furthermore, it is urged that treating statutory fee awards as income to plaintiffs would undermine the effectiveness of fee-shifting statutes in deputizing plaintiffs and their lawyers to act as private attorneys general.

We need not address these claims. After Banks settled his case, the fee paid to his attorney was calculated solely on the basis of the private contingent-fee contract. There was no court-ordered fee award, nor was there any indication in Banks' contract with his attorney, or in the settlement agreement with the defendant, that the contingent fee paid to Banks' attorney was in lieu of statutory fees Banks might otherwise have been entitled to recover. Also, the amendment added by the American Jobs Creation Act redresses the concern for many, perhaps most, claims governed by fee-shifting statutes. . . .

For the reasons stated, the judgments of the Courts of Appeals for the Sixth and Ninth Circuits are reversed, and the cases are remanded for further proceedings consistent with this opinion.

Notes and Questions

1. *Is* Lucas v. Earl *really on point?* Is the Court correct in applying the "anticipatory assignment doctrine" from *Lucas v. Earl* and the other classic assignment of income cases to the cases decided here? The classic assignment of

income cases are about the shifting of income within a family to lower bracket taxpayers. In those cases, there is no argument about the total amount to be taxed or how many times it should be taxed, but only about the identity of the proper taxpayer. What do those cases have to do with the attorneys' fees disputes, in which the issue is not the rate at which income should be taxed, but whether it should be taxed twice (to the taxpayer and his attorney) or only once (to the attorney), and there is no attempt to shift income within a family?

2. *Double taxation.* On the other hand, is it really significant, as taxpayers here argued, that the attorney will be taxed on the fees? Does it follow from the fact that the fees will be included in the attorney's income that they should not be included in the taxpayer's? Suppose you pay $1,000 out of your earned income to your gardener for taking care of your yard. Are you entitled to a $1,000 deduction (or an exclusion of $1,000 of your salary from gross income) because the $1,000 will be taxed to the gardener, and unless you are allowed a deduction you and the gardener will both be taxed on the same income?

3. *Economic benefit and §61.* Is it possible that the government is right on the gross income issue, even if *Lucas v. Earl* and the other assignment of income cases are not really on point? What about "economic benefit" cases, which hold that a taxpayer has received a taxable economic benefit when a liability of his is paid by another, despite the fact that the taxpayer never received (and perhaps never even had a right to receive) the cash with which the debt was paid? *See, e.g.,* Diedrich v. Commissioner, 457 U.S. 191 (1982). In *Diedrich,* the taxpayer made a gift of appreciated property on the condition that the donee pay the donor's gift tax liability resulting from the gift. The Supreme Court held that the donor realized a taxable gain to the extent the donor's gift tax liability paid by the donee exceeded the donor's basis in the transferred property. Is *Diedrich* relevant to the attorneys' fees cases? Notice that the *Diedrich* facts and the contingent attorneys' fees cases share the same peculiar feature: The taxpayer's debt is created and discharged more or less simultaneously. In *Diedrich,* the gift tax liability did not exist until the gift was made, and in the attorneys' fees cases the client does not owe the attorney the contingent fee until the defendant pays. The Supreme Court held in *Diedrich* that there was no difference in the legal analysis between the discharge of the newly created gift tax liability and the discharge of a preexisting obligation. Should that also be true in the attorneys' fee cases?

4. *The disparate treatment of exclusions and deductions.* Why did it matter whether the proper treatment of the fees was exclusion, or inclusion followed by deduction? As the Court explains, it mattered because the deduction was subject to significant limitations under the regular tax and disallowance under the AMT, but no such restrictions applied to exclusions. Although not every deduction is as disfavored as miscellaneous itemized deductions, it is generally true that deductions have to contend with all sorts of hoops and hurdles — floors, phaseouts, disallowance to non-itemizers, AMT disallowance, and so on — and exclusions do not. It is not obvious why the tax laws should be tougher on deductions than on exclusions. Is it simply that deductions tend to be more *visible* than exclusions, and thus more obvious targets for restrictions imposed by revenue-hungry legislators?

5. *Only a partial solution.* The new provision added to the Code in 2004 (§62(a)(20), described in part II of the *Banks* opinion) allows many taxpayers who obtain taxable tort recoveries (not excluded by §104(a)(2)) to effectively deduct their attorneys' fees for AMT purposes as well as for regular tax purposes. But because the relief provision is limited to actions involving "a claim of unlawful discrimination" it leaves some successful plaintiffs (in defamation cases, for example) still in the box in which the taxpayers in *Banks* found themselves. Is there any reason why the statutory relief could not have been provided more comprehensively?

6. *Assignment of income and charitable fundraising events.* There is another situation in the assignment of income area in which an exclusion produces a better result than an inclusion only partly offset by a deduction. Suppose an entertainer is hired, at fee of $100,000, to do a show at a casino. The casino has ticket sales of $250,000, and other show-related expenses (besides the performer's fee) of $60,000. The proper tax treatments of the performer and the casino are clear. The performer is like the law firm associate discussed earlier; he has only $100,000 (not $250,000) of gross income. The casino has $250,000 of gross income, but only $90,000 of taxable income after its business expense deductions. Now suppose a charity wants the entertainer to be the headliner at its annual fundraising gala, and the entertainer agrees to perform for free. The charity has sales of $250,000 and expenses of $60,000. Does the entertainer have $250,000 of gross income, $100,000 of gross income (his usual fee for a show), or no gross income? So long as the gala is organized and controlled by the charity, the entertainer will not be taxed on anything. *See* Reg. §1.61-2(c), providing that "[t]he value of services is not includible in gross income when such services are rendered directly and gratuitously to [a charitable organization]."[6] *Lucas v. Earl* does not apply because the entertainer has not assigned to the charity a right to receive compensation for his services; rather, he has donated the services themselves to the charity. But now suppose the entertainer is on a national tour, organized and controlled by himself, and he designates one tour performance as "Red Cross Night," with all profits from that performance to be donated to the Red Cross. Although the non-tax difference between this situation and the charity's annual gala may seem slight, the tax difference is considerable. In this case the entertainer is *not* viewed as donating the services themselves to the charity. Instead, he has made an anticipatory assignment of earned income (i.e., his profits from the performance) to a lower (zero) bracket taxpayer with whose economic interests he identifies. This is enough to bring *Lucas v. Earl* into play. The entertainer will have to include the profits in income. He can claim a deduction under §170 for the donation. If he is a very generous performer, however, his deduction may be for considerably less than the full amount of the donation. Section 170(b) imposes "percentage limitations" on the charitable deduction;

---

6. The charity will also not be taxed on any amount. Although §512 imposes a tax on the unrelated business income of charities, the tax applies only to income from businesses *regularly* carried on, and the regulations provide that an "annual dance or fund raising event for charity" is not a business regularly carried on. Reg. §1.513-1(c)(2)(iii). This applies even to "The Big Dance" — the NCAA Division I basketball tournament, which unfolds over the course of three gripping weeks each March. *See* NCAA v. Comm'r, 914 F.2d 1417 (10th Cir. 1990).

basically, one cannot deduct contributions to the extent they exceed 50 percent of one's adjusted gross income.[7] In addition, his §170 deduction may be reduced under the §68 "overall limitation on itemized deductions."[8]

3.   *The Effect of the Taxpayer's Inability to Receive Income He Earns*

TESCHNER v. COMMISSIONER

38 T.C. 1003 (1962) (*nonacq.*)

TRAIN, J: The sole question is whether petitioners are taxable on a prize received by their daughter. . . .

Sometime prior to October 2, 1957, Johnson & Johnson, Inc. (hereinafter referred to as Johnson & Johnson), in cooperation with the Mutual Benefit Life Insurance Company of Newark, New Jersey (hereinafter referred to as Mutual), announced a contest called the "Annual Youth Scholarship Contest" (hereinafter referred to as the contest). An entrant was required to complete in fifty additional words or less the statement "A good education is important because. . . ." . . .

The prizes consisted of annuity policies in the face amount of the respective prizes. Rule 4 of the contest stated that:

> Only persons under age 17 years and 1 month (as of May 14, 1957) are eligible to receive the policies for education. A contestant over that age must designate a person below the age of 17 years and 1 month to receive the policy for education. In naming somebody else, name, address and age of both contestant and designee must be filled in on entry blank.

As of May 14, 1957, both petitioners were over the age of 17 years and 1 month.

The preclusion of Paul [Teschner] from eligibility to receive any of the policies was neither directly nor indirectly attributable to any action taken by him. He had not suggested such a contest to anyone; had never discussed such a contest with representatives of either Johnson & Johnson or Mutual; and had no knowledge of the contest until the official announcement of it was first brought to his attention. Neither at the time Paul prepared and submitted the entry nor at any other time has there been any arrangement or agreement between petitioners and their daughter to divide or share in anything of value she might receive.

Paul, an attorney, entered the contest, submitting two statements on the form supplied by Johnson & Johnson. At that time, he designated his daughter, Karen Janette Teschner (hereinafter referred to as Karen), age 7, as the recipient should either of the entries be selected.

One of the statements submitted by Paul was selected, and on October 2, 1957, petitioners' daughter received the following telegraph notification addressed to her:

JOHNSON & JOHNSON AND THE MUTUAL BENEFIT LIFE INSURANCE COMPANY TAKE GREAT PLEASURE IN INFORMING YOU THAT YOU HAVE BEEN AWARDED THE FOURTH PRIZE OF A ONE

---

7. For §170(b), see section A.5 of Chapter 4.
8. For §68, see section G of Chapter 5, and the Chapter 1 cell on understanding tax rates.

THOUSAND FIVE HUNDRED DOLLAR PAID-UP INSURANCE POLICY IN THEIR NATIONAL YOUTH
SCHOLARSHIP CONTEST. YOU WILL BE CONTACTED WITH FURTHER DETAILS AS SOON AS POSSIBLE—
NATIONAL YOUTH SCHOLARSHIP COMMITTEE

Thereafter, Johnson & Johnson filed an application and paid Mutual $1,287.12. As the result thereof, petitioners' daughter received from Mutual, during 1957, a fully paid-up annuity policy, having a face value of $1,500. This policy contained no limitation whatsoever on the manner in which Karen would be entitled to use the proceeds or any other benefits available under the policy. Specifically, the use of these proceeds or benefits was not limited to educational or similar purposes.

Petitioners did not include any amount in their 1957 income tax return with regard to the foregoing annuity policy. Respondent determined that the policy constituted gross income to petitioners, and assigned a value thereto of $1,287.12, the consideration paid by Johnson & Johnson.

OPINION

While the taxability of prizes and awards may have been in doubt prior to the enactment of the Internal Revenue Code of 1954, it is now clear that they are includible in gross income, with certain exceptions not here applicable. Sec. 74. The sole question in this case is whether the prize (annuity policy) is taxable to petitioners.

Respondent, relying on Lucas v. Earl, 281 U.S. 111 (1930), and Rev. Rul. 58-127, 1958-1 C.B. 42, contends that the annuity policy which Karen received is includible in petitioners' gross income. Respondent states on brief that the issue here "is whether a prize attributable to a taxpayer's contest efforts, which, if received by him, would constitute taxable income in the nature of compensation for services rendered, may be excluded by him because paid to his designee." Respondent declares his theory of the case to be "that whenever A receives something of value attributable to services performed by B, B, the earner, is the proper taxpayer."

Petitioners contend that the value of the annuity policy should not be included in their gross income because they did not receive anything either actually or constructively and never had a right, at anytime, to receive anything that could have been the subject of an anticipatory assignment or similar arrangement.

We agree with the petitioners.

In the instant case, we are not confronted with the question of whether the prize is income. The sole question is whether it is the petitioners' income for tax purposes. Certainly, it was Paul's effort that generated the income, to whomever it is to be attributed. However, as we have found, he could not under any circumstances whatsoever receive the income so generated, himself. He had no right to either its receipt or its enjoyment. He could only designate another individual to be the beneficiary of that right. Moreover, under the facts of this case, the payment to the daughter was not in discharge of an obligation of petitioners. Cf. Douglas v. Willcutts, 296 U.S. 1 (1935). At age 18, Karen will be entitled to $1,500. She can use that money, in her uncontrolled and unfettered discretion, for any purpose she chooses. Nor does respondent here contend that petitioners received income by virtue of a satisfaction of an obligation to support. Finally, there is no evidence whatsoever that the arrangement here involved was a sham or the product of connivance.

As pointed out above, respondent relies, in part, on Rev. Rul. 58-127, *supra*, and a consideration of that ruling is useful because it reveals the error into which the respondent has here fallen. Under the circumstances stated by that ruling, the taxpayer prepared and submitted a winning entry in an essay contest. Pursuant to the terms of that contest, the taxpayer received a check payable to his child, the use of which was entirely without restriction imposed by the sponsors of the contest. The respondent ruled that, under such circumstances, the amount of the prize was includible in the gross income of the taxpayer. While the facts set out in that ruling do not disclose whether the taxpayer could himself have received the prize, it would seem that in all salient respects the facts therein are identical to those before us.

In his ruling, the respondent declared, "The basic rule in determining to whom an item of income is taxable is that income is taxable to the one who earns it." If by this statement the respondent means that income is in all events includible in the gross income of whomsoever generates or creates the income by virtue of his own effort, the respondent is wrong. If this were the law, agents, conduits, fiduciaries, and others in a similar capacity would be personally taxable on the proceeds of their efforts. The charity fund-raiser would be taxable on sums contributed as the result of his efforts. The employee would be taxable on income generated for his employer by his efforts. Such results, completely at variance with every accepted concept of Federal income taxation, demonstrate the fallacy of the premise.

If, on the other hand, the respondent used the term "earn," not in such a broad sense, but in the commonly accepted usage of "to acquire by labor, service, or performance; to deserve and receive compensation" (*Webster's New International Dictionary*), then the rule is intelligible but does not support the conclusion reached by the respondent either in the ruling in question or in the case before us. The taxpayer there, as here, acquired nothing himself; he received nothing nor did he have a right to receive anything. . . .

In Lucas v. Earl, 281 U.S. 111 (1930), upon which respondent heavily relies, the Supreme Court refused to allow a husband to escape taxes on his income by way of salaries and attorney fees through a contractual arrangement by which he and his wife were to receive, hold, and own such earnings as joint tenants. The Court declared that tax on a salary could not be avoided by the person earning the salary by anticipatory arrangements and contracts. Shortly thereafter, in Poe v. Seaborn, 282 U.S. 101, 117 (1930), the Supreme Court stated:

> In the *Earl* case . . . the husband's professional fees, earned in years subsequent to the date of the contract, were his individual income. . . . The very assignment in that case was bottomed on the fact that the earnings would be the husband's property, else there would have been nothing on which it could operate. That case presents quite a different question from this, because here, by law, the earnings are never the property of the husband. . . .

It cannot be argued that Paul voluntarily gave up his right to get the annuity policy and designated his daughter to receive it in his place. There was no discretion on his part; the choice was to accept the terms of the contest or reject them.

In the case before us, the taxpayer, while he had no power to dispose of income, had a power to appoint or designate its recipient. Does the existence or exercise of such a power alone give rise to taxable income in his hands? We think clearly not. In Nicholas A. Stavroudes, 27 T.C. 583, 590 (1956), we found it to be settled doctrine that a power to direct the distribution of trust income to others is not alone sufficient to justify the taxation of that income to the possessor of such a power. *See also* Bateman v. Commissioner, 127 F.2d 266 (C.A. 1, 1942).

Granted that an individual cannot escape taxation on income to which he is entitled by "turning his back" upon that income, the fact remains that he must have received the income or had a right to do so before he is taxable thereon. . . .

Section 1(a) of the 1954 Code imposes a tax on the "income of every individual." Where an individual neither receives nor has the right to receive income, he is not the taxable individual within the contemplation of the statute. There is no basis in the statute or in the decided cases for a construction at variance with this fundamental rule.

Decision will be entered for the petitioners.

[Concurring opinion by Dawson, J., is omitted.]

ATKINS, J., dissenting: It is a well-settled principle of our income tax law that personal earnings are taxable to the earner, and that cases involving the taxation of personal earnings are not to be decided by attenuated subtleties. Lucas v. Earl, 281 U.S. 111, in which the Supreme Court held an anticipatory assignment of future personal earnings to be ineffective to relieve the earner of tax. . . .

The annuity policy which Paul won resulted from his personal efforts. The fruit of his labor consisted of the payment of the award to his designee, his daughter. His efforts alone generated the income in question; and it is a matter of no consequence that, under the rules of the contest, such income could not be paid to him, for he had the power to control its disposition. He in fact exercised that power when he entered the contest, by designating the natural object of his bounty, his daughter, as the recipient of any prize which he might win. The exercise of such power, with resultant payment to the daughter, constituted the enjoyment and hence the realization of the income by Paul. In the circumstances he should be fully charged with the income. Cf. Helvering v. Horst, 311 U.S. 112 (1940), and Helvering v. Eubank, 311 U.S. 122 (1940). There is no more basis here for narrowing the broad scope of the holding in Lucas v. Earl than there was in the *Horst* and *Eubank* cases. The decision of the majority herein rests upon "attenuated subtleties" similar to those disapproved, first in Lucas v. Earl and then again in Burnet v. Leininger, 285 U.S. 136 (1932), Helvering v. Horst, Helvering v. Eubank, Hanison v. Schaffner, 312 U.S. 579 (1941), and Commissioner v. P. G. Lake, Inc., 356 U.S. 260 (1958).

Notes and Questions

1. *A controversial opinion.* Seven judges dissented in *Teschner,* and the nonacquiescence noted in the citation means that the IRS disagrees with and will not follow the opinion (with respect to other taxpayers). On the other hand, the Supreme Court cited *Teschner* with approval in Commissioner v. First Security Bank of Utah, 405 U.S. 394 (1972) (holding that the assignment of income doctrine cannot be used to tax a taxpayer on income that it did not

receive and that it was prohibited by law from receiving, even if the taxpayer was in economic reality the earner of the income).

Problem 1. A taxpayer is informed by her new employer that the employer has a special program that applies to all employees with children under the age of 18. For every minor child of an employee, the employee's annual cash salary is reduced by $5,000, and $5,000 is put into a college savings trust fund for the child's benefit. This is a mandatory program; for as long as one remains an employee one has no choice but to participate. To whom—employee or child—should the $5,000 annual payments be taxed?

C. INCOME FROM PROPERTY

1. *Unrealized Appreciation in Gifted Property*

TAFT v. BOWERS
278 U.S. 470 (1929)

Mr. Justice MCREYNOLDS delivered the opinion of the Court.

Abstractly stated, this is the problem — In 1916 *A* purchased 100 shares of stock for $1,000 which he held until 1923 when their fair market value had become $2,000. He then gave them to *B* who sold them during the year 1923 for $5,000. The United States claim that, under the Revenue Act of 1921, *B* must pay income tax upon $4,000, as realized profits. *B* maintains that only $3,000 — the appreciation during her ownership — can be regarded as income; that the increase during the donor's ownership is not income assessable against her within intendment of the Sixteenth Amendment.

[The applicable statute, the predecessor of current §1015, clearly required a donee of property to use the donor's basis in the property for purposes of calculating gain on the sale of the property. Thus the statute called for a $1,000 basis for *B*, which would result in a $4,000 gain on the sale. — EDS.]

The only question subject to serious controversy is whether Congress had power to authorize the exaction.

It is said that the gift became a capital asset of the donee to the extent of its value when received and, therefore, when disposed of by her no part of that value could be treated as taxable income in her hands.

The Sixteenth Amendment provides —

> The Congress shall have power to lay and collect taxes on incomes from whatever source derived, without apportionment among the several States, and without regard to any census or enumeration.

Income is the thing which may be taxed — income from any source. The Amendment does not attempt to define income or to designate how taxes may be laid thereon, or how they may be enforced.

Under former decisions here the settled doctrine is that the Sixteenth Amendment confers no power upon Congress to define and tax as income without apportionment something which theretofore could not have been properly regarded as income.

Also, this Court has declared — "Income may be defined as the gain derived from capital, from labor, or from both combined, provided it be understood to include profit gained through a sale or conversion of capital assets." Eisner v. Macomber, 252 U.S. 189, 207. The "gain derived from capital," within the definition, is "not a gain accruing to capital, nor a growth or increment of value in the investment, but a gain, a profit, something of exchangeable value proceeding from the property, severed from the capital however invested, and coming in, that is, received or drawn by the claimant for his separate use, benefit and disposal." United States v. Phellis, 257 U.S. 156, 169.

If, instead of giving the stock to petitioner, the donor had sold it at market value, the excess over the capital he invested (cost) would have been income therefrom and subject to taxation under the Sixteenth Amendment. He would have been obliged to share the realized gain with the United States. He held the stock — the investment — subject to the right of the sovereign to take part of any increase in its value when separated through sale or conversion and reduced to his possession. Could he, contrary to the express will of Congress, by mere gift enable another to hold this stock free from such right, deprive the sovereign of the possibility of taxing the appreciation when actually severed, and convert the entire property into a capital asset of the donee, who invested nothing, as though the latter had purchased at the market price? And after a still further enhancement of the property, could the donee make a second gift with like effect, etc.? We think not.

In truth the stock represented only a single investment of capital — that made by the donor. And when through sale or conversion the increase was separated therefrom, it became income from that investment in the hands of the recipient subject to taxation according to the very words of the Sixteenth Amendment. By requiring the recipient of the entire increase to pay a part into the public treasury, Congress deprived her of no right and subjected her to no hardship. She accepted the gift with knowledge of the statute and, as to the property received, voluntarily assumed the position of her donor. When she sold the stock she actually got the original sum invested, plus the entire appreciation; and out of the latter only was she called on to pay the tax demanded.

The provision of the statute under consideration seems entirely appropriate for enforcing a general scheme of lawful taxation. To accept the view urged in behalf of petitioner undoubtedly would defeat, to some extent, the purpose of Congress to take part of all gain derived from capital investments. To prevent that result and insure enforcement of its proper policy, Congress had power to require that for purposes of taxation the donee should accept the position of the donor in respect of the thing received. And in so doing, it acted neither unreasonably nor arbitrarily. . . .

There is nothing in the Constitution which lends support to the theory that gain actually resulting from the increased value of capital can be treated as taxable income in the hands of the recipient only so far as the increase occurred while he owned the property. And Irwin v. Gavit, 268 U.S. 161, 167 (1925), is to the contrary.

The judgments below are affirmed.

Notes and Questions

1. *A permissible kind of income-shifting.* The tax treatment of unrealized appreciation in gifted property, approved by the Supreme Court in *Taft v. Bowers*, remains the same today. The donor is not taxed on the appreciation when the gift is made, and the donee generally takes the property with a transferred basis under §1015.[9] Although the taxpayer challenged this statutory scheme in *Taft v. Bowers*, the scheme is actually quite taxpayer-friendly, in that it permits the shifting of a particular type of income to a lower bracket taxpayer. Suppose a father owns appreciated stock. If he sells the stock, he will have to pay tax on the appreciation at his capital gains rate of 15 percent.[10] But if he gives the stock to his daughter and she later sells the stock, the tax liability on the appreciation is shifted to the daughter, whose capital gain tax rate may be zero percent (if she has little other income).[11] Why is Congress willing to allow income-shifting with respect to unrealized appreciation in gifted property, when it is not willing to allow it with respect to earned income?

2. Income Streams from Income-Producing Property

a. In General

Even more significant than the permitted income-shifting with respect to unrealized appreciation is the fact that a taxpayer can shift the tax liability on a future stream of investment income by making a gift of the income-producing property. The general rule is that income from property is taxed to the owner of the property. If a higher bracket donor gives stocks, bonds, or rental real estate to a lower bracket donee, the subsequent income stream (dividends, interest, or rent, as the case may be) will be taxed at the donee's lower rates.

At first glance, the income attribution rules for earned income and for investment income seem inconsistent. Why are taxpayers allowed to use gifts to shift the tax liability on investment income, when they are not allowed to use gifts to shift the tax liability on earned income? Actually, both rules are consistent with the principle that income should be taxed to the person with the strongest connection with, or control over, the source of the income. With earned income, that person is always the earner. Even if the earner makes a legally binding assignment of his right to compensation for future services, he still controls the income stream because he can choose whether to earn the income. By contrast, it is possible to sever one's control over income-producing property by the simple expedient of giving it away.

While the rule that investment income is taxed to the owner of the income-producing property is easy to apply in most cases, problems arise when taxpayers make gifts of the right to receive income from property for several years, while retaining the property itself. Suppose a father gives his daughter the right to

---

9. For a more detailed examination of §1015, see section F.1 of Chapter 3.
10. *See* §1(h)(1)(C).
11. *See* §1(h)(1)(B). This assumes the daughter is old enough that the "kiddie tax" of §1(g) does not apply.

receive the income from certain income-producing property, but only for the next five years. Should the daughter's income interest be treated as property in its own right, so that the father has made a tax-effective gift of income-producing property? Or should the father's retention of the property itself and of the right to income after five years make the father the proper taxpayer on the income received by the daughter? The leading case in this area is Helvering v. Horst, 311 U.S. 112 (1940) (which the Supreme Court relied on in *Banks*), in which a father detached an interest coupon from a bond, shortly before the coupon matured, and gave the coupon to his son. The Supreme Court ruled that the father was taxable on the interest when the son received it, because the father had retained control of the income-producing property (the bond). Our hypothetical is a slightly harder case, because the father has parted with a longer (five-year) income stream, but it is nevertheless clear that the father would be taxed on the income received by the daughter under the authority of *Horst*.

But what if the father had given away the right to the income from the property for so many years that the daughter's rights were more valuable than the rights retained by the father? For example, if the applicable discount rate is 6 percent, the right to the income from property for the next 12 years is worth slightly more than the remainder interest in the property. If that tipping point has been reached, should the gift then be effective to shift the income tax liability to the daughter for those 12 years? Under current law, that would not be good enough; the father would still be taxed. The grantor trust rules[12] provide that income from a trust will be taxed to the grantor of the trust (rather than to the trust itself or to the beneficiaries of the trust) if the grantor retains certain powers over the trust or certain economic interests in the trust. The relevant provision here is §673, which provides that a grantor who retains a reversion in property transferred to a trust will be taxed on the income from that property during the term of the trust, unless the reversion is worth no more than 5 percent of the value of the property at the time of the transfer. Suppose the father transferred the income-producing property to a trust, with the income payable to the daughter for a term of years and with the property reverting to the father at the end of that term. Still assuming an applicable discount rate of 6 percent, the trust would have to have a term of a little more than 51 years, before the value of the father's reversion would fall below the magic 5 percent figure. Although §673 is applicable by its terms only to transfers in trust, it is clear that the father could not receive more lenient treatment by giving his daughter a shorter income interest outside of a trust arrangement.

This rather strict treatment applies only to gifts of *carved-out* income interests, in which the high bracket taxpayer makes a gift of less than his entire temporal interest in income-producing property. If the taxpayer's own interest is temporally limited—for example, a life estate—and the taxpayer makes a gift covering the entire period of his interest, the taxpayer will succeed in transferring the tax liability on future income. *See* Blair v. Commissioner, 300 U.S. 5 (1937).

Problem 2.   Mother transfers income-producing property to a trust. The trust income is payable to Son (an adult) for the next 30 years, after which the property will revert to Mother. Assuming the applicable discount rate (for purposes of valuing Mother's reversion) is 5 percent, will Mother be taxed on the income from the property during the 30-year term of the trust?

---

12. Sections 671 et seq., described in more detail in section C.2.f of this chapter.

Problem 3. The facts are similar to those in Problem 2, except that Mother does not use a trust. Instead, she simply makes a gift to Son of the right to receive the income from the property for the next 30 years. Who will be taxed on the income from the property during the 30 years in which Son has the right to the income?

Problem 4. The facts are the same as in Problem 2, except the applicable discount rate (for purposes of valuing the reversion) is 12 percent. Will Mother be taxed on the income from the property during the 30-year term of the trust?

Problem 5. The facts are similar to those in Problem 4, except that Mother does not use a trust. Instead, she simply makes a gift to Son of the right to receive the income from the property for the next 30 years. Who will be taxed on the income from the property during the 30 years in which Son has the right to the income?

b. Stripped Bonds

Section 1286 applies a special rule when a taxpayer owning a debt instrument makes a gift of the right to receive some or all of the interest payments on the instrument, while retaining the instrument itself. Suppose a father buys a newly issued $100,000 bond, which bears 8 percent interest (the market rate) and matures in ten years. Shortly after buying the bond, he partially "strips" the bond, by giving his daughter the right to collect the interest on the bond for the next six years. Under the "common law" approach of *Horst*, the stripping of the bond would have no tax effect; the father would be taxed on all the interest collected by the daughter. Section 1286, however, takes a different approach. What the father gives away and what he retains are treated as two separate assets, and the father's total basis ($100,000) is allocated between the two assets according to their relative fair market values on the date the bond is stripped. Using an 8 percent discount rate, the daughter's right to receive $8,000 per year for the next six years is worth $36,983; the father's right to the remainder is worth $63,017. Accordingly, the daughter takes a basis of $36,983 in her rights, and the father has a basis of $63,017 in what he retains. The interest income taxable to each will then be determined under original issue discount (OID) principles.[13] Without going into all the gory details, the daughter will be taxed on $11,017 of original issue discount over the next six years,[14] and the father will be taxed on $68,983 of original issue discount over the next ten years.[15] Together, they will be taxed on exactly $80,000 of interest over the ten-year period, at the rate of $8,000 per year; this is the same amount of interest that would have been taxed to the father over the ten-year period if he had not stripped the bond. Unlike the *Horst* approach, §1286 does permit a limited amount of income-shifting for an interest-stripping donor. This is hardly a tax bonanza, however. On the facts of the hypothetical, §1286 simply

13. For a detailed explanation of the OID rules, see the Chapter 3 cell on original issue discount, §483 unstated interest, and market discount.

14. Treating each of the six rights to annual interest payments as a separate OID instrument, the daughter holds debt instruments with a combined "stated redemption price" of $48,000 ($8,000 × 6). Her total OID is the excess of the $48,000 stated redemption price over her $36,983 basis in the rights.

15. Treating the right to the principal upon maturity and each of the four rights to annual interest payments as five separate OID instruments, the father holds debt instruments with a combined "stated redemption price" of $132,000 ($100,000 + [$8,000 × 4]). His total OID is the excess of the $132,000 stated redemption price over his $63,017 basis in the rights.

replicates the results that would have been obtained if the father had (1) invested $63,107 at 8 percent for ten years, and (2) made an outright gift of $36,983 to the daughter, which the daughter had then invested at 8 percent for six years.

c.   Labor Embodied in Property

What if a parent builds a house with his own labor, and makes a gift of the house to his adult child, who rents it out to tenants? Is the rental income taxable to the child because this is a gift of income-producing property, or is it taxable to the parent because the parent's own labor created the income-producing property? The IRS has long taken the position that gifts of taxpayer-created income-producing property are effective in transferring tax liability to the donee.[16] In practice, this most often involves intangible assets, such as patents and copyrights. This is good news for inventors and writers, but is there any way for lawyers (for example) to take advantage of this rule? Could a lawyer hired to draft a contract for a client make a gift of the contract to his child (who is old enough that the "kiddie tax," described immediately below, does not apply), have the child sell the contract to the client, and thereby transfer the tax liability on the client's payment to his lower-bracket child? Sad to say, it is clear that this would not work. The labor-embodied-in-property rule applies only to items that are ordinarily considered property — and are bought and sold as such — for non-tax purposes. Houses, patents, and copyrights all qualify, but drafted-to-order contracts do not.

d.   The "Kiddie Tax"

Section 1(g) provides (oversimplifying a little) that the investment income of a child under the age of 18 is taxed to the child, but that it is taxed at the marginal tax rate of the child's parents. Section 1(g) also applies to the investment income of an adult child, if the child's earned income does not exceed half of the amount of the child's support, and the child either (1) has not reached age 19 before the end of the year, or (2) is a full-time student and has not reached age 24 before the end of the year. The effect of these rules is to tax the investment income of an adult child at the parents' marginal tax rate if the parents are able to claim a dependency exemption for the child. Since the child remains the taxpayer under §1(g), the "kiddie tax" is not literally an exception to the general rule that income from property is taxed to the owner of the property. Recall, however, that the real point of income-shifting is not the identity of the person who technically pays the tax, but the rate at which the income is taxed. Taxing the income at the parents' marginal tax rate generally takes the tax fun out of making gifts of investment property to children. The "kiddie tax" uses the marginal tax rate of the child's parents, regardless of whether the parents are the source of the child's income-producing property. If a grandparent makes a gift of income-producing property to a ten-year-old grandchild, the income is taxed at the parents' marginal tax rate, not at the grandparent's. If the parents are in a lower tax bracket than the grandparents, the gift will not have been wholly ineffective from an income-shifting standpoint.

---

16. *See, e.g.,* Rev. Rul. 54-599, 1954-2 C.B. 52 (involving an assignment of a copyright).

e. Interest-free Gift Loans and §7872

Parents have $500,000 invested at 5 percent interest, and they want to use the $25,000 of annual interest income to help finance the law school education of their 24-year-old son. They realize that more of the $25,000 will be available for tuition if the interest income is taxed to their son than if it is taxed to them. They also realize that they could shift the tax liability to their son by simply giving him the $500,000 and letting him invest it. The problem is that they do not want to give him permanent control over the $500,000; they only want to give him the income it will generate over the next three years. Is there any way they can give him only the right to the interest for the next three years, and still succeed in transferring the tax liability to him? It won't work to transfer the $500,000 to a trust, with the income payable to the son for three years followed by a reversion to the parents; under §673 of the grantor trust rules (described earlier), the reversion will cause the income to be taxed to the parents. It also will not work to strip the right to the next three years' worth of interest payments from an existing $500,000 debt instrument; under §1286 (also described above), the bulk of the interest would still be taxed to the parents. But the parents have another idea. What if they make an interest-free *loan* of $500,000 to their son, the son invests the $500,000 at 5 percent for the next three years, and the son then repays the loan? That would accomplish their non-tax objective of regaining control of the $500,000 principal at the end of three years, and at first glance it would also seem to accomplish their income-shifting goal, because the $25,000 interest income would now belong to the son. Section 7872, however, ruins this plan. In the case of a "gift loan" — defined as a loan bearing a below-market rate of interest when the forgoing of interest is in the nature of a gift — the statute creates a deemed interest payment from the borrower (here, the son) to the lender (the parents). The amount of the deemed interest payment is the difference between interest at the "applicable federal rate" (AFR) and the actual interest charged (here, zero). Assuming the AFR is 5 percent, §7872 creates a deemed annual interest payment of $25,000 from the son to his parents. The deemed interest income is taxable to the parents, thus foiling their attempt to shift the tax liability on $25,000 to their son. The deemed interest payment is deductible by the son, subject to the various limitations imposed on interest expense deductions under §163. If the son is able to deduct the entire $25,000,[17] the effect of §7872 will be to put the parents and the son in the same position as if the gift loan had never been made: The parents will have $25,000 of taxable income, and the son will have no taxable income.

Problem 6.   An interest-free "gift loan" (as defined in §7872(f)(3)) of $1 million from Parents to Daughter (a 24-year-old law student) is outstanding for the entire year. Daughter has invested the loan proceeds and has earned $40,000 of net investment income for the year. If the applicable federal rate (AFR) is 5 percent, what are the income tax consequences of this loan for Parents and for Daughter under §7872? Note: To make the arithmetic easier in this and the following two problems, apply §7872(f)(2) as if it called for annual compounding, rather than semi-annual compounding.

Problem 7.   An interest-free "gift loan" (as defined in §7872(f)(3)) of $100,000 from Parents to Daughter (a 24-year-old law student) is outstanding for the entire year. Daughter has invested the loan proceeds and has earned $4,000 of net

---

17. On these facts, the entire $25,000 should be deductible as investment interest under §§163(a) and 163(d).

investment income for the year. If the AFR is 5 percent, what are the income tax consequences of this loan for Parents and for Daughter under §7872? Hint: Take a look at §7872(d).

Problem 8.   An interest-free "gift loan" (as defined in §7872(f)(3)) of $10,000 from Parents to Daughter (a 24-year-old law student) is outstanding for the entire year. Daughter used the loan proceeds in the previous year to pay for some of her living expenses. Daughter owns no income-producing assets. If the AFR is 5 percent, what are the income tax consequences of this loan for Parents and for Daughter under §7872? Hint: Take a look at §7872(c)(2).

f. Grantor Trusts

Ordinarily, the income of a trust is taxed either to the beneficiaries of the trust (if the income is distributed to the beneficiaries) or to the trust itself (if the income is accumulated by the trust).[18] Thus, a taxpayer who makes a gift of income-producing property to a trust can shift to the trust or its beneficiaries the tax liability on future investment income. Two statutory provisions, however, limit the tax-saving potential of this strategy. First, the "kiddie tax" (§1(g)) will tax distributions to a child under the age of 18 at the marginal tax rate of the child's parents. Second, §1(e) provides a very compressed rate schedule for accumulated income taxed to the trust. In 2010, for example, the top individual marginal tax rate applies to all trust income in excess of $11,200. In many cases, a "successful" shifting of tax liability from a grantor to a trust will be a pyrrhic victory, because the trust's marginal tax rate will be higher than the grantor's.

Under current law, then, gifts of income-producing property to trusts provide only modest income-shifting opportunities. In earlier decades, however — before the enactment of the "kiddie tax" and the compression of the tax rate schedule for trusts — gifts to trusts were a major tax-reduction strategy for wealthy taxpayers. A taxpayer making a transfer to a trust can design the trust so that he has a right to receive distributions of corpus or income from the trust, or so that he has control over the timing and destination of trust distributions (even if he retains no right to distributions himself). In the days when the shifting of income to a trust could produce major tax savings, the crucial question was whether a grantor had retained sufficient interest in, or control over, trust property, so that he should continue to be treated as the owner of the property for tax purposes. The question reflects the "bundle of sticks" conception of property. If the grantor of a trust holds certain ownership sticks with respect to trust property — because of his beneficial interest in or control over the trust — he should be taxed on the trust income under the rule that income from property is taxed to the owner of the property; tax liability should be governed by the grantor's retained sticks, rather than by the trust's legal title. During this era, Congress enacted the grantor trust rules (currently codified at §§671 et seq.) to specify which retained sticks would cause the grantor of a trust to be taxed on trust income.

---

18. *See* subchapter J of the IRC, §§641 et seq.

A brief description cannot do justice to the complexity of the grantor trust rules, but with that caveat here is a summary of the rules.[19] Under §673, the grantor will be treated as the owner of trust property if he retains a reversionary interest in the trust, unless the present value of the reversion (at the time of the transfer to the trust) is not greater than 5 percent of the value of the transferred property. If the grantor retains any power to decide who will have beneficial enjoyment of trust income or corpus, the grantor will generally be taxed as the owner of the trust under §674. It is no defense to the application of §674 that the grantor retained no power to make trust distributions to himself. Section 674 does not apply, however, to a power exercisable only with the consent of an "adverse party." Suppose a grantor (G) transfers property to a trust, income to daughter (D), but income to son (S) if D displeases G (as determined at G's unfettered discretion). G would be taxed on trust income under §674. On the other hand, if the change of income beneficiary from D to S requires D's consent, G will not be taxed on the trust's income, because D is an adverse party with respect to the exercise of G's power. In addition to the adverse party exception, §674 provides a number of exceptions for certain limited grantor-retained powers to affect beneficial enjoyment. Section 675 treats the grantor as the owner of trust property with respect to which he retains specified "administrative powers," including the power to deal with trust property for less than adequate and full consideration, and the power to borrow from the trust without adequate interest or security. Some of the §675 administrative powers are the functional equivalent of the power to revoke the trust. Section 676 tackles revocation head-on; the grantor is generally taxable on trust income if he retains the power to revoke the trust. Under §677, the grantor is generally taxable if the trust income *may* be distributed to the grantor or the grantor's spouse, regardless of whether the trust income actually *is* so distributed.

The elaborateness of the grantor trust rules is an artifact of an era predating the "kiddie tax" and the compressed tax rate schedule for trusts, when the stakes in this area were much higher. One suspects Congress would not have felt the need for such complex rules if §§1(e) and 1(g) had existed when the grantor trust provisions were being drafted. The grantor trust rules remain in the Code in all their grandeur, however, even if they have outlived the circumstances that called them into existence.

g. Controlled Corporations

A corporation is ordinarily a taxpayer in its own right. The overall tax burden on corporate income depends on whether the corporation retains its after-tax earnings or distributes its after-tax earnings to its shareholders. If a corporation earns income and does not distribute the income to its shareholders, the income is taxed to the corporation — and *only* to the corporation — at rates set forth in §11. Under §11, the first $50,000 of corporate taxable income is taxed at the rate of 15 percent;

---

19. For brevity and ease of comprehension, the summary refers to powers retained by the grantor himself. For the most part, however, a power vested in a "nonadverse party" has the same effect as a power vested in the grantor himself. The statute defines a nonadverse party as a party who does not have an economic interest in the trust that would be adversely affected by the exercise or nonexercise of the power. The assumption underlying this treatment of powers held by nonadverse parties is that a nonadverse party given a power by the grantor will usually be happy to do the grantor's bidding.

the next $25,000 is taxed at 25 percent; and additional income is taxed at 34 and 35 percent rates. Suppose you are an individual with a marginal tax rate of 35 percent. The bulk of your income comes from your very successful law practice, but you also own a small business on the side, which produces about $75,000 of taxable income annually. If you incorporate the business (and do not have the corporation pay you a salary), you can shift the tax on the business income from your 35 percent bracket to the corporation's 15 and 25 percent brackets. This is true even if you are the sole owner of the corporation and in complete control of it; there is no corporate analogue to the grantor trust rules. If this sounds too good to be true, it is. The catch is that *distributed* corporate earnings are subject to a double tax. The corporation is taxed on its earnings regardless of whether it retains or distributes its income, but the nontaxation of shareholders on corporate earnings lasts only as long as the earnings remain in the corporation. Sooner or later, shareholders will want corporations to distribute earnings to them, and the distributions will then be taxable to the shareholders (without any offsetting deduction for the corporation). Before 2003, dividends were taxable to shareholders as ordinary income. Temporary legislation, however, provides that most dividends received in 2003 through 2012 are taxed at the rate applicable to long-term capital gains (15%, for most dividend-receiving taxpayers).[20] There are some situations in which a controlled corporation is an attractive income-shifting device, despite the eventual imposition of the second tax, especially with the temporary reduction in the tax imposed on dividends. For example, the combination of a 15 percent corporate tax rate (on the first $50,000 of corporate income) and a 15 percent dividend tax rate is obviously less burdensome than the 35 percent top individual income tax rate.[21] In many cases, however, the second tax takes all the fun — and then some — out of the game of shifting income to controlled corporations.

For taxpayers who want the non-tax advantages of incorporation, but who want to avoid the double tax, Congress has provided an alternative corporate tax regime. If a closely held corporation meets certain eligibility requirements, its taxpayers may elect taxation under the rules of subchapter S (§§1361 et seq.). S corporations ordinarily pay no tax, but their income is taxed to their shareholders (at whatever tax rates apply to the shareholders under §1), regardless of whether the income is retained or distributed. Since shareholders are taxed on their shares of undistributed S corporation income, distributions from S corporations are ordinarily tax-free to shareholders. As is apparent from this description, a taxpayer cannot shift income away from himself by transferring income-producing property to a 100-percent-owned S corporation.

---

20. *See* §1(h)(11). In addition to the temporary favorable treatment of dividends, some nondividend corporate distributions are eligible for capital gains treatment. *See, e.g.,* §302 (treating some corporate redemptions as nondividend distributions eligible for capital gains treatment).

21. The combined burden of the two 15 percent taxes is actually less than 30 percent, because the second tax (on the dividend) is not imposed on the portion of the corporate income used to pay the first (i.e., corporate) tax. Suppose a corporation earns $50,000. After paying a tax of $7,500 (15% of $50,000), the corporation is able to distribute a dividend of $42,500. The 15 percent dividend tax is imposed on $42,500, rather than on $50,000. The dividend tax is $6,375 (15% of $42,500). The sum of the two taxes is $13,875, which is 27.75 percent (*not* 30%) of the $50,000 of corporate income.

Cell

INTEREST ON CLIENT TRUST ACCOUNTS: OF TECHNICAL RULES AND PUBLIC RELATIONS

General Counsel Memorandum 38374

Rev. Rul. 81-209

GENERAL COUNSEL MEMORANDUM 38374

(1980)

ISSUES

I. Whether interest earned on clients' funds that are placed in an interest-bearing trust savings account by an attorney is includible in the gross income of the clients for Federal income tax purposes where the interest is automatically paid to a designated tax exempt fund under the fact situation described below.

II. Additionally the G.C.M. considers . . . whether the clients can obtain an I.R.C. §170 charitable deduction equal to the amount of interest earned on their funds and paid to. . . . [1]

CONCLUSIONS

I. The proposed revenue ruling holds that the interest earned on clients' funds that are placed in the interest-bearing trust savings account by the attorney is includible in the gross income of the clients for federal income tax purposes. We agree.

II. . . . We think that the facts of the proposed revenue ruling indicate that the clients therein are eligible for a section 170 charitable deduction equal to the amount of interest earned on their funds and paid to the foundation.

---

1. [The version of the GCM released to the public has been redacted to avoid revealing the identity of the program discussed in the document. — EDS.]

FACTS

The proposed revenue ruling is based on the following fact situation. Attorneys in . . . often hold funds received from their clients in connection with litigation costs, filing fees, expenses of real estate transactions, and other expenses for which the client must reimburse the attorney. Under the code of ethics adopted by . . . an advance is the property of the client held by the attorney in a fiduciary capacity, and has had to be segregated from the attorney's other funds into clearly labeled "trust accounts" subject to established accounting procedures. In the past, attorneys have ordinarily deposited clients' funds in noninterest-bearing commercial bank checking accounts to avoid extensive accounting problems associated with apportioning earnings on commingled funds among individual clients.

In 1980, the . . . authorized a program (the Program) which allows attorneys voluntarily to put commingled clients' funds in interest-bearing trust savings accounts without accounting to the clients for the interest earned, provided the interest monies are periodically paid to the . . . (the Foundation), which is a non-profit foundation associated with the . . . (the Association). An attorney who participates in the program may not withdraw the interest, but must instruct the depository to pay the interest directly to the Foundation. Those attorneys participating in the Program must send to each client a notice advising the client that his funds will be deposited in the trust savings account unless the client specifically gives written instructions to the contrary, in which case, the client's funds are placed in a noninterest-bearing trust checking account.

Even though the funds are in "trust," they remain the property of the client. Immediate availability of funds deposited in trust savings accounts is assured because the Foundation guarantees the immediate payment to the client, upon demand, of the amounts in a trust savings account allocable to the client in the event that requirements legally imposed by the depository bank with respect to such accounts preclude immediate payment. Moreover, the sums which are left in the account after the attorney has been reimbursed for all expenses are returned to the client.

ANALYSIS

I. Section 61 provides that, except as otherwise provided by law, gross income means all income from whatsoever source derived, and includes interest income.

Taxpayers will generally be required to include an income item in their gross income even though they have assigned the income interest to another. Thus the Supreme Court concluded in Lucas v. Earl, 281 U.S. 111 (1930), that a taxpayer's entire salary was includible in his gross income even though the taxpayer had by contract assigned half of all his future income to his spouse. This decision rested essentially on the ground that the realization of income by the assignee required the future rendition of services by the assignor-taxpayer, and thus, the income was controlled by the taxpayer who could defeat the gift by failing to perform the services. In Helvering v. Horst, 311 U.S. 112 (1940), the Court held that the interest income on bond interest coupons was includible in the gross income of a taxpayer who had transferred the coupons by gift shortly before their due date, because the taxpayer had control over the coupons and their payment, by virtue of the taxpayer's ownership and control of the bonds themselves. The Court reasoned that full enjoyment of the income accrued to the taxpayer, who owned the bonds, the source of the income, but who did not actually receive the interest income, because the taxpayer's desire to benefit another was satiated by the assignment.

The proposed revenue ruling holds that the interest earned on clients' funds that are placed in interest-bearing trust accounts by attorneys, under the Program described above, is includible in the gross income of the client for federal income tax purposes where the interest is automatically paid to a designated tax exempt fund, the Foundation. We agree.

Representatives of the Foundation . . . argue that the assignment of income principle does not apply to the Program because (1) the client can never receive the income, (2) the client is not attempting to avoid taxation and (3) the client has no control over the advances, the source of the income.

(1) The Representatives argue that the assignment of income doctrine is only applicable in situations where the taxpayer could have received the income. They cite Commissioner v. First Security Bank of Utah, 405 U.S. 394 (1972), Poe v. Seaborn, 282 U.S. 101 (1930), and Corliss v. Bowers, 281 U.S. 376 (1930), as cases supportive of their position. We disagree with the Representatives concerning whether the Program comes within the principles of *Poe* and *First Security Bank of Utah*. The Court in those cases refused to apply the assignment of income doctrine only in those instances where the taxpayer was prohibited by law from receiving the income.

Here, the client is not prohibited by law from receiving the interest income as the taxpayers in *First Security Bank of Utah* and *Poe* were. The . . . simply recognized that it is impractical timewise and expensewise for the attorney, who is the trustee of the accounts, to tabulate each client's interest income with respect to commingled trust savings account funds. In the conference the Representatives agreed that if an industrious attorney actually tabulated each client's interest income with respect to commingled trust savings account funds then the attorney would be required to distribute to each client his portion of the interest income and each client's portion of the interest income would be includible in his gross income. This follows from the fact that the . . . only allows donations of interest to the Foundation where it is impractical to make the interest available to clients.

It also appears that if an attorney put funds into an interest-bearing account and failed to properly notify the client, then the client would have a legal claim to the interest. In fact until the Program was created the attorney would have had to distribute even the interest on commingled funds; this prompted attorneys to ordinarily put commingled funds into noninterest-bearing accounts because tabulation of individual clients' interest was a both time-consuming and expensive practice. However, where individual clients have bargaining power or a substantial advance, their funds have always been placed in individual savings accounts, and there is no doubt that the income on the account belongs to them. Thus because the client is not legally prohibited from receiving interest income, *First Security Bank of Utah* and *Poe* are not applicable here. . . .

[T]he fact that clients in the Program have a veto power over attorneys' commingling their funds in interest-bearing accounts whose interest is payable only to the Foundation, indicates that it is the clients who ultimately designate the Foundation as the recipient of the interest. . . .

(2) The Representatives argue that because the Program was not implemented to alter the tax of clients, the assignment of income principle does not apply.

Although many cases involving the assignment of income principle encompass situations where the taxpayer is attempting to split income, we do not believe that tax avoidance motive is a necessary element of the assignment of income principle.

Although this is not an explicit trust situation, there is a fiduciary relationship between the attorney and client which could be analyzed as such. Using such an analysis, we believe that the Service would have to conclude that the client as grantor of the trust has sufficient control or command over the funds "in trust" to make the income taxable to him under the grantor trust provisions.

The attorney holds the client's funds in "trust," and if the client allows him to, the attorney keeps the client's funds in an interest-bearing trust savings account, directing the income to . . . Foundation[.] The client then is the grantor; the attorney is the trustee; and the Foundation is the designated income beneficiary of the income-producing trust. Under such a characterization and given the facts described above, such a "trust" must be found to be a grantor trust with income taxable to the grantor-client because the client has retained a reversionary interest in the "trust" within the meaning of section 673, a power to alter beneficial enjoyment of "trust" income within the meaning of section 674, and a power of revocation in the "trust" within the meaning of section 676. The client has a reversionary interest in the "trust" since the funds in the "trust" will revert to him as soon as all expenses, for which the client must reimburse the attorney, have been paid out of the fund. The client can stop the flow of income to the beneficiary and thus change the beneficial enjoyment of the income or entirely revoke the trust; he can require that the funds, the corpus of the trust[,] be immediately paid to him at any time, or he can at any time direct the attorney to deposit his funds in a noninterest-bearing checking account. Thus section 671, together with sections 673, 674, and 676, would require the client to include the interest income in his gross income, and thus be consistent with the conclusion of the proposed revenue ruling.

(3) Finally, the Representatives argue that the assignment of income principle is not applicable here because clients' control over income earned by advances is not only limited, but nonexistent as well. In essence the Representatives maintain that there is no point in time in which the clients themselves have a property right in the interest income which permits them to have the interest paid to themselves; thus, the clients have nothing to assign. We think that this position is contradicted by the very fact that the . . . requires attorneys participating in the Program to inform their clients that their funds have been placed in interest-bearing accounts and that they have the right to veto this arrangement; in essence, the attorney [must] obtain a waiver from each client. If the interest did not belong to the client, there would be no need to get such a waiver since the client's property rights in the account would be the same whether or not the account is interest-bearing. . . .

Accordingly although the attorney makes the initial decision to put the funds in an interest-bearing account, we think that it is the client who has made the ultimate decision to place the funds in that account because the client has the power to veto the attorney's decision. Moreover the fact that the interest income of each client may be *de minimus* [sic] or that it is impractical to distribute the interest income of each client, does not provide the Service with a legal basis for concluding that the interest income is not earned by and taxable to the client though these factors appear to be the primary ones weighed by the . . . when that . . . approved the Program.[2] We thus agree with the proposed revenue ruling which concludes that the interest income accruing on the funds of a Program client is includible in that client's gross income.

II. . . . The facts of the ruling indicate that the interest is paid to a "non-profit foundation." This raises the question concerning whether the client can receive a section 170 charitable deduction for the amount of interest that is paid to the Foundation and includible in the client's gross income. . . . Although the phrase "contribution or gift" is not defined either in the Code or in the underlying regulations, it is well-established that in order to be deductible under section 170 a contribution must qualify as a gift in the common law sense of being a voluntary transfer of money or property made by the transferor without receipt or expectation of a financial or economic benefit therefrom. . . . We believe that the client's contributions satisfy this criteria [sic]. . . .

Notes and Questions

1. *General Counsel Memoranda.* A General Counsel Memorandum (GCM) is an internal IRS document that is made available to the public (in redacted form) pursuant to §6110. Although GCMs and other documents covered by §6110 "may not be used or cited as precedent" (§6110(k)(3)), they provide valuable insight into the IRS's thinking. (And courts do sometimes cite these informal documents as authority, notwithstanding §6110(k)(3). See the *Niles* case in Chapter 4.B, *supra.*)

2. *Much ado about nothing?* In light of the GCM's conclusion that clients could claim charitable contribution deductions for trust account interest included in their gross income, is the inclusion issue much ado about nothing? For some taxpayers, the deduction will completely offset the inclusion, but that will not be true for all taxpayers. The deduction will be unavailable to taxpayers who claim the standard deduction instead of itemizing. Even taxpayers who do itemize may find their §170 deduction limited by §68's overall limitation on itemized deductions, or by the percentage limitations of §170(b).

3. *The better part of valor?* Imagine you are the Commissioner of the Internal Revenue Service, you have just read GCM 38374, and you have to decide whether to approve the issuance of the proposed revenue ruling. You believe the analysis in the GCM is technically sound, but you also believe that the situation described in the revenue ruling does not involve tax avoidance and is far removed from the core concerns of the assignment of income doctrine. You also know that the IRS will take a major public

---

2. We recognize that the . . . has social benefits and that, as a result of the Program, the Foundation would be able to contribute large sums of money to various programs for the benefit of the public. At the same time we must recognize that this is not an isolated case. In fact, you have informed us that there is a ruling request pending from a group of real estate brokers who want to set up a similar program which would allow their clients to waive their rights to interest payments on escrow deposits in favor of the . . . , which is a tax-exempt entity. While in each program the interest accruing on any one client's funds may be *de minimus* [sic], the amount of income accruing, in the aggregate, on clients' funds is not at all negligible.

relations blow if it stands in the way of such a worthy program. What would you do? Read on to see what the IRS actually did.

REV. RUL. 81-209

1981-2 C.B. 16

ISSUE

Whether interest earned on client advances deposited in "trust accounts" under the circumstances described below is includible in the gross income of the clients.

FACTS

Attorneys in state X who are retained to render legal service must place in trust accounts monetary advances received in the ordinary course of their business. In many cases these advances are too small in amount and are on deposit for too short a time to permit, as a practical matter, deposit of funds in separate accounts for each client, or deposit in a commingled account with interest allocated to each client. As a consequence, the long standing practice of attorneys in state X is to deposit these small and short-term advances in commingled noninterest bearing checking accounts.

In 1981 the Supreme Court of state X reviewed this practice regarding client advances as a matter within its original jurisdiction regarding the discipline and practice of attorneys. The court concluded that for practical reasons interest could not be made available to the clients on advances that were nominal and held for short duration, and continued the practice of allowing attorneys to deposit these advances in noninterest bearing checking accounts. However, the court also concluded that such funds could be productive of income for charitable purposes, and could be invested without violating the fiduciary relationship between attorney and client. Accordingly, the court established a program whereby an attorney could elect to commingle the nominal and short-term advances of all clients in an interest bearing trust account instead of a noninterest bearing checking account. Interest earned on amounts deposited in these trust accounts will be paid to the bar foundation of state X, a non-profit charitable organization described in section 501(c)(3) of the Internal Revenue Code.

The rights of the clients with respect to these advances will not be changed by the program; and no client may individually elect whether to participate in the program. If the attorney elects to participate in the program, the attorney must do so with respect to nominal and short-term advances of all clients. As with advances deposited in noninterest bearing checking accounts, advances deposited under the program continue to be readily available to attorneys for disbursement on behalf of clients. Under the program, all these disbursements for clients are in fact paid out of these trust accounts. The program bars clients from receiving the benefit of any interest earned on the commingled advances; and, because of their fiduciary responsibility to their clients with respect to any advances, it is illegal for the attorneys to receive any benefit from the interest earned on the commingled advances. Furthermore, under the program, clients cannot compel attorneys to invest the advances on the clients' behalf.

HOLDING

Under the unique facts described herein, interest earned on clients' nominal and short-term advances and paid over to the bar foundation pursuant to the program established by the Supreme Court of *X* is not includible in the gross incomes of the clients.

Notes and Questions

1. *A ruling literally devoid of analysis.* Something is missing from Rev. Rul. 81-209. Ordinarily, the heart of a revenue ruling is a section in between the facts and the holding, labeled "Analysis." When a ruling is issued without any analysis and the holding is expressly limited to "the unique facts described herein," the obvious inference is that the IRS felt politically compelled to issue a technically indefensible ruling, and attempted to minimize the precedential effect by omitting any analysis and by making the holding as narrow as possible.

2. *Distinguishing the GCM.* Rev. Rul. 81-209 is not, however, flatly inconsistent with the GCM, because the facts are not identical. In the situation described in the GCM, each client was entitled to opt out of the program (in favor of simply having the client's funds deposited in a noninterest-bearing account). In the revenue ruling, however, "no client may individually elect whether to participate in the program." According to GCM 38854 (1982), because of this factual distinction, "[W]e do not believe that the revenue ruling and the GCM [38374] are inconsistent." The argument in defense of the revenue ruling is that, in the absence of a veto power, the client does not have the control over the interest income necessary to bring the assignment of income doctrine into play. The attempted distinction is not very persuasive, however. Although the revenue ruling is silent on this point, presumably the client has the right to demand the return of his trust account principal at any time. Should not that be enough to make the client taxable on the interest income attributable to his funds, either under general assignment of income principles, or specifically under §676 (taxing the grantor on the income of a revocable trust)? Even if you think the revenue ruling is technically dubious (or worse), do you agree with the decision to issue it in light of the public relations implications?

3. *The Fifth Amendment issue.* In Brown v. Legal Foundation of Washington, 538 U.S. 216 (2003), the Supreme Court ruled (by a vote of 5 to 4) that Washington State's interest on lawyer's trust accounts (IOLTA) program did not violate the Just Compensation Clause of the Fifth Amendment. The Washington IOLTA program directs a lawyer to deposit a client's trust funds into a pooled IOLTA account (with the interest destined for the Washington State Legal Foundation) only if the funds could not be invested to pay a positive net return to the client, after taking into account the costs

of establishing and administering the fund. The Supreme Court assumed that the program constituted a technical taking of the *gross* interest earned by a client's funds. The Court held, however, that no compensation was required, because just compensation is measured by the client's loss, and the client's loss was zero — the amount of *net* interest the client could have earned on the trust funds were it not for the IOLTA program. What are the implications, if any, of *Brown* for the income taxation of clients whose funds are deposited into IOLTA accounts?

Chapter 11

RETIREMENT SAVINGS AND CONSUMPTION TAXATION

A. INDIVIDUAL RETIREMENT ACCOUNTS AND QUALIFIED PLANS

1. Individual Retirement Accounts, Deductible and Roth

Section 219 permits a taxpayer who meets certain eligibility requirements to deduct up to $5,000 contributed to an individual retirement account (IRA).[1] The deduction is allowed in arriving at adjusted gross income, so it is available even to taxpayers who claim the standard deduction.[2] If you contribute $5,000 of your earned income to a deductible IRA, the deduction offsets the inclusion of the $5,000 in gross income, with the result that the earned income is not taxed. Moreover, the return on your IRA investment (such as interest and dividends) is not taxed so long as the money remains in the IRA. When you retire and begin receiving distributions from your IRA, the distributions will be fully taxable as ordinary income.[3]

Instead of making a contribution to a deductible IRA, a taxpayer may choose to make a nondeductible contribution to a Roth IRA, described in §408A.[4] The ceiling on contributions to a Roth IRA is also $5,000, but the ceiling is reduced by the amount of the taxpayer's contribution to a deductible IRA for the same year.[5] Thus, a taxpayer can contribute $5,000 to a deductible IRA, or $5,000 to a Roth IRA, or $2,500 to each, but he cannot contribute $5,000 to each. What is the attraction of a Roth IRA, if there is no deduction? Any "qualified distribution" from a Roth IRA — which includes any distribution made after the taxpayer reaches the age of 59½ — is excluded from gross income. The tax on investment return is merely deferred in the case of a regular IRA, but the investment return on a Roth IRA is *never* taxed.

---

1. The ceiling, which is imposed by §219(b), is adjusted annually to reflect post-2007 inflation, but with the adjustment rounded down to the next lower multiple of $500. Because of this rounding rule, the ceiling for 2011 remains $5,000. Section 219(b)(5)(B) increases the ceiling by $1,000 for a taxpayer 50 or older.

2. *See* §62(a)(7).

3. *See* §408(d)(1).

4. The Roth IRA is named in honor of the late Senator William Roth, the former chairman of the Senate Finance Committee. Apparently there was a shortage of unnamed post offices and federal office buildings.

5. *See* §408A(c)(2).

Suppose you want to devote $5,000 of this year's wages to savings for your retirement, and you meet the eligibility requirements for both a deductible IRA and a Roth IRA. Which tax break is more valuable—the immediate deduction (and deferral of tax on investment return) under a regular IRA, or the permanent exclusion for investment return under a Roth IRA? The answer depends on tax rates, so we'll need to make some assumptions. Suppose your marginal tax rate this year is 30 percent, and your best guess is that your marginal tax rate in retirement will also be 30 percent. (Predicting your marginal tax rate in retirement can never be more than a rough guess; even if somehow you knew exactly what your taxable income would be in 30 years, you would not know what the tax rate schedule would be.) Let's also estimate that whatever you invest this year will triple in value by the time you retire and take the money out of the IRA.

With a regular IRA, you would invest $5,000, it would grow to $15,000 over the next few decades, and you would then receive a $15,000 distribution from the IRA. The 30 percent tax on the distribution would be $4,500, leaving you with $10,500. If you take the Roth route instead, you will not be able to invest the entire $5,000 in the Roth IRA, because without an IRA deduction you will owe $1,500 tax on the $5,000 of earnings. After paying the tax, you will have $3,500 left to invest. Over the decades, that $3,500 grows to $10,500. You then receive a tax-free distribution of $10,500 from the Roth IRA, leaving you with the entire $10,500 available for consumption—exactly the same result as if you had chosen a deductible IRA.

The result in the example generalizes. So long as your marginal tax rate is the same in the year you make the IRA contribution and in the year you receive the IRA distribution, it doesn't make any difference whether you choose a deductible IRA or a Roth IRA. If this is surprising, consider the formula for each result. With the deductible IRA, the after-tax amount available in retirement is

$$\$5,000 \times 3 \times (1-.3) = \$10,500$$

In the above equation, $5,000 is the amount invested, 3 is the investment return multiple (representing a tripling of the original investment), and .3 is the tax rate in retirement. With the Roth IRA, the amount available in retirement is

$$\$5,000 \times (1 -.3) \times 3 = \$10,500$$

In this equation, $5,000 is the amount to be devoted to retirement savings (before reduction by the tax imposed in the initial year), .3 is the tax rate in the initial year, and 3 is again the investment return multiple. In both equations, the $10,500 figure is the result of multiplying the same three numbers; the only difference is the order in which the three numbers are multiplied. Since multiplication is commutative—that is, the order in which the operations are performed does not affect the result—the final number is the same. Notice that the equivalency of the results under the two types of IRAs is independent of the rate of return on the IRA investment, so long as the rate of return is the same for an investment in either type of IRA—as it normally would be, since you can invest in the assets of your choice regardless of the type of IRA. Whether you expect your original investment merely to double, or to increase tenfold, the deductible IRA and Roth IRA bottom lines will be identical, *if* the marginal tax rates in the two years are identical.

The two equations above also make it clear when there *would* be a reason to prefer one type of IRA over the other: when you expect your marginal tax rate in retirement to be different from your marginal tax rate in the current year. You want the multiplier, *1 – tax rate*, to be as large as possible, which means you want the tax rate in the equation to be as low as possible. Thus, you should opt for a deductible IRA if you expect your tax rate in retirement to be lower than your current rate, and you should choose a Roth IRA if you think your retirement tax rate will be higher than this year's rate. Typically, taxable income is higher during working years than in retirement. If you expect your experience to be typical, you should prefer a deductible IRA (unless you think Congress will significantly increase tax rates across the board by the time you retire). A law student with a limited amount of income from a summer job, however, might reasonably expect to be in a higher bracket in retirement than she is in this year, and might therefore choose a Roth IRA.

Suppose your best guess is that your marginal tax rate in retirement will be about the same as this year's rate, but (unlike the previous example) you want to devote as much of this year's earnings as possible to tax-favored retirement savings. Will you still be indifferent between the two types of IRAs? You shouldn't be, because the $5,000 ceilings for the two types are only nominally equivalent. The above example demonstrated that $3,500 in a Roth IRA is the equivalent of $5,000 in a deductible IRA, because the tax has already been paid in the Roth but not in the deductible IRA. If you take the Roth to the limit, and invest $5,000, you will have the equivalent of substantially more than $5,000 in a deductible IRA. Using the same assumption of a tripling of your original investment, $5,000 in a Roth will leave you with $15,000 to spend in retirement, compared with only $10,500 from $5,000 in a deductible IRA. It would take about $7,143 in a deductible IRA to produce a $15,000 after-tax retirement distribution[6] — but you can't put $7,143 in a deductible IRA.

What if your best guess is that your marginal tax rate will be a little lower in retirement than it is now *and* you want to save as much this year as possible? The expected rate difference favors a regular IRA, but the desire to save as much as possible favors a Roth, and you must do some serious number crunching (based, unfortunately, largely on guesswork) to decide which is the better choice.

Up to this point, we have assumed you have a choice between the two types of IRAs. Many taxpayers, however, are eligible for a Roth IRA but not for a deductible IRA. Eligibility to make deductible IRA contributions is phased out for taxpayers who are active participants in employer-sponsored tax-favored retirement plans.[7] In 2011, the phaseout begins at $56,000 AGI for an unmarried taxpayer, and is completed at $66,000 AGI. There is also an AGI phaseout of Roth IRA eligibility, but in 2011 it does not begin (for an unmarried taxpayer) until $107,000 AGI — regardless of whether the taxpayer participates in an employer-sponsored retirement plan.[8] For example, the IRA choice is no choice at all for an unmarried taxpayer who has $75,000 AGI and participates in an employer-sponsored plan. She is eligible for a Roth, but not eligible for a deductible IRA.

A taxpayer whose high AGI makes him ineligible for either a deductible IRA or a Roth IRA can still make a contribution to a §408(*o*) nondeductible, non-Roth, IRA. The only tax advantage in that case is the deferral of tax on the investment return

---

6. Let *z* equal the amount that you need to invest in a deductible IRA to leave you with $15,000 in retirement, after tax. Then $z \times 3 \times (1 - .3) = \$15,000$. Solving for *z*, $z = \$7,143$.

7. *See* §219(g).

8. *See* §408A(c)(3).

until the taxpayer receives retirement distributions from the IRA. Unlike a taxpayer owning a deductible IRA, a taxpayer will have basis in a §408(*o*) IRA, and part of each distribution will be treated as a tax-free return of basis.[9]

The following three problems are exercises in reading and applying some of the technical intricacies of the IRA provisions.

Problem 1.   The year is 2011, and Fred is 51 years old and unmarried. Fred's AGI is $60,000. Although Fred is an active participant in his employer's qualified pension plan, he is concerned that he is not saving enough for retirement through his employer's plan. How much, if anything, can he contribute to a deductible IRA? *See* §§219(b) and (g).

Problem 2.   The facts are the same as in the previous problem. What is the maximum amount Fred can contribute to a Roth IRA for 2011, assuming he makes no contribution to a deductible IRA? *See* §408A(c)(2).

Problem 3.   The year is 2011. Rob and Laura are married, and file a joint income tax return. Rob's annual salary is $100,000. Rob is an active participant in his employer's pension plan, so he is not eligible to make a deductible IRA contribution. *See* §219(g). He could make a contribution to a Roth IRA, or to a nondeductible, non-Roth IRA, but he has not done so and does not plan on doing so. Laura, who is 35 years old, is a full-time homemaker, with no earned income. Rob and Laura would like to make a deductible contribution to an IRA for Laura. Can they do so? If they can, what is the largest deductible contribution they can make? *See* §219(c).

2.   Income Tax or Consumption Tax?

There is a long-standing political and philosophical debate, which heats up from time to time, over whether income or consumption is the better tax base. The current "income" tax, however, already has very significant consumption tax features. This section explains the hybrid income-consumption character of the current system, and provides an introduction to the great tax base debate.

Basically, there are only two things you can do with your income (apart from paying taxes)—consume it now or save it. It follows that we can define income, in terms of its uses, as

$$\text{Income} = \text{Consumption} + \text{Savings, or, I} = \text{C} + \text{S}$$

A consumption tax can take several different forms, of which the retail sales tax is most familiar to Americans. Another form of consumption tax is suggested by the above equation. If $I = C + S$, then we can subtract S from both sides of the equation to produce $C = I - S$. This means that the income tax could be converted to a consumption tax simply by allowing taxpayers to deduct all their savings.[10] It also means that deductible IRAs are already afforded consumption tax treatment, and

---

9. *See* §408(d).

10. Dissavings—that is, spending out of savings—would figure into the equation as negative savings, and would thus be taxable. Consumption financed by borrowing—another form of negative savings—would also be taxable.

that removing the dollar ceiling on deductible IRAs (by repealing §219(b)) would come close to converting the income tax to a consumption tax.[11] As will be explained more fully in the next section, current law also provides consumption tax treatment for retirement savings in employer-sponsored pension plans. Considering both deductible IRAs and employer-sponsored pensions, the vast majority of private (non–social security) retirement savings is already subject to a consumption tax, rather than to an income tax.

A roughly accurate description of current law is that it is an income-consumption tax hybrid, with the bulk of retirement savings receiving consumption tax treatment, but with income tax treatment as the norm for other savings. Even with respect to other savings, current law has important consumption tax features. Most significantly, current law provides an exclusion—the equivalent of an inclusion and an offsetting deduction—for income saved in the form of unrealized appreciation. Various nonrecognition provisions extend this treatment to some forms of realized gain.

In forming your own opinion on the merits of replacing the "income" tax with a consumption tax, here are several points to keep in mind:

(1) *The real stakes.* Because the consumption tax features of the income tax are so significant, there is less at stake in the income-versus-consumption tax debate than is often supposed. Since the bulk of the savings of the middle class is in tax-favored retirement savings (or in owner-occupied housing, which gets its own very favorable tax treatment[12]), replacing the income tax with a consumption tax is primarily about eliminating the taxation of saved income for the non-retirement savings of affluent taxpayers. Affluent taxpayers can already obtain consumption tax treatment for most or all of their *retirement* savings, through employer-sponsored plans, but their *bequest* savings—amounts saved for transfer to younger generations—are subject to income tax treatment (to the extent they do not take the form of unrealized appreciation). Thus, the major tax savings from the replacement of the current tax system with a consumption tax would be with respect to the intergenerational savings of the most affluent families.

(2) *Consumption taxes and wage taxes.* Just as a deductible IRA is a limited version of a consumption tax, a Roth IRA is a limited version of a wage tax. Under a Roth IRA, labor income is taxed when earned, but investment income is never taxed. That is, of course, the definition of a wage tax. The demonstration that a deductible IRA and a Roth IRA are equivalent, when the tax rate is constant across time, can be generalized to show that consumption taxation and wage taxation are equivalent, given a constant tax rate.[13] If you would not be in favor of replacing the

11. A complete conversion of the income tax to a consumption tax would require a few more changes. Most significantly, (1) IRA-type tax treatment would have to be made available for savings for all purposes, rather than only for retirement savings, and (2) debt-financed consumption would have to be taxable.
12. Income invested in owner-occupied housing is basically given wage tax treatment. That is, there is no deduction for wages invested in housing, but the return on the investment is tax-free. Return in the form of rental value is tax-free imputed income from property, and return in the form of appreciation is usually never taxed—not even on a deferred basis—because of §§121 and 1014. As noted later in the text, Roth IRAs are another example of wage tax treatment, and wage tax treatment is closely related to consumption tax treatment.
13. In addition to requiring a constant tax rate, the strict equivalency of a consumption tax and a wage tax holds only if there is no existing wealth in a society at the time the tax system is introduced. A consumption tax would tax spending out of wealth that existed at the time the

income tax with a wage tax, perhaps you should also not favor replacing the income tax with a consumption tax.

(3) *Distinguishing the tax base and tax rate questions.* In political debates about fundamental tax reform, the question of income versus consumption base is usually mixed up with the question of a "flat" tax (with one positive tax rate, above a zero rate for poverty-level income) versus a tax with progressive marginal rates. Some forms of consumption taxation are imposed on businesses rather than on individuals. This category includes the retail sales tax and the closely related value-added tax (VAT), which is common outside the United States. Since consumption taxes of this sort do not keep track of individuals' total consumption, they cannot impose higher marginal rates on those who consume more. Consumption taxes of this sort are thus "naturally" flat. But consider a cash-flow consumption tax, based on the equation $C = I - S$. Under this kind of consumption tax — basically current law, as it would be modified by the repeal of §219(b) — the tax is imposed on an individual according to his total consumption. This individualized tax base is perfectly compatible with progressive marginal rates. The so-called flat tax, popularized by Steve Forbes, is another form of consumption tax that is imposed (in part) on individuals, and thus could accommodate a progressive rate structure.[14] In short, there is no technical — as distinguished from political — connection between the base and rate issues. Although the usual associations are of income tax and progressive rates, and of consumption tax and a flat rate, there is no technical barrier to either a flat rate income tax or a progressive consumption tax.

3. *Employer-Sponsored Retirement Savings*

Employer-sponsored retirement savings — often referred to as qualified plans — are afforded the same basic consumption tax treatment as deductible IRAs. There is no tax at the time the employer makes the contribution (this is accomplished by an exclusion, rather than a deduction), but distributions are fully taxable. The details of the rules for qualified plans are beyond the scope of a basic income tax course, but there are two crucial differences between such plans and deductible IRAs. First, the ceilings on the annual amount of retirement savings eligible for consumption tax treatment are much higher for qualified plans than for IRAs. In the case of a defined contribution plan (i.e., a plan that defines the amount to be contributed each year by the employer on the employee's behalf, as contrasted with a defined benefit plan that defines the annual benefits to be received by the employee in retirement), the inflation-adjusted limitation imposed by §415(c)(1)(A) for 2011 is $49,000. Second, qualified plans are subject to non-discrimination requirements, under which "the contributions or benefits provided under the plan [must] not discriminate in favor of highly compensated employees."[15] Can you discern the policy behind these two differences? The idea is that

---

consumption tax was introduced, but a wage tax would not tax spending out of wealth that existed at the time the wage tax was introduced.

14. The flat tax is actually a bifurcated VAT, with a portion of the tax imposed on businesses and a portion imposed on wage earners. For an explanation, see Lawrence Zelenak, *Flat Tax vs. VAT: Progressivity and Family Allowances,* 69 Tax Notes 1129 (1995).

15. Section 401(a)(4). Another difference is that an employer-sponsored plan may either (1) define the amount to be contributed by the employer on behalf of the employee, with the amount

highly compensated employees will want large amounts of tax-favored retirement savings, and thus will demand employer-sponsored pensions to avoid the low ceiling on IRAs. When highly compensated employees insist on tax-favored employer-sponsored pensions, the employer can comply only by also providing pensions for rank-and-file employees, who otherwise might not make adequate provision for their own retirements. In short, the nondiscrimination rules are a way of using highly compensated employees to put pressure on employers to provide pensions for non–highly compensated employees. Unfortunately, this strategy has not worked very well. Most low and moderate wage workers do not have adequate retirement savings. Part of the explanation for the failure is in the details of the so-called nondiscrimination rules; in fact, the rules permit considerable discrimination in favor of highly compensated employees.

In a classic employer-sponsored retirement plan, the employee has no option to receive taxable cash compensation instead of a tax-favored pension contribution; the plan simply specifies the amount the employer is to contribute to a particular employee's pension, and the employer makes the contribution. Under the doctrine of constructive receipt,[16] an employee who did have the option to receive cash, but turned his back on the cash in favor of a pension contribution, would be taxed just as if he had actually received the cash. However, §401(k) overrides the constructive receipt doctrine for certain "cash or deferred arrangements," under which an employee may choose between taxable cash and a tax-deferred employer contribution to his pension.[17] Section 401(k) contributions closely resemble deductible IRAs. In both cases, the taxpayer has the choice to consume now and pay tax, or to save for retirement and defer tax. Nevertheless, the ceiling is much higher for §401(k) contributions than for IRAs (and nondiscrimination rules apply under §401(k), but not with respect to IRAs).

4. Limiting Consumption Tax Treatment to Retirement Savings

If the basic idea behind deductible IRAs and employer-sponsored pensions is to provide consumption tax treatment *for retirement savings*, there should be rules to prevent taxpayers (1) from consuming tax-favored retirement savings before retirement, and (2) from oversaving, so that much of their savings remains in an IRA or qualified plan at death, with the deferral then extending to the savings in the hands of the next generation. There are Code provisions designed to police both of these areas, but they have not been particularly effective, apparently because Congress does not want the rules to be very effective.

Section 72(t) imposes a 10 percent penalty tax on "early distributions" from IRAs and employer-sponsored plans. A distribution is not early if it is made no sooner than the date on which the taxpayer reaches age 59½. There are numerous exceptions to the penalty tax, but the two exceptions least consistent with the basic

---

of the eventual retirement distributions depending on the employee's investment choices, or (2) define the benefits the employee will be entitled to receive in retirement, leaving the employee with no investment decisions and no investment risk. By contrast, IRAs are always defined-contribution savings.

16. See section B.1 of Chapter 7.

17. Section 403(b) provides a similar rule for employees of governments and tax-exempt organizations.

retirement savings rationale for tax deferral are for distributions to pay for "qualified higher education expenses," and for distributions to finance the purchase of the taxpayer's first home.[18]

To some extent, concerns about excessive tax-favored retirement savings are addressed by the ceilings on the annual amount of contributions eligible for deferral. Roughly speaking, these limits are supposed to deny consumption tax treatment for savings beyond reasonable retirement needs. In fact, however, the limits — at least the limits on employer-sponsored plans — are far too generous to achieve that purpose. In any event, no *contribution* limit could control excessive *accumulations*, when the accumulations result from spectacular investment returns. As an additional constraint on excessive deferral, the Code requires that taxable distributions from an IRA or a qualified plan must begin in the year after the taxpayer reaches age 70½ (or in the year after he retires, if later).[19] Finally, the Code imposes minimum distribution requirements with respect to annual payments after distributions have begun. The entire interest of a taxpayer in an IRA or a qualified plan must be distributed "over the life of such employee or over the lives of such employee and a designated beneficiary (or over a period not extending beyond the life expectancy of such employee or the life expectancy of such employee and a designated beneficiary)."[20] If this sounds complicated, it is. The important point to note, however, is that in many cases this rule permits deferral to continue well beyond the taxpayer's death, both because the taxpayer may die earlier than the actuarial tables predicted, and because of the ability to extend distributions over the life or life expectancy of a younger designated beneficiary. The designated beneficiary may be anyone at all, although the typical designated beneficiary is the spouse or child of the taxpayer. The Treasury has issued, to rave reviews, taxpayer-favorable regulations interpreting the minimum distribution requirements.[21]

B. "NONQUALIFIED" DEFERRED COMPENSATION

From the point of view of a highly compensated executive, neither an IRA nor an employer-sponsored plan is an ideal retirement savings vehicle. The IRA contribution ceiling is far too low. Even the employer plan limits are too low, and one has to deal with those pesky nondiscrimination rules as well. In the case of a cash method taxpayer — and all employees are cash method taxpayers with respect to their employment — a mere unsecured contractual right to receive payment in a future year is not currently includible in gross income. Thus, an executive can avoid all dollar ceilings on tax-favored retirement savings, and avoid all nondiscrimination rules, if he is willing to accept his deferred compensation (which may be deferred until retirement, or for some shorter period) in the form of the employer's unsecured contractual obligation to pay deferred compensation in a

---

18. *See* §§72(t)(2)(E) and (F).
19. *See* §§408(a)(6) (IRAs), 401(a)(9)(C) (employer-sponsored pensions).
20. Section 401(a)(9)(A)(ii), made applicable to IRAs by §408(a)(6).
21. Reg. §1.401(a)(9).

later year. This is known as "nonqualified" deferred compensation, because it does not meet the statutory requirements for qualified plans. The non-tax risk to the executive is that the employer may not be able to make the required payments when they become due. Some amelioration of this risk is made possible by Rev. Proc. 92-64, 1992-2 C.B. 422, which permits the employer's obligation to pay nonqualified deferred compensation to be funded by a trust without triggering immediate taxation of the employee under the constructive receipt doctrine, but only if the trust is subject to the claims of the employer's creditors.[22] The extent of the risk of never being paid one's nonqualified deferred compensation varies tremendously from one situation to another, depending on the creditworthiness of the employer and the length of the deferral. An unsecured obligation of Exxon, payable in five years, may be almost as safe as an obligation of the federal government. An unsecured obligation of some dot.com, payable in 30 years, may be a very different story.

Congress tightened the rules governing nonqualified deferred compensation considerably in the American Jobs Creation Act of 2004, which added §409A to the Code. The rules of §409A are applicable to nonqualified deferred compensation plans, a concept that is defined quite broadly. (Even an agreement between one employee and her employer providing for a single deferred compensation payment qualifies as a "plan.") If the plan fails to conform to the new statutory rules, any deferred compensation will be immediately taxable unless it is subject to a "substantial risk of forfeiture" if certain conditions stated in the contract are not fulfilled.[23] The rules generally bar distribution of the deferred compensation earlier than the first of several dates: the date of the participant's separation from service (or six months following separation in certain cases, typically involving corporate officers and the like), death, or disability; a time specifically identified in the plan; a time of change in ownership or control of the party paying the deferred compensation; or the occurrence of an unforeseeable emergency, such as the illness or injury of the participant or a spouse, or casualty loss of the participant's property. This leaves a fair amount of freedom to the parties in structuring the nonqualified plan, but substantially limits their flexibility to adjust the plan once it is in place.

Consistently with that approach, the rules of §409A specifically bar acceleration of the deferred compensation under ordinary circumstances, and contain a considerable volume of detail regarding when and how deferral elections may be made, how plans may be funded, and the like. These details are beyond the scope of an introductory course, but they certainly take much of the fun out of nonqualified deferred compensation as it was known prior to 2004. If the arrangements don't comply with the §409A rules governing what might be called "qualified nonqualified deferred compensation," then the compensation simply won't be deferred (unless it is made on the basis of contingencies that ordinarily will not be acceptable to the participant).

Apart from the complexities of §409A, the tax problem with nonqualified deferred compensation is that §404(a)(5) imposes a matching requirement. The employer may not claim a business expense deduction for nonqualified deferred

22. For historical reasons, the kind of trust sanctioned by the revenue procedure is commonly referred to as a "rabbi trust."

23. See discussion of this concept in the cell following Chapter 2 entitled, "Restricted Property and Stock Options."

compensation until the year that the employee is required to include the compensation in income. By contrast, an employer may immediately deduct a contribution to a qualified plan, even though the employee will not be taxed for several years or even decades. The following case involves an employer's creative attempt to circumvent the matching requirement.

ALBERTSON'S, INC. v. COMMISSIONER
42 F.3d 537 (9th Cir. 1994), *cert. denied*, 516 U.S. 807 (1995)

REINHARDT, Circuit Judge: On December 30, 1993, we filed an opinion concerning various disputes between Albertson's and the Internal Revenue Service. 12 F.3d 1529 (9th Cir. 1993). We granted the government's petition for rehearing as to Part II.B of the opinion, which concerned the appropriate tax treatment of deferred compensation agreements. Today we vacate Part II.B of the original opinion and affirm the Tax Court's decision.

I. BACKGROUND

Deferred compensation agreements ("DCAs") are agreements in which certain employees and independent contractors ("DCA participants") agree to wait a specified period of time ("deferral period") before receiving the annual bonuses, salaries, or director's fees that they would otherwise receive on a current basis. During the deferral period, the employer uses the basic amounts of deferred compensation ("basic amounts"), which accumulate on an annual basis, as a source of working capital. At the end of the deferral period, the employer pays the participating individuals the basic amounts and an additional amount for the time value of the deferred payments that have accumulated on the basic amounts ("additional amount"). The time-value-of-money sums are also computed on a yearly basis. The total of these basic amounts and the amounts attributable to compensation for the delay in payment of those amounts constitutes the whole of the deferred compensation ("deferred compensation"). The time-value-of-money component may be measured by interest rate indices, equity fund indices, or cost of living increases, or it may simply be included within a lump-sum payment.

Prior to 1982, Albertson's entered into DCAs with eight of its top executives and one outside director. The parties agreed that their deferred compensation would include the annual basic amounts plus additional amounts calculated annually in accordance with an established formula. The DCA participants would be eligible to receive the deferred compensation (the total sum) upon their retirement or termination of employment with Albertson's. The DCA participants also had the option of further deferring payment for up to fifteen years thereafter. During that extra period, the additional amounts would continue to accrue on an annual basis.

In 1982, Albertson's requested permission from the IRS to deduct the additional amounts (but not the basic amounts) during the year in which they accrued instead of waiting until the end of the deferral period. In 1983, the IRS granted Albertson's request. Accordingly, Albertson's claimed deductions of $667,142 for the additional amounts that had already accrued, even though it had not yet paid the DCA participants any sums under the deferred compensation agreements. In 1987, the

IRS changed its policy, however, and sought a deficiency for the additional amounts, contending that all amounts provided for in the deferred compensation agreements were deductible only when received by Albertson's employees. Albertson's filed a petition with the Tax Court, claiming that the additional amounts constituted "interest" and thus could be deducted as they accrued.

In a sharply divided opinion, the Tax Court rejected Albertson's position. Albertson's, Inc. v. Commissioner, 95 T.C. 415 (1990). The court found that the additional amounts represented compensation, not interest, and were therefore not deductible until the end of the deferral period under I.R.C. §404(a)(5) & (d).

We reversed the decision of the Tax Court. We held that the additional amounts constituted interest within the definition of I.R.C. §163(a) and that interest payments were not governed by the timing restrictions of section 404. The government petitioned for rehearing due to the significant fiscal impact of the panel's opinion which it estimates will cause a $7 billion loss in tax revenues.

II. REHEARING

We agreed to rehear this issue after lengthy consideration and reflection. In our original opinion, we stated that the plain language of the statute strongly supported Albertson's interpretation and, accordingly, we adopted it. Nevertheless, we expressed sympathy for the Commissioner's argument that Congress intended the timing restrictions of I.R.C. §404 to apply to all payments made under a deferred compensation plan and recognized that our plain language interpretation seemed to undercut Congress' purpose.

We have now changed our minds about the result we reached in our original opinion and conclude that our initial decision was incorrect. The question is not an easy one, however. We have struggled with it unsuccessfully at least once, and it may, indeed, ultimately turn out that the United States Supreme Court will tell us that it is this opinion which is in error. This is simply one of those cases — and there are more of them than judges generally like to admit — in which the answer is far from clear and in which there are conflicting rules and principles that we are forced to try to apply simultaneously. Such accommodation sometimes proves to be impossible. In some cases, as here, convincing arguments can be made for both possible results, and the court's decision will depend on which of the two competing legal principles it chooses to give greater weight to in the particular circumstance. Law, even statutory construction, is not a science. It is merely an effort by human beings, albeit judges, to do their best with imperfect tools to arrive at a correct result. . . .

In its petition for rehearing, the government, far more forcefully and clearly than it did originally, has articulated the purpose of the timing restrictions outlined in I.R.C. §404: to encourage employers to invest in qualified compensation plans by requiring inclusions and deductions of income and expense to be "matched" for nonqualified plans. . . . As the Commissioner forcefully argues, our original interpretation of I.R.C. §404 undercut the essential purpose of that provision by violating the matching principle and creating a taxation scheme that favors the type of plan that Congress intended to discourage. For this reason, we granted the Commissioner's petition for rehearing. We now withdraw the portion of our earlier opinion that dealt with deferred compensation agreements, and affirm the Tax Court's decision, although not for the reasons upon which the Tax Court majority relied.

III. ANALYSIS

Albertson's again urges this court (1) to characterize the additional amounts as interest as defined by I.R.C. §163(a), and (2) to find that such "interest" payments are deductible under I.R.C. §404.[24] However, we have now concluded that, notwithstanding the statutory language on which Albertson's relies, to hold the additional amounts to be deductible would contravene the clear purpose of the taxation scheme Congress created to govern deferred compensation plans. As the Supreme Court noted in Bob Jones University v. United States, 461 U.S. 574 (1983), a term in the Code "must be analyzed and construed within the framework of the Internal Revenue Code and against the background of the congressional purposes." *Id.* at 586 (emphasis added).

A. A COMPARISON OF QUALIFIED AND NONQUALIFIED PLANS

An examination of the differences between qualified and nonqualified plans is essential to an understanding of the purpose of the congressional scheme governing deferred compensation agreements. Congress has imposed few restrictions upon nonqualified deferred compensation plans. An employer may limit participation in a nonqualified plan to highly paid executives, and it need not guarantee equal benefits for all participants. In addition, the employer is not required to set aside any funds or provide any guarantees (beyond the initial contractual promise) that its employees will receive the compensation. Thus, promised benefits for unfunded, nonqualified plans are subject to the claims of the employer's general creditors.

Under a qualified plan, in contrast, an employer may not discriminate in favor of officers, shareholders, or highly compensated employees. I.R.C. §401(a)(4) & (a)(5). In addition, a qualified plan must satisfy minimum participation and coverage standards concerning eligibility and actual rates of participation. I.R.C. §§401(a)(2) & (a)(26), 410. The amounts which an employer may contribute to qualified plans and the benefits which qualified plans may provide are also restricted. I.R.C. §§401(a)(17), 415.

---

24. The relevant provisions, at the time Albertson's filed its 1983 tax return, were as follows:

Sec. 404. Deductions for . . . compensation under a deferred-payment plan.
(a) General rule. — . . . If compensation is paid or accrued on account of any employee under a plan deferring the receipt of such compensation, such . . . compensation shall not be deductible under section 162 (relating to trade or business expenses) or section 212 (relating to expenses for the production of income); but if they satisfy the conditions of either such sections, they shall be deductible subject, however, to the following limitations as to the amounts deductible in any year. . . .
(5) If the plan is not one included in paragraph (1), (2), or (3) [relating to pension trusts, annuities, and stock bonus and profit-sharing trusts], in the taxable year in which an amount attributable to the contribution is includible in the gross income of employees participating in the plan. . . .
(d) Deductibility of payments of deferred compensation, etc., to independent contractors. — If a plan would be described [as above] . . . [the] compensation —
(1) shall not be deductible by the payor thereof under section 162 or 212, but
(2) shall . . . be deductible under this subsection for the taxable year in which an amount attributable to the . . . compensation is includible in the gross income of the persons participating in the plan.

A qualified plan also provides significant guarantees that employees will receive the compensation promised to them. It generally must be funded through a trust. I.R.C. §401(a). Neither the corpus nor the income of the trust may be diverted for any purpose; they can only be used for the exclusive benefit of the participants. I.R.C. §§401(a)(2). . . . It is clear that few employers would adopt a qualified deferred compensation plan, with all of its burdensome requirements, if the taxation scheme favored nonqualified plans or treated nonqualified and qualified plans similarly. Although qualified plans provide significant benefits to employees, they allow employers little flexibility in structuring a plan, require them to provide extensive coverage, prevent them from discriminating in favor of highly compensated employees, and involve a significant initial outlay of funds. Thus, the extensive regulations Congress has imposed upon qualified plans would serve little purpose unless employers had an incentive to adopt such plans. As we discuss in the next part, section 404 provides the incentive necessary to encourage employers to adopt qualified plans by providing significantly more favorable tax treatment of qualified plans than of nonqualified ones. . . .

B. THE PURPOSE OF SECTION 404

Congress enacted section 23(p), the forerunner to section 404, in 1942. Prior to 1942, corporations were allowed to deduct DCA-related expenses as they accrued each year, even though employees did not recognize any income until a subsequent taxable year. In 1942, Congress eliminated this favorable treatment for deductions relating to "nonqualified" deferred compensation agreements, such as the DCAs at issue in this case. In so doing, Congress forced employers who chose to retain their funds for their own use to wait until the end of the deferral period, when these amounts were includible in plan participants' taxable income, before they could take deductions for deferred compensation payments. However, employers who maintained a "qualified" plan that met the rigorous requirements of the Internal Revenue Code (and now ERISA), including turning over the sums involved to a trust fund (or purchasing an annuity), were allowed to continue to take the annual deductions even though their employees would not receive the deferred compensation until a later year. *See, e.g.*, I.R.C. §§404(a) & (d); 29 U.S.C. §1082 (1988).

1. *The Matching Principle*

Congress provided a single explanation for the timing restrictions of section 404: to ensure matching of income inclusion and deduction between employee and employer under nonqualified plans. As both the House and Senate Reports note, "if an employer on the accrual basis defers paying any compensation to the employee until a later year or years . . . he will not be allowed a deduction until the year in which the compensation is paid." H.R. Rep. No. 2333, 77th Cong., 2d Sess. (1942), 1942-2 Cum. Bull. 372, 452; S. Rep. No. 1631, 77th Cong., 2d Sess. (1942), 1942-2 Cum. Bull. 504, 609. . . .

2. *The Significance of the Matching Principle*

The significance of section 404's matching principle becomes evident when one compares the treatment of qualified and nonqualified plans under that section. Because section 404 requires employer deductions for contributions to nonqualified plans to be "matched," an employer cannot take tax deductions for payments to its employees until the DCA participants include those payments in their taxable income — that is, until the employees actually receive the compensation promised to them.

Qualified plans, in contrast, are not governed by the matching principle and consequently generate concurrent tax benefits to employers. Although employees are not taxed upon the benefits they receive from the plan until they actually receive them, an employer's contributions to a qualified plan are deductible when paid to the trust. I.R.C. §§402(a)(1) & 404(a). Thus, the employer may take an immediate, unmatched deduction for any contribution it makes to a qualified plan.[25]

By exempting contributions to qualified plans from the matching principle, Congress compensates employers for meeting the burdensome requirements associated with qualified plans by granting them favorable tax treatment. The current taxation scheme thus creates financial incentives for employers to contribute to qualified plans while providing no comparable benefits for employers who adopt plans that are unfunded or that discriminate in favor of highly compensated employees.

C. THE EFFECTS OF ALBERTSON'S PROPOSAL

Albertson's maintains that section 404 only requires that the basic amounts of compensation be matched; it argues that all additional amounts paid to compensate an employee for the time value of money represent "interest" payments for which an employer may take an immediate deduction. In light of the clear purpose underlying section 404 — to encourage employers to create qualified plans for their employees — we decline to ascribe such an intention to Congress.

First, Albertson's proposal appears to undermine the effectiveness of the timing restrictions by reducing the significance of the incentive structure created by section 404. In order to adopt Albertson's proposal and allow employers to take current deductions for additional "interest" payments, we would be required to conclude that Congress created a system in which employers could deduct a substantial portion of the nonqualified deferred compensation package long before its employees had received any of those funds. For example, when the additional amounts are calculated for a compensation package deferred over a fifteen-year period using an interest rate similar to that used by Albertson's, an employer can classify more than seventy percent of the deferred compensation package as "interest payments."[26] . . .

---

25. In addition, the earnings of a trust established by a qualified plan are not taxable to the trust. I.R.C. §§401(a) & 501(a).

26. According to the record, it appears that Albertson's employees were compensated at a 14.8% interest rate, compounded monthly.

Albertson's has been unable to explain why Congress, in designing a taxation scheme to encourage the creation of qualified plans, would require an employer that maintains a nonqualified plan to defer taking a deduction on the basic amounts of a promised compensation package but nevertheless allow that employer to take current deductions on amounts that constitute a substantial portion of the compensation package, merely because that portion is classified as "interest." Given that the interest payments will often constitute the bulk of the total compensation package that an employee under a nonqualified plan ultimately receives, it would make little sense to impose a matching requirement upon "basic" payments but not upon "interest" payments. Albertson's interpretation of section 404 would seriously undermine the incentive structure designed by Congress to encourage employers to establish qualified plans.

An additional reason to reject Albertson's statutory interpretation of section 404 is that, in certain cases, Albertson's approach might actually create an incentive for employers to establish nonqualified plans. Whereas an employer who maintains a qualified plan may only take a current deduction for the basic amounts of promised compensation, an amount it actually has paid out, under Albertson's approach an employer that maintains a nonqualified plan could take current deductions for "interest" payments that substantially exceed the basic amounts even though it has paid out none of these funds. Moreover, the employer could take advantage of these tax benefits without being constrained by the burdensome requirements associated with qualified plans. For this reason, characterizing the additional amounts as deductible interest, as Albertson's suggest, would encourage employers to maintain nonqualified plans and thus directly contradict the statutory purpose underlying I.R.C. §404.[27]

Thus, Albertson's proposal runs counter to the congressional scheme. It undermines Congress' attempts to encourage employers to adopt qualified plans and, in some cases, directly contradicts the purpose of section 404 by creating an incentive to create nonqualified plans.

D. ALBERTSON'S RESPONSE

Albertson's has not been able to refute the argument that its interpretation of section 404 undercuts the provision's central purpose. Equally important, it offers us no reason why Congress would have wanted to treat the "interest" part of the deferred compensation package differently from the basic amounts for tax purposes.

---

27. We also note the government's argument concerning the possible consequences of a finding in favor of Albertson's. According to the Commissioner, under a long-standing administrative practice, employees are currently not taxed upon the benefits they receive from deferred compensation plans until they actually receive them, precisely because employers have not taken deductions for those amounts. Because section 404 only exempts payments under qualified plans from the matching principle, were we to uphold Albertson's approach, the Commissioner suggests that we would be required to conclude that employer deductions for interest accruing under nonqualified plans must be "matched" by the inclusion of those amounts in employees' current taxable income. As is clear from the foregoing discussion, such an unrealized addition to the employees' income for tax purposes would indeed be substantial and, as far as the employees are concerned, harshly inequitable. We express no opinion about the merits of the government's argument.

Instead, Albertson's rests its argument upon its contention that, because the plain language of §404 only refers to "compensation" rather than "interest," the employers have a statutory right to deduct the additional amounts as interest under §163. In this connection, Albertson's points out that section 404 prohibits deduction under sections 162 and 212 but not under section 163, and it is the latter section that governs the deduction of interest.[28] Albertson's argument as to the plain language of the statute is a strong one. We certainly agree that the additional payments resemble "interest" and that, under a literal reading of the statutory language, the deduction of interest is not affected by section 404. However, holding such payments to be deductible "interest" under section 404 would lead to an anomalous result: a taxation scheme designed to make nonqualified plans less attractive would in many cases provide incentives for adopting such plans, and a provision intended to apply the matching principle to nonqualified deferred compensation agreements would exempt substantial portions of DCA payments from its application.

In the end we are forced, therefore, to reject Albertson's approach. We may not adopt a plain language interpretation of a statutory provision that directly undercuts the clear purpose of the statute. . . . In reaching our conclusion, we follow[] the Supreme Court's approach in United States v. American Trucking Ass'ns., 310 U.S. 534 (1940). There the Court noted that "when [a given] meaning has led to absurd results . . . this Court has looked beyond the words to the purpose of the act. Frequently, however, *even when the plain meaning did not produce absurd results but merely an unreasonable one 'plainly at variance with the policy of the legislation as a whole,' this Court has followed that purpose, rather than the literal words.*" *American Trucking Ass'ns.*, 310 U.S. at 543 (emphasis added; citations omitted). . . .

For the reasons we have expressed, we conclude that, despite the literal wording of the statute, Congress could not have intended to exclude interest payments, a substantial part of the deferred compensation package, from the rule prohibiting deductions until such time as the employee receives the benefits. Indeed, the matching principle would not be much of a principle if so substantial a part of the deferred compensation package were excluded from its operation.

IV. Conclusion

In sum, we decline to adopt Albertson's interpretation of I.R.C. §404. Whether or not the additional amounts constitute interest, allowing Albertson's to deduct them prior to their receipt by their employees would contravene the clear purpose of the taxation scheme governing deferred compensation agreements. Accordingly, we vacate the portion of our original opinion dealing with deferred compensation agreements and affirm the Tax Court's holding that Albertson's may not currently deduct the additional amounts.

---

28. [Section 404(a) was amended in 1986, replacing the specific deferral of deductions under §§162 and 212 with a general deferral of deductions "under this chapter." The change did not apply to the pre-1986 tax years at issue in *Albertson's*. Like the pre-1986 version of the statute, the post-1986 version defers employer deductions only for "compensation," so even if the post-1986 version had applied Albertson's could have argued that interest is not "compensation," and thus is not subject to §404(a). — Eds.]

Notes and Questions

1. Albertson's *and the tax shelter cases.* Many tax practitioners would not consider *Albertson's* a tax shelter case. They would reserve the tax shelter label for transactions in which the tax-saving motivation is clearly dominant. In *Albertson's*, by contrast, the taxpayer was seeking highly favorable tax treatment for a transaction that it might well have entered into even if it had known it would not be allowed to deduct "interest" as it accrued. Nevertheless, the statutory interpretation problem in *Albertson's* has much in common with the statutory interpretation problems addressed in the tax shelter cases set forth in section B.4 of Chapter 8, and in the Chapter 8 cell on corporate tax shelters.

2. *Literal statutory interpretation versus purposive interpretation.* The court is almost certainly right that Congress would have wanted to apply the matching principle to interest on nonqualified deferred compensation, if the question had been brought to Congress's attention. But the question did not occur to Congress, and the statutory language does not seem to apply to interest (especially the pre-1986 version of the statute at issue in *Albertson's*). Should a court clean up Congress's messes, or should it simply apply the statute as written and let Congress amend the statute (prospectively) if it wants to? Should it make a difference that $7 billion of tax revenue is riding on the court's interpretation? As the Ninth Circuit's flip-flop in *Albertson's* demonstrates, there is no well-settled answer to these questions. At times a court will apply the literal language of the statute even though it produces results Congress could not have intended; at other times a court will push aside the statutory language in favor of an interpretation based on the court's understanding of Congress's policy objectives or the "deep structure" of the Code. In Gitlitz v. Commissioner, 531 U.S. 206 (2001), the Supreme Court took a literalist approach to interpreting the Code, in sharp contrast with the Ninth Circuit's purposive interpretive approach in *Albertson's*. The *Gitlitz* Court considered a technical issue involving the interaction between the income tax rules governing S corporations and §108 (excluding certain discharges of indebtedness from gross income).[29] The taxpayers argued for a highly taxpayer-favorable interpretation, based on the literal language of the Code. The government countered that the taxpayers' interpretation was not intended by Congress and made no policy sense. The Court was not impressed with the government's response, and ruled for the taxpayers: "Because the Code's plain text permits the taxpayers here to receive these benefits, we need not address [the government's] policy concern." *Id.* at 220. Contrast this with the Ninth Circuit's statement in *Albertson's*: "We may not adopt a plain language interpretation of a statutory provision that directly undercuts the clear purpose of the statute."

---

29. By the standard expressed in Note 1 (immediately above), *Gitlitz* was also not a tax shelter case.

Chapter 12

CAPITAL GAINS AND LOSSES

A. INTRODUCTION

One of the central insights of the Haig-Simons income definition discussed in Chapter 1 is that changes in the value of a taxpayer's portfolio of assets should be reflected in income: increasing asset values add to income; decreasing values reduce income over the (annual) accounting period. However, as we have seen (in Chapter 3), our tax system applies this insight only to closed transactions. The realization doctrine generally requires a sale or other disposition of the asset before a gain is included in income or a loss is deducted.

There is a facial neutrality in a rule that defers recognition of both gains (deferral of which generally favors taxpayers) and losses (deferral of which generally disfavors taxpayers). In practice, however, this combination is to the great advantage of taxpayers, because taxpayers typically control the timing of the realization events. They can create realization events when they want them, and largely avoid them when they don't. The fact that, in normal economic circumstances, there are many more investment assets that tend to increase in value than there are ones that tend to decline adds to the taxpayer-favorable nature of the treatment of capital transactions. Land, for example, has shown a strong tendency to appreciate over time, reflecting its increasing scarcity relative to a growing population. Corporate stock tends to increase in value because corporations pay out less than half of their profits as dividends to shareholders, retaining the rest for internal reinvestment that makes the corporation (and each of its shares of stock) more valuable. Even as to physical assets (like machinery) that do tend to lose value, generous depreciation deductions frequently mean that their values will remain high relative to their declining tax bases. Add, finally, the fact that §1014 allows decedents' estates to pass assets to their heirs at a fair market value basis, thus avoiding any tax at all on the gain that accrued over the decedents' lives, and the picture that emerges is one in which investment assets receive tax treatment that is quite favorable indeed.

It may come as a bit of a surprise then to learn that Congress has also decided, at various times and to various degrees, that gains from sales of assets should be taxed at lower rates than apply to other forms of income. At the present time, for individual (and other noncorporate) taxpayers, the top rate for most types of capital gain income is 15 percent, rather than the rates of up to 35 percent that might otherwise apply.[1] (Corporate taxpayers currently enjoy no rate preference

---

1. The top rate applicable to most long-term capital gains is scheduled to rise to 20 percent after the end of 2012, but it will not be at all surprising if Congress extends the 15 percent rate beyond its scheduled demise.

on their capital gain income, though they too benefitted from favorable rates on capital gains before 1986.)

This favorable treatment doesn't apply to all assets, under all circumstances. The asset in question must be a "capital asset," and, generally, that asset must have been held for more than one year. The definition of "capital asset" will be examined in some detail later in this chapter, but it will suffice for the moment to be aware that most of the assets that are generally considered investments — stocks, bonds, real estate, interests in partnerships or other unincorporated businesses — are usually capital assets. In contrast, property that constitutes the inventory of a business is not a capital asset. Real estate and depreciable equipment used in a business are technically not capital assets, but such property ordinarily falls, after it has been owned by the taxpayer for a year, into a category referred to as "quasi-capital assets." Gains with respect to such property are eligible for favorable treatment in much the way that gains on the disposition of capital assets are. Generally, then, the 15 percent rate will apply to most investment assets, so long as an individual taxpayer has held those assets for at least one year.

Many justifications have been offered for this treatment. Several of these have come to be less persuasive over time, as other features of the tax laws or economic conditions have changed. Others have never been very persuasive under any conditions. At best, one or two of the possible justifications may be entitled to some weight. See what you think of the following.

(1) *Capital gains are capital, not income.* One early argument for favorable treatment of capital gains income was based on the widely held view that capital gains were not really income at all. This view was derived from the distinction between income interests and remainder interests in trust law, under which capital gains and losses were treated as affecting the principal balance of the trust fund (held for ultimate distribution to the holder of the remainder interest), rather than the amount of distributable income. Under this view, of course, complete exemption of capital gains would have been the only appropriate rule. However, favorable rates on capital gains were to some an acceptable compromise between regular tax treatment of gains and complete exemption.

Over time, however, the view of gains as reflecting a change of wealth (as expressed, for example, in the Haig-Simons income definition), came to predominate. No responsible commentator today defends favorable capital gains rates as a concession to the now discredited argument that capital gains are not properly taxable at all.

(2) *Inflation.*[2] The consumer price index was 31.5 in 1965.[3] By December 2010, that index had reached 219.2. This means that an asset acquired in 1965 at a price of $1,000 represented the same purchasing power (in consumer goods markets) as an asset worth about $6,960 in 2010. Yet the tax system would treat a sale in 2010 at that price as generating a gain of $5,960. Imposing a special low tax rate on that gain relieves, at least partially, the overtaxation that may result from failure to adjust the taxpayer's basis for inflation.

But this argument is defective in two ways: First, as an adjustment for inflation, this device is extremely crude, providing insufficient relief in some cases and excessive relief in others. The purchase and sale described in the preceding

2. For a general discussion of inflation and the income tax, see the cell on this topic, associated with Chapter 1.
3. The base of the CPI was restated at 100 for the 1982-1984 period, and earlier index numbers were rescaled at that time to represent their ratios to that new baseline.

paragraph should not have resulted in any tax liability at all; so a favorable tax rate leaves the taxpayer still aggrieved at being taxed at any rate. In contrast, $1,000 invested in a NASDAQ index fund in 1990 would have been worth nearly $11,000 in 1999, with only a small part of that $10,000 gain (about $300) being attributable to inflation. Here the favorable rate dramatically reduces the tax bill with little justification.

Further, inflation tends to result in overtaxation of investment income more generally. If a certificate of deposit pays an 8 percent return while the inflation rate is 5 percent, the holder of the certificate is fully taxed on the 8 percent return, even though only the excess of the nominal rate over the inflation rate is economic income.[4] But no comparable relief is offered by the Code in this case. If inflation were the primary concern, an inflation-indexing mechanism would clearly be preferable to a special capital gains rate.

(3) *Bunching.* Irregular income flows generally result in higher levels of tax, because of the effects of graduated rates. For example, a single taxpayer with an income of $500,000 will pay about 57 percent more tax if that income is earned in a single year than if the same income is earned in equal increments over five years.[5] Capital gains income tends to be irregular, so more favorable rates operate to relieve some of the unfairness associated with the natural, but unpurposeful, overtaxation of lumpy incomes.

Again, there are several problems with this argument; First, most taxpayers who enjoy large capital gains are in, or near, the top bracket year after year. But income lumpiness that merely shifts income from the top bracket in one year to the top bracket in another year will generally not penalize the taxpayer at all. Further, the income "lump" from a capital gain always comes at the end of the holding period. In many cases, the benefits of deferral are likely to offset all, or most, of the lumpiness penalty. Finally, the taxpayer can choose the time of the gains tax through his control of the realization decision. In at least some cases, the taxpayer could use this control to offset lumpiness from other income sources. That is, a strategy of realizing gains during relatively low-income years could actually result in smoothing income fluctuations over a period of years.

(4) *Incentives.* Some defenders of favorable capital gains rates argue that the favoritism is justified as an incentive to make investments that involve more risk than ordinary investments. In some versions of this argument, the desired incentive effect is quite general, reflecting a view that any reasonable accommodation through the tax system that will encourage entrepreneurial risk is worth doing. Other versions of this argument begin by noting that limitations on capital losses (discussed below) lead to tax asymmetries, under which gains face tax penalties, while losses go largely uncompensated by the tax system. Under this argument, lower rates on capital gains do no more than restore a balance between the

---

4. By contrast with the investment income measurement problems created by inflation, inflation does not normally create income measurement problems with respect to labor income, because all the relevant dollars involved in the measurement of labor income are current-year dollars. The "bracket creep" issue (discussed in the Chapter 1 cell on inflation) affects labor income, but involves a question of applicable tax rates rather than one of income measurement.

5. The taxpayer with the income of $100,000 in 2011 would take a personal exemption of $3,700 and (if unmarried and not claiming itemized deductions) a standard deduction of $5,800, leaving a taxable income of $90,500, on which a tax liability of $18,957 would be imposed. If repeated over five years, the total tax on this individual's total income of $500,000 would be $94,785. An income of $500,000 earned by a single individual in 2011 would yield a taxable income of $490,500 (taking the same standard deduction), on which a tax liability of $148,989 would be imposed.

treatments of gains and losses on investments. Yet another variant notes the unfortunate effects of the "double taxation" of corporate income at both the corporate and shareholder levels. Favorable capital gain rates, it is argued, can partially compensate for this alleged defect in our tax system.[6]

As to the first of the three versions of the incentive argument, there is presumably an optimal level of risk taking, and no very convincing evidence that a lower capital gains rate is necessary to get to that level. As to the second argument, there is little evidence suggesting that large numbers of investors go to their graves with unused capital loss carryovers; if that seldom happens, it seems doubtful that this possibility looms large in the minds of would-be entrepreneurs. As to the third argument, the current capital gains rate favoritism is too broad to be justified by this double-tax problem, because favorable rates are also available on gains from noncorporate assets. If relief from the so-called double tax problem is what we want, much more accurate targeting could be achieved by any of several methods of integrating the corporate and individual tax rules.

(5) *Lock-in and the Laffer curve.* Taxes on capital gains are easily avoided if the taxpayer eschews realization of those gains. Of course, a taxpayer likewise can avoid employment, and by so doing avoid taxes on wages; but avoidance of the tax on wages requires avoidance of the wages as well. In contrast, in the case of capital gains, one can enjoy the benefit of the increased wealth in a variety of ways without subjecting oneself to a realization event and the consequent tax; little is ordinarily forgone by retaining the capital asset. It may go up or down in value in the future, but on average the asset value will simply move with market trends.

Faced with the negative and largely avoidable tax consequences of realizing gains, many taxpayers are reluctant to part with assets in which they have accrued gains. This reluctance is sometimes called the "lock-in" effect associated with a capital gains tax that can be dodged simply by retention of the asset. This effect is exacerbated by the additional incentive presented by §1014, which gives the heirs of the taxpayer a basis in assets equal to their fair market value at the taxpayer's death (or alternate valuation date). The message to taxpayers is that retention of assets not only *defers* taxation of gains, but can make those gains *disappear* altogether for tax purposes when the basis for computing gain or loss is reset at death.

Because of the lock-in effect, some economists believe that the government actually raises more money taxing capital gains at 15 percent than would be raised by taxing gains at regular rates above 30 percent. Try a thought experiment. If the capital gain rate is now 15 percent, what might be the effect on tax revenues if the rate were increased to 35 percent (the top rate on ordinary income)? There would be two types of effects, working in opposite directions;

1. The government would collect more tax from taxpayers who sold their assets and realized capital gains.
2. But some taxpayers who would have sold and paid a 15 percent tax would be deterred from selling by a 35 percent rate; they would decide to continue to hold their assets and thus pay no tax on their unrealized appreciation.

As tax rates on capital gains are increased, sooner or later the second effect will dominate, and the increased tax rate will actually cause a decrease in tax revenues.

---

6. The temporary special rate of 15 percent that applies to most dividend income (from 2003 through 2012) diminishes the force of this argument; it remains true, however, that the combined corporate and individual rates that apply to income earned by a corporation often exceed the rate that applies to individual taxation of noncorporate income.

This is the lesson of the so-called Laffer curve, named after the economist Arthur Laffer (who had a profound influence on the tax policies of the Reagan administration).

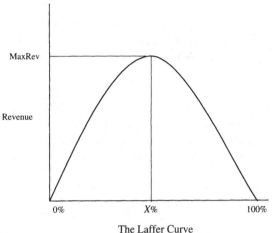

The Laffer Curve

As the curve illustrates, the government collects no revenue when the tax rate is zero (for obvious reasons). The government will also collect little or no revenue when the rate is 100 percent. If the government confiscates all gains, taxpayers will make great efforts to avoid realizing any gains; they will also be dissuaded from investing in the first place. As the rate rises from 0 to X percent, the first effect dominates and revenues increase. As the rate rises from X to 100 percent, however, the second effect dominates and revenues decline. Laffer curves are not unique to capital gains taxation. There is also, for example, a Laffer curve for the taxation of labor income. Congress does not necessarily want to set tax rates as high as X percent (the revenue-maximizing rate), since that may produce more revenue than the government needs. It seems clear, however, that there is no good reason to set the tax rate above X percent.[7] The problem is finding X percent — locating the top of the Laffer curve — for any given type of tax. For income taxes on labor income, economists estimate that X percent is very high — somewhere around 70 or 80 percent. High tax rates on labor income do not greatly deter people from working for money, because alternative uses of their time are not good substitutes for cash wages. The top of the Laffer curve for capital gains, however, is much lower. This is because the alternative to paying capital gains tax — simply holding onto unrealized appreciation — is reasonably attractive. If 35 percent (for example) is lower than X percent for labor income but higher than X percent for capital gains, it could make sense to tax affluent taxpayers' labor income at 35 percent but to tax their capital gains at a lower rate.

Whatever conclusions the reader might draw from these arguments, the congressional response has been, almost invariably, to extend some rate preference to certain kinds of capital gain income. At present, the preference cuts the tax on capital gains by more than 50 percent of what the rate would otherwise have been,

7. The exception would be a tax the main purpose of which was not to raise revenue but to discourage the taxed behavior. For example, an antismoking legislature might intentionally set a cigarette tax at above the revenue maximizing rate, because it was more intent on discouraging smoking than on raising revenue. Congress has no desire, however, to discourage either capital gains or labor income.

in some cases. The details of this tax treatment are explained in the following section of this chapter.

B. MECHANICS OF NET CAPITAL GAIN COMPUTATION

The rate preference for gains on the sale or exchange of certain capital assets in the current Code is embodied in the basic rate provisions in §1(h). In language of mind-numbing complexity, it provides favorable treatment for a taxpayer's "net capital gain" for the tax year. Several steps are necessary to compute this amount.

1. Capital Gain: The Long and Short of It

A critical variable in obtaining favorable rate treatment is the duration of the taxpayer's "holding period" with respect to the particular capital asset. Only assets held for more than one year can qualify for favorable treatment.

Generally, a taxpayer's holding period includes the holding period of prior owner(s) of the capital asset if the asset was acquired in a transaction in which recognition of the prior owner's gain or loss was deferred by operation of law. (§1223(1).) Thus, property acquired by inter vivos gift, or in connection with a marital property settlement, where the transferee typically takes the transferor's basis, is accompanied into the transferee's hands by the transferor's holding period. Similarly, property acquired in a like-kind exchange under §1031, property acquired to replace property lost due to an involuntary conversion under §1033, and stock of a corporation received in exchange for other stock surrendered in a corporate reorganization under §354, are all considered to have been held by the taxpayer from the time the taxpayer had acquired the original property.[8] Under a special holding-period rule applying to transfers at death, even property that receives a new basis in the hands of an heir under §1014 is treated as though the heir had held the property for more than one year from the moment she receives it. (§1223(11).)

Gains and losses from property held for (or considered to have been held for) more than one year are referred to as "long-term" capital gains or losses, respectively. Property held for one year or less generates "short-term" capital gains or losses, as the case may be.[9]

---

8. All of these are examples of what is called "substituted basis property," which is defined in §7701(a)(42). The examples involving receipt of property by gift or in connection with a marital property settlement are in a subcategory of substituted basis property referred to as "transferred basis property," in which the transferor, in effect, transfers her basis along with the property itself. §7701(a)(43). The examples involving exchanges are in a subcategory of substituted basis property that is referred to, logically enough, as "exchanged basis property." §7701(a)(44).

9. The "more than one year" language of §1222(3), defining long-term capital gain, suggests that property held for exactly one year is not long-term property. However, the case law does not provide much detail on how finely this distinction is sliced. Might a taxpayer, knowing that he bought an asset in the morning of February 12, 2011, sell the asset for a long-term gain on the afternoon of February 12, 2012? Presumably so, but it would certainly be safer to wait until the following morning.

2. *Netting of Long and Short Gains and Losses*

Once a taxpayer has ascertained her holding periods with respect to all capital assets sold or exchanged during a tax year, she can categorize them into four groups, according to whether the dispositions produced gain or loss and whether the assets were held for more or less than one year. The four groups are then netted against one another according to the following rules (which are contained in §1222, and which loosely resemble the NCAA basketball "Final Four" determination):

1. Long-term gains are netted against long-term losses.
2. Short-term gains are netted against short-term losses.
3. If the results of the first two netting procedures have the same sign (that is, both are losses or both are gains), then the taxpayer has that amount of each type of net gain or loss, and each is treated accordingly.[10] But if the results of the first two netting procedures have opposite signs (that is, if one is a net gain and the other a net loss), those two outcomes are netted against each other in the championship game.

This final result has the character of whatever type of gain or loss "sticks out" after the netting procedures. Suppose, for example, that the taxpayer sold assets that produced the following four categories of long- and short-term gain and loss:

1. Long-term gain: $10,000
2. Long-term loss: $6,000
3. Short-term gain: $2,000
4. Short-term loss: $5,000

In this case, the netting of long-term assets produces a net long-term gain of $4,000. The netting of the short-term assets produces a net short-term loss of $3,000. Since those semifinal outcomes have opposite signs, they are netted against each other; and because the net long-term gain is greater than the net short-term loss, the net result—$1,000 in this case—takes the character of net long-term capital gain, or "net capital gain" in the terminology of the Code.[11]

If, in the previous example, the taxpayer had had short-term gains of $6,000, then he would have had, after the first two netting procedures, net long-term gains of $4,000 and net short-term gains of $1,000. In such a case, no further netting could be done, and he would obtain a favorable rate with respect to the $4,000 of long-term gain, but not with respect to the short-term gain. Since capital gains are explicitly included in the list of income items recited in §61, the effect of receiving no favoritism on the short-term gains is that they are taxed at the same rate that would apply to the ordinary income items of this taxpayer.

---

10. There are, however, significant limitations on the immediate deduction of net capital losses, which are described in section B of this chapter.

11. The statutory terminology on this is somewhat confusing; it refers to the outcome of this netting as "net capital gain." (§1222(11).) And "net capital gain" is what entitles the taxpayer to favorable rate treatment under §1(h). However, despite the fact that "long-term" does not appear in the name of this category, a taxpayer will never have "net capital gain" unless his long-term capital gains exceed both his long-term capital losses (if any) and his net short-term capital losses (if any).

These netting procedures can produce some surprising results, especially at the margin; that is, in cases where some capital gain or loss transactions have already been completed during the tax year, and others are (or might be) added. For example, suppose a taxpayer with the gains and losses listed in the indented paragraph above has another asset that he is thinking about selling at the end of the tax year. It is an asset in which the taxpayer has a "gain position" of $3,000 (meaning simply that its fair market value exceeds its basis by this amount). But the taxpayer has held the asset less than a year, and so is reluctant to sell it now because he knows that if he can hold it for more than a year, he will qualify for the favorable long-term capital gains rate.

In this case, he actually needn't worry about that. If he realizes another $3,000 of short-term capital gain, what impact does that have on the netting process described above? Now his short-term gains and short-term losses are in equipoise, resulting in no net short-term gain or loss. But he still has $4,000 of net gain in the long-term category. Thus, by realizing an additional *short-term* gain of $3,000 at the end of a year in which all these other transactions had taken place, he has increased his net *long-term* capital gain from $1,000 to $4,000.

This somewhat magical effect can work in the opposite direction as well, converting apparent long-term gain to short-term, thereby disappointing a taxpayer who expected to benefit by realizing one last long-term gain at the end of the year. For example, if a taxpayer already has a $4,000 long-term loss and a $4,000 short-term gain, she has neither net gains nor losses to report at the end of the year. But if, just before the end of the year, she realizes another $4,000 of gains, this time on assets held for more than one year, look what happens: her long-term gains and long-term losses are now netted against each other, cancelling each other perfectly. Now what "sticks out" of the final calculation is a $4,000 net short-term capital gain, which will be taxed at the same rate that ordinary income would have been.

The clear lesson in this is simply that marginal transactions must be evaluated at the margin; they must be viewed taking into account all previous capital asset transactions in the same year, as well as any others that are planned before the year ends.[12] Without that full context, one cannot say definitively whether any marginal realization event will or will not receive favorable rate treatment. Lawyers refer to this sort of phenomenon as a "trap for the unwary," and the tax law is full of such traps. The only safe approach is to make sure that you and your clients are among the wary.

3. The Several Capital Gains Rates

Tax advisors often speak loosely of "the capital gains rate." At the moment, 15 percent is the rate that they generally have in mind. In fact, there is now a panoply of rates that may apply in particular instances. Characteristics of the assets, of the taxpayers, of the holding periods, and of the year the gain is realized, all come into play in setting these various rates. Looking first at the categories of gains that are based on the types of assets that generate them, the following have less attractive rates than the basic capital gains rate of 15 percent:

"Collectibles gain" for which a gains rate of 28 percent is provided, In 1997, when Congress extensively rewrote the capital gains rules, it decided that the 28 percent rate that then applied to capital gains generally should continue to apply to assets that fall into the

12. The taxpayer will also need to consider the effects of capital loss carryovers from prior years, if he has any. See section C below.

"collectibles" category. The committee reports do not fully explain the reasoning for this, but it was presumably some combination of the fact that such assets have considerable personal consumption elements associated with their ownership and the fact that stimulating investment in such assets was thought to have few if any positive macroeconomic consequences. Borrowing from the definition of such assets for purposes of pension rules (under which investments in these assets are generally proscribed), the Code defines "collectibles" to include works of art, rugs and antiques, stamps and coins, metals and jewels, alcoholic beverages, and anything else that the Secretary of the Treasury may decide from time to time to include in this category. (§§408(m); 1(h)(6).)

"Section 1202 gains," for which the 28 percent rate also applies. This is a special category of small-business corporate stock. Since the basic rules of §1202 allow exclusion of half of the gain from sale or exchange of this stock, Congress apparently felt that the remaining gain should be taxed at 28 percent.[13] The effect is the same, of course, as including all the gain in income and taxing it at 14 percent.

"Unrecaptured §1250 gains," for which a 25 percent rate applies. As explained elsewhere,[14] §1250, which applies to dispositions of depreciable real property, recaptures only the excess of depreciation claimed over the allowable straight-line depreciation. This permits gain that is attributable to depreciation at the straight-line rate to be taxed as capital gain, rather than being recaptured as ordinary income. The "unrecaptured §1250 gain" category leaves that basic result undisturbed, but applies a higher capital gains rate to such gains. Since 1986, only straight-line methods have been available for improved real estate; thus, for sales of such real estate now, gains will be unrecaptured §1250 gains up to the full amount of depreciation deductions taken.

In addition to special capital gains rates based on asset types, there are also special rates based on taxpayers' income levels. If the capital gain income, when stacked on top of the taxpayer's ordinary income, would have been taxed at marginal tax rates below 25 percent, then and to that extent such gains will be taxed at the following rates;

	Normal Capital Gains Rate	**Rate for Low Rate Taxpayer**
Residual capital gains	15%	0%[15]
§1202 gain	28%	Regular rate[16]
§1250 gain	25%	Regular rate
Collectibles gain	28%	Regular rate

The date of the realization may also affect the rate applied to the gains. The background capital gains rate of 15 percent and the low bracket capital gains rate of 0 percent are effective generally with respect to gains realized on or before December 31, 2012. Gains realized after that date are generally subject to a tax rate of 20 percent (or 10 percent, in the case of a low bracket taxpayer). It would not be

---

13. In the case of §1202 stock acquired after September 27, 2010, and before January 1, 2012, 100 percent of the gain is excluded (thereby mooting the question of the tax rate applicable to non-excluded gain).

14. See the discussion of recapture in section A of Chapter 6.

15. As the law now stands, the zero rate applies only through the end of 2012. After that, the rate on residual capital gains of low rate taxpayers is scheduled to rise to 5 percent.

16. That is, the taxpayer simply pays tax on these gains as if they were ordinary income; so if the taxpayer is in the 15 percent bracket, that will be the rate that she pays. The capital gains provisions thus never have the effect of *increasing* the tax rate applied to any sort of capital gain income.

surprising if Congress extended the lower temporary rates or made them permanent. However, nothing is perfectly predictable in tax legislation, so careful planning with respect to realization dates continues to be wise.

4. *Netting the Special Rate Categories*

Suppose that a taxpayer has a net short-term capital loss of $5,000 and net long-term capital gains of $8,000, of which $3,000 are §1202 gains and $5,000 are gains on other stock, which would normally fall into the 15 percent residual category. How is the loss netted against the two gains?

The statutory scheme is quite pro-taxpayer on this point. It mandates netting the loss first against the category of gain that would be more highly taxed. Thus, in this case, the $5,000 of loss would first offset the $3,000 of §1202 gain, and then $2,000 of the $5,000 of residual long-term gain. The taxpayer would be taxed at 15 percent on the "net capital gain" of $3,000.

C. LIMITATIONS ON DEDUCTIONS OF CAPITAL LOSSES

1. *Rationale*

As noted above, taxpayers have a good deal of control over the timing of their capital asset transactions. Realization events are rarely forced on taxpayers; and when they are, such as by condemnation or accidental destruction of their property, §1033 generally allows reinvestment of the proceeds of the realization event without recognition of the gain for tax purposes.

If there were no limitation on loss deductions against ordinary income, many wealthy people would be able to use their control of their realization events to offset income with realized losses, and thus to pay little or no tax. For example, imagine a taxpayer with a portfolio of $10 million, which generates an average total return on investment of 6 percent, or $600,000 per year, of which, let us say, $200,000 is in the form of taxable dividends, and $400,000 is the net unrealized appreciation on the assets in the portfolio. If the portfolio is aggressively invested, it may be that the net unrealized gain is the sum of unrealized gains of $700,000 on some assets and unrealized losses of $300,000 on others. Under such circumstances, the taxpayer could, toward the end of her tax year, arrange to realize enough of her losses through sale of some of these loss assets that she would produce $200,000 of losses. If she does so, can she use these losses to offset her $200,000 of dividend income, and thus avoid paying any tax, despite the fact that she has earned $600,000 of economic income and received $200,000 of that income in cash?

2. *The Capital Loss Limitation Rule*

We know the hypothetical taxpayer we just described had an income, in Haig-Simons terms, of $600,000. We are resigned to the idea that only the $200,000 of this that has been realized in the form of dividend distributions will be currently taxable. But the tax rules will not go much further than that; they will not allow a taxpayer who has overall gains of $400,000, but $200,000 of realized losses, to manipulate the realization requirement to avoid being taxed at all on her rather sizable income. Section 1211 thus imposes some severe limits on the deductibility of capital losses. For noncorporate taxpayers, the rule is that capital losses are allowed up to the amount of capital gains in the same year, plus $3,000.[17] Thus, if a taxpayer had $10,000 of losses in a particular tax year, and $5,000 of capital gains in the same year, he would be allowed to deduct $8,000 of his capital losses: $5,000 of losses to offset his gains plus the $3,000 net loss deduction permitted by §1211. For corporate taxpayers, the limitation is even more severe: They can deduct losses only to the extent of gains in the same year.

3. A Big Exception for Small Business Stock

In certain circumstances, §1244 allows an important exception to the loss limitation rules for losses realized with respect to investments in small businesses. Qualifying losses are allowed up to $50,000 per year (or up to $100,000 for a couple filing a joint return) on the sale of stock of a corporation that was capitalized with less than $1 million of capital contributions, so long as several conditions specified in §1244 are met.

4. Capital Loss Carryback and Carryover

The undeductible capital losses a taxpayer might have in any particular year do not simply disappear, however. Under §1212, corporate taxpayers may carry back those capital losses for up to the three preceding taxable years, to offset any net capital gains the corporation might have enjoyed (and been taxed on) in those prior years. In such a case, an immediate refund of the taxes paid with respect to those earlier net gains can be sought, to the extent that those gains are now offset retrospectively by the new net losses. If the losses cannot be absorbed by prior gains, then those losses may be carried over to any of the five taxable years following the year the loss was sustained.

For noncorporate taxpayers, there is no carryback provision. However, losses that are nondeductible because of the §1211 limitations may be carried over to future years indefinitely. In each of those years, the carried over losses are treated as if they arose in that subsequent year. If the net loss was a short-term loss, it is treated as a short-term loss in that subsequent year; if it was a long-term loss, it is so treated in the subsequent year.

Problem 1. Suzanne has the following transactions in capital assets during 2011: In January 2011, she sells 400 shares of Starbucks stock for $10,000. She bought the stock in 1998 for $1,000. In September 2011, she also sells for $10,000 some undeveloped land that she bought in April of the same year for $8,000. Finally, in

---

17. Although most dividends are taxed at the same rate as long-term capital gains (from 2003 through 2012), dividends are not technically capital gains. As a result, the rule permitting capital losses to offset an unlimited amount of capital gains does *not* permit capital losses to offset an unlimited amount of dividend income.

October 2011, she sells, for $10,000, some Treasury bonds that she bought in December 2010 for $14,000. She is a taxpayer whose income will place her in the top income tax bracket for 2011. What will be the effect of the capital transactions described, assuming that all of the assets are capital assets in her hands?

Problem 2. If, in December 2011, Suzanne sells, for $13,000, a vintage automobile that she bought earlier in 2011 for $10,000, how would it change the answer to Problem 1 (assuming all other facts of that problem continue to apply)?

Problem 3. Sabine has the following transactions in capital assets during 2011: In January, she sells 600 shares of Barnes & Noble stock for $12,000. She bought the stock in 2003 for $10,000. She also sold, in July, an antique oriental rug for $10,000. The carpet was a gift from her father earlier that year. Her father bought the carpet for $5,000 in 1997. Finally, in September, Sabine sold some stock in a high-tech start-up company for $4,000. She had bought this stock for $7,000 at its initial public offering in May of 2011. Sabine is a graduate student who has some income from teaching and other part-time employment, but her regular income that year will put her within the 15 percent tax bracket. How will she be taxed on the capital transactions described, assuming that all of the assets are capital assets in her hands, and that the stock is not §1244 stock?

Problem 4. Assume all the facts of Problem 3, except that Sabine had invested $24,000 in the start-up company stock, and sold it for only $12,000 in 2011. How will she be taxed? Would the result be different if §1244 applied to the stock?

Problem 5. Assume all the facts of Problem 4 (under the initial, non-§1244 variant). Suppose further that in February of 2012 Sabine sells a University of North Carolina tax-exempt bond for $12,000, having purchased the bond in 2006 for $9,000; and that in August she sells, for $5,000, Lucent stock that her father bought in April of 2012 for $2,000, and gave to her in July, when it had a value of $4,000. How will Sabine be taxed in 2012?

D.   DEFINITION OF A CAPITAL ASSET

Capital assets are defined in §1221(a). The somewhat unusual (though less so in the Internal Revenue Code than in most other legal materials[18]) syntax of the definition makes it virtually a definition by exclusion — rather like defining the hole instead of the doughnut. Capital assets are "property held by the taxpayer" that is *not* property described in one of the eight paragraphs immediately following the quoted phrase. Those paragraphs take out of the capital asset category assets that are:

1. Stock-in-trade, inventory, or property held primarily for sale to customers in the ordinary course of a trade or business. This important category has generated a good deal of controversy, and will be explored in depth in some of the cases below.

---

18. *See, e.g.,* §§67(b), 163(h)(2), and 509(a), to mention a few Code sections discussed earlier in this book that are structurally similar to §1221.

2. Trade or business property that is either real estate or depreciable property. After the taxpayer holds such property for one year, it becomes a "§1231 asset," sometimes referred to colloquially as a "quasi-capital asset." These assets generally receive very favorable treatment, because they are typically treated as though they were capital assets when their sale or exchange generates a gain (when the taxpayer generally wants them to be capital assets, to benefit from the favorable rates), but they are treated as non-capital, ordinary assets when their sale or exchange generates a loss (when the taxpayer generally wants them to be ordinary assets, to avoid the limitations on the deduction of net capital losses). Even though corporations hold a considerable share of the business property owned by U.S. taxpayers, and even though corporations no longer enjoy lower rates on capital gain income, the treatment of §1231 gains as capital is still significant, both because much business property is held by individuals or partnerships, and because even corporations can use §1231 gains to absorb otherwise nondeductible capital losses.

3. Copyrights, personal papers, artistic creations, and the like, in the hands of the person who created them.[19] In a way, these resemble inventory property; one could, by only a slight stretch, say that an artist's paintings are his inventory. However, prior to the addition of this paragraph to §1221 in 1969, that view had not always prevailed.

4. Accounts or notes receivable acquired in the ordinary course of business for assets described in item 1 above. This simply prevents the taxpayer from converting an ordinary asset into a capital asset by exchanging it for a note.

5. Publications of the U.S. government received by the taxpayer at no cost or at a discount.

6. Certain commodities future contracts held by dealers.

7. Certain hedging transactions.

8. Supplies regularly used by the taxpayer in the ordinary course of business.

1. Property Held for Sale to Customers

UNITED STATES v. WINTHROP

417 F.2d 905 (5th Cir. 1969)

GOLDBERG, Circuit Judge: We must emerge with a solution to the "old, familiar, recurring, vexing and ofttimes elusive" problem described by Judge Brown in Thompson v. Commissioner of Internal Revenue, 5 Cir. 1963, 322 F.2d 122, concerning capital gains versus ordinary income arising out of the sale of subdivided real estate. Finding ourselves engulfed in a fog of decisions with gossamer like distinctions, and a quagmire of unworkable, unreliable, and often irrelevant tests, we take the route of ad hoc exploration to find ordinary income.

---

19. Section 1221(b)(3) allows a taxpayer to elect to treat a musical composition or a copyright in a musical work as a capital asset, despite the fact the taxpayer was the asset's creator. What is the policy justification for treating writers of music more favorably than (for example) writers of fiction? (Don't try too hard to think of an answer; the question is mostly rhetorical.)

I

The taxpayer, Guy L. Winthrop, was the owner of certain property in the environs of Tallahassee, Florida, known as Betton Hills. The property had been in his family since 1836. Winthrop first received a share of the property in 1932 upon the death of his mother. Additional portions of the property were received by him in 1946, 1948, and 1960 through inheritance and partition. As the city of Tallahassee expanded, its city limits were extended to incorporate most of the Winthrop property and the taxpayer began to sell lots for homesites. The first subdivision was undertaken in 1936, and the first sales were made in that year. Thereafter, eight other subdivisions were platted and developed by the taxpayer. Each subdivision was platted separately and the taxpayer endeavored to sell most of the lots in one subdivision before another was developed. The process was one of gradual orderly development of the property through the various subdivisions. Each was surveyed and platted. The streets were graded and paved at Winthrop's expense. Electricity and water facilities were installed; and in some subdivisions sewer lines were built, again at Winthrop's expense, although this was eventually repaid out of the utility bills incurred by homeowners who moved into the subdivisions. Moreover, the taxpayer participated in building five houses for sale in the addition in order to assist other purchasers in obtaining FHA loans to finance their homes.

In selling the lots Winthrop neither advertised nor engaged brokers. The customers primarily came to his home to conduct the sale negotiations since he did not even have an office. He did however, purchase an annual occupational license as a real estate broker from the City of Tallahassee from 1948 through 1963. Despite this low pressure and informal selling technique, the parties stipulated that Winthrop was primarily engaged in selling the Betton Hills property and that though he was a civil engineer by profession, he did little work of this type during the period in question save that done on the Betton Hills property. Furthermore, Winthrop's technique, although unorthodox, was apparently effective. Commencing with the year 1945 and ending in December, 1963, approximately 456 lots were sold in Betton Hills. The profit and other income realized by Winthrop from the sale of these lots from 1951 through 1963 was $483,018.94 or 52.4% of his total income during that period.

The taxpayer reported the profits from these sales as capital gains up until 1953. In that year the Commissioner determined that Winthrop was liable for self employment taxes with respect to his real estate sales. His accountant thereafter listed the sales of Betton Hills property, and expenses connected with those sales, as profits from a business or profession and for the years 1953 through 1963 the taxpayer and his wife paid taxes on these profits at ordinary income rates. In addition, the taxpayer paid self employment taxes for these years on the income derived from the sale of Betton Hills real estate, and such a tax was paid for him in 1963 by his executrix. On his income tax returns for the years 1953 through 1962 the taxpayer listed his occupation as "real estate and engineer." He also listed his occupation in a similar manner on motel registration cards during his extensive travels within the period in question.

After Mr. Winthrop's death in 1963, Mrs. Winthrop, individually and as executrix of Mr. Winthrop's estate, filed claims for a refund for the years 1959 through 1963 in the amount of $57,630.96, asserting that the gains from the sale of the subdivided properties should have been treated as capital gains rather than ordinary income, as originally reported on the tax returns for those years. The Commissioner disallowed these claims and this suit followed. The court below agreed with Mrs. Winthrop's contention and ordered the refund. From this adverse judgment the government appeals. Agreeing with the government, we reverse the decision of the district court and hold that the profits received by the taxpayer from the sales of the property in question were ordinary income.

II

The government's first argument in support of its contention that the district court erred in granting capital gains treatment to the taxpayer is founded upon the proposition that capital gains treatment is available only where the appreciation in value is the result of external market changes occurring over a period of time. In other words, the government argues that where the appreciation is due to the taxpayer's efforts, all profit should be reported as ordinary income. In statutory terms the government argues that the subdivided land ceased to be a "capital asset" when the taxpayer improved the land through his own efforts by platting the lots, paving streets, and installing utilities. Although recognizing that subdivided land is not expressly removed from the "capital asset" category by the exclusionary provisions of I.R.C. §1221 unless such land is held primarily for sale to customers in the ordinary course of business, the government, nevertheless, maintains that its taxpayer efforts rule has, in effect, been read into the statute by the courts. In support of this argument the government relies principally on the following language from Corn Products Refining Co. v. Commissioner of Internal Revenue, 1955, 350 U.S. 46.

> Congress intended that profits and losses arising from the everyday operation of a business be considered as ordinary income or loss rather than capital gain or loss. The preferential treatment provided by [§1221] applies to transactions in property which are not the normal source of business income. It was intended "to relieve the taxpayer from . . . excessive tax burdens on gains resulting from a conversion of capital investments, and to remove the deterrent effect of those burdens on such conversions." Burnet v. Harmel, 287 U.S. at page 106. *Id.* at 52.

We think the preceding language from *Corn Products* fails to support the taxpayer efforts rule advanced by the government. The case does support the proposition that an asset may not be a capital asset for tax purposes even though not expressly excluded from that status by I.R.C. §1221, but the opinion neither mentions nor deals with assets improved by the taxpayer's effort. Rather, it dealt with daily operational profits in the ordinary course of the taxpayer's business. Further, the other cases discussed in the government's brief in support of this novel interpretation of *Corn Products* do not adopt the taxpayer efforts rule. In Commissioner of Internal Revenue v. Gillette Motor Transport, Inc., 1960, 364 U.S. 130, the court held that the fair rental value of facilities taken over temporarily by the government was ordinary income. In United States v. Midland-Ross Corp., 381 U.S. 54, also relied on by the government, the gain on the sale of non-interest bearing notes purchased at a discount was held to be ordinary income. In neither case did the court have before it property which had been improved by the taxpayer's effort. In both cases what was really sold was the right to receive income, one in the form of rentals, the other in the form of interest. The lump sum payments were, therefore, held to be ordinary income to the recipient. These decisions hardly support the government's argument that Betton Hills was not a capital asset merely because its increase in value was due in part to the taxpayer's efforts.

If the universality and sweep which the government reads into the *Corn Products* message is in fact the gospel word in capital gains cases, it has not yet come through nor been heard by the Fifth Circuit. Indeed, the cases are many where taxpayer efforts have contributed to value and have been accorded capital gains treatment. As this court said in *Barrios' Estate* [265 F.2d 517 (5th Cir. 1955)],

> The idea of selling a large tract of land in lots embraces necessarily the construction of streets for access to them, the provision of drainage and the furnishing of access to such a necessity as water. It is hardly conceivable that taxpayer could have sold a lot without doing these things. To contend that reasonable expenditures and efforts, in such necessary undertakings are not entitled to capital gains treatment is to reject entirely the established principle that a person holding lands under such circumstances may subdivide it for advantageous sale. 265 F.2d at 520.

We therefore conclude that this blanket interdiction of capital gains treatment where there has been any laying on of hands is belied by the past decisions of this court.

III

While we are in disagreement with the government's first argument concerning taxpayer efforts, we find its second argument, that the land in question was primarily held for sale in the ordinary course of business and, therefore, was not a capital asset under §1221, persuasive. In holding against the government on this point the court below appears to have placed particular emphasis upon the following facts: (1) The proceeds from the sales of the property were not reinvested in real estate; (2) the taxpayer had other investments, none of which involved the sale of real estate; (3) the subdivided property was acquired by inheritance, not by purchase for the purpose of resale; (4) the taxpayer's holding period was twenty-five years; (5) the taxpayer maintained no office, made most of the sales from his home, spent no time whatever promoting sales and did not advertise; and (6) the purchasers came to him and he was selective in making the sales.

In relying on these factors the court below was obviously following earlier suggestions by this court that such facts are relevant in determining the ultimate question of whether or not the land in question was held primarily for sale to customers in the ordinary course of business. In condensed form the tests mentioned most often are: (1) the nature and purpose of the acquisition of the property and the duration of the ownership; (2) the extent and nature of the taxpayer's efforts to sell the property; (3) the number, extent, continuity and substantiality of the sales; (4) the extent of subdividing, developing, and advertising to increase sales; (5) the use of a business office for the sale of the property; (6) the character and degree of supervision or control exercised by the taxpayer over any representative selling the property; and (7) the time and effort the taxpayer habitually devoted to the sales.

Despite their frequent use, this court has often declared that these seven pillars of capital gains treatment "in and of themselves . . . have no independent significance, but only form part of a situation which in the individual case must be considered in its entirety to determine whether or not the property involved was held primarily for sale in the ordinary course of business." Cole v. Usry, [294 F.2d

426, 427]. Moreover, in Thompson v. Commissioner, [322 F.2d 122, 127 (5th Cir. 1963)], this court remarked concerning these "tests":

> Essential as they are in the adjudication of cases, we must take guard lest we be so carried away by the proliferation of tests that we forget that the statute excludes from capital assets "property held by the taxpayer primarily for sale to customers in the ordinary course of his trade or business."

In the instant case the trial court found that these test facts, about which there is no disagreement, compelled a finding of the ultimate fact that the holding was not primarily for sale in the ordinary course of the taxpayer's business. In weighing the arguments on this point this court recognizes that the characterization of the taxpayer's manner of holding lands is a question of fact. The district court's finding on this ultimate issue, however, is not to be garrisoned by the clearly erroneous rule. Though it has factual underpinnings this ultimate issue is inherently a question of law. . . .

[O]ur analysis of the undisputed facts leads us to the contrary conclusion, that the taxpayer did hold the land in question primarily for sale to customers in the ordinary course of business, and thus, under I.R.C. §1221 is not eligible for capital gains treatment on the profits made from the sale of this land.

In analyzing a case of this sort no rubrics of decision or rubbings from the philosopher's stone separate the sellers garlanded with capital gains from those beflowered in the garden of ordinary income. Each case and its facts must be compared with the mandate of the statute. In so doing we note that the enunciations of the Supreme Court are clarion as they enjoin us to construe narrowly the definition of a capital asset and as a corollary interpret its definitional exclusions broadly. We therefore approach first the issue of whether or not Winthrop held the property "primarily for sale" as that phrase is used in §1221.

It is undisputed that Winthrop inherited the first portion of the Betton Hills land in 1932. By 1936 the first sales had been made and further subdivisions were under way. Mrs. Winthrop's testimony indicates that, except for the subdividing and selling, the land was not used by the taxpayer. . . . On the other hand, her testimony was equally clear in showing that the taxpayer's activities regarding the land, such as paving the streets and having utilities installed, were done with the express purpose of making it more saleable. She testified that he built houses on some of the lots in order to make FHA financing available to prospective purchasers of other lots. Moreover, she [sic] built some houses on the lots because "if a person built a house and there was a house nearby, somebody wanted the lot, because people like neighbors."

There were, therefore, no multiple, dual, or changes of purpose during the relevant years of Winthrop's Betton Hills sales. The taxpayer, long before the tax years in question, had as his sole motivation the sale of Betton Hills, lot by lot, year by year, transaction by transaction. The evidence is clear and uncontradicted that the lots were at all times held by Winthrop "primarily for sale" as that phrase was interpreted by the Supreme Court in Malat v. Riddell, 1966, 383 U.S. 569.

Holding primarily for sale, however, is by itself insufficient to disqualify the taxpayer from capital gains privileges. The sales must also be made in the ordinary course of the taxpayer's trade or business. The next issue, therefore, is whether the taxpayer's activities constituted a trade or business. We think that they did. The magnitude and continuity of his operations and design all point to these sales being part of a business. This was a planned program of subdividing and selling, lasting over a quarter of a century. It constituted Winthrop's principal activity and produced over one-half of his income during the years in question. This was no minuscule operation in terms of transactions or profits. Unlike the sellers in Smith v. Dunn, [224 F.2d 353 (5th Cir. 1955)], the taxpayer here devoted a substantial amount of his time, skill and financial resources to developing and selling the property. He thereby became engaged in the business of subdividing real estate for sale. One need not be a static holder to qualify for capital gains treatment, but the flexing of commercial muscles with frequency and continuity, design and effect does result in disqualification because it indicates one has entered the business of real estate sales.

The taxpayer has made much over the fact that no office was used, no brokers were employed, no time was spent promoting sales, and no advertising was used. While advertising, solicitation and staff are the usual components of a business, they are not a necessary element in either the concept or the pragmatics of selling. Here it is evident that the taxpayer was quite successful in selling the lots without the assistance of these usual props. It is not necessary that customers be actively and fervently and frenetically sought. Winthrop had lots to sell and not mousetraps, so they beat a way to his door to buy his lots. As the court remarked in *Thompson v. Commissioners, supra,* which involved a similar lack of promotional activity, "merely because business was good, indeed brisk, does not make it any less in the ordinary course of such a good business." 322 F.2d at 124. Winthrop was in the business of selling lots in Betton Hills, even though his salesmanship was unorthodox and low pressure. The sales were out of his lots, and were made to customers, though these customers sought him out rather than having been pursued.

In addition, we think the sales were ordinary in the course of this business. The concept of normalcy requires for its application a chronology and a history to determine if the sales of lots to customers were the usual or a departure from the norm. History and chronology here combine to demonstrate that Winthrop did not sell his lots as an abnormal or unexpected event. He began selling shortly after he acquired the land; he never used the land for any other purpose; and he continued this course of conduct over a number of years. Thus, the sales were not only ordinary, they were the sole object of Winthrop's business. It is this singleness of purpose which distinguishes Winthrop's sales from those in *Barrios' Estate* [and others cited], *supra,* all relied on by the taxpayer. It is true, as the taxpayer asserts, that in each of these cases there was considerable sales activity. However, in each the property had been used for some other purpose and the sales ensued only when this primary purpose was abandoned. Here there was no change of purpose.

Winthrop's subdividing was not adventitious, but on the contrary was consistently advertent. While Winthrop probably would not have qualified as the salesman of the year in any of the years in controversy in Tallahassee and its environs, the sales were routine and ordinary, not a result of an abandoned activity on the land. Sale was the prime purpose of the holding and the sales were made in the ordinary course of the taxpayer's business. We conclude, therefore, that the taxpayer is not entitled to capital gains treatment on the profit made from the sales of land during the years 1959 through 1963. The judgment of the district court is reversed.

Notes and Questions

1. *Allocation or all-or-nothing?* The numerous real estate development cases arising under §1221(a)(1) (a remarkable proportion of which have originated in the Fifth Circuit) usually involve some market appreciation of the sort that typically is considered to generate capital gain. That is, the profit occurs not because of any business activity by the taxpayer, but rather because of changes in market conditions, the most common of which is precisely the one involved in *Winthrop:* the growth of an urban area into its surrounding countryside. In developing the property for sale, however, owners of real estate do engage in activities that have the qualities of a trade or business, such as obtaining residential or commercial zoning and/ or plat approval from local land regulating authorities; subdividing the property into individual lots; arranging for the construction of streets and sewers; and the like. Some, but in most cases probably a modest amount, of the total profit on the sales of the lots thus reflects the business activities of the seller.

   Ideally, one might wish to allocate the profit between the two sources from which it arises, giving capital gain treatment to the part of the gain that resulted from changes in the market price of the completely undeveloped land, and characterizing the residual as ordinary business profits. Sometimes this result has been achieved by negotiation and settlement between a taxpayer who has claimed all the profit was capital gain and an IRS that has claimed that all was ordinary income. For example, the record in Biedenharn Realty Co. v. United States, 526 F.2d 409 (5th Cir.), *cert. denied,* 429 U.S. 819 (1976), indicated that for a number of years prior to the litigation of this issue, the IRS and the taxpayer had settled their differences under an agreement that allowed 40 percent of the profit to receive capital gain treatment, while the other 60 percent was treated as ordinary income.

   The statute, however, is decidedly uncongenial to this outcome. At the time of sale, the property either is or is not a capital asset under the definition in §1221(a)(1). If it is, then all the gain is capital gain; if it is not, then it is all ordinary. This may present the taxpayer with a dilemma if she holds highly appreciated land: develop it and risk having all the gain taxed at ordinary income rates, or sell it without doing anything that resembles real estate development, thereby sacrificing the profits that might be obtained, in some cases rather easily, from those activities.

   Occasionally, however, taxpayers have managed to do some development activities without adverse results on the capital asset issue. *See, e.g.,* Scheuber v. Commissioner, 371 F.2d 996 (7th Cir. 1967), in which the taxpayer obtained capital gain status despite being a real estate dealer, and Byram v. United States, 705 F.2d 1418 (5th Cir. 1983), in which a taxpayer who sold 22 lots over a three-year period managed to convince the district court that the assets retained their capital character. (The Fifth Circuit had by that time changed its view on the standard of review in such cases, following the Supreme Court decision in Pullman-Standard v. Swint, 456 U.S. 273 (1982), and so sustained the district court findings, rather than treating them as a matter of law, as it did in *Winthrop.*)

2. *Real estate versus securities.* While the real estate cases are flatly internally inconsistent, even within the same circuit, the general pattern is one that is unfavorable to taxpayers. If the owner does much of anything to develop his property, he is likely to find that the property has lost capital asset status. This stands in noticeable contrast to the treatment of taxpayers who buy and sell stocks, bonds, and other securities. In those cases, capital asset status is generally assumed, unless the taxpayers are stockbrokers or dealers. *See* Higgins v. Commissioner, 312 U.S. 212 (1941). In the securities cases, courts seem to pay a good deal more attention to the "to customers" phrase of §1221(a)(1). If the securities in question are simply sold on an exchange for the account of the taxpayer, they will usually be considered capital assets, for lack of an identifiable customer (or perhaps for the taxpayer's lack of privity with the ultimate customer). This strong presumption may be due in part to the fact that, unlike land, stocks and bonds frequently are sold at a loss. If capital asset status could be avoided by a particular manner of sale — such as by advertising the asset for sale and engaging in other sales efforts — then taxpayers might try to engage in such efforts when markets were depressed, but avoid them when markets were good, thereby avoiding capital loss limitations on their loss assets, but qualifying for favorable capital gains rates on their profitable investments.

3. *Limited statutory relief.* Sections 1236 and 1237 provide some relief for taxpayers who are able to comply with the conditions of those sections. Section 1236 essentially allows dealers in securities to designate at the time of acquisition those investments that they wish to hold as capital assets, thereby avoiding §1221(a)(1) status as to those assets. Section 1237 allows taxpayers to subdivide certain real estate while retaining capital asset status. The real estate in question must have been held for at least five years and must not have been substantially improved. Even then, only the first five parcels sold from a larger tract of land retain complete capital asset status; the sixth and subsequent sales from the same tract generate ordinary income equal to 5 percent of the gross proceeds (*not* the net profits) of the sale, with capital gain treatment available for the balance (if any) of the gain.

4. *Factoring again. Winthrop* recites a list of factors, such as we have seen in earlier cases. Recall Judge Posner's disparaging remarks about such tests in the *Exacto Spring* case in Chapter 5, regarding the reasonable compensation issue, and note the contrast to Judge Goldberg's more amiable view. Do the factors in this area seem any more workable than the factors in *Exacto Spring*? Are the results any more determinative, once you have applied the factors? Or is the difference mostly one of the expectations that the judge brings to the ways in which the factors may prove useful?

Problem 6.   Many years ago, Rita bought several dozen acres of undeveloped land as an investment, paying $200,000. A real estate developer has just offered her $1 million for the land. Rita is considering the offer, but she is also considering going into the real estate development business herself. Under this alternative, she would subdivide the property into lots for single family homes, put in roads and sewers, and sell the lots one by one. She anticipates development costs of $100,000 under this approach, and total sales proceeds of $1,300,000. Aside from taxes, this would leave her with $1,200,000 at the end of the day

($1,300,000 amount realized minus $100,000 expenses), which would be a $200,000 improvement over the sale to the developer. How do the numbers change once taxes are figured into the equation? Analyze Rita's situation under the following set of assumptions: (1) the undeveloped land is a capital asset, (2) if Rita develops the land herself it will lose its capital asset status, (3) Rita's tax rate for long-term capital gains is 15 percent, and (4) Rita's marginal tax rate for ordinary income is 35 percent.

2. Property Used in a Trade or Business

CORN PRODUCTS REFINING CO. v. COMMISSIONER
350 U.S. 46 (1955)

Mr. Justice CLARK delivered the opinion of the Court.

This case concerns the tax treatment to be accorded certain transactions in commodity futures.[20] In the Tax Court, petitioner Corn Products Refining Company contended that its purchases and sales of corn futures in 1940 and 1942 were capital-asset transactions under §[1221] of the Internal Revenue Code of 1939. . . . [B]oth the Tax Court and the Court of Appeals for the Second Circuit, 215 F.2d 513, held that the futures were not capital assets under §[1221]. We granted certiorari because of an asserted conflict with holdings in the Courts of Appeal for the Third, Fifth, and Sixth Circuits. Since we hold that these futures do not constitute capital assets in petitioner's hands, we do not reach the issue of whether the transactions were "wash sales."

Petitioner is a nationally known manufacturer of products made from grain corn. It manufactures starch, syrup, sugar, and their by-products, feeds and oil. Its average yearly grind of raw corn during the period 1937 through 1942 varied from thirty-five to sixty million bushels. Most of its products were sold under contracts requiring shipment in thirty days at a set price or at market price on the date of delivery, whichever was lower. It permitted cancellation of such contracts, but from experience it could calculate with some accuracy future orders that would remain firm. While it also sold to a few customers on long-term contracts involving substantial orders, these had little effect on the transactions here involved.

In 1934 and again in 1936 droughts in the corn belt caused a sharp increase in the price of spot corn. With a storage capacity of only 2,300,000 bushels of corn, a bare three weeks' supply, Corn Products found itself unable to buy at a price which would permit its refined corn sugar, cerelose, to compete successfully with cane and beet sugar. To avoid a recurrence of this situation, petitioner, in 1937, began to establish a long position in corn futures "as a part of its corn buying program" and "as the most economical method of obtaining an adequate supply of raw corn" without entailing the expenditure of large sums for additional storage facilities. At harvest time each year it would buy futures when the price appeared favorable. It would take delivery on such contracts as it found necessary to its manufacturing

---

20. A commodity future is a contract to purchase some fixed amount of a commodity at a future date for a fixed price. Corn futures, involved in the present case, are in terms of some multiple of five thousand bushels to be delivered eleven months or less after the contract. Cf. Hoffman, *Future Trading* (1932), 118.

operations and sell the remainder in early summer if no shortage was imminent. If shortages appeared, however, it sold futures only as it bought spot corn for grinding. In this manner it reached a balanced position with reference to any increase in spot corn prices. It made no effort to protect itself against a decline in prices.

In 1940 it netted a profit of $680,587.39 in corn futures, but in 1942 it suffered a loss of $109,969.38. In computing its tax liability Corn Products reported these figures as ordinary profit and loss from its manufacturing operations for the respective years. It now contends that its futures were "capital assets" under §[1221] and that gains and losses therefrom should have been treated as arising from the sale of a capital asset. In support of this position it claims that its futures trading was separate and apart from its manufacturing operations and that in its futures transactions it was acting as a "legitimate capitalist." It denies that its futures transactions were "hedges" or "speculative" dealings as covered by the ruling of General Counsel's Memorandum 17322, XV-2 Cum. Bull. 151, and claims that it is in truth "the forgotten man" of that administrative interpretation.

Both the Tax Court and the Court of Appeals found petitioner's futures transactions to be an integral part of its business designed to protect its manufacturing operations against a price increase in its principal raw material and to assure a ready supply for future manufacturing requirements. Corn Products does not level a direct attack on these two court findings but insists that its futures were "property" entitled to capital-asset treatment under §[1221] and as such were distinct from its manufacturing business. We cannot agree.

We find nothing in this record to support the contention that Corn Products' futures activity was separate and apart from its manufacturing operation. On the contrary, it appears that the transactions were vitally important to the company's business as a form of insurance against increases in the price of raw corn. Not only were the purchases initiated for just this reason, but the petitioner's sales policy, selling in the future at a fixed price or less, continued to leave it exceedingly vulnerable to rises in the price of corn. Further, the purchase of corn futures assured the company a source of supply which was admittedly cheaper than constructing additional storage facilities for raw corn. Under these facts it is difficult to imagine a program more closely geared to a company's manufacturing enterprise or more important to its successful operation.

Likewise the claim of Corn Products that it was dealing in the market as a "legitimate capitalist" lacks support in the record. There can be no quarrel with a manufacturer's desire to protect itself against increasing costs of raw materials. Transactions which provide such protection are considered a legitimate form of insurance. However, in labeling its activity as that of a "legitimate capitalist" exercising "good judgment" in the futures market, petitioner ignores the testimony of its own officers that in entering that market the company was "trying to protect a part of [its] manufacturing costs"; that its entry was not for the purpose of "speculating and buying and selling corn futures" but to fill an actual "need for the quantity of corn [bought] . . . in order to cover . . . what [products] we expected to market over a period of fifteen or eighteen months." It matters not whether the label be that of "legitimate capitalist" or "speculator"; this is not the talk of the capital investor but of the far-sighted manufacturer. For tax purposes petitioner's purchases have been found to "constitute an integral part of its manufacturing business" by both the Tax Court and the Court of Appeals, and on essentially factual questions the findings of two courts should not ordinarily be disturbed.

Petitioner also makes much of the conclusion by both the Tax Court and the Court of Appeals that its transactions did not constitute "true hedging." It is true that Corn Products did not secure complete protection from its market operations. Under its sales policy petitioner could not guard against a fall in prices. It is clear, however, that petitioner feared the possibility of a price rise more than that of a price decline. It therefore purchased partial insurance against its principal risk, and hoped to retain sufficient flexibility to avoid serious losses on a declining market.

Nor can we find support for petitioner's contention that hedging is not within the exclusions of §[1221]. Admittedly, petitioner's corn futures do not come within the literal language of the exclusions set out in that section. They were not stock in trade, actual inventory, property held for sale to customers or depreciable property used in a trade or business. But the capital-asset provision of §[1221] must not be so broadly applied as to defeat rather than further the purpose of Congress. Congress intended that profits and losses arising from the everyday operation of a business be considered as ordinary income or loss rather than capital gain or loss. The preferential treatment provided by §[1221] applies to transactions in property which are not the normal source of business income. It was intended "to relieve the taxpayer from . . . excessive tax burdens on gains resulting from a conversion of capital investments, and to remove the deterrent effect of those burdens on such conversions." Since this section is an exception from the normal tax requirements of the Internal Revenue Code, the definition of a capital asset must be narrowly applied and its exclusions interpreted broadly. This is necessary to effectuate the basic congressional purpose. This Court has always construed narrowly the term "capital assets" in §[1221].

The problem of the appropriate tax treatment of hedging transactions first arose under the 1934 Tax Code revision. Thereafter the Treasury issued G.C.M. 17322, *supra*, distinguishing speculative transactions in commodity futures from hedging transactions. It held that hedging transactions were essentially to be regarded as insurance rather than a dealing in capital assets and that gains and losses therefrom were ordinary business gains and losses. The interpretation outlined in this memorandum has been consistently followed by the courts as well as by the Commissioner. While it is true that this Court has not passed on its validity, it has been well recognized for twenty years; and Congress has made no change in it though the Code has been re-enacted on three subsequent occasions. This bespeaks congressional approval. Furthermore, Congress has since specifically recognized the hedging exception here under consideration in the short-sale rule of §1233(a) of the 1954 Code.

We believe that the statute clearly refutes the contention of Corn Products. Moreover, it is significant to note that practical considerations lead to the same conclusion. To hold otherwise would permit those engaged in hedging transactions to transmute ordinary income into capital gain at will. The hedger may either sell the future and purchase in the spot market or take delivery under the future contract itself. But if a sale of the future created a capital transaction while delivery of the commodity under the same future did not, a loophole in the statute would be created and the purpose of Congress frustrated.

The judgement is affirmed.

Notes and Questions

1. *A narrow rule or a broad exception?* The Court says that, to protect the integrity of the income tax, "the definition of a capital asset must be narrowly applied, and its exclusions must be interpreted broadly." Does the opinion apply a narrow reading of the flush language of §1221, or a broad reading of one of the exceptions? Or is there, just possibly, no actual act of interpretation of any part of §1221 involved here?

2. *Butterflies are (tax-)free?* Commodity futures contracts have been used in other ways to game the tax rules. For example, in the 1980s, a transaction sometimes known as a "butterfly straddle" (because of its appearance in some diagrams of the transaction) was introduced as a popular means of deferring tax on large capital gains. If a taxpayer had a large gain on a capital transaction in a particular tax year, he might be encouraged by a promoter of butterfly transactions to enter into very large, but offsetting, long and short commodity futures positions. In effect, the taxpayer would bet that the price of some commodity — orange juice, pork bellies, cocoa, whatever — would rise over the term of the contract, and would simultaneously make a bet of similar magnitude that the price of the same commodity would fall over the same period. As time passed, one of the bets would show a profit while the other showed a loss, due to the movement of the underlying price of the commodity. At some point before the end of the tax year, the loss position (the losing bet) would be closed out, generating a loss that could be used to offset the capital gain on the unrelated transaction earlier in the year. Just after the new tax year, the gain position (the winning bet) of the transaction would also be liquidated. This would, of course, produce a large gain in that second year; but that only meant that this taxpayer would likely be in the market for another butterfly straddle in the second year. And so on. (We note in passing that, although we refer casually to these futures contracts as "bets," they are not subject to the limitations on gambling losses. It is not always clear why that is so, but the rules themselves are clear.)

   The addition of §1256 to the Code in 1986 put an end to this by requiring that the gain side of such transactions be "marked to market" at the end of the year — one of the most glaring of exceptions to the general principle of waiting until a "sale or other disposition" occurs to calculate gains or losses.

3. *Whipsawing the Commissioner.* The taxpayer in *Corn Products* appears to have reported, on an amended return, both gains and losses from transactions in corn futures as capital transactions. However, the Court is correct that a contrary outcome in this case would have given the taxpayer the ability to make its gains or losses capital or ordinary, at its option, by either selling the futures contracts or by accepting delivery of the corn under the contract at maturity. Generally speaking, if the price of corn went up between the time the futures contract was executed and the delivery date of the corn, the contract could be sold at a profit, and capital gain would result. The taxpayer could then use the proceeds of the contract to purchase corn on the "spot market," at prices that would increase costs, and diminish ordinary business profits, by about the amount of the gain on the futures contracts. In other words, a clean conversion of ordinary income to capital gain would be the likely result.

But if the price of corn went down, "sale" of the futures contract would produce a loss.[21] Under these circumstances, it would be possible simply to accept delivery of the high-priced corn, and use it in operations. In effect, the loss on the contract would get built into the cost structure of the taxpayer's operations, and end up being deducted as a cost of the goods sold, where it would function as an ordinary loss rather than as a disfavored capital loss.

4. *A pyrrhic victory for the government?* This decision cut off the taxpayer's opportunity to use commodities futures contracts to "whipsaw" the tax collector on the capital asset question. But the notion that investment instruments could be converted from capital assets to ordinary, noncapital assets if they were involved somehow in the taxpayer's business raised an intriguing possibility for a whipsaw of another sort. It was especially helpful for aggressive taxpayers that the Court in *Corn Products* had been so vague about what exactly in the language of §1221 dictated the Court's conclusion. As a result, the succeeding years witnessed many attempts, some of which were successful, to deduct as ordinary the losses that were realized on investments in stock or other assets that would normally have been thought to be capital in nature. The following case provides an example, and an antidote.

ARKANSAS BEST CORP. v. COMMISSIONER

485 U.S. 212 (1987)

Justice MARSHALL delivered the opinion of the Court.

The issue presented in this case is whether capital stock held by petitioner Arkansas Best Corporation (Arkansas Best) is a "capital asset" as defined in §1221 of the Internal Revenue Code regardless of whether the stock was purchased and held for a business purpose or for an investment purpose.

Arkansas Best is a diversified holding company. In 1968 it acquired approximately 65% of the stock of the National Bank of Commerce (Bank) in Dallas, Texas. Between 1969 and 1974, Arkansas Best more than tripled the number of shares it owned in the Bank, although its percentage interest in the Bank remained relatively stable. These acquisitions were prompted principally by the Bank's need for added capital. Until 1972, the Bank appeared to be prosperous and growing, and the added capital was necessary to accommodate this growth. As the Dallas real estate market declined, however, so too did the financial health of the Bank, which had a heavy concentration of loans in the local real estate industry. In 1972, federal examiners classified the Bank as a problem bank. The infusion of capital after 1972 was prompted by the loan portfolio problems of the bank.

Petitioner sold the bulk of its Bank stock on June 30, 1975, leaving it with only a 14.7% stake in the Bank. On its federal income tax return for 1975, petitioner claimed a deduction for an ordinary loss of $9,995,688 resulting from the sale of the stock. The Commissioner of Internal Revenue disallowed the deduction,

21. Futures contracts are usually not "sold" in the usual sense; they are disposed of by buying a matching contract. Thus, if one is obligated to buy corn at a specified price, one disposes of that obligation by buying another contract requiring another party to buy the same amount of corn at the same price. If the price of corn has fallen, it will be expensive to buy the second contract.

finding that the loss from the sale of stock was a capital loss, rather than an ordinary loss, and that it therefore was subject to the capital loss limitations in the Internal Revenue Code.

Arkansas Best challenged the Commissioner's determination in the United States Tax Court. The Tax Court, relying on cases interpreting Corn Products Refining Co. v. Commissioner, 350 U.S. 46 (1955), held that stock purchased with a substantial investment purpose is a capital asset which, when sold, gives rise to a capital gain or loss, whereas stock purchased and held for a business purpose, without any substantial investment motive, is an ordinary asset whose sale gives rise to ordinary gains or losses. The court characterized Arkansas Best's acquisitions through 1972 as occurring during the Bank's "'growth' phase," and found that these acquisitions "were motivated primarily by investment purpose and only incidentally by some business purpose." The stock acquired during this period therefore constituted a capital asset, which gave rise to a capital loss when sold in 1975. The court determined, however, that the acquisitions after 1972 occurred during the Bank's "'problem' phase," and, except for certain minor exceptions, "were made exclusively for business purposes and subsequently held for the same reasons." These acquisitions, the court found, were designed to preserve petitioner's business reputation, because without the added capital the Bank probably would have failed. The loss realized on the sale of this stock was thus held to be an ordinary loss.

The Court of Appeals for the Eighth Circuit reversed the Tax Court's determination that the loss realized on stock purchased after 1972 was subject to ordinary-loss treatment, holding that all of the Bank stock sold in 1975 was subject to capital-loss treatment. The court reasoned that the Bank stock clearly fell within the general definition of "capital asset" in Internal Revenue Code §1221, and that the stock did not fall within any of the specific statutory exceptions to this definition. The court concluded that Arkansas Best's purpose in acquiring and holding the stock was irrelevant to the determination whether the stock was a capital asset. We granted certiorari, and now affirm.

II

Section 1221 of the Internal Revenue Code defines "capital asset" broadly, as "property held by the taxpayer (whether or not connected with his trade or business)," and then excludes five specific classes of property from capital-asset status. . . . Arkansas Best acknowledges that the Bank stock falls within the literal definition of capital asset in section 1221, and is outside of the statutory exclusions. It asserts, however, that this determination does not end the inquiry. Petitioner argues that in Corn Products Refining Co. v. Commissioner, this Court rejected a literal reading of section 1221, and concluded that assets acquired and sold for ordinary business purposes rather than for investment purposes should be given ordinary-asset treatment. Petitioner's reading of *Corn Products* finds much support in the academic literature and in the courts. Unfortunately for petitioner, this broad reading finds no support in the language of section 1221.

In essence, petitioner argues that "property held by the taxpayer (whether or not connected with his trade or business)" does not include property that is acquired and held for a business purpose. In petitioner's view an asset's status as "property" thus turns on the motivation behind its acquisition. This motive test, however, is not only nowhere mentioned in section 1221, but it is also in direct conflict with the parenthetical phrase "whether or not connected with his trade or business." The broad definition of the term "capital asset" explicitly makes irrelevant any consideration of the property's connection with the taxpayer's business, whereas petitioner's rule would make this factor dispositive.

In a related argument, petitioner contends that the five exceptions listed in section 1221 for certain kinds of property are illustrative, rather than exhaustive, and that courts are therefore free to fashion additional exceptions in order to further the general purposes of the capital-asset provisions. The language of the statute refutes petitioner's construction. Section 1221 provides that "capital asset" means "property held by the taxpayer[,] . . . but does not include" the five classes of property listed as exceptions. We believe this locution signifies that the listed exceptions are exclusive. The body of §1221 establishes a general definition of the term "capital asset," and the phrase "does not include" takes out of that broad definition only the classes of property that are specifically mentioned. The legislative history of the capital asset definition supports this interpretation, *see* H.R. Rep. 704, 73d Cong., 2d Sess., 31 (1934) ("The definition includes all property, except as specifically excluded"). . . .

Petitioner's reading of the statute is also in tension with the exceptions listed in §1221. These exclusions would be largely superfluous if assets acquired primarily or exclusively for business purposes were not capital assets. Inventory, real or depreciable property used in the taxpayer's trade or business, and accounts or notes receivable acquired in the ordinary course of business, would undoubtedly satisfy such a business-motive test. Yet these exceptions were created by Congress in separate enactments spanning 30 years. Without any express direction from Congress, we are unwilling to read §1221 in a manner that makes surplusage of these statutory exclusions.

In the end, petitioner places all reliance on its reading of Corn Products Refining Co. v. Commissioner — a reading we believe is too expansive. In *Corn Products*, the Court considered whether income arising from a taxpayer's dealings in corn futures was entitled to capital-gains treatment. . . . In evaluating the company's claim that the sales of corn futures resulted in capital gains and losses, this Court stated:

> Nor can we find support for petitioner's contention that hedging is not within the exclusions of [§1221]. Admittedly, petitioner's corn futures do not come within the literal language of the exclusions set out in that section. They were not stock in trade, actual inventory, property held for sale to customers or depreciable property used in a trade or business. But the capital-asset provision of [§1221] must not be so broadly applied as to defeat rather than further the purpose of Congress. Congress intended that profits and losses arising from the everyday operation of a business be considered as ordinary income or loss rather than capital gain or loss. . . . Since this section is an exception from the normal tax requirements of the Internal Revenue Code, the definition of a capital asset must be narrowly applied and its exclusions interpreted broadly.

The Court went on to note that hedging transactions consistently had been considered to give rise to ordinary gains and losses, and then concluded that the corn futures were subject to ordinary-asset treatment.

The Court in *Corn Products* proffered the oft-quoted rule of construction that the definition of capital asset must be narrowly applied and its exclusions interpreted broadly, but it did not state explicitly whether the holding was based on a narrow reading of the phrase "property held by the taxpayer," or on a broad reading of the inventory exclusion of §1221. In light of the stark language of §1221, however, we believe that *Corn Products* is properly interpreted as involving an application of §1221's inventory exception. Such a reading is consistent both with the Court's reasoning in that case and with §1221. The Court stated in *Corn Products* that the company's futures transactions were "an integral part of its business designed to protect its manufacturing operations against a price increase in its principal raw material and to assure a ready supply for future manufacturing requirements." The company bought, sold, and took delivery under the futures contracts as required by the company's manufacturing needs. As Professor Bittker notes, under these circumstances, the futures can "easily be viewed as surrogates for the raw material itself." 2 B. Bittker, *Federal Taxation of Income, Estates and Gifts* para. 51.10.3, p. 51-62 (1981). The Court of Appeals for the Second Circuit in *Corn Products* clearly took this approach. That court stated that when commodity futures are "utilized solely for the purpose of stabilizing inventory cost[,] . . . [they] cannot reasonably be separated from the inventory items," and concluded that "property used in hedging transactions properly comes within the exclusions of [§1221]." This Court indicated its acceptance of the Second Circuit's reasoning when it began the central paragraph of its opinion, "Nor can we find support for petitioner's contention that hedging is not within the exclusions of [§1221]." In the following paragraph, the Court argued that the Treasury had consistently viewed such hedging transactions as a form of insurance to stabilize the cost of inventory, and cited a Treasury ruling which concluded that the value of a manufacturer's raw-material inventory should be adjusted to take into account hedging transactions in futures contracts. This discussion, read in light of the Second Circuit's holding and the plain language of §1221, convinces us that although the corn futures were not "actual inventory," their use as an integral part of the taxpayer's inventory-purchase system led the Court to treat them as substitutes for the corn inventory such that they came within a broad reading of "property of a kind which would properly be included in the inventory of the taxpayer" in §1221.

Petitioner argues that by focusing attention on whether the asset was acquired and sold as an integral part of the taxpayer's everyday business operations, the Court in *Corn Products* intended to create a general exemption from capital-asset status for assets acquired for business purposes. We believe petitioner misunderstands the relevance of the Court's inquiry. A business connection, although irrelevant to the initial determination of whether an item is a capital asset, is relevant in determining the applicability of certain of the statutory exceptions, including the inventory exception. The close connection between the futures transactions and the taxpayer's business in *Corn Products* was crucial to whether the corn futures could be considered surrogates for the stored inventory of raw corn. For if the futures dealings were not part of the company's inventory-purchase system, and instead amounted simply to speculation in corn futures, they could not be considered substitutes for the company's corn inventory, and would fall outside even a broad reading of the inventory exclusion. We conclude that *Corn Products* is properly interpreted as standing for the narrow proposition that hedging transactions that are an integral part of a business' inventory-purchase system fall within the inventory exclusion of §1221. Arkansas Best, which is not a dealer in securities, has never suggested that the Bank stock falls within the inventory exclusion. *Corn Products* thus has no application to this case.

It is also important to note that the business-motive test advocated by petitioner is subject to the same kind of abuse that the Court condemned in *Corn Products*. The Court explained in *Corn Products* that unless hedging transactions were subject to ordinary gain and loss treatment, taxpayers engaged in such transactions could "transmute ordinary income into capital gain at will." The hedger could garner capital-asset treatment by selling the future and purchasing the commodity on the spot market, or ordinary-asset treatment by taking delivery under the future contract. In a similar vein, if capital stock purchased and held for a business purpose is an ordinary asset, whereas the same stock purchased and held with an investment motive is a capital asset, a taxpayer such as Arkansas Best could have significant influence over whether the asset would receive capital or ordinary treatment. Because stock is most naturally viewed as a capital asset, the Internal Revenue Service would be hard pressed to challenge a taxpayer's claim that stock was acquired as an investment, and that a gain arising from the sale of such stock was therefore a capital gain. Indeed, we are unaware of a single decision that has applied the business-motive test so as to require a taxpayer to report a gain from the sale of stock as an ordinary gain. If the same stock is sold at a loss, however, the taxpayer may be able to garner ordinary-loss treatment by emphasizing the business purpose behind the stock's acquisition. The potential for such abuse was evidenced in this case by the fact that as late as 1974, when Arkansas Best still hoped to sell the Bank stock at a profit, Arkansas Best apparently expected to report the gain as a capital gain.

III

We conclude that a taxpayer's motivation in purchasing an asset is irrelevant to the question whether the asset is "property held by a taxpayer (whether or not connected with his business)" and is thus within §1221's general definition of "capital asset." Because the capital stock held by petitioner falls within the broad definition of the term "capital asset" in §1221 and is outside the classes of property excluded from capital-asset status, the loss arising from the sale of the stock is a capital loss. Corn Products Refining Co. v. Commissioner, *supra*, which we interpret as involving a broad reading of the inventory exclusion of §1221, has no application in the present context. Accordingly, the judgment of the Court of Appeals is affirmed.

Notes and Questions

1. *The law of Moses' rod.* As the last paragraph of part II of the opinion explains, the government's victory in *Corn Products* closed one whipsaw opportunity, only to open another in a slightly different place. It thus illustrates the "Law of Moses' Rod": Every stick crafted by the government to beat on the head of a taxpayer will, sooner or later, metamorphose into a large snake that will bite the Commissioner on the hind part.[22]

   Justice Marshall's admirable insistence on interpreting the actual words of the statute remedied some of the damage that the looser language of

---

22. The authors owe this formulation to the late Professor Martin Ginsburg.

Corn Products may have caused. In effect, he explains the result of *Corn Products* as stemming from a broad interpretation of §1221(1) (now §1221(a)(1)), making the futures contracts quasi-inventory property in the hands of a taxpayer like the one in that case. Since the taxpayer in *Arkansas Best* has no similar claim to quasi-inventory status as to its stock in the bank subsidiary, it cannot fall within the *Corn Products* exception to capital asset status.

2. *Hedging today.* Section 1221(a)(7), added to the Code in 1999, adds "hedging transactions" to the list of exclusions from capital asset status. The legislation confirms the Supreme Court's position in *Arkansas Best* that there are no "common law" exclusions from the capital asset definition. However, the definition of hedging transactions contained in §1221(h)(2) (and elaborated upon in Reg. §1.1221-2) is somewhat broader that the inventory-substitute rule enunciated by the Court in that opinion. As in the case of §1236 assets, the whipsaw possibilities are blocked by requiring the taxpayer to elect ordinary status by identifying the transaction as a hedge at the time the contract is entered into.

E.   SUBSTITUTES FOR FUTURE ORDINARY INCOME

Bonds sometimes come with "coupons" attached to them, each of which permits the owner of the bond to demand payment of the interest on the bond upon surrender (typically to a bank) of the coupon, which has been clipped from its attached bond.[23] Suppose that a taxpayer, immediately before each coupon matures, sells the coupon to another for approximately the amount of the interest that will be payable the next day. Has he sold a capital asset? If so, a nice question may arise as to the seller's basis, if any, in the coupon. But even in the worst case, where the basis is zero, the taxpayer would still likely be better off selling the coupon if he can obtain capital gain treatment of the sum received, since the full amount of that sum would be taxed at ordinary income rates if he had waited a day and received it as interest income.

This seems too easy a game, and it is. Courts have adopted a number of strategies for denying capital gain treatment in transactions of this sort, under the general rubric of "substitutes for future (ordinary) income." As in so many areas, the extreme cases seem easy, but drawing lines between the close cases has proven more difficult. In this, there is a particularly difficult conceptual question to deal with: It is generally thought that the value of most investment assets inheres in the flow of income that they will produce in the future. Indeed, in the case of a bond, the value is usually expressed as the discounted present value of all the remaining interest payments, plus the repayment of the principal. One of the implications of this theory of value is that a sale of any asset always involves, at its

---

23. This is, by the way, the basis of the term *coupon-clipper*, which is sometimes used to refer to wealthy people who live off the interest on their invested assets. The term has the opposite meaning of what some might expect: that it refers to people so thrifty (and perhaps so poor) that they need to watch each day's newspaper for coupons entitling them to a few cents off on a loaf of bread.

heart, payments that are in lieu of the ordinary income the asset would have produced had the seller continued to hold it.

Nevertheless, in a system that differentiates between ordinary income and capital gain income, lines must be drawn. A number of classic cases from the formative years of our income tax explore this question. The following is an example.

HORT v. COMMISSIONER

313 U.S. 28 (1941)

Mr. Justice MURPHY delivered the opinion of the Court.

We must determine whether the amount petitioner received as consideration for cancellation of a lease of realty in New York City was ordinary gross income as defined in [§61(a)] and whether, in any event, petitioner sustained a loss through cancellation of the lease which is recognized in [§165].

Petitioner acquired the property, a lot and ten-story office building, by devise from his father in 1928. At the time he became owner, the premises were leased to a firm which had sublet the main floor to the Irving Trust Co. In 1927, five years before the head lease expired, the Irving Trust Co. and petitioner's father executed a contract in which the latter agreed to lease the main floor and basement to the former for a term of fifteen years at an annual rental of $25,000, the term to commence at the expiration of the head lease.

In 1933, the Irving Trust Co. found it unprofitable to maintain a branch in petitioner's building. After some negotiations, petitioner and the Trust Co. agreed to cancel the lease in consideration of a payment to petitioner of $140,000. Petitioner did not include this amount in gross income in his income tax return for 1933. On the contrary, he reported a loss of $21,494.75 on the theory that the amount he received as consideration for the cancellation was $21,494.75 less than the difference between the present value of the unmatured rental payments and the fair rental value of the main floor and basement for the unexpired term of the lease. He did not deduct this figure, however, because he reported other losses in excess of gross income.

The Commissioner included the entire $140,000 in gross income, disallowed the asserted loss, made certain other adjustments not material here, and assessed a deficiency. The Board of Tax Appeals affirmed. The Circuit Court of Appeals affirmed *per curiam* on the authority of Warren Service Corp. v. Commissioner, 110 F.2d 1023. Because of conflict with Commissioner v. Langwell Real Estate Corp., 47 F.2d 841, we granted certiorari limited to the question whether, "in computing net gain or loss for income tax purposes, a taxpayer [can] offset the value of the lease canceled against the consideration received by him for the cancellation."

Petitioner apparently contends that the amount received for cancellation of the lease was capital rather than ordinary income and that it was therefore subject to [the several provisions] which govern capital gains and losses. Further, he argues that even if that amount must be reported as ordinary gross income he sustained a loss which [§165] authorizes him to deduct. We cannot agree.

The amount received by petitioner for cancellation of the lease must be included in his gross income in its entirety. Section [61(a)] expressly defines gross income to include "gains, profits, and income derived from . . . rent, . . . or gains or profits and income derived from any source whatever." Plainly this definition reached the rent paid prior to cancellation just as it would have embraced subsequent payments if the lease had never been canceled. It would have included a prepayment of the discounted value of unmatured rental payments whether received at the inception of the lease or at any time thereafter. Similarly, it would have extended to the proceeds of a suit to recover damages had the Irving Trust Co. breached the lease instead of concluding a settlement. That the amount petitioner received resulted from negotiations ending in cancellation of the lease rather than from a suit to enforce it cannot alter the fact that basically the payment was merely a substitute for the rent reserved in the lease. So far as the application of §[61(a)] is concerned, it is immaterial that petitioner chose to accept an amount less than the strict present value of the unmatured rental payments rather than to engage in litigation, possibly uncertain and expensive.

The consideration received for cancellation of the lease was not a return of capital. We assume that the lease was "property," whatever that signifies abstractly. Presumably the bond in Helvering v. Horst, 311 U.S. 112, and the lease in Helvering v. Bruun, 309 U.S. 461, were also "property," but the interest coupon in Horst and the building in Bruun nevertheless were held to constitute items of gross income. Simply because the lease was "property" the amount received for its cancellation was not a return of capital, quite apart from the fact that "property" and "capital" are not necessarily synonymous in the Revenue Act of 1932 or in common usage. Where, as in this case, the disputed amount was essentially a substitute for rental payments which §[61(a)] expressly characterizes as gross income, it must be regarded as ordinary income, and it is immaterial that for some purposes the contract creating the right to such payments may be treated as "property" or "capital."

For the same reasons, that amount was not a return of capital because petitioner acquired the lease as an incident of the realty devised to him by his father. Theoretically, it might have been possible in such a case to value realty and lease separately and to label each a capital asset. But that would not have converted into capital the amount petitioner received from the Trust Co., since §[102] would have required him to include in gross income the rent derived from the property, and that section, like §[61(a)], does not distinguish rental payments and a payment which is clearly a substitute for rental payments.

We conclude that petitioner must report as gross income the entire amount received for cancellation of the lease, without regard to the claimed disparity between that amount and the difference between the present value of the unmatured rental payments and the fair rental value of the property for the unexpired period of the lease. The cancellation of the lease involved nothing more than relinquishment of the right to future rental payments in return for a present substitute payment and possession of the leased premises. Undoubtedly it diminished the amount of gross income petitioner expected to realize, but to that extent he was relieved of the duty to pay income tax. Nothing in §[165] indicates that Congress intended to allow petitioner to reduce ordinary income actually received and reported by the amount of income he failed to realize. We may assume that petitioner was injured insofar as the cancellation of the lease affected the value of the realty. But that would become a deductible loss only when its extent had been fixed by a closed transaction.

The judgment of the Circuit Court of Appeals is affirmed.

Notes and Questions

1. *The lost loss deduction.* A taxpayer establishes the existence and amount of a loss by comparing the amount realized on an asset disposition with the asset's adjusted basis, which in the case of a loss will be larger than the amount realized. How did the taxpayer in this case propose to show an adjusted basis that was larger than the amount he received in settlement of the lease? Indeed, how could the taxpayer show any basis at all? He expected to receive rent over the remaining term of the lease of some $161,000, but did this represent an investment by the taxpayer? Does it represent an amount that the tax rules would have previously taxed? These are the two events that typically give rise to a taxpayer's basis, but neither seems an accurate description of what went on in this case.

   There is one other source of basis, and it creates an intriguing possibility in this very case: An heir receives a basis in an asset he inherits that is equal to the fair market value of the asset at the date of the testator's death.[24] Does this give the younger Mr. Hort a claim that he had a basis in the lease payments based on the value of those lease payments as of the death of his father in 1928? Would this argument have had a better chance of success if the elder Mr. Hort had died in 1932?

2. *The importance of basis.* In some cases that arguably involve a payment that is a substitute for ordinary income, a claim to some basis is more plausible. For example, if a taxpayer pays $1,000 for a 30-year bond that has an annual interest rate of 5 percent, he has in effect bought the benefit of 31 promises made by the debtor: 30 promises to pay interest in each of 30 years, and a promise to repay the principal of $1,000 at the end of the thirtieth year. The value of that last promise, if discounted to present value (at 5%) as of the purchase of the bond, is only $231.[25] The other $769 of value inheres in the right to receive thirty annual interest payments. Might a taxpayer plausibly claim under these circumstances that he has a basis of $769 in the interest payments and a basis of $231 in the repayment of principal? Or, to slice the bologna even more finely, could the taxpayer claim to have a basis in each interest coupon, representing the discounted present value of the promise to pay each year's interest? If so, the first interest coupon, due one year later, would get a basis of $47.62; the second year's payment would get a basis of $45.35; the third year's payment would get a basis of $43.19; and so on.

   In such a case, the allowance of basis may be much more significant in dollar terms than the question of whether the character of any gain is ordinary or capital. Imagine, for example, that shortly after the bond described above is issued, long-term interest rates drop to 4 percent. The market will now value the several promises contained in the bond indenture using a discount rate equal to the new market rate of 4 percent. This means that the first three interest payments of $50 each will now be valued at $48.08, $46.23, and $44.45, respectively. If the owner of the bond were to sell the first three coupons for their combined value of

---

24. Section 1014. If the executor elects the alternate valuation date under §2032, then the basis is fixed at the fair market value as of the date exactly six months after the death of the testator.

25. You can verify this calculation by reference to the present value table presented in Chapter 1.

$138.76, could he claim that his income is only $2.60, after subtracting as his basis the $136.16 that was the value of the coupons at the time he originally bought the bond? He might also claim that his gain of $2.60 was a capital gain, but it is clear that whether that amount is taxed as ordinary income or capital gain is much less important than the question of whether the taxpayer is allowed to claim a basis with respect to the interest coupons. *Hort* would imply that the full amount received would be ordinary income; but in 1982 Congress added special rules to the Code covering such "stripped" bonds. Under §1286(b), the seller of coupons in this situation would be allowed to allocate his basis between the bond itself and its various coupons in much the manner described.[26] However, any interest that had already accrued prior to the sale would be taxed as ordinary income.

3. *Subsequent cases.* Some years later, the Supreme Court applied the *Hort* analysis to a case involving mineral rights. *See* Commissioner v. P.G. Lake, Inc., 356 U.S. 260 (1958). The taxpayer in that case assigned a right to $600,000 of payments under its "working interests" in two oil leases to another party in exchange for cancellation of that amount of debt owed by the taxpayer to the third party. The total amount and duration of the payments to be received by the taxpayer under the working interests was uncertain, but the parties believed that the obligation to pay $600,000 would be satisfied within about three years, and that the working interests would continue to produce value well beyond that period. The Supreme Court said that what was received was no more than payment for the right to receive future income, which was therefore taxable in full, and as ordinary income.

Some courts have limited the "substitutes for ordinary income" doctrine to cases involving an interest that was "carved out" of some larger interest that the taxpayer held prior to the transaction. For example, in McAllister v. Commissioner, 157 F.2d 235 (2d Cir. 1946), a divided court held that the sale of a testamentary life estate in a trust for $55,000 was subject to an offset equal to the discounted present value of the life estate at the time of the testator's death, which had been $63,000. Much as in *Hort*, the taxpayer had argued (successfully, this time) that a capital loss of $8,000 should be allowed, while the Commissioner had argued that the full amount received, $55,000, was ordinary income. The court found that, because the taxpayer had sold her entire interest in the trust, the *Hort* doctrine did not apply. The majority of the court applied instead the principle underlying an earlier income attribution case, Blair v. Commissioner, 300 U.S. 5 (1937), which held that assignment of an entire interest in a trust effectively transferred (for tax purposes as well as property law purposes) the future income to the transferee.

The analogy to the income attribution problem is dubious, and the result in *McAllister* was overturned by Congress when it added §1001(e) to the Code in 1969. That provision denies any basis to a taxpayer who sells a term or life estate; it does not, however, deny that such a sale may qualify as the sale of a capital asset. And, while courts are generally vigilant about

---

26. See section C.2.b of Chapter 10 for a more detailed discussion of §1286.

taxpayer attempts to convert ordinary income to capital gain by selling the right to the income before it is realized, exceptional cases can be found in which the taxpayer may have done just that, and gotten away with it.[27]

While most of the cases outlining the substitutes for ordinary income were decided long ago, the doctrine continues to have some vitality. In particular, Justice Marshall's analysis in *Arkansas Best*, by emphasizing the actual language of §1221(a), may have given some hope to taxpayers that items not plausibly covered by any of the exceptions to capital asset status might remain capital assets (as the statutory definition suggests). But as the following case suggests, some notion of common-law (or perhaps just common-sense) exclusions from capital asset status still apply.

UNITED STATES v. MAGINNIS

356 F.3d 1179 (9th Cir. 2004)

FISHER, Circuit Judge: . . .

FACTUAL AND PROCEDURAL BACKGROUND

Maginnis, his wife and three sons won a total prize of $23 million in the Oregon state lottery in July 1991. They divided the prize among themselves, with Maginnis and his wife each receiving $9 million and their sons dividing the remainder. Maginnis' $9 million share was payable in 20 equal installments of $450,000, paid to Maginnis via an annuity policy purchased by the State of Oregon. . . .

In January 1996, Maginnis assigned his right to receive the remaining 15 installments of his lottery prize to the Woodbridge Financial Corporation for a lump sum payment of $3,950,000. Maginnis successfully petitioned the Oregon court to approve his assignment to Woodbridge. Maginnis reported the $3,950,000 payment on his joint tax return for 1996 as ordinary income and paid the full amount of tax liability shown on that return. He also reported the lump sum payment as taxable income for the purposes of state income tax.

Maginnis and his wife filed an amended federal return in 1998 for the 1996 tax year, seeking a refund of $305,043. They claimed that they had realized capital gain, not ordinary income, on the lump sum payment from Woodbridge. The IRS paid this amount back in full, including interest.

On March 20, 2001, the United States filed a complaint in the District of Oregon, asserting that the IRS had erroneously granted Maginnis and his wife a refund for the 1996 tax year. The government claimed that the sale of the lottery right produced only ordinary income, and that Maginnis was judicially estopped from claiming otherwise because of prior arguments in a separate Oregon state case involving the Oregon income tax, in which he characterized the lump sum payment from Woodbridge as ordinary income. Both parties moved for summary judgment. The district court granted the government's motion, noting that

---

27. Possible examples may include a pair of 1962 cases; Nelson Weaver Realty Co. v. Commissioner, 307 F.2d 897 (5th Cir. 1962), and Commissioner v. Ferrer, 304 F.2d 125 (2d Cir. 1962). However, both of these cases are quite complex (which may have worked to the taxpayers' advantage) and arguably did not represent substitutes for ordinary income. At least the courts in those cases so found, in full in *Nelson Weaver*, and in part in *Ferrer*.

"capital gains treatment is not appropriate here because no asset appreciated." (emphasis removed). We have jurisdiction pursuant to 28 U.S.C. §1291, and we affirm the district court. . . .

DISCUSSION

I.

Whether the sale of a lottery right by a lottery winner is a long-term capital gain under the Internal Revenue Code ("I.R.C.") is a novel question of statutory interpretation. Fundamental principles of tax law lead us to conclude that Maginnis' assignment of his lottery right produced ordinary income.

A long-term capital gain or loss is generated when there is a "sale or exchange of a capital asset." §1222(3). A capital asset, in turn, is "property held by the taxpayer (whether or not connected to his trade or business)," subject to several statutory exceptions not relevant here. §1221.

The definition of capital asset has, however, never been read as broadly as the statutory language might seem to permit, because such a reading would encompass some things Congress did not intend to be taxed as capital gains. For example, an employee's right to be paid for work to be performed in the future is (for some purposes) "property" not subject to any of the enumerated exceptions in I.R.C. §1221, but it is doubtful that Congress would intend the sale of a right to future employment income to be taxed as a capital gain. If the statutory term capital asset is defined too broadly, taxpayers might use simple accounting devices to convert all ordinary income into capital gains.

To avoid this problem, in a series of cases that have established what is commonly known as the "substitute for ordinary income" doctrine, the Supreme Court has narrowly construed the term capital asset when taxpayers have made transparent attempts to transform ordinary income into capital gain in ways that undermine Congress' reasons for differentially taxing capital gains. "[N]ot everything which can be called property in the ordinary sense and which is outside the statutory exclusions qualifies as a capital asset" because

> the term "capital asset" is to be construed narrowly in accordance with the purpose of Congress to afford capital-gains treatment only in situations typically involving the realization of appreciation in value accrued over a substantial period of time, and thus to ameliorate the hardship of taxation of the entire gain in one year.

Comm'r v. Gillette Motor Transport, Inc., 364 U.S. 130, 134 (1960).

The Court has instructed that "lump sum consideration [that] seems essentially a substitute for what would otherwise be received at a future time as ordinary income" may not be taxed as a capital gain. *Comm'r v. P.G. Lake, Inc.*, 356 U.S. 260, 265 (1958).

However, there are limits to the substitute for ordinary income doctrine, as well. Many assets, including common stock, are typically valued on the basis of the present value of their future income stream, so an approach that took the substitute for ordinary income doctrine too far, and defined the term capital asset too narrowly, would hold that no sale of an asset that produces revenue, even common stock, could be taxed as a capital gain. Because we must eschew both an approach that could potentially convert all capital gains into ordinary income and one that could convert all ordinary income into capital gains, we must make case-by-case judgments as to whether the conversion of income rights into lump-sum payments reflects the sale of a capital asset that produces a capital gain, or whether it produces ordinary income. . . .

Maginnis' "lottery right" was his right to future payments from the State of Oregon in return for his lottery win. We hold that this right is not a "capital asset" within the meaning of §§1221 and 1222, and that Maginnis therefore received ordinary income from its assignment. Two factors are crucial to our conclusion, although we do not hold that they will be dispositive in all cases.[28] Maginnis (1) did not make any underlying investment of capital in return for the receipt of his lottery right, and (2) the sale of his right did not reflect an accretion in value over cost to any underlying asset Maginnis held. . . .

Concerning the first factor, the Supreme Court has indicated that the substitute for ordinary income doctrine will apply when there is no evidence of a sale of an underlying capital investment. *Gillette,* 364 U.S. at 135 (holding that the right to determine the use to which certain facilities were put was "not something in which [the taxpayer] had any investment" and thus was not a capital asset giving rise to a capital gain.); *P.G. Lake,* 356 U.S. at 265, ("We do not see here any conversion of a capital investment."); *Hort v. Comm'r,* 313 U.S. 28, 31 (holding that a substitute for ordinary income occurred when "[t]he consideration received . . . was not a return of capital"). Similarly, the Court has stressed the importance of the second factor, instructing that the substitute for ordinary income doctrine should apply to a transaction "manifestly not of the type which gives rise to the hardship of the realization in one year of an advance in *value over cost* built up in several years, which is what Congress sought to ameliorate by the capital-gains provisions." *Gillette,* 364 U.S. at 135 (emphasis added).

A. Underlying Investment of Capital

Maginnis made no underlying investment in exchange for a right to future payments. First, Maginnis does not—and cannot—argue that the purchase of a lottery ticket is a "capital investment," the return from which should be treated as a capital gain. Lottery prizes are treated by the tax code as gambling winnings, which are taxed as ordinary income. The lottery prize would have been taxed at ordinary income rates, reflecting the Revenue Code's general position that gambling winnings are not treated as capital gains. Therefore, the purchase of a lottery ticket is no more an underlying investment of capital than is a dollar bet on the spin of a roulette wheel.

That Maginnis sold his right to accrued lottery winnings to Woodbridge for a lump sum payment did not somehow create a capital investment. Under Oregon law a person *already entitled* to lottery winnings could petition for a judicial order to convert his lottery winnings into an alienable property interest. Absent such a judicial order—that is, without already having won the lottery—Maginnis could not sell his right to receive future accrued income from his lottery prize. Because Maginnis had no right to an alienable lottery interest until he had already won the

---

28. We do not decide whether a purchaser (such as Woodbridge) of a lottery right from a lottery winner who then sells that right to a third party would receive ordinary income or capital gain on that sale.

lottery, and because he made no capital investment before winning the lottery, no investment of capital was involved in creating the lottery right. Therefore, the assignment of the lottery right is better understood as the pure assignment of a gambling winning, rather than as the assignment of a capital asset, the sale of which could create a capital gain.

B.   Change in Value Over Cost

Because Maginnis did not make any capital investment in exchange for his lottery right — because there was no "cost" in the relevant sense to Maginnis for the right to receive accrued future payments from the Oregon lottery — the money he received for the sale of his right cannot plausibly be seen as reflecting an increase of value above the cost of any underlying capital asset. Although the amount a purchaser such as Woodbridge might pay for the right might be subject to some uncertainty, there was no sense in which the purchase price for the lottery right compensated Maginnis for an increase in value over cost. Therefore, the sale of Maginnis' lottery winning to Woodbridge lacks the requisite "realization of appreciation in value accrued over a substantial period of time" that is typically necessary for capital gains treatment.

C.   Other Considerations

There is no other reason to believe that Maginnis' lottery right assumed the characteristics of a capital asset such that he could recover capital gain from its assignment. Indeed, Maginnis' sale of his lottery right is almost indistinguishable from the paradigmatic situation in which the substitute for ordinary income doctrine removes a right to future income from the definition of a capital asset, which occurs when a taxpayer assigns his right to future income from employment to a third party for a lump sum. As explained above, the Revenue Code treats gambling winnings essentially as ordinary income, and Maginnis has done no more than sell his gambling winnings to a third party.

Moreover, treating the sale of Maginnis' lottery right as a capital gain would reward lottery winners who elect to receive periodic payments in lieu of a direct lump sum payment from the state, and then sell that payment right to a third party. Those who would do so would receive a tax advantage as compared to those taxpayers who would simply choose originally to accept their lottery winning in the form of a lump sum payment. Nothing in the Revenue Code compels the creation of such a dichotomous system for the taxation of lottery winnings. The purpose of narrowly construing the term capital asset under the substitute for ordinary income doctrine is to "protect the revenue against artful devices" that undermine the Revenue Code's standard treatment of ordinary income and capital gains. That is precisely what Maginnis has attempted here.

II.

Maginnis argues that whatever our analysis of the nature of his transaction, the substitute for ordinary income doctrine should not apply, and that the sale of his lottery right should be treated as the sale of a capital asset. He claims that the substitute for ordinary income doctrine has been limited to specific fact situations, none of which is present here, and that we must therefore read §1221 broadly and construe the sale of his lottery right as the sale of a capital asset.

Maginnis claims that Arkansas Best Corp. v. Comm'r, 485 U.S. 212 (1988), mandates this approach. He reads *Arkansas Best* as having largely invalidated the substitute for ordinary income doctrine, and having limited its application to two circumstances only: first, "carve out" transactions in which the taxpayer retains some underlying interest in the property sold (which we discuss below); and second, rights to future income from personal services, which—according to Maginnis—are not covered by the substitute for ordinary income doctrine at all but fall within §1221's exclusion of "inventory" from the definition of a capital asset. Other sales of property, he suggests, must be treated as sales of a "capital asset" and therefore treated as capital gains for the purposes of I.R.C. §1222.

Despite Maginnis' argument, it is certain that *Arkansas Best* did not affect the substitute for ordinary income doctrine's constraints on the construction of the term capital asset. *Arkansas Best* dealt with a different subject entirely: it rejected the "motive" test, under which lower federal courts had excluded some property acquired or held for a "business purpose" from the definition of capital asset under §1221. The Court expressly held that its decision did not affect the way in which the substitute for ordinary income doctrine modifies the term capital asset. . . .

Regardless of *Arkansas Best*, we shall address the underlying merits of Maginnis' argument about carve out transactions. Maginnis claims that because he sold his *entire* right to the lottery payments . . . instead of merely a carve out right to an income stream (. . . in which he would have retained some underlying interest in the right sold), we must treat the income he received from the sale as a capital gain. We reject this argument, and hold that a transaction in which a taxpayer sells his entire interest in an underlying asset without retaining any property right does not *automatically* prevent application of the substitute for ordinary income doctrine.

Maginnis is correct that transactions in which a taxpayer transfers an income right without transferring his entire interest in an underlying asset will often be occasions for applying the substitute for ordinary income doctrine. As Maginnis notes, finding a capital gain where a taxpayer sells an income right while retaining a property interest in the underlying asset could encourage "all taxpayers owning stock or income-producing property . . . to convert their ordinary investment income into capital gain." Marvin A. Chirelstein, *Federal Income Taxation* ¶17.03 (7th ed. 1994). For example, if an owner of common stock could sell his right to dividends without selling the underlying stock and realize a capital gain on that sale, he could escape from the tax code's treatment of stock dividends as ordinary income through a simple accounting device.[29]

This does not mean, however, that the substitute for ordinary income doctrine will apply only where a taxpayer has retained some underlying right in the property interest sold. Such an approach is foreclosed, because we have previously applied the substitute for ordinary income doctrine in cases where the taxpayer has sold a property interest in its entirety. Rather, we must make an independent determination as to whether a transaction presents a suitable occasion for applying the substitute for ordinary income doctrine and narrowly construing the definition of a capital asset.

---

29. [Note that the example is now somewhat inapt, in view of the temporary treatment (through 2012) of dividend income as subject to the same special rates as those that apply to capital gains. — Eds.]

Here, we conclude that the fact that Maginnis sold his entire interest in his lottery winning is not a persuasive reason to treat the sale of that right as a capital gain. Because, as discussed above, Maginnis' lottery right did not reflect an underlying capital investment or an increase in value over cost, and because there is no other compelling reason to treat the assignment of the lottery right as an assignment of a capital asset, we shall apply the substitute for ordinary income doctrine. . . .

CONCLUSION

For the reasons stated above, we conclude that the sale of Maginnis' lottery right should be taxed as ordinary income. The district court correctly granted the government summary judgment.

Notes and Questions

1. *Income clumping*. Note that the taxpayer here received nearly four million dollars in a single tax year, instead of the $450,000 per year that he would have received in each of the following 15 years without the sale of his rights. If the purpose of special treatment of capital gains is, as the court says (quoting *Gillette Motor Transport*), to give capital gain rate breaks "to ameliorate the hardship of taxation of the entire gain [which accrues over a substantial period of time] in one year," then why wouldn't the taxpayer here qualify?

2. *The Ninth Circuit's test*. The first of two prongs in the Ninth Circuit's test for capital asset status requires that the taxpayer make an "underlying investment of capital." But were it not for the provisions §1221(a)(3), creators of "literary, musical, or artistic compositions" would presumably be allowed to treat the sale of rights to those works as capital assets, despite the difficulties their authors, composers, and artists would have had showing any investment of significance other than their time.[30] Doesn't the question of how much, if any, investment has been made shed light on the *amount* of gain or loss experienced by the taxpayer, rather than on the nature of that gain or loss?

3. *The Woodbridge question*. The court expressly refuses to provide any guidance as to how Woodbridge Financial Corporation, the purchaser of Maginnis' rights, would be treated on any subsequent sale of those rights to a third party. But what do you suppose the *Maginnis* court would in fact decide in such a case? Does that hypothetical decision shed any light on the soundness of the decision in this case?

4. *Full circle*. This opinion nicely captures the essential difficulty in treating capital gains and ordinary income differently: The value of a capital asset is, almost invariably, determined by its potential to produce future income. In light of that quandary, we might conclude this chapter with the rhetorical question with which we began; is it conceptually sensible to try to make any distinction between these two types of income?

---

30. The creators of such work would have used ink, paper, paints, etc. in making those works. These, however, are generally of trivial value, and better characterized as supplies than as "investments of capital." No doubt Mr. Maginnis could show some trivial costs of this type as well, such as the purchase of a newspaper to determine if he had won the lottery.

TABLE OF CASES

References are to page numbers or page numbers and note numbers. Italics indicate principal cases and the locations of major discussions of these cases.

929

TABLE OF INTERNAL REVENUE CODE SECTIONS

References are to page numbers or page numbers and note numbers.

933

TABLE OF TREASURY REGULATIONS

References are to page numbers or page numbers and note numbers.

TABLE OF REVENUE RULINGS

References are to page numbers or page numbers and note numbers. Italic type indicates rulings that are reprinted and the pages where they are reprinted.

TABLE OF MISCELLANEOUS IRS PRONOUNCEMENTS

References are to page numbers or page numbers and note numbers. Italic type indicates the reference is reprinted.

INDEX

References are to page numbers.